USING INFORMATION Technology

USING INFORMATION Technology

Tenth Edition

A Practical Introduction to Computers & Communications

Complete Version

BRIAN K. WILLIAMS | STACEY C. SAWYER

The McGraw-Hill Companies

USING INFORMATION TECHNOLOGY: A PRACTICAL INTRODUCTION TO COMPUTERS & COMMUNICATIONS, COMPLETE VERSION

Published by McGraw-Hill, a business unit of The McGraw-Hill Companies, Inc., 1221 Avenue of the Americas, New York, NY, 10020.

This book is printed on acid-free paper.

1 2 3 4 5 6 7 8 9 0 DOW/DOW 1 0 9 8 7 6 5 4 3 2

ISBN 978-0-07-351683-7
MHID 0-07-351683-X

Vice president/Director of marketing: *Alice Harra*
Publisher: *Scott Davidson*
Sponsoring editor: *Paul Altier*
Director, digital products: *Crystal Szewczyk*
Digital product manager: *Thuan Vinh*
Development editor: *Alan Palmer*
Freelance development: *Burrston House*
Editorial coordinator: *Allison McCabe*
Marketing manager: *Tiffany Russell*
Digital development editor: *Kevin White*
Director, Editing/Design/Production: *Jess Ann Kosic*
Project manager: *Jean R. Starr*
Senior buyer: *Kara Kudronowicz*
Senior designer: *Marianna Kinigakis*
Senior photo research coordinator: *Jeremy Cheshareck*
Photo researcher: *Judy Mason*
Manager, digital production: *Janean A. Utley*
Media project manager: *Brent dela Cruz*
Media project manager: *Cathy L. Tepper*
Cover design: *Cody Wallis*
Interior design: *Ellen Pettengell*
Typeface: *10/12 New Aster*
Compositor: *Laserwords Private Limited*
Printer: *R. R. Donnelley*
Credits: The credits section for this book begins on page 561 and is considered an extension of the copyright page.

Library of Congress Cataloging-in-Publication Data

Williams, Brian K.
Using information technology : a practical introduction to computers & communications / Brian K. Williams, Stacey C. Sawyer.—Complete version, 10th ed.
p. cm.
Includes index.
ISBN 978-0-07-351683-7 (alk. paper)—ISBN 0-07-351683-X (alk. paper)
1. Computers. 2. Telecommunication systems. 3. Information technology. I. Sawyer, Stacey C. II. Title.
QA76.5.W5332 2013
004—dc23

2011046153

www.mhhe.com

Brief Contents

UIT 10e App

Download the free UIT 10e App for:

- Key term flash cards

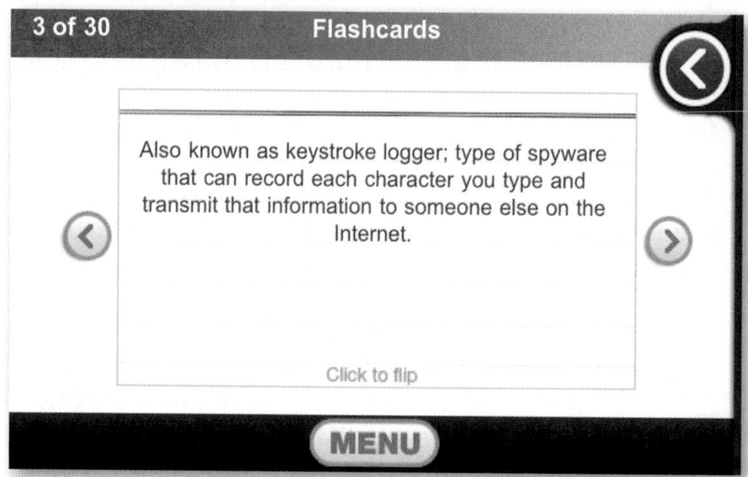

- Quizzes

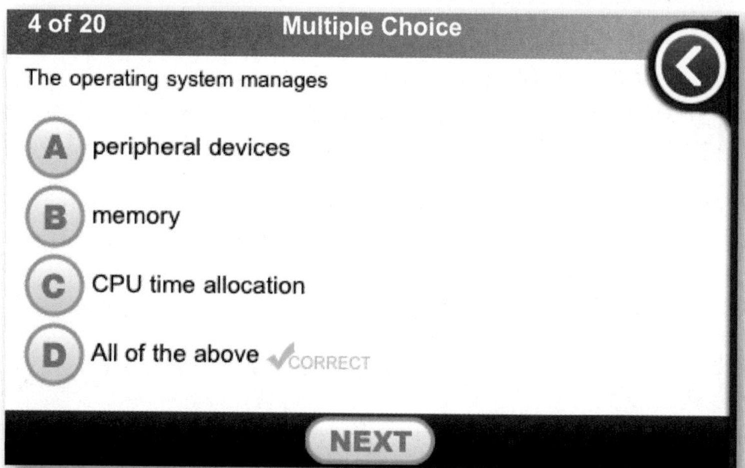

4 of 20
Multiple Choice
The operating system manages
A peripheral devices
B memory
C CPU time allocation
D All of the above
CORRECT
NEXT

- Game, *Over the Edge*

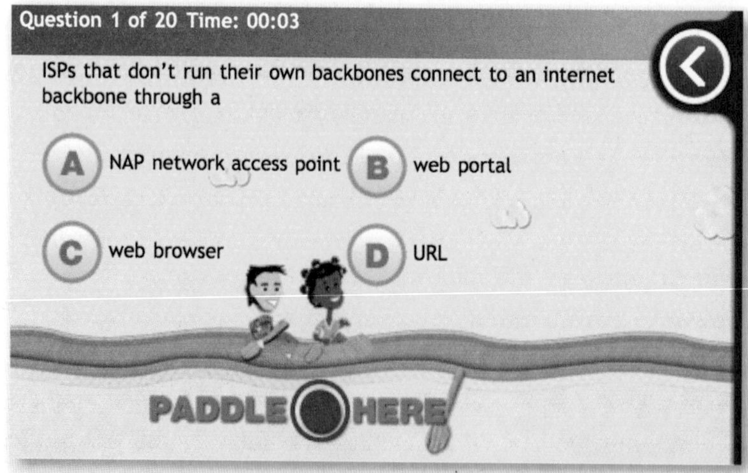

To the Instructor

INTRODUCTION Teaching the "Always On" Generation

If there is anything we have learned during the 19 years of writing and revising this computer concepts book, it is this: *Not only does the landscape of computer education change, but so do the students.*

USING INFORMATION TECHNOLOGY (abbreviated *UIT)* was written and revised around three important benchmarks:

- **The impact of digital convergence:** The First Edition was the first text to foresee the impact of digital convergence—the fusion of computers and communications—as the new and broader foundation for the computer concepts course.
- **The importance of cyberspace:** The Fourth Edition was the first text to acknowledge the new priorities imposed by the Internet and World Wide Web and bring discussion of them from late in the course to near the beginning (to Chapter 2).
- **The ascendancy of the "Always On" generation:** The Seventh Edition addressed another paradigm change: Because of the mobility and hybridization of digital devices, **an "Always On" generation of students has come of age that's at ease with digital technology but—and it's an important "but"—not always savvy about computer processes, possibilities, and liabilities.**

The appearance of this new generation imposes additional challenges on professors: **Instructors are expected to make the course interesting and challenging to students already at least somewhat familiar with information technology while teaching people of widely varying computer sophistication.**

ADDRESSING INSTRUCTORS' TWO MOST IMPORTANT CHALLENGES

As we embark on our eighteenth year of publication, we are extremely pleased at the continued reception to *USING INFORMATION TECHNOLOGY,* which has been used by well more than a half million students and adopted by instructors in over 850 schools. One reason for this enthusiastic response may be that we've tried hard to address professors' needs. We've often asked instructors—in reviews, surveys, and focus groups—

"What are your most significant challenges in teaching this course?"

Instructors generally have two answers:

The First Most Important Challenge: "Motivating Students & Making the Course Interesting"

One professor at a state university seems to speak for most when she says: "Making the course interesting and challenging." Others echo her with

QUOTES

What instructors say is the most significant challenge in teaching this course:

". . . Students lose interest in definitions and technical details unless they can see an immediate practical benefit."
—Melinda White, Seminole State College of Florida

"Keeping student interest and attention."
—Biswadip Ghosh, Metropolitan State College of Denver

remarks such as "Keeping students interested in the material enough to study" and "Keeping the students engaged who know some, but not all, of the material." Said one professor, "Many students take the course because they must, instead of because the material interests them." Another speaks about the need to address a "variety of skill/knowledge levels while keeping the course challenging and interesting"—which brings us to the second response.

> **QUOTE**
> "This will always be a difficult course to teach, since the students in any given class come from very different backgrounds and have vastly different levels of computer expertise."
> —Laurie Eakins, East Carolina University

The Second Most Important Challenge: "Trying to Teach to Students with a Variety of Computer Backgrounds"

The most significant challenge in teaching this course "is trying to provide material to the varied levels of students in the class," says an instructor at a large Midwestern university. Another says the course gets students from all backgrounds, ranging from "Which button do you push on the mouse?" to "Already built and maintain a web page with html." Says a third, "mixed-ability classes [make] it difficult to appeal to all students at the same time." And a fourth: "How do you keep the 'techies' interested without losing the beginners?"

Motivating the Unmotivated & Teaching to a Disparity of Backgrounds

As authors, we find information technology tremendously exciting, but we recognize that many students take the course reluctantly. And we also recognize that many students come to the subject with attitudes ranging from complete apathy and unfamiliarity to a high degree of experience and technical understanding.

To address the problem of **motivating the unmotivated and teaching to a disparity of backgrounds,** *UIT* offers unequaled treatment of the following:

1. **Practicality**
2. **Readability**
3. **Currentness**
4. **Three-level critical thinking system.**

We explain these features on the following pages.

> **QUOTE**
> About *UIT*'s practicality
> "[This] book is well written, interesting, and readable. It is a pleasure to read. It covers everything a new computer user needs to become computer literate."
> —Bonnie Smith, Fresno City College

FEATURE #1: Emphasis on Practicality

This popular feature received overwhelming acceptance by both students and instructors in past editions. **Practical advice,** of the sort found in computer magazines, newspaper technology sections, and general-interest computer books, is expressed not only in the text but also in the following:

The Experience Box

Appearing at the end of each chapter, the Experience Box is optional material that may be assigned at the instructor's discretion. However, students will find the subjects covered are of immediate value.

Examples: "Web Research, Term Papers, & Plagiarism." "Getting Help from Tech Support." "How to Buy a Laptop." "Preventing Your Identity from Getting Stolen." "Virtual Meetings: Linking Up Electronically." "The 'Always On' Generation."

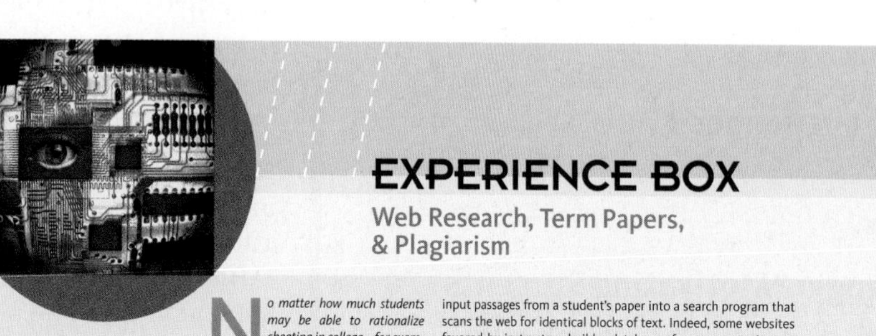
EXPERIENCE BOX

Web Research, Term Papers, & Plagiarism

No matter how much students may be able to rationalize cheating in college—for example, trying to pass off someone else's term paper as their own (plagiarism)—ignorance of the consequences is not an excuse. Most instructors announce the penalties for cheating at the beginning of the course—usually a failing grade in the course and possible suspension or expulsion from school.

input passages from a student's paper into a search program that scans the web for identical blocks of text. Indeed, some websites favored by instructors build a database of papers over time so that students can't recycle work previously handed in by others. Special software programs, such as CopyScape.com, Plagiarism-Checker.com, grammarly.com, SplaT, and academicplagiarism.com, are available for instructors to use to check students' work and for students to check their own work before turning it in.

Practical Action Box

See the list of Experience Boxes and Practical Action Boxes on the inside front cover.

This box consists of optional material on practical matters.

Examples: "How to Be a Good Online Student." "Evaluating & Sourcing Information Found on the Web." "Tips for Avoiding Spyware." "Utility Programs." "Social Networking: Worth the Convenience?" "Help in Building Your Web Page." "Storing Your Stuff: How Long Will Digitized Data Last?" "Starting Over with Your Hard Drive: Erasing, Reformatting, & Reloading." "WikiLeaks & DDoS." "Ways to Minimize Virus Attacks." "How to Deal with Passwords." "Online Viewing & Sharing of Digital Photos." "Database Research: Accuracy & Completeness." "Is the Boss Watching You? Trust in the Workplace."

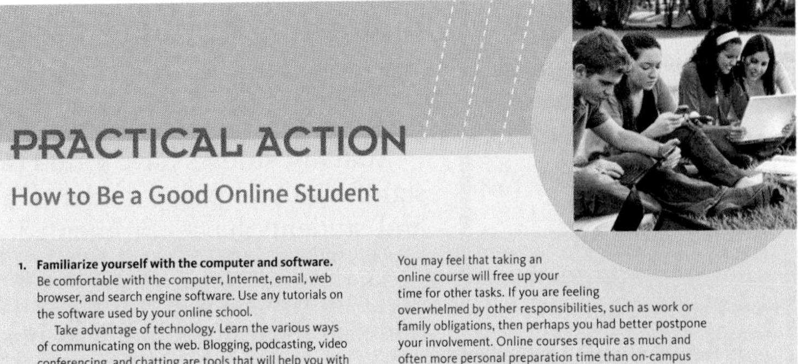

Survival Tips

> **Survival Tip**
>
> **New Software & Compatibility**
>
> Pay attention to compatibility requirements when you obtain new software. The system requirements for running the software will be listed on the box or included with the downloaded information. When it is time to update the software, you can usually do that by paying a small upgrade fee to the software manufacturer and then downloading the new version and/or obtaining a new CD/DVD.

In the margins throughout we present utilitarian **Survival Tips** to aid students' explorations of the infotech world.

See the list of Survival Tips on the inside front cover.

Examples: "Broadband: Riskier for Security." "Connection Speeds." "Finding Things on a Web Page or in a Web Document." "Urban Legends & Lies on the Internet." "Social-Networking Privacy." "Control Those Cookies!" "New Software & Compatibility." "What RAM for Your PC?" "ATMs & Fraud/Safety." "Firewalls." "E-Book Cautions." "Reporting Software Pirates." "Alleviating Info-Mania." "Fraud Baiters." "What Happens to Your Smartphone Data?"

> **QUOTE**
>
> About *UIT*'s practicality
>
> "I am particularly impressed with the pedagogical and the visual elements of the text. The 'more info!' and 'Survival Tip' have practical use that is beneficial and easy to locate in the margins."
> —Beata Lovelace, Pulaski Technical College

How to Understand a Computer Ad

In the hardware chapters (Chapters 4 and 5), we explain important concepts by showing students **how to understand the hardware components in a hypothetical PC ad.**

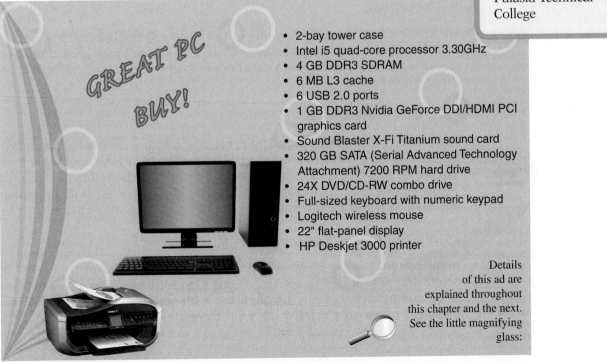

GREAT PC BUY!
• 2-bay tower case
• Intel i5 quad-core processor 3.30GHz
• 4 GB DDR3 SDRAM
• 6 MB L3 cache
• 6 USB 2.0 ports
• 1 GB DDR3 Nvidia GeForce DDI/HDMI PCI graphics card
• Sound Blaster X-Fi Titanium sound card
• 320 GB SATA (Serial Advanced Technology Attachment) 7200 RPM hard drive
• 24X DVD/CD-RW combo drive
• Full-sized keyboard with numeric keypad
• Logitech wireless mouse
• 22" flat-panel display
• HP Deskjet 3000 printer

Details of this ad are explained throughout this chapter and the next. See the little magnifying glass:

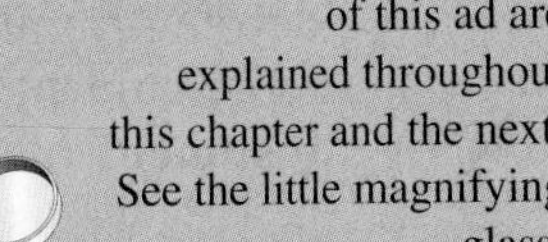

QUOTES

About *UIT*'s readability

"It discusses the software development in a down-to-earth manner without resorting to terminology that would deter non-programmers."
—Phillip Nielson, Salt Lake Community College

"Judging from the students' feedback, very easy to read and logically organized. I also like going from the general to the specific in each topic. I would rate the writing style excellent."
—David Pence, Moberly Area Community College

"I think it is better than any of the other intro books I've read; and I've read a great many of them in the last 14 years."
—Sandra Week, University of Nevada-Reno

FEATURE #2: Emphasis on Readability & Reinforcement for Learning

We offer the following features for reinforcing student learning:

Interesting Writing—Based on Good Scholarship

Where is it written that textbooks have to be boring? Can't a text have personality?

Actually, studies have found that textbooks **written in an imaginative style** significantly improve students' ability to retain information. Both instructors and students have commented on the distinctiveness of the writing in this book. We employ a number of journalistic devices—colorful anecdotes, short biographical sketches, interesting observations in direct quotes—to make the material as approachable as possible. We also use real anecdotes and examples rather than fictionalized ones.

Finally, **unlike most computer concepts books, we provide references for our sources—see the endnotes in the back of the book. Many of these are from the year preceding publication.** We see no reason why introductory computer books shouldn't practice good scholarship by revealing their information sources. And we see no reason why good scholarship can't go along with good writing—scholarship need not mean stuffiness.

Key Terms AND Definitions Emphasized

To help readers avoid confusion about important terms and what they actually mean, we print each key term in ***bold italic underscore*** and its definition in **boldface.** ***Example*** (from Chapter 1): "***Data*** **consists of raw facts and figures that are processed into information.**"

Material in Easily Manageable Portions

Major ideas are presented in **bite-size form,** with generous use of advance organizers, bulleted lists, and new paragraphing when a new idea is introduced. Most **sentences have been kept short,** the majority not exceeding 22–25 words in length.

"What's in It for Me?" Questions—to Help Students Read with Purpose

We have **crafted the learning objectives as Key Questions** to help readers focus on essentials. These are expressed as "I" and "me" questions, of the type students ask. These questions follow both first-level and second-level headings throughout the book.

Emphasis Throughout on Ethics

See ethics examples pp. 40, 90, 103, 243, 391, 452, 465

Many texts discuss ethics in isolation, usually in one of the final chapters. We believe this topic is too important to be treated last or lightly, and users have agreed. Thus, **we cover ethical matters throughout the book,** as indicated by the special icon shown at left. ***Example:*** We discuss such all-important questions as online plagiarism, privacy, computer crime, and netiquette.

Emphasis Throughout on Security

See Security icons on pp. 40, 87, 103, 444, 484

SECURITY

In the post 9-11 era, security concerns are of gravest importance. Although we devote several pages (in Chapters 2, 6, and 9) to security matters, we also reinforce student awareness by **highlighting with page-margin Security icons instances of security-related material throughout the book.** ***Example:*** On p. 103, we use the special icon shown at left to highlight the advice that one should pretend that every email message one sends "is a postcard that can be read by anyone."

Eight Timelines to Provide Historical Perspective

Some instructors like to see coverage of the history of computing. Not wishing to add greatly to the length of the book, we decided on **a student-friendly approach: the presentation of eight pictorial timelines showing the most significant historical IT events.** These timelines, which occur in most chapters, appear along the bottom page margin. (See the example at the bottom of this page.) Each timeline repeats certain "benchmark" events to keep students oriented, but **each one is modified to feature the landmark discoveries and inventions appropriate to the different chapter material.** ***Examples:*** In Chapter 4, "System Software," the timeline features innovations in operating systems. In Chapter 7, "Telecommunications," the timeline highlights innovations in data transmission.

See timelines beginning on pp. 17, 52, 168, 200, 262, 312, 416, 530

2004	2005	2006	2007	2008	2010	2013	2015	2030–2045
IBM PC sold to Lenovo Group Flickr	YouTube Wii	Twitter	Skype; Apple introduces iPhone	Netbooks become popular	Apple releases iPad	Foldable computers	Teleportation?; self-aware machine intelligence	The singularity

FEATURE #3: New to This Edition

Reviewers have applauded previous editions of UIT for being **more up to date than other texts.** For example, we have traditionally ended many chapters with a forward-looking section that offers a preview of technologies to come—some of which are realized even as students are using the book.

Among the new topics and terms covered in this edition are: *tablet computers, multitouch screens, Windows 8, Apple OS X Lion, Google Chrome, Adobe Flash, HTML5, CSS, Internet Exchange Points (IXP), Android, HDMI, mesh networks, Cat5 and Cat7 cable, 5G, WikiLeaks, blended threats, rootkits, zombies, bots and botnets, ransomware, keylogging, time bombs and logic bombs, computer forensics, and UML.* In this edition, we have updated the PC advertisement on page 203 and we have also updated the screen shots of software in Chapter 3. Material has also been updated on the following: *Internet usage statistics, how to buy a computer, distance (online) learning, e-books, robotics, uses of computers in medicine and many other professions and jobs, infrastructure of the Internet, types of computers, including supercomputers, hardware speeds and capacities, future of information technology, cloud computing, The Singularity, ethics of computer use, ecology of computer use, social networking, connectivity speeds and capacities, Wi-Fi and other wireless technologies, IP addresses and domain names, browsers, Internet search techniques, operating systems, utilities, applications, building a web page, processors and other motherboard components, ports and connectors, storage technologies, display screens, cellphone radiation, printers and other peripherals, security, networks (including advantages and disadvantages), switches, bridges, gateways, and routers, GPS, 4G, USB, malware, smartphones and their use, online search techniques, problems of multitasking, PMP/MP3 players, Internet radio and TV, digital cameras, sensor, batteries, flash memory, texting, databases, dirty data, types of files, identity theft, ethics, plagiarism, fair use and copyright infringement, computer crimes, ergonomics, environmental issues, Internet overuse and dangers, productivity and "information overload," information systems, programming and languages, markup and scripting languages.*

> **QUOTE**
> About *UIT*'s currentness
>
> "Very current . . . Lots of Internet references in the chapters. . . . Also, [the text] asks students lots of questions instead of just giving out material to memorize."
> —Linda Kliston, Broward College

"More Info!" Feature Helps Students Find Their Own Answers to Questions

In addition, **we have taken the notion of currentness to another level through the use of the "MoreInfo!" feature to encourage students to obtain their own updates** about material.

Examples: "How to Set Up Your Computer for Speech Recognition in Windows 7." "RFID Identity Theft." "Laptop Buying Guides." "What's Your Cellphone's Radiation Level?" "Mouse-Pointer Systems for the Disabled." "Hobbes's Internet Timeline." "Finding Wi-Fi Hot Spots." "Where Are the IXPs?" "The Internet Traffic Report." "Your IP Address." "Generalized Lists of Search Engines." "FTP Clients & Servers." "How VoIP Works." "Blog Search Engines." "Comparison of the Top 10 Social Networking Sites." "Verifying Valid Websites." "How to Get Rid of a Browser Hijacker." "Safe Mode." "More on OS Comparisons." "Rules for Upgrading Your Operating System." "Shareware & Freeware." "Software Installation Basics." "System Crashes."

"Online Storage." "Nanotechnology Dangers?" "Internet Backbone Maps." "Geocaching." "Choosing CDMA or GSM." "Texting while Driving." "Latest Bluetooth Devices." "Beginners Guide to Going Wireless." "Cyber Security Tips." "Programming Language Popularity." "What's an Applet?" "JavaScript Tutorial." "Phone Apps." "Thinking about Majoring in IT?" "Mashup Sites." "What Kind of Battery Is Best?" "Ethics & Digital Photography." "Downloads for Handhelds." "What Is Computer Forensics?" "More on Interpol & Cybercrime." "Where to Learn More about Freeware & Shareware." "More about Watermarks."

Cellphone Tracking

Cellphone companies may be tracking your every move and compiling information about you . . .

http://current.com/news/93106962_it-s-tracking-your-every-move-and-you-may-not-even-know-it.htm

http://answers.yahoo.com/question/index?qid=20110508105144AAi1Cs1

http://online.wsj.com/article/SB10001424052748703467304575383522318244234.html

www.livephonetracking.com/cell-phone-gps-tracking.html

FEATURE #4: Three-Level System to Help Students Think Critically about Information Technology

This feature, which has been in place for the preceding three editions, has been warmly received. More and more instructors seem to have become familiar with Benjamin Bloom's *Taxonomy of Educational Objectives,* describing a hierarchy of six critical-thinking skills: (a) two lower-order skills—*memorization* and *comprehension;* and (b) four higher-order skills—*application, analysis, synthesis,* and *evaluation.* Drawing on our experience in writing books to guide students to college success, we have implemented Bloom's ideas in a three-stage pedagogical approach, using the following hierarchical approach in the Chapter Review at the end of every chapter:

Stage 1 Learning—Memorization: "I Can Recognize & Recall Information"

Using self-test questions, multiple-choice questions, and true/false questions, we enable students to test how well they recall basic terms and concepts.

Stage 2 Learning—Comprehension: "I Can Recall Information in My Own Terms & Explain It to a Friend"

Using open-ended short-answer questions, we enable students to re-express terms and concepts in their own words.

Stage 3 Learning—Applying, Analyzing, Synthesizing, Evaluating: "I Can Apply What I've Learned, Relate These Ideas to Other Concepts, Build on Other Knowledge, & Use All These Thinking Skills to Form a Judgment"

In this part of the Chapter Review, we ask students to put the ideas into effect using the activities described. The purpose is to help students take possession of the ideas, make them their own, and apply them realistically to their own ideas. **Our web exercises are also intended to spur discussion in the classroom and other contexts.**

QUOTES

About *UIT*'s critical thinking emphasis

"[It] is very important because it helps students comprehend and make sound decisions." —Maryann Dorn, Southern Illinois University

"A critical thinking emphasis is very important because . . . it represents a higher level of understanding." —Evelyn Lulis, DePaul University

Examples: "Learn about Wikis." "Communicating in Times of Emergencies." "Starting your Own B2B Business." "What's Wrong with Using Supermarket Loyalty Cards?"

RESOURCES FOR INSTRUCTORS

Online Learning Center

The Online Learning Center *(www.mhhe.com/uit10e)* is designed to provide students with additional learning opportunities and instructors with additional teaching tools. For instructors, the website includes PowerPoint presentations for each chapter. For the convenience of instructors, all the following resources are available for download.

Instructor's Manual

The electronic Instructor's Manual, available as part of the Instructor's Resource Kit, helps instructors to create effective lectures. The Instructor's Manual is easy to navigate and simple to understand. Each chapter contains a chapter overview, lecture outline, teaching tips, additional information, and answers to end-of-chapter questions and exercises.

Testbank

The Testbank format allows instructors to effectively pinpoint areas of content within each chapter on which to test students. The text questions include learning level, answers, and text page numbers.

EZ Test

McGraw-Hill's EZ Test is a flexible and easy-to-use electronic testing program. The program allows instructors to create tests from book-specific items. It accommodates a wide range of question types, and instructors may add their own questions. Multiple versions of the test can be created and any test can be exported for use with course management systems such as WebCT, BlackBoard, or PageOut. EZ Test Online is a new service and gives you a place to easily administer your EZ Test created exams and quizzes online. The program is available for Windows and Macintosh environments.

PowerPoint Presentation

The PowerPoint presentation includes additional material that expands on important topics from the text, allowing instructors to create interesting and engaging classroom presentations. Each chapter of the presentation includes illustrations, to enable instructors to emphasize important concepts in memorable ways.

ACKNOWLEDGMENTS

This book has only two names on its title page, but we are extraordinarily grateful for the many others who have been important contributors to its development. First we wish to thank Paul Altier, our sponsoring editor, and Alan Palmer, development editor, for their in helping to roll out this edition, which, because of the surge in technological change, now compels an updating on a frequent basis. Thanks also go to our marketing manager, Tiffany Russell, and we were extremely delighted to once again have Jean Starr as our project manager, who was instrumental in keeping the project on track—we are grateful to her for her professionalism. We also thank Kevin White, Thuan Vinh, and Brent dela Cruz for their media and digital support. Thanks are also due Jess Ann Kosic, Kay Lieberherr, and Jeremy Cheshareck.

Outside McGraw-Hill, we were fortunate to have the services of Glenn and Meg Turner of New Jersey-based Burrston House, a research and development firm who worked on earlier editions of this book, as well as on Brian's successful McGraw-Hill *Management* book (with Angelo Kinicki) and our *Business* text (with Susan Berston). We appreciate the market-driven focus of their evidence-based approach to book development. We also want to state our appreciation for the contributions of Judy Mason, our San Francisco Bay Area photo researcher, whose history with us goes back many, many years and who did her usual always reliable, always superb job in photo research. Peter deLissovoy copyedited the text, Alyson Platt was our able proofreader, and James Minkin, who has been a stalwart and sensitive indexer on many of our projects, did his usual satisfying and predictably outstanding job.

Finally, we are grateful to the following reviewers for helping to make this the most market-driven book possible.

Beverly Bohn
Park University–Parkville

Ronald E. Conway
Bowling Green State University

Dale Craig
Fullerton College

Nancy Jo Evans
Indiana University–Purdue University Indianapolis

Bob Grill
College of Alameda

Dorothy G. Harman
Tarrant County College, Northeast Campus

Carson Haury
Central Oregon Community College

Richard Hauser
East Carolina University

Cheryl R. Heemstra
Anne Arundel Community College

Marilyn Hibbert
Salt Lake Community College

Linda Kavanaugh Varga
Robert Morris University

Linda Kliston
Broward College–North

Paul Koester
Tarrant County College

Kurt W. Kominek
Northeast State Community College

Shawn Krest
Genesee Community College

Jackie Althea Lamoureux
Central New Mexico Community College

David Lee Largent
Ball State University

Dawn D. Laux
Purdue University–West Lafayette

Janet D. Lindner
Midlands Technical College

Donna Lohn
Lakeland Community College

Beata Lovelace
Pulaski Technical College

Roberta Mae Marvel
Casper College

Sue A. McCrory
Missouri State University

Veronica F. McGowan
Delaware Valley College

Alanah Mitchell
Appalachian State University

Philip H. Nielson
Salt Lake Community College

James Gordon Patterson
Paradise Valley Community College

David E. Pence
Moberly Area Community College

Teresa Marie Peterman
Grand Valley State University

Carol B. Reed
Mount Wachusett Community College

Glen Sagers
Illinois State University

Harry D. Shea
Missouri State University

Bonnie Sue Specht Smith
Fresno City College

Kathleen Tamerlano
Cuyahoga Community College

Kasia Taylor
Anne Arundel Community College

Michelle Vlaich-Lee
Greenville Technical College

Sandra M. (Sandy) Week
University of Nevada–Reno

Melinda White
Seminole State College of Florida

Pauline White
Siena College

Nancy Ann Woolridge
Fullerton College

Mary Ann Zlotow
College of DuPage

Reviewers & Other Participants in Previous Editions

We are grateful for the magnificent help over the past 15 years from all the instructors who have given us the benefit of their opinion, as follows:

Nancy Alderdice
Murray State University

Margaret Allison
University of Texas–Pan American

Angela Amin
Great Lakes Junior College

Leon Amstutz
Taylor University, Upland, Indiana

Sharon Anderson
Western Iowa Tech

Anderson
Marymount College

Hashem Anwari
Northern Virginia Community College–Loudoun Campus

Connie Aragon
Seattle Central Community College

Tahir Azia
Long Beach City College, California

Bonnie Bailey,
Morehead State University

Don Bailey
Plymouth State University, New Hampshire

David Brent Bandy
University of Wisconsin–Oshkosh

Robert L. Barber
Lane Community College

Vic Barbow
Purdue University

Robert Barrett
Indiana University and Purdue University at Fort Wayne

Anthony Baxter
University of Kentucky

Gigi Beaton
Tyler Junior College

Virginia Bender
William Rainey Harper College

Hossein Bidgoli
California State University–Bakersfield

Warren Boe
University of Iowa

Beverly Bohn
Park University

Randall Bower
Iowa State University

Russell Breslauer
Chabot College

Bob Bretz
Western Kentucky University

William C. Brough
University of Texas–Pan American

Phyllis Broughton
Pitt Community College

Charles Brown
Plymouth State College

Bidi Bruno
Portland Community College, Oregon

David Burris
Sam Houston State University

Jeff Butterfield
University of Idaho

J. Wesley Cain
City University, Bellevue

Patrick Callan
Concordia University

Anthony Cameron
Fayetteville Technical Community College, North Carolina

Judy Cameron
Spokane Community College

Ralph Caputo
Manhattan College

Robert Caruso
Santa Rosa Junior College

Joe Chambers
Triton College

Kris Chandler
Pikes Peak Community College

William Chandler
University of Southern Colorado

John Chenoweth
East Tennessee State University

Ashraful Chowdhury
Dekalb College

Erline Cocke
Northwest Mississippi Community College

Jennifer Cohen
Southwest Florida College, Fort Myers

Robert Coleman
Pima County Community College

Helen Corrigan-McFadyen
Massachusetts Bay Community College

Paulette Comet
Community College of Baltimore County, Maryland

Ron Conway
Bowling Green State University, Indiana

Jami Cotler
Siena College

Glen Coulthard
Okanagan University

Rebecca Cunningham
Arkansas Technical University, Russellville

Robert Crandall
Denver Business School

Hiram Crawford
Olive Harvey College

Thad Crews
Western Kentucky University

Martin Cronlund
Anne Arundel Community College

Jim Dartt
San Diego Mesa College

Joseph DeLibro
Arizona State University

Edouard Desautels
University of Wisconsin–Madison

William Dorin
Indiana University–Northwest

Maryan Dorn
Southern Illinois University

Patti Dreven
Community College of Southern Nevada

John Durham
Fort Hays State University

Laura A. Eakins
East Carolina University

Bonita Ellis
Wright City College

John Enomoto
East Los Angeles College

Ray Fanselau
American River College

Pat Fenton
West Valley College

Eleanor Flanigan
Montclair State University

Ken Frizane
Oakton Community College

James Frost
Idaho State University

Susan Fry
Boise State University

Susan Fuschetto
Cerritos College, Norwalk, California

Bob Fulkerth
Golden Gate University

Janos Fustos
Metropolitan State College

Saiid Ganjalizadeh
Catholic University of America, Washington, D.C.

Yaping Gao
College of Mount St. Joseph

Enrique Garcia
Laredo Community College

JoAnn Garver
University of Akron

Jill Gebelt
Salt Lake Community College

Charles Geigner
Illinois State University

David German
Cerro Coso Community College

Candace Gerrod
Red Rocks Community College

Julie Giles
DeVry Institute of Technology

Bish Ghosh
Metropolitan State College, Denver

Frank Gillespie
University of Georgia

Mindy Glander
North Metro Technical College, Acworth, Georgia

Myron Goldberg
Pace University

Dwight Graham
Prairie State College

Fillmore Guinn
Odessa College

Norman P. Hahn
Thomas Nelson Community College

Sallyann Hanson
Mercer County Community College

Debra Harper
Montgomery County Community College–North Harris

Albert Harris
Appalachian State University

Jan Harris
Lewis & Clark Community College

Michael Hasset
Fort Hays State University

Julie Heine
Southern Oregon State College

Lonnie Hendrick
Hampton University, Hampton, Virginia

Richard Hewer
Ferris State University

Ron Higgins
Grand Rapids Community College

Martin Hochhauser
Dutchess Community College

Don Hoggan
Solano Community College

James D. Holland
Okaloosa-Waltoon Community College

Mary Carole Hollingsworth
Georgia Perimeter College, Clarkston

Stan Honacki
Moraine Valley Community College

Wayne Horn
Pensacola Junior College

Tom Hrubec
Waubonsee Community College

Jerry Humphrey
Tulsa Junior College

Christopher Hundhausen
University of Oregon

Alan Iliff
North Park College

Washington James
Collin County Community College–Plano

John Jansma
Palo Alto College, San Antonio, Texas

Jim Johnson
Valencia Community College

Linda Johnsonius
Murray State University, Murray, Kentucky

Julie Jordahl
Rock Valley College

Laleh Kalantari
Western Illinois University

Jan Karasz
Cameron University

Hak Joon Kim
Southern Connecticut State University, New Haven

Jorene Kirkland
Amarillo College

Victor Lafrenz
Mohawk Valley Community College

Sheila Lancaster
Gadsden State Community College

Dana Lasher
North Carolina State University

Stephen Leach
Florida State University

Paul Leidig
Grand Valley State University

Mary Levesque
University of Nebraska–Omaha

Andrew Levin
Delaware Valley College, Doylestown, Pennsylvania

Nicholas Lindquist
Arizona State University

Gina Long
Southwestern Community College

John Longstreet
Harold Washington College

Paul Lou
Diablo Valley College

Pamela Luckett
Barry University

Deborah Ludford
Glendale Community College

Evelyn Lulis
DePaul University

Peter MacGregor
Estrella Mountain Community College

Donna Madsen
Kirkwood Community College

Ed Mannion
California State University–Chico

Warren Mack
Northwest Vista College, San Antonio, Texas

Alan Maples
Cedar Valley College

Kenneth E. Martin
University of North Florida

Thomas Martin
Shasta College

Jerry Matejka
Adelphi University

Elizabeth McCarthy
Kirkwood Community College, Cedar Rapids, Iowa

Jacob McGinnis
Park University, Parkville, Missouri

Todd McLeod
Fresno City College

Curtis Meadow
University of Maine

Jennifer Merritt
Park University

Timothy Meyer
Edinboro University

Michael Michaelson
Palomar College

Cindy Minor
John A. Logan College

Norman Muller
Greenfield Community College

Rebecca Mundy
University of California, Los Angeles, and University of Southern California

Paul Murphy
Massachusetts Bay Community College

Kathleen Murray
Drexel University

Marry Murray
Portland Community College

Sonia Nayle
Los Angeles City College

Charles Nelson
Rock Valley College

Bruce Neubauer
Pittsburgh State University

Wanda Nolden
Delgado Community College

E. Gladys Norman
Linn-Benton Community College

George Novotny
Ferris State University

Janet Olpert
Cameron University

Pat Ormond
Utah Valley State College

John Panzica
Community College of Rhode Island

Rajesh Parekh
Iowa State University

Bettye Jewel Parham
Daytona Beach Community College

Merrill Parker
Chattanooga State Technical Community College

Michelle Parker
Indiana Purdue University

Marie Planchard
Massachusetts Bay Community College

Jim Potter
California State University–Hayward

Tammy Potter
West Kentucky Community & Technical College

Leonard Presby
William Patterson State College

William Pritchard
Wayne State University

Delores Pusins
Hillsborough Community College

Janak Rajani
Howard Community College Columbia, Maryland

Eugene Rathswohl
University of San Diego

Alan Rea
Western Michigan University

Jerry Reed
Valencia Community College

John Rezac
Johnson County Community College

Pattie Riden
Western Illinois University

Jane Ritter
University of Oregon

Fernando Rivera
University of Puerto Rico–Mayaguez Campus

Donald Robertson
Florida Community College–Jacksonville

Stan Ross
Newbury College

Russell Sabadosa
Manchester Community College

Behrooz Saghafi
Chicago State University

Greg Saxon
New Jersey Institute of Technology, Teaneck, New Jersey

Barbara Scantlebury
Mohawk Valley Community College, Utica, New York

Judy Scheeren
Westmoreland County Community College

Al Schroeder
Richland College

Dick Schwartz
Macomb County Community College

Earl Schweppe
University of Kansas

Susan Sells
Wichita State University

Tom Seymour
Minot State University

Naj Shaik
Heartland Community College

Morgan Shepherd
University of Colorado–Colorado Springs

Elaine Shillito
Clark State Community College

Jack Shorter
Texas A&M University

James Sidbury
University of Scranton

Stephanie Spike
Tallahassee Community College, Florida

Maureen Smith
Saddleback College

Diane Mayne-Stafford
Grossmont College

Esther Steiner
New Mexico State University

Randy Stolze
Marist College

Susan Taylor
Mount Wachusett Community College, Gardner, Massachusetts

Charlotte Thunen
Foothill College

Denis Tichenell
Los Angeles City College

Angela Tilaro
Butte College

Martha Tillman
College of San Mateo

David Trimble
Park University, Parkville, Missouri

DeLyse Totten
Portland Community College

Jack VanDeventer
Washington State University

Sue VanBoven
Paradise Valley Community College, Phoenix

James Van Tassel
Mission College

Jim Vogel
Sanford Brown College

Dale Walikainen
Christopher Newport University

Reneva Walker
Valencia Community College

Ron Wallace
Blue Mountain Community College

Nancy Webb
San Francisco City College

Steve Wedwick
Heartland Community College

Patricia Lynn Wermers
North Shore Community College

Cora Lee Whitcomb
Bentley College

Doug White
Western Michigan University

Anita Whitehill
Foothill College

Edward Winter
Salem State College

Floyd Winters
Manatee Community College

Chang-Yang Lin
Eastern Kentucky University

Israel Yost
University of New Hampshire

Alfred Zimermann
Hawai'i Pacific University

Eileen Zisk
Community College of Rhode Island.

Contents

1

INTRODUCTION to INFORMATION TECHNOLOGY: Your Digital World

Chapter Topics & Key Questions

1.1 **The Practical User: How Becoming Computer Savvy Benefits You** What does being *computer savvy* mean, and what are its practical payoffs?

1.2 **Information Technology & Your Life: The Future Now** What is information technology, and how does it affect education, health, money, leisure, government, and careers?

1.3 **Information Technology Is All-Pervasive: Cellphones, Email, the Internet, & the E-World** How does information technology facilitate email, networks, and the use of the Internet and the web; what is the meaning of the term *cyberspace?*

1.4 **The "All-Purpose Machine": The Varieties of Computers** What are the different sizes of computers, and what are clients and servers?

1.5 **Understanding Your Computer** What four basic operations do all computers use, and what are some of the devices associated with each operation? How does communications affect these operations?

1.6 **Where Is Information Technology Headed?** What are three directions of computer development and three directions of communications development?

Download the free UIT 10e App for key term flash cards, quizzes, and a game, *Over the Edge*

Information technology has blurred the line between professional and private lives.

Many people are "always on," accustomed to spending 8 hours or more a day looking at various screens—on cellphones, on computers, on TVs.[1] You are a "digital native," as one anthropologist put it, constantly busy with text messaging, email, and the Internet.[2] On the average, Americans spend about 13 hours a week watching TV and 12 hours a week on the Internet. That leaves about 31 hours a week for cellphone and various types of computer use.[3]

Panel 1.1 shows some statistics from 2010 about how people spend their time online.

What are the developments that have encouraged these kinds of behavior? The answer is *information technology*. Of the top 30 innovations from 1969 to 2009, according to a 2009 panel of judges at the University of Pennsylvania's Wharton School, *most were related to information technology.*[4] The first four items on the list, for example, are the Internet, broadband, and the World Wide Web; PC and laptop computers; mobile phones; and email. *(See • Panel 1.2.)* Indeed, semiconductors (processors) and the Internet rank among the 15 greatest innovations in all history, along with the invention of the number zero, money, printing, and participatory democracy.[5] And what are some of the hottest jobs for the future? Among others, CareerPlanner.com lists computer systems analyst, computer engineer, web specialist, network support technician, information technology manager, web developer, and database manager.

Unlike previous generations, you live in a world of *pervasive computing* or *ubiquitous computing*.

Central to this concept is the Internet—the "Net," or "net," that sprawling global connection of smaller computer networks that enable data transmission at high speeds. Everything that presently exists on a personal computer,

panel 1.1

Internet timeshares

Top 10 Sectors by Share of U.S. Internet Time

Rank	Subcategory	Share of Time June 2010	Share of Time June 2009	% Change in Share of Time
1	Social Networks	22.7%	15.8%	43%
2	Online Games	10.2%	9.3%	10%
3	Email	8.3%	11.5%	−28%
4	Portals	4.4%	5.5%	−19%
5	Instant Messaging	4.0%	4.7%	−15%
6	Videos/Movies	3.9%	3.5%	−12%
7	Search	3.5%	3.4%	−1%
8	Software Manufacturers	3.3%	3.3%	−0%
9	Multicategory Entertainment	2.8%	3.0%	−7%
10	Classified/Auctions	2.7%	2.7%	−2%
	Other	34.3%	37.3%	−8%

Source: The Nielsen Company
http://mashable.com/2010/08/02/stats-time-spent-online/

1.	Internet, broadband, World Wide Web	16.	Media file compression
2.	PC and laptop computers	17.	Microfinance
3.	Mobile phones	18.	Photovoltaic solar energy
4.	Email	19.	Large-scale wind turbines
5.	DNA testing and sequencing	20.	Internet social networking
6.	Magnetic resonance imaging	21.	Graphic user interface
7.	Microprocessors	22.	Digital photography
8.	Fiber optics	23.	RFID and applications
9.	Office software	24.	Genetically modified plants
10.	Laser/robotic surgery	25.	Bio fuels
11.	Open-source software	26.	Barcodes and scanners
12.	Light-emitting diodes	27.	ATMs
13.	Liquid crystal display	28.	Stents
14.	GPS devices	29.	SRAM flash memory
15.	E-commerce and auctions	30.	Antiretroviral treatment for AIDS

*To be more than just a new invention, an event was defined as an innovation if it created more opportunities for growth and development and if it had problem-solving value.

Source: Adapted from "A World Transformed: What Are the Top 30 Innovations of the Last 30 Years?" *Knowledge@Wharton*, February 18, 2009, *http://knowledge.wharton.upenn.edu/article.cfm?articleid=2163* (accessed May 28, 2009).

panel 1.2

Top innovations in recent years

The majority (23 of the 30) are in the field of information technology.*

experts suggest, will move onto the Internet, giving us greater mobility and wrapping the Internet around our lives. "We are using the Internet more and more to access applications that are provided to us over the Internet. . . . When all our essential software is provided to us through the Internet, all we'll need is an Internet connection, a monitor, keyboard, and a mouse."[6]

In this chapter we begin by discussing how becoming computer savvy can benefit you and how computing and the Internet affect your life. We then discuss cellphones, the Internet, the World Wide Web, and other aspects of the electronic world (e-world). Next we describe the varieties of computers that exist. We then explain three key concepts behind how a computer works and what goes into a personal computer, both hardware and software. We conclude by describing three directions of computer development and three directions of communications development. All these concepts are discussed in greater detail in subsequent chapters.

"Just keeping busy." Multiple electronic devices allow people to do multiple tasks simultaneously—multitasking.

1.1 THE PRACTICAL USER: How Becoming Computer Savvy Benefits You

Be computer savvy to win practical payoffs.

There is no doubt now that for most of us information technology is becoming like a second skin—an extension of our intellects and even emotions, creating almost a parallel universe of "digital selves." Perhaps you have been using computers a long time and in a multitude of ways, or perhaps not. In either case this book aims to deliver important practical rewards by helping you become "computer streetwise"—that is, computer savvy. Being *computer savvy* means knowing what computers can do and what they can't, knowing how

Competence. To be able to choose a computer system or the components to build one, you need to be computer savvy.

they can benefit you and how they can harm you, knowing when you can solve computer problems and when you have to call for help.

Among the practical payoffs are these:

MAKE BETTER BUYING DECISIONS No matter how much computer prices come down, you will always have to make judgments about quality and usefulness when buying equipment and software ("apps"). In fact, we start you off in this chapter by identifying the parts of a computer system, what they do, and about how much they cost. (Computer-based appliances, such as cellphones, cameras, and so on, are covered in later chapters.)

FIX ORDINARY COMPUTER PROBLEMS Whether it's replacing a printer cartridge, obtaining a software improvement ("patch" or "upgrade"), or pulling photos from your digital camera or cellphone's camera, we hope this book gives you the confidence to deal with the continual challenges that arise with computers—and know when and how to call for help.

UPGRADE YOUR EQUIPMENT & INTEGRATE NEW TECHNOLOGY New gadgetry and software are constantly being developed. A knowledgeable user learns under what conditions to upgrade, how to do so, and when to start over by buying a new machine.

USE THE INTERNET EFFECTIVELY The sea of data that exists on the Internet and other online sources is so great that finding what's best or what's really needed can be a hugely time-consuming activity. We hope to show you the most workable ways to approach this problem.

PROTECT YOURSELF AGAINST ONLINE DANGERS The online world poses real risks to your time, your privacy, your finances, and your peace of mind—spammers, hackers, virus developers, identity thieves, and companies and agencies constructing giant databases of personal profiles—as we will explain. This book aims to make you streetwise about these threats.

KNOW WHAT KINDS OF COMPUTER USES CAN ADVANCE YOUR CAREER Top executives use computers, as do people in careers ranging from police work to politics, from medicine to music, from retail to recreation. We hope you will come away from this book with ideas about how the technology can benefit you in whatever work you choose.

From now on, whenever you see the **more info!** icon in the margin, you'll find information about Internet sites to visit and how to search for terms related to the topic just discussed.

Along the way—in the Experience Boxes, Practical Action Boxes, Survival Tips, and More Info!s—we offer many kinds of practical advice that we hope will help you become truly computer savvy in a variety of ways, large and small.

1.2 INFORMATION TECHNOLOGY & YOUR LIFE: The Future Now

Information technology affects almost all aspects of our lives, including education, health, finance, recreation and entertainment, government, and jobs and careers.

This book is about computers, of course. But not just about computers. It is also about the way computers communicate with one another. When computer and communications technologies are combined, the result is *information*

technology, or "infotech." ***Information technology (IT)* is a general term that describes any technology that helps to produce, manipulate, store, communicate, and/or disseminate information.** IT merges computing with high-speed communications links carrying data, sound, and video. Examples of information technology include personal computers but also new forms of telephones, televisions, appliances, and various handheld devices.

Two Parts of IT: Computers & Communications

Information technology comprises both computer technology and communications technology.

Note that there are two important parts to information technology—computers and communications.

COMPUTER TECHNOLOGY You have certainly seen and probably used a computer. Nevertheless, let's define what it is. **A *computer* is a programmable, multiuse machine that accepts data—raw facts and figures—and processes, or manipulates, it into information we can use,** such as summaries, totals, or reports. Its main purpose is to speed up problem solving and increase productivity.

COMMUNICATIONS TECHNOLOGY Without question you've been using communications technology for years. ***Communications technology*, also called *telecommunications technology*, consists of electromagnetic devices and systems for communicating over long distances.** The principal examples are telephone, radio, satellite, broadcast television, and cable TV. We also have communication among computers—which is what happens when people "go online" on the Internet. In this context, ***online* means using a computer or some other information device, connected through a network, to access information and services from another computer or information device. A *network* is a communications system connecting two or more computers; the Internet is the largest such network.**

Information technology is already affecting your life in exciting ways and will do so even more in the future. Let's consider how.

Education: The Promise of More Interactive & Individualized Learning

Education has become heavily involved in information technology.

In her physics classes at the Massachusetts Institute of Technology, professor Gabriella Sciolla's high-tech classroom has white boards and huge display screens instead of blackboards. The professor can make brief presentations of general principles, then throw out multiple-choice questions that students "vote" on, using wireless "personal response clickers." These devices transmit the answers to a computer monitored by the professor, helping her gauge the level of understanding in the room. "You know where they are," she says. She can then adjust, slow down, or engage students in guided discussions of their answers.[7] Some sociology instructors have used similar technology to get students to answer questions about themselves—race, income, political affiliation—showing how,

Six-year-old girl plays a Sesame Street interactive program at Maxwell Memorial Library in Camilluis, New York.

Online Colleges

The following websites provide detailed information about getting college degrees online:

www.onlinecollegedegrees.net/

www.earnmydegree.com/index.html

www.classesusa.com/indexall/?campusType=online

www.guidetoonlineschools.com

www.usdla.org

http://distancelearn.about.com/ (includes information about bad programs, called diploma mills)

www.distancelearning.com/

www.elearners.com/resources/

Survival Tip

Choosing Online Colleges: Use Caution

Before signing up with an online college, make sure that you have the needed hardware, software, and connectivity. Make sure that you don't have to rely mostly on libraries. Be alert for deceptive marketing. Don't take on large loans and allow yourself to be kept enrolled in online programs as you amass more loan debt. Understand the time requirements. Make sure that the material is not too advanced and that you can get a degree in a reasonable amount of time. Ask for career counseling and help in finding a job after you have your degree.

for example, the class is skewed toward wealthier or poorer students, an event that can stir up a half hour of excited class discussion.[8]

Maybe the classrooms at your school haven't reached this level of interactivity yet, but there's no question that information technology is universal on college campuses, and at some levels the Internet has penetrated almost 100% of schools.[9] Most college students have been exposed to computers since the lower grades.

When properly integrated into the curriculum and the classroom, information technology can (1) allow students to personalize their education, (2) automate many tedious and rote tasks of teaching and managing classes, and (3) reduce the teacher's workload per student, so that the teacher can spend more time on reaching individual students.[10] For instance, ***email*, or "electronic mail," messages transmitted over a computer network, most often the Internet,** are used by students to set up appointments (62%) with professors, discuss grades (58%), or get clarification of an assignment (75%).[11]

Besides using the Internet to help in teaching, today's college instructors also use *presentation graphics software* such as PowerPoint to show their lecture outlines and other materials on classroom screens (as we discuss in Chapter 3). In addition, they use Blackboard (*www.blackboard.com*), It's Learning, Inc. (*www.itslearning.net/company*), and other *course-management software (CMS)* (or learning management systems) for administering online assignments, individual learning plans, schedules, examinations, and grades. One of the most intriguing developments in education at all levels, however, is the rise of ***distance learning*, or *e-learning*, the name given to online education programs,** which has gone from under 2 million online students in 2003, to 12.36 million in 2010, to an expected 25 million students in 2015.[12]

E-learning has had some interesting effects. For example, the availability of the Internet has helped to propel the home-schooling movement, in which children are taught at home, usually by parents, to expand from 1.7% of all school-age children in 1999 to 2.9% in 2007.[13] E-learning has also propelled the rise of for-profit institutions, such as Strayer University, Kaplan University, Colorado Technical Institute, and the University of Phoenix. More than a third of institutions of higher education—and 97% of public universities—offer online courses, and many have attracted on-campus students, who say they like the flexibility of not having to attend their classes at a set time.[14]

E-learning has been put to such varied uses as bringing career and technical courses to high school students in remote prairie towns, pairing gifted science students with master teachers in other parts of the country, and helping busy professionals obtain further credentials outside business hours. But the reach of information technology into education has only begun. "Intelligent tutoring systems" software is now available that gives students individualized instruction when personal attention is scarce—such as the software Cognitive Tutor, which not only helps high school students to improve their performance in math but also sparks them to enjoy a subject they might have once disliked. In colleges, more students may use interactive simulation games, such as McGraw-Hill's Business Strategy Game, to apply their knowledge to real-world kinds of problems. And employees in company training programs may find themselves engaged in mock conversations with ***avatars*—computer depictions of humans,** as are often found in online videogames—that represent imaginary customers and coworkers, combining the best parts of computer-based learning with face-to-face interaction.

Avatar. The simulated depictions of humans are a staple not only of videogames but also of computerized training programs. (What culture does "avatar" come from? See *www.answers.com/topic/avatar?cat=technology.*)

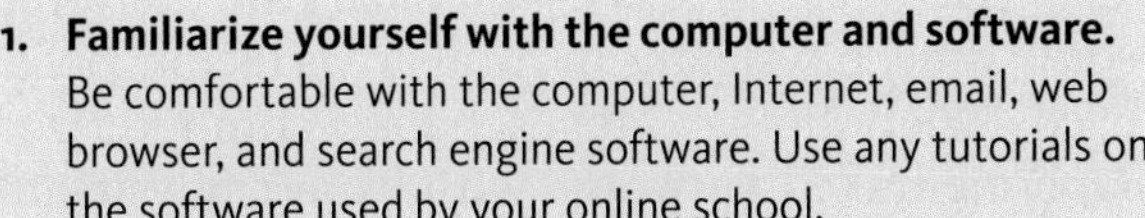

PRACTICAL ACTION

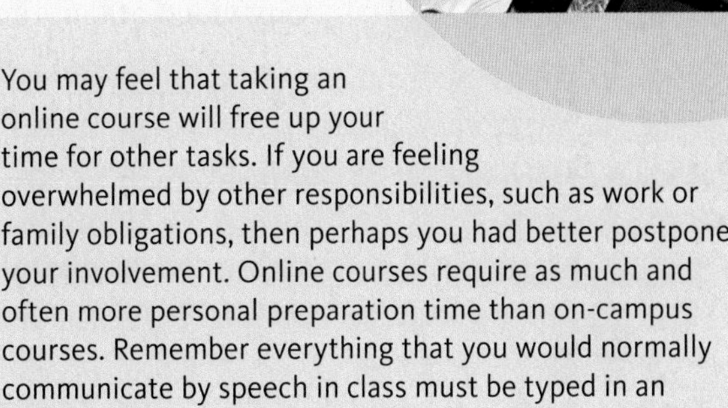

How to Be a Good Online Student

1. **Familiarize yourself with the computer and software.** Be comfortable with the computer, Internet, email, web browser, and search engine software. Use any tutorials on the software used by your online school.

   Take advantage of technology. Learn the various ways of communicating on the web. Blogging, podcasting, video conferencing, and chatting are tools that will help you with online studying.

2. **Do you have regular access to the Internet?** Do you have your own email account? It is necessary to maintain regular communication with the instructor with whom you are taking the course. *You must be able to answer your email quickly* during the school week, which means within 24 hours after receipt. And you should be able to successfully send and receive email with attachments. Students must have a reliable Internet Service Provider (ISP) and email account before the start of class. (Students are often required to use a school email account.)

3. **Read every document within your syllabus within the first five days of your online course.** This is usually the time to begin introducing yourself to your classmates and instructor and to start asking questions concerning the expectations described in the syllabus. You need to know what is expected of you.

   Know how to find assignments and course material, as well as be able to participate in and post to discussions and send emails with attachments.

4. **Are you comfortable working on your own? Are you self-motivated?** You will have flexible use of the time to spend on course work. Due dates are set by the instructor. Flexibility and independence are agreeable to some, but for others it is difficult to self-start. Be honest with yourself about your capabilities.

   It is the student's responsibility to take the course seriously and to be able to budget time to receive a successful grade. Make a schedule and stick to it.

5. **Can you make deadlines?** Your instructor is counting on you to finish your work on time. Your communication may be virtual (online), but your tasks and assigned deadlines are not.

   Be consistent in the amount of time you take to read and study. Every week you will be expected to read a chunk of pages from your textbook.

   Try not to get behind in your class work; try to stay on course or ahead. Some online learning programs move at an advanced rate, missing one week is like missing two in a traditional classroom.

6. **Is this the right time for you to take an online class?** You should be confident that you can set enough time aside for your online course assignments and study time. You may feel that taking an online course will free up your time for other tasks. If you are feeling overwhelmed by other responsibilities, such as work or family obligations, then perhaps you had better postpone your involvement. Online courses require as much and often more personal preparation time than on-campus courses. Remember everything that you would normally communicate by speech in class must be typed in an online course.

7. **You will need good written communication skills.** Remember, your primary means of communication is through writing. Being able to send well-structured messages and essays will help with the communication process.

8. **Pay attention to detail, particularly when following written directions.** Assignments, projects, and so on are posted in written form. Grades are drawn from work accomplished as directed. When grading assignments the instructor will look for competence in the work submitted. This means that all the required steps were followed and presented in a professional manner.

9. **Create a private study area.** This will help you focus on your studies without distractions and ensure that others do not disturb you while you are in your study area. Keep all your study materials here, so you know where to look for them.

10. **Interact with your peers.** Contribute and exchange your ideas, perspective, and comments with your virtual (online) classmates. Join online student communities and blogs.

11. **Interact with your faculty.** Constantly stay in touch with your professors. Consult them if you have technical difficulties or problems in understanding something related to the course. Since your professors cannot see you, you must be absolutely clear in expressing your ideas and needs.

12. **Evaluate and test yourself.** Take tests after thorough preparations. Don't hurry to take the tests; time them carefully. Have your work evaluated by fellow classmates.

13. **Netiquette: remember the dos and don'ts.** When you are online, be careful of netiquette (online etiquette). Both the real world and the virtual world are inhabited by people, so the same rules apply. Never be rude or disrespectful. Respect the privacy of other people.

Adapted from *www.olhcc.edu/Documents/academics/1%20Online%20Courses%20Are%20You%20Ready.pdf, www.brighthub.com/education/online-learning/articles/26877.aspx*, and *www.onlinedegreedirect.com/onlinedegreedirect-articles/10-Easy-Ways-to-Become-a-Good-Online-Student.htm.*

Health: High Tech for Wellness

Computers are now often used in the fields of health and medicine.

Neurologist Bart Demaerschalk of Phoenix, Arizona, was at home enjoying his Thanksgiving dessert when he received a message that a woman 200 miles away had developed drooping facial muscles and slurred speech. Within a few minutes, Demaerschalk was looking at her, asking questions, reviewing her brain scan, and confirming a diagnosis of stroke—all with the help of a two-way video and audio connection set up for just this kind of consultation.[15]

Damaerschalk's story is an example of *telemedicine*—medical care delivered via telecommunications. For some time, physicians in rural areas lacking local access to radiologists have used "teleradiology" to exchange computerized images such as X rays via telephone-linked networks with expert physicians in metropolitan areas. Now telemedicine is moving to an exciting new level, as the use of digital cameras and sound, in effect, moves patients to doctors rather than the reverse.

Carnegie Learning's Cognitive Tutor software:

www.carnegielearning.com/specs/cognitive-tutor-overview/

Computer technology is radically changing the tools of medicine. All medical information, including that generated by X ray, lab test, and pulse monitor, can be transmitted to a doctor in digital format. Image transfer technology allows radiologic images such as CT scans and MRIs to be immediately transmitted to electronic charts and physicians' offices. Patients in intensive care, who are usually monitored by nurses during off-times, can also be watched over by doctors in remote "control towers" miles away. Electronic medical records and other computerized tools enable heart attack patients to get follow-up drug treatment and diabetics to have their blood sugar measured. Software can compute a woman's breast cancer risk.[16]

Various ***robots*—automatic devices that perform functions ordinarily performed by human beings,** with names such as ROBO DOC, RoboCart,

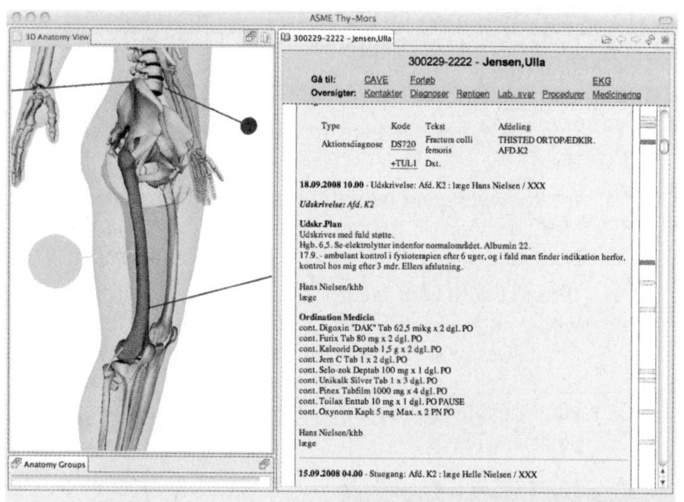

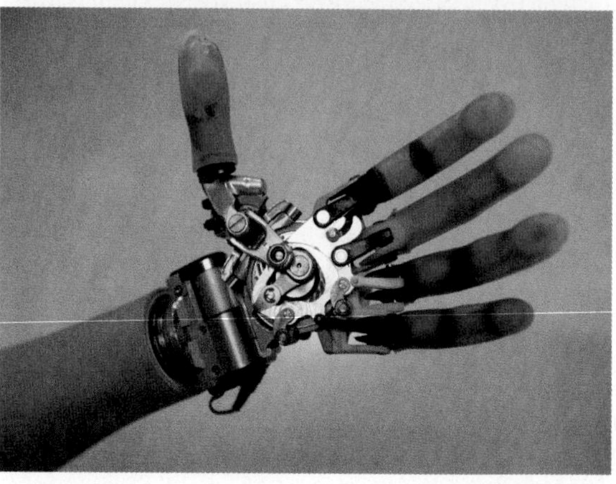

High-tech medicine. (*left*) Screenshot of the visual patient record software pioneered at Thy-Mors hospital. This patient has had a fracture of the femur in the right leg. This computer-based image shows a close-up view of the treated area. A click on the arrow or the highlighted femur would show the pertinent medical information from the record on the right panel. The tool allows doctors to easily zoom in and out on a particular body region or part and choose between many different views, for example, the cardiovascular system, the central nervous system, or the muscular system. (*right*) Open heart surgery is seen on a computer monitor as an Israeli medical team repairs a congenital defect in a boy's heart at the Wolfson Medical Center in Tel Aviv. (*bottom*) The Proto 1 bionic arm, created by Johns Hopkins University, a prototype of the first fully integrated prosthetic arm that can be controlled naturally and provide sensory feedback.

TUG, and HelpMate—help free medical workers for more critical tasks; the four-armed da Vinci surgical robot, for instance, can do the smallest incisions and stitches for complex surgery deep inside the body, so that surgery is less traumatic and recovery time faster. Hydraulics and computers are being used to help artificial limbs get "smarter,"[17] and pressure-sensitive artificial skin made of tiny circuits is expected to improve limbs' effectiveness.[18] An international team of researchers at the university of Tel Aviv is working on a biomimetic computer chip for brain stimulation that is programmable, responsive to neural activity, and capable of bridging broken connections in the brain. This device could be used to replace diseased or damaged brain tissue, restore brain functions lost to aging, and even treat epilepsy, chronic pain, and Parkinson's Disease.[19]

Want to calculate the odds on how long you will live? Go to *www.livingto100 .com*, an online calculator developed by longevity researchers at Harvard Medical School and Boston Medical Center. Want to gather your family health history to see if you're at risk for particular inherited diseases? Go to *www.hhs.gov/familyhistory* to find out how. These are only two examples of health websites available to patients and health consumers. Although online health information can be misleading and even dangerous (for example, be careful about relying on Wikipedia for health advice), many people now tap into health care databases, email health professionals, or communicate with people who have similar conditions.

Health Websites

Some reliable sources:

www.medlineplus.gov
www.nimh.nih.gov
www.womenshealth.gov/
www.mayoclinic.com
www.nationalhealthcouncil.org
www.yourdiseaserisk.wustl.edu/

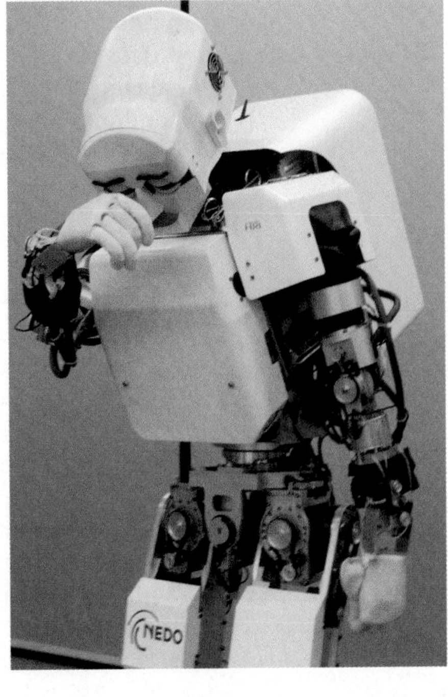

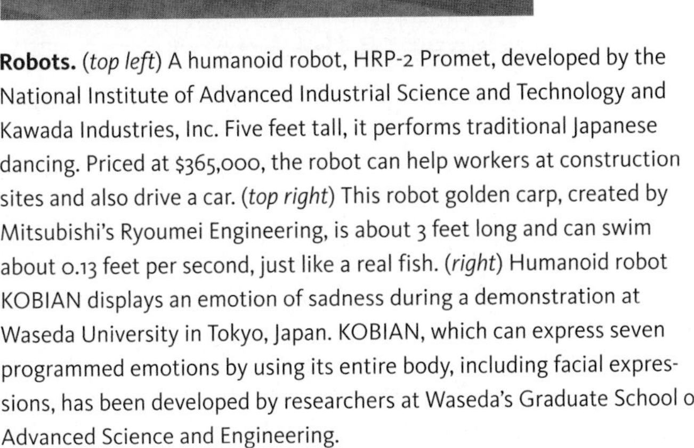

Robots. (*top left*) A humanoid robot, HRP-2 Promet, developed by the National Institute of Advanced Industrial Science and Technology and Kawada Industries, Inc. Five feet tall, it performs traditional Japanese dancing. Priced at $365,000, the robot can help workers at construction sites and also drive a car. (*top right*) This robot golden carp, created by Mitsubishi's Ryoumei Engineering, is about 3 feet long and can swim about 0.13 feet per second, just like a real fish. (*right*) Humanoid robot KOBIAN displays an emotion of sadness during a demonstration at Waseda University in Tokyo, Japan. KOBIAN, which can express seven programmed emotions by using its entire body, including facial expressions, has been developed by researchers at Waseda's Graduate School of Advanced Science and Engineering.

Money: Toward the Cashless Society

Information technology is reducing the use of traditional money.

Financial Information

The Internet contains lots of financial information. Some of the better sources:

www.financialcalculators.com/

www.mindpicnic.com/course/finance-for-beginners/

www.finance.yahoo.com

www.fool.com

www.ragingbull.com

www.usatoday.com/money/default.htm

"The future of money is increasingly digital, likely virtual, and possibly universal," says one writer.[20] ***Virtual* means that something is created, simulated, or carried on by means of a computer or a computer network—but that it is almost real**—and we certainly have come a long way toward becoming a cashless—and virtual money—society. The number of electronic (debit card, credit card, online checking, and automatic deductions) and regular check transactions taking place have reached record levels, surpassing 100 billion at the end of 2009, according to Moebs Services, an economic research firm. In the United States, online shoppers spent about $29 billion in 2009.[21]

Besides currency, paper checks, and credit and debit cards, the things that serve as "money" include cash-value cards (such as subway fare cards), automatic transfers (such as direct-deposit paychecks), and digital money ("electronic wallet" accounts such as PayPal).

You probably already have engaged in online buying and selling, purchasing DVDs, music, books, airline tickets, or computers. But what about groceries? After several years of slow growth, online groceries are expected to reach $7.5 billion in U.S. sales by 2012.[22] To change decades of shopping habits, e-grocers such as netgrocer.com and aulsuperstore.com try to keep their delivery charges low and delivery times convenient, although their product prices are generally higher than average.

Studies indicate that more than 70% of all workers in the United States receive their pay through direct deposit. Eighty percent of large companies (companies that employ more than 500 employees) offer direct deposit of employee wages. Many employers and employees consider direct deposit an important employee benefit. Educational institutions, state and federal governmental agencies, and retirement administrators often require direct deposit. Over 85% of people receiving social security benefits use direct deposit. Direct deposit is even more common outside the United States. Almost all European and Japanese workers receive their pay by direct deposit.[23]

But this is sure to change as Americans discover that direct deposit is actually safer and faster. Online bill paying is also picking up steam. For more than two decades, people have been able to pay bills online.

Some banks and other businesses are backing an electronic-payment system that allows Internet users to buy goods and services with *micropayments,* electronic payments of as little as 25 cents in transactions for which it is uneconomical to use a credit card. The success of Apple Computer's iTunes online music service, which sells songs for 69–99 cents each, suggests that micro sales are now feasible. All kinds of businesses and organizations, from independent songwriters to comic book writers to legal aid societies, now accept micropayments, using intermediaries such as One Pass, Pay Pal, and Carrot.org. Thus, you could set up your own small business simply by constructing a website (we show you how later in the book) and accepting micropayments.

Leisure: Infotech in Entertainment & the Arts

Information technology is transforming entertainment and the arts.

Information technology is being used for all kinds of entertainment, ranging from videogames to movies and streaming concerts. It is also being used in the arts, from painting to photography. Let's consider just two examples, music and film.

Computers, the Internet, and the World Wide Web are standing the system of music recording and distribution on its head—and in the process are changing the financial underpinnings of the music industry. Because of their high overhead, major record labels typically need a band to sell half a million CDs in order to be profitable, but independent bands, using online marketing,

can be reasonably successful selling 20,000 or 30,000 albums. Team Love, a small music label established in 2003, found it could promote its first two bands, Tilly and the Wall and Willy Mason, by offering songs online free for ***downloading*—transferring data from a remote computer to one's own computer**—so that people could listen to them before paying $12 for a CD. It also puts videos online for sharing and uses quirky websites to reach fans. "There's something exponential going on," says one of Team Love's founders. "The more music that's downloaded, the more it sells."[24] Many independent musicians are also using the Internet to get their music heard, hoping that giving away songs will help them build audiences.

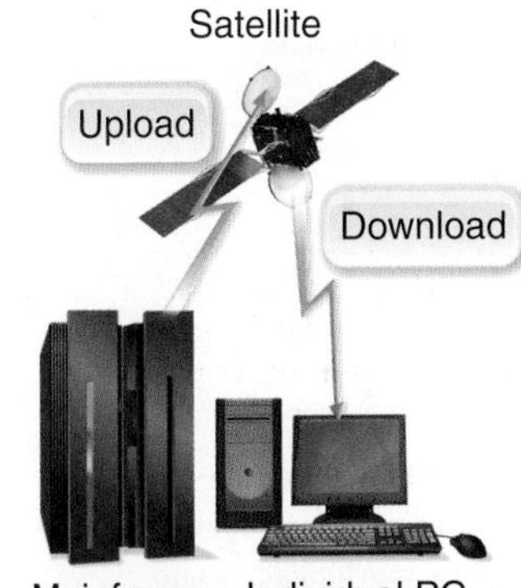

Download
(reverse the direction of data transmission to **upload**)

The web also offers sources for instantly downloadable sheet music (see *www.everynote.com, www.musicnotes.com, www.sheetmusicdirect.com,* and *www.freehandmusic.com/*). One research engineer has devised a computerized scoring system for judging musical competitions that overcomes the traditional human-jury approach, which can be swayed by personalities and politics.[25] And a Spanish company, Polyphonic HMI, has created Hit Song Science software, which they say can analyze the hit potential of new songs by, according to one description, "reference to a finely parsed universe of attributes derived from millions of past songs."[26] (Since 2005, some of the senior management team left HMI and formed Platinum Blue Music Intelligence, a competing company based in New York City.)

Movies are also downloadable on a pay-per-view basis to user's computers, TVs, and handheld devices via such companies as Netflix, iDownloadMoviesOnline.net, Apple iTunes, YouTube, and starz.com.

As for movies, now that blockbuster movies routinely meld live action and animation, computer artists are in big demand. Already in 1999 the film *Star Wars: Episode I*, for instance, had fully 1,965 digital shots out of about 2,200 shots. Even when film was used, it was scanned into computers to be tweaked with animated effects, lighting, and the like. Entire beings were created on computers by artists working on designs developed by producer George Lucas and his chief artist.[27] The 2009 film *Avatar* required 4,000 Hewlett-Packard computers with 35,000 microprocessors to create the special effects.[28]

What is driving the demand for computer artists? One factor is that animation, though not cheap, can look like a bargain, because hiring movie actors costs so much—some make $20 million or more a film. Moreover, special effects are readily understood by audiences in other countries, and major studios increasingly count on revenues from foreign markets to make a film profitable. Digital manipulation also allows a crowd of extras to be multiplied into an army of thousands. It can also be used to create settings: in the film *Sky Captain and the World of Tomorrow,* the actors—Gwyneth Paltrow, Angelina Jolie, and Jude Law—shot all their scenes in front of a blue screen, and computer-generated imagery was then used to transport them into an imaginary world

more info!

Free Music Online

Places to look for free—and legal—music online:

new.music.yahoo.com

www.epitonic.com

http://memory.loc.gov/ammem/audio.html

www.archive.org

Entertainment. (*left*) Computer-generated special effects shot from the movie *Avatar.* (*right*) The computer-controlled ski center at the Mall of the Emirates, Dubai City, United Arab Emirates.

Online Movie Tickets

Three sites offer movie tickets, as well as reviews and other materials. In some cities you can print out tickets at home.

www.fandango.com
www.moviefone.com
www.movietickets.com

of 1939.[29] Computer techniques have even been used to develop digitally created actors—called "synthespians." (Thespis was the founder of ancient Greek drama; thus, a thespian works in drama as an actor.) Actors ranging from the late James Dean to the late John Wayne, for instance, have been recruited for new television commercials. And computerized animation is now so popular that Hollywood studios and movie directors are finding they can make as much money from creating videogames as from making movies.[30]

But animation is not the only area in which computers are revolutionizing movies. Digital editing has radically transformed the way films are assembled. Whereas traditional film editing involved reeling and unreeling spools of film and cutting and gluing pieces of highly scratchable celluloid together, nearly burying the editor in film, today an editor can access 150 miles of film stored on a computer and instantly find any visual or audio moment, allowing hundreds of variations of a scene to be called up for review. Even nonprofessionals can get into movie making as new computer-related products come to market. Now that digital video capture-and-edit systems are available for under $1,000, amateurs can turn home videos into digital data and edit them. Also, digital camcorders, which offer outstanding picture and sound quality, have steadily dropped in price.

Government & Electronic Democracy: Participating in the Civic Realm

Information technology is changing voting procedures and affecting the spread of political movements.

The Internet and other information technology have helped government deliver better services and have paved the way for making governmental operations more transparent to the public. For instance, during a health crisis involving salmonella-tainted peanut butter, the U.S. Food and Drug Administration sent out information 707 times per minute in response to citizens seeking information about it.[31] The U.S. State Department has a "DipNote" blog read by more than 2 million readers, and it holds press conferences on YouTube.[32] Congress has a publicly searchable website for all federal contracts and grants over $25,000, and a growing number of states are putting everything from budgets to contracts to travel expenses online for the public to look

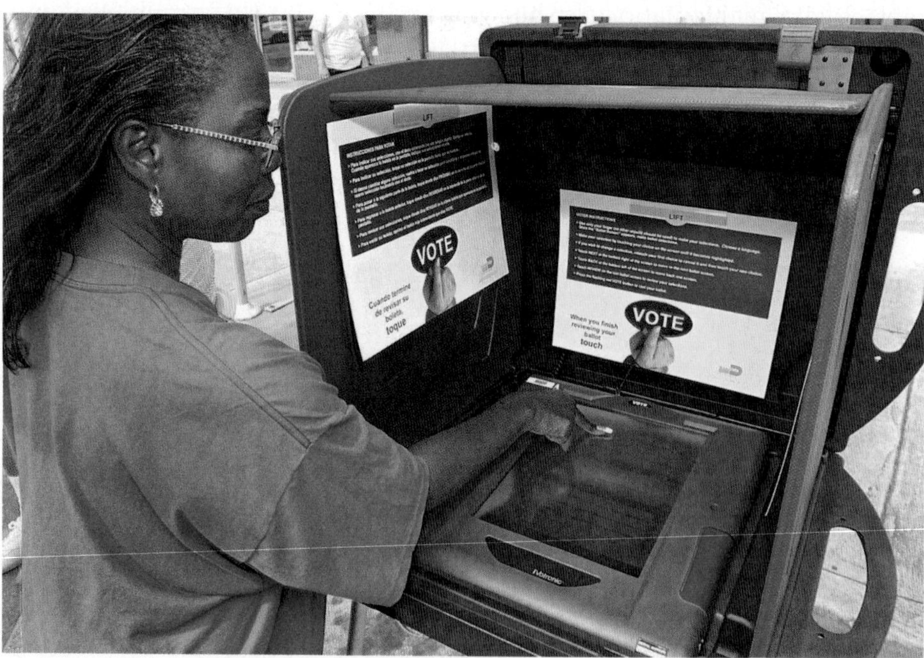

Electronic voting. Voting using computer technology and a touch screen to vote.

at. The White House also has its own website (*www.whitehouse.gov*) with its Open Government Dialogue blog. Many local and state governments also have websites through which citizens can deal with everything from paying taxes and parking tickets, to renewing vehicle registration and driver's licenses, viewing birth and marriage certificates, and applying for public sector jobs.

The Internet is also changing the nature of politics, enabling political candidates and political interest groups to connect with voters in new ways, to raise money from multiple small donors instead of just wealthy groups, and (using cellphones and text messaging) to organize street protests. Yet information also has its downside, as computers have helped incumbent legislators to design (gerrymander) voting districts that make it nearly impossible for them to be dislodged; electronic tools have also made it easier for political parties to skirt campaign laws, and computerized voting machines still don't always count votes as they are supposed to. Still, websites and bloggers have become important watchdogs on government. The website E-Democracy (*http://forums.e-democracy.org/*), for instance, can help citizens dig up government conflicts of interest, and websites such as Project Vote Smart (*www.votesmart.org*) outline candidates' positions.

Online Government Help

You can gain access to government agencies through the following websites:

www.usa.gov/

www.govspot.com

www.info.gov

Jobs & Careers

People now use computers to post résumés and find jobs.

Today almost every job and profession requires computer skills of some sort. Some are ordinary jobs in which computers are used as ordinary tools. Others are specialized jobs in which advanced computer training combined with professional training gives people dramatically new kinds of careers.

Consider:

- In the hotel business, even front-desk clerks need to know how to deal with computer-based reservation systems. Some hotels, however, also have a so-called computer concierge, someone with knowledge of computer systems who can help computer-carrying guests with online and other tech problems. And guests can check themselves in at many hotels, at computer desks.
- In law enforcement, police officers need to know how to use computers while on patrol or at their desks to check out stolen cars, criminal records, outstanding arrest warrants, and the like. However, investigators with specialized computer backgrounds are also required to help solve fraud, computer break-ins, accounting illegalities, and many other high-tech crimes.
- In entertainment, computers are used for such ordinary purposes as budgets, payroll, and ticketing. However, there are also new careers in virtual set design, combining training in architecture and 3-D computer modeling, and, as we discussed, in creating cinematic special effects.
- In the restaurant business, small computer-based devices are used tableside for menu display and ordering options. The new Hard Rock Cafe restaurant in Las Vegas has an 18-feet wide by 4-feet tall interactive touch wall that acts as a touch screen *(see next page)*. A guest can access and expand a single image or video to be as large as the wall itself; or up to six guests can explore their own collections in dynamic "zones" simultaneously. The restaurant chain also provides incredible graphics on a touch-based interface for 38 of the cafe's booths, where guests can explore memorabilia, look at merchandise, and vote on what video plays next in the cafe. Guests can also plug in to the in-house music video system to cast their vote on the next song.

Interactive touch wall at the Hard Rock Cafe in Las Vegas. This 18-feet wall provides a 6-person multitouch experience that allows visitors to browse the growing database of Hard Rock memorabilia. The experience is designed to have touch "stalls" where 1 to 6 users can stand and select an image to be zoomed into and pull up related information.

Careers. Front-desk workers at many hotels use computers to check guests in.

Clearly, information technology is changing old jobs and inventing new ones. To prosper in this environment, you need to combine a traditional education with training in computers and communications. You also need to be savvy about job searching, résumé writing, interviewing, and postings of employment opportunities. Advice about careers, job hunting, occupational trends, and employment laws is available at Yahoo!, Google, and other websites. Some average salaries for college and postgraduate graduates are shown in the chart; we discuss the information-technology-related jobs later in the book. (● *See Panel 1.3.)*

Police work. Syracuse, New York: An Onondaga County sheriff's deputy enters information into a laptop in his squad car as he issues a ticket for an uninspected vehicle.

Discipline (bachelor's degree)	Current average starting salary
Family practice physician	$172,740
Computer systems manager	$133,194
Website designer/graphics creator	$102,794
Computer science professor	$97,060
Entry-level attorney	$88,450
Petroleum engineer	$86,220
History professor	$84,823
University English professor	$79,612
Registered nurse	$71,692
Chemical engineer	$65,142
Computer science job	$61,205
Computer engineer	$60,879
Electrical/electronics engineer	$59,131
Mechanical engineer	$58,392
Industrial/manufacturing engineer	$57,734
Management information systems job	$54,038
High school teacher	$53,504
Computer equipment repair job	$50,291
Finance worker	$49,607
Accountant	$47,982
Business administrator/manager	$45,200
Computer game designer	$44,211
Marketing/marketing manager	$43,485
Crime lab analyst	$39,568
Preschool teacher	$38,413

panel 1.3

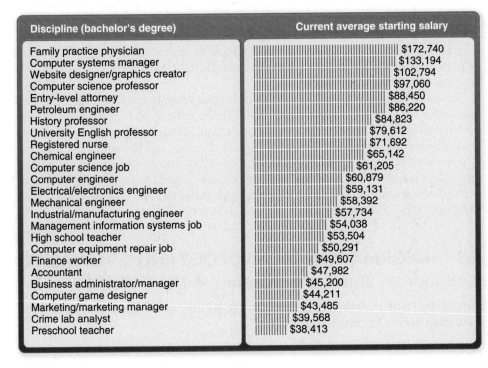

Entering the job market
Average 2010 salaries (data from National Association of Colleges and Employers; TheProfessionalEngineer.com; SalaryExpert.com; MySalary.com)

Computers can be used both for you to find employers and for employers to find you.

WAYS FOR YOU TO FIND EMPLOYERS As you might expect, the first to use cyberspace as a job bazaar were companies seeking people with technical backgrounds and technical people seeking employment. However, as the public's interest in commercial services and the Internet exploded, the focus of online job exchanges broadened. Now, interspersed among ads for programmers on the Internet are openings for forest rangers in Idaho, physical therapists in Atlanta, models in Florida, and English teachers in China. Most websites are free to job seekers, although many require that you fill out an online registration form. *(• See Panel 1.4.)*

Survival Tip

Some Basic Computer Skills Needed for Office Jobs

Keyboarding (typing)
Microsoft Word
Microsoft Excel
Internet browser and email (communications both on the Internet and within a business environment)
File sharing

WAYS FOR EMPLOYERS TO FIND YOU Posting your résumé online for prospective employers to view is attractive because of its low (or zero) cost and wide reach. But does it have any disadvantages? Certainly it might if the employer who sees your posting happens to be the one you're already working for. In addition, you have to be aware that you lose control over anything broadcast into cyberspace. You're putting your credentials out there for the whole world to see, and you need to be somewhat concerned about who might gain access to them.

If you have a technical background, it's definitely worth posting your résumé with an electronic jobs registry, since technology companies in particular find this an efficient way of screening and hiring. However, posting may also benefit

panel 1.4

Some websites that post job listings

Career Builder: *www.careerbuilder.com*
Career One Stop: *www.careeronestop.org*
College Grad Job Hunter: *www.collegegrad.com*
Experience: *www.experience.com*
FedWorld (U.S. Government jobs): *www.fedworld.gov*
Indeed.com: *www.indeed.com*
Jobs.com: *www.jobs.com*
Jobs on Line: *www.jobsonline.com*
MonsterCollege: *www.jobtrak.com*
Monster.com: *www.monster.com*
Monster + Yahoo! Hot Jobs: *http://hotjobs.yahoo.com*
NationJob Network: *www.nationjob.com*
Simply Hired: *www.simplyhired.com*
U.S. Dept. of Labor: *www.bls.gov/oco/*

Computer Basic Skills Test

A computer basic skills test is usually a prerequisite for a job or placement companies:

www.cvtips.com/interview/computer-basic-skills-test-job-interview-tips.html

people with less technical backgrounds. Online recruitment is popular with companies because it prescreens applicants for at least basic computer skills. If you've mastered the Internet, you're likely to know something about word processing, spreadsheets, and database searching as well, knowledge required in most good jobs these days.

A number of websites allow you to post your résumé for free. But you often can pay a fee to move your résumé higher in the listings so that it will stand out compared with competing résumés. For example, Careerbuilder.com will move your résumé listing toward the top of the search heap, and the company says that employers click on upgraded résumés 25%–190% more often than on regular ones, depending on the level of exposure the user wishes to pay for (up to $150).

And always remember: lack of computer skills will get in the way of your finding a job—almost any job.

1.3 INFORMATION TECHNOLOGY IS ALL-PERVASIVE: Cellphones, Email, the Internet, & the E-World

Email, networks, Internet, web, smartphone, ***and*** **cyberspace** ***are now common terms in many languages.***

One of the first computers, the outcome of military-related research, was delivered to the U.S. Army in 1946. ENIAC (short for "Electronic Numerical Integrator And Calculator") weighed 30 tons and was 80 feet long and two stories high, but it could multiply a pair of numbers in the then-remarkable time of three-thousandths of a second. (• *See Panel 1.5.*) This was the first general-purpose, programmable electronic computer, the grandparent of today's lightweight handheld machines—including the smart cellphone. Some of the principal historical developments are illustrated in the timeline below. (• *See Panel 1.6.*)

The Phone Grows Up

The telephone is not what it used to be.

Cellphone e-mania has swept the world. All across the globe, people have acquired the portable gift of gab, with some users making 45 or more calls a day. Strategy Analytics has estimated that worldwide mobile phone subscriptions will rise to 3.9 billion in 2013; more than half the world's population are using mobile phones in 2010.[33] And about 82% of Americans own a cellphone.[34] It has taken more than 100 years for the telephone to get to this point—getting smaller, acquiring push buttons, losing its cord connection. In 1964 the * and # keys were added to the keypad. In 1973 the first cellphone call was processed.

In its most basic form the telephone is still so simply designed that even a young child can use it. However, it is now becoming more versatile and complex—a way of connecting to the Internet and the World Wide Web. Indeed, Internet

4000–1200 BCE	3500 BCE–2900 BCE	3000 BCE	1270 BCE	900 BCE	530 BCE	100 CE
Inhabitants of the first known civilization in Sumer keep records of commericial transactions on clay tablets	Phoenicians develop an alphabet; Sumerians develop cuneiform writing; Egyptians develop hierogylphic writing	Abacus is invented in Babylonia	First encyclopedia (Syria)	First postal service (China)	Greeks start the first library	First bound books

panel 1.5

Grandparent and offspring
ENIAC (*left*) is the grandparent of today's iPads (*right*).

smartphones—such as the Apple iPhone, Android, T-Mobile and LG models, the Samsung Infuse, the Blackberry, and the Motorola Atrix—represent another giant step for information technology. Now you no longer need a personal computer to get on the Internet. Smartphones in their various forms enable you not only to make voice calls but also to send and receive email and text messages, take and send photos and videos, browse the World Wide Web, get map directions, and obtain news, research, music, photos, movies, and TV programs.

"You've Got Mail!" Email's Mass Impact

Email revolutionized communication, but it is not without problems and may already be dying out.

It took the telephone 40 years to reach 10 million customers, and fax machines 20 years. Personal computers made it into that many American homes 5 years after they were introduced. Email, which appeared in 1981, became popular far more quickly, reaching 10 million users in little more than a year.[35] No technology has ever become so universal so fast. Thus, one of the first things new computer and Internet users generally learn is how to send and receive email.

Until 1998 hand-delivered mail was still the main means of correspondence. But in that year the volume of email in the United States surpassed the volume of hand-delivered mail. In 2009 the total number of email messages sent daily was estimated at 247 billion worldwide.[36]

Using electronic mail clearly is different from calling on a telephone or writing a conventional letter. As one writer puts it, email "occupies a psychological space all its own. It's almost as immediate as a phone call, but if you need to, you

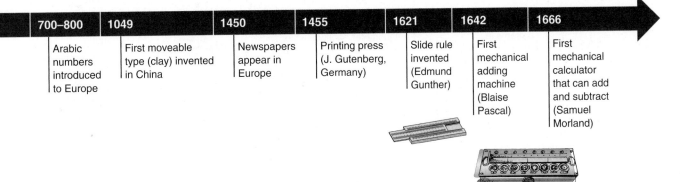

panel 1.6

Timeline
Overview of some of the historical developments in information technology. In upcoming chapters we modify the timelines to show you more about the people and advances contributing to developments in information technology.

700–800	1049	1450	1455	1621	1642	1666
Arabic numbers introduced to Europe	First moveable type (clay) invented in China	Newspapers appear in Europe	Printing press (J. Gutenberg, Germany)	Slide rule invented (Edmund Gunther)	First mechanical adding machine (Blaise Pascal)	First mechanical calculator that can add and subtract (Samuel Morland)

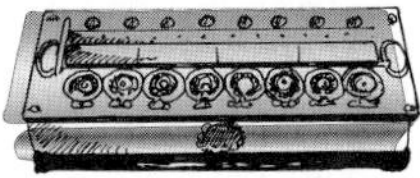

Smartphones. (*left*) Apple 4G iPhone; (*middle*) EVO 4G smartphone; (*right*) Nexus smartphone

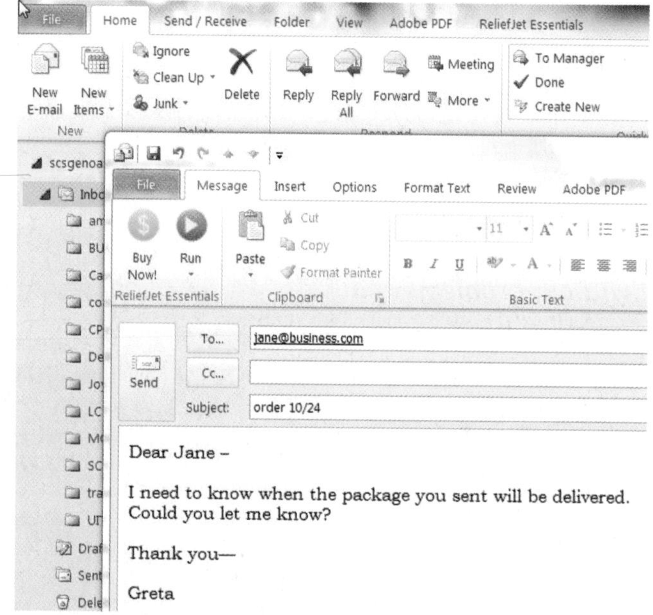

can think about what you're going to say for days and reply when it's convenient."[37] Email has been popular, points out another writer, not because it gives us more immediacy but because it gives us *less*. "The new appeal of email is the old appeal of print," he says. "It isn't instant; it isn't immediate; it isn't in your face." Email has succeeded for the same reason that the videophone—which allows callers to see each other while talking—has been so slow to catch on: because "what we actually want from our exchanges is the minimum human contact commensurate with the need to connect with other people."[38] However, the lack of face-to-face contact and communication has proven to be isolating and a problem for many people, as we discuss in a later chapter.

In 2010 email started to lose in popularity to texting and such social networking sites as Twitter and Facebook, which we discuss in Chapter 2.

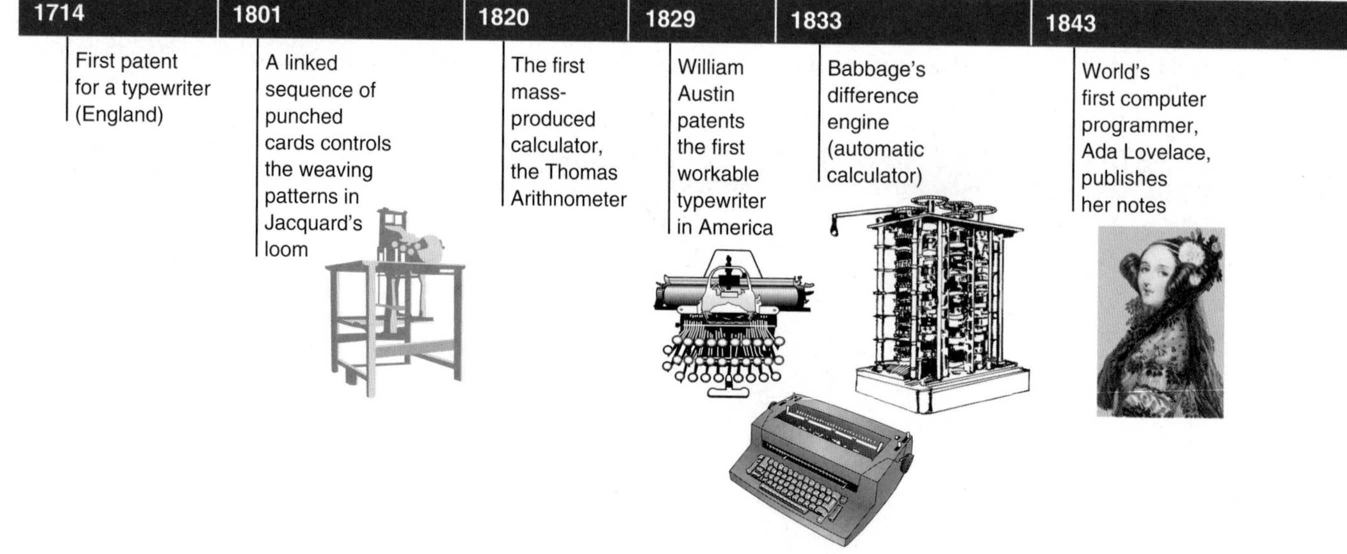

1714
First patent for a typewriter (England)
1801
A linked sequence of punched cards controls the weaving patterns in Jacquard's loom
1820
The first mass-produced calculator, the Thomas Arithnometer
1829
William Austin patents the first workable typewriter in America
1833
Babbage's difference engine (automatic calculator)
1843
World's first computer programmer, Ada Lovelace, publishes her notes

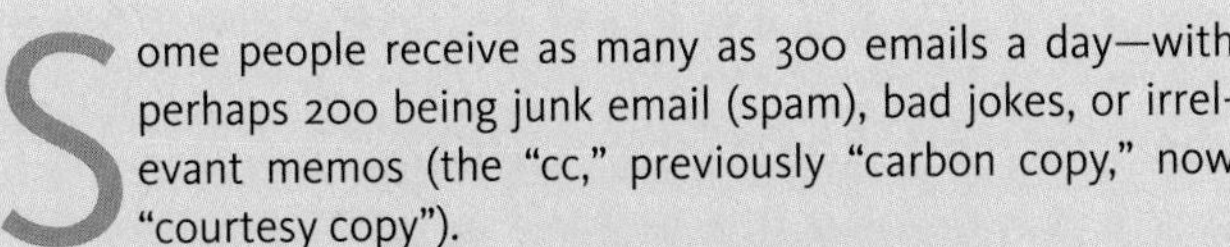

PRACTICAL ACTION

Managing Your Email

Some people receive as many as 300 emails a day—with perhaps 200 being junk email (spam), bad jokes, or irrelevant memos (the "cc," previously "carbon copy," now "courtesy copy").

It's clear, then, that email increases productivity only if it is used properly. Overuse or misuse just causes more problems and wastes time. The following are some ideas to keep in mind when using email:

- *Do your part to curb the email deluge:* Put short messages in the subject line so that recipients don't have to open the email to read the note. Don't reply to every email message you get. Avoid "cc:ing" (copying to) people unless absolutely necessary. Don't send chain letters or lists of jokes, which just clog mail systems.
- *Be helpful in sending attachments:* Attachments—computer files of long documents or images attached to an email—are supposed to be a convenience, but often they can be an annoyance. Sending large files to a 500-person mailing list creates 500 copies of those files—and that many megabytes can clog the mail system.
- *Be careful about opening attachments you don't recognize:* Some dangerous computer viruses—renegade programs that can damage your computer—have been spread by email attachments that automatically activate the virus when they are opened.
- *Use discretion about the emails you send:* Email should not be treated as informally as a phone call. Don't send a message electronically that you don't want some third party to read. Email messages are not written with disappearing ink; they remain in a computer system long after they have been sent. Worse, recipients can easily copy and even alter your messages and forward them to others without your knowledge.
- *Make sure emails to bosses, coworkers, and customers are literate:* It's okay to be informal when emailing friends, but employers and customers expect a higher standard. Pay attention to spelling and grammar.
- *Don't use email to express criticism and sarcasm:* Because email carries no tone or inflection, it's hard to convey emotional nuances. Avoid criticism and sarcasm in electronic messaging. Nevertheless, you can use email to provide quick praise, even though doing it in person will take on greater significance.
- *Be aware that email you receive at work is the property of your employer:* Be careful of what you save, send, and back up.
- *Realize that deleting email messages doesn't totally get rid of them:* "Delete" moves the email from the visible list, but the messages remain on your hard disk and can be retrieved by experts. (Special software, such as Spytech Eradicator and Window Washer, can completely erase email from the hard disk; we cover this later.)

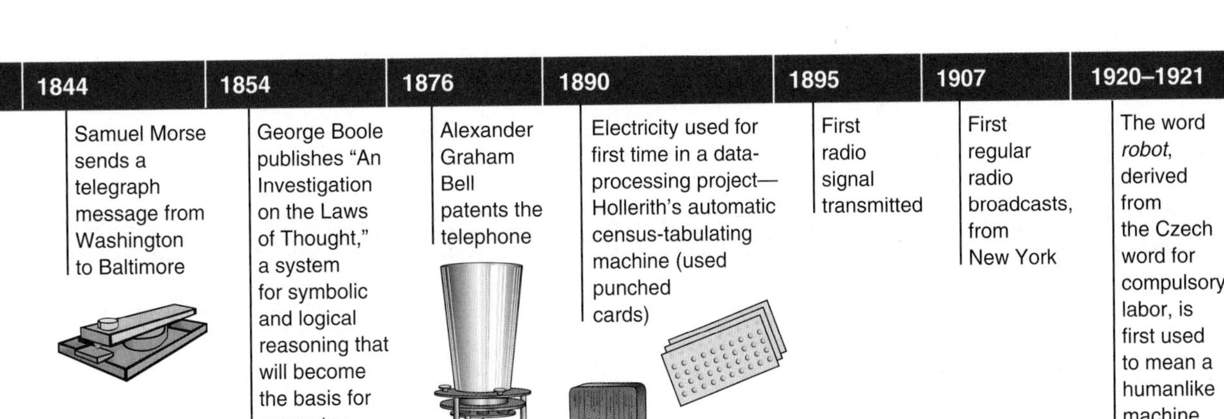

1844
Samuel Morse sends a telegraph message from Washington to Baltimore
1854
George Boole publishes "An Investigation on the Laws of Thought," a system for symbolic and logical reasoning that will become the basis for computer design
1876
Alexander Graham Bell patents the telephone
1890
Electricity used for first time in a data-processing project—Hollerith's automatic census-tabulating machine (used punched cards)
1895
First radio signal transmitted
1907
First regular radio broadcasts, from New York
1920–1921
The word *robot*, derived from the Czech word for compulsory labor, is first used to mean a humanlike machine

What is interesting, though, is that in these times, when images often seem to overwhelm words, email is actually *reactionary*. "The Internet is the first new medium to move decisively backward," points out one writer, because it essentially involves writing. Twenty years ago, "even the most literate of us wrote maybe a half a dozen letters a year; the rest of our lives took place on the telephone."[39] Email has changed all that—and has put pressure on businesspeople in particular to sharpen their writing skills. (A countertrend, unfortunately, is that the informal style of electronic messages, especially texting, is showing up in schoolwork.)[40]

The Internet, the World Wide Web, & the "Plumbing of Cyberspace"

The net, the web, and cyberspace are not the same things.

As the success of the cellphone shows, communications has extended into every nook and cranny of civilization (with poorer nations actually the leaders in cellphone growth), a development called the "plumbing of cyberspace." The term *cyberspace* was conceived by William Gibson in his novel *Neuromancer* (1984) to describe a futuristic computer network into which users plug their brains. (*Cyber* comes from "cybernetics," a term coined in 1948 to apply to the comparative study of automatic control systems, such as the brain/nervous system and mechanical-electrical communication systems.) In everyday use, this term has a rather different meaning.

Always on. Most of today's students don't remember a time before the existence of cyberspace.

Today many people equate cyberspace with the Internet. But it is much more than that. Cyberspace includes not only the web, chat rooms, online diaries (blogs), and member-based services such as America Online—all features we explain in this book—but also such things as conference calls and automatic teller machines. We may say, then, that ***cyberspace*** **encompasses not only the online world and the Internet in particular but also the whole wired and wireless world of communications in general**—the nonphysical terrain created by computer and communications systems. Cyberspace is where you go when you go online with your computer.

THE NET & WEB DEFINED The two most important aspects of cyberspace are the Internet and that part of the Internet known as the World Wide Web. To give them formal definition:

- **The Internet—"the mother of all networks":** The Internet is at the heart of the Information Age. Called "the mother of all networks," the ***Internet*** **(the "net") is a worldwide computer network that connects hundreds**

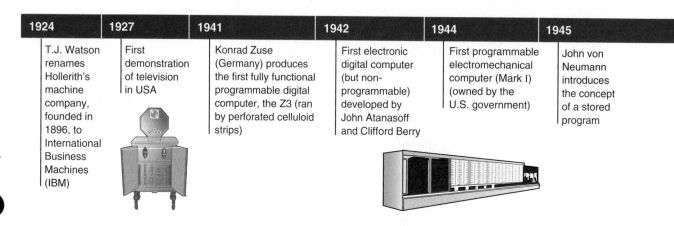

1924	1927	1941	1942	1944	1945
T.J. Watson renames Hollerith's machine company, founded in 1896, to International Business Machines (IBM)	First demonstration of television in USA	Konrad Zuse (Germany) produces the first fully functional programmable digital computer, the Z3 (ran by perforated celluloid strips)	First electronic digital computer (but non-programmable) developed by John Atanasoff and Clifford Berry	First programmable electromechanical computer (Mark I) (owned by the U.S. government)	John von Neumann introduces the concept of a stored program

of thousands of smaller networks. These networks link educational, commercial, nonprofit, and military entities, as well as individuals.

- **The World Wide Web—the multimedia part of the Internet:** The Internet has been around for more than 40 years. But what made it popular, apart from email, was the development in the early 1990s of the ***World Wide Web*, often called simply the "Web" or the "web"—an interconnected system of Internet computers (called *servers*) that support specially formatted documents in multimedia form.** The word *multimedia*, from "multiple media," refers to technology that presents information in more than one medium, such as text, still images, moving images, and sound. In other words, the web provides information in more than one way.

Brief History of the Internet

We cover the Internet in more detail in the next chapter, But if you would like a brief history of the Internet now, go to:

www.isoc.org/internet/history/brief.shtml

THE INTERNET'S INFLUENCE There is no doubt that the influence of the net and the web is tremendous. At present, about 74% of American adults use the Internet, according to the Pew Internet & American Life Project.[41] Seventy-two percent of American adult Internet users use the net on an average day, with 60% using it to send or read email.[42] But just how revolutionary is the Internet? Is it equivalent to the invention of television, as some technologists say? Or is it even more important—equivalent to the invention of the printing press? "Television turned out to be a powerful force that changed a lot about society," says *USA Today* technology reporter Kevin Maney. "But the printing press changed everything—religion, government, science, global distribution of wealth, and much more. If the Internet equals the printing press, no amount of hype could possibly overdo it."[43]

College Students & the E-World

Students use information technology in different ways—for study and research, for entertainment, for communication and social interaction.

One thing we know already is that cyberspace is saturating our lives. The worldwide Internet population was 1.97 billion (or nearly 28% of the world's population in 2010). About 266 million of those users were in North America, representing a penetration of 77% of the population. While the average age of users is rising, there's no doubt that people ages 18–29 love the Internet, with about 87% of them using it; among all users with a college education, 95% use the net.[44]

Teens and young adults (age 18–32) are the most likely of all groups to use the Internet for communicating with friends and family; for entertainment—especially online videos, online games, and virtual worlds (such as for multiplayer online role-playing games)—and for obtaining music. They are also considerably more likely than older users to use social networking sites—online communities, such as Facebook and Twitter, that allow members to

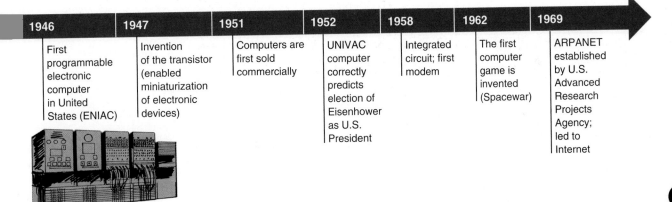

1946	1947	1951	1952	1958	1962	1969
First programmable electronic computer in United States (ENIAC)	Invention of the transistor (enabled miniaturization of electronic devices)	Computers are first sold commercially	UNIVAC computer correctly predicts election of Eisenhower as U.S. President	Integrated circuit; first modem	The first computer game is invented (Spacewar)	ARPANET established by U.S. Advanced Research Projects Agency; led to Internet

keep track of their friends and share photos, videos, and the like. In addition, young people are more apt to send instant messages and to do text messaging (texting) with friends—send brief written messages between cellphones.[45] We consider all these technologies later in the book.

1.4 THE "ALL-PURPOSE MACHINE": The Varieties of Computers

Computers come in different sizes; they also function as clients and/or servers.

When the ★alarm clock blasts you awake, you leap out of bed and head for the kitchen, where you check the ★coffee maker. After using your ★electronic toothbrush and showering and dressing, you stick a bagel in the ★microwave, and then pick up the ★TV remote and click on the ★TV to catch the weather forecast. Later, after putting dishes in the ★dishwasher, you go out and start up the ★car and head toward campus or work. Pausing en route at a ★traffic light, you turn on your ★iPod to listen to some music. And you might use your ★GPS system to get to your destination.

You haven't yet touched a PC, a personal computer, but you've already dealt with at least 11 computers—as you probably guessed from the ★s. All these familiar appliances rely on tiny "computers on chips" called *microprocessors*. Maybe, then, the name "computer" is inadequate. As computer pioneer John von Neumann has said, the device should not be called the computer but rather the "all-purpose machine." It is not, after all, just a machine for doing calculations. The most striking thing about it is that it can be put to *any number of uses*.

What are the various types of computers? Let's take a look.

All Computers, Great & Small: The Categories of Machines

There are five basic computer sizes.

At one time, the idea of having your own computer was almost like having your own personal nuclear reactor. In those days, in the 1950s and 1960s, computers were enormous machines affordable only by large institutions. Now they come in a variety of shapes and sizes, which can be generally classified according to their processing power: *supercomputers, mainframe computers, workstations, microcomputers,* and *microcontrollers*. We also consider *servers*.

Supercomputers

Supercomputers are used in very special situations.

Typically priced from $1 million to more than $350 million, ***supercomputers*** **are high-capacity machines with thousands of processors that can**

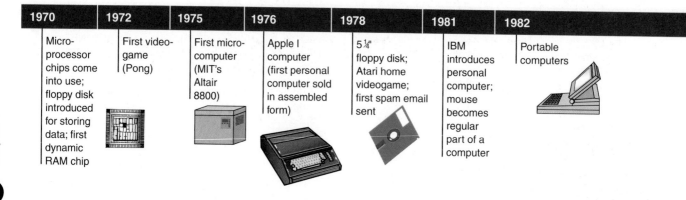

1970	1972	1975	1976	1978	1981	1982
Microprocessor chips come into use; floppy disk introduced for storing data; first dynamic RAM chip	First videogame (Pong)	First microcomputer (MIT's Altair 8800)	Apple I computer (first personal computer sold in assembled form)	5¼" floppy disk; Atari home videogame; first spam email sent	IBM introduces personal computer; mouse becomes regular part of a computer	Portable computers

Chapter 1

Supercomputer Maker or Lab	Top Speed, Teraflops	Location
K Computer	8–10 petaflops	Japan
NUDT Tianhe-1A	2.57 petaflops	China
Cray XT5 Jaguar	1.76 petaflops	U.S.A.
Nebulae	1.27 petaflops	China
Tsubame 2.0	1.19 petaflops	Japan
Cray Cielo	1.11 petaflops	U.S.A.
Cray XE6 Hopper	1.05 petaflops	U.S.A.
Tera 100	1.05 petaflops	France
IBM Roadrunner	1.04 petaflops	U.S.A.

panel 1.7

Top 10 Supercomputers

more info!

FLOPS

In computing, FLOPS is an abbreviation of Floating-point Operations Per Second. Flops is used as a measure of a computer's performance, especially in fields of scientific calculations. Using floating-point encoding, extremely long numbers can be handled relatively easily. Computers operate in the trillions of flops; for comparison, any response time below 0.1 second is experienced as instantaneous by a human operator, so a simple pocket calculator could be said to operate at about 10 flops. Humans are even worse floating-point processors. If it takes a person a quarter of an hour to carry out a pencil-and-paper long division with 10 significant digits, that person would be calculating in the milliflops range.

perform more than several trillion calculations per second. These are the most expensive and fastest computers available. "Supers," as they are called, have been used for tasks requiring the processing of enormous volumes of data, such as doing the U.S. census count, forecasting weather, designing aircraft, modeling molecules, and breaking encryption codes. More recently they have been employed for business purposes—for instance, sifting demographic marketing information—and for creating film animation. The fastest computer in the world, costing $1.25 billion to build and $10 million for annual electrical power usage, with roughly the computing power of 1 million desktop computers, is Japan's Fujitsu K Computer. The K Computer system comprises 672 computer cabinets filled with system boards (motherboards). K Computer's speed is 8–10 petaflops (8–10 quadrillion calculations per second). *(• See Panel 1.7.)*

Supercomputers are still the most powerful computers, but a new generation may be coming that relies on ***nanotechnology*, in which molecule-size nanostructures are used to create tiny machines for holding data or performing tasks.** (*Nano* means "one-billionth.") Computers the size of a pencil eraser could become available that work 10 times faster than today's fastest supercomputer. Eventually nanotech could show up in every device and appliance in your life.

Japan's K Computer. This is the world's fastest supercomputer.

1984	1990	1994	1998	2000	2001	2002	2003
Apple Macintosh; first personal laser printer	Laptops become very popular	Apple and IBM introduce PCs with full-motion video built in; wireless data transmission for small portable computers; first web browser invented	PayPal is founded	The "Y2K" nonproblem; the first U.S. presidential webcast	Dell computers becomes the largest PC maker	Friendster	Facebook MySpace

IBM zEnterprise mainframe computer

Mainframe Computers

Mainframe computers are used in many large businesses.

The only type of computer available until the late 1960s, ***mainframes*** **are water- or air-cooled computers that cost $5,000–$5 million and vary in size from small, to medium, to large, depending on their use.** Small mainframes ($5,000–$200,000) are often called *midsize computers;* they used to be called *minicomputers,* although today the term is seldom used. Mainframes are used by large organizations—such as banks, airlines, insurance companies, and colleges—for processing millions of transactions. Often users access a mainframe by means of a ***terminal*, which has a display screen and a keyboard and can input and output data but cannot by itself process data.** Mainframes process billions of instructions per second.

Workstations

Workstations are used for graphics, special effects, and certain professional applications.

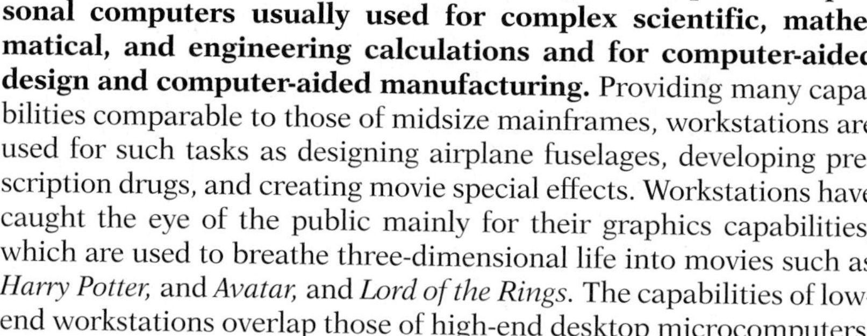

Introduced in the early 1980s, ***workstations*** **are expensive, powerful personal computers usually used for complex scientific, mathematical, and engineering calculations and for computer-aided design and computer-aided manufacturing.** Providing many capabilities comparable to those of midsize mainframes, workstations are used for such tasks as designing airplane fuselages, developing prescription drugs, and creating movie special effects. Workstations have caught the eye of the public mainly for their graphics capabilities, which are used to breathe three-dimensional life into movies such as *Harry Potter,* and *Avatar,* and *Lord of the Rings.* The capabilities of low-end workstations overlap those of high-end desktop microcomputers.

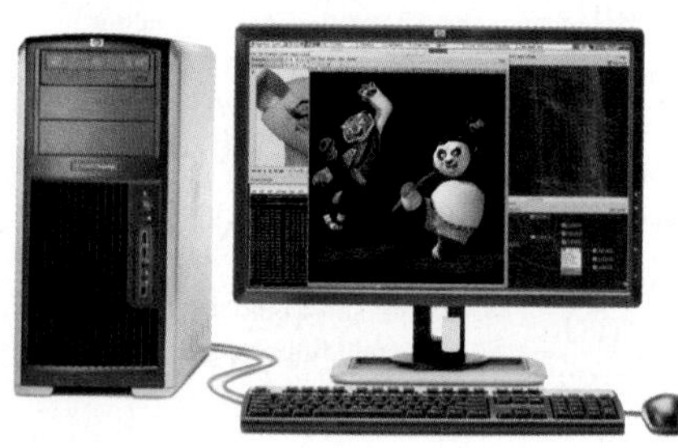

Workstation

Microcomputers

Microcomputers are used by individuals as well as businesses, and they can be connected to networks of larger computers. There are many types of microcomputers.

***Microcomputers*, also called *personal computers* (*PCs*), which cost $500 to over $5,000, can fit next to a desk or on a desktop or can be carried around.** They either are stand-alone machines or are connected to a computer network, such as a local area network. **A *local area network (LAN)* connects, usually by special cable, a group of desktop PCs and other devices, such as printers, in an office or a building.**

Microcomputers are of several types: desktop PCs, tower PCs, notebooks (laptops), netbooks and tablets, mobile Internet devices (MIDs), and personal digital assistants—handheld computers or palmtops. Also, some microcomputers are powerful enough to be used as workstations.

DESKTOP PCS ***Desktop PCs*** **are the original style of microcomputers whose case or main housing sits on a desk, with keyboard in front and monitor (screen) often on top.**

2004	2005	2006	2007	2008	2010	2013	2015	2030–2045
IBM PC sold to Lenovo Group Flickr	YouTube Wii	Twitter	Skype; Apple introduces iPhone	Netbooks become popular	Apple releases iPad	Foldable computers	Teleportation?; self-aware machine intelligence	The singularity

Small. The Mac Mini has the smallest desktop microcomputer case, just 6.5 inches square and 1.25 inches tall.

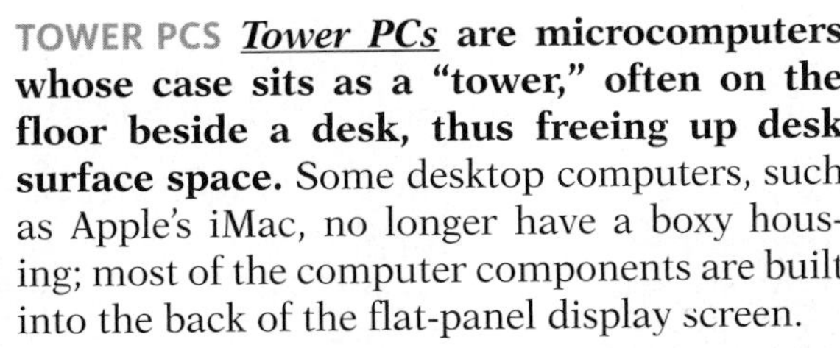

TOWER PCS ***Tower PCs* are microcomputers whose case sits as a "tower," often on the floor beside a desk, thus freeing up desk surface space.** Some desktop computers, such as Apple's iMac, no longer have a boxy housing; most of the computer components are built into the back of the flat-panel display screen.

Tower PC (with speakers, keyboard, and mouse)

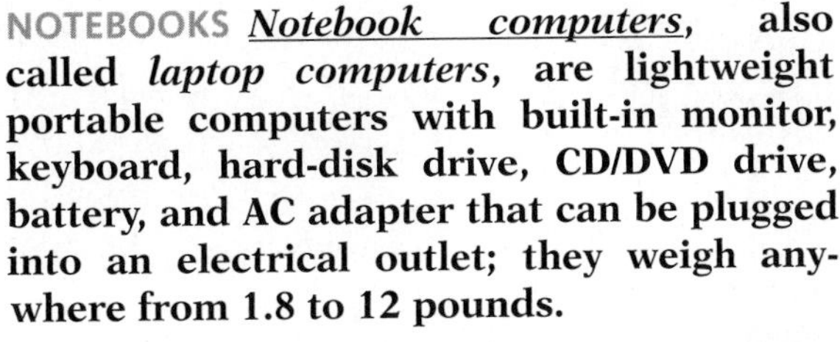

NOTEBOOKS ***Notebook computers*, also called *laptop computers*, are lightweight portable computers with built-in monitor, keyboard, hard-disk drive, CD/DVD drive, battery, and AC adapter that can be plugged into an electrical outlet; they weigh anywhere from 1.8 to 12 pounds.**

Notebook computers: Macbooks

NETBOOKS AND TABLET COMPUTERS ***Netbooks* are mini-notebooks—low-cost, lightweight, small computers with functions designed for basic tasks, such as web searching, email, and word processing.** They weigh anywhere from 2.25 to 3.2 pounds, cost generally between $200 and $400, have less processing power than notebooks (laptops), and have screens between 7 and 10 about inches wide diagonally. Netbooks fill a technological category between notebooks and handheld devices.

Hewlett-Packard Touchsmart. This tablet allows users to move items around on the screen with their hands, to open and close files, and to perform other functions manually.

***Tablet computers*, such as Apple's iPad and Amazon's Fire, are a combination of smartphone and laptop computer with wireless connections.** The screen is a 9–10-inch touch screen (one can manipulate the screen contents directly with one's hand.) Tablet computers support multimedia.

Netbooks: (*top*) Apple iPad2, (*left*) the MacBook Air, and (*below*) Dell Inspiron mini netbooks

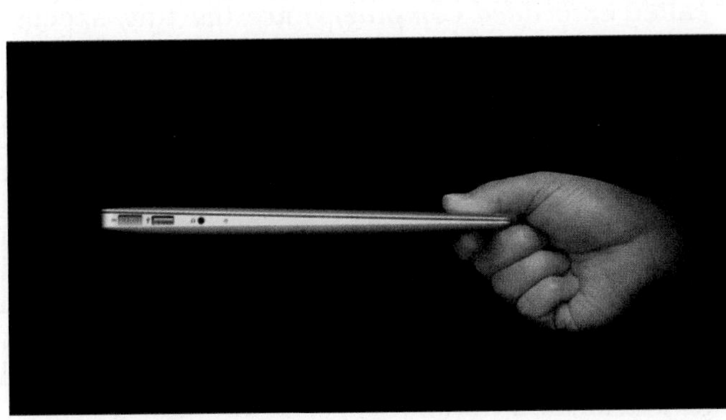

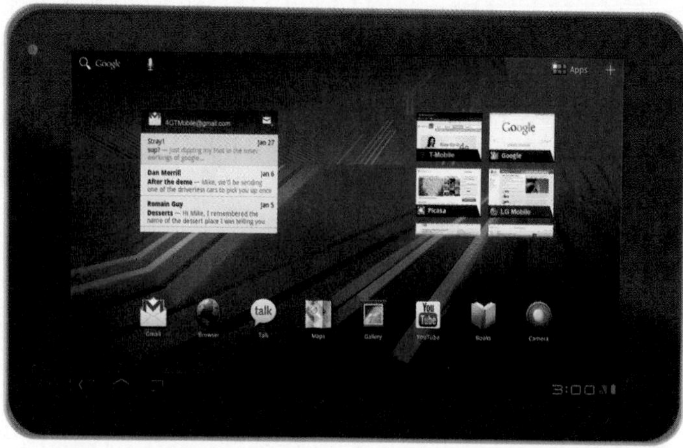

LG Mobile Internet Devices (MIDs): PanTech (*left*) and T-Mobile G-Slate

MOBILE INTERNET DEVICES (MIDS) **Smaller than notebook and netbook computers but larger and more powerful than PDAs and cellphones, *mobile Internet devices (MIDs)* are multimedia devices for consumers and business professionals.** Fully Internet integrated, they are highly compatible with desktop microcomputers and laptops.

Kindle 3 e-reader

PERSONAL DIGITAL ASSISTANTS AND E-READERS ***Personal digital assistants (PDAs)*, also called *handheld computers* or *palmtops*, combine personal organization tools—schedule planners, address books, to-do lists—with the ability in some cases to send email and faxes.** Some PDAs have touch-sensitive screens. Some also connect to desktop computers for sending or receiving information. (For now, we are using the word *digital* to mean "computer based.") The range of handheld wireless devices, such as multipurpose cellphones (smartphones, which can also act as PDAs and small netbooks and e-readers) has surged in recent years, and we consider these later in the book (Chapters 6 and 7).

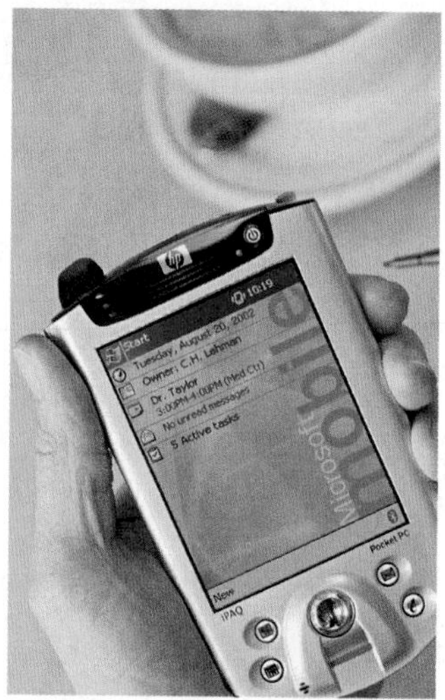

Personal digital assistant (PDA)

***E-readers* are electronic devices that can download e-books, digital versions of regular books, articles, and magazines from various suppliers**, such as Amazon.com, Barnes & Noble, and Google. Many e-readers are book-size and can easily be put in a purse or a pocket.

Microcontrollers

What gadgets do I have that might contain microcontrollers?

***Microcontrollers*, also called *embedded computers*, are the tiny, specialized microprocessors installed in "smart" appliances and automobiles.** These microcontrollers enable microwave ovens, for example, to store data about how long to cook your potatoes and at what power setting. Microcontrollers have been used to develop a new universe of experimental electronic appliances—e-pliances. For example, they are behind single-function products such as digital cameras, MP3 and MP4 players, and organizers, which have been developed into hybrid forms such as gadgets that store photos and videos as well as music. They also help run tiny web servers embedded in clothing, jewelry, and household appliances such as refrigerators. In addition, microcontrollers are used in blood-pressure monitors, air bag sensors, gas and chemical sensors for water and air, and vibration sensors.

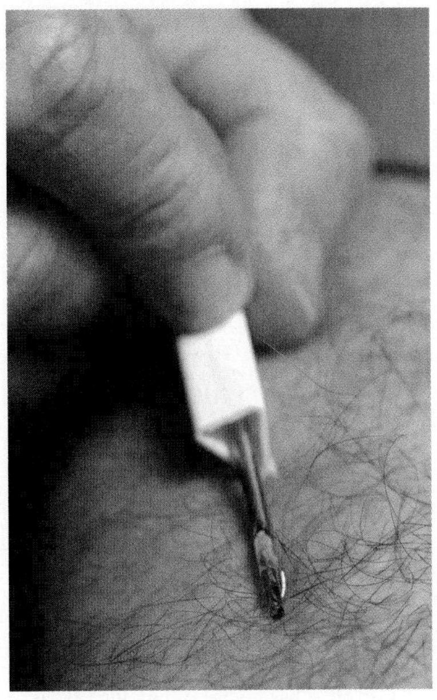

Microcontroller. *(left)* The microcontroller pressure sensor from Motorola reduces tire blowouts and improves gas mileage. This embedded computer notifies drivers, via a dashboard display, when tire pressure is not optimal. *(right)* Injection of a VeriChip, which, when implanted in a person's forearm or shoulder, can provide medical and identity information when scanned.

Servers

Servers are computers and special software dedicated to providing services to other computers

The word *server* describes not a size of computer but rather a particular way in which a computer is used. Nevertheless, because servers have become so important to telecommunications, especially with the rise of the Internet and the web, they deserve mention here. (Servers are discussed in detail in Chapters 2, 6, and 7.)

A *server*, or *network server*, is a central computer that holds collections of data (databases) and programs for connecting or supplying services to PCs, workstations, and other devices, which are called *clients*. These clients are linked by a wired or wireless network. The entire network is called a *client/server network*. In small organizations, servers can store files, provide printing stations, and transmit email. In large organizations, servers may also house enormous libraries of financial, sales, and product information.

Servers. A group of networked servers that are housed in one location is called a *server farm* or a *server cluster*.

You may never lay eyes on a supercomputer or mainframe or even a tiny microcontroller. But most readers of this book will already have laid eyes and hands on a personal computer. We consider this machine next.

1.5 Understanding Your Computer

All computers use four basic operations and can be connected to various types of devices.

Perhaps you know how to drive a car. But do you know what to do when it runs badly? Similarly, you've probably been using a personal computer. But do you know what to do when it doesn't act right—when, for example, it suddenly "crashes" (shuts down)?

Cars are now so complicated that professional mechanics are often required for even the smallest problems. With personal computers, however, there are still many things you can do yourself—and should learn to do, so that, as we've suggested, you can be effective, efficient, and employable. To do so, you first need to know how computers work.

How Computers Work: Three Key Concepts

All computer users must understand three basic principles: (1) data is turned into information; (2) hardware and software have their own specific functions; (3) all computers involve input, processing, storage, and output plus communications.

Do you always have to buy an off-the-shelf computer? No. Could you customize your own personal computer? Yes. Many ordinary users order their own customized PCs. Let's consider how you might do this.

We're not going to ask you to actually order a PC—just to pretend to do so. The purpose of this exercise is to give you a basic overview of how a computer works. This information will help you when you go shopping for a new system. It will also help you to understand how your existing system works, if you have one.

Before you begin you need to understand three key concepts.

1. PURPOSE OF A COMPUTER: **TURNING DATA INTO INFORMATION** Very simply, the purpose of a computer is to process data into information.

- Data: ***Data*** **consists of the raw facts and figures that are processed into information**—for example, the votes for different candidates being elected to student-government office.
- Information: ***Information*** **is data that has been summarized or otherwise manipulated for use in decision making**—for example, the total votes for each candidate, which are used to decide who won.

2. DIFFERENCE BETWEEN HARDWARE & SOFTWARE What is the difference between hardware and software?

- Hardware: ***Hardware*** **consists of all the machinery and equipment in a computer system.** The hardware includes, among other devices, the keyboard, the screen, the printer, and the "box"—the computer or processing device itself. Hardware is useless without software.
- Software: ***Software*****, or *programs*, consists of all the electronic instructions that tell the computer how to perform a task.** These instructions come from a software developer in a form (such as a CD, or compact disk) that will be accepted by the computer. Examples are Microsoft Windows 7, Microsoft Office 2010, Mac OS X Snow Leopard and Lion, and Microsoft Home and Office 2011 for the Mac.

3. THE BASIC OPERATIONS OF A COMPUTER Regardless of type and size, all computers use the same four basic operations: (1) input, (2) processing, (3) storage, and (4) output. To this we add (5) communications.

- **Input operation: *Input* is whatever is put in ("input") to a computer system.** Input can be nearly any kind of data—letters, numbers, symbols, shapes, colors, temperatures, sounds, pressure, light beams, or whatever raw material needs processing. When you type some words or numbers on a keyboard, those words are considered input data.
- **Processing operation: *Processing* is the manipulation a computer does to transform data into information.** When the computer adds 2 + 2 to get 4, that is the act of processing. The processing is done by the *central processing unit*—frequently called just the *CPU*—a chip device consisting of electronic circuitry that executes instructions to process data.
- **Storage operation:** Storage is of two types—temporary (primary) storage and permanent (secondary) storage. ***Primary storage*, or *memory*, is the internal computer circuitry (chips) that temporarily holds data waiting to be processed. *Secondary storage*, simply called *storage*, refers to the devices and media that store data or information permanently.** A hard disk or CD/DVD is an example of this kind of storage. (Storage also holds the software—the computer programs.)
- **Output operation: *Output* is whatever is output from ("put out of") the computer system—the results of processing, usually information.** Examples of output are numbers or pictures displayed on a screen, words printed out on paper by a printer, digital files stored on a CD, and music piped over some loudspeakers.
- **Communications operation:** These days, most computers have communications ability, which offers an extension capability—in other words, it extends the power of the computer. With wired or wireless communications connections, data may be input from afar, processed in a remote area, stored in several different locations, and output in yet other places.

These five operations are summarized in the illustration on the next page. *(• See Panel 1.8.)*

Survival Tip

Input is covered in detail in Chapter 5.

Survival Tip

Processing is covered in detail in Chapter 4.

Survival Tip

Storage is covered in detail in Chapter 4.

Survival Tip

Output is covered in detail in Chapter 5.

Survival Tip

Communications is covered in detail in Chapters 2, 6, and 7.

Pretending to Customize a Desktop Computer: Basic Knowledge of How a Computer Works

Customizing a computer is not as hard as you might think.

Now let's see how to order a custom-built desktop PC. Remember, the purpose of this is to help you to understand the internal workings of a computer so that you'll be knowledgeable about buying one and using it. Although prices of components are always subject to change, we have indicated general ranges of prices for basic equipment current as of 2011 so that you can get a sense of the relative importance of the various parts. ("Loaded" components—the most powerful and sophisticated equipment—cost more than the prices given here.)

Note: All the system components you or anyone else chooses *must be compatible*—in other words, each brand must work with other brands. If you work with one company—such as Dell or Hewlett-Packard—to customize your system, you won't have to worry about compatibility. If you choose all the components yourself—for example, by going to a computer-parts seller such as ComputerGeeks.com (*www.geeks.com*)—you will have to check on compatibility as you choose each component. And you'll have to make sure each component comes with any necessary cables, instructions, and component-specific software (called a *driver*) that allows the component to run (the software "drives" the device).

Survival Tip

Hardware Info

For a listing of virtually all types of hardware, their descriptions, ratings, and prices, and the names of sellers go to:

http://computers.bizrate.com/computers_software/

http://reviews.cnet.com/

www.juggle.com/computers/hardware-and-software

www.itreviews.co.uk/

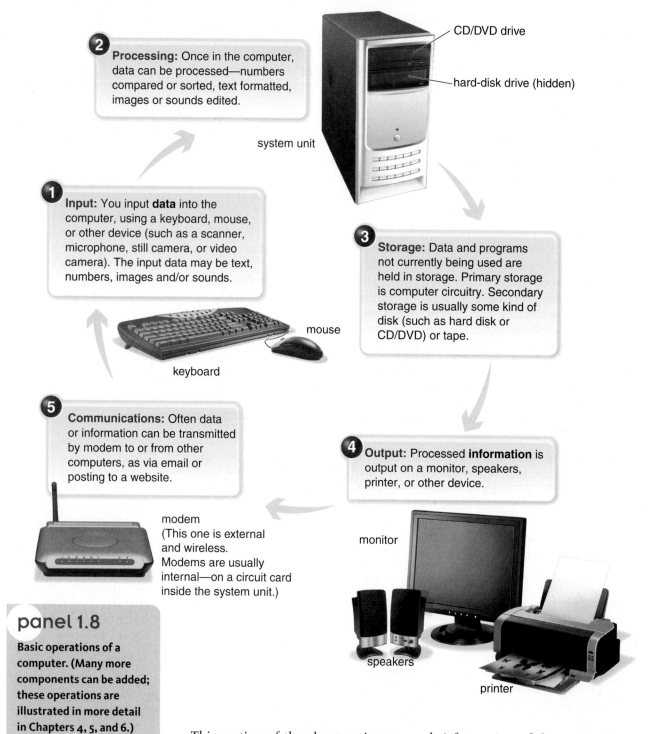

2 **Processing:** Once in the computer, data can be processed—numbers compared or sorted, text formatted, images or sounds edited.

CD/DVD drive

hard-disk drive (hidden)

system unit

1 **Input:** You input **data** into the computer, using a keyboard, mouse, or other device (such as a scanner, microphone, still camera, or video camera). The input data may be text, numbers, images and/or sounds.

3 **Storage:** Data and programs not currently being used are held in storage. Primary storage is computer circuitry. Secondary storage is usually some kind of disk (such as hard disk or CD/DVD) or tape.

mouse

keyboard

5 **Communications:** Often data or information can be transmitted by modem to or from other computers, as via email or posting to a website.

4 **Output:** Processed **information** is output on a monitor, speakers, printer, or other device.

modem (This one is external and wireless. Modems are usually internal—on a circuit card inside the system unit.)

monitor

speakers

printer

panel 1.8

Basic operations of a computer. (Many more components can be added; these operations are illustrated in more detail in Chapters 4, 5, and 6.)

This section of the chapter gives you a brief overview of the components, which are all covered in detail in Chapters 2–6. We describe them in the following order: (1) input hardware—keyboard and mouse; (2) processing and memory hardware; (3) storage hardware—disk drives; (4) output hardware—video and sound cards, monitor, speakers, and printer; (5) communication hardware—the modem; and (6) software—system and application.

Input Hardware: Keyboard & Mouse

The two principal input devices are the keyboard and the mouse.

Input hardware consists of devices that allow people to put data into the computer in a form that the computer can use. Usually, you will need two things: a *keyboard* and a *mouse*.

Keyboard

KEYBOARD (Cost: $10–$400) On a microcomputer, a keyboard is the primary input device. **A *keyboard* is an input device that converts letters, numbers, and other characters into electrical signals readable by the processor.** A microcomputer keyboard looks like a typewriter keyboard, but besides having keys for letters and numbers it has several keys (such as *F* keys and *Ctrl, Alt,* and *Del* keys) intended for computer-specific tasks. After other components are assembled, the keyboard will be plugged into the back of the computer in a socket intended for that purpose. (Cordless keyboards work differently.)

Mouse

MOUSE ($5–$400) **A *mouse* is a nonkeyboard input device ("pointing device") that is used to manipulate objects viewed on the computer display screen.** The mouse cord is plugged into the back of the computer or into the back of the keyboard after the other components are assembled. (Cordless mice are also available.)

Processing & Memory Hardware: Inside the System Cabinet

A computer's processing and memory devices are inside the computer case on the main circuit board, called the motherboard.

The brains of the computer are the *processing* and *memory* devices, which are installed in the case, also called the system cabinet or system unit.

Case

CASE & POWER SUPPLY (about $10–$200) **Also known as the *system unit*, the *case* or *system cabinet* is the box that houses the *processor chip (CPU)*, the memory chips, and the motherboard (main circuit board) with power supply, as well as some secondary-storage devices**—hard-disk drive and CD or DVD drive, as we will explain. The case generally comes in desktop or tower models. It includes a power supply unit and a fan to keep the circuitry from overheating.

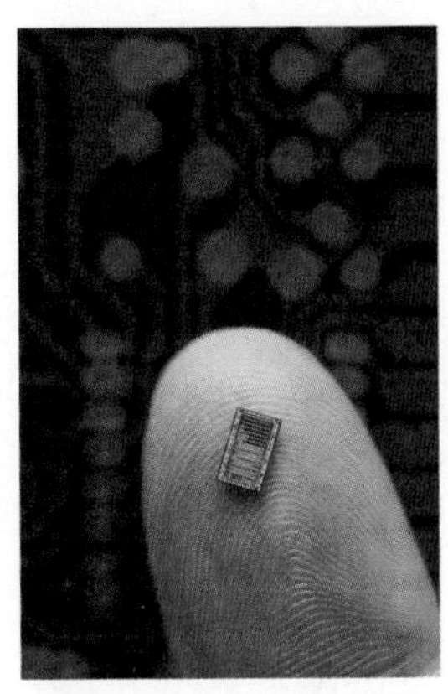

PROCESSOR CHIP ($20–$1,000 or more) It may be small and not look like much, but it could be the most expensive hardware component of a build-it-yourself PC—and doubtless the most important. **A *processor chip (CPU, for central processing unit)* is a tiny piece of silicon that contains millions of miniature electronic circuits.** The speed at which a chip processes information is expressed in *megahertz (MHz),* millions of processing cycles per second, or *gigahertz (GHz),* billions of processing cycles per second. The faster the processor, the more expensive it is. For $100, you might get a 2-GHz chip, which is adequate for most student purposes. For $200, you might get a 3-GHz chip, which you would want if you're running software with spectacular graphics and sound, such as those with some new videogames.

Processor chip

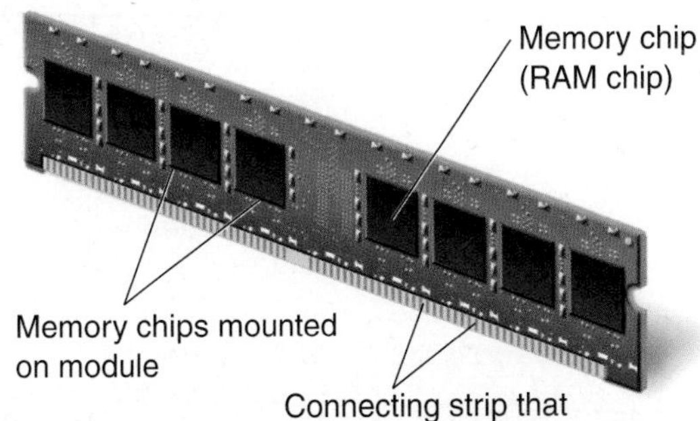

MEMORY CHIPS ($20–$600) ***Memory chips*, also known as *RAM (random access memory) chips*, represent *primary* storage, or temporary storage; they hold data before processing and information after processing, before it is sent along to an output or storage device.** You'll want enough memory chips to hold at least 2–4 gigabytes, or roughly 2–4 billion characters, of data, which is adequate for most student purposes. (Students into heavy graphics use and game playing will need more memory. We will explain the numbers used to measure storage capacities in a moment.)

MOTHERBOARD (about \$45–\$500) **Also called the *system board*, the *motherboard* is the main circuit board in the computer.** This is the big (usually) green circuit board to which everything else—such as the keyboard, mouse, and printer—attaches through connections (called *ports*) in the back of the computer. The processor chip and memory chips are also installed on the motherboard.

The motherboard has ***expansion slots*—for expanding the PC's capabilities—which give you places to plug in additional circuit boards,** such as those for video, sound, and communications (modem). *(● See Panel 1.9.)*

PUTTING THE COMPONENTS TOGETHER Now the components can be put together. As the illustration below shows, ❶ the memory chips are plugged into the motherboard. Then ❷ the processor chip is plugged into the motherboard. Now ❸ the motherboard is attached to the system cabinet. Then ❹ the power supply unit is connected to the system cabinet. Finally, ❺ the wire for the power switch, which turns the computer on and off, is connected to the motherboard.

panel 1.9

Putting the components together

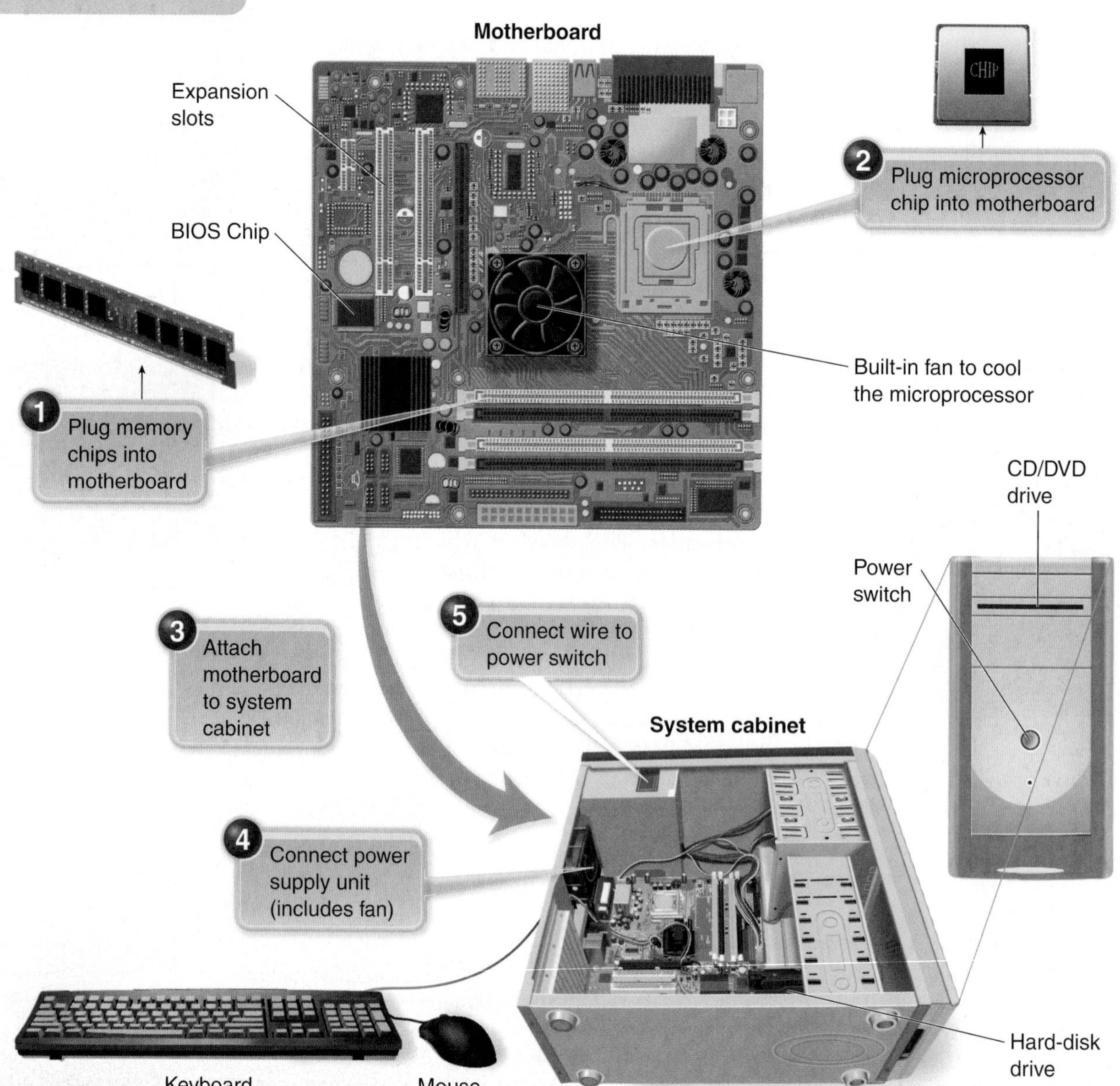

Storage Hardware: Hard Drive & CD/DVD Drive

Computers can have several types of storage devices.

With the motherboard in the system cabinet, the next step is installation of the storage hardware. Whereas memory chips deal only with temporary storage, *secondary storage*, or *permanent storage*, stores your data for as long as you want.

For today's student purposes, you'll need a hard drive and a CD/DVD drive. These storage devices slide into the system cabinet from the front and are secured with screws. Each drive is attached to the motherboard by a cable. Also, each drive must be hooked up to a plug extending from the power supply.

A computer system's data/information storage capacity is represented by bytes, kilobytes, megabytes, gigabytes, terabytes, petabytes, exabytes, and zettabytes, as follows:

1 byte	= *1 character of data* (A character can be alphabetic —A, B, or C—or numeric—1, 2, or 3—or a special character—!, ?, *, $, %.)
1 kilobyte	= *1,024 characters* (about ½ of a double-space typed page of text)
1 megabyte	= *1,048,576 characters* (about 768 pages of text)
1 gigabyte	= *more than 1 billion characters* (about 786,432 pages of text)
1 terabyte	= *more than 1 trillion characters* (a stack of typed pages about 52 miles high)
1 petabye	= *about 1 quadrillion characters* (a stack of typed pages about 52,000 miles high)
1 exabyte	= *about 1 quintillion characters* (a stack of typed pages about 52 million miles high)
1 zettabyte	= *about 1 sextillion characters* (a stack of typed pages about 52 billion miles high)

Hard-disk drive (goes inside the computer case)

HARD-DISK DRIVE ($60–$100, depending on storage capacity) **A *hard-disk drive* is a storage device that stores billions of characters of data on a nonremovable disk platter.** With 500 gigabytes of storage, you should be able to handle most student needs. (Many hard-disk drives store up to 2 terabytes of data.)

CD/DVD DRIVE ($30–$180) **A *CD (compact-disk) drive*, or its more recent variant, a *DVD (digital video-disk) drive*, is a storage device that uses laser technology to read data from optical disks.** (Some companies call a DVD a "digital versatile disk.") Today new software is generally supplied on CDs or via the net.

The system cabinet has lights on the front that indicate when these drives are in use. (You must not remove a disk from the drive until its light goes off, or else you risk damage to both disk and drive.) The wires for these lights need to be attached to the motherboard.

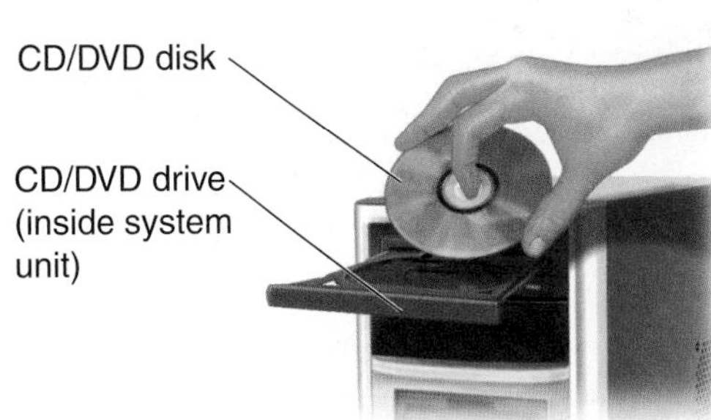

Output Hardware: Video & Sound Cards, Monitor, Speakers, & Printer

Output hardware provides users with the information they need.

Output hardware consists of devices that translate information processed by the computer into a form that humans can understand—print, sound, graphics, or video, for example. Now a video card and a sound card need to be installed in the system cabinet. Next the monitor, speakers, and a printer are plugged in.

This is a good place to introduce the term *peripheral device*. **A *peripheral device* is any component or piece of equipment that expands a computer's input, storage, and output capabilities.** In other words, a peripheral device is not part of the essential computer. Peripheral devices can be inside the computer or connected to it from the outside. Examples include printers and disk drives.

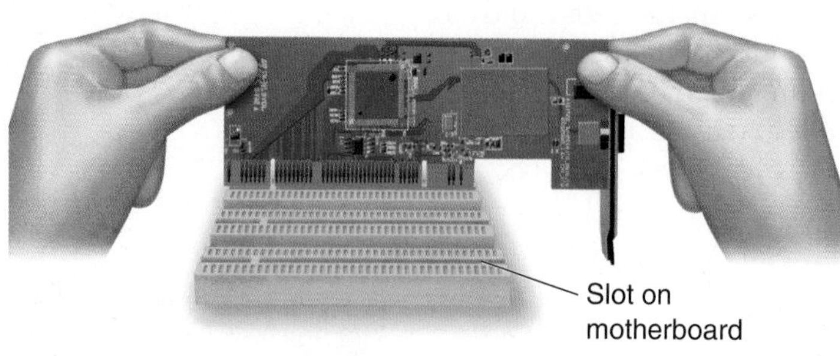

VIDEO CARD ($30–$1,400) You will certainly want your monitor to display color (rather than just black-and-white) images. Your system cabinet will therefore need to have a device to make this possible. **A *video card* converts the processor's output information into a video signal that can be sent through a cable to the monitor.** Remember the expansion slots we mentioned? The video card is plugged into one of these on the motherboard.

SOUND CARD ($15–$300 and higher) To listen to music and sound effects on your PC, you'll need a ***sound card*, which enhances the computer's sound-generating capabilities by allowing sound to be output through speakers,** either built into the computer or connected externally. This card, too, would be plugged into an expansion slot on the motherboard. With the CD drive connected to the card, you can listen to music CDs.

Monitor

MONITOR ($100–$300 or higher for a 17-inch model or a 19-inch model; $300–$1,200 or more for larger displays) As with television sets, the inch dimension on monitors is measured diagonally corner to corner. **The *monitor* is the display device that takes the electrical signals from the video card and forms an image using points of colored light on the screen.** Later, after the system cabinet has been closed up, the monitor will be connected by means of a cable to the back of the computer, using the clearly marked connector. The power cord for the monitor will be plugged into a wall plug

External speakers

SPEAKERS ($25–$250) ***Speakers* are the devices that play sounds transmitted as electrical signals from the sound card.** They may not be very sophisticated, but unless you're into high-fidelity recordings they're probably good enough. The speakers are either built into the computer or connected to a single wire that is plugged into the back of the computer.

PRINTER ($50–$1,000) Especially for student work, you certainly need a ***printer*, an output device that produces text and graphics on paper.** There are various types of printers, as we discuss later. The printer has two connections. One, which relays signals from the computer, goes to the back of the PC, where it connects with the motherboard. The other is a power cord that goes to a wall plug. Color printers are more expensive than black-and-white printers, and fast printers cost more than slow ones.

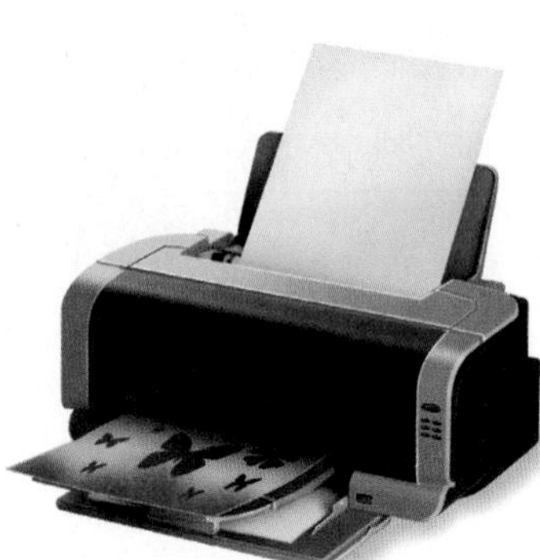

Printer

Communications Hardware: Modem

Computers often need some kind of modem in order to communicate and become part of a network.

Computers can be stand-alone machines, unconnected to anything else. If all you're doing is word processing to write term papers, you can do it with a stand-alone system. As we have seen, however, the communications component of the computer system vastly extends the range of a PC. Thus, while the system cabinet is still open, there is one more piece of hardware to install.

MODEM ($10–$100) **A standard *modem* is a device that sends and receives data over telephone lines, or wirelessly via a network, to and from computers.** The modem is sometimes mounted on an expansion card, which is fitted into an expansion slot on the motherboard; sometimes the modem is wired directly into the motherboard. (Other types of computer communications connections are discussed in Chapters 2 and 6.)

Modem expansion card

Now the system cabinet is closed up. The person building or customizing the system will plug in all the input and output devices and turn on the power "on" button. Your microcomputer system will look similar to the one shown in Panel 1.10. (● *See Panel 1.10.*) Are you now ready to roll? Not quite.

Software

Computers use two basic types of software: system software and application software.

After the computer has been assembled, it will be tested. But first the software, the electronically encoded instructions that tell the computer hardware what to do, must be installed. (*Installation* is the process of copying software programs from a main secondary-storage source onto the system's hard disk and some special chips, so that you can have direct access to your hardware.)

Software is what makes the computer worthwhile, what makes it functional for the user. There are two types—*system software* and *application software*.

Mac OS X Snow Leopard
The world's most advanced operating system. Finely tuned.
Mac OS X Snow Leopard

System software—a version of Apple's OS X system software for the Macintosh

SYSTEM SOFTWARE First, system software must be installed. ***System software*** **helps the computer perform essential operating tasks and enables the application software to run.** System software consists

panel 1.10

Completely assembled basic PC hardware system

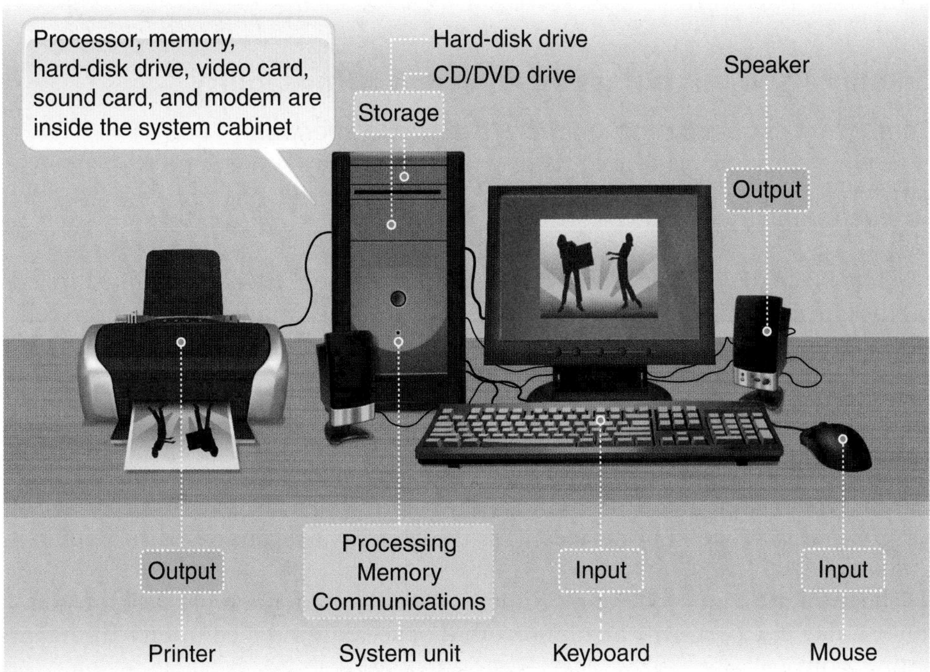

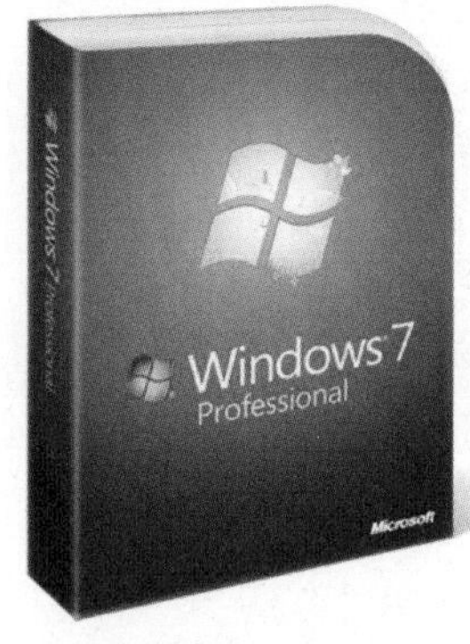

System software for the PC—a version of Microsoft 7

of several electronically coded programs. The most important is the *operating system*, the master control program that runs the computer. Examples of operating system (OS) software for the PC are various Microsoft programs (such as Windows XP, Vista, 7, and 8), Unix, and Linux. The Apple Macintosh microcomputer is another matter altogether. As we explain in Chapter 3, it has its own software.

After the system software is installed, setup software for the hard drive, the video and sound cards, and the modem must be installed. These setup programs (*drivers*, discussed in Chapter 3) often come on CDs and can also be downloaded from the Internet.

APPLICATION SOFTWARE Now we're finally getting somewhere! After the application software has been installed, the computer can be used for various activities. ***Application software*** **enables you to perform specific tasks—solve problems, perform work, or entertain yourself.** For example, when you prepare a term paper on your computer, you will use a word processing program. (Microsoft Word and Corel WordPerfect are two brands.) *Application software is specific to the system software you use.* If you want to run Microsoft Word for the PC, for instance, you'll need to first have Microsoft Windows system software on your system, not Unix or Linux or Apple OS X (without modifications).

Application software comes on CDs packaged in boxes that include instructions, or it can also be downloaded from manufacturers' websites on the Internet.

We discuss software in more detail in Chapter 3.

Application software: Adobe Creative Suite, which among other things is used to create art, manipulate photos, and build websites

1.6 Where Is Information Technology Headed?

Computers are headed in three basic directions—miniaturization, higher speeds, and greater affordability—and communications is improving connectivity, interactivity, and support of multimedia.

How far we have come. At the beginning of the 20th century, most people thought they would live the same life their parents did. Today most people aren't surprised by the prediction that the Information Age will probably transform their lives beyond recognition. Let's consider the trends in the development of computers and communications and, most exciting, the area where they intersect.

Computers: Miniaturization, Speed, & Affordability

Computers are becoming smaller, faster, and cheaper.

Since the days of ENIAC, computers have developed in three directions—and are continuing to do so.

MINIATURIZATION Everything has become smaller. ENIAC's old-fashioned radio-style vacuum tubes gave way after 1947 to the smaller, faster, more reliable transistor. A *transistor* is a small device used as a gateway to transfer electrical signals along predetermined paths (circuits).

The next step was the development of tiny *integrated circuits*. Integrated circuits are entire collections of electrical circuits or pathways that are now etched on tiny squares (chips) of silicon half the size of your thumbnail. *Silicon* is a natural element found in sand. In pure form, it is the base material for computer processing devices. (All these items are discussed in detail in Chapter 4.)

The miniaturized processor, or microprocessor, in a personal desktop computer today can perform calculations that once required a computer filling an entire room.

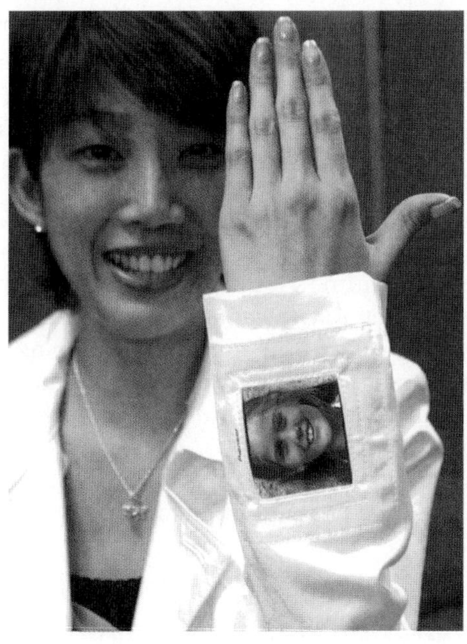

Miniaturization. (*left*) A woman tries on a prototype of a wearable computer, a jacket with a built-in display in its sleeve. This type of computer, from Pioneer, is expected to aid medical, firefighting, and farm workers. (*right*) M2A Imaging Capsule, a miniature camera and transmitter that can be swallowed by a patient to give physicians a wireless real-time view of the patients digestive tract. The capsule transmits the images to a device, worn on the patient's belt, which can be downloaded into a specially configured computer.

SPEED Thanks to miniaturization and new material used in making processors, computer makers can cram more hardware components into their machines, providing faster processing speeds and more data storage capacity.

AFFORDABILITY Processor costs today are only a fraction of what they were 15 years ago. A state-of-the-art processor costing less than $1,000 provides the same processing power as a huge 1980s computer costing more than $1 million.

These are the three major trends in computers. What about communications?

Communications: Connectivity, Interactivity, & Multimedia

Information technology systems are becoming more connected and interactive, and they support more and more kinds of multimedia.

Once upon a time, we had the voice telephone system—a one-to-one medium. You could talk to your Uncle Joe and he could talk to you, and with special arrangements (conference calls) more than two people could talk with one another. We also had radio and television systems—one-to-many media (or mass media). News announcers could talk to you on a single medium such as television, but you couldn't talk to them.

Three recent developments in communications include:

CONNECTIVITY ***Connectivity* refers to the connection of computers to one another by a communications line in order to provide online information access and/or the sharing of peripheral devices.** The connectivity resulting from the expansion of computer networks has made possible email and online shopping, for example.

INTERACTIVITY ***Interactivity* refers to two-way communication; the user can respond to information he or she receives and modify what a computer is doing.** That is, there is an exchange or dialogue between the user and the computer, and the computer responds to user requests. A

Interactivity. A dashboard computer allows drivers to request information about the car's operation, location, and nearby services.

noninteractive program, once started, continues without requiring human contact, or interaction. The ability to interact means users can be active rather than passive participants in the technological process. On the television networks MSNBC or CNN, for example, you can immediately go on the Internet and respond to news from broadcast anchors. Today, most application software is interactive. We already have cars that respond to voice commands and/or have computers built into the dashboard.

MULTIMEDIA Radio is a single-dimensional medium (sound), as is most email (mainly text). As mentioned earlier in this chapter, ***multimedia*** **refers to technology that presents information in more than one medium—such as text, pictures, video, sound, and animation—in a single integrated communication.** The development of the World Wide Web expanded the Internet to include pictures, sound, music, and so on, as well as text.

Exciting as these developments are, truly mind-boggling possibilities have emerged as computers and communications have cross-pollinated.

When Computers & Communications Combine: Convergence, Portability, Personalization, Collaboration, & Cloud Computing

Information technology systems are moving away from standard personal hardware to more extensive networks and smaller devices.

Sometime in the 1990s computers and communications started to fuse together, beginning a new era within the Information Age. The result has been five additional developments.

CONVERGENCE *Convergence* describes the combining of several industries through various devices that exchange data in the format used by computers. The industries are computers, communications, consumer electronics, entertainment, and mass media. Convergence has led to electronic products that perform multiple functions, such as TVs with Internet access, cellphones that are also digital cameras, and a refrigerator that allows you to send email.

PORTABILITY In the 1980s portability, or mobility, meant trading off computing power and convenience in return for smaller size and weight. Today, however, we are close to the point where we don't have to give up anything. As a result, experts have predicted that small, powerful, wireless personal electronic devices will transform our lives far more than the personal computer has done so far. "The new generation of machines will be truly personal computers, designed for our mobile lives," wrote one journalist back in 1992. "We will read office memos between strokes on the golf course and answer messages from our children in the middle of business meetings."[46] Today such activities are commonplace, and smartphones are taking on other functions. The risk they bring is that, unless we're careful, work digital activities will completely take over our personal time.

PERSONALIZATION Personalization is the creation of information tailored to your preferences—for instance, programs that will automatically cull recent news and information from the Internet on just those topics you have designated. Companies involved in e-commerce can send you messages about forthcoming products based on your pattern of purchases, usage, and other criteria. Or they will build products (cars, computers, clothing) customized to your heart's desire.

COLLABORATION A more recent trend is mass collaboration. Says *New York Times* technology writer John Markoff, "A remarkable array of software systems makes it simple to share anything instantly, and sometimes enhance it along the way."[47] *BusinessWeek* writer Robert Hof observed that the huge numbers of people "online worldwide—along with their shared knowledge, social contacts, online reputations, computing power, and more—are rapidly becoming a collective force of unprecedented power."[48] Examples are file-sharing, photo-sharing websites, calendar-sharing services, group-edited informational (encyclopedic) sites called *wikis*, social networking services, and so-called citizen-journalism sites, in which average people write their own news items on the Internet and comment on what other people post—an interactive, democratic form of mass media.[49] Pooled ratings, for instance, enable people to create personalized net music radio stations or Amazon.com's millions of customer-generated product reviews.

According to inventor and futurist, Raymond Kuzweil, technological change will become so rapid and so profound that human bodies and brains will merge with machines.

CLOUD COMPUTING: THE GLOBAL COMPUTER Not everyone agrees on exactly what "cloud computing" means.[50] Previously called *on-demand computing, grid computing,* or *software as a service,* ***cloud computing*** **basically means that, instead of storing your software and/or data on your own PC or your own company's computers, you store it on servers on the Internet.** You don't care where the servers are located; they're out there somewhere—"in the cloud"—run by special cloud-service businesses. The idea here is that companies can tap into computers as they are needed, just as they do now with the electric power grid, splitting their computing workload among data centers in different parts of the world. The hope of technology people is that companies will find cloud computing cheaper and more reliable than managing their own microcomputers, servers, and software.[51]

Examples of cloud companies are Qriocity, which supplies music and movies to Internet-enabled Sony devices, and 3Tera, which frees businesses from having to operate their own servers and buy their own software; instead they subscribe to 3Tera and pay only for the services they use, which include all types of software and storage space on 3Tera servers.

In a later chapter, we discuss an even more involved concept known as *the singularity.*

More on Cloud Computing

www.20thingsilearned.com/cloud-computing/1

www.20thingsilearned.com/cloud-computing/1

http://searchcloudcomputing.techtarget.com/definition/cloud-computing

www.wikinvest.com/concept/Cloud_Computing

Illuminated plastic balls meant to graphically represent cloud computing (servers in the "cloud") go up and down on metal cables at the IBM stand at the CeBIT technology trade fair in Hanover, Germany. CeBIT is the world's largest computer and IT trade fair.

"E" Also Stands for Ethics

Many important ethical issues are involved in the use of information technology.

Every computer user will have to wrestle with ethical issues related to the use of information technology. ***Ethics*** **is defined as a set of moral values or principles that govern the conduct of an individual or a group.** Because ethical questions arise so often in connection with information technology, we will note them, wherever they appear in this book, with the symbol shown at left. Below, for example, are some important ethical concerns pointed out by Tom Forester and Perry Morrison in their book *Computer Ethics*.[52] These considerations are only a few of many; we'll discuss others in subsequent chapters.

SPEED & SCALE Great amounts of information can be stored, retrieved, and transmitted at a speed and on a scale not possible before. Despite the benefits, this has serious implications "for data security and personal privacy," as well as employment, Forester and Morrison say, because information technology can never be considered totally secure against unauthorized access.

UNPREDICTABILITY Computers and communications are pervasive, touching nearly every aspect of our lives. However, at this point, compared to other pervasive technologies—such as electricity, television, and automobiles—information technology seems a lot less predictable and reliable.

COMPLEXITY Computer systems are often incredibly complex—some so complex that they are not always understood even by their creators. "This," say Forester and Morrison, "often makes them completely unmanageable," producing massive foul-ups or spectacularly out-of-control costs.

Ethics and security can often be talked about in the same breath, since secure computer systems obviously go a long way toward keeping people ethical and honest. When we discuss security, you will see the icon below.

SECURITY

The 10 Commandments of Computer Ethics

The Computer Ethics Institute says:

1. Thou shalt not use a computer to harm other people.
2. Thou shalt not interfere with other people's computer work.
3. Thou shalt not snoop around in other people's computer files.
4. Thou shalt not use a computer to steal.
5. Thou shalt not use a computer to bear false witness.
6. Thou shalt not copy or use proprietary software for which you have not paid.
7. Thou shalt not use other people's computer resources without authorization or proper compensation.
8. Thou shalt not appropriate other people's intellectual output.
9. Thou shalt think about the social consequences of the program you are writing or the system you are designing.
10. Thou shalt always use a computer in ways that ensure consideration and respect for your fellow humans.

http://computerethicsinstitute.org/images/TheTenCommandmentsOfComputerEthics.pdf

Survival Tip

Be Ethical about Disposing of Old Computer Equipment

Just got a new computer? Where to donate or recycle your old one? Check with schools, after-school programs, churches, and the following websites:

www1.us.dell.com/content/topics/segtopic.aspx/dell_reycling?c=us&cs=19&l=en&s=dhs

www.crc.org

www.youthfortechnology.org/frames.html

http://earth911.com/recycling/electronics/computers/

www.epa.gov/epawaste/conserve/materials/ecycling/

www.recycles.org/

http://ww1.pcdisposal.com/

www.computerhope.com/disposal.htm

EXPERIENCE BOX

Better Organization & Time Management: Dealing with the Information Deluge in College—& in Life

An Experience Box appears at the end of each chapter. Each box offers you the opportunity to acquire useful experience that directly applies to the Digital Age. This first box illustrates skills that will benefit you in college, in this course and others. (Students reading the first nine editions of our book have told us they received substantial benefit from these suggestions.)

"How on earth am I going to be able to keep up with what's required of me?" you may ask yourself. "How am I going to handle the information glut?" The answer is: *by learning how to learn.* By building your skills as a learner, you certainly help yourself do better in college, and you also train yourself to be an information manager in the future.

Using Your "Prime Study Time"

Each of us has a different energy cycle. The trick is to use it effectively. That way, your hours of best performance will coincide with your heaviest academic demands. For example, if your energy level is high during the evenings, you should plan to do your studying then.

To capitalize on your prime study time, take the following steps: (1) Make a study schedule for the entire term, and indicate the times each day during which you plan to study. (2) Find some good places to study—places where you can avoid distractions. (3) Avoid time wasters, but give yourself frequent rewards for studying, such as a TV show, a favorite piece of music, or a conversation with a friend.

Learning to Focus

Multitasking is shifting focus from one task to another in rapid succession. When you read this textbook while listening to music and watching TV, you may think you're simultaneously doing three separate tasks, but you're really not. "It's like playing tennis with three balls," says one expert.[53] Today multitasking is easy and focus is hard because of all the things demanding our attention—phone calls, email, text messages, music, radio, TV, Twitter, MySpace, Facebook, various blogs and websites. "You can drive yourself crazy trying to multitask and answer every email message instantly," says one writer. "Or you can recognize your brain's finite capacity for processing information."[54]

Here are some tips on learning to concentrate:[55]

Choose What to Focus On. "People don't realize that attention is a finite resource, like money," one expert says. "Do you want to invest your cognitive cash on endless Twittering or Net surfing or couch potatoing [watching TV]?" She adds, "Where did the idea come from that anyone who wants to contact you can do so at any time? You need to take charge of what you pay attention to instead of responding to the latest stimuli."[56] For example, to block out noise, you can wear earplugs while reading.

Devote the First 1½ Hours of Your Day to Your Most Important Task. Writing a paper? Studying a hard subject? Make it your first task of the day, and concentrate on it for 90 minutes. After that, your brain will probably need a rest, and you can answer email, return phone calls, and so on. But until that first break, don't do anything else, because it can take the brain 20 minutes to refocus.

Improving Your Memory Ability

Memorizing is, of course, one of the principal requirements for succeeding in college. And it's a great help for success in life afterward. Some suggestions:

Space Your Studying, Rather than Cramming. Cramming—making a frantic, last-minute attempt to memorize massive amounts of material—is probably the least effective means of absorbing information. Research shows that it's best to space out your studying of a subject over successive days. A series of study sessions over several days is preferable to trying to do it all during the same number of hours on one day. It is *repetition* that helps move information into your long-term memory bank.

Review Information Repeatedly—Even "Overlearn" It. By repeatedly reviewing information—known as "rehearsing"—you can improve both your retention and your understanding of it. Overlearning is continuing to review material even after you appear to have absorbed it. Also, recent research studies show that taking a test after reading a block of material improves recall of the material, even a week later. This method seems to work better than simple reading, reading the block in segments, and concept-mapping (creating a diagram of the concepts after one has finished reading the block of material).[57]

Use Memorizing Tricks. There are several ways to organize information so that you can retain it better. For example, you can make drawings or diagrams (as of the parts of a computer system). Some methods of establishing associations between items you want to remember are given in Panel 1.11. (• *See Panel 1.11.*)

How to Improve Your Reading Ability: The SQ3R Method

SQ3R stands for "survey, question, read, recite, and review."[58] The strategy behind the method is to break down a reading assignment into small segments and master each before moving on. The five steps of the SQ3R method are as follows:

1. *Survey the chapter before you read it:* Get an overview of the chapter before you begin reading it. If you have a sense of what the material is about before you begin reading it, you can predict where it is going. In this text, we offer on the first page of every chapter a list of the main heads and accompanying key questions. At the end of each chapter we

- **Mental and physical imagery:** Use your visual and other senses to construct a personal image of what you want to remember. Indeed, it helps to make the image humorous, action-filled, or outrageous in order to establish a personal connection. Example: To remember the name of the 21st president of the United States, Chester Arthur, you might visualize an author writing the number "21" on a wooden chest. This mental image helps you associate chest (Chester), author (Arthur), and 21 (21st president).
- **Acronyms and acrostics:** An acronym is a word created from the first letters of items in a list. For instance, *Roy G. Biv* helps you remember the colors of the rainbow in order: red, orange, yellow, green, blue, indigo, violet. An acrostic is a phrase or sentence created from the first letters of items on a list. For example, *Every Good Boy Does Fine* helps you remember that the order of musical notes on the treble staff is *E-G-B-D-F.*
- **Location:** Location memory occurs when you associate a concept with a place or imaginary place. For example, you could learn the parts of a computer system by imagining a walk across campus. Each building you pass could be associated with a part of the computer system.
- **Word games:** Jingles and rhymes are devices frequently used by advertisers to get people to remember their products. You may recall the spelling rule "I before E except after C or when sounded like A as in *neighbor* or *weigh*." You can also use narrative methods, such as making up a story.

panel 1.11

Some memorizing tricks

offer a Summary, which recalls what the chapter's terms and concepts mean and why they are important.

2. *Question the segment in the chapter before you read it:* This step is easy to do, and the point, again, is to get you involved in the material. After surveying the entire chapter, go to the first segment—whether a whole section, a subsection, or even just paragraph, depending on the level of difficulty and density of information. Look at the topic heading of that segment (or first sentence of a very difficult paragraph). In your mind, restate the heading as a question. In this book, to help you do this, following each section head we present a Key Question. An example in this chapter was "What are three directions of computer development and three directions of communications development?"

   After you have formulated the question, go to steps 3 and 4 (read and recite). Then proceed on to the next segment of the chapter and restate the heading there as a question, and so on.
3. *Read the segment about which you asked the question:* When you read the segment you asked the question about, read with purpose, to answer the question you formulated. Underline or color-mark sentences that you think are important, if they help you answer the question. Read this portion of the text more than once, if necessary, until you can answer the question. In addition, determine whether the segment covers any other significant questions, and formulate answers to these, too. After you have read the segment, proceed to step 4. (Perhaps you can see where this is all leading. If you read in terms of questions and answers, you will be better prepared when you see exam questions about the material later.)
4. *Recite the main points of the segment:* Recite means "say aloud." Thus, you should speak out loud (or softly) the answer to the principal question or questions about the segment and any other main points.
5. *Review the entire chapter by repeating questions:* After you have read the chapter, go back through it and review the main points. Then, without looking at the book, test your memory by repeating the questions and answers you formulated.

Clearly the SQ3R method takes longer than simply reading with a rapidly moving color marker or underlining pencil. However, the technique is far more effective because it requires your involvement and understanding. These are the keys to all effective learning.

Learning from Lectures

Does attending lectures really make a difference? Research shows that students with grades of B or above were more apt to have better class attendance than students with grades of C- or below.[59]

Some tips for getting the most out of lectures:

Take Effective Notes by Listening Actively. Research shows that good test performance is related to good note taking.[60] And good note taking requires that you listen actively—that is, participate in the lecture process. Here are some ways to take good lecture notes:

- *Read ahead and anticipate the lecturer:* Try to anticipate what the instructor is going to say, based on your previous reading. Having background knowledge makes learning more efficient.
- *Listen for signal words:* Instructors use key phrases such as "The most important point is . . . ," "There are four reasons for . . . ," "The chief reason . . . ," "Of special importance . . . ," "Consequently . . . ." When you hear such signal phrases, mark your notes with a ! or *.
- *Take notes in your own words:* Instead of just being a stenographer, try to restate the lecturer's thoughts in your own words, which will make you pay attention more.
- *Ask questions:* By asking questions during the lecture, you necessarily participate in it and increase your understanding.

Review Your Notes Regularly. Make it a point to review your notes regularly—perhaps on the afternoon after the lecture, or once or twice a week. We cannot emphasize enough the importance of this kind of reviewing.

TERMS & EXPLANATIONS

application software (p. 36) Software that has been developed to solve a particular problem, perform useful work on general-purpose tasks, or provide entertainment. Why it's important: *Application software such as word processing, spreadsheet, database management, graphics, and communications packages are commonly used tools for increasing people's productivity.*

avatar (p. 6) Computer depiction of a human, often found in online videogames. Why it's important: *Avatars can be helpful in training, such as by representing imaginary customers.*

case (p. 31) Also known as the *system unit* or *system cabinet;* the box that houses the processor chip (CPU), the memory chips, and the motherboard with power supply, as well as storage devices—floppy-disk drive, hard-disk drive, and CD or DVD drive. Why it's important: *The case protects many important processing and storage components.*

CD (compact-disk) drive (p. 33) Storage device that uses laser technology to read data from optical disks. Why it's important: *New software is generally supplied on CDs rather than diskettes. And even if you can get a program on floppies, you'll find it easier to install a new program from one CD than to repeatedly insert and remove many diskettes. The newest version is called DVD (digital video disk). The DVD format stores even more data than the CD format.*

central processing unit (CPU) *See* **processor chip.**

chip *See* **processor chip.**

clients (p. 27) Computers and other devices connected to a server, a central computer. Why it's important: *Client/server networks are used in many organizations for sharing databases, devices, and programs.*

cloud computing (p. 39) Concept of storing your software and/or data not on your own PC or company's computers but rather on servers on the Internet. Why it's important: *Users could tap into computers as they are needed, distributing computing workload among data centers in different parts of the world, perhaps making computing cheaper and more reliable.*

communications technology (p. 5) Also called *telecommunications technology;* consists of electromagnetic devices and systems for communicating over long distances. Why it's important: *Communications systems using electronic connections have helped to expand human communication beyond face-to-face meetings.*

computer (p. 5) Programmable, multiuse machine that accepts data—raw facts and figures—and processes (manipulates) it into useful information, such as summaries and totals. Why it's important: *Computers greatly speed up problem solving and other tasks, increasing users' productivity.*

connectivity (p. 37) Ability to connect computers to one another by communications lines, so as to provide online information access and/or the sharing of peripheral devices. Why it's important: *Connectivity is the foundation of the advances in the Information Age. It provides online access to countless types of information and services. The connectivity resulting from the expansion of computer networks has made possible email and online shopping, for example.*

cyberspace (p. 20) Term used to refer to not only the online world and the Internet in particular but also the whole wired and wireless world of communications in general. Why it's important: *More and more human activities take place in cyberspace.*

data (p. 28) Raw facts and figures that are processed into information. Why it's important: *Users need data to create useful information.*

desktop PC (p. 25) Microcomputer unit that sits on a desk, with the keyboard in front and the monitor often on top. Why it's important: *Desktop PCs and tower PCs are the most commonly used types of microcomputer.*

distance learning (p. 6) Also known as *e-learning*; name given to online education programs. Why it's important: *Provides students increased flexibility because they do not have to be in an actual classroom.*

download (p. 11) To transfer data from a remote computer to one's own computer. Why it's important: *Allows text, music, and images to be transferred quickly by telecommunications.*

DVD (digital video-disk) drive *See* **CD drive.**

e-readers (p. 26) Devices that can download e-books, digital versions of regular books, articles, and magazines from various suppliers, such as Amazon.com, Barnes & Noble, and Google. Why it's important: *E-books are cheaper than print books and are easy to obtain. Most e-readers are book-size and can easily be put in a purse or a pocket.*

email (electronic mail) (p. 6) Messages transmitted over a computer network, most often the Internet. Why it's important: *Email has become universal; one of the first things new computer users learn is how to send and receive email.*

ethics (p. 40) Set of moral values or principles that govern the conduct of an individual or a group. Why it's important: *Ethical questions arise often in connection with information technology.*

expansion slots (p. 32) Internal "plugs" used to expand the PC's capabilities. Why it's important: *Expansion slots give you places to plug in additional circuit boards, such as those for video, sound, and communications (modem).*

hard-disk drive (p. 33) Storage device that stores billions of characters of data on a nonremovable disk platter usually inside the computer case. Why it's important: *Hard disks have a very large storage capacity . Nearly all microcomputers use hard disks as their principal secondary-storage medium.*

hardware (p. 28) All machinery and equipment in a computer system. Why it's important: *Hardware runs under the control of software and is useless without it. However, hardware contains the circuitry that allows processing.*

information (p. 28) Data that has been summarized or otherwise manipulated for use in decision making. Why it's important: *The whole purpose of a computer (and communications) system is to produce (and transmit) usable information.*

information technology (IT) (p. 5) Technology that helps to produce, manipulate, store, communicate, and/or disseminate information. Why it's important: *Information technology is bringing about the fusion of several important industries dealing with computers, telephones, televisions, and various handheld devices.*

input (p. 29) Whatever is put in ("input") to a computer system. Input devices include the keyboard and the mouse. Why it's important: *Useful information cannot be produced without input data.*

interactivity (p. 37) Two-way communication; a user can respond to information he or she receives and modify the process. Why it's important: *Interactive devices allow the user to actively participate in a technological process instead of just reacting to it.*

Internet (the "net") (p. 20) Worldwide computer network that connects hundreds of thousands of smaller networks linking computers at academic, scientific, and commercial institutions, as well as individuals. Why it's important: *Thanks to the Internet, millions of people around the world can share all types of information and services.*

keyboard (p. 31) Input device that converts letters, numbers, and other characters into electrical signals readable by the processor. Why it's important: *Keyboards are the most common kind of input device.*

local area network (LAN) (p. 24) Network that connects, usually by special cable, a group of desktop PCs and other devices, such as printers, in an office or a building. Why it's important: *LANs have replaced mainframes for many functions and are considerably less expensive.*

mainframe (p. 24) Second-largest computer available, after the supercomputer; capable of great processing speeds and data storage. Costs $5,000–$5 million. Small mainframes are often called *midsize computers.* Why it's important: *Mainframes are used by large organizations (banks, airlines, insurance companies, universities) that need to process millions of transactions.*

memory chip (p. 31) Also known as *RAM* (for "random access memory") *chip;* represents primary storage or temporary storage. Why it's important: *Holds data before processing and information after processing, before it is sent along to an output or storage device.*

microcomputer (p. 24) Also called *personal computer;* small computer that fits on or next to a desk or can be carried around. Costs $500–$5,000. Why it's important: *The microcomputer has lessened the reliance on mainframes and has provided more ordinary users with access to computers. It can be used as a stand-alone machine or connected to a network.*

microcontroller (p. 26) Also called an *embedded computer;* the smallest category of computer. Why it's important: *Microcontrollers are the tiny, specialized microprocessors built into "smart" electronic devices, such as appliances and automobiles.*

mobile Internet device (MID) (p. 26) Fully Internet integrated, handheld computer highly compatible with desktop microcomputers and laptops. The initial models focus on data communication, not voice communication. Why it's important: *Some mobile devices are too small to adequately view images on screen, but viewers still want more pocket-size portability than is possible with a laptop.*

modem (p. 35) Device that sends and receives data over telephone lines or cable lines, or wirelessly over a network, to and from computers. Why it's important: *A modem enables users to transmit data from one computer to another by using standard telephone lines instead of special communications equipment.*

monitor (p. 34) Display device that takes the electrical signals from the video card and forms an image using points of colored light on the screen. Why it's important: *Monitors enable users to view output without printing it out.*

motherboard (p. 32) Also called the *system board;* main circuit board in the computer. Why it's important: *This is the big green circuit board to which everything else—such as the keyboard, mouse, and printer—is attached. The processor chip and memory chips are also installed on the motherboard.*

mouse (p. 31) Nonkeyboard input device, called a "pointing device," used to manipulate objects viewed on the computer display screen. Why it's important: *For many purposes, a mouse is easier to use than a keyboard for inputting commands. Also, the mouse is used extensively in many graphics programs.*

multimedia (p. 38) From "multiple media"; technology that presents information in more than one medium—including text, graphics, animation, video, and sound—in a single integrated communication. Why it's important: *Multimedia is used increasingly in business, the professions, and education to improve the way information is communicated.*

nanotechnology (p. 23) Technology whereby molecule-size nanostructures are used to create tiny machines for holding data or performing tasks. Why it's important: *Could result in tremendous computer power in molecular-size devices.*

netbook (p. 25) Low-cost, lightweight computer with tiny dimensions and with functions designed for basic tasks, such as web searching, email, and word processing; weighs 2.25–3.2 pounds. Why it's important: *Cheaper computers that fill a technological category between notebooks and handheld devices.*

network (p. 5) Communications system connecting two or more computers. Why it's important: *Networks allow users to share applications and data and to use email. The Internet is the largest network.*

notebook computer (p. 25) Also called *laptop computer;* lightweight portable computer with a built-in monitor, keyboard, hard-disk drive, battery, and adapter; weighs 1.8–9 pounds. Why it's important: *Notebook and other small computers have provided users with computing capabilities in the field and on the road.*

online (p. 5) Using a computer or some other information device, connected through a network, to access information and services from another computer or information device. Why it's important: *Online communication is widely used by businesses, services, individuals, and educational institutions.*

output (p. 29) Whatever is output from ("put out of") the computer system; the results of processing. Why it's important: *People use output to help them make decisions. Without output devices, computer users would not be able to view or use the results of processing.*

peripheral device (p. 34) Any component or piece of equipment that expands a computer's input, storage, and output capabilities. Examples include printers and disk drives. Why it's important: *Most computer input and output functions are performed by peripheral devices.*

personal digital assistant (PDA) (p. 26) Also known as *handheld computer* or *palmtop;* used as a schedule planner and address book and to prepare to-do lists and send email and faxes. Why it's important: *PDAs make it easier for people to do business and communicate while traveling.*

primary storage (p. 29) Also called *memory* (RAM); internal computer circuitry that temporarily holds data waiting to be processed. Why it's important: *By holding data, primary storage enables the processor to process.*

printer (p. 34) Output device that produces text and graphics on paper. Why it's important: *Printers provide one of the principal forms of computer output.*

processing (p. 29) The manipulation a computer does to transform data into information. Why it's important: *Processing is the essence of the computer, and the processor is the computer's "brain."*

processor chip (p. 31) Also called the *processor*, the *CPU (central processing unit)*, or simply *chip;* tiny piece of silicon that contains millions of miniature electronic circuits used to process data. Why it's important: *Chips have made possible the development of small computers.*

robot (p. 8) Automatic device that performs functions ordinarily performed by human beings. Why it's important: *Robots help perform tasks that humans find difficult or impossible to do.*

secondary storage (p. 29) Also called *storage;* devices and media that store data and programs permanently—such as disks and disk drives, tape and tape drives, CDs and CD drives. Why it's important: *Without secondary storage, users would not be able to save their work. Storage also holds the computer's software.*

server (p. 27) Central computer in a network that holds collections of data (databases) and programs for connecting PCs, workstations, and other devices, which are called *clients*. Why it's important: *Servers enable many users to share equipment, programs, and data.*

software (p. 28) Also called *programs;* step-by-step electronically encoded instructions that tell the computer hardware how to perform a task. Why it's important: *Without software, hardware is useless.*

sound card (p. 34) Special circuit board that enhances the computer's sound-generating capabilities by allowing sound to be output through speakers. Why it's important: *Sound is used in multimedia applications. Also, many users like to listen to music CDs on their computers.*

speakers (p. 34) Devices that play sounds transmitted as electrical signals from the sound card. Speakers are connected to a single wire plugged into the back of the computer, or they built into the computer. Why it's important: *See* **sound card.**

supercomputer (p. 22) High-capacity computer with thousands of processors that is the fastest calculating device ever invented. Costs up to $350 million or more. Why it's important: *Supercomputers are used primarily for research purposes, airplane design, oil exploration, weather forecasting, and other activities that cannot be handled by mainframes and other less powerful machines.*

system software (p. 35) Software that helps the computer perform essential operating tasks. Why it's important: *Application software cannot run without system software. System software consists of several programs. The most important is the operating system, the master control program that runs the computer. Examples of operating system software for the PC are various Microsoft programs (such as Windows 95, 98, NT, Me, XP, and Vista), Unix, Linux, and the Macintosh operating system.*

system unit *See* **case.**

tablet computer (p. 25) Tablet computers, such as Apple's iPad, are a combination of smartphone and laptop computer with wireless connections. Why it's important: *Tablet computers are easy to use and easy to carry around, and they don't require a keyboard to use. The screen is a 9–10-inch touch screen (one can manipulate the screen contents directly with one's hand.) Tablet computers support multimedia.*

terminal (p. 24) Input and output device that uses a keyboard for input and a monitor for output; it cannot process data. Why it's important: *Terminals are generally used to input data to and receive data from a mainframe computer system.*

tower PC (p. 25) Microcomputer unit that sits as a "tower," often on the floor, freeing up desk space. Why it's important: *Tower PCs and desktop PCs are the most commonly used types of microcomputer.*

video card (p. 34) Circuit board that converts the processor's output information into a video signal for transmission through a cable to the monitor. Why it's important: *Virtually all computer users need to be able to view video output on the monitor.*

virtual (p. 10) Something that is created, simulated, or carried on by means of a computer or a computer network. Why it's important: *Allows actual objects to be represented in computer-based form.*

workstation (p. 24) Smaller than a mainframe; expensive, powerful computer generally used for complex scientific, mathematical, and engineering calculations and for computer-aided design and computer-aided manufacturing. Why it's important: *The power of workstations is needed for specialized applications too large and complex to be handled by PCs.*

World Wide Web (the "web") (p. 21) The interconnected system of Internet servers that support specially formatted documents in multimedia form—sounds, photos, and video as well as text. Why it's important: *The web is the most widely known part of the Internet.*

CHAPTER REVIEW

More and more educators are favoring an approach to learning (presented by Benjamin Bloom and his colleagues in *Taxonomy of Educational Objectives)* that follows a hierarchy of six critical-thinking skills: (a) two lower-order skills—memorization and comprehension; and (b) four higher-order skills—application, analysis, synthesis, and evaluation. While you may be able to get through many introductory college courses by simply memorizing facts and comprehending the basic ideas, to advance further you will probably need to employ the four higher-order thinking skills.

In the Chapter Review at the end of each chapter, we have implemented this hierarchy in a three-stage approach, as follows:

- *Stage 1 learning—memorization:* "I can recognize and recall information." Self-test questions, multiple-choice questions, and true/false questions enable you to test how well you recall basic terms and concepts.
- *Stage 2 learning—comprehension:* "I can recall information in my own terms and explain it to a friend." Using open-ended short-answer questions, we ask you to reexpress terms and concepts in your own words.
- *Stage 3 learning—applying, analyzing, synthesizing, evaluating:* "I can apply what I've learned, relate these ideas to other concepts, build on other knowledge, and use all these thinking skills to form a judgment." In this part of the Chapter Review, we ask you to put the ideas into effect using the activities described, some of which include Internet activities. The purpose is to help you take possession of the ideas, make them your own, and apply them realistically to your life.

LEARNING MEMORIZATION

"I can recognize and recall information."

Self-Test Questions

1. The __________ __________ __________ refers to the part of the Internet that presents information in multimedia form.
2. "__________ technology" merges computing with high-speed communications.
3. A(n) __________ is an electronic machine that accepts data and processes it into information.
4. The __________ is a worldwide network that connects hundreds of thousands of smaller networks.
5. __________ refers to information presented in nontextual forms such as video, sound, and graphics.
6. __________ are high-capacity machines with thousands of processors.
7. Embedded computers, or __________, are installed in "smart" appliances and automobiles.
8. The kind of software that enables users to perform specific tasks is called __________ software.
9. RAM is an example of __________ storage, and a hard drive is an example of __________ storage.
10. A(n) __________ is a communications system connecting two or more computers.
11. The four basic operations of all computers are __________, __________, __________, and __________.
12. The first programmable computer in the USA, which appeared in 1946, was called __________.
13. The __________ is the display device that takes the electrical signals from the video card and forms an image using points of colored light on the screen.
14. The base material for computer processing devices is __________, a natural element found in sand.
15. The general term for all the machinery and equipment in a computer system is __________.
16. The __________ and the __________ are the two most common input devices.
17. The processor chip, commonly called the __________ or a __________, is a tiny piece of silicon that contains millions of miniature electronic circuits.
18. One gigabyte is approximately __________ characters.
19. __________ refers to two-way communication; the user can respond to information he/she receives via the computer and modify what the computer is doing.

Multiple-Choice Questions

1. Which of the following devices converts computer output into displayed images?
   a. printer
   b. monitor
   c. floppy-disk drive
   d. processor
   e. hard-disk drive
2. Which of the following computer types is the smallest?
   a. mainframe
   b. microcomputer
   c. microcontroller
   d. supercomputer
   e. workstation
3. Which of the following is a secondary-storage device?
   a. processor
   b. main memory chip
   c. hard-disk drive
   d. printer
   e. monitor

4. Since the days when computers were first made available, computers have developed in three directions. What are they?
   a. increased expense
   b. miniaturization
   c. increased size
   d. affordability
   e. increased speed
5. Which of the following operations constitute the four basic operations followed by all computers?
   a. input
   b. storage
   c. programming
   d. output
   e. processing
6. Supercomputers are used for
   a. breaking codes.
   b. simulations for explosions of nuclear bombs.
   c. forecasting weather.
   d. keeping planets in orbit.
   e. all of these
   f. only a, b, and c.
7. What is the leading use of computers?
   a. web surfing
   b. email and social networking
   c. e-shopping
   d. word processing
8. Which is the main circuit board in the computer?
   a. RAM chip (random access memory)
   b. CPU processor chip (central processing unit)
   c. motherboard (system board)
   d. hard drive
9. A terabyte is approximately
   a. one million characters.
   b. one billion characters.
   c. one trillion characters.
   d. one quadrillion characters.
10. Speakers are an example of
   a. an input device.
   b. an output device.
   c. a processor.
   d. a storage device.

True/False Questions

T F 1. Mainframe computers process faster than microcomputers.

T F 2. Main memory is a software component.

T F 3. The operating system is part of the system software.

T F 4. Processing is the manipulation by which a computer transforms data into information.

T F 5. Primary storage is the area in the computer where data or information is held permanently.

T F 6. The keyboard and the mouse are examples of input devices.

T F 7. Movies are a form of multimedia.

T F 8. Computers are becoming larger, slower, and more expensive.

T F 9. Modems store information.

T F 10. A hard disk is an example of software.

T F 11. Computers continue to get smaller and smaller.

T F 12. Supercomputers are particularly inexpensive.

T F 13. Online education programs are called *computer learning.*

T F 14. PDAs are devices that can download books in digital form.

stage 2 LEARNING **COMPREHENSION**

"I can recall information in my own terms and explain it to a friend."

Short-Answer Questions

1. What does *online* mean?
2. What is the difference between system software and application software?
3. Briefly define *cyberspace.*
4. What is the difference between software and hardware?
5. What is a local area network?
6. What is multimedia?
7. What is the difference between microcomputers and supercomputers?
8. What is the function of RAM?
9. What does *downloading* mean?
10. What is meant by *connectivity?*
11. Describe some ways that information technology can be used to help people find jobs and to help jobs find people.
12. Compare the use of email to the use of the telephone and of conventional letters sent via the postal system. Which kinds of communications are best suited for which medium?
13. What is the basic meaning of *cloud computing?*

stage 3 LEARNING APPLYING, ANALYZING, SYNTHESIZING, EVALUATING

"I can apply what I've learned, relate these ideas to other concepts, build on other knowledge, and use all these thinking skills to form a judgment."

Knowledge in Action

1. Do you wish there was an invention to make your life easier or better? Describe it. What would it do for you? Come up with ideas on how that device may be constructed.
2. Determine what types of computers are being used where you work or go to school. In which departments are the different types of computer used? Make a list of the input devices, output devices, and storage devices. What are they used for? How are they connected to other computers?
3. Imagine a business you could start or run at home. What type of business is it? What type(s) of computer(s) do you think you'll need? Describe the computer system in as much detail as possible, including hardware components in the areas we have discussed so far. Keep your notes, and then refine your answers after you have completed the course.
4. Has reality become science fiction? Or has science fiction become science fact? First, watch an old futuristic movie, such as *2001—A Space Odyssey*, and take note of the then-futuristic technology displayed. Classify what you see according to input, output, processing, storage, and communications. Then watch a recent science fiction movie, and also list all the futuristic technology used according to the given categories. What was futuristic in the old movie that is now reality? What in the new movie is not yet reality but seems already feasible?
5. From what you've read and what you have experienced and/or observed in your life, do you have a positive, negative, or impartial view of our rapidly converging technological society? Why? Reevaluate your answers at the end of the course.
6. Computer prices are constantly falling. Whatever you pay for a computer today, you can be certain that you will be able to buy a more powerful computer for less money a year from now, and quite possibly even just a month from now. So how can you decide when it's a good time to upgrade to a better computer? Paradoxically, it seems that no matter how you time it, you'll always lose, because prices will go down again soon, and yet you will also always gain, because, since you were going to upgrade sooner or later anyway, you will reap the benefits of having the more powerful equipment that much longer.

   Discuss the benefits and costs, both material and psychological, of "waiting until prices drop." Gather more information on this topic by asking friends and colleagues what choices they have made about upgrading equipment over the years and whether they feel satisfaction or regret about the timing when they finally did upgrade.
7. Computers are almost everywhere, and they affect most walks of life—business, education, government, military, hobbies, shopping, research, and so on. What aspects of your life can you think of that still seem relatively unaffected by computers and technology? Is this a good thing or a bad thing, and is it likely to last? What aspects of your life have been the most conspicuously affected by technology? Has anything been made worse or harder in your life by the advance of computers? What about things that have been made better or easier?
8. Have you become extremely dependent on some technologies? Some people no longer write down telephone numbers anywhere; instead, they simply program them into their cellphones. Some people feel helpless in a foreign country unless they have a calculator in hand to compute currency conversions. Many people rely on their email archive or cellphone to hold essential information, such as addresses and appointments. When any of these technologies fails us, we can feel lost.

   Make a list of technologies that have become indispensable to your life. Imagine the consequences if any of these technologies should fail you. What can you do to protect yourself against such failure?
9. It has been said that the computer is a "meta medium" because it can simulate (behave as) any other medium. Thus a computer can present text that can be read from virtual "pages" as if it were a book; it can let you compose and print text as if it were a typewriter; it can play music as if it were a boombox; it can display video as if it were a television set; it can make telephone calls as if it were a telephone; it can let you "draw" and "paint"; it can be programmed to serve as an answering machine; and so forth.

   Imagine a future in which computers have replaced all the things they can emulate: instead of books and magazines and newspapers, we would have text only on computers. Telephones, PDAs, television sets, VCRs, DVD players, stereo sets, and other electronic devices would all be gone or, rather, subsumed by computers. What benefits to your life can you see in such a future? What things might be worse? What dangers can you see? Do you think this kind of radical convergence is likely? If so, how long do you think it will take?

Web Exercises

If you are not yet familiar with web surfing, wait until you have finished Chapter 2 to do the following web exercises.

1. Are computers, cellphones, and other electronic devices bad for our health? You may have heard the term *electromagnetic radiation* and dismissed it as an obscure scientific term not worth understanding. Visit the links below to become educated on a topic that will be discussed more seriously and frequently when our society becomes completely wireless.

   www.csmonitor.com/Innovation/Latest-News-Wires/2011/0225/Cell-phone-radiation-Is-it-harmful

   www.npr.org/2011/02/25/134059267/cell-phone-radiation-affects-brain-study-says

   www.howstuffworks.com/cell-phone-radiation.htm

   www.fda.gov/Radiation-EmittingProducts/RadiationEmittingProductsandProcedures/HomeBusinessandEntertainment/CellPhones/ucm116282.htm

   http://jama.ama-assn.org/content/305/8/828.extract

2. List some pros and cons of a "paperless" environment. Do you believe that a paperless environment is something worth striving for in the workplace? In the home? In the classroom? In banking? Run a web search to see what others are doing to implement this idea.
3. Computer pioneer John Von Neumann was one of a group of individuals who conceived the idea of the "stored program." He could also divide two 8-digit numbers in his head. Spend a few hours researching this remarkable man; at online bookstores, look up some of the books he wrote and read the reviews.
4. Looking for legally free programs? Some great places to start:

   www.download.com

   www.shareware.com

   www.freewarefiles.com/

   www.freedownloadscenter.com/
5. Visit the following websites to become aware of some topics of interest in the computing world. Full comprehension of these topics isn't necessary at this time; this is only to familiarize you with subject matter you may come in contact with.

   www.sciencedaily.com/news/computers_math/computer_science/

   www.computeruser.com/

   www.infoworld.com/

   http://slashdot.org

   www.slideshare.net/dheerajmehrotra/basic-concepts-of-information-technology-it-presentation
6. "Moore's Law" predicts the rate at which computers will continue to get smaller (and hence faster). The "law" has proved to be astonishingly accurate over many years. Do a web search for Moore's Law, and see if you can find answers to the following questions:
   a. Who is Moore, and when did he make the prediction we know as Moore's Law?
   b. What is the simplest statement of the law's prediction?
   c. How has the law changed over time?
   d. Is the law still valid? If yes, how much longer is the law expected to hold true?
   e. How does the law affect business projections?
7. A Wiki is a website on which authoring and editing can be done very easily by anyone, anywhere, anytime using a web browser such as Internet Explorer or Mozilla Firefox, with no need for special software or other special requirements. (*Wiki* is Hawaiian for "quick.") Most web pages are less than perfect. If it is a Wiki-page and you are annoyed by something, you can just hit the Edit button and change it! Over time, the site gets better (people hope)!

   Here are some examples of Wikis that deal with general knowledge:

   http://en.wikipedia.org

   www.wikimedia.org/

   http://wiki.ehow.com/Main-Page

   And here are some specialized Wikis:

   http://raw.wikia.com/wiki/Main_Page

   http://webtrends.about.com/od/wikilists/tp/list_of_wiki_sites.htm

   www.wikispaces.com/

   www.wikia.com/Wikia

   http://wikisineducation.wetpaint.com/

   a. Make a small change on a page on one of the listed sites or on some other Wiki site you have identified. Submit your change, and note the results. Anyone navigating to that site will now see your change. Did you know that website authoring could be that easy? Are you surprised that someone would unconditionally open up his or her website for anyone to edit?
   b. Since you can make any change you wish, even something totally nonsensical or simply wrong, it's obviously possible for incorrect or misleading content to appear on a Wiki. Given that, why do you think that Wikis have become so popular and so widespread?
   c. How significant a problem do you think vandalism and other acts of poor citizenship might be on "open" Wikis? How can you find out?
   d. Some Wikis contend with the threat of vandalism by requiring that a password be provided before a user is allowed to make changes. What advantages can you see to this approach? What disadvantages? Do you think the advantages of password protection outweigh the disadvantages? What do the Wikis you browse through have to say about this issue?
   e. What measures do you think an online shared space can take to limit the potential damage from vandalism, while not being overly restrictive?
   f. If you knew that a particular person was defacing a Wiki, what would you do about it? Report the person? Wait for the vandal to get bored and turn his or her mischief elsewhere? Or try to reform the person? Are the basic ethical considerations here the same as those regarding other forms of vandalism in our society?
   g. Do you think that open-access systems such as unrestricted Wikis will become more common over time, or do you think that abuse of such systems will destroy their usefulness and that Wikis will eventually disappear?

2

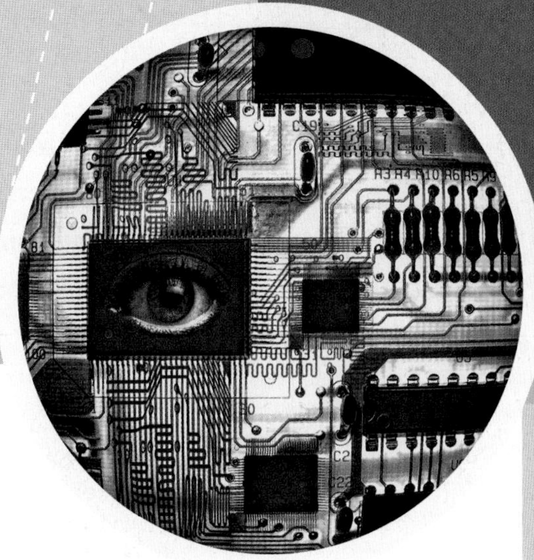

THE INTERNET & THE WORLD WIDE WEB

Exploring Cyberspace

Chapter Topics & Key Questions

2.1 **Connecting to the Internet: Narrowband, Broadband, & Access Providers** What are the means of connecting to the Internet, and how fast are they? What are three kinds of Internet access provider?

2.2 **How Does the Internet Work?** What is the basic structure of the Internet, and who controls it?

2.3 **The World Wide Web** How do the following work: websites, web pages, browsers, URLs, web portals, search tools, and search engines? What are HTML and hyperlinks?

2.4 **Email & Other Ways of Communicating over the Net** What are email and webmail, attachments, instant messaging, FTP, newsgroups, listservs, and netiquette?

2.5 **The Online Gold Mine: Telephony, Multimedia, Webcasting, Blogs, E-Commerce, & Social Networking** What are Internet telephony, various kinds of multimedia, RSS, and different web feeds (webcasting, blogging, podcasting), types of e-commerce, and social networking?

2.6 **The Intrusive Internet: Snooping, Spamming, Spoofing, Phishing, Pharming, Cookies, & Spyware** How can I protect myself against the various kinds of Internet dangers, such as snoopers, spam, spoofing, phishing, pharming, cookies, and spyware—adware, browser and search hijackers, and key loggers?

Download the free UIT 10e App for key term flash cards, quizzes, and a game, *Over the Edge*

The immensity of the changes wrought—and still to come—cannot be underestimated," says futurist Graham Molitor. "This miraculous information channel—the Internet—will touch and alter virtually every facet of humanity, business, and all the rest of civilization's trappings."[1]

Today the world of the Internet provides activities hardly imaginable 15 years ago. (● *See Panel 2.1 on the next page.*) Indeed, pervasive computing, ubiquitous computing, is already an established fact, with "everything connected to everything," from cellphones to cameras to car navigation systems. Because of its standard interfaces and low rates, the Internet has been the great leveler for communications—just as the personal computer was for computing.

The basis for the Internet began in 1969 as ARPANET (for ARPA, the Advanced Research Projects Agency of the U.S. Department of Defense), with four linked-together computers at different universities and defense contractors. From there the network expanded to 62 computers in 1974, 500 computers in 1983, and 28,000 in 1987. However, it still remained the domain of researchers and academics, and it was still all text—no graphics, video, or sound. Not until the development of the World Wide Web in the early 1990s, which made multimedia available on the Internet, and the first browser (for locating web pages), which opened the web to commercial uses, did the global network really take off. (● *See Panel 2.2 for a brief history of telecommunications.*) In 2010 almost 2 billion people were using the Internet, with people in the United States making up 24.8% of the world's total users. China had the highest numbers of users, followed by the United States, Japan, India, and Brazil.[2] By 2015, 5 billion people may be connected to the Internet.[3]

How does one become a participant in this network of networks? What is the first step? To connect to the Internet, you need three things: an *access device,* such as a personal computer with a modem, a cable modem, or other device; a *means of connection,* such as a telephone line, cable hookup, or wireless capability; and an *Internet access provider,* such as an Internet service provider (ISP), a commercial online service provider, or a wireless Internet service provider. We cover these subjects in the next section. We then describe how the Internet works.

more info!

Hobbes's Internet Timeline

For more detailed Internet timelines, go to:

www.computerhistory.org/internet_history

www.davesite.com/webstation/net-history5.shtml

www.webopedia.com/quick_ref/timeline.asp

www.factmonster.com/ipka/A0193167.html

www.zakon.org/robert/internet/timeline

panel 2.2

Timeline: Brief graphical history of telecommunications and the Internet

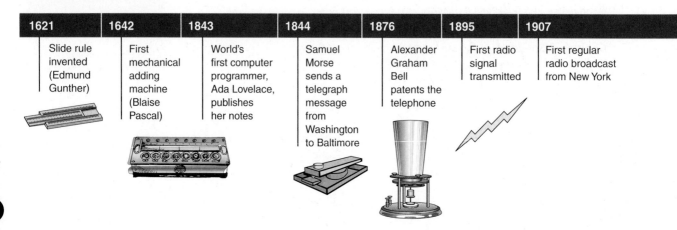

1621	1642	1843	1844	1876	1895	1907
Slide rule invented (Edmund Gunther)	First mechanical adding machine (Blaise Pascal)	World's first computer programmer, Ada Lovelace, publishes her notes	Samuel Morse sends a telegraph message from Washington to Baltimore	Alexander Graham Bell patents the telephone	First radio signal transmitted	First regular radio broadcast from New York

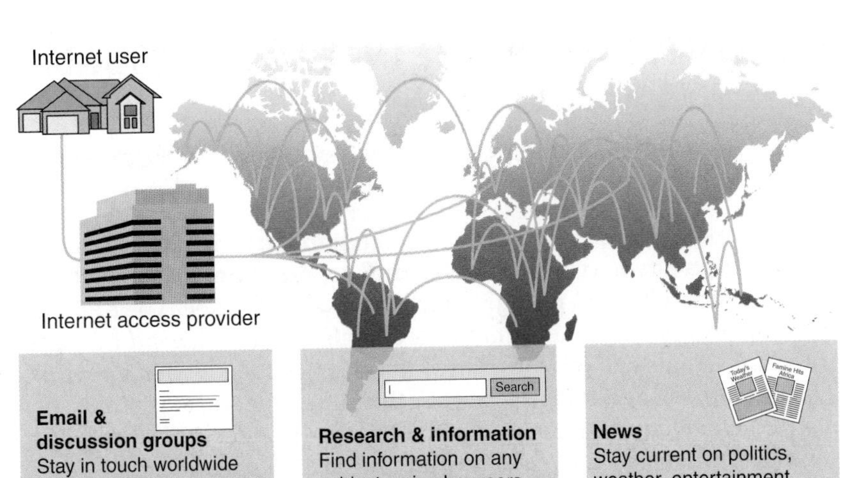

panel 2.1

Some areas in the world of the Internet

Email & discussion groups
Stay in touch worldwide and do business via email.

Research & information
Find information on any subject, using browsers and search tools.

News
Stay current on politics, weather, entertainment, sports, and financial news.

Entertainment
Amuse yourself with internet games, music, videos, and movies.

Download files
Get software, music, and documents such as e-books.

E-shopping
Price anything from plane tickets to cars; order anything from books to sofas.

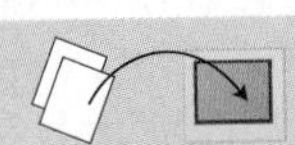

Financial matters
Do investing, banking, and bill paying online.

Auctions
Sell old stuff, acquire more stuff, with online auctions.

Telephony & conferencing
Make inexpensive phone calls; have online meetings.

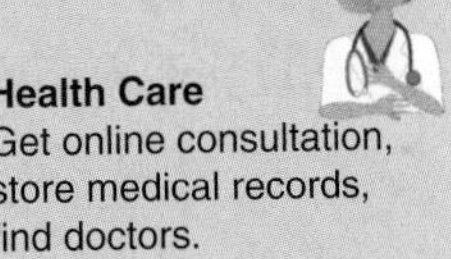

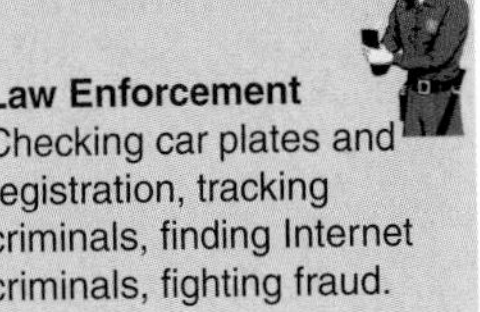

Career advancement
Search job listings, post résumés, interview online.

Distance learning
Attend online lectures, have discussions, write research papers, earn degrees.

E-business
Connect with coworkers, buy supplies, support customers, conduct negotiations, do marketing.

Social Networking
Facebook, Twitter, Myspace, Flickr, blogging

Health Care
Get online consultation, store medical records, find doctors.

Law Enforcement
Checking car plates and registration, tracking criminals, finding Internet criminals, fighting fraud.

1927 First demonstration of television in USA

1944 First electro-mechanical computer (Mark I)

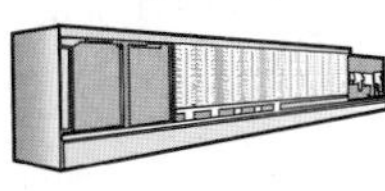

1946 First programmable electronic computer in United States (ENIAC)

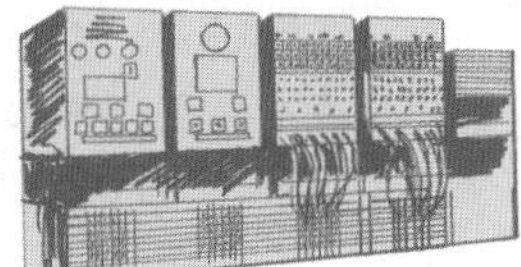

1947 Vannevar Bush proposes hypertext; mobile phones first invented (cellphones not sold commercially until 1983)

1958 Eisenhower administration creates the Advanced Research Projects Agency (ARPA) as part of the U.S. Department of Defense

1962 First commercially available modem (developed in the 1950s)

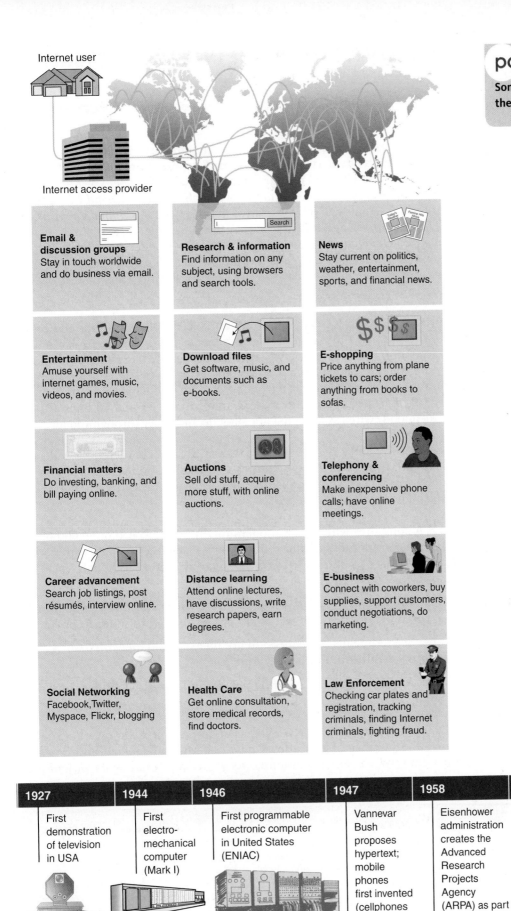

2.1 CONNECTING TO THE INTERNET: Narrowband, Broadband, & Access Providers

However you connect to the Internet, the bandwidth will determine the speed of your connection.

In general terms, ***bandwidth***, **or *channel capacity*, is an expression of how much data—text, voice, video, and so on—can be sent through a communications channel in a given amount of time.** The type of data transmission that allows only one signal at a time is called *baseband transmission*. When several signals can be transmitted at once, it's called *broadband transmission*. ***Broadband*—high-speed—connections** include various kinds of high-speed wired connections (such as coaxial and fiber optic, described in Chapter 6), as well as DSL, cable, and satellite and other wireless connections, discussed shortly. Today about two-thirds (66%) of all adult Americans have broadband Internet connections at home.[4]

THE PHYSICAL CONNECTION: WIRED OR WIRELESS? What are your choices of a *physical connection*—the wired or wireless means of connecting to the Internet? A lot depends on where you live. As you might expect, urban and many suburban areas offer more broadband connections than rural areas do. Among the principal means of connection are (1) telephone (dial-up) modem (used mostly in rural areas); (2) high-speed phone lines—DSL modem and T1 and T3 lines; (3) cable modem; and (4) wireless modem—for satellite and other through-the-air links.

DATA TRANSMISSION SPEEDS Data is transmitted in characters or collections of bits. A *bit*, as we will discuss later, is the smallest unit of information used by computers. Today's data transmission speeds are measured in *bits, kilobits, megabits,* and *gigabits* per second:

- **bps:** A computer with an old modem might have a speed of 56,000 bps, which is considered the minimum speed for visiting websites with graphics. The ***bps*** **stands for *bits per second*** (Eight bits equals one character, such as A, 3, or #.)
- **Kbps: *Kilobits per second*, or *Kbps*, are 1 thousand bits per second.** The speed of a modem that is 56,000 bps might be expressed as 56 Kbps.
- **Mbps:** Faster means of connection are measured in ***megabits per second*, or *Mbps*—1 million bits per second.**
- **Gbps:** At the extreme are ***gigabits per second*, *Gbps*—1 billion bits per second.**

UPLOADING & DOWNLOADING Why is it important to know these terms? Because the number of bits affects how fast you can upload and download information from a remote computer. As we've said (Chapter 1), ***download*** **is**

1969	1970	1971	1973	1974	1975	1976
ARPANET established at 4 U.S. universities (4 computers linked by leased lines); led to Internet (4 hosts)	Microprocessor chips come into use; 15 ARPANET sites established (universities/research), each with own address; 13 hosts on network	Email invented by computer engineer Ray Tomlinson; 23 hosts on network	ARPANET becomes international; 35 hosts on network	TCP (Transmission Control Protocol) specification developed by U.S. Dept. of Defense; 62 hosts on network; first use of the word *Internet*	First microcomputer (MITS Altair 8800)	Queen Elizabeth sends the first royal email

the transmission of data from a remote computer to a local computer, as from a website to your own PC—for example, downloading a movie. ***Upload*** **is the transmission of data from a local computer to a remote computer,** as from your PC to a website you are constructing or putting one of your videos on YouTube.

Satellite
Upload
Download
Mainframe
Individual PC

Narrowband (Dial-Up Modem): Low Speed but Inexpensive

Dial-up modems are used primarily in rural areas, where broadband connections are not always available.

The telephone line that you use for voice calls is still the cheapest means of online connection and is available everywhere. Although the majority of U.S. adults favor broadband Internet connections, many rural home users still use what are called ***narrowband,*** **or low-bandwidth,** connections. This mainly consists of ***dial-up connections*****—use of telephone modems to connect computers to the Internet.**

CONNECTING THE MODEM As we mentioned in Chapter 1, **a *modem* is a device that sends and receives data over telephone lines to and from computers.** A dial-up modem is attached to the telephone wall outlet. *(• See Panel 2.3, next page.)* (We discuss modems in a bit more detail in Chapter 6.)

Most dial-up modems today have a maximum speed of 56 Kbps. That doesn't mean, however, that dial-up users will be sending and receiving data at that rate. The modem in the computer must negotiate with the modems used by the *Internet service provider (ISP),* the regional, national, or wireless organization or business that connects you to the Internet. Downloading a 16 megabyte (MB) movie via a 56 Kbps dial-up connection would take about 31 minutes and 45 seconds.

High-Speed Phone Lines: More Expensive but Available in Most Cities

Dial-up connections are becoming obsolete, in favor of high-speed connections.

Waiting while your computer's modem takes 25 minutes to transmit a 1-minute low-quality video from a website may have you pummeling the desk in frustration. To get some relief, you could enhance your ***POTS*****—"plain old telephone system"**—connection with a high-speed adaptation. The choices are DSL and T1/T3, available in most major cities, though not in many rural areas.

DSL LINE ***DSL (digital subscriber line)*** **uses regular phone lines, a DSL modem, and special technology to transmit data in megabits per second.** Incoming data is significantly faster than outgoing data. That is, your computer can *receive* data at the rate of 1.5–10 Mbps, but it can *send* data at only

1976	1978	1979	1981	1983	1984	1986	1987
Apple I computer (first personal computer sold in assembled form)	TCP/IP developed (released in 1983) as standard Internet transmission protocol; 111 hosts on Internet; first spam email	First Usenet newsgroups; 188 hosts on Internet	IBM introduces personal computer; 213 hosts on Internet	TCP/IP use required	Apple Macintosh; first personal laser printer; William Gibson coins term *cyberspace*; Domain Name System (DNS) introduced	NSFNET (National Science Foundation Network) backbone established	Digital cellular phones invented; first email message sent from China

panel 2.3

Telephone dial-up modem connection

You connect the modem inside your computer from a port (socket) in the back of your computer to a line that is then connected to a wall jack. Your telephone is also connected to your computer so that you can make voice calls. (Note that this kind of connection, if using only one telephone number, cannot be used to make voice calls and connect to the Internet at the same time.)

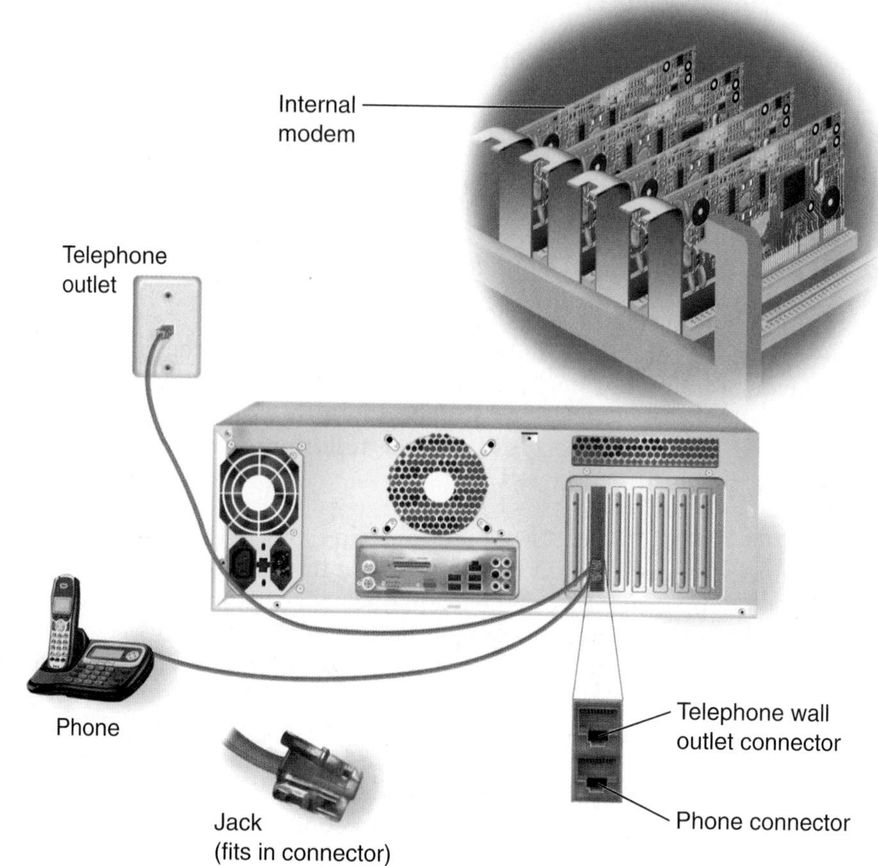

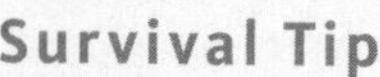

Survival Tip

Broadband: Riskier for Security

Unlike dial-up services, broadband and DSL services, because they are always switched on, make your computer vulnerable to over-the-Internet security breaches. Solution: Install firewall software, which prevents most unauthorized users from accessing a private network that is connected to a public network, such as the Internet. (Firewalls must be continually updated.)

128 Kbps–1.5 Mbps. This arrangement may be fine, however, if you're principally interested in obtaining very large amounts of data (video, music) rather than in sending such data to others. With DSL, you could download that 16 MB movie in about 8 minutes and 45 seconds. A big advantage of DSL is that it is always on (so you don't have to make a dial-up connection) and, unlike cable (discussed shortly), its transmission rate is relatively consistent. Also, you can talk on the phone and send data at the same time.

1989	1990	1984	1989–1991	1992	1993	1994
World Wide Web established by Tim Berners-Lee while working at the European Particle Physics Laboratory in Geneva, Switzerland; first home trials of fiber communications network; number of Internet hosts breaks 100,000; first commercial dial-up Internet availability	ARPANET decommissioned; first ISP comes on-line (dial-up access); Berners-Lee develops first web browser, WorldWideWeb; 313,000 hosts on Internet (9,300 domains)	9.6 K modem	14.4 K modem	"Surfing the Internet" coined by Jean Armour Polly; 1,136,000 hosts on Internet (18,1000 domains)	Multimedia desktop computers; IXPs replace NSFNET; first graphical web browser, Mosaic, developed by Marc Andreessen; the U.S. White House goes online; Internet talk radio begins broadcasting; 2,056,000 hosts on Internet (28,000 domains)	Apple and IBM introduce PCs with full-motion video built in; wireless data transmission for small portable computers; Netscape Navigator released; 28.8 K modem; the Japanese Prime Minister goes online; 3,864,000 hosts on Internet (56,000 domains)

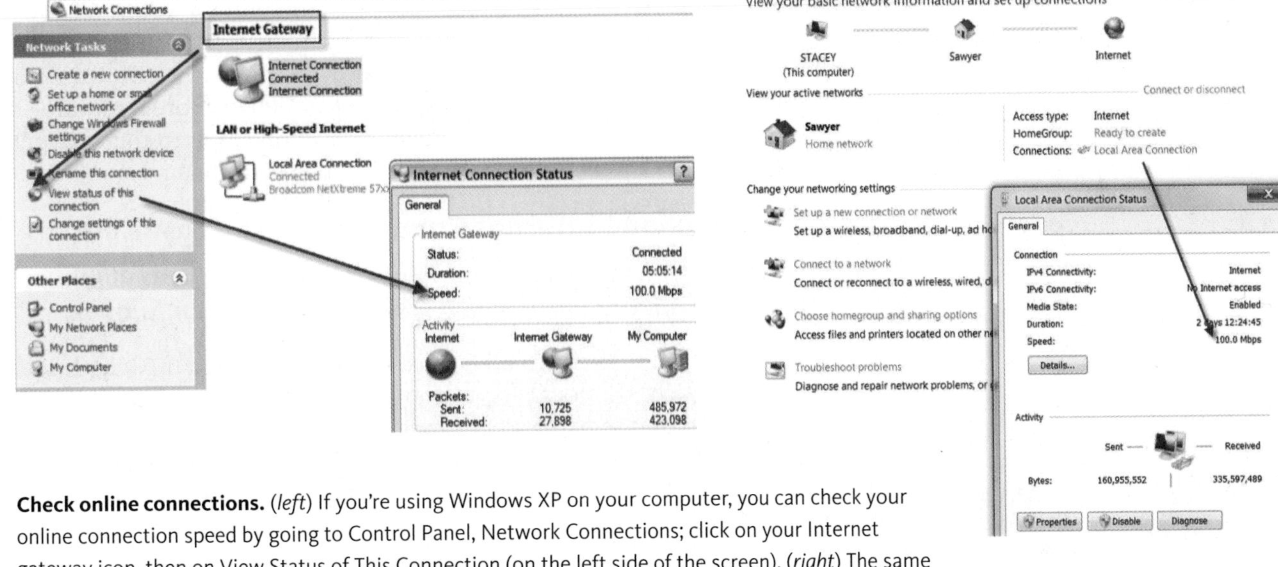

Check online connections. (*left*) If you're using Windows XP on your computer, you can check your online connection speed by going to Control Panel, Network Connections; click on your Internet gateway icon, then on View Status of This Connection (on the left side of the screen). (*right*) The same procedure shown in Windows 7: go to Control Panel, click on Network and Sharing Center, then click on Local Area Connection.

There is one big drawback to DSL: You have to live within 4.5 miles of a phone company central switching office, because the access speed and reliability degrade with distance. However, DSL is becoming more popular, and phone companies are building thousands of remote switching facilities to enhance service throughout their regions. Another drawback is that you have to choose from a list of Internet service providers that are under contract to the phone company you use, although other DSL providers exist. (DSL service costs users about $50 to $250 per month.) Still, the real problem for DSL—or any other kind of broadband—is that it is not available to many rural Americans, who thus lack the sort of high-speed services and opportunities, such as distance learning and web-based commerce, that urban dwellers take for granted.[5]

T1 LINE How important is high speed to you? Is it worth $550–$1,200 a month? Then consider getting a ***T1 line*****, essentially a traditional trunk line, a fiber-optic or copper line separate from the phone line, that carries**

1995	1996	1998	1999	2000	2001	2002	2003
NSFNET reverts to research project; Internet now in commercial hands; the Vatican goes online	Microsoft releases Internet Explorer; 56 K modem invented; cable modem introduced; 12,881,000 hosts on Internet (488,000 domains); Internet 2	Google is funded	Wi-Fi is standardized	Web surpasses 1 billion indexable pages; 93,047,785 hosts on Internet	AOL membership surpasses 28 million; Wikipedia is launched	Blogs become popular; Friendster	First official Swiss online election; flash mobs start in New York City; Facebook; MySpace; iTunes

24 normal telephone circuits and has a transmission rate of 1.5 to 6 Mbps. Generally, T1 lines are leased by corporate, government, and academic sites. Another high-speed line, the T3 line, transmits at 6–45 Mbps (the equivalent of about 672 simultaneous voice calls) and costs about $4,000 or more a month. T1 and T3 lines are also commonly used by businesses connecting to the Internet, by Internet access providers, and in the Internet high-speed transmission lines.

Problem for Telephone Internet Connections: The Last Mile

The medium that connects homes and business to the central switching office is usually old copper wire, which slows data movement down.

The length of the connections from all homes and businesses to the telephone's central switching office, the local loop, is often called the "last mile." As we mentioned earlier, if you are using POTS for your initial Internet connection—even if you use DSL—data must pass back and forth between you and your telephone switching station. (This distance is usually more than a mile; it is shorter than 20 miles and averages about 3 miles in metropolitan areas.) This "last mile" of old, often poor-quality copper wire is what really slows things down. This problem can be solved by installing newer transmission media, but communications companies are slow to incur this cost. There are about 130 million phone lines in the United States that use 650 million miles of copper wire. Considering that our planet is only about 93 million miles from the sun, 650 million miles of wire represents a huge challenge to replace!

Cable modem

Cable Modem: Close Competitor to DSL

Cable connections can be faster than DSL and are more popular in the United States.

DSL can download a 6-minute video in about 11 minutes; cable can often do it in 2 minutes. Cable modems can transmit outgoing data at about 1.4 Mbps and incoming data at up to 30 Mbps. (The common residential transmission rate is 3 Mbps.) **A *cable modem* connects a personal computer to a cable-TV system that offers an Internet connection.** The cable runs underground from a street cable-box connection to the house or business; it is separate from the phone line.

The advantage of a cable modem is that, like a DSL connection, it is always on. However, unlike DSL, you don't need to live near a telephone switching station. (• *See Panel 2.4.*) A disadvantage, however, is that you and your cable-TV-viewing-Internet-surfing neighbors are sharing the system and consequently, during peak-load times, your service may be slowed to the speed of a regular dial-up modem. Also, using an Internet connection that is always on—and that, in the case of cable, you share with other people—invites outside interference with your computer, a risk that we discuss later in the book.

Cable companies may contract you to use their own Internet service provider, but more commonly you may choose your own. (Some cable companies also supply voice phone service.)

Survival Tip

Connection Speeds

To test the speed of your Internet connection, go to:

www.speedtest.net

http://reviews.cnet.com/internet-speed-test

www.testmyspeed.com

www.computerhope.com/issues/ch000539.htm

www.auditmypc.com/speedtest.asp

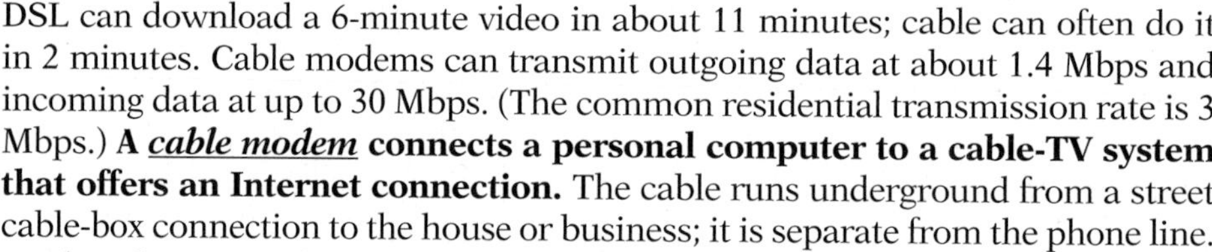

2004
More than 285,000,000 hosts on Internet; Facebook launched
2005
YouTube; Wii
2006
Twitter
2007
Skype
2010
More than 131,000,000 hosts on the Internet—top 10 are USA, China, UK, Japan, Germany, S. Korea, France, Canada, Australia, Italy; Asia has the most Internet users
2012
3D processing chip; 5G phones
2030–2045
The singularity

panel 2.4

Basic DSL/cable-PC system

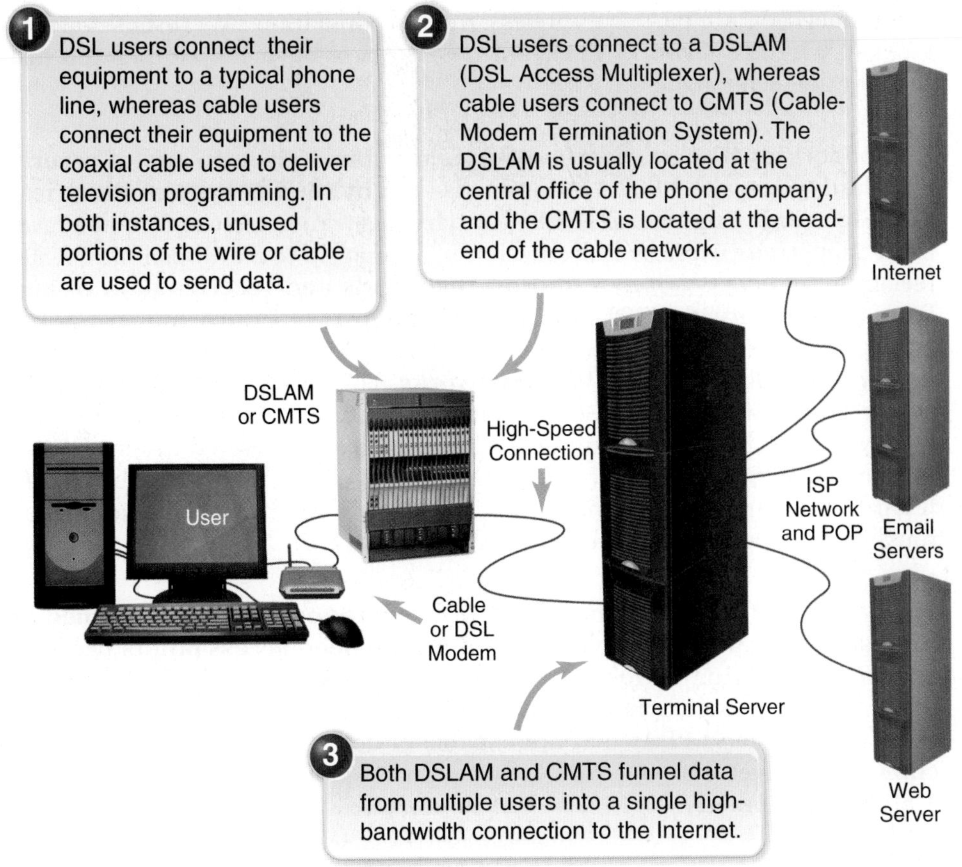

1. DSL users connect their equipment to a typical phone line, whereas cable users connect their equipment to the coaxial cable used to deliver television programming. In both instances, unused portions of the wire or cable are used to send data.

2. DSL users connect to a DSLAM (DSL Access Multiplexer), whereas cable users connect to CMTS (Cable-Modem Termination System). The DSLAM is usually located at the central office of the phone company, and the CMTS is located at the head-end of the cable network.

3. Both DSLAM and CMTS funnel data from multiple users into a single high-bandwidth connection to the Internet.

User
DSLAM or CMTS
Cable or DSL Modem
High-Speed Connection
Terminal Server
ISP Network and POP
Internet
Email Servers
Web Server

Satellite Wireless Connections

Satellite connections provide Internet access without telephone lines or cables; however, satellite connection involves signal delay.

If you live in a rural area and are tired of the molasses-like speed of your cranky local phone system, but you have no DSL or cable access, you might—if you have an unobstructed view of the southern sky—consider taking to the air. With a pizza-size satellite dish on your roof or on the side of your house, you can send data at the rate of about 200 to 512 Kbps and receive data at speeds up to about 1 to 5 Mbps from a ***communications satellite*****, a space station that transmits radio waves called *microwaves* from earth-based stations.**

Satellite Internet connections, which cost about $50 to $120 per month, are always on. To surf the Internet using this kind of connection, you need an Internet access provider that supports two-way satellite transmission. You will also have to lease or purchase satellite-access hardware, such as a dish and satellite modem and have the dish connected by cable to at least one computer inside your house or office, along with the modem. Note that satellite connectivity providers often impose use quotas on their customers. If you exceed your usage quota for the month, the service provider may slow you down significantly. (We cover satellites in more detail in Chapter 6.)

Sky connection. Setting up a home satellite dish.

Other Wireless Connections: Wi-Fi, 3G, & 4G

Newer mobile wireless connections are becoming the most popular type of connectivity.

More and more people are using laptop computers, tablet computers, smart cellphones, and personal digital assistants to access the Internet through ***wireless networks*****, which use radio waves to transmit data.** Indeed, about 85%

How much do you know about Wi-Fi? Take a quiz:

http://computer.howstuffworks.com/wifi-quiz.htm

Finding Wi-Fi Hot Spots

www.openwifispots.com/
www.wififreespot.com/
www.wifihotspotlist.com/
www.wifinder.com/

of all Americans are part of a wireless, mobile population.[6] We discuss various types of wireless networks in detail in Chapter 6, but here we mention just three of the technologies:

WI-FI Short for *Wireless Fidelity,* ***Wi-Fi*** **is the name given to any of several standards—so-called 802.11 standards—set by the Institute of Electrical and Electronic Engineers (IEEE) for wireless transmission.** One standard, 802.11b, permits wireless transmission of data at up to 54 Mbps for 300–500 feet from an ***access point,*** **a station that sends and receives data to and from a Wi-Fi network;** 802.11n can transmit up to 140 Mpbs. Many airports, hotels, libraries, convention centers, and fast-food facilities offer so-called ***hotspots*****—public access to Wi-Fi networks.** The hotspot can get its Internet access from DSL, cable modem, T1 local area network, dial-up phone service, or any other method. (Communications technology is covered in more detail in Chapter 6.) Once the hotspot has the Internet connection, it can broadcast it wirelessly. Laptops are commonly used for Wi-Fi Internet connections (they must be equipped with the necessary Wi-Fi hardware).

3G WIRELESS ***3G,*** **which stands for "third generation," is loosely defined as high-speed wireless technology that does not need access points because it uses the existing cellphone system.** This technology, which is found in many tablet PCs, smartphones (Internet-enabled cellphones that run applications, or apps), and PDAs that are capable of delivering downloadable video clips and high-resolution games, is being provided by AT&T, Sprint, Verizon, T-Mobile, and others.

4G LTE Galaxy Tab

4G WIRELESS ***4G,*** **which stands for "fourth generation," is a successor to 3G and 2G standards, with the aim to provide a wide range of data rates up to ultra-broadband (gigabit-speed) Internet access to mobile as well as stationary users.** Neither standards bodies nor service carriers have yet concretely defined or agreed on what exactly 4G will be. In general, "3G networks carry voice and Internet traffic. 4G networks are built specifically for Internet content, so cell sites don't include equipment to route phone calls, reducing their footprint and creating energy efficiencies. That also positions 4G networks to better handle high-bandwidth activities."[7] But carriers can claim whatever they want, because "the International Telecommunciations Union, the wireless industry standards body, hasn't set a firm 4G definition."[8] In the meantime the term 4G is basically being applied to existing 3G technologies.

4G smartpones have been released by Motorola, Samsung, HTC Evo, Sprint, T-Mobile, Verizon, Apple, and a few other companies. (Apple has also released 4S, and 5G is on the way.)

Internet Access Providers (ISPs): Three Kinds

Users need to know how to choose an ISP just right for them.

As we mentioned, in addition to having an access device and a means of connection, to get on the Internet you need to go through an *Internet access provider.* There are three types of such providers: *Internet service providers, commercial online services,* and *wireless Internet service providers.*

Survival Tip

Some Free ISPs

www.dailyedeals.com/free_internet/free_isp.htm
http://home.pacbell.net/dbk4297/freeisp.html
www.freei.com

INTERNET SERVICE PROVIDERS (ISPS) As we mentioned earlier, an ***Internet service provider (ISP)*** **is a local, regional, or national organization that provides access to the Internet for a fee.** The ISP may own the facilities that it uses to deliver services, or it may lease the facilities of another provider. Examples of national providers are EarthLink, Comcast, and Hughesnet; there are many others. There are also some free ISPs.

COMMERCIAL ONLINE SERVICES A *commercial online service* is a members-only company that provides not only Internet access but other specialized content as well, such as news, games, and financial data. The two best-known subscriber-only commercial online services are AOL (America Online) and MSN (Microsoft Network).

WIRELESS INTERNET SERVICE PROVIDERS A *wireless Internet service provider (WISP)* enables users with computers containing wireless modems—mostly laptops/notebooks/tablets—and web-enabled smartphones and personal digital assistants to gain access to the Internet. A WISP offers public wireless network services and Internet access. WISPs typically install Wi-Fi wireless hotspots in airports, hotels, cafes, and other public businessplaces. (A hotspot is a public location where Wi-Fi Internet access can be obtained.)

To use a WISP, you must subscribe to their wireless service. Some WISPs offer free Internet service, but many others charge fees and/or require service contracts. When choosing a WISP, you should ensure that the provider's equipment and software are compatible with your own system. WISPs also vary in the speed and security features they offer.

Examples of WISPs are AT&T, Sprint, T-Mobile, and Verizon.

Finding ISPs

For comparison shopping, go online to:

www.thelist.com

www.theispguide.com/

These sites list ISPs from all over the world and guide you through the process of finding one that's best for you.

2.2 How Does the Internet Work?

The Internet is basically a huge network that connects hundreds of thousands of smaller networks.

The *inter*national *network* known as the *Internet* consists of hundreds of thousands of smaller networks linking educational, commercial, nonprofit, and military organizations, as well as individuals. Central to this arrangement is the client/server network. **A *client* computer is a computer requesting data or services. A *server*, or *host computer*, is a central computer supplying data or services requested of it.** When the client computer's request—for example, for information on various airline flights and prices—gets to a server computer, that computer sends the information back to the client computer.

Internet Connections: POPs, IXPs, Backbone, & Internet2

The foundation of the Internet is the backbone, the fastest part, which links to slower types of connections, such as those of ISPs.

Your journey onto the Internet starts with connecting your client computer's modem or your wireless device to your Internet service provider (ISP). *(• See Panel 2.5, next page.)* This is the slowest part of the entire Internet connection. An ISP's headquarters and network servers may be located almost anywhere.

POINT OF PRESENCE ISPs provide each customer with a ❶ ***point of presence (POP)*—a local access point to the Internet—a collection of modems and other equipment in a local area.** The POP acts as a local gateway to the ISP's network.

INTERNET EXCHANGE POINT (IXP) The ISP in turn connects to an ❷ ***Internet Exchange Point (IXP)*, a routing computer at a point on the Internet where several connections come together.** IXPs are run by private companies that control physical infrastructures that allow different ISPs to exchange Internet traffic.

Where Are the IXPs?

For a map of IXP locations, go to:

www.datacentermap.com/ixps.html

INTERNET BACKBONE Each IXP has at least one computer, whose task is simply to direct Internet traffic from one IXP to the next. IXPs are connected by the equivalent of interstate highways, known collectively as the ❸ ***Internet backbone*, high-speed, high-capacity transmission lines, usually fiber-optic**

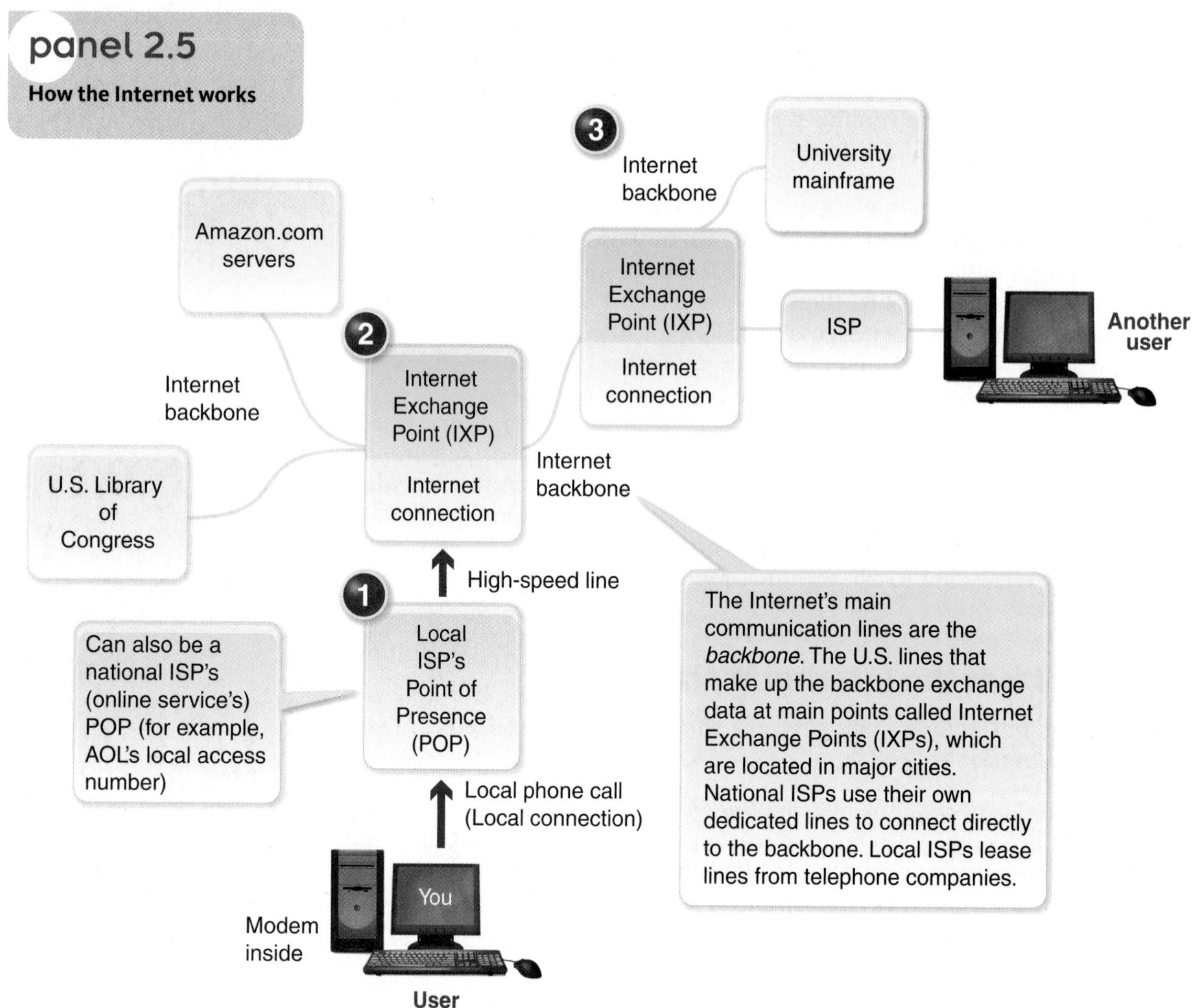

lines, that use the newest communications technology to transmit data across the Internet. Backbone connections are supplied by Internet backbone providers such as AT&T, British Telecom (BT), Sprint, VSNL, Verizon, Qwest, and Deutsche Telekom.

INTERNET2 ***Internet2*** **is a not-for-profit cooperative university/business education and research project that enables high-end users to quickly and reliably move huge amounts of data over high-speed networks.** In effect, Internet2 adds "toll lanes" to the older Internet to speed things up. The purpose is to advance videoconferencing, research, and academic collaboration—to enable a kind of "virtual university." By bringing research and academia together with technology leaders from industry, government, and the international community, Internet2 promotes collaboration and innovation that have a fundamental impact on the future of the Internet. Beyond just providing network capacity, Internet2 actively engages in the development of important new technology including security, network research and performance measurement capabilities, which are critical to the progress of the Internet.[9]

Internet Communications: Protocols, Packets, & Addresses

The data transmitted over the Internet must be set up to follow certain rules so that all the computers on the network can understand it.

When you connect to your ISP's POP location, the two entities go through a process called *handshaking,* whereby the fastest-available transmission speed is established. Then *authentication* occurs: your ISP needs to know you are who you say you are, so you need to provide a user name and a password. These two items will have been established when you opened your account with your ISP.

PROTOCOLS How do computers understand the data being transmitted? The key lies in the ***protocol*, or set of rules, that computers must follow to transmit data electronically. The protocol that enables all computers to use data transmitted on the Internet is called *Transmission Control Protocol/Internet Protocol*, or *TCP/IP*,** which was developed in 1978 by ARPA. TCP/IP is used for all Internet transactions, from sending email to downloading pictures off a friend's website. Among other things, TCP/IP determines how the sending device indicates that it has finished sending a message and how the receiving device indicates that it has received the message.[10]

The Internet Traffic Report

The Internet Traffic Report monitors the flow of data around the world. It displays values between 0 and 100 for many networks. Higher values indicate faster and more reliable connections. Check out your area at:

www.internettrafficreport.com

PACKETS Most important, perhaps, TCP/IP breaks the data in a message into separate ***packets*, fixed-length blocks of data for transmission.** This allows a message to be split up and its parts sent by separate routes yet still all wind up in the same place. IP is used to send the packets across the Internet to their final destination, and TCP is used to reassemble the packets in the correct order. The packets do not have to follow the same network routes to reach their destination because all the packets have the same *IP address*, as we explain next.

IP ADDRESSES When you type an Internet address such as www.mycollege.com into your computer, your computer converts it to an Internet Protocol (IP) address in order to take you to the website that you want to go to. To do this conversion, the computer uses the Internet connection and checks an online DNS (Domain Name System) server (Chapter 1) run by your ISP that is a database of regular Internet addresses and IP addresses. **An *Internet Protocol (IP) address* uniquely identifies every computer and device connected to the Internet.** An IP address consists of four sets of numbers between 0 and 255 separated by decimals (called a *dotted quad*)—for example, 1.160.10.240. An IP address is similar to a street address, but street addresses rarely change, whereas IP addresses often do. Each time you connect to your Internet access provider, it assigns your computer a new IP address, called a *dynamic IP address*, for your online session. When you request data from the Internet, it is transmitted to your computer's IP address. When you disconnect, your provider frees up the IP address you were using and reassigns it to another user.

A dynamic IP address changes each time you connect to the Internet. A *static IP address* is the same every time a person logs on to the Internet. Established organizational websites—such as your ISP's—have their own static IP addresses, which they pay for.

It would be simple if every computer that connects to the Internet had its own static IP number, but when the Internet was first conceived, the architects didn't foresee the need for an unlimited number of IP addresses. Consequently, there are not enough IP numbers to go around. To get around that problem, many Internet access providers limit the number of static IP addresses they allocate and economize on the remaining number of IP addresses they possess by temporarily assigning an IP address from a pool of IP addresses.

If your computer is constantly connected to the Internet, through a local network at work or school, most likely you have a static IP address. If you are using a computer that gets connected to the Internet intermittently, you're most likely picking up a dynamic IP address from a pool of possible IP addresses at your Internet access provider's network during each log-in.

This approach to determining IP addresses, created in the early 1980s, is called *IPv4* (*Internet Protocol Version 4*). After Internet use exploded in the 1990s, it became apparent that even with this approach of using dynamic, reusable IP addresses, the world would soon run out of IP addresses. Thus the Internet Engineering Task Force (IETF) started some years ago to develop *IPv6*

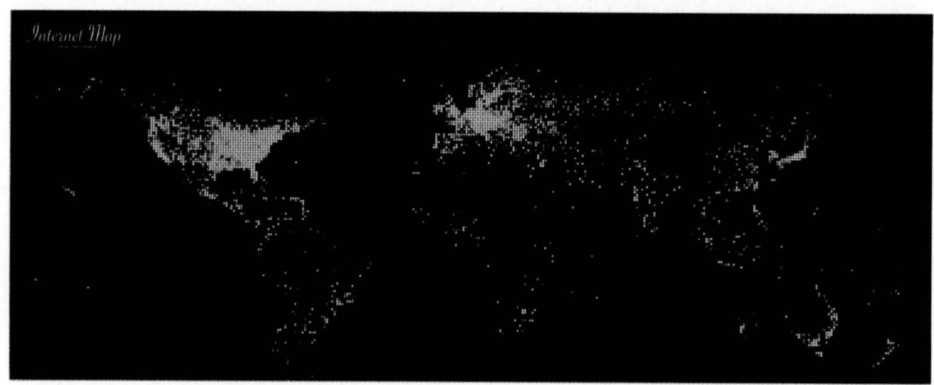

Relative densities of Internet connectivity around the globe

(*Internet Protocol Version 6*). An IPv6 address would have this format, and use both numbers and characters: 0000:0000:0000:0000:0000:0000:0000:0000. This approach is designed to facilitate an unlimited number of IP addresses and to make the connection of non-personal-computer devices, such as smartphones and digital home devices, easier. IPv4 had about 4.3 billion addresses; IPv6 will have enough spots for 340 trillion, trillion, trillion unique IP addresses.[11]

After your connection has been made, your Internet access provider functions as an interface between you and the rest of the Internet. If you're exchanging data with someone who uses the same provider, the data may stay within that organization's network. Large national Internet access providers operate their own backbones that connect their POPs throughout the country. Usually, however, data travels over many different networks before it reaches your computer.

Your IP Address

Want to find out what your IP address is while you're online? Go to:

http://whatismyipaddress.com

Who Runs the Internet?

Although no one really "owns" the Internet, several global and U.S. organizations establish standards for it.

Although no one owns the Internet, everyone on the net adheres to standards overseen by the international Board of Trustees of ISOC, the *I*nternet *Soc*iety (*www.isoc.org*). ISOC is a professional, nonprofit society with more than 100 organizational and 44,000 individual members in more than 80 chapters around the world. The organizations include companies, governments, and foundations. ISOC provides leadership in addressing issues that confront the future of the Internet and is the organizational home for groups responsible for Internet infrastructure standards, including the Internet Engineering Task Force (IETF), the Internet Architecture Board (IAB), and The World Wide Web Consortium.

In June 1998 the U.S. government proposed the creation of a series of nonprofit corporations to manage such complex issues as fraud prevention, privacy, and intellectual-property protection. The first such group, the ***Internet Corporation for Assigned Names and Numbers (ICANN)*, was established to regulate human-friendly Internet domain names—those addresses ending with *.com, .org, .net,* and so on, that overlie IP addresses and identify the website type.** (These domain names are discussed in more detail shortly.)

ICANN (which can be accessed at *www.icann.org*) is a global, private-sector, nonprofit corporation that has no statutory authority and imposes policies through contracts with its world members. Criticized for inefficiency, in 2003 it outlined what it called ICANN 2.0, intended to be a more responsive and agile agency that would consult better with the world Internet community about the adoption of standards. One of its improvements is the ICANN Whois Database, which returns the name and address of any domain name entered (entering *microsoft.com,* for instance, returns the name and address of Microsoft Corp.). ICANN doesn't control content on the Internet. It cannot stop spam and it doesn't deal with access to the Internet. But through its coordination role of the Internet's naming system, it does have an important influence on the expansion and evolution of the Internet.[12]

2.3 The World Wide Web

The World Wide Web brought multimedia to the Internet.

The Internet and the World Wide Web, as we have said, are not the same. The Internet is a massive network of networks, connecting millions of computers via protocols, hardware, and communications channels. It is the infrastructure that supports not only the web but also other communications systems such as email, instant messaging, newsgroups, and other activities that we'll discuss. The part of the Internet called the *web* is a *multimedia-based* technology that enables you to access more than just text. That is, you can also download art, audio, video, and animation and engage in interactive games.

Japan's machinery maker Hitachi Zosen and Shimadzu's wearable computer, which consists of a full-color head mount display (HMD) with a built-in camera and a palm-sized Windows PC with a pointing device

The Face of the Web: Browsers, Websites, & Web Pages

A browser is software that gets you to websites and their individual web pages.

If the storybook character Rip Van Winkle had fallen asleep in 1989—the year computer scientist Tim Berners-Lee developed the web software—and awoke today, he would be completely baffled by much of the vocabulary that we now encounter on a daily basis: *browser, website, web page, www.* Let's see how we would explain to him what these and similar web terms mean.

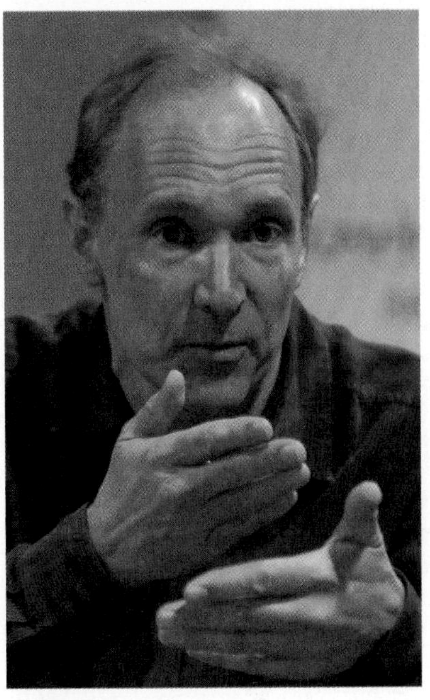

Sir Tim Berners-Lee

Tim Berners-Lee, British engineer and computer scientist, was born in London, England; his parents, both mathematicians, were employed together on the team that built the Manchester Mark I, one of the earliest computers. Berners-Lee graduated from the Queen's College of Oxford University, where he built a computer with a soldering iron. In 1980, while an independent contractor at CERN (European Organization for Nuclear Research), Berners-Lee proposed a project based on the concept of hypertext, to facilitate sharing and updating information among researchers. With other researchers, he built a prototype system named Enquire.

After leaving CERN he used ideas similar to those used in Enquire to create the WorldWideWeb, for which he designed and built the first browser. Berners-Lee built the first website at *http://info.cern.ch/,* and it was first put online on August 6, 1991. It provided an explanation about what the WorldWideWeb was, how one could own a browser, how to set up a web server, and so on.

In 1994 Berners-Lee founded the WorldWideWeb Consortium (W3C) at the Massachusetts Institute of Technology. It comprised various companies willing to create standards and recommendations to improve the quality of the Internet. It was not until 2000 and 2001 that popular browsers began to support this standard.

In 2004 Berners-Lee was knighted by Queen Elizabeth II for his pioneering work. In 2009 he was elected as a member of the United States National Academy of Sciences based in Washington, D.C.

BROWSERS: SOFTWARE FOR SURFING THE WEB **A <u>*browser*</u>, or *web browser*, is software that enables you to find and access the various parts of the web.** The two best-known browsers are *Microsoft Internet Explorer* (*IE*), more commonly used in the United States, and *Mozilla Firefox*, more commonly used in Europe.[13] IE has a 48.92% share of the North American market, followed by Firefox at 26.7%, Google's Chrome at 12.82%, and Safari (for the Mac) at 10.16%.[14] (● *See Panel 2.6, next page.*) The small remaining number of users have Microsoft's Bing as their browser. These and other browsers allow you, like riding a wave with a surfboard, to surf the web. **<u>*Surf*</u> means to explore the web by using your mouse to move via a series of connected paths, or links, from one location, or website, to another.**

Whence the Word *Web?*

Why did people perceive the need for a "web," and how did Berners-Lee develop what they needed? Go to:

www.ibiblio.org/pioneers/lee.html

http://en.wikipedia.org/wiki/Tim_Berners-Lee

panel 2.6

Internet Explorer, Mozilla Firefox, Google's Chrome, and Apple's Safari.
Note the different toolbar and tool setups.

WEBSITE: THE LOCATION ON THE COMPUTER **A *website,* or simply *site,* is a location on a particular computer on the web that has a unique address** (called a *URL,* for Uniform Resource Locator, as we'll explain). If you decided to buy books online from bookseller Barnes & Noble, you would visit its website, *www.barnesandnoble.com;* the website is the location of a computer or group of computers somewhere on the Internet. The computers might be located in Barnes & Noble's offices, but they might be located somewhere else entirely.

WEB PAGES: THE DOCUMENTS ON A WEBSITE A website is composed of a web page or collection of related web pages. **A *web page* is a document on the World Wide Web that can include text, pictures, sound, and video.** The first page you see at a website is like the title page of a book. This is the ***home page,* the starting point, or the main page, of a website that contains links to other pages at the site.** *(• See Panel 2.7.)* This page usually has some sort of table of contents on it and often describes the purpose of the site. If you have your own personal website, it might consist of just one page—the home page. Large websites have scores or even hundreds of pages.

Survival Tip

Do Home Pages Endure?

The contents of home pages often change. Or they may disappear, and so the connecting links to them in other web pages become links to nowhere. To find out how to view "dead" pages, go to:

http://web.ticino.com/multilingual/Search.htm

www.searchengineshowdown.com/others/archive.shtml

How the Browser Finds Things: URLs

URLs are Uniform Resource Locators, or web addresses.

Now let's look at the details of how the browser finds a particular web page.

URLS: ADDRESSES FOR WEB PAGES Before your browser can interpret a website and get you there, it needs to know the site's address, the URL. **The *URL (Uniform Resource Locator)* is a string of characters that points to a specific piece of information anywhere on the web.** In other words, the URL is the website's unique address.

A URL consists of (1) the web *protocol,* (2) the *domain name* or web server name, (3) the *directory name* (or folder) on that server, and (4) the *file* within

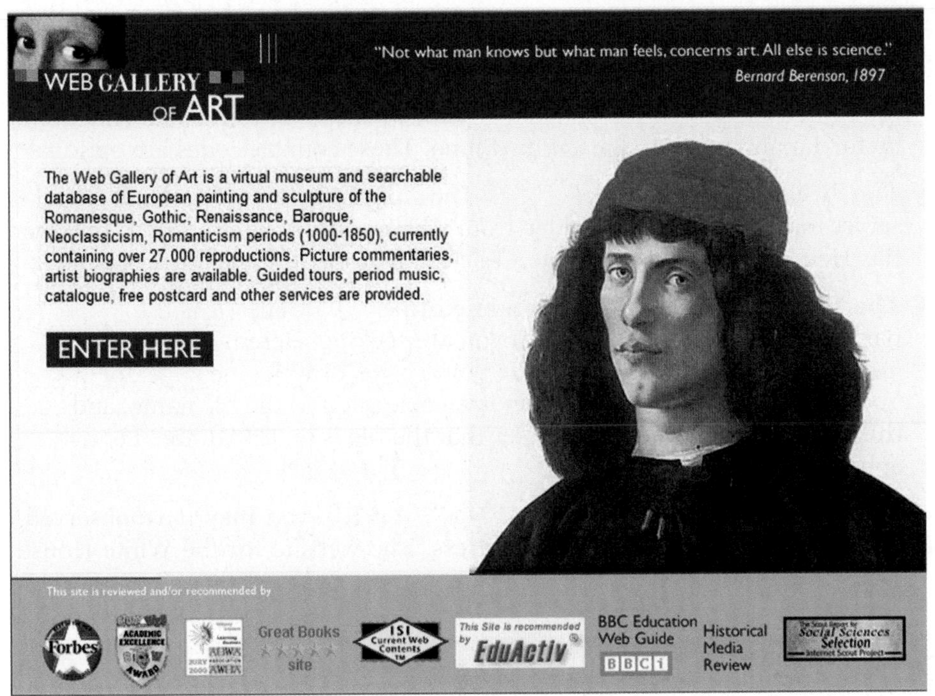

panel 2.7

Home page

This is a website's first page, or welcome page.

that directory (perhaps with an extension, such as *html* or *htm*). Consider the following example of a URL for a website offered by the National Park Service for Yosemite National Park:

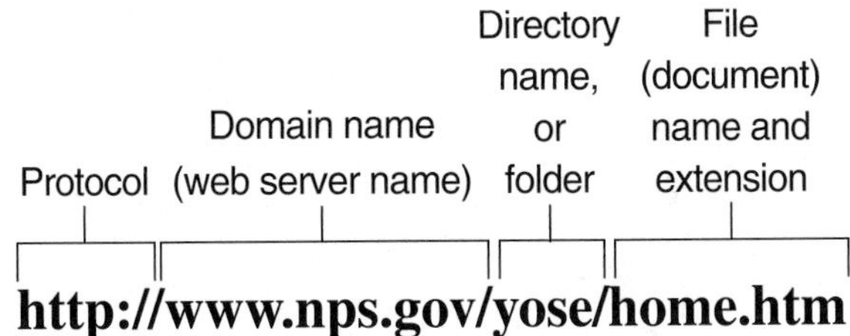

Let's look at these elements.

- **The protocol: http://** As mentioned, a protocol is a set of communication rules for exchanging information. The web protocol, HTTP, was developed by Tim Berners-Lee, and it appears at the beginning of some web addresses (as in *http://www.mcgraw-hill.com*). It stands for ***HyperText Transfer Protocol (HTTP)*, the communications rules that allow browsers to connect with web servers.** (Note: Most browsers assume that all web addresses begin with *http://,* and so you don't need to type this part; just start with whatever follows, such as *www.*)

  Often you will see https://, which refers to a secure, encrypted form of information transfer on the Internet. (Encryption is discussed in Chapter 6.)

- **The domain name (web server name): www.nps.gov/** **A *domain* is simply a location on the Internet, the particular web server.** Domain names tell the location and the type of address. Domain-name components are separated by periods (called "dots"). The last part of the domain, called the *top-level domain,* is usually a three-letter extension that describes the domain type: *.gov, .com, .net, .edu, .org, .mil, .int*—government, commercial, network, educational, nonprofit, military, or international organization. (Some extensions are longer.) In our example, the *www* stands for "World Wide Web," of course; the *.nps* stands for "National Park Service," and *.gov* is the top-level domain name indicating that this is a government website.

The meanings of other Internet top-level domain abbreviations appear in the box on the next page. (• *See Panel 2.8.*) Some top-level domain names also include a two-letter code extension for the country—for example, *.us* for United States, *.ca* for Canada, *.mx* for Mexico, *.uk* for United Kingdom, *.jp* for Japan, *.in* for India, *.cn* for China. These country codes are optional.

- **The directory name: yose/** The *directory* name is the name on the server for the directory, or folder, from which your browser needs to pull the file. Here it is *yose* for "Yosemite." For Yellowstone National Park, it is *yell*.
- **The file name and extension: home.htm** The *file* is the particular page or document that you are seeking. Here it is *home.htm,* because you have gone to the home page, or welcome page, for Yosemite National Park. The *.htm* is an extension to the file name, and this extension informs the browser that the file is an HTML file. Let us consider what HTML means.

URLS & EMAIL ADDRESSES: NOT THE SAME A URL, you may have observed, is *not* the same thing as an email address. The website for the White House

panel 2.8

Internet top-level domain abbreviations and users

Domain Name	Authorized Users	Example
.aero	air-transport industry	*director@bigwings.aero*
.biz	businesses	*ceo@company.biz*
.com	originally commercial; now anyone can use	*editor@mcgraw-hill.com*
.coop	cooperative associations	*buyer@greatgroceries.coop*
.edu	postsecondary accredited educational and research institutions	*professor@harvard.edu*
.gov	U.S. government agencies and bureaus	*president@whitehouse.gov*
.info	generic information service providers	*contact@research.info*
.int	organizations established by international treaties between governments	*sectretary_general@unitednations.int*
.jobs	human resources managers	*AnnChu@Personnel.jobs*
.mil	U.S. military organizations	*chief_of_staff@pentagon.mil*
.mobi	providers of mobile products and services	*user@phonecompany.mobi*
.museum	museums	*curator@modernart.museum*
.name	individuals	*joe@smith.name*
.net	generic networking organizations	*contact@earthlink.net*
.org	generic organizations, often nonprofit and professional (noncommercial)	*director@redcross.org*
.post	Universal Postal Union	*manager@UPS.post*
.pro	credentialed professionals and related entities	*auditor@accountant.pro*
.tel	For businesses and individuals to publish their contact data	*OurCorporationInfo@MyInc.tel*
.travel	travel industry	*JoeAgent@flyright.travel*
.xxx	adults-only website	*proprietor@badtaste.xxx*

Note: The number of domain names is expanding; for a list of current domain names, go to *www.iana.org/gtld/gtld.htm.*
Some groups pay $45,000 or more to ICANN for a particular domain name.

(which includes presidential information, history, a tour, and a guide to federal services) is *www.whitehouse.gov.* Some people might type *president@whitehouse.gov* and expect to get a website, but that won't happen. We explain email addresses in another few pages.

The Nuts & Bolts of the Web: HTML & Hyperlinks

HTML is the Internet's formatting language, and links allow users to jump easily among web pages.

The basic communications *protocol* that makes the Internet work, as we described, is *TCP/IP.* The communications protocol used to access that part of the Internet called the World Wide Web, we pointed out, is called *HyperText Transfer Protocol (HTTP).* A hypertext document uses *hypertext markup language (HTML),* which uses *hypertext links* to connect with other documents. The foundations of the World Wide Web, then, are HTML and its hypertext links.

HYPERTEXT MARKUP LANGUAGE (HTML) ***Hypertext markup language (HTML)*** **is the set of special instructions (called "tags" or "markups") that are used to specify document structure, formatting, and links to other multimedia documents on the web.** Extensible hypertext markup language (XHTML) is the successor to and the current version of HTML. The need for a stricter version of HTML was perceived primarily because World Wide Web content now needs to be delivered to many devices (such as mobile phones) that have fewer resources than traditional computers have.

HYPERTEXT LINKS ***Hypertext links*—also called *hyperlinks, hotlinks,* or just *links*—are HTML connections to other documents or web pages that contain related information; a word or phrase in one document becomes a connection to a document in a different place.** Hyperlinks usually appear as underlined or colored words and phrases. On a home page, for instance, the hyperlinks serve to connect the main page with other pages throughout the website. Other hyperlinks connect to pages on other websites, whether located on a computer next door or one on the other side of the world.

An example of an HTML document with hyperlinks is shown below. *(• See Panel 2.9.)*

Do You Need to Know HTML to Build a Website?

Most general web users do not need to know HTML. If you want to convert a word-processed document to HTML so that someone can post it on a website, applications such as Microsoft Word will convert it for you (for example, using the options Save as, Web page). Also, many website builders offer their services on the web; you can hire them to build a website for you. Many ISPs supply help with building websites and offer website storage on their servers to their subscribers.

If you want to learn more about HTML formatting, try these websites:

www.htmlcodetutorial.com/

www.make-a-web-site.com/

www.w3schools.com/html/default.asp

Using Your Browser to Get around the Web

A browser is software that interprets HTML and thus allows you to move around the web and to access, retrieve, and post information, including multimedia.

You can find almost anything you want on the approximately 30 billion indexed web pages available around the world.[15] Among the droplets of what amounts to a Niagara Falls of information: Weather maps and forecasts. Guitar chords. Recipe archives. Sports schedules. Daily newspapers in all languages. Nielsen television ratings. The Alcoholism Research Data Base. U.S. government phone numbers. The Central Intelligence Agency world map. The daily White House press releases. Radio stations. And on and on. But it takes a browser

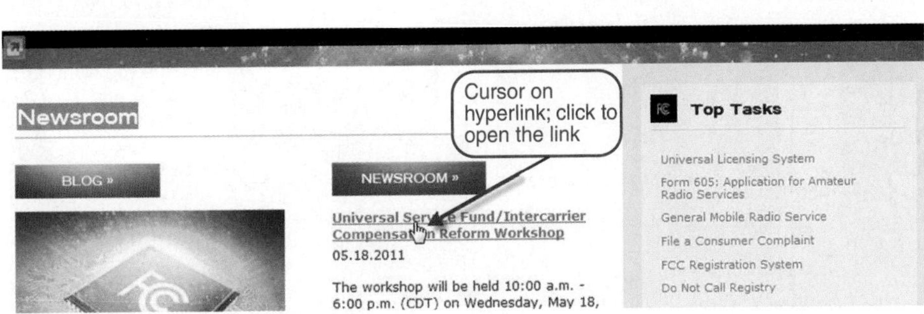

panel 2.9

An HTML document and hyperlinks

Using the mouse to click on the hyperlinked text connects to another location in the same website or at a different site.

and various kinds of search tools to find and make any kind of sense of this enormous amount of data.

BASIC ELEMENTS OF THE BROWSER If you buy a new computer, it will come with a browser already installed. Most browsers have a similar look and feel and similar navigational tools. Note that many web browser screens have a few basic elements: *menu bar, toolbar, address bar, workspace,* and *status bar.* To execute menu-bar and toolbar commands, you use the mouse to move the pointer over the word, known as a *menu selection,* and click the left button of the mouse. This will result in a pull-down menu of other commands for other options. *(● See Panel 2.10.)*

STARTING OUT FROM HOME: THE HOME PAGE The first page you see when you start up your browser is the *home page* or *start page*. (You can also start up from just a blank page, if you don't want to wait for the time it takes to connect with a home page.) You can choose any page on the web as your start page, but a good start page offers links to sites you want to visit frequently. Often you may find that the Internet access provider with which you arrange your Internet connection will provide its own start page. However, you can customize it to make it your own personal home page—just follow your browser's instructions for personalizing.

GETTING AROUND: BACK, FORWARD, HOME, & SEARCH FEATURES Driving in a foreign city (or even Boston or San Francisco) can be an interesting experience in which street names change, turns lead into unknown neighborhoods, and signs aren't always evident, so that soon you have no idea where you are. That's what the Internet is like, although on a far more massive scale. Fortunately, unlike being lost in Rome, here your browser toolbar provides navigational aids. *(● See Panel 2.11.) Back* takes you back to the previous page. *Forward* lets you look again at a page you returned from. If you really get lost, you can start over by clicking on *Home*, which returns you to your home page. *Search* lists various other search tools, as we will describe. Other navigational aids are *history lists* and *favorites* or *bookmarks*.

HISTORY LISTS If you are browsing through many web pages, it can be difficult to keep track of the locations of the pages you've already visited. The *history list* allows you to quickly return to the pages you have recently visited. *(● See Panel 2.12.)*

FAVORITES OR BOOKMARKS One great helper for finding your way is the Favorites or Bookmarks feature, which lets you store the URLs of web pages you frequently visit so that you don't have to remember and retype your

panel 2.10

Common tools and functions used by several browsers

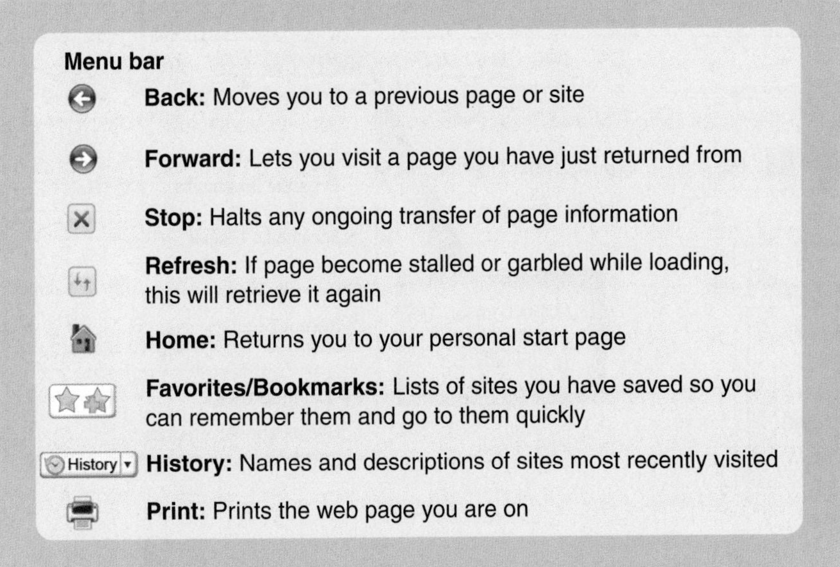

panel 2.11

More information on common browser functions

favorite addresses. (● *See Panel 2.13, next page.*) Say you're visiting a site that you really like and that you know you'd like to come back to. You click on *Favorites* (in Internet Explorer) or *Bookmarks* (in Firefox), which displays the URL on your screen, and then click on *Add,* which automatically stores the address. Later you can locate the site name on your Favorites menu and click on it, and the site will reappear. (When you want to delete it, you can use the right mouse button and select the *Delete* command.)

INTERACTIVITY: HYPERLINKS, RADIO BUTTONS, & TEXT BOXES For any given web page that you happen to find yourself on, there may be several ways to interact with it. (● *See Panel 2.14, next page.*) Here are three common ways:

1. By using your mouse to click on the hyperlinks, which will transfer you to another web page (p. 69).
2. By using your mouse to click on a *radio button* and then clicking on a *Submit* command or pressing the *Enter* key. ***Radio buttons*** **are little**

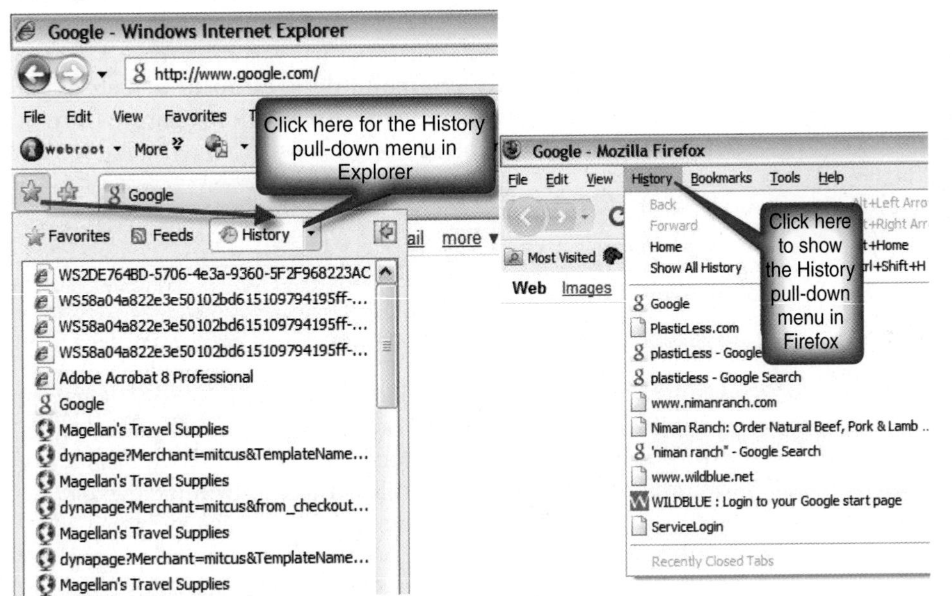

panel 2.12

History list

If you want to return to a previously viewed site in Internet Explorer or Firefox, click on *History.*

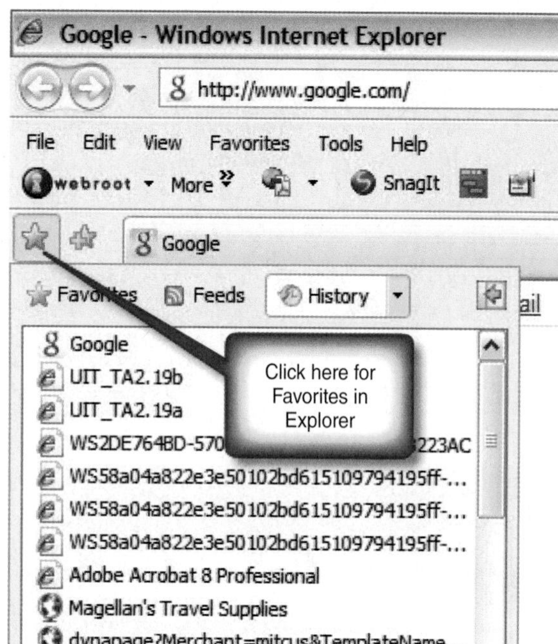

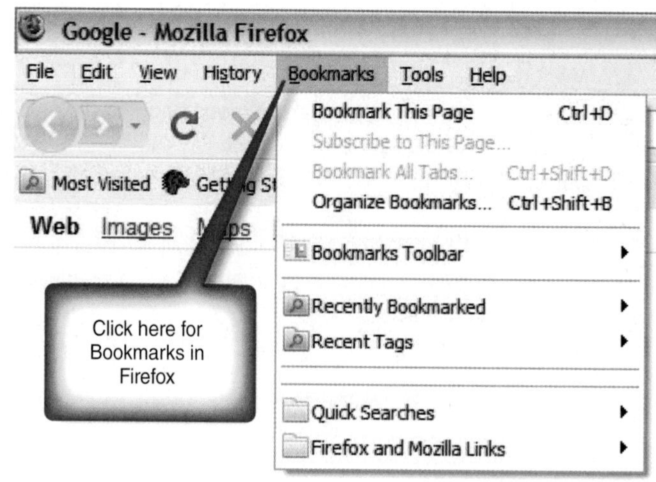

panel 2.13

Favorites

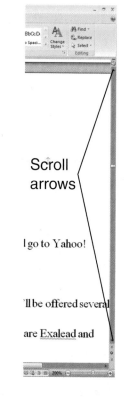

If you are at a website you may want to visit again, click on *Favorites* (in Internet Explorer, *left*) or *Bookmarks* (in Firefox, *right*) and choose *Add to Favorites* or *Add to Bookmark.* Later, to revisit the site, go to the Favorites menu, and the site's URL will reappear.

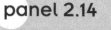

circles located in front of various options; selecting an option with the mouse places a dot in the corresponding circle.

3. By typing text in a ***text box*** and then hitting the *Enter* key or clicking on a *Go* or *Continue* command, which will transfer you to another web page.

Scroll arrows

SCROLLING & FRAMES To the bottom and side of your screen display you will note ***scroll arrows,*** **small up/down and left/right arrows. Clicking on scroll arrows with your mouse pointer moves the screen so that you can see the rest of the web page, a movement known as *scrolling*.** You can also use the arrow keys on your keyboard for scrolling.

Some web pages are divided into different rectangles known as *frames,* each with its own scroll arrows. **A *frame* is an independently controllable section of a web page.** A web page designer can divide a page into separate frames, each with different features or options.

panel 2.14

Radio buttons and text box

Radio buttons

Act like station selector buttons on a car radio

Page range
All
Current page
Selection
Pages:
Enter page numbers and/or page ranges separated by commas. For example, 1,3,5–12

Search (text) boxes

Require you to type in information

Pages: 17-33

Web Portals: Starting Points for Finding Information

Web portals can act as organizers for web activities.

Using a browser is sort of like exploring an enormous cave with flashlight and string. You point your flashlight at something, go there, and at that location you can see another cave chamber to go to; meanwhile, you're unrolling the ball of string behind you so that you can find your way back.

But what if you want to visit only the most spectacular rock formations in the cave and skip the rest? For that you

need a guidebook. There are many such "guidebooks" for finding information on the web, sort of Internet superstations known as *web portals*.

> **Survival Tip**
>
> **Finding Things on a Web Page or in a Web Document**
>
> When you are on a web page or in a document, type Ctrl+F to bring a text box up on your screen. Type in a word or words that relate to what you are looking for, and hit Enter. You will be taken to the first occurrence of the words. Keep hitting Enter, and you will be taken to subsequent appearances of the words.

TYPES OF WEB PORTALS **A *web portal,* or simply *portal,* is a type of gateway website that functions as an "anchor site," a major starting point, for users when they connect to the web.** It generally offers a broad array of resources and services, online shopping malls, email support, community forums, current news and weather, stock quotes, travel information, a search engine, and links to other popular subject categories. Portals are also called *links pages* or *gateways*.

In addition, there are *wireless portals,* designed for web-enabled portable devices. An example is Yahoo! Mobile, which offers Yahoo! oneSearch, Yahoo! Maps, Yahoo! Entertainment, and so on. Yahoo! Mobile users can access not only email, calendar, news, and stock quotes but also Yahoo!'s directory of wireless sites, movies, and auctions.

Portals may be general public portals (horizontal portals or megaportals), such as Yahoo!, Google, Bing (formerly MSN), Lycos, and AOL. There are also specialized portals—called *vertical portals*, or *vortals,* which focus on specific narrow audiences or communities—such as PoliceAuctions.com for buying seized property and unclaimed property from police departments and the government, Fool.com for investors, Burpee.com for gardeners, and Searchnetworking.techtarget.com for network administrators.

LOGGING ON TO A PORTAL In general, ***logon* is the procedure used to get access to an operating system, an application, or a website.** A logon procedure reguires a user ID and a password. When you log on to a portal, you can do three things: (1) check the home page for general information, (2) use the subject guide to find a topic you want, and (3) use a keyword to search for a topic. (• *See Panel 2.15.*)

- **Check the home page for general information:** You can treat a portal's home or start page as you would a newspaper—for example, to get news headings, weather forecasts, sports scores, and stock-market prices.

panel 2.15

Yahoo! home page

You can read headlines for news and weather, use the directory to find a topic, or use keywords in the Web Search text box to research specific topics.

Survival Tip

Urban Legends & Lies on the Internet

To check the veracity of material on the Internet, go to *www.snopes.com*, which lists, according to category, information circulated on the Internet that isn't true. Each category includes a key to color-coded bullets that precede each entry; the color lets you know how much truth there is to each item: green = true; red = false; yellow = undetermined; white = unclassifiable. Also check out *www.suite101.com/content/debunking-internet-rumors-and-political-lies-a158511.*

- **Use the subject guide to find a topic:** Before they acquired their other features, many of these portals began as a type of search tool known as a *subject guide,* providing lists of several categories of websites classified by topic, such as (with Yahoo!) "Business" or "Entertainment." Such a category is also called a *hypertext index*, and its purpose is to allow you to access information in specific categories by clicking on a hypertext link.
- **Use search box and keywords to search for a topic:** Often at the top of each portal's home page is a search text box, a blank space into which you can type a ***keyword*****, the subject word or words of the topic you wish to find.** If you want a biography on Apple Computer founder Steve Jobs, then *Steve Jobs* is the keyword. This way you don't have to plow through menu after menu of subject categories. The results of your keyword search will be displayed in a summary of documents containing the keyword you typed.

Search Services & Search Engines & How They Work

Many web portals act as search services and provide search engines. Search engines collect and organize information from all over the web.

Search services **are organizations that maintain databases accessible through websites to help you find information on the Internet.** Examples are not only parts of portals such as Yahoo! and Bing/MSN but also Google, Ask.com, and Gigablast, to name just a few. Search services also maintain ***search engines*****, programs that enable you to ask questions or use keywords to help locate information on the web.**

Search services compile their databases by using special programs called ***spiders*****—also known as *crawlers, bots* (for "robots"), or *agents*—that crawl through the World Wide Web, following links from one web page to another and indexing the words on that site.** Spiders are used to feed pages to search engines.

This method of gathering information has two important implications:

The Search Engine List

The Search Engine List is the web's most comprehensive list of major and minor search engines:

www.thesearchenginelist.com/

A SEARCH NEVER COVERS THE ENTIRE WEB Whenever you are doing a search with a search engine, you are never searching the entire web. As one writer points out: "You are actually searching a portion of the web, captured in a fixed index created at an earlier date."[16] (An exception: Some news databases, such as Yahoo! News and Google Breaking News, offer up-to-the-minute reports on a number of subjects.) In addition, you should realize that there are a lot of databases whose material is not publicly available. Finally, a lot of published material from the 1970s and earlier has never been scanned into databases and made available.

SEARCH ENGINES DIFFER IN WHAT THEY COVER Search engines list their results according to some kind of relevance ranking, and different search engines use different ranking schemes. Some search engines, for instance, rank web pages according to popularity (frequency of visits by people looking for a particular keyword), but others don't.

Four Web Search Tools: Individual Search Engines, Subject Directories, Metasearch Engines, & Specialized Search Engines

Web users should learn how to use the main types of search tools.

There are many types of search tools, but the most popular versions can be categorized as (1) *individual search engines,* (2) *subject directories,* (3) *metasearch engines,* and (4) *specialized search engines.* The most popular search sites, measured in share of visitors, are Google, Yahoo!, Bing, and Ask.

INDIVIDUAL SEARCH ENGINES An ***individual search engine*** **compiles its own searchable database on the web.** You search for information by typing one or more keywords, and the search engine then displays a list of web pages, or "hits," that contain those key words, ordered from most likely to least likely to contain the information you want. ***Hits*** **are defined as the sites that a search engines returns after running a keyword search.**

Examples of this kind of search engine are Ask, Bing, Google, and Yahoo!, as well as Gigablast, and Lycos. *(● See Panel 2.16.)* The search engine Ask allows users to ask questions in a natural way, such as "What is the population of the United States?" Answers.com is a site-and-software combination providing instant "one-click" reference answers rather than lists of search engine links.

SUBJECT DIRECTORIES Unlike a search engine, **a *subject directory* is created and maintained by human editors, not electronic spiders, and allows you to search for information by selecting lists of categories or topics,** such as "Health and Fitness" or "Science and Technology." Directories tend to be smaller than search engine databases, usually indexing only the top-level pages of a website. Subject directories are best for browsing and for searches of a more general nature.

Examples of subject directories are Beaucoup!, Galaxy, Google Directory, LookSmart, Open Directory Project, and Yahoo! Directory. *(● See Panel 2.17.)*

METASEARCH ENGINES **A *metasearch engine* allows you to search several search engines simultaneously.** Metasearch engines are very fast and can give you a good picture of what's available across the web and where it can be found. Examples are Yippy!, Dogpile, Mamma, MetaCrawler, and Webcrawler. *(● See Panel 2.18, next page.)*

SPECIALIZED SEARCH ENGINES There are also *specialized search engines*, which help locate specialized subject matter, such as material about movies, health, and jobs. These overlap with the specialized portals, or vortals, we discussed above. *(● See Panel 2.19, next page.)*

Generalized Lists of Search Engines

http://searchenginewatch.com/2156241

www.20search.com/

panel 2.16

Some individual search engines (see also *www.searchengineguide.com/*)

Search Tool	Site
Answers.com	*www.answers.com*
Ask	*www.ask.com*
Bing	*www.bing.com*
Gigablast	*www.gigablast.com*
Lycos	*www.lycos.com*
Technorati	*www.technorati.com*
Yahoo!	*www.yahoo.com*

panel 2.17

Some subject directories

Search Tool	Site
Beaucoup!	*www.beaucoup.com*
Galaxy	*www.galaxy.com/directory*
Google Directory	*http://directory.google.com*
Open Directory Project	*www.dmoz.org*
Yahoo! Directory	*http://dir.yahoo.com*

panel 2.18

Some metasearch engines

Search Tool	Site
Dogpile	*www.dogpile.com*
ixquick	*www.ixquick.com*
Kartoo	*www.kartoo.com*
Mamma	*www.mamma.com*
MetaCrawler	*www.metacrawler.com*
Webcrawler	*www.webcrawler.com*
Yippy!	*www.searchyippy.com*
Zuula	*www.zuula.com*

panel 2.19

Some specialized search engines

Search Tool	Site
Career.com (jobs)	*www.career.com*
Expedia (travel)	*www.expedia.com*
Internet Movie Database (movies)	*www.imdb.com*
Monster Board (jobs)	*www.monster.com*
Motley Fool (personal investments)	*www.fool.com*
U.S. Census Bureau (statistics)	*www.census.gov*
WebMD (health)	*www.webmd.com*

Smart Searching: Three General Strategies

Learn a few searching basics to help speed up your searches.

The phrase "trying to find a needle in a haystack" will come vividly to mind the first time you type a word into a search engine and back comes a response on the order of "63,173 listings found." Clearly, it becomes mandatory that you have a strategy for narrowing your search. The following are some tips.

IF YOU'RE JUST BROWSING—TWO STEPS If you're just trying to figure out what's available in your subject area, do as follows:

- **Try a subject directory:** First try using a subject directory, such as Yahoo! Directory or Open Directory Project.
- **Try a metasearch engine:** Next enter your search keywords into a metasearch engine, such as Dogpile or Mamma—just to see what else is out there.

Example: You could type *"search engine tutorial."*

IF YOU'RE LOOKING FOR SPECIFIC INFORMATION If you're looking for specific information, you can try Answers.com "one-click" search *(www.answers.com).* Or you can go to a major search engine such as Google or Yahoo! and then go to a specialized search engine.

Example: You could type *"Life expectancy in U.S."* first into Google and then into the Centers for Disease Control and Prevention's search engine (*www.cdc.gov*).

IF YOU'RE LOOKING FOR EVERYTHING YOU CAN FIND ON A SUBJECT If you want to gather up everything you can find on a certain subject, try the same search on several search engines.

Example: You could type *pogonip* (a type of dense winter fog) into more than one search tool. (Of course, you will probably get some irrelevant responses, so it helps to know how to narrow your search, as explained in the box on page 79.)

PRACTICAL ACTION

Evaluating & Sourcing Information Found on the Web

Want to know what a term means? You could try the immensely popular Wikipedia (*http://en.wikipedia.org*), a free online encyclopedia that anyone around the world can contribute to or edit. It has more than 3.5 million articles in more than 240 languages.

A *wiki,* which founding programmer Ward Cunningham got from the Hawaiian term for "quick" ("wiki wiki") when he created the WikiWiki Web in 1995, is a simple piece of software that can be downloaded for free and used to make a website that can be edited by anyone you like (or don't like). Thus, for example, corporations such as Kodak use business wikis for cross-company collaboration, such as a Word document memo that is worked on by several coworkers simultaneously. That use of wikis is valuable.

But note that *Wikipedia is not considered reliable or authoritative by academics and librarians.* As Larry Sanger, Wikipedia's former editor-in-chief, who now lectures at Ohio State University, says: "The wide-open nature of the Internet encourages people to disregard the importance of expertise." As a result, Sanger does not allow his students to use Wikipedia for their papers.[17] One of the primary concerns about Wikipedia is that it is openly edited —anyone can change or update entries. Although many "Wikipedians" spend hours of volunteer time maintaining the site, even Jimmy Wales, the site's cofounder, says that neither Wikipedia—nor any other encyclopedia—should be used as an academic source.[18]

"You can expect to find everything on the web," points out one library director, "silly sites, hoaxes, frivolous and serious personal pages, commercials, reviews, articles, full-text documents, academic courses, scholarly papers, reference sources, and scientific reports."[19] It is "easy to post information on the Internet, usually with no editorial oversight whatsoever, and that means it is often of questionable quality," adds a Columbia University instructor. "Few students are able to separate the good research from the bad, which is less of a problem with printed texts."[20] In general, Wikipedia should be regarded only as a starting point for additional specialized research.

An alternative to Wikipedia is Google's *Knol.* This is a "monetizable" creation, whereby authors are held accountable for the articles they write (and their names appear). The authors can share in revenue from ads on their page.

If you're relying on web sources for research for a term paper, how do you determine what's useful and what's not? And what is the form for citing web-based research?

Guidelines for Evaluating Web Resources

Anyone (including you) can publish anything on the World Wide Web—and all kinds of people do. Here are some ways to assess credibility of the information you find there:[21]

- ***On what kind of website does the information appear?*** Websites may be *professional sites,* maintained by recognized organizations and institutions. They may be *news and journalistic sites,* which may be anything from *The New York Times* to e-zines (electronic magazines, or small web-based publications) such as *Network Audio Bits.* They may be *commercial sites,* sponsored by companies ranging from the Disney Company to The Happy House Painter. They may be *special-interest sites,* maintained by activists ranging from those of the major political parties to proponents of legalization of marijuana. They may be *blogs* or *personal home pages,* maintained by individuals of all sorts, from professors to children to struggling musicians.
- ***Does the website author appear to be a legitimate authority?*** What kind of qualifications and credentials does the author have, and what kind of organization is he or she associated with? Does a web search show that the author published in other scholarly and professional publications?
- ***Is the website objective, complete, and current?*** Is the website trying to sell you on a product, service, or point of view? Is the language balanced and objective, or is it one-sided and argumentative? Does the author cite sources, and do they seem to come from responsible publications?

A variant on these guidelines has been framed by Butler University librarian Brad Matthies as CRITIC. (• *See Panel 2.20, next page.*)

Multimedia Search Tools: Image, Audio, & Video Searching

Text-based information is not the only thing that you can do Internet searches for.

Most web searches involve text, but there are many nontext kinds of resources as well, including videos and still images. (• *See Panel 2.21, next page.*)

STILL IMAGES Interested in particular still photos? You could go to Yahoo! Search—Image Search (*images.search.yahoo.com*), Google Image Search (*http://images.google.com*), or Bing Images (*www.bing.com/images*), where

Want to Write a Knol?

Here's what you need to know if you are knowledgeable on a particular subject and want to write a knol:

http://knol.google.com/k/basics-of-writing-knols#

panel 2.20

CRITIC

These guidelines will help you think critically about the reliability of online information.

Source: Adapted from Brad Matthies, "The Psychologist, the Philosopher, and the Librarian: The Information-Literacy Version of CRITIC," *Skeptical Inquirer,* May/June 2005, pp. 49–52.

- ***C—Claim:*** Is the source's claim clear and reasonable, timely and relevant? Or is there evidence of motivationally based language?
- ***R—Role of the claimant:*** Is the author of the information clearly identifiable? Are there reasons to suspect political, religious, philosophical, cultural, or financial biases?
- ***I—Information backing the claim:*** Is evidence for the claim presented? Can it be verified, or is the evidence anecdotal or based on testimony? Does the author cite credible references?
- ***T—Testing:*** Can you test the claim, as by conducting your own quantitative research?
- ***I—Independent verification:*** Have reputable experts evaluated and verified the claim?
- ***C—Conclusion:*** After taking the preceding five steps, can you reach a conclusion about the claim?

panel 2.21

Some multimedia search engines

Search Tool	Site
altavista	*www.altavista.com/image/default*
Blinkx	*www.blinkx.com*
Digital Library System	*http://digitalmedia.fws.gov/*
Find Sounds	*www.findsounds.com/types.html*
Google Video	*http://video.google.com*
Internet Archive for Audio	*www.archive.org/details/audio*
Internet Archive for Moving Images	*www.archive.org/details/movies*
Picsearch	*www.picsearch.com*
The University of Delaware Library	*www2.lib.udel.edu/subj/film/resguide/streamingweb.htm*
Yahoo! Video	*http://video.yahoo.com*

you'll be offered several thousand choices of photos and other still images. Other good image search engines are Exalead and Picsearch.

Citing Web Sources in College Papers

The four principal kinds of styles for citing sources—books, articles, and so on—are (1) the Modern Language Association (MLA) style (for some humanities and for languages), (2) the American Psychological Association (APA) style (for social science subjects), (3) the University of Chicago Manual of Style (CMS), and (4) the Turabian style. To learn the format of these styles—including those for Internet sources—go to:

www.apastyle.org/apa-style-help.aspx

http://owl.english.purdue.edu/owl/resource/747/01

http://citationmachine.net

www.easybib.com

www.libraries.psu.edu/psul/researchguides/citationstyles.html

AUDIO & VIDEO Other multimedia search engines offer audio as well as image and video searching. If you go to ShadowTV can provide continuous access to live and archived television content via the web. Yahoo! allows users to search for closed captioning associated with a broadcast and then to click for full-motion video of the words being spoken.

Among the audio search engines available are Yahoo! Music, Lycos MP3 Search, AltaVista Audio Search, BlogDigger, FindSounds, and Blinkx. Among video search engines you can select from are AOL.video, AlltheWeb, the Open Video Project, AltaVista Video, Yahoo! Video Search, Google Video Search, and Blinkx Video Search.

SCHOLARLY Google offers Google Scholar *(http://scholar.google.com/advanced_scholar_search),* described as "a one-stop shop of scholarly abstracts, books, peer-reviewed papers, and technical papers intended for academics and scientists."[22]

Google has also launched an ambitious project, the Google Books Library Project (*www.google.com/googlebooks/library.html*), in which it is scanning page by page more than 50 million books (at a cost of about $10 for each book scanned) from many libraries—for example, at Harvard, Stanford, Oxford, Columbia University, the Austrian National Library, the University of Michigan, Keio University Library (Japan), and the New York Public Library. Because of copyright issues, most scanned books are those that are out of copyright; however, Google Books is known to scan books still protected under copyright unless the publisher specifically excludes them. Thus the Google Project is being studied by the U.S. Justice Department to see if massive book scanning violates antitrust laws, since authors, campus researchers, and library groups have expressed serious concerns over the move.[23]

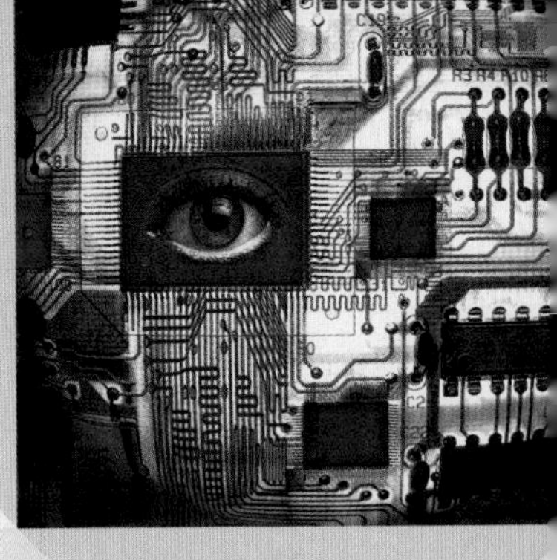

PRACTICAL ACTION

Serious Web Search Techniques

You type *Bill Gates* into Google and get around 20,000,000 hits; in Yahoo!, 32,000,100. How useful is that? Following are some tips for efficient searching:

- ***Choose your search terms well, and watch your spelling:*** Use the most precise words possible. If you're looking for information about novelist Thomas Wolfe (author of *Look Homeward Angel,* published 1929) rather than novelist/journalist Tom Wolfe (author of *I Am Charlotte Simmons*, 2005), details are important: *Thomas*, not *Tom*; *Wolfe*, not *Wolf*. Use *poodle* rather than *dog*, *Maui* rather than *Hawaii*, *Martin guitar* rather than *guitar*, or you'll get thousands of responses that have little or nothing to do with what you're looking for. You may need to use alternate words and spellings to explore the topic you're investigating: *e-mail, email, electronic mail.* And remember that searching is repetitive (iterative)—that is, you may have to do many searches to narrow down your search terms efficiently in order to get the kind of results you want.
- ***Type words in lowercase:*** Typing words in lowercase will help you find both lowercase and capitalized variations.
- ***Use phrases with quotation marks rather than separate words:*** If you type *ski resort*, you could get results of (1) everything to do with skis, on the one hand, and (2) everything to do with resorts—winter, summer, mountain, seaside—on the other. Sometimes it's better to put your phrase in quotation marks—*"ski resort"*—to narrow your search.
- ***Put unique words first in a phrase:*** Better to have *"Tom Wolfe novels"* rather than *"Novels Tom Wolfe."* Or if you're looking for the Hoagy Carmichael song rather than the southern state, indicate "Georgia on My Mind."
- ***Use Boolean operators—AND, OR, and NOT:*** Although some new search tools eliminate the need for operators, most search sites use symbols called *Boolean operators* to make searching more precise. To illustrate how they are used, suppose you're looking for the song "Strawberry Fields Forever."[24] (Boolean, or boolean logic, is a subset of algebra used for creating true/false statements. Boolean expressions use the operators AND, OR, and NOT to compare values and return a true or false result. [*www.techterms.com/definition/boolean*].)

  AND connects two or more search words or terms and means that all of them must appear in the search results. Example: *Strawberry AND Fields AND Forever.*

  OR connects two or more search terms but indicates that either of the two may appear in the results. Example: *Strawberry Fields OR Strawberry OR Fields.*

  NOT, when inserted before a word, excludes that word from the results. Example: *Strawberry Fields NOT Sally NOT W. C.* (to distinguish from the actress Sally Field and long-ago comedian W. C. Fields).
- ***Use inclusion and exclusion operators—plus (+) and minus (−):*** With many search engines you can use the *inclusion operator,* the plus sign, and the *exclusion operator,* the minus sign, to take the place of AND and NOT.

  The plus sign (+), like AND, precedes a word that must appear. Example: + Strawberry + Fields.

  The minus sign (−), like *NOT,* excludes the word that follows it. Example: *Strawberry Fields – Sally.*
- ***Use wildcards—asterisks (*) and question marks (?):*** If you want as many results as possible on a keyword, use an asterisk (*) or question mark (?) to mean "anything/everything."

  Example: Type *dance** and you will get hits for *dance, dances, dancers, dancing, dancewear*, and so on.

  If you can't remember how to spell something, use the question mark (?). Example: If you type *Solzhe?,* you will get page matches for the Russian author *Solzhenitsyn.*
- ***Read the Help or Search Tips section:*** All search sites provide a Help section and tips. This could save you time later.
- ***Try an alternate general search site or a specific search site:*** As we indicated in the text, if you're looking for very specific information, a general type of search site such as Yahoo! may not be the best way to go. Instead, you should turn to a specific search site. Examples: For news stories, try Yahoo News (*http://news.yahoo.com*) or CNN (*www.cnn.com*). For pay-per-view information from all sorts of articles, journals, and reports, try LexisNexis (*www.lexisnexis.com*) and Factiva (Dow Jones and Reuters at *www.factiva.com*).

Desktop Search: Tools for Searching Your Computer's Hard Disk

Sometimes we all lose things on our computer and need help finding them.

If we're storing text from magazine pages with 5,000 characters per page on a computer that uses 1 byte per character, 1 terabyte (TB) of hard disk space could hold 220 million pages of text! But what if you lost track of everything you have stored on your computer—on your hard disk—and you need help finding something in the midst of all that data?

panel 2.22

Some desktop search tools

Search Tool	Site
Archivarius	*www.likasoft.com/document-search*
Ask Jeeves Desktop Search	*http://dl.uk.ask.com/ajds20/docs/faq.html*
Blinkx Pico	*www.blinkx.com/pico*
Copernic Desktop Search	*www.copernic.com/*
Everything	*www.snapfiles.com/get/everything.html*
Google Desktop 5	*http://googledesktop.com*
Yahoo! Desktop Search	*http://info.yahoo.com/legal/us/yahoo/desktopsearch/desktopsearch-300.html*

The solution: a *desktop search engine,* a tool that extends searching beyond the web to the contents of your personal computer's hard disk. Desktop search allows users to quickly and easily find words and concepts stored on the hard-disk drive, using technology similar to that in web search engines. Desktop tools must be downloaded from the Internet, often as part of a toolbar (a bar across the top of the display window on your computer screen, offering frequently executed options or commands). The tools remain in the background on your computer screen until you want to use them. Separate searches are usually required for the web and for the desktop.

AltaVista premiered a version called Discovery in 1998, but the technology failed to catch on. Now all the principal search engine services offer it. *(• See Panel 2.22.)*

Tagging: Saving Links for Easier Retrieval Later

Tags help you find your favorite websites again.

Once you've found favorite websites, how do you keep them found so that you can get back to them easily? You can always use the bookmarking or favorites feature, but there is also another way called *tagging.* ***Tags*** **are do-it-yourself labels that people can put on anything found on the Internet, from articles to photos to videos.** Using so-called social-bookmarking websites such as delicious.com or BlinkList or photo-sharing services such as Flickr, users can tag anything for easy retrieval later. Unlike bookmarks or favorites, these tags can be shared easily with other people, which allows people to share similar interests and ideas.

Collaborative Categorization

Some "social bookmarking" or photo-sharing web services with tagging features:

BlinkList
www.blinklist.com

delicious
www.delicious.com

eBiz
www.ebizmba.com/articles/social-bookmarking-websites

squidoo
www.squidoo.com

Flickr
www.flickr.com

2.4 Email & Other Ways of Communicating over the Net

Email has many uses, in many different contexts; other ways of communicating on the Internet include FTP, newsgroups, listservs, and chat.

Once connected to the Internet, many people want to immediately join the millions of users who send and receive electronic mail, or email, one of the principal uses of the Internet. Your incoming mail is stored in your mailbox on the access provider's computer, usually a server called a *mail server.* Outgoing mail is sent to a *Simple Mail Transfer Protocol (SMTP) server.* *(• See Panel 2.23.)* When you use your email software to retrieve your messages, the email is sent from the server to your computer using Post Office Protocol version 3 (POP3—not the same as "point of presence," p. 61) or Internet Message Access Protocol (IMAP), which has expanded functions compared to POP3. For example, if your access provider and email software support IMAP, you can use your browser to search through your email messages while they are still on the access provider's server—*before* you download them. Then you can choose which messages to download on your machine, using your email program.

Jake's ISP (SMTP server)
Internet Exchange Point (IXP)
Cable company
Maria's ISP
Regional network
Routers
Routers
POP3
POP
Telephone company
Internet Exchange Point (IXP)
Jake
Maria

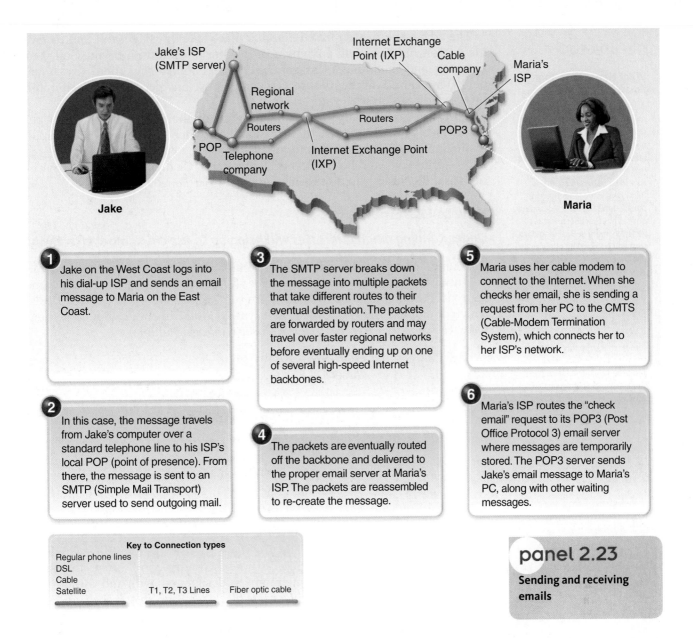

1 Jake on the West Coast logs into his dial-up ISP and sends an email message to Maria on the East Coast.

2 In this case, the message travels from Jake's computer over a standard telephone line to his ISP's local POP (point of presence). From there, the message is sent to an SMTP (Simple Mail Transport) server used to send outgoing mail.

3 The SMTP server breaks down the message into multiple packets that take different routes to their eventual destination. The packets are forwarded by routers and may travel over faster regional networks before eventually ending up on one of several high-speed Internet backbones.

4 The packets are eventually routed off the backbone and delivered to the proper email server at Maria's ISP. The packets are reassembled to re-create the message.

5 Maria uses her cable modem to connect to the Internet. When she checks her email, she is sending a request from her PC to the CMTS (Cable-Modem Termination System), which connects her to her ISP's network.

6 Maria's ISP routes the "check email" request to its POP3 (Post Office Protocol 3) email server where messages are temporarily stored. The POP3 server sends Jake's email message to Maria's PC, along with other waiting messages.

Key to Connection types

Regular phone lines DSL Cable Satellite	T1, T2, T3 Lines	Fiber optic cable

panel 2.23

Sending and receiving emails

Two Ways to Send & Receive Email

You can use email via software on your own computer or via web-based services, using a browser.

There are two ways to send and receive email—via *email program* or via *web-based email.*

EMAIL PROGRAM **An *email program* enables you to send email by running email software on your computer, which interacts with an email server at your Internet access provider to send and receive email.** Your incoming mail is stored on the server in an electronic mailbox. When you access the email server, your incoming messages are sent to your software's *inbox,* where they are ready to be opened and read. Examples of such programs are Microsoft's Outlook Express and Apple's Mail.

The advantage of standard email programs is that you can easily integrate your email with other applications, such as calendar, task list, and contact list.

WEB-BASED EMAIL **With *web-based email,* or *webmail,* you send and receive messages by interacting via a browser with a website.** The big four email carriers are Yahoo! Mail, Windows Live Hotmail, Gmail (Google), and AOL Mail.

Free Email

For discussion of free email services, go to:

www.emailaddresses.com

Survival Tip

What Happens to Your Smartphone Data?

Blackberry data is encrypted, meaning that it is very difficult to decipher if it's intercepted; encryption scrambles the text of messages, then unscrambles the text when the messages reach their destination. Also, BlackBerry data is stored on secure private servers that the company owns. Thus BlackBerry data is generally more secure than data sent and received by other smartphones and cellphones. Apple and HTC, among others, leave it up to the wireless providers (carriers) to manage data—in the cloud.

When you start using a cellphone or a smartphone, be sure to check the manufacturer's and wireless carrier's privacy and security policies. And purchase some cellphone security software.

The advantage of web-based email is that you can easily send and receive messages while traveling anywhere in the world. Moreover, because all your outgoing and incoming messages and folders for storing them (explained below) are stored on the mail server, you can use any personal computer and browser to keep up with your email.

Many users rely mostly on an email program on their personal computer, but when traveling without their regular PCs, they switch over to web-based email (using tablets or iPhones or computers belonging to friends or available—for a fee—in airports and hotels) to check messages. Or they use portable devices such as a BlackBerry to do text messaging. (• *See Panel 2.24.*)

How to Use Email

Understanding email addresses will help you to use email more effectively.

Of course, to use email you'll need an email address, a sort of electronic mailbox used to send and receive messages. All such addresses follow the same approach: *username@domain.* These are somewhat different from web URLs, which do not use the "@" (called "at") symbol. You can check with your Internet access provider to see if a certain user name is available.

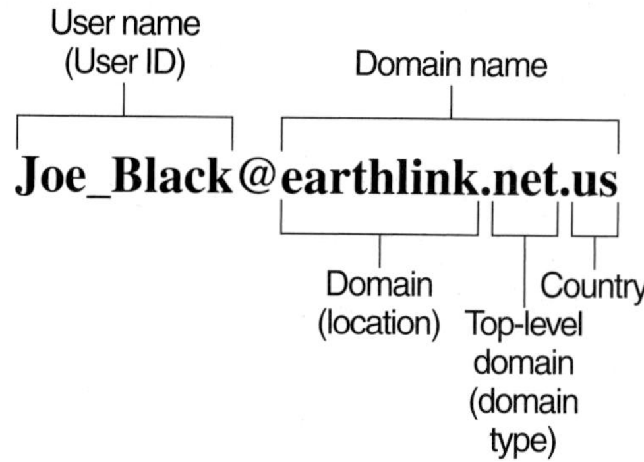

panel 2.24

Mobile mail

Portable devices such as this BlackBerry Bold wireless handheld smartphone allow you to send and receive email messages from many locations.

- **The user name: Joe_Black** The *user name,* or *user ID,* identifies who is at the address—in this case, *Joe_Black* (note the underscore). There are many ways that Joe Black's user name might be designated, with and without capital letters: *Joe_Black, joe_black, joe.black, joeblack, jblack, joeb,* and so on. If someone in your ISP's customer base has not already chosen the user name format that you want to use, then you will be able to sign up for it.
- **Domain name: @earthlink** The *domain name,* which is located after the @ ("at") symbol, tells the location and type of address. Domain-name components are separated by periods (called "dots"). The domain portion of the address (such as *Earthlink,* an Internet service provider) provides specific information about the location—where the message should be delivered.
- **Top-level domain: .net** The *top-level domain,* or *domain code,* is usually a three-letter extension that describes the domain type: *.net, .com, .gov, .edu, .org, .mil, .int*—network, commercial, government, educational, nonprofit, military, or international organization (p. 67).
- **Country: .us** Some domain names also include a two-letter extension for the country—for example, *.us* for United States, *.ca* for Canada, *.mx* for Mexico.

The illustration on the next page shows some generic basics about sending, receiving, and replying to email. (• *See Panel 2.25.*) Here are some tips about using email:

TYPE ADDRESSES CAREFULLY You need to type the address exactly as it appears, including all underscores and periods. If you type an email address incorrectly (putting in spaces, for example), your message will be returned to you labeled "undeliverable."

Sending email

Address Book: Lists email addresses you use most; can be attached automatically to messages

Send: Command for sending messages

cc: For copying ("carbon/ courtesy copy") message to others

bcc: For copying others ("blind carbon copy") without the primary recipient knowing it

Message area

You can conclude every message with a custom "signature"

Subject line: Preview incoming email by reviewing the subject lines to see if you really need to read the messages

Receiving email

Reply, Reply All, Forward, Delete: For helping you handle incoming email

Inbox lists messages waiting in email box. (Unopened envelope icon shows unread mail.)

Selected message displayed here

Replying to email

Use the **Reply** command icon, and the email program automatically fills in the To, From, and Subject lines in your reply.

panel 2.25

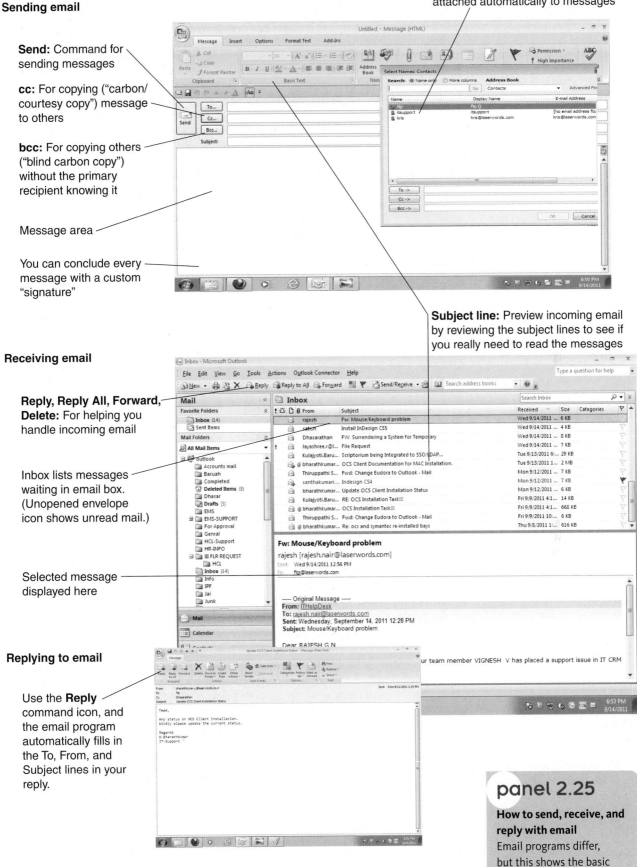

How to send, receive, and reply with email

Email programs differ, but this shows the basic principles.

Country Abbreviations

What do you think the country abbreviations are for Micronesia? Botswana? Saint Lucia? Go to:

www.eubank-web.com/William/Webmaster/c-codes.htm

www.thrall.org/domains.htm

History of the @ Sign

In 1972 Ray Tomlinson sent the first electronic message using the @ symbol to indicate the location or institution of the recipient. Tomlinson knew that he had to use a symbol that would not appear in anyone's name. Before the @ sign became a character on the keyboard, where was it used? Some linguists believe that the symbol dates back to the 6th or 7th centuries, when Latin scribes adapted the Latin word ad, meaning "at," "to," or "toward." Other linguists say that @ dates to its use in the 18th century as a symbol in commerce to indicate price per unit, as in 4 CDs @ $5 [each]. In 2000 a professor of history in Italy discovered some original 14th-century documents clearly marked with the @ sign to indicate a measure of quantity, based on the word amphora, meaning "jar." The amphora was a standard-size earthenware jar used by merchants for wine and grain. In Florence, the capital "A" was written with a flourish and later became @ ("at the price of").
Other countries have different names for this symbol. For example:

South Africa—*aapstet*, or "monkey's tail"
Czech Republic—*zavinac*, or "pickled herring"
Denmark—*snable-a*, or "elephant's trunk"
France—*petit escargot*, "little snail"
Greece—*papaki*, "little duck"
Hungary—*kukac*, "worm"
Taiwan—*xiao lao-shu*, "mouse sign"
Norway—*grisehale*, "pig's tail"
Russia—*sobachka*, "little dog"
Turkey—*kulak*, "ear"

Source: *www.pcwebopedia.com*, January 28, 2003, and www.webopedia.com, August 2005.

USE THE REPLY COMMAND When responding to an e-message someone has sent you, the easiest way to avoid making address mistakes is to use the Reply command, which will automatically fill in the correct address in the "To" line. *Be careful not to use the Reply All command unless you want your reply to be sent to all the original email's recipients!*

USE THE ADDRESS-BOOK FEATURE You can store the email addresses of people sending you messages in your program's "address book." This feature also allows you to organize your email addresses according to a nickname or the person's real name so that, for instance, you can look up your friend Joe Black under his real name, instead of under his user name, *bugsme2,* which you might not remember. The address book also allows you to organize addresses into various groups—such as your friends, your relatives, club members—so that you can easily send all members of a group the same message with a single command.

DEAL WITH EACH EMAIL ONLY ONCE When a message comes in, delete it, respond to it, or file it away in a folder. Avoid using your inbox for storage.

DON'T "BLOAT" YOUR EMAIL Email messages loaded with fancy typestyles, logos, and background graphics take longer to download. Keep messages simple.

Sorting Your Email

Keep your email organized in folders.

On an average day, billions of business and personal emails are sent in North America. If, as some people do, you receive 50–150 emails per day, you'll have to keep them organized so that you don't lose control.

One way to stay organized is by using instant organizers, also called *filters* or *rules,* which sort mail on the basis of the name of the sender or the mailing list and put particular emails into one folder. (• *See Panel 2.26.*) Then you can read emails sent to this folder later when you have time, freeing up your inbox for mail that needs your more immediate attention. Instructions on how to set up such organizers are in your email program's Help section.

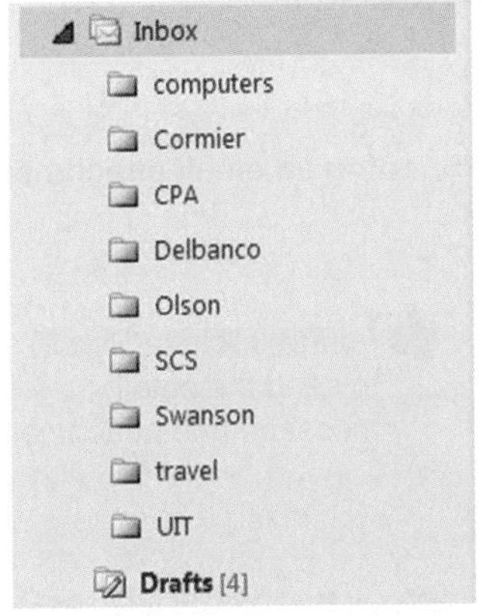

panel 2.26

Sorting email

Email folders keep you organized.

Attachments

In addition to typing a message and sending it as email, you can attach a separate file to the email and send that, too.

You have written a great research paper and you immediately want to show it off to someone. If you were sending it via the Postal Service, you would write a cover note—"Look at this great paper I wrote about globalization! See attached"—then attach it to the paper, and stick it in an envelope. Email has its own version of this. If the file of your paper exists in the computer from which you are sending email, you can write your email message (your cover note) and then use the Attach File command to attach the document. (• *See Panel 2.27, next page.*) (Note: It's important that the person receiving the email attachment have exactly the same software that created the attached file, such as Microsoft Word, or have software that can read and convert the attached file.) Downloading attachments from the mail server can take a lot of time—so you may want to discourage friends from sending you many attachments. Also, many email services have size limitations on attachments, so you may also want to use compression software to reduce the size of your attachments. (Compression is covered in detail in Chapter 3.)

(Note that sending yourself an email with an attached file is a good way to back up that file when you have no other back-up methods available—or even when you do.)

While you could also copy your document into the main message and send it that way, some email software loses formatting options such as **bold** or *italic* text or special symbols. And if you're sending song lyrics or poetry, the lines of text may break differently on someone else's display screen than they do on yours. Thus, the benefit of the attachment feature is that it preserves all such formatting, provided the recipient is using the same word processing software that you used. You can also attach pictures, sounds, videos, and other files to your email message.

Important Note: Many *viruses*—those "malware" programs that can seriously damage your PC or programs—ride along with email as attached files. Thus, you should *never open an attached file from an unknown source.* (We describe viruses in detail in Chapter 6.) (Latin *mal* or *malus* means "bad.")

Survival Tip

Accessing Email while Traveling Abroad

To access your email while traveling abroad, get a free email account with Yahoo! (*http://mail.yahoo.com*), Windows Live Hotmail (*www.hotmail.com*), Gmail (*www.mail.google*.com), or Mail.com (*www.mail.com*).

Instant Messaging

Instant messaging is a type of communications service that enables you to communicate in real time over the Internet, similar to a telephone conversation but using text-based, not voice-based, communication.

Instant messages are like a cross between email and phone, allowing communication that is far speedier than conventional email. With ***instant messaging (IM),*** **any user on a given email system can send a message and have it pop up instantly on the screen of anyone else logged onto that system.** (Instant messaging should not be confused with *text messaging,* or *texting,* the exchange of messages between mobile phones, as we discuss in Chapter 7. Nor should it be confused with *twittering,* the sending of text-based messages of up to 140 characters.)

As soon as you use your computer or portable device to connect to the Internet and log on to your IM account, you see a *buddy* list (or *contacts* list), a list you have created that consists of other IM users you want to communicate with. If all parties agree, they can initiate online typed conversations in real time

Sending an email attachment

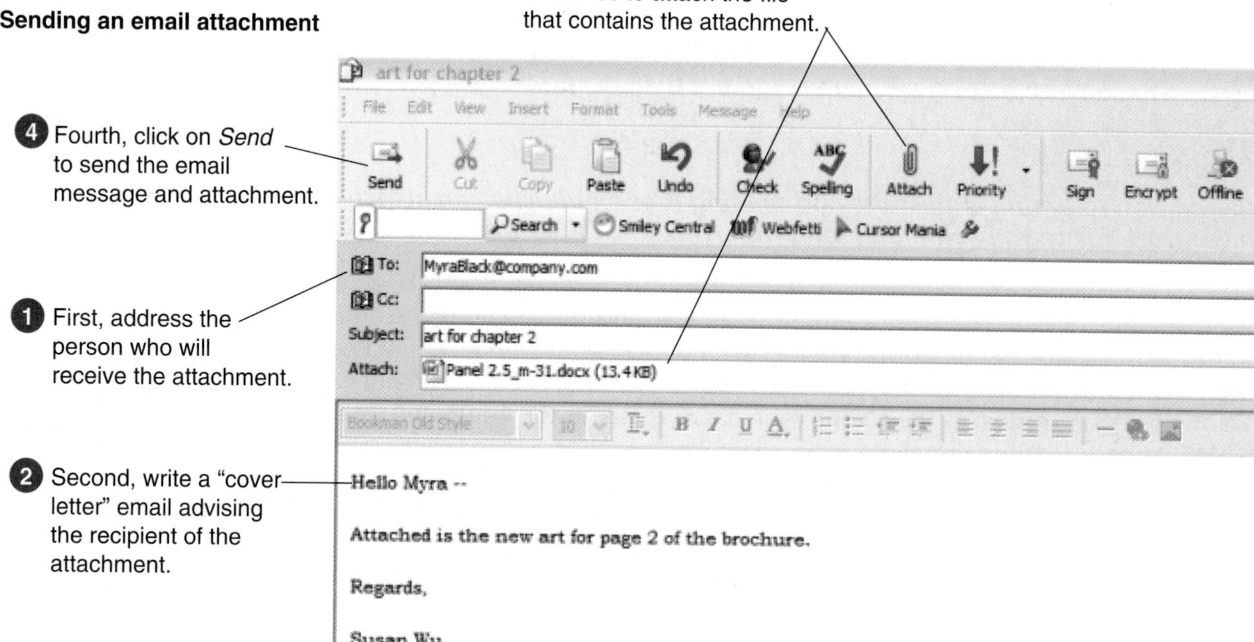

3 Third, use your email software's toolbar buttons or menus to attach the file that contains the attachment.
4 Fourth, click on *Send* to send the email message and attachment.
1 First, address the person who will receive the attachment.
2 Second, write a "cover-letter" email advising the recipient of the attachment.
art for chapter 2
File Edit View Insert Format Tools Message Help
Send Cut Copy Paste Undo Check Spelling Attach Priority Sign Encrypt Offline
Search Smiley Central Webfetti Cursor Mania
To: MyraBlack@company.com
Cc:
Subject: art for chapter 2
Attach: Panel 2.5_m-31.docx (13.4 KB)
Hello Myra --
Attached is the new art for page 2 of the brochure.
Regards,
Susan Wu

Receiving an email attachment

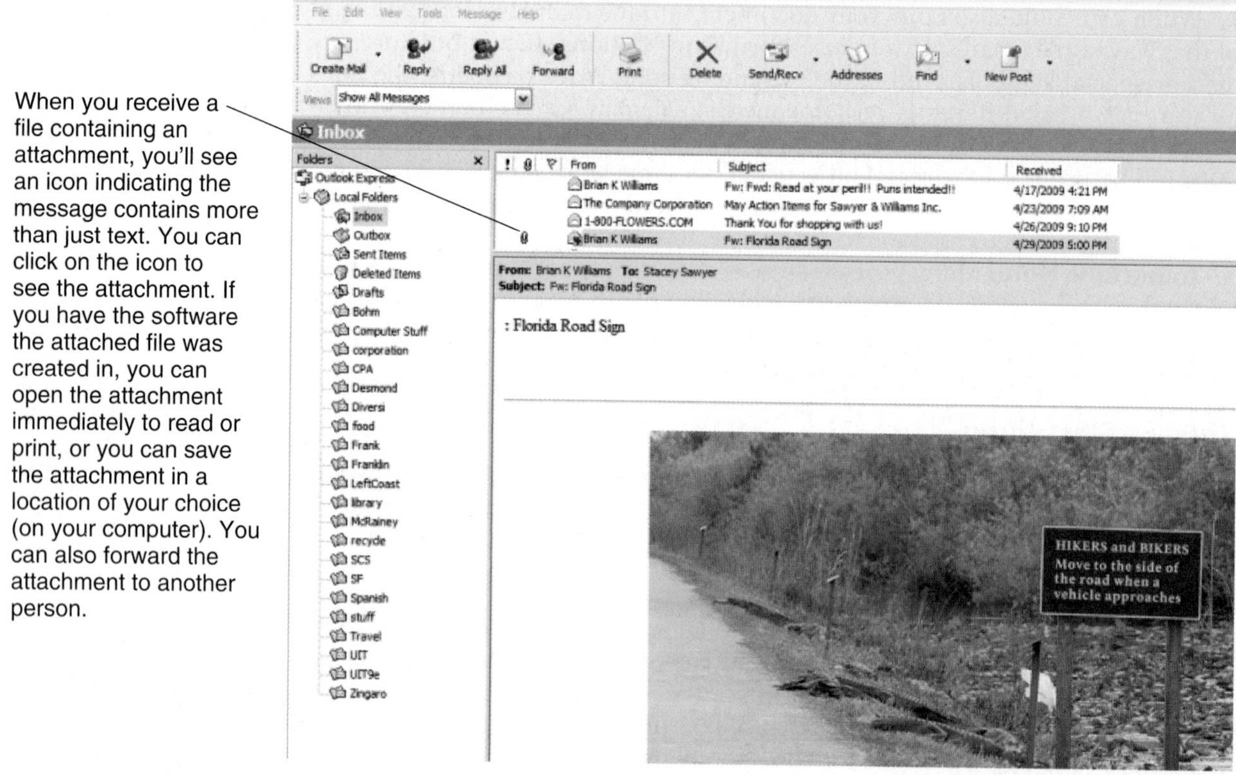

When you receive a file containing an attachment, you'll see an icon indicating the message contains more than just text. You can click on the icon to see the attachment. If you have the software the attached file was created in, you can open the attachment immediately to read or print, or you can save the attachment in a location of your choice (on your computer). You can also forward the attachment to another person.
Inbox - Outlook Express
Create Mail Reply Reply All Forward Print Delete Send/Recv Addresses Find New Post

From: Brian K Williams To: Stacey Sawyer
Subject: Fw: Florida Road Sign
: Florida Road Sign

panel 2.27

Attach File function

(in a "chat room"). The messages appear on the display screen in a small ***window*—a rectangular area containing a document or activity**—so that users can exchange messages almost instantaneously while operating other programs.

GETTING INSTANT-MESSAGING CAPABILITY Examples of present instant-message systems are AOL/AIM, MSN, Google Talk, MySpace, Facebook, and Yahoo! Messenger. To get instant messaging, which is often free, you download software and register with the service, providing it with a user name and password. When your computer or portable device is connected to the Internet, the software checks in with a central server, which verifies your identity and looks to see if any of your "buddies" are also online. You can then start a conversation by sending a message to any buddy currently online.

THE DOWNSIDE OF IM Instant messaging is especially useful in the workplace as a way of reducing long-distance telephone bills when you have to communicate with colleagues who are geographically remote but with whom you must work closely. However, you need to be aware of a few drawbacks:

SECURITY

- **Lack of privacy:** Most IM services lack the basic privacy that most other forms of communication provide. Efforts are under way to develop IM security software and procedures, but for now IM users should be aware that they have virtually no privacy.
- **Time wasters when you have to get work done:** An instant message is like a ringing phone, because it pops up on the recipient's screen right away. Some analysts suggest that, because of its speed, intrusiveness, and ability to show who else is online, IM can destroy workers' concentration in some offices. You can put off acknowledging email, voice mail, or faxes. But instant messaging is "the cyber-equivalent of someone walking into your office and starting up a conversation as if you had nothing better to do," says one critic. "It violates the basic courtesy of not shoving yourself into other people's faces."[25]

You can turn off your instant messages, but that is like turning off the ringer on your phone; after a while people will wonder why you're never available. Buddy lists or other contact lists can also become very in-groupish. When that happens, people are distracted from their work as they worry about staying current with their circle (or being shut out of one).

FTP—for Copying All the Free Files You Want

FTP makes it easy to transfer large files between computers.

Many net users enjoy "FTPing"—cruising the system and checking into some of the tens of thousands of FTP sites, which predate the web and offer interesting free or inexpensive files to download. ***FTP (File Transfer Protocol)* is a software standard for transferring files between computers with different operating systems. You can connect to a remote computer called an *FTP site* and transfer files to your own microcomputer's hard disk via TCI/IP over the Internet.** Free files offered cover nearly anything that can be stored on a computer: software, games, photos, maps, art, music, books, statistics. (• *See Panel 2.28, next page.*)

You can also set up your own private ftp site (for example, through ShareFile.com) to enable you and other people you allow to use your site to upload and download files that are too large to send as email attachments.

Some files on FTP sites are open to the public (at *anonymous FTP sites*); some are not. For instance, a university might maintain an FTP site with private files (such as lecture transcripts) available only to professors and students with assigned user names and passwords. It might also have public FTP files open to anyone with an email address. You can download FTP files using either your web browser or special software (called an *FTP client program*), such as Fetch and CuteFTP.

FTP Clients & Servers

FTP software programs, called *FTP clients*, come with many operating systems. Web browsers also come with FTP clients. For lists of FTP clients and FTP servers, go to:

www.answers.com/topic/comparison-of-ftp-clients

panel 2.28

FTP software

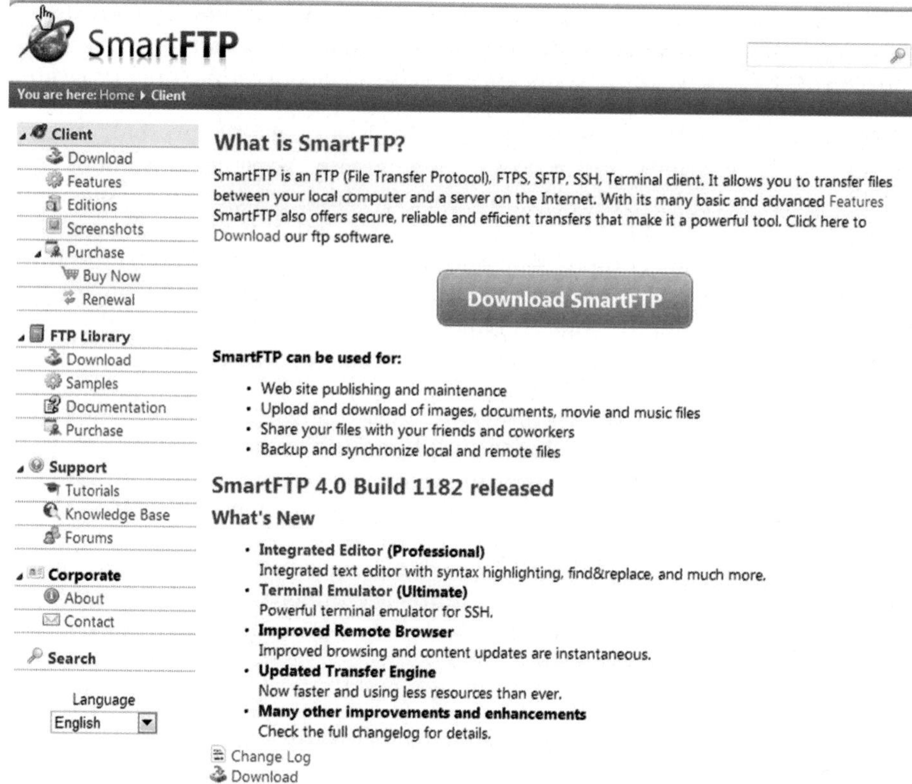

SmartFTP
You are here: Home ▸ Client
Client
Download
Features
Editions
Screenshots
Purchase
Buy Now
Renewal
FTP Library
Download
Samples
Documentation
Purchase
Support
Tutorials
Knowledge Base
Forums
Corporate
About
Contact
Search
Language
English
What is SmartFTP?
SmartFTP is an FTP (File Transfer Protocol), FTPS, SFTP, SSH, Terminal client. It allows you to transfer files between your local computer and a server on the Internet. With its many basic and advanced Features SmartFTP also offers secure, reliable and efficient transfers that make it a powerful tool. Click here to Download our ftp software.
Download SmartFTP
SmartFTP can be used for:
• Web site publishing and maintenance
• Upload and download of images, documents, movie and music files
• Share your files with your friends and coworkers
• Backup and synchronize local and remote files
SmartFTP 4.0 Build 1182 released
What's New
• Integrated Editor (Professional)
Integrated text editor with syntax highlighting, find&replace, and much more.
• Terminal Emulator (Ultimate)
Powerful terminal emulator for SSH.
• Improved Remote Browser
Improved browsing and content updates are instantaneous.
• Updated Transfer Engine
Now faster and using less resources than ever.
• Many other improvements and enhancements
Check the full changelog for details.
Change Log
Download

Newsgroups—for Online Typed Discussions on Specific Topics

Newsgroups are like bulletin boards.

panel 2.29

Newsgroup message board from the Blogger Help Group, a Google group

A ***newsgroup*** (or ***forum***) **is a giant electronic bulletin board on which users conduct written discussions about a specific subject.** (● *See Panel 2.29.*) There are thousands of Internet newsgroups—which charge no fee—and they

Blogger Search Blogger Help

Help forum

Help articles

Help forum

Post a question

Help forum > Blogger > Blogger Feature Suggestions & Feedback

Blogger Feature Suggestions & Feedback

Display all questions sorted by recent activity

Topic	Asked By	Replies	Last Reply
Should Blogger Become More Like YouTube and Wordpress Community-Wise? Answered	4/22/11 TheSwagtrician	25	5/17/11
Would LOVE a way to hide comments, but still allow them!	10:13 AM bridget350	0	--
Can we think about a short film like kerala cafe with 5 or 10 minutes film ?	10:07 AM ukcochin	0	--
Re: Virtual Feed Jar. How come only US and UK is enabled?	9:30 AM HerrMozart	0	--
Can I export the built-in blogger analytics stats to a real analytics account?	5/10/11 jajanowicz	2	9:05 AM ntcherno
My blog page won't list my followers	9:05 AM Bionicear	0	--
my blog cannot display, but fleedy.com always interupt when i open my blog, why?	6:44 AM qistina filzah	1	9:02 AM Martins
some of the misleading blogs can't be reported, including this : http://subwayspecial.blogspot.com/	8:29 AM Zlato Ku	1	9:01 AM Martins
Hi everybody, I really want to get more followers on blogger. My blog is http://alineolivson.blogspot.com/	8:59 AM alines blog	0	--
blogger changing date of draft posts	8:17 AM moffett sarah	0	--
Please Answer! Blog from 5/11/11 is still missing!!	7:12 AM tz_satchels	0	--

cover an amazing array of topics. In addition, for a small fee, services such as Meganetnews.com and CoreNews.com will get you access to more than 100,000 newsgroups all over the world. Newsgroups take place on a special network of computers called ***Usenet*,** **a worldwide public network of servers that can be accessed through the Internet** (*www.usenet.com*). To participate, you need a ***newsreader*,** **a program included with most browsers that allows you to access a newsgroup and read or type messages.** (Messages, incidentally, are known as *articles*.)

One way to find a newsgroup of interest to you is to use a portal such as Yahoo! or Bing to search for specific topics. Or you can use Google's Groups (*http://groups.google.com/grphp?hl+en&ie=UTF*), which presents the newsgroups matching the topic you specify. About a dozen major topics, identified by abbreviations ranging from *alt* (alternative topics) to *talk* (opinion and discussion), are divided into hierarchies of subtopics.

Listservs: Email-Based Discussion Groups

A listserv is a type of electronic mailing list, allowing for distribution of email to many subscribers.

Want to receive email from people all over the world who share your interests? You can try finding a mailing list and then "subscribing"—signing up, just as you would for a free newsletter or magazine. **A *listserv* is an automatic mailing-list server that sends email to subscribers who regularly participate in discussion topics.** *(● See Panel 2.30.)* Listserv companies include L-Soft's Listserv (*www.lsoft.com*), Email Universe.com (*http://emailuniverse.com/*), and *http://listserve.com/*. To subscribe, you send an email to the listserver moderator and ask to become a member, after which you will automatically receive email messages from anyone who responds to the server.

Mailing lists are one-way or two-way. A one-way list either accepts or sends information, but the user interacts only with the list server and not other users. Most one-way mailing lists are used for announcements, newsletters,

panel 2.30

Listserv mailing list software site

and advertising (and "spam," discussed shortly). Two-way lists, which are limited to subscribers, let users interact with other subscribers to the mailing list; this is the discussion type of mailing list.

Netiquette: Appropriate Online Behavior

Even in the often anonymous world of the Internet, civility and politeness—netiquette—are still required.

ethics

You may think etiquette is about knowing which fork to use at a formal dinner. Basically, though, etiquette has to do with politeness and civility—with rules for getting along so that people don't get upset or suffer hurt feelings.

New Internet users may accidentally offend other people in a discussion group or in an email simply because they are unaware of ***netiquette*, or "network etiquette"—appropriate online behavior.** In general, netiquette has two basic rules: (1) Don't waste people's time, and (2) don't say anything to a person online that you wouldn't say to his or her face.

Some more specific rules of netiquette are these:

- **Consult FAQs:** Most online groups post ***FAQs (frequently asked questions)*** **that explain expected norms of online behavior for a particular group.** Always read these first—before someone in the group tells you you've made a mistake.
- **Avoid flaming:** A form of speech unique to online communication, ***flaming*** **is writing an online message that uses derogatory, obscene, or inappropriate language.** Flaming is a form of public humiliation inflicted on people who have failed to read FAQs or have otherwise not observed netiquette (although it can happen just because the sender has poor impulse control and needs a course in anger management). Something that smooths communication online is the use of *emoticons,* keyboard-produced pictorial representations of expressions, such as :-) (smile), ;-) (wink), :-((frown).
- **Don't SHOUT:** Use of all-capital letters is considered the equivalent of SHOUTING. Avoid, except when they are required for emphasis of a word or two (as when you can't use italics in your e-messages).
- **Be careful with jokes:** In email, subtleties are often lost, so jokes may be taken as insults or criticism.
- **Avoid sloppiness, but avoid criticizing others' sloppiness:** Avoid spelling, punctuation, and grammatical errors. But don't criticize those same errors in others' messages. (After all, they may not speak English as a native language.) Most email software comes with spell-checking capability, which is easy to use. Also be sure to sign your messages.
- **Don't send huge file attachments, unless requested:** Your cousin living in the country may find it takes minutes rather than seconds for his or her computer to download a massive file (as of a video that you want to share). Better to query in advance before sending large files as attachments. Also, whenever you send an attachment, be sure the recipient has the appropriate software to open your attachment. If your attachments are large, use an application such as WinZip or Stuffit to reduce file sizes before attaching them.
- **When replying, quote only the relevant portion:** If you're replying to just a couple of matters in a long email posting, don't send back the entire message. This forces your recipient to wade through lots of text to find the reference. Instead, edit his or her original text down to the relevant paragraph and then put in your response immediately following.
- **Don't "overforward":** Don't automatically forward emails to your friends without checking if the contents are true and appropriate.

Good Websites on Netiquette, including a Quiz

http://netforbeginners.about.com/od/netiquetteonlineculture/l/bl_netiquette_quiz.htm

www.albion.com/netiquette

http://email.about.com/od/emailnetiquette/tp/core_netiquette.htm

www.networketiquette.net

2.5 THE ONLINE GOLD MINE: Telephony, Multimedia, Webcasting, Blogs, E-Commerce, & Social Networking

The Internet and the web are offering more new services every day. Social networking is currently one of the most popular activities.

Blogs used to be regarded as web-based "daily diaries of people with no real lives to chronicle in the first place."[26] But the December 2004 Indian Ocean calamity that resulted in over 143,000 people killed and more than 146,000 missing also showed how quickly and effectively this form of web technology could be in spreading instant news, often beating out the mainstream news media. In particular, the tsunami spurred the distribution of *video blogs,* or *vblogs* or *vlogs,* consisting of video footage mostly shot by vacationing foreign tourists during and after the disaster.

The opportunities offered by the Internet and the web seem inexhaustible. Here we'll examine several resources available to you.

Telephony: The Internet Telephone & Videophone

Internet telephony can enable you to make international phone calls and video connections for free.

As we stated earlier (p. 63), the Internet breaks up conversations (as it does any other transmitted data) into "information packets" that can be sent over separate lines and then regrouped at the destination, whereas conventional voice phone lines carry a conversation over a single path. Thus, the Internet can move a lot more traffic over a network than the traditional telephone link can.

With ***Internet telephony,* or *VoIP phoning* (short for *Voice over Internet Protocol*)—using the net to make phone calls, either one to one or for audioconferencing**—you can make long-distance phone calls that are surprisingly inexpensive or even free. (• *See Panel 2.31.*) Indeed, it's possible to do

panel 2.31

Internet telephony

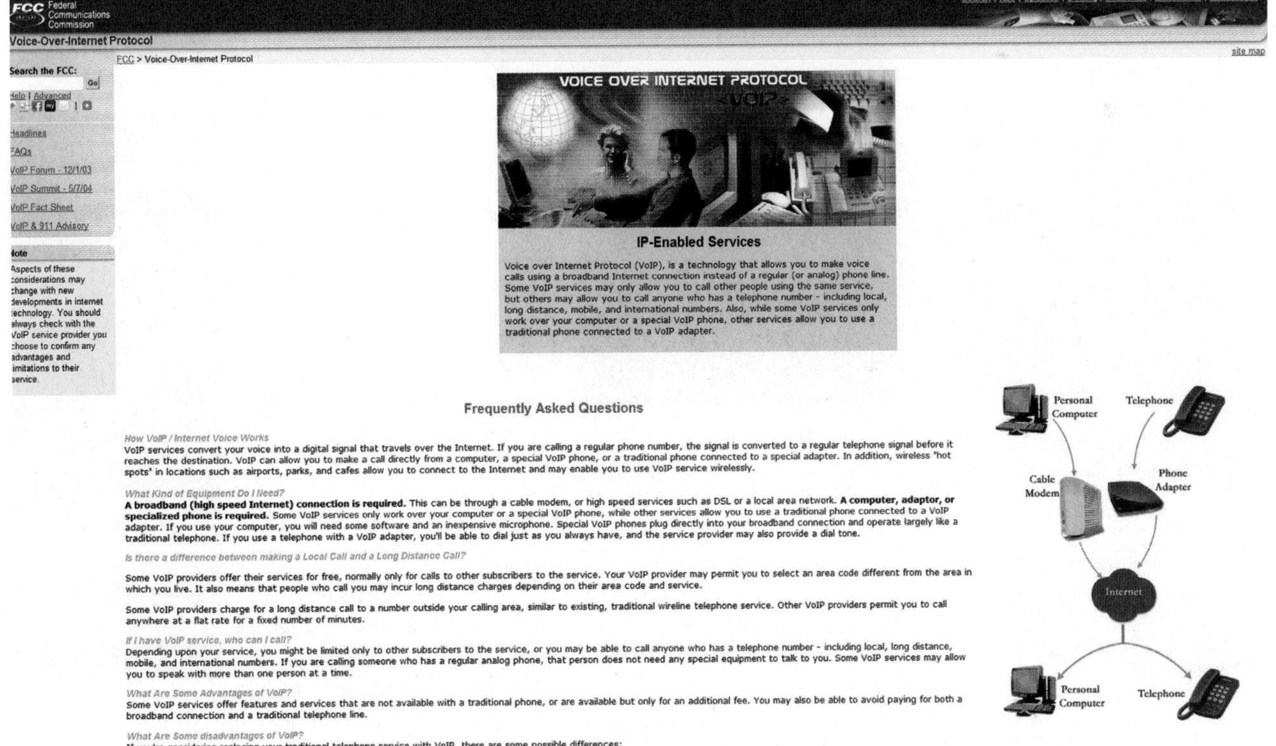

more info!

How VoIP Works

http://communication.howstuffworks.com/ip-telephony5.htm

http://mybusinessvoip.com/what-is-voip

http://pma101.com/101/howdoesvoipwork.html

this without owning a computer, simply by picking up your standard telephone and dialing a number that will "packetize" your conversation. However, people also can use a PC with a sound card and a microphone, and a modem linked to a standard Internet service provider. VoIP is offered by AT&T, Google Voice, Skype, Vonage, Yahoo! Voice, and scores of other companies. Although sound quality used to be a problem with VoIP systems, the widespread availability of broadband has improved call quality somewhat.

Be aware, however, that many VoIP companies cannot handle 911 emergency calls because they are not locally based. Also, if your ISP is having problems, then you may not be able to place calls until the problems are fixed. Local or distant power outages can also shut down VoIP service.

Besides carrying voice signals, Internet telephone software also allows videoconferencing, in which participants are linked by a videophone that will transmit their pictures, thanks to a video camera attached to their PCs.

Multimedia on the Web

Multimedia on the web is usually handled by plug-ins and small, special programs (software).

Many websites (especially those trying to sell you something) employ complicated multimedia effects, using a combination of text, images, sound, video, and animation. While most web browsers can handle basic multimedia elements on a web page, eventually you'll probably want more dramatic capabilities.

PLUG-INS In the 1990s, as the web was evolving from text to multimedia, browsers were unable to handle many kinds of graphic, sound, and video files. To do so, external application files called *plug-ins* had to be loaded into the system. **A *plug-in* is a program that adds a specific feature to a browser, allowing it to play or view certain files.**

For example, to view certain documents, you may need to download Adobe Acrobat Reader. (• *See Panel 2.32.*) To view high-quality video and hear radio, you may need to download RealPlayer. (• *See Panel 2.33.*) QuickTime is a media player for the Apple Macintosh. Plug-ins are required by many websites if you want to fully experience their content.

panel 2.32

Adobe Acrobat Reader

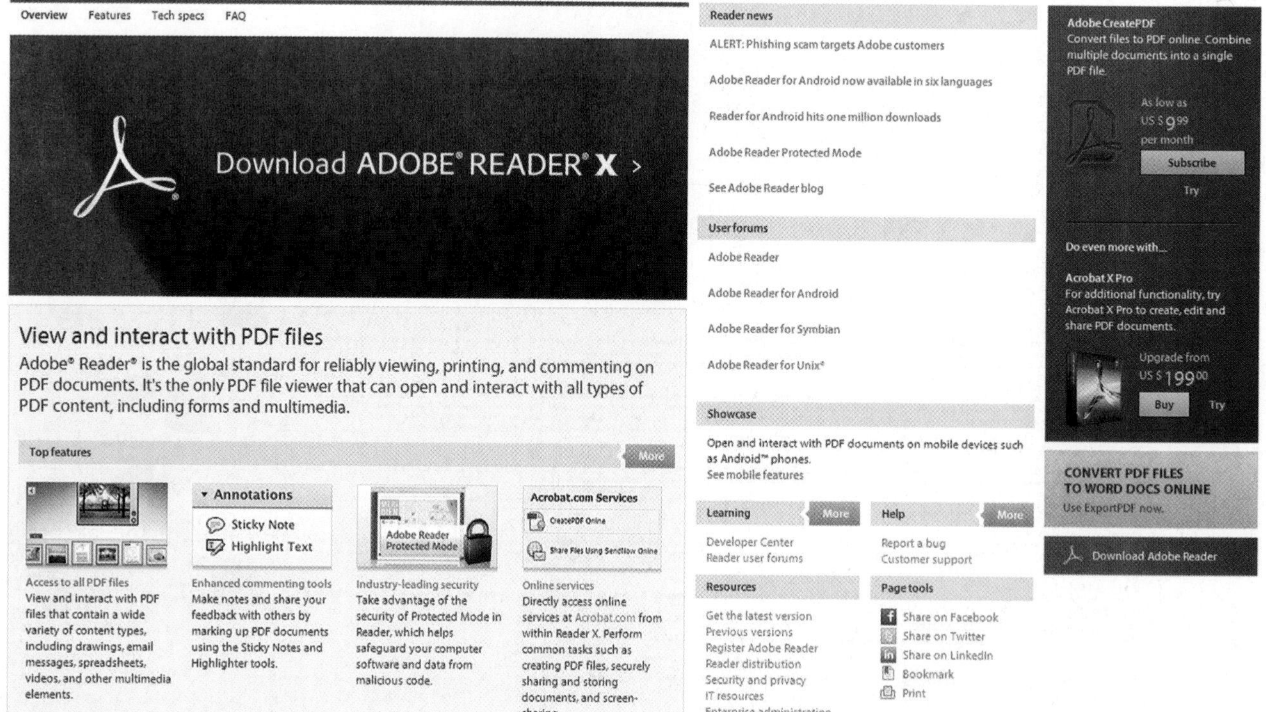

Adobe Acrobat /
Adobe Reader X
Overview Features Tech specs FAQ
Download ADOBE® READER® X >
View and interact with PDF files
Adobe® Reader® is the global standard for reliably viewing, printing, and commenting on PDF documents. It's the only PDF file viewer that can open and interact with all types of PDF content, including forms and multimedia.
Top features
More
Annotations
Sticky Note
Highlight Text
Adobe Reader Protected Mode
Acrobat.com Services
Access to all PDF files
View and interact with PDF files that contain a wide variety of content types, including drawings, email messages, spreadsheets, videos, and other multimedia elements.
Enhanced commenting tools
Make notes and share your feedback with others by marking up PDF documents using the Sticky Notes and Highlighter tools.
Industry-leading security
Take advantage of the security of Protected Mode in Reader, which helps safeguard your computer software and data from malicious code.
Online services
Directly access online services at Acrobat.com from within Reader X. Perform common tasks such as creating PDF files, securely sharing and storing documents, and screen-sharing.
Reader news
ALERT: Phishing scam targets Adobe customers
Adobe Reader for Android now available in six languages
Reader for Android hits one million downloads
Adobe Reader Protected Mode
See Adobe Reader blog
User forums
Adobe Reader
Adobe Reader for Android
Adobe Reader for Symbian
Adobe Reader for Unix®
Showcase
Open and interact with PDF documents on mobile devices such as Android™ phones.
See mobile features
Learning
More
Help
More
Developer Center
Reader user forums
Report a bug
Customer support
Resources
Page tools
Get the latest version
Previous versions
Register Adobe Reader
Reader distribution
Security and privacy
IT resources
Enterprise administration
Adobe PDF history
Share on Facebook
Share on Twitter
Share on LinkedIn
Bookmark
Print
Adobe CreatePDF
Convert files to PDF online. Combine multiple documents into a single PDF file.
As low as US $9.99 per month
Subscribe
Try
Do even more with...
Acrobat X Pro
For additional functionality, try Acrobat X Pro to create, edit and share PDF documents.
Upgrade from US $199.00
Buy
Try
CONVERT PDF FILES TO WORD DOCS ONLINE
Use ExportPDF now.
Download Adobe Reader

Recent versions of Microsoft Internet Explorer and Firefox (p. 65) can handle a lot of multimedia. Now if you come across a file for which you need a plug-in, the browser will ask whether you want it and then tell you how to go about downloading it, usually at no charge.

DEVELOPING MULTIMEDIA: APPLETS, JAVA, & VISUAL STUDIO.NET How do website developers get all those nifty special multimedia effects? Often web pages contain links to ***applets,*** **small programs (software) that can be quickly downloaded and run by most browsers.** Applets ("little applications") are written in ***Java,*** **a programming language that enables programmers to create animated and interactive web pages.** Java applets enhance web pages by playing music, displaying graphics and animation, and providing interactive games. Java-compatible browsers such as Internet Explorer automatically download applets from the website and run them on your computer so that you can experience the multimedia effects. Microsoft offers Visual Studio to compete with Java.

TEXT & IMAGES Of course, you can call up all kinds of text documents on the web, such as newspapers, magazines, famous speeches, and works of literature. You can also view images, such as scenery, famous paintings, and photographs. Most web pages combine both text and images.

One interesting innovation is that of aerial maps. Google Earth (*www.google.earth.com*) is a satellite imaging program that Google has described as "part flight simulator, part search tool."[27] You type in your ZIP (Zone Improvement Plan) code or street address and it feels like you're looking down on a high-resolution aerial view of your house from a plane at 30,000 feet. And you

Skype Interviews

1. Do a tech check: make sure you have what's needed.
2. Practice
3. Dress appropriately for the video
4. Check your background (for the video)
5. Pay attention to lighting
6. Minimize the chance of interruptions
7. Look at the camera
8. Sit still
9. Take notes
10. Make sure you completely hang up when you are done

(www.poughkeepsiejournal.com/article/20111002/BUSINESS/110020352/10-must-dos-Skype-interviews)

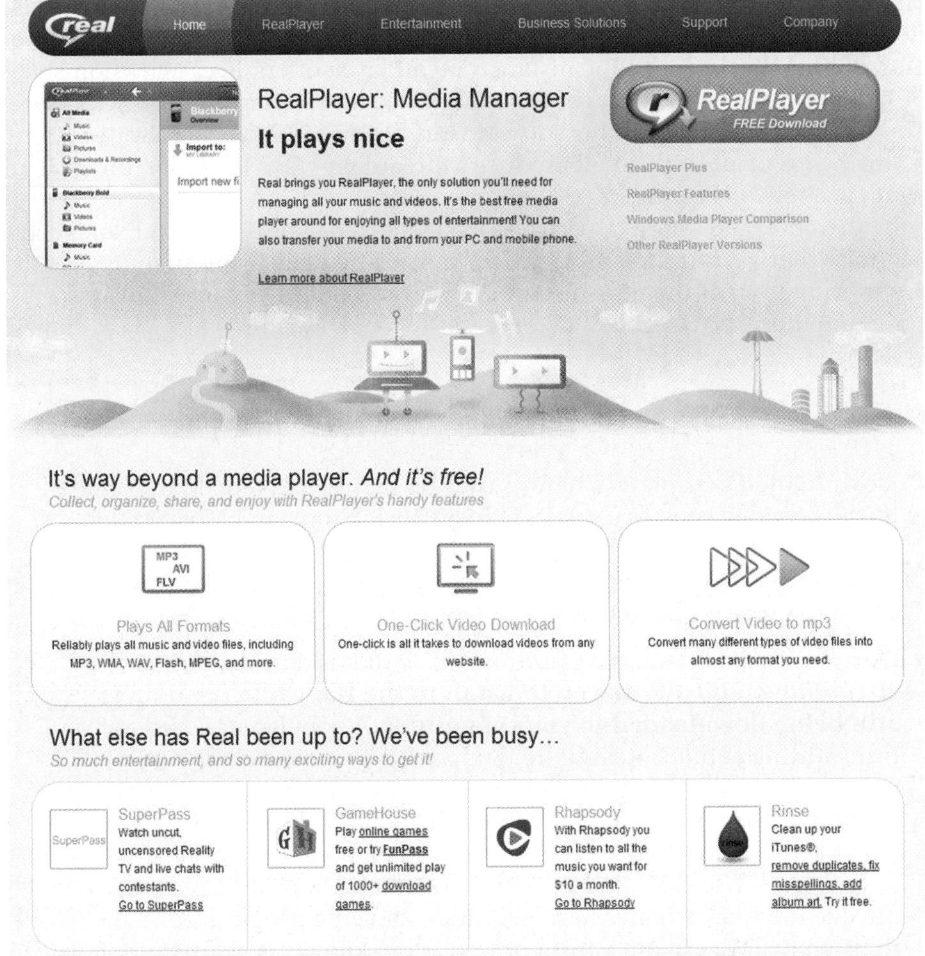

panel 2.33
RealPlayer

can also use Google Earth to look at the moon and Mars. Using Google Local Search, you can search for a business or other attraction in some city, and you'll get an indicator on your satellite image; if you click again, the establishment's web page opens. "Google sightseers can zoom in close enough to see airplanes parked in the desert, the baseball diamond at Wrigley Field, and cars in the Mall of America parking lot," says one writer.[28] Google Earth also extends under the sea. In 2009 the company released a 3-D mapping service "that lets users explore the ocean as if they were dolphins, swimming past submerged volcanoes and through underwater canyons."[29]

Google Earth also provides street views taken by camera-equipped cars that roam the streets taking 360-degree photographs "for display to anyone who types in the correct address, or latitude and longitude, or any number of other ways to indicate a location that Google can figure out."[30] Google's online map service, Street View, has been accused of taking pictures and coming too close inside people's private homes and/or to people who walk down the street not knowing they are being watched on Google's service. At the end of 2010 the German government was considering making it illegal for Google Street View to use camouflaged or hidden cameras in their videotaping of residential properties and to allow citizens to opt out of the privacy-invasive technology.

ANIMATION ***Animation*** **is the rapid sequencing of still images to create the appearance of motion,** as in most video games as well as in moving banners displaying sports scores or stock prices.

VIDEO Video can be transmitted in two ways. (1) A file, such as a movie or video clip, may have to be completely downloaded before you can view it. This may take several minutes in some cases. (2) A file may be displayed as streaming video and viewed while it is still being downloaded to your computer. ***Streaming video*** **is the process of transferring data in a continuous flow (in real time) so that you can begin viewing a file even before the end of the file is sent.** For instance, RealPlayer offers live, television-style broadcasts over the Internet as streaming video for viewing on your PC screen. You download and install this software and then point your browser to a site featuring RealVideo. That will produce a streaming-video television image in a window a few inches wide.

With more and more American households having the broadband connections that permit streaming video, movies-by-mail firms such as Netflix are moving toward the near-instant delivery of movies streamed to subscribers' computers, Net-enabled TV sets, set-top box systems, and Xbox games systems.

AUDIO Audio, such as sound or music files, may also be transmitted in two ways:

- **Downloaded completely before the file can be played:** Many online music services, such as eMusic, iTunes Music Store, and MusicMatch, offer music for a fee, either by subscription or by the song. Generally, music must be downloaded completely before the file can be played on a computer or portable music player.
- **Downloaded as streaming audio:** Music that is downloaded as ***streaming audio*** **allows you to listen to the file while the data is still being downloaded to your computer.** A popular standard for transmitting audio is RealAudio. Supported by most web browsers, it compresses sound so that it can be played in real time, even if sent over telephone lines. You can, for instance, listen to 24-hour-a-day net radio, which features "vintage rock," or English-language services of shortwave outlets from World Radio Network in London. Many large radio stations outside the United States have net radio, allowing people around the world to listen in. (We explain a form of web audio known as *podcasting* shortly.)

The Web Automatically Comes to You: Webcasting, Blogging, & Podcasting

You don't always have to search for what you want on the web; the web can also come to you.

PUSH TECHNOLOGY & WEBCASTING The trend of bringing web content to users without users doing any searching began in the late 1990s with ***push technology,*** **software that automatically downloads information to personal computers** (as opposed to *pull technology,* in which you go to a website and pull down the information you want—in other words, the web page isn't delivered until a browser requests or pulls it). One result of push technology was ***webcasting*** **("web broadcasting"), in which customized text, video, and audio are sent to you automatically on a regular basis or live on demand.**

The idea here is that you choose the categories, or (in Microsoft Internet Explorer) the channels, of websites that will automatically send you updated information. Thus, webcasting saves you time because you don't have to go out searching for the information. Webcasting companies are also called *subscription services,* because they sell on-demand services. However, a lot of push technology fell out of favor because it clogged networks with information that readers often didn't want. Then along came RSS.

BLOGGING—RSS, XML, & THE RISE OF THE BLOGOSPHERE RSS was built to be simpler than push technology. ***RSS newsreaders,*** **or *RSS aggregators,* are programs that scour the web, sometimes hourly or more frequently, and pull together in one place web "feeds" from several websites.** The developers of RSS technology don't agree on what the abbreviation stands for, but some say it means "Really Simple Syndication" or "Rich Site Summary," although there are other variations as well. "RSS allows you to play news editor and zero in on the information you really need," says one account, "even as you expand the number of sites you sample."[31] This is because the information is so specifically targeted.

RSS is based on ***XML,*** **or *extensible markup language,* a web-document tagging and formatting language that is an advance over HTML** (p. 69) **and that two computers can use to exchange information.** XML, in the form of RSS, has allowed people to have access to a whole new universe of content. One of the earliest adopters, for instance, was the Mormon Church, which used the system to keep in touch with members. Now, however, it has morphed into something called the ***blogosphere,*** **the total universe of blogs—*blog* being short for *web log,* a diary-style web page.** (• *See Panel 2.34, next page.*)

"Blogs can be anything their creators want them to be, from newsy to deeply personal, argumentative to poetic," says one writer. "Some are written by individuals. Some are group projects. Some have readerships in the thousands and influence world media. Others are read by a handful of people—or not read at all, because they're all pictures. Bloggers are a new breed of homegrown journal writers and diarists who chronicle life as it happens, with words, photos, sound, and art."[32] Says another dedicated blogger, "Blogging is . . . to writing what extreme sports are to athletics: more free-form, more accident-prone, less formal, more alive. It is, in many ways, writing out loud."[33] Some people have succeeded in turning blogging into successful businesses, with those who receive 100,000 or more unique visitors a month earning an average of $75,000 a year (aided by online ads).[34] But 95% of blogs are essentially abandoned, so the key to building a successful audience for a blog seems to be a nonstop, work-every-day workweek.[35]

Among other variations are *video blogs,* or *vblogs,* which are video versions of blogs, a kind of Internet TV, and *moblogs,* or *mobile blogs,* in which picture blogs are posted to websites directly from camera-enabled cellphones.

Blogging Products

Some popular blogging products are these:

e-Blogger www.blogger.com

Moveable Type's TypePad www.typepad.com

quackit www.quackit.com/create-a-blog/

HowToMakeMyBlog.com www.howtomakemyblog.com/

Blog Search Engines

Some blog search engines:

Technorati www.technorati.com/blogs/directory

Bloglines www.bloglines.com

Blogdigger www.blogdigger.com

Blog Search Engine www.blogsearchengine.com/

Google Blog Search http://blogsearch.google.com/

panel 2.34

The blogosphere: one way to create your own blog

Create a blog. It's free.

Get started

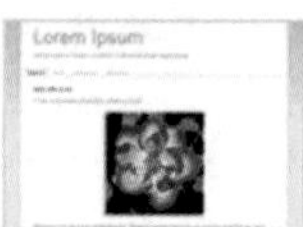
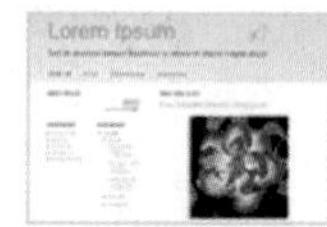

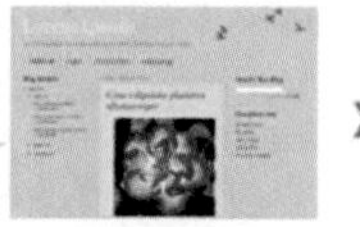

Beautiful, customizable templates and layouts. Try the template designer

Up to the minute stats

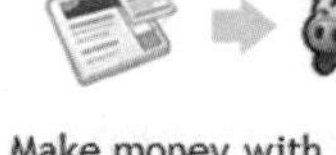
Make money with Adsense

Explore Blogs of Note

Want to learn more? Take a quick tour, watch a video tutorial or read Blogger Buzz.

PODCASTING ***Podcasting*** **involves the recording of Internet radio or similar Internet audio programs.** The term derives not only from *webcasting* but also from the Apple *iPod* portable music player and other mobile listening devices, such as MP3 players. In general, a podcast is an audio program in a compressed digital format, delivered via an RSS feed over the Internet to a subscriber and designed for playback on computers or portable digital audio players. Podcasts can also be posted on a website for downloading.

E-Commerce: B2B Commerce, Online Finance, Auctions, & Job Hunting

The Internet and the web are also important in the world of business and jobs.

The explosion in ***e-commerce (electronic commerce)*****—conducting business activities online—**is not only widening consumers' choice of products and services but also creating new businesses and compelling established businesses to develop Internet strategies. Many so-called brick-and-mortar retailers—those operating out of physical buildings—have lost business to such online companies as Amazon.com, seller of books, CDs, and many other products. As a result, traditional retailers from giant Walmart to very small one-person businesses now offer their products online.

Retail goods can be classified into two categories—hard and soft. *Hard goods* are those that can be viewed and priced online, such as computers, clothes, groceries, and furniture, but are then sent to buyers by mail or truck. *Soft goods* are those that can be downloaded directly from the retailer's site, such as music, software, travel tickets, and greeting cards.

Some specific forms of e-commerce are as follows:

B2B COMMERCE Of course, every kind of commerce has taken to the web, ranging from travel bookings to real estate. One of the most important variations is ***B2B (business-to-business) commerce*****, the electronic sale or exchange of goods and services directly between companies, cutting out traditional intermediaries.** Expected to grow even more rapidly than other forms of e-commerce, B2B commerce covers an extremely broad range of activities, such as supplier-to-buyer display of inventories, provision of wholesale price lists, and sales of closed-out items and used materials—usually without agents, brokers, or other third parties.

ONLINE FINANCE: TRADING, BANKING, & E-MONEY The Internet has changed the nature of stock trading. Anyone with a computer, a connection to the global network, and the information, tools, and access to transaction systems required to play the stock market can do so online. Companies such as E*Trade (*www.etrade.com*) have built one-stop financial supermarkets offering a variety of money-related services, including home mortgage loans and insurance.

AUCTIONS: LINKING INDIVIDUAL BUYERS & SELLERS Today millions of buyers and sellers are linking up at online auctions, where everything is available from comic books to wines. The Internet is also changing the tradition-bound art and antiques business (dominated by such venerable names as Sotheby's, Christie's, and Butterfield & Butterfield). There are generally two types of auction sites:

more info!
Some Auction Websites
eBay www.ebay.com
WeBidz www.webidz.com
Overstock.com http://auctions.overstock.com

- **Person-to-person auctions:** Person-to-person auctions, such as eBay, connect buyers and sellers for a listing fee and a commission on sold items. (● *See Panel 2.35.)*
- **Vendor-based auctions:** Vendor-based auctions, such as OnSale and Overstock.com, buy merchandise and sell it at discount. Some auctions are specialized, such as Priceline, an auction site for airline tickets and other items.

panel 2.35

eBay auction

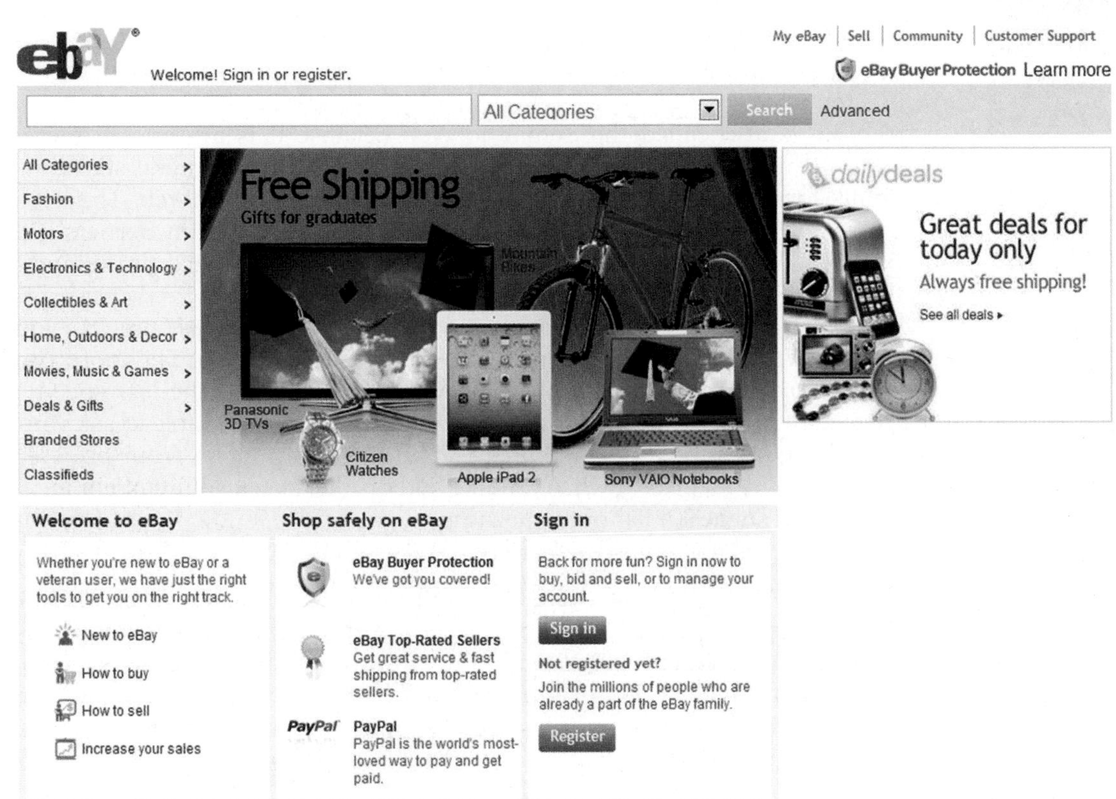

Some Top Social-Networking Websites

Bebo
BlackPlanet.com
Facebook
Flixster
Friendster
habbo
hi5
LinkedIn
MySpace
Netlog
Ning
Orkut
perfSpot
Xanga
Zorpia

Comparison of the Top 10 Social Networking Sites

http://social-networking-websites-review.toptenreviews.com/

Survival Tip

Social-Networking Privacy

Check your social-networking and messaging privacy options carefully:

http://mashable.com/2011/02/07/facebook-privacy-guide/

www.sophos.com/security/best-practice/facebook/

www.theatlantic.com/technology/archive/2011/02/10-facebook-privacy-settings-everyone-should-know/70868/

http://chronicle.com/blogs/profhacker/six-steps-for-checking-your-facebook-privacy/30402

http://arstechnica.com/security/news/2011/01/new-privacy-concerns-for-facebook-over-phone-numbers-addresses.ars

www.958.ibm.com/software/data/cognos/manyeyes/datasets/twitter-privacy-policy-jan-2011/versions/1

ONLINE JOB HUNTING There are more than 2,000 websites that promise to match job hunters with an employer. Some are specialty "boutique" sites looking for, say, scientists or executives. Some are general sites, the leaders being Monster.com, CareerPath.com, indeed.com, USAJOBS (U.S. government/federal jobs; *www.usajobs.opm.gov*), and CareerBuilder.com. Job sites can help you keep track of job openings and applications by downloading them to your own computer. Résumé sites such as Employment911.com help you prepare professional-quality résumés.

Web 2.0: Social Networking, Media Sharing, Social-Network Aggregation, & Microblogging

Web 2.0 refers to the web viewed as a medium in which interactive experience, in the form of blogs, wikis, forums, social networking, and so on, plays a more important role than simply accessing information.

Finally, we come to what is known as ***Web 2.0*, which can be defined as the move toward a more social, collaborative, interactive, and responsive web.**[36] As websites have become easier to use, they allow users to better harness the collective power of people, which has led to a "social web" or "social media," involving not only blogs and wikis (for sharing information) but also social networks and media sharing. The common theme of all these is human interaction.

What will Web 3.0, also called the Semantic Web, look like? Some Internet experts believe the next generation of the Web—Web 3.0—will make certain tasks, such as a search for movies and food, faster and easier. Instead of the multiple searches you would make now, you might type a complex sentence or two in your Web 3.0 browser, and the Web will do the rest. For example, you could type "I want to see a funny movie, and then eat at a good Mexican restaurant. What are my options?"[37] The Web 3.0 browser will analyze your response, search the Internet for all possible answers, and then organize the results for you.

Web 3.0 is also called the Semantic Web because it is a group of methods and technologies that supposedly will allow machines to understand the meaning—or "semantics"—of information on the World Wide Web. The term was coined by World Wide Web Consortium (W3C) director Tim Berners-Lee (p. 65), who defines it as a web of data that can be processed directly and indirectly by machines.

The Web 3.0 browser will probably also act as a personal assistant. As you search the Web, the browser learns what you are interested in. The more you use the Web, the more your browser learns about you and the less specific you'll need to be with your questions. Eventually you might be able to ask your browser open questions such as "where should I go for lunch?" Your browser would consult its records of what you like and dislike, check your current location, and then suggest a list of restaurants.

MYSPACE, FACEBOOK, & OTHER SOCIAL-NETWORKING WEBSITES **A *social-networking website* is an online community that allows members to keep track of their friends and share photos, videos, music, stories, and ideas with other registered members.** Social-networking websites are led by Facebook (400 million users) and MySpace (57 million users) but also include the business-contact site LinkedIn (60 million users).[38]

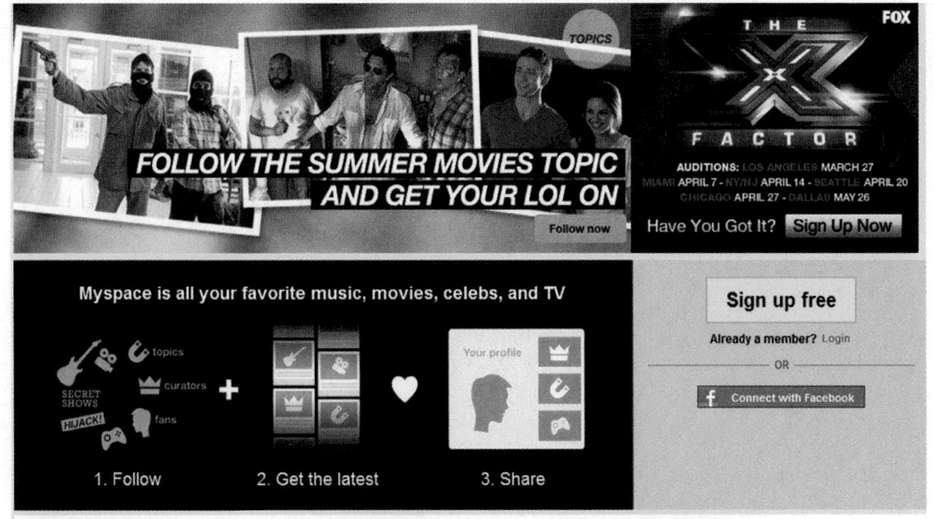

Music

"All In White"
The Vaccines
Video Premiere
Watch now

Our "Introducing..." rockers deliver a gut punch-of-a-video.

"Motivation" Ft. Lil Wayne
Kelly Rowland
Video Feature
Watch now

Kelly and Weezy. Sounds like a new rom-com. It's a hot video.

"Pumped Up Kicks"
Foster The People
Single Feature
Listen

Maybe it's the whistling. This track makes us smile.

Curators

Competition Reality w/Asha
664,122 Friends
+ Friend

Who will get kicked off 'Idol' tonight?

Blockbusters with Germain
210,326 Friends
+ Friend

Talk 'Hunger Games' with our movie man!

LOL with Claire
326,443 Friends
+ Friend

Someone's gone bananas for Bieber (Haven't we all?).

Topics

The Office
467,272 Fans
Follow

Dwight? Will Arnett? Jim Carrey? Who'll be the boss?

Beyoncé
76,064 Fans
Follow

This busy B really is running the world this week!

The Big Bang Theory
87,996 Fans
Follow

Will Sheldon get a new roommate in tonight's finale?

More in Music
Music Home
My Music
Music Videos
Charts
New Releases
Featured Playlists
Music News
Karaoke
Shows
Artists

More in Curators
Vinyl Toys with TB
Basketball with Barney
Street Art with Alana
Urban Culture with Adrienne
Memes with Amber
Fashion with Seojie
Movies with Marquis
WTF with Redux
Reality with Nikki
Photography with Paris

More in Topics
Arnold Schwarzenegger
The Voice
Two and a Half Men
Alexander McQueen
Ashley Greene
Beyoncé
Dancing with the Stars
Ralph Macchio
Justin Bieber
Kristen Wiig

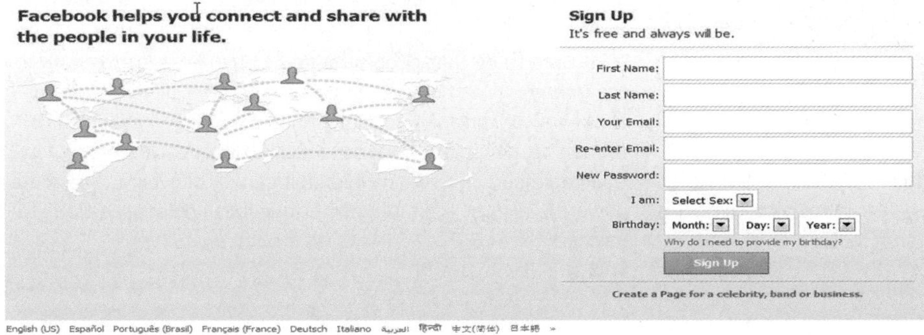

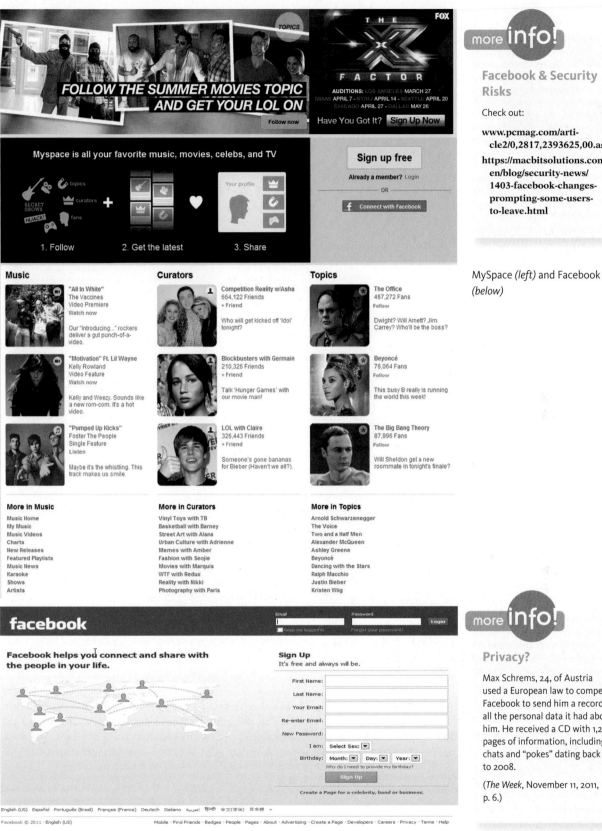

MySpace *(left)* and Facebook *(below)*

more info!

Facebook & Security Risks

Check out:

www.pcmag.com/article2/0,2817,2393625,00.asp

https://macbitsolutions.com/en/blog/security-news/1403-facebook-changes-prompting-some-users-to-leave.html

more info!

Privacy?

Max Schrems, 24, of Austria used a European law to compel Facebook to send him a record of all the personal data it had about him. He received a CD with 1,222 pages of information, including chats and "pokes" dating back to 2008.

(*The Week*, November 11, 2011, p. 6.)

YOUTUBE, FLICKR, & OTHER MEDIA-SHARING WEBSITES **A *media-sharing website* is a type of online social network in which members share media such as photos, videos, and music.** The most popular example is YouTube, but others are Hulu, Flickr, Shutterfly, Twango, and Yahoo! Video. Video-sharing sites include YouTube, Flickr, Photobucket, Imageshack, Vimeo, and Veoh.

PRACTICAL ACTION

Social Networking: Worth the Convenience?

According to many people, the Internet is supposed to be a global marketplace for the free exchange of ideas dedicated to truth. And social networking was supposed to make us closer. In some ways it has. Thanks to the Internet, many of us have gotten back in touch with old friends; shared photos, histories, and enthusiasms; and become better acquainted with some people whom we might never have gotten to know offline.

But there are dangers, too. Here are a few of them:

- For one thing, if we're not careful, our online interactions can hurt our real-life relationships. For example, many of us are too busy to pick up the phone or even write a decent email, yet we spend hours on social-networking sites, uploading photos of us and our friends, forwarding inane quizzes, posting quirky, sometimes nonsensical jokes, or tweeting unimportant information about our latest whereabouts. And how are our conversation skills? Typing leaves a lot to be desired as a communication tool; it lacks the nuances that can be expressed by body language and voice inflection. Are we losing some of the best human characteristics of interaction?
- And another thing: "If you use Facebook but don't want your personal information leaked all over the Web, you had better make sure you don't use any of Facebook's most popular apps."[39] And many of the most popular applications, or apps, on social-networking sites have been transmitting identifying information, including users' passwords, home addresses, phone numbers, and email addresses, to dozens of advertising and Internet tracking companies and other third-party entities, a *Wall Street Journal* investigation found.[40] This issue affects tens of millions of Facebook app users, including people who set their profiles to Facebook's strictest privacy settings. Indeed, many people feel that the main objective of social networking sites is the pursuit of profits, using their members' identities as products to sell. (See also "Are You Safe on Facebook?" *http://tech.fortune.cnn.com/2011/01/28/are-you-safe-on-facebook/*.)
- Also, "deleted" photos and messages may remain online for years, and employers are known to search social-networking sites for inappropriate photos and messages posted by potential and current employees. And e-crooks (hackers) quickly steal people's posted photos and use them on products sold around the world and in fraudulent schemes, such as using photos of babies to get money for faked adoptions. When Facebook's new email-similar messaging system becomes fully functional, users will not be able to delete messages, and non-Facebook people will be able to email you.
- And oppressive governments can use social messaging and networking sites such as Twitter and Facebook to identify photographs of protestors and find out their personal information and whereabouts. Crime gangs use such sites to gather information about their victims
- Social networking can spread incorrect and irresponsible information and offensive content. Martha Nussbaum, a professor of law and philosophy at the University of Chicago, refers, in a set of essays called *The Offensive Internet*, to the Internet as "a cesspool, a porn store, a form of pinkeye, a raunchy fraternity, a graffiti-filled bathroom wall, a haven for sociopaths, and the breeder of online mobs who are no better than 'masked Klan members' in their determination to 'interfere with victims' basic rights."[41]
- Social-networking sites can become platforms for anonymous bullying and other types of attacks. Anonymity, says Nussbaum, allows Internet bloggers and site users "to create for themselves a shame-free zone in which they can inflict shame on others." Their power "depends on their ability to insulate their Internet selves from responsibility in the real world, while ensuring real-world consequences" for the victims.[42] Many people believe that the Internet and social-networking sites would be better places if Internet providers were held accountable for the harmful and/or incorrect material that they disseminate. To this end, several U.S. states have passed laws about Internet bullying and victimizing.

It used to be that people wanted just to increase freedom on the Internet; now, however, more and more people are concerned about how to control it, to protect honest users. What kind of contributor are you to Internet content and social-networking activity?

Remember: "Every new technology will bite back. The more powerful its gifts, the more powerfully it can be abused. Look for its costs."[43]

FRIENDFEED, SPOKEO, & OTHER SOCIAL-NETWORK AGGREGATORS Cathy Brooks, of San Francisco is described as a "typically unapologetic Silicon Valley web addict." In one week alone, it's reported, "she produced more than 40 pithy updates on the text messaging service Twitter, uploaded two dozen videos to various video-sharing sites, posted seven graphs on . . . Flickr and one item to the online community calendar Upcoming."[44] She and her friends follow one another's activities by funneling them into a single information broadcast, a content-aggregation system known as FriendFeed.

YouTube | Search | Browse | Movies | Upload | Create Account | Sign In

LET'S PLAY With GAGA

Visit GagaVille and unlock Lady Gaga's music before her album release on May 23rd!

TAKE ME TO GAGAVILLE

Replay with Sound

zynga

Join the largest worldwide video-sharing community!

Create Account › Already have an account? Sign In

Recommended for You Learn More

Personalized video recommendations

Getting personalized recommendations is really easy, all you have to do is watch some videos then come back to this page to see what videos YouTube has recommended just for you!

Most Popular

Entertainment

Candy BBQ - Epic Meal Time
1,813,033 views
EpicMealTime

Music

DJ Khaled - I'm On One ft. Drake, Ric...
297,957 views
newdraketv

News & Politics

Vista aérea de la concentración en So...
427,378 views

Film & Animation

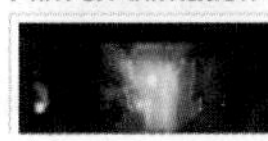

The Adventures of Tintin - Teaser
331,453 views

Spotlight

Your Highlight: Winner!

The votes are in and the winner of the YouTube + SportsCenter Your Highlight competition for best amateur sports video is (drum roll): "Middleton 3 Miracles"! Congratulations to Jay Nunnery, Shane Adler and Matt Everson of Middleton High School in Middleton, Wisconsin.

Presented by: ESPN

middleton 3 miracles
by MELancer34
6,570 views

Trends

Greatest Marriage Proposal EVER!!!
by MattandGinny
2,923,494 views

Raw Video: Gingrich Hit With Glitter in Minn.
by AssociatedPress
301,164 views

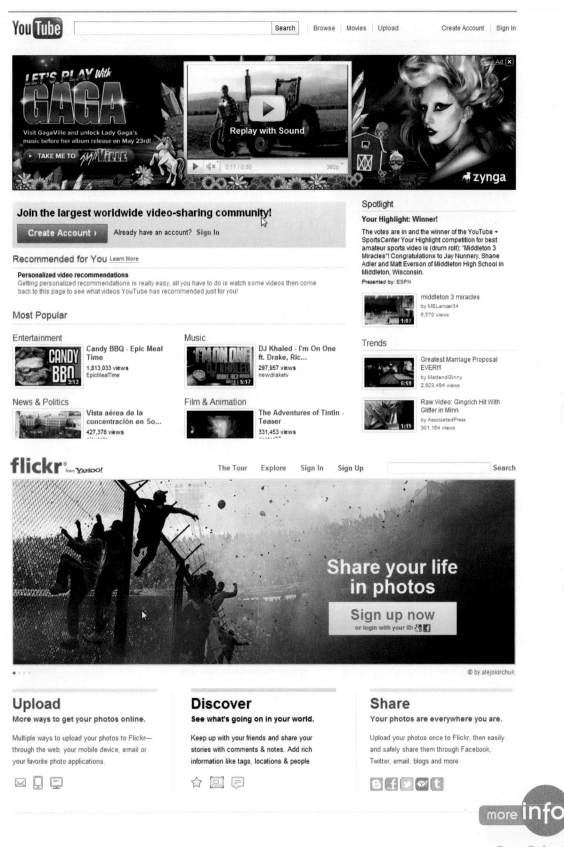

flickr from YAHOO! | The Tour | Explore | Sign In | Sign Up | Search

© by alejokirchuk

Upload
More ways to get your photos online.
Multiple ways to upload your photos to Flickr—through the web, your mobile device, email or your favorite photo applications.

Discover
See what's going on in your world.
Keep up with your friends and share your stories with comments & notes. Add rich information like tags, locations & people.

Share
Your photos are everywhere you are.
Upload your photos once to Flickr, then easily and safely share them through Facebook, Twitter, email, blogs and more.

Social-network aggregators, or *social aggregators,* collect content from all of a user's various social networks profiles into one place, then allow her or him to track friends and share other social network activities. Besides FriendFeed, other examples of "friend-tracking services" are Iminta, Plaxo, Readr, and Mugshot.

Does Being "Always On" Change Your Personality?

www.stanfordalumni.org/news/magazine/2011/janfeb/features/digital.html

Protest in Tahir Square, Cairo, Egypt, February 2011. Smartphone cameras and Facebook were instrumental in spreading news about the uprising.

TWITTER & TUMBLR SOCIAL NETWORKING & MICROBLOGGING SERVICES As you and your friends track each other's every moment, you can also use services such as Twitter and Tumblr to do "thoughtcasting" or "microblogging"—send a text message from your mobile phone, which your friends will receive on the web/IM or on their phones. (The phenomenon is called *microblogging,* because messages have to be short, 140 characters or less, owing to length restrictions on text messaging.) Tumblr lets you express yourself using multiple media, but in a way that's easier than using traditional blog software. Twitter co-owner Biz Stone has said that their site now has 105 million registered users. "Folks were tweeting 5,000 times a day in 2007. By 2008 that number was 300,000, and by 2009 it had grown to 2.5 million per day. Tweets grew 1,400% last year to 35 million per day. Today, we are seeing 50 million tweets per day—that's an average of 600 tweets per second."[45]

Twitter, Tumblr, and ReadWriteWeb

Email is still king at the office, but Twitter, Facebook, and other social media have overtaken email to become the most popular way people spend time online (after search, portals, and software applications).

2.6 THE INTRUSIVE INTERNET: Snooping, Spamming, Spoofing, Phishing, Pharming, Cookies, & Spyware

Protect your identity, your financial information, and your privacy while online and while using your computer.

The Internet is wide open. "The Internet is just too accessible, and it's too easy for people to make anything they want out of it."[46] Thus, although the Internet may be affected to a degree by governing and regulatory bodies, just like society in general, that doesn't mean that it doesn't have its pitfalls or share of users who can do you real harm.

We consider some of the other serious Internet issues (such as viruses, worms, crackers, pornography, and gambling) in Chapters 6 and 9, but here let us touch on a few of immediate concern that you should be aware of: snooping, spam, spoofing, phishing, pharming, cookies, and spyware.

> **Survival Tip**
>
> **Employers and Résumé Keyword Searches**
>
> Many employers search through online résumés using keywords; so the terminology you use in your résumé is very important! "If your document contains no mandatory keywords, the keyword search obviously will overlook your résumé. Those with the greatest 'keyword density' will be chosen for the next round of screening, this time by a human" (*www.quintcareers.com/resume_keywords.html*).

Snooping on Your Email: Your Messages Are Open to Anyone

Even if you delete your emails, they are not "gone." And they are not private.

The single best piece of advice that can be given about sending email is this: *Pretend every electronic message is a postcard that can be read by anyone.* Because the chances are high that it could be. (And this includes email on college campus systems as well.)

Think the boss can't snoop on your email at work? Well, you don't own your employee email account, your employer does. Thus anything included in your employee email account is fair game for human resources or your employer's lawyers—you have no defensible expectation of privacy on corporate systems. But what about *personal* email accounts you access on corporate computers on the corporate network via the corporate Internet connection? The law allows employers to "intercept" employee communications if *one* of the parties involved agrees to the "interception"; and the party "involved" is the employer. And in the workplace, email is typically saved on a server, at least for a while. Indeed, federal laws require that employers keep some email messages for years.

Think you can keep your email address a secret among your friends? You have no control over whether they might send your e-messages on to someone else—who might in turn forward them again. (One thing you can do for your friends, however, is delete their names and addresses before sending one of their messages on to someone.)

Think your Internet access provider will protect your privacy? Often service providers post your address publicly or even sell their customer lists.

If you're really concerned about preserving your privacy, you can try certain technical solutions—for instance, installing software that encodes and decodes messages (discussed in Chapter 6). But the simplest solution is the easiest: Don't put any sensitive or embarrassing information in your email. Even deleted email removed from the trash can still be traced on your hard disk. To guard against this, you can use software such as Spytech Eradicator and Webroot's Window Washer to completely eliminate deleted files. (Be aware, however: your email may already have been backed up on the company—or campus—server.)

> **Survival Tip**
>
> **Look for the Padlock Icon or the "s"**
>
> To avoid having people spying on you when you are sending information over the web, use a secure connection. This is indicated at the bottom of your browser window by an icon that looks like a padlock or key. Also, the "s" in "https://" indicates a secure site.

SECURITY

Spam: Electronic Junk Mail

Junk mail is unwanted mail, called spam.

Some years ago, Monty Python, the British comedy group, did a sketch in which restaurant customers were unable to converse because people in the background (a group of Vikings, actually) kept chanting "Spam, spam, eggs and spam . . ." The term *spam* was picked up by the computer world to describe another kind of "noise" that interferes with communication. Now ***spam*** **refers to unsolicited email, or junk mail, in the form of advertising or chain letters.** But the problem of spam has metastasized well beyond the stage of annoyance.

Spam has become so pestiferous that *Smart Computing* magazine referred to it as a "cockroach infestation."[47] In 2010 the number of spam messages sent daily was 262 billion, using enough electricity to power about 4 million homes for a year.[48] Spam plagues email users and social networks, such as Facebook. It is even migrating from computers to cellphones, messages that the recipients have to pay for.

Usually, of course, you don't recognize the spam sender on your list of incoming mail, and often the subject line will give no hint, stating something such as "The status of your application" or "It's up to you now." The solicitations can range from money-making schemes to online pornography. To better manage spam, some users get two email boxes. One is used for online shopping, business, research, and the like—which will continue to attract spam. The other is used (like an unlisted phone number) only for personal friends and family—and will probably not receive much spam.

Tips for Fighting Spam

http://ezinearticles.com/?Tips-to-Fight-SPAM&id=2321867

http://email.about.com/od/spamfightingtips/Spam_Fighting_Tips_Tricks_and_Secrets.htm

www.switched.com/2009/06/18/12-tips-to-fight-spam-on-your-cell-phone-and-computer/

www.toptenblogtips.com/10-ways-to-fight-spam/

Spoofing, Phishing, & Pharming: Phony Email Senders & Websites

Don't be fooled by real-looking but phony emails and websites.

A message shows up in your email supposedly from someone named "Sonia Saunders." The subject line reads "Re: Hey cutie." It could have been from someone you know, but it's actually a pitch for porn. Or you receive what appears to be an "Urgent notice from eBay," the online auction company, stating that "failure to update billing information will result in cancellation of service" and asking you to go to the web address indicated and update your credit-card information. In the first instance you've been *spoofed,* in the second you've been *phished.*[49]

SPOOFING—USING FAKE EMAIL SENDER NAMES ***Spoofing*** **is the forgery of an email sender name so that the message appears to have originated from someone or somewhere other than the actual source.** Spoofing is one of the main tactics used by spammers (and virus writers) to induce or trick recipients into opening and perhaps responding to their solicitations. Spoofing is generally not illegal and might even serve a legitimate purpose under some circumstances—say, a "whistle-blowing" employee fearful of retaliation who reports a company's illegalities to a government agency. It is illegal, however, if it involves a direct threat of violence or death.[50]

PHISHING—USING TRUSTED INSTITUTIONAL NAMES TO ELICIT CONFIDENTIAL INFORMATION ***Phishing*** **(pronounced "fishing" and short for *password harvesting fishing*) is (1) the sending of a forged email that (2) directs recipients to a replica of an existing web page, both of which pretend to belong to a legitimate company. The purpose of the fraudulent sender is to "phish" for, or entice people to share, their personal, financial, or password data.** The names may be trusted names such as Citibank, eBay, or Best Buy. A variant is *spear-phishing,* in which a message seems to originate within your company, as when a "Security Department Assistant" asks you to update your name and password or risk suspension. Thus, you should be suspicious of *any* email that directs you to a website that requests confidential information, such as credit-card info or Social Security number.

Deciphering Fake Email

For more about spoofing and how to identify origins of fake emails, go to:

www.mailsbroadcast.com/email.broadcast.faq/46.email.spoofing.htm

http://usgovinfo.about.com/cs/consumer/a/aaspoofing.htm

PHARMING—REDIRECTING YOU TO AN IMPOSTOR WEB PAGE Pharming is a newer kind of phishing that is harder to detect. **In *pharming*, thieves implant malicious software on a victim's computer that redirects the user to an impostor web page even when the individual types the correct address into his or her browser.** One way to protect yourself is to make sure you go to special secure web pages, such as any financial website, which begin with *https* (p. 103) rather than the standard *http* and which use encryption to protect data transfer.

Cookies: Convenience or Hindrance?

Cookies can make some Internet processes go faster, but they can also be used by companies to track your Internet use and your personal information.

Verifying Valid Websites

For more on verifying if you're dealing with a legitimate company website, go to:

www.ehow.com/how_2127435_choose-valid-websites.html

www.instantssl.com/ssl-certificate-products/addsupport/vengine.html

http://support.weebly.com/support/index.php?pg=kb.page&id=31

***Cookies* are little text files—such as your log-in name, password, and preferences—left on your hard disk by some websites you visit. The websites retrieve the data when you visit again.** A website that welcomes you by name uses cookies.

THE BENEFITS OF COOKIES Cookies can be a convenience. If you visit an online merchant—such as BarnesandNoble.com for a book—and enter all your address and other information, the merchant will assign you an identification number, store your information with that number on its server, and send the number to your browser as a cookie, which stores the ID number on your hard disk. The next time you go to that merchant, the number is sent to the server, which looks you up and sends you a customized web page welcoming you. "Cookies

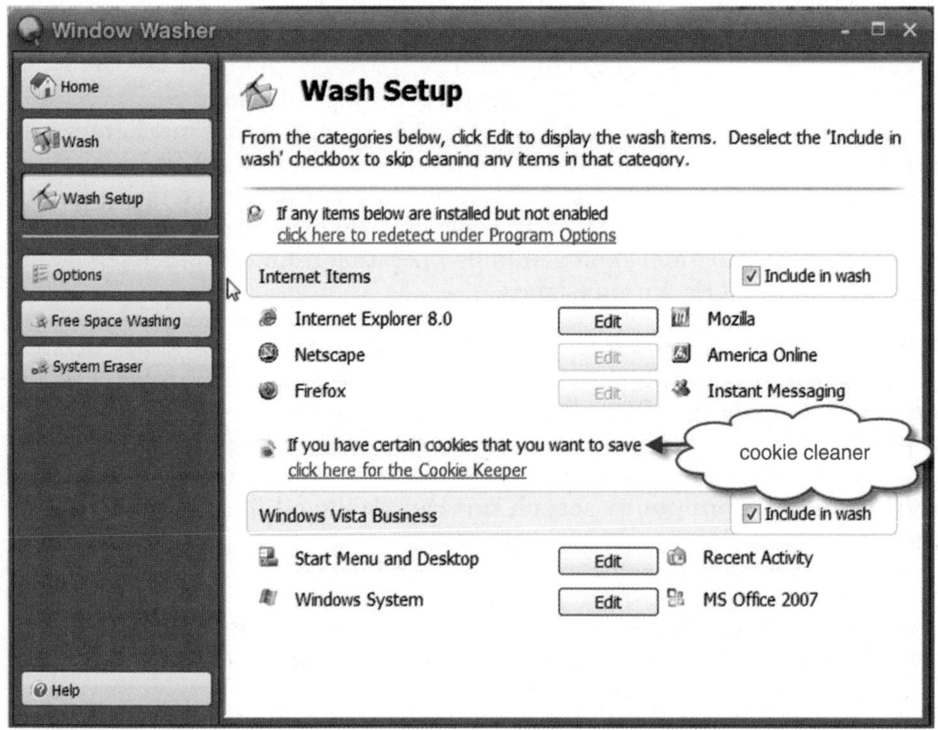

Webroot's Window Washer, among other programs, can clean your computer of cookies.

Survival Tip

Control Those Cookies!

You can use your browser's Help function to accept or reject cookies. For instance, in Internet Explorer, go to the Tools menu and click *Internet Options;* on the General tab, click *Settings;* then click *View files,* select the cookie you want to delete, and on the File menu click *Delete.* Software such as Cookie Pal (*www.kburra.com*) will also help block and control cookies, as will Webroot's Window Washer. Also read the *Wall Street Journal* article "How to Avoid Prying Eyes" at *http://online.wsj.com/article/SB100014240527487034673045753832030920 34876.html.*

How to Shop Safely on the Internet

www.wikihow.com/Shop-Online-Safely

www.microsoft.com/security/online-privacy/online-shopping.aspx

www.safeshopping.org/

http://usgovinfo.about.com/od/consumerawareness/l/blonlineshopsaf.htm

w http://www.microsoft.com/security/online-privacy/online-shopping.aspx wwww.kburra.com

Fighting Spyware

More information about ways to combat spyware may be found at:

www.microsoft.com/protect/terms/antispyware.aspx

http://antispyware.org/

www.pcpitstop.com

www.firewallguide.com/spyware.htm

www.webroot.com

www.cleansoftware.org

www.lavasoftusa.com/software/

actually perform valuable services," says technology writer and computer talk-radio-show host Kim Komando. "For instance, they can shoot you right into a site so you don't have to enter your password."[51] Says another writer: "They can also fill in a username on a site that requires logging in, or help a weather site remember a Zip code so that it can show a local forecast on return visits."[52]

THE DRAWBACKS OF COOKIES Cookies are not necessarily dangerous—they are not programs, and they can't transmit computer viruses, for example. However, some websites sell the information associated with your ID number on their servers to marketers, who might use it to target customers for their products. "Unsatisfactory cookies," in Microsoft's understated term, are those that might allow someone access to personally identifiable information that could be used without your consent for some secondary purpose. This can lead to *spyware,* as we describe next. Webroot's Window Washer, among other programs, can clean your computer of cookies.

Spyware—Adware, Browser & Search Hijackers, & Key Loggers: Intruders to Track Your Habits & Steal Your Data

Learn how to protect your data against intruders.

You visit a search site such as Yahoo! or Google and click on a text ad that appears next to your search results. Or you download a free version of some software, such as Kazaa, the popular file-sharing program. Or you simply visit some web merchant to place an order.

The next thing you know, you are getting ***pop-up ads*****, a form of online advertising in which, when you visit certain websites, a new window opens, or "pops up," to display advertisements.** You have just had an encounter with *spyware,* of which pop-up ads are only one form. ***Spyware*** **is deceptive software that is surreptitiously installed on a computer via the web; once installed on your hard disk, it allows outsiders to gather confidential information without your knowledge—**for example, keystrokes, passwords, your email address, your credit card numbers and Social Security number, and your history of website visits. Ways to avoid getting spyware are shown in the more info! feature opposite.

The most common forms of spyware are these:

ADWARE OR POP-UP GENERATORS ***Adware*****, or *pop-up generators,* is a kind of spyware that tracks web surfing or online buying so that marketers can send you targeted and unsolicited pop-up and other ads.** This is the most common, and benign, type of spyware. Adware can be developed by legitimate companies such as Verizon and Panasonic but also by all kinds of fly-by-night purveyors of pornography and gambling operating from computer servers in Russia, Spain, and the Virgin Islands.

BROWSER HIJACKERS & SEARCH HIJACKERS More damaging kinds of spyware are ***browser hijackers*****, which change settings in your browser without your knowledge, often changing your browser's home page and replacing it with another web page, and *search hijackers,* which intercept your legitimate search requests made to real search engines and return results from phony search services designed to send you to sites they run.**

How do you know if your browser has been hijacked?

- The Home page or other settings change on your computer. Links are added that point to websites that you'd usually avoid.
- You can't navigate to certain web pages, such as antispyware and other security software sites.
- A seemingly endless barrage of ads pops up on your screen.

PRACTICAL ACTION

Tips for Avoiding Spyware

You may not be able to completely avoid spyware, but doing the following may help:

- ***Be careful about free and illegal downloads:*** Be choosy about free downloads or illegal downloads of songs, movies, or TV shows. Often they use a form of spyware. File-sharing programs, which are popular with students, often contain spyware. Pornographic websites also are common carriers of spyware.
- ***Don't just say "I agree"; read the fine print:*** Sites that offer games, music-sharing videos, screen savers, and weather data often are paid to distribute spyware. When you install their software, you might be asked to agree to certain conditions. If you simply click "I agree" without reading the fine print, you may be authorizing installation of spyware. "People have gotten in the habit of clicking next, next, next, without reading" when they install software, says a manager at McAfee Inc., which tracks spyware and viruses.[54]
- ***Beware of unsolicited downloads:*** If while you're surfing the net your browser warns you a file is being downloaded and you're asked if you choose to accept, keep clicking *no* until the messages stop.

- New toolbars or Favorites are installed that give you icons and links to web pages that you don't want.
- Your computer runs sluggishly. Malicious software (malware) can slow down your computer.[53]

KEY LOGGERS ***Key loggers,* or *keystroke loggers,* can record each character you type and transmit that information to someone else on the Internet, making it possible for strangers to learn your passwords and other information.** For instance, some may secretly record the keystrokes you use to log in to online bank accounts and then send the information off to who knows where.

Internet access providers such as AOL and Earthlink offer spyware scan-and-removal tools, but you can also employ specialized antispyware software. Some of the good ones appear below. (• *See Panel 2.36.*)

One big problem with spyware is that overburdened PCs begin to run more slowly as the hard drives cope with random and uncontrollable processes. If none of the antispyware works, you will need to wipe your hard drive clean of programs and data and start from scratch—a complicated matter that we discuss in Chapter 4.

How to get Rid of a Browser Hijacker

www.ehow.com/how_4886023_remove-browser-hijacking-programs.html

And for information on combatting malware ("badware"):

www.stopbadware.org

Program Name	Site
Ad-Aware	*www.lavasoft.com/*
AntiSpyware	*http://us.mcafee.com*
ca Technologies	*www.pestpatrol.com*
PC Tools	*www.pctools.com/simple/*
Pest Patrol	*www.ca.com/products/pestpatrol*
Spybot Search & Destroy	*http://spywaresoftware.net*
SpyCatcher	*www.tenebril.com/consumer/spyware/spycatcher-express.php*
SpyCop	*www.spywareinfo.com/downloads.php*
SpyCatcher	*www.webroot.com*

panel 2.36

Some antispyware programs

EXPERIENCE BOX

Web Research, Term Papers, & Plagiarism

No matter how much students may be able to rationalize cheating in college—for example, trying to pass off someone else's term paper as their own (plagiarism)—ignorance of the consequences is not an excuse. Most instructors announce the penalties for cheating at the beginning of the course—usually a failing grade in the course and possible suspension or expulsion from school.

Even so, probably every student becomes aware before long that the World Wide Web contains sites that offer term papers, either for free or for a price. Some dishonest students may download papers and just change the author's name to their own. Others are more likely just to use the papers for ideas.

How the Web Can Lead to Plagiarism

Two types of term-paper websites are as follows:

- ***Sites offering papers for free:*** Such a site requires that users fill out a membership form and then provides at least one free student term paper. (Good quality is not guaranteed, since free-paper mills often subsist on the submissions of poor students, whose contributions may be subliterate.)
- ***Sites offering papers for sale:*** Commercial sites may charge \$6–\$10 or more a page, which users may charge to their credit card. (Expense is no guarantee of quality. Moreover, the term-paper factory may turn around and make your \$350 custom paper available to others—even fellow classmates working on the same assignment—for half the price.)

How Instructors Catch Cheaters

How do instructors detect and defend against student plagiarism? Professors are unlikely to be fooled if they tailor term-paper assignments to work done in class, monitor students' progress—from outline to completion—and are alert to papers that seem radically different from a student's past work.

Just as the Internet can be a source of cheating, it is also a tool for detecting cheaters. Search programs make it possible for instructors to locate texts containing identified strings of words from the millions of pages found on the web. Thus, a professor can input passages from a student's paper into a search program that scans the web for identical blocks of text. Indeed, some websites favored by instructors build a database of papers over time so that students can't recycle work previously handed in by others. Special software programs, such as CopyScape.com, Plagiarism-Checker.com, grammarly.com, SplaT, and academicplagiarism.com, are available for instructors to use to check students' work and for students to check their own work before turning it in.

How the Web Can Lead to Low-Quality Papers

Philosophy professor David Rothenberg, of New Jersey Institute of Technology, reported that as a result of students' doing more of their research on the web, he saw "a disturbing decline in both the quality of the writing and the originality of the thoughts expressed."[55] How can an instructor spot a term paper based primarily on web research? Rothenberg offers four clues:

- ***No books cited:*** The student's bibliography cites no books, just articles or references to websites. Sadly, says Rothenberg, "one finds few references to careful, in-depth commentaries on the subject of the paper, the kind of analysis that requires a book, rather than an article, for its full development."
- ***Outdated material:*** A lot of the material in the bibliography is strangely out of date, says Rothenberg. "A lot of stuff on the web that is advertised as timely is actually at least a few years old."
- ***Unrelated pictures and graphs:*** Students may intersperse the text with a lot of impressive-looking pictures and graphs that actually bear little relation to the precise subject of the paper. "Cut and pasted from the vast realm of what's out there for the taking, they masquerade as original work."
- ***Superficial references:*** "Too much of what passes for information online these days is simply advertising for information," points out Rothenberg. "Screen after screen shows you where you can find out more, how you can connect to this place or that." Other kinds of information are detailed but often superficial: "pages and pages of federal documents, corporate propaganda, snippets of commentary by people whose credibility is difficult to assess."

TERMS & EXPLANATIONS

access point (p. 60) Station that sends and receives data to and from a Wi-Fi network. Why it's important: *Many public areas, such as airports and hotels, offer hotspots, or access points, that enable Wi-Fi-equipped users to go online wirelessly.*

adware (p. 106) Also called *pop-up generators:* kind of spyware that tracks web surfing or buying online. Why it's important: *Adware enables marketers to send you targeted and unsolicited pop-up and other ads.*

animation (p. 94) The rapid sequencing of still images to create the appearance of motion, as in a cartoon. Why it's important: *Animation is a component of multimedia; it is used in online video games as well as in moving banners displaying sports scores or stock prices.*

applets (p. 93) Small programs that can be quickly downloaded and run by most browsers. Why it's important: *Web pages contain links to applets, which add multimedia capabilities.*

B2B (business-to-business) commerce (p. 97) Electronic sale or exchange of goods and services directly between companies, cutting out traditional intermediaries. Why it's important: *Expected to grow even more rapidly than other forms of e-commerce, B2B commerce covers an extremely broad range of activities, such as supplier-to-buyer display of inventories, provision of wholesale price lists, and sales of closed-out items and used materials—usually without agents, brokers, or other third parties.*

backbones *See* **Internet backbone.**

bandwidth (p. 54) Also known as *channel capacity;* expression of how much data—text, voice, video, and so on—can be sent through a communications channel in a given amount of time. Why it's important: *Different communications systems use different bandwidths for different purposes. The wider the bandwidth, the faster the data can be transmitted.*

bits per second (bps) (p. 54) Eight bits make up a character. Why it's important: *Data transfer speeds are measured in bits per second.*

blog (p. 95) Short for *web log,* an Internet journal. Blogs are usually updated daily; they reflect the personality and views of the blogger. Why it's important: *Blogs are becoming important sources of current information.*

blogosphere (p. 95) The total universe of blogs. Why it's important: *The blogosphere has allowed the rise of a new breed of homegrown journal writers and diarists to chronicle life as it happens.*

broadband (p. 54) High-speed connection. Why it's important: *Access to information is much faster than access with traditional phone lines, and multimedia such as movies and online games will not work well without broadband connectivity.*

browser *See* **web browser.**

browser hijacker (p. 106) A damaging kind of spyware that changes settings in your browser without your knowledge. Why it's important: *This spyware can reset your home page to a porn site or obscure search engine or change your home page and replace it with another web page.*

cable modem (p. 58) Device connecting a personal computer to a cable-TV system that offers an Internet connection. Why it's important: *Cable modems transmit data faster than do standard modems.*

client (p. 61) Computer requesting data or services. Why it's important: *Part of the client/server network, in which the server is a central computer supplying data or services requested of it to the client computer.*

communications satellite (p. 59) Space station that transmits radio waves called *microwaves* from earth-based stations. Why it's important: *An orbiting satellite contains many communications channels and receives signals from ground microwave stations anywhere on earth.*

cookies (p. 105) Little text files, such as your log-in name, password, and preferences, that are left on your hard disk by some websites you visit; the websites retrieve the data when you visit again. Why it's important: *Cookies can be beneficial in that they put you right into a website without having to enter your password. However, some websites sell the information associated with your ID number on their servers to marketers, who might use it to target you as a customer for their products.*

dial-up connection (p. 55) Use of a telephone modem to connect a computer to the Internet. Why it's important: *Cheapest means of online connection and available everywhere.*

domain (p. 67) A location on the Internet, the particular web server. Why it's important: *A domain name is necessary for sending and receiving email and for many other Internet activities.*

download (p. 54) To transmit data from a remote computer to a local computer. Why it's important: *Downloading enables users to save files on their own computers for later use, which reduces the time spent online and the corresponding charges.*

DSL (digital subscriber line) (p. 55) A hardware and software technology that uses regular phone lines to transmit data in megabits per second. Why it's important: *DSL connections are much faster than regular dial-up modem connections. It's often used in areas where cable and satellite are not available.*

e-commerce (electronic commerce) (p. 96) Conducting business activities online. Why it's important: *E-commerce not only is widening consumers' choice of products and services but is also creating new businesses and compelling established businesses to develop Internet strategies.*

email program (p. 81) Software that enables you to send email by running email software on your computer, which interacts with an email server at your Internet access provider to send and receive email. Why it's important: *With this standard email program, unlike web-based email, you can easily integrate your email with other applications, such as calendar, task list, and contact list.*

4G (p. 60) 4G stands for "fourth generation"; it is a successor to 3G and 2G cellphone standards, with the aim to provide a wide range of data rates up to ultra-broadband (gigabit-speed) Internet access to mobile as well as stationary users. Why it's important: 4G devices seek to improve broadband access to multimedia.

FAQs (frequently asked questions) (p. 90) Guides that explain expected norms of online behavior for a particular group. Why it's important: *Users should read a group's/site's FAQs to know how to proceed properly.*

flaming (p. 90) Writing an online message that uses derogatory, obscene, or inappropriate language. Why it's important: *Flaming should be avoided. It is a form of public humiliation inflicted on people who have failed to read FAQs or have otherwise not observed netiquette (although it can happen just because the sender has poor impulse control and needs a course in anger management).*

frame (p. 72) An independently controllable section of a web page. Why it's important: *A web page designer can divide a page into separate frames, each with different features or options.*

FTP (File Transfer Protocol) (p. 87) Method whereby you can connect to a remote computer called an *FTP site* and transfer publicly available files to your own microcomputer's hard disk via TCP/IP over the Internet. Why it's important: *The free files offered cover nearly anything that can be stored on a computer: software, games, photos, maps, art, music, books, statistics.*

gigabits per second (Gbps) (p. 54) 1 billion bits per second. Why it's important: *Gbps is a common measure of data transmission speed.*

hit (p. 75) Site that a search engine returns after running a keyword search. Why it's important: *The web pages, or hits, that a search engine returns after you type in a keyword are the beginning of the types of information you are looking for.*

home page (p. 66) The starting point, or the main page, of a website that contains links to other pages at the site. This page usually has some sort of table of contents on it and often describes the purpose of the site. Why it's important: *The first page you see at a website is the home page.*

host computer *See* **server.**

hotspot (p. 60) Public access to Wi-Fi networks. Why it's important: *Hotspots in airports, hotels, and the like enable wireless-equipped users to go online without a physical connection.*

hypertext links (p. 69) Also called *hyperlinks, hotlinks,* or just *links;* HTML connections to other documents or web pages that contain related information. Why it's important: *Allows a word or phrase in one document to become a connection to a document in a different place.*

hypertext markup language (HTML) (p. 69) Set of special instructions (called "tags" or "markups") used to specify web document structure, formatting, and links to other documents. Why it's important: *HTML enables the creation of web pages.*

HyperText Transfer Protocol (HTTP) (p. 67) Communications rules that allow browsers to connect with web servers. Why it's important: *Without HTTP, files could not be transferred over the web.*

individual search engine (p. 75) Type of Internet search tool that compiles its own searchable database on the web. You search for information by typing one or more keywords, and the search engine then displays a list of web pages, or "hits," that contain those key words, ordered from most likely to least likely to contain the information you want. Why it's important: *Examples of this kind of search engine are Ask, Bing, Google, and Yahoo!, as well as AllTheWeb, Gigablast, and Lycos. These are the search engines most commonly used by individual users.*

instant messaging (IM) (p. 85) Service that enables any user on a given email system to send a message and have it pop up instantly on the screen of anyone else logged onto that system. Why it's important: *People can initiate online typed conversations in real time. As they are typed, the messages appear on the display screen in a small window.*

Internet2 (p. 62) A cooperative university/business education and research project that enables high-end users to quickly and reliably move huge amounts of data over high-speed networks. Why it's important: *Internet2 creates a kind of "virtual university" by advancing videoconferencing, research, and academic collaboration.*

Internet backbone (p. 61) High-speed, high-capacity transmission lines that use the newest communications technology. Why it's important: *The Internet backbone transmits data across the Internet.*

Internet Corporation for Assigned Names and Numbers (ICANN) (p. 64) Global, private-sector, nonprofit corporation that was established to regulate human-friendly Internet domain names, those addresses ending with *.com, .org, .net,* and so on, that overlie IP addresses and identify the website type. Why it's important: *This organization helps humans organize and understand websites.*

Internet Exchange Point (IXP) (p. 61) A routing computer at a point on the Internet where several connections come together. Why it's important: *IXPs connect Internet service providers to the Internet backbone.*

Internet Protocol (IP) address (p. 63) Uniquely identifies every computer and device connected to the Internet; consists of four sets of numbers between 0 and 255 separated by decimals—for example, 1.160.10.240. This address is similar to a street address. However, street addresses rarely change, but IP addresses often do. Why it's important: *Each time you connect to your ISP, the ISP will assign your computer a new IP address, called a* dynamic IP address, *for your online session. When you request data from the Internet, it is transmitted to your computer's IP address. When you disconnect, your ISP frees up the IP address you were using and reassigns it to another user.*

Internet service provider (ISP) (p. 60) Company that connects you through your communications line to its servers, or central computer, which connects you to the Internet via another company's Internet Exchange Points (IXPs). Why it's important: *Unless they subscribe to an online information service (such as AOL) or have a direct network connection (such as a T1 line), microcomputer users need an ISP to connect to the Internet.*

Internet telephony (p. 91) Also known as *VoIP phoning,* short for *Voice over Internet Protocol:* using the Internet to make phone calls, either one-to-one or for audioconferencing. Why it's important: *Long-distance phone calls by this means are surprisingly inexpensive.*

Java (p. 93) Complex programming language that enables programmers to create animated and interactive web pages using applets. Why it's important: *Java applets enhance web pages by playing music, displaying graphics and animation, and providing interactive games.*

key logger (p. 107) Also known as *keystroke logger;* type of spyware that can record each character you type and transmit that information to someone else on the Internet. Why it's important: *A key logger can make it possible for strangers to learn your passwords and other information.*

keyword (p. 74) A keyword is the subject word or words that refer to the topic you wish to find. Why it's important: *You must use keywords to research topics on the Internet.*

kilobits per second (Kbps) (p. 54) 1,000 bits per second. Why it's important: *Kbps is a common measure of data transfer speed. The speed of a modem that is 28,800 bps might be expressed as 28.8 Kbps.*

listserv (p. 89) Automatic mailing-list server that sends email to subscribers who regularly participate in discussion topics. To subscribe, the user sends an email to the list-server moderator and asks to become a member, after which he or she automatically receives email messages from anyone who responds to the server. Why it's important: *Anyone connected to the Internet can subscribe to listserv services. Subscribers receive information on particular subjects and can post email to other subscribers.*

log on (p. 73) To gain access to an operating system, an application, or a website (remote computer). Why it's important: *Users must be familiar with log-on procedures to go online.*

media-sharing website (p. 99) Type of online social network, such as YouTube, Flickr, and Shutterfly, that allows members to share media. Why it's important: *Members can share their photos, videos, and music with others with great ease and convenience.*

megabits per second (Mbps) (p. 54) 1 million bits per second. Why it's important: *Mbps is a common measure of data transmission speed.*

metasearch engine (p. 75) Type of Internet search tool that allows you to search several search engines simultaneously. Why it's important: *A metasearch engine enables you to expand the range of your search.*

modem (p. 55) Device that sends and receives data over telephone lines, cables, or satellite to and from computers. Why it's important: *The modem was developed as a means for computers to communicate with one another using the standard copper-wire telephone network, an analog system that was built to transmit the human voice but not computer signals.*

narrowband (p. 55) Low-bandwidth connection, such as dial-up (telephone). Why it's important: *Narrowband connecting technology is inexpensive and widely available.*

netiquette (p. 90) "Network etiquette," or appropriate online behavior. Why it's important: *In general, netiquette has two basic rules: (1) Don't waste people's time, and (2) don't say anything to a person online that you wouldn't say to his or her face.*

newsgroup (p. 88) Also called *forum;* giant electronic bulletin board on which users conduct written discussions about a specific subject. Why it's important: *There are thousands of newsgroup forums—which charge no fee—and they cover an amazing array of topics.*

newsreader (p. 89) Program included with most browsers that allows users to access a newsgroup and read or type messages. Why it's important: *Users need a newsreader to participate in a newsgroup.*

packet (p. 63) Fixed-length block of data for transmission. Why it's important: *TCP/IP breaks data in a message into separate packets, which allows the message to be split up and its parts sent by separate routes yet still all wind up in the same place.*

pharming (p. 105) A type of phishing in which malicious software is implanted on a victim's computer that redirects the user to an impostor web page even when the individual types the correct address into his or her browser. Why it's important: *The purpose is to trick people into sharing their personal, financial, or password data.*

phishing (p. 104) Short for *password harvesting fishing;* (1) the sending of a forged email that (2) directs recipients to a replica of an existing web page, both of which pretend to belong to a legitimate company. Why it's important: *The purpose of the fraudulent sender is to "phish" for, or entice people to share, their personal, financial, or password data.*

plug-in (p. 92) Program that adds a specific feature to a browser, allowing it to play or view certain files. Why it's important: *To fully experience the contents of many web pages, you need to use plug-ins.*

podcasting (p. 96) Recording of Internet radio or similar Internet audio programs. Why it's important: *Podcasting is another expression of personalized media.*

point of presence (POP) (p. 61) Collection of modems and other equipment in a local area. Why it's important: *To avoid making their subscribers pay long-distance phone charges, ISPs provide POPs across the country. The POP acts as a local gateway to the ISP's network.*

pop-up ads (p. 106) Form of online advertising in which, when you visit certain websites, a new window opens, or "pops up," to display advertisements. Why it's important: *Pop-up ads are one form of the nuisance known as* spyware.

portal. *See* **web portal.**

POTS (plain old telephone system) (p. 55) Traditional kind of connection to the Internet. Why it's important: *Slowest method of connecting to the Internet.*

protocol (p. 63) Set of communication rules for exchanging information. Why it's important: *Transmission Control Protocol/Internet Protocol (TCP/IP) enables all computers to use data transmitted on the Internet. HyperText Transfer Protocol (HTTP) provides the communication rules that allow browsers to connect with web servers.*

push technology (p. 95) Software that automatically downloads information to your computer, as opposed to *pull technology,* in which you go to a website and pull down the information you want. Why it's important: *With little effort, users can obtain information that is important to them.*

radio buttons (p. 71). An interactive tool displayed as little circles in front of options; selecting an option with the mouse places a dot in the corresponding circle. Why it's important: *Radio buttons are one way of interacting with a web page.*

RSS newsreaders (p. 95) Also called *RSS aggregators;* programs that scour the web, sometimes hourly or more frequently, and pull together in one place web "feeds" from several websites. Why it's important: *RSS newsreaders give people access to a whole new universe of content and have led to the creation of the blogosphere.*

scroll arrows (p. 72) Small up/down and left/right arrows located to the bottom and side of your screen display. Why it's important: *Clicking on scroll arrows with your mouse pointer moves the screen so that you can see the rest of the web page, or the content displayed on the screen.*

scrolling (p. 72) Moving quickly upward or downward through text or some other screen display, using the mouse and scroll arrows (or the arrow keys on the keyboard). Why it's important: *Normally a computer screen displays only part of, for example, a web page. Scrolling enables users to view an entire document, no matter how long.*

search engine (p. 74) Search tool that allows you to find specific documents through keyword searches and menu choices, in contrast to directories, which are lists of websites classified by topic. Why it's important: *Search engines enable users to find websites of specific interest or use to them.*

search hijacker (p. 106) A damaging kind of spyware that can intercept your legitimate search requests made to real search engines and return results from phony search services. Why it's important: *Phony search services may send you to sites they run.*

search service (p. 74) Organization that maintains databases accessible through websites. Why it's important: *A search service helps you find information on the Internet.*

server (p. 61) Central computer supplying data or services. Why it's important: *Part of the client/server network, in which the central computer supplies data or services requested of it to the client computer.*

site (p. 66) *See* **website.**

social-network aggregator (p. 101) Also called *social aggregator;* this technology collects content from all of a user's various social network profiles into one place. Why it's important: *Aggregators such as FriendFeed and Spokeo are "friend tracking services" that allow members to track friends and share their other social network activities.*

social-networking website (p. 98) An online community that allows members to keep track of their friends and share ideas and media. Why it's important: *Social-networking websites such as MySpace, Facebook, and LinkedIn allow members to easily expand their circle of acquaintances and to exchange photos, videos, music, stories, and ideas with each other.*

spam (p. 104) Unsolicited email in the form of advertising or chain letters. Why it's important: *Spam filters are available that can spare users the annoyance of receiving junk mail, ads, and other unwanted email.*

spider (p. 74) Also known as *crawler, bot,* or *agent;* special program that crawls through the World Wide Web, following links from one web page to another. Why it's important: *A spider indexes the words on each site it encounters and is used to compile the databases of a search service.*

spoofing (p. 104) The forgery of an email sender name so that the message appears to have originated from someone or somewhere other than the actual source. Why it's important: *Spoofing is one of the main tactics used by spammers to induce or trick recipients into responding to their solicitations.*

spyware (p. 106) Deceptive software that is surreptitiously installed on a computer via the web. Why it's important: *Once spyware is installed on your hard disk, it allows an outsider to harvest confidential information, such as keystrokes, passwords, or your email address.*

streaming audio (p. 94) Process of downloading audio in which you can listen to the file while the data is still being downloaded to your computer. Why it's important: *Users don't have to wait until the entire audio is downloaded to the hard disk before listening to it.*

streaming video (p. 94) Process of downloading video in which the data is transferred in a continuous flow so that you can begin viewing a file even before the end of the file is sent. Why it's important: *Users don't have to wait until the entire video is downloaded to the hard disk before watching it.*

subject directory (p. 75) Type of search engine that allows you to search for information by selecting lists of categories or subjects. Why it's important: *Subject directories allow you to look for information by categories such as "Business and Commerce" or "Arts and Humanities."*

surf (p. 65) To explore the web by using your mouse to move via a series of connected paths, or links, from one location, or website, to another. Surfing requires a browser. Why it's important: *Surfing enables you to easily find information on the web that's of interest to you.*

3G (third generation) (p. 60) High-speed wireless technology that does not need access points because it uses the existing cellphone system. Why it's important: *The technology is found in many new smartphones and PDAs that are capable of delivering downloadable video clips and high-resolution games.*

T1 line (p. 57) Traditional trunk line that carries 24 normal telephone circuits and has a transmission rate of 1.5 Mbps to 6 Mbps. Why it's important: *High-capacity T1 lines are used at many corporate, government, and academic sites; these lines provide greater data transmission speeds than do regular modem connections.*

tags (p. 80) Do-it-yourself labels that people can put on anything found on the Internet, from articles to photos to videos. Why it's important: *A tag is more powerful than a bookmark, because tags can be shared easily with other people.*

text box (p. 72) Fill-in text box. Why it's important: *Text boxes are often used on the Internet for pages that require input from a user; allows interaction with a web page.*

Transmission Control Protocol/Internet Protocol (TCP/IP) (p. 63) Protocol that enables all computers to use data transmitted on the Internet by determining (1) the type of error checking to be used, (2) the data compression method, if any, (3) how the sending device will indicate that it has finished sending a message, and (4) how the receiving device will indicate that it has received a message. TCP/IP breaks data into *packets,* which are the largest blocks of data that can be sent across the Internet (less than 1,500 characters, or 128 kilobytes). IP is used to send the packets across the Internet to their final destination, and TCP is used to reassemble the packets in the correct order. Why it's important: *Internet computers use TCP/IP for all Internet transactions, from sending email to downloading stock quotes or pictures off a friend's website.*

upload (p. 55) To transmit data from a local computer to a remote computer. Why it's important: *Uploading allows users to easily exchange files over networks.*

URL (Uniform Resource Locator) (p. 66) String of characters that points to a specific piece of information anywhere on the web. A URL consists of (1) the web protocol, (2) the name of the web server, (3) the directory (or folder) on that server, and (4) the file within that directory (perhaps with an extension such as *html* or *htm*). Why it's important: *URLs are necessary to distinguish among websites.*

Usenet (p. 89) Worldwide network of servers that can be accessed through the Internet. Why it's important: *Newsgroups take place on Usenet.*

VoIP phoning. *See* **Internet telephony.**

Web 2.0 (p. 97) Defined as the move toward a more social, collaborative, interactive, and responsive World Wide Web. Why it's important: *As websites have become easier to use, they allow users to better harness the collective power of people, which has led to a "social web" or "social media," involving blogs, wikis, social networks, and media sharing. The common theme of all these is human interaction.*

web-based email (p. 81) Type of email in which you send and receive messages by interacting via a browser with a website. Why it's important: *Unlike standard email, web-based email allows you to easily send and receive messages while traveling anywhere in the world and to use any personal computer and browser to access your email.*

web browser (browser) (p. 65) Software that enables users to locate and view web pages and to jump from one page to another. Why it's important: *Users can't surf the web without a browser. Examples of browsers are Microsoft Internet Explorer, Netscape Navigator, Mozilla Firefox, Opera, and Apple Macintosh Browser.*

webcasting (p. 95) Service, based on push technology, in which customized text, video, and audio are sent to the user automatically on a regular basis or live on demand. Why it's important: *Users choose the categories, or the channels, of websites that will automatically send updated information. Thus, webcasting saves time because users don't have to go out searching for the information.*

web page (p. 66) Document on the World Wide Web that can include text, pictures, sound, and video. Why it's important: *A website's content is provided on web pages. The starting page is the home page.*

web portal (p. 73) Type of gateway website that functions as an "anchor site," a major starting point, for users when they connect to the web. Portals are also called *links pages* or *gateways*. The most popular portals are America Online, Yahoo!, Google, Bing, and Lycos. Why it's important: *Web portals provide an easy way to access the web. They generally offer a broad array of resources and services, online shopping malls, email support, community forums, current news and weather, stock quotes, travel information, a search engine, and links to other popular subject categories.*

website (site) (p. 66) Location of a web domain name in a computer somewhere on the Internet. Why it's important: *Websites provide multimedia content to users.*

Wi-Fi (p. 60) Short for "wireless fidelity." The name given to any of several standards—so-called 802.11 standards—set by the Institute of Electrical and Electronic Engineers for wireless transmission. Why it's important: *Wi-Fi enables people to use their Wi-Fi-equipped laptops to go online wirelessly in certain areas such as airports that have public access to Wi-Fi networks.*

window (p. 87) A rectangular area on a computer display screen that contains a document or activity. Why it's important: *In instant messaging, a window allows a user to exchange IM messages with others almost simultaneously while operating other programs.*

wireless network (p. 59) Network that uses radio waves to transmit data, such as Wi-Fi. Why it's important: *Wireless networks enable people to access the Internet without having a cabled or wired connection, using wireless-equipped laptops and smart cellphones.*

XML (extensible markup language) (p. 95) A Web-document tagging and formatting language that two computers can use to exchange information. Why it's important: *XML is an improvement over HTML and enables the creation of RSS newsreaders.*

CHAPTER REVIEW

1 LEARNING MEMORIZATION

"I can recognize and recall information."

Self-Test Questions

1. Today's data transmission speeds are measured in __________, Kbps, __________, and __________.
2. A(n) __________ __________ connects a personal computer to a cable-TV system that offers an Internet connection.
3. A space station that transmits data as microwaves is a __________.
4. A company that connects you through your communications connection to its server, which connects you to the Internet, is a(n) __________.
5. A rectangular area on the computer screen that contains a document or displays an activity is called a(n) __________.
6. __________ is writing an online message that uses derogatory, obscene, or inappropriate language.

7. A(n) __________ is software that enables users to view web pages and to jump from one page to another.
8. A computer with a domain name is called a(n) __________.
9. A(n) __________ comprises the communications rules that allow browsers to connect with web servers.
10. A(n) __________ is a program that adds a specific feature to a browser, allowing it to play or view certain files.
11. Unsolicited email in the form of advertising or chain letters is known as __________.
12. The expression of how much data—text, voice, video, and so on—can be sent through a communications channel in a given amount of time is known as __________.
13. A(n) __________ is a string of characters that points to a specific piece of information somewhere on the web.
14. Some websites may leave files on your hard disk that contain information such as your name, password, and preferences; they are called __________.
15. Using trusted institutional names to elicit confidential information is called __________.
16. The kind of spyware that can record each character you type and transmit that information to someone else on the Internet, making it possible for strangers to learn your passwords and other information, is called a(n) __________.

Multiple-Choice Questions

1. Kbps means how many bits per second?
   a. 1 billion
   b. 1 thousand
   c. 1 million
   d. 1 hundred
   e. 1 trillion
2. A location on the Internet is called a
   a. network.
   b. user ID.
   c. domain.
   d. browser.
   e. web.
3. In the email address *Kim_Lee@earthlink.net.us,* Kim_Lee is the
   a. domain.
   b. URL.
   c. site.
   d. user ID.
   e. location.
4. Which of the following is *not* one of the four components of a URL?
   a. web protocol
   b. name of the web server
   c. name of the browser
   d. name of the directory on the web server
   e. name of the file within the directory
5. Which of the following is the fastest method of data transmission?
   a. ISDN
   b. DSL
   c. modem
   d. T1 line
   e. cable modem
6. Which of the following is *not* a netiquette rule?
   a. Consult FAQs.
   b. Flame only when necessary.
   c. Don't shout.
   d. Avoid huge file attachments.
   e. Avoid sloppiness and errors.
7. Which protocol is used to retrieve email messages from the server to your computer?
   a. HTTP (HyperText Transfer Protocol)
   b. SMTP (Simple Mail Transfer Protocol)
   c. POP3 (Post Office Protocol version 3)
   d. POP (point of presence)
8. Who owns the Internet?
   a. Microsoft
   b. IBM
   c. Apple
   d. U.S. government
   e. No one owns the Internet; the components that make up the Internet are owned and shared by thousands of public and private entities.
9. Each time you connect to your ISP, it will assign your computer a new address called a(n)
   a. domain.
   b. IP address.
   c. plug-in.
   d. POP.
   e. URL (Universal Resource Locator).
10. ISPs that don't run their own backbones connect to an Internet backbone through a(n)
    a. Internet Exchange Point.
    b. web portal.
    c. web browser.
    d. URL.
    e. TCP/IP.
11. Which of the following is *not* a protocol?
    a. TCP/IP
    b. IE
    c. HTTP
    d. SMTP
12. The sending of phony email that pretends to be from a credit-card company or bank, luring you to a website that attempts to obtain confidential information from you, is called
    a. spoofing.
    b. phishing.

c. spamming.
d. keylogging.
e. cookies.

True/False Questions

T F 1. POP3 is used for sending email, and SMTP is used for retrieving email.

T F 2. A dial-up modem is an ISP (Internet service provider).

T F 3. Replying to spam email messages with the statement "remove" will always get spammers to stop sending you unsolicited email.

T F 4. All computer communications use the same bandwidth.

T F 5. A T1 line is the slowest but cheapest form of Internet connection.

T F 6. A dynamic IP address gives you faster Internet access than a static IP address does.

T F 7. A bookmark lets you return to a favorite website quickly.

T F 8. Radio buttons are used for listening to radio stations on the Internet.

T F 9. Spoofing means using fake email sender names.

T F 10. Hypertext refers to text presented with very large letters.

2 LEARNING COMPREHENSION

"I can recall information in my own terms and explain it to a friend."

Short-Answer Questions

1. Name three methods of data transmission that are faster than a regular modem connection.
2. What does *log on* mean?
3. What is netiquette, and why is it important?
4. Briefly define *bandwidth.*
5. Many web documents are "linked." What does that mean?
6. Compare and contrast a cable modem service to a DSL service.
7. Explain the basics of how the Internet works.
8. What expanded functions does IMAP (Internet Message Access Protocol) have?
9. Briefly explain what TCP/IP does.
10. Why was ICANN established?
11. What's the difference between a dynamic IP address and a static IP address?
12. Explain what a blog is.
13. State your answer to a person who asks you the question "Who owns the Internet?"
14. What is B2B commerce?
15. List and briefly describe three kinds of spyware.

3 LEARNING APPLYING, ANALYZING , SYNTHESIZING, EVALUATING

"I can apply what I've learned, relate these ideas to other concepts, build on other knowledge, and use all these thinking skills to form a judgment."

Knowledge in Action

1. Distance learning uses electronic links to extend college campuses to people who otherwise would not be able to take college courses. Are you, or is someone you know, involved in distance learning? If so, research the system's components and uses. What hardware and software do students need in order to communicate with the instructor and classmates? What courses are offered? Discuss the pros and cons of distance learning compared to classroom-based learning.
2. It's difficult to conceive how much information is available on the Internet and the web. One method you can use to find information among the millions of documents is to use a search engine, which helps you find web pages on the basis of typed keywords or phrases. Use your browser to go to the Google home page, and click in the *Search* box. Type the keywords *"personal computers"*; then click on *Google Search*, or press the *Enter* key. How many results did you get?
3. As more and more homes get high-speed broadband Internet connections, the flow of data will become exponentially faster and will open up many new possibilities for sharing large files such as video. What types of interactive services can you envision for the future?
4. Draw a diagram of what happens when you log onto your ISP; include all the connections you think possible for your situation.
5. How do the latest cellphones incorporate the Internet into their functions? What functions could be improved? Have any of these extra functions affected your daily life?
6. How does the Internet affect your life? Start keeping a list.
7. Email, instant messaging (IM), and texting are ways of sending text messages back and forth to other people on the Internet. They seem very similar: in all, you compose a message, and when it's ready, you send it; and when someone else sends something to you, you receive it on your device and can read it.

   But in practice, email, IM, and texting can be surprisingly different; each has its own rhythm, its own strengths and weaknesses, its own sociology, its own etiquette.

   As you use these messaging systems during the course of the term, watch for differences between them. Which medium is more appropriate for which kinds of relationships and communications? Which medium is more stressful to use? Which takes more time? Which is more convenient for you? Which one is more useful for getting real work done? Which one would you use if you knew that whatever you wrote was eventually going to be published in a book? If you were restricted to using only one of these communications methods, which would it be?

8. Internet service providers (ISPs) often place limits on upload speeds, thus making it take much longer to send (upload) a large file than it would take to receive (download) a file of the same size from someone else. Do a comparison between upload and download speeds on your Internet connection, perhaps by emailing yourself a file large enough to allow you to notice the difference. Why do you think there is a difference? (Consider both technological and economic factors.)
9. Imagine that a relative or friend wants to start using the Internet for the first time. You want to help this beginner get started, but you need to be careful not to overwhelm him or her with more information than he or she can use. What three or four things would you tell and show this person first? What things do you think will be hardest for him or her to master? How do you think using the Internet is likely to change this person's life?
10. As we have discussed in this chapter, the Internet is both a goldmine and a minefield. There are vast riches of information, entertainment, education, and communication to be found, but there are also snoopers, spam, spoofing, phishing, spyware, adware, browser hijackers, and key loggers. What should you do to avoid these threats?
11. Some websites require you to register before you are allowed to use them. Others require that you have a paid membership. Others allow limited free access to everyone but require payment for further content. Why do you think different sites adopt these different attitudes toward use of their material?

Web Exercises

1. Some websites go overboard with multimedia effects, while others don't include enough. Locate a website that you think makes effective use of multimedia. What is the purpose of the site? Why is the site's use of multimedia effective? Take notes, and repeat the exercise for a site with too much multimedia and one with too little.
2. If you have never done a search before, try this: Find out how much car dealers pay for your favorite cars, what they charge consumers for them, and what you should know about buying a new car. A company called Edmunds publishes a magazine with all that information, but you can get the same information on its website for free.

   Using the Google search engine (*www.google.com*), type *"automobile buyer's guide"* and *Edmunds* in the search box, and hit the *Google Search* button. How many entries did you get? Click on a link to the Edmunds website. Explore the site, and answer the questions at the beginning of this exercise.
3. Ever wanted your own dot-com in your name? Visit these sites to see if your name is still available:

   www.register.com

   www.namezero.com

   www.domainname.com

   www.checkdomain.com/

   www.domaindirect.com/
4. Interested in PC-to-phone calls through your Internet connection? Visit these sites and check out their services:

   http://voice.yahoo.com/

   www.net2phonedirect.com

   www.iconnecthere.com

   www.skype.com

   www.voip.com/
5. HTTP (HyperText Transfer Protocol) on the World Wide Web isn't the only method of browsing and transferring data. FTP is the original method and is still a useful Internet function. To use FTP, you'll need an FTP client software program, just as you need a web browser to surf the web. Download one of these shareware clients and visit its default FTP sites, which come preloaded:

CuteFtp	*www.globalscape.com/products/ftp_clients.aspx*
WS_FTP	*www.ipswitch.com*
FTP Voyager	*www.ftpvoyager.com*
SmartFTP	*www.smartftp.com*
FileZilla	*http://filezilla-project.org/*

   You will need an FTP client program to upload files to a server if you ever decide to build a website. Some online website builders have browser uploaders, but the conventional method has always been FTP.
6. There are many ways to have a website created or to do it yourself without learning HTML; but if you want to learn more about creating websites with HTML:

   www.make-a-web-site.com

   www.htmlgoodies.com/primers/html/

   www.htmlcodetutorial.com/

   www.w3schools.com/html/default.asp

   Or do an Internet search for "html primer," "learn html," or "html tutorial."
7. To learn more about Internet emoticon/symbol/acronym conventions, go to:

   http://members.tripod.com/~paandaa/smiley.htm

   http://research.microsoft.com/~mbj/Smiley/Smiley.html

   http://piology.org/smiley.txt

   www.cygwin.com/acronyms/

   www.netlingo.com/acronyms.php
8. Some hobbies have been dramatically changed by the advent of the World Wide Web. Particularly affected are the "collecting" hobbies, such as stamp collecting, coin collecting, antique collecting, memorabilia collecting, plate collecting, and so forth. Choose some such hobby that you know something about or have some interest in. Run a web search about the hobby and see if you can find:

   a. a mailing list about the hobby.

   b. an auction site that lists rare items and allows you to bid on them.

   c. a chat room or other discussion forum allowing enthusiasts to gather and discuss the hobby.

   d. a site on which someone's formidable collection is effectively displayed.

9. When the web first came into widespread use, the most popular search engine was AltaVista. For several years there were a variety of search engines available, but in recent years one search engine, Google, has become predominant, and the word *googling* has entered the language as a verb that means "to use a search engine to find information."

   Visit *http://searchenginewatch.com/links/* for a list of many alternative search engines, as well as explanations about how they work and how to get your site listed on them.

10. E-commerce is booming. For any given product you may wish to buy on the web, there may be hundreds or thousands of possible suppliers, with different prices and terms—and not all of them will provide equally reputable and reliable service. The choices can be so numerous that it may sometimes seem difficult to know how to go about choosing a vendor.

    Websites that do comparison shopping for you can be a great help. Such a service communicates with many individual vendors' websites, gathering information as it proceeds; it then presents its findings to you in a convenient form. Often, ratings of the various vendors are provided as well, and sales tax and shipping charges are calculated for you.

    Here are a few sites that can assist with comparison shopping:

    www.epinions.com/

    www.bizrate.com/

    http://shopper.cnet.com/

    Practice "catch-and-release e-commerce" by researching the best deals you can find for:

    a rare or at least out-of-print book that you'd like to have.

    a high-end digital video recorder (DVD).

    a replacement ink or toner cartridge for your laser or inkjet printer.

    a pair of athletic shoes exactly like the shoes you currently have.

    Pursue each transaction right up to the last step before you would have to enter your credit-card number and actually buy the item, and then quit. (Don't buy it. You can always do that another time.)

11. WebCams, or web cameras, are used by some websites to show pictures of their locations—either live video or still shots. To run your own WebCam site requires a suitable camera and a continuous Internet connection. But to look at other people's WebCam sites requires only a web browser.

    For example, try searching for "WebCam Antarctica." Or go to *www.webcam-index.com.*

    Find and bookmark at least one interesting WebCam site in each of the following places: Africa, Asia, South America, Europe, Australia, Antarctica, Hawai'i.

3

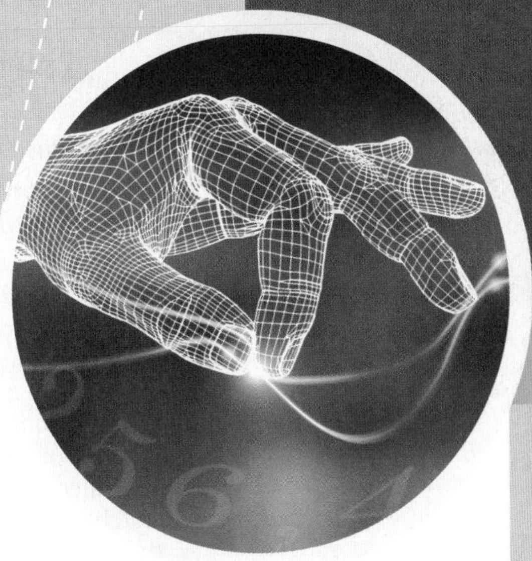

SOFTWARE

Tools for Productivity & Creativity

Chapter Topics & Key Questions

3.1 System Software: The Power behind the Power What are three components of system software, what does the operating system (OS) do, and what is a user interface?

3.2 The Operating System: What It Does What are the principal functions of the operating system?

3.3 Other System Software: Device Drivers & Utility Programs What are the characteristics of device drivers and utility programs?

3.4 Common Features of the User Interface What are some common features of the graphical software environment (GUI), and how do they relate to the keyboard and the mouse?

3.5 Common Operating Systems What are some common desktop, network, and portable (embedded) OSs?

3.6 Application Software: Getting Started What are five ways of obtaining application software, tools available to help me learn to use software, three common types of files, and the types of software?

3.7 Word Processing Software What can I do with word processing software that I can't do with pencil and paper?

3.8 Spreadsheet Programs What can I do with electronic spreadsheet worksheets that I can't do with pencil and paper and a standard calculator?

3.9 Database Software What is database software, and what is personal information management software?

3.10 Specialty Application Software What are some principal kinds of specialty software?

3.11 Filenames and File Extensions What are some common filename extensions, what purpose do they serve, and what is data compression?

Download the free UIT 10e App for key term flash cards, quizzes, and a game, *Over the Edge*

W hat we need is a science called practology, a way of thinking about machines that focuses on how things will actually be used."

So said Alan Robbins, a professor of visual communications, on the subject of *machine interfaces*—the parts of a machine that people actually manipulate.[1] An *interface* is a machine's "control panel," ranging from the volume and tuner knobs on an old radio to all the switches and dials on the flight deck of a jetliner. You may have found that on too many of today's machines—digital watches, cameras, even stoves—the interface is often designed to accommodate the machine or some engineering ideas rather than the people actually using it. Good interfaces are intuitive—that is, based on previous knowledge and experience—like the twin knobs on a 1950s radio, immediately usable by both novices and sophisticates. Bad interfaces, such as a software program with a bewildering array of menus and icons, force us to relearn the required behaviors every time.

So how well are computer hardware and software makers doing at giving us useful, helpful interfaces? The answer is, they're getting better all the time. Improving interfaces is the province of *human-computer interaction (HCI),* which is concerned with the study, design, construction, and implementation of human-centric interactive computer systems. HCI goes beyond improving screens and menus into the realm of adapting interfaces to human reasoning and studying the long-term effects that computer systems have on humans. HCI encompasses the disciplines of information technology, psychology, sociology, anthropology, linguistics, and others. As computers become more pervasive in our culture, HCI designers are increasingly looking for ways to make interfaces easier, safer, and more efficient.

HCI innovations are also extremely important for people with disabilities, including blindness and limited mobility. Google is working on an Android OS add-on that will make the mobile phone operating system much easier for blind people to use. One idea is to disable the touchscreen and add buttons with holes or other manually discernable dintinctions. Another is to develop GPS-based phones for the blind that can read street signs and directions aloud and sophisticated screen-reader software that can turn documents and web pages into synthesized speech. Amazon is now working on new features such as an audible menu system for its e-reader, Kindle.[2]

Note that the 2010 U.S. government standards according to the American Disabilities Act of 1990 require accessibility options for computer hardware and software in various government and public education venues (*www.ada.gov/regs2010/2010ADAStandards/2010ADAStandards.pdf*).

In time, as interfaces are refined, computers may become no more difficult to use than a car. Until then, however, for smoother computing you need to know something about how software works. Today people communicate one way, computers another. People speak words and phrases; computers process bits and bytes. For us to communicate with these machines, we need an intermediary, an interpreter. This is the function of software, particularly system software.

more info!

HCI Careers!

Could you make a career in HCI-associated areas? Go to:

www.sigchi.org

www.hfcareers.com/Default.aspx

Do you see some HCI-related areas that you might consider as a major?

more info!

Who Was John Tukey?

The term *software* was coined by John Tukey. Who was he? Did he coin any other important computer terms? Do a keyword search on his name and see what you can find out.

3.1 SYSTEM SOFTWARE: The Power behind the Power

System software is the platform for running application software.

As we mentioned in Chapter 1 (p. 28), *software,* or *programs,* consists of all the electronic instructions that tell the computer how to perform a task. These instructions come from a software developer in a form (such as a CD or DVD,

USB drive, or an Internet download) that will be accepted by the computer. ***Application software*** **is software that has been developed to solve a particular problem for users—to perform useful work on specific tasks or to provide entertainment. *System software* enables the application software to interact with the computer and helps the computer manage its internal and external resources.** We interact mainly with the application software, which interacts with the system software, which controls the hardware.

New microcomputers are equipped not only with system software but usually also with some application software. There are three basic components of system software that you need to know about. (● *See Panel 3.1.*)

- **Operating systems:** An operating system is the principal component of system software in any computing system.
- **Device drivers:** Device drivers help the computer control peripheral devices.
- **Utility programs:** Utility programs are generally used to support, enhance, or expand existing programs in a computer system.

A fourth type of system software, *language translators*, is briefly described in Chapter 10.

3.2 THE OPERATING SYSTEM: What It Does

The operating system manages the entire computer system.

The *operating system (OS)* consists of the low-level, master system of programs that manage the basic operations of the computer. These programs provide resource management services of many kinds. In particular, they handle the control and use of hardware resources, including disk space, memory, CPU

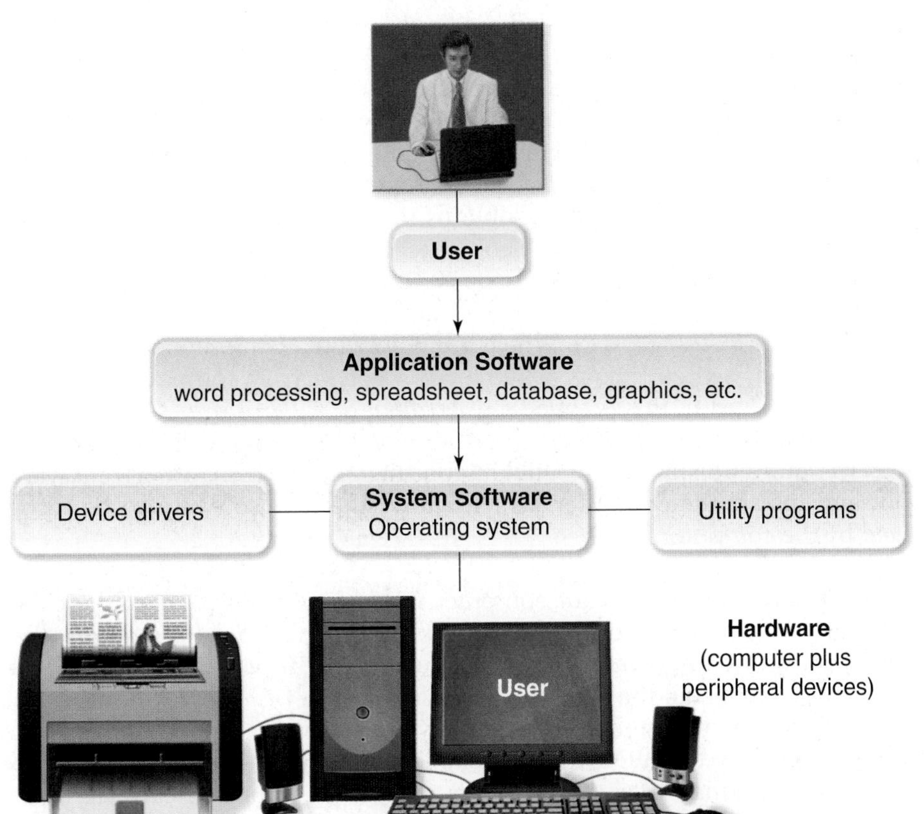

panel 3.1

Three components of system software

In general, system software is the interface between the user/application software and the computer hardware. (Occasionally users interact directly with the system software—for example, when setting security options, organizing files, and installing and launching application software.)

time allocation, and peripheral devices. Every general-purpose computer must have an operating system to run other programs. The operating system, through its interface, allows you to concentrate on your own tasks or applications rather than on the complexities of managing the computer. Each application program is written to run on top of a particular operating system.

Different sizes and makes of computers have their own operating systems. For example, Cray supercomputers use UNICOS and COS; IBM mainframes use MVS and VM; PCs run Windows or Linux and Apple Macintoshes run the Macintosh OS. Cellphones have their own operating systems, such as Apple's iPhone OS 3 or 4, which works with iPhones, or Google and the Open Handset Alliance's Android operating system for smartphones and other mobile devices. With a few exceptions, an operating system written for one kind of hardware will not be able to run on another kind of machine.

But before we discuss the different kinds of operating systems, we should have an idea of what operating systems do. We consider:

- Booting
- CPU management
- File management
- Task management
- Security management

Survival Tip

New Software & Compatibility

Pay attention to compatibility requirements when you obtain new software. The system requirements for running the software will be listed on the box or included with the downloaded information. When it is time to update the software, you can usually do that by paying a small upgrade fee to the software manufacturer and then downloading the new version and/or obtaining a new CD/DVD.

Booting

When you turn on a computer, you boot it, meaning that the operating system starts to load.

The work of the operating system begins as soon as you turn on, or "boot," the computer. ***Booting*** (from "bootstrapping") **is the process of loading an operating system into a computer's main memory.** This loading is accomplished automatically by programs stored permanently in the computer's electronic circuitry (called *read-only memory*, or *ROM*, described in Chapter 4). When you turn on the machine, programs called *diagnostic routines* test the main memory, the central processing unit, and other parts of the system to make sure they are running properly. Next, BIOS (for "basic input/output system") programs are copied to main memory and help the computer interpret keyboard characters or transmit characters to the display screen or to a disk. Then the boot program obtains the operating system, usually from the hard disk, and loads it into the computer's main memory, where it remains until you turn the computer off. *(• See Panel 3.2.)*

COLD BOOTS & WARM BOOTS When you power up a computer by turning on the power "on" switch, this is called a *cold boot*. If your computer is already on and you restart it, this is called a *warm boot* or a *warm start*.

After installing new software on your computer, you will usually see a "Restart" button displayed; by clicking on this button, you authorize a warm boot and restart the computer, which allows the new software to be recognized by the computer.

THE BOOT DISK Normally, your computer would boot from the hard drive, but if that drive is damaged, you can use a disk called a *boot disk* (or a *restore disk*) to start up your computer. A boot disk is usually a CD or a flash drive (Chapter 4) that contains all the files needed to launch the OS. When you insert the boot disk into your computer's CD drive, you answer the displayed queries to feed the OS files to the BIOS, thereby enabling it to launch the OS and complete the start-up routine. After the OS loads completely, you then can access the contents of the hard drive, run basic drive maintenance utilities, and perform troubleshooting tasks that will help you resolve the problem with the drive.

If Windows doesn't boot properly, it may go into Safe Mode. You can also get into Safe Mode by pressing the F8 key during the boot process. Safe Mode is used for diagnosing problems and fixing them. When the system is in Safe Mode, only the essential parts of the system work—monitor, mouse, keyboard—and there are no fancy interface graphics on the screen.

www.computerhope.com/issues/chsafe.htm

http://computer.howstuffworks.com/question575.htm

Once you are in Safe Mode, you use the Device Manager to fix problems:

https://kb.wisc.edu/helpdesk/page.php?id=502

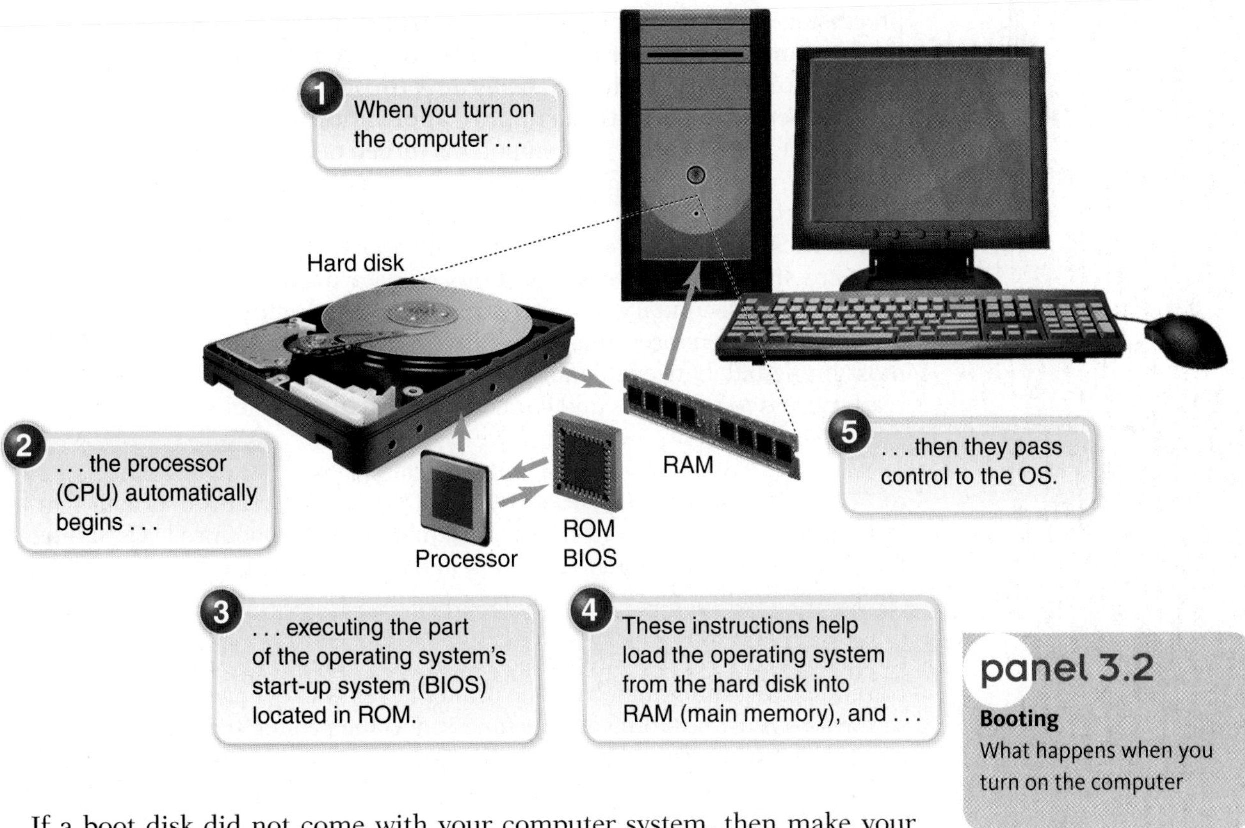

1 When you turn on the computer . . .
Hard disk
2 . . . the processor (CPU) automatically begins . . .
Processor
ROM BIOS
RAM
5 . . . then they pass control to the OS.
3 . . . executing the part of the operating system's start-up system (BIOS) located in ROM.
4 These instructions help load the operating system from the hard disk into RAM (main memory), and . . .

panel 3.2

Booting

What happens when you turn on the computer

If a boot disk did not come with your computer system, then make your own by following the instructions in the online user's manual on your system manufacturer's website (which you can also download to your computer).

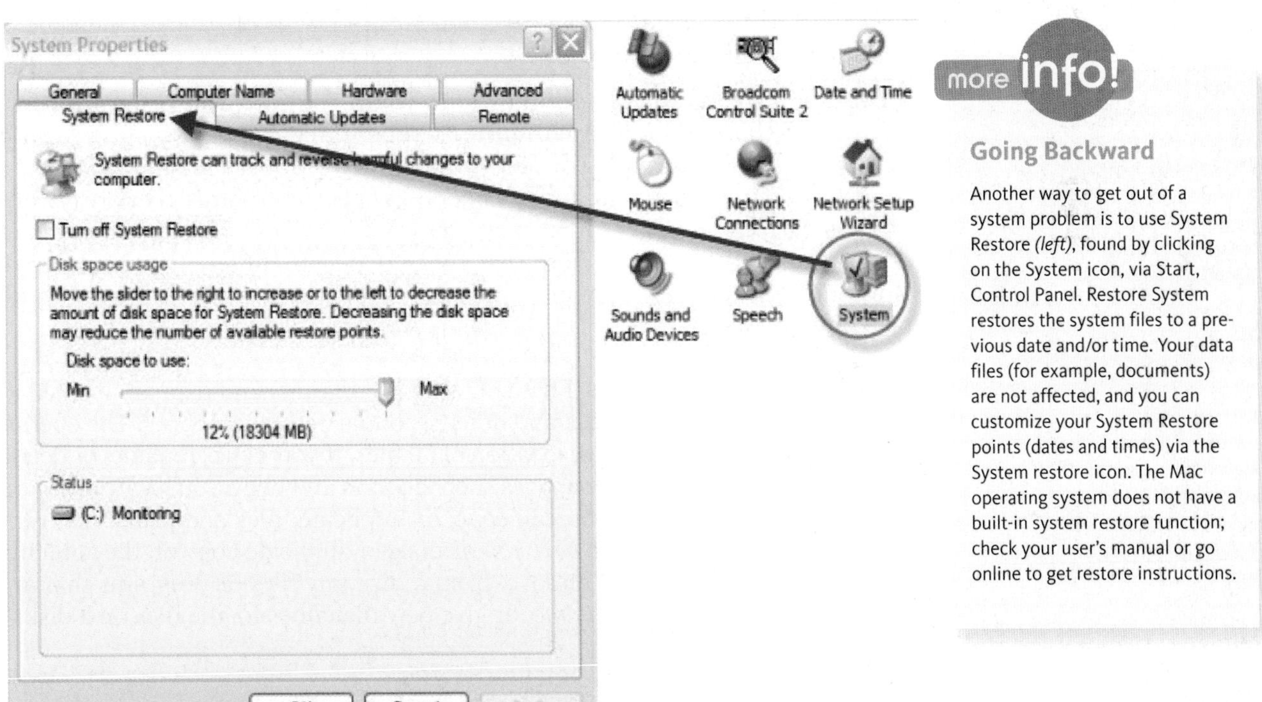

System Properties
General
Computer Name
Hardware
Advanced
System Restore
Automatic Updates
Remote
System Restore can track and reverse harmful changes to your computer.
Turn off System Restore
Disk space usage
Move the slider to the right to increase or to the left to decrease the amount of disk space for System Restore. Decreasing the disk space may reduce the number of available restore points.
Disk space to use:
Min
Max
12% (18304 MB)
Status
(C:) Monitoring
OK
Cancel
Apply
Automatic Updates
Broadcom Control Suite 2
Date and Time
Mouse
Network Connections
Network Setup Wizard
Sounds and Audio Devices
Speech
System

more info!

Going Backward

Another way to get out of a system problem is to use System Restore *(left)*, found by clicking on the System icon, via Start, Control Panel. Restore System restores the system files to a previous date and/or time. Your data files (for example, documents) are not affected, and you can customize your System Restore points (dates and times) via the System restore icon. The Mac operating system does not have a built-in system restore function; check your user's manual or go online to get restore instructions.

CPU Management

The CPU is the central processing unit.

The central component of the operating system is the supervisor. Like a police officer directing traffic, the ***supervisor,*** **or *kernel,* manages the CPU** (the central processing unit or processor, Chapter 1, p. 29). **It remains in memory (main memory or primary storage) while the computer is running and copies into memory other "nonresident" programs (programs that were not in memory) to perform tasks that support application programs.** The supervisor remains in memory until the computer is turned off.

MEMORY MANAGEMENT The operating system also manages memory—it keeps track of the locations within main memory, where the programs and data are stored. It can swap portions of data and programs between main memory and secondary storage, such as your computer's hard disk, as so-called *virtual memory.* This capability allows a computer to hold only the most immediately needed data and programs within main memory. Yet it has ready access to programs and data on the hard disk, thereby greatly expanding memory capacity.

GETTING IN LINE: QUEUES, BUFFERS, & SPOOLING Programs and data that are to be executed or processed wait on disk in *queues* (pronounced "Qs"). A queue is a first-in, first-out sequence of data and/or programs that "wait in line" in a temporary holding place to be processed. The disk area where the programs or documents wait is called a *buffer.* Print jobs are usually *spooled*—that is, placed—into a buffer, where they wait in a queue to be printed. This happens because the computer can send print jobs to the printer faster than the printer can print them, so the jobs must be stored and then passed to the printer at a rate it can handle. Once the CPU has passed a print job to the buffer, it can take on the next processing task. (The term *spooling* dates back to the days when print jobs were reeled, or copied, onto spools of magnetic tape, on which they went to the printer.)

File Management

Every operating system or program uses a file management system to organize and keep track of files.

A *file* is (1) a named collection of data (data file) or (2) a program (program file) that exists in a computer's secondary storage, such as a hard disk or CD/DVD. Examples of data files are a word processing document, a spreadsheet, images, songs, and the like. Examples of program files are a word processing program or a spreadsheet program. (We cover files in more detail at the end of the chapter; note that files created by different programs are stored in different file formats, which is why some files will not open in all programs.)

FINDING & HANDLING FILES Files containing programs and data are located in many places on your hard disk and other secondary storage devices. The operating system records the storage location of all files. If you move, rename, or delete a file, the operating system manages such changes and helps you locate and gain access to it. For example, you can *copy,* or duplicate, files and programs from one disk to another. You can *back up,* or make a duplicate copy of, the contents of a disk. You can *erase,* or remove, from a disk any files or programs that are no longer useful. You can *rename,* or give new filenames to, the files on a disk.

ORGANIZING FILES: DIRECTORIES/FOLDERS, SUBFOLDERS, & PATHS The operating system's file system arranges files in a hierarchical manner, first into folders (also called *directories*) and then into subfolders (subdirectories). *(• See Panel 3.3.)* The topmost folder/directory is called the *root directory;* a folder below another folder is called a *subfolder* (*subdirectory*)*;* any folder above a subfolder is called its *parent folder* (*parent directory*).

To find a particular file in an operating system's file system, you type in the file's *pathname.* The *path* is the route through the file system. A simple example of a pathname in Windows is *C:\mydocuments\termpaper\section1.doc*

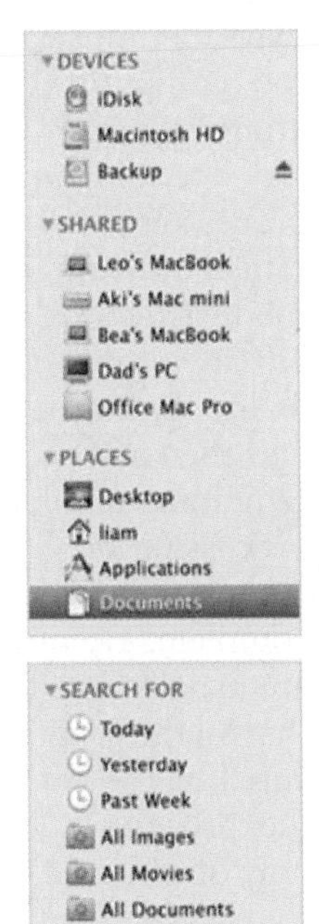

Windows XP (*left*), Windows 7 (*middle*), and the Mac operating system (*right*) provide a Find (Search) function for finding files if you don't know the pathname.

"C" refers to the hard disk (the root directory); "mydocuments" is the main (or primary) folder, the parent folder to "termpaper," which is a subfolder; "section 1" is the name of the file (filename); and "doc" is a file extension that indicates what type of file it is (.doc = document). (Note that in Unix-based operating systems and the Mac OS X operating system, the pathnames use a forward slash [/] instead of a backward slash [\ ].)

Root Directory
C:
Folders
My Music
My Documents
My Pictures
Subfolders
Files
Term Paper
Letters
Section 1 . . .

panel 3.3

Directories/folders, and subfolders, and files

Task Management

The operating system is the manager of the tasks that the computer performs.

A computer is required to perform many different tasks at once (multitasking). In word processing, for example, it accepts input data, stores the data on a disk, and prints out a document—seemingly simultaneously. Most desktop and laptop operating systems are single-user systems that can handle more than one program at the same time—word processing, spreadsheet, database searcher. Each program is displayed in a separate window on the screen. Other operating systems (multiuser systems) can accommodate the needs of several different users at the same time. All these examples illustrate *task management.* A *task* is an operation such as storing, printing, or calculating.

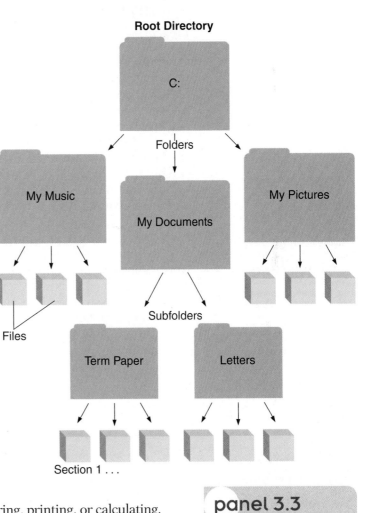

MULTITASKING: HANDLING MORE THAN ONE PROGRAM CONCURRENTLY ***Multitasking*** **is the execution of two or more programs by one user almost at the same time on the same computer with one or two central processors**; that is, the programs are sharing the same processing resources. You may be writing a report on your computer with one program while another program

more info!

Task Manager

If you want to see a list of processes being executed by your system, open the Task Manager *(right)* in Windows by holding down the Ctrl, Alt, and Del keys.

plays a music CD. How does the computer handle both programs at once? The answer is that the operating system directs the processor(s) to spend a predetermined amount of time executing the instructions for each program, one at a time. Thus, a small part of the first program is processed, and then a processor moves to the remaining programs, one at a time, processing small parts of each. The cycle is repeated until processing is complete. Because the processors are usually very fast, it may appear that all the programs are being executed at the same time. However, the processors are still executing only one instruction at a time.

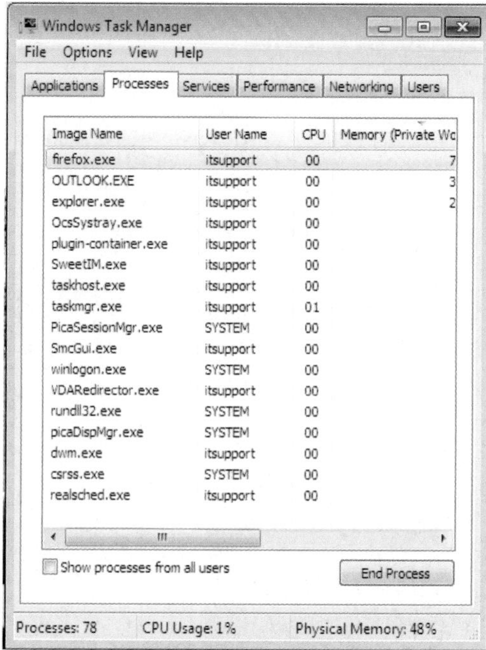

Security Management

Operating systems also take care of some security management.

Operating systems allow users to control access to their computers—an especially important matter when several people share a computer or the same computer network. Users gain access in the same manner as accessing their email—via a user name (user ID) and a password. As we stated in Chapter 2, a *password* is a special word, code, or symbol required to access a computer system. When you first boot up a new personal computer, the OS will prompt you to choose a user name and a password. Then, every time after that, when you boot up your computer, you will be prompted to type in your user name and password. Some OSs even allow you to protect individual files with separate access passwords. (The Help feature explains how to change or turn off your password.)

Survival Tip

Is Your Password Guessable?

Don't choose a password that could be easily guessed. Examples of weak passwords are birth date, anniversary date, boyfriend/girlfriend name, city/town name, pet's name, fad words/expressions, or names of celebrities or famous movie/book characters. Instead, use meaningless letters and numbers. The longer the password, the better—and don't use the same password for everything that requires passwords.

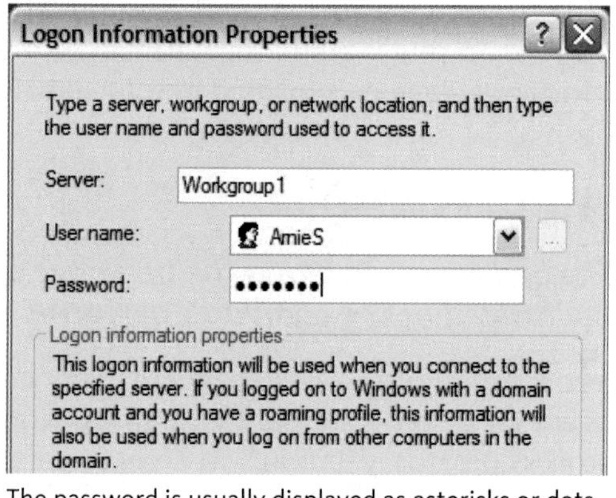

The password is usually displayed as asterisks or dots, so that anyone looking over your shoulder—a "shoulder surfer"—cannot read it.

Computer systems and security issues have become complicated

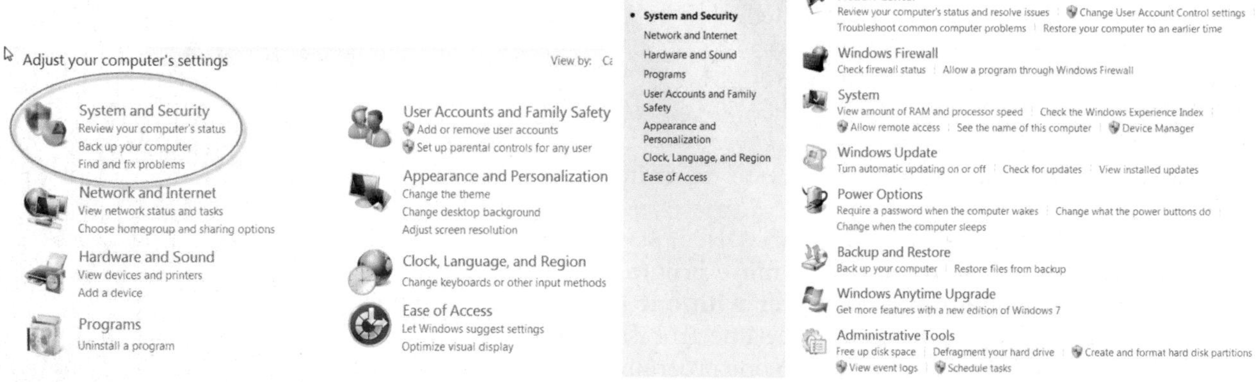

In Windows, you can access the Security Center (*left*) via the Control Panel to control additional security features (*right*).

and critically important. We discuss this subject in more detail in Chapters 6, 8, and 9.

3.3 OTHER SYSTEM SOFTWARE: Device Drivers & Utility Programs

Drivers and utility programs add functionality to your computer and help it perform better.

We said that the three principal parts of system software are the operating system, device drivers, and utility programs. Let's now consider the last two.

Device Drivers: Running Peripheral Hardware

Device drivers communicate with peripherals (usually input/output devices).

Device drivers **are specialized software programs that allow input and output devices to communicate with the rest of the computer system.** Each device's brand and model are supported by a different driver that works with only one operating system. Many basic device drivers come with the system software when you buy a computer, and the system software will guide you through choosing and installing the necessary drivers. If, however, you buy a new peripheral device, such as a mouse, a scanner, or a printer, the package will include a device driver for the device (probably on a CD or DVD, or downloaded from the Internet).

Most new operating systems recognize many new hardware devices on their own and automatically install them. If your OS does not recognize your new hardware, it will display a message and ask you to install the driver from the CD that came with your hardware. (• *See Panel 3.4.*)

Survival Tip

Update Your Drivers

You should regularly (once a year, say) update your drivers. To do so, visit the websites of your peripheral devices' manufacturers and download any updates. You can also buy utilities for backing up and restoring drivers, such as 3D2F.com Software Directory (*http://3d2f.com/programs/54-281-my-drivers-download.shtml*) or Driver-Soft.com's Driver Genius (*www.driver-soft.com*).

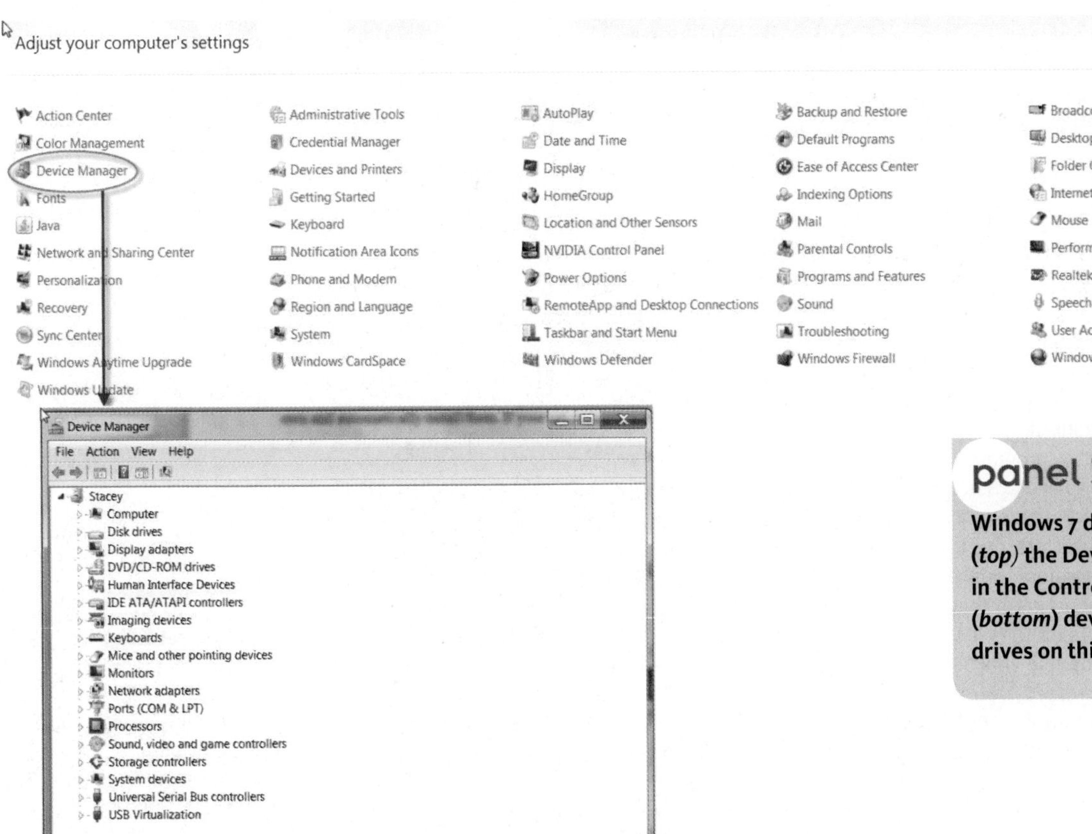

panel 3.4

Windows 7 device drivers; (*top*) the Device Manager in the Control panel; (*bottom*) devices with drives on this computer

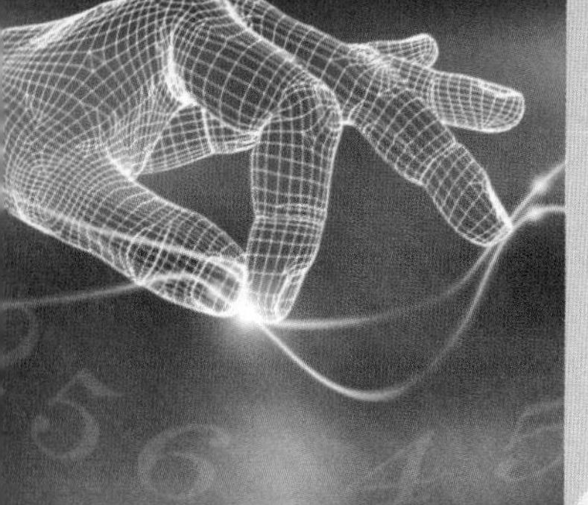

PRACTICAL ACTION

Utility Programs

Utility programs are incorporated into the operating system. Others, such as antivirus programs, are sold as standalone programs. Some important utility programs are as follows:

Backup

Suddenly your hard-disk drive fails, and you have no more programs or files. Fortunately, we hope, you have used a *backup utility* to make a backup, or duplicate copy, of the information on your hard disk. The backup can be made to an external hard drive, an off-site networked (online, or "cloud") site, or other choices discussed later in the book. Examples of freestanding backup utilities are Norton Ghost (from Symantec) and DT Utilities PC Backup.

Data Recovery

One day in the 1970s, so the story goes, programming legend Peter Norton was working at his computer and accidentally deleted an important file. This was, and is, a common enough error. However, instead of reentering all the information, Norton decided to write a computer program to recover the lost data. He called the program "The Norton Utilities." Ultimately it and other utilities made him very rich.

A *data-recovery utility* is used to restore data that has been physically damaged, deleted, or corrupted. Data can be damaged by viruses (see following), bad software, hardware failure, and power fluctuations that occur while data is being written/recorded.

Virus Protection

If there's anything that can make your heart sink faster than the sudden failure of your hard disk, it may be the realization that your computer system has been invaded by a virus. A *virus* consists of hidden programming instructions that are buried within an application or system program. Sometimes viruses copy themselves to other programs, causing havoc. Sometimes the virus is merely a simple prank that pops up in a message. Other times, however, it can destroy programs and data and wipe your hard disk clean. Viruses are spread when people exchange CDs and flash drives, download information from the Internet and other computer networks, or open files attached to email. (• *See Panel 3.5, p. 130.)*

You should, therefore, install antivirus software. *Antivirus software* is a utility program that scans all disks and memory to detect viruses. Some utilities destroy the virus on the spot. Others notify you of possible viral behavior. Because new viruses are constantly being created, you need the type of antivirus software that can constantly update itself against newly discovered viruses. Examples of antivirus software are Symantec's Norton AntiVirus, Webroot Antivirus, and McAfee AntiVirus. New viruses appear every day, so it's advisable to look for an antivirus utility that offers frequent online updates without additional cost.

We discuss viruses again in more detail in Chapter 6.

Data Compression

As you continue to store files on your hard disk, it may eventually fill up. You then have several choices: You can delete old files to make room for the new. You can add a second hard-disk drive, externally or internally. Or you can use a data compression utility, such as PK Zip, ZipIt, WinZip, or StuffIt. (As a result of the name "Zip," people have come to refer to compressing a file as "zipping" and decompressing a file as "unzipping.") ("Zip" programs are often included with an OS.)

Data compression utilities remove redundant elements, gaps, and unnecessary data from computer files so that less space (fewer bits) is required to store or transmit data. (Also see the end of the chapter.) With a data compression utility, files can be made more compact for storage on your hard-disk drive. With the increasing use of large graphic, sound, and video files, data compression is necessary both to reduce the storage space required and to reduce the time required to transmit such large files over a network.

As the use of sophisticated multimedia becomes common, compression and decompression are being increasingly taken over by built-in hardware boards that specialize in this process. That will leave the main processor free to work on other things, and compression/decompression software utilities will become obsolete.

File Defragmentation

Over time, as you delete old files from your hard disk and add new ones, something happens: the files become fragmented. *Fragmentation* is the scattering of portions of files about the disk in nonadjacent areas, thus greatly slowing access to the files.

When a hard disk is new, the operating system puts files on the disk contiguously (next to one another).

More on Utilities

For some unusual utilities, go to:

NimiVisuals
www.mynimi.net

Piriform
www.piriform.com/defraggler

FileAlyzer
www.safer-networking.org/en/filealyzer

Edgeless
www.fxc.btinternet.co.uk/assistive.htm

Fences
www.stardock.com/products/fences

PCWorld
www.pcworld.com/downloads/file/fid,114526-order,4/description.html

File Guru
www.fileguru.com/DetectSatan/info

FreeOTFE
www.freeotfe.org

DoubleKiller
www.bigbangenterprises.de/en/doublekiller

JPEGsnoop
www.impulseadventure.com/photo/jpeg-snoop.html

Top Ten Reviews
http://pc-system-utilities-software-review.toptenreviews.com/

PC Tune-Up: Stop at the Pitstop

To find out what problems your PC has and to learn which utilities might improve its performance, go to:

www.pcpitstop.com/default.asp

and try their free computer scans.

However, as you update a file over time, new data for that file is distributed to unused spaces. These spaces may not be contiguous to the older data in that file. It takes the operating system longer to read these fragmented files. A *defragmenter* utility program, commonly called a "defragger," will find all the scattered files on your hard disk and reorganize them as contiguous files. Defragmenting the disk will speed up the drive's operation. So, if you notice your computer slowing down, it might be a good idea to "defrag" the disk. Computer users who use their machines for hours every day might want to defrag every few days.

Disk Scanner (ScanDisk or Check Disk) & Disk Cleanup

These utilities detect and correct certain types of common problems on hard drives and CDs and search for and remove unnecessary files, such as temporary files, or "temp files." Both Windows and the applications you run create temp files needed only for short tasks and system restore (return to normal operating conditions) after certain types of system problems. These files are stored in the Temp folder. For example, when you create a Word document, Word stores a temp file version of it in the Temp folder. When you save this document, Word saves it to the location you designated and then deletes the temp file. The computer should delete temp files when a program is closed, but this doesn't always happen. Also, files will be left in the Temp folder if the computer crashes. Thus temp files can accumulate in the Temp folder and take up space.

Note that the Mac with OS X does not use temp files in the manner of Windows. OS X has its own Disk Utility feature that will take care of many of the utility functions that we have discussed. Also, OnyX is a freeware utility available separately for conducting routine maintenance and tweaking the interface on the Mac.

Many other utilities exist, such as those for transferring files back and forth between a desktop microcomputer and a laptop and for troubleshooting various types of system problems. Generally, the companies selling utilities do not manufacture the operating system. OS developers usually eventually incorporate the features of a proven utility as part of their product. (Note: Independent, or external, utilities must be compatible with your system software; check the software packaging and user documentation.)

Survival Tip

Temp File Removal

In Windows, to remove temporary and unnecessary files from your hard drive, Click *Start, All Programs, Accessories, System Tools,* and *Disk Cleanup*. Put checks in the boxes next to the types of file you want to delete, and click *OK*.

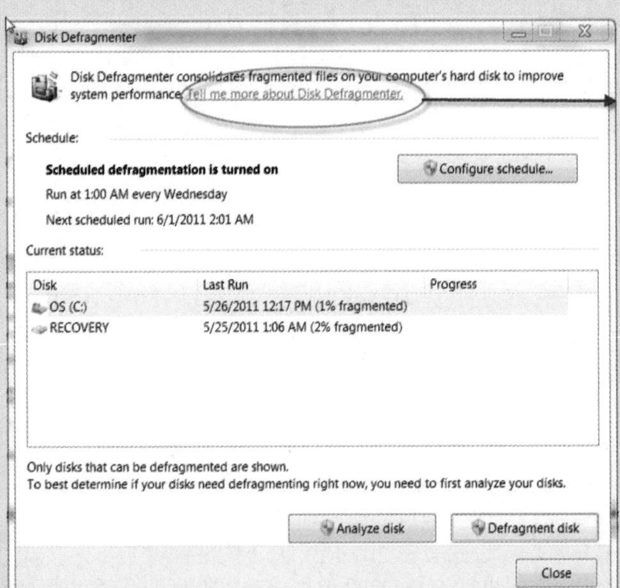

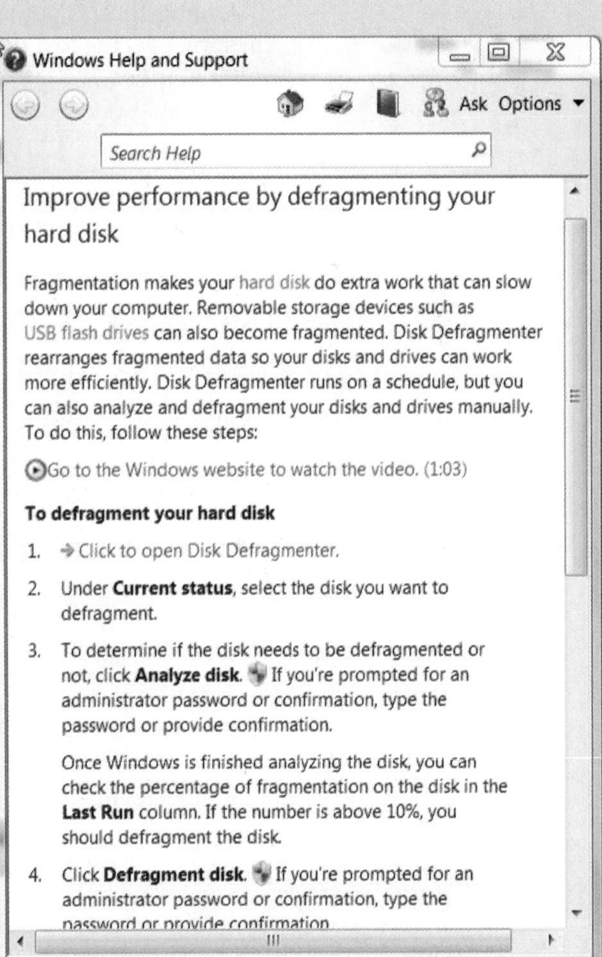

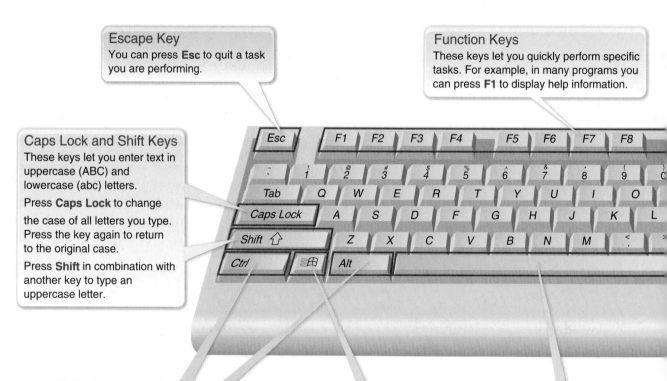

panel 3.5

Preventing viruses

- If you download or install software from a network server (including the Internet), or an online service, always run virus scanning software on the folder/directory you place the new files in before you run/execute them.

- Make sure that you have a disk (e.g., CD) with your virus program so that you can reinstall the software if necessary. Or print out your purchase ID information and the link to the manufacturer's website so that you can re-download your software if you need to.

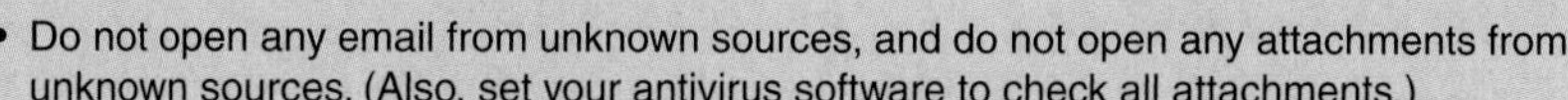

- Do not open any email from unknown sources, and do not open any attachments from unknown sources. (Also, set your antivirus software to check all attachments.)

- If your Internet connection is always on (e.g., cable), purchase firewall software or make sure that your OS is set properly to protect you from unauthorized intrusion.
- Never start your computer from an unknown CD or flash drive, and make sure secondary storage drives are empty before you boot your computer.

Survival Tip

Free Antivirus Software

For a list of free antivirus software, see:

www.thefreecountry.com/security/antivirus.shtml

www.pcworld.com/reviews/collection/1597/free_antivirus_software.html

www.freebyte.com/antivirus/

Utilities: Service Programs

Utilities are small programs that play supporting roles.

***Utility programs*, also known as *service programs*, perform tasks related to the control, allocation, and maintenance of computer resources.** (See preceding Practical Action box.) They enhance existing functions or provide services not supplied by other system software programs. Most computers come with built-in utilities as part of the system software. However, they may also be bought separately as external utility programs (such as Norton SystemWorks and McAfee Utilities).

Among the tasks performed by utilities are backing up data, compressing files, recovering lost data, and identifying hardware problems. *(See the Practical Action box.)*

Escape Key
You can press **Esc** to quit a task you are performing.
Function Keys
These keys let you quickly perform specific tasks. For example, in many programs you can press **F1** to display help information.
Caps Lock and Shift Keys
These keys let you enter text in uppercase (ABC) and lowercase (abc) letters.
Press **Caps Lock** to change the case of all letters you type. Press the key again to return to the original case.
Press **Shift** in combination with another key to type an uppercase letter.
Esc
F1
F2
F3
F4
F5
F6
F7
F8
Tab
Caps Lock
Shift
Ctrl
Alt
Ctrl and Alt Keys
You can use the **Ctrl** or **Alt** key in combination with another key to perform a specific task. For example, in some programs, you can press **Ctrl** and **S** to save a document.
Windows Key
You can press the **Windows** key to quickly display the Start menu when using many Windows operating systems.
Spacebar
You can press the **Spacebar** to insert a blank space.

3.4 Common Features of the User Interface

User-interface features use graphics to facilitate a person's interaction with the computer.

The first thing you look at when you call up any system software on the screen is the ***user interface*—the user-controllable graphic display screen that allows you to communicate, or interact, with the computer.** Like the dashboard on a car, the user interface has gauges that show you what's going on and switches and buttons for controlling what you want to do. From this screen, you choose the application programs you want to run or the files of data you want to open.

You can interact with the display screen using the keys on your keyboard. As well as having letter, number, and punctuation keys and often a calculator-style numeric keypad, computer keyboards have special-purpose and function keys. (● *See Panel 3.6.*)

***Special-purpose keys* are used to enter, delete, and edit data and to execute commands.** An example is the Esc (for "Escape") key, which tells the computer to cancel an operation or leave ("escape from") the current mode of operation. The Enter, or Return, key, which you will use often, tells the computer to execute certain commands and to start new paragraphs in a document. *Commands* are instructions that cause the software to perform specific actions.

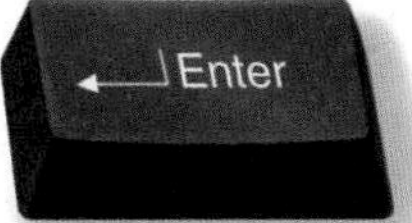

Special-purpose keys are generally used the same way regardless of the application software package being used. Most keyboards include the following special-purpose keys: *Esc, Ctrl, Alt, Del, Ins, Home, End, PgUp, PgDn, Num Lock,* and a few others. (For example, *Ctrl* means "Control," *Del* means "Delete," *Ins* means "Insert.")

***Function keys,* labeled "F1," "F2," and so on, are usually positioned along the top of the keyboard. They are used to execute commands specific to the software being used.** For example, one application software package may use F6 to exit a file, whereas another may use F6 to underline a word.

panel 3.6

Keyboard functions

Some keyboards include other ("dedicated") keys, such as for direct Internet connection and email connection.

Backspace Key
You can press **Backspace** to remove the character to the left of the cursor.

Status Lights
These lights indicate whether the **Num Lock** or **Caps Lock** features are on or off.

Delete Key
You can press **Delete** to remove the character to the right of the cursor.

Numeric Keypad
When the **Num Lock** light is on, you can use the number keys (0 through 9) to enter numbers. When the **Num Lock** light is off, you can use these keys to move the cursor around the screen. To turn the light on or off, press **Num Lock.**

Arrow Keys
These keys let you move the cursor around the screen.

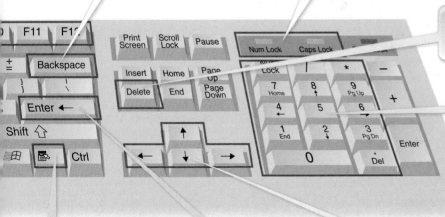

Application Key
You can press the **Application** key to quickly display the shortcut menu for an item on your screen. Shortcut menus display a list of commands commonly used to complete a task related to the current activity.

Enter Key
You can press **Enter** to tell the computer to carry out a task. In a word processing program, press this key to start a new paragraph.

Common Shortcuts (Macros)

Instead of using the mouse and menus to select options and perform functions—for example, to save, to print, to boldface a word, to copy text—you can often use 2-key shortcuts:

Windows:

www.microsoft.com/enable/products/KeyboardSearch_xp.aspx

http://support.microsoft.com/kb/126449

http://windows.microsoft.com/en-US/windows7/Keyboard-shortcuts

www.windows7news.com/2009/03/22/master-list-of-windows-7-keyboard-shortcuts/

Mac:

http://support.apple.com/kb/ht1343

www.danrodney.com/mac/

Sometimes you may wish to reduce the number of keystrokes required to execute a command. To do this, you use a macro. **A *macro,* also called a *keyboard shortcut,* is a single keystroke or command—or a series of keystrokes or commands—used to automatically issue a longer, predetermined series of keystrokes or commands.** Thus, you can consolidate several activities into only one or two keystrokes. The user names the macro and stores the corresponding command sequence; once this is done, the macro can be used repeatedly. (To set up a macro, pull down the Help menu and type in *macro*.)

Although many people have no need for macros, individuals who find themselves continually repeating complicated patterns of keystrokes say they are quite useful.

You will also frequently use your mouse to interact with the user interface. The mouse allows you to direct an on-screen pointer to perform any number of activities. **The *pointer* usually appears as an arrow, although it changes shape depending on the application. The mouse is used to move the pointer to a particular place on the display screen or to point to little symbols, or icons.** You can activate the function corresponding to the symbol by pressing ("clicking") buttons on the mouse. Using the mouse, you can pick up and slide ("drag") an image from one side of the screen to the other or change its size. (● *See Panel 3.7.*)

The GUI: The Graphical User Interface

The GUI's use of graphics makes it easy for computer users to interact with their machine.

Personal computers used to have *command-driven interfaces,* which required that you type in complicated-looking instructions (such as *copy a:\filename c:*

panel 3.7

Mouse language

Term	Action	Purpose
Point	Move mouse across desk to guide pointer to desired spot on screen. The pointer assumes different shapes, such as arrow, hand, or I-beam, depending on the task you're performing.	To execute commands, move objects, insert data, or similar actions on screen.
Click	Press and quickly release left mouse button.	To select an item on the screen.
Double-click	Quickly press and release left mouse button twice.	To open a document or start a program.
Drag and drop	Position pointer over item on screen, press and hold down left mouse button while moving pointer to location in which you want to place item, then release.	To move an item on the screen.
Right-click	Press and release right mouse button.	To display a shortcut list of commands, such as a pop-up menu of options.

to copy a file from an old floppy disk to a hard disk). In the next version, they also had *menu-driven interfaces,* in which you could use the arrow keys on your keyboard (or a mouse) to choose a command from a menu, or a list of activities.

Today the computer's "dashboard" is usually a ***graphical user interface (GUI)*** (pronounced "gooey"), **which allows you to use a mouse or keystrokes to select icons (little graphic symbols) and commands from menus or menu bars (lists of activities).** The GUIs on the PC and on the Apple Macintosh (which was the first easy-to-use personal computer available on a wide scale) are somewhat similar. Once you learn one version, it's fairly easy to learn the other. However, the best-known GUI is that of Microsoft Windows system software. (● *See Panel 3.8, next page.)*

DESKTOP, ICONS, & MENUS Three features of a GUI are the desktop, icons, and menus.

- **Desktop:** After you turn on the computer, the first screen you will encounter is the *desktop (Panel 3.8),* a term that embodies the idea of folders of work (memos, schedules, to-do lists) on a businessperson's desk. **The *desktop,* which is the system's main interface screen, displays pictures (icons) that provide quick access to programs and information.**

- **Icons and rollovers:** We're now ready to give a formal definition: ***Icons*** **are small pictorial figures that represent programs, data files, or procedures.** For example, a trash can represents a place to dispose of a file you no longer want. If you click your mouse pointer on a little picture of a printer, you can print out a document. One of the most important icons is the *folder,* a representation of a manila folder; folders hold the files in which you store your documents and other data.

  Of course, you can't always be expected to know what an icon or graphic means. **A *rollover* feature (also called a *tooltip*), a small text box explaining the icon's function, appears when you roll the mouse pointer over the icon. A rollover may also produce an animated graphic.**

Icon: Symbol representing a program, data file,or procedure. Icons are designed to graphically communicate their function, such as a little disk for the "Save" icon.

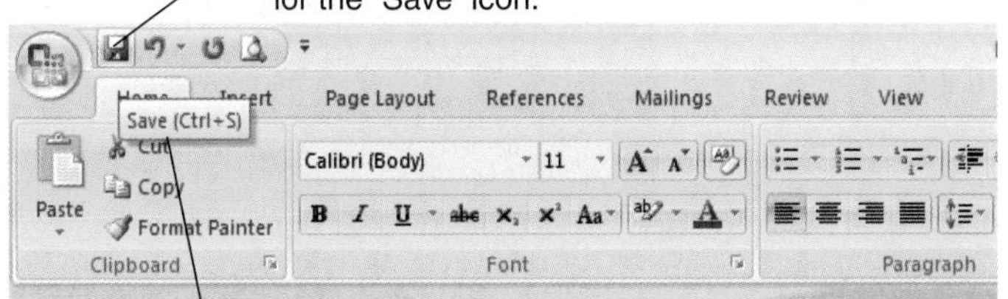

Rollover: When you roll your mouse pointer over an icon (in this case, the "Save" icon), a small box with explanatory text appears

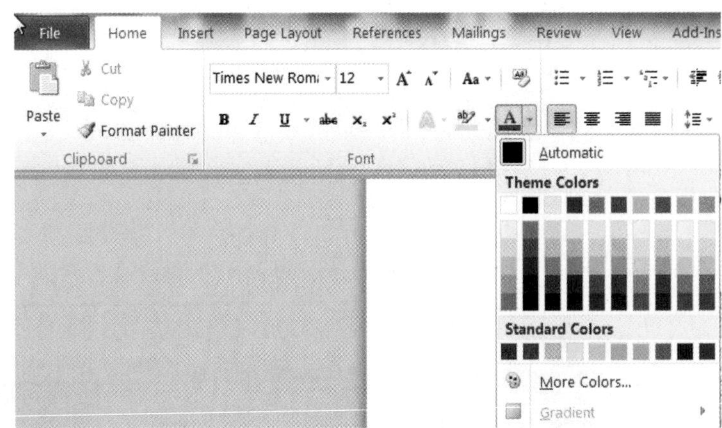

When you click the mouse on the menu bar, a list of options appears or pulls down like a shade—for example, the color choices menu on the right.

- **Menus:** Like a restaurant menu, a ***menu*** **offers you a list of options to choose from**—in this case, a list of commands for manipulating data, such as Print or Edit. Menus are of several types. Resembling a pull-down window shade, a *pull-down menu,* also called a *drop-down menu,* is a list of options that pulls down from the menu bar at the top of the screen. For example, if you use the mouse to "click on" (activate) a command (for example, File) on the menu bar, you will see a pull-down menu offering further commands.

OutlookExpress: Window's email program.

Microsoft Network: Click here to connect to Microsoft Network (MSN), the company's online service.

My Documents: Where your documents are stored (unless you specify otherwise), in folders you create and name.

Network Neighborhood: If your PC is linked to a network, click here to get a glimpse of everything on the network.

My Computer: Gives you a quick overview of all the files and programs on your PC, as well as available drives (A:, C:, D:, E:).

Documents: Multitasking capabilities allow users to smoothly run more than one program at once.

The opening screen is the **desktop.**

Menu bar

Title bar

Minimize Maximize Close

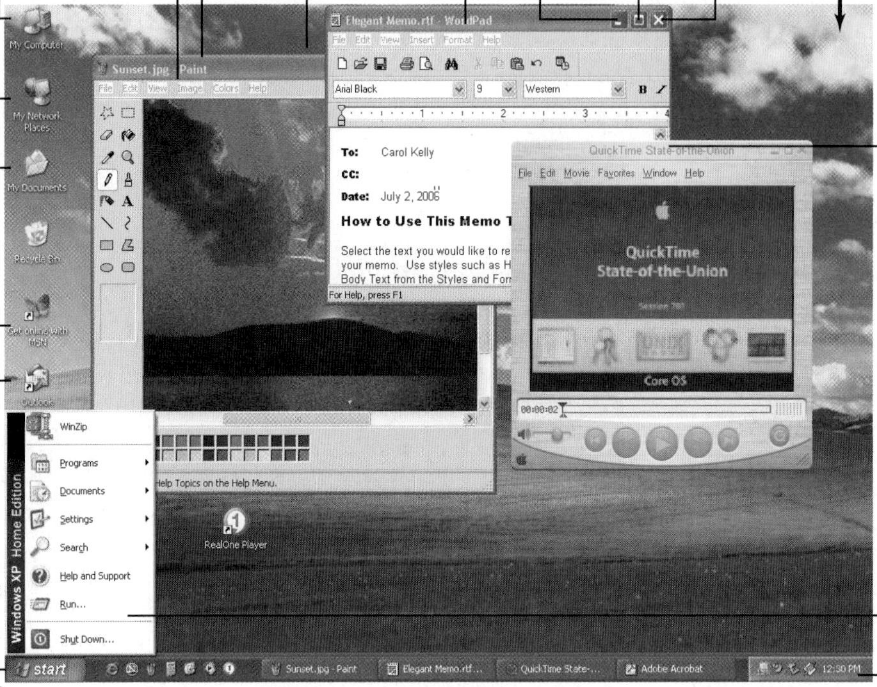

Multimedia: Windows XP features sharp graphics and video capabilities.

Taskbar: Gives you a log of all programs you have opened. To switch programs, click on the icon buttons on the taskbar.

Start menu: After clicking on the Start button, a menu appears, giving you a quick way to handle common tasks. You can launch programs, call up documents, change system settings, get help, and shut down.

Start button: Click for an easy way to start using the computer.

OutlookExpress: Window's email program.

Computer: Gives you a quick overview of all the files and programs on your PC, as well as available drives (A:, C:, D:, E:).

Documents: Multitasking capabilities allow users to smoothly run more than one program at once.

The opening screen is the **desktop.**

Menu bar

Title bar

Minimize Maximize Close

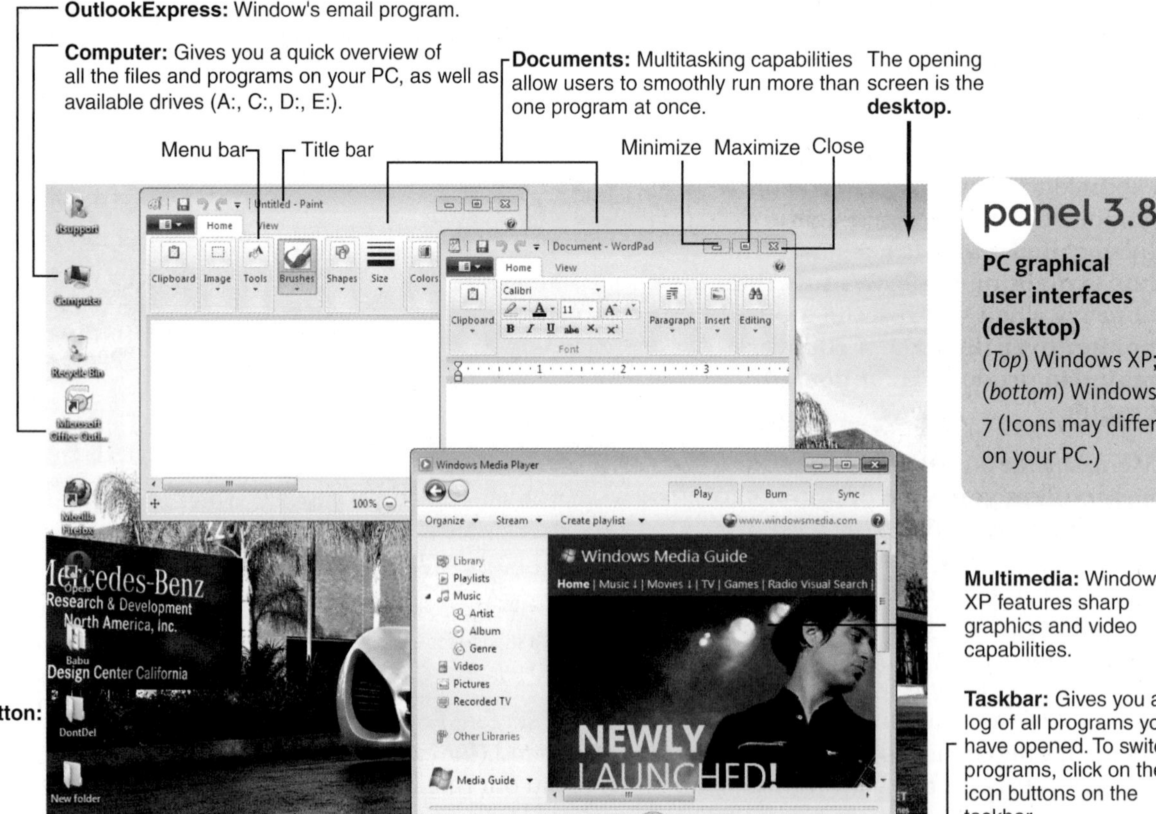

panel 3.8

PC graphical user interfaces (desktop)

(*Top*) Windows XP; (*bottom*) Windows 7 (Icons may differ on your PC.)

Multimedia: Windows XP features sharp graphics and video capabilities.

Taskbar: Gives you a log of all programs you have opened. To switch programs, click on the icon buttons on the taskbar.

Start button: Click for an easy way to start using the computer.

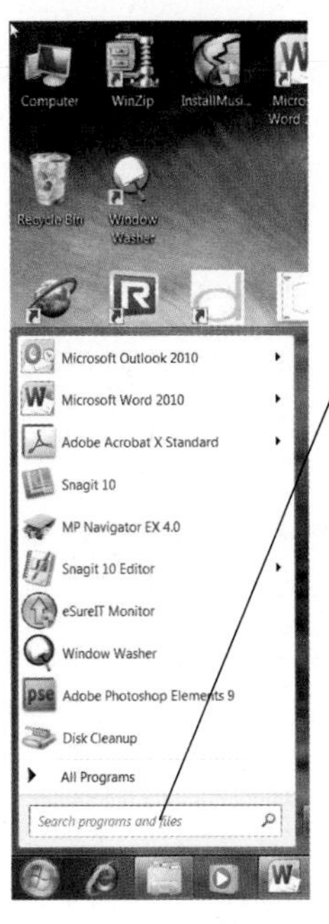

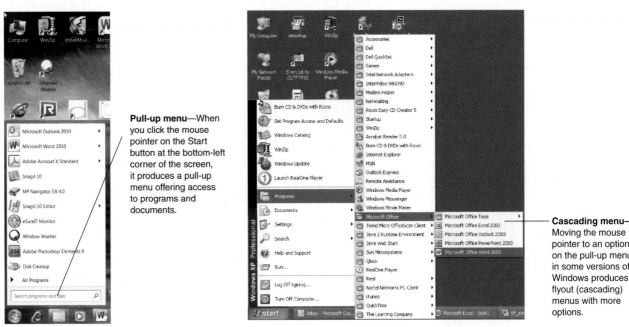

Pull-up menu—When you click the mouse pointer on the Start button at the bottom-left corner of the screen, it produces a pull-up menu offering access to programs and documents.

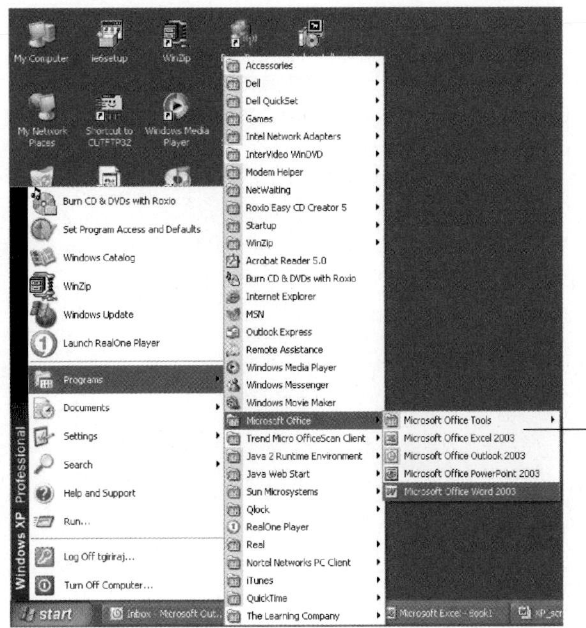

Cascading menu—Moving the mouse pointer to an option on the pull-up menu in some versions of Windows produces flyout (cascading) menus with more options.

Choosing one of these options may produce further menus called *cascading menus (top right),* menus that seem to fly back to the left or explode out to the right, wherever there is space.

DOCUMENTS, TITLE BARS, MENU BARS, TOOLBARS, TASKBARS, & WINDOWS (SMALL "W") If you want to go to a document, there are three general ways to begin working from a typical Microsoft Windows GUI desktop: (1) You can click on the *Start* button at the lower left corner and then make a selection from the pull-up menu that appears. (2) Or you can click on the *My Computer* (just *Computer* in Windows 7) icon on the desktop and pursue the choices offered there. (3) Or click on the *My Documents* icon (a folder icon with your name under it in Windows 7) and then on the folder that contains the document you want. In each case, the result is the same: the document is displayed in the window. *(● See Panel 3.9, next page.)*

Once past the desktop—which is the GUI's opening screen—if you click on the *My Computer* icon, you will encounter various "bars" and window functions. *(● See Panel 3.10, p. 137.)*

- Title bar: **The *title bar* runs across the very top of the display window and shows the name of the folder you are in**—for example, "My Computer."
- Menu bar: Below the title bar is the ***menu bar*, which shows the names of the various pull-down menus available.** Examples of menus are File, Edit, View, Favorites, Tools, and Help.
- Toolbar: **The *toolbar*, below the menu bar, displays menus and icons representing frequently used options or commands.** An example of an icon is the picture of two pages in an open folder with a superimposed arrow, which issues a *Copy to* command.
- Taskbar: In Windows, the ***taskbar* is the bar across the bottom of the desktop screen that contains the Start button and that appears by default.** Small boxes appear here that show the names of open files. You can switch among the files by clicking on the boxes.
- Windows: When spelled with a capital "W," Windows is the name of Microsoft's system software (Windows XP, Vista, 7, and so on). When spelled with a lowercase "w," a ***window* is a rectangular frame on the computer display screen. Through this frame you can view a file of data—such as a document, spreadsheet, or database—or an application program.**

FROM MY COMPUTER

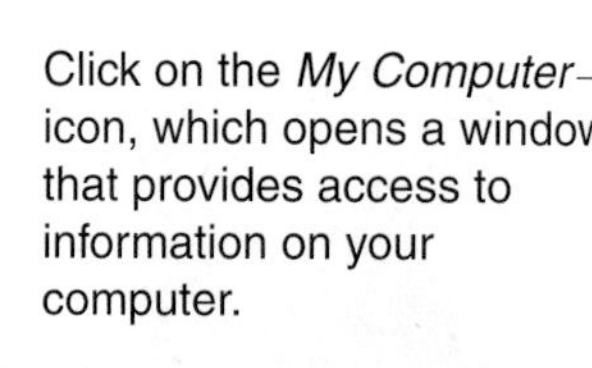

Click on the *My Computer* icon, which opens a window that provides access to information on your computer.

FROM START MENU

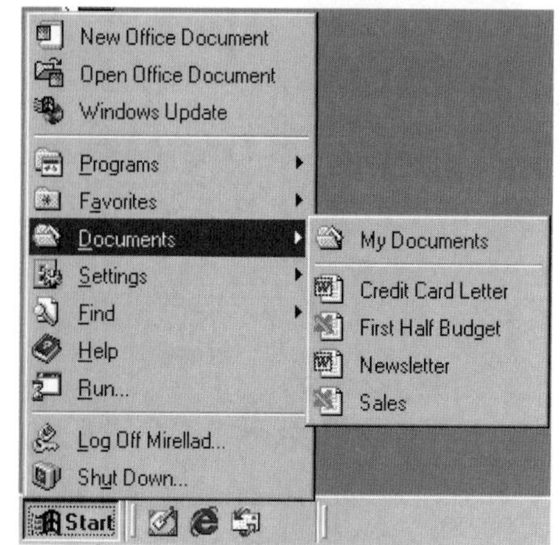

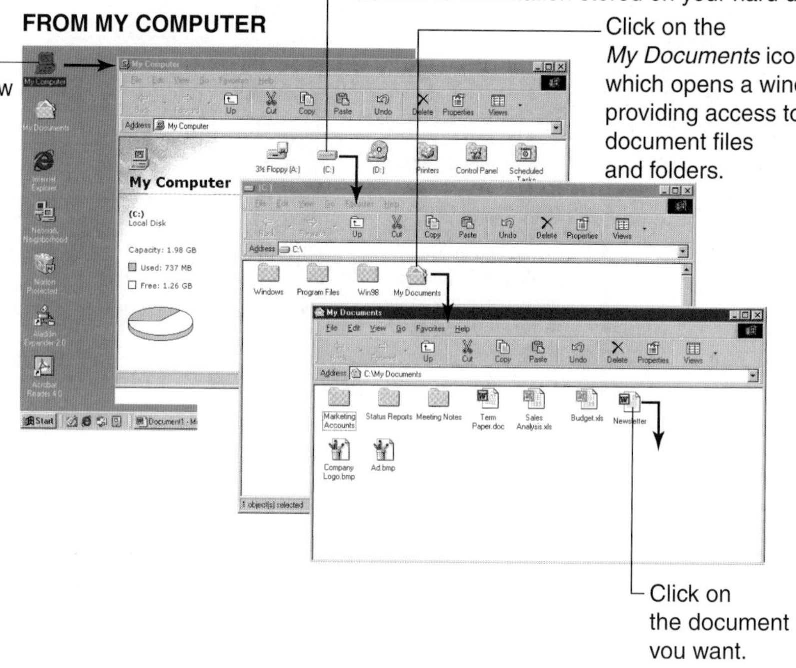

FROM MY DOCUMENTS ICON

panel 3.9

Three ways to go to a document in Windows XP and three ways in Windows 7 (*bottom*)

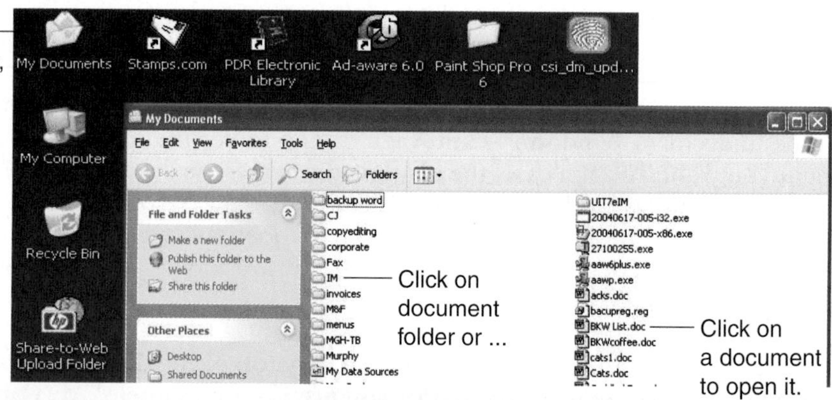

IN WINDOWS 7

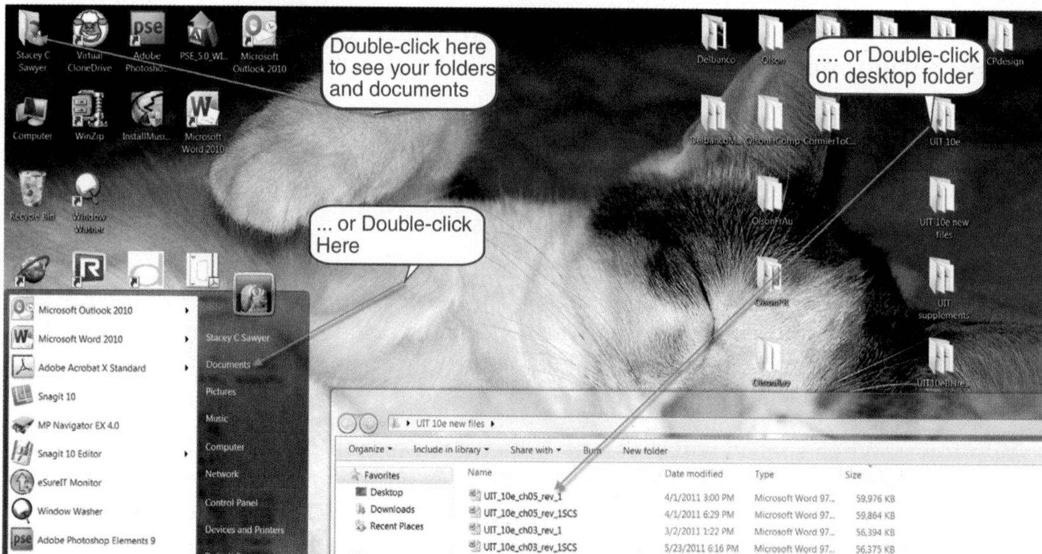

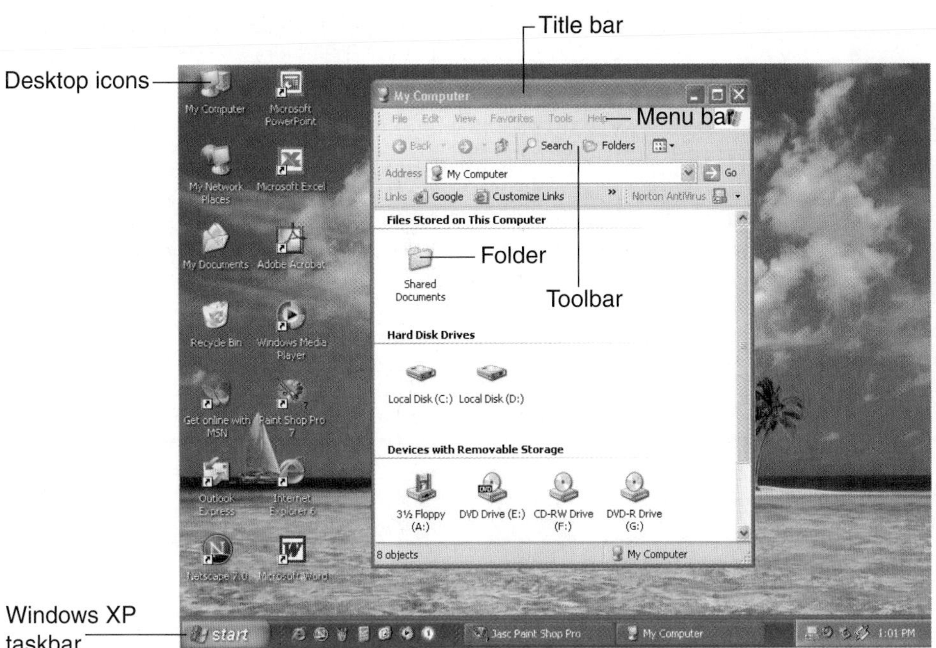

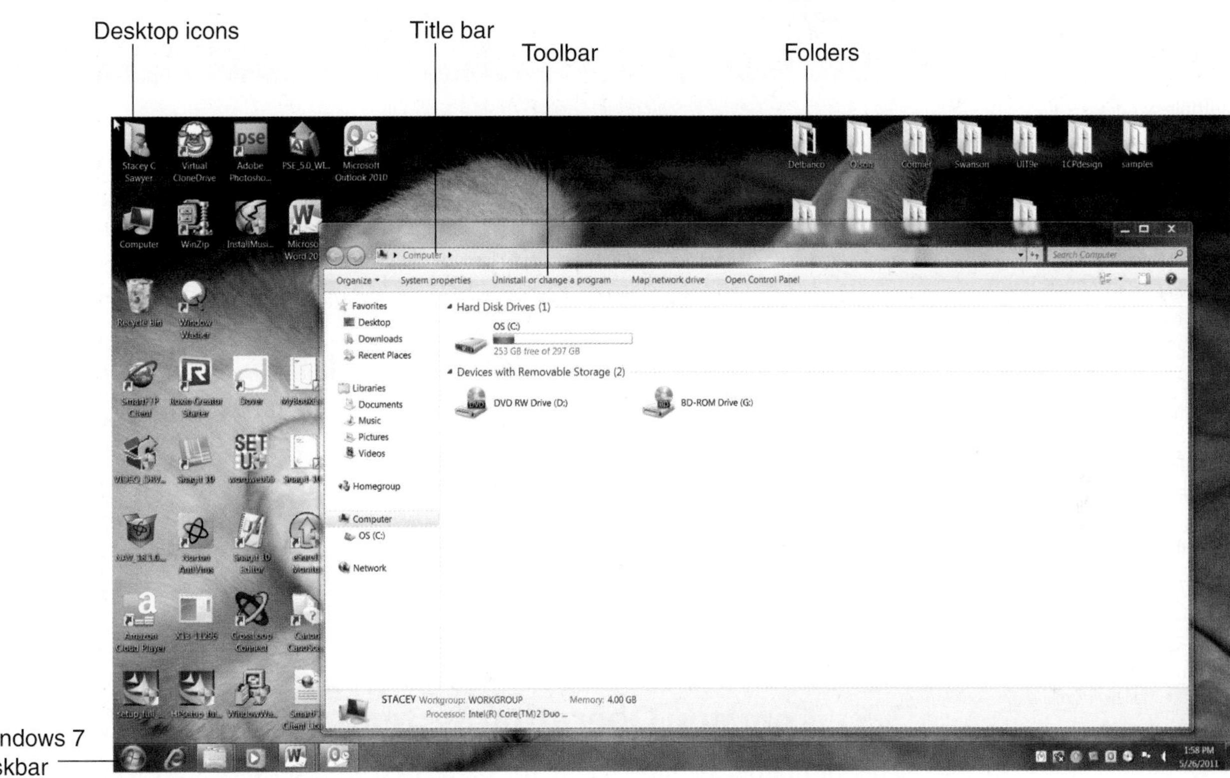

panel 3.10

"Bars" and windows functions (*top*) Windows XP; (*bottom*) Windows 7

In the upper right-hand corner of the Windows title bar are some window controls—three icons that represent *Minimize, Maximize and Restore Down,* and *Close.* By clicking on these icons, you can *minimize* the window (shrink it down to an icon at the bottom of the screen), *make the application window fill the entire desktop window (maximize) or restore the application window to its original size (restore down),* or *close* it (exit the file and make the window disappear).You can also use the mouse to move the window around the desktop, by clicking on and dragging the title bar.

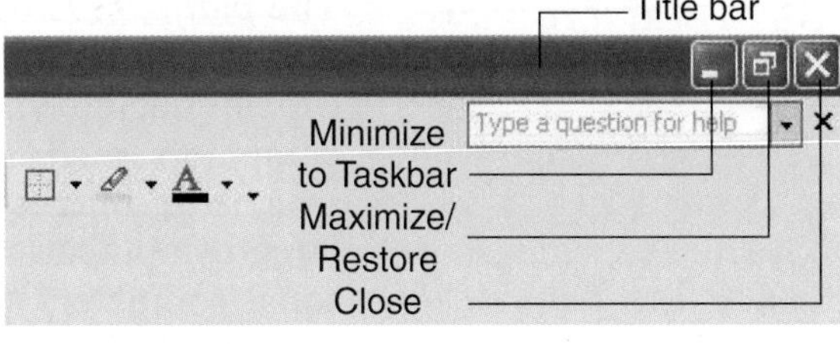

Finally, you can create *multiple windows* to show programs running concurrently. For example, one window might show the text of a paper you're

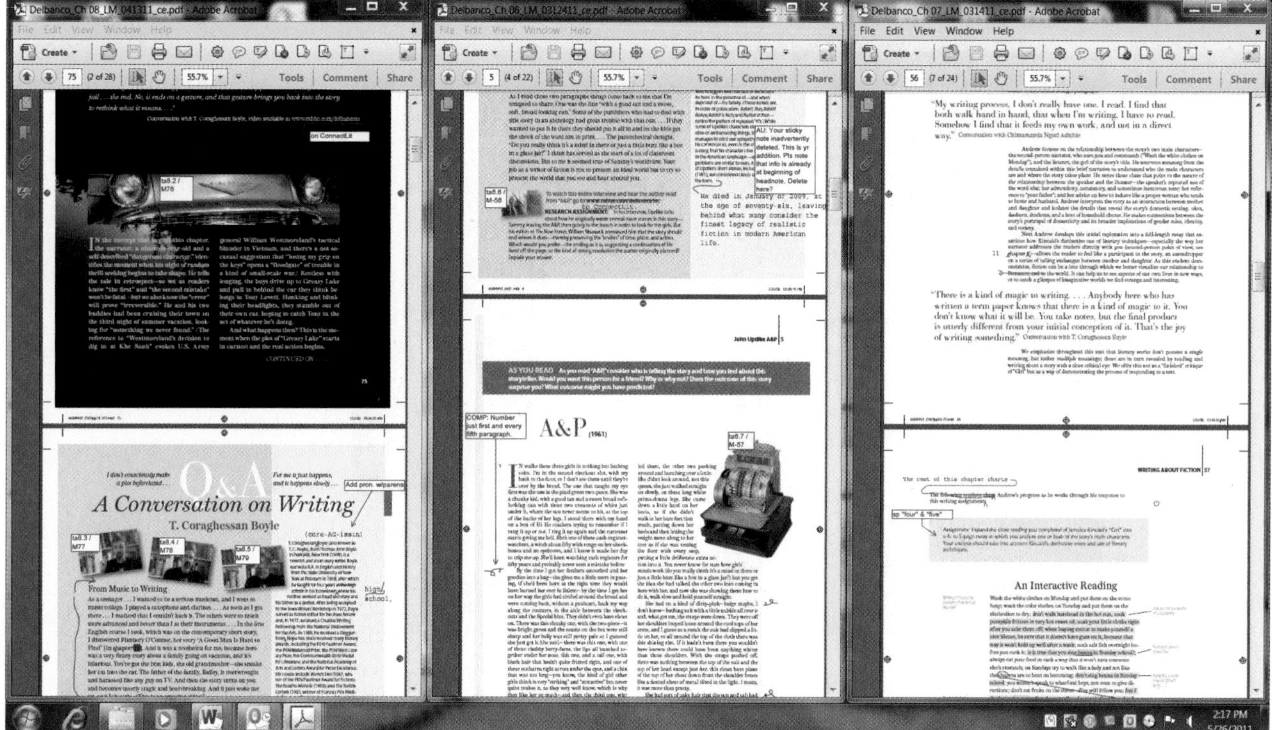

Multiple windows

working on, another might show the reference section for the paper, and a third might show something you're downloading from the Internet. If you have more than one window open, click on the Maximize button of the window you want to be the main window to *restore* it.

> **Survival Tip**
>
> **Don't Trash Those Icons**
>
> In Windows, don't delete unwanted software programs by using the mouse to drag their icons to the recycle bin. This might leave behind system files that could cause problems. Instead, use an "uninstall" utility. In Windows, go to *Start, Settings, Control Panel;* double-click *Add/Remove Programs.* Find the program you want to delete, and click the *Add/Remove* button. (In the Mac OS, one can often—but not always—uninstall programs by dragging icons into the trash; see the Mac user's manual.)

The Help Command

The Help function solves problems for you when you've forgotten how to do something on the computer.

Don't understand how to do something? Forgotten a command? Accidentally pressed some keys that messed up your screen layout and you want to undo it? Most toolbars contain a ***Help command*—a command generating a table of contents, an index, and a search feature that can help you locate answers**, often on the web**.** In addition, many applications have *context-sensitive help,* which leads you to information about the task you're performing. *(• See Panel 3.11.)*

3.5 Common Operating Systems

The main operating systems for general computer users are Windows, Mac OS, and Unix/Linux.

The *platform* is the particular processor model and operating system on which a computer system is based. For example, there are "Mac platforms" (Apple Macintosh), "Windows platforms" and "PC platforms" (for personal computers such as Dell, Compaq, Lenovo, Gateway, and Hewlett-Packard, which run Microsoft Windows), and "Unix/Linux platforms," often used on large computer systems. (Note: Although all computers can be called "personal computers," "PC" still generally refers to Microsoft-based computers, because "PC" evolved from "PC-DOS" as described next.)

> **Survival Tip**
>
> **Getting Help**
>
> On Windows computers, you can find the Help area by pressing the *F1* key. Or use the mouse to click on *Start* in the lower left screen; then click on *Help.* On the Macintosh, Help is located under the main menu bar.

Despite the dominance of these platforms, some so-called *legacy systems* are still in use. A legacy system is an older, outdated, yet still functional technology, such as the *DOS operating system. DOS* (rhymes with "boss")—for *Disk Operating System*—was the original operating system produced by Microsoft

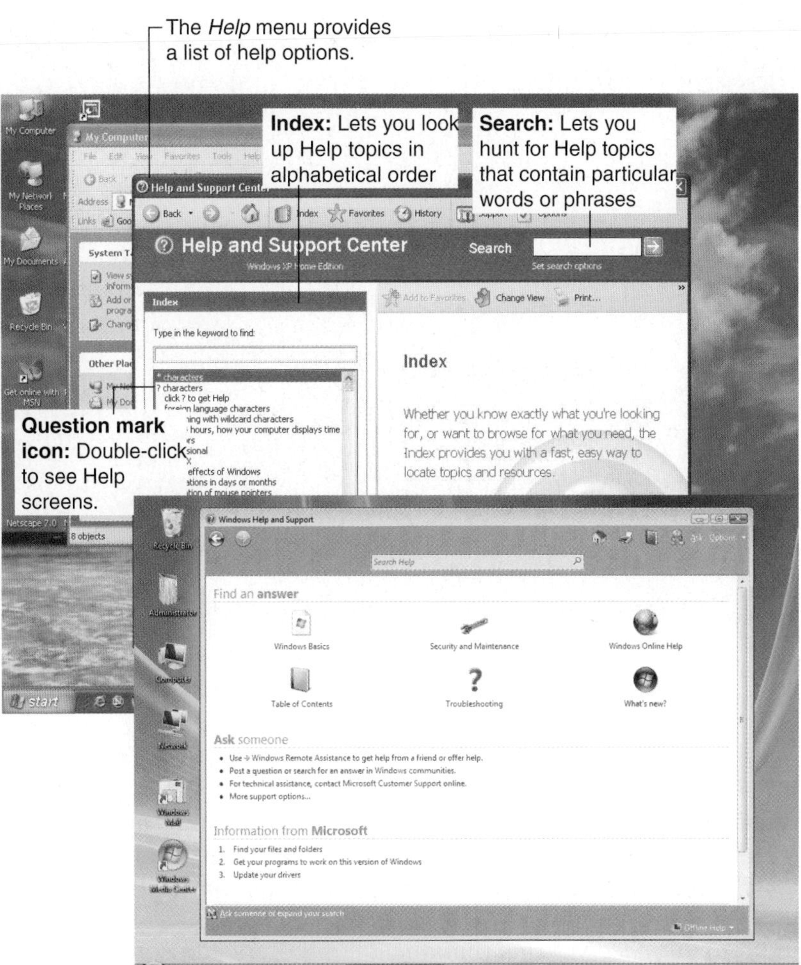

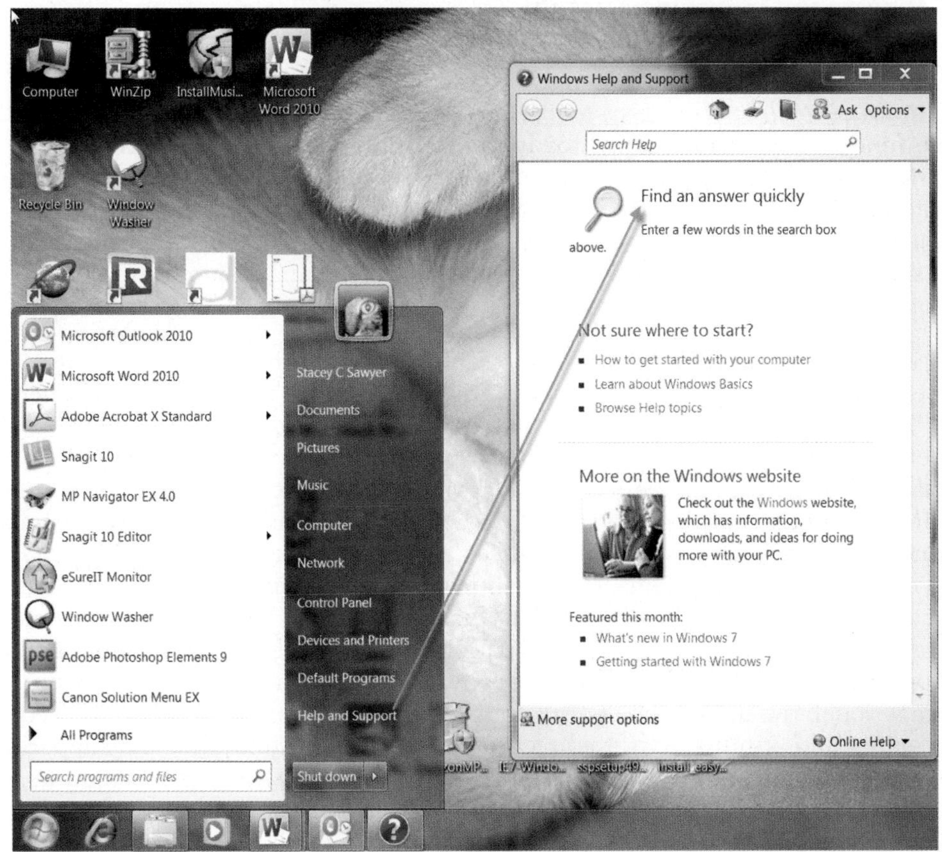

panel 3.11

Help features

(*Top*) The XP Help command yields a pull-down menu; (*bottom*) the Help screen for Windows 7, reached from the Start button at the bottom-left corner of the screen.

panel 3.12

DOS screen: command-line user interface

```
C:\WINDOWS\System32\cmd.exe
(C) Copyright 1985-2001 Microsoft Corp.

C:\Documents and Settings\Stacey C. Sawyer>
C:\Documents and Settings\Stacey C. Sawyer>DIR
 Volume in drive C has no label.
 Volume Serial Number is B0EB-7091

 Directory of C:\Documents and Settings\Stacey C. Sawyer

04/25/2003  07:14 PM    <DIR>          .
04/25/2003  07:14 PM    <DIR>          ..
03/01/2003  12:58 PM    <DIR>          .java
03/01/2003  12:58 PM    <DIR>          .jpi_cache
04/25/2003  07:17 PM             1,106 .plugin140_01.trace
08/23/2003  03:31 PM    <DIR>          Desktop
02/11/2003  11:35 AM               831 Eudora.lnk
08/23/2003  03:29 PM    <DIR>          Favorites
08/25/2003  11:48 AM    <DIR>          My Documents
08/25/2003  10:45 AM         3,145,728 ntuser.dat
07/17/2003  10:24 AM    <DIR>          Start Menu
02/28/2002  09:31 PM    <DIR>          WINDOWS
               3 File(s)      3,147,665 bytes
               9 Dir(s)  29,842,452,480 bytes free

C:\Documents and Settings\Stacey C. Sawyer>_
```

and had a hard-to-use command-driven user interface. *(● See Panel 3.12.)* Its initial 1982 version was designed to run on the IBM PC as PC-DOS. Later Microsoft licensed the same system to other computer makers as MS-DOS.

Here we briefly describe the principal platforms used on *single-user, standalone* computers today, both desktops and laptops: the Apple Macintosh OS and Microsoft Windows. We discuss operating systems for *networks* (servers) and for *embedded systems* (handheld computers and some consumer devices) in a few pages.

Macintosh Operating System

The Mac had a GUI before Windows did.

The *Macintosh operating system (Mac OS)*, which runs on Apple Macintosh computers, set the standard for icon-oriented, easy-to-use graphical user interfaces. Apple based its new interface on work done at Xerox, which in turn had based its work on early research at Stanford Research Institute (now SRI International). (See the timeline starting on page 170.) The software generated a strong legion of fans shortly after its launch in 1984 and inspired rival Microsoft to upgrade DOS to the more user-friendly Windows operating systems.

MAC OS X The Mac OS is *proprietary,* meaning that it is privately owned and controlled by a company. Some Mac users still use System 9, introduced in October 1999, which added an integrated search engine, updated the GUI, and improved networking services. The next version of the operating system, Mac OS X ("ex" or "10"), broke with 15 years of Mac software to use Unix (discussed shortly) to offer a dramatic new look and feel. *(● See Panel 3.13.)* Many Apple users claim that OS X won't allow software conflicts, a frequent headache with Microsoft's Windows operating systems. (For example, you might install a game and find that it interferes with the device driver for a sound card. Then, when you uninstall the game, the problem persists. With Mac OS X, when you try to install an application program that conflicts with any other program, the Mac simply won't allow you to run it.) Mac OS X also offers free universal email services, improved graphics and printing, improved security, easier ways to find files, and support for building and storing web pages. Also, new Macs can also support Windows, using a built-in utility called Boot Camp—meaning that it lets you boot up the computer using either the Mac OS or Windows.

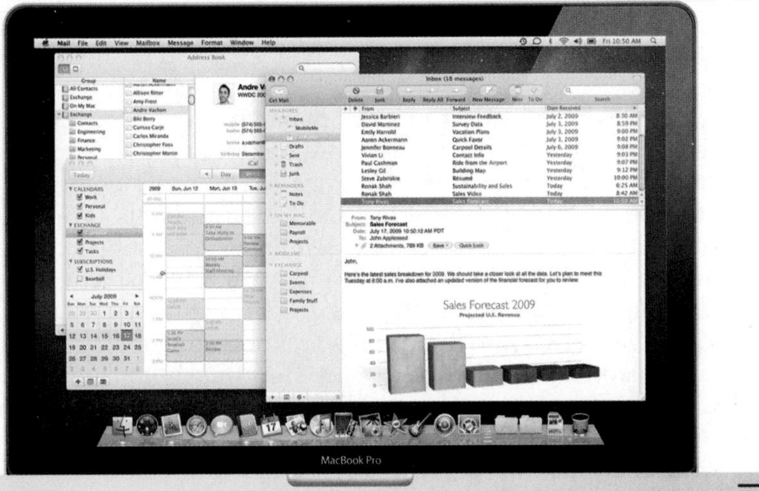

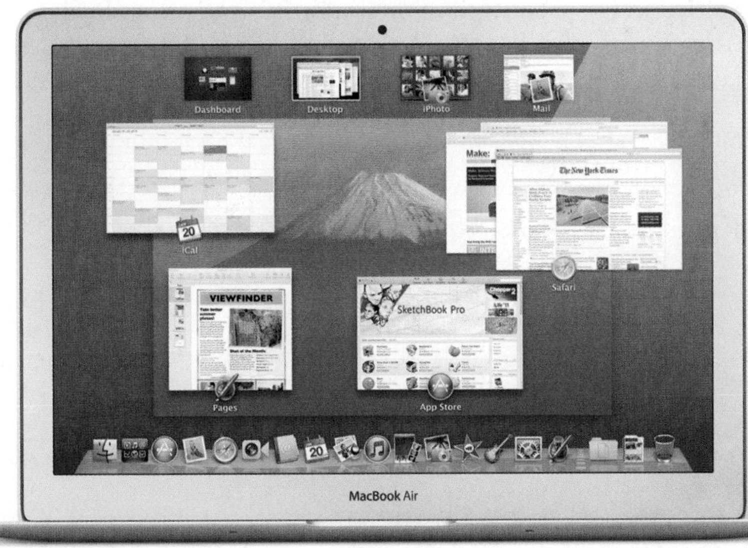

panel 3.13

Mac OS X screens—graphical user interface

Mac Apps

To see the wide variety of applications available to download for the Mac, go to:

www.apple.com/downloads/macosx/

The latest version of OS X, 10.7, or Lion, was released in 2010 and for now is available only via download or on a USB flash drive. Lion offers several new features, including increased support for gesture control of the computer via a multitouch screen. To take full advantage of all Lion's features, users must purchase applications written specifically for Lion.

As of 2011 Mac OS X is the second most popular general-purpose operating system in use (about 8%), after Microsoft Windows (about 85%). (● *See Panel 3.14.*)

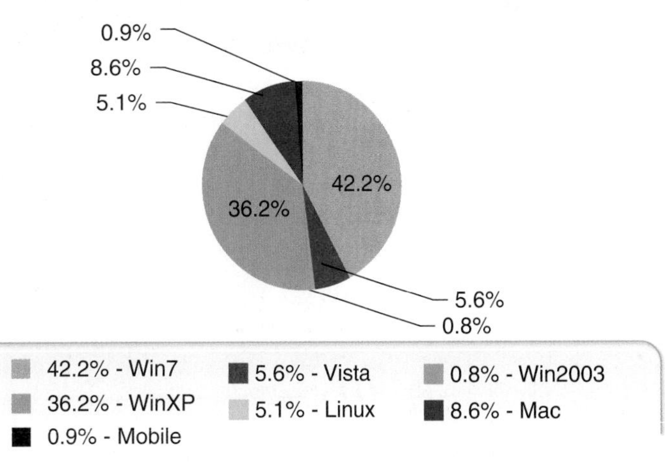

panel 3.14

OS market shares September 2011

(*www.w3schools.com/browsers/browsers_os.asp*)

WHERE IS MAC MOST POPULAR? Macintosh is considered king in areas such as desktop publishing and graphics, and Macs are still favored in many educational settings. For very specialized applications, most programs are written for the Windows platform. However, programs for games and for common business uses such as word processing and spreadsheets are also widely available for the Mac.

Note that many Macs can work with Microsoft PC (Windows) applications, such as Word.

Microsoft Windows

Another graphical user interface.

In the 1980s, taking its cue from the popularity of Mac's easy-to-use GUI, Microsoft began working on Windows to make DOS more user-friendly. Also a proprietary system, ***Microsoft Windows*** **is the most common operating system for desktop and portable PCs.** Early attempts (Windows 1.0, 2.0, 3.0) did not catch on. However, in 1992 *Windows 3.X* emerged as the preferred system among PC users. (Technically, Windows 3.X wasn't a full operating system; it was simply a layer or "shell" over DOS.)

Windows 3.X evolved into the *Windows 95* operating system, which was succeeded by *Windows 98* and *Windows Me* (for *Millennium Edition*). *Microsoft Windows XP*, introduced in 2001, combined elements of Windows networking software and Windows Me with a new GUI. *(• See Panel 3.15.)*

Windows Vista was introduced to consumers in January 2007. *(• See Panel 3.16.)* It is the equivalent of Windows version 12—preceded by 1.0, 2.0, 3.0, 3.1, NT, 95, NT 4.0, 98, 2000, ME, XP. So much computing power was required to run Vista that many people found their new PCs ran more slowly than their

Aerial view of Microsoft's Redmond, Washington, main corporate campus, which spreads over several square miles of the Seattle suburb.

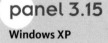

panel 3.15

Windows XP

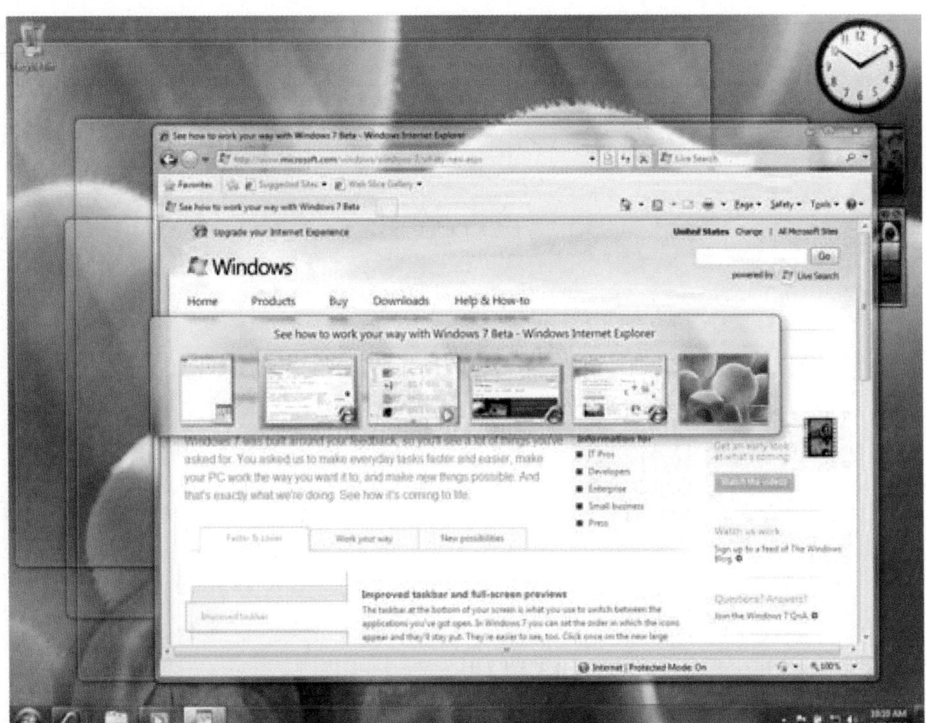

panel 3.16

Vista desktop screen showing a computer's various storage locations

older, less powerful XP machines. Vista was also criticized for software and hardware incompatibility issues with office suites and some printers, digital cameras, and other devices. So, many businesses decided that, given the downturn in the economy, they wouldn't be upgrading from XP to Vista, because they saw no value in it and because it required buying more powerful PCs and new software. To spur Vista sales, Microsoft announced it would stop selling Windows XP in June 2008. However, in spite of this change, Vista did not sell well, so Microsoft moved on to Windows 7.

Windows 7, currently the most widely used version of Microsoft Windows, was released during the 2009 holiday season. The new operating system supports iPhone-like touchscreen applications called Microsoft Surface, an alternative to the computer mouse. Thus, if you download the software for it, you can manipulate objects on the screen with your hands, such as enlarge and shrink photos or navigate a city map by stroking the screen. (• *See Panel 3.17, next page.)* Windows 7 is less power-hungry than Vista, boots up more quickly than previous Windows systems, and has improved networking and security features. It is used on desktops, laptops, notebooks, and tablets. Also, with the addition of Windows Media Center, you can turn your PC into a TV. (Windows 8 is expected to be released in 2012. Technology writers expect Windows 8 to move from the WIMP [windows, icons, menus, pointing devices) generation to the MPG (multitiouch, physics, and gestures) generation of computing, currently represented by Apple's OS X Lion operating system.)

A problem for any version of Windows, however, is that it builds on the same core architecture that represents more than 20 years of legacies. Some believe that Microsoft needs to do what Apple did when it introduced its Mac OS X in 2001: start over from scratch. Although this risked alienating some Macintosh users, since it forced them to buy new versions of their existing Mac applications software, it also made the system less vulnerable to crashes. "A monolithic operating system like Windows perpetuates an obsolete design," said one critic. "We don't need to load up our machines with bloated layers we won't use."[3]

Windows 7 comes in various versions:

- **Home Premium:** For general PC users; includes basic multimedia functions
- **Professional:** Mainly for small businesses but appropriate for the advanced home user; can run XP applications

Survival Tip

New Installation

Every time you install or reinstall Windows, you will have to get Microsoft's permission to activate it. You can do this over the Internet or via the phone.

Survival Tip

OEM

If you buy a computer with Windows (or any other operating system) already installed, the OS is called an *OEM (original equipment manufacturer) version*. If you buy your OS off the shelf, it is called a *retail version*. These two versions are almost identical, except an OEM version will install only on the *specific* machine for which it was intended. A retail version will install on any compatible machine. If you have an OEM version, you have to call the computer manufacturer, not the OS producer, for technical support. Because a retail version is not specifically tailored for your particular computer, Microsoft recommends that, before you buy a retail version of an OS, you run a compatibility check at its website (*http://support.microsoft.com*).

To explore Windows 7 on videos, go to:

www.microsoft.com/windows/explore/default.aspx

Windows 7 desktop screen
New feature: You can pin a program directly to the taskbar so you can open it quickly and conveniently, rather than looking for the program in the Start menu.

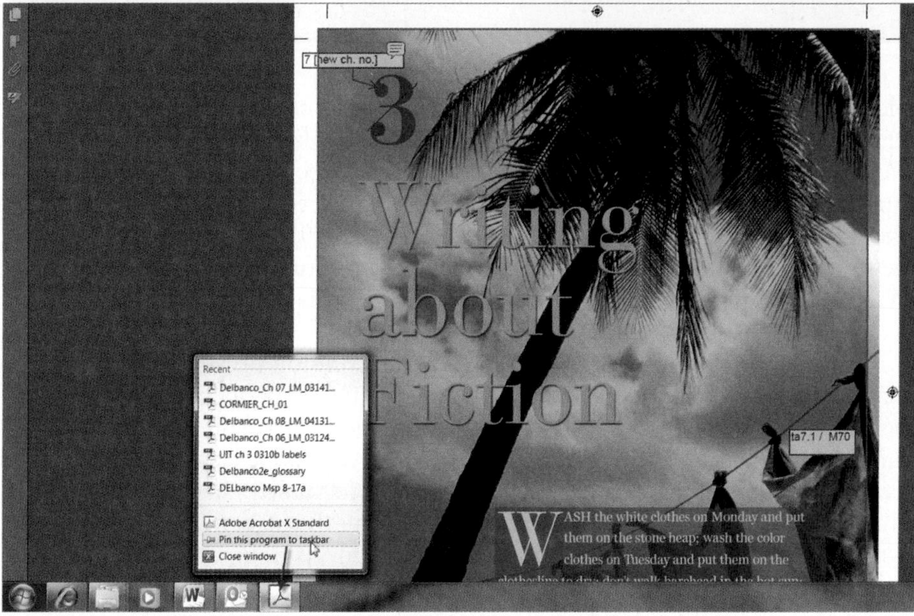

Windows vs. Mac

To compare Windows to the Mac, go to:

www.laptopmag.com/mobile-life/snow-leopard-vs-windows-7.aspx

www.guidenet.net/resources/win_vs_mac.html

http://windows.about.com/b/2010/02/05/windows-vs-mac-which-is-safer.htm

or do keyword searches for "Mac vs. Windows" and "Mac vs. PC."

- **Enterprise:** For multiuser businesses
- **Ultimate:** For advanced PC users, gamers, multimedia professionals; users can switch among 35 languages; can run XP applications

Network Operating Systems: OES, Windows Server, Unix, & Linux

Abbreviated NOS, a network operating system includes special functions for connecting computers and devices into a local-area network (LAN).

The operating systems described so far were principally designed for use with stand-alone desktop and laptop machines. Now let's consider the important operating systems designed to work with sizeable networks—OES, Windows Server, Unix/Solaris, and Linux.

NOVELL'S OPEN ENTERPRISE SERVER *NetWare,* now called *Open Enterprise Server (OES),* has long been a popular network operating system for coordinating microcomputer-based local area networks (LANs) throughout a company or a campus. LANs allow PCs to share programs, data files, and printers and other devices. A network OS is usually located on a main server (see Chapter 1, p. 27), which controls the connectivity of connected smaller networks and individual computers. Novell, the maker of OES, thrived as corporate data managers realized that networks of PCs could exchange information more cheaply than the previous generation of mainframes and midrange computers.

WINDOWS SERVER Windows desktop operating systems (XP/Vista/7) can be used to link PCs in small networks in homes and offices. However, something more powerful was needed to run the huge networks linking a variety of computers—PCs, workstations, mainframes—used by many companies, universities, and other organizations, which previously were served principally by Unix and NetWare operating systems. ***Microsoft Windows Server*** **is the company's multitasking operating system designed to run on network servers in businesses of all sizes.** It allows multiple users to share resources such as data, programs, and printers and to build web applications and connect to the Internet.

The Windows Server networking OS comes in various versions and some of its functions are built into XP, Vista, and Windows 7.

UNIX, SOLARIS, & BSD Unix (pronounced "*you*-nicks") was developed at AT&T's Bell Laboratories in 1969 as an operating system for minicomputers. By the 1980s AT&T entered into partnership with Sun Microsystems to develop a standardized version of Unix for sale to industry. Today ***Unix*** **is a proprietary multitasking operating system for multiple users that has built-in networking capability and versions that can run on all kinds of computers.** (Note: it is a common misconception that Unix is open-source software [p. 146]; only a few versions of Unix-like OSs are open source.) It is used mostly on mainframes, workstations, and servers, rather than on microcomputers. Government agencies, universities, research institutions, large corporations, and banks commonly use Unix for everything from designing airplane parts to currency trading. Because it is particularly stable and reliable, Unix is also used for website management and runs the backbone of the Internet. The developers of the Internet built their communications system around Unix because it has the ability to keep large systems (with hundreds of processors) churning out transactions day in and day out for years without fail.

- **Versions of Unix:** Sun Microsystem's *Solaris* is a version of Unix that is popular for handling large e-commerce servers and large websites. Another interesting variant is *BSD,* free software derived from Unix. BSD began in the 1970s in the computer science department of the University of California, Berkeley, when students and staff began to develop their own derivative of Unix, known as the Berkeley Software Distribution, or BSD. And there are many other versions of Unix. Like MS-DOS, Unix uses a command-line interface (but the commands are different for each system). (● *See Panel 3.18.*) Some companies market Unix systems with graphical interface shells that make Unix easier to use.

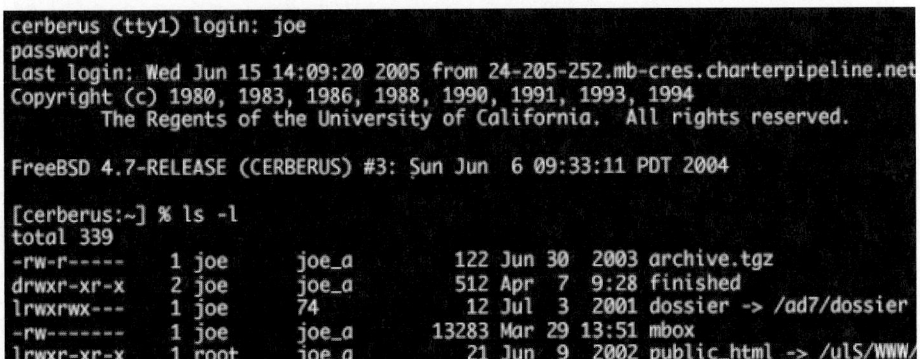

```
cerberus (tty1) login: joe
password:
Last login: Wed Jun 15 14:09:20 2005 from 24-205-252.mb-cres.charterpipeline.net
Copyright (c) 1980, 1983, 1986, 1988, 1990, 1991, 1993, 1994
        The Regents of the University of California.  All rights reserved.

FreeBSD 4.7-RELEASE (CERBERUS) #3: Sun Jun  6 09:33:11 PDT 2004

[cerberus:~] % ls -l
total 339
-rw-r-----    1 joe      joe_a          122 Jun 30  2003 archive.tgz
drwxr-xr-x    2 joe      joe_a          512 Apr  7  9:28 finished
lrwxrwx---    1 joe      74              12 Jul  3  2001 dossier -> /ad7/dossier
-rw-------    1 joe      joe_a        13283 Mar 29 13:51 mbox
lrwxr-xr-x    1 root     joe_a           21 Jun  9  2002 public_html -> /ulS/WWW/
```

panel 3.18

Partial Unix screen

Some Common Unix Commands

^h, [backspace]	erase previously typed character
^u	erase entire line of input typed so far
cp	copy files
whoami	who is logged on to this terminal
mkdir	make new directory
mv	change name of directory
mail	read/send email
gzip, gunzip	compress, recompress a file
lpr	send file to printer
wc	count characters, words, and lines in a file
head	show first few lines of a file
tail	show last few lines of a file
find	find files that match certain criteria

LINUX It began in 1991 when programmer Linus Torvalds, a graduate student in Finland, posted his free Linux operating system on the Internet. Linux (pronounced "*linn*-uks") is the rising star of network software. ***Linux*** **is a free (nonproprietary) version of Unix, and its continual improvements result from the efforts of tens of thousands of volunteer programmers.** *(• See Panel 3.19.)* Whereas Windows Server is Microsoft's proprietary product, Linux is ***open-source software*****—meaning any programmer can download it from the Internet for free and modify it with suggested improvements.** The only qualification is that changes can't be copyrighted; they must be made available to all and remain in the public domain.

panel 3.19

Linux screen (Linux Mint)

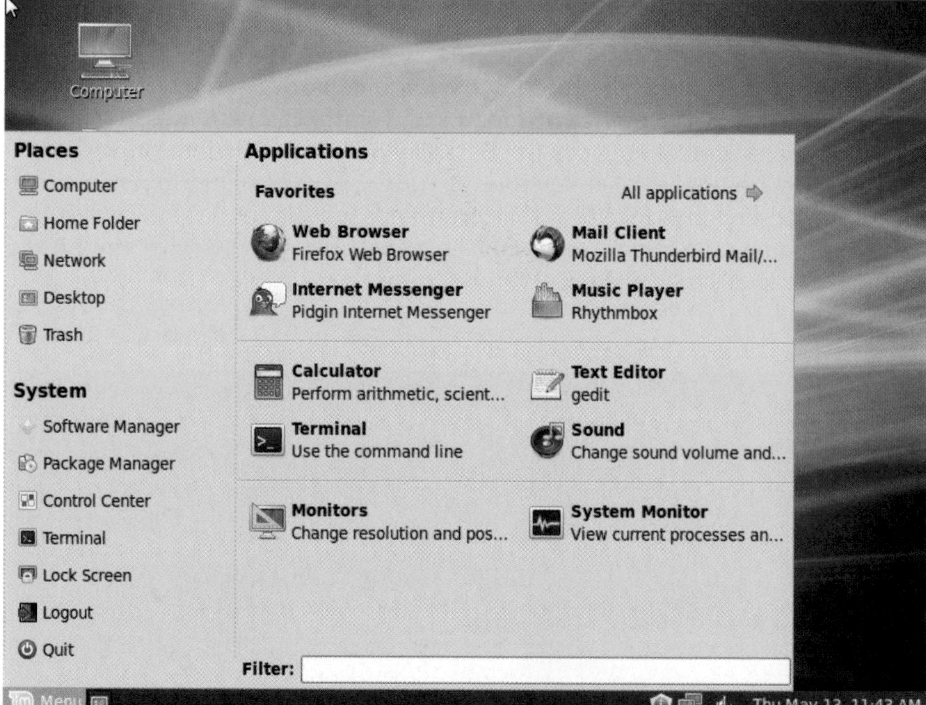

Linux is available with a command-line interface or a GUI. It is used on a wide range of computers and devices, including mobile phones. It is a leading server operating system and runs some of the fastest supercomputers in the world.

- **Linux and China:** In 2000 the People's Republic of China announced that it was adopting Linux as a national standard for operating systems because it feared being dominated by the OS of a company of a foreign power—namely, Microsoft. In 2005 Red Flag Software Company, Ltd., the leading developer of Linux software in China, joined the Open Source Development Labs, a global consortium dedicated to accelerating the adoption of Linux in the business world. In 2007 OSDL and the Free Standards Group merged to form The Linux Foundation (*http://osdl.org/en/Main_Page*), narrowing their respective focuses to that of promoting Linux in competition with Microsoft Windows.

more info!

China's Red Flag

To learn more about China's Red Flag Software Company, go to:

www.redflag-linux.com/en/

http://en.wikipedia.org/wiki/Red_Flag_Linux

- **The permutations of Linux:** If Linux belongs to everyone, how do companies such as Red Hat Software—a company that bases its business on Linux—make money? Their strategy is to give away the software but then sell services and support. Red Hat, for example, makes available an inexpensive application software package that offers word processing, spreadsheets, email support, and the like for users of its PC OS version. It also offers more powerful versions of its Linux OS for small and medium-size businesses, along with applications, networking capabilities, and support services.

- **Google Chrome and Android:** In late 2008 Google launched its Chrome Internet browser. Based on Linux, this browser is intended for people who do most of their computer activities on the web. However, most of the operating systems that computers run on were designed in an era when there was no web; so in July 2009 Google introduced the Chrome OS. This operating system is a lightweight, open-source Linux-based system with a new windowing arrangement that has initially been targeted at netbooks. The user interface is minimal, and Internet connection is fast and secure. As with Chrome, this OS has been created for people who spend most of their computer time on the web. Chrome does not support Microsoft Office, which will limit its usability in business, educational, and professional environments, but it does support OpenOffice, Google email, Google Docs, and cloud computing. Also, Google has developed the Linux-based Android OS for mobile phones and netbooks.

Chrome

For a video on how Google Chrome OS works, go to:

www.youtube.com/watch?v=0QRO3gKj3qw

- **Ubuntu & Debian:** Dell Computers offers a Linux-based operating system, Ubuntu (the Zulu word for "humanity"), on some of its products. The Debian Project is an association of individuals who created the free operating system called Debian GNU/Linux, or simply Debian for short. Debian comes with over 29,000 applications—all of it free. Debian will run on almost all personal computers, including most older models; it is used by a wide range of organizations, large and small, as well as many thousands of individuals.

- **Linux in the future:** Because it was originally built for use on the Internet, Linux is more reliable than Windows for online applications. Hence, it is better suited to run websites and e-commerce software. Its real growth, however, may come as it reaches outward to other applications and, possibly, replaces Windows in many situations. IBM, Red Hat, Motorola Computing, Panasonic, Sony, and many other companies have formed the nonprofit, vendor-neutral Embedded Linux Consortium, which now, as part of The Linux Foundation, is working to make Linux a top operating system of choice for developers designing embedded systems, as we discuss next.

More on OS Comparisons

For more details on OS comparisons, go to:

www.operating-system.org/

www.pcmag.com/category2/0,2806,2362,00.asp

The three major microcomputer operating systems are compared in the box on the next page. (● *See Panel 3.20.)*

panel 3.20

Brief OS comparison

Windows	Linux	Mac OS X
Pros:	*Pros:*	*Pros:*
Runs on a wide range of hardware	Is very stable and can be easily updated.	Easy to install
Has largest market share	Runs on a wide range of hardware	Best GUI
Has many built-in utilities	Has largest number of user interface types	Secure and stable
Cons:	Can be used as server or desktop PC open source software; anyone can fix bugs	*Cons:*
Security problems	*Cons:*	Fewer applications are available for the Mac than for Windows.
Not efficient used as a server OS	Limited support for games	Base hardware more expensive than other platforms
Have to reboot every time a network configuration is changed	Limited commercial applications available	Fewer utilities available
Proprietary software; only company programmers can fix bugs	Can be difficult to learn	Fewer games than for Windows
		Proprietary software; only company programmers can fix bugs

Rules for Upgrading Your Operating System

http://blog.macsales.com/1411-the-golden-rules-of-upgrading-tips-from-the-owc-technical-support-team

www.youtube.com/watch?v=T2xnLpuAyCE

www.ehow.com/how_2157557_upgrade-computers-operating-system.html

Embedded Systems

For updates on smartphone OSs try:

www.palm.com/us/products/phones/

www.android.com/

www.apple.com/ios/

http://us.blackberry.com/apps-software/blackberry6/

www.symbianos.org/intro

http://windows.microsoft.com/en-US/windows/products/windows-phone

Embedded Operating Systems for Handhelds

In general, embedded operating systems are used in small or specialized devices.

An ***embedded system*** (also called a real-time operating system) **is any electronic system that uses a CPU chip but that is not a general-purpose workstation, desktop, or laptop computer. It is a specialized computer system that is part of a larger system or a machine.** Embedded systems are used, for example, in automobiles, planes, trains, toasters, coffee machines, traffic lights, barcode scanners, fuel pumps, space vehicles, machine tools, watches, appliances, cellphones, MP3 players, PDAs, high-definition TV, and robots. Handheld computers and personal digital assistants also rely on specialized operating systems. Such operating systems include Android, Symbian, Apple iPhone, Windows Phone, BlackBerry OS, Palm OS, Embedded Linux, and many others.

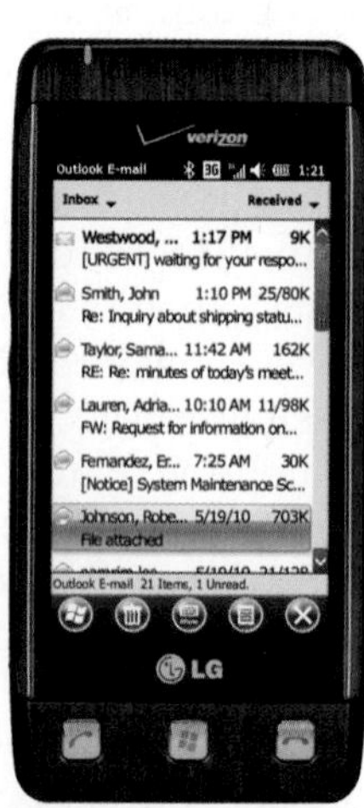

Droid Pro, Apple iPhone, and LG Fathom Windows phone

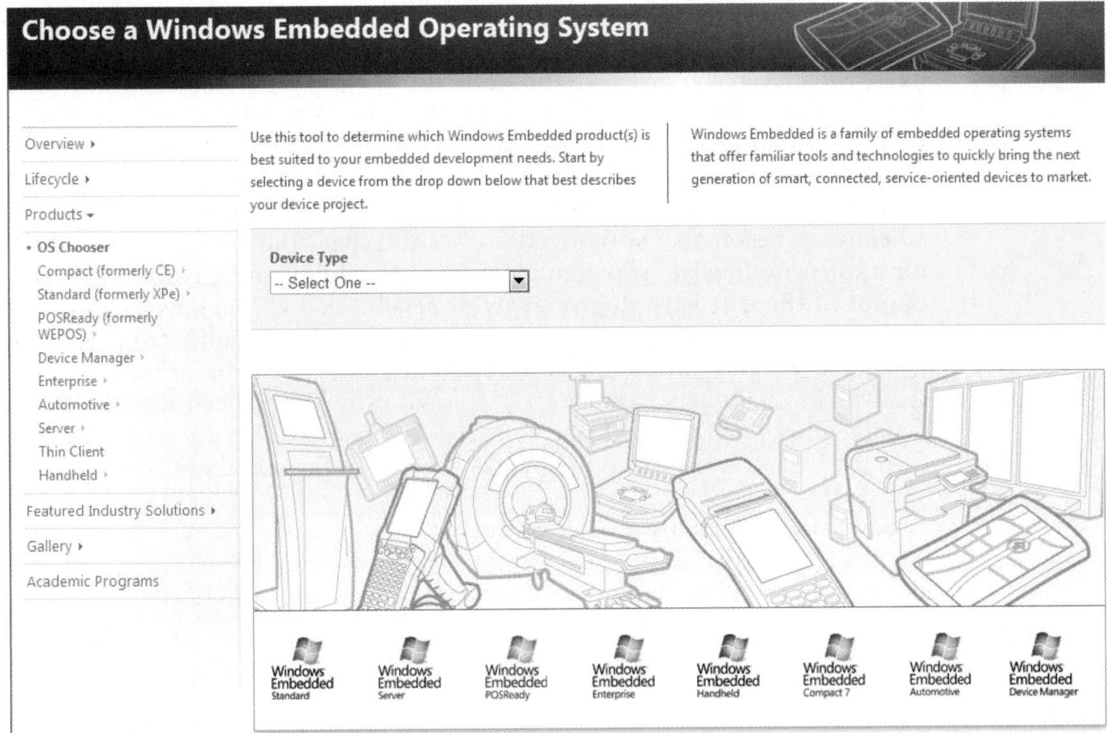

3.6 APPLICATION SOFTWARE: Getting Started

Application software comprises the programs that do the work that users are directly interested in.

Application software is designed to enable users to accomplish specific tasks—whether related to serious work or to entertainment. But before we discuss some of the common types of application software, we cover the ways to obtain application software—issues of licensure.

For Sale, For Free, or For Rent?

Software licensing protects the copyright by placing restrictions on the user.

Although most people pay for application software—popular brands that they can use with similar programs owned by their friends and coworkers—it's possible to rent programs or get them free. (• *See Panel 3.21.*) Let's consider these categories.

COMMERCIAL SOFTWARE *Commercial software,* also called *proprietary software* or *packaged software,* is software that's offered for sale, such as Microsoft Word, Microsoft Office, or Adobe PhotoShop. Although some such software

panel 3.21

Choices among application software

Types	Definition
Commercial software	Copyrighted. If you don't pay for it, you can be prosecuted.
Public-domain software	Not copyrighted. You can copy it for free without fear of prosecution.
Shareware	Copyrighted. Available free, but you should pay to continue using it.
Freeware	Copyrighted. Available free.
Rentalware	Copyrighted. Lease for a fee.

may have been preinstalled on your new PC and may not show up on the bill of sale when you buy it, you've paid for it as part of the purchase. And, most likely, whenever you order a new game or other commercial program, you'll have to pay for it. This software is copyrighted. A *copyright* is the exclusive legal right that prohibits copying of intellectual property without the permission of the copyright holder.

Software manufacturers don't sell you their software; rather, they sell you a license to become an authorized user of it. What's the difference? In paying for a ***software license***, **you sign a contract in which you agree not to make copies of the software to give away or resell.** That is, you have bought only the company's permission to use the software and not the software itself. This legal nicety allows the company to retain its rights to the program and limits the way its customers can use it. The small print in the licensing agreement usually allows you to make one copy *(backup copy* or *archival copy)* for your own use. (Each software company has a different license; there is no industry standard.)

Several types of software licenses exist:

- *Site licenses* allow the software to be used on all computers at a specific location.
- *Concurrent-use licenses* allow a certain number of copies of the software to be used at the same time.
- *A multiple-user license* specifies the number of people who may use the software.
- *A single-user license* limits software use to one user at a time.

Important: Use of the enclosed software is subject to the license agreement included on this CD-ROM. You must read and agree to these terms and conditions before using the software. Any other use, copying, or distribution of the software is strictly prohibited.

Part of a software license

Most personal computer software licenses allow you to run the program on only one to three personal machines and make copies of the software only for personal backup purposes. If you buy software in shrink-wrapped packages, once you have opened the shrink-wrap, you have accepted the terms of the software license. When you download software, you will be required to check boxes next to licensure statements, indicating that you have accepted the licensing conditions.

Every year or so, software developers find ways to enhance their products and put forth new versions or new releases. A *version* is a major upgrade in a software product, traditionally indicated by numbers such as 1.0, 2.0, 3.0—for example, Adobe 9.0 and Adobe 10.0. More recently, other notations have been used. After 1995 Microsoft labeled its Windows and Office software versions by year instead of by number, as in Microsoft's Office 2000, Office 2003, Office 2007, and Office 2010. A *release,* which now may be called an "add" or "addition," is a minor upgrade. Often this is indicated by a change in number after the decimal point. (For instance, 8.0 may become 8.1, 8.2, and so on.) Some releases are now also indicated by the year in which they are marketed. And, unfortunately, some releases are not clearly indicated at all. (These are "patches," which may be downloaded from the software maker's website, as can version updates.) Once you have purchased an application, the manufacturer will usually allow you to download small patches for free but will charge for major new versions.

More recently, Apple Inc. has enjoyed huge success with its online App Store, offering more than 350,000 downloadable applications ("apps") for the iPhone, iPad, and iPod and more than 1,000 applications for the Mac computer. Other "stores" offering downloadable applications are BlackBerry App World, Google Android Market, Palm OS Apps Store, and Microsoft's Windows Phone.

For information on public domain software and where to obtain it, go to:

www.gnu.org/philosophy/categories.html

www.webcrawler.com/webcrawler301/ws/results/web/public+domain+software/1/417/topnavigation/relevance/iq=true/zoom=off/_iceurlflag=7?_iceurl=true&gclid=ckik1ifjspscfrwdagodtafvpa

PUBLIC-DOMAIN SOFTWARE ***Public-domain software*** **is not protected by copyright and thus may be duplicated by anyone at will.** Public-domain programs—sometimes developed by government agencies or universities—have been donated to the public by their creators. They are often available through sites on the Internet. You can download and duplicate public-domain software without fear of legal prosecution.

SHAREWARE ***Shareware* is copyrighted software that is distributed free of charge, but users are required to make a monetary contribution, or pay a registration fee, to continue using it**—in other words, you can try it before you buy it. Once you pay the fee, you usually get supporting documentation, access to updated versions, and perhaps some technical support. Shareware is distributed primarily through the Internet, but because it is copyrighted, you cannot use it to develop your own program that would compete with the original product. If you copy shareware and pass it along to friends, they are expected to pay the registration fee also, if they choose to use the software.

Shareware & Freeware

What kinds of shareware and freeware are available? To find out, go to:

www.searchalot.com/?p=&q=shareware

www.searchalot.com/?p=&q=freeware

www.shareware.com

www.tucows.com

www.freewarehome.com

www.download.com

FREEWARE ***Freeware* is copyrighted software that is distributed free of charge,** today most often over the Internet. Why would any software creator let his or her product go for free? Sometimes developers want to see how users respond, so that they can make improvements in a later version. Sometimes they want to further some scholarly or humanitarian purpose—for instance, to create a standard for software on which people are apt to agree. In its most recent form, freeware is made available by companies trying to make money some other way—actually, by attracting viewers to their advertising. (The web browsers Internet Explorer and Mozilla Firefox are of this type.) Freeware developers generally retain all rights to their programs; technically, you are not supposed to duplicate and redistribute the programs. (Freeware is different from free software, or public-domain software, which has no restrictions on use, modification, or redistribution.)

RENTALWARE: ONLINE SOFTWARE ***Rentalware* is online software that users lease for a fee and download whenever they want it.** This is the concept behind *application service providers (ASPs)*, or *software-as-a-service (SaaS) technology,* the idea of leasing software over the Internet. The ASP stores the software on its servers and supplies users with support and other services. Today online software accounts for only a small part of business-software sales, but it could represent the wave of the future, because it frees businesses from having to buy computer servers and hire a staff to maintain them. Some business owners find that present-day online software isn't as good as the traditional software available. However, online software represents a stage in what in Chapter 1 we called "cloud computing," the idea of obtaining computing resources from the network of computers sitting beyond a user's own four walls.[4] Some experts believe that future software is more apt to be available in a variety of ways: through traditional licensing, through online rentalware, through ad-supported online means, and even through open-source means.

More about ASPs

If you want to learn more about ASPs, go to:

www.aspnews.com

www.business.com/directory/internet_and_online/application_service_providers_asps/

http://dir.yahoo.com/business_and_economy/business_to_business/communications_and_networking/internet_and_world_wide_web/application_service_providers__asps_/

PIRATED SOFTWARE ***Pirated software* is software obtained illegally,** as when you get a CD/DVD from a friend who has made an illicit copy of, say, a commercial video game. Sometimes pirated software can be downloaded off the Internet. Sometimes it is sold in retail outlets in foreign countries. If you buy such software, not only do the original copyright owners not get paid for their creative work, but you risk getting inferior goods and, worse, picking up a virus. To discourage software piracy, many software manufacturers, such as Microsoft, require that users register their software when they install it on their computers. If the software is not registered, it will not work properly.

ABANDONWARE "Abandonware" does not refer to a way to obtain software. It refers to software that is no longer being sold or supported by its publisher. U.S. copyright laws state that copyrights owned by corporations are valid for up to 95 years from the date the software was first published. Copyrights are not considered abandoned even if they are no longer enforced. Therefore, abandoned software does not enter the public domain just because it is no longer supported. Don't copy it.

Make the switch to Access 2010
Make the switch to PowerPoint 2010
Make the switch to SharePoint 2010

Office 2010 online training

Access 2010 | Outlook 2010 | SharePoint 2010
Excel 2010 | PowerPoint 2010 | SharePoint Workspace 2010
OneNote 2010 | Project 2010 | Visio 2010
Word 2010

Office 2007 online training

Access 2007 | OneNote 2007 | Publisher 2007
Communicator 2007 | Outlook 2007 | SharePoint Server 2007
Excel 2007 | PowerPoint 2007 | Visio 2007
Live Meeting 2007 | Project 2007 | Word 2007

Office 2003 online training

Access 2003 | OneNote 2003 | Publisher 2003
Excel 2003 | Outlook 2003 | Visio 2003
FrontPage 2003 | PowerPoint 2003 | Word 2003
InfoPath 2003 | Project 2003

Tutorial: Microsoft Office training for versions 2010, 2007, and 2003

CUSTOM SOFTWARE Occasionally companies or individuals need software written specifically for them, to meet unique needs. This software is called *custom software,* and it's created by software engineers and programmers.

Tutorials & Documentation

Application software documentation is the same as a user's manual; tutorials, often on video, take you through practice learning sessions.

How are you going to learn a given software program? Most commercial packages come with tutorials and documentation.

TUTORIALS A *tutorial* is an instruction book or program that helps you learn to use the product by taking you through a prescribed series of steps. For instance, our publisher offers several how-to books that enable you to learn different kinds of software. Tutorials may also be included in the software package.

For information on new and unusual software applications and where to obtain them, go to:

www.appscout.com/about_appscout/

DOCUMENTATION *Documentation* is all information that describes a product to users, including a user guide or reference manual that provides a narrative and graphical description of a program. Although documentation may be print-based, today it is usually available on CD, as well as downloaded from the Internet. Documentation may be instructional, but features and functions are usually grouped by category for reference purposes. For example, in word processing documentation, all features related to printing are grouped together so that you can easily look them up.

A Few Facts about Files & the Usefulness of Importing & Exporting

Program files contain software instructions that process data; data files contain the data that program files use. There are several types of data files—three common ones are document, spreadsheet, and database files—and you will often have to import and export them.

Before we discuss some of the commonly used application software types, we need to briefly discuss file types. (A bit more detail is given at the end of the chapter, in Section 3.11.)

There is only one reason for having application software: to take raw data and manipulate it into useful files of information. A *file,* as we said earlier, is (1) a program (program file) (p. 124) that exists in a computer's secondary storage, such as hard disk, flash drive, or CD/DVD, or (2) a named collection of data (data file).

Program files **are files containing excutable software instructions.** Examples are word processing or spreadsheet programs, which are made up of several different program files. The two most important are source program files and executable files.

Source program files contain high-level computer instructions in the original form written by the programmer. Some source program files have the extension of the language in which they are written, such as *.bas* for BASIC, *.pas* for Pascal, or *.jav* for Java.

For the processor to use source program instructions, they must be translated into an *executable file*, which contains the instructions that tell the computer how to perform a particular task. You can identify an executable file by its extension, *.exe* or *.com*. You use an executable file by running it—as when you select Microsoft Excel from your on-screen menu and run it. (There are some executable files, called *runtime libraries*, that you cannot run—other programs cause them to execute. These are identified by such extensions as *.dll* [dynamic link library], *.drv* [*driver file*], *.ocx* [*object control extension*], *.sys* [*system file*], and *.vbx* [*Visual Basic extension*].) (Extensions are covered in more detail at the end of the chapter.)

***Data files* are files that contain data—**words, numbers, pictures, sounds, and so on. Unlike program files, data files don't instruct the computer to do anything. Rather, data files are there to be acted on by program files. Some data files are readable only by the software application that created them, whereas other data files (such as *.txt*, or "text," files) can be accessed by many different software applications.

THREE TYPES OF DATA FILES Three well-known types of data files are these:

- **Document files:** Document files are created by word processing programs and consist of documents such as reports, letters, memos, and term papers. (For example, *.doc* and *.docx* files are created by Microsoft Word.)
- **Workbook files:** Workbook files are created by electronic spreadsheets and usually consist of collections of numerical data such as budgets, sales forecasts, and schedules. (For instance, *.xls* files are created by Microsoft Excel spreadsheet software.)
- **Database files:** Database files are created by database management programs and consist of organized data that can be analyzed and displayed in various useful ways. Examples are student names and addresses that can be displayed according to age, grade-point average, or home state. (For example, *.mdb* files are created by Microsoft Access.)

EXCHANGING FILES: IMPORTING & EXPORTING It's useful to know that often files can be exchanged—that is, imported and exported—between programs.

- **Importing: *Importing* is defined as getting data from another source and then converting it into a format compatible with the program in which you are currently working.** For example, you might write a letter in your word processing program and include in it—that is, import—a column of numbers from your spreadsheet program. The ability to import data is very important in software applications because it means that one application can complement another.
- **Exporting: *Exporting* is defined as transforming data into a format that can be used in another program and then transmitting it.** For example, you might work up a list of names and addresses in your database program and then send it—export it—to a document you wrote in your word processing program. Exporting implies that the sending application reformats the data for the receiving application; importing implies that the receiving application does the reformatting.

Types of Application Software

There are many types of application software; productivity software is the type used in business and in many educational situations.

Application software can be classified in many ways—for entertainment, personal, education/reference, productivity, and specialized uses. *(● See Panel 3.22.)*

In the rest of this chapter we discuss types of ***productivity software*****—such as word processing programs, spreadsheets, and database managers—whose purpose is to make users more productive at particular tasks.** Some productivity software comes in the form of an *office suite,* which bundles several applications together into a single large package. Microsoft Office, for example, includes (among other things) Word, Excel, PowerPoint, and Access—word processing, spreadsheet, presentation, and database programs, respectively. (Office is available for both the PC and the Mac platforms.) Corel Corp. offers similar programs, such as the WordPerfect word processing program. Other productivity software, such as Lotus Notes, is sold as *groupware*—online software that allows several people to collaborate on the same project and share some resources. Google offers a free suite of applications called Google Apps (from *www.google.com/apps*).

Note that all these types of programs must be *installed* on your computer before you can use them. For example, if you buy Microsoft Office, you need to install it on your computer before you can run any of the included programs such as Word or Excel. You can install software from a CD or DVD, an external hard drive, or a networked computer, or install a downloaded version from the Internet.

panel 3.22

Some types of application software

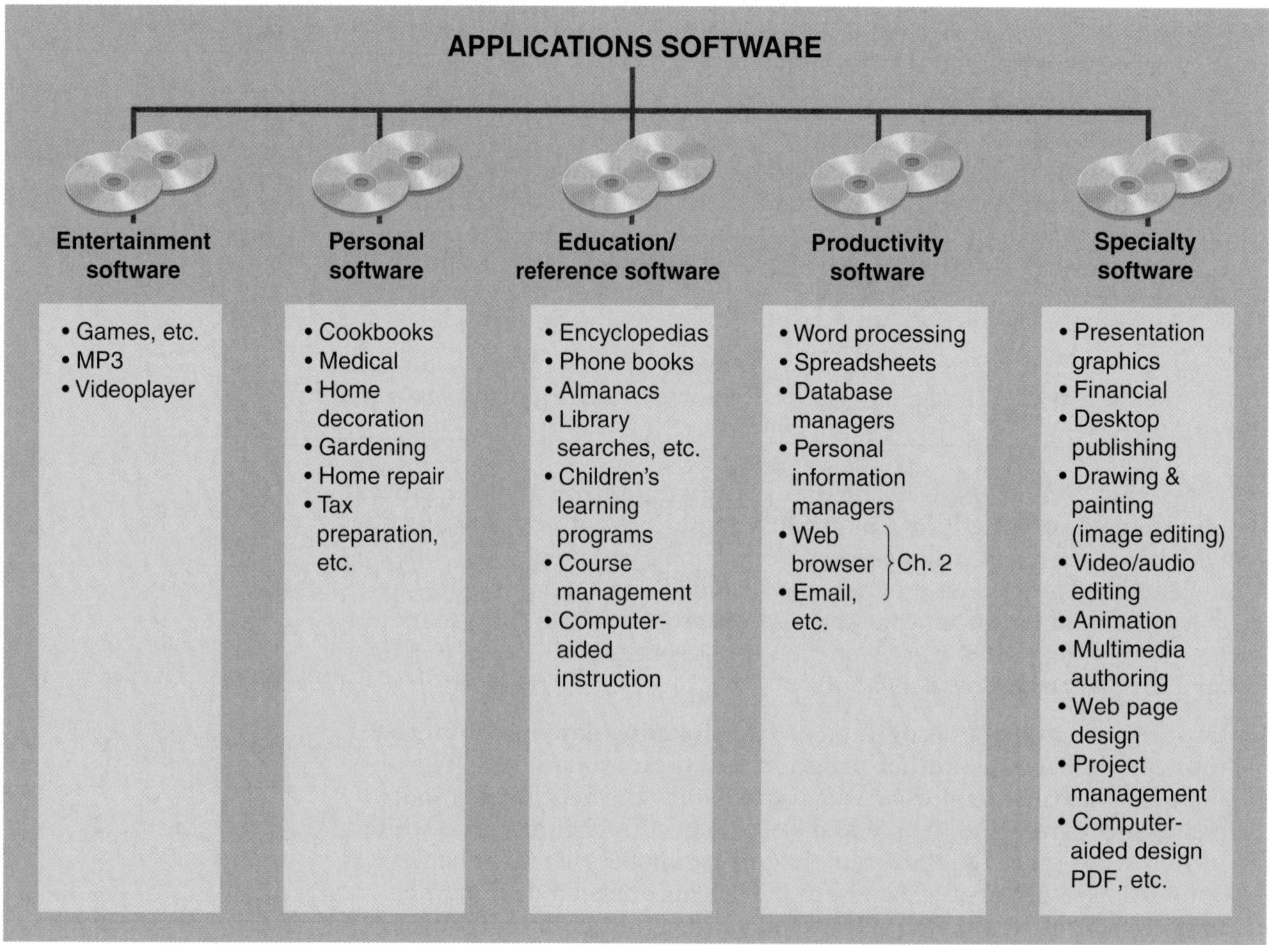

Installing a software program writes the necessary data instructions for running the program on your hard drive. Often the installer program will decompress the data included with the installer immediately before writing the information to your hard drive. Software updates, which are typically downloaded from the Internet, work the same way. When you run the update, the installer file decompresses the data and then updates the correct program.

Installing software is usually a simple process. It involves double-clicking an installer icon and then clicking "I Agree" when the license agreement displays. You may have to choose what directory on your hard disk you would like to install the software in, but often the installer will choose that for you. A *clean install* is a software installation in which any previous version is erased. The alternative to a clean install is an *upgrade*, in which elements of the previous version remain and new elements are added. An upgrade is typically less expensive, but because some elements of the earlier version remain, any existing problems may remain as well, and new compatibility-related issues may arise. A clean install should make the computer's software run like new.

We now consider the three most important types of productivity software: word processing, spreadsheet, and database software (including personal information managers). We then discuss more specialized software: presentation graphics, financial, desktop-publishing, drawing and painting, project management, computer-aided design, web page design, image/video/audio editing, and animation software.

more info!

Software Installation Basics

http://windows.microsoft.com/en-US/windows-vista/Install-a-program

www.installsoftware.com/

http://support.apple.com/kb/HT1148

OpenOffice.org · home of the world's leading open-source office suite

Why OpenOffice.org

Why | Great Software | Easy to use | and it's free

Great Software...
... Easy to Use ...
... and it's Free!
OpenOffice.org

OpenOffice.org 3 is the leading **open-source office software suite** for **word processing, spreadsheets, presentations, graphics, databases** and more. It is available in **many languages** and works on all **common computers**. It stores all your data in an **international open standard format** and can also read and write files from other common office software packages. It can be downloaded and used completely **free of charge** for **any purpose**.

Get OpenOffice.org 3 now

Governments

Education

Businesses

Not for profits

IT Businesses

F/OSS advocates

Great software

OpenOffice.org 3 is the result of over twenty years' software engineering. Designed from the start as a single piece of software, it has a consistency other products cannot match. A completely open development process means that anyone can report bugs, request new features, or enhance the software. The result: OpenOffice.org 3 does everything you want your office software to do, the way you

Easy to use

OpenOffice.org 3 is easy to learn, and if you're already using another office software package, you'll take to OpenOffice.org 3 straight away. Our world-wide native-language community means that OpenOffice.org 3 is probably available and supported in your own language. And if you already have files from another office package - OpenOffice.org 3 will probably read them with no difficulty.

and it's free

Best of all, OpenOffice.org 3 can be downloaded and used entirely free of any licence fees. OpenOffice.org 3 is released under the LGPL licence. This means you may use it for any purpose - domestic, commercial, educational, public administration. You may install it on as many computers as you like. You may make copies and give them away to family, friends, students, employees - anyone you like.

more info!

OpenOffice

Commercial Office suites are fairly expensive—but there is a free alternative, available for a number of different OSs: OpenOffice.org (*www.openoffice.org*). It can read most other file formats, including Microsoft Office, and it has most of the same features as MS Office.

3.7 Word Processing Software

Word processing mostly involves the creation of text documents.

Word processing software **allows you to use computers to create, edit, format, print, and store text material,** among other things. Word processing is the most common software application. The best-known word processing program is Microsoft Word, but there are others, such as Corel WordPerfect, Apple iWork Pages, Google Apps (a free download from *www.google.com/apps),* and Zoho Writer (a free download from *www.zoho.com*). There is even a full-fledged office suite for word processing, known as Quickoffice, that can be used on Android phones, Apple iPhones, BlackBerries, and Symbian OS devices. Word processing software allows users to work through a document and *delete, insert,* and *replace* text, the principal edit/correction activities. It also offers such additional features as *creating, formatting, printing,* and *saving.*

Of course, creating a document means entering text using the keyboard or the dictation function associated with speech-recognition software. Word processing software has three features that affect this process—the *cursor, scrolling,* and *word wrap.*

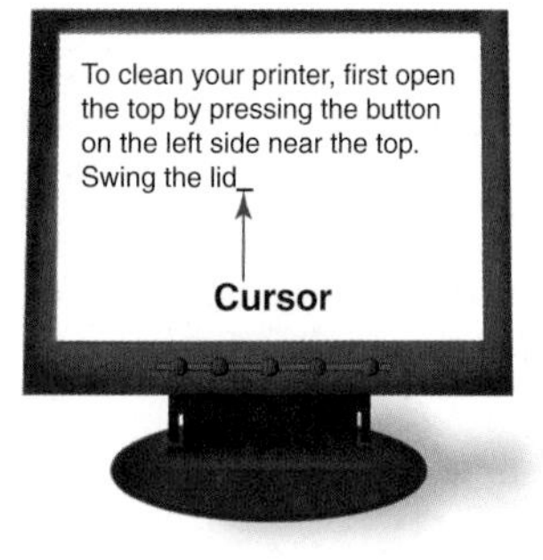

CURSOR **The *cursor* is the movable symbol on the display screen that shows you where you may next enter data or commands.** The symbol is often a blinking rectangle or an I-beam. You can move the cursor on the screen using the keyboard's directional arrow keys or a mouse. The point where the cursor is located is called the *insertion point.*

SCROLLING ***Scrolling*** **means moving quickly upward, downward, or sideways through the text or other screen display.** A standard computer screen displays only 20–22 lines of standard-size text. Of course, most documents are longer than that. Using the directional arrow keys, or the mouse and a scroll bar located at the side of the screen, you can move ("scroll") through the display screen and into the text above and below it.

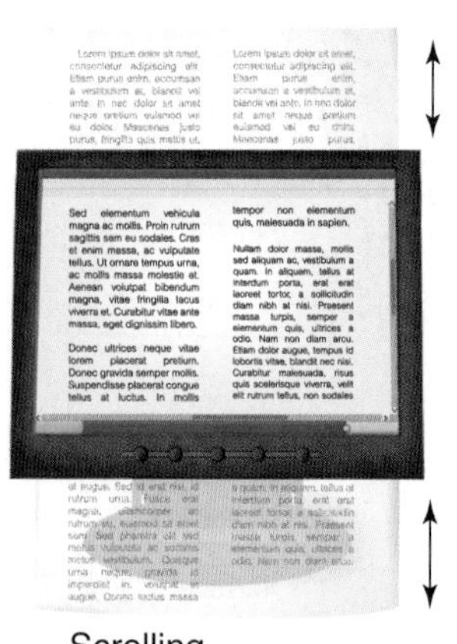
Scrolling

WORD WRAP ***Word wrap*** **automatically continues text to the next line when you reach the right margin.** That is, the text "wraps around" to the next line. You don't have to hit a "carriage-return" key or Enter key, as was necessary with a typewriter.

SOME OTHER FEATURES To help you organize term papers and reports, the *Outline View* feature puts tags on various headings to show the hierarchy of heads—for example, main head, subhead, and sub-subhead. Word processing software also allows you to insert footnotes that are automatically numbered and renumbered when changes are made. The basics of word processing are shown in the accompanying illustration. *(• See Panel 3.23.)*

Editing is the act of making alterations in the content of your document. Some features of editing, as we will discuss briefly, are *insert* and *delete, undelete, find and replace, cut/copy and paste, spelling checker, grammar checker,* and *thesaurus.*

Inserting is the act of adding to the document. Simply place the cursor wherever you want to add text and start typing; the existing characters will be pushed along. If you want to write over (replace) text as you write, press the *Insert* key before typing. When you're finished typing, press the *Insert* key again to exit Insert mode.

Deleting is the act of removing text, usually using the *Delete* key or the *Backspace* key.

The *Undo command* allows you to change your mind and undo your last action (or several previous actions) and restore text that you have deleted.

The *Find,* or *Search, command* allows you to find any word, phrase, or number that exists in your document. The *Replace command* allows you to automatically replace it with something else.

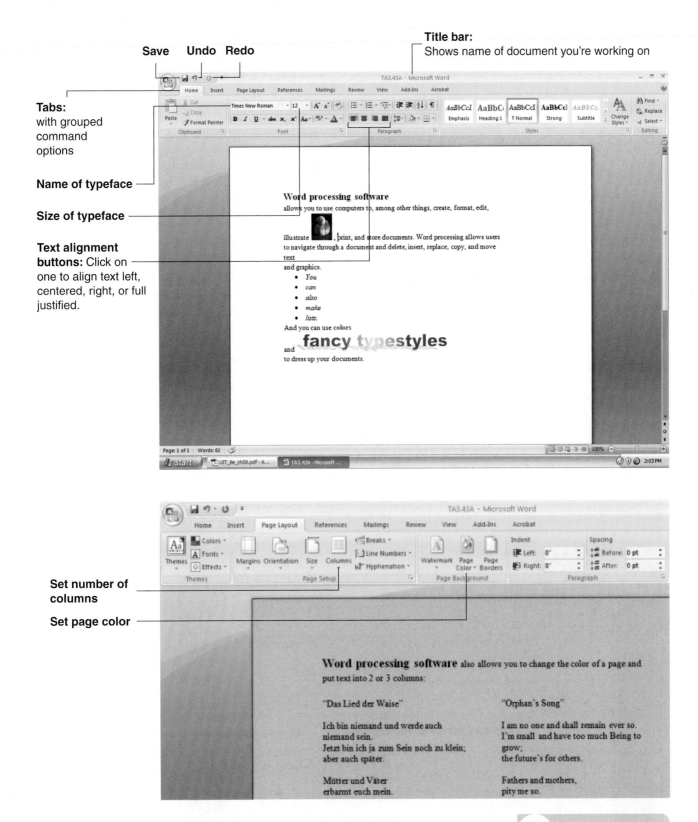

Save **Undo** **Redo**

Title bar: Shows name of document you're working on

Tabs: with grouped command options

Name of typeface

Size of typeface

Text alignment buttons: Click on one to align text left, centered, right, or full justified.

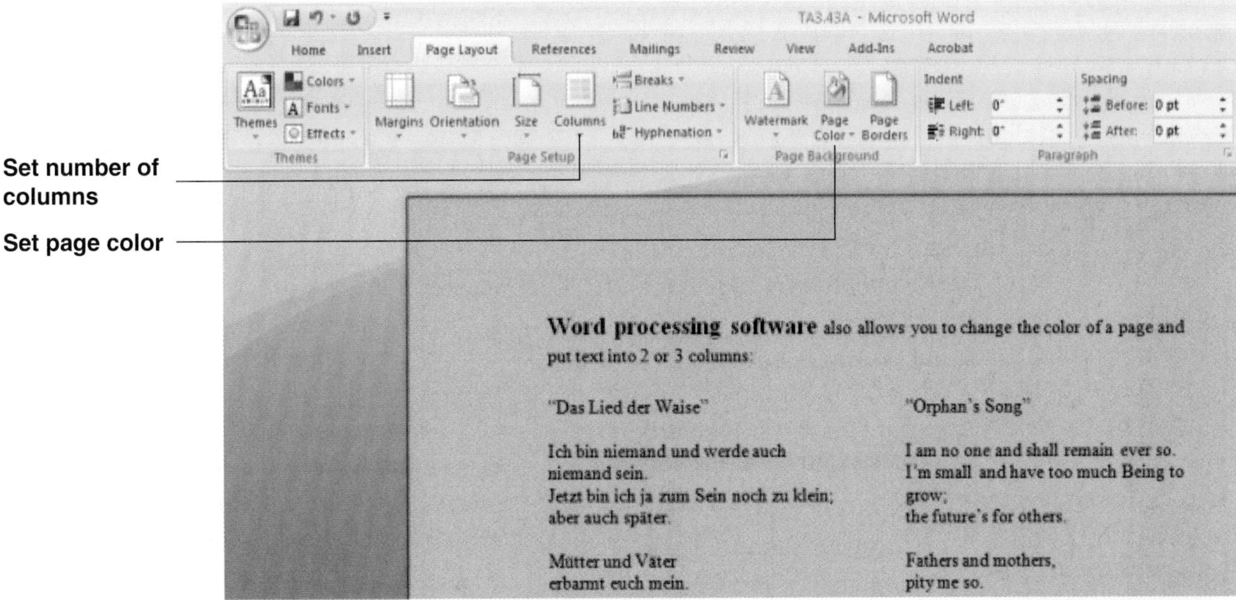

panel 3.23

Some word processing functions in Word 2007

Typewriter users who wanted to move a paragraph or block of text from one place to another in a manuscript used scissors and glue to "cut and paste." With word processing, moving text takes only a few keystrokes. You select (highlight with the mouse) the portion of text you want to copy or move. Then you use the *Copy* or *Cut command* to move it to the *clipboard,* a special holding area in the computer's memory. From there, you use *Paste* to transfer the material to any point (indicated with the cursor) in the existing document or in a new document. The clipboard retains its material, so repeated pastes of the same item will work without your having to recopy each time.

Most word processors have a *spelling checker,* which tests for incorrectly spelled words. As you type, the spelling checker indicates (perhaps with a squiggly line) words that aren't in its dictionary and thus may be misspelled. *(● See Panel 3.24.)* Special add-on dictionaries are available for medical, engineering, and legal terms.

In addition, programs such as Microsoft Word have an Auto Correct function that automatically fixes such common mistakes as transposed letters—replacing "teh" with "the," for instance.

A *grammar checker* highlights poor grammar, wordiness, incomplete sentences, and awkward phrases. The grammar checker won't fix things automatically, but it will flag (perhaps with a different-color squiggly line) possible incorrect word usage and sentence structure. *(● See Panel 3.25.)*

If you find yourself stuck for the right word while you're writing, you can call up an on-screen *thesaurus,* which will present you with the appropriate word or alternative words. You can also purchase more comprehensive thesaurus add-on programs, such as WordWeb55.

In the context of word processing, *formatting* means determining the appearance of a document. You can always format your documents manually, but word processing programs provide a helpful device to speed the process up and make it more sophisticated. **A *template* is a preformatted document that provides basic tools for shaping a final document**—the text, layout, and style for a letter, for example. Simply put, it is a style guide for documents. Because most documents are fairly standard in format, every word processing program comes with at least a few standard templates. When you use a template, you're actually opening a copy of the template. In this way you'll always have a fresh copy of the original template when you need it. After you open a copy of the template and add your text, you save this version of the template

panel 3.24

Spelling checker in Word 2007
How a word processing program checks for misspelled words and offers alternatives.

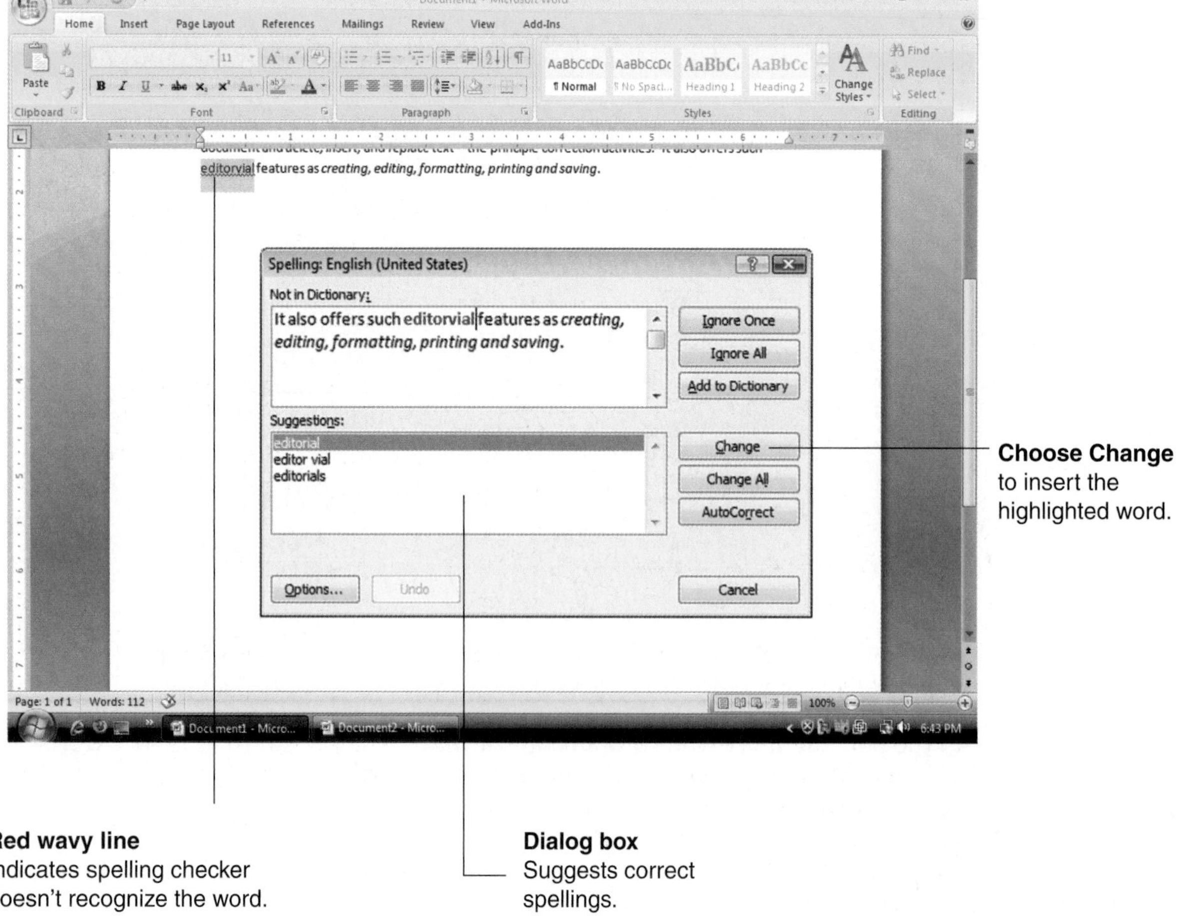

Choose Change to insert the highlighted word.

Red wavy line Indicates spelling checker doesn't recognize the word.

Dialog box Suggests correct spellings.

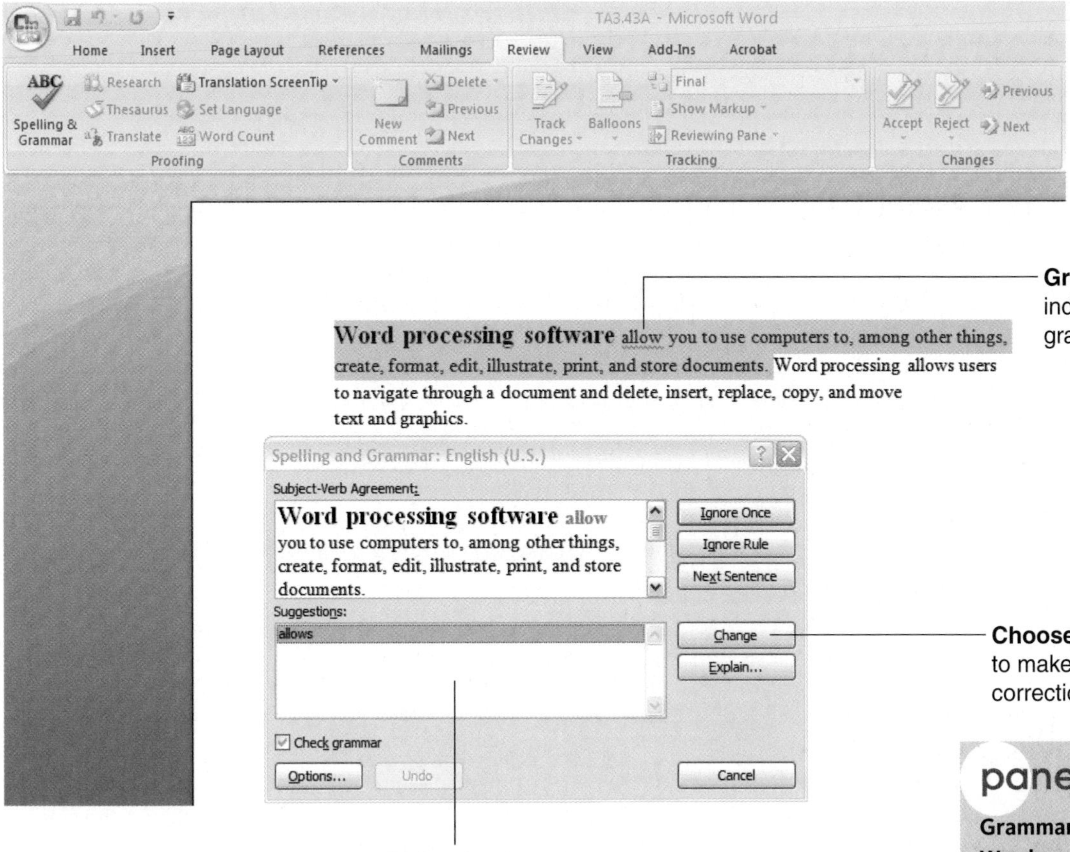

Green wavy line indicates a possible grammar error.

Choose Change to make the suggested correction.

Dialog box suggests a correction.

panel 3.25

Grammar checker in Word 2007

This program points out possible errors in sentence structure and word usage and suggests alternatives.

under the filename of your choice. In this way, for example, in a letterhead template, your project's name, address, phone number, and web address are included every time you open your letterhead template file.

Among the many aspects of formatting are these:

Fonts

- You can decide what *font*—typeface and type size—you wish to use. For instance, you can specify whether it should be Times Roman, Arial, or Courier. You can indicate whether the text should be, say, 10 points or 12 points in size and the headings should be 14 points or 16 points. (There are 72 points—6 picas—in an inch.) You can specify what parts should be underlined, *italic*, or **boldface.**
- You can choose whether you want the lines to be *single-spaced* or *double-spaced* (or something else). You can specify whether you want text to be *one column* (like this page), *two columns* (like many magazines and books), or *several columns* (like newspapers).
- You can indicate the dimensions of the margins—left, right, top, and bottom—around the text. You can specify the text *justification*—how the letters and words are spaced in each line. To *justify* means to align text evenly between left and right margins, as in most newspaper columns and the preceding two paragraphs. To *left-justify* means to align text evenly on the left. (Left-justified text has a "ragged-right" margin, as do many business letters and this paragraph.) *Centering* centers each text line in the available white space between the left and right margins.

Justification

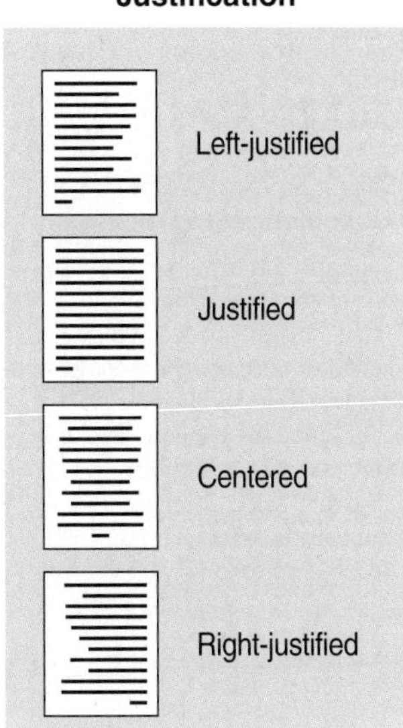

Where do I find templates?

Need to find a template on your computer?

Templates are files designed to be interesting, compelling, and professional-looking documents. All the formatting is complete; you add what you want to them. Examples are resumes, invitations, and newsletters. Your Office applications come with several templates already installed. To locate them, use the following instructions.

1. Click the **File** tab, and then select **New**.
2. All the templates currently installed on our computer will be listed under **Available Templates**.
3. Highlight the template you want to use and click **Create**. A new file will open in the template you've selected.

NOTE To select a template that you have created, or downloaded to your computer, select **My Templates**, and then choose your template from the **Personal Templates** window.

Want to find and download a new template?

Do you want to create a resume, budget, fax cover sheet, presentation, or invitation? To get free templates for these and other areas, go to the Templates home page on Office.com. You can use these free templates, or modify them to match what you need to create.

You can also download these templates from within your Office program by following Step 1, in the previous section. Under **Office.com Templates**, you can search the online template library, or select a template type from the list to filter your search, and download the template directly to your computer.

Have a template you want to share?

Do you have a template that you created and are proud of? If you want to share your template with other people, you can submit a template to Office.com.

TOP OF PAGE

See Also

Learn about templates in Office 2010

Word can help you choose templates.

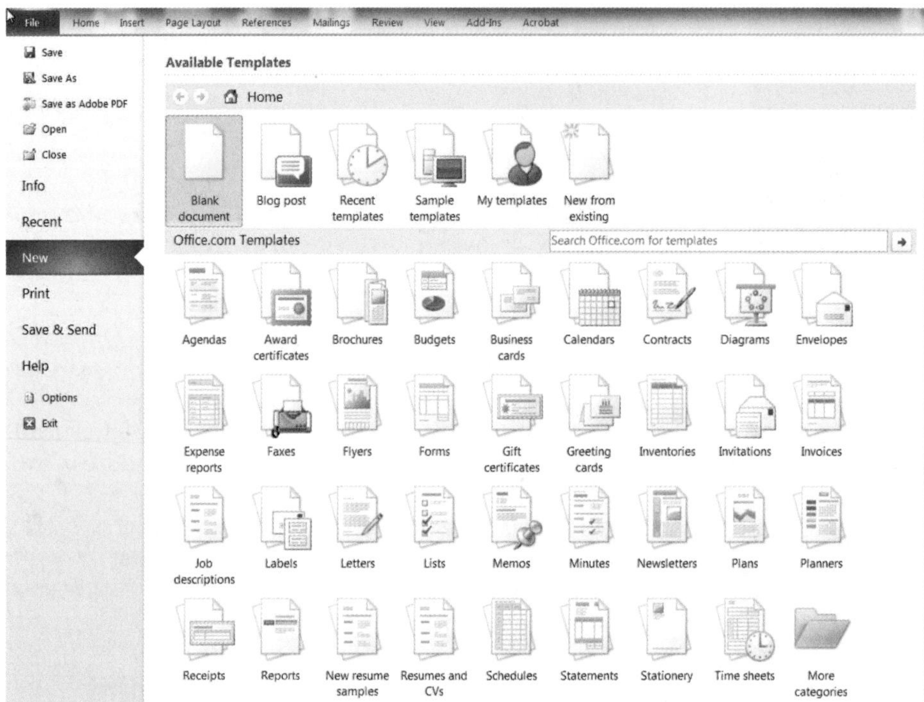

Survival Tip

When Several Word Documents Are Open

You can write with several Word documents open simultaneously. To go ("toggle") back and forth, hold down *Ctrl* and press *F6*. To display several documents at once, go to the Windows menu (2003) or the View tab (2007, 2010) and select *Arrange All*. You can cut and paste text from one document to another.

- You can indicate headers or footers and include page numbers. A *header* is common text (such as a date or document name) printed at the top of every page. A *footer* is the same thing printed at the bottom of every page. If you want page numbers, you can determine what number to start with, among other things.
- You can specify *borders* or other decorative lines, *shading, tables,* and *footnotes*. You can even import *graphics* or drawings from files in other software programs, including *clip art*—collections of ready-made pictures and illustrations available online or on CDs/DVDs.

Note that word processing programs (and indeed most forms of application software) come from the manufacturer with default settings. ***Default settings*** **are the settings automatically used by a program unless the user specifies otherwise, thereby overriding them.** Thus, for example, a word processing program may automatically prepare a document single-spaced, left-justified, with 1-inch right and left margins, unless you alter these default settings.

Most word processing software gives you several options for printing. For example, you can print *several copies* of a document. You can print *individual pages* or a *range of pages*. You can even preview a document before printing it out. *Previewing (print previewing)* means viewing a document on-screen to see what it will look like in printed form before it's printed. Whole pages are displayed in reduced size.

You can also send your document off to someone else by fax or email attachment if your computer has the appropriate communications link.

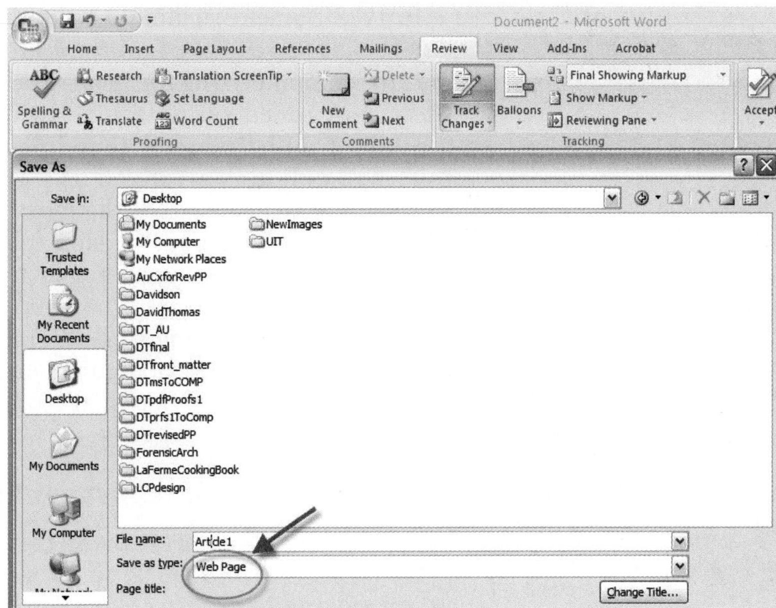

Saving a document as a web page in Word 2007

Of course, you must also be able to save your work. ***Saving* means storing, or preserving, a document as an electronic file permanently**—on your hard disk, a CD, or online. You need only retrieve the document from storage and make the changes you want. Then you can print it out or save it again—or email it. (*Always save your documents often while you are working; don't wait!*)

Most word processing programs allow you to automatically format your documents into HTML (p. 179) so that they can be used on the web. To do this in Microsoft Word, open *File, Save As, Save As Type: Web page (*.htm, *.html).*

disciples. These are discussed particularly in light of the use of aboriginal collections.

The last 15 years have seensaw significant advances in the field. These nNew developments in the discipline, such as advances in education and training, are briefly discussed, and the roules of various forensic societies and associations in the development of *forensic anthropology* are also examined. Employment of forensic anthropologists is outlineds, along with examples of court cases in whichwhere forensic anthropologists acted as expert witnesses.

Forensic anthropology is sometimes comprised ofcomprises many different points

Comment [SCS1]: 20?

Formatted: Font: Italic

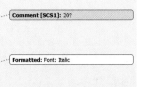

Tracking in Word 2010

Word processing programs also have *tracking* features. What if you have written an important document and have asked other people to edit it? Word processing software allows editing changes to be tracked by highlighting them, underlining additions, and crossing out deletions. Each person working on the document can choose a different color so that you can tell who's done what and when. An edited document can be printed out showing all the changes, as well as a list of comments keyed to the text by numbers. Or it can be printed out "clean," showing the edited text in its new form, without the changes.

3.8 Spreadsheet Programs

A spreadsheet program uses rectangular grids for laying out linked, usually financial, data in a very organized fashion.

What is a spreadsheet? Traditionally, it was simply a grid of rows and columns, printed on special light-green paper, that was used to produce financial projections and reports. A person making up a spreadsheet spent long days and weekends at the office penciling tiny numbers into countless tiny rectangles. When one figure changed, all other numbers on the spreadsheet had to be erased and recomputed. Ultimately, there might be wastebaskets full of jettisoned worksheets.

In 1978 Daniel Bricklin was a student at the Harvard Business School. One day he was staring at columns of numbers on a blackboard when he got the idea for computerizing the spreadsheet. He created the first electronic spreadsheet, now called simply a worksheet. **The *worksheet* allows users to create tables and financial schedules by entering data and formulas into rows and columns arranged as a grid on a display screen.** Before long the electronic spreadsheet was the most popular small business program. Unfortunately for Bricklin, his version (called VisiCalc) was quickly surpassed by others. Today the principal spreadsheet programs are Microsoft Excel, Corel Quattro Pro, Apple iWork Numbers, and IBM's Lotus 1-2-3. These programs are used for maintaining student grade books, tracking investments, creating and tracking budgets, calculating loan payments, estimating project costs, and creating other types of financial reports.

The Basics: How Spreadsheet Programs Work

Spreadsheet programs provide tools for collecting and calculating data of all types. Beyond working with numerical data, worksheets can be formatted to create clear, concise reports and can be easily sorted and updated.

A worksheet is arranged as follows. (• *See Panel 3.26.)*

HOW A SPREADSHEET FILE IS ORGANIZED The word *spreadsheet* usually refers to the type of application program. A spreadsheet file is called a *workbook.* A workbook's grid arrangement of columns, rows, and labels is called a

panel 3.26

Spreadsheet program worksheet

This program is Microsoft Excel 2007.

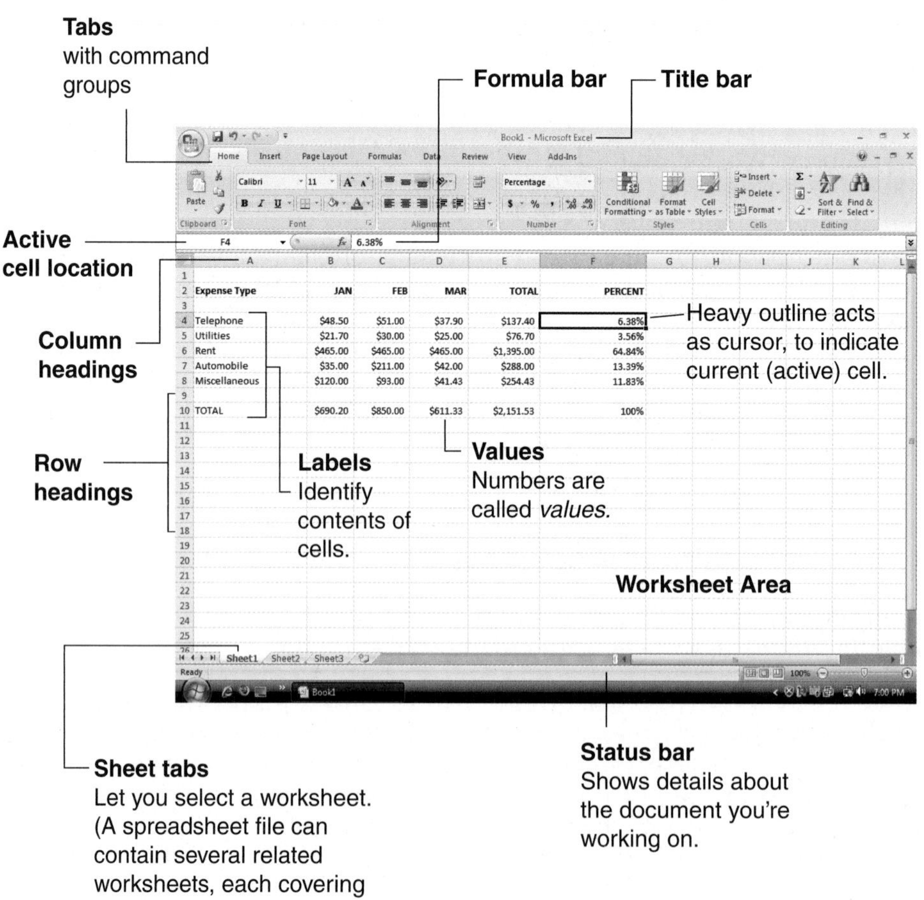
Tabs
with command groups
Formula bar
Title bar
Active cell location
Column headings
Row headings
Labels
Identify contents of cells.
Values
Numbers are called *values.*
Heavy outline acts as cursor, to indicate current (active) cell.
Worksheet Area
Sheet tabs
Let you select a worksheet. (A spreadsheet file can contain several related worksheets, each covering a different topic.)
Status bar
Shows details about the document you're working on.

worksheet. So, for example, when you open the Excel spreadsheet program, it loads an empty workbook file consisting of three blank worksheets for you to use. The worksheets have columns, rows, and labels:

- **Column headings:** In the worksheet's frame area (work area), lettered *column headings* appear across the top ("A" is the name of the first column, "B" the second, and so on).
- **Row headings:** Numbered *row headings* appear down the left side ("1" is the name of the first row, "2" the second, and so forth).
- **Labels:** *Labels* are any descriptive text that identifies categories, such as APRIL, RENT, or GROSS SALES.

Use your keyboard to type in the various headings and labels. Each Microsoft Office Excel worksheet has 16,384 columns and 1,048,576 rows, and each spreadsheet file (workbook) can technically hold up to 650 related worksheets—but the computer's memory (RAM, p. 31) will not likely hold more than about 200.

CELLS: WHERE COLUMNS & ROWS MEET Each worksheet has more than 17 million cells.

- **Cells & cell addresses: A *cell* is the place where a row and a column intersect; its position is called a *cell reference* or *cell address.*** For example, "A1" is the cell address for the top left cell, where column A and row 1 intersect. (The column letter is always listed first.)
- **Ranges: A *range* is a rectangular group of adjacent cells**—for example, B5 to D10. Ranges are identified by the cell references of the cells in the upper left and lower right corners of the range. The two cell references used for a range are separated by a colon (:), which tells Excel to include all the cells between these start and end points—B5:D10.
- **Values: A number or date entered in a cell is called a *value*.** The values are the actual numbers used in the spreadsheet—dollars, percentages, grade points, temperatures, or whatever. Headings, labels, and formulas also go into cells.
- **Cell pointer:** A *cell pointer,* or *spreadsheet cursor,* indicates where data is to be entered. The cell pointer can be moved around like a cursor in a word processing program.

How to Plan Worksheets

For a start on how to set up a worksheet, try:

http://spreadsheets.about.com/od/excel101/ss/enter_data.htm

FORMULAS, FUNCTIONS, RECALCULATION, & WHAT-IF ANALYSIS Why has the spreadsheet program become so popular? The reasons lie in the features known as formulas, functions, recalculation, and what-if analysis.

- **Formulas: *Formulas* are instructions for calculations; they define how one cell relates to other cells.** For example, a formula might be =SUM(A5:A15) or @SUM(A5:A15), meaning "Sum (that is, add) all the numbers in the cells with cell addresses A5 through A15."
- **Functions: *Functions* are built-in formulas that perform common calculations.** For instance, a function might average a range of numbers or round off a number to two decimal places.
- **Recalculation:** After the values have been entered into the worksheet, the formulas and functions can be used to calculate outcomes. However, what was revolutionary about the electronic spreadsheet was its ability to easily do recalculation. ***Recalculation* is the process of recomputing**

values, either as an ongoing process as data is entered or afterward, with the press of a key. With this simple feature, the hours of mind-numbing work required to manually rework paper spreadsheets have become a thing of the past.

- **What-if analysis:** The recalculation feature has opened up whole new possibilities for decision making. In particular, ***what-if analysis* allows the user to see how changing one or more numbers changes the outcome of the calculation.** That is, you can create a worksheet, putting in formulas and numbers, and then ask, "What would happen if we change that detail?"—and immediately see the effect on the bottom line.

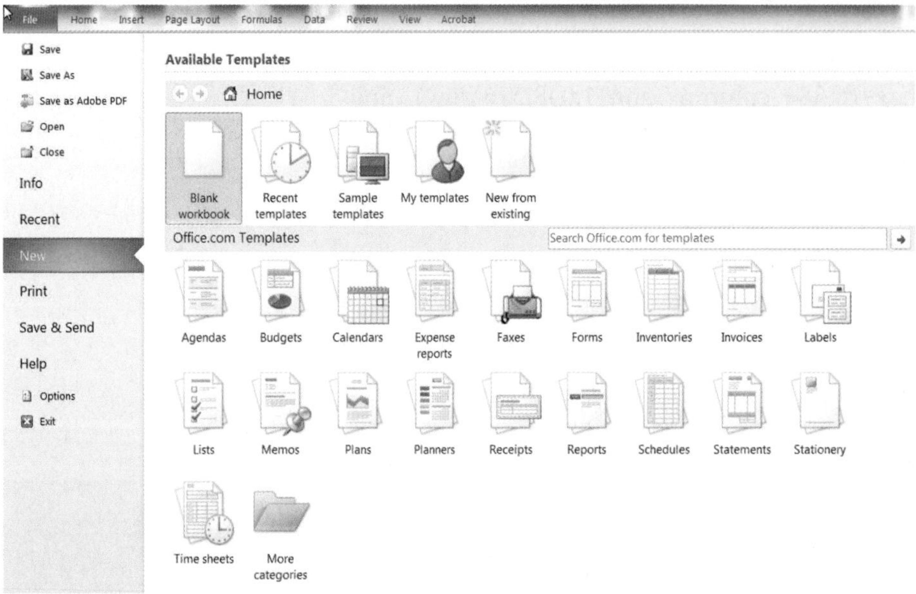

Microsoft Excel worksheet templates

WORKSHEET TEMPLATES You may find that your spreadsheet software makes worksheet templates available for specific tasks. *Worksheet templates* are forms containing formats and formulas custom-designed for particular kinds of work. Examples are templates for calculating loan payments, tracking travel expenses, monitoring personal budgets, and keeping track of time worked on projects. Templates are also available for a variety of business needs—providing sales quotations, invoicing customers, creating purchase orders, and writing a business plan.

Analytical Graphics: Creating Charts

Worksheet and workbook data can be displayed in graphic form.

You can use spreadsheet packages to create analytical graphics, or charts. ***Analytical graphics*, or *business graphics*, are graphical forms that make numeric data easier to analyze than it is when organized as rows and columns of numbers.** Whether viewed on a monitor or printed out, analytical graphics help make sales figures, economic trends, and the like easier to comprehend and visualize. In Excel, you enter your data to the worksheet, select the data, and use the chart-formatting tools to step through the process of choosing the chart type and various options.

Examples of analytical graphics are *column charts, bar charts, line graphs, pie charts,* and *scatter charts*. (*• See Panel 3.27.*) If you have a color printer, these charts can appear in color. In addition, they can be displayed or printed out so that they look three-dimensional.

Most spreadsheet applications are *multidimensional,* meaning that you can link one spreadsheet file to another. A three-dimensional spreadsheet model is like a stack of worksheets all connected by formulas. A change made in one worksheet automatically affects the others. Looking at data in several dimensions could include, for example, sales by region, sales by sales rep, sales by product category, sales by month, and so on. A spreadsheet program's multidimensional view might take on a 3D graphics form.

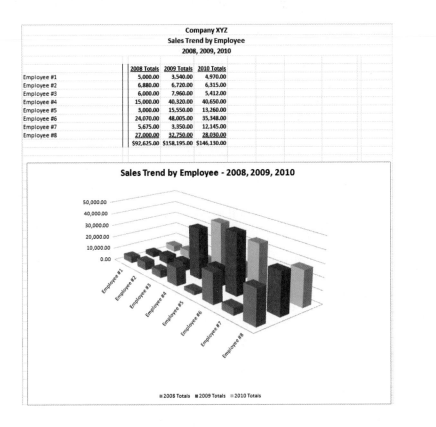

	Company XYZ Sales Trend by Employee 2008, 2009, 2010		
	2008 Totals	2009 Totals	2010 Totals
Employee #1	5,000.00	3,540.00	4,970.00
Employee #2	6,880.00	6,720.00	6,315.00
Employee #3	6,000.00	7,960.00	5,412.00
Employee #4	15,000.00	40,320.00	40,650.00
Employee #5	3,000.00	15,550.00	13,260.00
Employee #6	24,070.00	48,005.00	35,348.00
Employee #7	5,675.00	3,350.00	12,145.00
Employee #8	27,000.00	32,750.00	28,030.00
	$92,625.00	$158,195.00	$146,130.00

Sales Trend by Employee - 2008, 2009, 2010

50,000.00
40,000.00
30,000.00
20,000.00
10,000.00
0.00

Employee #1 Employee #2 Employee #3 Employee #4 Employee #5 Employee #6 Employee #7 Employee #8

■ 2008 Totals ■ 2009 Totals ■ 2010 Totals

panel 3.27

Analytical graphics

Bar charts, line graphs, and pie charts are used to display numbers in graphical form.

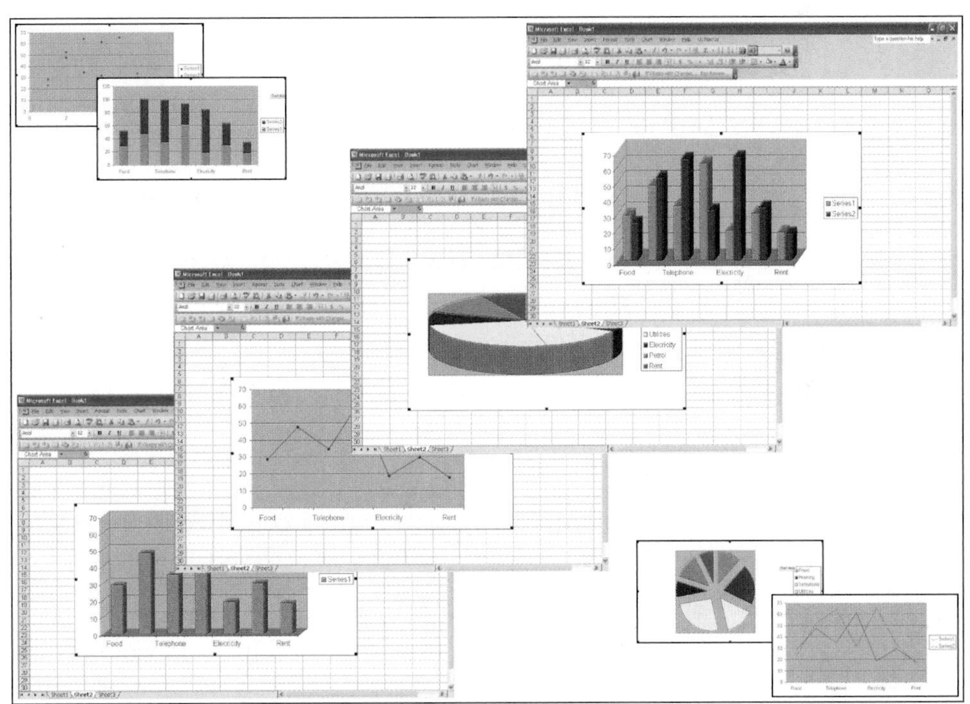

3.9 Database Software

A database is a collection of data that is organized so that its contents can easily be accessed, managed, and updated.

In its most general sense, a database is any electronically stored collection of data in a computer system. In its more specific sense, a ***database*** **is a collection of interrelated files in a computer system.** These computer-based files are organized according to their common elements, so that they can be retrieved easily. Sometimes called a *database manager* or *database management system (DBMS)*, ***database software*** **is a program that sets up and controls the structure of a database and access to the data.**

The Benefits of Database Software

The correct set-up and use of databases can improve the reliability of data.

When data is stored in separate files, the same data will be repeated in many files. In the old days, each college administrative office—registrar, financial aid, housing, and so on—might have a separate file on you. Thus, there was *redundancy*—your address, for example, was repeated over and over. This means that when you changed addresses, all the college's files on you had to be updated separately. Thus, database software has two advantages.

INTEGRATION With database software, the data is not in separate files. Rather, it is *integrated*. Thus, your address need only be listed once, and all the separate administrative offices will have access to the same information.

INTEGRITY For that reason, information in databases is considered to have more *integrity*. That is, the information is more likely to be accurate and up to date.

Databases are a lot more interesting than they used to be. Once they included only text. Now they can also include pictures, sound, animation, and video. It's likely, for instance, that your personnel record in a company database will include a picture of you and even a clip of your voice. If you go looking for a house to buy, you can view a real estate agent's database of video clips of homes and properties without leaving the realtor's office or your own computer.

Today the principal microcomputer database programs are Microsoft Access and FileMaker Pro. (In larger systems, Oracle, Advantage Database Server, and SQL Anywhere are major players.)

The Basics: How Databases Work

The main type of microcomputer database program is the relational database.

Let's consider some basic features of databases:

HOW A RELATIONAL DATABASE IS ORGANIZED: TABLES, RECORDS, & FIELDS The most widely used form of database, especially on PCs, is the ***relational database*****, in which data is organized into related tables.** Each table contains rows and columns; the rows are called *records,* and the columns are called *fields*. An example of a record is a person's address—name, street address, city, and so on. An example of a field is that person's last name; another field would be that person's first name; a third field would be that person's street address; and so on. *(• See Panel 3.28.)*

Just as a spreadsheet program may include a workbook with several worksheets, so a relational database program might include a database with several tables. For instance, if you're running a small company, you might have one database headed *Employees,* containing three tables—*Addresses, Payroll,* and *Benefits*. You might have another database headed *Customers,* with *Addresses, Orders,* and *Invoices* tables.

LINKING RECORDS, USING A KEY In relational databases a ***key*****—also called *key field, sort key, index,* or *keyword*—is a field used to sort data.** For example, if you sort records by age, then the age field is a key. The most frequent key field used in the United States is the Social Security number, but any unique identifier, such as employee number or student number, can be

panel 3.28

Some database functions

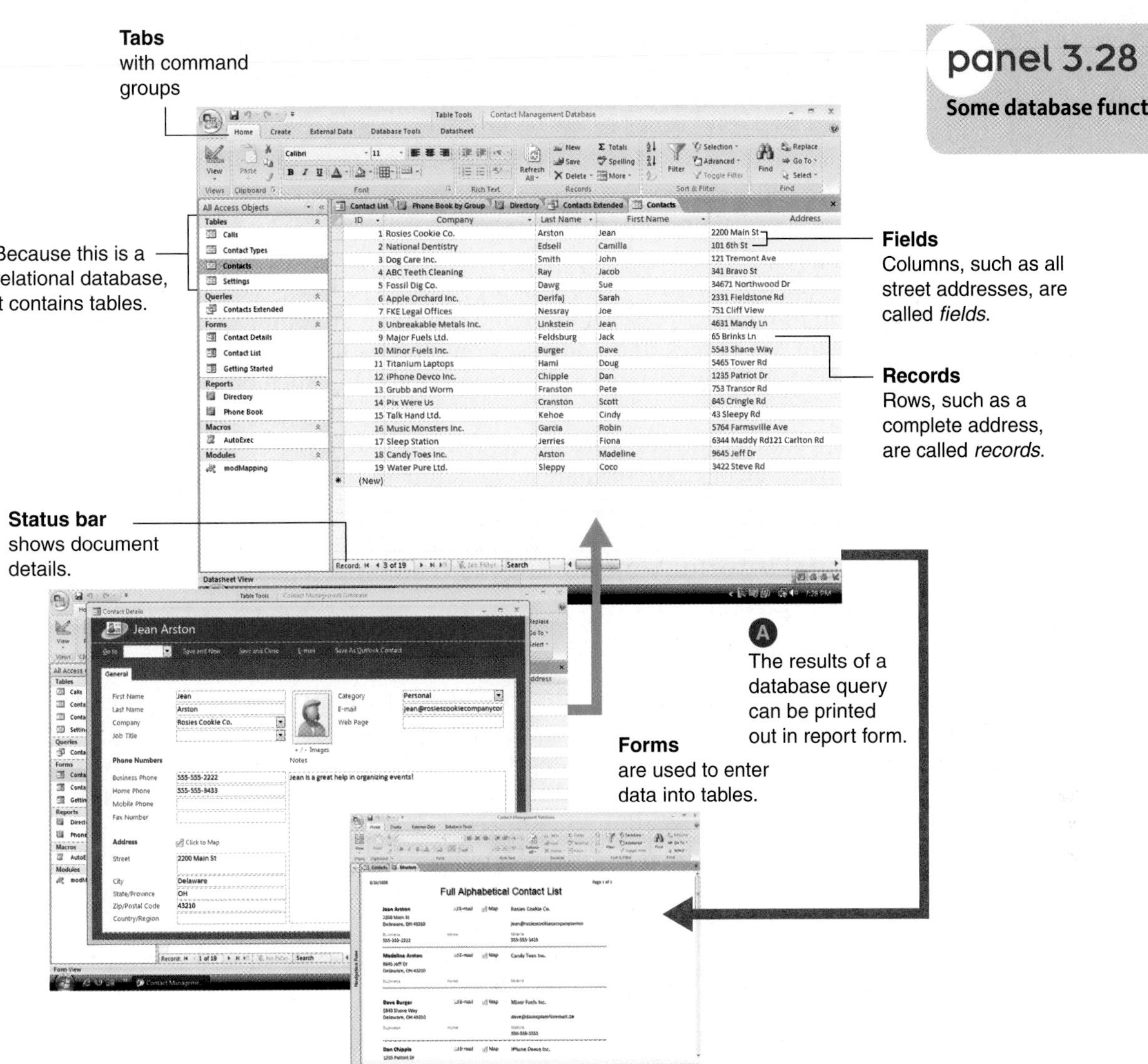

Tabs
with command groups
Because this is a relational database, it contains tables.
Fields
Columns, such as all street addresses, are called *fields*.
Records
Rows, such as a complete address, are called *records*.
Status bar
shows document details.
A
The results of a database query can be printed out in report form.
Forms
are used to enter data into tables.
Full Alphabetical Contact List
Jean Arston

used. Most database management systems allow you to have more than one key so that you can sort records in different ways. One of the keys is designated the *primary key* and must hold a unique value for each record. A key field that identifies records in different tables is called a *foreign key*. A foreign key is a field in a relational table that matches the primary key of another table. Foreign keys are used to cross-reference data among relational tables.

FINDING WHAT YOU WANT: QUERYING & DISPLAYING RECORDS The beauty of database software is that you can locate records quickly. For example, several offices at your college may need access to your records but for different reasons: registrar, financial aid, student housing, and so on. Any of these offices can *query records*—locate and display records—by calling them up on a computer screen for viewing and updating. Thus, if you move, your address field will need to be corrected for all relevant offices of the college. A person making a search might make the query, *"Display the address of [your name]."* Once a record is displayed, the address field can be changed. Thereafter, any office calling up your file will see the new address.

SORTING & ANALYZING RECORDS & APPLYING FORMULAS With database software you can easily find and change the order of records in a table—in other words, they can be *sorted* in different ways—arranged alphabetically, numerically, geographically, or in some other order. For example, they can be rearranged by state, by age, or by Social Security number.

In addition, database programs contain built-in mathematical *formulas* so that you can analyze data. This feature can be used, for example, to find the grade-point averages for students in different majors or in different classes.

PUTTING SEARCH RESULTS TO USE: SAVING, FORMATTING, PRINTING, COPYING, OR TRANSMITTING Once you've queried, sorted, and analyzed the records and fields, you can simply save them to your hard disk, CD, or other secondary storage medium. You can format them in different ways, altering headings and typestyles. You can print them out on paper as reports, such as an employee list with up-to-date addresses and phone numbers. A common use is to print out the results as names and addresses on *mailing labels*—adhesive-backed stickers that can be run through your printer and then stuck on envelopes. You can use the Copy command to copy your search results and then paste them into a paper produced on your word processor. You can also cut and paste data into an email message or make the data an attachment file to an email, so that it can be transmitted to someone else.

Personal Information Managers (PIMs)

A PIM is software that serves as a planner, notebook, and address book all in one. PIMs are especially popular for PDAs

Many people find ready uses for specialized types of database software known as personal information managers. **A *personal information manager (PIM)* is software that helps you keep track of and manage information you use on a daily basis, such as addresses, telephone numbers, appointments, to-do lists, and miscellaneous notes.** Some programs feature phone dialers, outliners (for roughing out ideas in outline form), and ticklers (or reminders). With a PIM, you can key in notes in any way you like and then retrieve them later based on any of the words you typed.

Popular PIMs are Microsoft Outlook, Lotus Notes, Contactizer Pro, and Yojimbo. Microsoft Outlook, for example, has sections such as Inbox, Calendar, Contacts, Tasks (to-do list), Journal (to record interactions with people), Notes (scratchpad), and Files. *(• See Panel 3.29, next page.)*

3.10 Specialty Application Software

There's an app for that!

After learning some of the productivity software just described, you may wish to become familiar with more specialized programs. For example, you might first learn word processing and then move on to desktop publishing, or first learn spreadsheets and then learn personal-finance software. We consider the following kinds of software, although they are but a handful of the thousands

Timeline
Developments in software

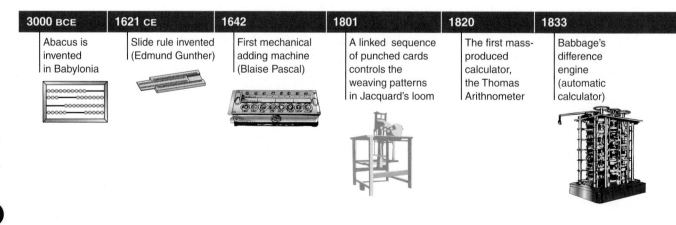

3000 BCE	1621 CE	1642	1801	1820	1833
Abacus is invented in Babylonia	Slide rule invented (Edmund Gunther)	First mechanical adding machine (Blaise Pascal)	A linked sequence of punched cards controls the weaving patterns in Jacquard's loom	The first mass-produced calculator, the Thomas Arithnometer	Babbage's difference engine (automatic calculator)

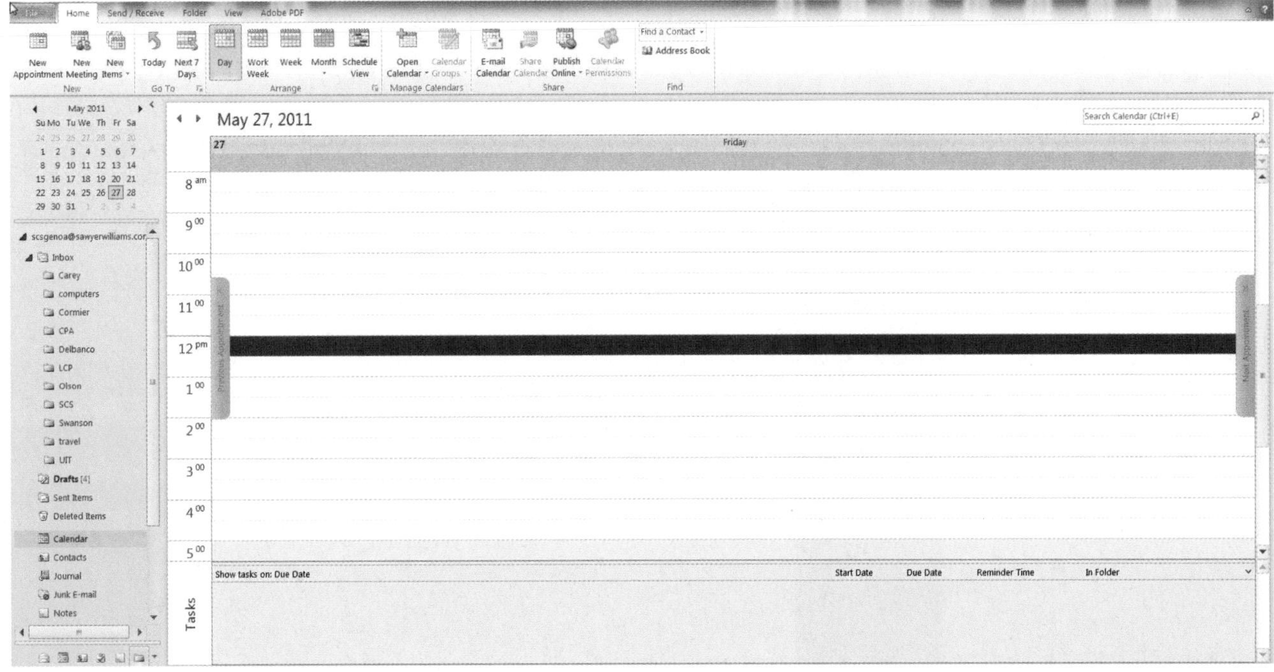

panel 3.29

Personal information manager

Microsoft Outlook 2007

of specialized programs available: *presentation graphics, financial, desktop-publishing, drawing and painting, project management, computer-aided design, video/audio editing, animation,* and *web page design software.*

Presentation Graphics Software

Presentation graphics make information more accessible.

Presentation graphics software is intended primarily for creating slide-show presentations, reports, portfolios, and training materials. ***Presentation graphics software*** **uses graphics, animation, sound, and data or information to make visual presentations.** Presentation graphics are much more fancy and complicated than are analytical graphics. Pages in presentation software are often referred to as *slides,* and visual presentations are commonly called *slide shows.* They can consist, however, not only of slides but also of paper copies, video, animation, and sound. Completed presentations are frequently published in multiple formats, which may include print, the web, and electronic files.

Most often, presentation projects are used in live sessions and commonly projected onto large screens or printed as handouts to accompany the live presentation. Slides are generally intended to be followed in an ordered sequence,

1843 World's first computer programmer, Ada Lovelace, publishes her notes

1854 George Boole publishes "An Investigation on the Laws of Thought," a system for symbolic and logical reasoning that will become the basis for computer design

1890 Electricity used for first time in a data-processing project — Hollerith's automatic census-tabulating machine (used punched cards)

1924 T.J. Watson renames Hollerith's machine company, founded in 1896, to International Business Machines (IBM)

1930 General theory of computers (MIT)

1944 First electro-mechanical computer (Mark I)

Getting started in Microsoft Office PowerPoint 2007: [1] Tabs are designed to be task-oriented; [2] groups within each tab break a task into subtasks; [3] command buttons in each group carry out a command or display a menu of commands.

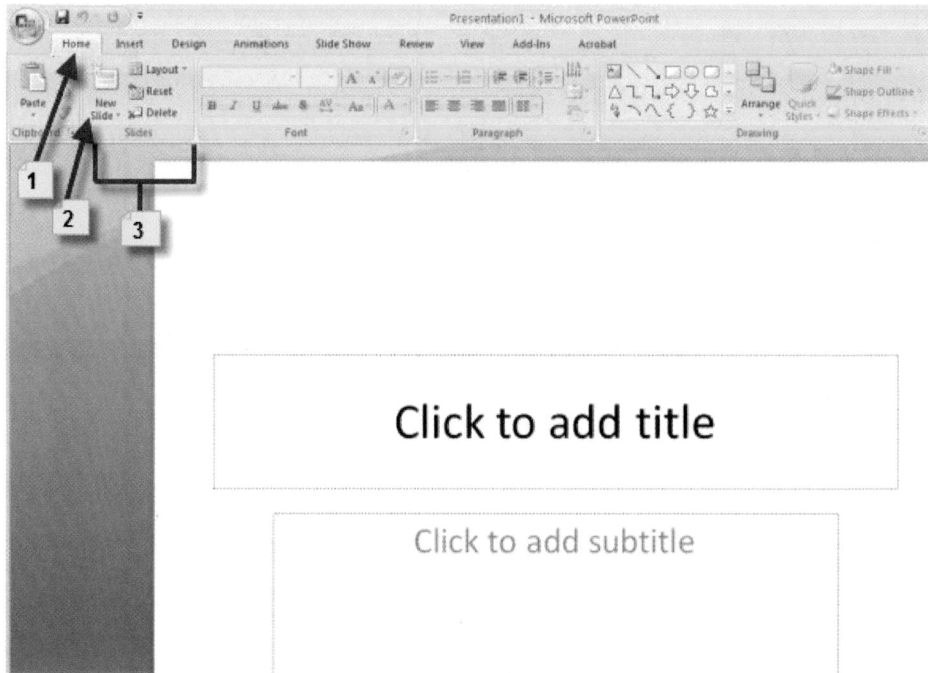

although some presentations may utilize interactive forms of navigation. This software also has the ability to export to HTML (p. 179) for posting presentations on the web.

You may already be accustomed to seeing presentation graphics, because many college instructors now use such software to accompany their lectures. Well-known presentation graphics packages include Microsoft PowerPoint, Corel Presentations, Harvard Graphics, and Presentation Graphics SDK. (*• See Panel 3.30.*) Companies such as Presentation Load (*www.presentationload.de/powerpoint-templates/?cur=1&force_sid=jv036tse7rr9ki9abgvf436qj4*) specialize in professional templates for sophisticated business presentations.

Just as word processing programs offer templates for faxes, business letters, and the like, presentation graphics programs offer templates to help you organize your presentation, whether it's for a roomful of people or over the Internet. Templates are of two types: design and content.

- **Design templates:** These offer formats, layouts, background patterns, and color schemes that can apply to general forms of content material.
- **Content templates:** These offer formats for specific subjects. For instance, PowerPoint offers templates for "Selling Your Ideas," "Facilitating a Meeting," and "Motivating a Team."

DRESSING UP YOUR PRESENTATION Presentation software makes it easy to dress up each visual page ("slide") with artwork by pulling in ("dragging and dropping") clip art from other sources. Although presentations may make use of some

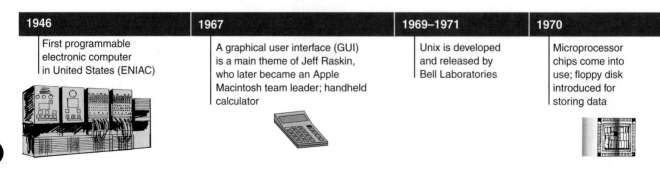

1946	1967	1969–1971	1970
First programmable electronic computer in United States (ENIAC)	A graphical user interface (GUI) is a main theme of Jeff Raskin, who later became an Apple Macintosh team leader; handheld calculator	Unix is developed and released by Bell Laboratories	Microprocessor chips come into use; floppy disk introduced for storing data

panel 3.30

Presentation graphics

Microsoft PowerPoint 2007

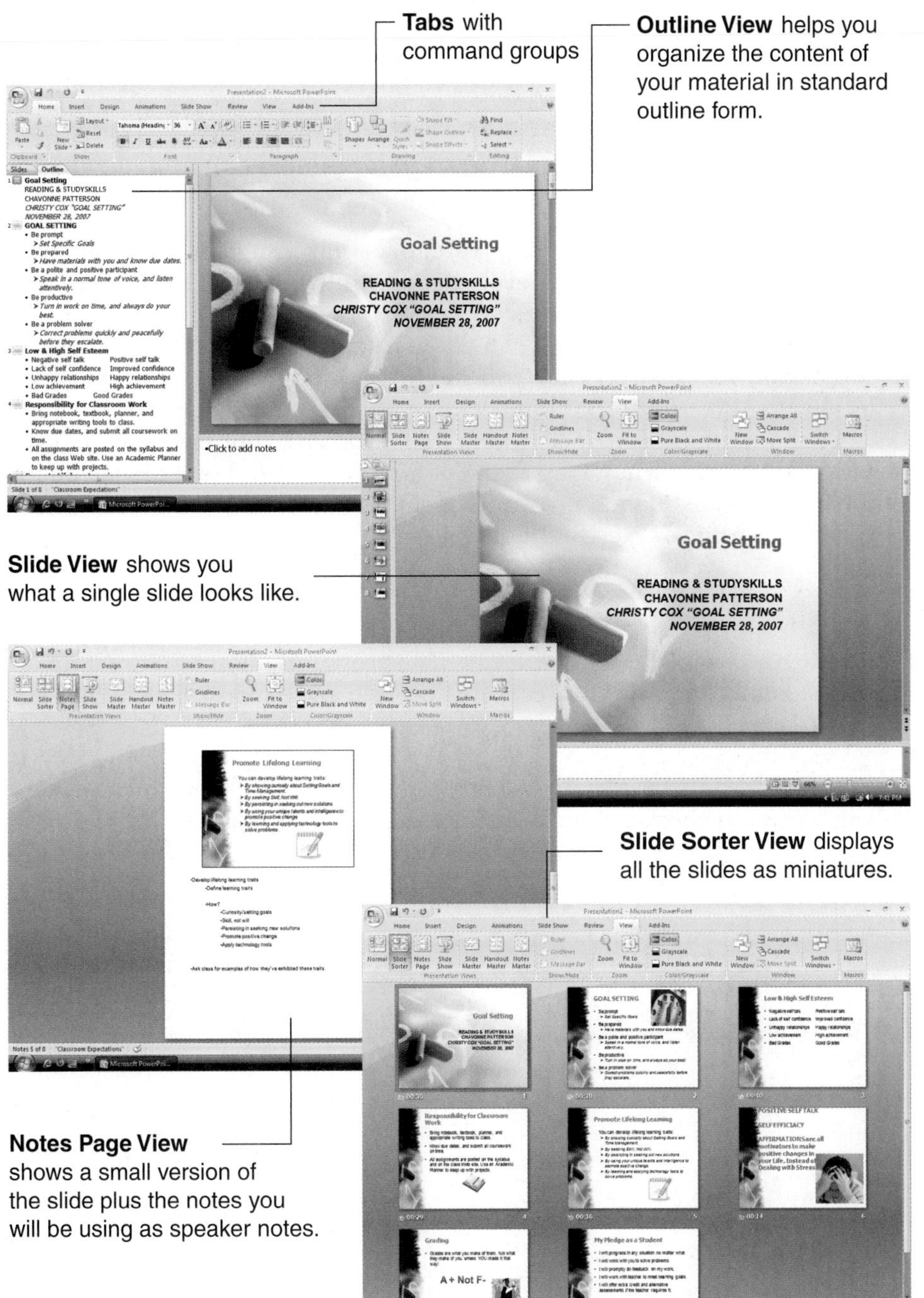
Tabs with command groups
Outline View helps you organize the content of your material in standard outline form.
Slide View shows you what a single slide looks like.
Slide Sorter View displays all the slides as miniatures.
Notes Page View shows a small version of the slide plus the notes you will be using as speaker notes.
Goal Setting
READING & STUDYSKILLS
CHAVONNE PATTERSON
CHRISTY COX "GOAL SETTING"
NOVEMBER 28, 2007

basic analytical graphics—bar, line, and pie charts—they generally use much more sophisticated elements. For instance, they may display different textures (speckled, solid, cross-hatched), color, and three-dimensionality. In addition, you can add sound clips, special visual effects (such as blinking text), animation, and

1973	1975	1976	1977
Xerox PARC develops an experimental PC that uses a mouse and a GUI	Bill Gates and Paul Allen start Microsoft in Albuquerque, N.M. (move to Seattle in 1979); first microcomputer (MITS Altair 8800)	Apple I computer (first personal computer sold in assembled form)	Apple II's floppy disk drive leads to writing of many software programs

Adding Clip Art

For information on adding clip art to presentation slides, check out:

www.thinkoutsidetheslide.com/articles/using_clip_art_photo.htm

www.clipartpress.com/43

http://presentationsoft.about.com/od/nextstepsinpowerpoint/ss/add_pics.htm

http://webclipart.about.com/library/weekly/bluse.htm

www.ideabook.com/tutorials/illustrations/how_to_choose_and_use_clip_art.html

For information on obtaining clip art, go to:

www.clipartinc.com

http://dir.yahoo.com/Computers_and_Internet/Graphics/Clip_art/

http://office.microsoft.com/en-us/images

video clips. (You can, in fact, drag and drop art and other enhancements into desktop-publishing, word processing, or other standard PC applications.)

Financial Software

Financial software can help you with regular budgets and bill paying, as well as taxes and financial planning.

Financial software **is a growing category that ranges from personal-finance managers to entry-level accounting programs to business financial-management packages.**

Consider the first of these, which you may find particularly useful. ***Personal-finance managers*** **let you keep track of income and expenses, write checks, do online banking, and plan financial goals.** *(• See Panel 3.31.)* Such programs don't promise to make you rich, but they can help you manage your money. They may even get you out of trouble. Popular microcomputer personal finance programs include Quicken, Ace Money, Moneydance, and YNAB (You Need A Budget).

FEATURES OF FINANCIAL SOFTWARE The principal features are these:

1. TRACKING OF INCOME & EXPENSES: The programs allow you to set up various account categories for recording income and expenses, including credit card expenses.

2. CHECKBOOK MANAGEMENT: All programs feature checkbook management, with an on-screen check-writing form and check register that look like the ones in your checkbook. Checks can be purchased to use with your computer printer.

panel 3.31

Financial software

Moneydance can be used for all sorts of money-related management. It includes guidance tips for setting up your accounts.

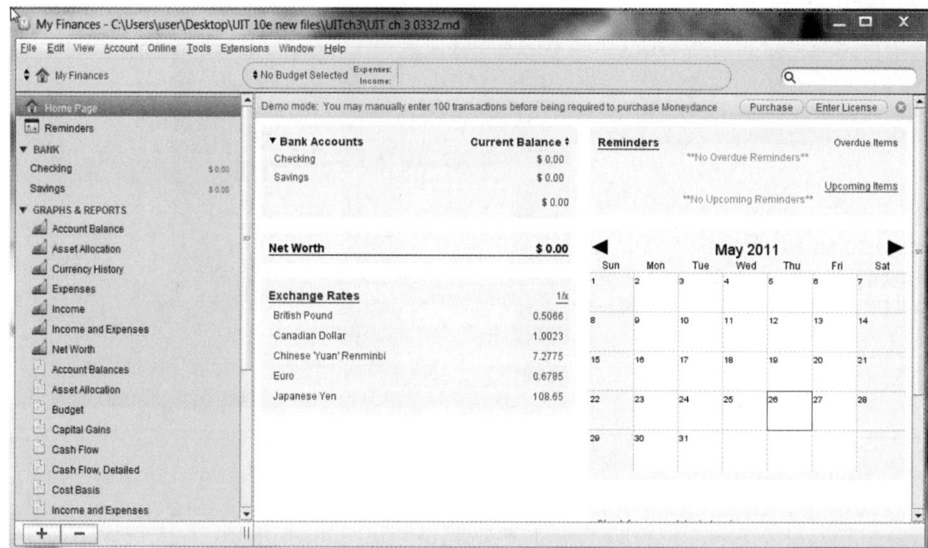

1978	1980	1981	1982	1983	1984
The first electronic spreadsheet, VisiCalc, is introduced; WordStar, the first commercial word processor for consumers, is introduced	Microsoft obtains DOS version that becomes PC-DOS for IBM PC.	Xerox introduces mouse-operated icons, buttons, and menus on the Star computer; IBM introduces personal computer (IBM PC)	Portable computers	Bill Gates announces the first version of the Windows operating system (and releases it two years later)	Apple Macintosh; first personal laser printer; the Apple Macintosh introduces the first widely used GUI; Mac System 1.0 is introduced

3. REPORTING: All programs compare your actual expenses with your budgeted expenses. Some will compare this year's expenses to last year's.

4. INCOME TAX: All programs offer tax categories, for indicating types of income and expenses that are important when you're filing your tax return.

5. OTHER: Some of the more versatile personal-finance programs also offer financial-planning and portfolio-management features.

GOING BEYOND PERSONAL FINANCE Besides personal-finance managers, financial software includes small business accounting and tax software programs, which provide virtually all the forms you need for filing income taxes. Tax programs such as TaxCut and TurboTax make complex calculations, check for mistakes, and even unearth deductions you didn't know existed. Tax programs can be linked to personal-finance software to form an integrated tool.

Many financial software programs may be used in all kinds of enterprises. For instance, accounting software such as Intuit Quickbooks and Sage Software's Peachtree automates bookkeeping tasks, while payroll software keeps records of employee hours and produces reports for tax purposes.

Some programs go beyond financial management and tax and accounting management. For example, Business Plan Pro and Small Business Management Pro can help you set up your own business from scratch.

Finally, there are investment software packages, such as StreetSmart Pro from Charles Schwab, as well as various retirement-planning programs.

Desktop Publishing

Desktop publishing software can make all types of documents look professional.

Adobe Systems was founded in 1982, when John Warnock and Charles Geschke began to work on solving some of the long-standing problems that plagued the relationship between microcomputers and printers. Collaboration with Apple Computers produced the first desktop-publishing package, using Adobe PostScript, a printer language that can handle many fonts and graphics, in 1984. By 1987 Adobe had agreements with IBM, Digital, AST Research, Hewlett-Packard, and Texas Instruments for them to use PostScript in their printers.

Desktop publishing (DTP) **involves mixing text and graphics to produce high-quality output for commercial printing, using a microcomputer and mouse, scanner, digital cameras, laser or ink-jet printer, and DTP software.** Often the printer is used primarily to get an advance look before the completed job is sent to a typesetter service bureau or a professional printer for even higher-quality output. Service bureaus and printers have special machines that convert the DTP files to film, which can then be used to make plates for offset printing or be used to go straight to digital printing. Offset printing produces higher-quality documents, especially if color is used, but is generally more expensive than digital printing.

1985	1986	1987	1988	1990	1991
Aldus PageMaker becomes the first integrated desktop publishing program; Microsoft Windows 1.0 is released; Mac System 2.0	Mac System 3.0	Microsoft's Excel program introduced; Mac system 4.0, then 5.0	Mac System 6.0	Microsoft introduces Windows 3.0 in May, intensifying its legal dispute with Apple over the software's "look and feel" resemblance to the Macintosh operating system	Linus Torvalds introduces Linux; Mac System 7.0

Desktop-publishing software. Adobe InDesign CS5 allows users to create interactive documents with sound, video, graphics, colors, text, and photos, all ready to go to a professional printer. (For an InDesign CS5 video overview, go to *http://tv.adobe.com/watch/cs5-design-premium-feature-tour/indesign-cs5-overview.*)

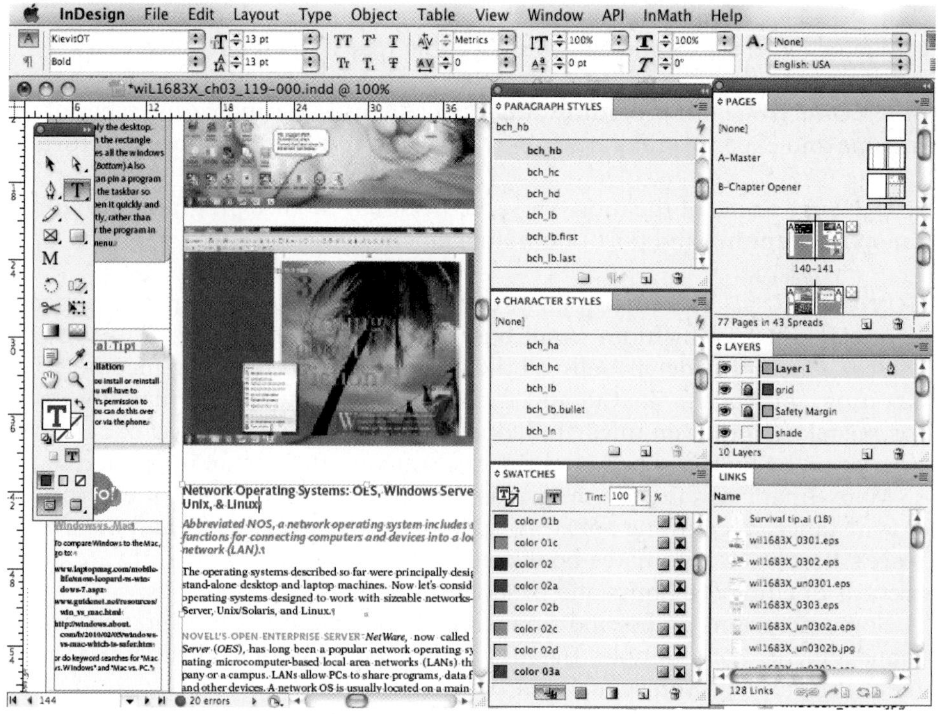

FEATURES OF DESKTOP PUBLISHING Desktop publishing has these characteristics:

- **Mix of text with graphics:** Desktop-publishing software allows you to precisely manage and merge text with graphics. As you lay out a page on-screen, you can make the text "flow," liquidlike, around graphics such as photographs. You can resize art, silhouette it, change the colors, change the texture, flip it upside down, and make it look like a photo negative.
- **Varied type & layout styles:** As do word processing programs, DTP programs support a variety of fonts, or typestyles, from readable Times Roman to staid Tribune to wild Jester and Scribble. Additional fonts can be purchased on disk or downloaded online. You can also create all kinds of rules, borders, columns, and page-numbering styles.
- **Use of files from other programs:** It's usually not efficient to do word processing, drawing, and painting with the DTP software. As a rule, text is composed on a word processor, artwork is created with drawing and painting software, and photographs are input using a scanner and then modified and stored using image-editing software. Prefabricated art to illustrate DTP documents may be obtained from clip-art sources. The DTP program is used to integrate all these files. You can look at your work on the display screen as one page, as two facing pages (in reduced size), or as "thumbnails." Then you can see it again after it has been printed out. (● *See Panel 3.32.*)

1992	1993	1994	1995	1997	1998	1999	2000
Microsoft's Access database program released	Multimedia desktop computers PDF software	Apple and IBM introduce PCs with full-motion video built in; wireless data transmission for small portable computers; Netscape's first web browser is introduced (based on Mosaic, introduced in 1993)	Windows 95 is released	Mac OS 8 sells 1.25 million copies in its first two weeks	Windows 98 is released	Adobe InDesign	Windows 2000 (ME) is released; Mac System 9.0

4 The files created in Steps 1, 2, 3 are imported into a DTP document.
5 DTP software is used to make up pages (arrange page content).
6 A black-and-white or color printer, usually a laser printer, prints out the pages.
3 Images scanned to disk by a scanner or Input from a digital camera
2 Art created with drawing or painting software.
1 Text created with word processing software.

panel 3.32

How desktop publishing uses other files

BECOMING A DTP PROFESSIONAL Not everyone can be successful at desktop publishing, because many complex layouts require experience, skill, and knowledge of graphic design. Indeed, use of these programs by nonprofessional users can lead to rather unprofessional-looking results. Nevertheless, the availability of microcomputers and reasonably inexpensive software has opened up a career area formerly reserved for professional typographers and printers.

QuarkXPress and Adobe InDesign are "high-end" professional DTP programs. Microsoft Publisher 2010 is a "low-end," consumer-oriented DTP package. Some word processing programs, such as Word and WordPerfect, also have many DTP features, although still not at the sophisticated level of the specialized DTP software. DTP packages, for example, give you more control over typographical characteristics and provide more support for full-color output.

Drawing & Painting Programs

There are several types of software for illustrators.

Commercial artists and fine artists have largely abandoned the paintbox and pen-and-ink for software versions of palettes, brushes, and pens. However, even nonartists can produce good-looking work with these programs.

2001	2003	2007	2008	2009	2012	2012/2013?	2014?
Windows XP becomes available; Mac OS X ships	Microsoft Vista OS (Pre-Beta) first introduced; Windows Mobile released	Windows Vista commercially available; Mac OS X.5 (Leopard) available	Cloud computing starts to take off	Windows 7	Web has a greater reach than TV	Windows 8 released	Most software will be open-source; 3-D user interface

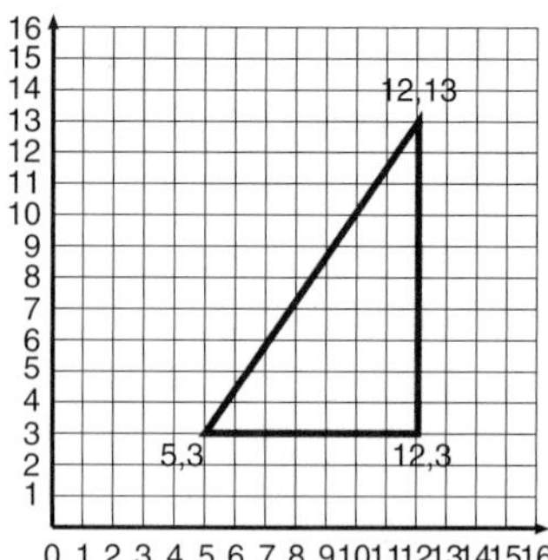

Vector image

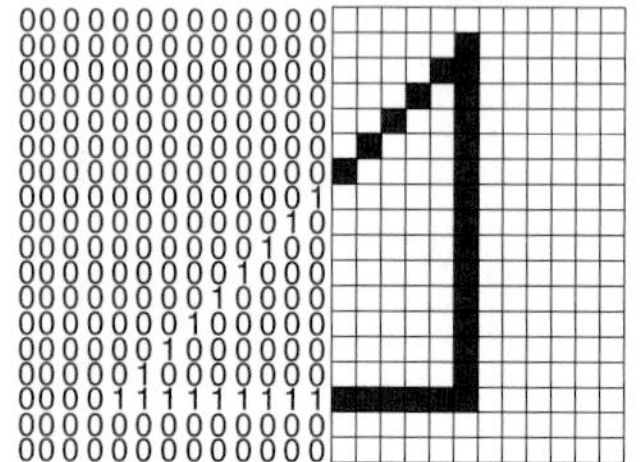
Bit-mapped image

There are two types of computer art programs, also called *illustration software*—drawing and painting.

DRAWING PROGRAMS A *drawing program* is graphics software that allows users to design and illustrate objects and products. Some drawing programs are CorelDRAW, Adobe Illustrator, and SmartDraw.

Drawing programs create *vector images*—images created from geometrical formulas. Almost all sophisticated graphics programs use vector graphics.

PAINTING PROGRAMS *Painting programs* are graphics programs that allow users to simulate painting on-screen. A mouse or a tablet stylus is used to simulate a paintbrush. The program allows you to select "brush" sizes, as well as colors from a color palette. Examples of painting programs are Adobe PhotoShop, Microsoft Digital Image Pro, Corel Photopaint, and JASC's PaintShop Pro.

Painting programs produce *bit-mapped images,* or *raster images,* made up of little dots.

Painting software is also called *image-editing software* because it allows you to retouch photographs, adjust the contrast and the colors, and add special effects, such as shadows.

SOME GRAPHICS FILE FORMATS When you create an image, it's important to choose the most appropriate graphics file format, which specifies the method of organizing information in a file. Among the most important graphics formats you are apt to encounter are these (more formats are covered in Chapter 8):

- **.bmp (BitMaP):** This bitmap graphic file format is native to Microsoft Windows and is used on PCs. Microsoft Paint creates .bmp file formats.
- **.gif (Graphic Interchange Format):** This format is used in web pages and for downloadable online images.
- **.jpeg (Joint Photographic Experts Group):** Pronounced *"jay-peg,"* this bitmapped format is used for websites and for photos and other high-resolution images.
- **.tiff (Tagged Image File Format):** This bitmapped format is used on both PCs and Macs for high-resolution files that will be printed.
- **.png (Portable network Graphics):** This file format was specifically created for web page images and can be used as a public domain alternative to .gif for compression.

File Formats

For a complete list of file formats, go to:

http://en.wikipedia.org/wiki/List_of_file_formats

Video/Audio Editing Software

Video and audio editing has become easier to do on microcomputer systems.

The popularity of digital camcorders ("camera recorders") has caused an increase in sales of video-editing software. This software allows you to import video footage to your PC and edit it, for example, deleting parts you don't want, reordering sequences, and adding special effects. Popular video-editing software packages include Adobe Premiere Elements, Corel Video Studio, Sony Pictures Digital Vegas, Magix Movie Edit Pro, Roxio Creator, Apple Final Cut Express, Pinnacle Studio DV, CyberLink Power Director, and Ulead VideoStudio.

Audio-editing software provides similar capabilities for working with sound tracks, and you can also clean up background noise (called *artifacts*) and emphasize certain sound qualities. Sound-editing software includes Windows Sound Recorder, Sony Pictures Sound Forge, Audacity (freeware), Felt Tip Software's Sound Studio (shareware), GoldWave, and WavePad.

Video and audio are covered in more detail in Chapter 5.

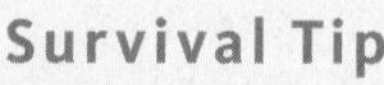

Compressing Web & Audio Files

Video and audio files tend to be very large, so they need to be edited down and compressed to be as short as possible, especially if they are to be used on web pages. Your software documentation will explain how to do this.

Sophisticated application software. Animation artist at work at the Studio Ghibli, Mitaka, Japan.

About Animation

For sources about animation, go to:

http://animation.about.com/od/referencematerials/a/freesoftware.htm

www.sciencedaily.com/articles/c/computer_animation.htm

http://entertainment.howstuffworks.com/computer-animation.htm

www.edb.utexas.edu/minliu/multimedia/Computer%20Animation.pdf

For schools offering training in computer-based graphics, including animation, check out:

www.computertrainingschool.com/?googleanimation=y&got=3d_animation_training&t=30

Animation Software

Animation is usually a part of multimedia presentations.

Animation **is the simulation (illusion) of movement created by displaying a series of still pictures, or frames, very quickly in sequence.** *Computer animation* refers to the creation of moving images by means of a computer. Whereas video devices record continuous motion and break it up into discrete frames, animation starts with independent pictures and puts them together to

Microsoft Gif Animator

Monday, January 10, 2011, 2:38   Software   Add a comment

Microsoft Gif Animator is a free and recommended gif animation creator.

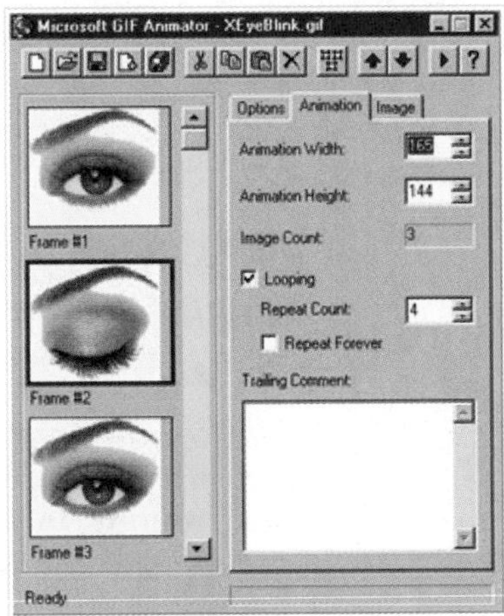

MICROSOFT GIF ANIMATOR

Microsoft Gif Animator was released by Microsoft long back but still it is popular as it works on all the popular versions of Windows, and **no installation** is required, simply select the picture and that's it.

Microsoft Gif Animator provides a very easy to use freeware. To create GIF animation you need to select all the images that you want in your animation and arrange them in the required order simple Microsoft Gif Animator will create GIF animation for you.

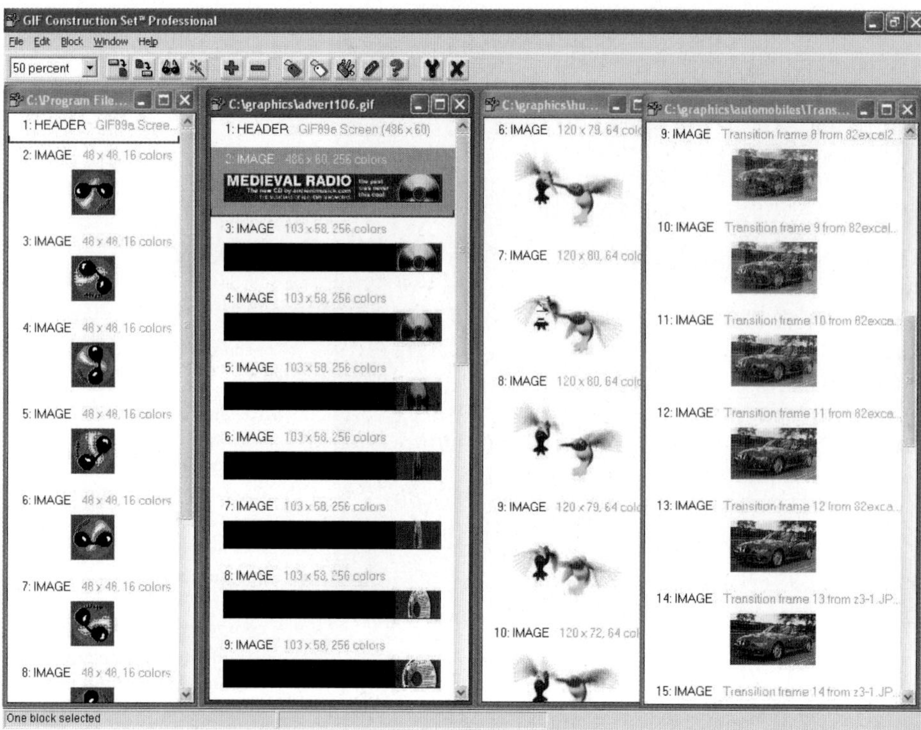

Screen from a GIF animation program

form the illusion of continuous motion. Animation is one of the chief ingredients of multimedia presentations and is commonly used on web pages. There are many software applications that enable you to create animations that you can display on a computer monitor.

The first type of animation to catch on for web use was called *GIF* (for Graphics Interchange Format) animation, and it is still very popular today. GIF files contain a group of images that display very quickly to simulate movement when a web page viewer clicks on the file icon. Animated GIF Construction Professional enables users to easily create animation via the use of a wizard. It allows the creation of many special effects and supports compression, as well as offering tutorials. Among the many other GIF animation software packages are Ulead Gif Animator and Easy Gif Animator.

Multimedia authoring software

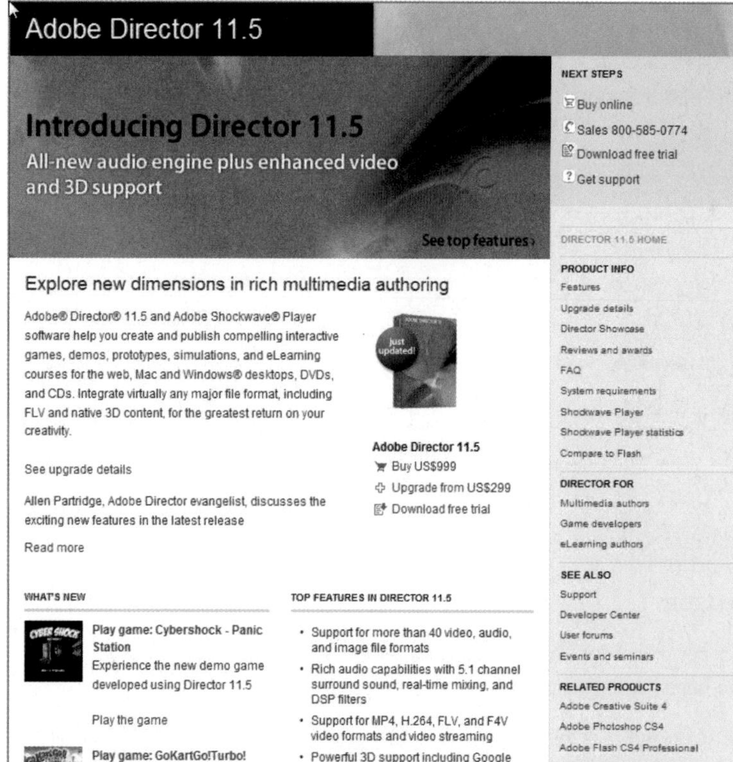

Multimedia Authoring Software

Multimedia software brings together many components.

<u>Multimedia authoring software</u> **combines text, graphics, video, animation, and sound in an integrated way to create stand-alone multimedia applications.** Content can be burned to CDs/DVDs or delivered via the web. Until the mid-1990s, multimedia applications were relatively uncommon, owing to the expensive hardware required. With increases in performance and decreases in price, however, multimedia is now commonplace. Nearly all microcomputers are capable of displaying video, though the resolution available depends on the power of the computer's video adapter and CPU. Macromedia Director and Macromedia Authorware are two popular multimedia authoring packages.

Many websites, as well as business training centers and educational institutions, use multimedia to develop interactive applications.

Web Page Design/Authoring Software

Software that allows you to create your own websites.

Web page design/authoring software **is used to create web pages with sophisticated multimedia features.** A few of these packages are easy enough for beginners to use. Some of the best-known are Adobe Dreamweaver, Seamonkey, Adobe Flash, Coffee Cup Visual Site Designer, RealMac Rapid Weaver, Microsoft Expression Web 4, and Dynamic HTML Editor. These tools generate the necessary HTML coding (p. 69) (and other, newer language coding) based on the user's design and content and present everything to the design in a WYSIWYG ("what you see is what you get") form. *(● See Panel 3.33.)*

Reall's HTML/WYSIWYG Editor IE5.5+ only

to use this free html editor..... wait until page loads fully......

```
<p><font face="Verdana" size="2">Reall's HTML Editor is an online
html/WYSIWYG editor to use for editing our templates.<br /><br />If
you're not a customer of ours, then please feel free to use this editor
if it helps you understand and learn HTML.</font> </p><p /><p /><p><font
face="Verdana" size="2">To start using our Editor, you need to highlight
all of the text here and then delete it. </font></p><p /><p /><p><font
face="Verdana" size="2">At the moment you are viewing this html in <font
color="#ff0000" size="2"><strong>WYSIWYG</strong></font> mode. If you
have a template of ours, simply delete this and then in code view paste
your template. To see how it looks, toggle back to the WYSIWYG
mode.</font></p><p /><p /><p><font face="Verdana" size="2">To see your
template in html view, you need to find and push the &lt; &gt; icon
button above (bottom row - right hand side) to see your html source
code.</font></p><p /><p /><p><font face="Verdana" size="2">If you get
stuck at any stage, just hit refresh in your browser window and this
text will appear again. With our Editor you can change images, insert
hyperlinks, add tables and so on, you could even create an entire
website..</font></p><p /><p /><p><font face="Verdana" size="2">Then
simply right click and then copy and paste this code into your file for
the page, and upload it to your server.</font><font
```

You are in TEXT MODE. Use the [<>] button to switch back to WYSIWYG.

Reall's HTML/WYSIWYG Editor IE5.5+ only

to use this free html editor..... wait until page loads fully......

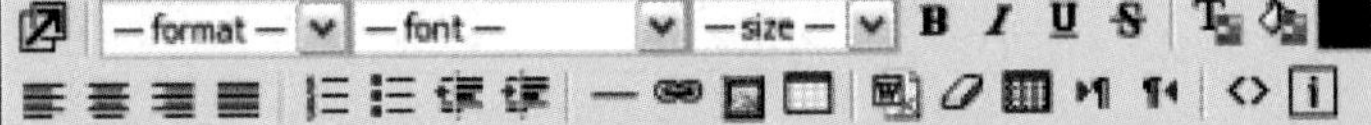

Reall's HTML Editor is an online html/WYSIWYG editor to use for editing our templates.

If you're not a customer of ours, then please feel free to use this editor if it helps you understand and learn HTML.

To start using our Editor, you need to highlight all of the text here and then delete it.

At the moment you are viewing this html in **WYSIWYG** mode. If you have a template of ours, simply delete this and then in code view paste your template. To see how it looks, toggle back to the WYSIWYG mode.

To see your template in html view, you need to find and push the < > icon button above (bottom row - right hand side) to see your html source code.

Web Authoring

This site offers a lot of information on web authoring tools:

http://webdesign.about.com/od/htmleditors/HTML_Editors_Web_Page_Authoring_Tools.htm

For some basic steps of web design, go to:

www.grantasticdesigns.com/5rules.html

www.chromaticsites.com/blog/12-steps-to-creating-a-professional-web-design/

www.rcaguilar.com/html-design.htm

http://ezinearticles.com/?Basic-Steps-For-Website-Design&id=5462320

For information on becoming a professional website designer, try:

www.wikihow.com/Become-a-Professional-Web-Designer-and-Programmer

http://designeducation.allgraphicdesign.com/

http://websitetips.com/business/education/

www.tuj.ac.jp/newsite/main/cont-ed/certificate/graphic_design.html

http://webdesign.about.com/od/jobs/p/aa031703a.htm

http://jobsearchtech.about.com/od/careerplanning/l/aa070201.htm

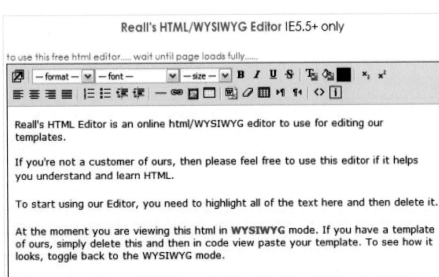

panel 3.33

(*Top*) HTML coded text; (*bottom*) the same text translated into WYSIWYG form by Reall's HTMLWYSIWYG Editor

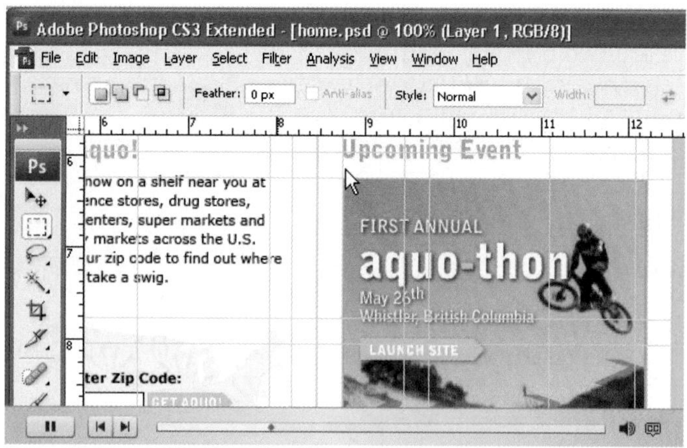

Inserting an Adobe Photoshop photo file into a Dreamweaver web page that is being designed

Internet access providers also offer some free, easy-to-use web-authoring tools for building simple websites. They help you create web pages, using icons and menus to automate the process; you don't need to know hypertext markup language to get the job done. These automated tools let you select a prepared, template web page design, type a few words, add a picture or two—and you're done. To save the pages and make them accessible on the Internet, the provider grants you a certain amount of space on its web servers.

Website design can include much more than text: for example, animation, video, sound, interactivity, search-engine functions. But before creating a website, the designer must first plan exactly what is needed in the website—define the audience, as well as the purpose and the content. Once a website is completed, it must be uploaded (published) in order to be available to Internet users via a browser. Some people with powerful personal computers and an always-on Internet connection, such as cable, leave their websites on their own computers; the website is accessed by users typing in the site's URL (web address; Chapter 2, p. 66) in their browsers. Most people, however, use ftp software (covered shortly) to upload their website files to a server host, where, for a fee, the website is stored for access.

Complicated business websites are created and maintained by professional website developers.

more info!

Social Media Management Software

There is also software for managing your social networking and media activities:

http://workawesome.com/software/social-media-management/

www.vivalogo.com/vl-resources/open-source-social-networking-software.htm

www.web-strategist.com/blog/2010/03/19/list-of-social-media-management-systems-smms/

www.crowdcontrolhq.com/social-media-management-software/

Project Management Software

Software can be very helpful in managing large projects.

As we have seen, a personal information manager (PIM) can help you schedule your appointments and do some planning. That is, it can help you manage your own life. But what if you need to manage the lives of others in order to accomplish a full-blown project, such as steering a political campaign or handling a nationwide road tour for a band? Strictly defined, a *project* is a one-time operation involving several tasks and multiple resources that must be organized toward completing a specific goal within a given period of time. The project can be small, such as an advertising campaign for an in-house advertising department, or large, such as construction of an office tower or a jetliner.

Project management software **is a program used to plan and schedule the people, costs, and resources required to complete a project on time.** (● *See Panel 3.34.*) For instance, the associate producer on a feature

panel 3.34

Project management software: Tenrox

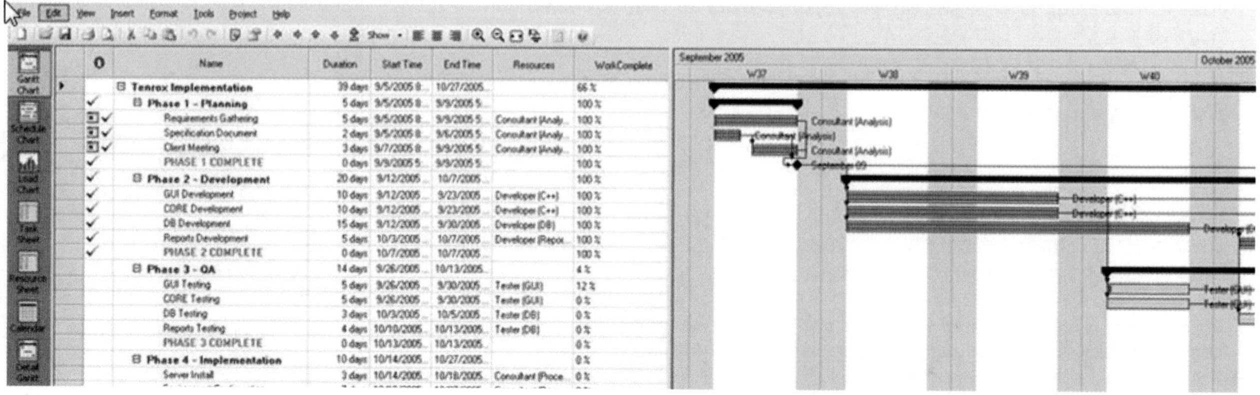

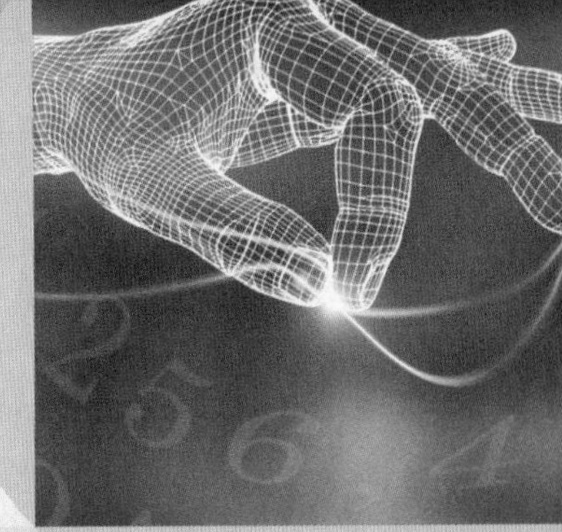

PRACTICAL ACTION

Help in Building Your Web Page

Local and national Internet access providers often offer web-page-building tools, as well as space on their servers for storing your web page. Other sources of information for designing and building web pages are these:

For Novices

- ***Yahoo!:*** Yahoo! offers web-page-building tools and templates under the name SiteBuilder (*http://webhosting.yahoo.com/ps/sb/index.php*), which enables you to add music and other special effects to your web pages and have components that track how many people visit your site. For a fee, Yahoo! offers unlimited storage for your website and will help you determine your URL (website address).
- ***Lycos:*** Lycos offers templates and tools, and it also offers tutorials to help you get started if you want to build your own pages from scratch. Lycos also offers free space in its Tripod area (*www.tripod.lycos.com*). As with Yahoo!, you will have advertisements on your pages unless you pay a small fee to get rid of them.
- ***Google Sites:*** Google offers this free online tool that makes it easy for anyone to create and publish web pages in just minutes. You can see what your pages will look like, and you can edit your pages right in your browser. Google will host your web pages on your own site at *www.google.com/accounts/ServiceLogin?continue=http%3A%2F%2Fsites.google.com%2F&followup=http%3A%2F%2Fsites.google.com%2F&service=jotspot&passive=true&ul=.1*

Once you've created your website, you'll need to "publish" it—upload it to a web server for viewing on the Internet. You can get upload instructions from your online service or Internet access provider, which may also provide space (for free or for a fee) on its servers. (Or, as we mentioned earlier, if you have a powerful, large-storage-capacity microcomputer that has an always-on Internet connection, you can use it to host your own website.)

For much more information about building and storing your own web pages, just do a keyword search using "build web page" or "website design" in any good search engine.

film might use such software to keep track of the locations, cast and crew, materials, dollars, and schedules needed to complete the picture on time and within budget. The software would show the scheduled beginning and ending dates for a particular task—such as shooting all scenes on a certain set—and then the date that task was actually completed. Examples of project management software are Mindjet MindManager Pro 9, MindView, Intuit Eclipse, Microsoft Project, FastTrackSchedule, and Project KickStart.

Integrated Software & Software Suites

Some programs combine several applications in one package.

Integrated software, for personal computers, combines several applications in one program, typically providing at least word processing, spreadsheet, and database management. Presentation graphics, page layout, paint, calendar, address book, email, and other applications may also be included. Microsoft Works and AppleWorks are two primary examples of integrated software packages. One of the benefits of integrated software is that it eliminates the need to open a separate software application for reference purposes or to perform a few quick tasks. However, integrated software programs have been scaled back from their full-fledged versions and do not offer all the features and functions of each program.

Software suites are not the same as integrated software packages; they are bundled software—several programs available together in a single package. Although there are suites for graphics, mathematics, and other applications, the most popular are "office suites." Also known as "productivity suites," they are a set of basic programs that use a single user interface. The primary programs

more info!

Top-Selling Software 2009–2010

1. Microsoft Office 2007 Home & Student (Windows)
2. Turbo Tax 2009 Deluxe (Windows/Mac)
3. Microsoft Office 2008 Home & Student (Mac)
4. Microsoft Windows 7 Home Premium Upgrade
5. Norton 360 3.0 (Windows)
6. iWork 2009 (Mac)
7. Microsoft Office 2007 (Windows)
8. QuickBooks 2010 Pro (Windows)
9. Turbo Tax 2009 Home & Business Federal + State (Windows/Mac)
10. MobileMe (Windows/Mac)

(The NPD Group/Retail Tracking Service, *The World Almanac and Book of Facts, 2011*)

are word processing, spreadsheet, presentation graphics, database, and email, although other programs and utilities may also be included; examples of software suites are Microsoft Office, WordPerfect Office, Lotus SmartSuite, StarOffice, OpenOffice.org, Google Apps, and Zoho.

Survival Tip

Try before You Buy

Free trial versions of software are often offered as downloads from company sites.

Portable Document Format (PDF)

PDF is a multiplatform file format that allows documents to be used with any operating system.

Short for ***Portable Document Format,* PDF is a file format developed by Adobe Systems that preserves most attributes (including text, color, formatting, graphics, layout, and more) of a source document no matter which application, platform, and hardware type was originally used to create it.** PDF captures information from a variety of applications on different platforms making it possible to send documents and have them appear on the recipient's monitor (or printer) as they were intended to be viewed. *(• See Panel 3.35.)*

Originally PDF was mostly used by graphic artists, designers, and publishers for producing color page proofs. Today, however, PDF is used for virtually any data that needs to be exchanged among applications and users. Individuals, businesses, and government agencies around the world trust and rely on PDF to communicate. PDF files are widely used on websites and are also used to distribute electronic documents over networks and via email.

A PDF file can be shared, viewed, and printed by anyone using the free downloadable Adobe Reader software regardless of the operating system and original application used. PDF can also be used on mobile devices. In addition, many applications, such as Microsoft Word, enable users to save their files in a PDF version. To be able to create and work with all of Adobe's PDF features, you need to purchase the complete Adobe Acrobat Suite.

Computer-Aided Design (CAD)

CAD uses computer programs to design two- and three-dimensional models.

The Ultimate CAD Directory

This directory has information about all sorts of CAD products to suit every type of need:

www.tenlinks.com/CAD

Computers have long been used in engineering design. ***Computer-aided design (CAD)* programs are intended for the design of products, structures, civil engineering drawings, and maps.** CAD programs, which are available for microcomputers, help architects design buildings and workspaces and help engineers design cars, planes, electronic devices, roadways, bridges, and subdivisions. CAD and drawing programs are similar. However, CAD programs provide precise dimensioning and positioning of the elements being drawn, so they can be transferred later to computer-aided manufacturing (CAM) programs. Also, CAD programs lack some of the special effects for illustrations that come with drawing programs. One advantage of CAD software is that the product can be drawn in three dimensions and then rotated on the screen, so the designer can see all sides. *(• See Panel 3.36, p. 184.)* Examples of popular CAD programs are Autodesk, AutoCAD, TurboCAD, Alibre Design, and PowerCADD.

Computer-aided design/computer-aided manufacturing (CAD/CAM) software allows products designed with CAD to be input into an automated manufacturing system that makes the products. For example, CAD/CAM systems brought a whirlwind of enhanced creativity and efficiency to the fashion industry. The designs and specifications are then input into CAM systems that enable robot pattern-cutters to automatically cut thousands of patterns from fabric with only minimal waste. Whereas previously the fashion industry worked about a year in advance of delivery, CAD/CAM has cut that time to less than 8 months—a competitive edge for a field that feeds on fads.

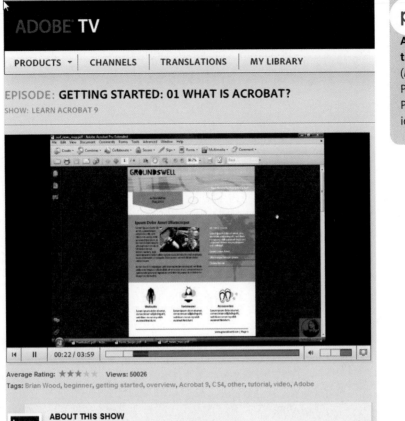

ADOBE TV

PRODUCTS | CHANNELS | TRANSLATIONS | MY LIBRARY

EPISODE: **GETTING STARTED: 01 WHAT IS ACROBAT?**

SHOW: LEARN ACROBAT 9

00:22 / 03:59

Average Rating: ★★★★★ **Views: 50026**

Tags: Brian Wood, beginner, getting started, overview, Acrobat 9, CS4, other, tutorial, video, Adobe

Learn

ABOUT THIS SHOW

LEARN ACROBAT 9

Learn how to use Acrobat 9 Pro with tutorials selected by experts at Adobe.There's everything from Getting Started for beginners, to New Features, Workflows, and Overviews.

MORE EPISODES IN THIS SHOW ▾

panel 3.35

Adobe Acrobat PDF tutorial screens

(*lower right corner*) Adobe PDF file icon. Any file in the PDF format will have this icon next to the filename.

Learn Acrobat X

These tutorials and learning resources from Adobe and community experts will give beginners and experienced users a core overview of Adobe® Acrobat® X.

Getting started

Setup
Downloading, installing, and setting up

Overview
Getting started with Acrobat X (video 5:19)
Creating simple PDFs with Acrobat (HTML)

Tutorials
25 How-To Tutorials-Acrobat X (PDF)
Getting Started (GS) tutorials, Learn Acrobat X show (video series)

What's new in Acrobat X

What's new in Acrobat X Pro (HTML)
What's new in Acrobat X Standard (HTML)

Creating PDF files from Microsoft Office (video 5:23)
Converting scanned PDF files to other file formats (video 5:23)
Recognizing text in scanned PDF documents (video 4:41)
How to customize your PDF Portfolio (video 5:46)

How to create actions (video 4:59)
Using SharePoint with Acrobat X (video 3:45)
How to track your review in Acrobat (video 5:13)
Using Adobe SendNow (video 3:00)
Saving search results in Acrobat (video 5:21)

Learn more

Create and combine files
Creating PDF files from a web browser (video 3:58)
Converting PDF files to other file formats (video 5:45)
What is a PDF Portfolio? (video 4:55)
Working in PDF Portfolios (video 5:09)

Collaboration
The basics of commenting (video 5:03)

Forms
Managing form data (video 5:19)

Editing tools
Adding interactivity to PDF files (video 4:51)
Adding rich media to PDF files (video 7:37)
Manipulating pages in Acrobat (video 5:34)
Comparing documents (video 5:30)

Security
How to protect PDF documents (video 8:23)
Removing sensitive information (video 6:46)
How to remove hidden information (video 4:41)
Using digital signatures in a PDF file (video 7:53)

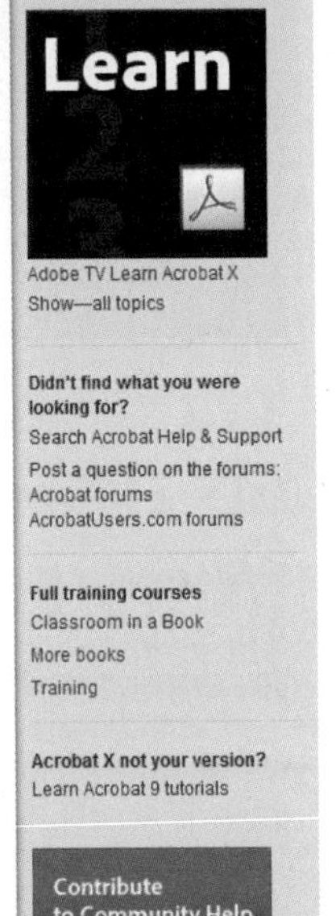

Learn

Adobe TV Learn Acrobat X Show—all topics

Didn't find what you were looking for?
Search Acrobat Help & Support
Post a question on the forums:
Acrobat forums
AcrobatUsers.com forums

Full training courses
Classroom in a Book
More books
Training

Acrobat X not your version?
Learn Acrobat 9 tutorials

Contribute to Community Help
Learn how›

panel 3.36

CAD

CAD software is used for nearly all three-dimensional designing. (*Top*) TurboCAD; (*bottom*) Autodesk

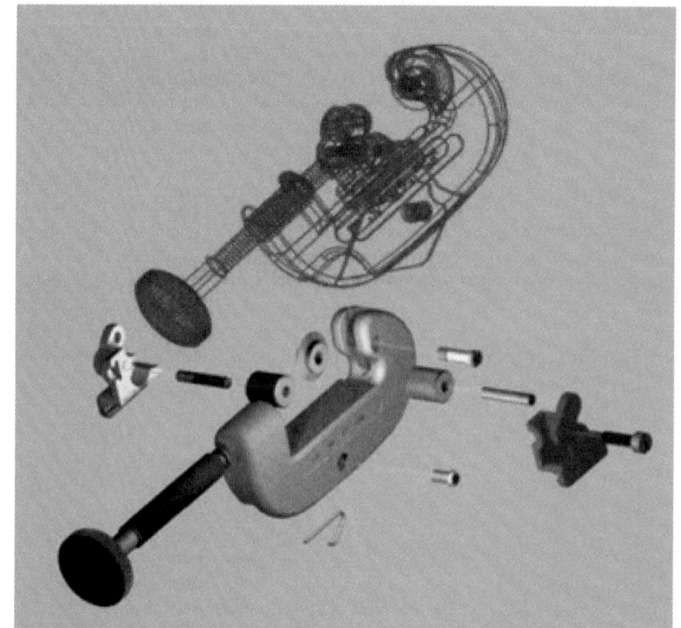

3.11 Filenames & Extensions

A filename is a name given to a computer file to distinguish it from other computer files. A file extension is the suffix preceded by a dot at the end of a filename that indicates what type of file it is.

Survival Tip

Some Records Have to Be Hardcopy

You could scan your birth certificate, will, or car ownership title into your computer to make a digital record. But such records printed off a hard drive aren't always legally acceptable. Original documents are often required by government agencies and the court system.

An applications file—such as a Word document and an Excel spreadsheet document—is the collection of data or information that is treated as a unit by the computer; as we noted earlier, it is a data file. **Data files are given names—*filenames*.** If you're using a word processing program to write a psychology term paper, you might name it "Psychreport." In a database, a filename might be "AccountingPersonnel."

Filenames also have *extensions,* or *extension names,* usually three or four letters added after a period following the filename. For example, the *.doc* in *Psychreport.doc* is recognized by Microsoft Word as a "document," as is *.docx,* which refers to a Word 2007 or 2010 document. Extensions are usually inserted automatically by the application software.

Three types of data files worth particular attention are graphics, audio, and video files.

- **Graphics files:** Some important ones are *.bmp, .tiff, .gif, .jpeg,* and *.png.*
- **Audio files:** The ones you're most apt to encounter are *.mp3, .wav,* and *.mid.*
- **Animation/video files:** Common files are *.qt, .mpg, .wmv, .avi.,* and *.rm.*

The box on the next page describes these and other common types of files. (● *See Panel 3.37.*)

Data Compression: Putting More Data in Less Space

Data compression methods enable devices to transmit or store the same amount of data in fewer bits.

The vast streams of text, audio, and visual information threaten to overwhelm us. To fit large multimedia files into less space and increase the speed of data transmission, a technique called compression/decompression, or *codec,* is used. ***Compression*** **is a method of removing repetitive elements from a file so that the file requires less storage space and therefore less time to transmit.** Later the data is decompressed—the repeated patterns are restored.

There are two principal methods of compressing data—lossless and lossy. In any situation, which of these two techniques is more appropriate will depend on whether data quality or storage space is more critical.

Lossless compression uses mathematical techniques to replace repetitive patterns of bits with a kind of coded summary. During decompression, the coded summaries are replaced with the original patterns of bits. In this method, the data that comes out is exactly the same as what went in; it has merely been repackaged for purposes of storage or transmission. Lossless techniques are used when it's important that nothing be lost—for instance, for computer data, database records, spreadsheets, and word processing files.

Lossy compression techniques permanently discard some data during compression. Lossy data compression involves a certain loss of accuracy in exchange for a high degree of compression (to as little as 5% of the original file size). This method of compression is often used for graphics files and sound files. Thus, a lossy codec might discard subtle shades of color or sounds outside the range of human hearing. Most users wouldn't notice the absence of these details. Examples of two lossy compression file formats are *.jpeg* and *.mpeg.*

More Types of Application Software

Gaming software examples:

BioShock Infinite
Batman: Arkham City
NBA 2K12
Insanely Twisted Shadow Planet
Super Mario 3DS

Educational software examples:

SAT
GMAT
LSAT
MCAT
lumosity.com
brainage.com

Simulation program examples:

Flight Simulator X
Physion (physics simulation software)
CCENT 640-822 Network Simulator

Course management software examples:

Learning Management LMS
Blackboard
Moodle

Reference & encyclopedia examples:

Britannia Ultimate Reference Suite
Oxford World Encyclopedia
Reference Point Software (for MLA and APA scholarly writing)

panel 3.37

Common types of files

Graphic files

- *.bmp (BitMap):* Bitmapped graphic format native to Microsoft Windows. Some Macintosh programs can also read .bmp files.
- *.gif (Graphic Interchange Format):* Pronounced "Jiff." Format used on web pages and downloadable images.
- *.jpeg or .jpg (Joint Photographic Experts Group):* Pronounced "*Jay-peg.*" Used for web images and for digital photography, especially for high-resolution images.
- *.pcx:* Format introduced for PC Paintbrush. Used for other graphics packages as well.
- *.pict (PICTure):* Format used by Apple for use on Macintosh computers.
- *.png (Portable Network Graphic):* Pronounced "ping." Patent-free alternative to *.gif.*
- *.tiff or .tif (Tagged Image File Format):* High-resolution bitmapped graphics file widely used on both Macintosh and PC computers. Used in exchanging bit-mapped files that will be printed.

Audio files

- *.au:* Low-fidelity monaural format now often used to distribute sample sounds online.
- *.mid (MIDI, Musical Instrument Digital Interface):* Format meant to drive music synthesizers.
- *.mp3 (MPEG-3):* File format used to compress CD-quality music while preserving much of the original sound quality. (Also *.mp4.*)
- *.wav (WAVe):* Waveform file format that contains all the digital information needed to play speaker-quality music.

Video files

- *.avi (Audio Video Interleaved):* Video file format recognized by Windows Media Player. Not good for broadcast-quality video.
- *.mov or .qt (QuickTime):* Video file formats developed by Apple for QuickTime video player. Can play broadcast-quality video.
- *.mpg or .mpeg (Motion Picture Experts Group):* Video formats for full-motion video. MPEG-2 format used by DVD-ROM disks. MPEG-4 recognized by most video player software.
- *.rm (RealMedia):* Popular file format for streaming video.
- *.wmv (Windows Media Video):* Video format recognized by Windows Media Player.

Other files

- *ASCII files:* Text-only files containing no graphics and no formatting such as boldface or italic. ASCII format is used to transfer documents between computers, such as PC and Macintosh. Such files may use the *.txt* (for text) extension.
- *Web files:* Files carried over World Wide Web. Extensions include *.html, .htm, .xml, and .asp* (active server page).
- *Desktop publishing files:* Include PostScript commands, which instruct a PostScript printer how to print a file and use *.eps* (encapsulated PostScript).
- *Drivers:* Software drivers often have the extension *.drv.*
- *Windows operating system files:* Files such as *Autoexec.bat* and *Config.sys* relate to OS setup.
- *PDF (Portable Document Format) files:* Files that use Adobe Acrobat's format for all types of document exchange as well as for publishing documents on the web that are downloaded and read independently of the HTML pages. These files use the extension *.pdf.* Editable PDF files are created with Adobe's Acrobat software. Acrobat can convert a wide variety of document types on Windows, Mac, and Unix to PDF format.

EXPERIENCE BOX

Getting Help from Tech Support

Your screen flashes "Fatal Error." Your new software upgrade totals your printer. You can't connect to your Internet access provider. No wonder one online survey found that nearly 20% of the respondents admitted they'd dropped a computer on the floor out of anger.[5] *Because of the complicated mesh of elements—software, hardware, communications, people—Murphy's Law ("If anything can go wrong, it will") seems to apply in computing as almost nowhere else. Information technology is becoming more complex. The more personal computers and other infotech devices are expected to do—music, video, photos, DVDs, home networking, email, and so on—the more complex the interaction between the components and the harder it is to figure out what's wrong. Also, the proliferation of viruses, worms, spyware, and other types of malware makes the support task more daunting. Thus, one of the most valuable tasks you can learn is how to deal with tech support—getting technical help on the phone or online (via email or websites) when things don't work.* (• *See Panel 3.38 on the next page.*)

Improving Your Chances with Tech Support

Here are three things that you can do in advance to improve your chances of success:

- *Use the web to research a manufacturer's tech support before you buy:* If you decide to purchase or upgrade, go to the manufacturer's website and look at tech support resources to see how coherent and easily accessible they are. This will also give you some feel for the kinds of problems customers are having. Also check out some online comment forums on the item you are planning to buy/upgrade (for example, *www.techsupportforum.com/forums*). Another good idea is to print out some articles on tech help, such as *PC Magazine*'s "Top Tips for Tech Support Success" (*www.pcmag.com/article2/0,2817,2192075,00.asp*), and keep them on hand for when you can't get online for help.
- *Call tech support before you buy:* Calling tech support in advance of purchasing may cost you something in long-distance charges, but you'll also find out how confusing the voice menu is and how long it takes to reach a live human.
- *Create a fact sheet with your computer's important specs:* When you get a computer or new software, create a fact sheet listing the important technical specifications and attach it to the outside of the computer case. This will provide you with the kind of information that tech support personnel will ask should you call them. Take a copy along with you whenever you buy a game or other video- and sound-intensive application to make sure it is compatible with the rest of your system.
- *If you have a communication problem, ask to be referred to another person:* Many companies now hire people in offshore call centers as tech support specialists, and sometimes you may have trouble with unfamiliar accents. If this happens to you, don't give up your place in line; ask to be connected to another service representative.

Other Sources of Help

Although usually less specific in solving your problem, other sources of help are available:

- *Help programs: instruction manuals, software, and online:* User guides or instruction manuals printed on paper have traditionally accompanied software. Now most software publishers rely more on Help programs on a CD/DVD or in downloadable PDF manuals. Help programs are also available through the Internet. The problem with this approach, of course, is—How do you go online to solve the problem of your computer not working if your computer isn't working? (It helps to have two computers.)
- *Commercial how-to books:* How-to books are the kind of books found both in computer stores and in general bookstores such as Barnes & Noble and on Amazon.com. Examples are the "For Dummies" or "Complete Idiot's" books (such as *PCs for Dummies* and *The Complete Idiot's Guide to Microsoft Office*).
- *Knowledgeable friends:* Nothing beats having a knowledgeable friend: your instructor, a student more advanced than you, or someone with a technical interest in computers. We can't stress enough how important it is to get to know people—from your classes, from computer user groups (including online Internet groups), from family friends, or whatever—who can lend aid and expertise when your computer software or hardware gives you trouble.

Company	Price	Services
Ask Dr. Tech 1-888-592-8843 *www.AskDrTech.com*	$98 per year, $39 per month, $24 per call	Phone, email, or online chat support for PCs and Macs and peripherals
geeks to go! Toll free: 888-433-5435 *www.geekstogo.com/*	Free	Live chat support with consultants and forums for numerous software and hardware problems
Geek Squad 1-800-433-5778 *www.geeksquad.com*	From $29 to about $300, depending on the problem; at your location, one of their stores, or at a Best Buy store	Almost any problem related to computers, electronics, and networks
Geeks on Call 1-800-905-GEEK *www.geeksoncall.com*	Varies, depending on the problem	Same as above
Nerds On Site 1-877-696-3737 *www.nerdsonsite.us*	Same as above	Same as above
iYogi 1-877-570-2965 *www.iyogi.com*	$169 per year	24/7 PC and peripherals support
Just Answer *www.justanswer.com/Geek*	Name your price and place a deposit Free online chat, email, text message	PCs and Macs
itok 1-866-515-itok *www.itokhelp.com*	$40 per incident and up, or $20 per month (gold membership) or $35 per month (platinum membership)	PCs, Macs, and peripherals
firedog 1-877-505-3714 *www.firedog.com*	$25–$50 per month, depending on the number of computers	All kinds of support

panel 3.38

Some individual technical support services

800 and 888 numbers are toll-free. Most services are available 24 hours a day, 7 days a week. Note that not all operations serve Macintosh users, and not all have a phone option—which can be a handicap when you're not able to go online.

KEY TERMS & EXPLANATIONS

analytical graphics (p. 164) Also called *business graphics;* graphical forms that make numeric data easier to analyze than it is when organized as rows and columns of numbers. The principal examples of analytical graphics are bar charts, line graphs, and pie charts. Why it's important: *Whether viewed on a monitor or printed out, analytical graphics help make sales figures, economic trends, and the like easier to comprehend and analyze.*

animation (p. 177) The simulation (illusion) of movement created by displaying a series of still pictures, or frames, very quickly in sequence. Why it's important: *Animation is used in video games, movies, special-effects presentations, and even in email, to make it more interesting.*

application software (p. 121) Software that has been developed to solve a particular problem for users—to perform useful work on specific tasks or to provide entertainment. Why it's important: *Application software consists of most of the software you are familiar with and use on a daily basis.* (Compare ***system software.***)

booting (p. 122) Loading an operating system into a computer's main memory. Why it's important: *Without booting, computers could not operate. The programs responsible for booting are stored permanently in the computer's electronic circuitry. When you turn on the machine, programs called* diagnostic routines *test the main memory, the central processing unit, and other parts of the system to make sure they are running properly. Next, BIOS (basic input/output system) programs are copied to main memory and help the computer interpret keyboard characters or transmit characters to the display screen or to a diskette. Then the boot program obtains the operating system, usually from the hard disk, and loads it into the computer's main memory, where it remains until you turn the computer off.*

cell (p. 163) Place where a row and a column intersect in a spreadsheet worksheet; its position is called a *cell reference or a cell address.* Why it's important: *The cell is the smallest working unit in a spreadsheet. Data and formulas are entered into cells. Cell addresses provide location references for worksheet users.*

compression (p. 185) Method of removing repetitive elements from a file so that the file requires less storage space, then later decompressing the removed data, or restoring the repeated patterns. Why it's important: *Compression/decompression makes storage and transmission of large files, such as multimedia files, more feasible.*

computer-aided design (CAD) (p. 182) Programs intended for the design of products, structures, civil engineering drawings, and maps. Why it's important: *CAD programs, which are available for microcomputers, help architects design buildings and workspaces and help engineers design cars, planes, electronic devices, roadways, bridges, and subdivisions. While similar to drawing programs, CAD programs provide precise dimensioning and positioning of the elements being drawn, so they can be transferred later to computer-aided manufacturing programs; however, they lack special effects for illustrations. One advantage of CAD software is that three-dimensional drawings can be rotated on-screen, so the designer can see all sides of the product.*

cursor (p. 156) Movable symbol on the display screen that shows where the user may next enter data or commands. The symbol is often a blinking rectangle or an I-beam. You can move the cursor on the screen using the keyboard's directional arrow keys or a mouse. The point where the cursor is located is called the *insertion point.* Why it's important: *All application software packages use cursors to show the current work location on the screen.*

data files (p. 153) Files that contain data—words, numbers, pictures, sounds, and so on. Why it's important: *Unlike program files, data files don't instruct the computer to do anything. Rather, data files are there to be acted on by program files. Examples of common extensions in data files are* .txt *(text) and* .xls *(spreadsheets). Certain proprietary software programs have their own extensions, such as* .html *for Hypertext Markup Language,* .ppt *for PowerPoint, and* .mdb *for Access. (Extensions are three or more letters.)*

database (p. 165) Collection of interrelated files in a computer system. These computer-based files are organized according to their common elements, so that they can be retrieved easily. Why it's important: *Businesses and organizations build databases to help them keep track of and manage their affairs. In addition, online database services put enormous resources at the user's disposal.*

database software (p. 166) Also called *database manager* or *database management system (DBMS);* application software that sets up and controls the structure of a database and access to the data. Why it's important: *Database software allows users to organize and manage huge amounts of data.*

default settings (p. 160) Settings automatically used by a program unless the user specifies otherwise, thereby overriding them. Why it's important: *Users need to know how to change default settings in order to customize documents.*

desktop (p. 133) The operating system's main interface screen. Why it's important: *The desktop displays pictures (icons) that provide quick access to programs and information.*

desktop publishing (DTP) (p. 173) Application software and hardware system that involves mixing text and graphics to produce high-quality output for commercial printing, using a microcomputer and mouse, scanner, digital cameras, laser or ink-jet printer, and DTP software (such as QuarkXPress and InDesign or, at a more consumer-oriented level, Microsoft Publisher). Often the printer is used primarily to get an advance look before the completed job is sent to a typesetter for even higher-quality output. Some word processing programs, such as Word and WordPerfect, have rudimentary DTP features. Why it's important: *Desktop publishing has reduced the number of steps, the time, and the money required to produce professional-looking printed projects.*

device drivers (p. 127) Specialized software programs—usually components of system software—that allow input and output devices to communicate with the rest of the computer system. Why it's important: *Drivers are needed so that the computer's operating system can recognize and run peripheral hardware.*

embedded system (p. 148) Operating system for any electronic system that uses a CPU chip but that is not a general-purpose workstation, desktop, or laptop computer. It is a specialized computer system that is part of a larger system or a machine. Why it's important: *Embedded systems are used, for example, in automobiles, planes, trains, barcode scanners, fuel pumps, space vehicles, machine tools, watches, appliances, cellphones, and robots. Handheld computers and personal digital assistants also rely on specialized operating systems. Such operating systems include Android, Symbian, iPhone, Windows Phone, BlackBerry OS, Embedded Linux, and many others.*

exporting (p. 153) Transforming data into a format that can be used in another program and then transmitting it. Why it's important: *Users need to know how to export many types of files.*

file (p. 124) A named collection of data (data file) or a program (program file) that exists in a computer's secondary storage, such as on a hard disk or CD. Why it's important: *Dealing with files is an inescapable part of working with computers. Users need to be familiar with the different types of files.*

filename (p. 184) The name given to a file. Why it's important: *Files are given names so that they can be differentiated. Filenames also have extension names of three or four letters added after a period following the filename.*

financial software (p. 172) Application software that ranges from personal-finance managers to entry-level accounting programs to business financial-management packages. Why it's important: *Financial software provides users with powerful management tools (personal-finance managers) as well as small business programs. Moreover, tax programs provide virtually all the forms needed for filing income taxes, make complex calculations, check for mistakes, and even unearth deductions you didn't know existed. Tax programs can also be integrated with personal finance software to form an integrated tool. Accounting software automates bookkeeping tasks, while payroll software keeps records of employee hours and produces reports for tax purposes. Some programs allow users to set up a business from scratch. Financial software also includes investment software packages and various retirement planning programs.*

formulas (p. 163) In a spreadsheet, instructions for calculations entered into designated cells. Why it's important: *When spreadsheet users change data in one cell, all the cells linked to it by formulas automatically recalculate their values.*

freeware (p. 151) Copyrighted software that is distributed free of charge, today most often over the Internet. Why it's important: *Freeware saves users money.*

function keys (p. 131) Keys labeled "F1," "F2," and so on, positioned along the top of the keyboard. Why it's important: *They are used to execute commands specific to the software being used.*

functions (p. 163) In a spreadsheet, built-in formulas that perform common calculations. Why it's important: *After the values have been entered into the worksheet, formulas and functions can be used to calculate outcomes.*

graphical user interface (GUI) (p. 133) User interface in which icons and commands from menus may be selected by means of a mouse or keystrokes. Why it's important: *GUIs are easier to use than command-driven interfaces.*

Help command (p. 138) Command generating a table of contents, an index, and a search feature that can help users locate answers to questions about the software. Why it's important: *Help features provide a built-in electronic instruction manual.*

icons (p. 133) Small pictorial figures that represent programs, data files, or procedures. Why it's important: *Icons have simplified the use of software. The feature represented by the icon can be activated by clicking on the icon.*

importing (p. 153) Getting data from another source and then converting it into a format compatible with the program in which the user is currently working. Why it's important: *Users will often have to import files.*

key (p. 166) Also called *key field, primary key, sort key, index,* or *keyword;* field used to sort data in a database. For example, if users sort records by age, then the age field is a key. Why it's important: *Key fields are needed to identify and retrieve specific items in a database. Most database management systems allow you to have more than one key so that you can sort records in different ways. One of the keys is designated the primary key and must hold a unique value for each record. A key field that identifies records in different tables and relates them to the primary key is called a foreign key. Foreign keys are used to cross-reference data among relational tables. The most frequent key field used in the United States is the Social Security number, but any unique identifier, such as employee number or student number, can be used.*

Linux (p. 146) Free (open-source) version of the Unix OS, supported by the efforts of thousands of volunteer programmers. Why it's important: *Linux is an inexpensive, open-source operating system useful for online applications and to PC users who have to maintain a web server or a network server.*

Macintosh operating system (Mac OS) (p. 140) System software that runs only on Apple Macintosh computers. Why it's important: *Although Macs are not as common as PCs, many people believe they are easier to use. Macs are often used for graphics and desktop publishing.*

macro (p. 132) Also called *keyboard shortcut;* a single keystroke or command—or a series of keystrokes or commands—used to automatically issue a longer, predetermined series of keystrokes or commands. Why it's important: *Users can consolidate several activities into only one or two keystrokes. The user names the macro and stores the corresponding command sequence; once this is done, the macro can be used repeatedly.*

menu (p. 133) Displayed list of options—such as commands—to choose from. Why it's important: *Menus are a feature of GUIs that make software easier to use.*

menu bar (p. 135) Bar across the top of the display window, below the title bar. Why it's important: *It shows the names of the various pull-down menus available.*

Microsoft Windows (p. 142) Most common operating system for desktop and portable microcomputers. Windows 95 was succeeded by Windows 98, Windows 2003, Windows Me, Windows XP, Vista, Windows 7, and Windows 8. Why it's important: *Windows supports the most applications written for microcomputers.*

Microsoft Windows Server (p. 145) Microsoft's multitasking OS designed to run on network servers in businesses of all sizes. Why it's important: *It allows multiple users to share resources such as data, programs, and printers and to build web applications and connect to the Internet.*

multimedia authoring software (p. 178) Application software that combines text, graphics, video, animation, and sound in an integrated way to create stand-alone multimedia applications. Why it's important: *Multimedia is now commonplace and an important feature of the web and many software application, including those for mobile devices.*

multitasking (p. 125) Feature of OS software that allows the execution of two or more programs concurrently by one user almost at the same time on the same computer with one or two CPUs. For instance, you might write a report on your computer with one program while another plays a music CD. Why it's important: *Multitasking allows the computer to switch rapidly back and forth among different tasks. The user is generally unaware of the switching process and thus can work in more than one application at a time.*

open-source software (p. 146) Software that any programmer can download from the Internet free and modify with suggested improvements. The only qualification is that changes can't be copyrighted; they must be made available to all and remain in the public domain. Why it's important: *Because this software is not proprietary, any programmer can make improvements, which can result in better-quality software.*

operating system (OS) (p. 121) Low-level master system of programs that manage the basic operations of the computer. Why it's important: *These programs provide resource management services of many kinds. In particular, they handle the control and use of hardware resources, including disk space, memory, CPU time allocation, and peripheral devices. The operating system allows users to concentrate on their own tasks or applications rather than on the complexities of managing the computer.*

PDF *See* **portable document format.**

personal-finance manager (p. 172) Application software that lets users keep track of income and expenses, write checks, do online banking, and plan financial goals. Why it's important: *Personal-finance software can help people manage their money more effectively.*

personal information manager (PIM) (p. 168) Software that helps users keep track of and manage information they use on a daily basis, such as addresses, telephone numbers, appointments, to-do lists, and miscellaneous notes. Some programs feature phone dialers, outliners (for roughing out ideas in outline form), and ticklers (or reminders). Why it's important: *PIMs can help users better organize and manage daily business activities.*

pirated software (p. 151) Software that is obtained illegally. Why it's important: *If you buy such software, not only do the original copyright owners not get paid for their creative work but you risk getting inferior goods and, worse, picking up a virus. To discourage software piracy, many software manufacturers require that users register their software when they install it on their computers. If the software is not registered, it will not work properly.*

platform (p. 138) Particular processor model and operating system on which a computer system is based. Why it's important: *Generally, software written for one platform will not run on any other. Users should be aware that there are Mac platforms (Apple Macintosh) and Windows platforms, or "PC platforms" (for personal computers such as Dell, Acer, Inovo, Toshiba, Hewlett-Packard, and others that run Microsoft Windows).*

pointer (p. 132) Indicator that usually appears as an arrow, although it changes shape depending on the application. The mouse is used to move the pointer to a particular place on the display screen or to point to little symbols, or icons. Why it's important: *Manipulating the pointer on the screen by means of the mouse is often easier than typing commands on a keyboard.*

portable document format (PDF) (p. 182) File format developed by Adobe Systems. PDF captures text, graphic, and formatting information from a variety of applications on different platforms making it possible to send documents and have them appear on the recipient's monitor (or printer) as they were intended to be viewed. Why it's important: *A properly prepared PDF file maintains the original fonts (type styles and type sizes), images, colors, and graphics, as well as the exact layout of the file. A PDF file can be shared, viewed, and printed by anyone using the free downloadable Adobe Reader software. PDF can also be used on mobile devices. With the complete Adobe Acrobat suite, users can also edit PDF files.*

presentation graphics software (p. 169) Software that uses graphics, animation, sound, and data or information to make visual presentations. Why it's important: *Presentation graphics software provides a means of producing sophisticated graphics.*

productivity software (p. 154) Application software such as word processing programs, spreadsheets, and database managers. Why it's important: *Productivity software makes users more productive at particular tasks.*

program files (p. 152) Files containing software instructions. Why it's important: *Contrast* ***data files.***

project management software (p. 180) Program used to plan and schedule the people, costs, and resources required to complete a project on time. Why it's important: *Project management software increases the ease and speed of planning and managing complex projects.*

public-domain software (p. 150) Software, often available on the Internet, that is not protected by copyright and thus may be duplicated by anyone at will. Why it's important: *Public-domain software offers lots of software options to users who may not be able to afford much commercial software. Users may download such software from the Internet free and make as many copies as they wish.*

range (p. 163) A group of adjacent cells in a spreadsheet—for example, A1 to A5. Why it's important: *Ranges help sort data for calculation or reports.*

recalculation (p. 163) The process of recomputing values in a spreadsheet, either as an ongoing process as data is entered or afterward, with the press of a key. Why it's important: *With this simple feature, the hours of mind-numbing work required to manually rework paper spreadsheets have become a thing of the past.*

relational database (p. 166) Database in which data is organized into related tables. Each table contains rows and columns; the rows are called *records,* and the columns are called *fields.* An example of a record is a person's address—name, street address, city, and so on.

An example of a field is that person's last name; another field would be that person's first name; a third field would be that person's street address; and so on. Why it's important: *The relational database is the most common type of database.*

rentalware (p. 151) Software that users lease for a fee and download whenever they want it. Why it's important: *This is the concept behind application service providers (ASPs).*

rollover (p. 133) Icon feature, also called a tooltip, in which a small textbox explaining the icon's function appears when you roll the mouse pointer over the icon. A rollover may also produce an animated graphic. Why it's important: *The rollover gives the user an immediate explanation of an icon's meaning.*

saving (p. 161) Storing, or preserving, a document as an electronic file permanently—on hard disk, flash drive, CD, or online (in the cloud) for example. Why it's important: *Saving is a feature of nearly all application software. Having the document stored in electronic form spares users the tiresome chore of retyping it from scratch whenever they want to make changes. Users need only retrieve it from the storage medium and make the changes, then resave it and print it out again.*

scrolling (p. 156) Moving quickly upward, downward, or sideways through the text or other screen display. Why it's important: *A standard computer screen displays only 20–22 lines of standard-size text; however, most documents are longer than that. Using the directional arrow keys, or the mouse and a scroll bar located at the side of the screen, users can move ("scroll") through the display screen and into the text above and below it.*

shareware (p. 151) Copyrighted software that is distributed free of charge but requires that users make a monetary contribution in order to continue using it. Shareware is distributed primarily through the Internet. Because it is copyrighted, you cannot use it to develop your own program that would compete with the original product. Why it's important: *Like public-domain software and freeware, shareware offers an inexpensive way to obtain new software.*

software license (p. 150) Contract by which users agree not to make copies of software to give away or resell. Why it's important: *Software manufacturers don't sell people software; they sell them licenses to become authorized users of the software.*

special-purpose keys (p. 131) Keys used to enter, delete, and edit data and to execute commands. For example, the *Esc* (for "Escape") key tells the computer to cancel an operation or leave ("escape from") the current mode of operation. The Enter, or Return, key tells the computer to execute certain commands and to start new paragraphs in a document. Why it's important: *Special-purpose keys are essential to the use of software.*

spreadsheet program (p. 161) Application software that allows users to create tables and financial schedules by entering data and formulas into rows and columns arranged as a grid on a worksheet display screen. A spreadsheet file is called a workbook. Why it's important: *When data is changed in one cell, values in other cells in the linked worksheets are automatically recalculated.*

supervisor (p. 123) Also called *kernel;* the central component of the operating system that manages the CPU. Why it's important: *The supervisor remains in main memory while the computer is running. As well as managing the CPU, it copies other nonresident programs into memory to perform tasks that support application programs.*

system software (p. 121) The software that helps the computer perform essential operating tasks and enables the application software to run. The most important component of system software is the *operating system*, the master control program that runs the computer. Examples of operating system software for the PC are various Microsoft programs (such as Windows XP, Vista, and 7), Apple Macintosh OS X, Unix, and Linux. Why it's important: *Computers cannot run application software without having system software.*

taskbar (p. 135) Graphic toolbar that appears at the bottom of the Windows screen. Why it's important: *The taskbar presents the applications that are running.*

template (p. 158) In word processing, a preformatted document that provides basic tools for shaping a final document—the text, layout, and style for a letter, for example. Why it's important: *Templates make it very easy for users to prepare professional-looking documents, because most of the preparatory formatting is done.*

title bar (p. 135) Bar across the very top of the display window. Why it's important: *It shows the name of the folder the user is in.*

toolbar (p. 135) Bar across the top of the display window, below the menu bar. It displays menus and icons representing frequently used options or commands. Why it's important: *Toolbars make it easier to identify and execute commands.*

Unix (p. 145) Proprietary multitasking operating system for multiple users that has built-in networking capability and versions that can run on all kinds of computers. Why it's important: *Government agencies, universities, research institutions, large corporations, and banks all use Unix for everything from designing airplane parts to currency trading. Unix is also used for website management. The developers of the Internet built their communication system around Unix because it has the ability to keep large systems (with hundreds of processors) churning out transactions day in and day out for years without fail.*

user interface (p. 131) User-controllable graphic display screen that allows the user to communicate, or interact, with his or her computer. Why it's important: *The interface determines the ease of use of hardware and software. The three types of user interface are command-driven, menu-driven, and graphical (GUI), which is now the most common. Without user interfaces, no one could operate a computer system.*

utility programs (p. 130) Also known as *service programs;* system software components that perform tasks related to the control, allocation, and maintenance of computer resources. Why it's important: *Utility programs enhance existing functions or provide services not supplied by other system software programs. Most computers come with built-in utilities as part of the system software; they usually include backup, data recovery, virus protection, data compression, and file defragmentation, along with check (scan) disk and disk cleanup.*

value (p. 163) A number or date entered in a spreadsheet cell. Why it's important: *Values are the actual numbers used in the spreadsheet—dollars, percentages, grade points, temperatures, or whatever.*

web page design/authoring software (p. 179) Software used to create web pages with sophisticated multimedia features. Why it's important: *Allows beginners as well as professional web designers to create web pages, which have become extremely important communications tools on the Internet, for all sorts of purposes.*

what-if analysis (p. 164) Spreadsheet feature that employs the recalculation feature to investigate how changing one or more numbers changes the outcome of the calculation. Why it's important: *Users can create a worksheet, putting in formulas and numbers, and then ask, "What would happen if we change that detail?"—and immediately see the effect.*

window (p. 135) Rectangular frame on the computer display screen. Through this frame users can view a file of data—such as a document, spreadsheet, or database—or an application program. Why it's important: *Using windows, users can display at the same time portions of several documents and/or programs on the screen.*

word processing software (p. 156) Application software that allows users to use computers to format, create, edit, print, and store text material, among other things. Why it's important: *Word processing software allows users to maneuver through a document and delete, insert, and replace text, the principal correction activities. It also offers such additional features as creating, editing, formatting, printing, and saving.*

word wrap (p. 156) Special feature that automatically continues text to the next line by "wrapping around" when the user reaches the right margin. Why it's important: *You don't have to hit a "carriage-return" key or Enter key to move to the next line.*

worksheet (p. 162) See **spreadsheet program.**

CHAPTER REVIEW

1 LEARNING MEMORIZATION

"I can recognize and recall information."

Self-Test Questions

1. ________ software enables the computer to perform essential operating tasks.
2. ________ ________ is the term for programs designed to perform specific tasks for the user.
3. ________ is the activity in which a computer works on more than one process at a time.
4. ________ is the scattering of portions of files about the disk in nonadjacent areas, thus greatly slowing access to the files.
5. Windows and Mac OS are generally used on ________ computers.
6. ________ is the process of loading an operating system into a computer's main memory.
7. A(n) ________ is a utility that will find all the scattered files on your hard disk and reorganize them as contiguous files.
8. The ________ is the component of system software that comprises the master system of programs that manage the basic operations of the computer.
9. The ________ is the user-controllable display screen that allows you to communicate, or interact, with your computer.
10. Disk scanner and disk cleanup utilities detect and correct certain types of common problems on hard disks, such as removing unnecessary files called ________ files that are created by Windows only for short tasks and system restore after system problems.
11. OSs allow users to control access to their computers via use of a(n) ________ and a(n) ________.
12. Software or hardware that is ________ means that it is privately owned and controlled by a company.
13. Linux is ________-________ software—meaning any programmer can download it from the Internet for free and modify it with suggested improvements.
14. When you power up a computer by turning on the power "on" switch, this is called a ________ boot. If your computer is already on and you restart it, this is called a ________ boot.
15. ________ software allows you to create and edit documents.
16. ________ is the activity of moving upward or downward through the text or other screen display.
17. Name four editing features offered by word processing programs: ________, ________, ________, ________.
18. In a spreadsheet, the place where a row and a column intersect is called a(n) ________.
19. The ________ is the movable symbol on the display screen that shows you where you may next enter data or commands.
20. When you buy software, you pay for a ________, a contract by which you agree not to make copies of the software to give away or resell.
21. Records in a database are sorted according to a(n) ________.
22. ________ involves mixing text and graphics to produce high-quality output for commercial printing.
23. A(n) ________ allows users to create tables and do "what-if" financial analyses by entering data and formulas into rows and columns arranged as a grid on a display screen.
24. ________ automatically continues text to the next line when you reach the right margin.

25. Settings that are automatically used by a program unless the user specifies otherwise are called ________ ________.

26. ________-________ software is not protected by copyright and may be copied by anyone.

27. ________ ________ are specialized software programs that allow input and output devices to communicate with the rest of the computer system.

28. The ________ format allows documents to be sent to almost any platform and be opened without losing any of their characteristics (text, colors, graphics, formatting).

29. ________ files contain software instructions; ________ files contain words, numbers, pictures, sounds, and so on.

Multiple-Choice Questions

1. Which of the following are functions of the operating system?
   a. file management
   b. CPU management
   c. task management
   d. booting
   e. all of these

2. Which of the following was the first major microcomputer OS?
   a. Mac OS
   b. Windows
   c. DOS
   d. Unix
   e. Linux

3. Which of the following is a prominent network operating system?
   a. Linux
   b. Ubuntu
   c. OES
   d. DOS
   e. Mac OS

4. Which of the following is the newest Microsoft Windows operating system?
   a. Windows Vista
   b. Windows XP
   c. Windows 7
   d. Windows NT
   e. Windows CE

5. Which of the following refers to the execution of two or more programs by one user almost at the same time on the same computer with one central processor?
   a. multitasking
   b. multiprocessing
   c. time-sharing
   d. multiprogramming
   e. coprocessing

6. Which of the following are specialized software programs that allow input and output devices to communicate with the rest of the computer system?
   a. multitasking
   b. boot-disks
   c. utility programs
   d. device drivers
   e. service packs

7. Which of the following is *not* an advantage of using database software?
   a. integrated data
   b. improved data integrity
   c. lack of structure
   d. elimination of data redundancy

8. Which of the following is *not* a feature of word processing software?
   a. spelling checker
   b. cell address
   c. formatting
   d. cut and paste
   e. find and replace

9. What is the common consumer computer interface used today?
   a. command-driven interface
   b. graphical user interface
   c. menu-driven interface
   d. electronic user interface
   e. biometric user interface

10. Which type of software can you download and duplicate without any restrictions whatsoever and without fear of legal prosecution?
    a. commercial software
    b. shareware
    c. public-domain software
    d. pirated software
    e. rentalware

11. Which of these is not a common file extension?
    a. .doc
    b. .nos
    c. .docx
    d. .xls
    e. .jpeg

True/False Questions

T F 1. The supervisor manages the CPU.

T F 2. The first graphical user interface was provided by Microsoft Windows.

T F 3. All operating systems are mutually compatible.

T F 4. *Font* refers to a preformatted document that provides basic tools for shaping the final document.

T F 5. Unix crashes often and thus is not normally used for running important large systems.

T F 6. Windows NT is the most recent Microsoft OS.

T F 7. Spreadsheet software enables you to perform what-if calculations.

T F 8. Public-domain software is protected by copyright and so is offered for sale by license only.

T F 9. The records within the various tables in a database are linked by a key field.

T F 10. QuarkXPress and Adobe InDesign are professional desktop-publishing programs.

T F 11. The best-known graphical user interface is the command-driven one.

T F 12. Microsoft PowerPoint is an example of financial software.

T F 13. Drawing programs create vector images, and painting programs produce bit-mapped images.

T F 14. General computer users can design their own web pages using Adobe Dreamweaver, Adobe Flash, and Microsoft FrontPage.

T F 15. Data files are identified by filenames.

2 LEARNING COMPREHENSION

"I can recall information in my own terms and explain it to a friend."

Short-Answer Questions

1. Briefly define *booting*.
2. What is the difference between a command-driven interface and a graphical user interface (GUI)?
3. Why can't you run your computer without system software?
4. Why is multitasking useful?
5. What is a device driver?
6. What is a utility program?
7. What is a platform?
8. What are the three components of system software? What is the basic function of each?
9. What is open-source software?
10. What does defragmenting do?
11. What is an embedded system?
12. What are the following types of application software used for?
    a. project management software
    b. desktop-publishing software
    c. database software
    d. spreadsheet software
    e. word processing software
13. Which program is more sophisticated, analytical graphics or presentation graphics? Why?
14. How are the following different from one another? Pop-up menu; pull-down menu; cascading menu.
15. What is importing? Exporting?
16. Briefly compare drawing programs and painting programs.
17. Explain what computer-aided design (CAD) programs do.
18. Discuss the various software licenses: site licenses, concurrent-use licenses, multiple-user licenses, single-user license.

3 LEARNING APPLYING, ANALYZING, SYNTHESIZING, EVALUATING

"I can apply what I've learned, relate these ideas to other concepts, build on other knowledge, and use all these thinking skills to form a judgment."

Knowledge in Action

1. Here's a Windows 7 exercise in defragmenting your hard-disk drive. Defragmenting is a housekeeping procedure that will speed up your system and often free up hard-disk space.

   Click on the Start button at the bottom left corner of your screen. Click on All Programs, then Accessories, then System Tools, Disk Defragmenter. Click on the Analyze Disk button to find out how much of your hard disk is fragmented, and click on Defragment Disk to run the defragmentation utility.

   Many times when your PC isn't performing well, such as when it's sluggish, running both ScanDisk and Defragment will solve the problem.

2. Ray Kurzweil is, among other things, the author of *The Age of Intelligent Machines; The Age of Spiritual Machines, When Computers Exceed Human Intelligence;* and *The Singularity Is Near: When Humans Transcend Biology*. He has said: "We are entering a new era. I call it 'the Singularity.' It's a merger between human intelligence and machine intelligence that is going to create something bigger than itself. It's the cutting edge of evolution on our planet" (*www.edge.org/3rd_culture/kurzweil_singularity/kurzweil_singularity_index.html;* accessed July 1, 2009). He envisions a future in which information technologies have advanced so far that they enable humans to transcend their biological limitations (*www.singularity.com*).

   What is "singularity"? Will it hurt? Will we hate it? Will we be able to notice it? Search the terms "Kurzweil" and "Singularity" on *www.singularity.com, www.kurzweilai.net*, and other sites, and see if you can explain the concept to friends within 5 minutes or so.

3. What do you think is the future of Linux? Experts currently disagree about whether Linux will become a serious competitor to Windows. Research Linux on the web. Which companies are creating application software to run on Linux? Which businesses are adopting Linux as an OS? What are the predictions about Linux use?

4. How do you think you will obtain software for your computer in the future? Explain your answer.

5. Design your own handheld. Draw what your ideal handheld would look like, and draw screens of what your user interface would look like. Describe the key features of your handheld.

6. What sorts of tasks do operating systems *not* do that you would like them to do?
7. If you were in the market for a new microcomputer today, what application software would you want to use on it? Why? What are some "dream" applications that you would like that have not yet been developed?
8. Several websites include libraries of shareware programs. Visit the *www.5star-shareware.com* site and identify three shareware programs that interest you. State the name of each program, the operating system it runs on, and its capabilities. Also, describe the contribution you must make to receive technical support. What about freeware? Check out *www.freewarehome.com*.
9. What is your opinion of downloading free music from the web to play on your own computer and/or CDs? Much attention has been given lately to music downloading and copyright infringement. Research this topic in library magazines and newspapers or on the Internet, and take a position in a short report.
10. How do you think you could use desktop publishing at home? For personal items? Family occasions? Holidays? What else? What hardware and software would you have to buy?
11. Think of three new ways that software companies could prevent people from pirating their software.
12. What is your favorite application software program of all? Why?
13. Did your computer come with a Windows Startup disk, and have you misplaced it? If your computer crashes, you'll need this disk to reinstall the operating system.

    To learn the benefits of having a Startup disk, visit *www.microsoft.com*. Type *startup* in the "search for" box; then click on the links that interest you.

Web Exercises

1. Go to *http://list.driverguide.com/list/company243/* and identify the drivers that correspond to equipment you use. How does this website let you know which devices the drivers are for and which operating systems are compatible with them? If you own your own computer, go to the manufacturer's website and locate its resource for updating drivers. Does the manufacturer recommend any driver updates that you could use?
2. Use a web search tool such as Google or Yahoo! to find some online antivirus sites—sites where users can regularly download updates for their antivirus software. Do you know what kind of antivirus software is installed on your computer?
3. Microsoft offers "patches," or updates, for its Windows OS. Go to *www.microsoft.com* and search for the list of updates. What kinds of problems do these updates fix? Do you need any?
4. The History of Operating Systems: Visit the following websites to get an overview of the evolution and history of the theory and function of operating systems:

    www.microsoft.com/windows/winhistoryintro.mspx

    www.computinghistorymuseum.org/teaching/papers/research/history_of_operating_system_Moumina.pdf

    www.osdata.com/kind/history.htm

    www.answers.com/topic/history-of-operating-systems
5. Some people are fascinated by the error message commonly referred to as the "Blue Screen of Death" (BSOD) or "Doom." Run a search on the Internet and find websites that sell T-shirts with the BSOD image on it, photo galleries of public terminals displaying the BSOD, fictional stories of BSOD attacks, and various other forms of entertainment based on the infamous error message.

    Do a search on the web to find users' hypotheses of why the BSOD occurs, and find methods to avoid it. Here are a few sites:

    www.maximumpc.com/article/features/blue_screen_survival_guide

    http://bluescreenofdeathfixer.com/

    http://bsod.org/

    http://bbspot.com/News/2000/9/bsod_death.html

    http://technet.microsoft.com/en-us/library/cc750081.aspx
6. Using Microsoft Excel or another spreadsheet program, make a food shopping list incorporating the estimated price for each item, and then have Excel calculate the overall cost. Then go buy your groceries and compare Excel's price with the supermarket's price. What else could Excel help you with?
7. The Windows operating system comes with a basic word processing program called *WordPad*. Go to the Microsoft home page and to *http://en.wikipedia.org/wiki/WordPad* and find out how WordPad differs from Microsoft Word. Then use a keyword search in a search engine to get more information about these programs. Which one is right for you?
8. Curriculum Data Wales (CDW) is a public/private partnership that has been charged by the Welsh Assembly Government with the task of designing, building, and maintaining the National Grid for Learning Cymru as a bilingual service to schools and colleges in Wales. CDW's website includes some short tutorials on desktop-publishing (DTP), spreadsheet, word processing, and database management software:

    www.ngfl-cymru.org.uk/vtc-home/vtc-ks4-home/vtc-ks4-ict/vtc-ks4-ict-application_software.htm

    Work through the tutorials. Did they expand your knowledge of these applications?

    Do a search for *"application software" & tutorials*. What other useful tutorials did you find?

4

HARDWARE: THE CPU & STORAGE

How to Choose a Multimedia Computer System

Chapter Topics & Key Questions

4.1 **Microchips, Miniaturization, & Mobility** What are the differences between transistors, integrated circuits, chips, and microprocessors?

4.2 **The System Unit: The Basics** How is data represented in a computer, what are the components of the system cabinet, and what are processing speeds?

4.3 **More on the System Unit: What Supports the Processor?** How do the processor and memory work, and what are the control unit, ALU, registers, some important ports, buses, and cards?

4.4 **Secondary Storage** What are the features of hard disks, optical disks, magnetic tape, smart cards, flash memory, and online secondary storage?

4.5 **Future Developments in Processing & Storage** What are some forthcoming developments that could affect processing power and storage capacity?

Download the free UIT 10e App for key term flash cards, quizzes, and a game, *Over the Edge*

The microprocessor was "the most important invention of the 20th century," says Michael Malone, author of The Microprocessor: A Biography.[1]

Quite a bold claim, considering the incredible products that issued forth during those 100 years. More important than the airplane? More than television? More than atomic energy?

According to Malone, the case for the exalted status of this thumbnail-size information-processing device is demonstrated, first, by its pervasiveness in the important machines in our lives, from computers to transportation. Second, "The microprocessor is, intrinsically, something special," he says. "Just as [the human being] is an animal, yet transcends that state, so too the microprocessor is a silicon chip, but more." Why? Because it can be programmed to recognize and respond to patterns in the environment, as humans do. Malone writes: "Implant [a microprocessor] into a traditional machine—say an automobile engine or refrigerator—and suddenly that machine for the first time can learn, it can adapt to its environment, respond to changing conditions, become more efficient, more responsive to the unique needs of its user."[2]

4.1 Microchips, Miniaturization, & Mobility

Since the early 1970s, microchips have gotten smaller and smaller yet more and more powerful and faster.

The microprocessor has presented us with gifts that we may only barely appreciate—*portability* and *mobility* in electronic devices.

In 1955, for instance, portability was exemplified by the ads showing a young woman holding a Zenith television set over the caption: it doesn't take a muscle man to move this lightweight TV. That "lightweight" TV weighed a hefty 45 pounds. Today, by contrast, there is a handheld Axion 7-inch color TV weighing a mere 2 pounds.

Had the transistor not arrived, as it did in 1947, the Age of Portability and consequent mobility would never have happened. To us a "portable" telephone might have meant the 40-pound backpack radio-phones carried by some American GIs during World War II, rather than the 3-ounce shirt-pocket cellular models available today.

From Vacuum Tubes to Transistors to Microchips

The evolution of small electronic components has been relatively quick.

A *circuit* is a closed path followed or capable of being followed by an electric current. Without circuits, electricity would not be controllable, and so we would not have electric or electronic appliances. Old-time radios used vacuum tubes—small lightbulb-size electronic tubes with glowing filaments, or wire circuits, inside them—to facilitate the transmission (flow) of electrons.

One computer with these tubes, the ENIAC, was switched on in 1946 at the University of Pennsylvania and employed about 18,000 of them. Unfortunately, a tube failure occurred on average once every 7 minutes. Since it took more than 15 minutes to find and replace the faulty tube, it was difficult to get any useful computing work done—during a typical week, ENIAC was down for about one-third of the time. Moreover, the ENIAC was enormous, occupying 1,800 square feet and weighing more than 30 tons. ENIAC could perform about 5,000 calculations per second—more than 10,000 times *slower* than modern PCs. Yet even at that relatively slow speed, ENIAC took about 20 seconds to complete a problem that had taken experts 1 or 2 days to complete manually.

THE TRANSISTOR ARRIVES The transistor changed all that. **A *transistor* is essentially a tiny electrically operated switch, or gate, that can alternate between "on" and "off" many millions of times per second.** The transistor was developed by Bell Labs in 1947. The first transistors were one-hundredth the size of a vacuum tube, needed no warm-up time, consumed less energy, and were faster and more reliable. *(• See Panel 4.1.)* Moreover, they marked the beginning of a process of miniaturization that has not ended yet. In 1960 one transistor fit into an area about a half-centimeter square. This was sufficient to permit Zenith, for instance, to market a transistor radio weighing about 1 pound (convenient, the company advertised, for "pocket or purse"). Today up to about 781 million transistors can be squeezed onto one computer chip, and a headset radio weighs only 4.3 ounces. Hewlett-Packard is working on a transistor about 0.1 nanometer square. One nanometer is 1 billionth of a meter; a human hair is about 80,000 nanometers thick.

In the old days, transistors were made individually and then formed into an electronic circuit with the use of wires and solder. Today transistors are part of an ***integrated circuit*—an entire electronic circuit, including wires, formed on a single "chip," or piece, of special material, usually silicon,** as part of a single manufacturing process. Integrated circuits were developed by Jack Kilby at Texas Instruments, who demonstrated the first one in 1958. *(• See the timeline, Panel 4.2.)*

An integrated circuit embodies what is called solid-state technology. **In a *solid-state device*, the electrons travel through solid material with no moving parts**—in this case, silicon. They do not travel through a vacuum, as was the case with the old radio vacuum tubes.

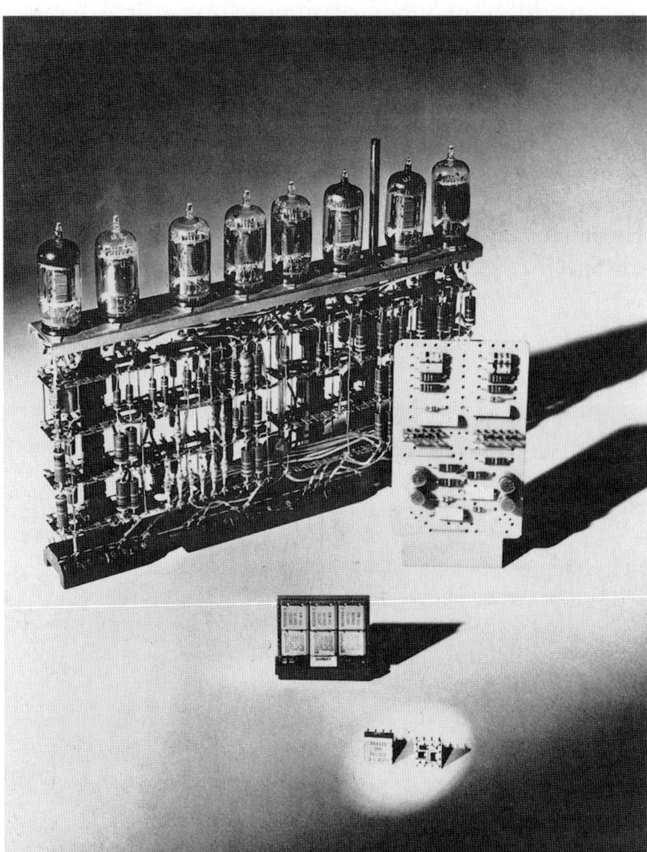

panel 4.1

Shrinking components

The lightbulb-size 1940s vacuum tube was replaced in the 1950s by a transistor one-hundredth its size. Many of today's transistors are much smaller, being microscopic in size.

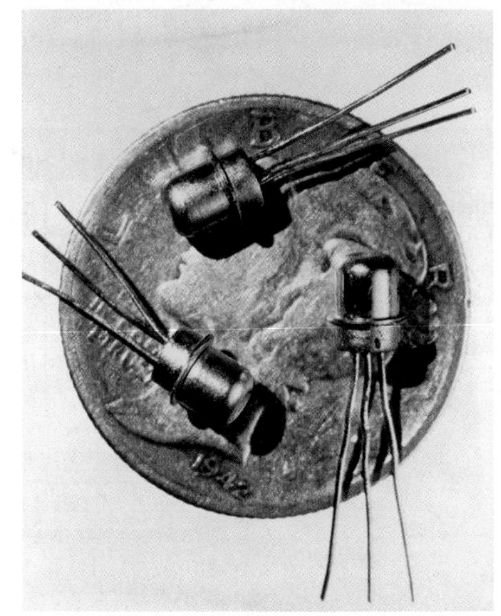

SILICON & SEMICONDUCTORS What is silicon, and why use it? ***Silicon*** **is an element that is widely found in clay and sand. It is used not only because its abundance makes it cheap but also because it is a semiconductor.**

A *semiconductor* is a material whose electrical properties are intermediate between a good conductor of electricity and a nonconductor of electricity. (An example of a good conductor of electricity is the copper in household wiring; an example of a nonconductor is the plastic sheath around that wiring.) Because it is only a semiconductor, silicon has partial resistance to electricity. As a result, highly conducting materials can be overlaid on the silicon to create the electronic circuitry of the integrated circuit. (• *See Panel 4.3.)*

Silicon alone has no processing power. **A *chip,* or *microchip,* is a tiny piece of silicon that contains millions of microminiature integrated electronic circuits.** Chip manufacturing requires very clean environments, which is why chip-manufacturing workers dress almost as though they are getting ready for a surgical operation. Such workers must also be highly skilled, which is why chip makers are not found everywhere in the world.

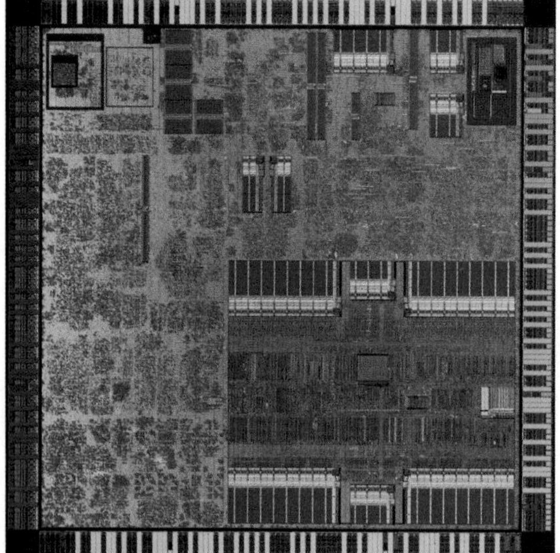

Chip with etched transistors. This chip would be about 1/2 inch by 1/2 inch and be several layers deep, with transistors etched on each level.

Miniaturization Miracles: Microchips & Microprocessors

There are different kinds of microchips; the microprocessor is one.

Microchips—"industrial rice," as the Japanese call them—are responsible for the miniaturization that has revolutionized consumer electronics, computers, and communications. They store and process data in all the electronic gadgetry we've become accustomed to—from microwave ovens to videogame controllers to music synthesizers to cameras to automobile fuel-injection systems to pagers to satellites.

There are different kinds of microchips—for example, microprocessor, memory, logic, communications, graphics, and math coprocessor chips. We discuss some of these later in this chapter. Perhaps the most important is the microprocessor chip. **A *microprocessor* ("microscopic processor" or "processor on a chip") is the miniaturized circuitry of a computer processor—the *CPU* (central processing unit), the part that processes, or manipulates, data into information.** When modified for use in machines other than computers, microprocessors are called *microcontrollers,* or *embedded computers*.

panel 4.2

Timeline: Developments in processing and storage

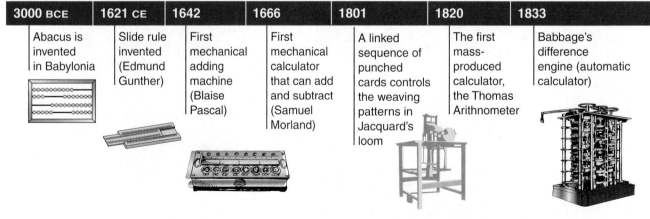

3000 BCE	1621 CE	1642	1666	1801	1820	1833
Abacus is invented in Babylonia	Slide rule invented (Edmund Gunther)	First mechanical adding machine (Blaise Pascal)	First mechanical calculator that can add and subtract (Samuel Morland)	A linked sequence of punched cards controls the weaving patterns in Jacquard's loom	The first mass-produced calculator, the Thomas Arithnometer	Babbage's difference engine (automatic calculator)

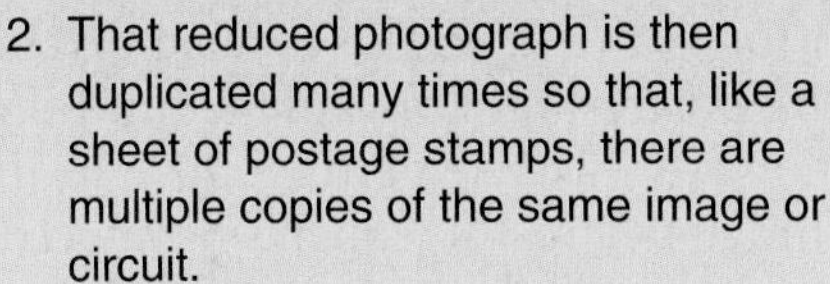

1. A large drawing of the electrical circuitry is made; it looks something like the map of a train yard. The drawing is photographically reduced hundreds of times, to microscopic size.
2. That reduced photograph is then duplicated many times so that, like a sheet of postage stamps, there are multiple copies of the same image or circuit.
3. That sheet of multiple copies of the circuit is then printed (in a printing process called *photolithography*) and etched onto a round slice of silicon called a *wafer.* Wafers have gone from 4 inches in diameter to 6 inches to 8 inches, and now are usually 12 inches and are moving toward 18 inches; this allows semiconductor manufacturers to produce more chips at lower cost.
4. Subsequent printings of layer after layer of additional circuits produce multilayered and interconnected electronic circuitry built above and below the original silicon surface.
5. Later an automated die-cutting machine cuts the wafer into separate *chips,* which are usually less than 1 centimeter square and about half a millimeter thick. A *chip,* or microchip, is a tiny piece of silicon that contains millions of microminiature electronic circuit components, mainly transistors. A 12-inch silicon wafer will have a grid of 600–800 chips, each with up to 781 million transistors.
6. After testing, each chip is mounted in a protective frame with protruding metallic pins that provide electrical connections through wires to a computer or other electronic device.

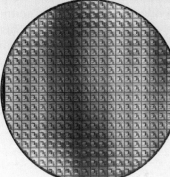

A wafer imprinted with many microprocessors.

Chip designers checking out an enlarged drawing of chip circuits

(above) Pentium 4 microprocessor chip mounted in a protective frame with pins that can be connected to the circuit board of an electronic device such as a microcomputer.

panel 4.3

Making of a chip

How microscopic circuitry is put onto silicon.

1843 World's first computer programmer, Ada Lovelace, publishes her notes

1854 George Boole publishes "An Investigation on the Laws of Thought," a system for symbolic and logical reasoning that will become the basis for computer design

1877 Thomas Edison invents the phonograph

1890 Electricity used for first time in a data-processing project – Hollerith's automatic census-tabulating machine (used punched cards)

1915 78 rpm record platters are introduced

Learning More about Computer Technology

Try the magazine *Smart Computing in Plain English* (*www.smartcomputing.com*). A more technical publication is *PC Magazine* (*www.pcmag.com*). See also:

www.webopedia.com

http://computer.howstuffworks.com

www.geek.com

At *www.pcpitstop.com* you can get all sorts of information about testing your system's performance and improving it.

Mobility

Microprocessors and microcontrollers have enabled mobility of electronic devices.

Smallness in TVs, phones, radios, camcorders, CD players, and computers is now largely taken for granted. In the 1980s portability, or mobility, meant trading off computing power and convenience in return for smaller size and less weight. Today, however, we are getting close to the point where we don't have to give up anything. As a result, experts have predicted that small, powerful, wireless personal electronic devices will transform our lives far more than the personal computer has done so far.

Choosing an Inexpensive Personal Computer: Understanding Computer Ads

Learn the terminology before you buy a computer.

You're in the market for a new PC and are studying the ads. What does "4 GB DDR3 SDRAM" mean? How about "320 GB SATA 7200 RPM Hard Drive"? Let's see how to interpret a typical computer ad. *(• See Panel 4.4.)*

Most desktop computers are *multimedia computers,* with sound and graphics capability. As we explained in Chapter 1, the word *multimedia* means "combination of media"—the combination of pictures, video, animation, and sound in addition to text. A multimedia computer features such equipment as a fast processor, DVD drive, sound card, graphics card, and speakers, and you may also wish to have headphones and a microphone. (Common peripherals are printer, scanner, sound recorder, and digital camera.)

Let us now go through the parts of a computer system so that you can understand what you're doing when you buy a new computer. First we look at how the system processes data. In the remainder of this chapter, we consider the *system unit* and *storage devices*. In Chapter 5, we look at *input devices* and *output devices*.

4.2 THE SYSTEM UNIT: The Basics

The system unit is the main part of a computer system.

Computers run on electricity. What is the most fundamental thing you can say about electricity? Electricity is either *on* or *off*. This two-state situation allows computers to use the binary system to represent data and programs.

The Binary System: Using On/Off Electrical States to Represent Data & Instructions

The binary numeral system uses two numbers: 0 and 1.

The decimal system that we are accustomed to has 10 digits (0, 1, 2, 3, 4, 5, 6, 7, 8, 9). By contrast, the ***binary system*** **has only two digits: 0 and 1.** Thus, in the

1924	1930	1936	1944	1945	1946	1947
T.J. Watson renames Hollerith's machine company, founded in 1896, to International Business Machines (IBM)	General theory of computers (MIT)	Konrad Zuse develops the concept of a computer memory to hold binary information	First electro-mechanical computer (Mark I)	John von Neumann introduces the concept of a stored program	First programmable electronic computer in United States (ENIAC)	Magnetic tape enters the U.S. market; the first transistor is developed

panel 4.4

Advertisement for a PC

The terminology in microcomputer ads generally does not change as quickly as the numbers; users will continue to need most of these components for a while, but the speeds and capacities change quickly, as do methods of connection.

computer, the 0 can be represented by the electrical current being off and the 1 by the current being on. Although the use of binary systems is not restricted to computers, *all data and program instructions that go into the computer are represented in terms of these binary numbers.* (● *See Panel 4.5, next page.*)

For example, the letter "G" is a translation of the electronic signal 01000111, or off-on-off-off-off-on-on-on. When you press the key for "G" on the computer keyboard, the character is automatically converted into the series of electronic impulses that the computer can recognize. Inside the computer, the character "G" is represented by a combination of eight transistors. Some are off, or closed (representing the 0s), and some are on, or open (representing the 1s).

MEASURING CAPACITY How many representations of 0s and 1s can be held in a computer or a storage device such as a hard disk? Capacity is denoted by *bits* and *bytes* and multiples thereof:

- **Bit:** In the binary system, **each 0 or 1 is called a *bit*, which is short for "binary digit."**
- **Byte:** To represent letters, numbers, or special characters (such as ! or *), bits are combined into groups. **A group of 8 bits is called a *byte*,**

1947–1948	1949	1952	1954	1956	1958	1962	1963
Magnetic drum memory is introduced as a data storage device for computers	45 rpm record platters are introduced	UNIVAC computer correctly predicts election of Eisenhower as U.S. President	Texas Instruments introduces the silicon transistor	First computer hard disk is used	Stereo records are produced	Integrated circuit is nicknamed the "chip"; timesharing becomes common	The American National Standards Institute accepts ASCII-7 code for information exchange

panel 4.5

Binary data representation
How the letters "G-R-O-W" are represented in one type of on/off, 1/0 binary code.

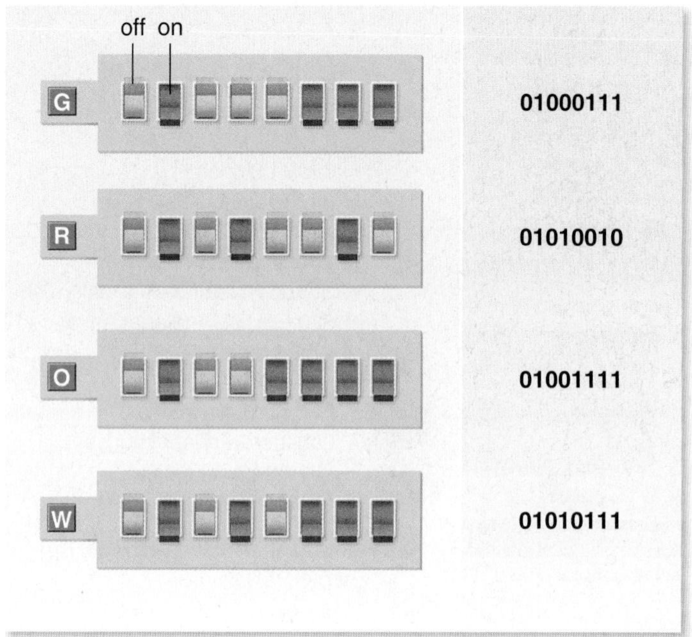

and a byte represents one character, digit, or other value. (As we mentioned, in one scheme, 01000111 represents the letter "G.") The capacity of a computer's memory or hard disk is expressed in numbers of bytes or multiples such as kilobytes, megabytes, and gigabytes. (There are 256 combinations of 8 bits available: $2^8 = 256$.)

- **Kilobyte: A *kilobyte (K, KB)* is about 1,000 bytes.** (Actually, it's precisely 1,024 bytes, but the figure is commonly rounded.) The kilobyte was a common unit of measure for memory (primary storage) or secondary storage capacity on older computers. 1 KB equals about one-half page of text.
- **Megabyte: A *megabyte ("meg"; M, MB)* is about 1 million bytes** (1,048,576 bytes). Measures of some microcomputer memory capacity today are expressed in megabytes. 1 MB equals about 500 pages of text.
- **Gigabyte: A *gigabyte ("gig"; G, GB)* is about 1 billion bytes** (1,073,741,824 bytes). This measure was formerly used mainly with "big iron" (mainframe) computers, but it is typical of the secondary storage (hard-disk) capacity and main memory (RAM) of today's microcomputers. One gigabyte equals about 500,000 pages of text.
- **Terabyte: A *terabyte (T, TB)* represents about 1 trillion bytes** (1,009,511,627,776 bytes). 1 TB equals about 500,000,000 pages of text. High-capacity disk storage is expressed in terabytes.

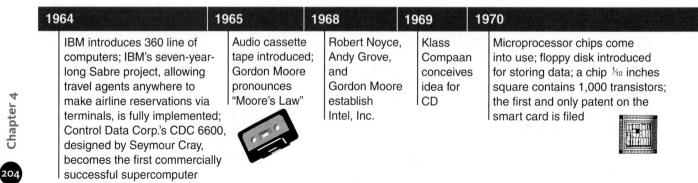

1964	1965	1968	1969	1970
IBM introduces 360 line of computers; IBM's seven-year-long Sabre project, allowing travel agents anywhere to make airline reservations via terminals, is fully implemented; Control Data Corp.'s CDC 6600, designed by Seymour Cray, becomes the first commercially successful supercomputer	Audio cassette tape introduced; Gordon Moore pronounces "Moore's Law"	Robert Noyce, Andy Grove, and Gordon Moore establish Intel, Inc.	Klass Compaan conceives idea for CD	Microprocessor chips come into use; floppy disk introduced for storing data; a chip ⅒ inches square contains 1,000 transistors; the first and only patent on the smart card is filed

- **Petabyte:** **A *petabyte* (*P, PB*) represents about 1 quadrillion bytes** (1,048,576 gigabytes). The huge storage capacities of modern databases are now expressed in petabytes.
- **Exabyte:** **An *exabyte* (*EB*) represents about 1 quintillion bytes**—that's *1 billion billion* bytes (1,024 petabytes—or 1,152,921,504,606,846,976 bytes). This number is seldom used. It is estimated that all the printed material in the world represents about 5 exabytes.[3]

Bigger Than an Exabyte?

How big is a zettabyte? A yottabyte? Do an online search to find out.

BINARY CODING SCHEMES Letters, numbers, and special characters are represented within a computer system by means of binary coding schemes. *(• See Panel 4.6.)* That is, the off/on 0s and 1s are arranged in such a way that they can be made to represent characters, digits, or other values.

- **ASCII:** Pronounced "*ask*-ee," ***ASCII (American Standard Code for Information Interchange)* is the binary code most widely used on microcomputers.** Depending on the version, ASCII uses 7 or 8 bits (1 byte) for each character. Besides having the more conventional characters, the version known as Extended ASCII includes such characters as math symbols and Greek letters. ASCII's 256 characters, however, are not enough to handle such languages as Chinese and Japanese, with their thousands of characters.

more info!

Want to Learn How to Count in Binary?

Try playing the Cisco Binary game at:

http://forums.cisco.com/CertCom/game/binary_game_page.htm

Character	ASCII-8	EBCDIC	Character	ASCII-8	EBCDIC
A	0100 0001	1100 0001	N	0100 1110	1101 0101
B	0100 0010	1100 0010	O	0100 1111	1101 0110
C	0100 0011	1100 0011	P	0101 0000	1101 0111
D	0100 0100	1100 0100	Q	0101 0001	1101 1000
E	0100 0101	1100 0101	R	0101 0010	1101 1001
F	0100 0110	1100 0110	S	0101 0011	1110 0010
G	0100 0111	1100 0111	T	0101 0100	1110 0011
H	0100 1000	1100 1000	U	0101 0101	1110 0100
I	0100 1001	1100 1001	V	0101 0110	1110 0101
J	0100 1010	1101 0001	W	0101 0111	1110 0110
K	0100 1011	1101 0010	X	0101 1000	1110 0111
L	0100 1100	1101 0011	Y	0101 1001	1110 1000
M	0100 1101	1101 0100	Z	0101 1010	1110 1001
0	0011 0000	1111 0000	5	0011 0101	1111 0101
1	0011 0001	1111 0001	6	0011 0110	1111 0110
2	0011 0010	1111 0010	7	0011 0111	1111 0111
3	0011 0011	1111 0011	8	0011 1000	1111 1000
4	0011 0100	1111 0100	9	0011 1001	1111 1001
!	0010 0001	0101 1010	;	0011 1011	0101 1110

panel 4.6

Binary coding schemes: ASCII (personal computers) and EBCDIC (large IBM computer systems) (This chart show uppercase [capital] letters; lowercase letters have different codes.)

1971	1972	1973	1974	1975	1976	1978
First pocket calculator; the Intel 4004 microprocessor is developed—a "computer on a chip"	Intel 8008 8-bit microprocessor	Large-scale integration: 10,000 components are placed on a 1-sq.-cm. chip	A DRAM chip becomes available	First microcomputer (MITS Altair 8800)	Apple I computer (first personal computer sold in assembled form); has 512 KB RAM	5¼" floppy disk; Atari home videogame; Intel's first 16-bit microprocessor, the 8086, debuts

- **Unicode:** Developed in the early 1990s, ***Unicode* uses 2 bytes (16 bits) for each character, rather than 1 byte (8 bits).** Instead of having the 256 character combinations of ASCII, Unicode can handle 65,536 character combinations. Thus, it allows almost all the written languages of the world to be represented using a single character set.
- **EBCDIC:** Pronounced "*eb*-see-dick," ***EBCDIC (Extended Binary Coded Decimal Interchange Code)* is a binary code used with large IBM and IBM-compatible computers, such as mainframes.** It was developed in 1963–1964 by IBM and uses 8 bits (1 byte) for each character.

Machine Language

Machine code is the computer's "native language."

Every brand of microprocessor has its own binary language, called *machine language*. ***Machine language* is a binary-type programming language built into the CPU that the computer can run directly.** The machine language is specific to the particular CPU model; this is why, for example, software written for a Macintosh will not run on a Dell PC. To most people, an instruction written in machine language, consisting only of 0s and 1s, is incomprehensible. To the computer, however, the 0s and 1s represent precise storage locations and operations.

How do people-comprehensible program instructions become computer-comprehensible machine language? Special system programs called *language translators* rapidly convert the instructions into machine language. This translating occurs virtually instantaneously, so you are not aware it is happening.

Because the type of computer you will most likely be working with is the microcomputer, we'll now take a look at what's inside the microcomputer's system unit.

The Computer Case: Bays, Buttons, & Boards

The computer case houses the main parts of the computer.

The system unit houses the motherboard (including the processor chip and memory chips), the power supply, and storage devices. (• *See Panel 4.7.*) In computer ads, the part of the system unit that is the empty box with just the power supply is called the *case* or *system cabinet*. For today's desktop PC, the system unit may be advertised as something like a "2-bay mini-tower case." A *bay* is a shelf or an opening used for the installation of electronic equipment, generally storage devices such as a hard drive or DVD drive. Empty bays are covered by a panel.

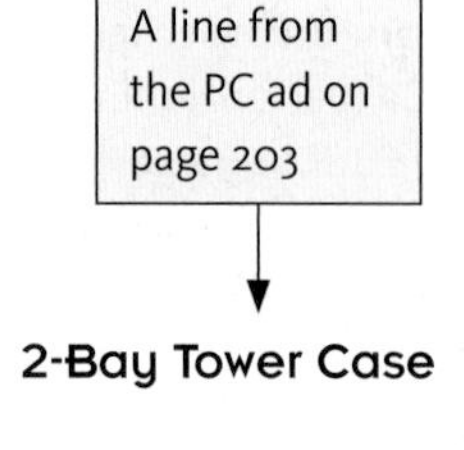

A *tower* is a cabinet that is tall, narrow, and deep (so that it can sit on the floor beside or under a table) rather than short, wide, and deep. Originally a tower (full tower) was considered to be 24 inches high. Mini- (micro) and mid-towers are smaller. At 6.5 inches square and 2 inches high, the Mac mini (Chapter 1, p. 25) is the smallest desktop microcomputer. The number

1979	1981	1982	1983	1984	1985
Motorola introduces the 68000 chip, which later will support the Mac	IBM introduces personal computer (with 8088 CPU and 16 KB RAM)	Portable computers	The capacity of floppy disks is expanded to 360 KB; CDs are introduced to U.S. market	Apple Macintosh; first personal laser printer; Sony and Philips introduce the CD-ROM; Intel's 80286 chip is released	Intel's 80386 32-bit microprocessor is introduced

panel 4.7

The system unit
Interior view of the box, or case. It includes the motherboard, power supply, and storage devices. (The arrangement of the components varies among models.)

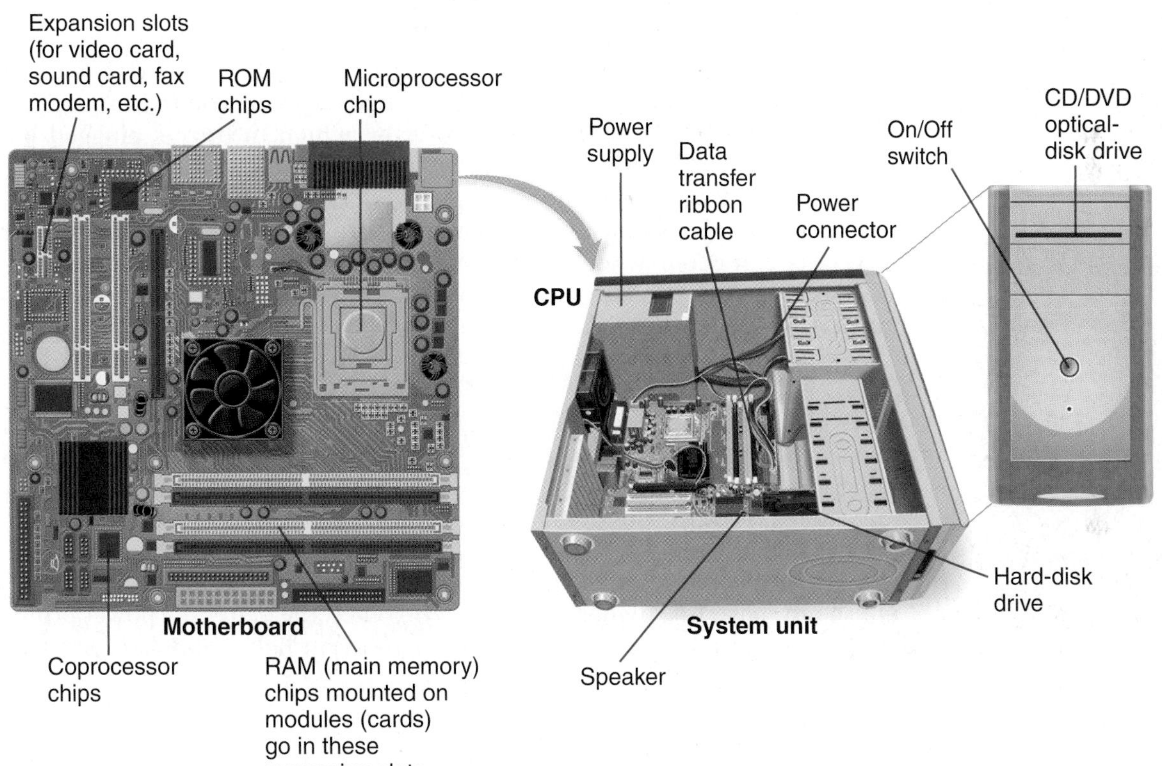

1986	1988	1989	1990
The 3½" diskette is introduced for the Mac and becomes popular for the PC as well	Motorola's 32-bit 88000 series of RISC microprocessors is introduced	Double-sided, double-density floppy disks come on the market, increasing the 5¼" diskette to 1.2 MB and the 3½" diskette to 1.4 MB; Intel's 80486 chip with 1.2 million transistors is introduced; first portable Mac	Motorola's 68040 and Intel's 1486 chips are released

of buttons on the outside of the computer case will vary, but the on/off power switch will appear somewhere, probably on the front. Inside the case—not visible unless you remove the cabinet—are various electrical circuit boards, chief of which is the motherboard, as we'll discuss.

Power Supply

The power supply unit provides power for the motherboard and other main components of the computer.

The electricity available from a standard wall outlet is alternating current (AC), but a microcomputer runs on direct current (DC). **The *power supply* is a device that converts AC to DC to run the computer.** The on/off switch in your computer turns on or shuts off the electricity to the power supply. Because electricity can generate a lot of heat, a fan inside the computer keeps the power supply and other components from becoming too hot.

Electrical power drawn from a standard AC outlet can be quite uneven. For example, a sudden surge, or "spike," in AC voltage can burn out the low-voltage DC circuitry in your computer ("fry the motherboard"). Instead of plugging your computer directly into a wall electrical outlet, it's a good idea to plug it into a power protection device. The three principal types are surge protectors, voltage regulators, and UPS units.

iGo Surge protector

SURGE PROTECTOR A *surge protector,* or *surge suppressor,* is a device that protects a computer from being damaged by surges (spikes) of high voltage. The computer is plugged into the surge protector, which in turn is plugged into a standard electrical outlet. *(See the Practical Action box on page 211.)* Surge protectors usually also operate *voltage regulators,* which protect a computer from being damaged by insufficient power—"brownouts" or "sags" in voltage. Brownouts can occur when a large machine such as a power tool starts up and causes the lights in your house to dim. They also may occur on very hot summer days when the power company has to lower the voltage in an area because too many people are running their air conditioners all at once.

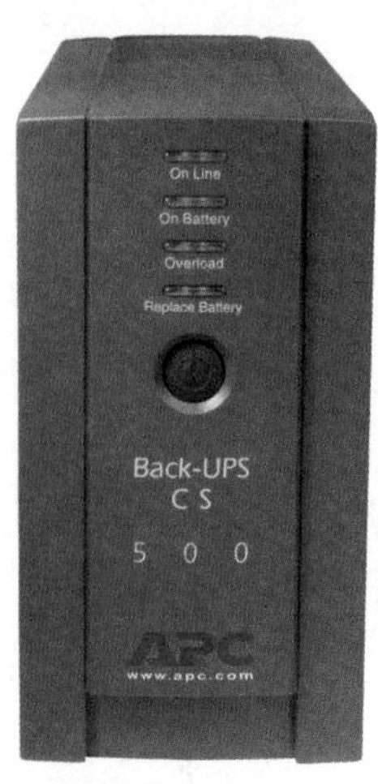

UPS

UPS A *UPS (uninterruptible power supply)* is a battery-operated device that provides a computer with electricity if there is a power failure. The UPS will keep a computer going for 5–30 minutes or more. It goes into operation as soon as the power to your computer fails. UPSs also act as surge protectors.

Power supply units are usually rated in *joules,* named after a 19th-century English physicist. The higher the number of joules, the better the power protection. (One hundred joules of energy keep a 100-watt light going for 1 second.)

1993	1994	1995	1997	1998	1999	2000
Multimedia desktop computers; Intel introduces its first Pentium chip; Motorola releases the Power PC CPU	Apple and IBM introduce PCs with full-motion video built in; wireless data transmission for small portable computers; Power Macintosh based on Motorola's Power PC 601 microprocessor; DNA computing proof of concept released	Intel's Pentium Pro	Intel's Pentium II and Pentium MMX for games and multimedia	Apple iMac	Intel's Pentium III; AMD's Athlon CPU (800 MHz); Power Mac G4 available; end of the floppy disk predicted	Intel's Pentium 4; AMD's Athlon CPU reaches 1 GHz

The Motherboard & the Microprocessor Chip

The motherboard is the computer's central printed circuit board.

As we mentioned in Chapter 1, the *motherboard,* or *system board,* is the main circuit board in the system unit. The motherboard consists of a flat board that fills one side of the case. It contains both soldered, nonremovable components and sockets or slots for components that can be removed—microprocessor chip, RAM chips, and various expansion cards, as we explain later. (● *See Panel 4.8, next page.)*

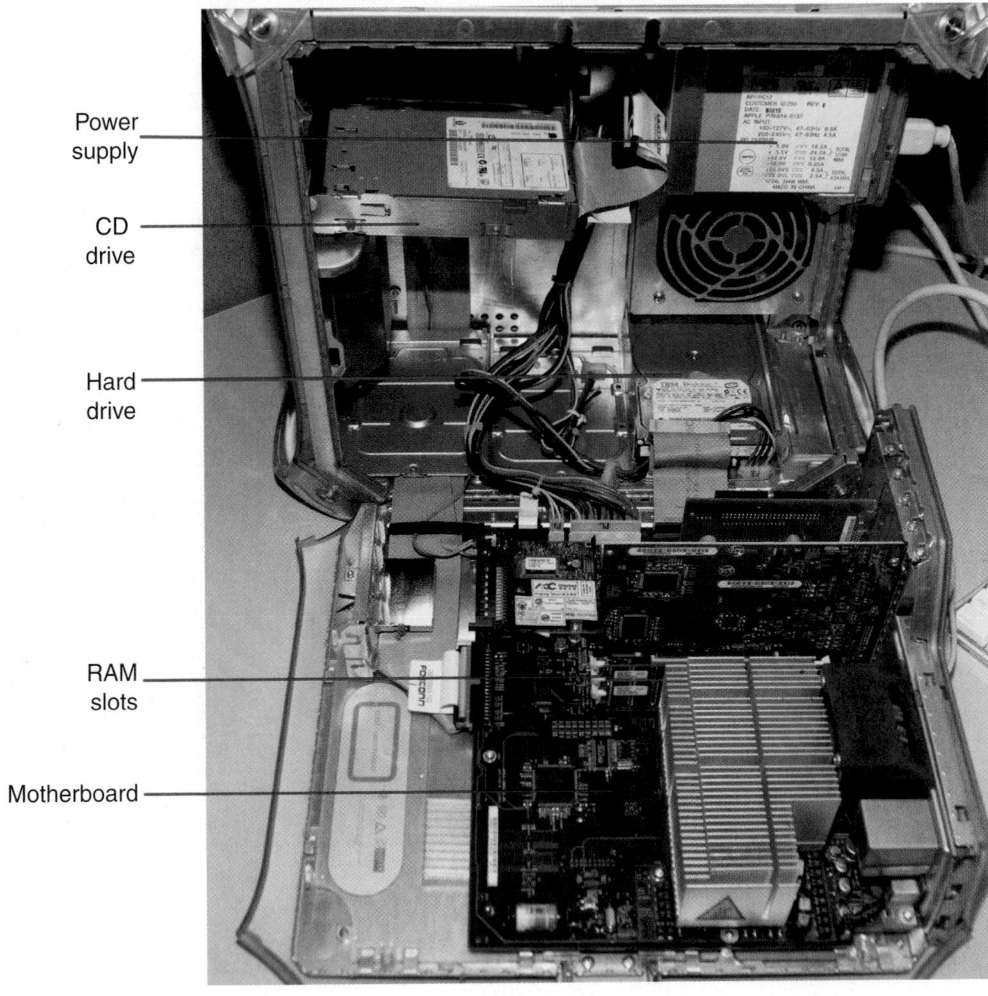

Mac motherboard
(*Mark Dierker*)

2001	2002	2003	2004	2005	2006	2009
Pentium 4 reaches 2 GHz; USB 2.0 is introduced	Pentium 4 reaches 3.06 GHz; Power Mac has 2 1-GHz Power PC CPUs; about 1 billion PCs have been shipped worldwide since the mid-70s	Intel's Pentium M/Centrino for mobile computing; 64-bit processors	Intel Express chipsets for built-in sound and video capabilities (no cards needed); IBM sells its PC computing division to Lenovo Group	Perpendicular recording for disk drives	Intel and AMD introduce dual core processors; 64-bit processors enter the market	Multi-core processors

panel 4.8

The motherboard and an expansion card

This example of a main board (*top*) offers slots or sockets for removable components: microprocessor chip, RAM chips, and various expansion cards, such as that shown at bottom.

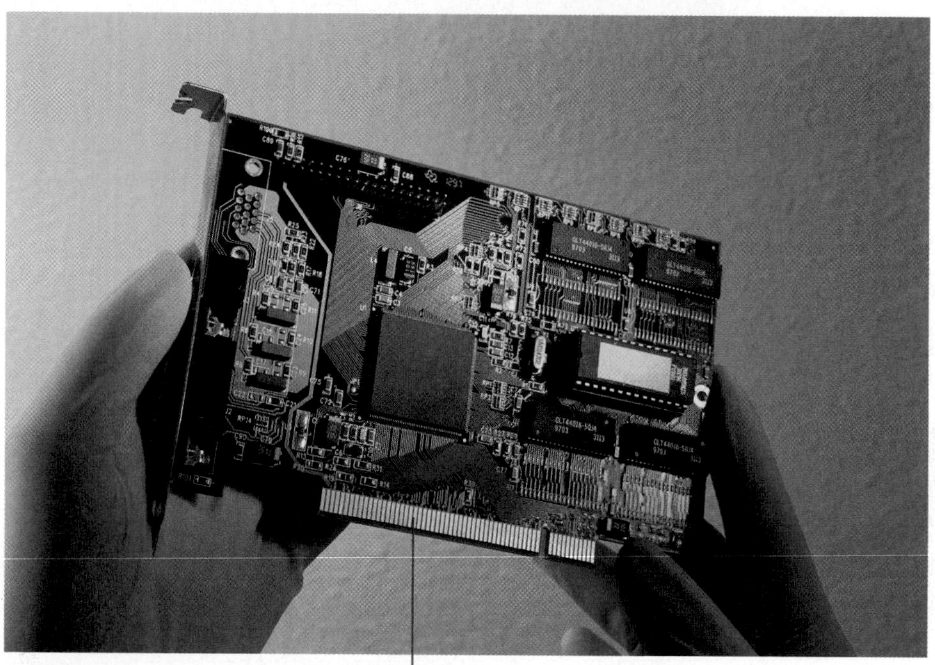

Making some components removable allows you to expand or upgrade your system. ***Expansion*** **is a way of increasing a computer's capabilities by adding hardware to perform tasks that are beyond the scope of the basic system.** For example, you might want to add video and sound cards. ***Upgrading***

2010	2013	2015?	2017?	2025?	2030	2030–2045
$1,000 buys a computer working at 10 quadrillion calculations per second; USB 3.0 available	Speech-to-speech translation available in cellphones; batteries that charge in seconds	Microcomputer storage in zettabytes; teleportation via nanotechnology; DNA computer; desktop computer as fast as human brain	Use of bacteria for processing and storage	Computers are able to simulate the entire human brain	$1,000 buys a computer more powerful than the human brain	The point of "singularity" is reached, when technical progress is so fast that unenhanced human intelligence can't follow it.

PRACTICAL ACTION

Power Issues: Problems with Electrical Power to Your Computer

Ben Veligdan, a Brooklyn, New York, music teacher, wondered why his monthly electric bill exceeded $100 a month when his household consisted only of him, his wife, and his cat. Then he looked around his modest one-bedroom apartment and thought, Could it be the computer? When he decided to unplug it while he was sleeping or not working, his electric bill fell almost immediately.[4]

You need power to run your computer, of course, but electricity can be very problematic: Leaving a computer turned on all the time is expensive, even in standby mode—because of "vampire power," the electric power consumed by electronic appliances while they are switched off or in a standby mode. Also, having a computer on your thighs can quickly become hot and uncomfortable. Sudden power surges can devastate your hardware. Sudden power drops can wipe out your data.

Here are a few things you can do to deal with these problems:

- ***To reduce your electricity bill, disconnect your computer when you're not using it for a significant length of time:*** It's not just your computer. Many electronic gadgets—cellphone chargers, microwave ovens, and so on—suck electricity when they're not being used. Indeed, it amounts to 5%–10% every year in American homes.[5] Leaving PCs on overnight costs U.S. companies $2.8 billion a year.[6] Devices are coming to market that can detect when an appliance is in standby mode (not working). But the best thing you can do is to plug your computer into some variant of a USB, so that you can turn off the on-off switch when your PC is not in use.
- ***If a laptop's heat on your thighs is uncomfortable, put it on a "cool tray":*** A computer on your lap can generate heat that can quickly make you uncomfortable. Some companies now offer pads and so-called cool trays ($30–$50) with fans or pads made from special materials that you can slide under your laptop and can cool off both the machine and your lap.
- ***Back up data regularly:*** You should faithfully make backup (duplicate) copies of your data every few minutes as you're working. Then, if your computer has power problems, you'll be able to get back in business fairly quickly once the machine is running again.
- ***Use a surge protector to protect against too much electricity:*** Plug all your hardware into a surge protector/voltage regulator, which will prevent damage to your equipment if there is a power surge. (You'll know you've experienced a power surge when the lights in the room suddenly get very bright.) Surge protectors cost $10–$35.
- ***Use a UPS to protect against complete absence of electricity:*** Consider plugging your computer into a UPS, or uninterruptible power supply (available at electronics stores for $35–$200). It will keep your computer running long enough (5–30 minutes) for you to save your data before you turn off the machine. It also acts as a surge protector.
- ***Turn ON highest-power-consuming hardware first:*** When you turn on your computer system, you should turn on the devices that use the most power first. This will avoid causing a power drain on smaller devices. The most common advice is to turn on (1) printer, (2) other external peripherals, (3) system unit, (4) monitor—in that order.
- ***Turn OFF lowest-power-consuming hardware first:*** When you turn off your system, follow the reverse order. This avoids a power surge to the smaller devices.
- ***Unplug your computer system during lightning storms:*** Unplug all your system's components—including phone lines—during thunder and lightning storms. If lightning strikes your house or the power lines, it can ruin your equipment.

means changing to newer, usually more powerful or sophisticated versions, such as a more powerful microprocessor or more memory chips.

THE MICROPROCESSOR CHIP The motherboard may be thought of as your computer's central nervous system. The brain of your computer is the microprocessor chip. As we described in Chapter 1, a *microprocessor* is the miniaturized circuitry of a computer processor, contained on a small silicon chip. It stores program instructions that process, or manipulate, data into information.

- **Transistors—key parts of a chip:** The key parts of the microprocessor are transistors. *Transistors,* we said, are tiny electronic devices that act as on/off switches, which process the on/off (1/0) bits used to represent data. According to *Moore's law,* named for legendary Intel cofounder Gordon Moore, the number of transistors that can be packed onto a

Microprocessor

chip doubles about every 18–24 months, while the price stays the same, which has enabled the industry to shrink the size and cost of things such as computers and cellphones while improving their performance. (This situation is expected to last until about 2015–2020.)

- **The chipset—chips for controlling information among system components: The _chipset_ consists of groups of interconnected chips on the motherboard that are designed to work together to control the flow of information between the microprocessor and other system components connected to the motherboard.** The chipset determines what types of processors, memory, and video card ports will work on the same motherboard. It also establishes the types of multimedia, storage, network, and other hardware the motherboard supports.

TRADITIONAL MICROCOMPUTER MICROPROCESSORS The leading chip makers today are Intel, AMD, IDT, Samsung, Toshiba, Texas Instruments, Renesas, and Micron Technology.

- **Intel-type processors for microcomputers—Intel and AMD chips:** Most PCs use CPUs manufactured by Intel Corporation or Advanced Micro Devices (AMD). Indeed, the Microsoft Windows operating system was designed to run on Intel chips. ***Intel-type chips*** **have a similar internal design and are made to run microcomputers.** They are used by manufacturers such as Dell, Lenovo, Toshiba, and Hewlett-Packard in their PC microcomputers. They are also now used in Macs, so that they can run both Microsoft- and Apple-based programs by supporting both Mac OS X and Windows.
- **Multicore processors for PCs—dual core and quadcore:** "You'll be typing along on an email when suddenly the PC stops responding to your keystrokes, then catches up a few seconds later," wrote *BusinessWeek*'s Stephen Wildstrom. "Or a program that used to load in a few seconds inexplicably takes three times as long. Processors are faster than ever, but the demands of even routine computing are overwhelming them."[7]

  The reason computers bog down is that, as Wildstrom explained, "no matter how fast a processor runs, it can do only one thing at a time." Adding more transistors doesn't help, because they generate too much heat. Enter a new kind of microcomputer chip—**the _multicore processor_, designed to let the operating system divide the work over more than one processor, with two or more processor "cores" on a single piece of silicon.**

  The concept is not new; large computer systems, such as IBM's Blue Gene/L supercomputer, have featured as many as 65,000 processors working

Intel i5 microprocessor and an ATI Radeon graphics chip.

in unison. But the beauty of having two or more cores is that chips can take on several tasks at once, eliminating the annoying pauses that Wildstrom mentioned. Common multicore processors for microcomputers today are *dual-core processors* (two cores—for example, AMD Athlon, Intel Core Duo), *quad-core processors* (four cores—for example, AMD Phenom II X4 and the Intel 2010 core, including the i5 and the i7 processors), and *hexa-core processors* (six cores—for example, AMD Phenom II X6, Intel Core i7 Extreme Edition 980X). (The multicore technology takes advantage of a technology called *hyperthreading,* explained in a few pages.) The new Intel Tri-Gate (3D) transistor, used in Intel's Atom line of CPUs, has doubled the transistor count in the same area space, thus making Tri-Gate chips even faster than multicore transistors.

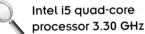

- **Processors for portable devices:** Chip makers have been rushing to produce processors for a new breed of portable devices—*mobile Internet devices* (Chapter 1, p. 26), *netbooks*, and other electronics, from cellphones to MP3 players to handheld game systems to household appliances. Among the contenders making processors for this market are Nvidia, Qualcomm, Texas Instruments, Via Technologies, Samsung (the iPad A4 microprocessor), and Intel. What all such chips have in common is energy efficiency; Nvidia's Tegra, for instance, can hold a battery charge five times longer than Intel's Atom.

- **Graphics processing units—specialized processors for 3-D graphics:** A ***graphics processing unit (GPU)*** **is a specialized processor used to manipulate three-dimensional (3-D) computer graphics.** Unlike a general-purpose CPU, a GPU is able to perform a range of complex algorithms (problem-solving steps). GPUs are found in personal computers, workstations, cellphones, and game consoles. The first company to develop the GPU was Nvidia.

  Some GPUs are integrated into the motherboard; high-powered GPUs are on the video cards and have their own RAM.

Tri-Gate Chip

Read about this new chip at:

www.pcmag.com/article2/0,2817,2384909,00.asp

http://newsroom.intel.com/docs/DOC-2032

www.ibtimes.com/articles/154773/20110531/intel-ultrabook-laptop-netbooks-ipad-macbook-air-sandybridge-ivy-bridge-trigate-usb3-0-cedar-trail-h.htm

Processing Speeds: From Megahertz to Picoseconds

A computer's main CPU is its fastest piece of processing hardware.

Often a PC ad will say something like "Intel i5 processor 3.30 GHz." *GHz* stands for "gigahertz," a measure of how fast the microprocessor can process data and execute program instructions.

Every microprocessor contains a ***system clock,*** **which controls how fast all the operations within a computer take place.** The system clock uses fixed vibrations from a quartz crystal to deliver a steady stream of digital pulses or "ticks" to the CPU. These ticks are called *cycles*. Faster *clock speeds* will result in faster processing of data and execution of program instructions, as long as the computer's internal circuits can handle the increased speed.

There are four main ways in which processing speeds are measured, as follows.

FOR MICROCOMPUTERS: MEGAHERTZ & GIGAHERTZ Older microcomputer microprocessor speeds are expressed in ***megahertz (MHz),*** **a measure of frequency equivalent to 1 million cycles (ticks of the system clock) per second.** The original IBM PC had a clock speed of 4.77 megahertz, which equaled 4.77 million cycles per second. The latest-generation processors from AMD and Intel operate in ***gigahertz (GHz)*****—a billion cycles per second.** Intel's Pentium i5 and i7 operate at up to 3.80 gigahertz, or 3.80 billion cycles per second. However, unfortunately, the faster a CPU runs, the more power it consumes and the more waste heat it produces. Thus, rather than increasing clock speeds, which requires smaller transistors and creates tricky engineering problems, chip makers such as Intel and AMD are now employing additional CPU cores and running them in parallel—dual core or multicore technology, as we've described.

As for you, since a new high-speed processor can cost many hundred dollars more than a previous-generation chip, experts often recommend that buyers fret less about the speed of the processor (since the work most people do on their PCs doesn't even tax the limits of the current hardware) and more about spending money on extra memory. (However, game playing *does* tax the system. Thus, if you're an avid computer game player, you may want to purchase the fastest processor.)

FOR WORKSTATIONS & MAINFRAMES: MIPS Processing speed can also be measured according to the number of instructions per second that a computer can process. ***MIPS*** **stands for "millions of instructions per second."** MIPS is used to measure processing speeds of mainframes and workstations. A workstation might perform at 100 MIPS or more; a mainframe at as much as 981,024 MIPS.

FOR SUPERCOMPUTERS: FLOPS The abbreviation ***flops*** **stands for "floating-point operations per second."** A *floating-point operation* is a special kind of mathematical calculation. This measure, used mainly with supercomputers, is expressed as *megaflops* (*mflops,* or millions of floating-point operations per second), *gigaflops* (*gflops,* or billions), *teraflops* (*tflops,* or trillions), and *petaflops* (*pflops,* or a thousand trillion calculations per second). IBM's Blue Gene/L (for "Lite") supercomputer cranks out 280.6 teraflops, or 280.6 trillion calculations per second. (A person able to complete one arithmetic calculation every second would take more than a million years to do what a 70.72 teraflop supercomputer could do in a single second.) As we mentioned in Chapter 1, Japan's K Computer is currently the world's fastest supercomputer, at 8–10 petaflops.

Comparison of Some Popular Recent Microcomputer Processors

Year	Processor Name	Clock Speed	Transistors
2011	Intel Xeon	3.47 GHz (each core)	2.3 billion (each core)
2010	Intel Core i7 995X	3.60 GHz (each core)	731 million (each core)
	AMD Phenom II X6		
	Intel 6-core i7		
2009	AMD Phenom II	3.2 GHz	1.17 billion (each core)
	Athlon 2	3.0 GHz (each core)	
2008	Intel Core i7	3.1 GHz (each core)	153–221 million
	Intel Tukwila Quad Core	3.0 GHz (each core)	410 million (each core)
		2.66 GHz (each core)	2 billion (each core)
		2 GHz (each core)	2 billion
2007	Intel Core Quad	2.4–2.7 HZ	582 million
2006	Intel Pentium EE 840 dual core	3.2 GHZ (each core)	230 million
2005	Intel Pentium 4 660	3.6–3.7 GHz	169 million
2005	AMD Athlon 64 X2 dual core	2 GHz (each core)	105.9 million
2005	Intel Itanium 2 Montecito dual core	2 GHz (each core)	1.7 billion
2004	IBM PowerPC 970FX (G5)	2.2 GHz	58 million
2003	AMD Opteron	2–2.4 GHz	37.5 million
2002	Intel Itanium 2	1 GHz and up	221 million
2002	AMD Athlon MP	1.53–1.6 GHz	37.5 million
2001	Intel Xeon	1.4–2.8 GHz	140 million
2001	Intel Mobile Pentium 4	1.4–3.06 GHz	55 million
2001	AMD Athlon XP	1.33–1.73 GHz	37.5 million
2001	Intel Itanium	733–800 MHz	25.4–60 million
2000	Intel Pentium 4	1.4–3.06 GHz	42–55 million
1999	Motorola PowerPC 7400 (G4)	400–500 MHz	10.5 million

FOR ALL COMPUTERS: FRACTIONS OF A SECOND Another way to measure cycle times is in fractions of a second. A microcomputer operates in microseconds, a supercomputer in nanoseconds or picoseconds—thousands or millions of times faster. A *millisecond* is one-thousandth of a second. A *microsecond* is one-millionth of a second. A *nanosecond* is one-billionth of a second. A *picosecond* is one-trillionth of a second.

4.3 MORE ON THE SYSTEM UNIT: What Supports the Processor?

The processor is connected by buses to the control unit, ALU, registers, main memory, ports, and expansion cards.

Once upon a time, the processor in a computer was measured in feet. A processing unit in the 1946 ENIAC (which had 20 such processors) was about 2 feet wide and 8 feet high. Today, as we have said, computers are based on *micro*processors, less than 1 centimeter square. It may be difficult to visualize components so tiny. Yet it is necessary to understand how microprocessors work if you are to grasp what PC advertisers mean when they throw out terms such as "4 GB DDR3 SDRAM" or "6 MB Level 2 Advanced Transfer Cache."

Word Size

Modern microcomputers computers usually have a word size of 32 or 64 bits.

Computer professionals often discuss a computer's word size. **Word size is the number of bits that the processor can process at any one time.** The more bits in a word, the faster the computer. A 32-bit computer—that is, one with a 32-bit-word processor—will transfer data within each microprocessor chip in 32-bit chunks, or 4 bytes at a time. (Recall there are 8 bits in a byte, which equals 1 character in ASCII and ½ character in Unicode.) A 64-bit-word computer is faster; it transfers data in 64-bit chunks, or 8 bytes at a time.

The Parts of the CPU

The control unit and the arithmetic/logic unit make up the CPU.

A processor is also called the *CPU,* and it works hand in hand with other circuits known as *main memory* to carry out processing. **The CPU (central processing unit) is the "brain" of the computer; it follows the instructions of the software (program) to manipulate data into information. The CPU consists of two parts—(1) the control unit and (2) the arithmetic/logic unit (ALU), both of which contain registers, or high-speed storage areas** (as we discuss shortly). All are linked by a kind of electronic "roadway" called a *bus*. (● *See Panel 4.9.*)

panel 4.9

The CPU and main memory

The two main CPU components on a microprocessor are the control unit and the ALU, which contain working storage areas called *registers* and are linked by a kind of electronic roadway called a *bus.*

CPU on motherboard
(enlarged representation)
Registers
High-speed storage areas used by control unit and ALU to speed up processing
Control unit
Directs electronic signals between main memory and ALU
Arithmetic/logic unit (ALU)
Performs arithmetic and logical operations
Buses
Electrical data roadways that transmit data within CPU and between CPU and main memory and peripherals
Bus
Main memory in expansion slot on the motherboard (Random Access Memory, or RAM)
Bus
Expansion slots on motherboard

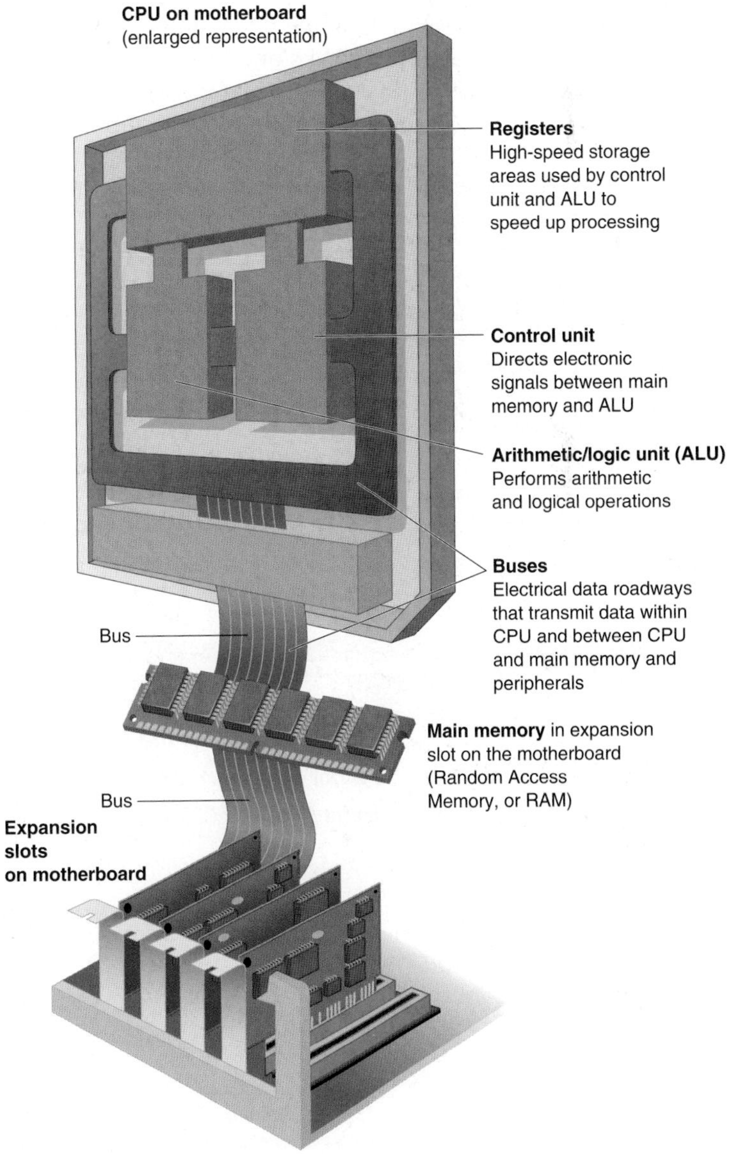

- **The control unit—for directing electronic signals: The *control unit* deciphers each instruction stored in the CPU and then carries out the instruction.** It directs the movement of electronic signals between main memory and the arithmetic/logic unit. It also directs these electronic signals between main memory and the input and output devices.

  For every instruction, the control unit carries out four basic operations, known as the *machine cycle*. In the ***machine cycle*, the CPU (1) fetches an instruction, (2) decodes the instruction, (3) executes the instruction, and (4) stores the result.** (● *See Panel 4.10.*)

- **The arithmetic/logic unit—for arithmetic and logical operations: The *arithmetic/logic unit (ALU)* performs arithmetic operations and logical operations and controls the speed of those operations.**

  As you might guess, *arithmetic operations* are the fundamental math operations: addition, subtraction, multiplication, and division.

  Logical operations are comparisons. That is, the ALU compares two pieces of data to see whether one is equal to (=), greater than (<), greater than or equal to (<=) less than (>), less than or equal to (>=), or not equal to (≠) the other.

- **Registers—special high-speed storage areas:** The control unit and the ALU also use registers, special CPU areas that enhance the computer's performance. ***Registers* are high-speed storage areas that temporarily store data during processing.** They may store a program instruction while it is being decoded, store data while it is being processed by the ALU, or store the results of a calculation.

  All data must be represented in a register before it can be processed. For example, if two numbers are to be multiplied, both numbers must be in registers, and the result is also placed in a register. (The register can contain the address of a memory location where data is stored rather than the actual data itself.)

  The number of registers that a CPU has and the size of each (number of bits) help determine the power and speed of a CPU. For example, a 32-bit CPU is one in which each register is 32 bits wide. Therefore, each CPU instruction can manipulate 32 bits of data. (There are several types of registers, including *instruction register, address register, storage register, general register,* and *accumulator register.*)

- **Buses—data roadways: *Buses*, or *bus lines*, are electrical data roadways through which bits are transmitted within the CPU and between the CPU and other components of the motherboard.** A bus resembles a multilane highway: The more lanes it has, the faster the bits can be

panel 4.10

The machine cycle

(Left) The machine cycle executes instructions one at a time during the instruction cycle and the execution cycle. *(Right)* Example of how the addition of two numbers, 50 and 75, is processed and stored in a single cycle.

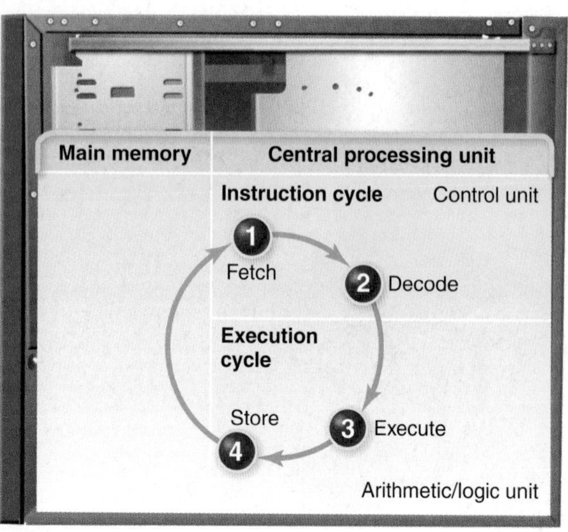

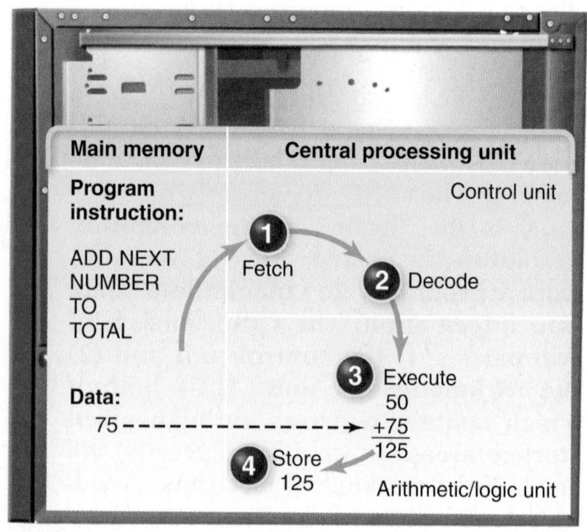

transferred. The old-fashioned 8-bit-word bus of early microprocessors had only eight pathways. Data is transmitted four times faster in a computer with a 32-bit bus, which has 32 pathways, than in a computer with an 8-bit bus. Most of Intel's newest chips are 64-bit processors, including their dual-core and quad-core processors. Supercomputers usually have 128-bit processors. (Microsoft has plans to make its upcoming operating system, Windows 8, a 128-bit system, for desktop microcomputers.)

We return to a discussion of buses in a few pages.

How Memory Works: RAM, ROM, CMOS, & Flash

As the CPU is on a chip, so are several kinds of memory.

So far we have described only the kinds of chips known as microprocessors. But other silicon chips called *memory chips* are attached to the motherboard. The four principal types of memory chips are *RAM, ROM, CMOS,* and *flash.*

RAM CHIPS—TO TEMPORARILY STORE PROGRAM INSTRUCTIONS & DATA Recall from Chapter 1 that there are two types of storage: primary and secondary (p. 29). Primary storage is temporary or working storage and is often called *memory* or *main memory.* Secondary storage, usually called just *storage,* is relatively permanent storage. *Memory* refers to storage media in the form of chips, and *storage* refers to media such as disks and tape.

RAM (random access memory) chips **temporarily hold (1) software instructions and (2) data before and after it is processed by the CPU.** Think of RAM as the primary workspace inside your computer. When you open a file, a copy of the file transfers from the hard disk to RAM, and this copy in RAM is the one that changes as you work with the file. When you activate the Save command, the changed copy transfers from RAM back to permanent storage on the hard drive.

Because its contents are temporary, RAM is said to be ***volatile*****—the contents are lost when the power goes off or is turned off.** This is why you should *frequently*—every 5–10 minutes, say—transfer (save) your work to a secondary storage medium such as your hard disk, in case the electricity goes off while you're working. (However, there is one kind of RAM, called *flash RAM,* that is not temporary, as we'll discuss shortly.)

Several types of RAM chips are used in personal computers—*DRAM, SDRAM, SRAM,* and *DDR SDRAM:*

- **DRAM:** The first type (pronounced "dee-ram"), *DRAM (dynamic RAM),* must be constantly refreshed by the CPU or it will lose its contents.
- **SDRAM:** The second type of RAM is *SDRAM (synchronous dynamic RAM),* which is synchronized by the system clock and is much faster than DRAM. Often in computer ads the speed of SDRAM is expressed in megahertz.
- **SRAM:** The third type, *static RAM,* or *SRAM* (pronounced "ess-ram"), is faster than DRAM and retains its contents without having to be refreshed by the CPU.
- **DDR-SDRAM:** The fourth type, *DDR SDRAM (double-data rate synchronous dynamic RAM),* is the current standard of RAM chip in PCs used at home; the speed is measured in megahertz. An even faster version is *DDR3 SDRAM* (up to 1,333 MHz). (Keep in mind that if you are running gaming programs and videos, you need fast RAM and a lot of it, as well as a fast processor.)

Microcomputers come with different amounts of RAM, which is usually measured in megabytes or gigabytes. An ad may list "256 MB SDRAM," but you will probably need more. The Mac Pro, for instance, can provide

Survival Tip

What RAM for Your PC?

Before adding more RAM to improve your computer's performance, check the manufacturer's website as to the type of RAM modules required for the motherboard. RAM slots and chipsets vary, and different computer models cannot work with all kinds of RAM chips.

Survival Tip

Need More RAM?

If your system is giving you low-system-resources messages, you may need more memory. For detailed information on your system, go to:

www.crucial.com

www.kingston.com

www.tomshardware.com

4 GB DDR3 SDRAM

RAM memory module.

up to 64 gigabytes of RAM. The more RAM you have, the more efficiently the computer operates and the better your software performs. *Having enough RAM is a critical matter.* Before you buy a software package, look at the outside of the box or check the manufacturer's website to see how much RAM is required. For Microsoft Office 2007 and 2010, for instance, a minimum of 256 megabytes of RAM is required, depending on the operating system, plus 8 megabytes of RAM for *each* application the user plans to run simultaneously. The Mac Pro OS X requires 2 GB of RAM plus 512 MB RAM per processor core.

- If you're short on memory capacity, you can usually add more RAM chips by plugging a RAM *memory module* into the motherboard. A memory module is a small fiberglass circuit board that can be plugged into a RAM slot on the motherboard. Most memory modules used in microcomputers are DIMMs. A *DIMM (dual inline memory module)* has RAM chips on both sides.

RAM-ifications

To find out more about how RAM works, go to:

http://computer.howstuffworks.com/ram.htm

http://pcsupport.about.com/od/componentprofiles/p/p_ram.htm

www.kb.iu.edu/data/ahty.html

ROM CHIPS—TO STORE FIXED START-UP INSTRUCTIONS Unlike RAM, to which data is constantly being added and removed, ***ROM (read-only memory)*** **cannot be written on or erased by the computer user without special equipment. ROM chips contain fixed start-up instructions.** That is, ROM chips are loaded, at the factory, with programs containing special instructions for basic computer operations, such as those that start the computer (BIOS) or put characters on the screen. These chips are nonvolatile; their contents are not lost when power to the computer is turned off.

In computer terminology, ***read*** **means to transfer data from an input source into the computer's memory or CPU. The opposite is *write*—to transfer data from the computer's CPU or memory to an output device.** Thus, with a ROM chip, *read-only* means that the CPU can retrieve programs from the ROM chip but cannot modify or add to those programs. A variation is *PROM (programmable read-only memory),* which is a ROM chip that allows you, the user, to load read-only programs and data. However, this can be done only once.

Survival Tip

RAM

Try to get a computer/laptop with a minimum of 2–4 GB RAM.

CMOS CHIPS—TO STORE FLEXIBLE START-UP INSTRUCTIONS Pronounced *"see-moss,"* ***CMOS (complementary metal-oxide semiconductor) chips*** **are powered by a battery and thus don't lose their contents when the power is turned off.** CMOS chips contain flexible start-up instructions—such as time, date, and calendar—that must be kept current even when the computer is turned off. Unlike ROM chips, CMOS chips can be reprogrammed, as when you need to change the time for daylight savings time. (Your system software may prompt you to do this; newer systems do it automatically.)

FLASH MEMORY CHIPS—TO STORE FLEXIBLE PROGRAMS Also a nonvolatile form of memory, ***flash memory chips*** **can be erased and reprogrammed more than once** (unlike PROM chips, which can be programmed only once). Flash memory, which doesn't require a battery and which can range from 2 gigabytes to 128 gigabytes in capacity, is used to store programs not only in personal computers but also in pagers, cellphones, MP3 players, printers, and digital cameras. Flash memory is also used in newer PCs for BIOS instructions; they can be updated electronically on flash memory—the chip does not need to be replaced, as a ROM chip would.

How Cache Works

A cache is a special storage space.

Because the CPU runs so much faster than the main system RAM does, it ends up waiting for information, which is inefficient. To reduce this effect, we have cache. Pronounced "cash," ***cache*** **temporarily stores instructions and**

data that the processor is likely to use frequently. Thus, cache speeds up processing. Cache memory is extremely fast memory that is built into the CPU or located next to it on a separate chip inserted into a special slot. The cache enhances the "horsepower" of the CPU by allowing faster receipt and delivery of data. The CPU uses cache memory to store instructions that are repeatedly required to run programs, improving overall system speed.

Currently processors can operate at speeds that are much greater than affordable, reliable main memory (RAM) can keep up with to supply the necessary data. Cache memory is much like main memory, except it can operate much faster, but it is much more expensive. Thus fast, expensive small cache memory bridges the gap between slower, less expensive but higher-capacity RAM and the processor. By giving the processor a small amount of fast memory to use, and then having that memory read in and write to main memory in "spare" time, the processor can operate at full speed much of the time.

THREE KINDS OF CACHE There are three kinds of cache, as follows:

- **Level 1 (L1) cache—part of the microprocessor chip:** *Level 1 (L1) cache,* also called *internal cache,* is built into the processor chip. Ranging from 8 to 256 kilobytes, its capacity is less than that of Level 2 cache, although it operates faster.
- **Level 2 (L2) cache—not part of the microprocessor chip:** This is the kind of cache usually referred to in computer ads. *Level 2 (L2) cache,* also called *external cache,* resides on a chip outside the processor chip. Capacities range from 64 kilobytes to 2 megabytes. L2 cache is generally quite a bit larger than L1 cache (most new systems have at least 1–6 megabytes of L2 cache) and is the most commonly cited type of cache for measuring PC performance.
- **Level 3 (L3) cache—on the motherboard:** *Level 3 (L3) cache* is also a cache chip separate from the processor chip on the motherboard. It holds 2–8 megabytes.

Without the cache memory, every time the CPU requested data it would have to send a request to main memory that would then be sent back across the memory bus to the CPU. This is a slow process in computing terms. When the microprocessor accesses main memory (RAM), it does it in about 60 nanoseconds (60 billionths of a second). That's pretty fast, but it is much slower than the typical microprocessor. Microprocessors can have cycle times as short as 2 nanoseconds, so to a microprocessor 60 nanoseconds seems like an eternity. Cache is not upgradable; it is set by the type of processor purchased with the system.

VIRTUAL MEMORY In addition to including cache, most current computer operating systems allow for the use of ***virtual memory*—that is, some free hard-disk space is used to extend the capacity of RAM.** The processor searches for data or program instructions in the following order: first L1, then L2, then RAM, then hard disk (or CD). In this progression, each kind of memory or storage is slower than its predecessor.

Other Methods of Speeding Up Processing

Interleaving, bursting, pipelining, superscalar architecture, and hyperthreading also speed up processing.

The placement of memory chips on the motherboard has a direct effect on system performance. Because RAM must hold all the information the CPU needs to process, the speed at which the data can travel between memory and the

CPU is critical to performance. And because the exchanges of data between the CPU and RAM are so intricately timed, the distance between them becomes another critical performance factor. Ways to speed up data traveling between memory and CPU are *interleaving, bursting, pipelining, superscalar architecture,* and *hyperthreading.* When you see these terms in a computer ad, you'll know that the processor's speed is being boosted.

INTERLEAVING The term *interleaving* refers to a process in which the CPU alternates communication between two or more memory banks. Interleaving is generally used in large systems such as servers and workstations. For example, SDRAM chips are each divided into independent cell banks. Interleaving between the two cell banks produces a continuous flow of data.

BURSTING The purpose of *bursting* is to provide the CPU with additional data from memory based on the likelihood that it will be needed. So, instead of the CPU retrieving data from memory one piece at a time, it grabs a block of information from several consecutive addresses in memory. This saves time because there's a statistical likelihood that the next data address the CPU will request will be sequential to the previous one.

PIPELINING *Pipelining* divides a task into a series of stages, with some of the work completed at each stage. That is, large tasks are divided into smaller overlapping ones. The CPU does not wait for one instruction to complete the machine cycle before fetching the next instruction. Pipelining is available in most PCs; each processor can pipeline up to four instructions.

SUPERSCALAR ARCHITECTURE & HYPERTHREADING *Superscalar architecture* means the computer has the ability to execute more than one instruction per clock cycle (a 200-MHz processor executes 200 million clock cycles per second). One type of such architecture is hyperthreading. With *hyperthreading,* software and operating systems treat the microprocessor as though it's two microprocessors. This technology lets the microprocessor handle simultaneous requests from the OS or from software, initially improving performance by around 30%–40%. A processor using hyperthreading technology manages the incoming data instructions in parallel by switching between the instructions every few nanoseconds, essentially letting the processor handle two separate threads of code at once.

Ports & Cables

A port is a socket for some kind of plug, of which there are many types.

A *port* is a connecting socket or jack on the outside of system unit into which are plugged different kinds of cables. (• *See Panel 4.11 and p. 225.)* A port allows you to plug in a cable to connect a peripheral device, such as a monitor, printer, scanner, or modem, so that it can communicate with the computer system.

Ports are of several types, as follows.

DEDICATED PORTS—FOR KEYBOARD, MOUSE, MONITOR, AUDIO, & MODEM/NETWORK CONNECTION *Dedicated ports* are ports for special purposes, such as the round ports for connecting the keyboard and the mouse (if they're not USB), the monitor port, the audio ports (green for speakers or headphones, pink for microphone, yellow for home stereo connection; see next page), the modem port to connect your computer to a phone line, and a network port for a high-speed Internet connection. (There is also one connector that is not a port at all—the power plug socket, into which you insert the power cord that brings electricity from a wall plug.)

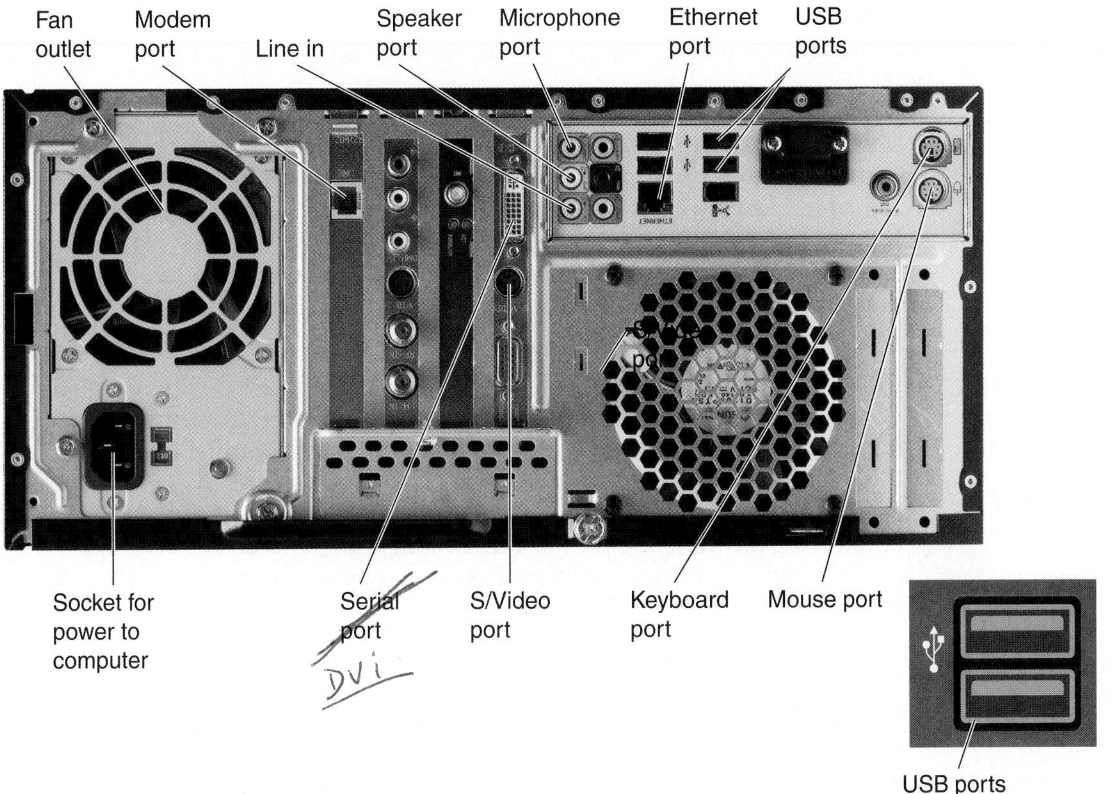

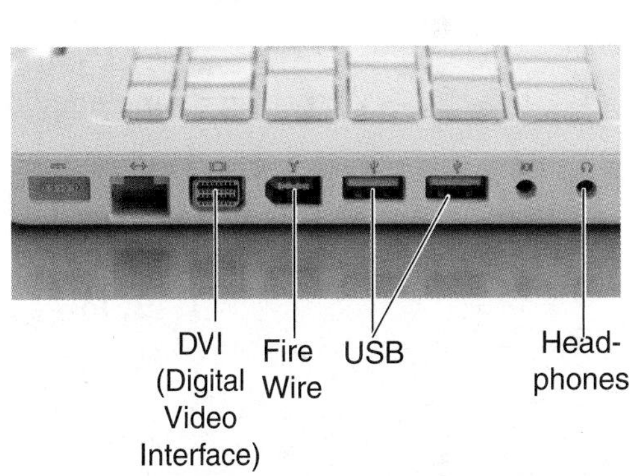

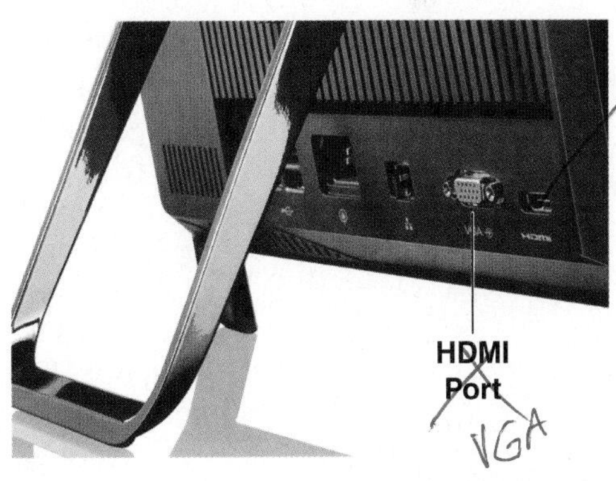

panel 4.11

Ports

The backs of a PC (*top*) and a Macintosh (*bottom*). Additional USB ports may be on the front or side of some system units.

SERIAL, PARALLEL, & USB PORTS Most ports other than the dedicated ones just described are generally multipurpose. We consider serial, parallel, and USB ports:

- **Serial ports—for transmitting slow data over long distances: A line connected to a *serial port* will send bits one at a time, one after another,** like cars on a one-lane highway. Because individual bits must follow each other, a serial port is usually used to connect devices that do not require fast transmission of data, such as keyboard, mouse, monitors, and dial-up modems. It is also useful for sending data over a long distance. New computers have eliminated older serial ports in favor of USB ports.
- **Parallel ports—for transmitting fast data over short distances: A line connected to a *parallel port* allows 8 bits (1 byte) to be transmitted simultaneously,** like cars on an eight-lane highway. Parallel lines move information faster than serial lines do, but they can transmit information efficiently only up to 15 feet. Thus, parallel ports are used principally for connecting printers or external disk or magnetic-tape backup storage devices (although these peripheral devices now generally use USB connections).
- **USB ports—The most widely used hardware interface for attaching peripherals to a computer: A *USB (universal serial bus) port* is a high-speed hardware standard for interfacing peripheral devices, such as scanners and printers, to computers without a need for special expansion cards or other hardware modifications to the computer.** USB is replacing many varieties of serial and parallel ports. USB ports are multipurpose, useful for all kinds of peripherals, and are included on all new computers.

6 USB 2.0 Ports

The designers of the USB standard had several goals in mind. They wanted it to . . .

1. Be low-cost so that it could be used in cheap peripherals such as mice and game controllers.
2. Be able to connect lots of devices and have sufficient speed that it could replace all the different ports on computers with a single standard.
3. Be "hot swappable" or "hot pluggable," meaning that it could allow USB devices to be connected or disconnected even while the PC is running.
4. Permit ***plug and play*—to allow peripheral devices and expansion cards to be automatically configured while they are being installed—** to avoid the hassle of setting switches and creating special files, as was required of early users.

USB has fulfilled these goals, so now just about every peripheral is available in a USB version, and it's expected that soon microcomputers will have nothing but USB ports.

You can also hook up a USB hub to one of the USB ports. You plug the hub into your computer, and then plug your devices—or other hubs—into that. By chaining hubs together, you can build up dozens of available USB ports on a single computer. However, using a hub weakens data signals, so some peripherals, such as cable modems, work better when plugged directly into one of the computer's USB ports.

Just about every peripheral made now comes in a USB version. Common USB standards are *USB 1.1, USB 2.0, and USB 3.0.* Nearly all new PCs have USB 2.0 ports or 3.0 ports. Users with an older PC with USB 1.1 ports will have to buy a 2.0 add-on upgrade card to be able to hook up 2.0 peripherals. (USB 2.0 data "throughput"—the speed at which data passes through the cable—is 2–13 times faster than USB 1.1.)

(*top*) USB hubs; (*bottom*) the USB symbol on USB connectors and USB port

> **Survival Tip**
>
> **Powered versus Unpowered USB Hubs**
>
> USB peripheral devices can draw their power from their USB connection. Printers and scanners have their own power supply. Mice and digital cameras draw power from the PC. If you have lots of self-powered devices (like printers and scanners), your hub need not be powered. If you have lots of unpowered devices (like mice and cameras), you probably need a powered hub.

SuperSpeed USB 3.0 was released by Intel and its partners in November 2008, and the first devices with USB 3.0 ports were released in 2010. USB 3.0 is about 10 times faster than USB 2.0 and can handle higher levels of power. With a special cable and adapter, 3.0 devices are compatible with 2.0 ports.

> **Survival Tip**
>
> **Are Your PC's USB Ports 2.0?**
>
> Find the USB port by looking for the icon. If there's a tiny + (plus sign) next to the icon, you have USB 2.0.

SPECIALIZED EXPANSION PORTS—FIREWIRE, DVI, HDMI, , BLUETOOTH, & ETHERNET Some specialized expansion ports are these:

- **FireWire ports—for camcorders, DVD players, and TVs:** FireWire was created by Apple Computer and later standardized as IEEE-1394 (IEEE is short for Institute of Electrical and Electronics Engineers). It actually preceded USB and had similar goals. The difference is that ***FireWire (IEEE-1394)*** **is intended for devices working with lots of data—not just mice and keyboards but digital video recorders, DVD players, gaming consoles, and digital audio equipment.** Like USB, FireWire is a serial bus. However, USB 2.0 is limited to 480 megabits per second (Mbps); FireWire 800 handles 800 megabits per second (Mbps). (USB 3.0 could be as fast as 4.8 gigabytes per second [Gbps].) USB can handle 127 devices per bus, while FireWire handles 63. Both USB and FireWire allow you to plug and unplug devices at any time.

  FireWire doesn't always require the use of a PC; you can connect a FireWire camcorder directly to a digital TV, for example, without a PC in the middle. Like USB devices, FireWire devices can be powered or unpowered, and they are also hot pluggable. FireWire requires a special card in the PC.

> **Survival Tip**
>
> **Types of USB Connectors**
>
> Different USB devices use different types of USB connectors. For a pictorial chart of all the connectors and descriptions of what devices they are used for, go to: **www.cablestogo.com/resources/usb.asp**

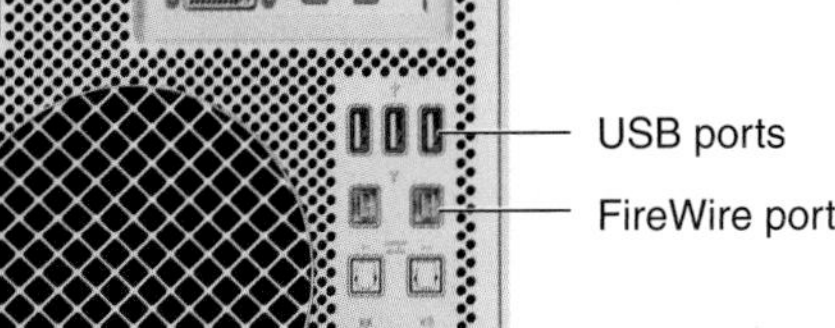

- **Multimedia ports—for connecting monitors and multimedia devices: Most newer monitors and multimedia devices such as TVs and DVD players connect via *DVI (digital video interface)* ports.**

Using a Bluetooth headset; Bluetooth logo

The digital interface standard was created by the Digital Display Working Group (DDWG) to convert analog signals into digital signals to accommodate both analog and digital monitors.

- **HDMI ports—for high-definition video and audio:** DVI can carry only video signals; however, ***HDMI (high-definition multimedia interface)*** **can carry both video and audio signals** and is used for HD TVs, DVD players, and game consoles.
- **Bluetooth ports—for wireless connections up to 30 feet:** ***Bluetooth*** **technology consists of short-range radio waves that transmit up to 30 feet.** It is used to connect cellphones to computers but also to connect computers to printers, keyboards, headsets, and other appliances (including refrigerators).
- **Ethernet—for LANs:** Developed by the Xerox Corporation in the mid-1970s, ***Ethernet*** **is a network standard for linking all devices in a local area network** (p. 24). (The name comes from the concept of "ether.") It's commonly used to connect microcomputers, cable modems, and printers and to connect to high-speed DSL (Chapter 2, p. 55) or cable Internet connections. To use Ethernet, the computer must have an Ethernet network interface card, and special Ethernet cables are required. (Bluetooth and Ethernet are also discussed in Chapter 6.)

Expandability: Buses & Cards

There are several ways to make a computer faster and more powerful.

Many microcomputer systems can be expanded. As mentioned earlier, *expansion* is a way of increasing a computer's capabilities by adding hardware to perform tasks that are not part of the basic system. *Upgrading* means changing to a newer, usually more powerful or sophisticated version. (Computer ads often make no distinction between expansion and upgrading. Their main interest is simply to sell you more hardware or software.)

CLOSED & OPEN ARCHITECTURE Whether a computer can be expanded depends on its "architecture"—closed or open. *Closed architecture* means a computer has no expansion slots; *open architecture* means it does have expansion slots. (An alternative definition is that closed architecture is a computer design whose specifications are not made freely available by the manufacturer.

COMPUTER HARDWARE CHART

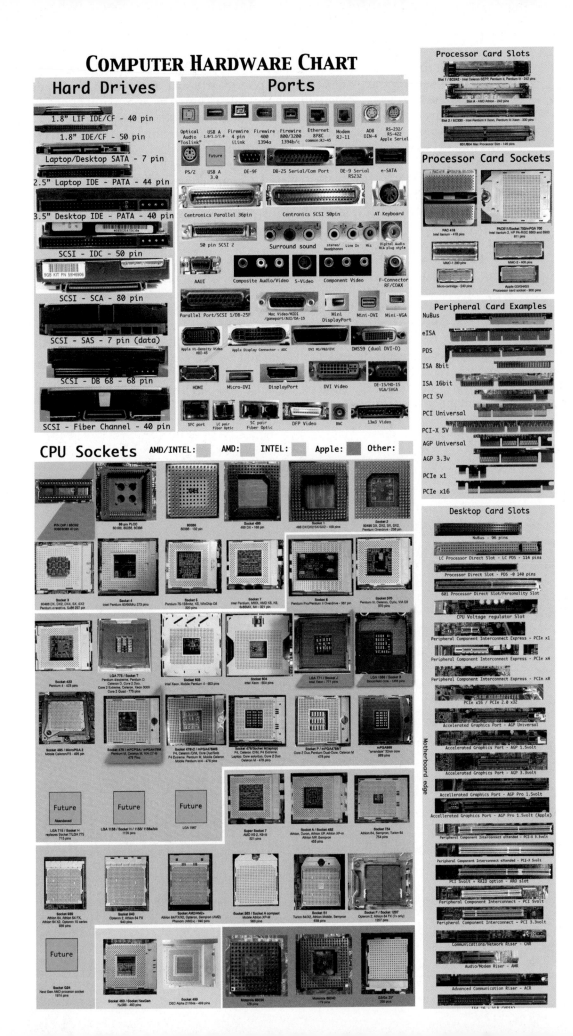

Hard Drives
1.8" LIF IDE/CF - 40 pin
1.8" IDE/CF - 50 pin
Laptop/Desktop SATA - 7 pin
2.5" Laptop IDE - PATA - 44 pin
3.5" Desktop IDE - PATA - 40 pin
SCSI - IDC - 50 pin
SCSI - SCA - 80 pin
SCSI - SAS - 7 pin (data)
SCSI - DB 68 - 68 pin
SCSI - Fiber Channel - 40 pin
Ports
Optical Audio "Toslink"
USB A 1.0/1.1/2.0
Firewire 4 pin ilink
Firewire 400 1394a
Firewire 800/3200 1394b/c
Ethernet 8P8C common:RJ-45
Modem RJ-11
ADB DIN-4
RS-232/ RS-422 Apple Serial
PS/2
Future
USB A 3.0
DE-9F
DB-25 Serial/Com Port
DE-9 Serial RS232
e-SATA
Centronics Parallel 36pin
Centronics SCSI 50pin
AT Keyboard
50 pin SCSI 2
Surround sound
stereo/ Headphones
Line In
Mic
Digital Audio RCA plug style
AAUI
Composite Audio/Video
S-Video
Component Video
F-Connector RF/COAX
Parallel Port/SCSI 1/DB-25F
Mac Video/MIDI /gameport/AUI/DA-15
Mini DisplayPort
Mini-DVI
Mini-VGA
Apple Hi-Density Video HDI-45
Apple Display Connector - ADC
DVI M1/P&D/EVC
DMS59 (dual DVI-D)
HDMI
Micro-DVI
DisplayPort
DVI Video
DE-15/HD-15 VGA/SVGA
SFC port
LC pair Fiber Optic
SC pair Fiber Optic
DFP Video
BNC
13w3 Video
CPU Sockets
AMD/INTEL:
AMD:
INTEL:
Apple:
Other:
Future
Future
Future
Future

Processor Card Slots
Processor Card Sockets
Peripheral Card Examples
NuBus
eISA
PDS
ISA 8bit
ISA 16bit
PCI 5V
PCI Universal
PCI-X 5V
AGP Universal
AGP 3.3v
PCIe x1
PCIe x16
Desktop Card Slots
NuBus - 96 pins
LC Processor Direct Slot - LC PDS - 114 pins
Processor Direct Slot - PDS -0 140 pins
601 Processor Direct Slot/Personality Slot
CPU Voltage regulator Slot
Peripheral Component Interconnect Express - PCIe x1
Peripheral Component Interconnect Express - PCIe x4
Peripheral Component Interconnect Express - PCIe x8
PCIe x16 / PCIe 2.0 x32
Accelerated Graphics Port - AGP Universal
Accelerated Graphics Port - AGP 1.5volt
Accelerated Graphics Port - AGP 3.3volt
Accellerated Graphics Port - AGP Pro 1.5volt
Accellerated Graphics Port - AGP Pro 1.5volt (Apple)
Peripheral Component Interconnect eXtended - PCI-X 3.3volt
Peripheral Component Interconnect eXtended - PCI-X 5volt
PCI 5volt + RAID option - ARO slot
Peripheral Component Interconnect - PCI 5volt
Peripheral Component Interconnect - PCI 3.3volt
Communications/Network Riser - CNR
Audio/Modem Riser - AMR
Advanced Communication Riser - ACR
Motherboard edge

Thus, other companies cannot create ancillary devices to work with it. With open architecture, the manufacturer shares specifications with outsiders.)

Expansion slots **are sockets on the motherboard into which you can plug expansion cards. *Expansion cards*—also known as *expansion boards, adapter cards, interface cards, plug-in boards, controller cards, add-ins,* or *add-ons*—are circuit boards that provide more memory or that control peripheral devices.** *(• See Panel 4.12.)*

COMMON EXPANSION CARDS & BUSES Common expansion cards connect to the monitor (graphics card), speakers and microphones (sound card), and network (network card), as we'll discuss. Most computers have four to eight expansion slots, some of which may already contain expansion cards included in your initial PC purchase.

Expansion cards are made to connect with different types of buses on the motherboard. As we mentioned, *buses* are electrical data roadways through which bits are transmitted, and every bus deals with a particular kind of traffic. The bus that connects the CPU within itself and to main memory is the *frontside bus,* also called the *memory bus* or the *local bus*. *(• See Panel 4.13.)* The buses that connect the CPU with expansion slots on the motherboard and thus with peripheral devices are *expansion buses*. We already described the universal serial bus (USB), whose purpose, in fact, is to *eliminate* the need for expansion slots and expansion cards, since you can just connect USB devices in a chain outside the system unit.

panel 4.12

Expandability

(Left) How an expansion card fits into an expansion slot. *(Right)* Types of cards.

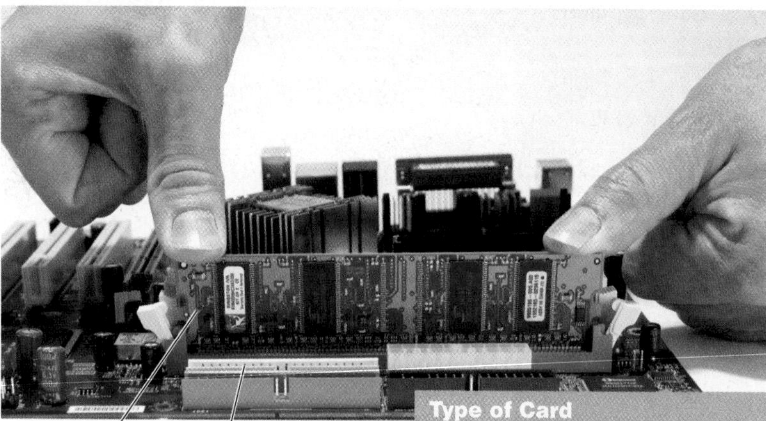

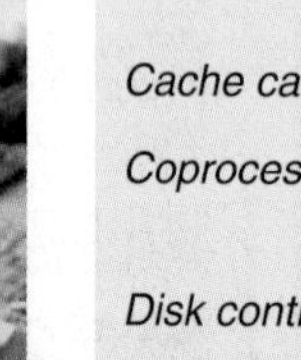

Memory expansion card

Type of Card (Board)	What It Does
Accelerator board	Speeds up processing; also known as turbo board or upgrade board
Cache card	Improves disk performance
Coprocessor board	Contains specialized processor chips that increase processing speed of computer system
Disk controller card	Allows certain type of disk drive to be connected to computer system
Emulator board	Permits microcomputer to be used as a terminal for a larger computer system
Fax modem board	Enables computer to transmit and receive fax messages and data over telephone lines; these days, modems are sometimes wired into the motherboard.
Graphics (video) adapter board	Permits computer to have a particular graphics standard
Memory expansion board	Enables additional RAM to be added to computer system
Sound board	Enables certain types of systems to produce sound output

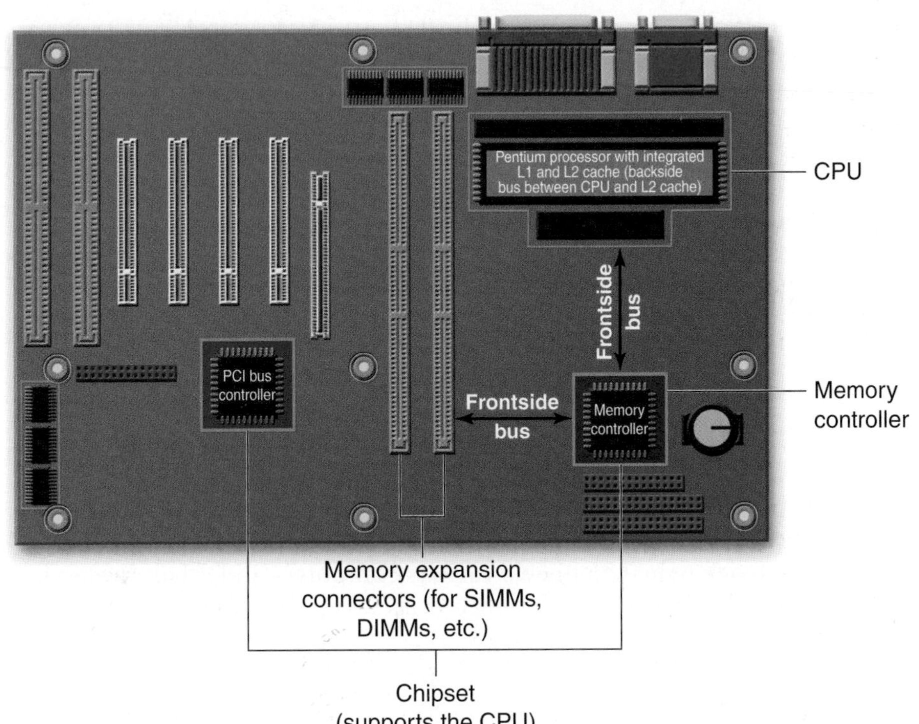

panel 4.13

Frontside bus

Some buses to be aware of are these:

- **PCI bus—for high-speed connections: At 32 or 64 bits wide, the *PCI (peripheral component interconnect) bus* is a high-speed bus** that has been widely used to connect PC graphics cards, sound cards, modems, and high-speed network cards. A more recent standard is the *PCI Express (PCIe),* as we explain below.
- **AGP bus—for even higher speeds and 3-D graphics:** The PCI bus was adequate for many years, providing enough bandwidth for all the peripherals most users wanted to connect—except graphics cards. In the mid-1990s, however, graphics cards were becoming more powerful, and three-dimensional (3-D) games were demanding higher performance. Because the PCI bus couldn't handle all the information passing between the main processor and the graphics processor, Intel developed the AGP bus. **The *AGP (accelerated graphics port) bus,* which transmits data at twice the speed of a PCI bus, is designed to support video and 3-D graphics.**
- **PCIe Express bus—for outperforming AGP:** In 2004, Intel developed the ***PCIe (PCI Express) bus,* which can outperform AGP and is more reliable.** PCIe is the latest standard for expansion cards available on mainstream personal computers.

TYPES OF EXPANSION CARDS Among the types of expansion cards are graphics, sound, modem, and network interface cards. A special kind of card is the PC card.

- **Graphics cards—for monitors:** Graphics cards are included in all PCs. **Also called a *video card, video RAM (VRAM),* or *video adapter,* a *graphics card* converts signals from the computer into video signals that can be displayed as images on a monitor.** Each graphics card has its own memory chips, a graphics BIOS ROM chip, and a dedicated processor, the graphics processing unit (GPU), discussed earlier. The GPU works in tandem with the computer's CPU to ease the load, resulting in faster overall speed.

1 GB DDR3 Nvidia GeForce DVI/HDMI Graphics

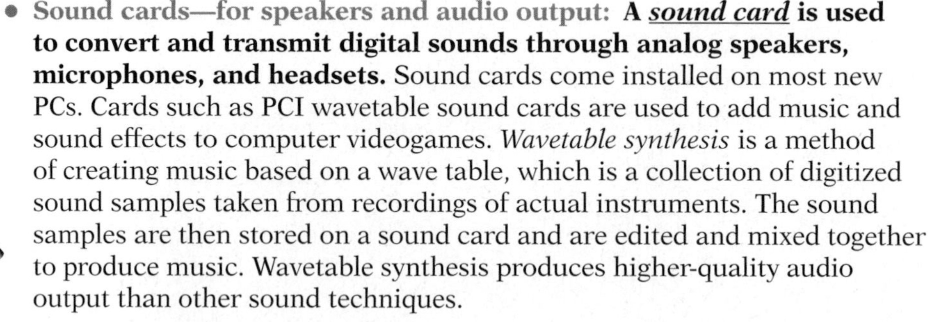

- **Sound cards—for speakers and audio output: A *sound card* is used to convert and transmit digital sounds through analog speakers, microphones, and headsets.** Sound cards come installed on most new PCs. Cards such as PCI wavetable sound cards are used to add music and sound effects to computer videogames. *Wavetable synthesis* is a method of creating music based on a wave table, which is a collection of digitized sound samples taken from recordings of actual instruments. The sound samples are then stored on a sound card and are edited and mixed together to produce music. Wavetable synthesis produces higher-quality audio output than other sound techniques.

Sound Blaster X-Fi Titanium Sound Card 

- **Modem cards—for remote communication via phone lines:** Occasionally you may still see a modem that is outside the computer. Most new PCs, however, come with internal modems—modems installed inside as circuit cards or wired directly into the motherboard.
- **Network interface cards—for remote communication via cable: A *network interface card (NIC)* allows the transmission of data over a cable network,** which connects various computers and other devices such as printers. (Various types of networks are covered in Chapter 6.)
- **PC cards—for laptop computers:** Originally called *PCMCIA cards* (for the Personal Computer Memory Card International Association), ***PC cards* are thin, credit card–size flash memory devices sometimes used on laptop computers to expand capabilities,** such as to access the Internet wirelessly. (• *See Panel 4.14.*)

more info!

System Crashes

What can you do if your system crashes? For information to print out and keep for emergencies, go to:

www.ehow.com/how_7434649_repair-system-error-crash.html

www.liutilities.com/how-to/fix-a-computer-crash/

www.techrepublic.com/blog/window-on-windows/how-do-i-create-and-use-a-windows-7-system-image-to-recover-from-a-crash/2829

www.windowsrecoverys.org/fix-missing-operating-system-crash.html

http://dlc.sun.com/osol/docs/content/SYSADV2/tsoverview-30557.html

www.whatsabyte.com/P1/HDD_Crash.html

4.4 Secondary Storage

Secondary storage is all data storage that is not currently in a computer's primary storage (main memory, or RAM).

You're on a trip with your laptop, or maybe just a cellphone or a personal digital assistant, and you don't have a crucial file of data. Or maybe you need to look up a phone number that you can't get through the phone company's directory assistance. Fortunately, you backed up your data online (in the cloud),

panel 4.14

PC card

Example of a PC card used in a laptop

using any one of several storage services (for example, iDrive, *www.idrive.com;* OpenDrive, *www.opendrive*.com; eSureIT, *www.intronis.com;* and SugarSync, *wwwsugarsync.com*), and are able to access it through your modem.

Here is yet another example of how the World Wide Web is offering alternatives to traditional computer functions that once resided within stand-alone machines. We are not, however, fully into the all-online era just yet. Let us consider more traditional forms of ***secondary storage hardware*****, devices that permanently hold data and information as well as programs.** We look at these types of secondary storage devices:

Relative size of a hard-disk drive

- Hard disks
- Optical disks
- Magnetic tape
- Smart cards
- Flash storage
- Online storage

Hard Disks

320 GB SATA 7200 RPM Hard Drive

Hard disks are still the major secondary storage device for desktop computers.

Hard disks **are thin but rigid metal, glass, or ceramic platters covered with a substance that allows data to be held in the form of magnetized spots.** Most hard-disk drives have at least two platters; the greater the number of platters, the larger the capacity of the drive. The platters in the drive are separated by spaces and are clamped to a rotating spindle that turns all the platters in unison. Hard disks are tightly sealed within an enclosed hard-disk-drive unit to prevent any foreign matter from getting inside. Data may be recorded on both sides of the disk platters. *(• See Panel 4.15.)*

panel 4.15

(*top*) Hard disk schematic; (*bottom*) Maxtor desktop computer hard drive

In a microcomputer, the hard disk is enclosed within the system unit. (SATA = Serial Advanced Technology Attachment, a computer bus interface for connecting mass storage devices such as hard-disk drives and optical drives.)

Tracks and sectors

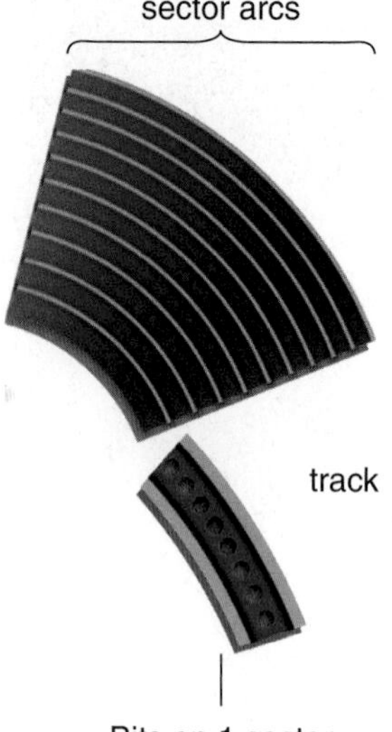

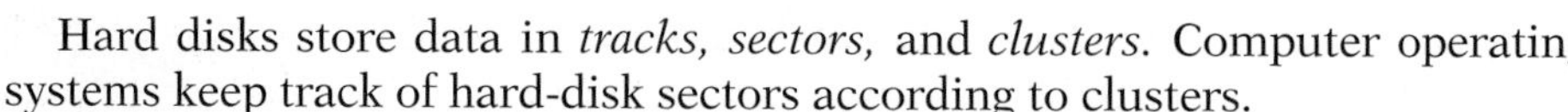

Hard disks store data in *tracks, sectors,* and *clusters.* Computer operating systems keep track of hard-disk sectors according to clusters.

- **Tracks, sectors, and clusters:** On the disk, **data is recorded in concentric recording bands called *tracks*.** Unlike on a vinyl phonograph record, these tracks are neither visible grooves nor a single spiral. Rather, they are closed concentric rings; each track forms a full circle on the disk. **When a disk is formatted, the disk's storage locations are divided into wedge-shaped sections, which break the tracks into small arcs called *sectors*.** When you save data from your computer to a disk, the data is distributed by tracks and sectors on the disk. That is, the system software uses the point at which a sector intersects a track to reference the data location. The smallest unit of disk space that can be written/read from is called a cluster. A *cluster* is a group of sectors on a storage device.
- **The read/write head:** Each disk is fixed in place over the spindle of the drive mechanism. **The *read/write head* is used to transfer data between the computer and the disk.** When the disk spins, the read/write head moves back and forth over the *data access area* on the disk.

The Windows operating system assigns a unique number to each cluster and then keeps track of files on a disk by using a kind of table, a *Virtual File Allocation Table (VFAT),* as a method for storing and keeping track of files according to which clusters they use. (The VFAT was called a FAT in earlier operating systems.) That is, the VFAT includes an entry for each cluster that describes where on the disk the cluster is located.

Occasionally, the operating system numbers a cluster as being used even though it is not assigned to any file. This is called a *lost cluster.* You can free up lost clusters and thus increase disk space in Windows by using the ScanDisk utility.

Storage in the Old Days

In 1978, a pioneering drive for home computers, the external Shugart SA4000, weighed 35 pounds, wholesaled for $2,550, and stored only 14.5 megabytes. Hard drives began to become popular with PC users in 1983, when Seagate made one that fit into the PC case. For more history, go to:

www.computerhistory.org/

HEAD CRASHES Hard disks are sensitive devices. The read/write head does not actually touch the disk but rather rides on a cushion of air about 0.000001 inch thick. *(● See Panel 4.16.)* The disk is sealed from impurities within a container, and the whole apparatus is manufactured under sterile conditions. Otherwise, all it would take is a human hair, a dust particle, a fingerprint smudge, or a smoke particle to cause what is called a head crash. A *head crash* happens when the surface of the read/write head or particles on its surface come into contact with the surface of the hard-disk platter, causing the loss of some or all of the data on the disk. A head crash can also happen when you bump a computer too hard or drop something heavy on the system cabinet. An incident of this sort could, of course, be a disaster if the data has not been backed up. There are firms that specialize in trying to retrieve data from crashed hard disks (for a hefty price), though this cannot always be done.

panel 4.16

Gap between hard-disk read/write head and platter

Were the apparatus not sealed, all it would take is a human hair, dust particle, fingerprint, or smoke particle to cause a head crash.

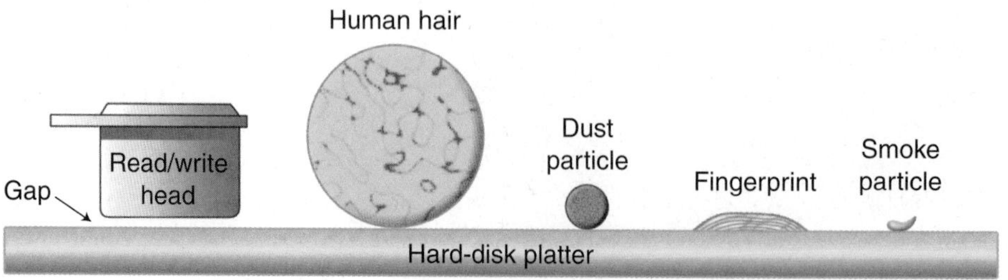

NONREMOVABLE HARD DISKS An internal *nonremovable hard disk,* also known as a *fixed disk,* is housed in the microcomputer system unit and is used to store nearly all programs and most data files. Usually it consists of several metallic or glass platters, from 1 to 5.25 inches (most commonly 3.5 inches) in diameter, stacked on a spindle, with data stored on both sides. Read/write heads, one for each side of each platter, are mounted on an access arm that moves back and forth to the right location on the platter. The entire apparatus is sealed within an airtight case to protect it from contaminants such as dust. The storage capacities of nonremovable hard drives for microcomputers range from 120 to 2,000 gigabytes.

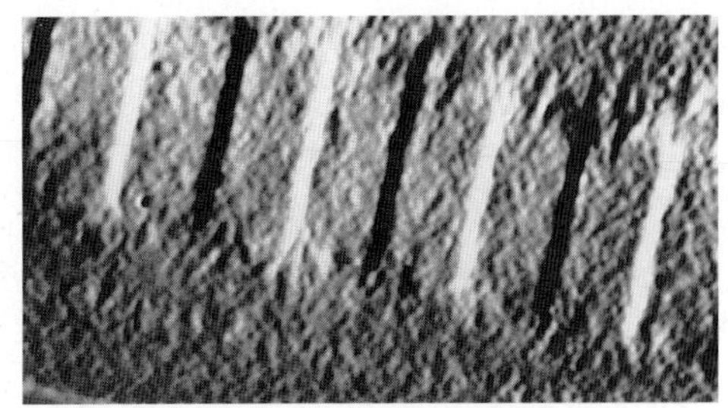

Bits on disk. Magnetic bits on a disk surface, caught by a magnetic force microscope. The dark stripes are 0 bits; the bright stripes are 1 bits.

PORTABLE HARD-DRIVE SYSTEMS: EXTERNAL HARD DISKS A *removable hard disk,* or *hard-disk cartridge,* consists of one or two platters enclosed along with read/write heads in a hard plastic case, which is inserted into a cartridge drive built into the microcomputer's system unit. Cartridges, which have storage capacities of 80 gigabytes–1 terabyte and more, are frequently used to back up and transport huge files of data, such as those for large spreadsheets or desktop-publishing files. These external hard drives are usually connected to the computer via USB.

Survival Tip

Data Recovery

Crashed your hard disk? Try these:

www.drivesavers.com

www.drivelabs.com

www.harddriverecovery.org

HARD-DISK TECHNOLOGY FOR LARGE COMPUTER SYSTEMS: RAID Large databases, such as those maintained by insurance companies or Google, require far bigger storage systems than the fixed-disk drives we've been describing, which send data to a computer along a single path. A *RAID (redundant array of independent disks) storage system,* which links any number of disk drives within a single cabinet or multiple cabinets, sends data to the computer along several parallel paths simultaneously. Response time is thereby significantly improved. RAID systems also store the same data in different places (thus, redundantly) on multiple hard disks; storing data redundantly also increases fault tolerance, meaning that the system can keep working in spite of a failure.

RAID, which connects to a computer system

Optical Disks: CDs & DVDs

The optical disk has become the preferred medium for music, movies, and software programs because of its advantages: compact, lightweight, durable, and digital.

Everyone who has ever played an audio CD is familiar with optical disks. **An *optical disk* is a removable disk, usually 4.75 inches in diameter and about .05 inch thick, on which data is written and read through the use of laser beams.** An audio CD holds up to 74 minutes (2 billion bits' worth) of high-fidelity stereo sound. Some optical disks are used strictly for digital data storage, but many are used to distribute multimedia programs that combine text, visuals, and sound.

more info!

History of Storage

For a short pictorial history of computer storage, go to:

http://royal.pingdom.com/?p=274

HOW OPTICAL-DISK STORAGE WORKS With an optical disk, there is no mechanical read/write arm, as with hard disks. Instead, a high-power laser beam is used to write data by burning tiny pits or indentations into the surface of a hard plastic disk. To read the data, a low-power laser light scans the disk surface: pitted areas are not reflected and are interpreted as 0 bits; smooth areas are reflected and are interpreted as 1 bits. (• *See Panel 4.17, next page.*) Because the pits are so tiny, a great deal more data can be represented than is possible in the same amount of space on a diskette and many hard disks. An optical disk can hold up to about 18 gigabytes of data, the equivalent of about 3.9 million typewritten pages. (High-density [HD] optical disks can hold up to 60 GB.)

All PCs marketed today contain a CD/DVD drive, which can also read audio CDs. These, along with their recordable and rewritable variations, are the two principal types of optical-disk technology used with computers.

Optical disk and disk drive in a laptop

panel 4.17

How a laser reads data on an optical disk

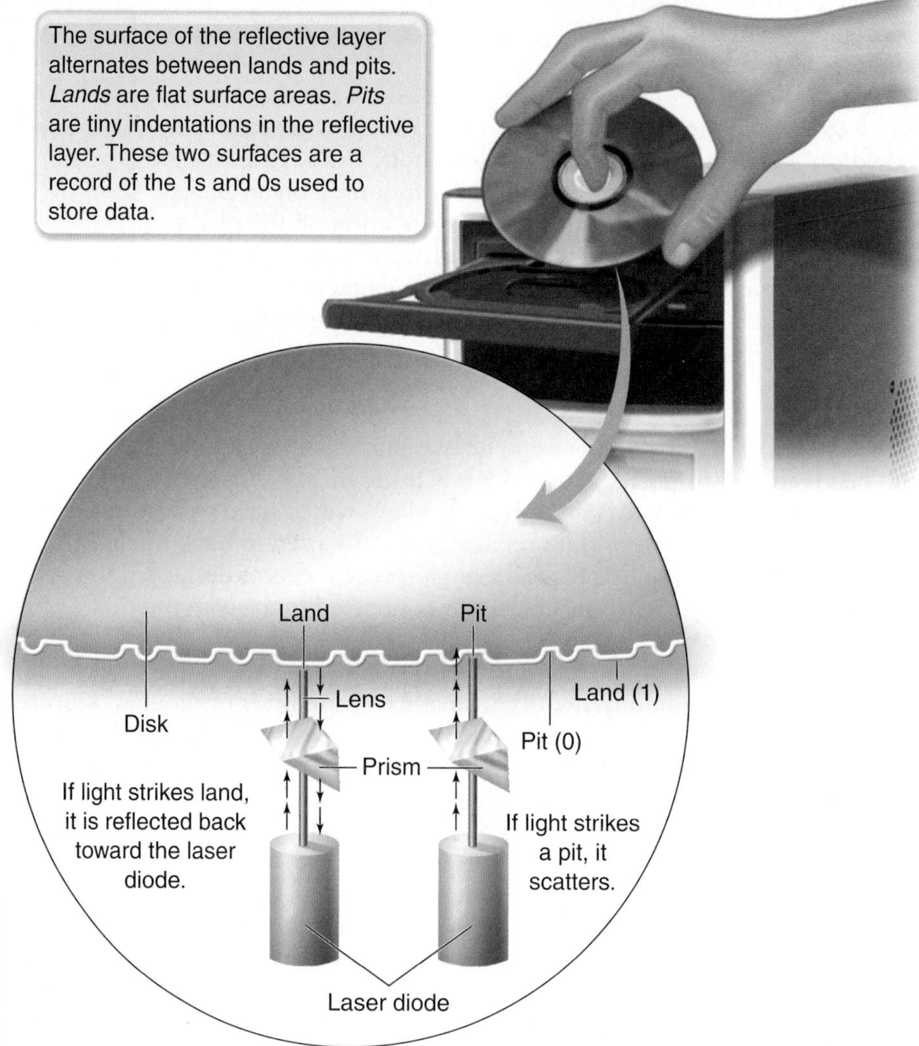

The surface of the reflective layer alternates between lands and pits. *Lands* are flat surface areas. *Pits* are tiny indentations in the reflective layer. These two surfaces are a record of the 1s and 0s used to store data.
Land
Pit
Lens
Land (1)
Disk
Pit (0)
Prism
If light strikes land, it is reflected back toward the laser diode.
If light strikes a pit, it scatters.
Laser diode

Survival Tip

CD Read, Write, & Rewrite Speeds

PC ads present CD speeds in different ways—for example, *44X/24X/24X* for "read/write/rewrite" or *48X/24X/48X* for "write/rewrite/read." To clarify, do a web search for the CD drive manufacturer, brand, and model. Click on *product details* or *specs*.

CD-ROM—FOR READING ONLY The first kind of optical disk for microcomputers was the CD-ROM. ***CD-ROM (compact disk read-only memory)*** **is an optical-disk format that is used to hold prerecorded text, graphics, and sound.** Like music CDs, a CD-ROM is a read-only disk. *Read-only* means the disk's content is recorded at the time of manufacture and cannot be written on or erased by the user. As the user, you have access only to the data imprinted by the disk's manufacturer. A CD-ROM disk can hold about 650 megabytes of data, equal to over 300,000 pages of text.

Lens on a CD/DVD drive on an Acer Aspire laptop

A CD-ROM drive's speed is important because, with slower drives, images and sounds may appear choppy. In computer ads, drive speeds are indicated by the symbol "X," as in "56X," which is a high speed. *X* denotes the original data-transfer rate of 150 kilobytes per second. The data-transfer rate is the time the drive takes to transmit data to another device. A 56X drive runs at 56 times 150, or 8,400 kilobytes (8.4 megabytes) per second. If an ad carries the word *Max*, as in "56X Max," this indicates the device's maximum speed. Common drive speeds are from 12X to 52X; the faster ones are more expensive.

24X DVD/CD-RW Combo Drive

CD-R—FOR RECORDING ONLY ONCE ***CD-R (compact disk–recordable) disks*** **can be written to only once but can be read many times.** This allows users to make their own CD disks. Once recorded, the information cannot be erased. CD-R is often used by companies for archiving—that is, to store vast amounts of information. If you're still using a film camera, for example, once you've shot a roll of color film, you can take it for processing to a photo shop, which can produce a disk containing your images. You can view the disk on any personal computer with a CD-ROM drive and the right software.

CD-RW—FOR REWRITING MANY TIMES **A *CD-RW (compact disk–rewritable) disk,* also known as an *erasable optical disk,* allows users to record and erase data, so the disk can be used over and over again.** CD-RW drives are common on microcomputers. CD-RW disks are useful for archiving and backing up large amounts of data or work in multimedia production or desktop publishing. CD-RW disks commonly have a capacity of 185–700 megabytes.

DVD-ROM—THE VERSATILE VIDEO DISK **A *DVD-ROM (digital versatile disk or digital video disk, with read-only memory)* is a CD-style disk with extremely high capacity, able to store 4.7–18 or more gigabytes (GB).** How is this done? Like a CD or CD-ROM, the surface of a DVD contains microscopic pits, which represent the 0s and 1s of digital code that can be read by a laser. The pits on the DVD, however, are much smaller and grouped more closely together than those on a CD, allowing far more information to be represented. Also, the laser beam used focuses on pits roughly half the size of those on current audio CDs. In addition, the DVD format allows for two layers of data-defining pits, not just one. Finally, engineers have succeeded in squeezing more data into fewer pits, principally through data compression.

How to hold a DVD/CD while inserting it

New computer systems come with a DVD drive as standard equipment. These drives can also take standard CD-ROM disks, so you can watch DVD movies and play CD-ROMs using just one drive. DVDs are replacing CDs for archival storage, mass distribution of software, and entertainment. They not only store far more data but are different in quality from CDs, because they can handle multiple dialogue tracks and screen formats, and high-quality sound and video.

Like CDs, DVDs have their recordable and rewritable variants:

- **DVD-R—recordable DVDs: *DVD-R (DVD-recordable) disks* allow one-time recording by the user.** That is, they cannot be reused—written on more than once.
- **DVD-RW, DVD-RAM, DVD+RW—reusable DVDs:** Three types of reusable disks are *DVD-RW (DVD-rewritable), DVD-RAM (DVD–random access memory),* and *DVD+RW (DVD+rewritable),* all of which can be recorded on and erased (except for video) many times.

BLU-RAY: THE NEXT-GENERATION OPTICAL DISK *Blu-ray,* also known as *Blu-ray Disc (BD),* is the name of a next-generation optical-disk format jointly developed by the Blu-ray Disc Association (BDA), a group of consumer electronics and PC companies (including Dell, Hitachi, HP, JVC, LG, Mitsubishi, Panasonic, Pioneer, Philips, Samsung, Sharp, Sony, TDK, and Thomson). **The *Blu-ray* optical format was developed to enable recording, rewriting, and playback**

Survival Tip

Did You Back Up Your Files?

According to the Consumer Electronics Association, a 2008 study ("Amassing Digital Fortunes: A Digital Storage Study") shows that nearly one in three (33%) of U.S. consumers don't see the need to back up their files, while nearly a quarter (22%) say they aren't backing up files because it's too time consuming. Generally, consumers don't know how to back up their data and if they do, they're failing to back up data because they claim it takes too much time. The average American adult has 1,800 digital files.[8] A more recent study showed that although significantly more people back up their data, 92% of computer users continue to not do *regular* backups. Photos, music, financial data, work documents, and more are lost every single day as the result of computers not being backed up.[9]

How about you? Will you be able to get your files back if something goes wrong with your computer system? For common mistakes people make regarding computer backup and other info, see:

www.datadoctors.com/help/columns/21736-The-most-common-backup-mistakes/

www.pcworld.com/article/101767/ultimate_backup_guide.html

What's a DVD Easter Egg?

DVDs often contain hidden features, called "Easter eggs," such as previews for movies, software, or music. For some great examples, go to:

www.eeggs.com

Audio-visual receiver with a Blu-ray Disc Player

of high-definition video, as well as storing of large amounts of data. The format offers more than five times the storage capacity of traditional DVDs and can hold up to 25 GB on a single-layer disc and 50 GB on a dual-layer disc.

Whereas current optical-disk technologies such as DVD, DVD-R, DVD-RW, and DVD-RAM use a red laser to read and write data, the new format uses a blue-violet laser instead, hence the name Blu-ray. Blu-ray products are backward-compatible and allow use of CDs and DVDs. The benefit of using a blue-violet laser is that it has a shorter wavelength than a red laser, which makes it possible to focus the laser spot with even greater precision. This allows data to be packed more tightly and stored in less space, so it's possible to fit more data on the disk even though it's the same size as a CD/DVD.

Not all the optical-disk drives and different types of optical media (read-only, rewritable, and so on) are mutually compatible. Thus, you need to check the product information before you buy to make sure you get what you want.

THE WORLD'S DVD ZONES As a way to maximize movie revenues, the film industry decided to split the world up into six DVD zones. This is to prevent the DVD version of a movie made in one country from being sold in another country in which the theater version has not yet opened. DVD disks with a particular region code will play only on DVD players with that region code. However, some of the newest DVD players are code-free—they are not "region locked." (Thus, if you plan to travel and use a DVD player for foreign movies, check out the compatibility restrictions.)

Smart Cards

A smart card is a pocket-sized card with integrated circuits.

Today in the United States, most credit cards are still the old-fashioned magnetic-strip cards. A *magnetic-strip card* has a strip of magnetically encoded data on its back and holds about 0.2–0.9 kilobytes (KB) of data. The encoded data might include your name, account number, and PIN (personal identification number). The strip contains information needed to use the card, but the strip also has drawbacks. First, it can degrade over time, making the data unreadable. Second, the magnetic strip doesn't hold much information. Third, such data as

Six DVD regions. The DVD world is basically divided into six regions. This means that DVD players and DVDs are encoded for operation in a specific geographical region. For example, the U.S. is in region 1; thus all DVD players sold in the U.S. are made to region 1 specifications. As a result, region 1 players can play only region 1 DVDs. On the back of each DVD package, you will find a region number (1 through 6).

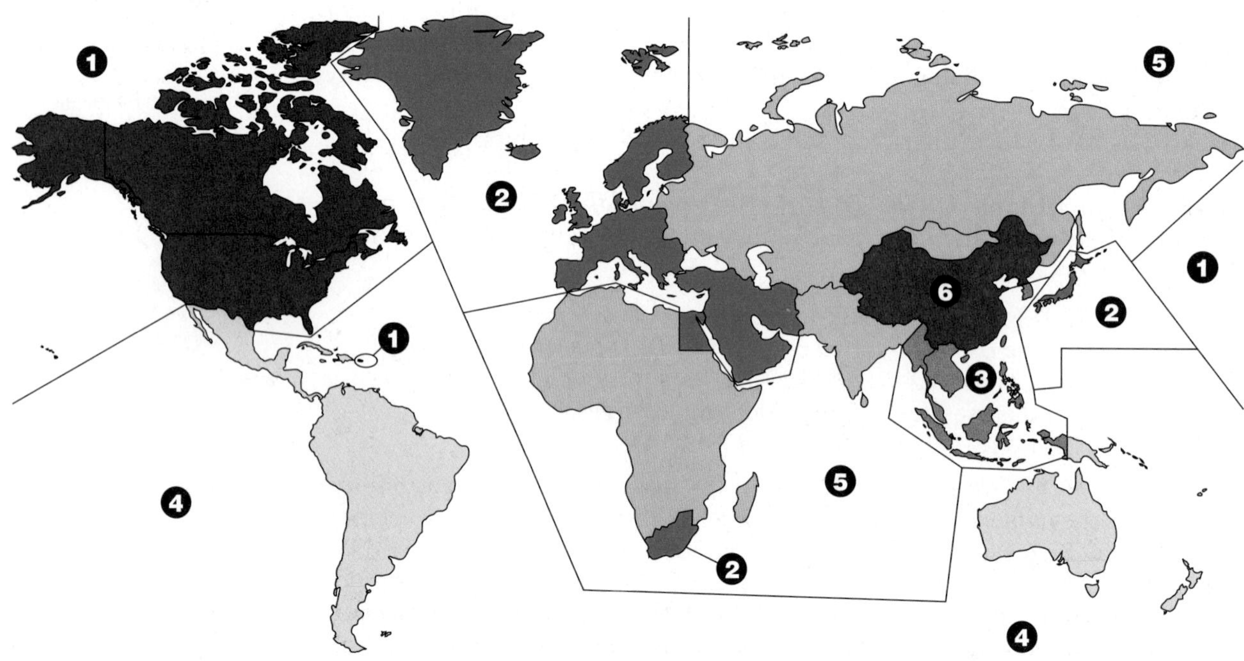

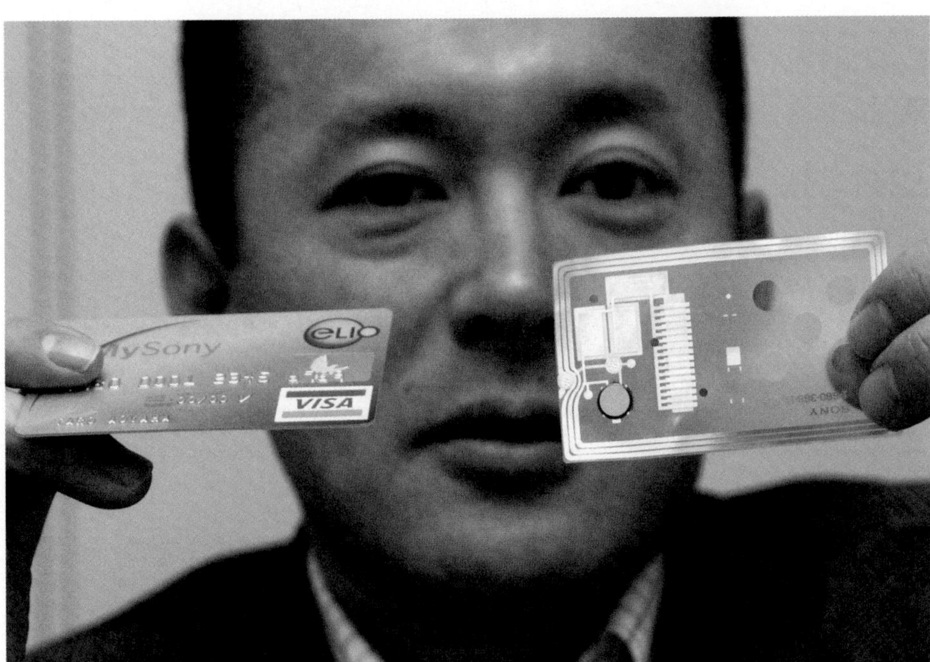

A smart card (*right*) compared to a regular credit card (*left*).

the magnetic strip does contain is easy to access and duplicate, raising the risk of fraud.

Two other kinds of cards, smart cards and optical cards, which hold far more information, are already popular in Europe. Manufacturers are betting they will become more popular in the United States.

SMART CARDS **A *smart card* is a plastic card the size of a credit card with an integrated circuit—a microprocessor and memory chips—built into it.** Most smart cards have been designed with the look and feel of a credit or debit card but can function on at least three levels: credit, debit, personal information. Smart cards include data storage capacity of around 10 megabytes. Owing to the portability and the size of smart cards, they are seen as the next generation of data exchange.

Smart cards contain an operating system just like personal computers. Smart cards can store and process information and are fully interactive. Advanced smart cards also contain a file structure. Some smart cards can be reloaded for reuse. When inserted into a reader, a smart card transfers data to and from a central computer. It is more secure than a magnetic-strip card and can be programmed to self-destruct if the wrong password is entered too many times. As a financial transaction card, it can be loaded with digital money and used as a traveler's check, except that variable amounts of money can be spent until the balance is zero.

Smart cards are well suited for prepaid, disposable applications such as cash cards or telephone debit cards. For example, when you're using a phone card, which is programmed to contain a set number of available minutes, you insert the card into a slot in the phone, wait for a tone, and dial the number. The length of your call is automatically calculated on the card, and the corresponding charge is deducted from the balance. Other uses of smart cards are as student cards, building-entrance cards, bridge-toll cards, and (as in Germany) national-health-care cards. They are also used in certain mobile phones.

Different forms of smart-card technology are available:

- **Contact smart cards:** These kinds of cards, which must be swiped through card readers or inserted in mobile phones, are less prone to misalignment and being misread, but they tend to wear out from the contact.

Website for the LaserCard

- **Contactless smart cards:** These cards, which are read when held in front of a low-powered laser or a radio-frequency reader, can be used in mobile applications, as by automated toll-collecting devices reading cards as drivers pass through toll booths without stopping. (Radio-frequency card use is discussed in more detail in Chapter 5.)

OPTICAL MEMORY CARDS Optical cards use the same type of technology as music compact disks but look like silvery credit cards. ***Optical memory cards* are plastic, laser-recordable, wallet-type cards used with an optical-card reader.** Optical health cards have room not only for the individual's medical history and health-insurance information but also for digital images, such as electrocardiograms.

One form of optical memory card technology, the LaserCard, is used by the U.S. Immigration and Naturalization Service as new Permanent Resident and Border Crossing cards because of its highly secure, counterfeit-resistant features. In addition, LaserCards containing shipping manifest data are attached to shipping containers and sea vans, speeding up receipt processing considerably.

Flash & Solid State Memory

Flash memory and solid-state memory have become the most important form of mobile secondary storage.

Disk drives, whether for hard disks or CDs/DVDs, all involve some moving parts—and moving parts can break. By contrast, *flash memory,* which is a variation on conventional computer memory chips (p. 31), has no moving parts; it is "solid state." Flash memory is also nonvolatile—it retains data even when the power is turned off. A drawback, however, is that flash memory circuits wear out after repeated use, limiting their life span.

Flash memory media are available in three forms: *flash memory cards, flash memory sticks,* and *flash memory drives.*

Smart (SD) card

FLASH MEMORY CARDS ***Flash memory cards***, **or *flash RAM cards*, are removable storage media that are inserted into a flash memory slot in a digital camera, handheld PC, smartphone, or other mobile device.** Unlike smart cards, flash memory cards have no processor; they are useful only for storage. Flash memory cards store up to 64 gigabytes.

SD (smart digital) cards are a kind of flash memory card; they are about the size of a postage stamp. SD technology is becoming the industry standard for mobile phones, digital cameras, MP3 music players, personal computers, printers, car navigation systems, electronic books, and other consumer electronic devices. And SDXC memory cards will increase SD storage capacity from about 32 GB up to 2 TB and also increase SD bus interface read/write speeds up to 104 MB–300 MB per second.

FLASH MEMORY STICKS Smaller than a stick of chewing gum, **a *flash memory stick* is a form of flash memory media that plugs into a memory stick port in a digital camera, camcorder, notebook PC, photo printer, and other devices.** It holds up to 2 gigabytes to 2 terabytes of data.

FLASH MEMORY DRIVES **A *flash memory drive*, also called a *USB flash drive, keychain drive, memory stick*, or *key drive*, consists of a finger-size module of flash memory that plugs into the USB ports of nearly any microcomputer.** It has storage capacities up to 256 gigabytes, making the device extremely useful if you're traveling from home to office, say, and don't want to carry a laptop. When you plug the device into your USB port, it shows up as an external drive on the computer screen. (Note: storage capacities keep increasing.)

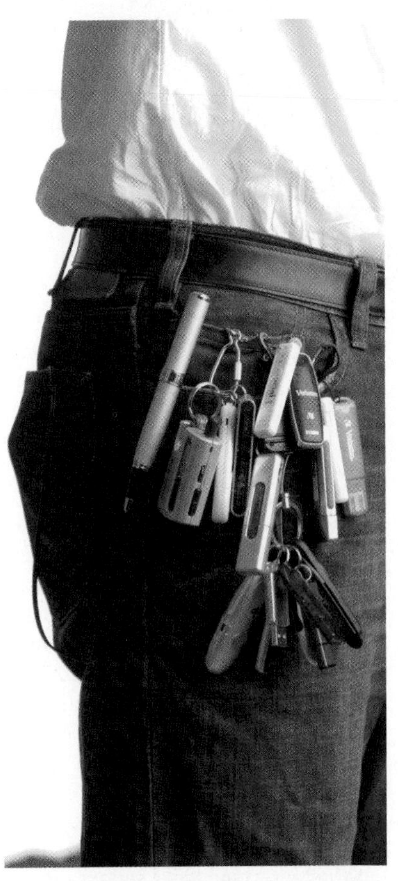

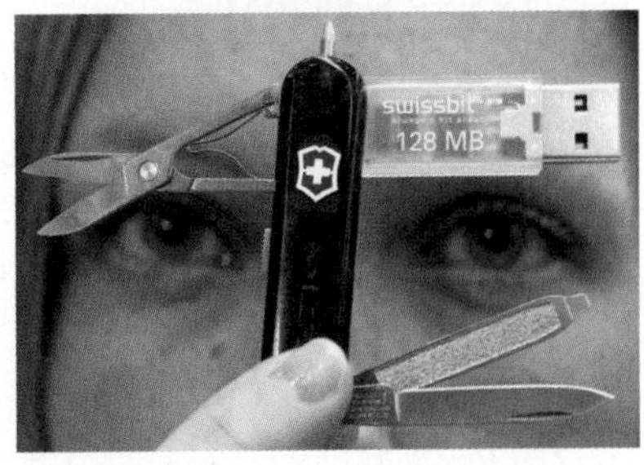

(*Top*) A collection of flash drives; (*bottom*) Swiss Army knife with a USB flash drive that folds out.

SOLID-STATE MEMORY DRIVES Instead of hard disk drives, some newer laptops (such as Apple's MacBook Air laptop) now feature ***solid-state drives*, which have far greater capacity** (128 gigabytes to 512 terabytes) **than flash memory drives or keychain drives; like flash drives, they have no moving parts to break down,** as hard disk drives do. Some solid-state drives use SDRAM instead of flash memory, but in either case such drives are lighter, faster, and use less power than conventional disk drives and can better withstand bumps and bangs. The drawback, however, is that so far solid-state drives are much more expensive than hard disk drives.[10]

Dangers of USB Drives

"Look at some of the most spectacular computer attacks in the last few years, and you'll usually find a USB stick at the center":

www.slate.com/toolbar.aspx?action=print&id=2270003

PRACTICAL ACTION

Storing Your Stuff: How Long Will Digitized Data Last?

How long are those CDs or flash drives on which you're storing your important documents going to last? Will you, or anyone else, be able to make use of them 15 or 25 or 50 years from now?

In 1982 software pioneer Jaron Lanier created a video game called *Moondust* for the then-popular Commodore 64 personal computer. Fifteen years later, when asked by a museum to display the game, he couldn't find a way to do it—until he tracked down an old microcomputer of exactly that brand, type, and age, along with a joystick and video interface that would work with it.

Would this have been a problem if Lanier had originally published a game in a *book*? Probably not. Books have been around since about 1453, when Johannes Gutenberg developed the printing press and used it to print 150 copies of the Bible in Latin. Some of these Gutenberg Bibles still exist—and are still readable (if you can read Latin).

Digital storage has a serious problem: It isn't as long-lived as older forms of data storage. Today's books printed on "permanent" (low-acid, buffered) paper may last up to 500 years. Even books printed on cheap paper that crumbles may still be readable.

By contrast, data stored on disks, magnetic tape, optical disks, and flash drives is subject to two hazards:

- ***Short life span of storage media:*** The storage media themselves have varying life expectancies, and often the degradation is not apparent until it's too late. Hard drives last 2–5 (occasionally up to 10) years, CDs/DVDs also 2–5 years. The maximum life of a CD-RW seems to be about 10 years. Very high-quality CD-Rs and DVD-Rs might last up to 100 years, but light (UV rays) can "kill" the disks way before that. (Optical disks commonly used for burning, such as CD-R and CD-RW, have a recording surface consisting of a layer of dye that can be modified by heat to store data. The degradation process can result in the data "shifting" on the surface and thus becoming unreadable to the laser beam.) USB drives last about 10 years, flash drives also about 10 years.
- ***Hardware and software obsolescence:*** As Jaron Lanier found out, even when disks and drives remain intact, the hardware and software needed to read them may no longer be available. Without the programs and computers used to encode data, digital information may no longer be readable.

  Eight-inch floppy disks and drives, popular 25 years ago, are now extinct, as are their 5¼-inch and 3½-inch successors. Optical and magnetic disks will be increasingly useless one day because of the lack of working equipment to read them.

What about the personal records you store on your own PC, such as financial records, inventories, genealogies, and photographs? Here are a few suggestions for preserving your data:

1. Choose your storage media carefully and research their longevity.
2. Store files in a standard format, such as simple text (.txt) files and uncompressed bitmapped files. (Compression schemes can change, as well as the software and hardware able to deal with them.)
3. Keep copies of the software that created the data that you are saving.
4. Keep two copies, stored in separate places, preferably cool, dry environments.
5. Use high-quality media, not off-brands.
6. When you upgrade to a new hardware or software product, have a strategy for migrating and/or resaving the old data. (However, keep in mind that migrating data can degrade the data; keeping electronic data pristine over many years is becoming an increasingly important problem.)

Remember that although the storage media might last some years, the devices used to read them may become obsolete during that time; so it's a good idea to transfer stored data to new media every couple of years. And don't store media in extreme temperatures or extreme levels of humidity. Keep disks in plastic jewel boxes and store them upright.

And remember that there are always printouts (paper!!); books from the 15th and 16th centuries are still around, as is the first photograph, dating from 1826.

Online Secondary Storage

Online secondary storage is cloud storage.

Online storage services, mentioned at the start of this section, allow you to use the Internet to back up your data. Some services are free; others charge a small fee. Examples are Syncplicity, Dropbox, Mozy, Carbonite, iDrive Pro, iDrive.com, and (for business) iBackup.com and eSureIt Business. ASUSTeK

PRACTICAL ACTION

Starting Over with Your Hard Drive: Erasing, Reformatting, & Reloading

There may come a time when your hard drive is so compromised by spyware and other parasites and slows down your computer so much it's as though you had lost two cylinders on your car engine. (This situation might have been avoided had you been running antispyware software, such as, for example, Ad-Aware, AntiSpyware, CounterSpy, PestPatrol, Spybot Search & Destroy, SpyCatcher, or Spy Sweeper. But many people don't do this, which is why one study found that more than 96% of the respondents felt protected from outside threats using traditional antivirus and firewall solutions, yet nearly 82% reported their desktops to be infected with spyware.[11])

Or perhaps you've installed a new application, such as a speech-recognition program or new piece of hardware, whose drivers have the effect of causing such chaos in your system that you wish you'd never acquired the new item.

What should you do now? Give up your computer, buy a new one (if you can afford it), and transfer all your old data to it? (Some people actually do this.) Or erase everything on your hard drive and reinstall your software and data files? Here's what to do.[12]

Make a List of Everything in Your System & Tech Support Phone Numbers

The first thing you need to do is take paper and pencil and make a list of all (1) hardware components, (2) software registration codes and product keys, and (3) technical support phone numbers for your computer maker and your Internet access provider, in case you run into problems while rebuilding your system.

Make Sure You Have Disks with Copies of Your Software

See if you have the original disks for all your software (your program files), including the operating system installation ("recovery" or "restore") disks that came with your computer. If you don't, create CD/DVD copies. Or contact your computer maker for new ones (for which the company will probably charge you). (You can also get download instructions for re-obtaining your application software after you have re-set up your system.)

Make Backup Copies of Your Data Files

There are several different ways to back up your data files—for example, those listed under My Documents, My Pictures, My Scans, and My Music:

- ***Copy to a server:*** If you're on a network, you can save all your data files to a networked folder.
- ***Copy to CDs or DVDs:*** Using a CD/DVD burner, you can back up your data files onto writable CDs or DVDs. (One DVD may be sufficient. Or you may use several CDs.)
- ***Copy to a keychain drive or an MP3 player:*** You can save all your data files to a keychain drive, an MP3 player, or another external hard drive and then transfer them to another computer to burn them onto CD/DVD disks.

You might wish to make two copies of your backed-up files—just in case.

Reformat Your Hard Drive & Reinstall Your Operating System

Insert your operating system CD-ROM installation disks into the CD drive. When your computer asks you if you want to reformat your hard drive, answer yes. When it advises that if you continue all files will be deleted, respond that this is okay. It will take perhaps 60 minutes to reformat the hard disk. You will then be asked to fill in your name, time zone, country, and type of Internet connection. Probably at this point you should also download any operating system updates (patches) from the manufacturer's website. Reboot your computer.

Reinstall Your Programs & Drivers

Reinstall all your applications, such as Microsoft Office, and all the drivers for your printer, camera, CD burner, and other peripherals. (Drivers may not be needed, because new OSs can recognize almost anything and find the driver online.)

Install Security Software & Firewall

To be sure you're starting over with a secure system, now you should install updated security software (such as McAfee Virus Protection, Norton AntiVirus, or ZoneAlarm Antivirus), which contains antivirus software and a firewall that prevents unauthorized users from gaining access to your network. Reboot your computer.

Reinstall All Your Data Files

Copy your saved data files from the backup source. Run virus and spyware scans on everything, using the security software. Reboot. By now, it's hoped, you will have gotten rid of all your spyware and other nuisances.

Computer, maker of the low-cost ($300–$400) Eee PC, offers free online storage. When you sign up, you obtain software that lets you upload whatever files you wish to the company's server. For security, you are given a password, and the files are supposedly encrypted to guard against unwanted access.

Online Storage

Examples of online storage services:

Backup, www.atbackup.com

Digital Iron Mountain, www.ironmountain.com/digital/

Driveway, www.driveway.com

eSureIT, www.intronis.com

Incidentally, you should know that if you lose your cellphone, all those phone numbers in your address book are wirelessly backed up on a regular schedule by your cellphone carrier.

4.5 Future Developments in Processing & Storage

Everyone agrees that computer developers are focused on speed and power, constantly seeking ways to promote faster processing and more main memory in a smaller area.

Not too long ago, IBM came up with a manufacturing process (called *silicon-on-insular*, or *SOI*) that had the effect of increasing a chip's speed and reducing its power consumption. This increasing power, said physicist Michio Kaku, is the reason you can get "a musical birthday card that contains more processing power than the combined computers of the Allied Forces in World War II."[13] But eventually transistors will become so tiny that their components will approach the size of molecules, and the laws of physics will no longer allow this kind of doubling predicted by Moore's Law (p. 211).

Scientists have assumed that silicon chips can't be made infinitely smaller because of leakage of electrons across boundaries that are supposed to serve as insulators. In addition, engineers are creating three-dimensional chips that consist of a multistory silicon stack that can run faster and cooler than ordinary chips. Still, chip makers continue to refine the technology. Intel, for example, has changed the materials used in its chips—using metal instead of silicon in a key component called a gate and replacing silicon dioxide as an insulating layer in its transistors with hafnium—to reduce energy consumption and increase processing speed.

Magnetic RAM

M-RAM is the focus of the website at:

www.mram-info.com

http://searchstorage.techtarget.com/sDefinition/0,,sid5_gci539346,00.html

For now, RAM is volatile, but researchers have developed new nonvolatile forms of RAM that may soon be available. One form is *M-RAM*—the *M* stands for "magnetic"—which uses minuscule magnets rather than electric charges to store the 0s and 1s of binary data. M-RAM uses much less power than current RAM, and whatever is in memory when the computer's power is turned off or lost will remain there. A second type, *OUM (ovonic unified memory)* or *phase-change memory*, stores bits by generating different levels of low and high resistance on a glossy material (*www.seminartopicsonline.com/2010/02/ovonic-unified-memory.html, http://discuss.itacumens.com/index.php?topic=23115.0, http://academic.research.microsoft.com/Paper/5270611*) .

Future Developments in Processing

Nanotechnology, optical computing, and DNA computing are already becoming realities.

What are the possible directions in which processors are going? Let us consider a few:

Application Virtualization

For more information about this kind of cloud computing, go to:

http://searchenterprisedesktop.techtarget.com/definition/application-virtualization

www.microsoft.com/systemcenter/appv/default.mspx

www.radware.com/Resources/Glossary/application_virtualization.aspx

SELLING PROCESSING POWER OVER THE INTERNET In 2002 IBM launched a service, Virtual Linux Service, selling computer processing power on an as-needed basis, in the same way that power companies sell electricity. When, for example, a company wants to update its email or other programs, instead of buying more servers or the latest hardware to provide processing power, it rents the processing time on Linux servers. By now, many companies have gone into the business of what is now called *application virtualization,* which is a kind of cloud computing (Chapter 1, p. 39).

NANOTECHNOLOGY Nanotechnology, nanoelectronics, nanostructures, nanofabrication—all start with a measurement known as a *nanometer,* a billionth of a meter, which means we are operating at the level of atoms and molecules. (● *See Panel 4.18.*) A human hair is between 100,000 and 200,000 nanometers thick,

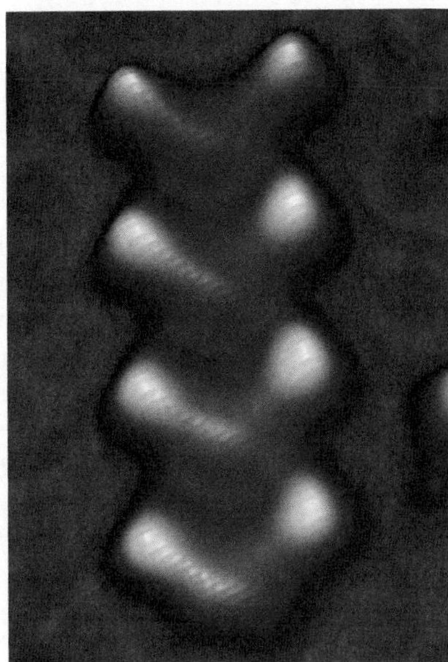

The smallest superconductor, measuring just .87 nanometer wide

The world of superconductors just became a much smaller place. Scientists taking part in an Ohio University led study have discovered the world's smallest superconductor— a sheet of four pairs of molecules measuring less than 1 nanometer (that's 0.000001 millimeter) wide, potentially paving the way for next-generation nanoscale electronics.

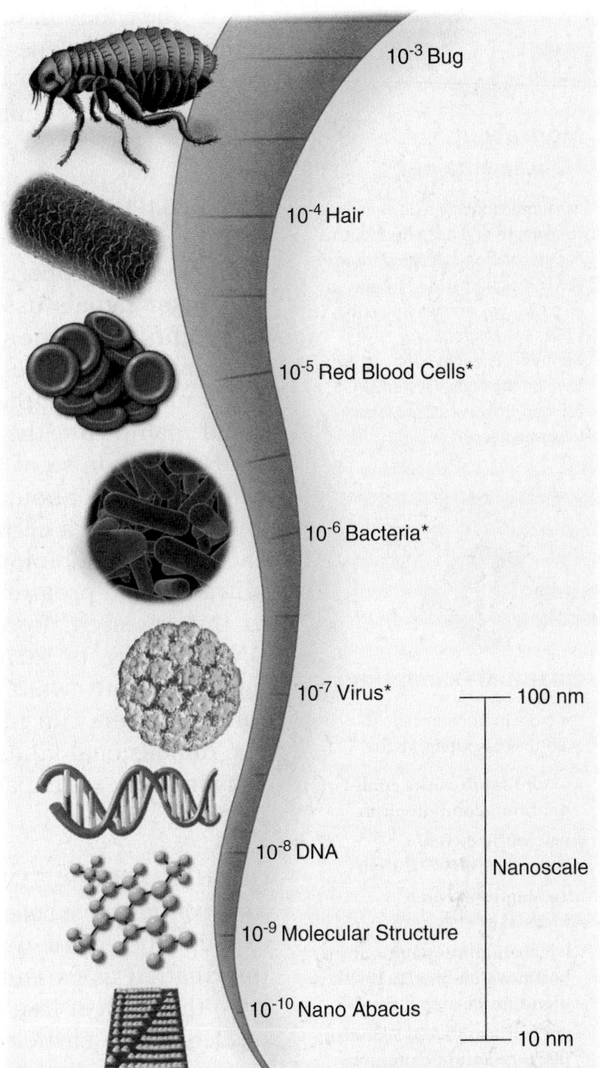

panel 4.18

Nanotechnology: A matter of scale

The world of nanotechnology is so small it defies imagination. (adapted from *www.discovernano.northwestern.edu/whatis/index_html/images/* and *www.mindfully.org/Technology/2004/Buckyball-Football1jul04.htm*).

Nokia's nanotech Morph telephone. The phone's theoretical feature list would include the ability to bend into numerous shapes, so it can be worn around the wrist or held up to the face; transparent electronics would allow the device to be see-through yet functional; self-cleaning surfaces could absorb solar energy to recharge the phone's battery.

while a typical virus can be just 100 nanometers wide. Atoms are typically between one-tenth and one-half of a nanometer wide. Line up 5 million carbon atoms, and the line would be as long as a grain of sand.

In *nanotechnology,* molecules are used to create tiny machines for holding data or performing tasks. Experts attempt to do nanofabrication by building tiny nanostructures one atom or molecule at a time. When applied to chips and other electronic devices, the field is called *nanoelectronics.*

OPTICAL COMPUTING Today's computers are electronic; tomorrow's might be optical, or opto-electronic—using light, not electricity. With optical technology, a machine using lasers, lenses, and mirrors would represent the on/off codes of data with pulses of light.

Light is much faster than electricity. Indeed, fiber-optic networks, which consist of hair-thin glass fibers instead of copper wire, can move information at speeds 3,000 times faster than conventional networks. However, the signals get bogged

More about Nanotechnology

Is nanotechnology really here? To begin to find out, check out nanotechnology's leading forum, the Foresight Institute (*www.foresight.org*), and leading critic, ETC (*www.etcgroup.org*). Also, what effects might nanoparticles have on the body's systems? Go to: <bbb_lu>*www.cdc.gov/niosh/topics/nanotech/*

Quantum Computing

For more information about quantum computing, go to:

www.howstuffworks.com/quantum-computer.htm

www.youtube.com/watch?v=5W4e7ZE0Nv0

http://bigthink.com/ideas/31615

www.theinquirer.net/inquirer/boffin-watch-blog/2029991/quantum-pc-step-closer

www.itpro.co.uk/631585/mit-plans-quantum-computer

down when they have to be processed by silicon chips. Optical chips would remove that bottleneck. It's suggested that mass-produced versions of optical chips could not only slash costs of voice and data networks but also become a new type of technology for delivering high-bandwidth movies, music, and games.

DNA COMPUTING Potentially, biotechnology could be used to grow cultures of bacteria that, when exposed to light, emit a small electrical charge, for example. The properties of this "biochip" could be used to represent the on/off digital signals used in computing. Or a strand of synthetic DNA might represent information as a pattern of molecules, and the information might be manipulated by subjecting it to precisely designed chemical reactions that could mark or lengthen the strand. For instance, instead of using binary, it could manipulate the four nucleic acids (represented by *A, T, C, G*), which holds the promise of processing big numbers. This is an entirely *nondigital* way of thinking about computing.[14] "Can you instruct a biomolecule to move and function in a certain way—researchers at the interface of computer science, chemistry, biology, and engineering are attempting to do just that," says Mitra Basu, a program director at NSF responsible for the agency's support to this research. Recent molecular robotics work has produced so-called DNA walkers, or strings of reprogrammed DNA with "legs" that enabled them to briefly walk. Now this research team has shown these molecular robotic spiders can in fact move autonomously through a specially created, two-dimensional landscape. The walkers acted in rudimentary robotic ways, showing they are capable of starting motion, walking for awhile, turning, and stopping.[15]

QUANTUM COMPUTING Sometimes called the "ultimate computer," the *quantum computer* is based on quantum mechanics, the theory of physics that explains the erratic world of the atom. Whereas an ordinary computer stores information as 0s and 1s represented by electrical currents or voltages that are either high or low, a quantum computer stores information by using states of elementary particles. Scientists envision using the energized and relaxed states of individual atoms to represent data. For example, hydrogen atoms could be made to switch off and on like a conventional computer's transistors by moving from low energy states (off) to high energy states (on).

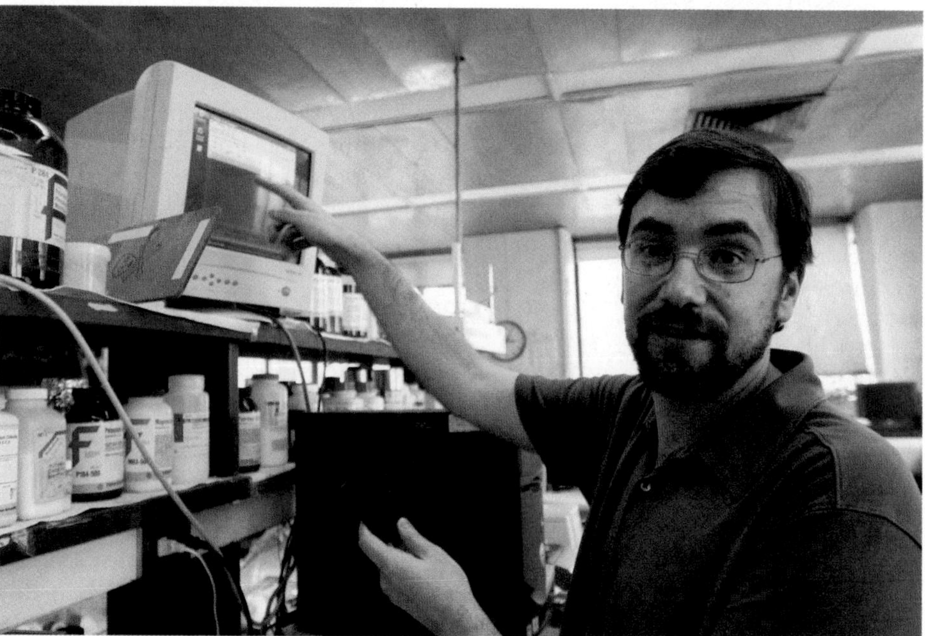

Dr. Milan Stojanovic of Columbia University developed the first game-playing DNA computer, called Maya.

EXTENDING BATTERY & RECHARGING TECHNOLOGY Where is the weak link in our high-tech world? Says one writer, "Computer chips double in speed every two years—your current BlackBerry is as powerful as your desktop computer once was—but the batteries powering these devices are improving only about 8% per year."[16] Laptop, cellphone, and iPod users are tired of having their devices run out of electric charge after only a few hours. And claims that a laptop will get up to 5 hours and 40 minutes of battery life are "not even close," says one expert.[17]

Among the areas of research: Intel is working on developing wireless charging, freeing gadgets from their recharging cords. Companies are also experimenting with developing new lithium-ion batteries, which may extend battery life. Silver-zinc batteries may provide up to 30% higher capacity compared to existing lithium-ion batteries. Tiny fuel-cell batteries, powered by combustible liquids or gases, could potentially power a laptop for days between refills. Marvell Technology Group, which makes chips, is promoting the idea of "plug computers," computing devices that plug into electrical sockets and that are about the same size yet would have enough power to manage people's digital media.[18] Direct methanol fuel cells (DMFCs) are another new technology planned for green, low-cost, and long-running batteries.

ETHICAL MATTERS Of these future developments, nanotechnology has probably received the most attention, and indeed the U.S. government has launched the National Nanotechnology Initiative. In fact, however, nanotechnology and other important fields have been melding into a new field of science vital to U.S. security and economic development. This field is known by the acronym *NBIC* (pronounced either "*en*-bick" or "*nib*-bick"; see, for example, *www.nanotech.upenn.edu/*, *www.futureforall.org/* and *http://convergentsystems.pbworks.com/w/page/16444399/NBIC-Converging-Technologies*), which represents the convergence of nanotechnology, biotechnology, information technology, and cognitive (brain) science.

But is there a possibility of "Gray Goo"? This is a scenario hypothesized in *Wired* magazine in which self-replicating molecule-size robots run amok and transform all earthly matter into nanobots.

Nanotechnology Dangers?

For more information, go to:

www.scientificamerican.com/article.cfm?id=government-fails-to-assess-dangers-of-nanotechnology

http://science.howstuffworks.com/nanotechnology5.htm

www.crnano.org/dangers.htm

Future Developments in Secondary Storage

New memory technology could sidestep all current RAM technologies.

As for developments in secondary storage, when IBM introduced the world's first disk drive in 1956, it was capable of storing 2,000 bits per square inch. Today the company is shipping hard disks with densities of 14.3 billion bits, or 1.43 gigabits, or more per square inch. But that, too, is changing.

HIGHER-DENSITY DISKS Hard drive makers have begun employing a technology known as *perpendicular recording technology,* which involves stacking magnetic bits vertically on the surface of a platter (instead of horizontally, as is usual). Based on this innovation, Seagate Technology makes a 3 terabyte (TB) hard drive, the Barracuda, for desktop PCs, servers, and external storage. Also using perpendicular recording, Hitachi Ltd's Ultrastar can store up to 3 terabytes. *(• See Panel 4.19, next page.)*

Another promising technology is the *microholographic* disk developed by General Electric Co. that stores 540 gigabytes, or the content of 100 standard DVDs, on a single DVD (equivalent to 20 single-layer Blu-ray disks). Holographic technology can store data beneath the surface of a disk, whereas CDs, DVDs, and Blu-ray disks store data only on the surface. A team of Australian researchers is going beyond this to develop "five-dimensional" storage, which would permit a 10-terabyte disk, the equivalent of storing 10,000 standard-definition movies on one disk.[19]

panel 4.19

Conventional versus perpendicular optical recording technologies

Conventional (Longitudinal) Recording

Each bit of information is represented by a collection of magnetized particles, with their north and south poles oriented in one direction or the other. In longitudinal recording, the particles' north and south poles are lined up parallel to the disk's surface in a ring around its center. Magnetic repulsion limits how closely packed those bits can be and still maintain data integrity.

Perpendicular Recording

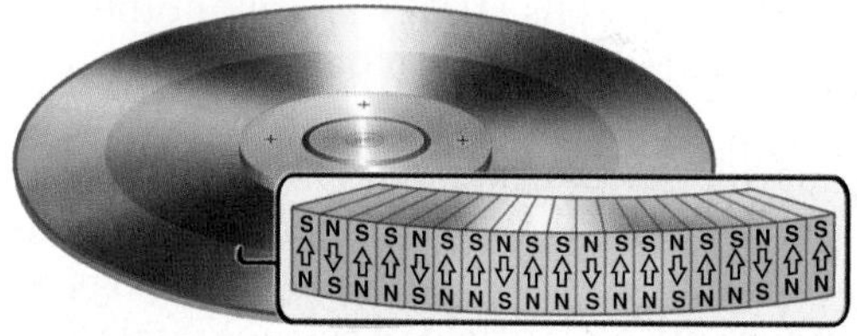

In this type of recording, the poles are arranged perpendicular to the disk's surface, which allows more bits to be packed onto a disk and reduces problems from magnetic interference.

Techno Life Skills

Tech writer Kevin Kelly says that "the older the technology, the more likely it will continue to be useful." And: "Every new technology will bite back. The more powerful its gifts, the more powerfully it can be abused. Look for its costs." Read his excellent article at:

www.kk.org/thetechnium/archives/2011/04/techno_life_ski.php

MOLECULAR ELECTRONICS—STORAGE AT THE SUBATOMIC LEVEL An emerging field, molecular electronics, may push secondary storage into another dimension entirely. Some possibilities include polymer memory, holograms, molecular magnets, subatomic lines, and bacteria.

Polymer memory involves developing an alternative to silicon to create chips that store data on polymers, or plastics, which are cheaper than silicon devices. A bonus with polymers is that, unlike conventional RAM memory, it is nonvolatile—it retains information even after the machine is shut off. Polymer memory involves storing data based on the polymer's electrical resistance. IBM is also developing so-called *probe storage* that uses tiny probes to burn pits in a Plexiglas-like polymer, in which each hole is about 10 nanometers wide, resulting in an experimental storage device of 200 gigabits per square inch. IBM has said that someday it expects as many as 25 million pages of text will be stored in an area no larger than a postage stamp.

EXPERIENCE BOX

How to Buy a Laptop

"Choosing a laptop computer is trickier than buying a desktop PC," says Wall Street Journal technology writer Walter Mossberg.[20] *The reason: laptops are more diverse and more personal and include "a mind-boggling array of computers, from featherweight models that are great for travel to bulky multimedia machines that double as TV sets." In addition, desktop "generic boxes" tend to be similar, at least within a price class. Trying to choose among the many Windows-based laptops is a particularly brow-wrinkling experience. Windows laptops cost less than Apple laptops, and they offer more variety; Macintosh laptops tend to be more straightforward and safer from malware attacks.*

Nevertheless, here are some suggestions:[21]

Purpose. What are you going to use your laptop for? You can get one that's essentially a desktop replacement and won't be moved much. If you expect to use the machine a lot in class, in libraries, or on airplanes, however, weight and battery life are important.

Whatever kind of computer you get (whether laptop or desktop), you want to be sure it works with your school's system. (Mossberg says that tablets are becoming more important, but they don't yet fully replace laptops.) Some departments within a college may require a specific computer configuration or software, so check beforehand. Certainly it should be up to date and able to get Internet access through Ethernet and wireless connections. "Don't bring clunkers [to college]," says one article. "Older computers tend to be buggy, and often lack protection against viruses and other malicious software."[22]

Basics. Most technology writers advise getting a 64-bit machine with 4 GB RAM for best performance, and a 320 GB hard drive. And make sure that you install antivirus and firewall software right away. (Macs can run well with only 2 GB, unless you are working with complex graphics.) Aim for newer processors, such as Intel's i3, i5, and i7 and new AMD chips, and make sure you have a new-model graphics chip. A few USB 2.0 ports are necessary (not all peripheral devices can use USB 3.0 yet), an HDMI port, an Ethernet port, and a CD/DVD slot and burner software. Of course, a Wi-Fi connection is necessary, and Bluetooth can be useful.

Budget & Weight. Laptops range from $300 (with rebates) to $3,000, with high-end brands aimed mainly at businesspeople, hard-core videogamers, and people doing video production. Weight can range from about 3 pounds to over 10 pounds. The general rule is not to buy more laptop than you need.

Batteries: The Life–Weight Trade-Off. Since laptops are designed to be used as a source of portable computing, one of their major features is the length of time the computer can be used away from an external power source. The battery is the only thing keeping the laptop running when it isn't plugged in with the ac adapter. As laptops have become more common and used in more situations, the battery technology used in laptops has become more sophisticated. You should find a laptop that will run for at least 3 hours on its battery.

Gadget Ownership, 2010

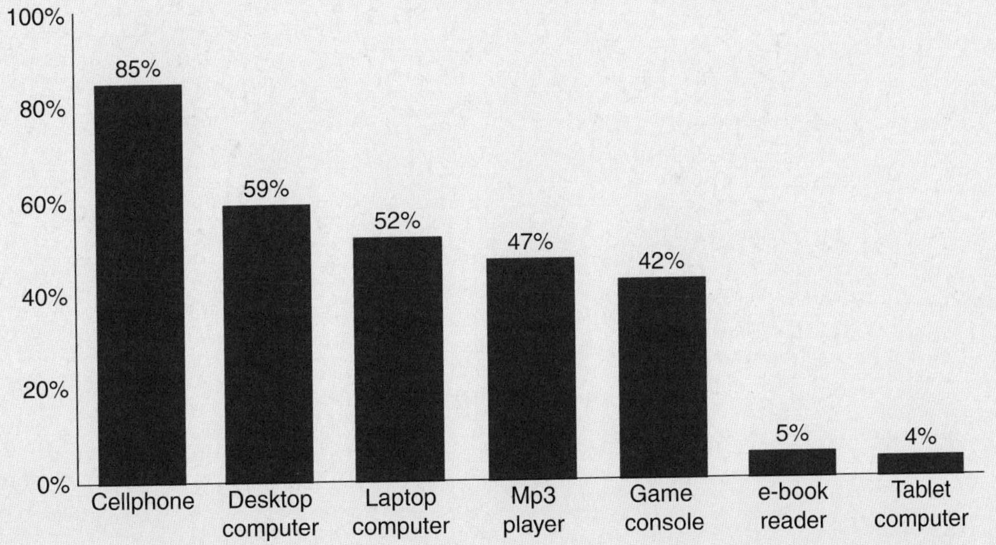

Source: Pew Research Center's Internet & American Life Project, August 9–September 13, 2010 Tracking Survey. N = 3,001 adults 18 and older, including 1,000 reached via cellphone.

A rechargeable lithium-ion battery lasts longer than a nickel-metal hydride battery. Even so, a battery in the less expensive machines will usually run continuously for only about 2¼ hours. (DVD players are particularly voracious consumers of battery power, so it's the rare laptop that will allow you to finish watching a 2-hour movie; a laptop with a bigger screen, faster processor, and better graphics will require more power from the battery.)

Heavier machines usually have longer battery life. The light-weight machines tend to get less than 2 hours, and toting extra batteries offsets the weight savings. (A battery can weigh a pound or so.)[23] (When shopping for a laptop you will often see manufacturers list the amount of cells contained within a laptop battery such as 6-cells and 9-cells. A 9-cell battery has 50% more capacity than a 6-cell, and a 12-cell battery more than a 6-cell battery, but more cells also increase the weight.)

For "22 Laptop Battery Life-Saving Tips & Tricks" go to *www.laptop-computer-comparison.com/laptop-battery-life.html.*

Software. Laptops might come with less software than you would get with a typical desktop, though what you get will probably be adequate for most student purposes. For instance, notebook PCs might offer Microsoft Works rather than the more powerful Microsoft Office to handle word processing, spreadsheets, databases, and the like. You will have to purchase most of your software separately.

Keyboards & Pointing Devices. The keys on a laptop keyboard are usually the same size as those on a desktop machine, although they can be smaller. However, the up-and-down action feels different, and the keys may feel wobbly. In addition, some keys may be omitted altogether, or keys may do double duty or appear in unaccustomed arrangements.

Most laptops have a small touch-sensitive pad in lieu of a mouse—you drag your finger across the touchpad to move the cursor. (But be sure to carry a regular USB wireless mouse with your laptop, so when you are working on a large flat surface, you can just plug the USB mouse connector into a USB port on the laptop and use it as you would on a desktop computer.)

Screens. If you're not going to carry the notebook around much, go for a big, bright screen. Most people find they are comfortable with a 13- to 15-inch display, measured diagonally, though screens can be as small as 8 inches and as large as 17 or 20 inches (which is better for viewing movies).

Memory, Speed, & Storage Capacity. If you're buying a laptop to complement your desktop, you may be able to get along with reduced memory, slow processor, small hard disk, and no CD-ROM. Otherwise, all these matters become important.

Memory (RAM) is the most important factor in computer performance, even though processor speed is more heavily hyped. Most laptops have at least 1 gigabyte of memory, but 4 gigabytes of high-speed DDR SDRAM is best. A microprocessor running 2.0 gigahertz should be adequate. (But if you plan to work with a lot of graphics and/or video, get more RAM and a higher-speed processor, as well as a laptop with a separate video card inside with its own additional memory.)

A hard drive of 320 gigabytes or more is sufficient for most people, and make sure that you have an internal CD/DVD drive, for backing up your files and to play movies and the like.

Wireless. Most laptops come with Wi-Fi for wireless networking; 802.11 technology is fine for ordinary use, but try to buy a laptop with the newer and faster "n" version.

For more information about buying a computer, go to

www.pcmag.com/article2/0,2817,2356818,00.asp
http://reviews.cnet.com/desktop-computer-buying-guide/
www.consumerreports.org/cro/electronics-computers/computers-internet/computers/computer-buying-advice/computer-getting-started/computer-getting-started.htm

Also, go green: look for manufacturers that sell Energy Star systems and provide instructions for recycling old computer equipment.

KEY TERMS & EXPLANATIONS

AGP (accelerated graphics port) bus (p. 227) Bus that transmits data at very high speeds; designed to support video and three-dimensional (3-D) graphics. Why it's important: *An AGP bus is twice as fast as a PCI bus and supports video and 3D graphics.*

arithmetic/logic unit (ALU) (p. 216) Part of the CPU that performs arithmetic operations and logical operations and controls the speed of those operations. Why it's important: *Arithmetic operations are the fundamental math operations: addition, subtraction, multiplication, and division. Logical operations are comparisons such as "equal to," "greater than," or "less than."*

ASCII (American Standard Code for Information Interchange) (p. 205) Binary code used on microcomputers. Besides having the more conventional characters, the Extended ASCII version includes such characters as math symbols and Greek letters. Why it's important: *ASCII is the binary code most widely used in microcomputers.*

binary system (p. 202) A two-state system used for data representation in computers; has only two digits—0 and 1. Why it's important: *In the computer, 0 can be represented by electrical current being off and 1 by the current being on. All data and program instructions that go into the computer are represented in terms of these binary numbers.*

bit (p. 203) Short for "binary digit," which is either a 0 or a 1 in the binary system of data representation in computer systems. Why it's important: *The bit is the fundamental element of all data and information processed and stored in a computer system.*

bluetooth (p. 223) Wireless technology that consists of short-range radio waves that transmit up to 30 feet. Why it's important: *It is used to connect cellphones to computers but also to connect computers to printers, keyboards, headsets, and other appliances.*

Blu-ray (p. 233) The Blu-ray optical format was developed to enable recording, rewriting, and playback of high-definition video, as well as storing of large amounts of data. Why it's important: *It's possible to fit more data on a Blu-ray disk even though it's the same size as a CD/DVD.*

bus (p. 216) Also called *bus line;* electrical data roadway through which bits are transmitted within the CPU and between the CPU and other components of the motherboard. Why it's important: *A bus resembles a multilane highway: The more lanes it has, the faster the bits can be transferred.*

byte (p. 203) Group of 8 bits. Why it's important: *A byte represents one character, digit, or other value. It is the basic unit used to measure the storage capacity of main memory and secondary storage devices (kilobytes and megabytes).*

cache (p. 218) Special high-speed memory area on a chip that the CPU can access quickly. It temporarily stores instructions and data that the processor is likely to use frequently. Why it's important: *Cache speeds up processing.*

CD-R (compact disk–recordable) disk (p. 233) Optical-disk form of secondary storage that can be written to only once but can be read many times. Why it's important: *This format allows consumers to make their own CD disks, though it's a slow process. Once recorded, the information cannot be erased. CD-R is often used by companies for archiving—that is, to store vast amounts of information. A variant is the Photo CD, an optical disk developed by Kodak that can digitally store photographs taken with an ordinary 35-millimeter camera.*

CD-ROM (compact disk read-only memory) (p. 232) Optical-disk form of secondary storage that is used to hold prerecorded text, graphics, and sound. Why it's important: *Like music CDs, a CD-ROM is a read-only disk. Read-only means the disk's content is recorded at the time of manufacture and cannot be written on or erased by the user. A CD-ROM disk can hold up to 650–700 megabytes of data, equal to over 300,000 pages of text.*

CD-RW (compact disk–rewritable) disk (p. 233) Also known as *erasable optical disk;* optical-disk form of secondary storage that allows users to record and erase data, so the disk can be used over and over again. Special CD-RW drives and software are required. Why it's important: *CD-RW disks are useful for archiving and backing up large amounts of data or work in multimedia production or desktop publishing; however, they are relatively slow.*

chip (p. 200) Also called a *microchip;* consists of millions of microminiature integrated electronic circuits printed on a tiny piece of silicon. Silicon is an element widely found in sand that has desirable electrical (or "semiconducting") properties. Why it's important: *Chips have made possible the development of small computers.*

chipset (p. 212) Groups of interconnected chips on the motherboard that control the flow of information between the microprocessor and other system components connected to the motherboard. Why it's important: *The chipset determines what types of processors, memory, and video-card ports will work on the same motherboard. It also establishes the types of multimedia, storage, network, and other hardware the motherboard supports.*

CMOS (complementary metal-oxide semiconductor) chips (p. 218) Battery-powered chips that don't lose their contents when the power is turned off. Why it's important: *CMOS chips contain flexible start-up instructions—such as time, date, and calendar—that must be kept current even when the computer is turned off. Unlike ROM chips, CMOS chips can be reprogrammed, as when you need to change the time for daylight savings time.*

control unit (p. 216) Part of the CPU that deciphers each instruction stored in it and then carries out the instruction. Why it's important: *The control unit directs the movement of electronic signals between main memory and the arithmetic/logic unit. It also directs these electronic signals between main memory and the input and output devices.*

CPU (central processing unit) (p. 200) The processor; it follows the instructions of the software (program) to manipulate data into information. The CPU consists of two parts—(1) the control unit and (2) the arithmetic/logic unit (ALU), both of which contain registers, or high-speed storage areas. All are linked by a kind of electronic "roadway" called a *bus.* Why it's important: *The CPU is the "brain" of the computer.*

DVD-R (DVD-recordable) disks (p. 233) DVD disks that allow one-time recording by the user. Why it's important: *Recordable DVDs offer the user yet another option for storing large amounts of data.*

DVD-ROM (digital versatile disk or digital video disk, with read-only memory) (p. 233) CD-type disk with extremely high capacity, able to store 4.7–18 or more gigabytes. Why it's important: *It is a powerful and versatile secondary storage medium.*

DVI (digital video interface) port (p. 223). A multimedia port on most newer monitors and multimedia devices such as TVs and DVD players. Why it's important: *The digital interface standard was created by the Digital Display Working Group (DDWG) to convert analog signals into digital signals to accommodate both analog and digital monitors.*

EBCDIC (Extended Binary Coded Decimal Interchange Code) (p. 206) Binary code used with large computers. Why it's important: *EBCDIC is commonly used in mainframes.*

Ethernet (p. 224) Network standard for linking all devices in a local area network (LAN). Why it's important: *It's commonly used to connect microcomputers, cable modems, and printers. (To use Ethernet, the computer must have an Ethernet network interface card, and special Ethernet cables are required.)*

exabyte (EB) (p. 205) Approximately 1 quintillion bytes—1 billion billion bytes (1,024 petabytes—or 1,152,921,504,606,846,976 bytes). Why it's important: *Although this number is seldom used, it is estimated that all the printed material in the world represents about 5 exabytes.*

expansion (p. 210) Way of increasing a computer's capabilities by adding hardware to perform tasks that are beyond the scope of the basic system. Why it's important: *Expansion allows users to customize and/or upgrade their computer systems.*

expansion card (p. 226) Also known as *expansion board, adapter card, interface card, plug-in board, controller card, add-in, or add-on;* circuit board that provides more memory or that controls peripheral devices. Why it's important: *Common expansion cards connect to the monitor (graphics card), speakers and microphones (sound card), and network (network card). Most computers have four to eight expansion slots, some of which may already contain expansion cards included in your initial PC purchase.*

expansion slot (p. 226) Socket on the motherboard into which the user can plug an expansion card. Why it's important: *See* ***expansion card.***

FireWire (p. 223) A specialized serial-bus port intended to connect devices working with lots of data, such as digital video recorders, DVD players, gaming consoles, and digital audio equipment. Why it's important: *Whereas the USB 2.0 port handles only 480 megabits per second, FireWire handles up to 800 megabits per second.*

flash memory card (p. 237) Also known as *flash RAM cards;* form of secondary storage consisting of circuitry on credit-card-size cards that can be inserted into slots connecting to the motherboard on notebook computers. Why it's important: *Flash memory is nonvolatile, so it retains data even when the power is turned off. Flash memory is used in digital cameras, smartphones, and other mobile devices.*

flash memory chip (p. 218) Chip that can be erased and reprogrammed more than once (unlike PROM chips, which can be programmed only once). Why it's important: *Flash memory, which can range from 2 to 128 gigabytes in capacity, is used to store programs not only in personal computers but also in pagers, cellphones, printers, and digital cameras. Unlike standard RAM chips, flash memory is nonvolatile—data is retained when the power is turned off.*

flash memory drive (p. 237) Also called a *USB flash drive, keychain drive, memory stick,* or *key drive;* a finger-size module of flash memory that plugs into the USB ports of nearly any PC or Macintosh. Why it's important: *They generally have storage capacities up to 256 gigabytes, making the device extremely useful if you're traveling from home to office and don't want to carry a laptop. When you plug the device into your USB port, it shows up as an external drive on the computer.*

flops (p. 214) Stands for "floating-point operations per second." A *floating-point operation* is a special kind of mathematical calculation. This measure, used mainly with supercomputers, is expressed as *megaflops* (*mflops*, or millions of floating-point operations per second), *gigaflops* (*gflops*, or billions), and *teraflops* (*tflops*, or trillions). Why it's important: *The measure is used to express the processing speed of supercomputers.*

gigabyte (G, GB) (p. 204) Approximately 1 billion bytes (1,073,741,824 bytes); a measure of storage capacity. Why it's important: *This measure was formerly used mainly with "big iron" (mainframe) computers but is typical of the secondary storage (hard-disk) capacity of today's microcomputers.*

gigahertz (GHz) (p. 213) Measure of speed used for the latest generation of processors: 1 billion cycles per second. Why it's important: *Since a new high-speed processor can cost many hundred dollars more than a previous-generation chip, experts often recommend that buyers fret less about the speed of the processor (since the work most people do on their PCs doesn't even tax the limits of the current hardware) and more about spending money on extra memory.*

graphics processing unit (GPU) (p. 213) Specialized processor used to minipulate three-dimensional (3-D) computer graphics. Why it's important: Unlike a general-purpose CPU, a GPU is able to perform a range of complex algorithms (problem-solving steps). GPUs are found in personal computers, workstations, cellphones, and game consoles.

graphics card (p. 227) Also called a *video card, video RAM (VRAM),* or *video adapter;* expansion card that converts signals from the computer into video signals that can be displayed as images on a monitor. Why it's important: *The power of a graphics card determines the clarity of the images on the monitor.*

hard disk (p. 229) Secondary storage medium; thin but rigid metal, glass, or ceramic platter covered with a substance that allows data to be stored in the form of magnetized spots. Hard disks are tightly sealed within an enclosed hard-disk-drive unit to prevent any foreign matter from getting inside. Data may be recorded on both sides of the disk platters. Why it's important: *All microcomputers use hard disks as their principal storage medium.*

HDMI (high-definition multimedia interface) (p. 223) Multimedia connection that can carry both video and audio signals. Why it's important: *HDMI is used for HD TVs, DVD players, and game consoles.*

integrated circuit (p. 199). An entire electronic circuit, including wires, formed on a single "chip," or piece, of special material, usually silicon. Why it's important: *In the old days, transistors were made individually and then formed into an electronic circuit with the use of wires and solder. An integrated circuit is formed as part of a single manufacturing process.*

Intel-type chip (p. 212) Processor chip originally made for microcomputers; made principally by Intel Corp. and Advanced Micro Devices (AMD), but also by Cyrix, DEC, and others. Why it's important: *These chips are used by manufacturers such as Dell, Hewlett-Packard, Toshiba, Samsung, and Lenovo. Since 1993, Intel has marketed its chips under the names "Pentium," "Pentium Pro," "Pentium MMX," "Pentium II," "Pentium III," "Pentium 4," "Xeon," "Itanium," and "Celeron." Many ads for PCs contain the logo "Intel inside" to show that the systems run an Intel microprocessor. Newer Apple Macs use 4- to 12-core Intel processors.*

kilobyte (K, KB) (p. 204) Approximately 1,000 bytes (1,024 bytes); a measure of storage capacity. Why it's important: *The kilobyte was a common unit of measure for memory or secondary storage capacity on older computers.*

machine cycle (p. 216) Series of operations performed by the control unit to execute a single program instruction. It (1) fetches an instruction, (2) decodes the instruction, (3) executes the instruction, and (4) stores the result. Why it's important: *The machine cycle is the essence of computer-based processing.*

machine language (p. 206) Binary code (language) that the computer uses directly. The 0s and 1s represent precise storage locations and operations. Why it's important: *For a program to run, it must be in the machine language of the computer that is executing it.*

megabyte (M, MB) (p. 204) Approximately 1 million bytes (1,048,576 bytes); measure of storage capacity. Why it's important: *Microcomputer primary storage capacity is expressed in megabytes.*

megahertz (MHz) (p. 213) Measure of microcomputer processing speed, controlled by the system clock; 1 million cycles per second. Why it's important: *Generally, the higher the megahertz rate, the faster the computer can process data. A 550-MHz Pentium III–based microcomputer, for example, processes 550 million cycles per second. Most new microcomputers operate in the gigahertz (GHz).*

microprocessor (p. 200) Miniaturized circuitry of a computer processor. It stores program instructions that process, or manipulate, data into information. The key parts of the microprocessor are transistors. Why it's important: *Microprocessors enabled the development of microcomputers.*

MIPS (p. 214) Stands for "millions of instructions per second"; a measure of processing speed. Why it's important: *MIPS is used to measure processing speeds of mainframes, minicomputers, and workstations. A workstation might perform at 100 MIPS or more, a mainframe at up to 981,024 MIPS.*

multicore processor (p. 212) Microcomputer chip such as Intel's dual-core and quad-core processors and AMD's Athlon X2 processor, with two or more processor "cores" on a single piece of silicon. Why it's important: *Chips can take on several tasks at once because the operating system can divide its work over more than one processor.*

network interface card (NIC) (p. 228) Expansion card that allows the transmission of data over a cable network. Why it's important: *Installation of a network interface card in the computer enables the user to connect with various computers and other devices such as printers.*

optical disk (p. 231) Removable disk, usually 4.75 inches in diameter and about .05 inch thick, on which data is written and read through the use of laser beams. Why it's important: *An audio CD holds up to 74 minutes (2 billion bits' worth) of high-fidelity stereo sound. Some optical disks are used strictly for digital data storage, but many are used to distribute multimedia programs that combine text, visuals, and sound.*

optical memory card (p. 236) Plastic, laser-recordable, wallet-type card used with an optical-card reader. Why it's important: *Because optical cards can cram so much data into so little space, they may become more popular in the future. For instance, a health card based on an optical card would have room not only for the individual's medical history and health-insurance information but also for digital images, such as electrocardiograms.*

parallel port (p. 222) A connector for a line that allows 8 bits (1 byte) to be transmitted simultaneously, like cars on an eight-lane highway. Why it's important: *Parallel lines move information faster than serial lines do. However, because they can transmit information efficiently only up to 15 feet, they are used principally for connecting printers or external disk or magnetic-tape backup storage devices. (Parallel ports are being replaced by USB ports.)*

PC card (p. 228) Thin, credit card-size hardware device. Why it's important: *PC cards are used principally on laptop computers to expand capabilities.*

PCI (peripheral component interconnect) bus (p. 227) High-speed bus; at 32- or 64-bits wide. Why it's important: *PCI has been widely used in microcomputers to connect graphics cards, sound cards, modems, and high-speed network cards. (PCI is being replaced by AGP and PCIe.)*

PCIe (PCi Express) (p. 227) Intel's PCI Express bus. Why it's important: *PCIe is the latest standard for expansion card available on mainstream personal computers and is faster and more reliable than AGP.*

petabyte (P, PB) (p. 205) Approximately 1 quadrillion bytes (1,048,576 gigabytes); measure of storage capacity. Why it's important: *The huge storage capacities of modern databases are now expressed in petabytes.*

plug and play (p. 222) USB peripheral connection standard that allows peripheral devices and expansion cards to be automatically configured while they are being installed. Why it's important: *Plug and play avoids the hassle of setting switches and creating special files, which plagued earlier users.*

port (p. 220) A connecting socket or jack on the outside of the system unit into which are plugged different kinds of cables. Why it's important: *A port allows the user to plug in a cable to connect a peripheral device, such as a monitor, printer, or modem, so that it can communicate with the computer system.*

power supply (p. 208) Device that converts AC to DC to run the computer. Why it's important: *The electricity available from a standard wall outlet is alternating current (AC), but a microcomputer runs on direct current (DC).*

RAM (random access memory) chips (p. 217) Also called *primary storage* and *main memory;* chips that temporarily hold software instructions and data before and after it is processed by the CPU. RAM is a volatile form of storage. Why it's important: *RAM is the working memory of the computer. Having enough RAM is critical to users' ability to run many software programs.*

read (p. 218) To transfer data from an input source into the computer's memory or CPU. Why it's important: *Reading, along with writing, is an essential computer activity.*

read/write head (p. 230) Mechanism used to transfer data between the computer and the hard disk. When the disk spins inside its case, the read/write head moves back and forth over the data access area on the disk. Why it's important: *The read/write head enables the essential activities of reading and writing data.*

registers (p. 216) High-speed storage areas that temporarily store data during processing. Why it's important: *Registers may store a program instruction while it is being decoded, store data while it is being processed by the ALU, or store the results of a calculation.*

ROM (read-only memory) (p. 218) Memory chip that cannot be written on or erased by the computer user without special equipment. Why it's important: *ROM chips contain fixed start-up instructions. They are loaded, at the factory, with programs containing special instructions for basic computer operations, such as starting the computer or putting characters on the screen. These chips are nonvolatile; their contents are not lost when power to the computer is turned off.*

secondary storage hardware (p. 229) Devices that permanently hold data and information as well as programs. Why it's important: *Secondary storage—as opposed to primary storage—is nonvolatile; that is, saved data and programs are permanent, or remain intact, when the power is turned off.*

sectors (p. 230) The small arcs created in tracks when a disk's storage locations are divided into wedge-shaped sections. Why it's important: *The system software uses the point at which a sector intersects a track to reference the data location.*

semiconductor (p. 200) Material, such as silicon (in combination with other elements), whose electrical properties are intermediate between a good conductor and a nonconductor of electricity. When highly conducting materials are laid on the semiconducting material, an electronic circuit can be created. Why it's important: *Semiconductors are the materials from which integrated circuits (chips) are made.*

serial port (p. 222) A connector for a line that sends bits one after another, like cars on a one-lane highway. Why it's important: *Because individual bits must follow each other, a serial port is usually used to connect devices that do not require fast transmission of data, such as keyboard, mouse, monitors, and modems. It is also useful for sending data over a long distance.*

silicon (p. 200) An element that is widely found in clay and sand and is used in the making of solid-state integrated circuits. Why it's important: *It is used not only because its abundance makes it cheap but also because it is a good semiconductor. As a result, highly conducting materials can be overlaid on the silicon to create the electronic circuitry of the integrated circuit.*

smart card (p. 235) Plastic card that looks like a credit card but has a microprocessor and memory chips embedded in it. When inserted into a reader, it transfers data to and from a central computer. Why it's important: *Unlike conventional credit cards, smart cards can hold a fair amount of data and can store some basic financial records. Thus, they are used as telephone debit cards, health cards, and student cards.*

solid-state device (p. 199) Electronic component, such as an integrated circuit, made of solid materials with no moving parts. Why it's important: *Solid-state integrated circuits are far more reliable, smaller, and less expensive than electronic circuits made from several components.*

solid-state drive (p. 237) Secondary storage device that has far greater capacity than flash memory drives or keychain drives; like flash drives, they have no moving parts to break down, as hard disk drives do. Why it's important: *Some newer laptops (such as Apple's MacBook Air laptop) now feature solid-state drives. These drives are lighter and use less power than conventional disk drives and can better withstand bumps and bangs.*

sound card (p. 228) Expansion card used to convert and transmit digital sounds through analog speakers, microphones, and headsets. Why it's important: *Cards such as PCI wavetable sound cards are used to add music and sound effects to computer video games.*

system clock (p. 213) Internal timing device that uses fixed vibrations from a quartz crystal to deliver a steady stream of digital pulses or "ticks" to the CPU. These ticks are called *cycles.* Why it's important: *Faster clock speeds will result in faster processing of data and execution of program instructions, as long as the computer's internal circuits can handle the increased speed.*

terabyte (T, TB) (p. 204) Approximately 1 trillion bytes (1,009,511,627,776 bytes); measure of storage capacity. Why it's important: *Some high-capacity disk storage is expressed in terabytes.*

tracks (p. 230) The rings on a hard disk along which data is recorded. Why it's important: *See* ***sectors.***

transistor (p. 199) Tiny electronic device that acts as an on/off switch, switching between "on" and "off" millions of times per second. Why it's important: *Transistors are part of the microprocessor.*

Unicode (p. 206) Binary coding scheme that uses 2 bytes (16 bits) for each character, rather than 1 byte (8 bits). Why it's important: *Instead of the 256 character combinations of ASCII, Unicode can handle 65,536 character combinations. Thus, it allows almost all the written languages of the world to be represented using a single character set.*

upgrading (p. 210) Changing to newer, usually more powerful or sophisticated versions, such as a more powerful microprocessor or more memory chips. Why it's important: *Through upgrading, users can improve their computer systems without buying completely new ones.*

USB (universal serial bus) port (p. 222) High-speed hardware standard for interfacing peripheral devices, such as scanners and printers, to computers without a need for special expansion cards or other hardware modifications to the computer. Why it's important: *USB is replacing many varieties of serial and parallel ports.USB ports are useful for peripherals such as digital cameras, digital speakers, scanners, high-speed modems, and joysticks. Being "hot pluggable" or "hot swappable" means that USB allows such devices to be connected or disconnected even while the PC is running.*

virtual memory (p. 219) Type of hard-disk space that is used to extend RAM capacity. Why it's important: *When RAM space is limited, virtual memory allows users to run more software at once, provided the computer's CPU and operating system are equipped to use it. The system allocates some free disk space as an extension of RAM; that is, the computer swaps parts of the software program between the hard disk and RAM as needed.*

volatile (p. 217) Temporary; the contents of volatile storage media, such as RAM, are lost when the power is turned off. Why it's important: *To avoid data loss, save your work to a secondary storage medium, such as a hard disk, in case the electricity goes off while you're working.*

word size (p. 215) Number of bits that the processor may process at any one time. Why it's important: *The more bits in a word, the faster the computer. A 32-bit computer—that is, one with a 32-bit-word processor—will transfer data within each microprocessor chip in 32-bit chunks, or 4 bytes at a time. A 64-bit computer transfers data in 64-bit chunks, or 8 bytes at a time.*

write (p. 218) To transfer data from the computer's CPU or memory to an output device. Why it's important: *See* **read.**

CHAPTER REVIEW

1 LEARNING MEMORIZATION

"I can recognize and recall information."

Self-Test Questions

1. A(n) __________ is about 1,000 bytes; a(n) __________ is about 1 million bytes; a(n) __________ is about 1 billion bytes.
2. The __________ is the part of the microprocessor that tells the rest of the computer how to carry out a program's instructions.
3. The process of retrieving data from a storage device is referred to as __________; the process of copying data to a storage device is called __________.
4. To avoid losing data, users should always __________ their files.
5. Formatted hard disks have __________ and __________ that the system software uses to reference data locations.
6. The __________ is often referred to as the "brain" of a computer.
7. The electrical data roadways through which bits are transmitted are called __________.
8. A cable connected to a __________ port sends bits one at a time, one after the other; a cable connected to a __________ port sends 8 bits simultaneously.
9. Part of the disk-drive mechanism, the __________ transfers data between the computer and the disk.
10. __________ chips, also called *main memory*, are critical to computer performance.
11. __________ operations are the fundamental math operations: addition, subtraction, multiplication, and division; __________ operations are comparisons such as "equal to," "greater than," or "less than."
12. A group of 8 bits is a __________.
13. A tiny electronic device that acts as an on/off switch, switching between "on" and "off" millions of times per second, is called a __________.
14. __________ is an element that is widely found in clay and sand. It is used not only because its abundance makes it cheap but also because it is a semiconductor.
15. The __________ system has only two digits: 0 and 1.
16. The specialized processor used to manipulate 3D graphics is the __________.
17. The most widely used hardware interface for attaching peripherals to a computer is __________.
18. __________ is an optical-disk format used to hold prerecorded text, graphics, and sound.

Multiple-Choice Questions

1. Which of the following is another term for primary storage?
   a. ROM
   b. ALU
   c. CPU
   d. RAM
   e. CD-R
2. Which of the following is *not* included on a computer's motherboard?
   a. RAM chips
   b. ROM chips
   c. keyboard
   d. microprocessor
   e. expansion slots
3. Which of the following is used to hold data and instructions that will be used shortly by the CPU?
   a. ROM chips
   b. peripheral devices
   c. RAM chips
   d. CD-R
   e. hard disk

4. Which of the following coding schemes is widely used on microcomputers?
   a. EBCDIC
   b. Unicode
   c. ASCII
   d. Microcode
   e. Unix
5. Which of the following is used to measure processing speed in microcomputers?
   a. MIPS
   b. flops
   c. picoseconds
   d. gigahertz
   e. millihertz
6. Which expansion bus specializes in graphics processing?
   a. PCI
   b. ROM
   c. CMOS
   d. AGP
   e. USB
7. Which element is commonly used in the making of solid-state integrated circuits?
   a. pentium
   b. lithium
   c. copper
   d. iron
   e. silicon
8. What are the high-speed areas called that *temporarily* store data during processing?
   a. control units
   b. registers
   c. machine cycles
   d. buses
   e. word banks
9. A __________, also called a USB drive or a keychain drive, plugs into the USB port of nearly any microcomputer and can store up to 256 gigabytes.
   a. CD
   b. DVD
   c. optical memory card
   d. flash memory drive
   e. smart card
10. Cloud storage is also called __________ storage.
   a. USB
   b. live
   c. online
   d. flash
   e. exabyte

True/False Questions

T F 1. A bus connects a computer's control unit and ALU.

T F 2. The machine cycle comprises the instruction cycle and the execution cycle.

T F 3. Virtual memory is hard-disk space used to expand RAM capacity.

T F 4. Main memory is nonvolatile.

T F 5. Pipelining is a method of speeding up processing.

T F 6. Today's laptop computers can perform more calculations per second than the ENIAC, an enormous machine occupying more than 1,800 square feet and weighing more than 30 tons.

T F 7. USB can theoretically connect up to 127 peripheral devices.

T F 8. A petabyte is approximately 1 quadrillion bytes.

T F 9. Online secondary storage services test your computer's RAM capacity.

T F 10. HDMI connections support both video and audio signals.

T F 11. A megabyte is bigger than a terabyte.

T F 12. ASCII is the binary code most widely used on microcomputers.

2 LEARNING COMPREHENSION

"I can recall information in my own terms and explain it to a friend."

Short-Answer Questions

1. What is ASCII, and what do the letters stand for?
2. Why should measures of capacity matter to computer users?
3. What's the difference between RAM and ROM?
4. What is the significance of the term *gigahertz*?
5. What is a motherboard? Name at least four components of a motherboard.
6. What are the most convenient forms of backup storage? Why?
7. Why is it important for your computer to be expandable?
8. What are three uses of a smart card?
9. What is nanotechnology?
10. What are the uses of a surge protector, voltage regulator, and UPS, and why are these devices important?
11. Explain the binary system.
12. What is Unicode?
13. Why is silicon used in the manufacture of microprocessors?
14. What is Blu-ray used for?

"I can apply what I've learned, relate these ideas to other concepts, build on other knowledge, and use all these thinking skills to form a judgment."

Knowledge in Action

1. If you're using Windows 7, you can easily determine what microprocessor is in your computer and how much RAM it has. To begin, click the *Start* button in the Windows desktop pull-up menu bar and then choose *Control Panel.* Then locate the System icon in the Control Panel window and double-click on the icon.

   The System Properties screen will appear, listing your system's specifications, including RAM capacity.

   Visit a local computer store and note the system requirements listed on five software packages. What are the requirements for processor? RAM? Operating system? Available hard-disk space? CD/DVD speed? Audio/video cards? Are there any output hardware requirements?
2. Develop a binary system of your own. Use any two objects, states, or conditions, and encode the following statement: "I am a rocket scientist."
3. The floppy disk drive no longer comes as a standard component of microcomputers. What do you think will be the next "legacy" device to be abandoned?
4. Storing humans: If the human genome is 800 million bytes (according to Raymond Kurzweil), how many humans could you fit on a 120-GB hard drive?
5. What are the predictions about how long Moore's Law will continue to apply? Do a web search for four opinions; list the website sources and their predictions, and state how reliable you believe the sites are, and why.

Web Exercises

1. The objective of this project is to introduce you to an online encyclopedia that's dedicated to computer technology. The *www.webopedia.com* website is a good resource for deciphering computer ads and clearing up difficult concepts. For practice, visit the site and type *processor* into the Search text box and then press the *Enter* key or click on the *Go!* button. Click on some of the links that are displayed. Search for information on other topics of interest to you.
2. You can customize your own PC through a brand-name company such as Dell or Hewlett-Packard, or you can create your own personal model by choosing each component on your own. Decide which method is best for you.

   Go to the following sites and customize your ideal PCs:

   www.dell.com

   http://shop.lenovo.com/us/products/

   www.hpshopping.com

   http://store.apple.com/us

   www.cyberpowerpc.com/landingpages/intel/i7/?gclid=CIzX-fSkmKkCFQQ7gwodWWYhuw

   Write down the prices for your ideal customized PCs. Then go to

   www.microcenter.com/storefronts/byopc/index.html

   www.pricewatch.com

   http://store.sysbuilder.com/desktop.html

   and see if you could save money by putting your own PC together piece by piece. (This includes purchasing each component separately and verifying compatibility of all components.)

   For a tutorial on building your own computer, go to *www.pcmech.com/build.htm* and *http://www.pcworld.com/article/203950/how_to_build_your_own_pc_part_1.html* (this includes a video).
3. DVD formats: DVD+R, DVD-R, DVD+RW, DVD-RW, so many formats! Are they all the same? Visit these websites to get current information on the issues surrounding recordable DVD media:

   www.webopedia.com/DidYouKnow/Hardware_Software/2003/DVDFormatsExplained.asp

   www.videohelp.com/dvd
4. What is a Qubit? You've learned about binary digits in this chapter; now learn about the Qubit, the basic unit of information in a quantum computer. Beware: When you step into the realm of quantum theory, things become bizarre.

   http://whatis.techtarget.com/wsearchResults/1,290214,sid9,00.html?query=qubit#

   www.thefreedictionary.com/quantum+bit

   www.qubit.org/

   www.answers.com/topic/qubit?method=6

   www.worldwidewords.org/turnsofphrase/tp-qub1.htm
5. DNA computing: Visit the following websites to learn more about DNA software and computing:

   www.arstechnica.com/reviews/2q00/dna/dna-1.html

   www.tribuneindia.com/2008/20080711/science.htm

   www.bbc.co.uk/news/science-environment-13626583

   http://computer.howstuffworks.com/dna-computer.htm

   www.britannica.com/EBchecked/topic/941575/DNA-computing

   http://bzupages.com/f33/dna-computing-technology-report-presentation-slides-7451/
6. Security issue—credit card fraud: When buying parts or making any kind of purchase over the Internet, always make sure that the web address says HTTPS to let you know it is an encrypted SSL (Secured Socket Layer) website. Visit these sites for safety tips when using your credit card online.

   www.microsoft.com/security/online-privacy/online-shopping.aspx

   http://securitygarden.blogspot.com/2010/11/online-shopping-safety-tips.html

   http://money.howstuffworks.com/personal-finance/debt-management/credit-card4.htm

   www.creditcards.com/credit-card-news/credit-card-fraud-and-online-shopping-1282.php

   http://idtheft.about.com/od/preventionpractices/a/OnlineShopping.htm

5

HARDWARE: INPUT & OUTPUT Taking Charge of Computing & Communications

Chapter Topics & Key Questions

5.1 **Input & Output** How is input/output hardware used by a computer system?

5.2 **Input Hardware** What are the three categories of input hardware, what devices do they include, and what are their features?

5.3 **Output Hardware** What are the two categories of output hardware, what devices do they include, and what are their features?

5.4 **Input & Output Technology & Quality of Life: Health & Ergonomics** What are the principal health and ergonomic issues relating to computer use?

5.5 **The Future of Input & Output** What are some trends of future input and output technology?

Download the free UIT 10e App for key term flash cards, quizzes, and a game, *Over the Edge*

"Automated teller machines have become so common, it now seems there are almost as many places to get cash as to spend it," says one account.[1]

Not only are *automated teller machines (ATMs)*, or cash machines, in office buildings, convenience stores, nightclubs, and even the lobbies of some big apartment buildings; they are also becoming something quite different from simple devices for people who need fast cash. They are migrating into different kinds of *kiosks* (pronounced *"key*-ahsks"), computerized booths or small standing structures providing any number of services, from electronic banking options to corporate job benefits, from tourism advice to garage-sale permits. (● *See Panel 5.1.)*

People in many places use kiosks to conveniently cash their paychecks. In New York City, kiosks can be used by citizens to pay parking tickets and check for building-code violations. In San Antonio, they provide information on animals available for adoption. In Seattle, commuters at car-ferry terminals view images of traffic conditions on major highways. In Nevada, motorists can use kiosks at the Department of Motor Vehicles to get a driver history printout. Many colleges and universities use kiosks to provide students with information about classes, schedules, activity locations, maps, and so on.

Kiosks also sell stamps, print out checks, and issue movie and plane tickets. Alamo car rental offices have kiosks at which travelers can print out directions, get descriptions of hotel services, and obtain restaurant menus and reviews—in four languages. At many hotels, guests may not even find front-desk clerks; kiosks have replaced them. Many kiosks have been transformed into full-blown multimedia centers, offering publicized corporate and governmental activities, job listings, and benefits, as well as ads, coupons, and movie previews.

The kiosk presents the two faces of the computer that are important to humans: it allows them to input data and to output information. For example, many kiosks use touch screens (and sometimes also keyboards) for input and thermal printers for output. In this chapter, we discuss what the principal input and output devices are and how you can make use of them.

panel 5.1

Kiosks

(*Left*) A wireless Internet kiosk at LaGuardia Airport, New York. Boingo Wireless launched its Wi-Fi wireless Internet access service at LaGuardia, where more than 20 million travelers who pass through the airport annually will have access to the largest aggregated hotspot network. (*Right*) Tourist purchasing rail tickets at the electronic kiosk in Kyoto's Central Station.

5.1 INPUT & OUTPUT

Without input/output devices, the computer would be simply a static display unit.

Recall from Chapter 1 that *input* refers to data entered into a computer for processing—for example, from a keyboard or from a file stored on disk. Input includes program instructions that the CPU receives after commands are issued by the user. Commands can be issued by typing keywords, defined by the application program, or pressing certain keyboard keys. Commands can also be issued by choosing menu options or clicking on icons. Finally, input includes user responses—for example, when you reply to a question posed by the application or the operating system, such as "Are you sure you want to put this file in the Recycle Bin?" *Output* refers to the results of processing—that is, information sent to the screen or the printer or to be stored on disk or sent to another computer in a network. Some devices combine input and output functions, examples being not only ATMs and kiosks, as we just mentioned, but also combination scanner-printer-fax devices.

This chapter focuses on the common input and output devices used with a computer. (• *See Panel 5.2.*) ***Input hardware*** **consists of devices that translate data into a form the computer can process.** The people-readable form of the data may be words like those on this page, but the computer-readable form consists of binary 0s and 1s, or off and on electrical signals.

Output hardware **consists of devices that translate information processed by the computer into a form that humans can understand.** The computer-processed information consists of 0s and 1s, which need to be translated into words, numbers, sounds, and pictures.

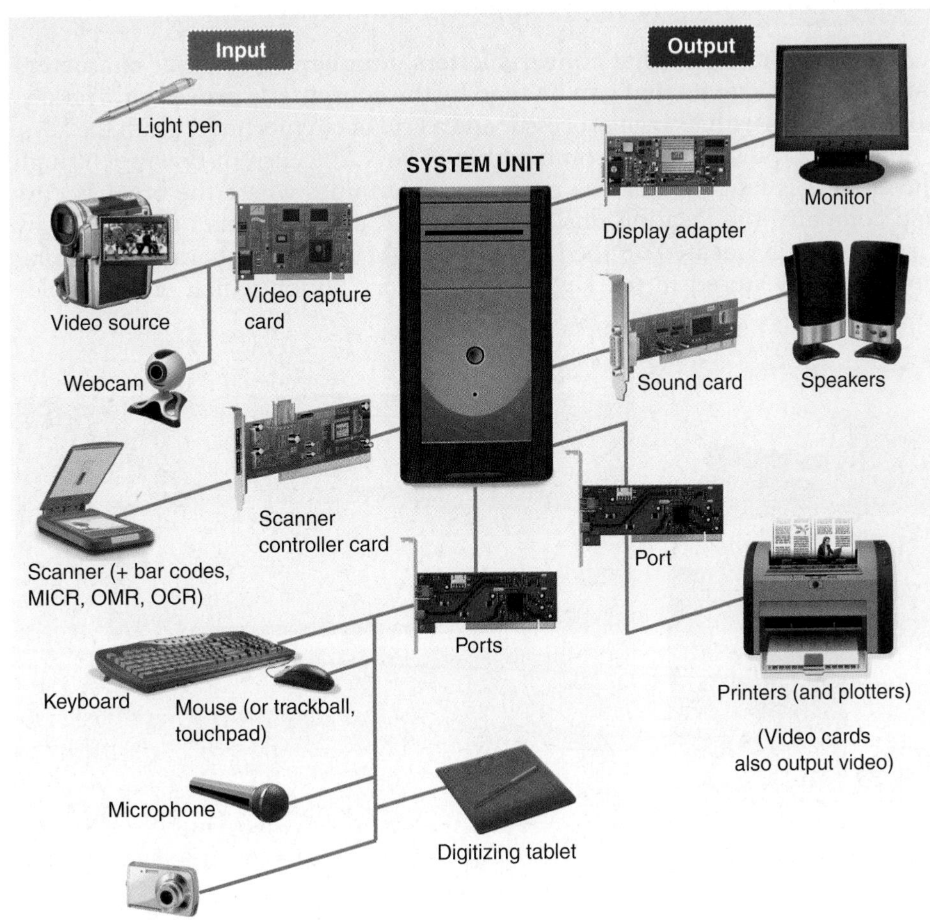

panel 5.2

Common input and output devices

Survival Tip

ATMs & Fraud/Safety

- Never use ATM machines at convenience stores.
- Change your identification number (PIN) number regularly, and use different PINs for different accounts.
- While shopping use credit cards over debit cards. Try to avoid using your PIN as much as possible.
- Never use your PIN under any circumstances while in online transactions.
- Memorize your PIN. Never write your PIN on your card or anything that you carry near your card.
- Check your account frequently and report any suspicious activity immediately.
- Be wary of an ATM scam called "skimming" in which a realistic-looking electronic device designed to capture your card information and PIN number is attached to the ATM by criminals. If an ATM card reader appears unusual or bulky compared to other ATMs, use another ATM.
- Never leave your receipt behind—even with an incomplete transaction. Discarded ATM receipts are a primary means of identity theft and account fraud. At home, shred receipts before discarding them.

From: *www.thepicky.com/how/atm-debit-card-safety-tips-riskiest-places-to-use/* and *www.liveoncash.com/blog/safety-tips-for-atm-use*

And for more on how to spot an ATM skimming device, try: **http://bucks.blogs.nytimes.com/2010/06/09/how-to-spot-an-a-t-m-skimming-device/ and http://krebsonsecurity.com**

Keyboards	Pointing Devices	Source Data-Entry Devices
Traditional computer keyboards Specialty keyboards and terminals: dumb terminals, intelligent terminals (ATMs, POS terminals), internet terminals	Mice, trackballs, touchpads Touch screens Pen-based computer systems, light pens, digitizers (digitizing tablets) Optical sensor technology remotes, such as for Wii	Scanner devices: imaging systems, bar-code readers, mark- and character-recognition devices (MICR, OMR, OCR), fax machines Audio-input devices Webcams and video-input devices Digital cameras Speech-recognition systems Sensors Radio-frequency identification Human-biology input devices

panel 5.3

Three types of input devices

5.2 INPUT HARDWARE

Input devices send data to the computer.

The three major types of input hardware devices are *keyboards, pointing devices,* and *source data-entry devices*. (● *See Panel 5.3.*) Quite often a computer system uses all three.

Keyboards

The keyboard is still the main computer input device.

A *keyboard* is a device that converts letters, numbers, and other characters into electrical signals that can be read by the computer's processor. The keyboard does this with its own processor and a grid of circuits underneath the keys.

When you press a key or combination of keys, the current flowing through the circuits is interrupted. The processor determines where the break occurs and compares the location information with a character map (organized by *x,y* coordinates) located on the keyboard's ROM chip. The character information is briefly stored in the keyboard's memory buffer, which usually holds

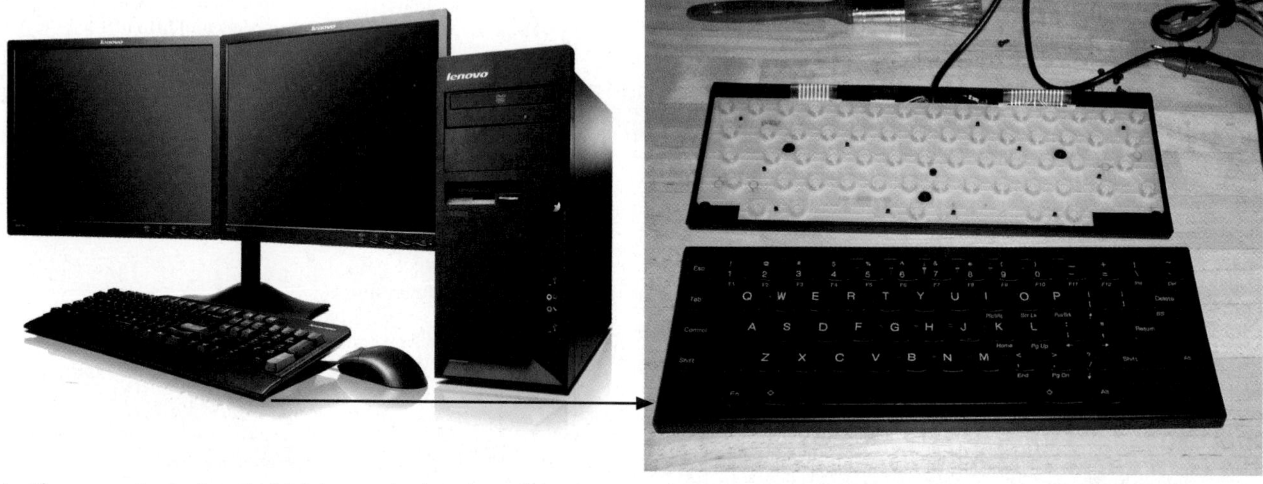

Inside a computer keyboard (*right*). In most keyboards, each key sits over a small, flexible rubber dome with a hard carbon center (*top part*). When the key (*bottom part*) is pressed, a plunger on the bottom of the key pushes down against the dome. This pushes the carbon center down, which presses against the keyboard circuitry to complete an electrical circuit and send a signal to the computer.

about 16 bytes. The keyboard then sends the data in a stream to the PC via a wired or wireless connection. (Laptops use an internal wired connection.) The computer has a keyboard controller, an integrated circuit whose job it is to process all the data that comes from the keyboard and forward it to the operating system. The operating system checks to see if the keyboard data is operating-system-specific or application-specific.

If, for example, you press *Ctrl+Alt+Delete*—the keyboard command for rebooting your computer—the OS will recognize the data as operating-system-specific and react accordingly (reboot or bring up the OS task manager). If, in contrast, you are doing word processing in Microsoft Word 2010 and press *Alt+F4* (close the file), the OS will recognize the data as application-specific and send it along to the current application, Word, to be executed. All this happens so quickly that you notice no time lapse between pressing keys and seeing results.

The keyboard may look like a typewriter keyboard to which some special keys have been added. Alternatively, it may look like the keys on a bank ATM or the keypad of a pocket computer. It may even be a Touch-Tone phone or cable-TV set-top box.

Let's look at *traditional computer keyboards* and various kinds of *specialty keyboards and terminals.*

TRADITIONAL COMPUTER KEYBOARDS Picking up where we left off with the PC ad presented in Chapter 4 (p. 203), we see that the seller lists a "full-sized keyboard with numeric keypad." Conventional computer keyboards have all the keys on old typewriter keyboards, plus other keys unique to computers. This generally totals 104–108 keys for desktop computers and 80–85 keys for laptops. Newer keyboards include extra keys for special activities such as instant web access, CD/DVD controls, and Windows shortcut keys.

Full-Sized Keyboard with Numeric Keypad

Wired keyboards connect a cable to the computer via a serial port or a USB port. Wireless keyboards use either infrared-light (IR) technology or radio frequency (RF) technology to transmit signals to a receiver device plugged into the computer, usually via a USB port. Infrared wireless keyboards have a transmission range of 6–10 feet and cannot have any obstacles in the transmission path (called the *line of sight*). Radio-based keyboards have a range of up to 100 feet and have no line-of-sight

Wireless keyboard

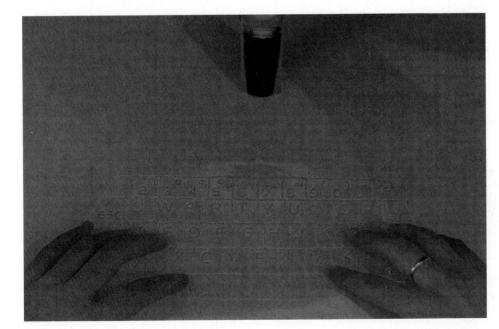

Seeing the light. The Virtual Keyboard uses light to project a full-size computer keyboard onto almost any surface. Used with smartphones and PDAs, this technology provides a way to do email, word processing, and other basic tasks without one's having to carry a notebook computer.

> **Survival Tip**
>
> **How Do I Use the Print Scrn key?**
>
> This PC key is a holdover from DOS days, before Windows. Then it sent the contents of the display screen to the printer. It still can, but in a roundabout way. The sole function of this key is to take a snapshot or picture of your computer screen and copy it to the clipboard (the clipboard is an invisible holding area for content that is copied). So, when you press the key, an image of the screen is placed on the Windows clipboard. Open a blank document in any program that accepts graphics and choose *Edit, Paste*. The image is inserted, and you can print it. (Some new keyboards have eliminated this key.)

problems. A final interesting variation is the VKB Virtual Keyboard. The size of a writing pen, it uses light (laser) to project a full-size computer keyboard onto almost any surface; the image disappears when not in use. The Virtual Keyboard can be used with PDAs and smartphones, allowing users a practical way to do email and word processing without having to take along a laptop computer.[2]

The keyboard illustration in Chapter 3 shows keyboard and numeric keypad functions. *(Refer back to Panel 3.6, pp. 131–132.)*

SPECIALTY KEYBOARDS & TERMINALS Specialty keyboards range from Touch-Tone telephone keypads to keyboards featuring pictures of food for use in fast-food restaurants. Here we will consider dumb terminals, intelligent terminals, and Internet terminals:

- **Dumb terminals: A *dumb terminal,* also called a *video display terminal (VDT),* has a display screen and a keyboard and can input and output but cannot process data.** Usually the output is text only. For instance, airline reservations clerks use these terminals to access a mainframe computer containing flight information. Dumb terminals cannot perform functions independent of the mainframe to which they are linked.
- **Intelligent terminals: An *intelligent terminal* has its own memory and processor, as well as a display screen and a keyboard.** Such a terminal can perform some functions independent of any mainframe to which it is linked. One example is the familiar *automated teller machine (ATM),* the self-service banking machine that is connected through a telephone network to a central computer. Another example is the *point-of-sale (POS) terminal,* used to record purchases at a store's checkout counter. Intelligent terminals can be connected to the main (usually mainframe) computer system wirelessly or via cables.

  A third example of an intelligent terminal is the *mobile data terminal (MDT),* a rugged notebook PC found in police cruisers, which must endure high-speed chases and nonstop use. MDTs may run Windows operating systems but use specialized software that lets officers track dispatch information, search for local and national warrants, verify license plate and vehicle registration, check criminal records, and more. Some systems let officers complete reports online to avoid time-consuming in-office paperwork.
- **Internet terminals: An *Internet terminal* provides access to the Internet**—that is, it powers up directly into a browser. There are several variants: (1) *Internet TV,* which distributes TV via the Internet; (2) *Internet-ready TV,* TV sets that allow viewers to also go online; (3) the *network computer,* a cheap, stripped-down computer that connects people to networks; and (4) the *online game player,* which not only lets the user play games but also connects to the Internet. (5) Smartphones, such as the iPhone and Android phones, also act as Internet terminals.

Terminals. (*Left*) A dumb terminal at an airline check-in counter. (*Middle and right*) A point-of-sale (POS) terminal at a retail store. It records purchases and processes the buyer's credit card.

Mobile personal Internet terminals—PDAs (*top*) and smartphones (*bottom*) iPhone and SonyEricsson Experia

Pointing Devices

Pointing devices are used to control the movement of a cursor or icon on a display screen.

One of the most natural of all human gestures, the act of pointing, is incorporated in several kinds of input devices. ***Pointing devices*** **control the position of the cursor or pointer on the screen and allow the user to select options displayed on the screen.** Pointing devices include the *mouse* and its variants, the *touch screen*, and various forms of *pen input*. We also describe recent innovations in *handwriting input.*

THE MOUSE The principal pointing tool used with microcomputers is the ***mouse*, a device that is moved about on a desktop mouse pad and directs a pointer on the computer's display screen.** Making its first appearance at a demonstration in San Francisco in 1968, the mouse's name is derived from the device's shape, which is a bit like a mouse, with the cord to the computer being the tail. The mouse went public in 1984 with the introduction

Special Mice

If your mouse is causing arm and wrist pain or other problems, you could try a special mouse model (including a vertical mouse):

www.fentek-ind.com/ergmouse.htm

www.thehumansolution.com/mice.html

www.evoluent.com/vm3.html

www.microsoft.com/hardware/mouseandkeyboard/productdetails.aspx?pid=086

www.consumersearch.com/computer-mice

of the Apple Macintosh. (● *See the timeline, Panel 5.4.*) Once Microsoft Windows 3.1 made the GUI (p. 133) the PC standard, the mouse also became a standard input device.

- **Mechanical versus optical mouse:** A mouse pad—a rectangular rubber/foam pad—provides traction for the old traditional mouse, often called a *mechanical mouse* or a *wheeled mouse*. Most mice now are *optical;* that is, they use light beams and special chips to encode data for the computer. Optical mice have no moving parts, have a smoother response, and don't require a mouse pad (unless you are working on a transparent glass surface).

  The optical mouse works by using an LED (light emitting diode), which is a very small diode that emits light underneath the mouse. The LED is red in color, and it bounces light off the desk surface or mouse pad onto a Complimentary Metal-Oxide Semiconductor (CMOS) sensor inside the mouse. With the recent development of laser-based optical mice, it is possible for the mice to detect even more surfaces than the LED technology.

  Once light is reflected onto the CMOS sensor, it sends each reflected image to the digital signal processor (DSP) mouse-chip for analysis. The DSP is then able to detect image patterns and analyze the movements of the patterns in relation to the previous image. It uses these patterns to determine if there has been mouse movement and if so, the distance and speed of the movement. It then sends the coordinates to the computer. The computer responds by moving the cursor according to the coordinates it receives from the mouse. Because of the high speed of these movements, the computer receives mouse coordinates hundreds of times per second, which ensures that the cursor movement is smooth.

Arrow

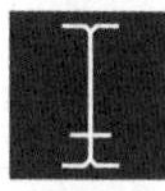

I-beam

- **Mouse pointers and buttons:** The *mouse pointer*—an arrow, a rectangle, a pointing finger—is the symbol that indicates the position of the mouse on the display screen or that activates icons. When the mouse pointer changes to the shape of an I-beam, it shows the place where text may be inserted or selected for special treatment.

  On the top side of the traditional mouse are one to five buttons. The first button is used for common functions, such as clicking and dragging. The functions of the other buttons are determined by the software you're using and can often be customized. Most mice have a scroll wheel on top to make it easier for you to scroll up and down the screen.

panel 5.4

Timeline: developments in input/output

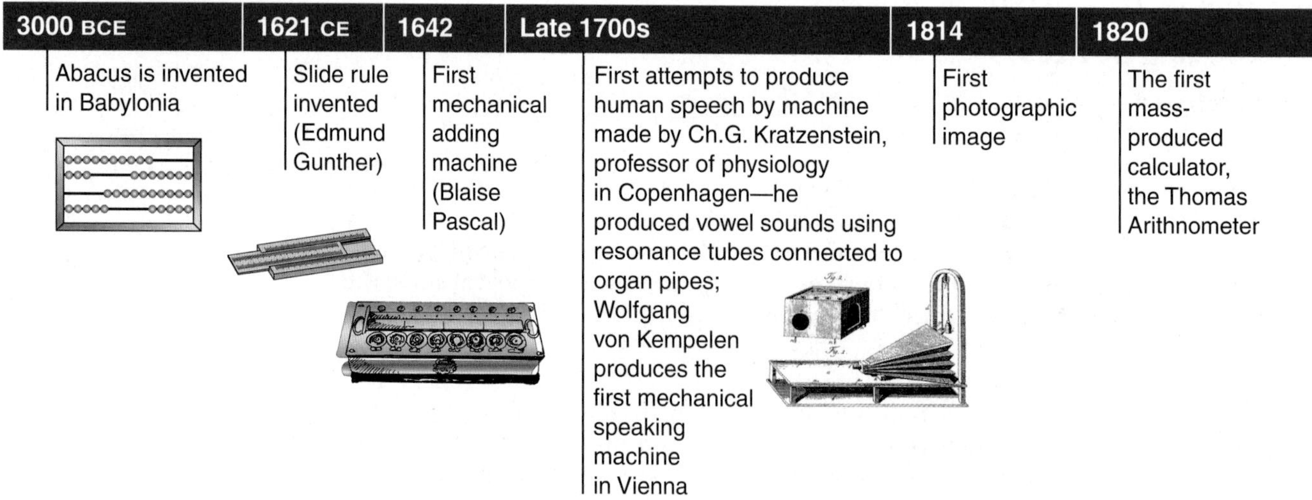

3000 BCE
Abacus is invented in Babylonia
1621 CE
Slide rule invented (Edmund Gunther)
1642
First mechanical adding machine (Blaise Pascal)
Late 1700s
First attempts to produce human speech by machine made by Ch.G. Kratzenstein, professor of physiology in Copenhagen—he produced vowel sounds using resonance tubes connected to organ pipes; Wolfgang von Kempelen produces the first mechanical speaking machine in Vienna
1814
First photographic image
1820
The first mass-produced calculator, the Thomas Arithnometer

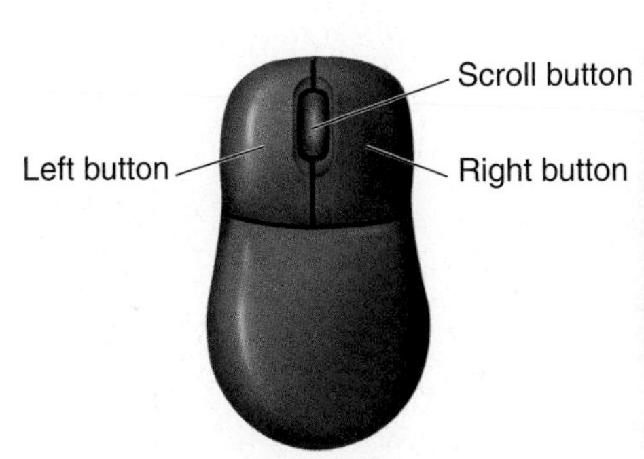

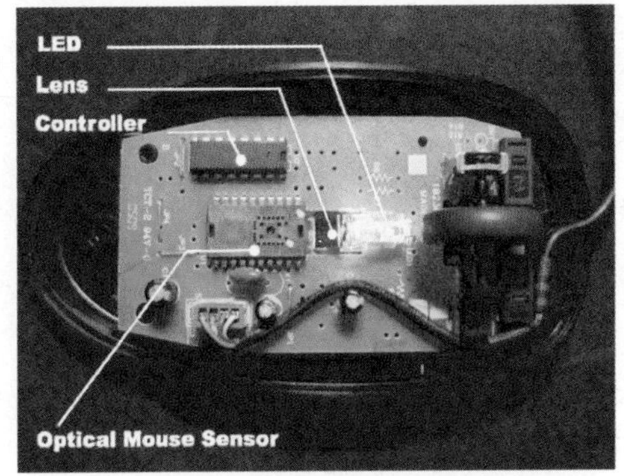

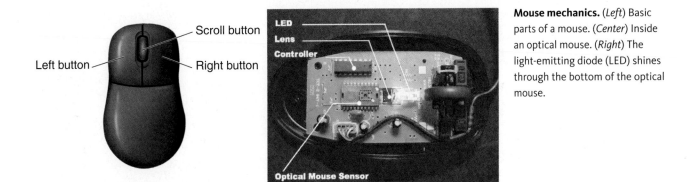

Mouse mechanics. (*Left*) Basic parts of a mouse. (*Center*) Inside an optical mouse. (*Right*) The light-emitting diode (LED) shines through the bottom of the optical mouse.

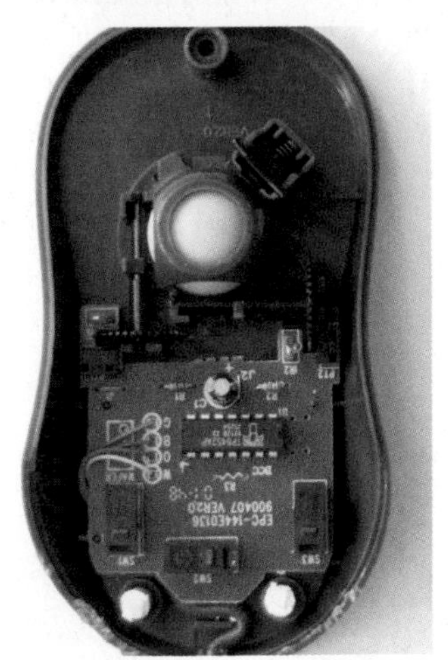

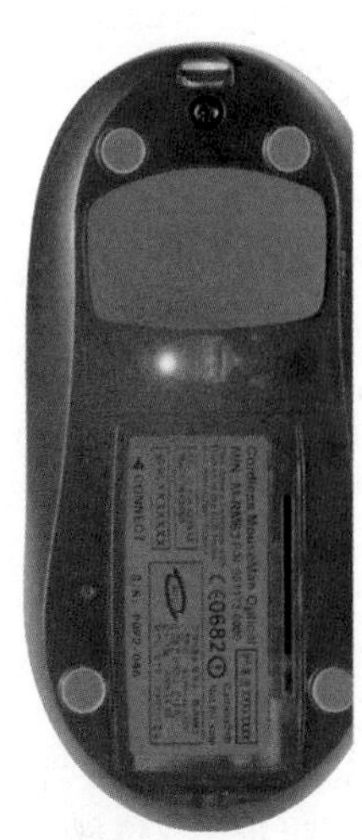

The MoGo Mouse BT is a business-card-sized, Bluetooth-enabled wireless mouse that stores and charges inside the laptop's PC Card slot

- **1821** First microphone
- **1829** William Austin patents the first workable typewriter in America
- **1843** World's first computer programmer, Ada Lovelace, publishes her notes; facsimile transmission (faxing) over wires invented by Alexander Bain, Scottish mechanic (via telegraph wires)
- **1844** Samuel Morse sends a telegraph message from Washington to Baltimore
- **1876** A. G. Bell patents the electric telephone
- **1877** Thomas Edison patents the phonograph

for your Mac. When you use gestures, it's as if you're touching what's on your screen. For instance, swiping through web pages in Safari gives you the feeling of flicking through pages in a magazine. And scrolling with Magic Mouse isn't your everyday scrolling. It supports momentum scrolling (similar to iPhone and iPod touch), where the scrolling speed is dictated by how fast or slowly you perform the gesture.

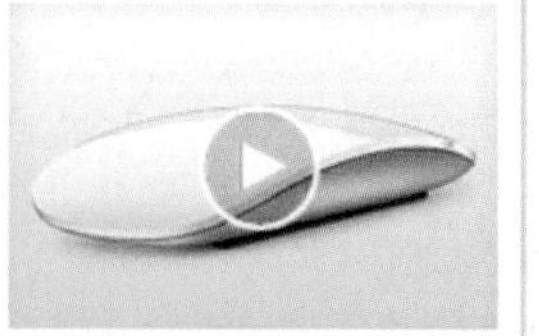

Watch the Magic Mouse video.
See Magic Mouse Multi-Touch gestures in action.
Watch the video

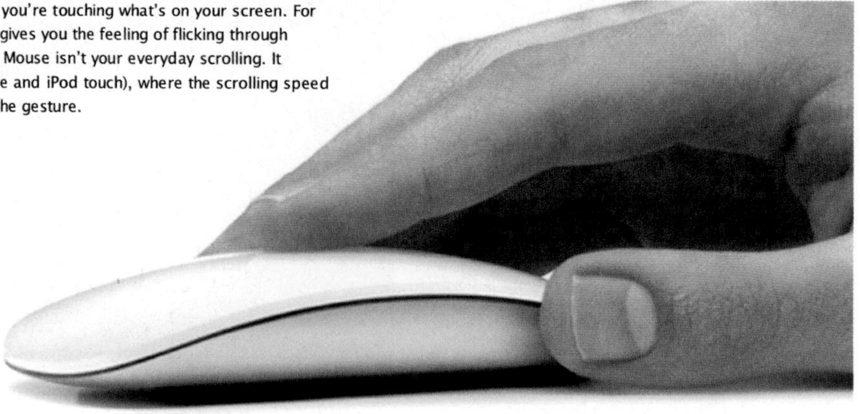

Click
Magic Mouse is an advanced point-and-click mouse that lets you click and double-click anywhere on its Multi-Touch surface.

Two-button click
Magic Mouse functions as a two-button mouse when you enable Secondary Click in System Preferences. Left-handed users can reassign left and right click, as well.

360° scroll
Brush one finger along the Multi-Touch surface to scroll in any direction and to pan a full 360 degrees.

Screen zoom
Hold down the Control key on your keyboard and scroll with one finger on Magic Mouse to enlarge items on your screen.

Two-finger swipe
Using two fingers, swipe left and right along the Multi-Touch surface to advance through pages in Safari or browse photos in iPhoto.

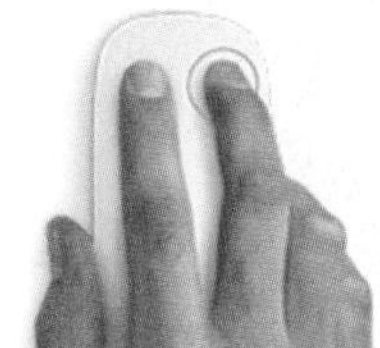
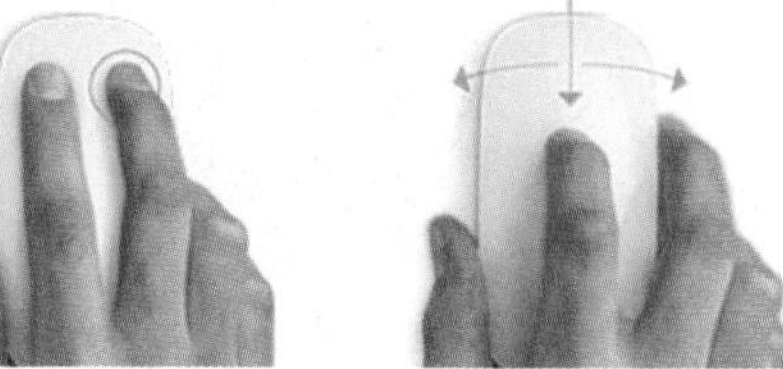
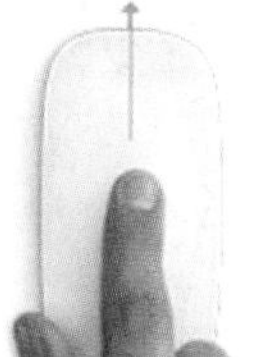
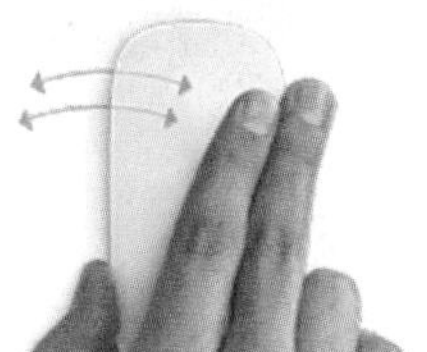

Apple's wireless Bluetooth multitouch Magic Mouse

Survival Tip

Setting Mouse Properties

From the Start menu in Windows, go to *Start, Control Panel, Mouse* to get a dialog box with several tabs that allow you to set mouse properties, such as setting the mouse buttons for left-handed use, adjusting the speed at which the pointer moves across the screen, and changing the shape of the mouse pointer.

One new type of mouse is Apple's Magic Mouse *(above)*, a multitouch mouse. The Multi-Touch area covers the top surface of Magic Mouse, and the mouse itself is the button. Use gestures to swipe through web pages and photos and to click and double-click anywhere. Inside Magic Mouse is a chip that tells it exactly what you want to do.

VARIATIONS ON THE MOUSE: TRACKBALL & TOUCHPAD There are two main variations on the mouse. (• *See Panel 5.5.*)

- Trackball: **The *trackball* is a movable ball, mounted on top or side of a stationary device, that can be rotated using your fingers or palm.** In fact, the trackball looks like the mouse turned upside down. Instead of moving the mouse around on the desktop, you move the trackball with the tips of your fingers. A trackball is not as accurate as a mouse, and it requires more frequent cleaning, but it's a good alternative when desktop space is limited. Trackballs come in wired and wireless versions, and newer trackballs use laser technology.

1897	1898	1912	1924	1927
Karl Ferdinand Braun, German physicist, invents the first cathode-ray tube (CRT), the basis of all early TV and computer monitors	First telephone answering machine	Motorized movie camera replaces hand-cranked movie camera	T. J. Watson renames Hollerith's machine company, founded in 1896, to International Business Machines (IBM); first political convention photos faxed via AT&T telephone fax technology	The first electronic TV picture is transmitted

Pros		Cons
• Relatively inexpensive • Very little finger movement needed to reach buttons	**Mouse**	• When gripped too tightly can cause muscle strain • Uses more desk space than other pointing devices • Must be cleaned occasionally
• Uses less desk space than mouse • Requires less arm and hand movement than mouse	**Trackball**	• Wrist is bent during use • More finger movement needed to reach buttons than with other pointing devices • Requires frequent cleaning because of finger oils
• Small footprint • Least prone to dust • Needs little cleaning	**Touchpad**	• Places more stress on index finger than other pointing devices do • Small active area makes precise cursor control difficult

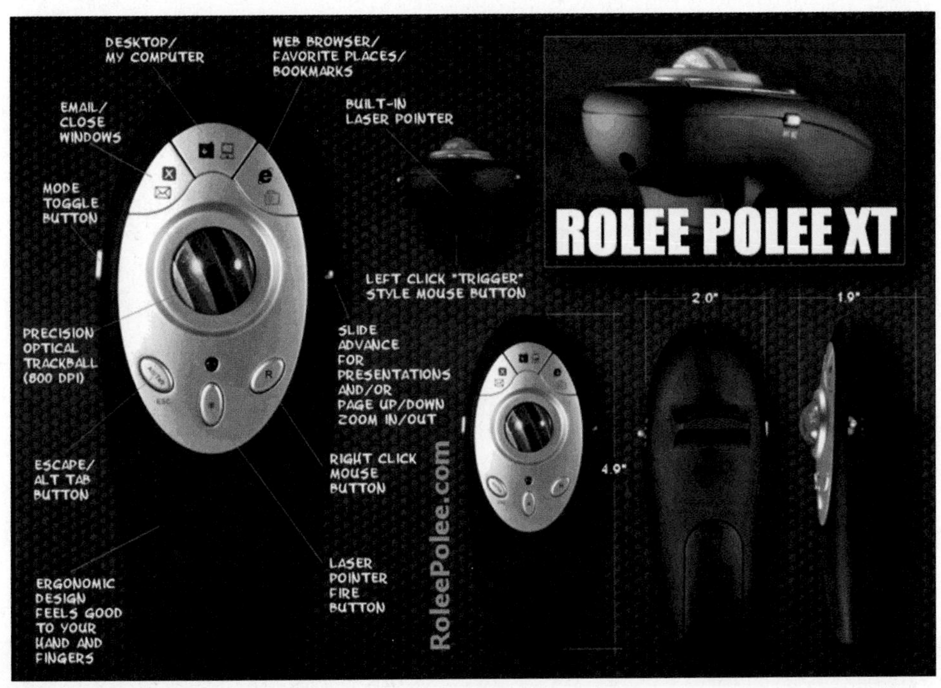

panel 5.5

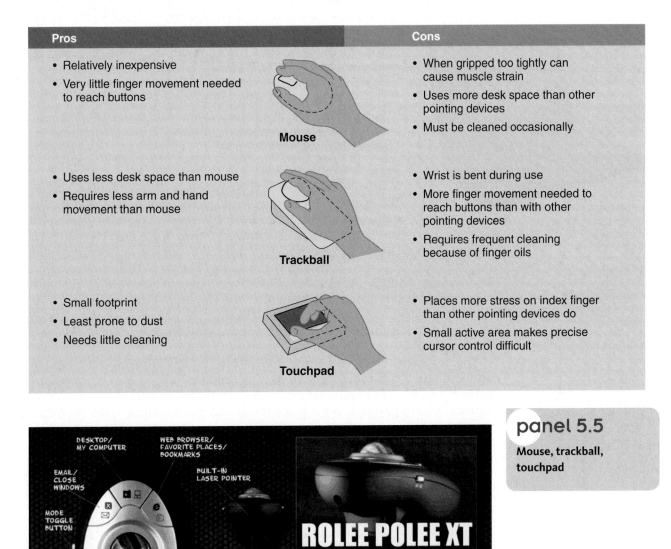

Mouse, trackball, touchpad

Rolee Polee wireless trackball with built-in laser pointer

1931	1936	1939	1944	1946	1959
Reynold B. Johnson, a Michigan high-school science teacher, invents a test-scoring machine that senses conductive pencil marks on answer sheets	Bell Labs invents the voice-recognition machine	First electrical speech-producing machine—New York World's Fair; computer technology takes over speech synthesis in about 1970	First electro-mechanical computer (Mark I)	First programmable electronic computer in United States (ENIAC)	General Electric produces the first system to process checks in a banking application via magnetic-ink character recognition (MICR)

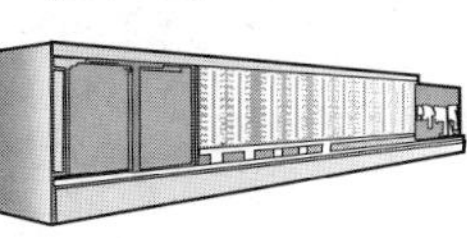

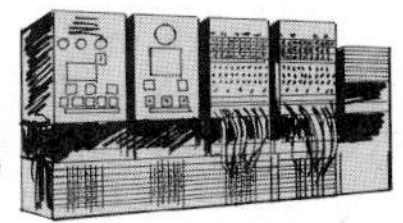

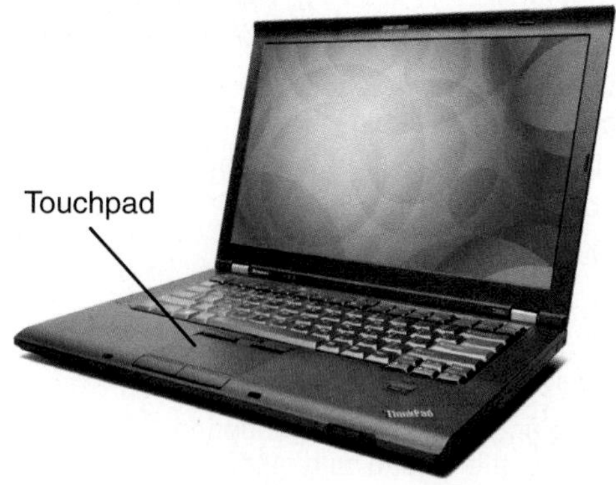

Touchpad on a Lenovo Thinkpad

- **Touchpad: A *touchpad* is a small, flat surface over which you slide your finger, using the same movements as you would with a mouse.** The cursor follows the movement of your finger. You "click" by tapping your finger on the pad's surface or by pressing buttons positioned close by the pad. Touchpads are most often found on laptop computers, but freestanding touchpads are available for use with PCs.

TOUCH SCREEN **A *touch screen* is a video display screen that has been sensitized to receive input from the touch of a finger.** (• *See Panel 5.6.*) The specially coated screen layers are covered with a plastic layer. Depending on the type of touch screen, the pressure of the user's finger creates a connection of electrical current between the layers, decreases the electrical charge at the touched point, or otherwise disturbs the electrical field. The change in electrical current creates a signal that is sent to the computer. You can input requests for information by pressing on displayed buttons or menus. The answers to your requests are then output as displayed words or pictures on the screen. (There may also be sound.)

Touch screens can also be *multitouch*. Multitouch—introduced by Apple on its iPhone—is a touchscreen input method that allows two or more fingers (or two hands) to be used on the screen at one time. It allows pinching and stretching gestures on the screen to control zooming—that is, pinch the screen to zoom in (make and image smaller) or spread the thumb and forefinger on the screen to zoom out, or spread images apart. This technology is now also used on some tablet computers and for large screen in technical settings.

panel 5.6

Touch screens

(*Left*) Touch screen menus at Inamo Restaurant, London; the entire table top is an interactive touch screen that can be used to order food items . (*Right*) Touch screen used to operate a sewing machine.

1960	1962	1963	1967	1968	1970
DEC introduces the PDP-1, the first commercial computer with a monitor for output and a keyboard for input	Bell Laboratories develops software to design, store, and edit synthesized music	Ivan Sutherland uses the first interactive computer graphics in his Ph.D. thesis, which used a light pen to create engineering graphics	Hand-held calculator	World debut of the computer mouse, in development since 1965 by Doug Engelbart at Stanford Research Institute (SRI)	Microprocessor chips come into use; floppy disk introduced for storing data; bar codes come into use; the daisy wheel printer makes its debut

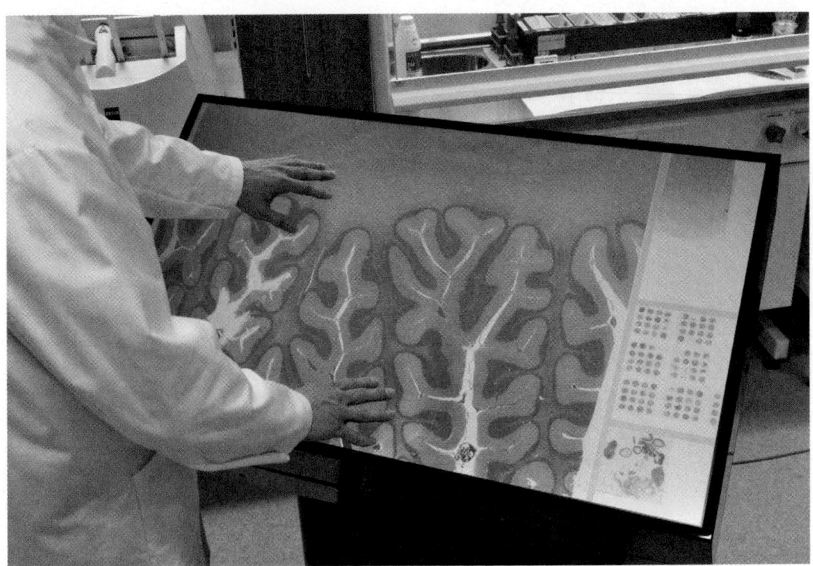

Multitouch screen at the Institute for Molecular Medicine, University of Helsinki, Finnland.

PEN INPUT Some input devices use variations on an electronic pen. Examples are *pen-based systems, light pens, digitizers,* and *digital pens:*

> **Survival Tip**
>
> **Games & Wireless Input**
>
> If you're a serious game fan, you're advised to stick with wired input devices. Wireless devices tend to lag during data transmission, which will slow down your game response. (The lag time is called *latency*.)

- **Pen-based computer systems:** ***Pen-based computer systems*** **allow users to enter handwriting and marks onto a computer screen by means of a penlike stylus rather than by typing on a keyboard.** A *stylus* is a penlike device that is used to write text or draw lines on a touch-sensitive surface as input to a computer. Pen computers use *handwriting-recognition* software that translates handwritten characters made by the stylus into data that is usable by the computer. ***Handwriting recognition*** **refers to the ability of a computer to receive intelligible written input.** The system requires special software that interprets the movements of the stylus across the writing surface and translates the resulting cursive writing into digital information. (Alternatively, written text may be scanned from a piece of paper, using optical character recognition, as we describe in the next section.)

  Handwriting recognition is commonly used as an input method for PDAs. A currently successful handwriting-recognition system is Microsoft's version of the Windows operating system for the Tablet PC. The Tablet PC is Microsoft's version of a *tablet PC,* a special notebook computer outfitted with a digitizer tablet and a stylus that allows a user to handwrite text on the unit's screen. (● *See Panel 5.7, next page.*) A Mac version is the Modbook from Axiotron. A stylus can take the place of a keyboard when users use an on-screen input panel or tap letters and numbers directly

1973	1974	1976	1984	1990
The Alto, an experimental PC that uses a mouse and a GUI, is developed at Xerox PARC	Simple version of optical character recognition (OCR) developed	IBM develops the ink-jet printer	Apple Macintosh; first personal laser printer	Dragon speech-recognition program recognizes 30,000 words; SVGA video standard

panel 5.7

Pen-based computer systems

Handheld tablet PCs: (*left*) HTC EVO 4G; (*right*) Axiotron Modbook

on an on-screen keyboard. Some tablets (such as ViewSonic and Motion Computing) also include a standard keyboard so that the computer can function as a laptop when the screen is repositioned.

Although handwriting recognition has become a popular input form, it is still generally accepted that keyboard input is both faster and more reliable.

- Light pen: **The *light pen* is a light-sensitive penlike device that uses a wired connection to a computer terminal.** The user brings the pen to a desired point on the display screen and presses the pen button, which identifies that screen location to the computer. Light pens are used by engineers, graphic designers, and illustrators. They also are used in the health, food service, and chemical fields in situations in which users' hands need to be covered. *(• See Panel 5.8.)*

panel 5.8

Light pen

This person is using a light pen to design circuitry.

- Digitizer: **A *digitizer* uses an electronic pen or a mouselike copying device called a *puck* that can convert drawings and photos to digital data.** One form of digitizer is **the *digitizing tablet*, used in engineering and architecture applications, in which a specific location on an electronic plastic board corresponds to a location on the screen.** *(• See Panel 5.9.)*

panel 5.9

Digitizing tablet

Such tablets are often used in engineering, art, and architectural applications.

1994	2005	2010	2011	2013?	2016?	2019?
Apple and IBM introduce PCs with full-motion video built in; wireless data transmission for small portable computers; web browser invented	Wireless desktop printers commercially available	Multitouch screens	Apple's Magic (multitouch) Mouse	TV can output odors; full voice interaction with PCs; digital X-ray glasses; 3-D technologies become widespread	Thought recognition as everyday input means; active wallpaper responds to people's moods	Bionic eyes are commercially available

- **Digital pen:** **A *digital pen* is a writing instrument that allows users to write on paper and send the writing as an image file to the computer.** (• *See Panel 5.10.*) Basically, there are two kinds of digital pens. The first version, such as Logitech's Io pen and Leapfrog's FLY Fusion pen, requires you to write on special paper that's been printed with millions of nearly invisible microdots. A tiny camera in the pen tip learns its position, and a microchip in the pen converts the pen to digital ink, which can be transmitted to a PC. Pens such as the LiveScribe Pulse and the Nokia Digital Pen SU-27W also require special paper. The second version, such as the Mobile Digital Scribe, captures natural handwriting from any surface, and stores it in the receiver for future use. No special digital notepad or ink is required. When the Mobile Digital Scribe is connected to a computer, handwritten text and drawings are displayed directly on the computer screen.

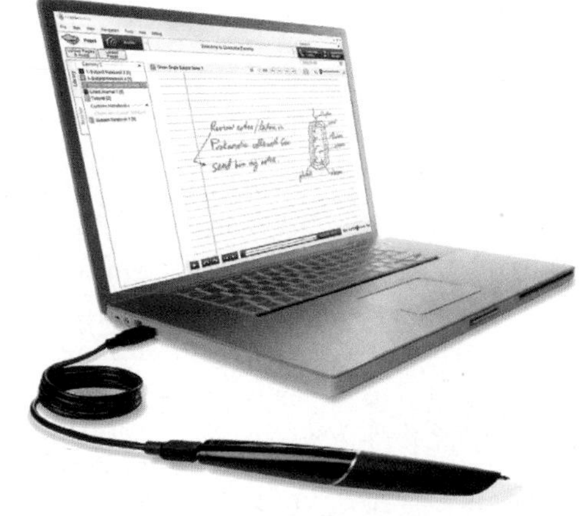

panel 5.10

Handwritten notes via digital pen (Echo SmartPen)

Scanning & Reading Devices

Scanning and reading devices are source data-entry devices.

In old-fashioned stores, checkout clerks read the price on every can and box and then entered those prices on the keyboard—a time-consuming, duplicated effort. In most stores now, of course, the clerks merely wave the products over a scanner, which automatically enters the price (from the bar code) in digital form. This is the difference between keyboard entry and source data entry.

Source data-input devices do not require keystrokes (or require only a few keystrokes) to input data to the computer. In most cases, data is entered directly from the source, without human intervention. ***Source data-entry devices*** **feed data into a computer system directly from its source, without the need for keyboard entry.** One type of source data-entry device includes scanning and reading devices—scanners, bar-code readers, mark- and character-recognition devices, and fax machines.

panel 5.11

Image scanners

(*Left*) Desktop scanner used in desktop publishing. (*Right*) Handheld scanner used to scan information from a hospital patient's ID bracelet.

SCANNERS ***Scanners,*** **or *optical scanners,* use light-sensing (optical) equipment to translate images of text, drawings, photos, and the like into digital form.** (• *See Panel 5.11.*) The images can then be processed by a computer, displayed on a monitor, stored on a storage device, or transmitted to another computer.

Scanners have led to a whole new industry called *electronic imaging,* the software-controlled integration and manipulation of separate images, using scanners, digital cameras, and advanced graphic computers. This technology has become invaluable for all kinds of reasons, such as to digitize and preserve old books and manuscripts that would otherwise fall into decay. PC users can get a decent

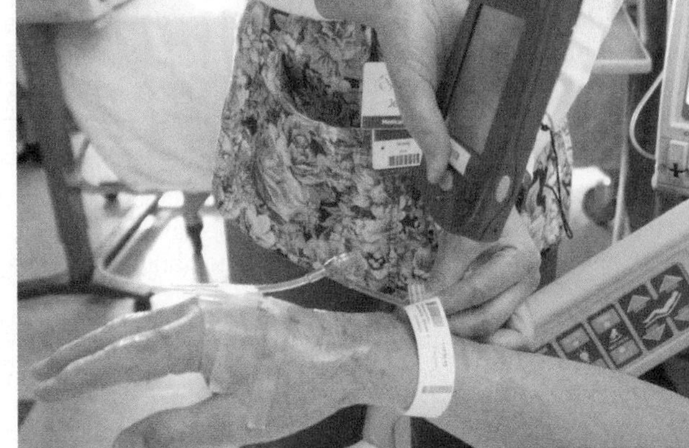

scanner with good software for less than $100 or a fantastic one for about $1,000.

- **Dots and bitmaps:** Scanners are similar to photocopy machines except they create electronic files of scanned items instead of paper copies. The system scans each image—color or black and white—with light and breaks the image into rows and columns of light and dark dots or color dots. Dots are stored in computer memory as digital code called a *bitmap,* a grid of dots. A *dot* is the smallest identifiable part of an image, and each dot is represented by one or more bits. The more bits in each dot, the more shades of gray and the more colors that can be represented. The amount of information stored in a dot is referred to as *color depth,* or *bit depth.* Scanners with higher bit depths tend to produce better color images. Today, most color scanners are at least 24-bit and are fine for normal use. For those wanting better image quality, 30- and 36-bit scanners are available. Really good scanners have a 48-bit color depth.

more info!

What Is TWAIN?

Maybe "Technology Without An Interesting Name"? It's a driver that's a go-between for a scanner and the applications on the computer. Borrowing from a Rudyard Kipling poem ("and never the twain [that is, two] shall meet," about Eastern and Western cultures), someone used the word *TWAIN* to express the difficulty, at the time, of connecting scanners and personal computers, although this is no longer the case.

Do a web search for *TWAIN.* When was it developed, and how does it work?

- **Resolution:** Scanners vary in resolution. In general, ***resolution*** **refers to the clarity and sharpness of an image and is measured in *dots per inch (dpi)*—the number of columns and rows of dots per inch.** The higher the number of dots, the clearer and sharper the image—that is, the higher the resolution. Popular color desktop scanners currently vary in dpi from 300 × 200 up to 2,400 × 2,400; some commercial scanners operate at 4,800 × 9,600 dpi. The quality of the scanner's optical equipment also affects the quality of the scanned images.

- **Types of scanners:** One of the most popular types of scanners is the ***flatbed scanner,*** **or *desktop scanner,* which works much like a photocopier—the image being scanned is placed on a glass surface, where it remains stationary, and the scanning beam moves across it.** Three other types of scanners are *sheet-fed, handheld,* and *drum.* The four types are compared below. *(• See Panel 5.12.)* Other single-purpose scanners are available, such as business-card, slide, and photo scanners. There are even scanner pens, such as the DocuPen, that can scan text from books and articles.

BAR-CODE READERS On June 26, 1974, a customer at Marsh's Supermarket in Troy, Ohio, made the first purchase of a product with a bar code—a pack

panel 5.12

Types of scanners compared

Flatbed: Costs $60–$400. The type most PC users have. Operates like a photocopier—image lies atop glass, which is scanned by scanning beam. Useful for single-sheet documents, books, photos. Some models scan transparencies, slides.

Sheet-fed: Costs $300–$500. Also popular for desktops because of compact size, which is smaller than flatbed. Operates similarly except sheet with image being scanned is fed into a slot and drawn past sensor. Useful only for single-page documents, photos; some accept slides; can also handle automatic feeding of many single-page documents.

Handheld: Costs $130–$160. Popular for use in factory and field settings and student and research use because of portability. Handheld scanners are physically dragged by hand across a document. Most models are pen-shaped and scan in swaths 5 inches wide or less, and special software "knits" strips of images together into a complete image. Some models translate single words into other languages. Images can be transmitted to a PC, PDA, or cellphone via serial, infrared (IR), or USB connection.

Drum: Costs in tens of thousands of dollars. Used by publishing industry to capture extremely detailed images. Image to be scanned is mounted on a glass cylinder, inside of which are sensors (photomultiplier tubes) that convert light signals into digital images.

Choosing a Scanner

- **What Do You Need to Scan?** Knowing what you expect to scan and how often you expect to scan it will tell you the most about the scanner features you'll need. The two most common choices are photos and documents (as single sheets), but there are other possibilities—books, business cards, film (slides and negatives), magazines, and easily damaged originals such as old photos and stamps. Somewhat less common are 3-D objects, such as coins or flowers. Also consider details like the maximum size of the originals and whether you'll need to scan both sides of document pages.
- **Do You Need a Flatbed?** For photos or other easily damaged originals, bound material, and 3-D objects, you need a flatbed. Some documents can go through a sheet feeder, but you risk damaging them. If you need to scan this sort of original only rarely, you may be able to make do with a sheet-fed scanner that comes with a plastic carrier to protect the originals. Keep in mind, however, that even brand-new, unscratched plastic carriers can degrade scan quality.
- **Do You Need a Sheet Feeder?** If you plan to scan documents on a regular basis—particularly documents longer than one or two pages—you almost certainly want a sheet feeder. Having to open a flatbed lid and set a page in it 10 times for a 10-page document is tiresome. Some sheet-fed scanners can also handle thick originals, such as health insurance ID cards. Also, some sheet feeders come with automatic feeding capability, for multi-page scanning jobs. An Automatic Document Feeder (ADF) will scan an entire stack of pages while you do something else. Pick an ADF capacity based on the number of pages in the typical document you expect to scan. If you occasionally have a longer document, you can add pages during the scan. Some ADFs can also handle stacks of business cards.
- **Do You Need to Duplex?** Duplexing means scanning both sides of a page at once. If you need a sheet feeder or ADF, and you expect to scan duplex documents (printed on both sides) on a regular basis, you'll want a duplexing scanner, duplexing ADF, or a scanner whose driver includes a manual duplex feature.
- **What Resolution Do You Need?** For most scanning, resolution isn't an issue. For documents, even a 200 dpi scan will give you good enough quality for most purposes; 300 dpi is almost always sufficient, and it's hard to find a scanner today with less than 600 dpi. For photos, unless you plan to crop in on a small part of the photo or print the photo at a larger size than the original, 600 dpi is usually fine.

  There are some kinds of originals, however, that require higher resolution. If you're scanning 35-mm slides or negatives, for example, you'll probably want to print them at a much larger size than the original, which means you'll need to scan them at a high resolution. Similarly, if you want to see the fine detail on an original like a stamp, you'll need to scan it at a high resolution. In these cases you'll want at least a 4,800 dpi optical resolution.
- **How Large Are Your Originals?** Pick a scanner that can handle the size of the originals you need to scan. For example, most flatbeds are letter size, which will be a problem if you occasionally need to scan legal-size pages. Most flatbeds with ADFs will scan legal-size pages with the ADF, but not all do, so be sure to check. You can also find scanners with larger flatbeds.
- **What Software Comes with the Scanner?** Most scanners will work with just about any scan-related program, but if the software you need already comes with the scanner, you won't have to pay extra for it. Depending on what you plan to scan, some of the software features you may want to look for include photo editing, optical character recognition (OCR), text indexing, the ability to create searchable PDF documents, and a business-card program.
- **Do You Need a Special-Purpose Scanner?** Finally, consider whether you need a special-purpose, rather than general-purpose, scanner. Among the most common special-purpose choices are scanners for business cards (small and highly portable), books (designed to let pages lie flat), and slides (smaller than flatbed scanners, but no better at scanning slides than flatbed scanners with equivalent features). Two other possibilities are portable scanners (general-purpose sheet-fed scanners small enough to fit in your laptop bag) and pen scanners (the size of a pen).

Adapted from *www.pcmag.com/article2/0,2817,2355771,00.asp.*

of Wrigley's Juicy Fruit chewing gum (which pack is now in the Smithsonian National Museum of National History in Washington, D.C.). ***Bar codes* are the vertical, zebra-striped marks you see on most manufactured retail products**—everything from candy to cosmetics to comic books. *(• See Panel 5.13, next page.)* In North America, supermarkets, food manufacturers, and many other businesses have agreed to use a bar-code system called the *Universal Product Code (UPC),* established by the Uniform Code Council (UCC). Other kinds of bar-code systems are used on everything from FedEx and Postal Service packages to railroad cars, video-store videos, and the jerseys of long-distance runners.

panel 5.13

Bar code and bar-code reader

This bar-code reader is being used to update inventory, by scanning in the information on the stickers put on the boxes coming into the warehouse.

***Bar-code readers* are photoelectric (optical) scanners that translate the symbols in the bar code into digital code.** In this system, the price of a particular item is set within the store's computer. Once the bar code has been scanned, the corresponding price appears on the salesclerk's point-of-sale terminal and on your receipt. Records of sales from the bar-code readers are input to the store's computer and used for accounting, restocking store inventory, and weeding out products that don't sell well.

Do-it-yourself checkout is an automated scanning process that enables shoppers to scan, bag, and pay for their purchases without human assistance. The self-scanning checkout lane looks like a traditional checkout lane except that the shopper interacts with a computer's user interface instead of a store employee. *(• See Panel 5.14.)* Self-scanning has become popular at many name-brand stores.

panel 5.14

Self-Scanning System

Self-service scanning systems allow consumers to check themselves out of the supermarket. The shopper begins the process by touching the computer's welcome screen. Then the computer's voice output provides the shopper with instructions about how to scan the items and where to place them once they've been scanned. When the shopper scans in an item, the item's bar code provides the computer with the information it needs to determine what item is being scanned, its weight, and its price. The system also deactivates any security tags on the items. The shopper places the items in shopping bags sitting on security scales, so the system can check that heavy items were not substituted for light ones.

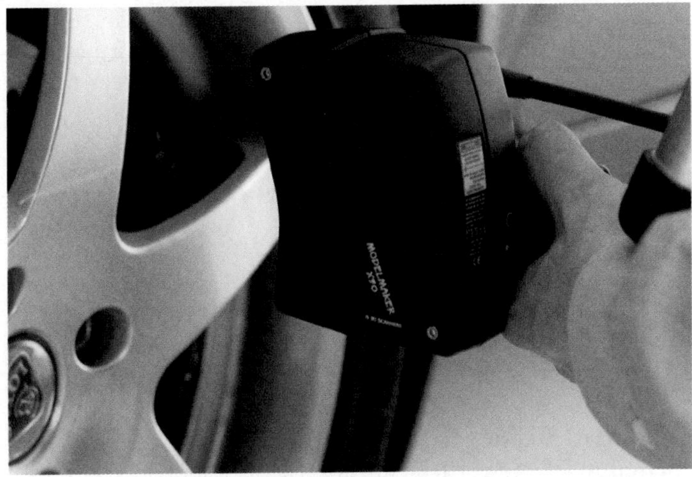

The Model Maker 3-D scanning system can scan all types of surfaces in all sorts of lighting. It is used, among other things, to scan cars and motorcycles, or specific components, into a CAD/CAM system so that new models can be created.

TYPES OF BAR CODES Bar codes may be 1-D, 2-D, or 3-D.

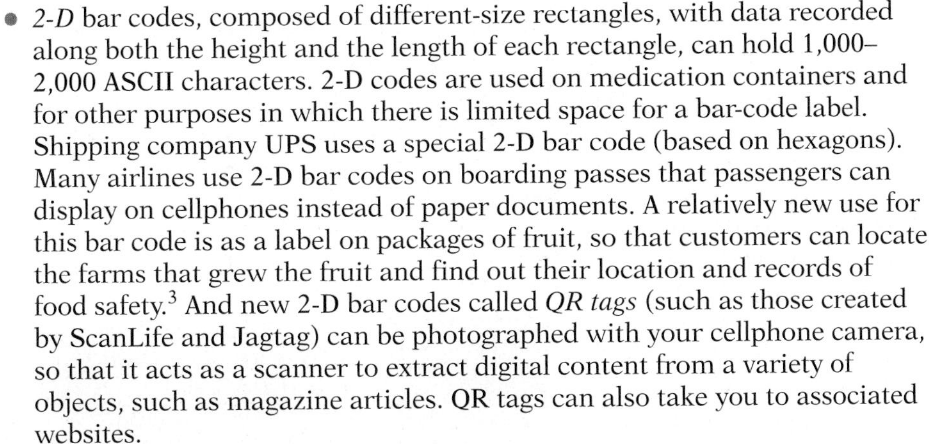

- *1-D* codes, today's ordinary vertical bar codes, can hold up to 16 ASCII characters. These are the bar codes commonly used by supermarkets.
- *2-D* bar codes, composed of different-size rectangles, with data recorded along both the height and the length of each rectangle, can hold 1,000–2,000 ASCII characters. 2-D codes are used on medication containers and for other purposes in which there is limited space for a bar-code label. Shipping company UPS uses a special 2-D bar code (based on hexagons). Many airlines use 2-D bar codes on boarding passes that passengers can display on cellphones instead of paper documents. A relatively new use for this bar code is as a label on packages of fruit, so that customers can locate the farms that grew the fruit and find out their location and records of food safety.[3] And new 2-D bar codes called *QR tags* (such as those created by ScanLife and Jagtag) can be photographed with your cellphone camera, so that it acts as a scanner to extract digital content from a variety of objects, such as magazine articles. QR tags can also take you to associated websites.
- *3-D* bar codes, used on items such as automobile tires, are called "bumpy" bar codes because they are read by a scanner that differentiates by symbol height. 3-D codes are used on metal, hard rubber, and other surfaces to which ordinary bar codes will not adhere.

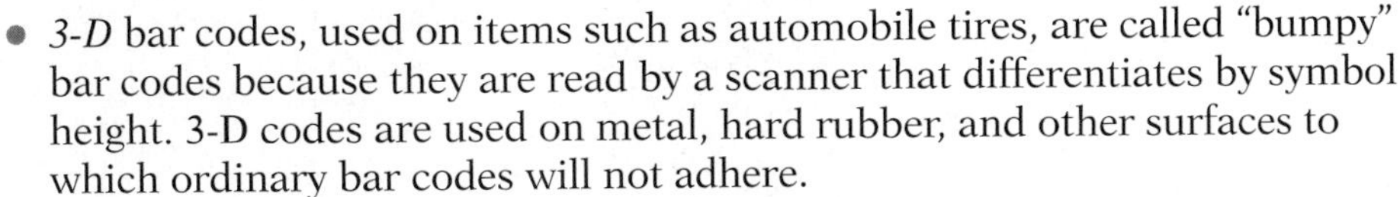

Soon store 1-D bar codes may yield to so-called *smart tags,* radio-frequency identification (RFID) tags already now employed for the tracking of cattle or of electronic components in a warehouse. We discuss RFID shortly.

Conventional 1-D bar code

2-D bar code

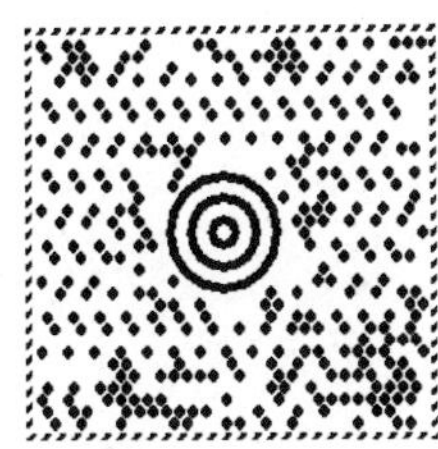

Maxicode is a 2-D bar code used by United Parcel Service (UPS).

More Types of Bar Codes

What are these proprietary bar codes used for: Aztec Code, Data Matrix, Code 1, Snowflake Code, QR Code? Go to:

www.mecsw.com/specs/speclist.html

www.agamik.co.uk/symbols.php/

MARK RECOGNITION/CHARACTER RECOGNITION DEVICES There are three types of scanning devices that sense marks or characters. They are usually referred to by their abbreviations—MICR, OMR, and OCR:

- **Magnetic-ink character recognition: *Magnetic-ink character recognition (MICR)* is a character-recognition system that uses magnetizable ink and special characters.** When an MICR document needs to be read, it passes through a special scanner that magnetizes the special ink and then translates the magnetic information into characters. MICR technology is used by banks. Numbers and characters found on the bottom of checks (usually containing the bank code number, check number, sort number, and account number) are printed with a laser printer that accepts MICR toner. MICR provides a secure, high-speed method of scanning and processing information.

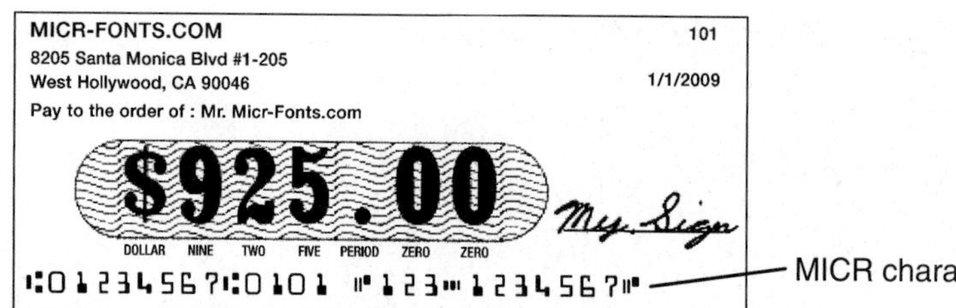

MICR-FONTS.COM
101
8205 Santa Monica Blvd #1-205
West Hollywood, CA 90046
1/1/2009
Pay to the order of : Mr. Micr-Fonts.com
$925.00
DOLLAR NINE TWO FIVE PERIOD ZERO ZERO
MICR characters

- **Optical mark recognition:** ***Optical mark recognition (OMR)*** **uses a special scanner that reads "bubble" marks and converts them into computer-usable form.** The best-known example is the OMR technology used to read students' answers to the College Board Scholastic Aptitude Test (SAT) and the Graduate Record Examination (GRE). In these cases, the scanner reads pencil marks that fill in circles, or bubbles, on specially designed documents. OMR is also used in forms and surveys.

- **Optical character recognition:** These days almost all scanners come with OCR software. ***Optical character recognition (OCR)*** **software converts scanned text from images (pictures of the text) to an editable text format (usually ASCII) that can be imported into a word processing application and manipulated.** Special OCR characters appear on utility bills and price tags on department-store merchandise. The wand reader is a common OCR scanning device. *(• See Panel 5.15.)*

OCR software can deal with nearly all printed characters, but script fonts and handwriting still present problems. In addition, OCR accuracy varies with the quality of the scanner—a text with 1,200 dpi will take longer to scan than one with 72 dpi, but the accuracy will be higher. Some OCR programs are better than others, with lesser versions unable to convert tables, boxes, or other extensive formatting; high-quality OCR software can read such complex material without difficulty. Users wanting to scan text with foreign-language (diacritical) marks, such as French accents, should check the OCR package to see if the program can handle this.

FAX MACHINES **A** ***fax machine*****—or** ***facsimile transmission machine*****— scans an image and sends it as electronic signals over telephone lines to a receiving fax machine, which prints out the image on paper.**

OCR-A
NUMERIC 0123456789
ALPHA ABCDEFGHIJ
SYMBOLS KLMNOPQRST
UVWXYZ
>$/-+-#"

OCR-B
NUMERIC 00123456789
ALPHA ACENPSTVX
SYMBOLS <+>-¥

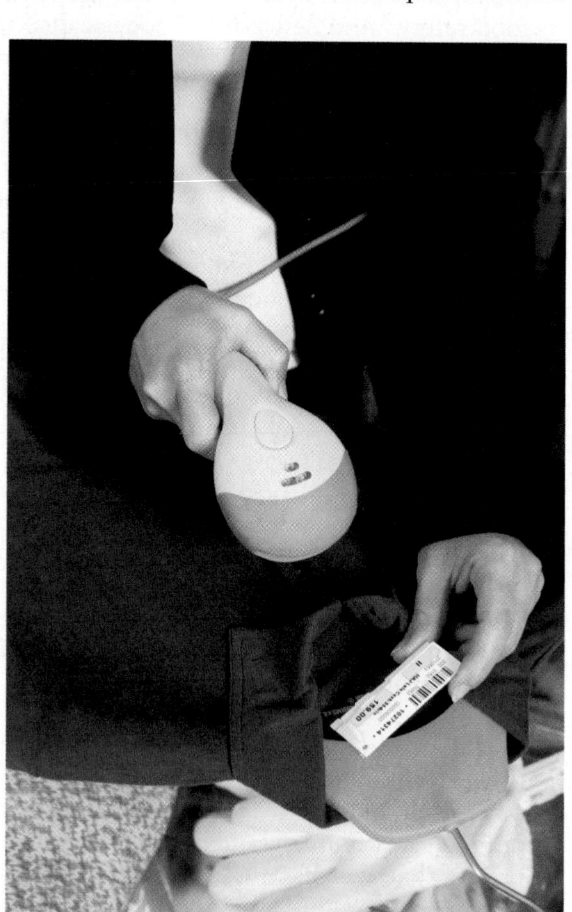

panel 5.15

Optical character recognition

OCR is often used in stores to encode and read price tags. A handheld wand is used as a reading device.

There are two types of fax machines—dedicated fax machines and fax modems:

Dedicated fax machine.

- **Dedicated fax machines:** *Dedicated fax machines* are specialized devices that do nothing except send and receive fax documents. These are what we usually think of as fax machines. They are found not only in offices and homes but also alongside regular phones in public places such as airports.

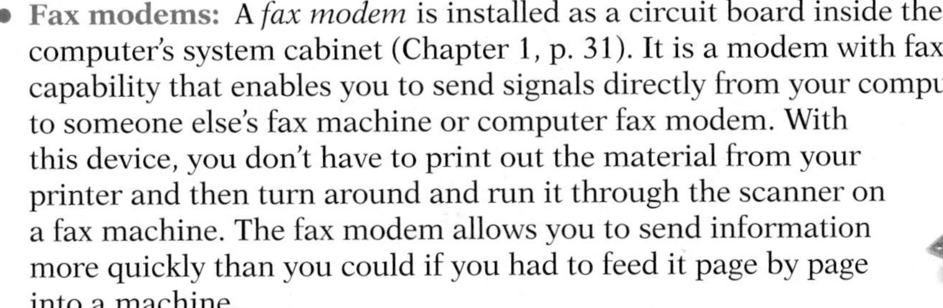

- **Fax modems:** A *fax modem* is installed as a circuit board inside the computer's system cabinet (Chapter 1, p. 31). It is a modem with fax capability that enables you to send signals directly from your computer to someone else's fax machine or computer fax modem. With this device, you don't have to print out the material from your printer and then turn around and run it through the scanner on a fax machine. The fax modem allows you to send information more quickly than you could if you had to feed it page by page into a machine.

  The fax modem is another feature of mobile computing; it's especially powerful as a receiving device. Fax modems are installed inside portable computers. If you link up a cellphone to a fax modem in your portable computer, you can send and receive wireless fax messages no matter where you are in the world.

Fax modem circuit board, which plugs into an expansion slot (p. 32) inside the computer.

Audio-Input Devices

Audio-input devices allow users to send audio signals to a computer for processing, storing, recording, or carrying out commands.

An *audio-input device* records analog sound and translates it for digital storage and processing. An analog sound signal is a continuously variable wave within a certain frequency range. For the computer to process them, these variable waves must be converted to digital 0s and 1s. The principal use of audio-input devices is to produce digital input for multimedia computers.

TWO WAYS OF DIGITIZING AUDIO An audio signal can be digitized in two ways—by a *sound board* or a *MIDI board:*

- **Sound board:** Analog sound—the kind of sound that exists in nature, for example, human voices, sounds from a musical instrument—from a cassette player or a microphone goes through a special circuit board called a *sound board*. **A *sound board* is an add-on circuit board in a computer that converts analog sound to digital sound** (binary computer language, 0s and 1s) **and stores it for further processing and/or plays it back, providing output directly to speakers or an external amplifier.** (Chapter 6 discusses analog and digital in more detail.)

- **MIDI board:** **A *MIDI board—MIDI,* pronounced "middie," stands for "Musical Instrument Digital Interface"—uses a standard for the interchange of musical information between musical instruments, synthesizers, and computers.**

MICROPHONES Also supporting audio input are *microphones,* devices that take varying air pressure waves created by voice or other sound sources and convert them into varying electric signals. Most new microcomputers and notebooks come with built-in microphones; stand-alone microphones can be connected via USB or some other connection. (Microphones are used in speech-recognition input, discussed shortly.)

Webcams & Video-Input Cards

Webcams download images to a computer for transmission over the Internet or other network.

A ***webcam*** **is a video camera attached to a computer to record live moving images that can then be posted on a website in real time.** *(• See Panel 5.16.)* Webcam connections require special software, usually included with the camera, and a USB or video cable or a wireless radio-frequency connection.

Laptops also come with webcams built in.

Initially intended for personal videoconferencing, the webcam has become popular with web users. You can join thousands of other webcam users out there who are hosting such riveting material as a live 24-hour view of the aquarium of a turtle named Pixel. Or you might show your living quarters or messy desk for all to see. Twenty20's VholdR Helmet Camera Camcorder is a digital video camera with a lens that straps onto your helmet—perfect for capturing your moves as you ski down a black-diamond trail.

Smartphones can also now be used as webcams, with special downloaded applications, such as WebCamera Plus and Mobiola Webcamera, that are installed on both the phone and on a computer. The video feeds into the phone are transmitted by wired (USB) or wireless transmission to the computer.

As with sound, most film and videotape traditionally has been in analog form; the signal is a continuously variable wave (Chapter 6). For computer use, the signals that come from a VCR or camcorder must be converted to digital form through a special digitizing card—a *video-capture card* or simply *video card*—that is installed in the computer. There are two types of video cards—frame-grabber and full-motion.

Coffee Pot Cam

The first webcam was the "Trojan room coffee pot cam." What was this? Search the web to find out.

Twenty20's VholdR helmet camcorder

FRAME-GRABBER VIDEO CARD The *frame-grabber video card* captures and digitizes only a single frame at a time. This type of video card is used less today than is the full-motion video card. It is still used by video enthusiasts and in certain professions, such as remote medical diagnosis and astronomy.

FULL-MOTION VIDEO CARD The *full-motion video (FMV) card* converts analog to digital signals at rates up to 30 frames per second, giving the effect of a continuously flowing motion picture. *(• See Panel 5.17.)* Motion pictures are run at 24 fps, which is the minimum frequency required to eliminate the perception of moving frames and make the images appear visually fluid to the eye.

The first use of FMV began in the early 1990s when personal computers and consoles became capable of using more than a few minutes' worth of movies in a game. Within a few years, FMV became a nearly mandatory component in computer games. Popular platforms for FMV include QuickTime, MPEG, and Smacker.

panel 5.16

Webcams in use

(*Left*) Webcam built into the top of a Lenovo IdeaPad; (*right*) an older externally attached model.

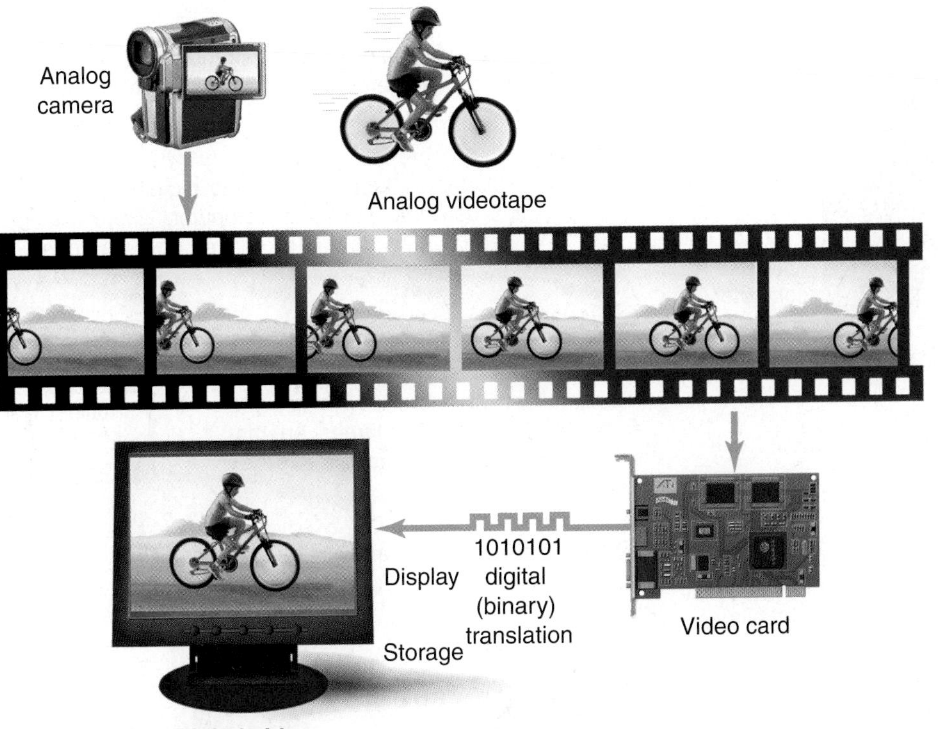

panel 5.17

How analog video input is changed to digital form

Video input: **Analog to Digital**
Full-motion video is accomplished by taking multiple pictures in sequence. Movie theater film uses 24 frames per second, which is the minimum frequency required to eliminate the perception of moving frames and make the images appear visually fluid to the eye. TV video generates 30 interlaced frames per second, which is actually transmitted as 60 half frames ("fields" in TV lingo) per second.

Video that has been digitized and stored in the computer can be displayed at varying frame rates, depending on the speed of the computer. The slower the computer, the jerkier the movement.

Survival Tip

Your Choice: More Colors or More Resolution?

You can't have the best of both. A video card may let you have 16.8 million colors at 800 × 600 resolution or 65,536 colors at 1,600 × 1,200 resolution.

Digital Cameras

A digital camera is a still camera that records images in digital form.

Digital cameras, which now greatly outsell film cameras in the United States, are particularly interesting because they have changed the entire industry of photography. The environmentally undesirable stage of chemical development required for conventional film is completely eliminated.

Instead of using traditional (chemical) film, **a *digital camera* uses a light-sensitive processor chip to capture photographic images in digital form and store them on a small diskette inserted into the camera or on flash memory cards.** (• *See Panel 5.18, next page.*) The bits of digital information can then be copied right into a computer's hard disk for manipulation, emailing, posting on websites, and printing out.

Many digital cameras can be connected to a computer by a USB or FireWire connection (Chapter 4), so your computer's operating system must support these connections to recognize the camera's driver. Most cameras store picture data on flash memory cards, memory sticks, and keychains (Chapter 4), from which later you can transmit photo data to your computer through a USB cable. Popular software applications for sophisticated digital photo manipulation include Adobe Photoshop, Corel Paint Shop Photo Pro, Xara Photo & Graphic Designer, Serif PhotoPlus, and Photo Explosion.

CAMERA PHONES Digital-camera technology has, of course, migrated to cellphones (which can also be used for web surfing, playing games, and

Digital-Camera Resource

For more information on digital cameras, go to:

http://reviews.cnet.com/digital-camera-buying-guide/

www.dcresource.com

http://reviews.cnet.com/digital-cameras/

www.digitalcamerareview.com/

www.digitaltrends.com/buying-guides/digital-camera-buying-guide/

Also be aware of limitations of storage media: If you store your photos on such secondary storage media as CDs, such media may very well not be usable by information technology equipment 10 or 20 years from now.

Memory

Interface cable connects to computer

Light

1 Light enters the camera through the lens.

2 The light is focused on the charge-coupled device (CCD), a solid-state chip made up of tiny, light-sensitive photosites. When light hits the CCD, it records the image electronically, just like film records images in a standard camera. The photosites convert light into electrons, which are then converted into digital information.

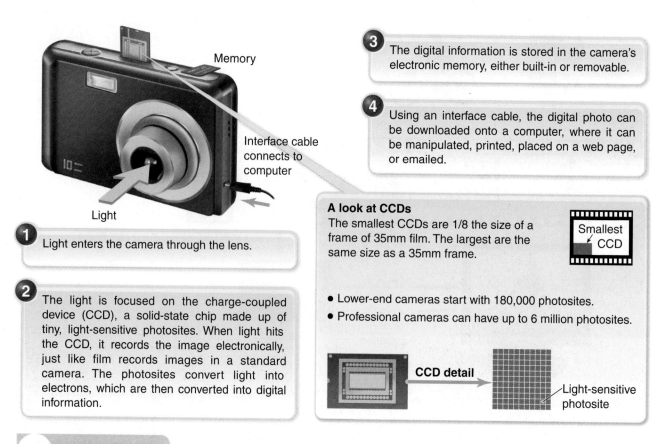

3 The digital information is stored in the camera's electronic memory, either built-in or removable.

4 Using an interface cable, the digital photo can be downloaded onto a computer, where it can be manipulated, printed, placed on a web page, or emailed.

A look at CCDs

The smallest CCDs are 1/8 the size of a frame of 35mm film. The largest are the same size as a 35mm frame.

- Lower-end cameras start with 180,000 photosites.
- Professional cameras can have up to 6 million photosites.

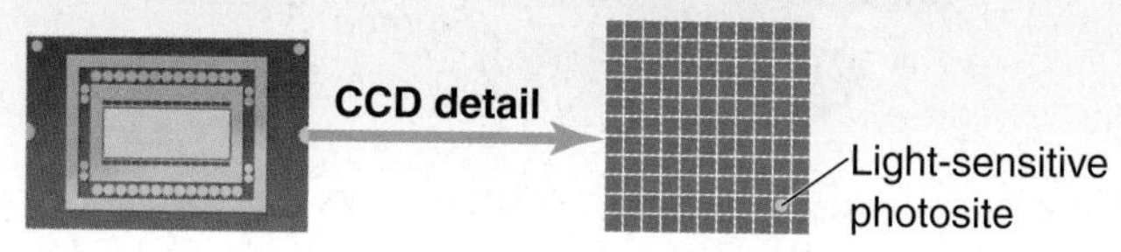

panel 5.18

How digital cameras work

downloading music), enabling you to visually share your vacation experiences in real time. You compose the shot on your phone's color LCD screen, point and shoot, then wait a minute or so for the picture to "develop," and then send it. We discuss camera phones further in Chapter 7.

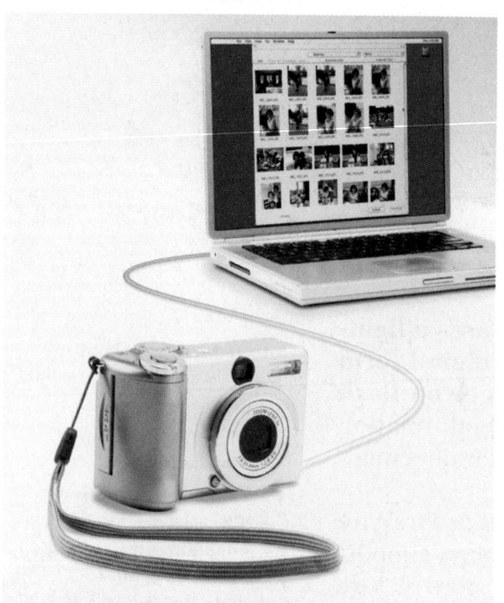

This digital camera is attached to a desktop computer in order to download its images to the computer via a USB connection.

Speech-Recognition Systems

Speech-recognition programs convert spoken words to text.

Can your computer tell whether you want it to "recognize speech" or "wreck a nice beach"? **A *speech-recognition system*, using a microphone (or a telephone) as an input device, converts a person's speech into digital signals by comparing the electrical patterns produced by the speaker's voice with a set of prerecorded patterns stored in the computer.** (• *See Panel 5.19, next page.*) Most of today's speech-recognition packages have a database of about 200,000 words from which they try to match the words you say. These programs let you accomplish two tasks: turn spoken dictation into typed text and issue oral commands (such as "Print file" or "Change font") to control your computer.

Speech-recognition systems have had to overcome many difficulties, such as different voices, pronunciations, and accents. Recently, however, the systems have measurably improved, at least up to a point. Major recognition systems are Dragon Naturally Speaking for the PC and for the Mac, Dragon Dictate for the Mac, and speech-recognition software built into the Windows OS and the Mac OS. Other systems are Talking Desktop, Fonix Speech, Aculab, and Verbio. Special speech-recognition

Speech
A person who's going to use speech recognition software usually must first go through an *enrollment*. This consists of the person dictating text that is already known to the software for 10 minutes to an hour. From this sampling, the software creates a table of *vocal references*, which are the ways in which the speaker's pronunciation of phonemes varies from models of speech based on a sampling of hundreds to thousands of people. *Phonemes* are the smallest sound units that combine into words, such as "duh," "aw," and "guh" in "dog." There are 48 phonemes in English. After enrollment, the speaker dictates the text he wants the software to transcribe into a microphone, preferably one that uses *noise-cancellation* to eliminate background sounds. The quality of the microphone and the computer's processing power are the most important hardware factors in speech recognition. The speaker can use continuous speech, which is normal speech without pauses between words.

Signal Processing
The sound wave is transformed into a sequence of codes that represent speech sounds.

1. Phonetic Models
Describe what codes may occur for a given speech sound.
In the word *how*, what is the probability of the "ow" sound appearing between an H and a D?

2. Dictionary
Defines the phonetic pronunciation (sequence of sounds) of each word.
How does it work
haw daz it werk

3. Grammar
Defines what words may follow each other, using parts of speech.
How does <it> [work]
adv vt pron v

Recognition Search
Using the data from 1, 2, and 3, the computer tries to find the best matching sequence of words as learned from a variety of examples.

Output
Computer recognizes word string and prints it on the screen.

panel 5.19
How a speech-recognition system works

software is available for specific professions, such as law, medicine, and public safety.

Speech-recognition systems are finding many uses. Warehouse workers are able to speed inventory taking by recording inventory counts verbally. Traders on stock exchanges can communicate their trades by speaking to computers. Radiologists can dictate their interpretations of X rays directly into transcription machines. Nurses can fill out patient charts by talking to a computer. Users can do online voice searches on their cellphones, using programs such as Google Mobile App, Yahoo! Search, Vlingo, and ChaCha. Speakers of Chinese can speak to machines that will print out Chinese characters. And for many individuals with disabilities, a computer isn't so much a luxury or a productivity tool as a necessity, providing freedom of expression, independence, and empowerment.

How to Set Up Your Computer for Speech Recognition in Windows 7

Go to:

http://windows.microsoft.com/en-US/windows7/Set-up-Speech-Recognition

Windows

Search this website

Home Explore Windows Products Shop Downloads Help & How-to

Windows 7 Help home Getting started Top solutions How-to videos Community

What can I do with Speech Recognition?

You can use your voice to control your computer. You can say commands that the computer will respond to, and you can dictate text to the computer.

Before you get started using Windows Speech Recognition, you'll need to connect a microphone to your computer. Once you've got the microphone set up, you can train your computer to better understand you by creating a voice profile that your computer uses to recognize your voice and spoken commands. For information about setting up your microphone, see Set up your microphone for Speech Recognition.

After you've got your microphone and voice profile set up, you can use Speech Recognition to do the following:

- **Control your computer.** Speech Recognition listens and responds to your spoken commands. You can use Speech Recognition to run programs and interact with Windows. For more information about the commands you can use with Speech Recognition, see Common commands in Speech Recognition.
- **Dictate and edit text.** You can use Speech Recognition to dictate words into word-processing programs or to fill out online forms in a web browser. You can also use Speech Recognition to edit text on your computer. For more information about dictating text, see Dictate text using Speech Recognition.

Sensors

A sensor is basically a device that receives and responds to a signal or a stimulus.

A *sensor* is an input device that collects specific data directly from the environment and transmits it to a computer. Although you are unlikely to see such input devices connected to a PC in an office, they exist all around us, often in nearly invisible form and as part of some larger electronic system. Sensors can be used to detect all kinds of things: speed, movement, weight, pressure, temperature, humidity, wind, current, fog, gas, smoke, light, shapes, images, and so on. An electronic device is used to measure a physical quantity such as temperature, pressure, or volume and convert it into an electronic signal of some kind (for instance, a voltage).

Nike markets a running shoe with a sensor that works with the Apple iPod or iPhone to customize and track your workouts. Building security systems use sensors to detect movement. Sensors are used to detect the speed and volume of traffic and adjust traffic lights. They are used on highways in wintertime in Iowa as weather-sensing devices to tell workers when to roll out snowplows and on Interstate 95 to give drivers from New Jersey to North Carolina access to real-time information on traffic flows, crashes, and travel time to help them anticipate delays.[4] In aviation, sensors are used to detect ice buildup on airplane wings or to alert pilots to sudden changes in wind direction. In California, sensors have been planted along major earthquake fault lines in an experiment to see whether scientists can predict major earth movements.[5]

Oceanic and land-based sensors alerted officials to the 2011earthquake and tsunami in Japan, allowing quicker broadcast of warnings, automatically shutting down some industrial facilities and saving hundreds of lives. As terrible as the devastation in Japan was, it could have been worse were it not for networks providing near-real-time alerts via Internet and wireless technologies. Even though the earthquake occurred close to the coastline—reducing the amount of time to effectively take action—the system still provided a crucial 10 minutes or so to activate a public warning system, allowing people to evacuate high-risk environments and get to higher ground. It also signaled activities such as hospital operations and energy production to revert to what is known as safe mode. Beyond Japan, the tsunami tracking network guided more accurate evacuations in Hawaii and elsewhere in the Pacific Basin.

After the earthquake and tsunami in the Indian Ocean in 2004, in which more than 230,000 people died as a result of unknown wave intensity, Japan and many other nations, including the United States, began deploying a network of sensors known as Deep-Ocean Assessment and Reporting of Tsunamis (DART) in suspected tsunami "hot spots" worldwide. The DART network

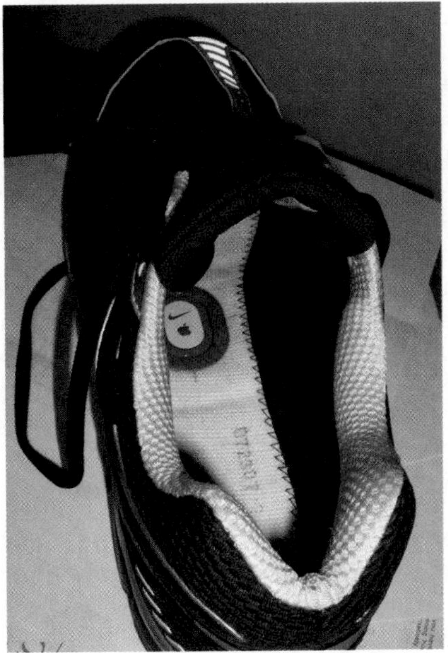

Sensors. (*Left*) On October 9, 2003, the 2,080-pound Liberty Bell made a 963-foot journey to a new home on Independence Mall in Philadelphia. High-tech sensors monitored the famous crack, to make sure it did not get larger. (*Middle*) Nike shoe with transmitter that tracks your time, distance, and pace while you run. Then you can upload your run data to Nike-plus.com, the world's largest running club, where you can monitor your progress. (*Right*) Mount Vesuvius, Italy. Perimeter of volcanic crater with seismic apparatus.

consists mostly of self-contained acoustic and pressure-sensitive buoys and sensors anchored to the ocean floor that are able to detect seismic activity as well as increases in size and height of wave activity. [6]

Radio-Frequency Identification Tags

RFID is a data collection technology that uses electronic tags for storing data.

Radio-frequency identification (RFID) tags **are based on an identifying tag bearing a microchip that contains specific code numbers. These code numbers are read by the radio waves of a scanner linked to a database.** *Active RFID tags* have their own power source and can transmit signals over a distance to a reader device. *Passive RFID tags* have no battery power of their own and must be read by some sort of scanner.

RFID tags of both types are used for a wide range of purposes and are starting to replace bar codes in many situations. Drivers with RFID tags breeze through tollbooths without having to even roll down their windows; the toll is automatically charged to their accounts. Radio-wave-readable ID tags are also used by the Postal Service to monitor the flow of mail, by stores for inventory control and warehousing, and in the railroad industry to keep track of rail cars. The Food and Drug Administration (FDA) and drug companies are working on tagging popular drugs with RFID devices to guard against counterfeit medicines. The technology is used to make supposedly "thief proof" keys in millions of automobiles. Gambling casinos have put RFID tags inside gambling chips to help them track the betting habits of high rollers. Visa and MasterCard "no-swipe" or "wave-and-pay" credit cards have been developed with embedded RFID technology that means cards don't have to be swiped across a magnetic-strip reader but can just be waved near a scanner, which could help speed up lines in stores. Walmart has required that all its vendors replace bar codes with RFID technology in order to improve inventory control. In the long run, the tags could end up on every product we buy, so that in the future we will no longer wait for a checkout counter but will breeze past readers that will scan our purchases in milliseconds.

All U.S. passports now must have RFID tags embedded in them. Machines can read the personal information in these passports—aiding customs and immigration officials but also, unfortunately making passport information vulnerable to terrorists and other criminals. Tiny transmitters have been

RFID Identity Theft

The use of RFID technology has increased the risk of identity theft; to find out more about this and what you can do, go to:

http://hubpages.com/hub/A-RFID-Blocking-Wallet-Can-Prevent-Identity-Theft

www.zdnet.com/blog/storage/rfid-passport-identity-theft-made-simple/713

www.popularmechanics.com/technology/how-to/4206464

www.ehow.com/how_4685750_yourself-hightech-rfid-identity-theft.html

www.wreg.com/wreg-electronic-pickpocketing-story,0,6289527.story

RFID as "Spytags"?

To find out:

www.spychips.com/devices/tag_images.html

www.spychips.com/what-is-rfid.html

http://theglobalawakening.wordpress.com/2010/08/18/tesco-is-leading-the-push-for-rfid-spying-chips-in-your-products/

installed in things ranging from cars to National Park Service cactuses to help authorities track thefts. Pet owners put RFID tags in their dogs and cats, to veterinarians with the right scanning equipment to identify the animals if they became separated from their owners. And an epidemic of kidnappings led wealthy and some middle-class Mexicans to start implanting geolocator tags that can pinpoint their location by satellite.

In the United States, the FDA approved implantation of an implantable chip, the VeriChip, for medical purposes, on the premise that patient-specific information stored in the chip could speed vital information about a person's medical history. (About twice the length of a dime, the device is typically implanted between the shoulder and elbow area of an individual's right arm.) However, privacy advocates fear that the technology could be used to track people's movements and put sensitive personal information at risk to hackers.

Human-Biology-Input Devices

In information technology, biometrics refers to technologies that measure and analyze human body characteristics.

Security concerns following the terrorist attacks of September 11, 2001, on the New York World Trade Center and the Pentagon made more people aware of ***biometrics*, the science of analyzing and measuring specific biological characteristics of an individual to create a unique digital identifier that can be electronically stored and subsequently matched against to verify or determine a person's identity.** Biometric security devices identify a person through a fingerprint; hand, eye, or facial characteristics; vein patterns;

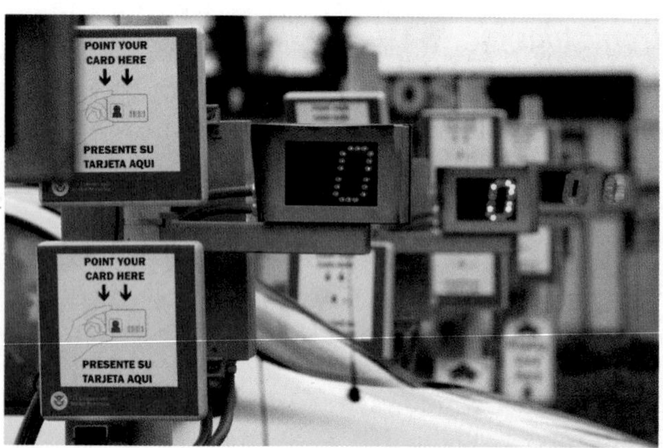

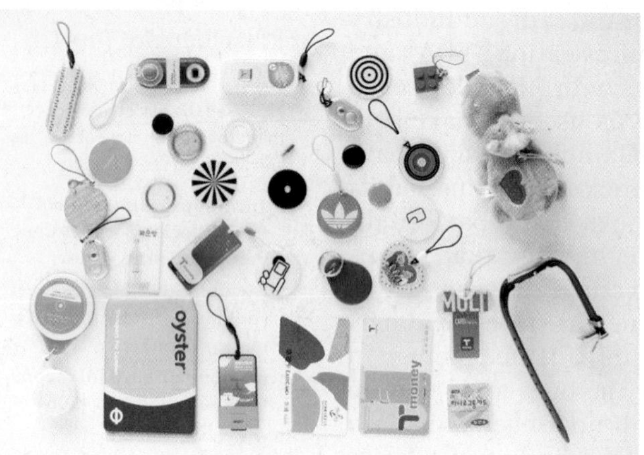

RFID. (*Top left*) Drivers can buy RFID tags to drive past tollbooths without having to stop; the tolls are automatically charged to their account, usually established with a credit card. FastTrack is a common tollbooth RFID program. (*Top right*) German passport with the RFID tag that will be embedded in the passport. (*Bottom left*) Assortment of RFID tags. (*Bottom right*) Sheep with RFID tags pass through a scanner or reader that scans the ear ID tag.

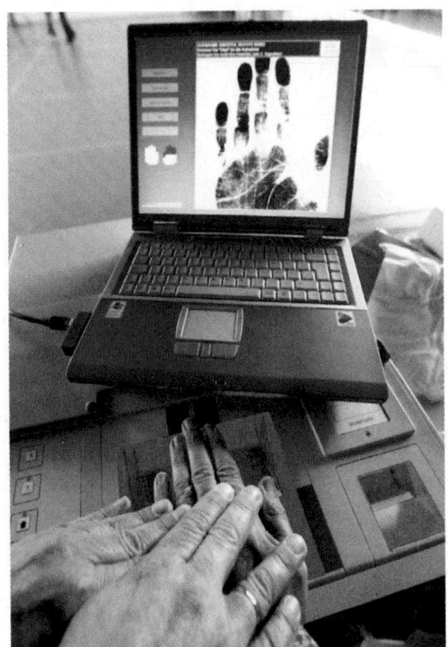

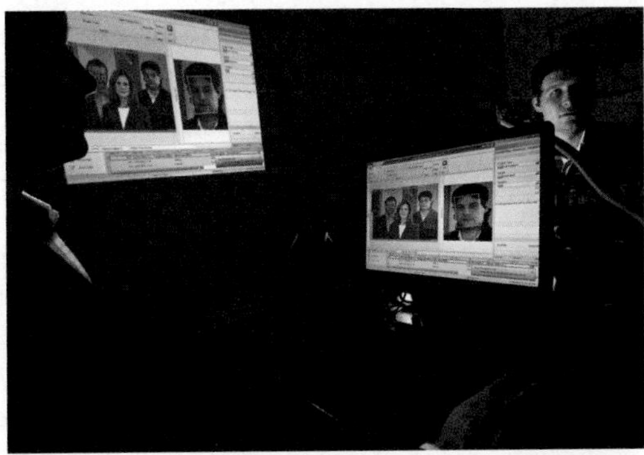

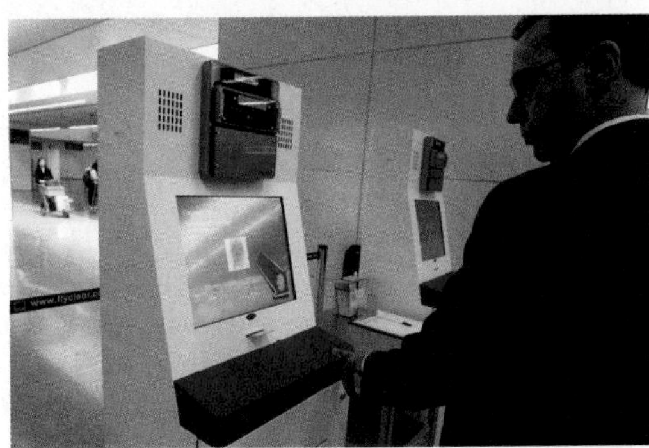

panel 5.20

Some types of biometric devices

(*Left*) Palm print recognition. (*Top right*) IView Systems has made a biometrics system for face recognition to be used in Ontario, Canada, casinos to help identify self-excluded gamblers. This system replaced the impractical use of security guards to ID the more than 15,000 people on the list. (*Bottom*) A representative from Clear demonstrates how biometrics is used at the Clear express security lane at San Francisco International Airport in San Francisco, which was the ninth airport in the U.S. to offer the express security lanes, which allows travelers, for a small fee, to bypass long security lines.

voice intonation; or some other biological trait. (● *See Panel 5.20.*) Many laptop, notebook, tablet, and smartphone manufacturers equip their devices with biometric sensors that read fingerprints, instead of passwords, before allowing access. And some U.S. travelers flying overseas avoid customs and security lines at some airports by swiping a digital ID card embedded with an image of the traveler's eye to verify his or her identity.

Software That Can Identify People from Any Photograph Anywhere on the Internet!?

How does this affect your privacy?

www.dailymail.co.uk/sciencetech/article-1305191/Facial-recognition-software-allow-ability-identify-people-photographs-internet.html

http://thementalmilitia.com/forums/index.php?topic=17433.0

www.techncoffee.com/25/the-facial-recognition-software/

5.3 OUTPUT HARDWARE

Output hardware communicates the results of data processing.

Computer output gets more innovative all the time. Ready to move up from one screen to two when you're working at your computer? With only a single display screen, you find yourself switching back and forth between, say, a word processing document, email, and Web searches. Multiple monitors reduce distractions. Indeed, a study shows that people who use *two* display screens, rather than one, are 44% more productive at certain text-editing operations.[7] "The study reveals that multiscreen users get on task quicker, work faster, and get more work done with fewer errors editing documents, spreadsheets, and graphic files in comparison with single screen users," said one of the study authors.[8] A cost-effective arrangement is to get two 22-inch monitors, one placed vertically, the other horizontally.[9]

In this section, we discuss monitors and other output hardware, devices that convert machine-readable information, obtained as the result of processing, into people-readable form. The principal kinds of output are softcopy and hardcopy.

- **Softcopy: *Softcopy* is data that is shown on a display screen or is in audio or voice form; it exists only electronically.** This kind of output is not tangible; it cannot be touched. It's like music: You can see musical scores and touch CDs and tapes, but the music itself is intangible. Similarly, you can touch disks on which programs are stored, but the software itself is intangible. *Soft* is also used to describe things that are easily changed or impermanent. In contrast, *hard* is used to describe things that are relatively permanent.

- Hardcopy: ***Hardcopy* is tangible output, usually printed.** The principal examples are printouts, whether text or graphics. Film, including microfilm and microfiche, is also considered hardcopy output.

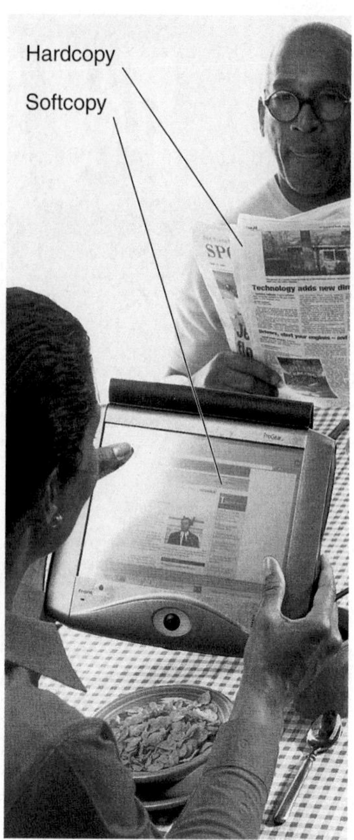

There are several types of softcopy and hardcopy output devices. In the following three sections, we discuss, first, traditional *softcopy* output—*display screens;* second, traditional *hardcopy* output—*printers;* and, third, *mixed* output—including *sound, voice,* and *video*.

Traditional Softcopy Output: Display Screens

Screens, or monitors, display visual processing output in electronic form.

***Display screens*—also variously called *monitors* or simply *screens*—are output devices that show programming instructions and data as they are being input and information after it is processed.** The monitor is the component that displays the visual output from your computer as generated by the video card. It does not do any real computing but rather shows the results of computing.

The most common type of display screen is the flat-panel monitor. ***Flat-panel displays* are made up of two plates of glass separated by a layer of a substance in which light is manipulated.** One flat-panel technology is *liquid crystal display (LCD),* in which molecules of liquid crystal line up in a way that alters their optical properties, creating images on the screen by transmitting or blocking out light. (● *See Panel 5.21.*)

22" Flat-Panel Display

New flat-panel displays

As with TV screens, the size of a computer screen is measured diagonally from corner to corner in inches. For desktop microcomputers, the most common sizes are 15 inches to 30 inches. For laptop computers, they are 12 inches to 18 inches. Increasingly, computer ads state the actual display area, called the *viewable image size (vis),* which may be an inch or so less. A 15-inch monitor may have a 13.8-inch vis; a 17-inch monitor may have a 16-inch vis. Many screens are wider than they are tall and are called *wide-screen monitors.*

Portable computers and smartphones have built-in LCD screens. Tablet screens are usually 8.4 to 14.1 inches; smartphones, 2.5 to 4.1 inches.

In deciding which display screen to buy, you will need to consider issues of screen clarity (dot pitch, resolution, color depth, and refresh rate) and color and resolution standards.

Pixels

SCREEN CLARITY: DOT PITCH, RESOLUTION, COLOR DEPTH, & REFRESH RATE Factors affecting screen clarity (often mentioned in ads) are *dot pitch, resolution, color depth,* and *refresh rate*. These relate to the individual dots on the screen known as *pixels,* which represent the images on the screen. **A *pixel,* for "*pic*ture *el*ement," is the smallest unit on the screen that can be turned on and off or made different shades.** Pixels are tiny squares, not circles.

Microprocessor on the motherboard sends digital video data to the video card.

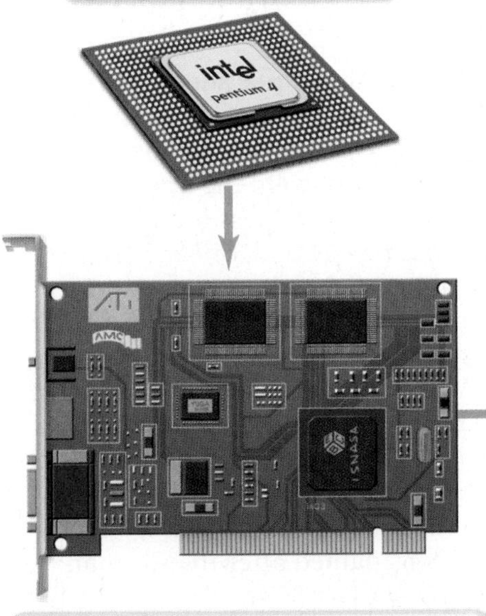

Video card on the motherboard converts digital signals to analog signals and sends them via a cable to the monitor.

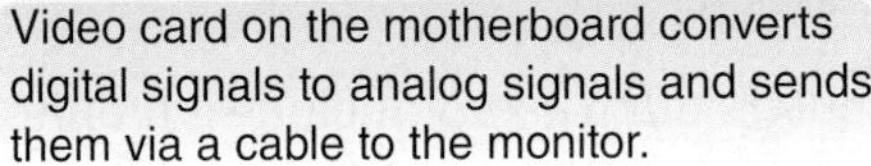

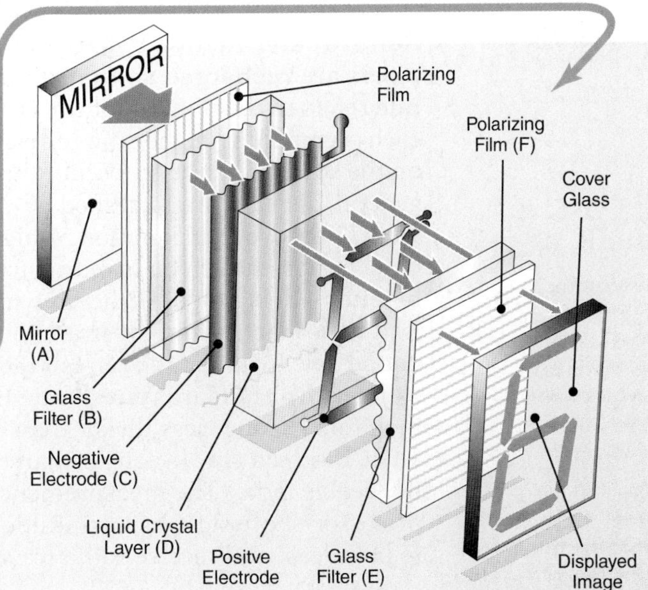

panel 5.21

How a monitor works

Flat-panel monitors are also called liquid crystal display (LCD) monitors. They are composed of two flat pieces of polarized glass. Inside the two pieces is liquid crystal that is backlit. When electrical currents are added to the crystal molecules, they allow certain colors and light to pass through them. They do this by aligning in specific patterns of either on or off, depending on the command. LCDs are used in a wide range of applications, including computer monitors, television, instrument panels, aircraft cockpit displays, and signage. They are common in consumer devices such as video players, gaming devices, clocks, watches, calculators, and telephones.

- **Dot pitch:** ***Dot pitch (dp)*** **(also called pixel pitch) is the amount of space between the centers of adjacent pixels; the closer the pixels, the crisper the image.** For a .25-dp monitor, for instance, the dots (pixels) are 25/100ths of a millimeter apart. Generally, a dot pitch of .25–.28 dp will provide clear images.

- **Resolution:** Here ***resolution*** **refers to the image sharpness of the display screen; the more pixels, or dots, there are per square inch, the finer the level of detail.** As with scanners, resolution is expressed in *dots per inch (dpi),* the number of columns and rows of dots per inch. The higher the number of dots, the clearer and sharper the image. Resolution clarity is measured by the formula *horizontal-row pixels* × *vertical-row pixels.* For example, a 1,024 × 768 screen displays 1,024 pixels on each of 768 lines, for a total of 786,432 pixels. On color monitors, each pixel is assigned some red, some green, some blue, or particular shades of gray.

- **Color depth:** As we said about scanners, ***color depth,*** **or *bit depth,* is the amount of information, expressed in bits, that is stored in a dot.** The more bits in a dot or pixel, the more shades of gray and colors can be represented. With 24-bit color depth, for example, 8 bits are dedicated

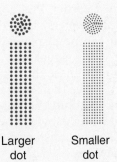

Larger dot pitch | Smaller dot pitch

The Letter " i "

Standard monitor resolutions, in pixels

1,024 x 768 — These are becoming obsolete
1,152 x 864 — These are becoming obsolete
1,280 x 960
1,400 x 1,050
1,600 x 1,200
2,048 x 1,536
3,200 x 2,400
4,000 x 3,000
6,400 x 4,800 >

Standard bit depths for color

8-bit—256 colors

16-bit—65,536 colors

24-bit—16,777,216 colors

to each primary color—red, green, and blue (3 × 8 = 24). If you're not doing anything professionally with graphic art, photography, or videos, then you'll most likely be content with a monitor color depth of only 8 bits, which is standard for most of computing; 24 bit, called *true color*, requires more resources, such as video memory.

- **Refresh rate: *Refresh rate* is the number of times per second that the pixels are recharged so that their glow remains bright.** That is, refresh rate refers to the number of times that the image on the screen is redrawn each second. The higher the refresh rate, the more solid the image looks on the screen and the smoother the video—that is, the less it flickers. In general, displays are refreshed 60–200 times per second, or *hertz (Hz)*, with 72 hertz being common. A high-quality monitor has a refresh rate of 90 hertz—the screen is redrawn 90 times per second. A low-quality monitor will be under 72 hertz, which will cause noticeable flicker and lead to headaches and eyestrain. If you have an LCD monitor, you may not be able to adjust the refresh rate. This is because most LCD monitors come with a standard refresh rate that is well above the flicker point. LCD monitors produce less flicker than older monitors because the pixels on an LCD screen stay lit longer than those in older monitors before they noticeably fade. (The measurement *hertz* was named after the German professor of physics Heinrich Rudolf Hertz [1847–1894], who was the first to broadcast and receive radio waves.)

Note: Advertisements for desktop computers often *do not* include a monitor as part of the system. You need to be prepared to spend a few hundred dollars extra for the monitor.

Survival Tip

Buying a New Monitor?

Be sure it can work with your computer and video card and has enough video RAM to support what you want to do. Also, screens come with a "native" resolution: its normal default setting. You often can change your resolution setting by going to the control panel's display setting. However, if you increase your resolution, the items on your computer's desktop, and the text type, will become smaller. You can fit more content on your screen that way, but the text may be difficult to read.

COLOR & RESOLUTION STANDARDS FOR MONITORS: SVGA & XGA As mentioned earlier, PCs come with *graphics cards* (also known as *video cards* or *video adapters*) that convert signals from the computer into video signals that can be displayed as images on a monitor. The monitor then separates the video signal into three colors: red, green, and blue signals. Inside the monitor, these three colors combine to make up each individual pixel. Video cards have their own memory, video RAM, or VRAM, which stores the information about each pixel. The more VRAM you have, which can range from 2 to 64 megabytes, the higher the resolution you can use. Video gamers and desktop publishers (Photoshop users) will want a video card with lots of VRAM.

The common resolution standards for monitors are *XGA, SXGA, UXGA, QXGA, WXGA, WSXGA+, and WUXGA.* (• *See Panel 5.22.*)

Laptop Buying Guides

http://reviews.cnet.com/4520-7602_7-1016082-3.html

http://laptopbuyingadvice.com/

www.laptop-computer-comparison.com/laptop-buying-guide.html

http://test1labs.com/2011/02/21/laptop-buying-guide-2011/

www.whatthetech.com/2011/02/28/laptop-buying-guide-springsummer-2011/

Traditional Hardcopy Output: Printers

Screens, or monitors, display visual processing output in hardcopy (printed) form.

The prices in ads for computer systems often do not include a printer. Thus, you will need to budget an additional $100–$1,000 or more for a printer. **A *printer* is an output device that prints characters, symbols, and graphics on paper or another hardcopy medium.** As with scanners, the resolution, or quality of sharpness, of the printed image is indicated by *dots per inch (dpi)*, a measure of the number of rows and columns of dots that are printed in a square inch. For microcomputer printers, the resolution is in the range of 600 × 600 to 5,760 × 1,440, with 1,200 × 1,200 being most common.

HP Deskjet 3000 printer 

Printers can be separated into two categories, according to whether or not the image produced is formed by physical contact of the print mechanism with the paper. *Impact printers* do have contact with paper; *nonimpact printers* do not. We also consider plotters and multifunction printers.

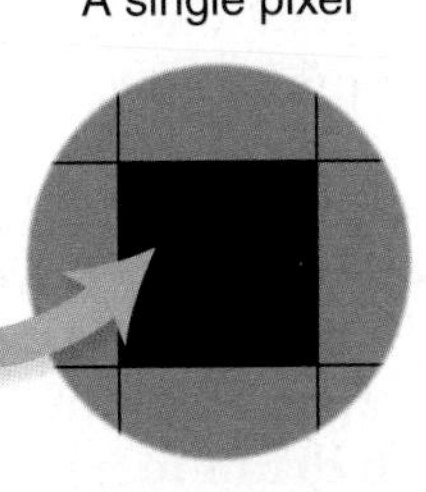

panel 5.22

Video graphics standards

Common Display Standards and Resolutions

Standard	Resolution	Typical Use
XGA (Extended Graphics Array)	1,024 x 768	15-inch LCD monitors
SXGA (Super XGA)	1,280 x 1,024	17- and 19-inch LCD monitors
UXGA (Ultra XGA)	1,600 x 1,200	20-inch LCD monitors
QXGA (Quad XGA)	2,048 x 1,536	20-inch and larger LCD monitors
WXGA (Wide XGA)	1,280 x 800	Wide-screen 15.4-inch laptop LCD displays
WSXGA+ (Wide SXGA plus)	1,680 x 1,050	Wide-screen 20-inch LCD monitors
WUXGA (Wide Ultra XGA)	1,920 x 1,200	Wide-screen 22-inch and larger LCD monitors

IMPACT PRINTERS Impact printers, an old printing technology, are most functional in specialized environments where low-cost printing is essential, such as for label printing, in shipping warehouses, and in hot factory conditions. **An *impact printer* forms characters or images one at a time by striking a mechanism such as a print hammer or wheel against an inked ribbon, leaving an image on paper.** The most common form of impact printer is the dot-matrix printer. A *dot-matrix printer* contains a print head of small pins that strike an inked ribbon against paper, to form characters or images. Print heads are available with 9, 18, or 24 pins; the 24-pin head offers the best quality. Dot-matrix printers can print *draft quality,* a coarser-looking 72 dpi; or *near-letter-quality (NLQ),* a crisper-looking 240 dpi. The machines print 40–300 characters per second and can handle graphics as well as text. A *line printer* is a high-speed impact printer that prints an entire line at a time; this type of printer is used in the automotive, logistic, and banking worlds for high-speed and bar-code printing.

Impact printers are the only desktop printers that can use multilayered forms to print "carbon copies." A disadvantage, however, is the noise they produce, because of the print head striking the paper. Nowadays such printers are more commonly used with mainframes than with personal computers.

NONIMPACT PRINTERS Nonimpact printers are usually faster and quieter than impact printers because no print head strikes paper. ***Nonimpact printers* form characters and images without direct physical contact between the**

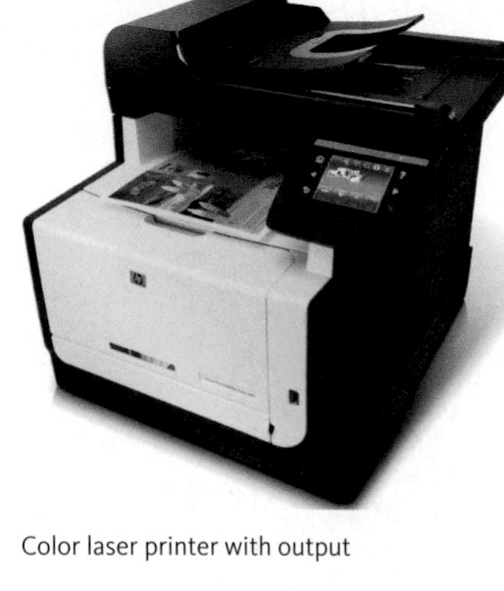

Color laser printer with output

printing mechanism and paper. Two types of nonimpact printers often used with microcomputers are *laser printers* and *inkjet printers*. A third kind, the *thermal printer,* is seen less frequently.

- **Laser printers:** Like a dot-matrix printer, a ***laser printer*** **creates images with dots. However, as in a photocopying machine, these images are produced on a drum, treated with a magnetically charged inklike toner (powder), and then transferred from drum to paper.** (• *See Panel 5.23.)*

  Laser printers run with software called a *page description language (PDL)*. This software tells the printer how to lay out the printed page, and it supports various fonts. A laser printer comes with one of two types of PDL: PostScript (developed by Adobe) or PCL (Printer Control Language, developed by Hewlett-Packard). In desktop publishing (p. 173), PostScript is the preferred PDL. Laser printers have their own CPU, ROM, and memory (RAM), usually 16 megabytes (expandable generally up to 512 megabytes for higher-cost printers). When you need to print out graphics-heavy color documents, your printer will need more memory.

There are good reasons that laser printers are among the most common types of nonimpact printer. They produce sharp, crisp images of both text and graphics. They are quiet and fast—able to print 11–33 pages per minute (ppm) in color and 10.5–37 black-and-white pages per minute for individual microcomputers and up to 200 pages per minute for mainframes. They can print in different *fonts*—that is, sets of typestyles

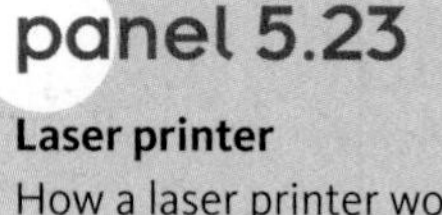

Laser printer
How a laser printer works.

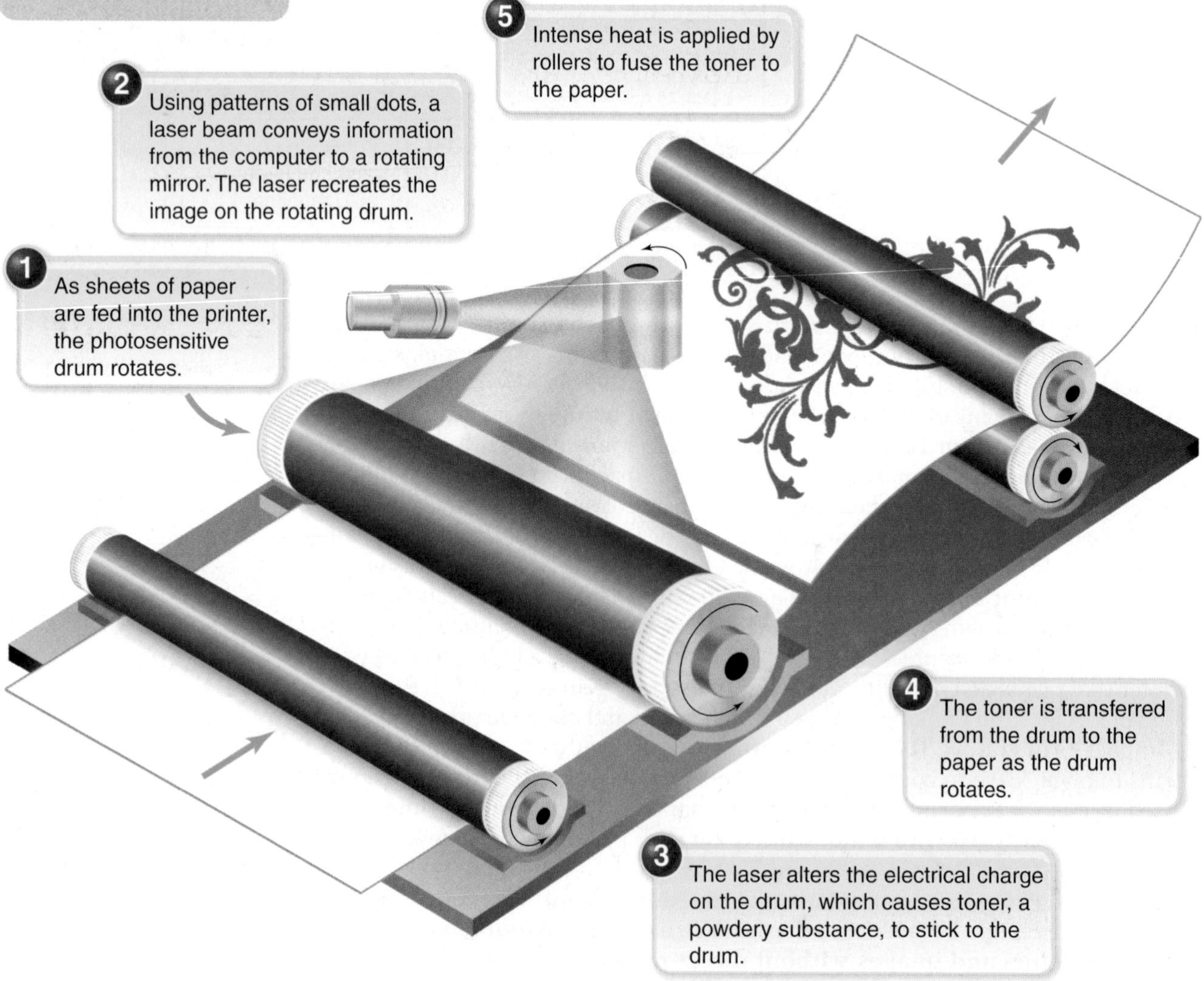

1 As sheets of paper are fed into the printer, the photosensitive drum rotates.

2 Using patterns of small dots, a laser beam conveys information from the computer to a rotating mirror. The laser recreates the image on the rotating drum.

3 The laser alters the electrical charge on the drum, which causes toner, a powdery substance, to stick to the drum.

4 The toner is transferred from the drum to the paper as the drum rotates.

5 Intense heat is applied by rollers to fuse the toner to the paper.

and type sizes. The more expensive models can print in different colors. Laser printers usually have a dpi of 1,200 × 1,200.

- **Inkjet printers:** ***Inkjet printers*** **spray onto paper small, electrically charged droplets of ink from four nozzles through holes in a matrix at high speed.** (• *See Panel 5.24.*) Like laser and dot-matrix printers, inkjet printers form images with little dots. Inkjet printers commonly have a dpi of 4,800 × 1,200 (but can be as high as 9,600 × 2,400); they spray ink onto the page a line at a time, in both high-quality black-and-white text and high-quality color graphics. (To achieve impressive color images, you should use high-quality, high-gloss paper, which prevents inkjet-sprayed dots from *feathering,* or spreading.) Inkjet cartridges come in various combinations: a single cartridge for black and all color inks, two separate black and color cartridges, or separate cartridges for black and each color. Some cartridges also include the print head, which is apt to wear out before the rest of the machine.

  The advantages of inkjet printers are that they can print in color, are quiet, and are generally less expensive than color laser printers. The disadvantages have been that they print a bit less precisely than laser printers do and traditionally they have been slower.

  Another disadvantage is that inkjet cartridges have to be replaced more often than laser-toner cartridges do and so may cost more in the long run. Moreover, a freshly inkjet-printed page is apt to smear unless handled carefully. For users who print infrequently, laser printers (which use toner, a dry powder) have the advantage of not drying out. Laser owners don't have to deal with dried-out cartridges clogging nozzles and wasting expensive ink and time—a common problem for inkjet users.

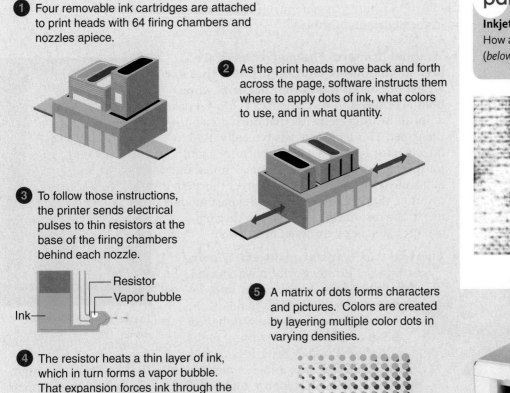

Survival Tip

Do I Have to Print the Whole Thing?

If you click on the shortcut icon on the Windows toolbar (the one that looks like a printer), your entire document will be printed. To print only a portion of your document, go to *File, Print* and check the option you want in the dialog box that appears.

Survival Tip

Digital Subscriptions

Overwhelmed by too many dead-tree (paper) print magazines and newspapers? Try digital subscriptions offered by NewsStand (*www.newsstand.com/?nsemc=nsiconvgo1*) and Zinio Systems (*www.zinio.com*) to read publications on your Tablet PC, desktop, e-reader, or PDA.

1 Four removable ink cartridges are attached to print heads with 64 firing chambers and nozzles apiece.

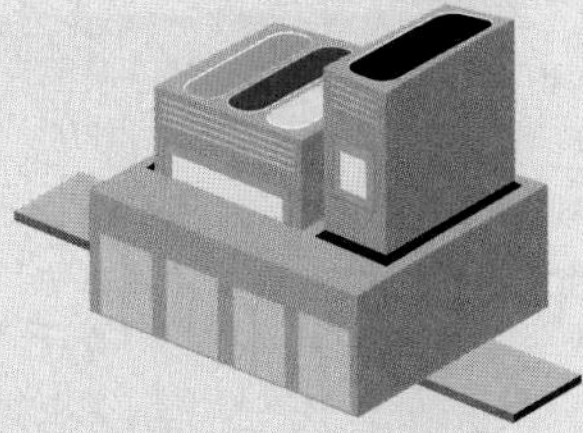

2 As the print heads move back and forth across the page, software instructs them where to apply dots of ink, what colors to use, and in what quantity.

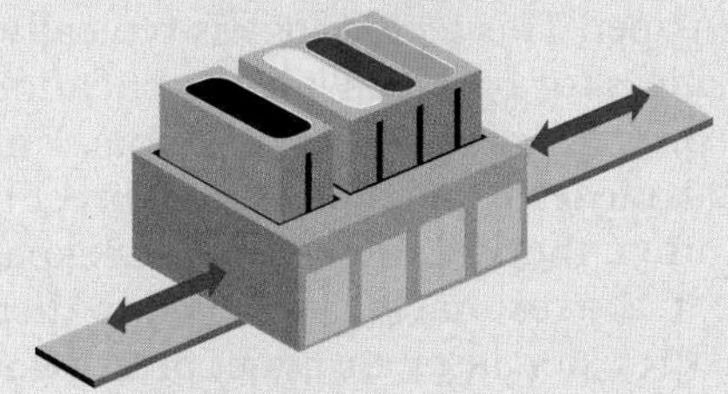

3 To follow those instructions, the printer sends electrical pulses to thin resistors at the base of the firing chambers behind each nozzle.

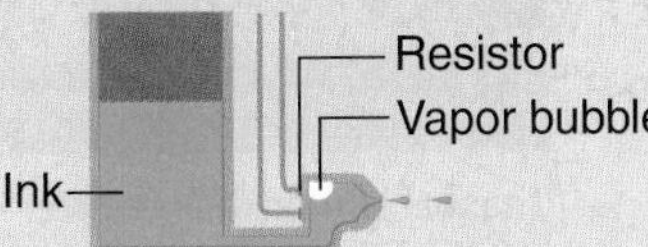

4 The resistor heats a thin layer of ink, which in turn forms a vapor bubble. That expansion forces ink through the nozzle and onto the paper at a rate of about 6,000 dots per second.

5 A matrix of dots forms characters and pictures. Colors are created by layering multiple color dots in varying densities.

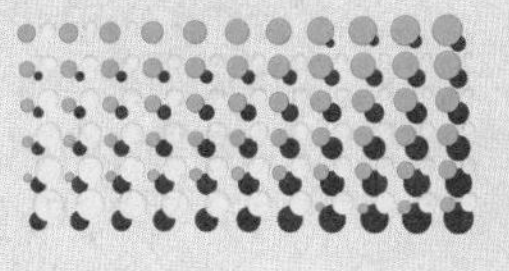

panel 5.24

Inkjet printer

How an inkjet printer works; (*below*) magnified ink dots.

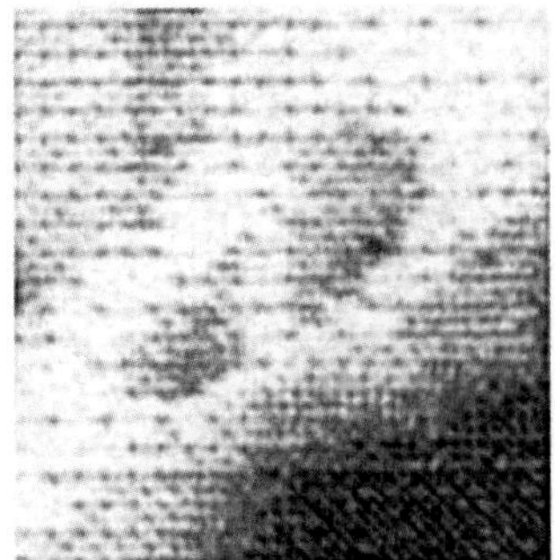

Homaro Cantu, chef-owner at Chicago's Moto Restaurant, prints sushi on a Canon inkjet printer using edible paper made of soybeans and cornstarch and food-based inks of his own concoction. He then flavors the back of the paper with powdered soy sauce and seaweed. Even Mr. Cantu's menu is edible; diners crunch it up into soups.

Survival Tip

Is Your Printer Telling the Truth?

Inkjet printers and laser printers display a message or a light when your ink/toner cartridges need to be replaced. But are they telling the truth? In general, no. Cartridge sales are profitable to the manufacturers. Your cartridges may have a much longer life than your printer is telling you. You can ignore the warning and wait until the toner really does run out; but you might be in the middle of a print job when that happens. Or you can locate the sensor and put a piece of black tape over it, and you may get much more printing out of your cartridges. But then you would not ever get any warning message at all. Before replacing a toner cartridge, try taking it out of the printer and shaking it a few times to redistribute the remaining toner inside the cartridge.

Still, experts maintain that users who want the best-quality photo output should get a photo inkjet printer. Laser printers in general are known for their mediocre photo output, with cheap personal laser printers often doing an especially poor job.

Laser printers are known for handling a much higher volume of printouts than inkjet printers. Buyers who do a lot of printing should pay close attention to a printer's monthly duty cycle, which determines how many printouts a printer can comfortably handle in a month. Going over this can often shorten the life of a printer. In general, cheaper printers have much lower duty cycles than the higher-end printers.

- **Thermal printers: *Thermal printers* are low- to medium-resolution printers that use a type of coated paper that darkens when heat is applied to it.** The paper is moved past a line of heating elements that burn dots onto the paper. This technology is typically used in business for bar-code label applications and for printing cash register receipts. Until about 2000, most fax machines used direct thermal printing, though now only the cheapest models use it, the rest having switched to thermal wax-transfer, laser, or inkjet printing.

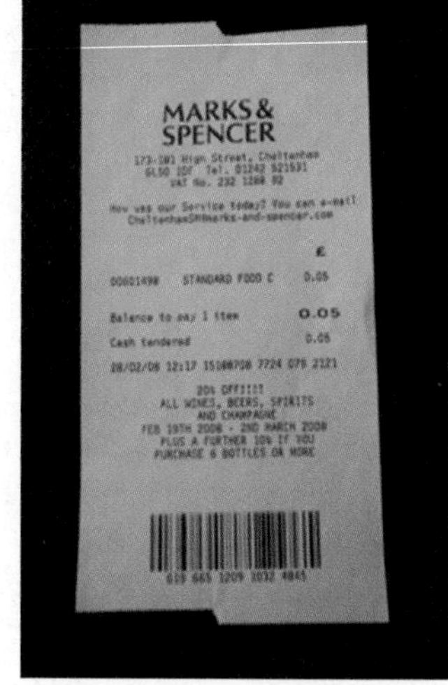

Thermal printed cash-register receipt

- **Thermal wax-transfer printers:** *Thermal wax-transfer printers* print a wax-based ink onto paper. As the paper and ribbon travel in unison beneath the thermal print head, the wax-based ink from the transfer ribbon melts onto the paper. After it becomes cool, the wax adheres permanently to the paper. Although such printers are highly reliable, they still don't compare with modern inkjet printers and color laser printers. However, because of their waterfastness, they find uses in industrial label printing.

Wax-transfer thermal printed label

Dye-sublimation photo printer

- **Photo printers:** *Photo printers* are specialized machines for printing continuous-tone photo prints (typically 3 × 5 or 4 × 6 inches), using special dye-receptive paper and ribbons with special transparent color dyes. Paper and ribbon pass together over the printhead, which contains thousands of heating elements producing varying amounts of heat. The hotter the element, the more dye is released, and as the temperature is varied, shades of each color can be overlaid on top of one another. The dyes are transparent and blend (sublimate) into continuous-tone color. Some inexpensive ($70–$200) photo printers are designed to be unplugged and taken on the go; in fact, they connect directly to a digital camera. These printers connect to the computer or digital camera via USB cable or wireless infrared.

panel 5.25

Multifunction device

This machine combines four functions in one—printer, copier, fax machine, and scanner.

MULTIFUNCTION PRINTERS: **Printers That Do More than Print *Multifunction printers* combine several capabilities, such as printing, scanning, copying, and faxing.** (• *See Panel 5.25.*) Brother, Canon, Epson, and Hewlett-Packard make machines in a price range of $100–$500 that combine a photocopier, fax machine, scanner, and inkjet printer. Several manufacturers offer all-in-one printers that also connect wirelessly to the Internet, allowing users to bypass their computer and print out Web content in paper form. Multifunction printers take up less space and can cost less than the four separate office machines that they replace.

PLOTTERS **A *plotter* is a specialized output device designed to produce large, high-quality graphics in a variety of colors.** (• *See Panel 5.26.*) Plotter lines are not made up of dots; they are actually drawn.

panel 5.26

Large-format plotters

PRACTICAL ACTION

Buying a Printer

Some questions to consider when you're buying a printer:

- *Do I need color, or will black-only do?* Are you mainly printing text, or will you need to produce color charts and illustrations (and, if so, how often)? If you print lots of black text, consider getting a laser printer. If you might occasionally print color, get an inkjet that will accept cartridges for both black and color. Unless you are in the publishing or design business, you will probably not need an expensive color laser printer.
- *Do I have other special output requirements?* Do you need to print envelopes or labels? Special fonts (type styles)? Multiple copies? Transparencies or on heavy paper? Unusual paper size? Find out if the printer comes with envelope feeders, sheet feeders holding at least 100 sheets, or whatever will meet your requirements.
- *Is the printer easy to set up?* Can you easily plug in the hardware, and adjust the software (the driver programs) to make the printer work with your computer?
- *Is the printer easy to operate?* Can you add paper, replace ink/toner cartridges or ribbons, and otherwise operate the printer without much difficulty?
- *Does the printer provide the speed and quality I want?* A laser printer prints about 11–37 pages per minute (ppm); a color inkjet prints about 17–34 ppm. Colors and graphics take longer to print. Are the blacks dark enough and the colors vivid enough?
- *Will I get a reasonable cost per page?* Special paper, ink or toner cartridges (especially color), and ribbons are all ongoing costs. Inkjet color cartridges, for example, may last 100–500 pages and cost $2–$30 new. Laser toner cartridges can cost up to $100 each but last much longer. Ask the seller what the cost per page works out to.
- *Is printer memory an issue?* Printers have their own dedicated memory, and you can install more printer memory to avoid problems and print larger files. All printers come with a certain amount of printer memory installed—usually 2 MB, 4 MB, or 16 MB—but most are upgradeable to handle more or larger print jobs. Printer memory is directly linked to two print characteristics: speed and print quality. More memory allows you to print faster and print larger, high-quality graphics at higher resolutions. (When you send a print job at a higher resolution than your printer cannot handle, your printer automatically drops your print job's resolution down to a resolution that it can handle.)

  Printer memory is used to store (buffer) print jobs after they are received from the computer. If it is overloaded, an error message saying "network printer is busy" will display. However, you shouldn't have to worry about memory unless you work in a crowded office with lots of print jobs.
- *What resolution do I need?* For general-purpose printing, 300 dpi should be sufficient; if you work in graphics, 600 (600 x 600) dpi is better; if you want high-quality photos, 1,200 dpi is preferred. Professionals in desktop publishing and graphics will probably want an even higher resolution.
- *Should I get a multifunction printer?* If you are short on space and have multiple tasks, then you should consider an all-in-one wireless printer: printer, scanner, fax machine, copier. Multifunction machines are good for people limited on space and money. Figuring out whether you need to go all-in-one or not is a matter of necessity. If you need to scan and print, then you need a multifunction machine, because getting a separate scanner and printer would be a waste of money and space. If all you do is print documents and random web articles and never scan pictures, then you should save money and get a single-function printer.
- *Do I need wireless printing?* Wireless printing (or Wi-Fi) is one of the best innovations applied to printers. If you don't like wires, if you have a laptop, or you are just short on space, then you might want Wi-Fi.
- *Does the manufacturer offer a good warranty and good telephone technical support?* Find out if the warranty for a printer lasts at least 2 years. See if the printer's manufacturer offers telephone support in case you have technical problems. The best support systems offer toll-free numbers and operate evenings and weekends as well as weekdays. (If you can, try calling tech support before you buy and see what happens.)

The plotter was the first computer output device that could not only print graphics but also accommodate full-size engineering, three-dimensional, and architectural drawings, as well as maps. Using different colored pens, it was also able to print in color long before inkjet printers became an alternative. Plotters are still the most affordable printing device for computer-aided design (CAD) and offer much higher resolutions than desktop printers do. Plotters are controlled by PCL and HPCL (Hewlett-Packard Control Language).

The three principal kinds of plotters are pen, electrostatic, and large-format:

- **Pen:** A *pen plotter* uses one or more colored pens to draw on paper or transparencies.
- **Electrostatic:** In an *electrostatic plotter,* paper lies partially flat on a tablelike surface, and toner is used in a photocopier-like manner.
- **Large-format:** *Large-format plotters* operate somewhat like an inkjet printer but on a much larger scale. This type of plotter is often used by graphic artists.

SPECIALTY PRINTERS Specialty printers exist for such purposes as printing certain types of labels, tickets, and text in Braille.

Mixed Output: Sound, Voice, & Video

Multimedia output requires several peripherals.

Most PCs are now multimedia computers, capable of displaying and printing not only traditional softcopy and hardcopy text and graphics but also sound, voice, and video, as we consider next.

SOUND OUTPUT ***Sound-output* devices produce digitized sounds, ranging from beeps and chirps to music.** To use sound output, you need appropriate software and a sound card. The sound card could be Sound Blaster or, since that brand has become a de facto standard, one that is "Sound Blaster–compatible." Well-known brands include Creative Labs, Diamond, and Turtle Beach. The sound card plugs into an expansion slot in your computer; on newer computers, it is integrated with the motherboard.

Not too long ago, the audio emerging from a computer had the crackly sound of an old vacuum-tube radio. Then, in 1997, audio in personal computers began to shift to three-dimensional sound. Now, a PC with two speakers can sound more like a "surround sound" movie house. Unlike conventional stereo sound, 3-D audio describes an expanded field of sound—a broad arc starting at the right ear and curving around to the left. Thus, in a video game, you might hear a rocket

Survival Tip

Customize Your Sounds

In Windows, open the Control Panel and click on the Sound icon, then the Sounds tab. Once there you can change all the sounds Windows outputs. Click on the event you want to alter the sound for, click the *Browse* button, and then select a new sound file. Don't assign long sound sequences to common events; they'll become annoying. Many websites offer "themes" for your computer—you can download sound bites from your favorite movies and TV shows.

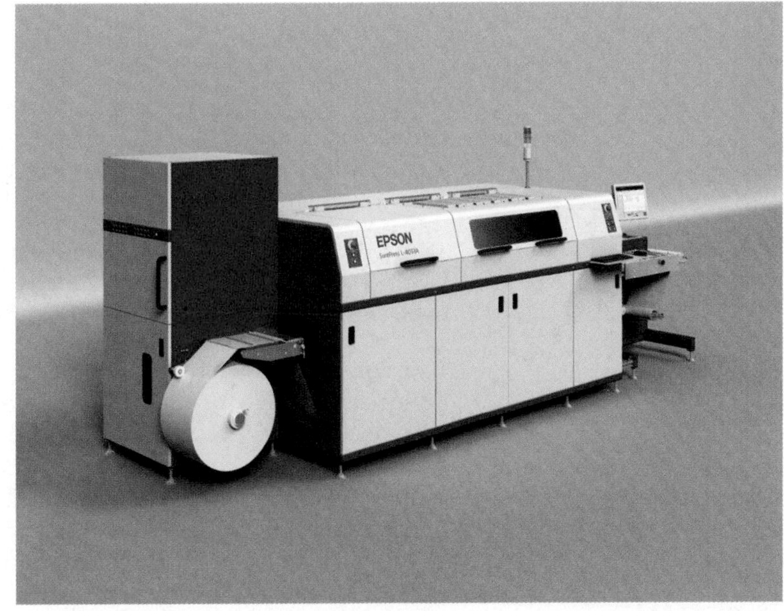

(*Left*) Proofreader Ed Kochanowski proofreads a Braille edition of *Beowulf* at the National Braille Press in Boston. (*Right*) SurePress digital label printer.

approach, go by, and explode off your right shoulder. The effect is achieved by boosting certain frequencies that provide clues to a sound's location in the room or by varying the timing of sounds from different speakers. You can augment your computer's internal speakers with external speakers for high-quality sound.

AT&T's TTS Program

To find out more about this program and listen to audio demonstrations, go to:

www.research.att.com/~ttsweb/tts/demo.php

VOICE OUTPUT ***Voice-output devices*** **convert digital data into speechlike sounds.** You hear such forms of voice output on telephones ("Please hang up and dial your call again"), in soft-drink machines, in cars, in toys and games, and in mapping software for vehicle-navigation devices. Voice portals read news and other information to users on the go.

One form of voice output that is becoming popular is *text-to-speech (TTS) systems,* which convert computer text into audible speech. TTS benefits not only the visually impaired but also anyone with a computer system sound card and speakers who wants to reduce reading chores (and eyestrain) and do other tasks at the same time. Windows offers a TTS program called Narrator; others are CoolSpeech, Balabolka, Natural Reader, NeoSpeech, and Digalo. AOL, Yahoo!, and MapQuest have licensed a high-quality TTS program developed by the AT&T Natural Voices Lab to read email, give driving directions, provide stock quotes, and more.

VIDEO OUTPUT ***Video*** **consists of photographic images, which are played at 15–29 frames per second to give the appearance of full motion.** Video is input into a multimedia system using a video camera or VCR and, after editing, is output on a computer's display screen. Because video files can require a great deal of storage—a 3-minute video may require 1 gigabyte of storage—video is often compressed. Good video output requires a powerful processor as well as a video card.

Another form of video output is ***videoconferencing*, in which people in different geographic locations can have a meeting—can see and hear one another—using computers and communications.** Videoconferencing systems range from videophones to group conference rooms with cameras and multimedia equipment to desktop systems with small video cameras, microphones, and speakers. (We discuss videoconferencing in more detail in Chapter 6.)

5.4 INPUT & OUTPUT TECHNOLOGY & QUALITY OF LIFE: Health & Ergonomics

Ergonomics studies the relationship between workers and their environments.

Danielle Weatherbee, a medical supplies saleswoman who's on the road constantly, spends much of her time hunched over the keyboard of her notebook computer on planes, in coffee shops, in bed, and even in taxicabs. Her neck and wrists constantly ache. Her doctor has said she has the skeletal health of a much older person. "But what can I do?" Weatherbee says. "My laptop is the only way to go for my work. I couldn't live without it."[10]

Health Matters

Information technology can affect the health of human beings.

The computer clearly has negative health consequences for some people. College students, for example, may be susceptible to back, shoulder, wrist, and neck aches because they often use laptops, which—unlike desktop computers—have keyboard and screen too close to each other. "When you use a laptop, you can make your head and neck comfortable, or you can make your hands and arms comfortable, but it's impossible to do both," says Tom Albin of the Human Factors and Ergonomics Society, an organization that issues standards on the use of computers.[11] Observes another expert about students,

"They sit in lecture halls with built-in tables, hunched over their laptops eight hours a day, and you can see it's very uncomfortable with them. Even if they could move their chairs, that would be a help."[12]

Let's consider some of the adverse health effects of computers. These may include repetitive strain injuries, eyestrain and headache, and back and neck pains. We will also consider the effects of electromagnetic fields and noise.

REPETITIVE STRESS INJURIES ***Repetitive stress (or strain) injuries (RSIs)*** **are wrist, hand, arm, and neck injuries resulting when muscle groups are forced through fast, repetitive motions.** Most victims of RSI are in dentistry, meatpacking, automobile manufacturing, poultry slaughtering, and clothing manufacturing, which require awkward wrist positions. Musicians, too, are often troubled by RSI (because of long hours of practice).

People who use computer keyboards—some superstar data-entry operators reportedly regularly average 15,000 keystrokes an hour—account for some RSI cases that result in lost work time. Before computers came along, typists would stop to make corrections or change paper. These motions had the effect of providing many small rest breaks. Today keyboard users must devise their own mini-breaks to prevent excessive use of hands and wrists (or install a computer program that uses animated characters to remind users to take breaks and provide suggestions for exercises). People who use a mouse for more than a few hours a day—graphic designers, desktop-publishing professionals, and the like—are also showing up with increased RSI injuries. The best advice is to find a mouse large enough so that your hand fits comfortably over it, and don't leave your hand on the mouse when you are not using it. You might also try using function keys instead of the mouse whenever possible.

RSIs

The United Food and Commercial Workers International Union provides detailed information about RSIs at:

www.ufcw.org/workplace_connections/retail/safety_health_news_and_facts/rep_stress_overview.cfm

Among the various RSIs, some, such as muscle strain and tendinitis, are painful but usually not crippling. These injuries may be cured by rest, anti-inflammatory medication, and change in typing technique. One type of RSI, carpal tunnel syndrome, is disabling and often requires surgery. ***Carpal tunnel syndrome (CTS)*** **is a debilitating condition caused by pressure on the median nerve in the wrist, producing damage and pain to nerves and tendons in the hands.** It is caused by short repetitive movements, such as typing, knitting, and using vibrating tools for hours on end. The lack of rest in between these motions irritates and inflames the flexor tendons that travel with the median nerve to the hand through an area in the wrist called the "carpal tunnel," which is surrounded by bones and a transverse ligament. The inflamed tendons squeeze the nerve against the ligament.

EYESTRAIN & HEADACHES Vision problems are actually more common than RSI problems among computer users. Computers compel people to use their eyes at close range for a long time. However, our eyes were made to see most efficiently at a distance. It's not surprising, then, that people develop what's called *computer vision syndrome.*

Computer vision syndrome (CVS) **consists of eyestrain, headaches, double vision, and other problems caused by improper use of computer display screens.** By "improper use," we mean not only staring at the screen for too long but also failing to correct faulty lighting and screen glare and using screens with poor resolution.

BACK & NECK PAINS Improper chairs or improper positioning of keyboards and display screens can lead to back and neck pains. All kinds of adjustable, special-purpose furniture and equipment are available to avoid or diminish such maladies.

ELECTROMAGNETIC FIELDS Like kitchen appliances, hairdryers, and television sets, many devices related to computers and communications generate low-level electromagnetic field emissions. ***Electromagnetic fields (EMFs)*** **are waves of electrical energy and magnetic energy.**

In recent years, stories have appeared in the mass media reflecting concerns that high-voltage power lines, cellphones, wireless mice, and old computer monitors might be harmful. There have been worries that old monitors might be linked to miscarriages and birth defects and that cellphones and power lines might lead to some types of cancers.

Is there anything to this? The answer, so far, is that no one is sure. The evidence is inconclusive whether weak electromagnetic fields, such as those used for cellphones and found near high-voltage lines, cause cancer. Still, handheld cellphones do put the radio transmitter next to the user's head. This causes some health professionals concern about the effects of radio waves entering the brain as they seek out the nearest cellular transmitter. Thus, in the United Kingdom, the Independent Expert Study Group on Mobile Phones recommended that children should use cellphones only when necessary, and Norway's Ombudsman for Children has said that children under the age of 13 should not have their own mobile phones. Dr. Lief Salford of Lund University in Sweden, who has called the evolution of wireless phones "the largest biological experiment in the history of the world," reported that cellphone radiation damaged neurons in the brains of young rats.[13] Another study found that cellphone users face a 50% greater risk of developing tumors of the parotid gland than do people who do not use cellphones.[14] However, an August 2005 study found no increased risk of brain tumors associated with using a cellphone for at least 10 years.[15] But recently, in May 2011, the World Health Organization reported that a 14-country study found enough evidence to categorize cellphone use as "possibly carcinogenic to humans"—they found some evidence of increase in certain kinds of brain cancers in cellphone users. "When you look at cancer development—particularly brain cancer—it takes a long time to develop. I think it is a good idea to give the public some sort of warning that long-term exposure to radiation from your cellphone could possibly cause cancer," said Dr. Henry Lai, research professor in bioengineering at University of Washington, who has studied radiation for more than 30 years.[16]

The Federal Communications Commission (FCC) has created a measurement called *Specific Absorption Rate (SAR)* to give consumers data on the radiation levels their phones produce.

What's Your Cellphone's Radiation level?

Cellphones' SAR levels are available at:

http://reviews.cnet.com/cell-phone-radiation-levels/

More on EMFs

Do you have CVS? What are computer eyeglasses? Find out at:

www.allaboutvision.com/cvs/faqs.htm

www.aoa.org/x5253.xml

www.doctorergo.com/

NOISE The chatter of impact printers or hum of fans in computer power units can be psychologically stressful to many people. Sound-muffling covers are available for impact printers. Some system units may be placed on the floor under the desk to minimize noise from fans. Of course, people talking on hands-free headsets and wireless mobile devices can cause noise problems, too.

Ergonomics: Design with People in Mind

People are any company's most important assets; if their work environment is poor, then their health and their work may be, too.

Previously, workers had to fit themselves to the job environment. However, health and productivity issues have spurred the development of a relatively new field, called *ergonomics,* that is concerned with fitting the job environment to the worker.

The purpose of *ergonomics* is to make working conditions and equipment safer and more efficient. It is concerned with designing hardware and software that are less stressful and more comfortable to use, that blend more smoothly with a person's body or actions. Examples of ergonomic hardware are tilting display screens, detachable keyboards, and keyboards hinged in the middle to allow the users' wrists to rest in a more natural position.

We address some additional ergonomic issues in the Experience Box at the end of this chapter.

Ergonomics for Kids

To learn how to set up an ergonomic workstation for children, go to:

www.businessweek.com/magazine/content/02_51/b3813121.htm

For more general government ergonomic guidelines, go to:

www.osha.gov

and then search for *computer workstations.*

5.5 THE FUTURE OF INPUT & OUTPUT

Input and output devices will become more useful for people with disabilities and for people working in nontraditional environments.

Science Sensors

Want to see how biologists study 30 acres of nature with wireless-network-linked sensors? Go to:

www.jamesreserve.edu

Toward More Input from Remote Locations

Data can be input from more and more remote locations.

The linkage of computers and telecommunications means that data may be input from nearly anywhere. For instance, X-ray machines are now going digital, which means that a medical technician in the jungles of South America can take an X ray of a patient and then transmit a perfect copy of it by satellite uplink to a hospital in Boston. Visa and MasterCard are moving closer to using "smart cards," or stored-value cards, for Internet transactions. Cell-PREVEN was created to allow access to real-time data to members of the healthcare ecosystem in Peru. This interactive voice response system enables health workers in the field to collect and transmit data via basic mobile phones. The data is aggregated in a centralized database and made available to medical professionals, and the system is designed to send text messages or email alerts if certain symptoms are recorded.

Mouse-Pointer Systems for the Disabled

To learn more about this subject, use the following keywords to search the web: *Eye Link 10000, faceLAB, Eye Gaze, CameraMouse, Quadjoy,* and *www.laesieworks.com/spinal/spinal-comp.html.* A laptop with eye-tracking input technology is already available: *www.nytimes.com/2011/03/27/business/27novel.html.*

Toward More Source Data Automation

The increased use of source-data entry will increase the reliability of data.

Increasingly, input technology is being designed to capture data at its source, which will reduce the costs and mistakes associated with copying or otherwise preparing data in a form suitable for processing. We mentioned some possible innovations in high-capacity bar codes, more sophisticated scanners, smarter smart cards, and widespread use of sensors. Some reports from elsewhere on the input-technology front:

INPUT HELP FOR THE DISABLED Some devices now available for people with physical disabilities, such as paraplegics, may portend new ways of entering and manipulating data input. For example, in one system a camera and special software enable users to operate the on-screen pointer with their eye movements instead of their hands. In another hands-free system, a camera tracks the user's body movements and the system converts them into mouse-pointer movements on the screen. In yet another system, the user's breathing controls the screen pointer. In a fourth, the nose is used to direct the cursor on a computer screen. There is also a system that can be attached to a baseball cap, enabling head movements to control the pointer. There is a web-based application called Web Anywhere that provides verbal feedback and enables blind people to use any Internet-connected computer, allowing them to type up a quick email at an Internet café or check a flight time on a public computer at the airport. Tongue movement alone, it's been suggested, could become an input device for assisting with computers, home appliances, and wheelchair control. Finally, there are ideas about implanting video cameras behind the fake eyeball of those who have lost an eye.

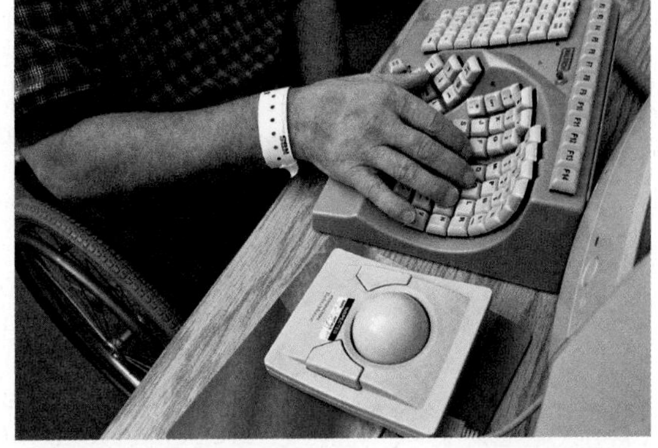

(*Top*) One-handed keyboard. (*Bottom*) Special mouse/digitizer and pointing stick to press keys.

MORE SOPHISTICATED TOUCH DEVICES As we mentioned, touch screens are becoming more and more popular. Microsoft, for instance, has developed the Surface tabletop computer, an interactive, 30-inch touch-responsive table that can be used to order meals or display maps. It is now in use at Harrah's Rio hotel in Las Vegas and in AT&T phone stores. Microsoft executives see surface computing as an alternative to the mouse and keyboard, one that could have far-reaching effects on the office, living room, and car.

Researchers in what is known as *hepatic*—active touch—systems are exploring how to create devices that will allow people to feel what isn't there. With this kind of "virtual touch," a dental student could train in drilling down into the decay of a simulated tooth without fear of destroying a real healthy tooth. Doctors would have new surgical tools, videogames would be made more realistic, and drivers would be able to manipulate dials and knobs without taking their eyes off the road.

BETTER SPEECH RECOGNITION It's possible that speech recognition may someday fulfill world travelers' fondest dream: You'll be able to speak in English, and a speech-recognition device will instantly translate your remarks into another language, whether French, Swahili, or Japanese. At the moment, translation programs such as Easy Translator can translate text on web pages (English to Spanish, French, and German and the reverse), although they do so imperfectly. Research is also going forward on speech-recognition software that can decode slight differences in pitch, timing, and amplitude, so that computers can recognize anger and pain, for example. And already voice-recognition techniques have been applied to animal sounds, so that, for instance, farmers can be alerted to unrest in the pigpen or cows in heat.

IMPROVED DIGITAL CAMERAS Microsoft has invented a wide-angle, fish-eye lens digital camera that can be worn like a badge, recording all the still and video images of the wearer's daily life. A boon to bird-watchers, sports spectators, and opera goers is the appearance of binoculars with built-in digital cameras, so that one can bring home photos or digital movies.

A future feature of cellphone cameras is exploitation of a branch of a field of computer science called *augmented reality*—which gave us yellow first-down lines (which really don't exist) on the field of televised football games—which will enable camera users to "see information about nearby restaurants, ATMs, and available jobs in front of buildings that house them," in one description.[17]

Gesture Recognition

For an update on the progress in gesture-recognition technology, go to:

www.youtube.com/watch?v=gTjV_BYUvtM

www.gesturecentral.com

www.gesturetek.com/

www.engineerlive.com/Asia-Pacific-Engineer/Automotive-Design/Gesture_%26lsquo%3Brecognition%26rsquo%3B_could_improve_automotive_safety/16927/gesture+recognition+automotive

www.igesture.org/

GESTURE RECOGNITION Researchers have been trying to apply gesturing to computing input devices for decades, and we have already seen the development of the *accelerometer,* a motion sensor that allows machines to respond to movement without waiting for humans to push a button. The Apple iPhone and Nintendo's Wii game console, for instance, currently feature similar technology, and many cellphones, computers, and other gadgets are being produced that are sensitive to motion.

Gesture recognition also is a key component in the idea of *pervasive computing,* which refers to having access to computing tools any place at any time. For example, a display could appear on a wall or wherever you want. To make pervasive computing work, however, users need to have an input device available wherever they are, a process often referred to as *human-centric computing.* Through human-centric computing, the user is always connected to computing tools. Gesture-recognition technology could provide the needed input capabilities for both types of computing.

PATTERN-RECOGNITION & BIOMETRIC DEVICES Would you believe a computer could read people's emotions from changes in their facial patterns, like surprise and sadness? Such devices are being worked on at Georgia Institute of Technology and elsewhere. (● *See Panel 5.27.*) Indeed, you can buy a face-recognition program so that you can have your computer respond only to your smile.

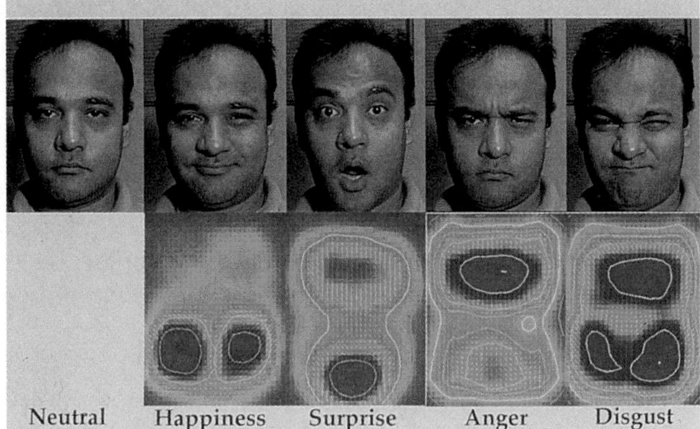

panel 5.27

Computers tuned to emotions

At Georgia Institute of Technology, researchers devised a computer system that can read people's emotions from changes in their faces. Expressions of happiness, surprise, and other movements of facial muscles are converted by a special camera into digitized renderings of energy patterns.

BRAINWAVE DEVICES Perhaps the ultimate input device analyzes the electrical signals of the brain and translates them into computer commands. In one experiment, 100 tiny sensors were implanted in the brain of a 25-year-old quadriplegic who, using just his thoughts, was able to control a computer well enough to operate a TV, open email, and play Pong with 70% accuracy. At the University of Pittsburgh, macaque monkeys with electrical sensors in their brains have learned to feed themselves with robotic arms, an experiment billed as the first successful use of a "brain-machine interface" to control a robotic limb for a practical function. Users have successfully moved a cursor on the screen through the sheer power of thought. Emotiv Systems of San Francisco even offers a noninvasive technology that allows players to manipulate objects in video games simply with their thoughts.

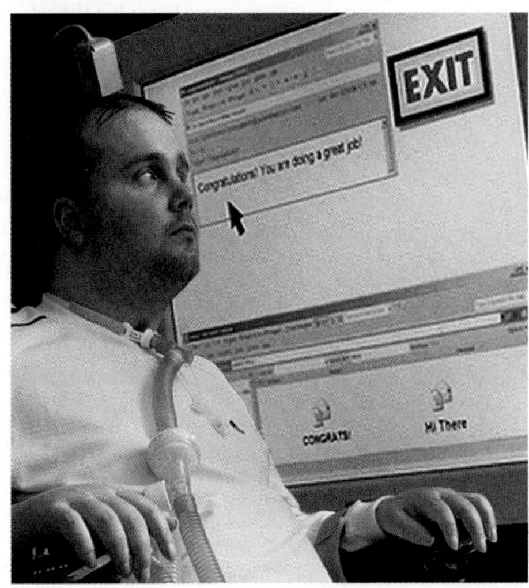

Quadriplegic Matt Nagle was the first person to use brain/computer interface called BrainGate—connected to a computer by a cable screwed into his head. The 4-millimeter square chip, placed on the surface of the motor cortex area of the brain, contained 100 electrodes, each thinner than a hair, that detected neural electrical activity. The sensor was connected to a computer via a small wire attached to a pedestal mounted on the skull. Nagle was able to check email and play computer games simply by using thoughts. He could also turn lights on and off and control a television, all while talking and moving his head.

Toward More Realistic Output

Output technology is getting more and more refined.

Another interesting new output technology: so-called *audio spotlight* or *directed-sound technology* projects sound in a focused beam so that only people in a certain spot can hear it. Court TV used the technology in New York and Atlanta bookstores to promote a murder mystery show. When customers tripped a motion sensor, they would suddenly hear a voice whispering a 30-second message that said in part: "Don't turn around. Do you ever think about murder? Committing the ultimate crime? I do. All the time." Directed-sound devices use narrow beams of ultrasound waves that can't be heard by human ears; the beam distorts air as it passes through, generating sound people can hear. The biggest use of such technology, unfortunately, is for advertising, so that messages could be sent to customers in grocery store checkout lines without disturbing the store's staff.

DISPLAY SCREENS: BETTER & CHEAPER New gas-plasma technology is being employed to build flat-panel hang-on-the-wall screens as large as 50 inches from corner to corner. Using a technique known as *microreplication,* researchers have constructed a thin transparent sheet of plastic prisms that allows builders of portable computer screens to halve the amount of battery power required.

E Ink's flexible display screen on 0.3-millimeter thick electronic "paper" with millions of tiny capsules with black-and-white pigment chips and transmitting electrodes (*www.youtube.com/watch?v=VO63-iYNAFo*).

PRINTERS: REDUCING PRINTER INK Xerox is hoping to help companies survive with fewer printers and copiers and less paper through a new technology they call *erasable paper.* The idea here is that you would print out a document you need only temporarily, then feed it through a machine with a heating element, which would make the document images disappear—so that you could reuse the paper for something else. Another company, called Zink (short for "zero ink"; *www.zink.com/how-ZINK-works*), is getting rid of ink entirely. Its approach is to encode paper with billions of dye crystals. To produce an image, a print head emits heat pulses that melt the dye crystals, turning them into the desired colors.

VIDEO: MOVIE QUALITY FOR PCS New technology based on digital wavelet theory, a complicated mathematical theory, has led to software that can compress digitized pictures into fewer bytes and do it more quickly than current standards. Indeed, the technology can display 30–38 frames a second—"real-time video." Images have the look and feel of a movie.

In addition, advanced graphics chips from firms such as Nvidia and NTI are increasing the realism of animation, making possible lifelike imagery through the use of geometric building blocks called *polygons*.

THREE-DIMENSIONAL OUTPUT In the 1930s radiologists tried to create three-dimensional images by holding up two slightly offset X rays of the same object and crossing their eyes. Now the same effects can be achieved by computers. With 3-D technology, flat, cartoonlike images give way to rounded objects with shadows and textures. Artists can even add "radiosity," so that a dog standing next to a red car, for instance, will pick up a red glow.

In the early 21st century, we have 3-D versions of films such as *Monsters vs. Aliens, My Bloody Valentine, Avatar, Alice in Wonderland, Tron,* and others in theaters. Indeed, for some of the top Hollywood filmmakers (such as *Titanic* director James Cameron, maker of the 2009 *Avatar*), digital 3-D looks like the future of movies.[18] But 3-D is also a reality in home theaters, with many companies selling what they call "3-D ready" TV sets.[19] In addition, Nvidia markets the GeForce 3D Vision system, which consists of software and special glasses that connect wirelessly to your PC, which can be used for existing games and other software as well as movies.[20]

But the same technology that makes images pop off movie screens is now being used for all kinds of other purposes as well.[21] Three-dimensional printers using inkjet printer heads are able to output layer after layer of images printed on starch or plaster, producing 3-D objects. In the future, this technology may be used to print on plastics and metals to produce electronic components, such as transistors. Military engineers have developed the Mobile Parts Hospital, in which technicians use workstations and robotic machine tools to fabricate replacement parts, such as bolts or machine-gun mounts, that lasers then will "print" as powdered metal, layer by layer. Medical researchers have even used 3-D printing technology to print layers of cells, building intricate tissue structures. And researchers have used older-model inkjet printers to spray cells onto a gauze scaffolding to create living tissue—artificial skin that may be of help to burn victims.

Using the Smithsonian

What kind of technology does the Smithsonian Museum in Washington, D.C., have on display? Find the museum's website and enter keywords of computer terms.

EXPERIENCE BOX

Good Habits: Protecting Your Computer System, Your Data, & Your Health

Whether you set up a desktop computer and never move it or carry a portable PC or smartphone from place to place, you need to be concerned about protecting not only your computer but yourself. You don't want your computer to get stolen or zapped by a power surge. You don't want to lose your data. And you certainly don't want to lose your health for computer-related reasons. Here are some tips for taking care of these vital areas.

Guarding against Hardware Theft & Loss

Portable computers are easy targets for thieves. Obviously, anything conveniently small enough to be slipped into your briefcase or backpack can be slipped into someone else's. Never leave a portable computer unattended in a public place. Also, never leave it in plain sight or in a very hot or very cold place; computers are sensitive to extreme temperatures.

It's also possible to simply lose a portable—for example, forgetting it's in the overhead luggage bin in an airplane. To help in its return, use a wide piece of clear tape to tape a card with your name and address to the outside of the machine. You should tape a similar card to the inside also. In addition, scatter a few such cards in the pockets of the carrying case. Desktop computers are also easily stolen. However, for under $25, you can buy a cable and lock, like those used for bicycles, and secure the computer, monitor, and printer to a work area.

Keep your laptop in the trunk of your car instead of the back seat, and use a locking device to attach it to the lid of the trunk or to a solid piece of furniture in your office or room. At airports or coffee shops, don't place your laptop down beside you while sitting or getting your ticket or a coffee, since this offers an opportunity for a thief to steal it. Consider purchasing a proximity device that attaches to your laptop; it sounds a loud alarm if it is moved more than a few feet from a device in your pocket. Not only does it prevent theft, it also ensures that you'll never absentmindedly leave your laptop behind. Some new laptops even have fingerprint readers built into the keyboard to prevent unauthorized use.

You can also purchase software programs that emit a signal when the thief uses your computer online. The software company's monitoring center will notify the local police of the laptop's location and even provide them with a map.

Flying to a conference? Never check laptops as luggage at the airport because they can disappear. The Federal Aviation Administration has issued a warning about an increasingly common scam—stealing laptops from the conveyor belts of metal detectors. At the security X-ray scanner two thieves get in line. The first one passes through the scanner quickly. The second person moves slowly, being delayed by pockets full of change, keys, or other items. Meanwhile, the travelers stuck behind the thief have already placed their belongings, including laptops, on the conveyor belt. The first thief picks up the laptop as if it were his or her own and walks away while the other thief continues to hold up the line. Put your laptop on the conveyer belt *only* when you are next in line, about to walk through the X-ray scanner. Keep your eye on your laptop as it comes off the conveyor belt. And alert security personnel right away if you think someone is attempting to steal your computer.

If your hardware does get stolen, its recovery may be helped if you have a bar code attached to it when you buy it. Finally, insurance to cover computer theft or damage is surprisingly cheap. Look for advertisements in computer magazines. (If you have standard tenants' or homeowners' insurance, it may not cover your computer. Ask your insurance agent.)

You can also purchase encryption software to protect your data. These programs are simple to use and install and can be purchased at most computer stores or online. If your laptop is stolen, an encryption program adds a strong layer of protection.

Guarding against Damage to Hardware

Because desktop computers aren't moved around much, they are less susceptible to damage. Laptops, however, are another story. According to a survey of 714 information technology managers, physical damage to laptops with data loss resulted from the following causes: 34% from spilled food or liquids on them, 28% from dropping them, 25% from not protecting them during travel, and 13% from worker anger.[22] (Special "ruggedized" laptops exist, such as the Hewlett-Packard EliteBook and the Panasonic Toughbook, which are built to be shock resistant.) So, it pays to take care when handling your laptop.

Guarding against Damage to Software

Systems software and applications software generally come on CD-ROM disks or are downloaded. The rule is simply this: copy the original software either onto other disks and/or flash memory devices; or back everything up on a cloud server. If your computer gets stolen or your software destroyed, you can retrieve the originals and make additional copies as needed.

Protecting Your Data

Computer hardware and commercial software are nearly always replaceable, although perhaps with some expense and difficulty. Data, however, may be major trouble to replace or even be irreplaceable. If your hard-disk drive crashes, do you have the same data on a backup disk? Almost every microcomputer user sooner or later has the experience of accidentally wiping out or losing material and having no copy. This is what makes people true believers in backing up their data—making a duplicate in some form. If you're working on a research paper, for example, it's easy to copy your work onto a CD, flash memory device, external backup hard drive, or a cloud server during and at the end of your work session.

In particular, you should also think about purchasing a flash drive. You could keep all important information on this drive instead of your laptop drive. The flash drive can be carried in your pocket away from your computer. You must be careful, however, not to misplace it. As an added protection measure, some flash drives now require your fingerprint to access the data. Some software programs, such as Laptop Sentry, allow you to remotely delete files if your laptop is stolen and use geo-location technology to track where your laptop is.

Protecting Your Health

Could a computer put you in the emergency room? Actually, the number of injuries caused by computers in the home, caused by people tripping over wires or getting hit by falling equipment, is significant. But injuries are also caused by not setting up computers correctly. Many people, for instance, set up their computers, particularly laptops, on a desk or table. This means "the keyboard is too high, which makes your arms reach up, your shoulders hunch and your wrists bend down," says one report. "The monitor is too low, which pulls your head and neck forward and down and puts a strain on your neck."[23]

With a computer, it's important to sit with both feet on the floor, thighs at right angles to your body. The chair should be adjustable and support your lower back. Your forearms should be parallel to the floor. You should look down slightly at the screen. (• *See Panel 5.28.*) This setup is particularly important if you are going to be sitting at a computer for hours at a time.

To avoid wrist and forearm injuries, keep your wrists straight and hands relaxed as you type. Instead of putting the keyboard on top of a desk, put it on a low table or in a keyboard drawer under the desk. Otherwise the nerves in your wrists will rub against the sheaths surrounding them, possibly leading to RSI pains. Or try setting an hourly alarm on your watch or on an alarm clock; when the alarm goes off, take a short break and rotate your wrists and hands a bit.

Eyestrain and headaches usually arise because of improper lighting, screen glare, and long shifts staring at the screen. Make sure that your windows and lights don't throw a glare on the screen and that your computer is not framed by an uncovered window.

Back and neck pains occur because furniture is not adjusted correctly or because of heavy computer use, especially of laptops. Adjustable furniture and frequent breaks should provide relief.

Also remember that sitting for long periods of time is simply not good for the human body. Many computer users have switched to standing desks. In addition to taking exercise breaks, try some of the ergonomic input devices mentioned earlier in this chapter.

Protecting Your Computer Devices

Go to these sites for more information about computer and data security, including smartphones:

http://gocsi.com/

www.cyberguys.com/product-listings/?categoryid=536

www.pcworld.com/businesscenter/article/216420/smartphone_security_how_to_keep_your_handset_safe.html

www.net-security.org/secworld.php?id=10774

Head Directly over shoulders, without straining forward or backward, about an arm's length from screen.

Neck Elongated and relaxed.

Shoulders Kept down, with the chest open and wide.

Back Upright or inclined slightly forward from the hips. Maintain the slight natural curve of the lower back.

Elbows Relaxed, at about a right angle, try to keep forearms parallel to floor.

Wrists Relaxed, and in a neutral position, without flexing up or down.

Knees Slightly lower than the hips.

Light source Should come from behind the head.

Screen At eye level or slightly lower. Use an anti-glare screen.

Fingers Gently curved.

Keyboard Best when kept flat (for proper wrist positioning) and at or just below elbow level. Computer keys that are far away should be reached by moving the entire arm, starting from the shoulders, rather than by twisting the wrists or straining the fingers. Take frequent rest breaks.

Feet Firmly planted on the floor. Shorter people may need a footrest.

Chair Sloped slightly forward to facilitate proper knee position.

Keep wrists above the pad, and tilt the keyboard downward.

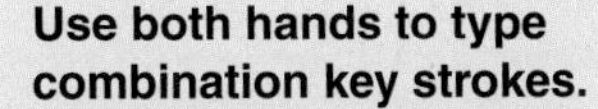

Yes

Use both hands to type combination key strokes.

Yes

Don't rest on the wrist pad.

No

Don't bend your hand in awkward angles to type key combinations.

No

Twisting your hands puts strain on them. Resting on a wrist rest, the table, or arm rests while typing forces you to twist your hand to reach some keys. Instead, keep your hands moving freely above the keyboard, letting the strong muscles of your arms move your hands.

It is also a bad idea to contort your hands in other ways. Your hand should be flat and parallel to the keyboard, without twisting. there should not be any pressure on your wrist or forearms while you type. You should NOT rest your wrists on a wrist rest except while taking a very short break from typing. A wrist rest of the proper height (level with the space bar) can serve as a reminder to keep your wrists straight. If you feel your wrist touching the rest, you know that your wrists are starting to dip.

panel 5.28

How to set up your computer work area

TERMS & EXPLANATIONS

audio-input device (p. 275) Hardware that records analog sound and translates it for digital storage and processing. Why it's important: *Analog sound signals are continuous variable waves within a certain frequency range. For the computer to process them, these variable waves must be converted to digital 0s and 1s. The principal use of audio-input devices is to produce digital input for multimedia computers. An audio signal can be digitized in two ways—by an audio board or a MIDI board.*

bar-code reader (p. 272) Photoelectric (optical) scanner that translates bar codes into digital codes. Why it's important: *With bar-code readers and the appropriate software system, store clerks can total purchases and produce invoices with increased speed and accuracy, and stores and other businesses can monitor inventory and services with increased efficiency.*

bar codes (p. 271) Vertical, zebra-striped marks imprinted on most manufactured retail products. Why it's important: *Bar codes provide a convenient means of identifying and tracking items. In North America, supermarkets, food manufacturers, and others have agreed to use a bar-code system called the* Universal Product Code (UPC). *Other kinds of bar-code systems are used on everything from FedEx packages to railroad cars to the jerseys of long-distance runners.*

biometrics (p. 282) Science of measuring individual body characteristics. Why it's important: *Biometric security devices identify a person through a fingerprint, voice intonation, or some other biological characteristic. For example, retinal-identification devices use a ray of light to identify the distinctive network of blood vessels at the back of the eyeball.*

carpal tunnel syndrome (CTS) (p. 295) Debilitating condition caused by pressure on the median nerve in the wrist, producing damage and pain to nerves and tendons in the hands. Why it's important: *CTS can be caused by overuse or misuse of computer keyboards.*

color depth (p. 285) Also called *bit depth;* the amount of information, expressed in bits, that is stored in a dot. Why it's important: *The more bits in a dot or pixel, the more shades of gray and colors can be represented. With 24-bit color depth, for example, 8 bits are dedicated to each primary color—red, green, and blue. Eight-bit color is standard for most of computing; 24-bit, called* true color, *requires more resources, such as video memory.*

computer vision syndrome (CVS) (p. 295) Eyestrain, headaches, double vision, and other problems caused by improper use of computer display screens. Why it's important: *CVS can be prevented by not staring at the display screen for too long, by correcting faulty lighting, by avoiding screen glare, and by not using screens with poor resolution.*

digital camera (p. 277) Electronic camera that uses a light-sensitive processor chip to capture photographic images in digital form and store them on a small diskette inserted into the camera or on flash memory chips (cards). Why it's important: *The bits of digital information—the snapshots you have taken, say—can be copied right onto a computer's hard disk for manipulation and printing out. The environmentally undesirable stage of chemical development required for conventional film is completely eliminated.*

digital pen (p. 269) Writing instrument that allows users to write on paper and send the writing as an image file to the computer. Why it's important: *You can easily store your handwritten notes in digital form.*

digitizer (p. 268) Input unit based on an electronic pen or a mouse-like copying device called a *puck* that converts drawings and photos to digital data. Why it's important: See ***digitizing tablet.***

digitizing tablet (p. 268) One form of digitizer; an electronic plastic board on which each specific location corresponds to a location on the screen. When the user uses a puck, the tablet converts his or her movements into digital signals that are input to the computer. Why it's important: *Digitizing tablets are often used to make maps and engineering drawings, as well as to trace drawings.*

display screen (p. 284) Also called *monitor* or simply *screen;* output device that shows programming instructions and data as they are being input and information after it is processed. Why it's important: *Screens are needed to display softcopy output.*

dot pitch (dp) (p. 285) Amount of space between the centers of adjacent pixels; the closer the pixels (dots), the crisper the image. Why it's important: *Dot pitch is one of the measures of display-screen crispness. For a .25dp monitor, for instance, the dots are 25/100ths of a millimeter apart. Generally, a dot pitch of .25–.28dp will provide clear images.*

dots per inch (dpi) (p. 270) Measure of the number of columns and rows of dots per inch. For microcomputer printers, resolution is usually in the range 1,200 × 1,200 dpi. Why it's important: *The higher the dpi, the better the resolution.* (See also ***resolution.***)

dumb terminal (p. 260) Also called *video display terminal (VDT);* display screen and a keyboard hooked up to a computer system. It can input and output but not process data. Why it's important: *Dumb terminals are used, for example, by airline reservations clerks to access a mainframe computer containing flight information.*

electromagnetic fields (EMFs) (p. 295) Waves of electrical energy and magnetic energy. Why it's important: *Some people have worried that CRT monitors might be linked to miscarriages, birth defects, and cancer and that cellphones and power lines might lead to some types of cancers.*

ergonomics (p. 296) Study, or science, of working conditions and equipment with the goal of improving worker safety and efficiency. Why it's important: *On the basis of ergonomic principles, stress, illness, and injuries associated with computer use may be minimized.*

fax machine (p. 274). Also called a *facsimile transmission machine;* input device that scans an image and sends it as electronic signals over telephone lines to a receiving fax machine, which prints the image on paper. Two types of fax machines are dedicated fax machines and fax modems. Why it's important: *Fax machines permit the transmission of text or graphic data over telephone lines quickly and inexpensively. They are found not only in offices and homes but also alongside regular phones in some public places such as airports.*

flat-panel display (p. 284) Most common type of display screen. Flat-panel (LCD) displays are made up of two plates of glass separated by a layer of a substance in which light is manipulated. Why it's important: *Flat-panel displays are essential to portable computers, and are commonly used for desktop computers as well.*

flatbed scanner (p. 270) Also called *desktop scanner;* the image being scanned is placed on a glass surface, where it remains stationary, and the scanning beam moves across it. Three other types of scanners are *sheet-fed, handheld,* and *drum.* Why it's important: *Flatbed scanners are one of the most popular types of general-use scanner.*

handwriting recognition (p. 267) System in which a computer receives intelligible written input, using special software to interpret the movement of a stylus across a writing service and translating the resulting cursive writing into digital information. Why it's important: *Handwriting recognition is a commonly used input method for PDAs, some handheld videogames, and tablet PCs.*

hardcopy (p. 284) Tangible output, usually printed. The principal examples are printouts, whether text or graphics, from printers. Film, including microfilm and microfiche, is also considered hardcopy output. Why it's important: *Hardcopy is an essential form of computer output.*

impact printer (p. 287) Printer that forms characters or images by striking a mechanism such as a print hammer or wheel against an inked ribbon, leaving an image on paper. Why it's important: *Nonimpact printers are more commonly used than impact printers, but dot-matrix printers are still used in some businesses.*

inkjet printer (p. 289) Printer that sprays onto paper small, electrically charged droplets of ink from four nozzles through holes in a matrix at high speed. Like laser and dot-matrix printers, inkjet printers form images with little dots. Why it's important: *Because they produce high-quality images on special paper, inkjet printers are often used in graphic design and desktop publishing. However, traditionally inkjet printers have been slower than laser printers and they print at a lower resolution on regular paper.*

input hardware (p. 257) Devices that translate data into a form the computer can process. Why it's important: *Without input hardware, computers could not function. The computer-readable form consists of 0s and 1s, represented as off and on electrical signals. Input hardware devices are categorized as three types: keyboards, pointing devices, and source data-entry devices.*

intelligent terminal (p. 260) Hardware unit with its own memory and processor, as well as a display screen and keyboard, hooked up to a larger computer system. Why it's important: *Such a terminal can perform some functions independent of any mainframe to which it is linked. Examples include the automated teller machine (ATM), a self-service banking machine connected through a telephone network to a central computer, and the point-of-sale (POS) terminal, used to record purchases at a store's customer checkout counter. Recently, many intelligent terminals have been replaced by personal computers.*

Internet terminal (p. 260) Terminal that provides access to the Internet. There are several variants of Internet terminal: (1) the set-top box or web terminal, which displays web pages on a TV set; (2) the network computer, a cheap, stripped-down computer that connects people to networks; (3) the online game player, which not only lets you play games but also connects to the Internet; (4) the full-blown PC/TV (or TV/PC), which merges the personal computer with the television set; and (5) smartphones. Why it's important: *In the near future, most likely, Internet terminals will be everywhere.*

keyboard (p. 258) Input device that converts letters, numbers, and other characters into electrical signals that can be read by the computer's processor. Why it's important: *Keyboards are the most popular kind of input device.*

laser printer (p. 288) Nonimpact printer that creates images with dots. As in a photocopying machine, images are produced on a drum, treated with a magnetically charged inklike toner (powder), and then transferred from drum to paper. Why it's important: *Laser printers produce much better image quality than do dot-matrix printers and can print in many more colors; they are also quieter. Laser printers, along with page description languages, enabled the development of desktop publishing.*

light pen (p. 268) Light-sensitive penlike device connected by a wire to the computer terminal. The user brings the pen to a desired point on the display screen and presses the pen button, which identifies that screen location to the computer. Why it's important: *Light pens are used by engineers, graphic designers, and illustrators.*

magnetic-ink character recognition (MICR) (p. 273) Scanning technology that reads magnetized-ink characters printed at the bottom of checks and converts them to digital form. Why it's important: *MICR technology is used by banks to sort checks.*

MIDI board (p. 275) *MIDI,* pronounced "middie," stands for "Musical Instrument Digital Interface." MIDI sound boards use this standard. Why it's important: *MIDI provides a standard for the interchange of musical information between musical instruments, synthesizers, and computers.*

mouse (p. 261) A pointing device that is moved about on a desktop mouse pad and directs a pointer on the computer's display screen. Why it's important: *The mouse is the principal pointing tool used with microcomputers.*

multifunction printer (p. 291) Hardware device that combines several capabilities, such as printing, scanning, copying, and faxing. Why it's important: *Multifunction printers take up less space and cost less than the four separate office machines that they replace.*

nonimpact printer (p. 287) Printer that forms characters and images without direct physical contact between the printing mechanism and paper. Two types of nonimpact printers often used with microcomputers are laser printers and inkjet printers. A third kind, the thermal printer, is seen less frequently. Why it's important: *Nonimpact printers are faster and quieter than impact printers.*

optical character recognition (OCR) (p. 274) Software technology that converts scanned text from images (pictures of the text) to an editable text format (usually ASCII) that can be imported into a word processing application and manipulated. Why it's important: *Special OCR characters appear on utility bills and price tags on department-store merchandise. The wand reader is a common OCR scanning device. These days almost all scanners come with OCR software.*

optical mark recognition (OMR) (p. 274) Scanning technology that reads "bubble" marks and converts them into computer-usable form. Why it's important: *OMR technology is used to read the College Board Scholastic Aptitude Test (SAT) and the Graduate Record Examination (GRE).*

output hardware (p. 257) Hardware devices that convert machine-readable information, obtained as the result of processing, into people-readable form. The principal kinds of output are softcopy and hardcopy. Why it's important: *Without output devices, people would have no access to processed data and information.*

page description language (PDL) (p. 288) Software that describes the shape and position of characters and graphics to the printer. PostScript and PCL are common page description languages. Why it's important: *Page description languages are essential to desktop publishing.*

pen-based computer system (p. 267) Input system that allows users to enter handwriting and marks onto a computer screen by means of a penlike stylus rather than by typing on a keyboard. Pen computers use handwriting-recognition software that translates handwritten characters made by the stylus into data that is usable by the computer. Why it's important: *Some PDAs and tablets have pen input, as do digital notebooks.*

pixel (p. 284) Short for "picture element"; the smallest unit on the screen that can be turned on and off or made different shades. Why it's important: *Pixels are the building blocks that allow text and graphical images to be displayed on a screen.*

plotter (p. 291) Specialized output device designed to produce high-quality graphics in a variety of colors. The inkjet plotter employs the same principle as an inkjet printer; the paper is output over a drum, enabling continuous output. In an electrostatic plotter, paper lies partially flat on a tablelike surface, and toner is used in a photocopier-like manner. Why it's important: *Plotters are used to create hardcopy items such as maps, architectural drawings, and three-dimensional illustrations, which are usually too large for regular printers.*

pointing device (p. 261) Hardware that controls the position of the cursor or pointer on the screen. It includes the mouse and its variants, the touch screen, and various forms of pen input. Why it's important: *In many contexts, pointing devices permit quick and convenient data input.*

printer (p. 286) Output device that prints characters, symbols, and perhaps graphics on paper or another hardcopy medium. Why it's important: *Printers provide one of the principal forms of computer output.*

radio-frequency identification (RFID) tags (p. 281) Source data-entry technology based on an identifying tag bearing a microchip that contains specific code numbers. These code numbers are read by the radio waves of a scanner linked to a database. Why it's important: *Drivers with RFID tags can breeze through tollbooths without having to even roll down their windows; the toll is automatically charged to their accounts. Radio-wave-readable ID tags are also used by the Postal Service to monitor the flow of mail, by stores for inventory control and warehousing, and in the railroad industry to keep track of rail cars.*

refresh rate (p. 286) Number of times per second that screen pixels are recharged so that their glow remains bright. In general, displays are refreshed 60–200 times per second (hertz), with 72 being common. Why it's important: *The higher the refresh rate, the more solid the image looks on the screen—that is, the less it flickers.*

repetitive stress (or strain) injuries (RSIs) (p. 295) Several wrist, hand, arm, and neck injuries resulting when muscle groups are forced through fast, repetitive motions. They include muscle strain and tendinitis, which are painful but usually not crippling, and carpal tunnel syndrome, which is disabling and often requires surgery. Why it's important: *People who use computer keyboards account for some of the RSI cases that result in lost work time and other problems.*

resolution (pp. 270, 285) Clarity or sharpness of display-screen/scanned/printed images; the more pixels (dots) there are per square inch, the finer the level of detail attained. Resolution is expressed in terms of the formula: horizontal pixels × vertical pixels. Each pixel can be assigned a color or a particular shade of gray. Standard screen resolutions are 1,024 × 768, 1,280 × 1,024, and 1,600 × 1,200 pixels. Common scanner resolutions are 300 × 200, 600 × 600, 600 × 1,200, 1,200 × 1,200, 1,200 × 2,400, 2,400 × 2,400. Why it's important: *Users need to know what resolution is appropriate for their purposes.*

scanner (p. 269) Source data-input device that uses light-sensing (optical) equipment to translate images of text, drawings, photos, and the like into digital form. Why it's important: *Scanners simplify the input of complex data. The images can be processed by a computer, displayed on a monitor, stored on a storage device, or communicated to another computer.*

sensor (p. 280) Input device that collects specific data directly from the environment and transmits it to a computer. Why it's important: *Although you are unlikely to see such input devices connected to a PC in an office, they exist all around us, often in nearly invisible form. Sensors can be used to detect all kinds of things: speed, movement, weight, pressure, temperature, humidity, wind, current, fog, gas, smoke, light, shapes, images, and so on. In aviation, for example, sensors are used to detect ice buildup on airplane wings and to alert pilots to sudden changes in wind direction.*

softcopy (p. 283) Data on a display screen or in audio or voice form. This kind of output is not tangible; it cannot be touched. Why it's important: *This term is used to distinguish nonprinted output from printed (hardcopy) output.*

sound board (p. 275) An add-on circuit board in a computer that converts analog sound to digital sound and stores it for further processing and/or plays it back, providing output directly to speakers or an external amplifier. Why it's important: *The sound board enables users to work with audible sound.*

sound-output device (p. 293) Hardware that produces digitized sounds, ranging from beeps and chirps to music. Why it's important: *To use sound output, the user needs appropriate software and a sound card. Such devices are used to produce the sound effects and music.*

source data-entry devices (p. 269) Data-entry devices that create machine-readable data on magnetic media or paper or feed it directly into the computer's processor, without the use of a keyboard. Categories include scanning devices (imaging systems, bar-code readers, mark- and character-recognition devices, and fax machines), audio-input devices, video input, photographic input (digital cameras), voice-recognition systems, sensors, radio-frequency identification devices, and human-biology-input devices. Why it's important: *Source data-entry devices lessen reliance on keyboards for data entry and can make data entry more accurate.*

speech-recognition system (p. 278) Input system that uses a microphone (or a telephone) as an input device and converts a person's speech into digital signals by comparing the electrical patterns produced by the speaker's voice with a set of prerecorded patterns stored in the computer. Why it's important: *Voice-recognition technology is particularly useful in situations in which people are unable to use their hands to input data or need their hands free for other purposes.*

thermal printer (p. 290) Low- to medium-resolution printer that uses a type of coated paper that darkens when heat is applied to it. The paper is moved past a line of heating elements that burn dots onto the paper. Why it's important: *This technology is typically used in business for bar-code label applications and for printing cash register receipts. Until about 2000, most fax machines used direct thermal printing, though now only the cheapest models use it, the rest having switched to thermal wax-transfer, laser, or inkjet printing.*

touch screen (p. 266) Video display screen that has been sensitized to receive input from the touch of a finger. The screen is covered with a plastic layer, behind which are invisible beams of infrared light. Why it's important: *Users can input requests for information by pressing on buttons or menus displayed. The answers to requests are displayed as output in words or pictures on the screen. (There may also be sound.) Touch screens are found in kiosks, ATMs, airport tourist directories, hotel TV screens (for guest checkout), and campus information kiosks making available everything from lists of coming events to (with proper ID and personal code) student financial-aid records and grades.*

touchpad (p. 266) Input device; a small, flat surface over which the user slides a finger, using the same movements as those used with a mouse. The cursor follows the movement of the finger. The user "clicks" by tapping a finger on the pad's surface or by pressing buttons positioned close by the pad. Why it's important: *Touchpads let users control the cursor/pointer with a finger and are installed on most laptops. (Thus no additional space is needed to use a mouse.)*

trackball (p. 264) Movable ball, mounted on top or side of a stationary device, that can be rotated by the user's fingers or palm. It looks like the mouse turned upside down. Instead of moving the mouse around on the desktop, you move the trackball with the tips of your fingers. Why it's important: *A trackball requires less space to use than a mouse does.*

video (p. 294) Output consisting of photographic images played at 15–29 frames per second to give the appearance of full motion. Why it's important: *Video is input into a multimedia system using a video camera or VCR and, after editing, is output on a computer's display screen. Because video files can require a great deal of storage—a 3-minute video may require 1 gigabyte of storage—video is often compressed.*

videoconferencing (p. 294) Form of video output in which people in different geographic locations can have a meeting—can see and hear one another—using computers and communications. Why it's important: *Many organizations use videoconferencing to take the place of face-to-face meetings. Videoconferencing systems range from videophones to group conference rooms with cameras and multimedia equipment to desktop systems with small video cameras, microphones, and speakers.*

voice-output device (p. 294) Hardware that converts digital data into speechlike sounds. Why it's important: *We hear such voice output on telephones ("Please hang up and dial your call again"), in soft-drink machines, in cars, in toys and games, and recently in mapping software for vehicle-navigation devices. Computers with voice output are particularly useful for people with physical challenges.*

webcam (p. 276) A video camera attached to a computer to record live moving images that can then be posted on a website in real time. Why it's important: *The webcam is an affordable tool that enables users to have videoconferencing capabilities and view real-time video recording on the web.*

CHAPTER REVIEW

1 LEARNING MEMORIZATION

"I can recognize and recall information."

Self-Test Questions

1. A(n) __________ terminal is entirely dependent for all its processing activities on the computer system to which it is connected.
2. The two main categories of printer are __________ and __________.
3. __________ is the study of the physical relationships between people and their work environment.
4. A(n) __________ is an input device that is rolled about on a desktop and directs a pointer on the computer's display screen.
5. __________ consists of devices that translate information processed by the computer into a form that humans can understand.
6. __________ is the science of measuring individual body characteristics.
7. A screen whose displayed contents can be manipulated by hand is called a(n) __________.
8. LCD is short for __________.
9. __________ is software that describes the shape and position of characters and graphics to the printer.

10. When people in different geographic locations can have a meeting using computers and communications, it is called __________.
11. __________ feed data directly into a computer system from its source, without the use of a keyboard.
12. A debilitating condition caused by pressure on the median nerve in the wrist, producing damage and pain to nerves and tendons in the hands, is called __________.
13. The measure of the number of dots that are printed in a linear inch is called __________ or __________.
14. A printer that forms characters or images by striking a mechanism such as a print hammer or wheel against an inked ribbon, leaving images on a paper, is called a(n) __________ printer.
15. __________ printers enabled the development of desktop publishing.

Multiple-Choice Questions

1. Which of the following is *not* a pointing device?
   a. mouse
   b. touchpad
   c. keyboard
   d. joystick
2. Which of the following is *not* a source data-entry device?
   a. bar-code reader
   b. sensor
   c. digital camera
   d. scanner
   e. mouse
3. Which of the following display standards has the highest screen resolution?
   a. XGA
   b. UXGA
   c. VGA
   d. SVGA
   e. QXGA
4. Which of the following *isn't* considered hardcopy output?
   a. spreadsheet printout
   b. microfilm
   c. fax report
   d. Word document computer file
   e. printed invoice
5. Which of the following factors does *not* affect the quality of a screen display?
   a. refresh rate
   b. speed
   c. resolution
   d. pixels
   e. color depth
6. A device with a microchip that contains code numbers that can be read by a scanner's radio waves is a(n) __________.
   a. digital pen
   b. nanotube
   c. pointing device
   d. RFID tag
   e. multifunction mouse

True/False Questions

T F 1. On a computer screen, the more pixels that appear per square inch, the higher the resolution.

T F 2. Photos taken with a digital camera can be downloaded to a computer's hard disk via a wired or wireless connection.

T F 3. Resolution is the amount of space between the centers of adjacent pixels.

T F 4. The abbreviation *dpi* stands for "dense pixel intervals."

T F 5. Pointing devices control the position of the cursor on the screen.

T F 6. Output hardware consists of devices that translate information processed by the computer into a form that humans can understand.

T F 7. Optical character-recognition software reads "bubble" marks and converts them into computer-usable form.

T F 8. The lower the refresh rate, the more solid the image looks on the screen.

T F 9. Bar codes are input with pointing devices.

T F 10. Computer users have no need to be concerned about ergonomics.

T F 11. It has been proven that electromagnetic fields pose no danger to human beings.

T F 12. Plotters are used to print architectural drawings and in computer-aided design.

2 LEARNING COMPREHENSION

"I can recall information in my own terms and explain it to a friend."

Short-Answer Questions

1. What is a common use of dumb terminals?
2. What characteristics determine the clarity of a computer screen?
3. Describe two situations in which scanning is useful.
4. What is source data entry?
5. What is *pixel* short for? What is a pixel?
6. Briefly describe RSI and CTS. Why are they problems?
7. What is a font?
8. Discuss the different types of printers and their features.
9. What is OCR used for?

3 LEARNING APPLYING, ANALYZING, SYNTHESIZING, EVALUATING

"I can apply what I've learned, relate these ideas to other concepts, build on other knowledge, and use all these thinking skills to form a judgment."

Knowledge in Action

1. Cut out several advertisements from newspapers or magazines that feature new microcomputer systems. Circle all the terms that are familiar to you now that you have read the first five chapters of this text. Define these terms on a separate sheet of paper. Is this computer expandable? How much does it cost? Is a monitor included in the price? A printer?
2. *Paperless office* is a term that has been around for some time. However, the paperless office has not yet been achieved. Do you think the paperless office is a good idea? Do you think it's possible? Why do you think it has not yet been achieved?
3. Compare and contrast the pros and cons of different types of monitors. Decide which one is best for you and explain why. Do some research on how each monitor type creates displayed images.
4. Do you have access to a computer with (a) speech-recognition software and (b) word processing software that determines writing level (such as eighth grade, ninth grade, and so on)? Dictate a few sentences about your day into the microphone. After your speech is encoded into text, use the word processing software to determine the grade level of your everyday speech.
5. A pixel is the smallest unit on the screen that can be turned on and off. In most high-quality digital photos, you can't see the pixilation unless you zoom in real close. However, even when you don't zoom in, you know that the pixilation is there, a series of different pixels all plotted on a grid. How can you relate this to our experience of reality? Via high-tech microscopes we see that everything is made of smaller particles not visible to the naked eye, such as atoms, subatomic particles, and quarks. How are the basic building blocks of computer imaging and the basic building blocks of physical matter alike, and how are they different?
6. Biometrics: Which form of biometric technology do you prefer for identification purposes: fingerprints, voice intonation, facial characteristics, or retinal identification? Which do you think will become most commonly used in the future? What problems do you foresee with biometric ID processes?

Web Exercises

1. Visit an online shopping site such as *www.yahoo.com.* Click on *Shopping;* then type *Printers* in the Shopping search box. Investigate five different types of printers by clicking on the printer names and then on Full Specifications. Note (a) the type of printer, (b) its price, (c) its resolution, and (d) its speeds for black-and-white printing and for color printing, if applicable. Which operating system is each printer compatible with? Which printer would you choose? Why?
2. There is an abundance of information about electronic devices on the Internet. People write all kinds of reviews either raving about the device that made their lives better or lamenting the device that became their evil nemesis. Go to *www.consumerreports.org/cro/search.htm?query=reviews* and find out how people at ConsumerReports.org rate some of your favorite electronic devices.
3. Go to *www.touchscreens.com* and find a touch screen that appeals to you. Is it multitouch?
4. Concerned about electromagnetic radiation? Search for discussions about the World Health Organizations' May 2011 report on the possibly of cellphone-caused brain cancer. Are you concerned enough to reduce your cellphone use?
5. Do you see any ethical problems involved with self-scanning checkout? Can people cheat the system? Are store jobs being lost to automation? Are people without credit cards and/or computer experience being excluded? Do a keyword search for *self-scanning* and *self-checkout* and other terms related to these issues. Do you think self-scanning is a good idea?
6. Research the development of Smart Labels. Do they offer more advantages than disadvantages? Visit these websites for more information on radio-frequency tagging:

   http://smart-labels.vista-files.org/

   www.answers.com/topic/rfid-tag

   http://electronics.howstuffworks.com/gadgets/high-tech-gadgets/rfid.htm

   http://www.intermec.com/products/rfid/tags_inserts_and_smart_labels/index.aspx
7. The human cyborg: Visit Professor Kevin Warwick's website to learn about the implant microchips he has been creating and surgically implanting in his body to allow it to communicate with a computer. Investigate the many applications he has been working on. After visiting his site, run a search on *"Kevin Warwick"* to read what others have to say about him and his ideas.

   www.kevinwarwick.com/
8. PostScript is the most important page description language in desktop publishing. Read the information at

   www.adobe.com/products/postscript/

   www.answers.com/topic/postscript-1?hl=postscript&hl=printing

   www.tailrecursive.org/postscript/postscript.html

   and find out why. You almost certainly will need some familiarity with PostScript.
9. When you prepare a paper or a presentation, do you know which fonts to use?

   http://justcreativedesign.com/2007/12/04/how-to-choose-a-font/

   http://desktoppub.about.com/cs/typography/f/choose_fonts.htmwww.powerframeworks.com/article-133

   www.serviceprinters.com/help/design/fonts.html

   http://webdesign.tutsplus.com/articles/choosing-the-right-font-a-practical-guide-to-typography-on-the-web/
10. How many images can the newest digital cameras hold? Do a web search and find out.

6

COMMUNICATIONS, NETWORKS, & SAFEGUARDS

The Wired & Wireless World

Chapter Topics & Key Questions

6.1 **From the Analog to the Digital Age** How do digital data and analog data differ, and what does a modem do?

6.2 **Networks** What are the benefits of networks, and what are their types, components, and variations?

6.3 **Wired Communications Media** What are types of wired communications media?

6.4 **Wireless Communications Media** What are types of wireless communications media, both long distance and short distance?

6.5 **Cyberthreats, Hackers, & Safeguards** What are areas I should be concerned about for keeping my computer system secure?

Download the free UIT 10e App for key term flash cards, quizzes, and a game, *Over the Edge*

The essence of all revolution, stated philosopher Hannah Arendt, is the start of a new story in human experience.

Before the 1950s, computing devices processed data into information, and communications devices communicated information over distances. The two streams of technology developed pretty much independently, like rails on a railroad track that never merge. Now we have a new story, a revolution.

For us, the new story has been ***digital convergence*—the gradual merger of computing and communications into a new information environment, in which the same information is exchanged among many kinds of equipment, using the language of computers.** (● *See Panel 6.1.*) At the same time, there has been a convergence of several important industries—computers, telecommunications, consumer electronics, entertainment, mass media—producing new electronic products that perform multiple functions.

panel 6.1

Digital convergence—the fusion of computer and communications technologies

Today's new information environment came about gradually from the merger of two separate streams of technological development—computers and communications.

Computer Technology

1621 CE	1642	1833	1843	1890
Slide rule invented (Edmund Gunther)	First mechanical adding machine (Blaise Pascal)	Babbage's difference engine (automatic calculator)	World's first computer programmer, Ada Lovelace, publishes her notes	Electricity used for first time in a data-processing project (punched cards); Hollerith's automatic census-tabulating machine (used punched cards)

Communications Technology

1562	1594	1639	1827	1835	1846	1857	1876	1888	1894
First monthly newspaper (Italy)	First magazine (Germany)	First printing press in North America	Photographs on metal plates	Telegraph (first long-distance digital communication system)	High-speed printing	Trans-atlantic telegraph cable laid	Telephone invented	Radio waves identified	Edison makes a movie

6.1 FROM THE ANALOG TO THE DIGITAL AGE

Analog is the process of taking an audio or video signal and translating it into electronic pulses; digital is breaking the signal into a binary format whereby the audio or video data is represented by a series of 1s and 0s.

Why have the worlds of computers and of telecommunications been so long in coming together? Because *computers are digital, but most of the world has been analog*. Let's take a look at what this means. We will elaborate on two subjects we introduced earlier—digital signals and modems.

The Digital Basis of Computers: Electrical Signals as Discontinuous Bursts

"Digital" describes electronic technology that generates, stores, and processes data in terms of two states: on (1) and off (0).

Computers may seem like incredibly complicated devices but, as we've seen, their underlying principle is simple. Because they are based on on/off electrical states, they use the *binary system,* which consists of only two digits—0 and 1. At their most basic level computers can distinguish between just these two values, 0 and 1, or off and on (Chapter 4). There is no simple way to represent all the values in between, such as 0.25. All data that a computer processes must be encoded digitally, as a series of 0s and 1s.

In general, *digital* means "computer-based." Specifically, ***digital*** **describes any system based on discontinuous data or events; in the case of computers, it refers to communications signals or information represented in a two-state (binary) way using electronic or electromagnetic signals. Each 0 and 1 signal represents a *bit.***

1930	1944	1946	1949	1952	1964	1967	1969
General theory of computers (MIT)	First electro-mechanical computer (Mark I)	First programmable electronic computer in United States (ENIAC)	First theories for self-replicating programs (viruses)	UNIVAC computer correctly predicts election of Eisenhower as U.S. President	IBM introduces 360 line of computers	Hand-held calculator	ARPANet established, led to Internet

1895	1907	1912	1915	1928	1939	1946	1947	1948	1950
Marconi develops radio; motion-picture camera invented	First regular radio broadcast from New York	Motion pictures become a big business	AT&T long-distance service reaches San Francisco	First TV demonstrated; first sound movie	Commercial TV broadcasting	Color TV demonstrated	Transistor invented	Reel-to-reel tape recorder	Cable TV

The Analog Basis of Life: Electrical Signals as Continuous Waves

"Analog" describes any fluctuating, evolving, or continually changing process; analog data is represented by continuously variable physical quantities

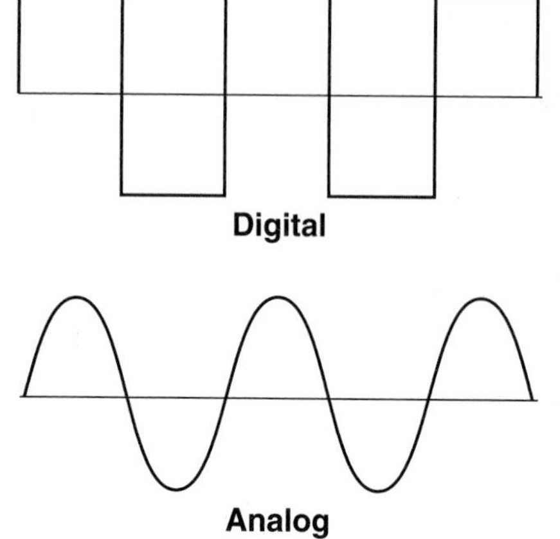

"The shades of a sunset, the flight of a bird, or the voice of a singer would seem to defy the black or white simplicity of binary representation," points out one writer.[1] Indeed, these and most other phenomena of the world are ***analog***, **continuously varying in strength and/or quality—fluctuating, evolving, or continually changing.** Sound, light, temperature, and pressure values, for instance, can be anywhere on a continuum or range. The highs, lows, and in-between states have historically been represented with analog devices rather than in digital form. Examples of analog devices are a speedometer, a thermometer, and a tire-pressure gauge, all of which can measure continuous fluctuations.

Humans experience most of the world in analog form—our vision, for instance, perceives shapes and colors as smooth gradations. But most analog events can be simulated digitally. A newspaper photograph, viewed through a magnifying glass, is made up of an array of dots—so small that most newspaper readers see the tones of the photograph as continuous (that is, analog).

Traditionally, electronic transmission of telephone, radio, television, and cable-TV signals has been analog. The electrical signals on a telephone line, for instance, have been analog-data representations of the original voices, transmitted in the shape of a wave. Why bother to change analog signals into digital ones, especially since the digital representations are only *approximations* of analog events? The reason is that *digital signals are easier to store and manipulate electronically.*

1970	1971	1973	1975	1976	1978	1981	1982	1984	1993
Microprocessor chips come into use; floppy disk introduced for storing data	First pocket calculator	FTP is developed	First microcomputer (MITS Altair 8800)	Apple I computer (first personal computer sold in assembled form); has 512 KB RAM	5$\frac{1}{4}$" floppy disk; Atari home video game	IBM introduces personal computer	Portable computers; TCP/IP is established as an internet standard; *Internet* is coined	Apple Macintosh; first personal laser printer; desktop publishing takes hold; Domain Name System (DNS) is introduced	Multimedia desktop computers; personal digital assistants (PDAs)

1952	1957	1961–1968	1968	1975	1977	1979	1981	1982	1985	1986
Direct-distance dialing (no need to go through operator); transistor radio introduced	First satellite launched (Russia's Sputnik)	Packet-switching networks developed	Portable video recorders; video-cassettes	Flat-screen TV; GPS	First interactive cable TV	3-D TV demonstrated	First viruses	Compact disks; European consortium launches multiple communications satellites	Cellular phone; Nintendo	First computer virus in the public sphere

Purpose of the Modem: Converting Digital Signals to Analog Signals & Back

Signals in the real world are analog—voice, light, sound. So, real-world signals must be converted into digital signals before they can be manipulated by digital equipment, and they must converted back to be handled by analog devices.

Consider a graphic representation of an on/off digital signal emitted from a computer. Like a regular light switch, this signal has only two states—on and off. Compare this with a graphic representation of a wavy analog signal emitted as a signal. The changes in this signal are gradual, as in a dimmer switch, which gradually increases or decreases brightness.

Because telephone lines have traditionally been analog, you need to have a modem if your computer is to send communications signals over a telephone line (or a cable line or a satellite connection). As we've seen (Chapter 2), older dial-up modems translate the computer's digital signals into the telephone line's analog signals. The receiving computer also needs a modem to translate the analog signals back into digital signals. (• *See Panel 6.2, next page.)*

How, in fact, does a modem convert the continuous analog wave to a discontinuous digital pulse that can represent 0s and 1s? The modem can make adjustments to the frequency—the number of cycles per second, or the number of times a wave repeats during a specific time interval (the fastness/slowness). Or it can make adjustments to the analog signal's amplitude—the height of the wave (the loudness/softness). Thus, in frequency, a slow wave might represent a 0 and a quick wave might represent a 1. In amplitude, a low wave might represent a 0 and a high wave might represent a 1. (• *See Panel 6.3.)*

Computer Technology

1994	1997	2000	2001	2003	2005	2009	2010	2012	2047?
Apple and IBM introduce PCs with full-motion video built in; wireless data transmission for small portable computers; web browser Mosaic invented	Network computers; Pathfinder robot lands on Mars	Microsoft .NET announced; BlackBerry	Windows XP; Mac OS X; MP3	Mac G5; iPod	Mac mini; Apple video iPod	Multicore processors	Windows 7	Windows 8	By this date, some experts predict, all electronically encodable information will be in cyberspace

Communications Technology

1991	1994	1997	2000	2001	2004	2005	2007	2010	2011	2012	2015?
CD-ROM games (Sega)	FCC selects HDTV standard	Internet telephone-to-telephone service	Napster popular; 3.8% of music sales online	2.5G wireless services; Wi-Fi and Bluetooth	Facebook launched; MySpace in operation	3G wireless services	112 million blogs are tracked	WikiLeaks controversy	4G	5G? Speech-to-speech translation for smartphones	Power rationing due to grid shortage

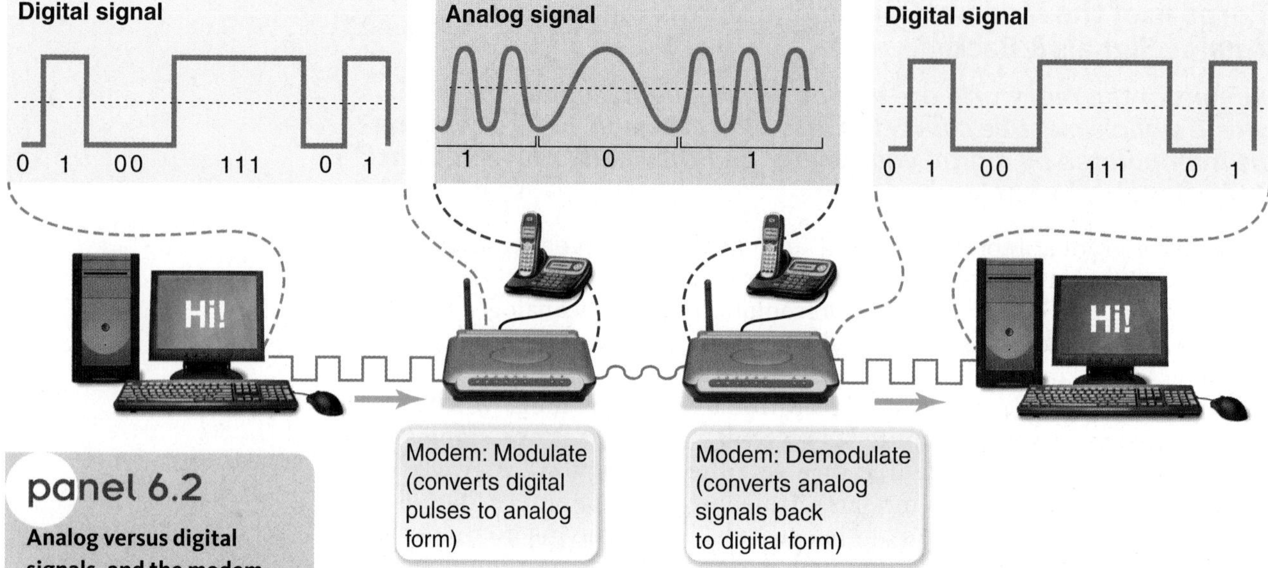

panel 6.2

Analog versus digital signals, and the modem

Note that an analog signal represents a continuous electrical signal in the form of a wave. A digital signal is discontinuous, expressed as discrete bursts of on/off electrical pulses.

Modem **is short for "*mo*dulate/*dem*odulate." A sending modem modulates digital signals into analog signals for transmission over phone lines or other transmission media. A receiving modem demodulates the analog signals back into digital signals.** The old dial-up modem provides a means for computers to communicate with one another using the standard copper-wire telephone network, an analog system that was built to transmit the human voice but not computer signals.

Our concern, however, goes far beyond telephone transmission. How can the analog realities of the world be expressed in digital form? How can light, sounds, colors, temperatures, and other dynamic values be represented so that they can be manipulated by a computer?

panel 6.3

Analog waves are modified to resemble digital pulses

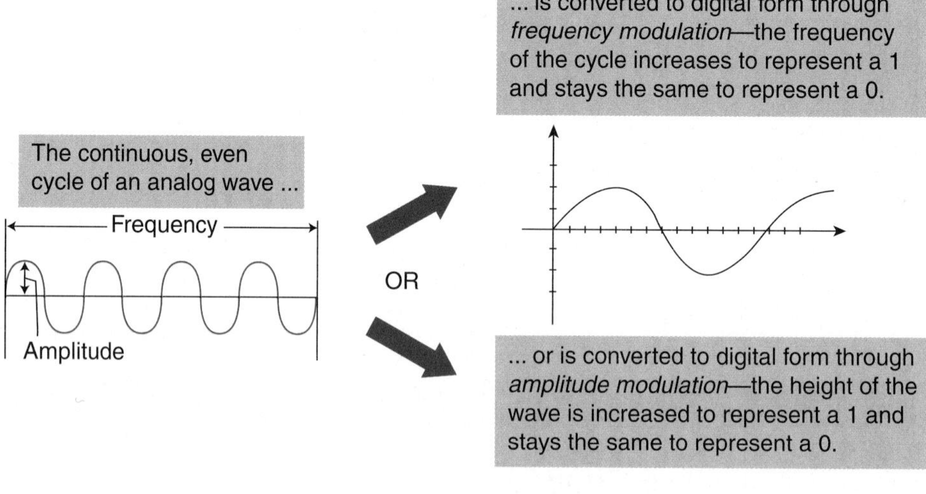

... is converted to digital form through *frequency modulation*—the frequency of the cycle increases to represent a 1 and stays the same to represent a 0.
The continuous, even cycle of an analog wave ...
Frequency
Amplitude
OR
... or is converted to digital form through *amplitude modulation*—the height of the wave is increased to represent a 1 and stays the same to represent a 0.

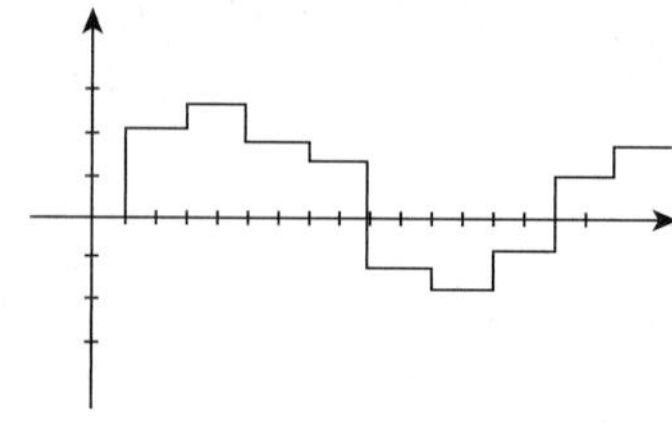

Converting Reality to Digital Form

Sampling is a process in which a continuous electrical signal is approximately represented by a series of discrete (binary) values, usually regularly spaced.

Suppose you are using an analog tape recorder to record a singer during a performance. The analog wave from the microphone, which is recorded onto the tape as an analog wave as well, will produce a near duplicate of the sounds—including distortions, such as buzzings and clicks, or electronic hums if an amplified guitar is used.

The digital recording process is different. The way that music is captured for digital audio CDs, for example, does not provide a duplicate of a musical performance. Rather, the digital process uses a device (called an *analog-to-digital converter*) to record *representative selections,* or *samples,* of the sounds and convert the analog waves into a stream of numbers that the computer then uses to express the sounds. To play back the music, the stream of numbers is converted (by a *digital-to-analog converter*) back into an analog wave. The samples of sounds are taken at regular intervals—nearly 44,100 times a second—and the copy obtained is virtually exact and free from distortion and noise. The sampling rate of 44,100 times per second and the high precision fool our ears into hearing a smooth, continuous sound.

Digital photography also uses sampling: a computer takes samples of values such as brightness and color. The same is true of other aspects of real-life experience, such as pressure, temperature, and motion.

Does digital sampling cheat us out of our experience of "reality" by allowing computers to sample sounds, images, and so on? Actually, people willingly made this compromise years ago, before computers were invented. Movies, for instance, carve up reality into 24 frames a second. Conventional television pictures (before high-definition TV) were drawn at 30 frames per second. These processes happen so quickly that our eyes and brains easily jump the visual gaps. Digital processing of analog experience is just one more way of expressing or translating reality.

Turning analog reality into digital form provides tremendous opportunities. One of the most important is that *all kinds of multimedia can now be changed into digital form and transmitted as data to all kinds of devices.*

Sampling

For detailed information, go to:

www.informit.com/articles/article.aspx?p=372009

http://en.wikipedia.org/wiki/Digitizing

http://electronics.howstuffworks.com/analog-digital3.htm

http://audacity.sourceforge.net/manual-1.2/tutorial_basics_1.html

Now let us examine the digital world of telecommunications. We begin with the subject of networks and then discuss how networks are connected—first by wired means, then by wireless means.

6.2 NETWORKS

In information technology, a network is a series of points interconnected by communications paths. Networks can interconnect with other networks and contain subnetworks.

Whether wired or wireless or both, **a *network,* or *communications network,* is a system of interconnected computers, telephones, or other communications devices that can communicate with one another and share applications and data.** The tying together of so many communications devices in so many ways is changing the world we live in.

Internet café in Laos

The Benefits of Networks

Computer networks are now a vital part of almost all organizations.

People and organizations use networks for the following reasons, the most important of which is the sharing of resources.

SHARING OF PERIPHERAL DEVICES Peripheral devices such as laser printers, disk drives, and scanners can be expensive. Consequently, to justify their purchase, management wants to maximize their use. Usually the best way to do this is to connect the peripheral to a network serving several computer users.

SHARING OF PROGRAMS & DATA In most organizations, people use the same software and need access to the same information. It is less expensive for a company to buy one word processing program licensed to serve many employees (site license; p. 150) than to buy a separate word processing program for each employee. Also, instead of using a disk or USB flash drive to carry files from one computer or office to another, you can share files directly using a network.

Moreover, if all employees have access to the same data on a shared storage device, the organization can save money and avoid serious problems; if each employee has a separate machine, some employees may update customer addresses while others remain ignorant of the changes. Updating information on a shared server is much easier than updating every user's individual system.

Finally, network-linked employees can more easily work together online on shared projects. A server manages network resources. Servers store data and share it with network users. Confidential or sensitive data can be protected and shared with the users who have permission to access that data. Document tracking software can be used to prevent users from overwriting files, or changing files that others are accessing at the same time, and users can access their files from any workstation.

Workgroup productivity software enables many users to contribute to a document concurrently. This allows for interactive teamwork.

BETTER COMMUNICATIONS One of the greatest features of networks is the support of electronic mail. With email, everyone on a network can easily keep others posted about important information. And when connected to the Internet, network users can communicate with people around the world via their network. Networks provide several different *collaboration tools* in addition to email: forums and chats, voice and video, and instant messaging. Special hardware devices allow the bandwidth of the connection to be easily allocated to individuals as they need it and permit an organization to purchase one high-speed connection instead of many slower ones.

CENTRALIZED COMMUNICATIONS Centralized administration reduces the number of people needed to manage the devices and data on the network, reducing time and cost to the company. Individual network users do not need to manage their own data and devices. One administrator can control the data, devices, and permissions of users on the network. Backing up data is easier because the data is stored in a central location.

SECURITY OF INFORMATION Before networks became commonplace, an individual employee might have been the only one with a particular piece of information, which was stored in his or her desktop computer. If the employee was dismissed—or if a fire or flood demolished the office—the company could have lost that information. Today such data would be backed up or duplicated on a networked storage device shared by others and backed up in the cloud (Chapter 1, p. 39; Chapter 4, pp. 238, 240). Specific directories can be password protected to limit access to authorized users. Also, files and programs on a network can be designated as "copy inhibit," so the organization doesn't have to worry about the illegal copying of programs.

ACCESS TO DATABASES Networks enable users to tap into numerous databases, whether private company databases or public databases available online through the Internet.

The National Science Foundation (NSF) created the first high-speed backbone in 1987. Called NSFNET, it was a T1 line (p. 329) that connected 170 smaller networks together and operated at 1.544 million bits per second (Mbps). IBM, MCI, and Merit worked with NSF to create the backbone and developed a T3 (45 Mbps) backbone the following year.

Backbones are typically fiber-optic trunk lines. The trunk line has multiple fiber-optic cables combined to increase the capacity. Fiber-optic cables are designated OC for optical carrier, such as OC-3, OC-12, or OC-48. An OC-3 line is capable of transmitting 155 megabits per second (Mbps); an OC-48 can transmit 2.4 gigabits per second (Gbps); OC-192 transmits 9.6 Gbps; and OC-768 39.8 Gbps. Compare that to a typical old dial-up 56 K modem transmitting 56,000 bps and you see just how fast a modern backbone is. Today there are many companies that operate their own high-capacity backbones, and all of them interconnect at various Internet Exchange Points (IXPs) (p. 61) around the world.

To see various Internet backbone maps, go to:

www.nthelp.com/images/agis.jpg

www.nthelp.com/maps.htm

www.haraswebs.com/about_us.php?page=1

www.telegeography.com/maps/index.php

A Few Disadvantages of Networks

Expense and security issues can be problems in setting up a network.

Although the advantages of networks are many and significant, there are a few potential problems that must be attended to.

- **Expense:** The initial set up cost of a computer network can be high depending on the number of computers to be connected and the number of connecting devices and NICs (Network Interface Cards, p. 329) for each of the workstations, in case they are not built in.
- **Security Issues:** One of the major drawbacks of computer networks is the security issues involved. If a computer is on a network, a computer hacker can get unauthorized access by using different tools. In case of big organizations, various types of network security software are used to prevent the theft of confidential and classified data.

  Sometimes (such as in medical equipment) a computer's software configuration must be predictable and stable. If a computer is connected to a network, it's easier to download and install software from the network onto the computer; this includes automatic software updates, which can happen automatically, without any human intervention. If the new software hasn't been tested, it could cause unpredictable behavior and possibly endanger lives.
- **Rapid Spread of Computer Viruses:** If any computer system in a network gets affected by computer virus, there is a possible threat of other systems getting affected, too. Viruses get spread on a network easily because of the interconnectivity of workstations.
- **Dependency on the Main File Server:** If the main file server of a computer network breaks down, the entire system can become useless. In case of big networks, the file server is often a powerful computer, which often makes a failure expensive—not to mention causing a service outage for many customers or system users. Computer networks can be so powerful and useful that it is common for them to be used for more and more purposes. A network might start out small, and so people may not pay any attention to what might happen if the network were to fail, even after the network grows and becomes indispensable. In such cases, all the computers in an organization might become completely useless if a single network component fails.

Types of Networks: WANs, MANs, & Others

Networks differ in size of coverage and degree of specialty of application.

Networks, which consist of various combinations of computers, storage devices, and communications devices, may be divided into several main categories, differing primarily in their geographic range and purposes.

WIDE AREA NETWORK **A *wide area network (WAN)* is a communications network that covers a wide geographic area, such as a country or the world.** Most long-distance and regional telephone companies are WANs. A WAN may use a combination of satellites, fiber-optic cable, microwave, and copper-wire connections and link a variety of computers, from mainframes to terminals. *(● See Panel 6.4.)*

WANs are used to connect local area networks (discussed shortly), so that users and computers in one location can communicate with users and computers in other locations. A wide area network may be privately owned or rented (or use both private and leased lines), but the term usually connotes the inclusion of public (shared-user) networks. The best example of a WAN is the Internet.

METROPOLITAN AREA NETWORK **A *metropolitan area network (MAN)* is a communications network covering a city or a suburb.** The purpose of a MAN is often to bypass local telephone companies when accessing long-distance services. Many cellphone systems are MANs, and some cities set up wireless MANs to connect local area networks to the Internet.

LOCAL AREA NETWORK **A *local area network (LAN)*, or *local net*, connects computers and devices in a limited geographic area, such as one office, one building, or a group of buildings close together.** *(● See Panel 6.5.)* LANs are the basis for most office networks. The LANs of different offices on a university campus may also be linked together into a so-called *campus-area network*. LANs are proprietary—that is, the organization that runs the LAN

panel 6.4

Wide area network (WAN)

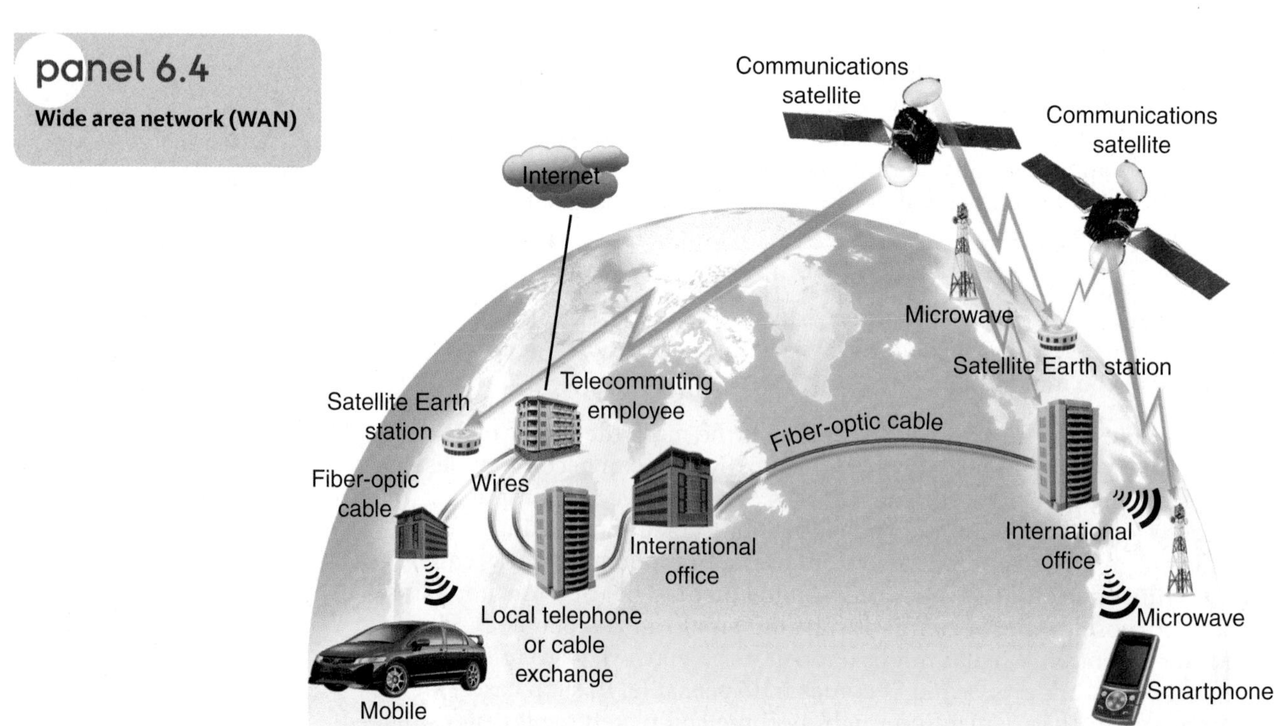

panel 6.5

Symbols used for diagramming networks, plus one example of a LAN

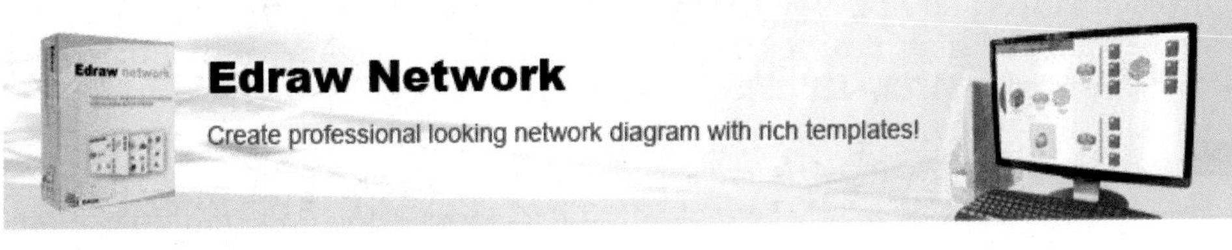

Edraw Network
Create professional looking network diagram with rich templates!

LAN Diagram Software

LAN Diagram (Local Area Network)

A network connecting computers in a relatively small area such as a building. A Local Area Network (LAN) delivers applications to local users, and provides the infrastructure for group collaboration, file sharing and transfer, printing and the rest of the user experience. Our LAN designs take into account the needs for resilience, security, Quality of service and scalability.

LAN Diagram Software

Edraw Network Diagram is ideal for network engineers and network designers who need to draw **LAN diagrams.** It had defined some common used **LAN diagram symbols** in drawing LAN diagrams. Just drag and drop pre-drawn shapes representing computers and network devices. Double click and set equipment data.

Free Download LAN Diagram Software and View All Examples

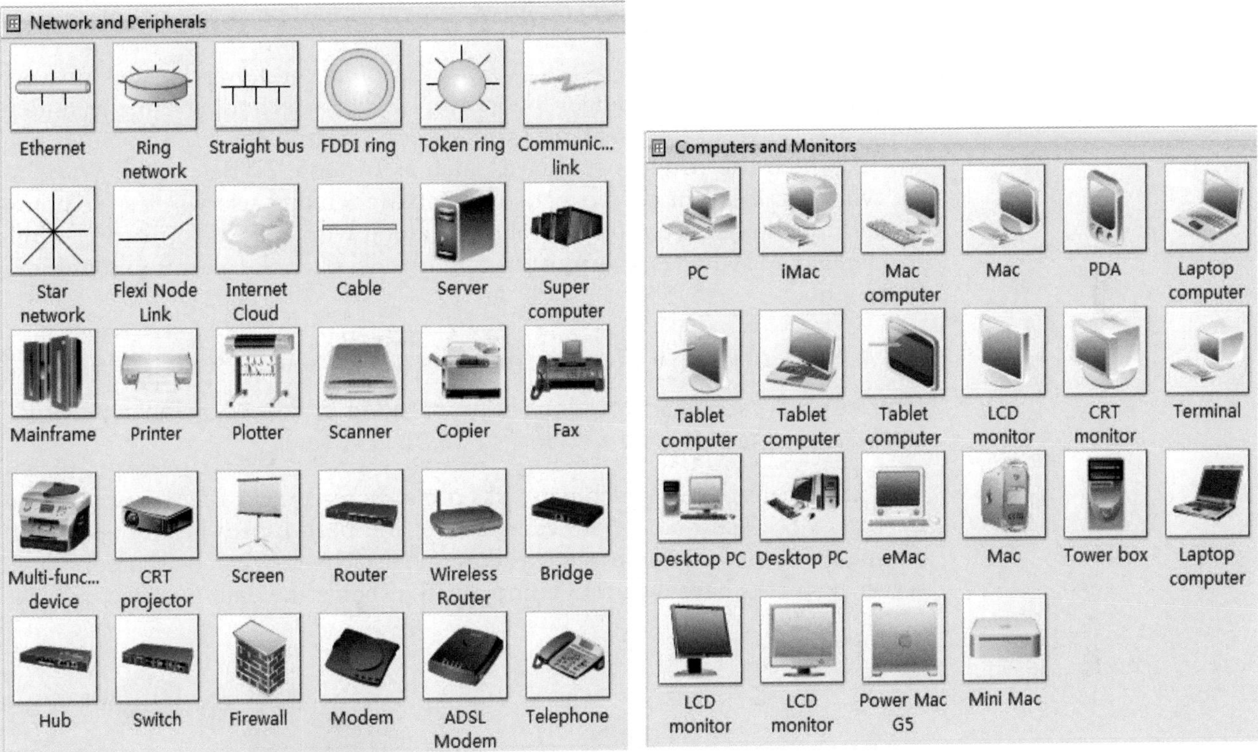

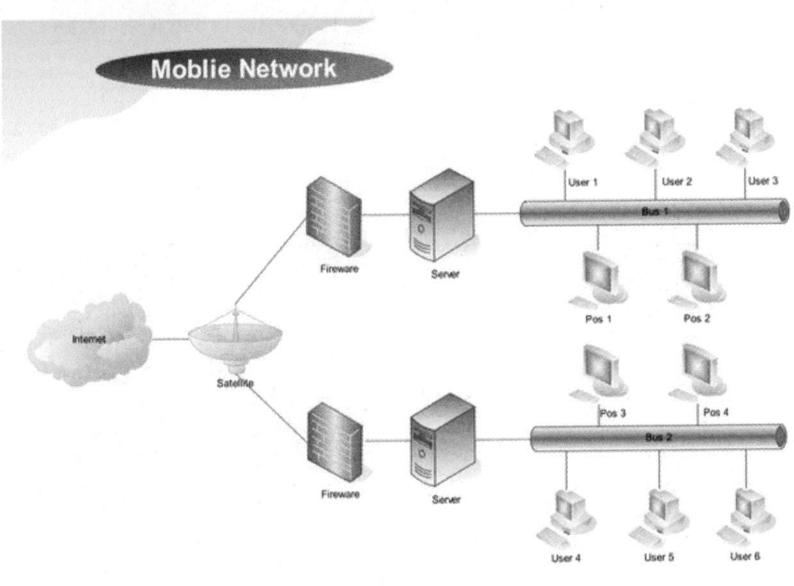

owns it. WANs and MANs generally use a common carrier—a telecommunications company that hires itself out to the public to provide communications transmission services—for at least part of its connections.

HOME AREA NETWORK A *home area network* uses wired, cable, or wireless connections to link a household's digital devices—not only multiple computers, printers, and storage devices but also VCRs, DVDs, televisions, fax machines, videogame machines, and home security systems. (A variant of the home area network is the garden area network—which can be used to link watering systems, outdoor lights, and alarm systems.)

PERSONAL AREA NETWORK Slightly different from a home area network because it doesn't use wires or cables, a *personal area network*, or *wireless personal area network*, uses short-range wireless technology to connect an individual's personal electronics, such as cellphone, MP3 player, notebook PC, and printer. These networks are made possible with such inexpensive, short-range wireless technologies as Bluetooth, ultra wideband, and wireless USB, which have a range of 30 feet or so, as we will describe.

HOME AUTOMATION NETWORK A *home automation network* relies on very inexpensive, very short-range, low-power wireless technology in the under-200-Kbps range to link switches and sensors around the house.[2] Such networks, which use wireless standards such as Insteon, ZigBee, and Z-Wave, as we will describe, run on inexpensive AA batteries and use wireless remotes, in-wall touch screens, and smartphones, along with special software, to control lights and switches, thermostats and furnaces, smoke alarms and outdoor floodlights.

How Networks Are Structured: Client/Server & Peer to Peer

Peer-to-peer networks are generally installed in homes or in very small businesses; client/server networks can be very large.

Two principal ways in which networks are structured are *client/server* and *peer to peer*. (• *See Panel 6.6.*) Both client/server and peer-to-peer networks connect computers so that resources such as files and applications can be shared. Client/server networks have a central computer that holds the data and manages the

Home area network

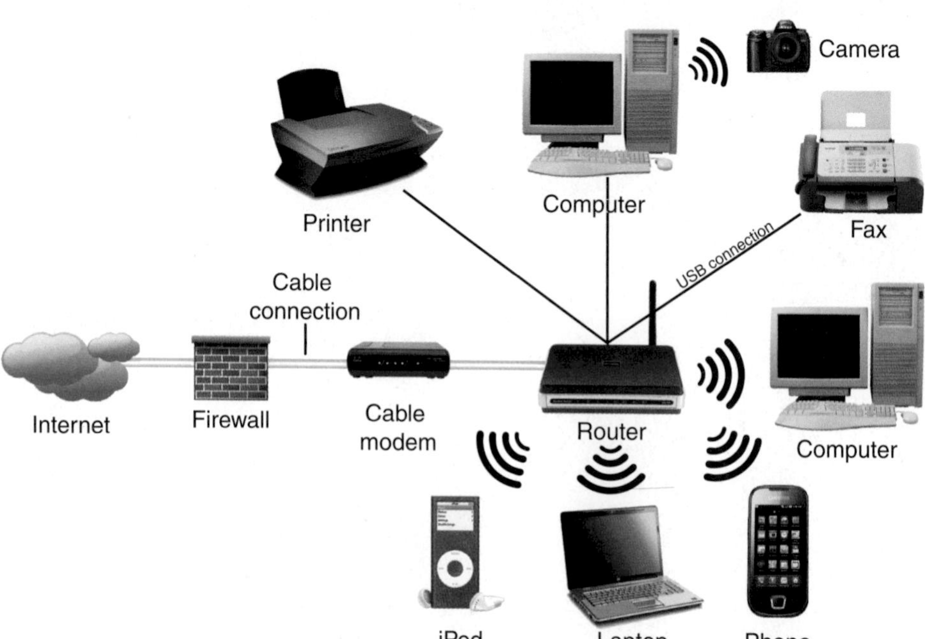

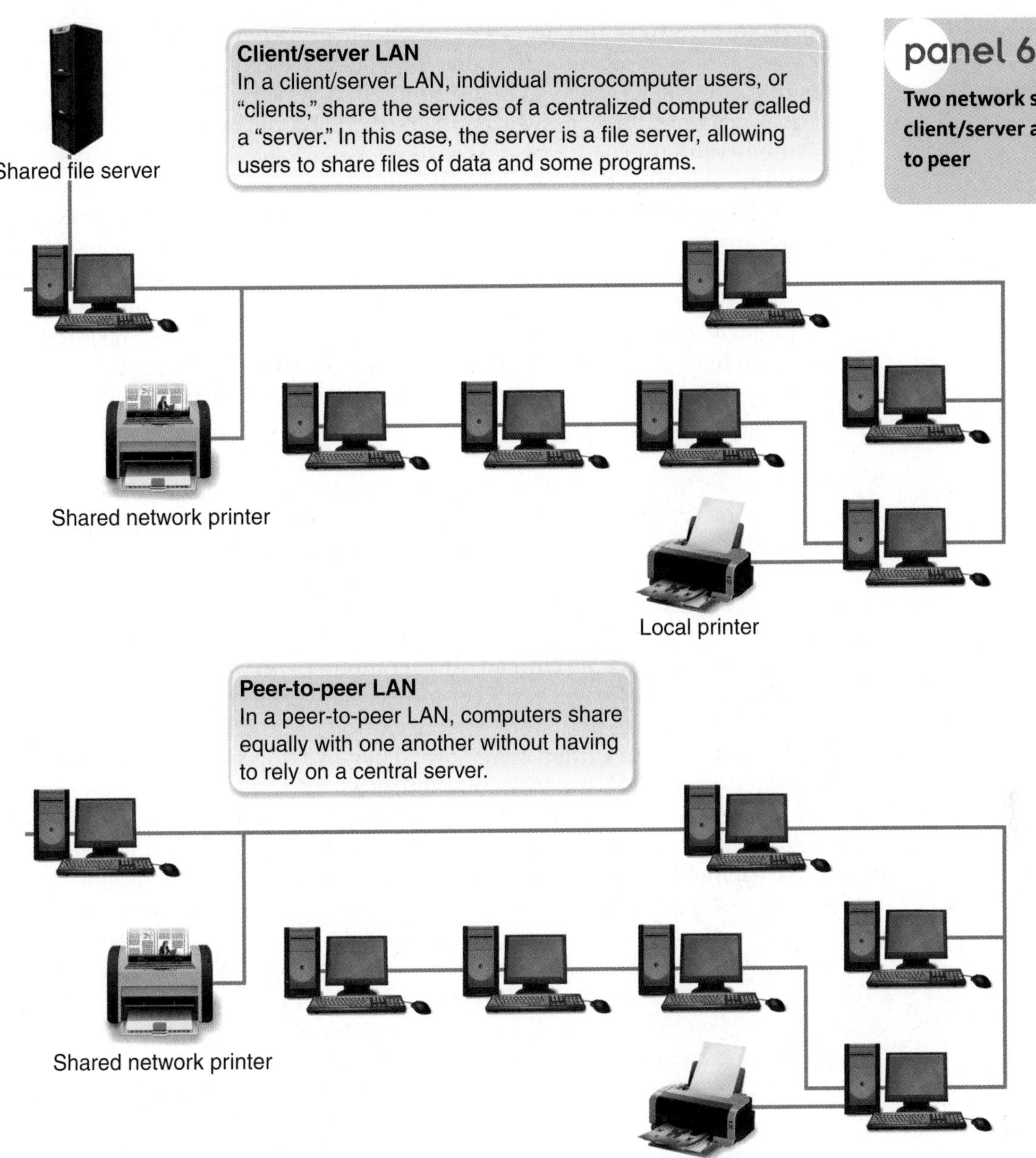

Shared file server
Client/server LAN
In a client/server LAN, individual microcomputer users, or "clients," share the services of a centralized computer called a "server." In this case, the server is a file server, allowing users to share files of data and some programs.
Shared network printer
Local printer
Peer-to-peer LAN
In a peer-to-peer LAN, computers share equally with one another without having to rely on a central server.
Shared network printer
Local printer

panel 6.6

Two network structures: client/server and peer to peer

resources. Peer-to-peer networks connect computers so that each computer shares all or part of its resources.

CLIENT/SERVER NETWORKS **A *client/server network* consists of *clients,* which are microcomputers that request data, and *servers,* which are central computers used to supply data.** In the client/server scheme, central servers handle all security and file transactions; they are powerful microcomputers that also manage shared devices. They may run server software for applications such as email and web browsing, or they may just host a database or be a file server or other kind of server; different servers may be used to manage different tasks.

A *file server* is a computer that acts like a disk drive, storing the programs and data files shared by users on a LAN. A *database server* is a computer in a LAN that stores data but doesn't store programs. A *print server* controls one or more printers and stores the print-image output from all the microcomputers on the system. *Web servers* contain web pages that can be viewed using a browser. *Mail servers* manage email.

There are an almost infinite variety of client/server networks, but all of them have some things in common. For one thing, all have centralized security databases that control access to shared resources on servers. Such servers contain lists of usernames and passwords. Users can't log on to the network unless they supply valid usernames and passwords. Once logged on, users may access only those resources that the network administrator allows them to access. Thus, client/server networks are more secure than peer-to-peer networks.

Client/server networks are more expensive to build than peer-to-peer networks, but client/server networks also tend to be much more stable. In a peer-to-peer network, certain shared resources reside on each user's machine. If users crash their computers, they could seriously affect their peer-to-peer network (where coworkers depend on resources that reside on other users' machines). On most client/server networks, however, shared resources reside on the server, where they're safe from careless users.

PEER-TO-PEER NETWORKS The word *peer* denotes one who is equal in standing with another (as in the phrases "peer pressure" and "jury of one's peers"). **In a *peer-to-peer (P2P) network*, all microcomputers on the network communicate directly with one another without relying on a server;** in peer-to-peer networks, which are relatively inexpensive to set up, each machine shares its own resources and handles its own security. Every computer can share files and peripherals with all other computers on the network, given that all are granted access privileges. Peer-to-peer networks are less expensive than client/server networks and work effectively for up to 25 computers. Beyond that, they slow down under heavy use. They are appropriate for small networks, such as small businesses and home networks.

The concept behind peer-to-peer networking is to share files and printers as inexpensively as possible; therefore, there's no main server on the network. Instead, each client functions both as a client and as a server simultaneously. Since users are allowed to control access to the resources on their own computers, however, security can become a problem; there's no central security or any way to control who shares what. Users are free to create any network share points on their computers—that is, they can create their own passwords for various resources available on their computers. Although this arrangement may sound somewhat secure, it isn't. The computer that contains the shared resources doesn't check on who's trying to access those resources. Any user can access them as long as the user knows the password.

more info!

Network Tutorials

For more on how various types of networks operate:

www.networktutorials.info/

Intranets, Extranets, & VPNs

Several types of networks use the Internet as their base.

Early in the Online Age, businesses discovered the benefits of using the World Wide Web to get information to customers, suppliers, or investors. For example, in the mid-1990s, FedEx found it could save millions by allowing customers to click through web pages to trace their parcels, instead of having FedEx customer-service agents do it. From there, it was a short step to the application of the same technology inside companies—in internal Internet networks called *intranets*.

INTRANETS: FOR INTERNAL USE ONLY **An *intranet* is an organization's internal private network that uses the infrastructure and standards** (technology, protocols, and hypertext links [Chapter 2]) **of the public Internet and web.** When a corporation develops a public website, it is making selected information available to consumers and other interested parties. When it creates an intranet, it enables employees to have quicker access to internal information and to share knowledge so that they can do their jobs better. The intranet is an in-house website (inside the firewall) on the company's local area network (LAN) that serves employees only. Although intranet pages may have links to websites on the Internet, the intranet is not exposed to, and is not accessed by,

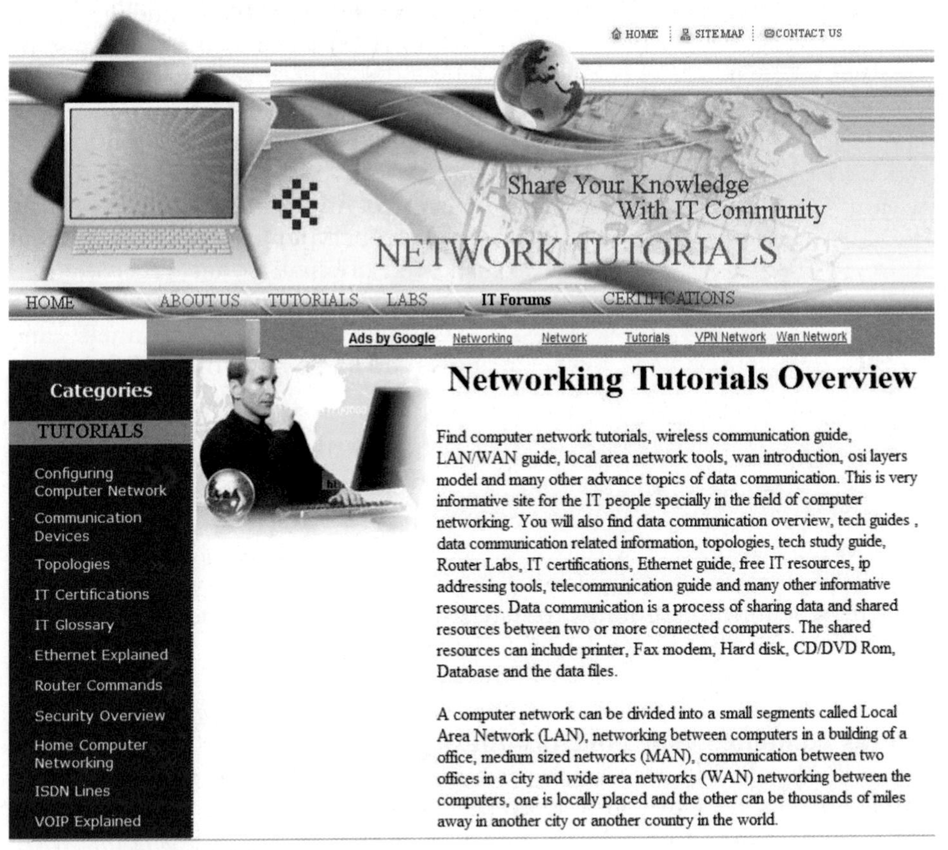

HOME | SITEMAP | CONTACT US
Share Your Knowledge With IT Community
NETWORK TUTORIALS
HOME ABOUT US TUTORIALS LABS IT Forums CERTIFICATIONS
Ads by Google Networking Network Tutorials VPN Network Wan Network
Categories
TUTORIALS
Configuring Computer Network
Communication Devices
Topologies
IT Certifications
IT Glossary
Ethernet Explained
Router Commands
Security Overview
Home Computer Networking
ISDN Lines
VOIP Explained
Networking Tutorials Overview
Find computer network tutorials, wireless communication guide, LAN/WAN guide, local area network tools, wan introduction, osi layers model and many other advance topics of data communication. This is very informative site for the IT people specially in the field of computer networking. You will also find data communication overview, tech guides, data communication related information, topologies, tech study guide, Router Labs, IT certifications, Ethernet guide, free IT resources, ip addressing tools, telecommunication guide and many other informative resources. Data communication is a process of sharing data and shared resources between two or more connected computers. The shared resources can include printer, Fax modem, Hard disk, CD/DVD Rom, Database and the data files.
A computer network can be divided into a small segments called Local Area Network (LAN), networking between computers in a building of a office, medium sized networks (MAN), communication between two offices in a city and wide area networks (WAN) networking between the computers, one is locally placed and the other can be thousands of miles away in another city or another country in the world.

(www.networktutorials.info/)

the general public. An intranet provides a standard in-company way to publish, for example, company policy, email addresses, news, schedules, medical and insurance forms, employee benefit information, jobs available within the company, and training manuals. Since a web browser is the primary interface, intranets offer cross-platform support for employees' Windows, Mac, and Linux desktops.

EXTRANETS: FOR CERTAIN OUTSIDERS Taking intranet technology a few steps farther, extranets offer security and controlled access. As we have seen, intranets are internal systems, designed to connect the members of a specific group or a single company. By contrast, ***extranets*** **are private intranets that connect not only internal personnel but also selected suppliers and other strategic parties via the public communications systems.** Most extranets use the Internet as the entry point for outsiders, a firewall configuration to limit access, and a secure protocol for authenticating users.

Extranets have become popular for standard transactions such as purchasing, supporting a mobile sales force, communicating product plans, obtaining customer feedback, and servicing law-firm clients. One way for a small business to provide an extranet is through hosted applications, like WebEx's WebOffice, Trichys' Work Zone, and Microsoft SharePoint Services.

VIRTUAL PRIVATE NETWORKS Because wide area networks use many leased lines, maintaining them can be expensive, especially as distances between offices increase. To decrease communications costs, some companies have established their own ***virtual private networks (VPNs)*****, private networks that use a public network (usually the Internet) to connect remote sites.** So, instead of using a dedicated connection such as leased line, a VPN uses "virtual" connections routed through the Internet from the company's private network to the remote site or employee. A VPN works by using the shared public infrastructure while maintaining privacy through security procedures and tunneling protocols

Virutal private network

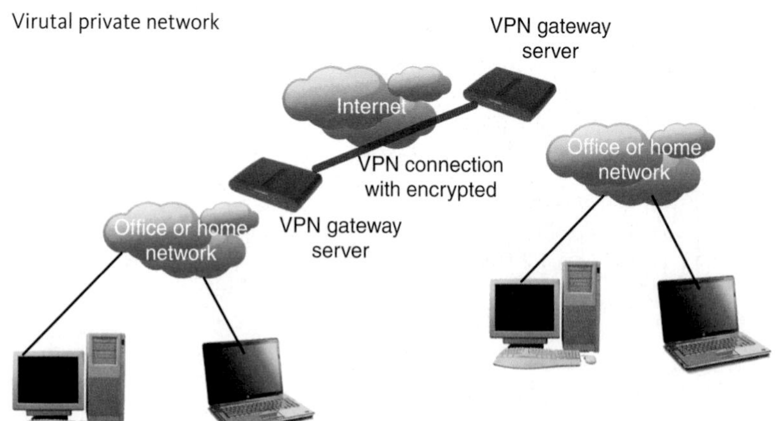

such as the Layer Two Tunneling Protocol (L2TP). In effect, the protocols, by encrypting data at the sending end and decrypting it at the receiving end, send the data through a "tunnel" that cannot be "entered" by data that is not properly encrypted. An additional level of security involves encrypting not only the data but also the originating and receiving network addresses.

Company intranets, extranets, and LANs can all be parts of a VPN.

Tunneling

For more on how VPNs work, go to:

http://computer.howstuffworks.com/vpn.htm

www.alliancedatacom.com/how-vpn-works.asp

www.ehow.com/how-does_4926227_a-vpn-work.html

http://hubpages.com/hub/How_do_VPNs_work

www.brightgreenvpn.com/what-is-a-vpn

Components of a Network

Regardless of size, networks all have several components in common.

Networks use a wired or wireless connection system. Wired connections may be twisted-pair wiring, coaxial cable, or fiber-optic cable, and wireless connections may be infrared, microwave (such as Bluetooth), broadcast radio (such as Wi-Fi), or satellite, as we describe shortly.

HOSTS & NODES The client/server type of network has a ***host computer*****, a central computer that controls the network.** The other devices on the network are called nodes. **A *node* is any device that is attached (wired or wireless) to a network—for example, a microcomputer, terminal, storage device, scanner, or printer.** A device called a *wireless access point (WAP)* when attached to a wired network essentially extends the range of the network by offering several wireless nodes, enabling you, say, to wirelessly connect a computer in a back bedroom to a network at the front of the house. Before wireless networks were available, setting up a computer network in a business, home, or school often required running many cables through walls and ceilings in order to deliver network access to all of the network-enabled devices in the building.

PACKETS Electronic messages are sent as packets. **A *packet* is a fixed-length block of data for transmission.** A sending computer uses a protocol (the TCP layer of TCP/IP, Chapter 2, p. 63) to break an electronic message apart into packets, each of which typically contains 1,000–1,500 bytes. The various packets are sent through a communications packet-switching network, such as the Internet—often using different (and most expedient) routes, at different speeds, and sandwiched in between packets from other messages. Once the packets arrive at their destination, the receiving computer reassembles them (called *packet switching*) into proper sequence to complete the message.

Most modern Wide Area Network (WAN) protocols are based on packet-switching technologies. In contrast, normal telephone service is based on a circuit-switching technology, in which a dedicated line is allocated for transmission between two parties. Circuit-switching is ideal when data must be transmitted quickly and must arrive in the same order in which it's sent. This is the case with most real-time data, such as live audio and video. Packet switching is more efficient and robust for data that can withstand some delays in transmission, such as email messages and web pages.[3]

PROTOCOLS **A *protocol*, or *communications protocol*, is a set of conventions governing the exchange of data between hardware and/or software components in a communications network** (Chapter 2, p. 63). Every device connected to a network has an Internet protocol (IP) address so that other computers on the network can properly route data to that address. Sending and receiving devices must follow the same set of protocols.

Protocols are built into the hardware or software you are using. The protocol in your communications software, for example, will specify how receiver devices will acknowledge sending devices, a matter called *handshaking*. Handshaking establishes the fact that the circuit is available and operational. It also establishes the level of device compatibility and the speed of transmission. In addition, protocols specify the type of electrical connections used, the timing of message exchanges, and error-detection techniques.

A packet, or electronic message, carries four types of information that will help it get to its destination—namely, the sender's address (the IP), the intended receiver's address, how many packets the message has been broken into, and the number of the individual packet. The packets carry the data in the protocols that the Internet uses—that is, TCP/IP.

NETWORK LINKING DEVICES: SWITCHES, BRIDGES, GATEWAYS, ROUTERS, & BACKBONES Networks are often linked together—LANs to MANs and MANs to WANs, for example. The means for connecting them are switches, bridges, routers, and gateways. (● *See Panel 6.7.)*

- **Switches: A *switch* is a device that connects computers to a network.** A switch is a *full-duplex* device, meaning data is transmitted back and forth at the same time, which improves the performance of the network.

panel 6.7

Components of a typical network

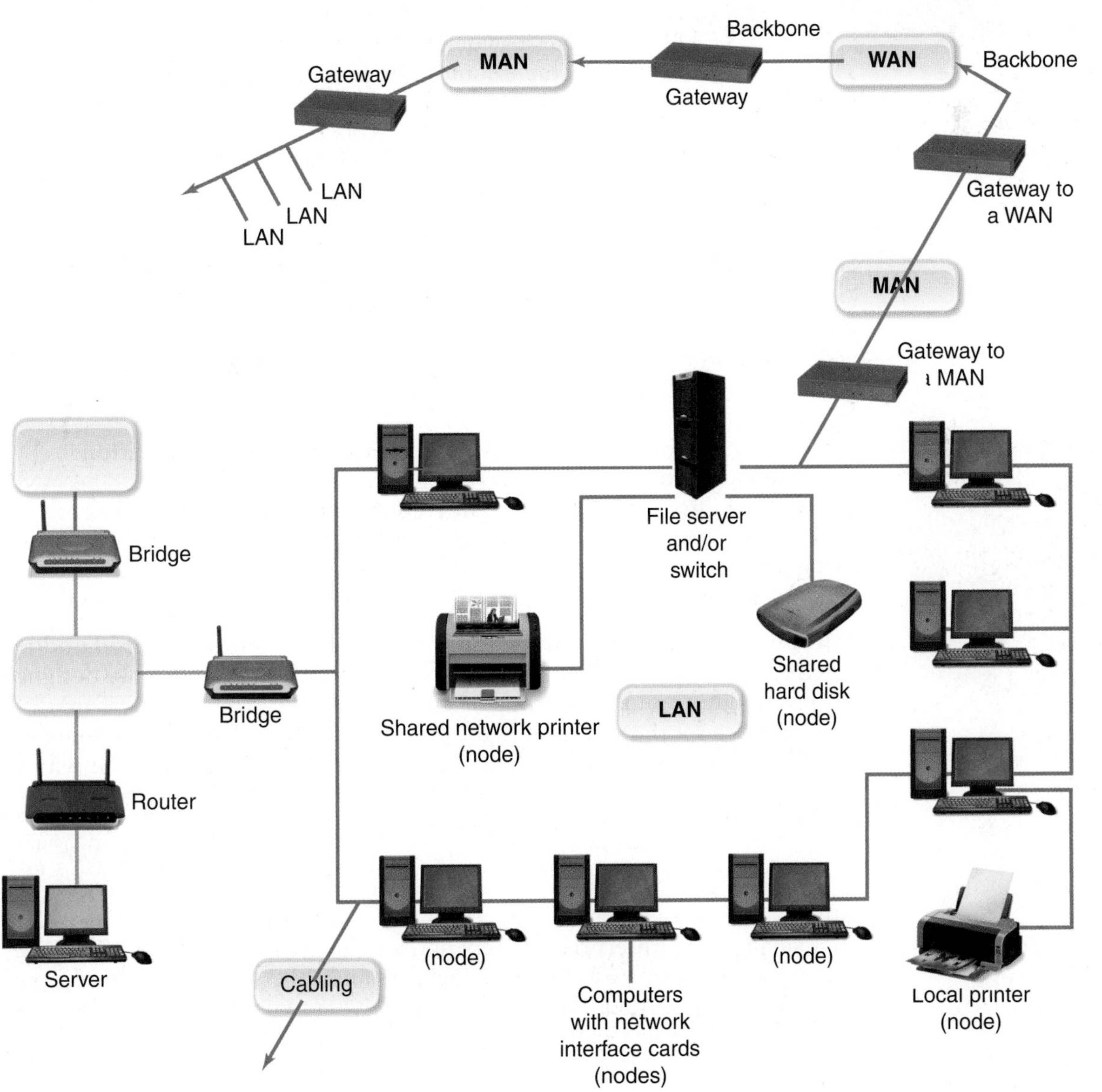

Belkin switch

Switches allow each component full use of the bandwidth (Chapter 2, p. 54). A network switch is charged with the job of connecting smaller segments of a single network into a connected whole. Network switches are capable of inspecting data packets as they are received, determining the source and destination device of each packet, and forwarding them appropriately. By delivering messages only to the connected device intended, a network switch conserves network bandwidth.

Ethernet implementations of network switches are the most common. Different models of network switches support differing numbers of connected devices. Most consumer-grade network switches provide either four or eight connections for Ethernet devices. Switches can be connected to each other, a so-called *daisy chaining* method to add progressively larger number of devices to a LAN.

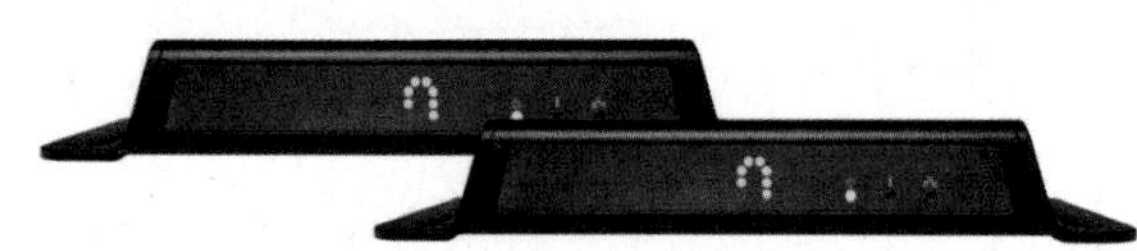
Sling Link Turbo bridge

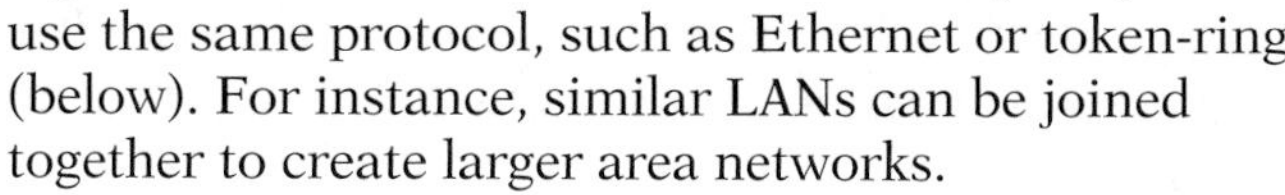

- **Bridges:** **A *bridge* is an interface used to connect the same types of networks** or two segments of the same local area network (LAN) that use the same protocol, such as Ethernet or token-ring (below). For instance, similar LANs can be joined together to create larger area networks.

  A network bridge is basically a type of switch. Whereas a switch has multiple connection ports, a bridge has a single connection port. You can envision a bridge as being a device that decides whether a message from you to someone else is going to the local area network in your building or to someone on the local area network in the building across the street.

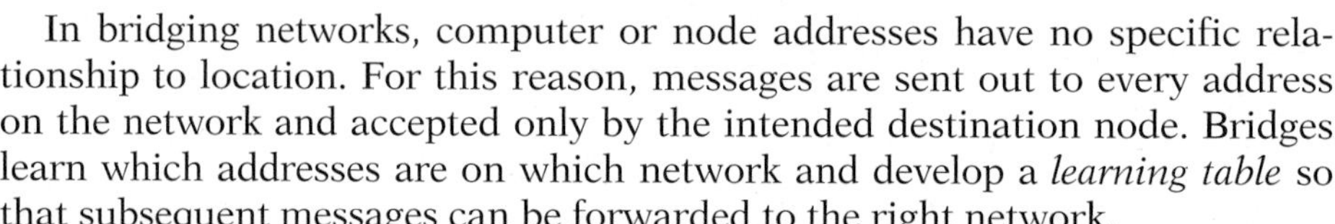

In bridging networks, computer or node addresses have no specific relationship to location. For this reason, messages are sent out to every address on the network and accepted only by the intended destination node. Bridges learn which addresses are on which network and develop a *learning table* so that subsequent messages can be forwarded to the right network.

A bridge is sometimes combined with a router (see below) in a product called a *brouter.*

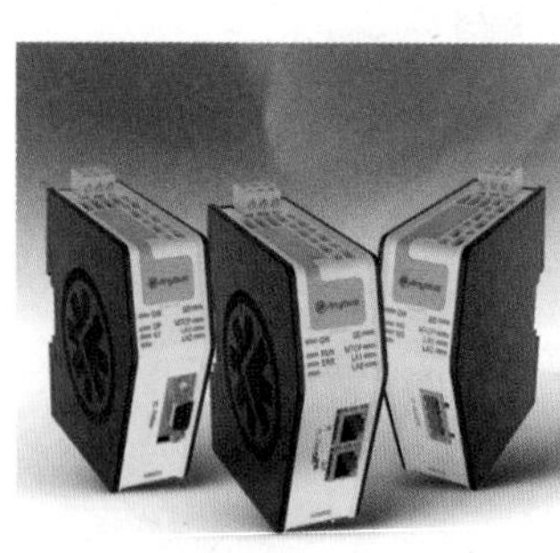
Anybus Gateways

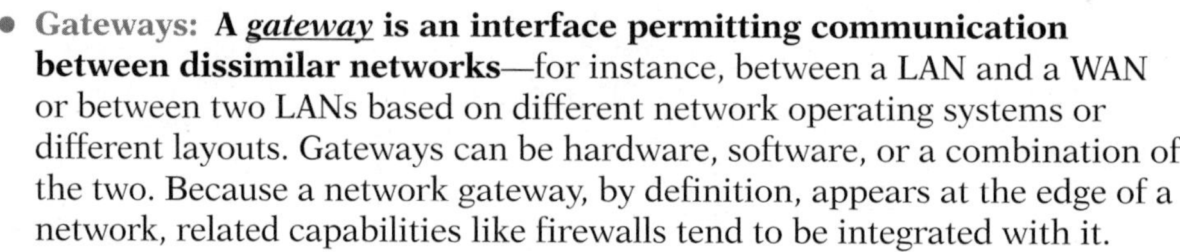

- **Gateways:** **A *gateway* is an interface permitting communication between dissimilar networks**—for instance, between a LAN and a WAN or between two LANs based on different network operating systems or different layouts. Gateways can be hardware, software, or a combination of the two. Because a network gateway, by definition, appears at the edge of a network, related capabilities like firewalls tend to be integrated with it.

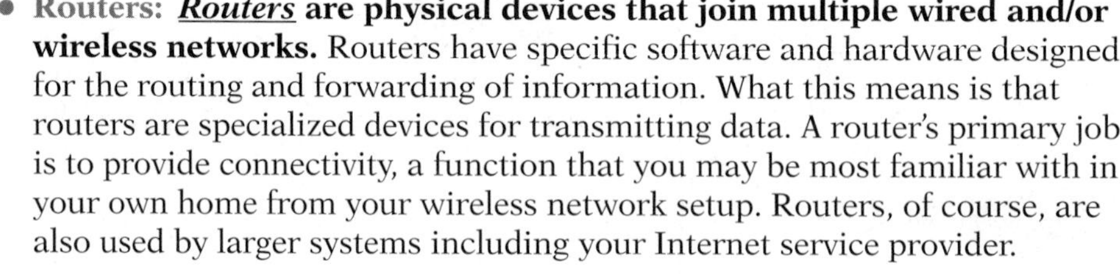

- **Routers:** ***Routers* are physical devices that join multiple wired and/or wireless networks.** Routers have specific software and hardware designed for the routing and forwarding of information. What this means is that routers are specialized devices for transmitting data. A router's primary job is to provide connectivity, a function that you may be most familiar with in your own home from your wireless network setup. Routers, of course, are also used by larger systems including your Internet service provider.

There are two main sizes of routers. The first are small office and home office connectivity routers. They allow you to connect to your cable or DSL on a small scale. Enterprise routers are usually confined to large companies and universities as well as research facilities and ISPs. Although these support basically the same function, they are infinitely more powerful.

High-speed routers can serve as part of the Internet backbone, or transmission path, handling the major data traffic, calculating the best possible

Network cables and computer switches

path for transmission of data packets between networks. The basis for routing of data through a router is the use of Internet protocol (IP) addresses. Most routers in the world sit in homes and small offices and just direct web, email and other Internet transactions from the local network to the cable or DSL modem, which is connected to the ISP and the Internet. Sitting at the edge of the network, they often contain a built-in firewall for security, and the firewall can serve all users in the network without requiring that the personal firewall in each computer be turned on and configured. However, in larger companies, routers are also used to separate local area networks (LANs) into subnetworks (subnets) in order to balance traffic within workgroups and to filter traffic for security purposes and policy management.

- Backbone: **The *backbone* consists of the main highway—including gateways, routers, and other communications equipment—that connects all computer networks in an organization.** People frequently talk about the *Internet backbone,* the central structure that connects all other elements of the Internet. As we discussed in Chapter 2, several commercial companies provide these major high-speed links across the country; these backbones are connected at Internet exchange points (IXPs; Chapter 2, p. 61).

NETWORK INTERFACE CARDS As we stated in Chapter 4, a *network interface card (NIC)* enables the computer to send and receive messages over a cable network. The network card can be inserted into an expansion slot in a microcomputer or is built into the motherboard. Alternatively, a network card in a stand-alone box may serve a number of devices. New computers often come with network cards already installed.

NETWORK OPERATING SYSTEM The *network operating system (NOS)* is the system software that manages the activity of a network. The NOS supports access by multiple users and provides for recognition of users based on passwords and terminal identifications. Depending on whether the LAN is client/server or peer-to-peer, the operating system may be stored on the file server, on each microcomputer on the network, or on a combination of both.

Network Topologies

Three popular network topologies are bus, ring, and star.

Networks can be laid out in different ways. **The layout, or shape, of a network is called a *topology*.** The three basic topologies, or configurations, are *bus, ring,* and *star,* from which other arrangements can be configured. In communication networks, a topology is a usually schematic description of the arrangement of a network, including its nodes and connecting lines. There are

Backbones

The National Science Foundation (NSF) created the first high-speed backbone in 1987. Called NSFNET, it was a T1 line that connected 170 smaller networks together. A T3 line was developed the following year. Backbones are typically fiber-optic trunk lines, with multiple fiber-optic cables combined to increase capacity. Some large companies that provide backbone connectivity are MCI, UUnet, British Telecom, AT&T, and Teleglobe. Scientists in the U.S. invented the Internet, and the computers that oversee the network are still controlled by the U.S. Department of Commerce. Some people believe that the Internet should be put under international control through the United Nations. What do you think?

What is the Open Systems Interconnection Model (OSI)?

For details on how the OSI model structures network set-ups:

www.networktutorials.info/osi_layers.html

http://compnetworking.about.com/cs/designosimodel/a/osimodel.htm

http://en.wikipedia.org/wiki/OSI_model

www.webopedia.com/quick_ref/OSI_Layers.asp

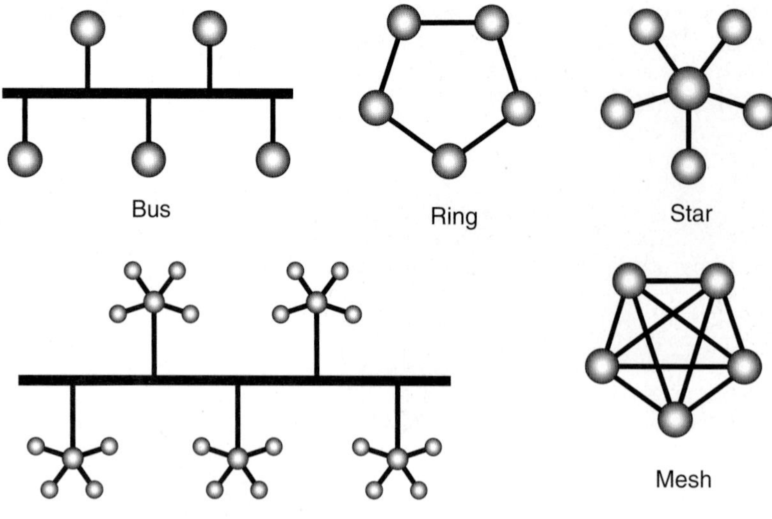

Some network topologies

two ways of defining network geometry: the physical topology and the logical (or signal) topology.

The physical topology of a network is the actual geometric layout of workstations—the physical design of a network including the devices, location, and cable installation. There are several common physical topologies, as described below and as shown in the illustration.

Logical (or signal) topology refers to how data actually transfers in a network as opposed to its design—that is, to the nature of the paths the signals follow from node to node. In many instances, the logical topology is the same as the physical topology. But this is not always the case. For example, some networks are physically laid out in a star configuration, but they operate logically as bus or ring networks.[4]

BUS NETWORK The bus network works like a bus system at rush hour, with various buses pausing in different bus zones to pick up passengers. In a bus network, all communications devices are connected to a common, linear channel. *(• See Panel 6.8.)* That is, **in a *bus network,* all nodes are connected to a single wire or cable, the *bus,* which has two endpoints, or terminators, which stop the network signal. Each communications device on the network transmits electronic messages to other devices.** If some of those messages collide, the sending device waits and tries to transmit again.

The advantages of a bus network are that it is relatively inexpensive, easy to use in peer-to-peer networks, and good for smaller networks not requiring high speeds. The disadvantages are that extra circuitry and software are needed to develop access methods in order to avoid collisions between messages and that the network is limited to 20 devices on a network segment that cannot exceed 185 meters in length. Also, if a connection in the bus is broken—as when someone moves a desk and knocks the connection out—the entire network may stop working.

With the increased use of client/server networks and the decreased cost of Ethernet networks (discussed shortly), bus networks are being used less and less.

panel 6.8

Bus network

A single channel connects all communications devices.

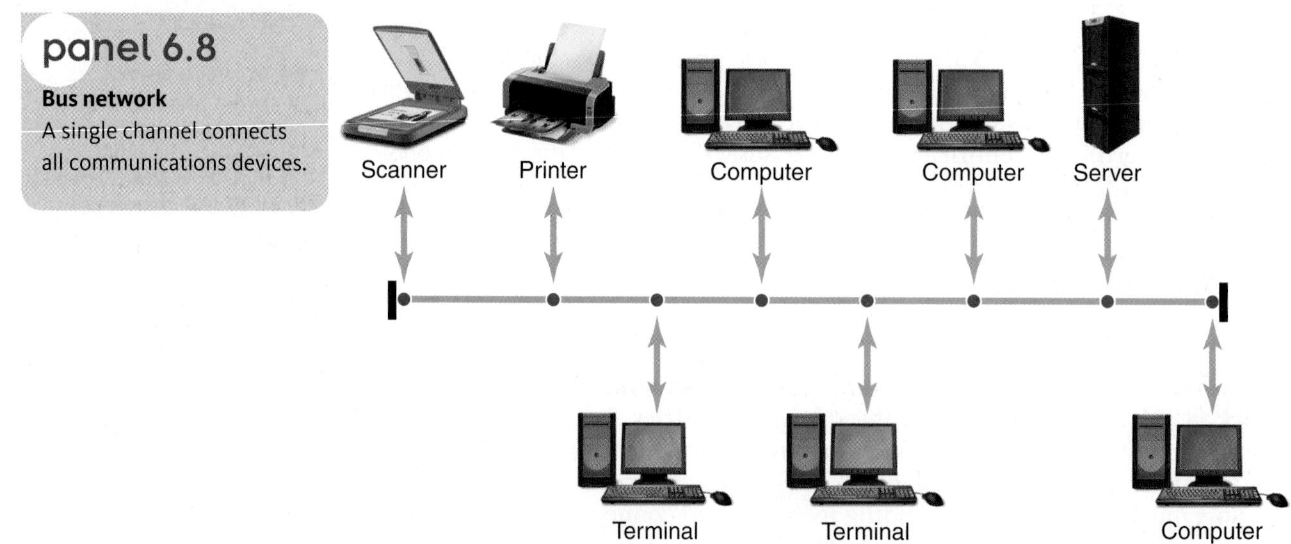

RING NETWORK **A *ring network* is one in which all microcomputers and other communications devices are connected in a continuous loop.** (● *See Panel 6.9.*) There are no endpoints.

Electronic messages are passed around the ring until they reach the right destination. There is no central server. An example of a ring network is IBM's Token Ring Network, in which a bit pattern (called a "token") determines which user on the network can send information.

The advantage of a ring network is that messages flow in only one direction. Thus, there is no danger of collisions. The disadvantage is that if one workstation malfunctions, the entire network can stop working.

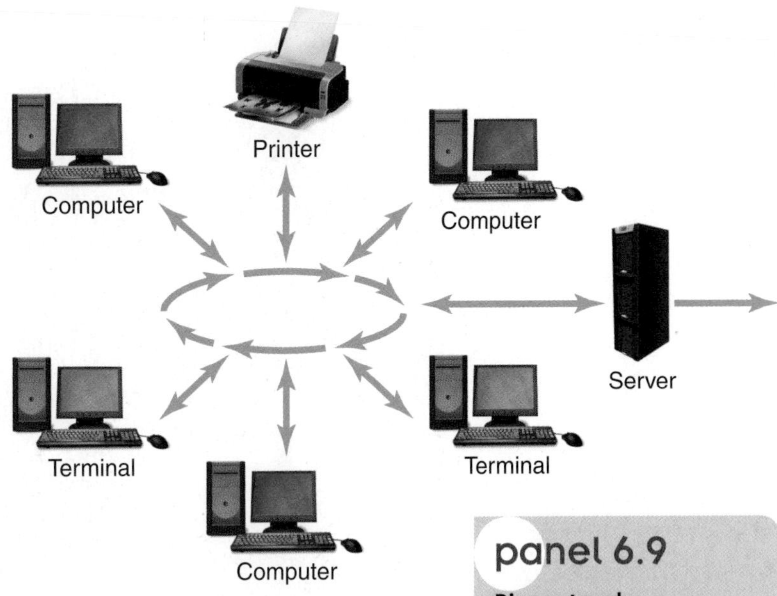

panel 6.9

Ring network

This arrangement connects the network's devices in a closed loop.

STAR NETWORK **A *star network* is one in which all microcomputers and other communications devices are directly connected to a central switch.** (● *See Panel 6.10.*) Electronic messages are routed through the central switch to their destinations. The central switch monitors the flow of traffic. A PBX system—a private telephone system, such as that found on a college campus, that connects telephone extensions to one another—is an example of a star network. Traditional star networks are designed to be easily expandable, because switches can be connected to additional switches of other networks.

Tree topologies (p. 330) are multiple star topologies on a bus. Star and tree networks are the topologies most commonly used today in LANs.

The advantage of a star network is that the switch prevents collisions between messages. Moreover, if a connection is broken between any communications device and the switch, the rest of the devices on the network will continue operating. However, if the switch goes down, the entire network stops.

panel 6.10

Star network

This arrangement connects all the network's devices to a central switch, through which all communications must pass.

MESH NETWORK **In a *mesh network topology*, messages sent to the destination can take any possible shortest, easiest route to reach its destination** (p. 330)**.** There must be at least two paths to any individual computer to create a mesh network. (Wireless networks are often implemented as a mesh.)

In the previous topologies, star and bus, messages are usually broadcast to every computer, especially in bus topology. In the ring topology, messages can travel in only one direction—clockwise or counterclockwise. The Internet employs the mesh topology, and the message, with the help of routers, finds its route for its destination.[5]

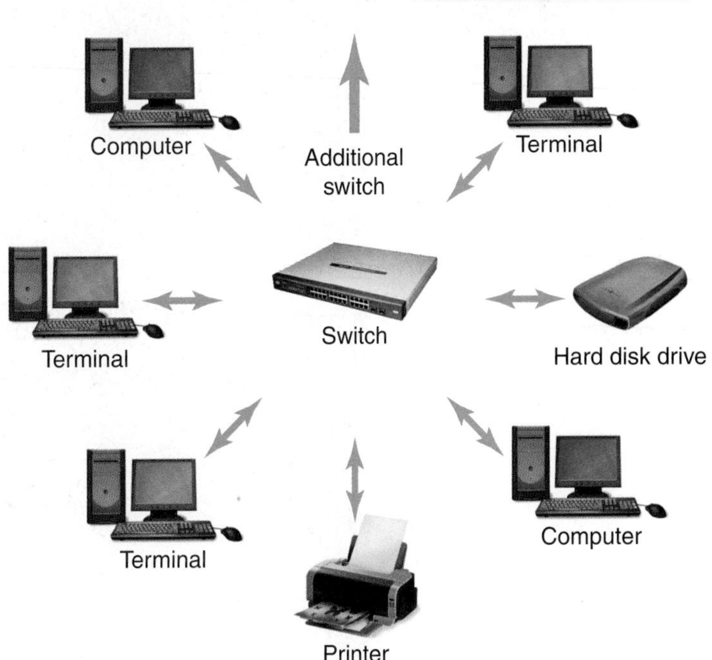

Ethernet

The Ethernet protocol prevents data collision on networks.

When you deal with small LANs, especially when they use wired or cable (twisted-pair, coaxial, or fiber-optic) connections, you may hear about Ethernet, a LAN protocol, or technology, used to keep messages from bumping into one another along the transmission line.

Traders work on the heavily networked floor of the New York Stock Exchange in New York.

ETHERNET In 1973, at Xerox Corporation's Palo Alto Research Center (more commonly known as PARC), researcher Bob Metcalfe designed and tested the first Ethernet network. While working on a way to link a particular computer to a printer, Metcalfe developed the physical method of cabling that connected devices on the Ethernet as well as the standards that governed communication on the cable. Ethernet has since become the most popular and most widely deployed network protocol technology in the world.

Ethernet **is a LAN technology that can be used with almost any kind of computer and that describes how data can be sent between computers and other networked devices usually in close proximity.** The Ethernet communications protocol is embedded in software and hardware devices intended for building a local area network (LAN), and it is commonly used in star topologies.

Inserting an Ethernet connector

- **Medium:** Ethernet devices attach to a common medium that provides a path along which the electronic signals will travel. Historically, this medium has been coaxial copper cable, but today it is more commonly a twisted-pair, fiber-optic cabling, or wireless connection.
- **Segment:** A single shared medium is called an Ethernet segment.
- **Node:** Devices that attach to that segment are stations, or nodes.
- **Frame:** The nodes communicate in short messages called *frames*, which are variably sized chunks of information.

Frames are analogous to sentences in human language. In English, we have rules for constructing our sentences; the Ethernet protocol specifies a set of rules for constructing frames. There are explicit minimum and maximum lengths for frames, and a set of required pieces of information that must appear in the frame. Each frame must include, for example, both a destination address and a source address that identify the recipient and the sender of the message. The address uniquely identifies the node, just as a name identifies a particular person. No two Ethernet devices should ever have the same address. Since a signal on the Ethernet medium reaches every attached node, the destination address is critical to identify the intended recipient of the frame.

Ethernet devices used to be able to have only a few hundred meters of cable between them, making it impractical to connect geographically dispersed locations. One version (called *10Base-T*) handles about 10 megabits per second. A newer version, *Fast Ethernet* (or *100Base-T*) transfers data at 100 megabits per second. The newest version, *Gigabit Ethernet* (or *1000Base-T*) transmits data at the rate of 1 gigabit (1,000 megabits) per second. Most new microcomputers come equipped with an Ethernet card and an Ethernet port (Chapter 4).

6.3 WIRED COMMUNICATIONS MEDIA

Communications media are the means of interchanging or transmitting and receiving information.

It used to be that two-way individual communications were accomplished mainly in two ways. They were carried by the medium of (1) a telephone wire or (2) a wireless method such as shortwave radio. Today there are many kinds of communications media, although they are still wired or wireless. ***Communications media*, or *communications channels*, carry signals over a *communications path*, the route between two or more communications media devices.** The speed, or data transfer rate, at which transmission occurs—and how much data can be carried by a signal—depends on the media and the type of signal.

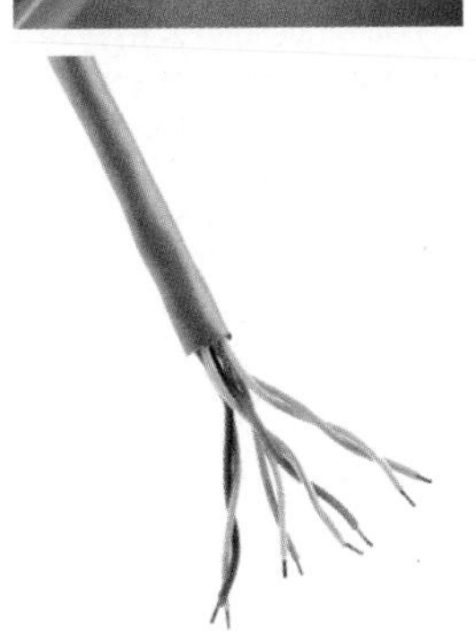

Twisted-pair wire

Wired Communications Media: Wires & Cables

There are three basic types of wired communications media.

Three types of wired communications media are *twisted-pair wire* (conventional telephone lines), *coaxial cable*, and *fiber-optic cable*. The various kinds of wired Internet connections discussed in Chapter 2—dial-up modem, DSL, cable modem, T1 lines, as well as Internet backbones—are created by using these wired communications media.

TWISTED-PAIR WIRE The telephone line that runs from your house to the pole outside, or underground, is probably twisted-pair wire. ***Twisted-pair wire* consists of two strands of insulated copper wire, twisted around each other. This twisted-pair configuration (compared to straight wire) somewhat reduces interference (called "crosstalk" or "noise") from electrical fields.** Twisted-pair is relatively slow, carrying data at the rate of 1–128 megabits per second (normally 56 Kbps). Moreover, it does not protect well against electrical interference. However, because so much of the world is already served by twisted-pair wire, it will no doubt be used for years to come, both for voice messages and for modem-transmitted computer data (dial-up connections).

(Category 5 [Cat5] is a newer kind of twisted-pair high-signal cable. This type of cable is generally used in cabling for computer networks such as Ethernet, for which it was designed, but is also sometimes used to carry many other signals such as telephony and video. Cat7 is the most recent version of this high-speed twisted-wire technology.)

The prevalence of twisted-pair wire gives rise to what experts call the "last-mile problem" (Chapter 2, p. 58). That is, it is relatively easy for telecommunications companies to upgrade the physical connections between cities and even between neighborhoods. But it is expensive for them to replace the "last mile" of twisted-pair wire that connects to individual houses.

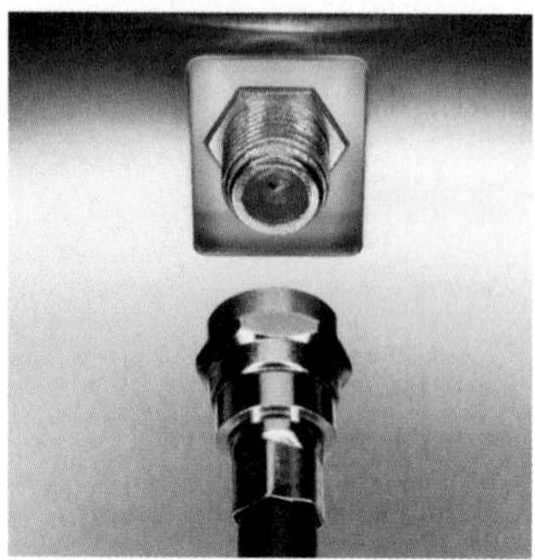

Coaxial cable

COAXIAL CABLE ***Coaxial cable*, commonly called "co-ax," is a high-frequency transmission cable that consists of insulated copper wire wrapped in a solid or braided metal shield and then in an external plastic cover.** Co-ax is widely used for cable television and cable Internet connections. Thanks to the extra insulation, coaxial cable is much better than twisted-pair wiring at resisting noise. Moreover, it can carry voice and data at a faster rate (up to 200 megabits per second; residential cable, 4–10 megabits per second). Often many coaxial cables are bundled together.

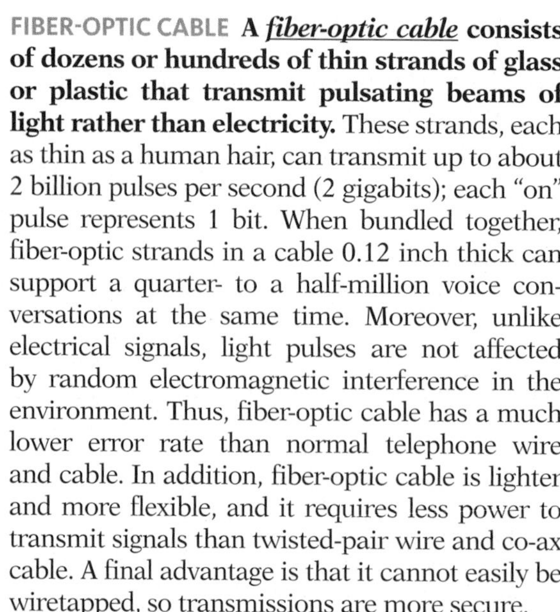

FIBER-OPTIC CABLE **A *fiber-optic cable* consists of dozens or hundreds of thin strands of glass or plastic that transmit pulsating beams of light rather than electricity.** These strands, each as thin as a human hair, can transmit up to about 2 billion pulses per second (2 gigabits); each "on" pulse represents 1 bit. When bundled together, fiber-optic strands in a cable 0.12 inch thick can support a quarter- to a half-million voice conversations at the same time. Moreover, unlike electrical signals, light pulses are not affected by random electromagnetic interference in the environment. Thus, fiber-optic cable has a much lower error rate than normal telephone wire and cable. In addition, fiber-optic cable is lighter and more flexible, and it requires less power to transmit signals than twisted-pair wire and co-ax cable. A final advantage is that it cannot easily be wiretapped, so transmissions are more secure.

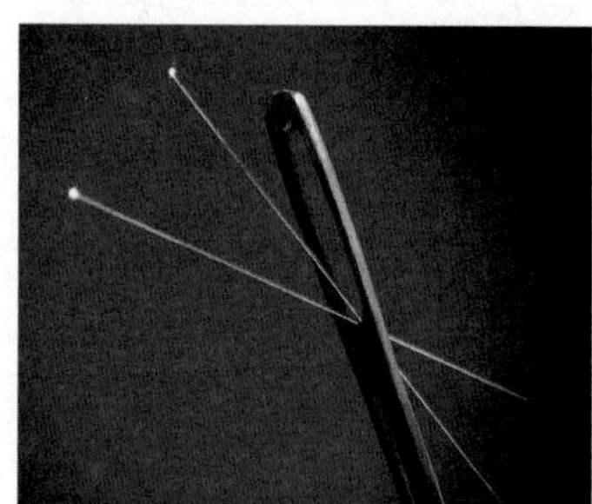

Fiber-optic strands

Do We Need More Fiber Optics?

Google has long been buying up data communications capacity, especially fiber optics. Its search engine works by making copies of nearly every page of the Internet in its own data centers. That requires Google to move a huge amount of data around the world on a regular basis. And its delivery of applications over the Internet uses even more bandwidth. So, it is planning to establish fiber-to-home service soon.

(www.google.com/appserve/fiberrfi/public/overview; http://latimesblogs.latimes.com/technology/2011/03/google-fiber-in-kansas-city-kan-free-to-schools-available-to-public-in-2012.html; http://gigaom.com/2010/04/22/hey-isps-google-wants-to-share-its-fiber-network/)

Wired Communications Media for Homes

Ethernet, HomePNA, and *HomePlug are three ways to create a home network.*

Many households now have more than one computer, and many have taken steps to link their equipment in a home network. Indeed, some new high-tech homes include network technology that links as many as 12 televisions positioned around the house plus computers, telephones, lights, audio, and alarm systems.

Traditionally, wired media have been used to connect equipment. Three wired network technologies are *Ethernet, HomePNA,* and *HomePlug.*

ETHERNET Most personal PCs come with Ethernet capability. Homes wanting to network with this technology generally use the kind of cabling (Cat5) that permits either regular Ethernet data speeds (10 megabits per second) or Fast Ethernet speeds (100 megabits per second). Besides cabling, which will have to be installed throughout the house (by you or by a professional installer), a home Ethernet network may require a few routers.

HOMEPNA: USING THE HOME'S EXISTING TELEPHONE WIRING Does your house have a phone jack in every room in which you have a computer? Then you might be interested in setting up a *phoneline network,* using conventional phonelines to connect the nodes in a network. The means for doing this is *HomePNA (HPNA)* technology, an alliance of leading technology companies working to ensure the adoption of a single, unified existing wire (telephone and cable) home-networking standard that transmits data at about 320 megabits per second.

HOMEPLUG: USING THE HOME'S EXISTING ELECTRIC-POWER WIRING Alternatively, you might want to set up a *power-line network,* using conventional power lines in a home to connect the nodes in a network, using HomePlug. *HomePlug* technology is a standard that allows users to send data over a home's existing electrical (AC) power lines, which can be transmitted at up to 200 megabits per second. This kind of communications medium has an advantage, of course, in that there is at least one power outlet in every room.

Some households have a combination of wired and wireless networks, but more are going over to all-wireless (covered later in the chapter).

6.4 WIRELESS COMMUNICATIONS MEDIA

The term "wireless" describes telecommunications in which electromagnetic waves (rather than wire or cable) carry the signal over part or all of the communication path.

Cellphone and wireless laptop Internet use each grew more prevalent in 2010, the last year for which we have data. Nearly half of all adults (47%) went online with a laptop using a Wi-Fi connection or mobile broadband card (up from the 39% who did so as of April 2009), and 40% of adults used the Internet, email or instant messaging on a mobile phone (up from the 32% of Americans who did this in 2009). This means that about 59% of adults now access the Internet wirelessly using a laptop or cell phone. That adds up to an increase from the 51% who used a laptop or cell phone wirelessly in April 2009.[6]

Cellphones and laptops are only two kinds of wireless communication. We consider (1) the electromagnetic spectrum, (2) the five types of long-distance wireless communications media, (3) long-distance wireless, and (4) short-distance wireless.

The Electromagnetic Spectrum, the Radio-Frequency (RF) Spectrum, & Bandwidth

The electromagnetic spectrum is the range of all possible frequencies of electromagnetic radiation that exist in the world and throughout the universe.

Often it's inefficient or impossible to use wired media for data transmission, and wireless transmission is better. To understand wireless communication, we need to understand transmission signals and the electromagnetic spectrum.

PRACTICAL ACTION

Telecommuting & Telework: The Nontraditional Workplace

Two offshoots of nontraditional office work are telecommuting and telework.

Telecommuting: Working from Home

Working at home while in telecommunication with the office is called *telecommuting*. In the United States, telecommuting has been gaining favor for several years. The number of U.S. telecommuters ranges between 2.8 million people (consider home their primary place of work, not including the self-employed) and 44.4 million (includes anyone who works at home at least once a year). Three million more teleworkers (180,000 more each year) are expected by 2015; in 2010, 79% of those polled would choose to telecommute if the opportunity were given to them.[7]

If these people worked from home 50% of the time, a company of 100 would gain approximately $576,000 per year; U.S. business would gain $235 billion in increased productivity, save $124 billion per year in office costs, save $46 billion in reduced absenteeism, and save $31 billion in reduced turnover.[8]

Telecommunication can have many benefits. The advantages to society are reduced traffic congestion, energy consumption, and air pollution. The advantages to employees are lower commuting and workplace-wardrobe costs and more choices about how they handle their time. The advantage to employers, it's argued, is increased productivity, because telecommuters may experience fewer distractions at home than in the office and can work flexible hours. Absenteeism may be reduced and the labor pool expanded, because hard-to-get employees don't have to uproot themselves from where they want to live. Costs for office space, parking, insurance, and other overhead are reduced.

Despite the advantages, however, telecommuting has some drawbacks. Employees sometimes feel isolated, "out of the loop," even deserted, or they are afraid that working outside the office will hinder their career advancement. They also find the arrangements blur the line between office and home, straining family life, and they also are often without IT support. Employers may feel telecommuting causes resentments among office-bound employees, and they may find it difficult to measure employees' productivity. In addition, with teamwork now more of a workplace requirement, managers may worry that telecommuters cannot keep up with the pace of change. Finally, some employers are concerned that telecommuters create more opportunities for security breaches by hackers or equipment thieves.[9]

Telework: Working from Anywhere

More recently, the term *telework* (or *virtual office*) has been adopted to replace the term "telecommuting," because it encompasses not just working from home but working from anywhere: a café, a client's office, an airport lounge, a commuter train, a car, a park. With smartphones, numerous broadband connections points, Wi-Fi, virtual private networks, instant messaging, and texting, telework has become easier than ever.

Employees at big high-tech companies work from their homes, cars, and other nontraditional work sites. Thus, the workplace exists more in virtual than physical space, and the actual office may be little more than a computer, a high-bandwidth connection, and a cellphone, with most communication with the outer world being through a voice mail system, an email address, a web page, and a post office box. (Indeed, you can live anywhere you want in the world but have a local business presence with a prestigious physical mailing address and local phone number by hiring a virtual office web service such as Officescape [*www.officescape.com*], whose staff can handle all your office information locally and forward your physical mail and packages.)

Despite the history of productivity, some managers fear losing control over employees who become teleworkers, picturing them at home watching TV instead of working. The way to avoid that, suggests Robert Smith, director of ITAC (Telework Advisory Group for WorldatWork), is for companies to install ways of measuring productivity. "Good organizations put into place performance requirements," he says. "They have a process in which managers can set performance goals and properly evaluate whether those goals are met. If you have that in place, you'll have a more effective organization, whether an employee is 10 feet or 10 miles away."[10] Smith stated later: "ITAC has developed several free and low-cost information resources that businesses affected directly by disasters such as Katrina can apply in advance to help shorten their recovery. At the same time employees affected today by gasoline's spiraling costs and threats of supply shortage can address this problem by reducing and possibly eliminating their commute when working from home or locations closer to home." ["ITAC Research Shows How to Combat High Gas Prices and GET Displaced Employees Back to Work," *www.prnewswire.com/news-releases/itac-research-shows-how-to-combat-high-gas-prices-and-get-displaced-employees-back-to-work-54702377.html* (accessed April 12, 2011).]

THE ELECTROMAGNETIC SPECTRUM Telephone signals, radar waves, microwaves, and the invisible commands from a garage-door opener all represent different waves on what is called the electromagnetic spectrum of radiation. The ***electromagnetic spectrum of radiation*** **is the basis for *all* telecommunications signals, carried by both wired and wireless media.**

Part of the electromagnetic spectrum is the ***radio-frequency (RF) spectrum*, fields of electrical energy and magnetic energy that carry most communications signals.** *(● See Panel 6.11, next page.)* Internationally, the RF spectrum is allocated by the International Telecommunications Union (ITU) in Geneva, Switzerland. Within the United States, the RF spectrum is further allocated to nongovernment and government users.

FM signals have a great advantage over AM signals. Both signals are susceptible to slight changes in amplitude. With an AM broadcast, these changes result in static. With an FM broadcast, slight changes in amplitude don't matter; since the audio signal is conveyed through changes in frequency, the FM receiver can just ignore changes in amplitude. The result: no static at all.

The Federal Communications Commission (FCC), acting under the authority of Congress, allocates and assigns frequencies to nongovernment users. The National Telecommunications and Information Administration (NTIA) is responsible for departments and agencies of the U.S. government.

Electromagnetic waves vary according to *frequency*—the number of times a wave repeats, or makes a cycle, in a second. The radio-frequency spectrum ranges from low-frequency waves, such as those used for garage-door openers (40 megahertz), through the medium frequencies for certain cellphones (824–849 megahertz) and air-traffic control monitors (960–1,215 megahertz), to deep-space radio communications (2,290–2,300 megahertz). Frequencies at the very ends of the spectrum take the forms of infrared rays, visible light, ultraviolet light, X rays, and gamma rays.

AM & FM: What's the Difference?

FM radio works the same way that AM radio works. The difference is in how the carrier wave is modulated, or altered. With AM radio, the amplitude, or overall strength, of the signal is varied to incorporate the sound information. With FM, the frequency (the number of times each second that the current changes direction) of the carrier signal is varied. (*See below.*)

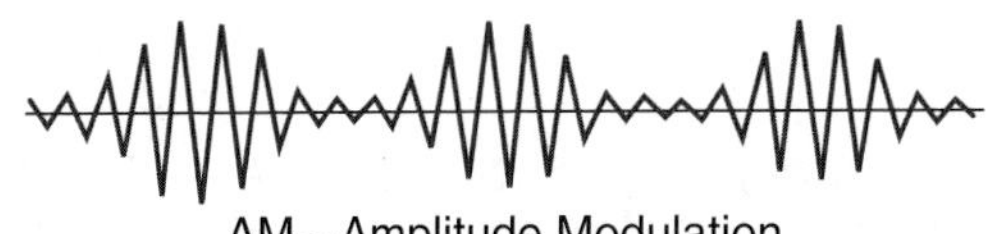

AM—Amplitude Modulation

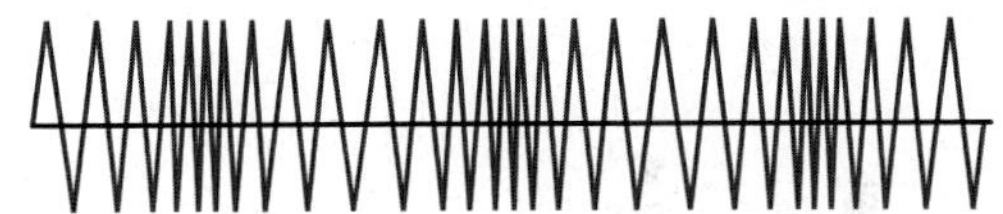

FM—Frequency Modulation

BANDWIDTH **The *bandwidth* is the range, or *band*, of frequencies that a transmission medium can carry in a given period of time.** For analog signals, bandwidth is expressed in *hertz (Hz)*, or *cycles per second*. For example, certain cellphones operate within the range 824–849 megahertz—that is, their bandwidth is 25 megahertz. *The wider a medium's bandwidth, the more frequencies it can use to transmit data and thus the faster the transmission.*

There are two general classes of bandwidth—narrow and broad—which can be expressed in hertz but also in *bits per second (bps)*:

- **Narrowband: *Narrowband*, also known as *voiceband*, is used for regular telephone communications**—that is, for speech, faxes, and data. Transmission rates are usually 1.5 megabits per second or less. Dial-up modems use this bandwidth.
- **Broadband:** In general, ***broadband* refers to telecommunications in which a wide band of frequencies is available to transmit information. Because a wide band of frequencies is available, information can be sent on many different frequencies or channels within the band concurrently, allowing more information to be transmitted in a given amount of time** (much as more lanes on a highway allow more cars to travel on it at the same time).[11] Thus

Waves in the electromagnetic spectrum vary in size from very long radio waves the size of buildings to very short gamma rays smaller than the size of the nucleus of an atom (*http://science.hq.nasa.gov/kids/imagers/ems/index.html*).

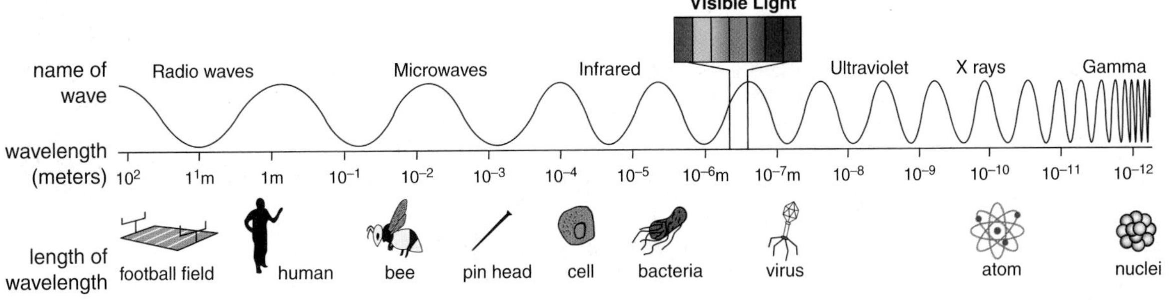

broadband is used to transmit high-speed data and high-quality audio and video. Transmission speeds are 1.5 megabits per second (Mbps) to (for super-broadband and ultra-broadband) 1 gigabit per second (Gbps) or more. In 2010 *average* download speed was 33.5 Mbps, an increase of 55% from 2009; average upload speed was 17 Mbps.[12]

In 2010, 48 countries (66%) were meeting the requirements to enjoy all the major services offered by the Internet today (defined in the study as social networking, low-definition video streaming, basic video-conferencing, small file sharing), as well as less demanding applications (such as instant messaging, email, web browsing). This adds 10 countries since 2009 and 18 since 2008. This is in spite of global Internet traffic volumes rising by 166% from 2008–2010. Following is the top-10 ranking of broadband leadership in 2010; the United States ranked 47.[13]

Ranking	Broadband Leadership 2010
1	South Korea
2	Hong Kong
3	Japan
4	Iceland
5	Switzerland, Luxemburg, Singapore
6	Malta
7	Netherlands
8	United Arab Emirates, Qatar
9	Sweden
10	Denmark

panel 6.11

The radio-frequency spectrum

The radio-frequency spectrum, which carries most communications signals, appears as part of the electromagnetic spectrum.

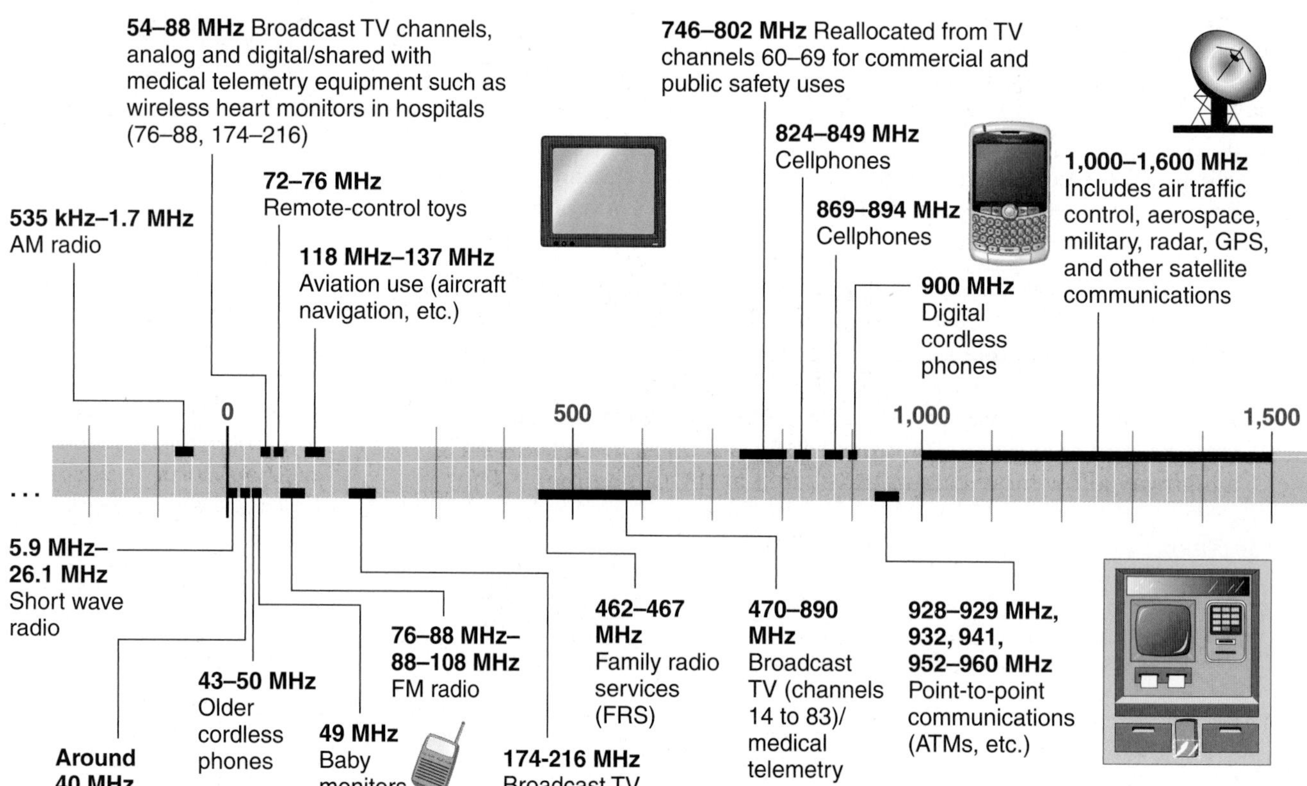

WAP: WIRELESS APPLICATION PROTOCOL Wireless handheld devices such as cellphones use the Wireless Application Protocol for connecting wireless users to the World Wide Web. Just as the protocol TCP/IP was designed to give you a wired connection to your Internet access provider, **the *Wireless Application Protocol (WAP)* is a standard designed to link nearly all mobile devices to your telecommunications carrier's wireless network and content providers.** WAP is supported by all operating systems, just as TCP/IP is. (Note that the acronym WAP is also used for wireless access point, p. 326.)

Five Types of Wireless Communications Media

The five types of wireless media are infrared transmission, broadcast radio, cellular radio, microwave radio, and communications satellite.

INFRARED TRANSMISSION ***Infrared wireless transmission*** **sends data signals using infrared-light waves at a frequency too low (1–16 megabits per second) for human eyes to receive and interpret.** Infrared ports can be found on some laptop computers, digital cameras, and printers, as well as wireless mice. TV remote-control units use infrared transmission. The drawbacks are that *line-of-sight* communication is required—there must be an unobstructed view between transmitter and receiver—and transmission is confined to short range.

BROADCAST RADIO When you tune in to an AM or FM radio station, you are using ***broadcast radio,*** **a wireless transmission medium that sends data over long distances at up to 2 megabits per second—between regions, states, or countries.** A transmitter is required to send messages and a receiver to receive them; sometimes both sending and receiving functions are combined in a *transceiver.*

In the lower frequencies of the radio spectrum, several broadcast radio bands are reserved not only for conventional AM/FM radio but also for broadcast television, CB (citizens band) radio, ham (amateur) radio, cellphones, and

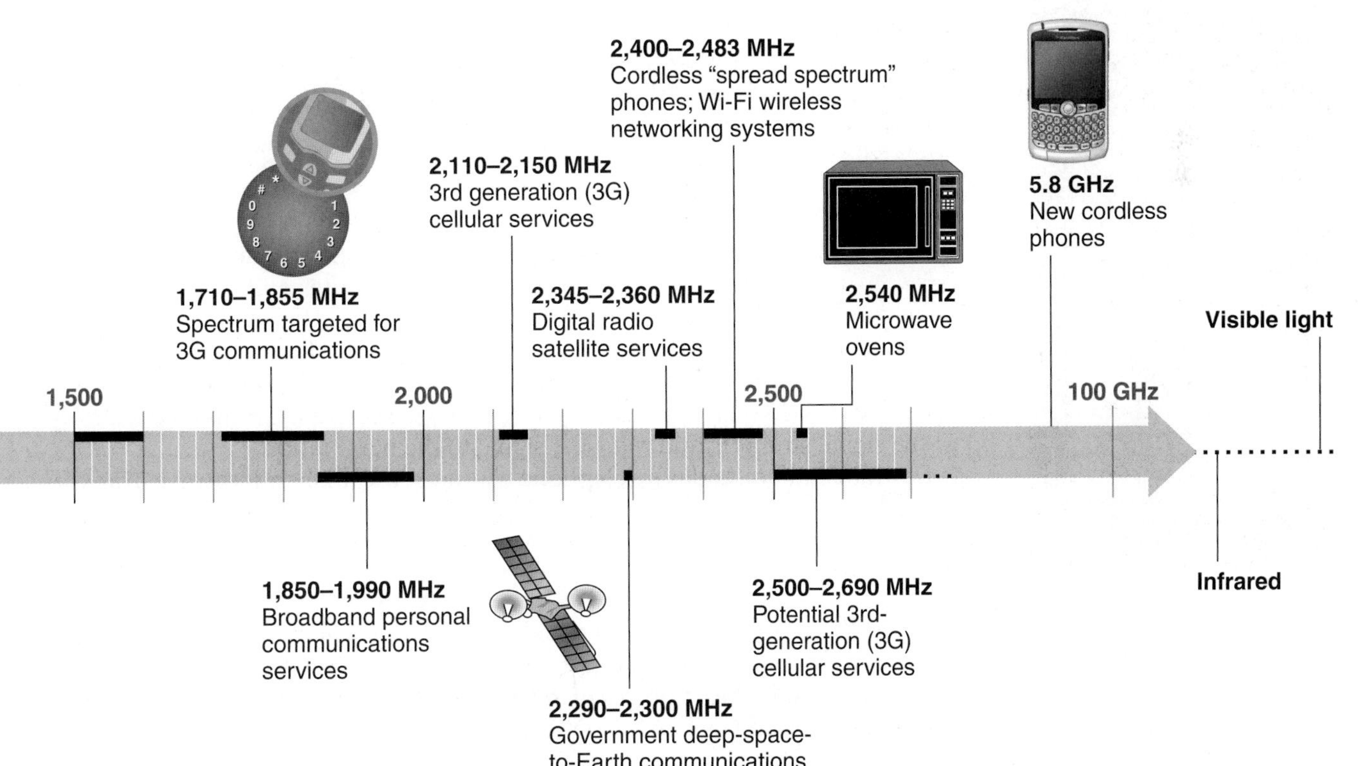

private radio-band mobile services (such as police, fire, and taxi dispatch). Some organizations use specific radio frequencies and networks to support wireless communications. For example, UPC (Universal Product Code) bar-code readers (p. 271) are used by grocery-store clerks restocking store shelves to communicate with a main computer so that the store can control inventory levels. In addition, there are certain web-enabled devices that follow standards such as Wi-Fi (wireless fidelity), as we discuss in a few pages.

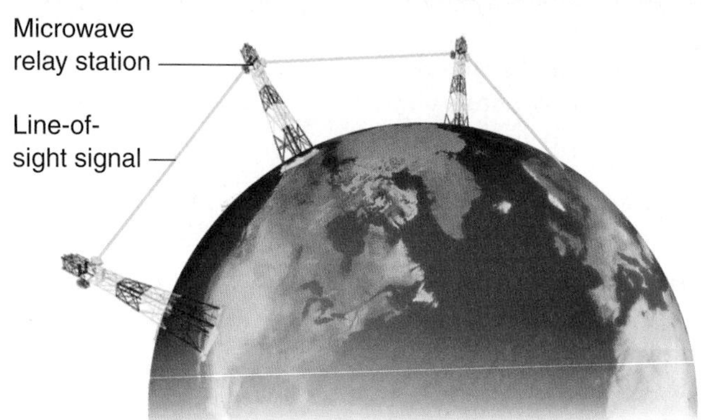

CELLULAR RADIO Actually a form of broadcast radio, ***cellular radio*** **is widely used for cellphones and wireless modems, using high-frequency radio waves to transmit voice and digital messages**. Unlike CB (citizens band) radio, used by truck drivers, which has a few radio channels that everyone must share, cellular radio channels are reused simultaneously in nearby geographic areas, yet customers do not interfere with one another's calls.

We discuss cellphones in more detail starting on p. 345.

MICROWAVE RADIO ***Microwave radio*** **transmits voice and data at 45 megabits per second through the atmosphere as superhigh-frequency radio waves called *microwaves,* which vibrate at 2.4 gigahertz (2.4 billion hertz) per second or higher.** These frequencies are used not only to operate microwave ovens but also to transmit messages between ground-based stations and satellite communications systems. One short-range microwave standard used for communicating data is *Bluetooth,* as we shall discuss.

Microwave towers on buildings in Shanghai.

Nowadays horn-shaped microwave reflective dishes, which contain transceivers and antennas, are nearly everywhere—on towers, buildings, and hilltops. Why, you might wonder, do we have to interfere with nature by putting a microwave dish on top of a mountain? As with infrared waves, microwaves are line-of-sight; they cannot bend around corners or around Earth's curvature, so there must be an unobstructed view between transmitter and receiver. Thus, microwave stations need to be placed within 25–30 miles of each other, with no obstructions in between. The size of the dish varies with the distance (perhaps 2–4 feet in diameter for short distances, 10 feet or more for long distances). In a string of microwave relay stations, each station will receive incoming messages, boost the signal strength, and relay the signal to the next station.

More than half of today's telephone systems use dish microwave transmission. However, the airwaves are becoming so saturated with microwave signals that future needs will have to be satisfied by other channels, such as satellite systems.

COMMUNICATIONS SATELLITES To avoid some of the limitations of microwave Earth stations, communications companies have added microwave "sky stations"—communications satellites. ***Communications satellites*** **are microwave relay stations in orbit around the earth.** Transmitting a signal from a ground station to a satellite is called *uplinking;* the reverse is called *downlinking*. The delivery process will be slowed if, as is often the case, more than one satellite is required to get the message delivered. Satellites cost from $300 million to $700 million each. A

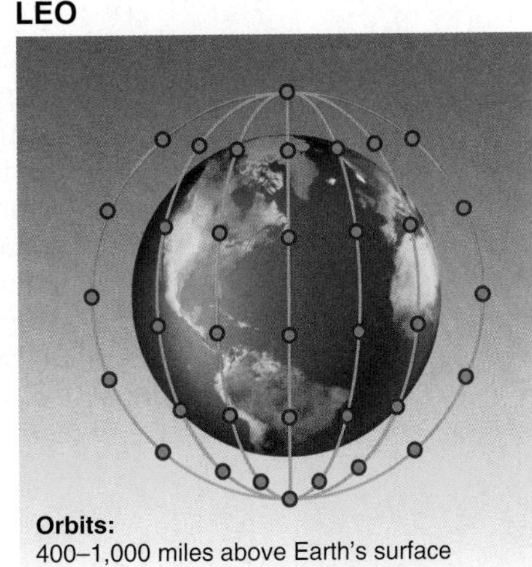

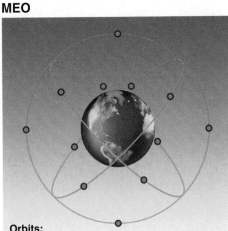

satellite launch costs between $50 million and $400 million. Communications satellites are the basis for the Global Positioning System (GPS), as we shall discuss.

Satellite systems may occupy one of three zones in space: *GEO, MEO,* and *LEO.*

- **GEO:** The highest level, known as *geostationary Earth orbit (GEO),* is 22,300 miles and up and is always directly above the equator. Because the satellites in this orbit travel at the same speed as the earth, they appear to an observer on the ground to be stationary in space—that is, they are geostationary. Consequently, microwave Earth stations are always able to beam signals to a fixed location above. The orbiting satellite has solar-powered transceivers to receive the signals, amplify them, and retransmit them to another Earth station. At this high orbit, fewer satellites are required for global coverage; however, their quarter-second delay (latency, or lag) makes two-way conversations and real-time online activities difficult.

  Broadband satellite Internet has a high latency problem owing to the signal having to travel to an altitude of 22,300 miles above sea level (from the equator) out into space to a satellite in geostationary orbit and back to Earth again. The signal delay can be as much as 500–900 milliseconds (MS), which makes this service unsuitable for applications requiring real-time user input such as certain multiplayer Internet games. Additionally, some satellite Internet providers do not support VPN owing to latency issues, and certain types of cellphone conversations can become difficult. However, latency problems are more than tolerable for just basic email access and web browsing and in most cases are barely noticeable.

- **MEO:** The *medium-Earth orbit (MEO)* is 5,000–10,000 miles up. It requires more satellites for global coverage than does GEO.

Communications satellites

- **LEO:** The *low-Earth orbit (LEO)* is 200–1,000 miles up and has no signal delay. LEO satellites may be smaller and are much cheaper to launch.

Long-Distance Wireless: One-Way Communication

GPS is an important one-way wireless communications technology.

Mobile wireless communications have been around for some time. The Detroit Police Department started using two-way car radios in 1921. Mobile telephones were introduced in 1946. Today, however, we are in the midst of an explosion in mobile wireless use that is making worldwide changes.

There are essentially two ways to move information through the air long distance on radio frequencies—one way and two way. *One-way communications,* discussed below, is typified by the satellite navigation system known as the Global Positioning System and by some pagers. *Two-way communications,* described on page 345, is exemplified by cellphones.

Satellite launch in India

THE GLOBAL POSITIONING SYSTEM Doreen Rosimos of Marlborough, New Hampshire, who heads a firm that funds micro-enterprises, sometimes brings along her Rottweiler, Zelda, when she takes business trips. One day in Kentucky when Zelda became sick, Rosimos quickly typed "veterinarian" in her car's global positioning device and found one nearby within minutes.[14]

A $10 billion infrastructure developed by the military, the ***Global Positioning System (GPS)*** **consists of 24–32 MEO Earth-orbiting satellites continuously transmitting timed radio signals that can be used to identify Earth locations.**

- **How GPS works:** The U.S. military developed and implemented this satellite network in the 1970s as a military navigation system, but on May 1, 2000, the federal government opened it up to everyone else. Each of these 3,000- to 4,000-pound, solar-powered satellites circles the earth twice a day at an altitude of 11,000 nautical miles. A GPS receiver—handheld or mounted in a vehicle, plane, or boat—can pick up transmissions from any four satellites, interpret the information from each, and pinpoint the receiver's longitude, latitude, and altitude. (*• See Panel 6.12.*) The system is accurate within 3–50 feet, with 10 feet being the norm. Most smartphones include a GPS.

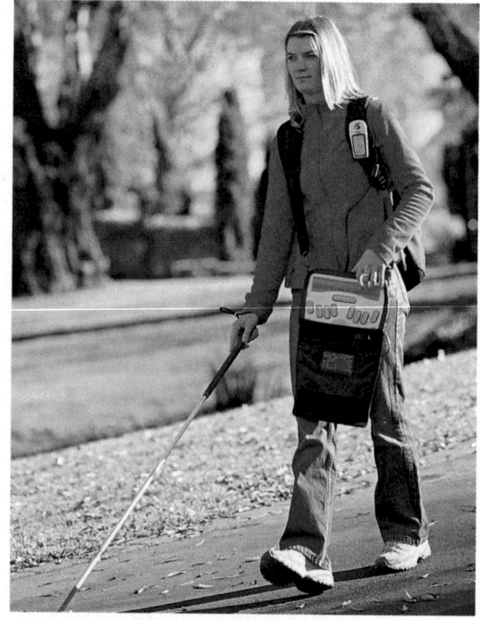

This woman is using a GPS unit with a Braille keyboard and voice output to find her way around a park.

Cellphone Tracking

Cellphone companies may be tracking your every move and compiling information about you . . .

http://current.com/news/93106962_it-s-tracking-your-every-move-and-you-may-not-even-know-it.htm

http://answers.yahoo.com/question/index?qid=20110508105144AAi1Cs1

http://online.wsj.com/article/SB10001424052748703467304575383522318244234.html

www.livephonetracking.com/cell-phone-gps-tracking.html

The ABCs of GPS

Developed by the U.S. military to aid ship and plane navigation, the Global Positioning System has evolved to serve a variety of purposes, with GPS receivers in everything from cars to handheld devices. The system has three main components—a satellite constellation, ground control, and receivers.

Space

There are about 24–32 satellites orbiting Earth at an altitude of 11,000 nautical miles. Each is equipped with an atomic clock that keeps time to three-billionths of a second. The satellites send time-stamped radio signals to Earth at the speed of light.The signals include information about each satellite's exact position.

Ground control

Five stations around the world monitor the satellites and send them information about their orbital position. The main control center is in Colorado Springs, Colorado.

The receiver

The receiver must pick up signals from at least four satellites. It calculates its distance from each satellite by comparing the time stamp of the signal to the time it reached the receiver. The receiver's clock isn't nearly as accurate as the atomic clocks in the satellites, but mathematical adjustments are made to account for inaccuracies.

Connect four

The basic premise of GPS is a concept called triangulation. Using this concept, the exact location of a golf ball on a two-dimensional course can be calculated by determining its distance from three pins.

The distance from pin 1 reveals possible locations anywhere along the edge of an imaginary circle.

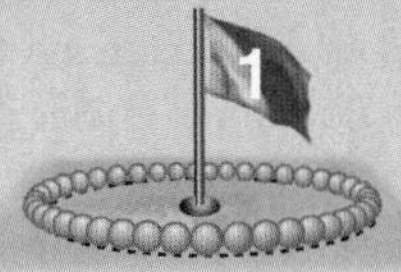

The distances from pins 1 and 2 reveal two possible ball locations—the point where the circles intersect.

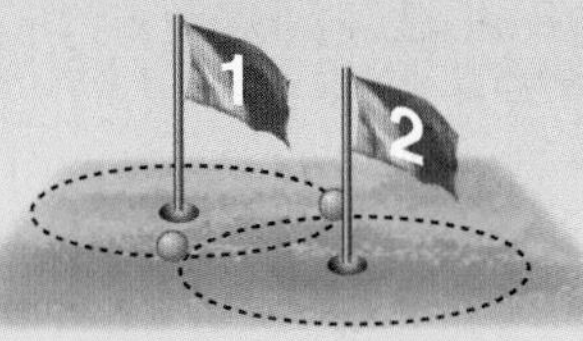

The distances from pins 1, 2, and 3 reveal one possible location—the point where all three circles intersect.

Triangulation works the same way in three-dimensional space, but with spheres instead of circles and a fourth reference point is needed.

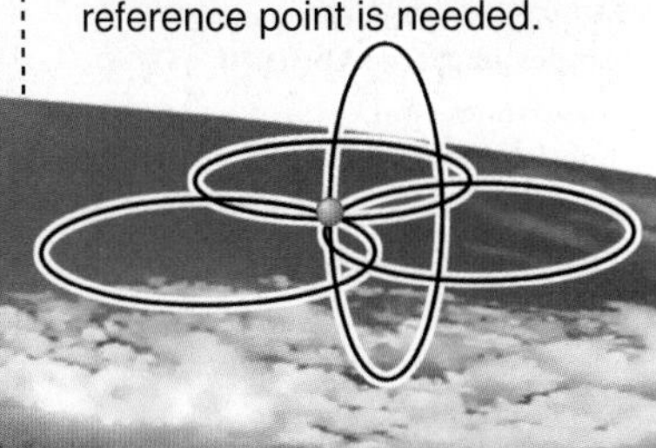

panel 6.12

GPS

The Global Positioning System uses 24 satellites, developed for military use, to pinpoint a location on the earth's surface.

GPS is used for geocaching, a high-tech treasure hunt in which items are stored in a waterproof container ("geocache") that can be located in the wilderness or in a public venue, typically not in plain view. The GPS coordinates of the cache are published on the geocaching website, and the object of the hunt is to locate the cache and enter your name in the log book as well as move objects from one cache to the next. In addition, geocachers may want to share their experiences online.

(Recall that smartphones are Internet-enabled cellphones that can run apps.)

- **The uses of GPS:** Besides being the technology behind car onboard navigation systems, the GPS is used for such activities as tracking trucks, buses, and taxis; locating stolen cars; orienting hikers; and aiding in surveying. An aerial camera connected to a GPS receiver can automatically tag photos with GPS coordinates, showing where the photograph was taken, which can be useful to surveyors, forestry managers, search-and-rescue teams, and archaeologists. GPS has been used by scientists to keep a satellite watch over a Hawaiian volcano, Mauna Loa, and to capture infinitesimal movements that may be used to predict eruptions. In one technology, cellular carriers have E911 (for "Enhanced 911") capability that is able to locate, through tiny GPS receivers embedded in users' digital cellphones, the position of every person making an emergency 911 call.[15]
- **The limitations of GPS:** Not all services based on GPS technology are reliable, as any frequent user of online mapping systems (such as those of MapQuest, MSN Maps and Directions, Google Earth, and Yahoo! Maps) knows by now. Indeed, about 1 in 50 computer-generated directions is a dud, according to Doug Richardson, previous executive director of the Association of American Geographers, mostly because of inaccurate road information. "You have to have the latest data about road characteristics—things like one-way streets, turns, and exits in order for it to generate accurate directions," he says.[16]

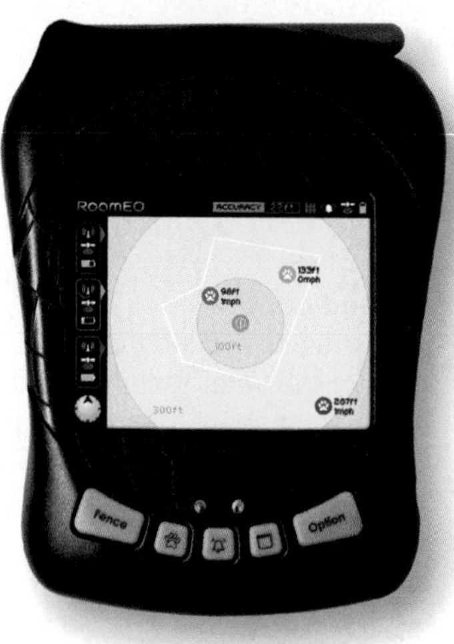

The RoamEO Location System is designed for pet owners to quickly and accurately locate their pets within a 1-mile radius by using GPS technology. Up to three dogs can each wear a GPS-equipped collar; the collars are tracked by the dog walker's handheld GPS unit.

more info!

Geocaching

For more details on how to go geocaching and what equipment is needed, try:

http://geocacher-u.com/?page_id=17

www.geocaching.com/about/logousage.aspx

http://photogeocaching.com/index.php?&width=1920

www.frontiernet.net/~techlady/GIS.html

www.youtube.com/watch?v=RxgcqgsU8ks

E911(Enhanced 911) is a location technology advanced by the Federal Communications Commission (FCC) that enables mobile phones to process 911 emergency calls and enable emergency services to locate the geographic position of the caller. Most 9-1-1 systems automatically report the telephone number and location of 9-1-1 calls made from wireline phones, and the FCC also requires wireless telephone carriers to provide

Many cars come with GPS units to guide users to their destinations.

9-1-1 and E9-1-1 capability.[17] However, emergency operators answering E911 cellphone calls have also often found some unsettling results, in which the information giving the caller's location either didn't appear or was inaccurate.

PAGERS Known as *beepers,* for the sound they make when activated, ***pagers* are simple radio receivers that receive data sent from a special radio transmitter.** The radio transmitter broadcasting to the pager sends signals over a specific frequency. All the pagers for that particular network have a built-in receiver that is tuned to the same frequency broadcast from the transmitter. The pagers listen to the signal from the transmitter constantly as long as the pager is turned on.

Although generally obsolete, because they are now built into smartphones, pagers are still used in areas where cellphones are unreliable or prohibited, such as large hospital complexes. They are also used to reach some emergency personnel and to control traffic signals and some irrigation systems.

Long-Distance Wireless: Two-Way Communication

There are four generations of cellular radio, used for two-way, long-distance communication.

Residential home phone users have been doing "cord cutting" to the point where in the United States in 2010 only about 1 in 7 homes still had landlines.[18] And 49% of adults ages 25–29 used cellphones only.[19]

Pager

Two-way wireless communications devices have evolved over time from two-way pagers and wireless email devices such as the original BlackBerry, which has become an all-in-one wireless data and voice device. The categories of long-distance wireless devices we discuss here use the transmission medium known as cellular radio (p. 340), which has several levels, or generations: 1G, 2G, 3G, and 4G.

Smartphone OS Comparison

www.techtree.com/India/Features/Smartphone_OS_Comparison/551-114322-899.html

www.popularmechanics.com/technology/gadgets/reviews/best_smartphone_operating_system

http://cell-phones.toptenreviews.com/smartphones/

1G (FIRST-GENERATION) CELLULAR SERVICE: ANALOG CELLPHONES "In the fall of 1985," wrote *USA Today* technology reporter Kevin Maney, "I went to Los Angeles to research a story about a new phenomenon called a cellphone. I got to use one for a day. The phones then cost $1,000 and looked like field radios from *M*A*S*H*. Calls were 45 cents a minute, and total cellphone users in the world totaled 200,000."[20] Digital cellphones are now ubiquitous. Mary Meeker, Morgan Stanley analyst, says that the world is currently in the midst of the fifth major technology cycle of the past half a century. The previous four were the mainframe era of the 1950s and 60s, the minicomputer era of the 1970s, and the desktop Internet era of the 80s. The current cycle is the era of the mobile Internet, she says—predicting that within the next five years "more users will connect to the Internet over mobile devices than desktop PCs."[21]

Cellphones are essentially two-way radios that operate using either analog or digital signals. *Analog cellphones* are designed primarily for communicating by voice through a system of ground-area cells. Each cell is hexagonal

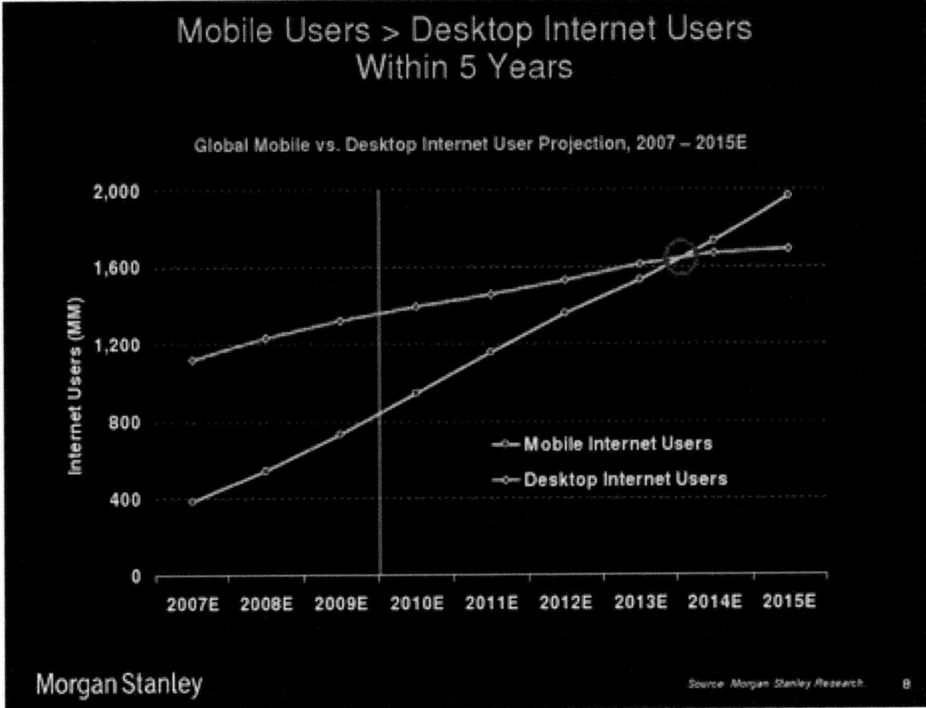

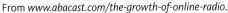

From *www.abacast.com/the-growth-of-online-radio.*

Texting while Driving

More dangerous than you think . . .

". . . from 2005 to 2008, distraction-related fatalities jumped from 10% to 16% of all traffic fatalities on American roads" . . . "tip of iceberg" . . . "number of text messages spiked from 7 billion per month in 2005 to about 173 billion per month in 2010." (Ray LaHood, Secretary, U.S. Department of Transportation, Washington, DC, *USA Today*, January 21, 2011, p. 6A), See also:

www.distraction.gov/stats-and-facts/

www.nationwide.com/newsroom/dwd-facts-figures.jsp

www.infographicsshowcase.com/wp-content/uploads/2010/02/driving-while-texting.png

www.intellicorp.net/marketing/texting-while-driving-statistics.aspx

www.mlive.com/news/jackson/index.ssf/2011/04/simulator_shows_teens_how_dang.html

in shape, usually 8 miles or less in diameter, and is served by a transmitter-receiving tower. Communications are handled in the bandwidth of 824–894 megahertz. Calls are directed between cells by a mobile-telephone switching office (MTSO). Movement between cells requires that calls be "handed off" by this switching office. (● *See Panel 6.13. next page.*) This technology is known as *1G*, for "first generation."

Handing off voice calls between cells poses only minimal problems. However, handing off data transmission (where every bit counts), with the inevitable gaps and pauses on moving from one cell to another, is much more difficult.

2G (SECOND-GENERATION) WIRELESS SERVICES: DIGITAL CELLPHONES & PDAS ***Digital wireless services*****—which support digital cellphones and personal digital assistants—use a network of cell towers to send voice communications and data over the airwaves in digital form.** Known as *2G* technology, digital cellphones began replacing analog cellphones during the 1990s as telecommunications companies added digital transceivers to their cell towers. 2G technology was the first digital voice cellular network; data communication was added as an afterthought, with data speeds ranging from 9.6 to 19.2 kilobits per second. 2G technology not only dramatically increased voice clarity; it also allowed the telecommunications companies to cram many more voice calls into the same slice of bandwidth.

3G (THIRD-GENERATION) WIRELESS SERVICES: SMARTPHONES 3G wireless digital services, often called *broadband technology*, are based either on the U.S. Code-Division Multiple Access (CDMA, currently the dominant network standard in North America) or Global System for Mobile Communications (GSM, used more widely in the rest of the world). They support devices that are "always on," carry data at high speeds (144 kilobits per second up to 3.1 megabits per

Inside a cellphone

panel 6.13

Cellular connections

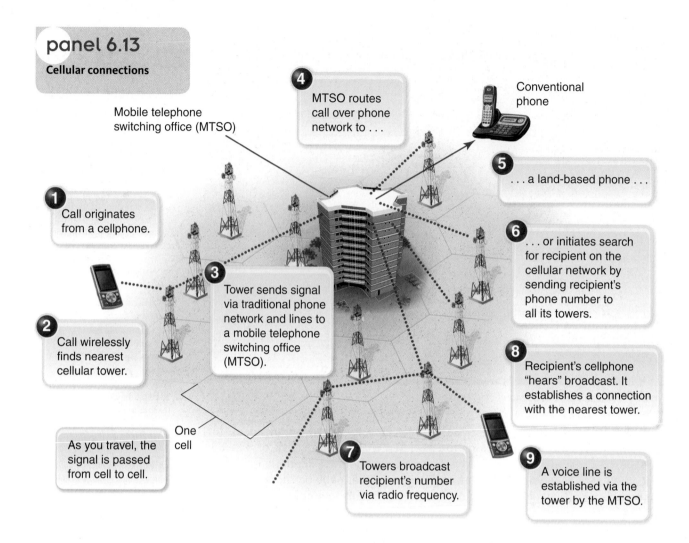

Mobile telephone switching office (MTSO)

4 MTSO routes call over phone network to . . .

Conventional phone

5 . . . a land-based phone . . .

1 Call originates from a cellphone.

6 . . . or initiates search for recipient on the cellular network by sending recipient's phone number to all its towers.

3 Tower sends signal via traditional phone network and lines to a mobile telephone switching office (MTSO).

2 Call wirelessly finds nearest cellular tower.

8 Recipient's cellphone "hears" broadcast. It establishes a connection with the nearest tower.

One cell

As you travel, the signal is passed from cell to cell.

7 Towers broadcast recipient's number via radio frequency.

9 A voice line is established via the tower by the MTSO.

Choosing CDMA or GSM

Many cellphones in the USA are CDMA; a few are GSM. Which one should you choose?

www.cellutips.com/gsm-vs-cdma-which-one-is-the-best-for-you/

Your Most Dangerous Possession?

Answer: Your smartphone.

http://money.cnn.com/2011/01/11/pf/smartphone_dangers/index.htm

second), accept emails with attachments, provide Internet and web access and videoconferencing capabilities, are able to display color video and still pictures, and play music. (CDMA was established earlier in North America and thus has a bit more coverage there than GSM. GSM is an international standard backed by an international organization, and the protocol is more mature and more robust. There is no clear winner in the CDMA vs. GSM debate; what you use depends on your needs. Just make sure that the carrier you want to use supports the standard of the phone that you want to use.)

4G (FOURTH-GENERATION) WIRELESS DIGITAL SERVICES: SMARTER PHONES In 2008 the ITU-R organization specified the IMT-Advanced (International Mobile Telecommunications Advanced) requirements for 4G standards, setting peak speed requirements for 4G service at 100 Mbps for high-mobility communication (such as from trains and cars) and 1 Gbps for low-mobility communication (such as pedestrians and stationary users).[22] (The ITU Radiocommunication Sector [ITU-R] is one of the three sectors [divisions or units] of the International Telecommunication Union [ITU] and is responsible for radio communication.)

4G does not include innovative applications but rather provides improved on-demand high quality video and audio services, better than 3G. Note that not all U.S. phone-service carriers support 4G as yet (late 2011); carriers' status regarding 4G will change rapidly in 2012 (*www.wired.com/gadgetlab/2011/01/4g-verizon-att-tmobile/* and *http://gcn.com/articles/2011/01/13/what-is-4g.aspx*). However, in spite of the lack of consistent 4G phone support, Apple has announced a prototype for a 5G phone—but it will not be available for a while (*www.new5gphone.net/; www.new5gphone.net/*).

Short-Range Wireless: Two-Way Communication

There are three basic types of short-range wireless technologies.

We have discussed the standards for high-powered wireless digital communications in the 800–1,900 megahertz part of the radio-frequency spectrum, which are considered long-range waves. Now let us consider low-powered wireless communications in the 2.4–7.5 gigahertz part of the radio spectrum, which are short-range and effective only within several feet of a wireless access point—generally between 30 and 250 feet. This band is available globally for unlicensed, low-power uses and is set aside as an innovation zone where new devices can be tested without the need for a government license; it's also used for industrial, scientific, and medical devices.

There are three kinds of networks covered by this range:

- **Local area networks—range 100–228 feet:** These include the popular Wi-Fi standards.
- **Personal area networks—range 30–32 feet:** These use Bluetooth, ultra wideband, and wireless USB.
- **Home automation networks—range 100–150 feet:** These use the Insteon, ZigBee, and Z-Wave standards.

Ideal Cellphone & Service

What's the ideal cellphone and service for your area? To compare plans, go to:

http://cell-phone-providers-review.toptenreviews.com/

http://reviews.cnet.com/cell-phone-buying-guide/

www.cellreception.com/

www.cellphonebattles.com/

SHORT-RANGE WIRELESS FOR LOCAL AREA NETWORKS: **WI-FI b, a, g, & n** Wi-Fi is known formally as an *802.11 network*, named for the wireless technical standard specified by the Institute of Electrical and Electronics Engineers (IEEE). As we mentioned in Chapter 2, *Wi-Fi*—short for *wi*reless *fi*delity—is a short-range wireless digital standard aimed at helping portable computers and handheld wireless devices to communicate at high speeds and share Internet connections at distances of 100–228 feet. You can find Wi-Fi connections, which operate at 2.4–5 gigahertz, inside offices, airports, and Internet cafés, and some enthusiasts have set up transmitters on rooftops, distributing wireless connections throughout their neighborhoods. *(• See Panel 6.14, next page.)*

Wi-Fi camera

- **802.11b**

  —Based on 2.4 GHz on the radio-frequency spectrum (pp. 338–339).

  —Typical throughput (bandwidth) 1–11 Mbps, comparable to traditional Ethernet.

  —Well established and low cost.

  —Good range.

  —Suffers interference from microwave ovens, some cordless phones, video senders, and other appliances using the same 2.4 GHz range.

While 802.11b was in development, IEEE created a second extension to the original 802.11 standard called *802.11a*. Because 802.11b gained in popularity much faster than did 802.11a, some folks believe that 802.11a was created

Wi-Fi symbol

Wi-Fi

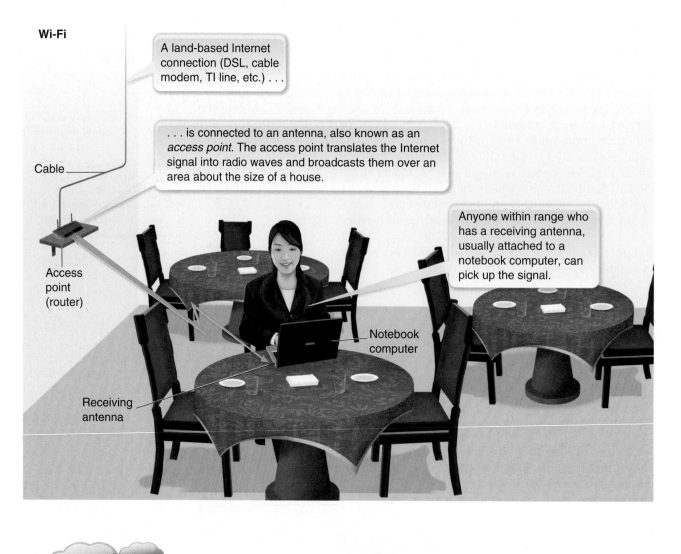

A land-based Internet connection (DSL, cable modem, TI line, etc.) . . .

. . . is connected to an antenna, also known as an *access point.* The access point translates the Internet signal into radio waves and broadcasts them over an area about the size of a house.

Anyone within range who has a receiving antenna, usually attached to a notebook computer, can pick up the signal.

Cable

Access point (router)

Notebook computer

Receiving antenna

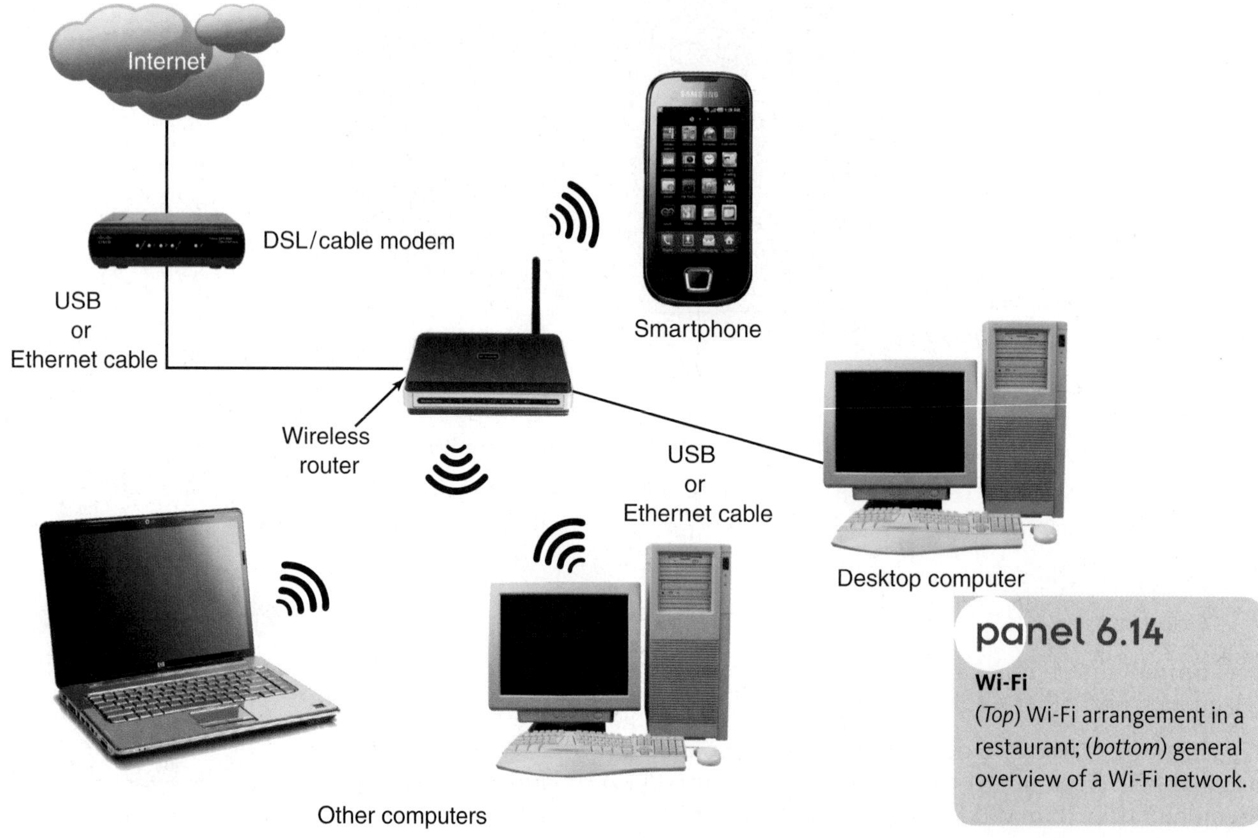

panel 6.14

Wi-Fi

(*Top*) Wi-Fi arrangement in a restaurant; (*bottom*) general overview of a Wi-Fi network.

after 802.11b. In fact, 802.11a was created at the same time. Because of its higher cost, 802.11a is usually found on business networks, whereas 802.11b better serves the home market.

- **802.11a**

  —Based on 5 GHz.

  —Expensive.

  —Typical throughput 6–54 Mbps.

  —Limited range in outdoor environments but similar ranges for indoor environments.

  —Much reduced interference problems.

  —Best suited for areas where there is a high density of radio LANs.

  —Signals are absorbed much more than at 2.4 GHz so it is less suitable for penetrating through more than thin walls—this can be overcome by using more access points.

  —This specification is not backward compatible with 802.11b/g and requires special wireless adapters.

- **802.11g**

  —Based on 2.4 GHz.

  —Backward compatible with 802.11b (meaning that 802.11g access points will work with 802.11b wireless network adapters and vice versa).

  —Same interference problems as 802.11b.

  —Similar throughput but at longer ranges as 802.11b.

  —Not easily obstructed.

  —Costs more than 802.11b.

- **802.11n**

  —Uses multiple transmitter and receiver antennas (MIMO) to allow for increased data throughput and range.

  —Designed to improve on 802.11g in the amount of bandwidth supported by utilizing multiple wireless signals and antennas (MIMO technology).

  —Throughput of up to 600 Mbps, with somewhat better range over earlier Wi-Fi standards, owing to its increased signal intensity.

  —802.11n equipment is backward compatible with 802.11g.

  —More resistant to signal interference from outside sources.

  —Costs more than 802.11g.

Wireless devices must use the same communications standard to communicate. Home and business networkers looking to buy wireless local area network (WLAN) gear face an array of choices. Many products conform to the 802.11a, 802.11b, 802.11g, or 802.11n wireless standards.

Increasingly, people are installing Wi-Fi networks in their homes, going online through wireless hot spots at Starbucks and other establishments, and connecting via free Wi-Fi networks in airports and hotels. Wherever the connection, it's extremely important to make sure the Wi-Fi connection is secure against cyberspying. If you're using a mobile connection, you may not even be aware that you're connected to an unverified access point because the

Setting up Wi-Fi in Windows 7

Some instructional tips:

http://forevergeeks.com/how-to-setup-a-wireless-profile-on-windows-7

www.windows7password.net/setup-wifi-in-windows-7/

www.howstuffworks.com/wireless-network.htm

www.brighthub.com/computing/hardware/articles/26291.aspx

connection can be made without your knowledge, so disable your Wi-Fi software, instead of leaving it on to auto connect, whenever you're not using it. This can keep you from unknowingly connecting to a fraudulent network. We give some more security tips in another few pages.

SHORT-RANGE WIRELESS FOR PERSONAL AREA NETWORKS: BLUETOOTH, ULTRA WIDEBAND, & WIRELESS USB As we stated, personal area networks use short-range wireless technology to connect personal electronics, such as cellphones, MP3 players, and printers in a range of 30–32 (sometimes up to 320) feet. The principal wireless technology used so far has been Bluetooth, which is now being joined by ultra wideband (UWB) and wireless USB.

- **Bluetooth:** ***Bluetooth*** **is a short-range wireless digital standard aimed at linking cellphones, computers, and peripherals up to distances of about 33 feet** in casual networks called *piconets*. Piconets are established dynamically and automatically as Bluetooth-enabled devices enter and leave radio proximity, meaning that you can easily connect whenever and wherever it's convenient for you. (The name comes from Harald Bluetooth, the 10th-century Danish king who unified Denmark and Norway.)

  Now transmitting up to 24 megabits (Mbps) per second, the original version of Bluetooth was designed to replace cables connecting PCs to printers and PDAs or wireless phones and to overcome line-of-sight problems with infrared transmission. When Bluetooth-capable devices come within range of one another, an automatic electronic "conversation" (called *pairing*) takes place to determine whether they have data to share, and then they form a mini-network to exchange that data. (• *See Panel 6.15.*)

panel 6.15

Bluetooth

Bluetooth allows two devices to interact wirelessly in sometimes novel ways. A Bluetooth-equipped notebook, for example, can connect through a similarly enabled cellphone or Internet access point to send and receive email. In addition to the links shown, Bluetooth can be used to network similar devices—for example, to send data from PC to PC, as long as they are not more than 33 feet apart (up to about 300 feet with special added equipment). Line of sight is not required.

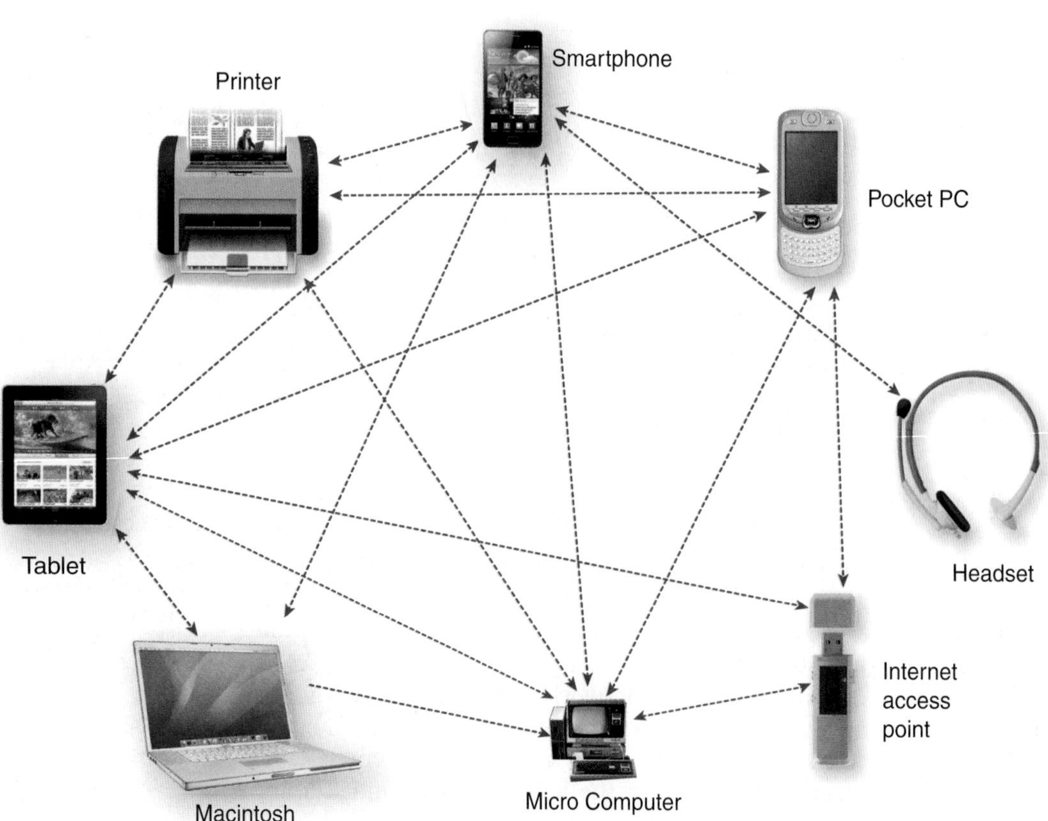

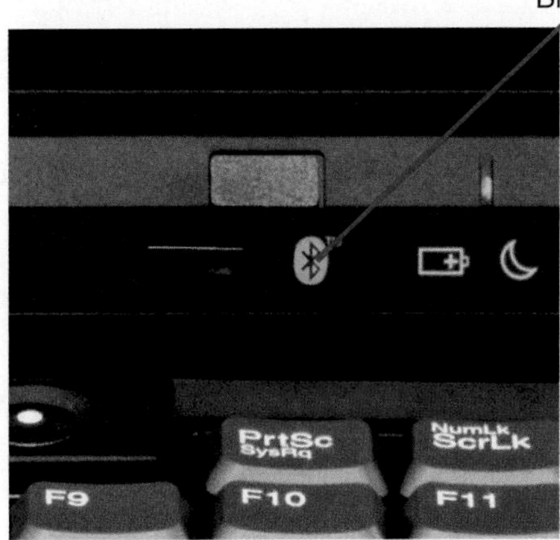

Bluetooth symbol on a notebook computer.

- **Ultra wideband (UWB):** Developed for use in military radar systems, ***ultra wideband (UWB)*** **is a technology operating in the range of 480 megabits per second up to 1.6 gigabytes per second up to about 30 feet that uses a low power source to send out millions of bursts of radio energy every second over many different frequencies, which are then reassembled by a UWB receiver.** It operates over low frequencies not used by other technologies, making it a candidate to replace many of the cables that now currently connect household and office devices. UWB systems tend to be short-range and indoor applications. High-data-rate UWB can enable wireless monitors, the efficient transfer of data from digital camcorders, wireless printing of digital pictures from a camera without the need for an intervening personal computer, and the transfer of files among cellphones and other handheld devices. Uses for ultra wideband technology in consumer networks include wireless USB, wireless high-definition video, medical imaging, next-generation Bluetooth, and peer-to-peer connections.

Latest Bluetooth Devices

What are the newest Bluetooth devices? See:

www.bluetooth.com

- **Wireless USB:** ***Wireless USB (WUSB) has*** **a typical range of 32 feet and a maximum data rate of 110–480 megabits per second.** Wireless USB is used in game controllers, printers, scanners, digital cameras, MP3 players, hard disks, and flash drives. With more than 2 billion legacy wired USB connections in the world today, USB is the de facto standard in the personal computing industry. Now these fast connections are available in the wireless world, with the introduction of Wireless USB. Wireless USB is the new wireless extension to USB (p. 222) that combines the speed and security of wired technology with the ease of use of wireless technology. Wireless USB supports robust high-speed wireless connectivity by utilizing the common WiMedia MB-OFDM Ultra-wideband (UWB) radio platform as developed by the WiMedia Alliance. Wireless USB will preserve the functionality of wired USB while also unwiring the cable connection and providing enhanced support for streaming media devices and peripherals.

  Shane Rau, research director of computing for International Data Corporation (IDC), states: "IDC believes that adoption of SuperSpeed [wireless] USB will accelerate in the second half of 2012, and we forecast that approximately 80% of mobile PCs will ship with SuperSpeed USB in 2013, with roughly equal penetration in commercial and consumer mobile PCs."[23]

Meshing

The following websites provide more information about these mesh technologies:

www.insteon.net
www.zigbee.org
www.z-wavealliance.com
http://communication.howstuffworks.com/how-wireless-mesh-networks-work1.htm
www.computerhope.com/jargon/m/mesh.htm
www.brainbell.com/tutorials/Networking/Mesh_Topology.html

SHORT-RANGE WIRELESS FOR HOME AUTOMATION NETWORKS: INSTEON, ZIGBEE, & Z-WAVE Home automation networks (smart homes)—those that link switches and sensors around the house and yard—use low-power, narrowband wireless technology, which operate in a range of 100–150 feet but at relatively slow data rates of 13.1–250 kilobits per second. The current standards are Insteon (*www.insteon.net/about-howitworks.html*), ZigBee (*www.zigbee.org/*), and Z-Wave (*www.zwaveproducts.com*). All three are so-called *mesh technologies*—networked devices equipped with two-way radios that can communicate with each other rather than just with the controller, the device that serves as central command for the network.

- **Insteon:** *Insteon* combines electric power line and wireless technologies and is capable of sending data at 13.1 kilobits a second at a typical range of 150 feet. With this kind of technology, you might drive up to your house, and the garage door device would recognize your car and open to let you in. The lights would come on and your favorite radio station would start playing.

Curious about Networked Homes?

For starters, try:

www.sciencedaily.com/releases/2007/12/071221215021.htm

www.technewsworld.com/story/Home-Automation-The-Unfulfilled-Promise-66973.html?wlc=1250196188

www.howstuffworks.com/home-network.htm

www.msichicago.org/whats-here/exhibits/smart-home/

www.youtube.com/watch?v=ZiodDkicRHw

Beginners' Guide to Going Wireless

For some tutorials on using wireless technology, go to:

www.palowireless.com/wireless/tutorials.asp

www.homeandlearn.co.uk/bc/beginnerscomputing.html

Some advantages of wireless:

Implementation cost is cheaper than wired network.

Ideal for the nonreachable places such as across river or mountain or rural area.

Ideal for temporary network setups.

Some disadvantages:

Lower speed compared to wired network.

Less secure, because hacker's laptop can act as access point and be able to read all your information.

More complex to configure than wired network.

Affected by surroundings—for example, walls (blocking), microwave oven (interference), far distance (attenuation and latency).

- **ZigBee:** *ZigBee* is an entirely wireless, very power-efficient technology that can send data at 128 kilobytes per second at a range of about 250 feet. It is primarily touted as sensor network technology and can be used in everything from automatic meter readers and medical sensing and monitoring devices to wireless smoke detectors and TV remote controls. One of the best features is that it can run for years on inexpensive batteries, eliminating the need to be plugged into an electric power line.
- **Z-Wave:** *Z-Wave* is also an entirely wireless, power-efficient technology, which can send data at 127 kilobits per second to a range of 100 feet. With a Z-Wave home, you could program the lights to go on when the garage door opens. You could program devices remotely, turning the thermostat up on the drive home from work.

6.5 CYBERTHREATS, HACKERS, & SAFEGUARDS

The content of a computer is vulnerable to few risks unless the computer is connected to other computers on a network. As the use of computer networks, especially the Internet, has become pervasive, the concept of computer security has expanded.

With improved communications and digital devices have come increased threats and dangers of many kinds, including viruses. Some people have gotten so fed up with virus-ridden computers that they have thrown them out and started all over with a new computer. Is throwing your virus-overrun computer in the dumpster a rational response? Many would disagree. However, there's no question that the ongoing dilemma of the Digital Age is balancing convenience against security. *Security* is a system of safeguards for protecting information technology against unauthorized access and systems failures that can result in damage or loss. Security matters are a never-ending problem, with attacks on computers and data becoming more powerful and more complex.[24]

We consider the following aspects of security as it relates to

- **Cyberthreats:** denial-of-service attacks, viruses, Trojan horses, worms, rootkits, zombies and bots, ransomware, and keylogger attacks
- **Perpetrators of cybercrime:** hackers and crackers
- **Computer safety:** antivirus software, firewalls, passwords, biometric authentication, and encryption

Cyberthreats

Some common cyberthreats are denial-of-service attacks, viruses, Trojan horses, worms, rootkits, zombies and bots, ransomware, and keylogger attacks.

Internet users, especially home users, are not nearly as safe as they believe, according to a study by McAfee and the nonprofit National Cyber Security Alliance.[25] Consumers suffer from complacency and a lack of expert advice on keeping their computer systems secure. The study found that 92% of 378 adults believed that they were safe from viruses; however, only 51% had up-to-date virus software. And 73% thought they had a firewall installed, but only 64% actually had it enabled. Little more than half had anti-spyware protection, and only about 12% had phishing protection. As we explain, these kinds of protections are musts in guarding against important cyberthreats such as denial-of-service attacks, viruses, worms, Trojan horses, rootkits, zombies and bots, ransomware, keylogger attacks, and other kinds of "malware."

PRACTICAL ACTION

WikiLeaks & DDoS

WikiLeaks, launched in 2006 under The Sunshine Press organization, "is a not-for-profit media organisation. Our goal is to bring important news and information to the public. We provide an innovative, secure and anonymous way for sources to leak information to our journalists (our electronic drop box). One of our most important activities is to publish original source material alongside our news stories so readers and historians alike can see evidence of the truth. . . . Publishing improves transparency, and this transparency creates a better society for all people. Better scrutiny leads to reduced corruption and stronger democracies in all society's institutions, including government, corporations and other organisations" (*http://wikileaks.org/About.html*). WikiLeaks, in spite of its professed goals of supporting transparency in a world of suppressed information, publishes submissions of private, secret, and classified media from anonymous news sources, news leaks, and whistleblowers, which has generated a storm of controversy. Julian Assange, an Australian Internet activist, is generally described as WikiLeaks' director. The site was originally launched as a user-editable wiki, but it no longer accepts user comments or edits.

Some of the topics that WikiLeaks focuses on are these:

- Brutality around the world (war, killings, torture, and detention—for example, treatment of prisoners at Guantanamo Bay: in April 2011 WikiLeaks began publishing 779 secret files relating to prisoners detained in the Guantanamo Bay detention camp).
- Suppression of free speech (for example, information on secret gag on U.K. *Times* preventing publication of 2009 report into toxic waste dumping; also information on how German intelligence infiltrated *Focus* magazine: illegal spying on German journalists).
- Government and corporate transparency (for example, international actions in Afghanistan and Iraq: in July 2010 WikiLeaks released Afghan War Diary, more than 76,900 documents about the War in Afghanistan not previously available to the public; in October 2010, the group released almost 400,000 documents called the Iraq War Logs, allowing every death in Iraq, and across the border in Iran, to be mapped; in November 2010, WikiLeaks began releasing U.S. State department diplomatic cables; WikiLeaks also covered U.S. profiteering after the Haiti earthquake in 2010).
- Ecology, climate, nature and sciences; corruption, finance, taxes, trading; censorship technology and Internet filtering; cults and other religious organizations; abuse, violence.

When WikiLeaks released the Afghan War Diary and the Iraq War Logs, several U.S. companies decided to cut off services to WikiLeaks. One of these companies was Mastercard. After they cut off services, their website was knocked offline by an organized denial-of-service attack. Also targeted was the Swiss payment transaction firm PostFinance, PayPal, and EveryDNS, all three of whom terminated services to WikiLeaks after the site published the leaked U.S. State Department cables. An attack was also launched against Amazon.com, but their server has massive server capacity that is almost impossible to crash.

A group of hackers calling themselves Anonymous have taken credit for the DoS attacks, which they called Operation Payback.

DENIAL-OF-SERVICE ATTACKS **A *denial-of-service (DoS) attack*, or *distributed denial-of-service (DDoS) attack*, consists of making repeated requests of a computer system or network, thereby overloading it and denying legitimate users access to it.** Because computers are limited in the number of user requests they can handle at any given time, a DoS onslaught will tie them up with fraudulent requests that cause them to shut down. The assault may come from a single computer or from hundreds or thousands of computers that have been taken over by those intending harm.

VIRUSES Viruses, worms, and Trojan horses are three forms of *malware*, or malicious software, that attack computer systems. (There are many forms of malware now.) The latest Symantec Internet Security Threat Report identified a 93% increase in the volume of web-based malware attacks in 2010 over the volume observed in 2009, and per *each single* data breach (unauthorized or unintentional exposure, disclosure, or loss of sensitive personal data), 260,000 personal identities were exposed.[26]

A *virus* attaches itself to a program or file (for example, attached to an email) enabling it to spread from one computer to another, leaving

Free Online Virus & Security Check

Go to Symantec.com at:

http://security.symantec.com/sscv6/home.asp?langid=ie&venid=sym&plfid=23&pkj=IHQYJABOKQYWTFVRHRM

and run the check. What are your results? What do you plan to do next?

Survival Tip

Keep Antivirus Software Updated

The antivirus software that comes with your computer won't protect you forever. To guard against new worms and viruses, visit the antivirus software maker's website frequently and enable your software's automatic update feature.

infections as it travels. Almost all viruses are attached to an executable file, which means the virus may exist on your computer but it cannot infect your computer unless you run or open the malicious program. Note that a virus cannot be spread without a human action (such as running an infected program) to keep it going. Because a virus is spread by human action, people will unknowingly continue the spread of a computer virus by sharing infected files or sending emails with viruses as attachments in the email.

There are millions of viruses circulating in the cyberworld. One famous email, Love Bug (its subject line was I LOVE YOU), which originated in the Philippines in May 2000 and did perhaps as much as $10 billion in damage worldwide, was both a worm and a virus, spreading faster and causing more damage than any other bug before it. The Love Bug was followed almost immediately by a variant virus. This new Love Bug didn't reveal itself with an I LOVE YOU line but changed to a random word or words each time a new computer was infected. More recent viruses have targeted Twitter, YouTube, website advertising, and digital photo-holding frames. A virus called Koobface attacked Facebook. Fast-spreading Clampi took aim at business financial accounts. A fired computer programmer embedded a malicious virus in servers run by financial institution Fannie Mae.

TROJAN HORSES If, as a citizen of Troy around 1200–1500 B.C.E., you looked outside your fortified city and saw that the besieging army of Greeks was gone but a large wooden horse was left standing on the battlefield, what would you think? Maybe you would decide it was a gift of the gods, as the Trojans did, and haul it inside the city gates—and be unpleasantly surprised when late at night several Greek soldiers climbed out of the horse and opened the gates for the invading army. This is the meaning behind the illegal program known as a Trojan horse, which, though not technically a virus, can act like one.

A *Trojan horse* is a program, a subclass of virus, that pretends to be a useful program, usually free, such as a game or screen saver, but carries viruses, or destructive instructions, that perpetrate mischief without your knowledge. The Trojan horse at first appears to be useful software but will do damage once installed or run on your computer. Those on the receiving end of a Trojan Horse are usually tricked into opening it, because they believe that they are receiving legitimate software or files from a legitimate source. When a Trojan is activated on your computer, the results can vary. Some Trojans are designed to be more annoying than malicious or they can cause serious damage by deleting files and destroying information on your system. One particularly malicious feature is that a Trojan horse may allow so-called backdoor programs to be installed. A *backdoor program* is an illegal program that allows illegitimate users to take control of your computer without your knowledge.

WORMS **A *worm* is a program, also a subclass of a virus, that copies itself repeatedly into a computer's memory or onto a disk or flash drive or USB device.** But unlike a virus, it has the capability to travel without any human action. A worm takes advantage of file or information transport features on your system, which is what allows it to travel unaided. Sometimes it will copy itself so often it will cause a computer to crash. Among some famous worms are Code Red, Nimda, Klez, Sasser, Bagle, Blaster, Sobig, Melissa, and Stuxnet. Klez spread its damage through Microsoft products by being inside email attachments or part of email messages themselves, so that merely opening an infected message could infect a computer running Outlook or Outlook Express. *(• See Panel 6.16.)*

In 2008–2010, a worm known as Conficker spread through a Microsoft Windows vulnerability that allowed guessing of network passwords, by people hand-carrying such gadgets as USB drives (thumb drives) and flash drives, and it infected millions of computers. The Conficker authors cleverly updated the worm through several versions, playing a cat-and-mouse game that kept them

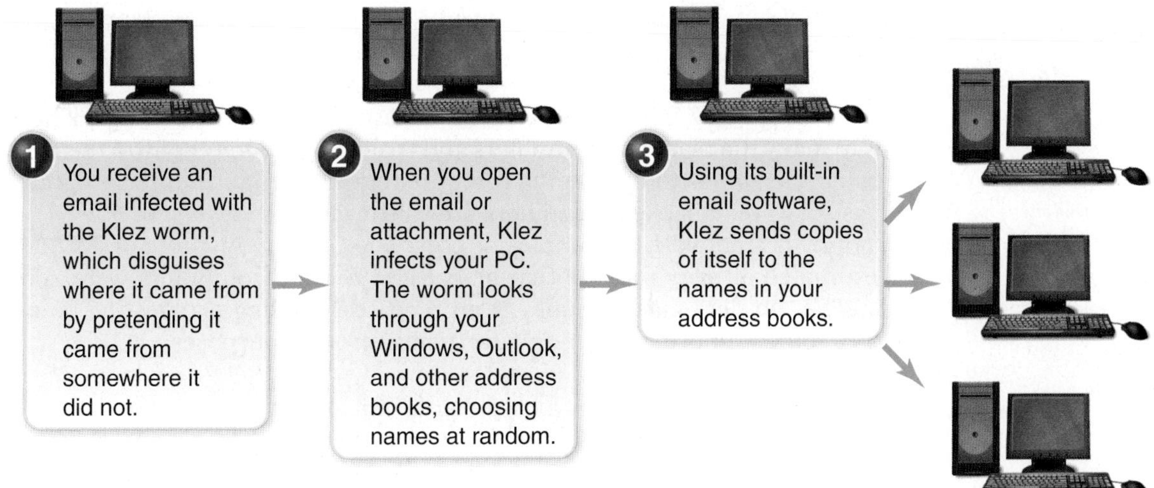

1
You receive an email infected with the Klez worm, which disguises where it came from by pretending it came from somewhere it did not.
2
When you open the email or attachment, Klez infects your PC. The worm looks through your Windows, Outlook, and other address books, choosing names at random.
3
Using its built-in email software, Klez sends copies of itself to the names in your address books.

panel 6.16

How one worm works

This is the Klez worm, but others work in similar ways. If you don't recognize the sender of an email message and you don't open the message, but instead just immediately delete it, your PC will not be infected.

one step ahead of security experts. Some researchers feared that Conficker could be turned into a powerful offensive weapon that could disrupt the Internet itself. April 1, 2009, was supposed to be the day the worm would launch a massive cyberattack, but the day came and went without incident. Nobody knows exactly what it's supposed to do, however. It seems to sit on people's computers and wait for instructions from websites. We can only speculate as to what the instructions will be if one of the websites has a hidden file that finally connects to Conficker.[27] Some experts believe, however, that Conficker will ultimately turn out to be a virus that has been written for profit.

We do know that the Conficker worm mostly spreads across networks. If it finds a vulnerable computer, it turns off the automatic backup service, deletes previous restore points, disables many security services, blocks access to a number of security websites, and opens infected machines to receive additional programs from the malware's creator. The worm then tries to spread itself to other computers on that same network.

When executed on a computer, Conficker disables a number of system services such as Windows Automatic Update, Windows Security Center, Windows Defender, and Windows Error Reporting.[28]

Stuxnet is a Windows computer worm discovered in July 2010 that targets industrial software and equipment. Stuxnet, which was first reported in mid-June by VirusBlokAda, a little-known security firm based in Belarus, gained notoriety a month later when Microsoft confirmed that the worm was actively targeting Windows PCs that managed large-scale industrial-control systems in manufacturing and utility firms. Iran was hardest hit by Stuxnet, according to Symantec researchers, who said in July 2010 that nearly 60% of all infected PCs were located in that country.

BLENDED THREATS Added into the mix, we also have what is called a blended threat. A blended threat is a more sophisticated attack that bundles some of the worst aspects of viruses, worms, Trojan horses, and other malware into one single threat. Blended threats can use server and Internet vulnerabilities to initiate, then transmit and also spread an attack.

To be considered a blended thread, the attack would normally serve to transport multiple attacks simultaneously. For example, it wouldn't just launch a DoS attack — it would also, for example, install a backdoor and maybe even damage a local system. Additionally, blended threats are designed to use multiple modes of transport—email, flash drives, USB thumb drives, networks, and so on.

ROOTKITS In addition to the preceding malware, we have the problem of *rootkits.* In many computer operating systems (OSs), the "root" is an account for system administration. A "kit" is the malware introduced into the computer.

Survival Tip

Risky Behavior

According to computer security experts, 20 minutes is the average time that an *unprotected* computer remains clean after connecting to the Internet. After that, the computer is infected with a virus or spyware or is hacked (*www.pc-st.com/us/index.htm*).

A *rootkit* gives an attacker "super powers" over computers—for example, the ability to steal sensitive personal information.

ZOMBIES AND BOTS In this situation, a *botmaster* uses malware to hijack hundreds to many thousands of computers and is able to remotely control them all, including the ability to update the malware and to introduce other programs such as spyware. Hijacked computers are called *zombies* (*robots,* or *bots*).

A *botnet* is a network of zombies or bots. The Georgia Institute of Technology estimated already in 2009 that globally 15% of all computers were zombies.[29] The "herder" makes money from repeatedly selling clandestine botnet access to others to use for pop-up advertising or other purposes.

RANSOMWARE Also known as a cryptovirus, *ransomeware* holds the data on a computer or the use of the computer hostage until a payment is made. Ransomware encrypts the target's files, and the attacker tells the victim to make a payment of a specified amount to a special account to receive the decryption key.

SPYWARE *Spyware* is a broad term that sometimes is used to mean the same thing as malware but more narrowly is thought of as a surveillance tool that spies on computer users and steals their information.

A keystroke logger, referred to as a *keylogger,* may be the most common form of spyware. A keylogger secretly "harvests" every keystroke that a computer user makes and so steals sensitive data for profit. Keyloggers may be hardware or software.

TIME, LOGIC, AND EMAIL BOMBS A *time bomb* is malware programmed to "go off" at a particular time or date. A *logic bomb* is "detonated" when a specific event occurs—for example, all personnel records are erased when an electronic notation is made that a particular person was fired. *Email bombs* overwhelm a person's email account by surreptitiously subscribing it to dozens or even hundreds of mailing lists.

more info!

Protect against Cellphone Viruses and Spyware

According to HowStuffWorks (*http://electronics.howstuffworks.com/cell-phone-virus4.htm*), the best way to protect yourself from cellphone viruses is the same way you protect yourself from computer viruses: never open anything if you don't know what it is, haven't requested it, or have any suspicions whatsoever that it's not what it claims to be. See also:

http://us.norton.com/products/library/article.jsp?aid=handheld_security

www.nospysoftware.com/spyware-articles/cell-phone-virus.php

http://news.discovery.com/tech/cell-phone-malware.html

http://cellphones.org/blog/keep-that-cell-phone-malware-and-spyware-free/

Now let's consider the people who perpetrate cyberthreats—hackers and crackers.

HOW MALWARE IS SPREAD Cyberthreats are passed in the following ways:

- **By infected disks, flash drives, and USB thumb drives:** The first way is via an infected disk or drive, perhaps from a friend or a repair person.
- **By opening unknown email attachments:** The second way is from an email attachment. This is why a basic rule of using the Internet is *Never click on an email attachment that comes from someone you don't know.* This advice also applies to unknown downloaded files, as for free video games or screen savers.
- **By clicking on infiltrated websites:** Some criminals "seed" web pages with contagious malware that enables them to steal personal data, so that by simply clicking on a website you can unwittingly compromise your PC or other device. The risk can be minimized if you have a firewall and keep antivirus software on your computer up to date, as we describe below.
- **Through infiltrated Wi-Fi hot spots:** As mentioned earlier, if you're a user of Wi-Fi wireless access points, or hot spots, you have to be aware that your laptop or device could be exposed to wireless transmitted diseases from illegal users. Many hot spots do not require passwords; which means that anyone with a wireless connection and hacking know-how can hop aboard the network. Here, too, having wireless firewalls can reduce risks.

Keep in mind that, although viruses and other malware for years attacked mostly Windows-based computers and devices, Apple computers and devices, as well as smartphones of all types, are now vulnerable to malware attacks.

PRACTICAL ACTION

Ways to Minimize Virus Attacks

Some tips for minimizing the chances of infecting your computer are as follows:

- Don't open, download, or execute any files, email messages, or email attachments if the source is unknown or if the subject line of an email is questionable or unexpected.
- Delete all spam and email messages from strangers. Don't open, forward, or reply to such messages.
- Use webmail (HTML email such as Hotmail and AOL email) sparingly, since viruses can hide in the HTML coding of the email. Even the simple act of previewing the message in your email program can activate the virus and infect your computer.
- Don't start your computer with a flash drive, USB thumb drive, or CD/DVD in place.
- Back up your data files regularly, and keep at least one backup device in a location separate from your computer (or use an online [cloud] backup service).
- Make sure you have virus protection software, such as McAfee VirusScan *(www.mcafee.com)* or Norton AntiVirus *(www.symantec.com/nav)* activated on your machine. You can download it from these companies; then follow the installation instructions. (Beware of antivirus software from unknown companies; they may be scamware; check well-known online computer magazines for antivirus software reviews.)
- Buying a new computer with antivirus software on it does not mean you are automatically protected. The software could be six months old and not cover new viruses. You have to register it with the manufacturer, and you need to activate automatic antivirus updates.
- Scan your entire system with antivirus software the first time it's installed; then scan it regularly after that. Often the software can be set to scan each time the computer is rebooted or on a periodic schedule. Also scan any new CDs and drives before using them.
- If you discover you have a virus, you can ask McAfee or Norton to scan your computer online. Then follow the company's directions for cleaning or deleting it.

CELLPHONE MALWARE Worms and viruses and other malware are now attacking cellphones. The most common type of cellphone infection right now occurs when a cellphone downloads an infected file from a PC or the Internet, but phone-to-phone viruses are on the rise. Infected files usually show up disguised as applications such as games, security patches, add-on functionalities, and, of course, erotica and free stuff.

Future possibilities include cellphone spyware—so someone can see every number you call and listen to your conversations—and viruses that steal financial information, which will become more serious as smartphones are used as common payment devices. Ultimately, more connectivity means more exposure to viruses and faster spreading of infection.

Cyber Security Tips

For more details about staying cybersafe, try:

www.cyber-safety.com/

www.haltabuse.org/resources/online.shtml

www.rferl.org/content/how_to_stay_safe_online/3544056.html

www.staysafeonline.org/ncsam

Some Cybervillains: Hackers & Crackers

All crackers are hackers, but not all hackers are crackers.

The popular press uses the word *hacker* to refer to people who break into computer systems and steal or corrupt data, but this is not quite the exact definition. Perhaps it helps to distinguish between hackers and crackers, although the term *cracker* has never caught on with the general public.

HACKERS **<u>*Hackers*</u> are defined (1) as computer enthusiasts, people who enjoy learning programming languages and computer systems, but also (2) as people who gain unauthorized access to computers or networks, often just for the challenge of it.**

Considering the second kind of hacker, those who break into computers for relatively benign reasons, we can say there are probably two types:

- **Thrill-seeker hackers:** *Thrill-seeker hackers* are hackers who illegally access computer systems simply for the challenge of it. Although they penetrate computers and networks illegally, they don't do any damage or steal anything; their reward is the achievement of breaking in.
- **White-hat hackers:** *White-hat hackers* are usually computer professionals who break into computer systems and networks with the knowledge of their owners to expose security flaws that can then be fixed.[30] (The term "white hat" refers to the hero in old Western movies, who often wore a white hat, as opposed to the villain, who usually wore a black hat—see below.)

CRACKERS As opposed to hackers, who do break-ins for more or less positive reasons, ***crackers*** **are malicious hackers, people who break into computers for malicious purposes**—to obtain information for financial gain, shut down hardware, pirate software, steal people's credit information, or alter or destroy data.

There seem to be four classes of crackers:

- **Script kiddies:** On the low end are *script kiddies,* mostly teenagers without much technical expertise who use downloadable software or source code to perform malicious break-ins.
- **Hacktivists:** *Hacktivists* are "hacker activists," people who break into a computer system for a politically or socially motivated purpose. For example, they might leave a highly visible message on the home page of a website that expresses a point of view that they oppose.
- **Black-hat hackers:** *Black-hat hackers* are those who break into computer systems to steal or destroy information or to use it for illegal profit. They are usually not bored, crafty teenagers but often professional criminals, for example, the people behind the increase in cyberattacks on corporate networks· Recently, such hackers have gone after cellphones and Twitter.
- **Cyberterrorists:** Cyberterrorism, according to the FBI, is any "premeditated, politically motivated attack against information, computer systems, computer programs, and data which results in violence against noncombatant targets by sub-national groups or clandestine agents."[31] Thus, *cyberterrorists* are politically motivated persons who attack computer systems so as to bring physical or financial harm to a lot of people or destroy a lot of information. Particular targets are power plants, water systems, traffic control centers, banks, and military installations.

Online Safety

Antivirus software, firewalls, passwords, biometric authentication, and encryption are methods to help preserve online safety.

Antivirus software

ANTIVIRUS SOFTWARE A variety of virus-fighting programs are available. ***Antivirus software*** **scans a computer's hard disk, other designated storage devices, and main memory to detect viruses and, sometimes, to destroy them.** Such virus watchdogs operate in two ways. First, they scan disk drives for "signatures," characteristic strings of 1s and 0s in the virus that uniquely identify it. Second, they look for suspicious viruslike behavior, such as attempts to erase or change areas on your disks.

Examples of antivirus programs, some of which we have already mentioned, are McAfee VirusScan, Norton AntiVirus, PC-cillin Internet Security, Avast!, and ZoneAlarm with Antivirus. Others worth considering are CA Internet Security Suite Plus, Panda Antivirus Platinum, and McAfee Virex for Macs.

Other ways of protecting your computer against viruses are given in the Practical Action box on page 359.

Survival Tip

Firewalls

Windows 7 has a built-in firewall. Many companies sell their own firewall versions. If you buy separate firewall software, turn off the operating system's firewall.

FIREWALLS **A *firewall* is a system of hardware and/or software that protects a computer or a network from intruders.** Firewalls are frequently used to prevent unauthorized Internet users from accessing private networks connected to the Internet, especially intranets. All messages entering or leaving the intranet pass through the firewall, which examines each message and blocks those that do not meet the specified security criteria.

Always-on Internet connections such as cable modem, satellite, and DSL, as well as some wireless devices, are particularly susceptible to unauthorized intrusion.

- **If you have one computer—software firewall:** If you have just one computer, a software firewall is probably enough to protect you while you're connected to the Internet. (Windows has a built-in software firewall that can be activated quickly.) Firewall software is also available for smartphones.
- **If you have more than one computer—hardware firewall:** If you have more than one computer and you are linked to the Internet by a cable modem or DSL, you probably need a hardware firewall, such as a router.

PASSWORDS When New York's World Trade Center was destroyed during the September 11, 2001, terrorist attack, debt-trading firm Cantor Fitzgerald lost 700 of its 1,000 employees—and no one knew the deceased workers' *passwords,* the special words, codes, or symbols required to access a computer system. Although records had been backed up and existed in another location, to maintain its customers' confidence, the company realized it had to be back up and running within two days. That meant discovering the passwords needed to get into essential files. What was it to do? According to one account, what surviving employees did was this: "They sat around in a group and recalled everything they knew about their colleagues, everything they had done, everywhere they had been, and everything that had ever happened to them. *And they managed to guess the passwords.*"[32]

As this story shows, protecting your Internet access accounts and files with a password isn't enough. Passwords (and PINs, too) can be guessed, forgotten, or stolen. To foil a stranger's guesses, experts say, you should never choose a real word or variations of your name, your birth date, or those of your friends or family. Instead you should mix letters, numbers, and punctuation marks in an oddball sequence of no fewer than eight characters. Examples of some good passwords are *2b/orNOT2b% and Alfred!E!Newman7.* Or you can also choose an obvious and memorable password but shift the position of your hands on the keyboard, creating a meaningless string of characters—the best kind of password. (Thus, *ELVIS* becomes *R:BOD* when you move your fingers one position right on the keyboard.)

More Password Tips

Get more password tips at:

www.us-cert.gov/cas/tips/ST04-002.html

www.phoronix.com/scan.php?page=article&item=213&num=1www.washington.edu/computing/windows/issue27/password.html

www.microsoft.com/protect/yourself/password/create.mspx

http://windows.microsoft.com/en-US/windows-vista/Tips-for-creating-a-strong-password

http://netsecurity.about.com/cs/generalsecurity/a/aa112103b.htm

BIOMETRIC AUTHENTICATION A hacker or cracker can easily breach a computer system with a guessed or stolen password. But some forms of identification can't be easily faked—such as your physical traits. ***Biometrics*, the science of measuring individual body characteristics,** tries to use these in security devices. *Biometric authentication devices* authenticate a person's identity by comparing his or her physical or behavioral characteristics with digital code stored in a computer system. (See also Chapter 5.)

There are several kinds of devices for verifying physical or behavioral characteristics that can be used to authenticate a person's identity. *(• See Panel 6.17.)*

- **Hand-geometry systems:** Also known as *full-hand palm scanners,* these are devices to verify a person's identity by scanning the entire hand, which, for each person, is as unique as a fingerprint and changes little over time.

panel 6.17

Biometric device

A soldier holds a HIIDE scanner during a mission in Afghanistan. HIIDE stands for Handheld Interagency Identity Detection Equipment enrollment and recognition device. It is a biometric security camera, used to identify unknown military people; it incorporates an iris scanner, fingerprint scanner, face scanner, and passport reader.

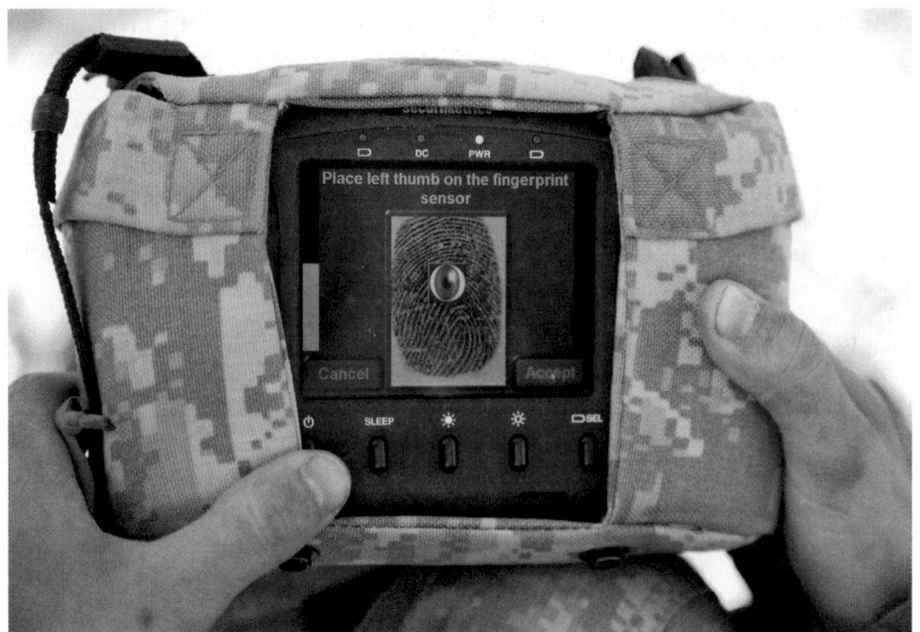

- **Fingerprint scanners:** These range from optical readers, in which you place a finger over a window, to swipe readers, such as those built into laptops and some handhelds, which allow you to run your finger across a barlike sensor. Microsoft offers optical fingerprint readers to go with Windows.
- **Iris-recognition systems:** Because no two people's eyes are alike, iris scans are very reliable identifiers. In Europe, some airports are using iris-scanning systems as a way of speeding up immigration controls. The Nine Zero, an upscale hotel in Boston, has experimented with letting guests enter one of its more expensive suites by staring into a camera that analyzes iris patterns.
- **Face-recognition systems:** Facial-recognition systems may come to play an important role in biometric photos embedded in U.S. passports and those of other industrialized nations during the next few years. The technology, which compares a live face image with a digitized image stored in a computer, is even used now as a security system for some notebook computers.
- **Voice-recognition systems:** These systems compare a person's voice with digitized voice prints stored in a computer, which the individual has previously "trained" to recognize his or her speech patterns.

ENCRYPTION ***Encryption*** **is the process of altering readable data into unreadable form to prevent unauthorized access.** Encryption is able to use powerful mathematical concepts to create coded messages that are difficult or even virtually impossible to break.

Suppose you wanted to send a message to a company colleague stating, "Our secret product will be revealed to the world on April 14." If you sent it in this undisguised, readable form, it would be known as *plain text.* To send it in disguised, unreadable form, you would *encrypt* that message into *cybertext,* and your colleague receiving it would then *decrypt* it, using an *encryption key*—a formula for encrypting and decrypting a coded message.

There are two basic forms of encryption—*private key* and *public key:*

- **Private key:** *Private-key (symmetric) encryption* means that the same secret key is used by both sender and receiver to encrypt and decrypt a message. The encryption system *DES* (for "Data Encryption Standard") was adopted as a federal standard for private-key encryption in 1976.

- **Public key:** *Public-key encryption* means that two keys are used—a *public key,* which the receiver has made known beforehand to the sender, who uses it to encrypt the message, and a *private key,* which only the receiver knows and which is required to decrypt the message. Examples of public-key encryption technologies are *PGP* (for "Pretty Good Privacy"), *RSA encryption,* and *Fortezza.*

Examples of the two types are shown below. *(● See Panel 6.18.)*

panel 6.18

Examples of two types of encryption

Private-key encryption

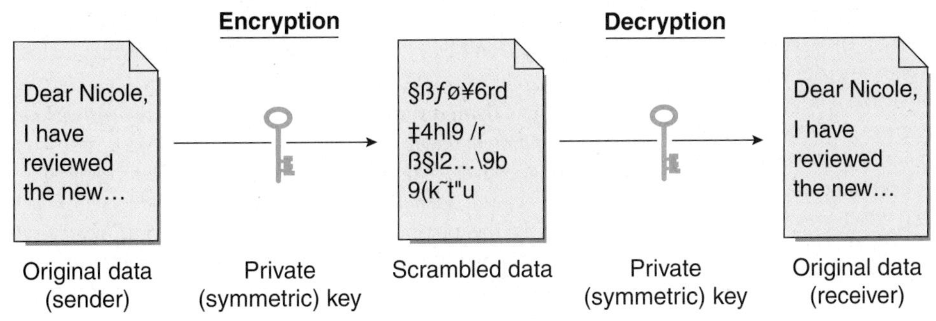

Public-key encryption

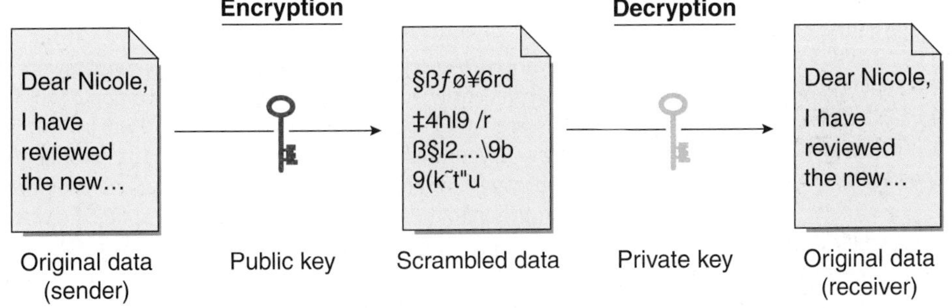

PRACTICAL ACTION

How to Deal with Passwords

Here's how easy it is to get someone's password: In 2005, 35 of 100 Internal Revenue Service (IRS) employees and managers contacted by U.S. Treasury Department inspectors posing as computer technicians provided their computer user name and their password. "With an employee's user account name and password," said the Treasury Department report, "a hacker could gain access to that employee's access privileges. Even more significant, a disgruntled employee could use the same . . . techniques and obtain another employee's username and password."[33] Employees complying with the request, which was in violation of IRS rules, said they were not aware of the hacking technique or they wanted to be as helpful as possible to the computer technicians. Some got approval from their managers to cooperate.

Rules in Creating Passwords

- ***Rule 1: Don't tell anyone your user name and password:*** Of course you shouldn't tell strangers. You also shouldn't even tell friends or relatives.
- ***Rule 2: Don't use passwords that can be easily guessed:*** Don't use "12345," the word "password," variations on your name, your nickname, your street address, mother's maiden name, pet's name, college name, or name of your favorite sports team.
- ***Rule 3: Avoid any word that appears in a dictionary:*** Instead, use weird combinations of letters, numbers, and punctuation. Mix uppercase and lowercase, along with special characters such as !, #, and %.
- ***Rule 4: Create long passwords, especially for sensitive sites:*** For financial accounts, for instance, 15-character passwords are recommended (which are 33,000 times harder to crack than an 8-character one).[34]
- ***Rule 5: Don't use the same password for multiple sites:*** Avoid reusing the same password at different sites, since if hackers or scammers obtain one account, they potentially have your entire online life. If you do use the same password for multiple purposes, use it only for low-risk sites, such as newspaper registrations.
- ***Rule 6: Change passwords often:*** Change passwords often, such as every 4 or 6 weeks or on a set schedule such as the first day of spring, summer, and so on. Change passwords when you use a computer in insecure locations such as libraries, airports, or Internet cafés.

Tips for Remembering Passwords

How on earth are you going to remember a dozen or more passwords of at least eight characters, mixing letters, numbers, and special characters—especially if you can't use words? First, Rules 7 and 8 below are things that people do that you *should not do.* Rule 9 offers some suggestions for memorizing your passwords.

- ***Rule 7: Don't write passwords on sticky notes, in a notebook, or in a handheld computer or tape them under your keyboard:*** Avoid writing out passwords on sticky notes (Post-its) and attaching them to your monitor or putting passwords in a notebook or personal information manager. And don't hide them under your keyboard—one of the first places a tech-knowledgeable person will look.
- ***Rule 8: Don't carry the passwords in your wallet:*** If you lose your wallet the consequences can be dire.
- ***Rule 9: Create a system for remembering passwords without writing them down:*** One technique is to think of a phrase from a song, such as, "Oh, say, can you see, by the dawn's early light," from *The Star-Spangled Banner.* Then use the last letter of each word in the phrase to construct the password: *hynueyesyt.* Mix it up by inserting a number or special character (#, ^, +) after each third letter or making every other letter uppercase. Another trick, says one writer, is to "begin with your random-looking string [of characters] and add a constant you memorize, such as '4!5.' End with something related to the website, such as the first four consonants of the domain name."[35]

Technical Tricks for Safeguarding Passwords

There are several technical solutions you can draw on for storing passwords. Two of the most available are these:

- ***Software with encrypted file:*** You can save all your passwords in a single, easily accessible encrypted file. Two popular programs are Any Password and PasswordSafe. PwdHash runs along with your web browsers; when you type a password into a web page, PwdHash encrypts the typed password before sending it on to the website (free test versions at *http://crypto.stanford.edu/PwdHash/*). Norton Confidential and Apple Computer's Keychain also help store keywords in secure encrypted form. Google, IBM, Microsoft, and Yahoo! are backing a system called OpenID (*http://openid.net/*), which, in one description, promotes "logging onto one OpenID website with one password, [which] will grant entrance during that session to all websites that accept OpenID credentials."[36]
- ***Fingerprint readers for master password:*** Microsoft offers fingerprint readers for Windows, and other fingerprint scanners are available such as BioMouse that are able to encrypt and keep track of all your various user names, passwords, and personal identification numbers (PINs). The fingerprint readers work only with the computer they are connected to, and the security of your various web accounts, bank accounts, frequent-flyer accounts, and so on depends on how unbreakable your passwords are. But at least you no longer have to memorize them.

Besides using encryption to secure email messages or transactions on e-commerce websites, you may also want to protect files on your computer—especially laptops and smartphones, in case you leave them behind on a train or bus. You can use special software to encrypt individual files, but experts recommend deploying whole-disk encryption, cloaking every file on your computer and granting access only to those with the proper password.

EXPERIENCE BOX

Virtual Meetings: Linking Up Electronically

Types of Virtual Meetings: Remote Conferencing

There are several ways in which people can conduct "virtual meetings"—meetings that don't entail physical travel—as follows.

Audioconferencing. *Audioconferencing* (or *teleconferencing*) is simply telephone conferencing. A telephone conference-call operator can arrange this setup among any three or more users. Users don't need any special equipment beyond a standard telephone. Audioconferencing is an inexpensive way to hold a long-distance meeting and is often used in business.

Computer-based audio, involving microphones, headsets or speakers, and Internet-based telephony, is also used for audioconferencing. (See VoIP and Skype in Chapter 2.)

Videoconferencing Using Closed-Circuit TV. Some of the more sophisticated equipment is known as telepresence technology, high-definition videoconference systems that simulate face-to-face meetings between users (for example, *www.tandberg.com/telepresence/* and *www.telepresenceoptions.com/*). Whereas traditional videoconferencing systems can be set up in a conventional conference room, telepresence systems require specially designed rooms with multiple cameras and high-definition video screens, simulating the sensation of two groups of people at identical tables facing each other through windows.

Videoconferencing Using a Webcam. A *webcam* is a tiny, often eyeball-shaped camera that sits atop a computer monitor or is built into the computer and that displays its output on a web page (Chapter 2, p. 66). Some cameras are able to automatically follow your face as you move. Headsets with built-in speakers and microphones are required. Yahoo! and MSN offer free video chatting through their instant-message programs. Webcams can also be used for VoIP and Skype conferences.

Videoconferencing Using Videophones. Videophones don't involve use of a PC, although the calls take place on the Internet. The Internet company 8×8 Inc., for example, makes a VoIP videophone.

Workgroup Computing or Web Conferencing. The use of groupware allows two or more people on a network to share information, collaborating on graphics, slides, and spreadsheets while linked by computer and telephone. Participants conduct meetings using tools such as "whiteboards," which can display drawings or text, along with group presentations (using PowerPoint, which displays slides on everyone's screen) and online chatting. Usually people do these things while talking to one another on the telephone. Users can collaborate by writing or editing word processing documents, spreadsheets, or presentations.

WHAT CAN REPLACE THE PASSWORD? Even if you make every effort to protect your password, there is nothing you can do if, say, hackers break into ATMs in convenience stores and steal customers' PIN codes, including yours. This actually happened in San Jose, California, where hackers got inside Citibank's network of ATMs inside 7-Eleven stores, netting themselves millions of dollars.[37] Thus, experts are suggesting users abandon passwords and use log-on systems that rely on cryptography, accessed with so-called information cards, bringing the concept of an identity card, like a driver's license, to the online world.[38]

Encryption Software

Some kinds of encryption software worth investigating:

PGP Personal Desktop (www.pgp.com)

WinMagic's SecureDoc (www.winmagic.com)

TERMS & EXPLANATIONS

analog (p. 314) Continuous and varying in strength and/or quality. An analog signal is a continuous electrical signal with such variation. Why it's important: *Sound, light, temperature, and pressure values, for instance, can fall anywhere on a continuum or range. The highs, lows, and in-between states have historically been represented with analog devices rather than in digital form. Examples of analog devices are a speedometer, a thermometer, and a tire-pressure gauge, all of which can measure continuous fluctuations. The electrical signals on a telephone line have traditionally been analog-data representations of the original voices, as have been telephone, radio, television, and cable-TV technologies—most of which are now digital.*

antivirus software (p. 360) Software that scans a computer's hard disk, flash drives, CDs, and main memory to detect viruses and, sometimes, to destroy them. Why it's important: *Antivirus software can protect your computer from disaster and from spreading viruses over networks.*

backbone (p. 329) The main highway—including gateways, routers, and other communications equipment—that connects all computer networks in an organization. Why it's important: *The Internet backbone is the central structure that connects all other elements of the Internet.*

bandwidth (p. 337) Also called *band;* range of frequencies that a transmission medium can carry in a given period of time and thus a measure of the amount of information that can be delivered. The bandwidth is the difference between the lowest and the highest frequencies transmitted. For analog signals, bandwidth is expressed in hertz (Hz), or cycles per second. For digital signals, bandwidth is expressed in bits per second (bps). In the United States, certain bands are assigned by the Federal Communications Commission (FCC) for certain purposes. Why it's important: *The wider the bandwidth, the faster the data can be transmitted. The narrower the band, the greater the loss of transmission power. This loss of power must be overcome by using relays or repeaters that rebroadcast the original signal.*

biometrics (p. 361) Science of measuring individual body characteristics. Why it's important: *Biometric devices authenticate a person's identity by comparing his or her physical identity with digital code stored in a computer system. Such devices can reduce attempts by unauthorized people to breach a computer system.*

Bluetooth (p. 352) Short-range wireless digital standard aimed at linking cellphones, PDAs, computers, and peripherals up to 33 feet. Why it's important: *Bluetooth technology can replace cables between PCs and printers and can connect PCs and wireless phones (hands-free).*

bridge (p. 328) Interface used to connect the same types of networks. Why it's important: *Similar networks (local area networks) can be joined together to create larger area networks.*

broadband (p. 337) Bandwidth characterized by very high speed; refers to telecommunications in which a wide band of frequencies is available to transmit information. Why it's important: *Because a wide band of frequencies is available, information can be sent on many different frequencies or channels within the band concurrently, allowing more information to be transmitted in a given amount of time. The wider a medium's bandwidth, the more frequencies it can use to transmit data and thus the faster the transmission. Broadband can transmit high-quality audio and video data. Compare with* **narrowband.**

broadcast radio (p. 339) Wireless transmission medium that sends data over long distances—between regions, states, or countries. A transmitter is required to send messages and a receiver to receive them; sometimes both sending and receiving functions are combined in a transceiver. Why it's important: *In the lower frequencies of the radio spectrum, several broadcast radio bands are reserved not only for conventional AM/FM radio but also for broadcast television, CB (citizens band) radio, ham (amateur) radio, cellphones, and private radio-band mobile services (such as police, fire, and taxi dispatch). Some organizations use specific radio frequencies and networks to support wireless communications.*

bus network (p. 330) Type of network in which all nodes are connected to a single linear wire or cable (the bus) that has two endpoints (terminators). Each device transmits electronic messages to other devices. If some of those messages collide, the device waits and then tries to retransmit. Why it's important: *The bus network is relatively inexpensive, but it's limited to 20 devices on the network and 185 meters in length.*

cellular radio (p. 340) Type of radio widely used for cellphones and wireless modems, using high-frequency radio waves to transmit voice and digital messages. Why it's important: *Unlike CB (citizens' band) radio, used by truck drivers, which has a few radio channels that everyone must share, cellular radio channels are reused simultaneously in nearby geographic areas, yet customers do not interfere with one another's calls.*

client/server network (p. 323) Local area network that consists of *clients,* which are microcomputers that request data, and *servers,* which are computers used to supply data. Why it's important: *In small organizations, servers can store files, provide printing stations, and transmit email. In large organizations, servers may also house enormous libraries of financial, sales, and product information. Compare with* **peer-to-peer network.**

coaxial cable (p. 334) Commonly called "co-ax"; insulated copper wire wrapped in a solid or braided metal shield and then in an external plastic cover. Why it's important: *Co-ax is widely used for cable television. Because of the extra insulation, coaxial cable is much better than twisted-pair wiring at resisting noise. Moreover, it can carry voice and data at a faster rate.*

communications medium (p. 333) Any medium (channel) that carries signals over a communications path, the route between two or more communications media devices. Why it's important: *Media may be wired or wireless. Three types of wired channels are twisted-pair wire (conventional telephone lines), coaxial cable, and fiber-optic cable. The speed, or data transfer rate, at which transmission occurs—and how much data can be carried by a signal—depends on the media and the type of signal.*

communications satellite (p. 340) Microwave relay station in orbit around the earth. Why it's important: *Transmitting a signal from a ground station to a satellite is called* uplinking; *the reverse is called* downlinking. *The delivery process will be slowed if, as is often the case, more than one satellite is required to get the message delivered.*

cracker (p. 360) Person who breaks into computers for malicious purposes—to obtain information for financial gain, shut down hardware, pirate software, steal people's credit information, or alter or destroy data. Why it's important: *Crackers can do major damage to computers and networks. Compare with* **hacker.**

denial-of-service (DoS) attack (p. 355) Also called *distributed denial of service (DDoS) attack*; form of technological assault that consists of making repeated fraudulent requests of a computer system or network, thereby overloading it. The assault may come from a single computer or from hundreds or thousands of computers that have been taken over by those intending harm. Why it's important: *A denial-of-service attack denies legitimate users access to the computer system.*

digital (p. 313) Communications signals or information represented in a discontinuous two-state (binary) way using electronic or electromagnetic signals. Why it's important: *Digital signals are the basis of computer-based communications.* Digital *is usually synonymous with* computer-based.

digital convergence (p. 312) The gradual merger of computing and communications into a new information environment, in which the same information is exchanged among many kinds of equipment, using the language of computers. Why it's important: *There has been a convergence of several important industries—computers, telecommunications, consumer electronics, entertainment, mass media—producing new electronic products that perform multiple functions.*

digital wireless services (p. 347) Two-way, second-generation (2G) wireless services that support digital cellphones and PDAs. They use a network of cell towers to send voice communications and data over the airwaves in digital form. Why it's important: *This technology was a dramatic improvement over analog cellphones. Voice clarity is better, and more calls can be squeezed into the same bandwidth. 2G has been supplanted by 3G and 4G services, and 5G is already a prototype.*

electromagnetic spectrum of radiation (p. 336) All the fields of electrical energy and magnetic energy, which travel in waves. This includes all radio signals, light rays, X rays, and radioactivity. Why it's important: *The part of the electromagnetic spectrum of particular interest is the area in the middle, which is used for communications purposes. Various frequencies are assigned by the U.S. federal government for different purposes.* See **radio frequency (RF) spectrum.**

encryption (p. 362) The process of altering readable data into unreadable form to prevent unauthorized access; coded messages are difficult or impossible to read. To send a message in disguised, unreadable form, you would *encrypt* that message into *cybertext*, and your colleague receiving it would then *decrypt* it, using an *encryption key*—a formula for encrypting and decrypting a coded message. Why it's important: *Using encryption to alter readable data into unreadable form can prevent unauthorized access.*

Ethernet (p. 332) LAN technology (protocol) that can be used with almost any kind of computer and that describes how data can be sent in between computers and other networked devices usually in close proximity. Why it's important: *Ethernet has become the most popular and most widely deployed network technology in the world; it is commonly used in star networks.*

extranet (p. 325) Private intranet that connects not only internal personnel but also selected suppliers and other strategic parties (outsiders). Why it's important: *Extranets have become popular for standard transactions such as purchasing.*

fiber-optic cable (p. 334) Cable that consists of dozens or hundreds of thin strands of glass or plastic that transmit pulsating beams of light rather than electricity. Why it's important: *These strands, each as thin as a human hair, can transmit up to 2 billion pulses per second (2 Gbps); each "on" pulse represents 1 bit. When bundled together, fiber-optic strands in a cable 0.12-inch thick can support a quarter-million to a half-million voice conversations at the same time. Moreover, unlike electrical signals, light pulses are not affected by random electromagnetic interference in the environment. Thus, they have much lower error rates than normal telephone wire and cable. In addition, fiber-optic cable is lighter and more durable than twisted-pair wire and co-ax cable. A final advantage is that it cannot easily be wiretapped, so transmissions are more secure.*

firewall (p. 361) System of hardware and/or software that protects a computer or a network from intruders. Always-on Internet connections such as cable modem and DSL, as well as some wireless devices, are particularly susceptible to unauthorized intrusion and so need a firewall. Why it's important: *The firewall monitors all Internet and other network activity, looking for suspicious data and preventing unauthorized access.*

gateway (p. 328) Interface permitting communication between dissimilar networks. Why it's important: *Gateways permit communication between a LAN and a WAN or between two LANs based on different network operating systems or different layouts.*

Global Positioning System (GPS) (p. 342) A series of Earth-orbiting satellites continuously transmitting timed radio signals that can be used to identify earth locations. Why it's important: *A GPS receiver—handheld or mounted in a vehicle, plane, or boat—can pick up transmissions from any four satellites, interpret the information from each, and calculate to within a few hundred feet or less the receiver's longitude, latitude, and altitude. Some GPS receivers include map software for finding one's way around, as with the Guidestar system available with some rental cars.*

hacker (p. 359) A hacker can be either (1) a computer enthusiast, a person who enjoys learning programming languages and computer systems; or (2) a person who gains unauthorized access to computers or networks, often just for the challenge of it. Why it's important: *Unlike crackers who have malevolent purposes, a hacker may break into computers for more or less positive reasons, but they may sometimes cause problems.*

host computer (p. 326) The central computer in a network that controls the network and the devices on it (such as a client/server network), called nodes. Why it's important: *The host computer controls access to the hardware, software, and all other resources on the network.*

infrared wireless transmission (p. 339) Transmission of data signals using infrared-light waves. Why it's important: *Infrared ports can be found on some laptop computers and printers, as well as wireless mice. The advantage is that no physical connection is required among devices. The drawbacks are that line-of-sight communication is required—there must be an unobstructed view between transmitter and receiver—and transmission is confined to short range.*

intranet (p. 324) An organization's internal private network that uses the infrastructure and standards of the Internet and the web. Why it's important: *When an organization creates an intranet, it enables employees to have quicker access to internal information and to share knowledge so that they can do their jobs better. Information exchanged on intranets may include employee email addresses and telephone numbers, product information, sales data, employee benefit information, and lists of jobs available within the organization.*

local area network (LAN) (p. 320) Communications network that connects computers and devices in a limited geographic area, such as one office, one building, or a group of buildings close together (for instance, a college campus). Why it's important: *LANs have replaced large computers for many functions and are considerably less expensive. They are the basis for most office networks.*

mesh network topology (p. 331) In *a mesh network* , messages sent to the destination can take any possible shortest, easiest route to reach its destination . There must be at least two paths to any individual computer to create a mesh network. (Wireless networks are often implemented as a mesh.) Why it's important: *The Internet employs the mesh topology.*

metropolitan area network (MAN) (p. 320) Communications network covering a city or a suburb. Why it's important: *The purpose of a MAN is often to bypass local telephone companies when accessing long-distance services. Many cellphone systems are MANs.*

microwave radio (p. 340) Transmission of voice and data through the atmosphere as superhigh-frequency radio waves called *microwaves*. These frequencies are used to transmit messages between ground-based stations and satellite communications systems. Why it's important: *Microwaves are line-of-sight; they cannot bend around corners or around Earth's curvature, so there must be an unobstructed view between transmitter and receiver. Thus, microwave stations need to be placed within 25–30 miles of each other, with no obstructions in between. In a string of microwave relay stations, each station receives incoming messages, boosts the signal strength, and relays the signal to the next station. Nowadays dish- or horn-shaped microwave reflective dishes, which contain transceivers and antennas, are nearly everywhere.*

modem (p. 316) Short for "modulate/demodulate"; device that converts digital signals into a representation of analog form (modulation) to send over phone lines. A receiving modem then converts the analog signal back to a digital signal (demodulation). Why it's important: *The modem provides a means for computers to communicate with one another using the standard copper-wire telephone network, an analog system that was built to transmit the human voice but not computer signals.*

narrowband (p. 337) Also known as *voiceband*. Bandwidth used for short distances. Transmission rates are usually 100 kilobits per second or less. Why it's important: *Narrowband is used in telephone modems and for regular telephone communications—for speech, faxes, and data. Compare with* **broadband.**

network (p. 317) Also called *communications network;* system of interconnected computers, telephones, or other communications devices that can communicate with one another and share applications and data. Why it's important: *The tying together of so many communications devices enables the Internet and in many ways is changing the world we live in.*

node (p. 326) Any device that is attached (wired or wireless) to a network. Why it's important: *A node may be a microcomputer, terminal, storage device, or peripheral device, any of which enhance the usefulness of the network.*

packet (p. 326) Fixed-length block of data for transmission. The packet also contains instructions about the destination of the packet. Why it's important: *By creating blocks, in the form of packets, a transmission system can deliver the data more efficiently and economically.*

pager (p. 345) Commonly known as *beeper;* simple radio receiver that receives data sent from a special radio transmitter. The pager number is dialed from a phone and travels via the transmitter to the pager. Why it's important: *Pagers are a way of receiving notification of phone calls so that the user can return the calls immediately; some pagers can also display messages of up to 80 characters and send preprogrammed messages. Pages are still used where cellphones are unreliable or prohibited, such as hospital complexes.*

peer-to-peer (P2P) network (p. 324) Type of network in which all computers on the network communicate directly with one another rather than relying on a server, as client/server networks do. Why it's important: *Every computer can share files and peripherals with all other computers on the network, given that all are granted access privileges. Peer-to-peer networks are less expensive than client/server networks and work effectively for up to 25 computers, making them appropriate for home networks.* Compare with **client/server network.**

protocol (p. 326) Also called *communications protocol;* set of conventions governing the exchange of data between hardware and/or software components in a communications network. Why it's important: *Protocols are built into hardware and software. Every device connected to a network must have an Internet protocol (IP) address so that other computers on the network can route data to that address.*

radio-frequency (RF) spectrum (p. 337) The part of the electromagnetic spectrum that carries most communications signals. Why it's important: *The radio spectrum ranges from low-frequency waves, such as those used for aeronautical and marine navigation equipment; through the medium frequencies for CB radios, cordless phones, and baby monitors; to ultrahigh-frequency bands for cellphones; and also microwave bands for communications satellites.*

ring network (p. 331) Type of network in which all communications devices are connected in a continuous loop and messages are passed around the ring until they reach the right destination. There is no central server. Why it's important: *The advantage of a ring network is that messages flow in only one direction and so there is no danger of collisions. The disadvantage is that if a workstation malfunctions, the entire network can stop working.*

router (p. 328) Device that joins multiple wired and wireless networks. Routers have specific software and hardware designed for routing and forwarding information. Why it's important: *High-speed routers serve as part of the Internet backbone, or transmission path, handling the major data traffic. They also provide small network connectivity.*

star network (p. 331) Type of network in which all microcomputers and other communications devices are connected to a central switch. Electronic messages are routed through the central switch to their destinations. The central switch monitors the flow of traffic. Why it's important: *The advantage of a star network is that the switch prevents collisions between messages. Moreover, if a connection is broken between any communications device and the switch, the rest of the devices on the network will continue operating.*

switch (p. 327) A device that connects computers to a network. Why it's important: *A switch is a full-duplex device, meaning data is transmitted back and forth at the same time, which improves the performance of the network.*

topology (p. 329) The logical layout, or shape, of a network. The three basic topologies are star, ring, and bus. Why it's important: *Different topologies can be used to suit different office and equipment network configurations.*

Trojan horse (p. 356) A subclass of virus program that pretends to be a useful program, such as a game or screen saver, but that carries viruses, or destructive instructions. Why it's important: *A Trojan horse can cause trouble without your knowledge, such as allow installation of backdoor programs, illegal programs that allow illegitimate users to take control of your computer without your knowledge.*

twisted-pair wire (p. 333) Two strands of insulated copper wire, twisted around each other. Why it's important: *Twisted-pair wire has been the most common channel or medium used for telephone systems. However, it is relatively slow and does not protect well against electrical interference.*

ultra wideband (UWB) (p. 353) A promising technology operating in the range of 480 megabits per second up to about 30 feet that uses a low power source to send out millions of bursts of radio energy every second over many different frequencies, which are then reassembled by a UWB receiver. Why it's important: *UWB operates over low frequencies not used by other technologies, making it a candidate to replace many of the cables that now currently connect household and office devices.*

virtual private network (VPN) (p. 325) Private network that uses a public network, usually the Internet, to connect remote sites. Why it's important: *Because wide area networks use leased lines, maintaining them can be expensive, especially as distances between offices increase. To decrease communications costs, some companies have established their own VPNs. Company intranets, extranets, and LANS can all be parts of a VPN.*

virus (p. 355) A virus attaches itself to a program or file enabling it to spread from one computer to another, leaving infections as it travels. Deviant program that can cause unexpected and often undesirable effects, such as destroying or corrupting data. Why it's important: *Viruses can cause users to lose data and/or files or can shut down entire computer systems.*

wide area network (WAN) (p. 320) Communications network that covers a wide geographic area, such as a country or the world. Why it's important: *Most long-distance and regional telephone companies are WANs. A WAN may use a combination of satellites, fiber-optic cable, microwave, and copper-wire connections and link a variety of computers, from mainframes to terminals.*

Wireless Application Protocol (WAP) (p. 339) Communications protocol designed to link nearly all mobile devices to your telecommunications carrier's wireless network and content providers. Why it's important: *Wireless devices such as cellphones use the Wireless Application Protocol for connecting wireless users to the World Wide Web.*

wireless USB (WUSB) (p. 353) Wireless standard with a typical range of 32 feet and a maximum data rate of 110–480 megabits per second. Why it's important: *Because USB is already the most used interface among PC users, the wireless version has immediately become very popular. It could be a natural replacement for USB cable links for printers, scanners, MP3 players, hard disks, and the like.*

worm (p. 356) Program that repeatedly copies itself into a computer's memory or onto a disk or flash drive or USB device drive until no space is left. Why it's important: *Worms can shut down computers and networks.*

CHAPTER REVIEW

LEARNING MEMORIZATION

"I can recognize and recall Information."

Self-Test Questions

1. A(n) __________ converts digital signals into analog signals for transmission over phone lines.
2. A(n) __________ network covers a wide geographic area, such as a state or a country.
3. __________ cable transmits data as pulses of light rather than as electricity.
4. __________ refers to waves continuously varying in strength and/or quality; __________ refers to communications signals or information in a binary form.
5. A(n) __________ is a private network that uses a public network (usually the Internet) to connect remote sites.
6. A(n) __________ is a computer that acts as a disk drive, storing programs and data files shared by users on a LAN.
7. The __________ is the system software that manages the activities of a network.
8. Modem is short for __________.
9. __________ is a short-range wireless digital standard aimed at linking cellphones, computers, and peripherals up to distances of 30 feet; it is often used for hands-free smartphone calls.
10. The __________ consists of the main highway—including gateways, routers, and other communications equipment—that connects all computer networks.
11. Any device that is attached to a network is called a(n) __________.

12. A set of conventions governing the exchange of data between hardware and software components in a communications network is called a(n) __________.
13. In a(n) __________ network topology, messages sent to the destination can take any possible shortest, easiest route to reach its destination; the Internet uses this toplogy.

Multiple-Choice Questions

1. Which of these best describes the regular telephone line that is used in most homes today?
   a. coaxial cable
   b. modem cable
   c. twisted-pair wire
   d. fiber-optic cable
   e. LAN
2. Which of these do local area networks enable?
   a. sharing of peripheral devices
   b. sharing of programs and data
   c. better communications
   d. access to databases
   e. all of these
3. Which of these is *not* a type of server?
   a. file server
   b. print server
   c. mail server
   d. disk server
   e. RAM server
4. Which of the following is *not* a short-distance wireless standard?
   a. Bluetooth
   b. PDA
   c. Wi-Fi
   d. WAP
5. Which type of local area network connects all devices through a central switch?
   a. bus network
   b. star network
   c. mesh network
   d. ring network
   e. router
6. Which is the type of local area network in which all microcomputers on the network communicate directly with one another without relying on a server?
   a. client/server
   b. domain
   c. peer to peer
   d. MAN
   e. WAN
7. How do fiber-optic cables transmit data?
   a. via copper wire
   b. via infrared
   c. via AC electric current
   d. via radio waves
   e. via pulsating beams of light
8. A(n) __________ is a system of hardware and/or software that protects a computer or a network from intruders.
   a. bridge
   b. firewall
   c. gateway
   d. router
   e. switch

True/False Questions

T F 1. In a LAN, a bridge is used to connect the same type of networks, whereas a gateway is used to enable dissimilar networks to communicate.

T F 2. Frequency and amplitude are two characteristics of analog carrier waves.

T F 3. A range of frequencies is called a *spectrum.*

T F 4. Twisted-pair wire commonly connects residences to external telephone systems.

T F 5. Wi-Fi signals can travel up to almost 250 feet.

T F 6. Microwave transmissions are a line-of-sight medium.

T F 7. 2G is the newest cellphone standard.

T F 8. Wi-Fi is formally known as an 802.11 network.

T F 9. A Trojan horse copies itself repeatedly into a computer's memory or onto a hard drive.

T F 10. Using Ethernet to alter readable data into unreadable form can prevent unauthorized access to transmitted messages.

2 LEARNING COMPREHENSION

"I can recall information in my own terms and explain it to a friend."

Short-Answer Questions

1. What is the difference between an intranet and an extranet?
2. What is the difference between a LAN and a WAN?
3. Why is bandwidth a factor in data transmission?
4. What is a firewall?
5. What do *2G* and *3G* mean?
6. Explain the differences between ring, bus, and star networks.
7. What is the electromagnetic spectrum?
8. What does a protocol do?
9. What are three basic rules for creating passwords?
10. What do we need encryption for?

3 LEARNING APPLYING, ANALYZING, SYNTHESIZING, EVALUATING

"I can apply what I've learned, relate these ideas to other concepts, build on other knowledge, and use all these thinking skills to form a judgment."

Knowledge in Action

1. Are the computers at your school connected to a network? If so, what kind of network(s)? What types of computers are connected? What hardware and software allow the network to function? What department(s) did you contact to find the information you needed to answer these questions?
2. Using current articles, publications, and/or the web, research cable modems. Where are they being used? What does a residential user need to hook up to a cable modem system?
3. Research the role of the Federal Communications Commission in regulating the communications industry. How are new frequencies opened up for new communications services? How are the frequencies determined? Who gets to use new frequencies?
4. Research the Telecommunications Act of 1996. Do you think it has had a positive or a negative effect? Why?
5. Would you like to have a job for which you telecommute instead of "going in to work"? Why or why not?
6. From your experience with cellphones, do you think it is wise to continue also paying for a "land-line" POTS phone line, or is cellphone service reliable enough and clear enough to use as your sole means of telephony? As cell service advances, how do you think the POTS infrastructure will be used?

Web Exercises

1. Compare digital cable and satellite TV in your area. Which offers more channels? Which offers more features? How much do the services cost? Do both offer Internet connectivity? What are the main differences between the two types of service?
2. Calculate the amount of airborne data transmission that travels through your body. To do this, research the amount of radio and television station broadcast signals in your area, as well as the estimated number of mobile-phone users. Imagine what the world would look like if you could see all the radio-wave signals the way you can see the waves in the ocean.
3. On the web, go to *www.trimble.com/gps/index.shtml* and work through some of the tutorial on GPS Technology. Then write a short report on the applications of a GPS system.
4. What is wardriving? Visit these sites to see what is being done to fix this security hole:

   www.wardriving.com/

   www.wordspy.com/words/wardriving.asp

   www.wardrive.net/

   http://searchmobilecomputing.techtarget.com/definition/war-driving
5. Test your ports and shields. Is your Internet connection secure, or is it inviting intruders to come in? Use the buttons at the bottom of the page at *https://grc.com/x/ne.dll?bhobkyd2* to test your port security and your shields and receive a full report on how your computer is communicating with the Internet.
6. Learn about the method of triangulation. This method helps when you use your cellphone to locate, for example, the nearest movie theater or restaurant. Visit the sites below to learn more. Run your own search on *triangulation*.

   www.qrg.northwestern.edu/projects/vss/docs/navigation/1-what-is-triangulation.html

   http://searchnetworking.techtarget.com/sDefinition/0,,sid7_gci753924,00.html

   www.al911.org/wireless/triangulation_location.htm

   www.ehow.com/how_2385973_triangulate-cell-phone.html

   www.securityfocus.com/columnists/376
7. TDMA, GSM, CDMA, and iDEN. What do these terms mean? The following websites do a good job of explaining these technologies and other cellphone-related issues.

   http://reviews.ebay.com/Cell-Phone-technologies-GSM- CDMA-TDMA-iDEN_W0QQugidZ10000000003636609

   www.dslreports.com/faq/5668

   http://e-articles.info/e/a/title/The-Role-of-Wireless-Application-Protocol-in-Web-Development/
8. Security issue—Wi-Fi security issues: As Wi-Fi becomes more widespread, how will users protect their networks? Wi-Fi is hacked almost as a harmless hobby to detect its vulnerabilities. Visit the following websites to learn about some issues of the Wi-Fi future.

   hwww.datapro.net/techinfo/wifi_security.html

   http://compnetworking.about.com/od/wirelesssecurity/tp/wifisecurity.htm

   www.slideshare.net/m9821735856/wifi-security-step-by-step-guide-1

   www.squidoo.com/what-is-wifi

   www.usatoday.com/tech/wireless/2007-08-06-wifi-hot-spots_N.htm

7

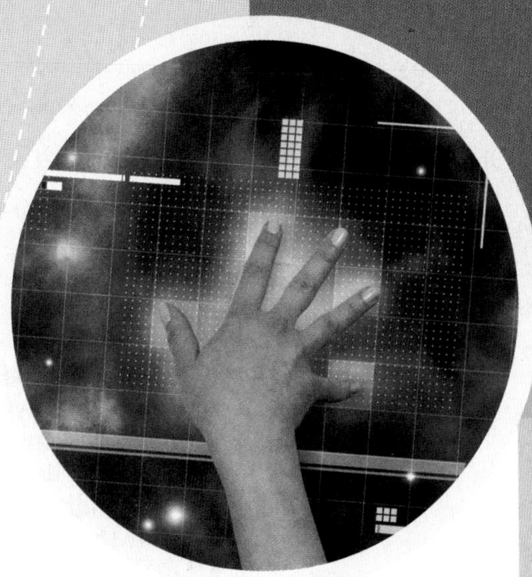

PERSONAL TECHNOLOGY: The Future Is You

Chapter Topics & Key Questions

- **7.1 Convergence, Portability, & Personalization** What are some of the pros and cons of the major trends in personal technology?
- **7.2 Portable Media Players** What should I know about portable media players?
- **7.3 High-Tech Radio: Satellite, High Definition, & Internet** How do the three forms of high-tech radio differ?
- **7.4 Digital Cameras: Changing Photography** What are some of the things I can do with digital cameras?
- **7.5 Digital Television** What's new about the new television?
- **7.6 E-Book Readers: The New Reading Machines** Can electronic books really improve on printed books?
- **7.7 Tablet PCs** How are tablet PCs useful?
- **7.8 Smartphones: More than Talk** How are smartphones different from basic cellphones?
- **7.9 Videogame Systems: The Ultimate Convergence Machine?** What are the principal videogame consoles?

Download the free UIT 10e App for key term flash cards, quizzes, and a game, *Over the Edge*

"The march of digital technologies through cameras, videos, and a flurry of gadgets is reshaping old standbys and broadening their use," says Gary McWilliams.

Cameras have turned into "slim wonders that beam images to a TV or printer. Television, which had evolved only gradually since the advent of color in the 1950s, is now a digital jungle of new screen types, shapes, and technologies," says *The Wall Street Journal* writer.[1]

It's all leading to what Jerry Yang and David Filo, the founders of Yahoo!, call the Internet's "second act," when broadband extends out to every electronic gadget. The Internet's first period, they say, involved shifting real-world activities such as shopping and dating into a virtual world, one dominated by the PC. In the net's second act, they believe, "creative power will shift into the hands of individuals, who will be just as likely to generate and share their own content as to consume someone else's."[2]

Indeed, this was readily demonstrated with the cellphone and blog-based outpouring of breaking news and shared information about the December 2004 tsunami in Asia, the July 2005 terrorist subway bombings in London, hurricane Katrina in 2005, and the demonstrations in Egypt, Syria, Libya, Algeria, Yemen, and Tunisia in 2011. It's also evident in the phenomenon known as *mashups* (blends), a creative combination of content or elements from different sources, including a web page that uses data combined from two or more sources to create new services or content and music created, for example, by overlaying two or more prerecorded songs or mixing up parts of different videos—part of an ongoing shift toward a more interactive and participatory web.

Mashup Sites

Information on various types of mashups:

www.mashuptown.com/

www.mashup-charts.com/

www.programmableweb.com/mashups

http://netforbeginners.about.com/od/m/f/What-Is-an-Internet-Mashup.htm

www.videomashups.ca/

7.1 Convergence, Portability, & Personalization

Three major trends in information technology continue to be convergence, portability, and personalization.

Is a phone with motion sensing really useful? What happens if you're calling while on a bumpy road? Regardless, the device seems to embody three principal results of the fusion of computers and communications that we mentioned in Chapter 1— *convergence, portability,* and *personalization.* Let's see what these developments, which began to build in strength during the 1990s, are like today.

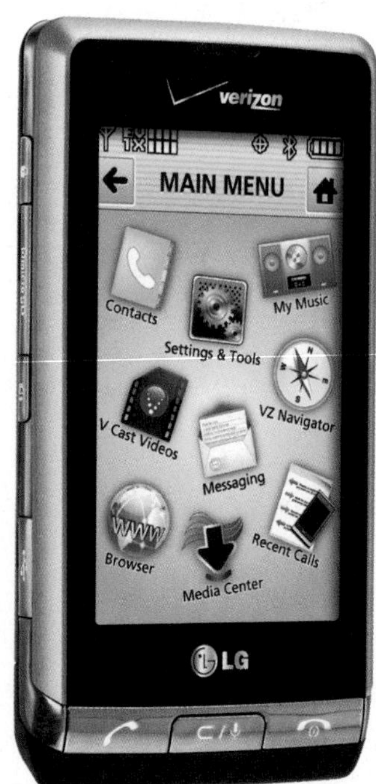

LG Dare, motion sensor cellphone

Convergence

The busiest area of convergence today is the merging of computers and consumer electronics.

As we said in Chapter 1, ***convergence,*** **or *digital convergence,* describes the combining of several industries—computers, communications, consumer electronics, entertainment, and mass media—through various devices that exchange data in digital form.** Long predicted but not fulfilled, convergence is now a reality. More and more households throughout the world have been going to broadband, with the faster Internet connections changing the computer, cable, phone, music, movie, and other businesses. Convergence, as we've pointed out, has led to electronic products that perform multiple functions, such as TVs with Internet access, cellphones that are also digital cameras and GPS units, and cars with various types of digital connection ports.

Convergence. Home entertainment centers bring together several electronic functions to access music, video, TV, and the Internet, as well as support some computer functions.

Of course, hybrid convergence devices have pros and cons, some of which are as follows.

CONVERGENCE: THE UPSIDE Over the past two decades, as computing and communications have migrated from expensive desktop computers, which were used mainly by upper-income people, to easier-to-use and more affordable cellphones, users have also changed, with a much greater diversity of people being involved. And they are using their handhelds for many more nonvoice data applications, such as taking pictures, accessing the Internet, playing music, retrieving email, watching movies, visiting social networking sites, and texting. Indeed, engineers have succeeded in designing the cellphone so you can use it as a universal remote to control your music, your TV, your PowerPoint presentation, or whatever.

All these capabilities have become accepted conveniences, keeping people connected to one another and many kinds of business and educational resources, information sources, and entertainment. But these conveniences carry some problems.

CONVERGENCE: THE DOWNSIDE Not all hybrid devices are necessarily practical. For one thing, just because companies can converge technologies into one appliance doesn't always mean that it's a good idea. Any device whose primary feature is compromised (weakened) by combining technologies is not necessarily a good device. For another thing, the more hardware capabilities that one loads onto one device, the more applications one uses it for—and the more apps and types of connections, the higher the risk of security breaches, ID theft, company tracking of personal data and locations, and the loss of focus on face-to-face communication.

Portability

A device that is portable is small, lightweight, and easy to carry.

Smart cellphones are, of course, an example of portability. Not all too long ago, having a phone in your car was a badge of affluence, affordable mainly by Hollywood movie producers and big-city real estate developers. Now, thanks to increasing miniaturization, faster speeds, and declining costs, more and more mobile phone and other electronic components can be crammed into smaller and smaller gadgets. But as today's students are well aware, a host

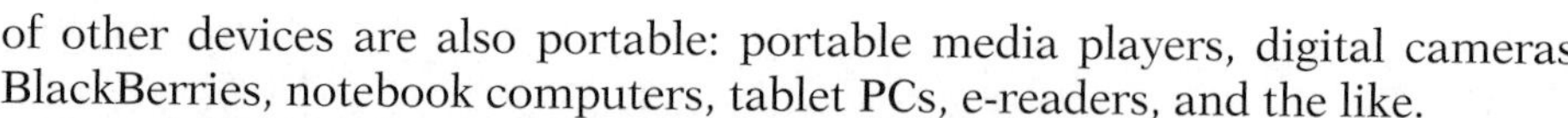

of other devices are also portable: portable media players, digital cameras, BlackBerries, notebook computers, tablet PCs, e-readers, and the like.

Portability also has its upside and downside.

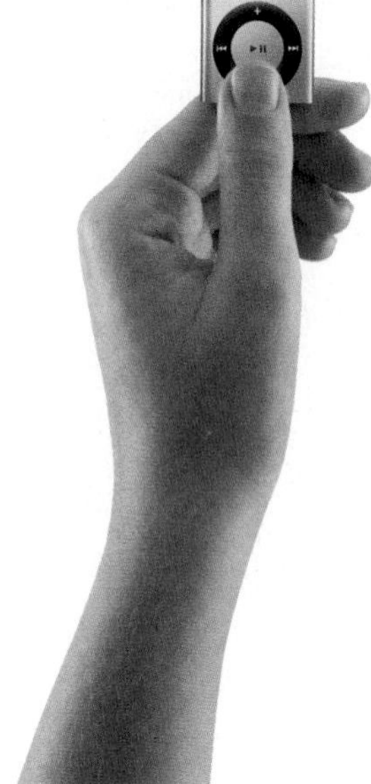

Portability: Apple iPod Shuffle

PORTABILITY: THE UPSIDE The advantages of portability seem obvious: being able to do phone calls and emails from anywhere that you can make a connection, keeping up with your social networks, listening to hundreds of songs on a digital music player such as an iPod, taking photos or video anywhere on a whim, watching TV anywhere anytime. One reason that manufacturers have targeted turning cellphones into hybrids, incidentally, is that people carry them wherever they go, unlike laptop computers, portable media players, and digital cameras.

PORTABILITY: THE DOWNSIDE The same portable technology that enables you to access information and entertainment anytime anywhere often means that others can find *you* equally conveniently (for them). Thus, you have to become disciplined about preventing others from wasting your time, as by screening your cellphone calls with *Caller ID,* a feature that shows the name and/or number of the calling party on the phone's display when you receive an incoming call. You may also find yourself bombarded throughout the day by unnecessary incoming emails, text messages, and web services known as RSS aggregators that automatically update you on new information from various sites.

iPod family

Nonstop connectivity may rain digital information on you, but it can also have the paradoxical result of removing you from real human contact. Consequently, the professor whose recommendation you may need someday for an employment or graduate school reference may never get to know you, because your interaction will never be face-to-face, for example, during his or her normal office hours. Businesses, incidentally, have recently had to deal with recurring complaints from employees about their inability to reach coworkers to get critical information they need—because their coworkers don't respond in timely fashion via email.

Personalization

Is personalization of media content possible without loss of privacy and restriction of information?

People on a telecommunications system are now not only consumers of information ("content") but also manipulators and possible providers of it. Consumers will soon expect each of their online experiences (on the web, mobile, email, Internet TV, and so forth) to be 100% relevant to them—BUT—while not infringing on their privacy.[3]

PERSONALIZATION: THE UPSIDE As a consumer, you may have downloaded hundreds or thousands of songs, so that you have your own personalized library of music on your computer and portable media player. You may also have created your own list of "favorites" or "bookmarks" on your PC so that you can readily access your favorite websites. And you may have accessed or contributed to certain blogs, or personalized online diaries. In addition, of course, PC software can be used to create all kinds of personal projects, ranging from artwork to finances to genealogy.

PERSONALIZATION: THE DOWNSIDE One of the downsides of personalization is that people may feel overburdened with *too much choice.* Indeed, Swarthmore College psychology professor Barry Schwartz, author of *The Paradox* *of Choice: Why More Is Less,* has identified several factors by which choice overload hurts us. As available options increase, he says, the following may happen:[4]

- **Regret:** People are more likely to regret their decisions.
- **Inaction:** People are more likely to anticipate regretting decisions, and the anticipated regret prevents people from actually deciding.
- **Excessive expectations:** Expectations about how good the decision will be go up. Thus, reality has a hard time living up to the expectations.
- **Self-blame:** When decisions have disappointing results, people tend to blame themselves, because they feel the unsatisfying results must be their fault.

Other possible problems caused by too much choice and "overpersonalization" of media devices and media content include these:

- **Paralysis:** Whatever one selects, the other option would have been better, so one chooses nothing.[5] "And even though we now have the capacity, via the Internet, to research choices endlessly, it doesn't mean we should. When looking, for example, for a new camera or a hotel, . . . limit yourself to three websites. . . . 'It is not clear that more choice gives you more freedom. It could decrease our freedom if we spend so much time trying to make choices.'"[6] As the French say: "Too much choice kills the choice."
- **Filtering:** Eli Pariser, of MoveOn fame, gave a talk on "the insidious encroachment of invisible filters on the web content we see and consume. Consider, Eli said, his own Facebook feed. He's got a number of friends who are liberal . . . and a number of friends who are conservative. One day, though, he noticed that his conservative friends' comments weren't showing up in his News Feed anymore. Facebook . . . had determined that, because Eli is more likely to click on a link from a liberal friend than on one from a conservative one, it would be easier for everybody concerned to show Eli *only* links from liberal friends. Without consulting Eli, the algorithm quietly hid all the apparently unwanted messages; thus this is a case of unwanted personalization."[7]
- **Facts are facts:** The news is the news, and it should reflect the world, not us. "One of the key requirements for a functioning democracy is a well-informed citizenry. A democracy demands that its people are active and informed from a variety of perspectives. As one of the most recent online fads, personalization poses a rather large threat to this."[8] Yet many consumers of online information customize its content to tell them what they basically already "know." But "your interests should not define what news you are exposed to."[9] The whole purpose of education is defeated by such an approach.

One result of having many choices is that people do ***multitasking*—performing several tasks at once, shifting focus from one task to another in rapid succession.** You may think you're one of those people who has no trouble juggling many tasks at once, but medical and learning experts say the brain has limits and can do only so much at one time. For instance, it has been found that people who do two demanding tasks simultaneously—drive in heavy traffic and talk on a cellphone, for example—do neither task as well as they do each alone.

Indeed, the result of constantly shifting attention is a sacrifice in quality for any of the tasks with which one is engaged. The phenomenon of half-heartedly talking to someone on the phone while simultaneously surfing the web, reading emails, or texting has been called "surfer's voice." Experts who study these things call it "absent presence."[10]

Research suggests many ways in which multitasking is inefficient or even harmful:[11]

- There is evidence that multitasking degrades short-term memory, not just for the topics being multitasked but possibly by affecting areas of the brain. Multitasking creates stress; stress invokes the more primitive parts of the brain that are concerned with personal safety, pulling energy from the more modern parts concerned with higher level thinking. Stress can also damage cells needed for new memories.
- We are more prone to errors when we multitask, so the quality of our work results goes down.
- Some parts of the brain are sequential processors, able to accept only one input at a time.
- The prefrontal cortex, the part of the brain most used for complex cognition and decision making, is the biggest energy consumer in the brain. The load from multitasking can lead to a quicker depletion of cognitive ability and more frequent need for recovery time.

Popular Personal Technologies

Have all the new personalized IT devices made our lives better or more complicated?

Where are you, technologically speaking, with the personal electronic devices you use every day? Let's explore what's out there (knowing full well that no textbook will be able to keep up with all the new devices constantly being marketed to consumers).

Now we consider the following kinds of personal technology:

- Portable media players
- Satellite, high-definition, and Internet radios
- Digital cameras
- The new television
- E-readers
- Tablet PCs
- Smartphones
- Videogame systems

7.2 Portable Media Players

Portable media players include MP3 players.

Exemplified by the Apple iPod, ***portable media players (PMPs)*** **are small portable devices that enable you to play digital audio, video, or still-image files.** PMPs are also known as *MP3 players*, or *digital music players,* portable devices for playing digital audio files. ***MP3*** **is a format that allows audio files to be compressed so they are small enough to be sent over the Internet or stored as digital files.** (MP3 is short for MPEG Audio Layer 3, an audio compression technology; MP4, or MPEG-4 Part 14, is used for audio and video; the iPod uses MP4 and can also play MP3.) MP3 files are about one-tenth the size of uncompressed audio files. For example, a 4-minute

Zen X-Fi2, a high-capacity personal media player (PMP) that adds Xtreme Fidelity (X-Fi) sound technology, a built-in speaker, built-in mic, and a few wireless functions.

MP3 player. Microsoft Zune HD

song on a CD takes about 40 megabytes of space, but an MP3 version of that song takes only about 4 megabytes.

PMPs differ from MP3 players, however, in that they can handle not only audio but also video and image files. Thus, you may be able to carry several hours of music or video—in the case of a 160-gigabyte Apple iPod Classic as many as 40,000 songs, 200 hours of video, or 25,000 still images. (For video, PMPs use MPEG-4 [Moving Picture Experts Group] video compression format and Windows Video Media [WMV].) Note that devices that serve *only* as audio MP3 players are becoming rare, as PMPs take over the market.

PMPs & MP3 Players

For reviews:

www.digitaltrends.com/mp3-media-player-reviews/

http://mp3-players.toptenreviews.com/flash-drive/

www.smart-review.com/portable-mp3-players.html

www.youtube.com/watch?v=6FCmrTrKDEo

How PMP/MP3 Players Work

PMP/MP3 players are small handheld devices that generally use small hard drives and/or solid-state flash memory for storing files.

The most famous of digital music players is Apple Computer's iPod, although there are many other players as well, such as Microsoft's Zune HD, Sony X Series Walkman, and Archos 32—with more coming along all the time. Basically, however, PMP/MP3 players can be divided into those that have hard-disk drives for storage (which store more songs) and those that have flash memory cards. For example, an 80GB hard-drive MP3 player that can hold roughly 20,000 songs will cost between $215 and $250 (about $2.91 per 1 GB of storage). An 8GB flash memory player that can hold about 2,000 songs will often cost $160 to $300 depending on how many features the device has (between $20 and $37.50 per 1 GB). Why is it more expensive for less storage capacity? Flash-based MP3 players are typically thinner and lighter and they get much longer battery life and have no moving parts, meaning zero potential for skipping music and fewer parts failures.[12] (If you want to run with your MP3 player, use a solid-state flash-based player.) Some players have both hard drives and flash memory cards.

Software for soft wear. Instead of wearing your heart on your sleeve, you can wear MP3, GPS, and cellphone technology incorporated into this German-made IO-jacket. The player is controlled through cloth buttons on the left sleeve, and the headphones are built into the collar.

SAMPLING RATE How many songs your PMP/MP3 player holds is affected not only by the storage capacity but also by the sound quality selected, which you can determine yourself when you're downloading songs from your computer to your player. Downloading and converting a digital audio track from a music CD to the MP3 format is called *ripping*. If you want high-quality sound when you're ripping (converting), the files will be relatively large, which means your PMP will hold fewer songs. If you're willing to have lower-quality sound, perhaps for the device you use while jogging or recording only voice in lectures,

Sampling Rate Guide for MP3 Players

Check out wiseGeek at:

www.wisegeek.com/what-is-a-good-bitrate-guideline-for-mp3-files.htm

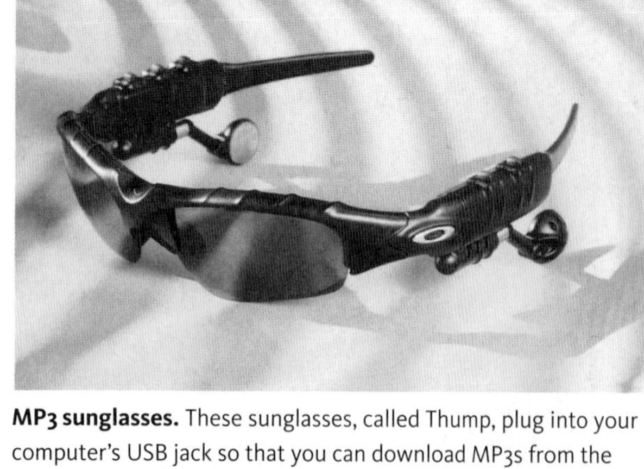

MP3 sunglasses. These sunglasses, called Thump, plug into your computer's USB jack so that you can download MP3s from the computer to the glasses. Then, just put on the glasses, put the earbuds in your ears, and enjoy the music.

you can carry more files on your player. The quality is determined by the ***sampling rate*****, the number of times, expressed in kilobits per second (kbps), that a song (file) is measured (sampled) and converted to a digital value** (p. 317). For instance, a song sampled at 192 kilobits per second is three times the size of a song sampled at 64 kilobits per second and is of better sound quality. Sampling choices that range from 32 kbps to 320 kbps will give good results. Many people simply use the highest sampling rate that their device allows.

TRANSFERRING FILES When you buy a PMP/MP3 player, it comes with software that allows you to transfer files to it from your personal computer, using a high-speed port such as a FireWire or universal serial bus port (USB 1.0, 2.0, or 3.0; p. 222), Bluetooth, or via Wi-Fi from a compatible website.

BATTERY LIFE Battery life varies. If you travel a lot, you will want the longest battery life possible before recharging is necessary. The best battery life (Cowan S9) is about 36 hours of music playback or 11 hours of video. The Sony X-Series Walkman offers 33 hours of audio playback or 9 hours of video. The Samsung P3, Apple iPod Touch and iPod Classic, and Microsoft Zune HD average 30 to 40 hours of audio or 6 to 8 hours of video.

DISPLAY SCREENS MP3 players come in a wide range of physical sizes—some so small that they can hang off a keychain and others almost too large to fit in your hand. The smallest players' screens are about 1.8–2 inches; midsize players' screens, 2–3.5 inches (these seem to be the most popular). Larger MP3 players have 4-inch or larger screens and have thicker, heavier bodies. Most PMP/MP3 screens these days are color.

OTHER FEATURES Many PMPs, particularly flash-based devices, offer FM radio reception. Many players also are able to make high-quality music recordings, using an extra microphone. Some also have a small internal microphone for voice recording, appropriate for capturing conversation or a lecture but usually unsuitable for music. All players come with earphones ("earbuds").

GETTING MUSIC AND VIDEO FILES Each MP3 player comes with software for managing your music (and video) library. You can copy an entire CD collection onto an MP3 player with almost no technical knowledge or experience. If you want to buy music online for an MP3 player, there are several services available.

PMP in a Ford Lincoln

The Apple iPod, for example, uses the iTunes program to manage music, and online music purchases are made through the iTunes website. There are millions of songs available, as well as thousands of movies, TV shows and other content. Non-iPod MP3 players connect to other websites or use amazon.com's MP3 Music Store and download files to their computer and then transfer the files to their player. Or they can store their purchased songs and so forth on amazon.com's Cloud Player and then download the files wirelessly to the device of their choice.

PMP IN YOUR CAR It's dangerous, and in most places illegal, to use earphones while driving. However, most new cars now come with ports/jacks for hands-free smartphones and PMP/MP3 players, as well as Bluetooth and Wi-Fi capabilities.

The Societal Effects of PMPs

PMPs are used almost everywhere by many people, but they do have the ability to damage hearing, so users should be careful with the volume controls.

"I've called the iPod the first cultural icon of the 21st century," says Michael Bull, an instructor in media and cultural studies at the University of Sussex in England. Bull has spent more than a decade researching the societal effects of portable audio devices, starting with Sony's Walkman portable cassette player and extending to Apple's iPod, which was introduced in 2001. The iPod, he says, "permits you to join the rhythm of your mind with the rhythm of the world," causing a cultural shift away from large communal areas—such as a cathedral, "a space we could all inhabit"—to the world of the iPod, "which exists in our heads."[13]

Nearly half of all adults (47%) own an MP3/MP4 player. Just about six years ago, only 11% of adults owned an MP3 player. Young people are the largest users of this form of technology. Fully three-fourths (75%) of adults 18–29 own an MP player.[14] It is true that MP listeners can control their own environment without intrusions from television and print advertisements, giving them the ability to express individuality. This technology also enables users to share files with their friends, creating a sense of community.[15]

But is the increase in the use of PMP/MP3/MP4 players a good thing? Many people believe that personalized digital media are making us all more isolated, with less and less face-to-face interaction, that they cut off individuals from the world. On the bus or train, at the gym, at work, at the grocery store, people are shutting out the world around them and are beginning to feel that each of them is the only person in the world. Some users also illegally download songs, effectively robbing creators of income.

Note: Hearing experts are concerned about the effect of hours of listening to audio players. A recent study has documented that listening with earbuds, or in-ear headphones, for 90 minutes a day at 80% volume is probably safe for long-term hearing. (Because earbuds are placed directly in the ear, they can boost the sound signal by as much as 6 to 9 decibels.) But softer is even better: you can safely tune in at 70% volume for about 4½ hours a day. The risk of permanent hearing loss, this study says, can increase with just 5 minutes of exposure a day to music at full volume. Over time, the noise can damage the delicate hair cells in the inner ear that transform sound waves to the electrical signals that the brain understands as sound.[16] A Northwestern University audiologist and professor found hearing loss in younger people with the use of iPods and earbuds that is similar to that found in aging adults. To avoid permanent hearing loss in the middle ranges—the range required to hear conversation in a noisy restaurant, for example—researchers recommend the older style, larger headphones that rest over the ear opening.[17]

Using PMPs in College

PMPs are useful for recording and replaying lectures, among other things.

College instructors and students have found ways to expand the uses of the iPod beyond just the enjoyment of music. For instance, PMPs can be used to store schedules, phone-number lists, and other personal information management software. "One of the most popular current uses of portable media players for educational purposes centers on the practice of recording and disseminating lectures. Through enabling students to use portable media players to store and play back digital copies of lectures, the intention is to make the lecture format more accessible for students and support student mobility and flexibility in their learning activities."[18] *(• See Panel 7.1, next page.)*

panel 7.1

Some college uses for portable media players

- Professors record lectures and post them online for students to download for later review, as when students have dead time (such as riding the bus).
- Interviews with guest speakers and messages from administrators may also be sent straight to students' portable media players.
- Some classes, such as those in music, foreign languages, or radio broadcasting, can especially benefit from use of audio players.
- Students record their own study group sessions and interviews, using their music players with microphones.
- Students record "audio web logs" during off-campus jobs to connect with people on campus.
- Students subscribe to feeds of frequently updated audio content from podcasts; students produce their own audio shows and podcast them. A "PodPage" website can be created that is devoted to such podcasts.

7.3 HIGH-TECH RADIO: Satellite, High Definition, & Internet

High-tech radio uses satellite, digital transmission on FM stations (HD radio), the Internet, and podcasting.

"The number of U.S. persons 12 and older listening to radio each week now reaches an estimated 241.6 million."[19] As its number of listeners grows, the radio industry has been transformed by a number of trends, which we discuss next.

Satellite Radio

Satellite radio is commercial-free digital radio transmitted via satellite and paid for by subscribers.

***Satellite radio*, also called *digital radio*, is a radio service in which digital signals are sent from satellites in orbit around the earth or by earth-based repeaters to subscribers owning special radios that can decode the encrypted signals.** (Satellite radio is also known as Satellite Digital Audio Radio Service [SDARS].) The CD-quality sound is much better than that of regular radio, and there are many more channels available than there are on regular radio. Unlike standard broadcasters, satellite radio broadcasters are for the most part not regulated by the Federal Communications Commission, although the FCC established the playing field back in the early 1990s when it began selling parts of the radio-wave spectrum for this class of service. Nearly all automobiles include satellite tuners in their radios, which typically provide a period of free service before requiring a paid subscription. Satellite TV carriers and Internet service providers also supply various satellite radio programs as part of their service. Most of the content is commercial-free, and it includes music, sports, talk shows, traffic, weather, and more. The major U.S. satellite radio company is Sirius XM, which offers more than 180 channels and supports itself by monthly subscription fees starting at $13 a month. In spring 2009, the company began streaming its service to the iPhone and iPod Touch devices.

The Sirius Starmate Replay, equipped to receive satellite radio

HD Radio

HD (hybrid digital) radio provides the digital technology for AM/FM stations in the U.S.

Traditional radio broadcasters "were quite nervous back in 1995 when the FCC was considering licensing two satellite digital audio radio service . . .

providers," says one account. "This was the potential death knell (or so they thought) of traditional radio. Something had to be done."[20] Enter ***HD (hybrid digital) radio*****, which provides CD-quality sound and allows broadcasters to squeeze one analog and two digital stations on the same frequency.** (• *See Panel 7.2.*) That is, HD Radio combines digital and analog broadcast signals, enabling stations to offer an analog main channel and digital "sidebands," so that multiple types of content can be broadcast from the same position on the dial. HD channels are called HD2/HD3 Channels, and are located on the FM dial. An additional advantage over satellite radio, at least so far, is that broadcasts are free; there are no subscription charges. HD radio is available in certain cars, as portable units for home use, and as add-ons for portable media players.

HD Radio Stations

Check HD radio availability in your state at:

www.hdradio.com/stations

Internet Radio

Internet radio is also called net radio, web radio, and streaming radio.

Internet radio **is the continuous streaming of audio over the Internet;** listeners have no control over the stream—just as with regular radio. Dedicated hardware devices, commonly called web radio or Internet radio appliances, can be purchased that connect to a home network and then to the Internet to play audio streams. Internet radio can also be played on computers and on portable

panel 7.2

How HD radio works

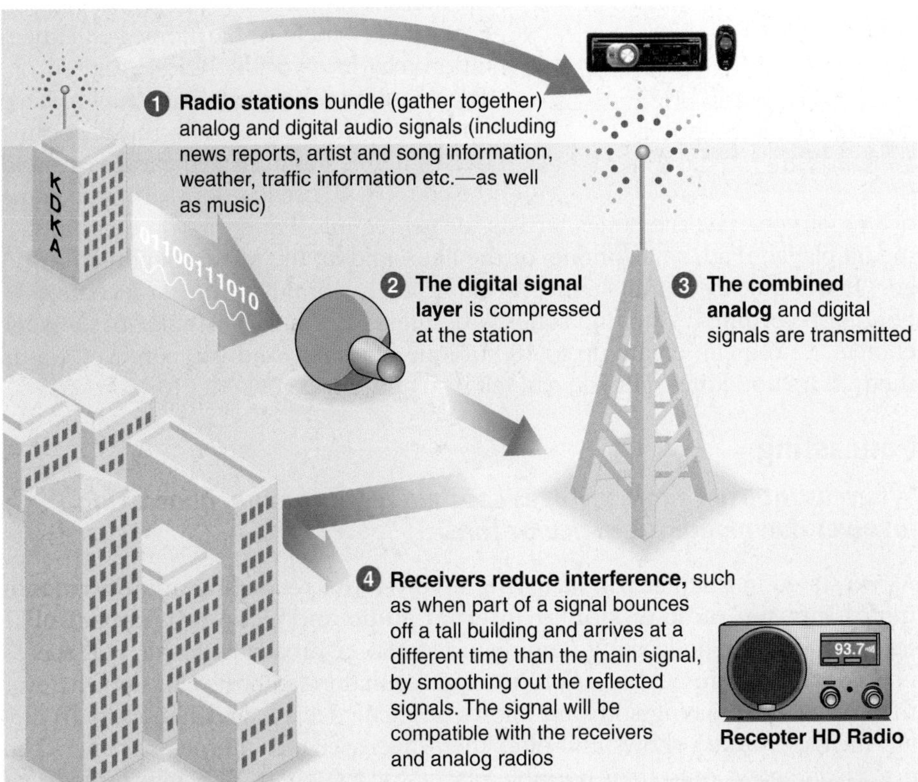

KDKA
1 Radio stations bundle (gather together) analog and digital audio signals (including news reports, artist and song information, weather, traffic information etc.—as well as music)
01100111010
2 The digital signal layer is compressed at the station
3 The combined analog and digital signals are transmitted
4 Receivers reduce interference, such as when part of a signal bounces off a tall building and arrives at a different time than the main signal, by smoothing out the reflected signals. The signal will be compatible with the receivers and analog radios
93.7
Recepter HD Radio

JVC HD radio

radio-locator

Welcome to Radio-Locator, the most comprehensive radio station search engine on the internet. We have links to over 10,000 radio station web pages and over 2500 audio streams from radio stations in the U.S. and around the world.

find unused frequencies on the FM dial

find US radio by city or zip go

find US radio by call letters go

find Internet streaming radio choose a format go

find world radio choose a country go

or search by: station format
U.S. state
Canadian province
city or location
advanced search

Are you a fan of Radio-Locator?

Check out some of our nifty merchandise in the Radio-Locator Online Store.

Looking for radio station email, phone or mailing addresses?

about radio-locator | frequently asked questions | what's new
contact us | partnership opportunities | login

devices, such as smartphones and media players, connected wirelessly to the Internet. If an Internet radio has built-in connectivity to a home wireless network, it is often called a Wi-Fi radio.

The most popular Internet-only radio sites are owned by online companies such as Yahoo!, AOL, and MSN. Yahoo!'s Musicmatch service, for instance, allows listeners to pick a category, such as alternative rock, and then play a number of songs in that genre, with fewer ads than are found on traditional radio. However, there are also numerous mom-and-pop web broadcasters, such as Radioparadise.com, which is run by a couple from their home in Paradise, California, as a commercial-free operation. Other popular Internet music services are Last.fm, Slacker, WCPE, Rhapsody, and Pandora, which uses its Music Genome Project: Pandora's "team of musician-analysts has been listening to music, one song at a time, studying and collecting literally hundreds of musical details on every track—melody, harmony, instrumentation, rhythm, vocals, lyrics," and so on. They continue this work every day to keep up with the flow of great new music coming from studios, stadiums and garages around the country. To use Pandora, drop the name of one of your favorite songs, artists, or genres into Pandora—on a computer, media player, iPad, smartphone, or the like—and let the Music Genome Project go. "It will quickly scan its entire world of analyzed music, almost a century of popular recordings . . . to find songs with interesting musical similarities to your choice. . . .You can create up to 100 unique 'stations.' And you can even refine them. If it's not quite right you can tell it so and it will get better for you."[21]

Podcasting

Whereas Internet radio involves continuous streaming, podcasting involves downloading particular files.

As we stated in Chapter 2, ***podcasting*** **involves the recording and downloading of Internet radio or similar Internet audio and video programs.** Unlike traditional radio, podcasting requires no studio or broadcast tower, and there's no Federal Communications Commission regulation (so hosts can say whatever they want). Podcasting software allows amateur deejays and hobbyists to create their own radio shows and offer them free over the Internet. Listeners can download shows onto their portable players or computer. Basically, in podcasting, providers create audio files that are available on their website, which people can then subscribe to and download to their iPods or other players and listen to. Podcasts are delivered through RSS (Rich Site Summary) feeds. With podcasts you choose what you want to listen to. (The word *podcast* is a play on the word *broadcast* combined with the word *iPod*; Apple did not invent the word *podcast.*)

Podcast audio files can be automatically received from the Internet and then synced to your MP3 player. Website users install a media *aggregator* program in their computers or media players, such as iTunes or Juice. Also called a "podcatcher," the application captures the audio feeds from the Internet for downloading to the music player.

Free Aggregators

Free podcast-receiving software is available at:

www.podcastingnews.com/topics/Podcast_Software.html

www.blogtalkradio.com

http://juicereceiver.sourceforge.net/

A tutorial on how to subscribe to a podcast is available at:

http://radio.about.com/od/podcastin1/a/aa030805a.htm

7.4 DIGITAL CAMERAS: Changing Photography

A digital camera takes video and still photographs and digitally converts the analog data by recording images via an electronic image sensor.

By now both professional and amateur photographers alike have pretty much abandoned film. "The evolution is having profound and unforeseen effects on society," says one analysis, "from changing the way that people record their daily lives to making it harder to trust the images we see."[22]

How Digital Cameras Work

Instead of film, a digital camera has a sensor that converts light into electrical charges.

We described general principles of digital cameras in Chapter 5. Here we consider the subject in more detail.

The most obvious statement to make about digital cameras is this: they do not use film. Instead, a digital camera uses a light-sensitive processor chip to capture photographic images in digital form and store them on a flash memory card. You can review your just-shot picture on the camera's LCD monitor, the little screen that displays what the camera lens sees, and decide whether to keep it or to try another angle in your next shot.

In general, digital cameras seem to be getting smaller, thinner (the size but not the thickness of a credit card), and less expensive, but they are also capable of performing more tricks. Product releases occur so frequently that it is impossible to present an up-to-date picture of the various models. However, we can outline certain general guidelines.

POINT-AND-SHOOT VERSUS SINGLE-LENS REFLEX (SLR) Point-and-shoot cameras are easy to carry around, but with SLR cameras produce a brighter and crisper picture.

Parts of a digital camera

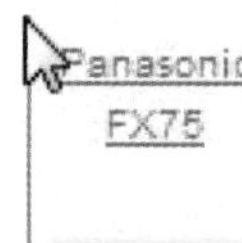

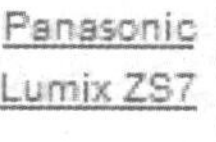

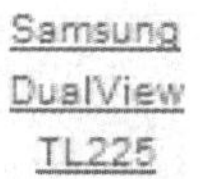

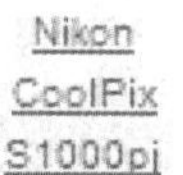

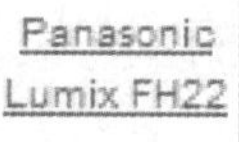

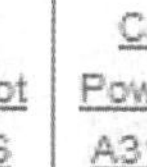

Canon PowerShot A3100 IS

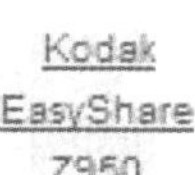

See It Now At
Sears

Nikon D7000 25468 Digital SLR Camera 16.2 Megapixel Body Only 18 - 105mm

(Write a Review) Compare Prices from 4 Stores

16.2 Megapixel, CMOS, Body Only, 18 - 105mm, F/3.3-5.6, Screen Size : 3 in, Automatic, ISO 100-6400

See It Now At
WolfCamera.com

Nikon D3100 25472 Digital SLR Camera 14.2 Megapixel With Lens 18 -55 mm

(Write a Review) Compare Prices from 3 Stores

14.2 Megapixel, CMOS, With Lens, 18 -55 mm, Optical Zoom : 3 x, Screen Size : 3 in, Automatic, ISO 100-3200

See It Now At
Best Buy

Canon EOS Rebel T2i 180-Megapixel Digital SLR Camera - Black

(Write a Review) Compare Prices from 2 Stores

This 18.0-megapixel digital SLR camera features a 18-55mm image-stabilized zoom lens for capturing stunning images from

See It Now At

Canon EOS 60D 4460B004 Digital SLR Camera 18 Megapixel With Lens 18 - 135mm

(Write a Review) Compare Prices from 2 Stores

18 Megapixel, CMOS, With Lens, Canon EF-S , 18 - 135mm, Optical Zoom : 7.5 x, F/3.5-5.6, Screen Size : 3 in, ISO 100-6400, ISO 12800, ISO auto

Point-and-shoot cameras (*top*) are less expensive than SLR cameras (*bottom*). SLR cameras are more sophisticated than point-and-shoot cameras.

- **Point-and-shoot:** A *point-and-shoot camera* is a camera, either film or digital, that automatically adjusts settings such as exposure and focus. Generally such cameras cost under $500. Manufacturers of digital point-and-shoots include Canon, Casio, Fuji, Hewlett-Packard, Kodak, Konika, Nikon, Olympus, Panasonic, Pentax, Samsung, Sony, and Vivitar, whose prices range from $100 to about $350. Point-and-shoots vary in size from subcompacts to compacts to superzooms.

  Although a point-and-shoot autofocus will do most of the work for you automatically, you may find it useful to get a camera that also has manual controls, so that you can take it over if you want. There are also disposable point-and-shoot cameras, such as the Kodak Plus Digital, selling for about $20, which are useful if you're afraid you might leave an expensive camera behind on the beach (and if you don't need high-quality images).

Note that point-and shoot cameras are becoming less popular owing to the use of camera-enabled smartphones and the rise in sales of single-lens reflex cameras.

- **Single-lens reflex:** A *single-lens reflex (SLR) camera* is a camera, either film or digital, that has a reflecting mirror that reflects the incoming light in such a way that the scene viewed by the viewer through the viewfinder is the same as what's framed by the lens. A digital SLR (DSLR), which may cost anywhere from $450 on up, is the choice of "prosumers" (professional consumers, such as professional photographers and serious amateurs) because it provides more manual options and better image quality and allows the use of interchangeable lenses, from wide angle to telephoto. Some manufacturers in this category include Canon, Nikon, Pentax, and Olympus, whose prices range from $450 to $1,300 (and $750–$2,700 for advanced SLRs). Some SLR cameras are also able to handle video recording.

Point and Shoot vs. SLR

For more details on the differences between these two types of camera:

http://electronics.howstuffworks.com/camera5.htm

http://manofthehouse.com/gadgets/cameras/point-and-shoot-vs-slr-cameras-what-are-the-real-differences

RESOLUTION: MEGAPIXELS & SENSORS *Resolution* refers to image sharpness. A digital camera's resolution is expressed in ***megapixels (mp)*, or millions of picture elements, the electronic dots making up an image.** The more megapixels a digital camera has, the better the resolution and the higher the quality of the image, and so the higher the price of the camera. The millions of pixels are tightly packed together on the camera's image sensor, a half-inch-wide silicon chip. When light strikes a pixel, it generates an electric current that is converted into the digital data that becomes your photograph.

- **How many megapixels are best?** Megapixels measure the maximum resolution of an image taken by the camera at its *top settings*. Megapixels are in the range of 7–14 for subcompact point-and-shoot cameras, 7–14 for compact cameras, and 12–18 for single-lens reflex cameras. If you shoot mainly 4 × 6s and rarely crop pictures, most cameras that have 7 or 8 megapixels should be adequate. But if you print poster-sized shots or do major cropping, a 14-megapixel camera makes more sense.
- **Don't forget sensor size:** But there's another consideration besides megapixels: sensor size. The best overall predictor of image quality is not megapixels but the size of the sensor inside the camera. "Big sensors absorb more light, so you get better color and sharper low-light images," points out one technology writer. "Small sensors pack too many light-absorbing pixels into too little space, so heat builds up, creating digital 'noise' (random speckles) on your photos."[23] Thus, in response to a reader who asks whether he should get 7 or 10–12 megapixels for a point-and-shoot, one technology expert points out that sensors in SLR digital cameras, such as those used by professional photographers, use sensors the size of a 35-mm negative, so they can easily handle more than 12 megapixels. However, he says, "most point-and-shoot sensors . . . are fingernail-size. If you cram too many pixels onto them, they produce interference (noise) that can hurt picture quality."[24] Thus, he suggests looking for a point-and-shoot with 7 or 8 megapixels.

Megapixels

Why a higher number of mexapixels is not always best:

www.photography101.org/basics/megapixels_explained.html

www.digital-slr-guide.com/compare-digital-slr-megapixels.html

Sensor Size

"If there's a single factor that predicts the quality of the photos you'll get from a camera, a single letter grade that lets you compare cameras, it's this: the sensor size":

http://sensor-size.com/

LENSES You also need to have a lens that ensures that your picture is properly focused and that pulls in enough light to get good exposure.

As for zoom lenses, you should be aware of the difference between digital zoom and optical zoom:

Digital camera memory card storage capacity (64 MB–2 GB) according to image file size and camera megapixel rating

Image resolutions	File Size*	64 MB	128 MB	256 MB	512 MB	1 GB	2 GB
2 megapixel	0.9 MB	71**	142	284	568	1,137	2,275
3 megapixel	1.2 MB	53	106	213	426	853	1,706
4 megapixel	2.1 MB	30	60	121	243	487	975
5 megapixel	3.2 MB	20	40	80	160	320	640
6 megapixel	3.5 MB	18	36	73	146	292	585
7 megapixel	3.7 MB	17	34	69	138	276	553
8 megapixel	3.9 MB	16	32	65	131	262	525

*Average size of compressed JPG format image with best image quality settings.
**Number of images.
From "Choosing the Right Memory Card for Your Digital Camera, *www.newegg.com/product/CategoryIntelligenceArticle.aspx?articleId=61* (accessed May 5, 2011).

- **Digital zoom:** Manufacturers like to tout *digital zoom,* but, says one description, it's just another way of saying "we'll crop the image for you in the camera."[25] Indeed, it actually lowers the resolution and often can produce a grainier photo. "Digital zoom is not really zoom, in the strictest definition of the term. What digital zoom does is enlarge a portion of the image, thus 'simulating' optical zoom. In other words, the camera crops a portion of the image and then enlarges it back to size. In so doing, you lose image quality."[26]
- **Optical zoom:** Only an *optical zoom* will bring you closer to your subject without your having to move. That is, the lens actually extends to make distant objects seem larger and closer. Optical zooms may be of the telescoping type or internal (untelescoping) type; the latter allows a camera to start up fast.

  Most subcompact and compact point-and-shoot cameras come with a 3X to 7X optical zoom, which is good for wide-angle, normal, and telephoto shots. If you're an experienced photographer, you should look for a superzoom camera with 10X to 20X optical zoom.

STORAGE Instead of being stored on film, the camera's digital images are stored on flash memory cards inside the camera. (• *See Panel 7.3.)* Cards come in a variety of formats, including Secure Digital (SD), Multimedia, Compact Flash (including MicroDrive), Memory Stick, and Smart Media. Most cameras come with "starter" cards, usually 16 or 32 megabytes, perhaps 64, which hold only a handful of photos. You'll need a card (which is reusable) with at least 512 MB to 1 GB. (Some cards store up to 8 GB of images.)

panel 7.3

Digital camera's flash memory card

The card's actual size is about 15 × 11 × 0.7 mm to 21.5 × 20 × 1.4 mm; it fits in a slot on the side of the camera. What you see here on the left side of the camera is the display screen.

OPTICAL VIEWFINDERS & LCD SCREENS The original digital cameras had tiny screens, which made it difficult to review photos before deciding whether to save or delete them. Now more cameras come with both optical viewfinders and LCD screens.

- **Optical viewfinders:** The *optical viewfinder* is the eye-level optical glass device on the camera that, when you look through it, shows the image to be photographed. Some digital cameras omit the viewfinder, forcing you to use only the LCD, which forces you to hold the camera with arms extended, making you more apt to shake the camera.
- **LCD screens:** The *LCD (liquid crystal display) screens* usually measure 2 inches or more diagonally and allow you to review the photos you take. It's best to get a camera with an LCD that can be seen well in daylight if you do a lot of outdoor shooting.

START-UP TIME, SHUTTER LAG, & CONTINUOUS SHOOTING A digital camera, like a PC, needs time to start up. You should look for one that takes no longer than a second or two, so that you won't miss that one-of-a-kind shot that suddenly appears out of nowhere. Another recommendation: You should look for a digicam with the least shutter lag, that annoying delay between the time you press the shutter-release button and the time the exposure is complete. Many digital cameras have a special setting called "burst" or "continuous" mode, which allows you to squeeze off a limited number of shots without pausing—helpful if you're taking pictures at sports events.

BATTERY LIFE Digital photographers obviously no longer have to worry about film—but they do have to worry about battery life. Some cameras come with rechargeable batteries, although they aren't always replaceable at the nearest drugstore (and replacements can be expensive, perhaps $40–$60). Some require you to recharge the battery inside the camera, by putting the camera in a charging unit; others, in both ways. Some cameras also require proprietary batteries, which also aren't as readily available. Regardless, you should be sure you have lots of batteries before setting out on a trip. Battery life varies depending on the size and quality of the images, how much of the time you use the flash, and whether you keep the LCD screen on all the time or use it sparingly; make sure that you can get at least a whole day's worth of shooting done off of one battery.

What Kind of Battery Is Best?

http://reviews.cnet.com/Digital_cameras/4520-7603_7-5023995-5.html

http://malektips.com/digital_camera_memory_help_and_tips.html

TRANSFERRING IMAGES Let's assume you've spent a day taking pictures. How do you get them out of your camera? Here are the principal methods:

- **Use a direct connection between your camera and your computer:** You'll need to have used the installation CD included with your digital camera to install the drivers and software on your PC. Then you can connect your camera to the computer using the USB or FireWire cable that came with it. (One end attaches to a slot on the camera, the other end to an open USB or FireWire port on the computer.) After connecting the camera (which must be turned on during the process), you open its software and use it to transfer the photos into the PC, typically placing the pictures into a default folder, such as My Pictures in the My Documents folder.
- **Wireless connection:** You can also connect your digital camera wirelessly. This makes it possible to download photos, save photos directly to a computer while you shoot, or print wirelessly (802.11 b and g; Chapter 6, pp. 349, 351). You can also connect to a cellphone network and share photos, just as you would with a camera smartphone. To enable your camera to work wirelessly, you need a wireless memory card, such as Eye-Fi, and a wireless-ready digital camera.

- **Insert the memory card into your computer or a card reader:** Assuming your PC has a built-in slot for your memory card (USB card) or has a card reader attached to a USB port, you can remove the memory card from the camera and insert it into the slot. External card readers cost $20 or so.
- **Put your camera in a cradle attached to your PC:** Many camera manufacturers include cradles ("docks") into which you can set your camera and use it to transfer photos to your PC. Some cradles also are able to charge your camera, if it has rechargeable batteries.
- **Use an online photo developer:** After downloading your photo to your computer, you can go online and send your images to an online photo developer, such as Shutterfly, KodakEasy Share, Flickr, or others mentioned in the Practical Action box on p. 391.
- **Use a photo printer with a built-in card slot:** If you've bought one of the newer photo printers, you can skip using a PC entirely and insert the memory card from your camera into a slot in the printer.
- **Use a photo-printing kiosk:** Various photo-printing kiosks are available at fast-food restaurants, big retailers, amusement parks, scrapbook-making stores, cruise ships, hospitals, and other high-traffic areas and can produce a standard 4 × 6 print in 4 seconds.
- **Use a photo lab:** Photo stores and labs, as well as Costco, Kinko's, Target, Walgreens, and Walmart, often sell inexpensive services (perhaps $3–$7) in which they will transfer the images on a memory card onto a CD and then clear the card for reuse. They will also print photos for you.
- **Bring along your own card reader and CDs and use others' computers:** If you bring along your own card reader and blank CDs, you can use other people's computers to store your images. These PCs could belong to friends, of course, but also to hotel business centers and Internet cafés.

The Societal Effects of Digital Cameras

Digital cameras have made it easier to take pictures and share them, but they have also devalued images and increased the ease of dishonestly manipulating images, the invasion of people's privacy, and the occurrence of voyeurism.

One result of the evolution in photography is that people are taking their cameras everywhere, either in backpacks or purses or as mobile phones with built-in cameras. (We describe cellphones and smartphones in another few pages.) Another is that people take far more pictures than they used to—perhaps 20 or more of a single scene, instead of three or four—since they don't have to worry about the cost of film and processing, and with digital it's easy to simply delete bad shots. A third consequence may be that photography is becoming more casual, with more off-the-cuff snapshots being taken instead of subjects being asked to pose for formal portraits. "Taking pictures used to be an event of sorts . . . Now they have camera phones—they email pictures, look at them once, and trash them. The image is not what it used to be. The value of the image is no longer what it was. . . . The rise of digital photography also raises questions about whether people will save these images for future generations, the same way they usually keep old prints."[27]

On the other hand, those photos that do end up being saved and treasured may have been so doctored to improve reality, with the help of photo-altering programs such as Apple's iPhoto or Adobe's Photoshop Elements, that tomorrow's generations may question their authenticity. Muses one writer, will future anthropologists wonder "Why do all those people look so good?"[28]

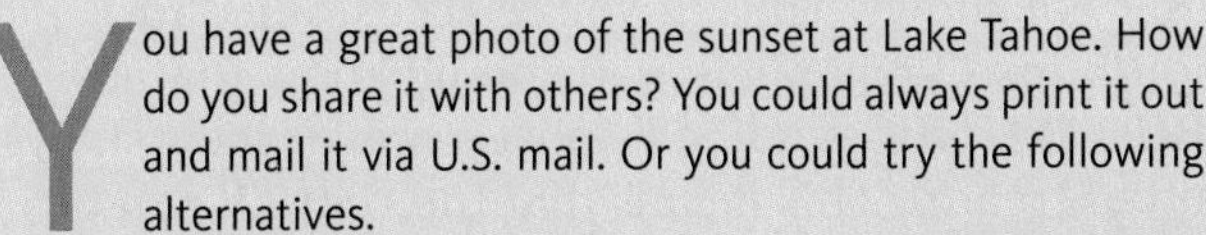

PRACTICAL ACTION

Online Viewing & Sharing of Digital Photos

You have a great photo of the sunset at Lake Tahoe. How do you share it with others? You could always print it out and mail it via U.S. mail. Or you could try the following alternatives.

- ***Send as an email attachment:*** You can download your photos to a PC and then send them as attached computer files to an email message. The drawback, however, is that if you have a lot of photos, it can quickly fill up the recipient's email inbox or take a lot of time if you are sending multiple images to multiple people. And some image files may be too large to send as email attachments.
- ***Use an online photo-sharing service:*** Web-based photo-sharing services provide online storage space for your photos and make it easier to share, especially if they are high-resolution files. Examples are Shutterfly, Kodak EasyShare Gallery, Snapfish, Flickr, American Greetings PhotoWorks, dotPhoto, Webshots, Fotki, Funtigo, Smugmug, and PhotoSite. No special software is required for you to upload from your computer, but a broadband connection is strongly recommended. Some charge fees, some do not.

Be sure to find out whether you have to renew membership or make a purchase in order to keep your photos from being deleted after a certain amount of time.

- ***If you have a camera with Wi-Fi transmitter, transmit your photos wirelessly:*** Many digital cameras are built with Wi-Fi transmitters for wireless networking. Thus, if you're within range of a Wi-Fi hotspot in a coffee shop or airport lounge, you can post pictures to your website, to a photo-sharing service such as Flickr, or to a social-networking site such as Facebook.

Digital cameras and smartphone cameras can also be used for public safety. For example, in 2007 New York's Mayor Bloomberg announced a plan encouraging people to use their camera phones to document crimes in progress and send the images or video directly to 911, making the camera phone a tool in crime prevention. Digital cameras are also used to document crime scenes (*www.policecentral.com/wp-digicam.htm*). In Kochi, India, a camera phone is supplied to all Police Control Room Vehicles, which allows the constables on patrol to immediately take a photo and send it to the Control Room. An intelligent system automatically tallies the total number of traffic accidents, traffic violations, drunken driving, and miscellaneous incidents in the city. This report is sent every morning to the police commissioner and other authorities.[29]

However, an obvious downside of all those digital cameras and smartphone cameras being used in all sorts of contexts is loss of privacy and abusive use of images, including voyeurism. Even where their use is prohibited, photos can often be taken in secret—and they can be shared or sent instantly and wirelessly.

As with any technology, the camera phone is neither good nor bad—its value depends on how it is used. Although the potential for abuse and invasion of privacy exists, the benefits of rapid information-sharing are real. But laws, courtesy, and basic etiquette must be respected.

Cellphones in School

Are cellphones disruptive in educational settings?

www.schoolsecurity.org/trends/cell_phones.html

http://viking.coe.uh.edu/~kbrooks/cuin3112/prod7.htm

Ethics & Digital Photography

Here is an article written by an online student of photography:

http://onlinestudentofphotography.blogspot.com/2010/04/ethics-of-digital-photography.html

And here is one about a university class on cellphone camera ethics:

www.ecampusnews.com/technologies/students-learn-the-ethics-of-cell-phone-snapshots/

7.5 Digital Television

Since 2009 full-power U.S. television stations have been broadcasting exclusively in a digital format.

Today there are many kinds of equipment available for watching TV, some of the more interesting of which are as follows.

- *Interactive TV* (*iTV*) lets you interact with the show you're watching, so that you can request information about a product or play along with a game show. We see this type of TV used with shows involving viewer voting, such as that for *American Idol* and *Dancing with the Stars*. BCM has developed the Clickable TV® interactive television service, which displays an icon on screen that indicates the programming or advertisement they are currently watching is interactive. These interactive opportunities are called Clickable Moments™, which enable viewers to press OK/Select on their remote to receive more information in their email about what they are watching on TV.[30]

- *Internet TV* is television distributed via the Internet, allowing users to choose shows from a library of shows. Thus, if you're accustomed to paying $40 or more a month for TV channels, you should know that all the major networks—ABC, CBS, NBC, and Fox—post many of their shows online (see Hulu.com and uStream). This means that Internet TV can be distributed via broadband, Wi-Fi, cable, or satellite. Thus, for example, you can use a Netflix set-top box (made by Roku), a BluRay player, a Wii box, an Xbox, an iPad or iPhone, a Windows phone, and some other devices to connect your broadband network to your TV and have access, for less than $10 a month, to Netflix's library of thousands of movies and TV shows on demand.
- *Internet-ready TV* (which some people also call "Internet TV") consists of television sets with broadband modems that allow viewers to watch TV shows as well as go online to get news, stream movies, view photos, and the like. The models introduced by LG, Panasonic, Samsung, Sony, and Toshiba feature a built-in Ethernet port, so that you can plug an Ethernet cable into the back of the TV. It's expected that 25% of high-definition (HD)TVs shipped in 2011 will be Internet-ready.[31] If you don't own an Internet-ready TV but want to send videos or photos from your PC screen onto your TV set's screen, you can do so by buying a $300 box called SlingCatcher. Some open-source software called Boxee, which you install on your computer, can act as a program guide to a lot of the video available on the Internet that you can view on your TV.

Three Kinds of Television: DTV, HDTV, SDTV

The HDTV screen is formatted much more closely than analog TV was to the way we see.

When most of us used to tune in our TV sets, we got analog television, a system of varying signal amplitude and frequency that represents picture and sound elements. Since 1996, however, things have become more complicated.

DIGITAL TELEVISION (DTV) In 1996, broadcasters and their government regulator, the Federal Communications Commission (FCC), adopted a standard called ***digital television (DTV)*, which uses a digital signal, or series of 0s and 1s.** DTV is much clearer and less prone to interference than the old analog TV, which disappeared on June 12, 2009, requiring viewers to acquire a converter box.

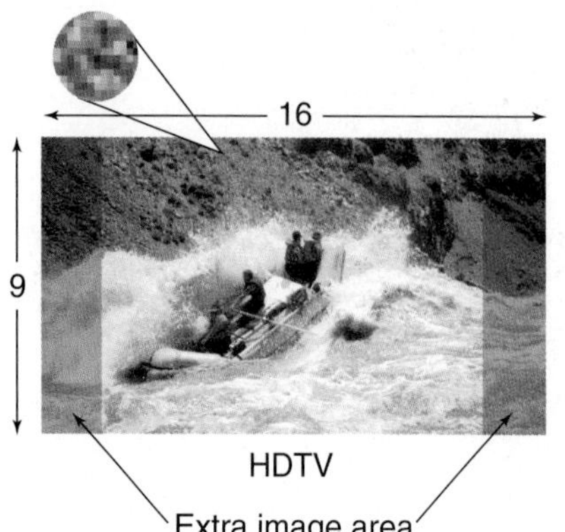

HIGH-DEFINITION TELEVISION (HDTV) A form of digital TV, ***high-definition television (HDTV)* works with digital broadcasting signals and has a wider screen and higher resolution than analog television had.** Whereas standard analog TV has a width-to-height ratio, or *aspect ratio,* of 4 to 3, HDTV has an aspect ratio of 16 to 9, which is similar to the wide-screen approach used in movies. In addition, compared to analog display screens, an HDTV display has 10 times more pixels on a screen—1,920 × 1,080 pixels or more. Thus, HDTV could have 1,080 lines on a screen, compared with 525-line resolution for analog TV.

STANDARD-DEFINITION TELEVISION (SDTV) HDTV takes a lot of bandwidth that broadcasters could use instead for ***standard-definition television (SDTV)*,** **which has a lower resolution, a minimum of 480 vertical lines, and a picture quality similar to that required to watch DVD movies.** What's important about the SDTV standard is that it enables broadcasters to transmit more information within the HDTV bandwidth. That is, broadcasters can *multicast* their products, transmitting up to five SDTV programs simultaneously—and getting perhaps five times the revenue—instead of just one HDTV program. "Multicast services piggyback on digital signals from local stations," says one report, "including those offering HDTV versions of ABC, CBS, Fox, NBC, and PBS. . . . Stations typically get multicast programming for free and sell five minutes an hour of air time. The networks sell an additional five minutes to national advertisers."[32] With so many extra channels, having enough content becomes a problem. Thus, we will no doubt see tons of reruns of vintage TV shows, from *The Lone Ranger* to *The Addams Family*.

Choosing a TV

For HDTV FAQs, go to

http://hometheater.about.com/od/televisionbasics/

http://electronics.howstuffworks.com/hdtv.htm

www.bestbuy.com/site/Electronics+Promotions/HDTV-Basics/pcmcat197600050000.c?id=pcmcat197600050000

The Societal Effects of the New TV

New technology has changed the way people experience television.

"The ethos of New TV can be captured in a single sweeping mantra," says Steven Levy, *"anything you want to see, any time, on any device"* (his emphasis).[33]

TIME SHIFTING: CHANGING WHEN YOU WATCH TV Digital video recorders (DVRs) such as those marketed by TiVo allow viewers to watch favorite shows at their own convenience rather than following a broadcast schedule. They also enable viewers to freeze-frame action sequences and to skip commercials. (What this could eventually do to advertising as the economic underpinning for free-to-viewers television can only be guessed at.)

Several manufacturers make TiVo sets, including TiVo itself, but they all have one thing in common—a hard drive. The hard drive is connected to the outside world through a variety of jacks on the back of the TV set, usually the typical connections that you would use to hook up, say, a cable box. (A subscription [monthly fee] is necessary to receive content.) The television signal comes into the TiVo set's built-in tuner usually through cable or satellite. Some TiVo sets have more than one tuner, which means the set can record programming from two channels at the same time. Then the signal is sent to the hard drive for storage. Digital cable customers will need a CableCARD for each tuner. CableCARDs are adapters that let your TiVo receive the digital signal from the cable company. Most cable companies require a technician to install the CableCARD in your TiVo.[34]

TiVo with TV and remote

The SlingPlayer is a companion to the Slingbox. SlingPlayer Mobile lets you watch and control your home TV and DVR, via your Slingbox, on your BlackBerry, iPhone, iPad, Windows phone, or other such device. (*Left*) SlingPlayer Mobile device; (*top*); back of Slingbox; (*bottom*) front of Slingbox.

Another technology affecting the "when" is ***video on demand* (VOD or VoD), which consists of a wide set of technologies that enable viewers to select videos or TV programs from a central server to watch when they want,** rather than when TV programmers offer them (*http://home.vod.com/*).

SPACE SHIFTING: CHANGING WHERE YOU WATCH TV Consumers can now download or receive TV programs, either stored or real-time, and watch them on some sort of handheld device. For instance, the SlingCatcher and the SlingPlayer Mobile from Sling Media enable you to watch a program playing on your living room TV on your laptop computer—anywhere in the world.

CONTENT SHIFTING: CHANGING THE NATURE OF TV PROGRAMS Perhaps the most important development is the movement of television to the Internet. This is made possible by *IPTV,* short for *Internet Protocol Television,* in which television and video signals are sent to viewers using Internet protocols (*http://iptv.tmcnet.com/*). Cable and satellite channels have limited capacity, but the Internet "has room for everything," Levy points out. As a consequence, you may be able to cram even *more* programs on your screen simultaneously—and what does that do to the human attention span? (Multiple-channel TV sets are available with what are known as "mosaic" screens that allow sports fans, for instance, to watch eight separate games on one screen.)

7.6 E-BOOK READERS: The New Reading Machines

One electronic device, the e-reader, can hold a library that you can take almost anywhere.

How much content could you comfortably read online? A few paragraphs from a Wikipedia entry? Some gossip about a celebrity? An entire novel? A textbook?

Many people find it difficult to read at length on a computer screen, which is why printed textbooks, for instance, remain more popular than online versions of the same thing. In recent years, however, e-books and e-book readers have begun to gain some ground over paper-and-print versions of the book.

As we described in Chapter 2, an ***e-book*, or *electronic book*, is an electronic text, the digital-media equivalent of a conventional printed book.**

(*Left*) Kindle 3; (*right*) Nook.

You can read an e-book on your personal computer, iPad, or smartphone (such as the iPhone or BlackBerry). Or you can read it on a specialized piece of hardware known as an ***e-book reader*, a device specifically designed to allow people to read electronic books.** The most well-known examples are Amazon's Kindle (in three versions) and Barnes & Noble's Nook. (Other e-book readers: Sony's Reader, Bookeen's Cybook, Elonex's eBook, Endless ideas's BeBook, Astak's Hanlin eReader and EZ Reader, Interead's COOL-ER, Samsung's Papyrus and SNE-50K, iRex's iLiad and Digital Reader, and FLEPia.)

How an E-Book Reader Works

E-readers use E Ink, the display portion of the reader—where the paper would be in a printed book, a screen that is composed of millions of tiny particles that display text.

Different e-book readers use different e-software formats. They include Adobe Acrobat, Microsoft Reader, and an open format called ePub. Amazon's Kindle uses a format called Topaz (which can be read on the iPod Touch and the iPhone as well). The Sony Reader uses ePub.

What makes e-book readers supposedly easier to read than e-books viewed on your PC monitor? Both Kindle and Sony use something called Vizplex (made by E Ink), the trademarked name of a layered substance that makes up the 6- to 10-inch-high display area that you read from. Vizplex is an "electronic paper" that was developed to act like real paper, to rely on reflected light, not the backlight used by computers and phone screens, which can be hard on the eyes. Thus, the Kindle 2 supports 16 shades of gray (but no color), to make photos sharp, and there's no glare, no eyestrain—and no battery consumption (you use power only when you actually turn the page; the rest of the time, the ink pattern remains on the screen without power).

Once you've acquired an e-book reader—for what at this time could be $149–199 (Nook), $120 (Kindle 2), or $379 (Kindle DX), for example—you may then download books by wireless access. In the case of the Kindle 2, this is more than 900,000 titles. The machine features control buttons (next/previous page, menu, and so on). Built-in batteries last about two weeks if the wireless capability is off, about four days if it's on. If you turn the DX on its side, the screen changes from portrait to landscape. The Kindle DX has a 9.7-inch screen (compared to Kindle 2's 6-inch), which is designed to be used with newspapers, magazines, and textbooks.

There are many benefits to having an e-book reader. One e-book reader can store hundreds or even thousands of books—1,500 books, in the case of the Kindle 2, 3,500 for the Kindle DX. Thus, instead of carrying several books around, you carry just a single gadget, which will be lighter and occupy less space than a conventional book or books. You can download e-books through a wireless connection (Wi-Fi and/or 3G). Type size and type faces can be adjusted. An e-book can be read in low light. The e-book will automatically open to the page where you left off. Text can be searched automatically and cross-referenced. You can bookmark pages, search within your library, look up definitions, and annotate text. Text-to-speech software can produce an audio version of an e-book. Some machines, such as the Kindle DX, also play MP3s and have a web browser.

Survival Tip

E-Book Cautions

Additional possible drawbacks of e-readers:

- They require electrical power; the battery can run down.
- They are more fragile than paper books.
- They can malfunction (hardware/software problems).
- They are more likely to be stolen than paper books.
- They can be easily hacked.
- Many publishers don't produce e-book versions of their printed books.
- The placement of illustrations can be problematic; it is not possible to place pictures exactly where they should be.
- Not all e-readers have color capability.
- You can't lend books to someone without lending your entire e-reader.
- Not all book formats are compatible with every e-reader.

The Drawbacks of E-Book Readers

As do all electronic devices, e-readers also have some drawbacks.

Some e-readers are expensive. Consumers have to weigh the risk of buying a reading appliance that may be easily lost, damaged, stolen, or hacked compared to buying a regular book at a tenth or less of its price (and that may be resold). One also has to consider that the reader doesn't actually own the e-books that are downloaded to the e-reader; rather, they are like licensing a piece of software—you can run them only on certain designated devices, and they usually can't be resold or passed on to someone else.

One writer also found fault with the way photographs, charts, diagrams, foreign characters, and tables appeared on the gray screen of the Kindle. The beautiful illustrations and drawings in the print version of one science book turned out to be hard to make out in the electronic version. Tables in a medical book were garbled and the color coding was lost. An elaborate chart in a highly expensive engineering book was totally illegible in its electronic form.[35]

Many students, both high school and college, are reportedly not always pleased with e-books as textbooks. Some complain that the e-texts cost too much at the outset, that they are awkward and inconvenient, that publishers make them difficult to share and print, that they can't be kept for future reference, and that they can't be resold.

Peter Fader, co-director of the Wharton Interactive Media Initiative, believes the e-book reader will probably go the way of other single-use machines. In an age in which cellphones double as cameras, music players, and computers, he suggests, it is only a matter of time before electronic readers will be embedded on mobile devices.[36] Growing numbers of people, however, have already turned to their tablets and mobile phones to do their reading.

7.7 Tablet PCs

Tablet PCs are smaller, and thus more convenient to use, than laptops; they are larger than smartphones and offer more features.

There you are in an unfamiliar city, looking for a restaurant. Fortunately, you have your tablet computer with software, Zagat to Go, that has not only a review of the restaurant but also a map of how to get there and even a formula for calculating tips. Maybe you also have an application ("app") called WorldMate, software (for Android, iPhone, and Blackberry) offering other tools for the sophisticated traveler, such as weather forecasts, fight alerts (flight delays and cancellations, rerouting), a clock that can display times around the world, hotel booking, currency converter, mapping functions, tax and tip calculator, meeting reminders, clothing size converters, and international dialing codes.

As we mentioned in Chapter 1, **a _tablet computer_ is a general-purpose computer contained in a single panel; it is a combination of smartphone and laptop computer with wireless connections and a 7- to 12-inch multitouch screen** (one can manipulate the screen contents directly with one's hand). Tablet computers support multimedia (music and movies), download e-books, access the Internet, play games, support email, and create and send documents. (• *See Panel 7.4.*) Most tablets also have online access to the huge variety of apps, allowing you to purchase, download, and then use them.

As of 2011 there are five tablet platforms: iPad, Android, BlackBerry, Windows, and HP WebOS.[37] Each platform runs apps written only for its operating system. However, all of them have web browsers for the web.

Tablet PCs—such as the iPad, the Acer Iconia, the Samsung Galaxy Tab, Amazon's Fire, the Asus Eee Pad Transformer, and about 45 other models—have become extremely popular. Tablets are lightweight, thin, web-enabled, and portable and yet powerful enough to provide the functionality of a laptop. And a tablet screen can be used both horizontally and vertically. Some will also work with a digital pen or stylus instead of fingertip touch.

Tablets come installed with an operating system and have some form of wireless connectivity to the Internet via 3G or 4G cellular, Wi-Fi, or both. The majority also have a virtual onscreen keyboard, and a few have an extendable keyboard.

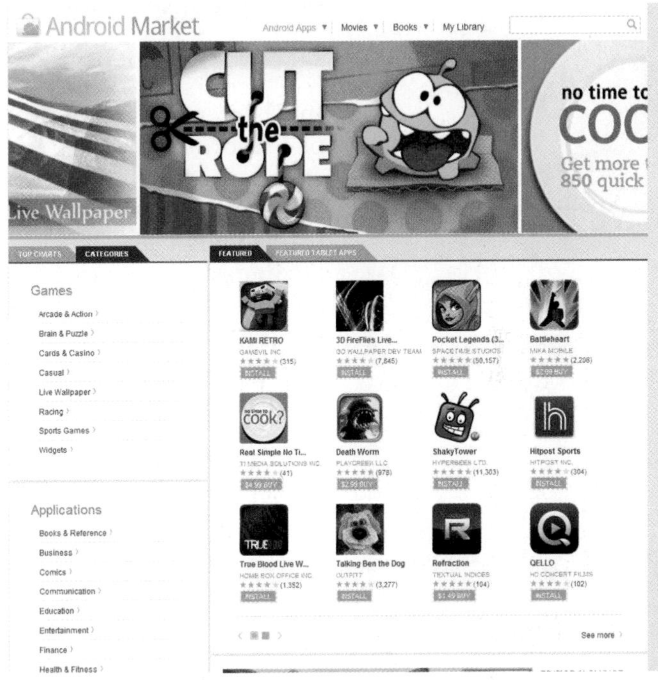

(*Top*) Apple iPad online app store; (*bottom*) Android tablet app store

panel 7.4

Android tablet PC

Downloads for Handhelds

Websites offering software downloads for smartphones and portable computers:

www.download.com
www.handango.com
www.pocketgear.com

7.8 SMARTPHONES: More Than Talk

A smartphone is a cellular telephone with software applications and Internet access.

"There's a digital land rush going on," says *New York Times* technology writer Steve Lohr, "driven by rapid advances in technology that make it possible to put more and more tools of higher and higher quality into phones."[38]

Lohr is referring to ***smartphones*****, cellular telephones with microprocessor, memory, display screen, and built-in modem** (Chapter 6). Smartphones provide digital voice service as well as text messaging, email, web browsing, search functions, GPS functions, still and video cameras, MP3 player, video viewing, and often video calling. In addition to their built-in functions, smartphones can store contact information and download and run many different applications.[39]

How a Mobile Phone Works

A cellphone is actually a radio.

In Chapter 6 (p. 347) we described how wireless services use their networks of cell towers to send voice and data over the airwaves in digital form to your cellphone, which is basically a sophisticated radio (p. 337), handing off your call from one cell to another as you move through a series of geographically overlapping cells. The cellphone or smartphone contains many of the same attributes as a personal computer: processor, memory, input/output devices, and operating system (such as Microsoft Windows Mobile OS or Mac OSx for the iPhone). The OS, which is stored in read-only memory (ROM) and is run by the processor, provides you with the interface that allows you to store data, change settings, and so on.

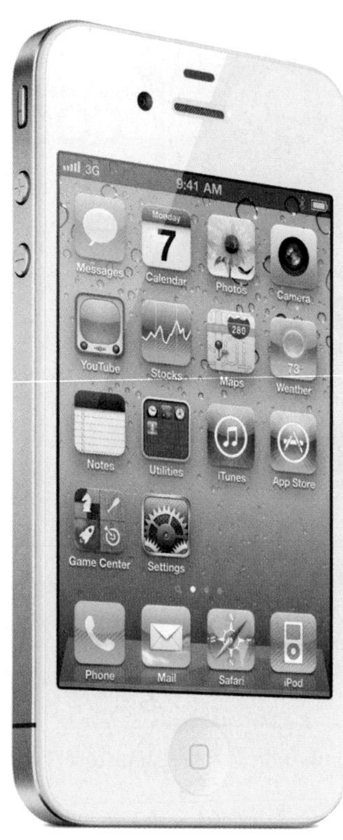

Apple 4G iPhone with touch-movable application icons

STORAGE The data you store in your phone, such as telephone numbers, is stored on flash memory cards, which means that when you turn off the phone, the data does not disappear. Smartphones come with 8, 16, or even 32 gigabytes of memory in which you can store your music, photos, videos, contact information, applications, and the like.

INPUT At minimum, basic cellphones have a keypad for entering numbers and text (and doing text messaging) and a microphone for picking up your voice. Some are also mobile speakerphones, giving you a hands-free option and offering voice-activated dialing. Smartphones also have a touch-sensitive screen or a screen with a stylus.

OUTPUT A cellphone includes a receiver or speaker, of course, for picking up voice calls. Mobile phones also have displays ranging from LCD to full-color, high-resolution plasma, suitable for watching TV and playing videogames, as we'll describe. Some phones act as MP3 players and offer FM radio and stereo sound. Others are also able to tap into Wi-Fi and Bluetooth networks.

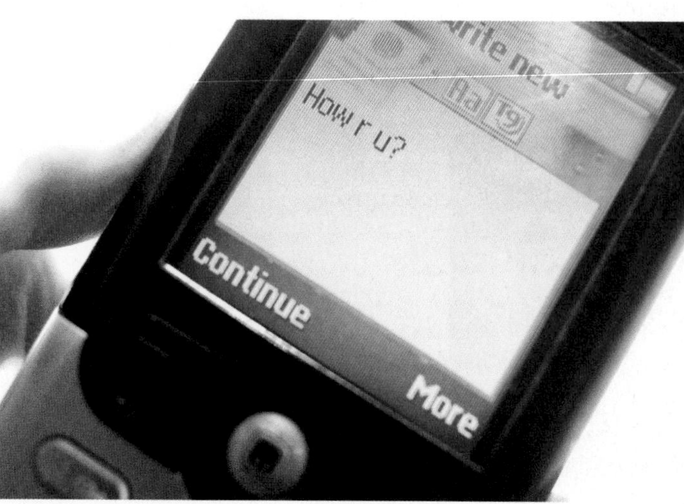

TEXT MESSAGING ***Text messaging*****, or *texting*, (*left*) is the sending of short messages, generally no more than 160 characters in length (including spaces), to a smartphone or other handheld device,** including notebook computers. (It is also called SMS, Short Message Service.) Text messages can also be sent to desktop computers and landline phones. Originally text messaging appeared during the days of mainframe computers, when workers sitting at terminals would send short text messages to one another. In the Internet world, these evolved into instant messaging and live text chat sessions. Today text messaging combines the portability of cellphones with the convenience of email and instant messaging. Text messaging is particularly appropriate for situations in which making a cellphone call is intrusive, as when you want to tell someone "I'm 15 minutes late."

Incidentally, texters need to be aware that it's unwise to assume that when they hit the Delete button, the messages are gone forever. Like email and instant messages, text messages are often saved on servers, at least for a while.

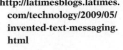

Why 160 Characters?

http://latimesblogs.latimes.com/technology/2009/05/invented-text-messaging.html

DOWNLOADED RINGTONES If your phone's ***ringtone*****, the audible sound a phone makes to announce that a call is coming in,** is still an old-fashioned "ring, ring," perhaps you have some catching up to do. Now your phone could be vibrating, flashing a photo of the caller across the phone's screen, and playing music. Ringtones include a variety of sound effects and melodies used to alert a phone owner of an incoming call. Most manufacturers design their phones so that users can not only choose from many musical ringtones but also program their own for a very personalized ringtone. Some ringtones may be had for free; others, which you may download from your wireless carrier (such as Verizon Wireless, Sprint, and AT&T, T-Mobile), may cost anywhere from about $1.25 to $4 per tune (not per ring).

Making Sense of Text Lingo

To translate regular English into text lingo, go to:

www.transl8it.com

EMAIL Until recently, the most well-known handheld device for sending wireless email was the BlackBerry, produced by Canadian company Research In Motion (RIM) Ltd., which practically created the industry. However, RIM has been joined by a host of rivals—most of which also offer telephone and other smartphone capabilities. As with text messaging, something that most email users need to pay attention to before buying is the layout and size of the keys. The BlackBerry 7100 series smartphones, for example, cram all letters and numbers onto just 14 keys. (As you type, built-in software anticipates the correct word, something that takes some getting used to.)

Incidentally, as we mentioned, many of the personal organizing functions formerly found in personal digital assistants—such as address book, schedule planner, and to-do list—have now migrated to smartphones. What happens if you break or lose your cellphone (as people do all the time)? How do you replace your built-in telephone numbers and contacts? Some carriers and technology companies offer services that, for free or a small monthly fee, back up such data wirelessly.

Downloading Ringtones

Some are free. Check if your phone is compatible with the site.

www.phonezoo.com/home.do

www.3gforfree.com/web/content3g/ringtones

www.mytinyphone.com/ringtones/

INTERNET ACCESS Many smartphone owners use their devices to perform web searches of one sort or another, accessing not only Yahoo! and Google but also such things as maps and directions, using the Global Positioning System (GPS). For instance, MapQuest enables you to pull up a map on your mobile phone while you're in transit and then navigate as you go along. Yahoo!, which also provides mapping services, has a local search system for cellphones. If you type in the word *pizza* and an address in Chicago, for example, your phone will display all pizza restaurants in that neighborhood, as well as maps showing their location and driving directions.

An important capability for wireless Internet access is the ability to make connections to Wi-Fi networks (some 4G phones do not need Wi-Fi to connect; they have 4G modems). For instance, some BlackBerry phones automatically detect when they are near a pre-set Wi-Fi network and use that network for voice calling or data instead of T-Mobile's cellphone connections. Phone calls started in the cellular network will switch over to Wi-Fi and vice versa. Other smartphones allow you to use the VoIP (voice-over IP) technology, which we described in Chapter 2 (p. 91), to make phone calls on the Internet. Thus, the device will work where cell service is offered as well as in Wi-Fi-accessible areas.

Example of QR code

Download a QR Reader

Most new smartphones have a QR code reader already installed. If your phone doesn't have a QR reader, you can download the reader and install it yourself—for example, from:

http://freenuts.com/best-5-free-online-qr-code-readers/

Be sure to check on the compatibility of QR readers with your phone—some readers work only on iPhones or Android phones. Some readers work on the Symbian OS, found on Nokia phones, and Java, found on lower-end smartphones.

Survival Tip

You Dropped Your Phone in Water? What to Do Next

Go to *www.wikihow.com/Save-a-Wet-Cell-Phone* to find out.

QR CODES QR codes, or tags, are a type of matrix barcode (two-dimensional code, Chapter 5, p. 273) designed to be read by smartphones; in other words, it is a "mobile barcode." (QR codes appear on the inside front cover of this book; you can scan them with your smartphone camera, using a QR code reader, and go via Internet connectivity directly to either the Apple or the Android store to download the app.)

QR, a registered trademark of Denso Wave, a subsidiary of Toyota, is short for Quick Response (they can be read quickly by a cellphone). QRs are used to take a piece of information from the web and put it into your cellphone. Once a code is in your cellphone, it can give you, for example, details about the website's business, or details about a particular person (QRs can be put on T-shirts), or show you a URL that you can click to see a trailer for a movie, or it may give you a coupon that you can use in a local business.

QR codes store more data than a regular 2D barcode can hold; they include URL links, geo-coordinates, and text.

PHOTOGRAPHY Camera phones are making the spontaneous snapshot an everyday part of life, and, says one observer, "turning ordinary citizens into documentarians, fine-art photographers, and, in cases such as hit-and-run accidents, community watchdogs."[40] And camera phone manufacturers are learning that consumers will take more pictures if the quality is improved and the printing made easier. Thus, there are now available 8-megapixel (mp) phones and phones that can connect directly to many home printers. Camera phones are also being made with memory card slots, so that images stored on a memory card can then be taken directly to a retailer to have prints made.

GAMES New smartphones have powerful graphics chips and good screen quality that allow three-dimensional images, fast computing capabilities, realistic drawings, and fast-moving action.

RADIO & MUSIC Some smartphones allow users to listen to FM radio. In addition, cellphones can store hundreds, if not thousands, of songs. An 8-gigabyte phone memory card, for instance, can store about 2,000 songs. Some of the biggest music companies and phone companies have been pairing up to make available song downloads—or songs and music videos to watch on mobile display screens—that customers may purchase through their phones.

Short-range wireless Bluetooth technology enables cellphone users to put on headphones so they can connect to their cellphones without cords.

TV & VIDEO TV programs and movies/videos made for a handheld mobile device with a 2-inch or 2¼-inch display screen pose particular challenges. For one thing, although cellphone screen quality has gotten better, there are still limitations in battery life, processing power, and storage capacity. In addition, most viewers don't have the patience to watch a 90-minute feature film on a screen this size. Whether it's a sitcom, news show, or sports highlights, TV programs designed for cellphones have to rely heavily on close-ups, more static shots, and little movement within the frame—the opposite of MTV video. In the end, then, the producers of such fare have to rely more on writing and storytelling.

OTHER FEATURES We have mentioned GPS locators and video cameras, but there seems to be no end of other features existing and forthcoming for smartphones. In the United States, students at the University of California, Santa Barbara, pay for parking stalls by charging the fee to an account through their cellphones. In Japan, customers can pay for purchases not with cash or credit cards but by making electronic payments through a

People are using electronic devices everywhere: digital cameras, computers, cellphones.

smartphone. Also in Japan, mobile phones have been turned into controllers for model racing cars, for use as television remotes, and as devices for fingerprint recognition. In South Korea, cellphones have been modified to allow diabetics to check their blood-sugar levels, and the data can be sent to their physicians.

The Societal Effects of Cellphones

The effects of cellphones are mixed.

We discussed many of the advantages, drawbacks, and dangers of smartphones in Chapter 6, and we noted that the effects of these phones are mixed. The positive attributes are many: parents can more easily monitor the safety of their children, police dispatchers can help people who are lost, information and amusements of all kinds are readily available, you can phone your apologies when you'll be late for an appointment, and so on.

However, people's personal behavior in using phones has not necessarily been improved. Cellphones regularly ring—and are answered—in theaters, despite movie screen advisories. Bus and train travelers become enraged by the loud conversations of fellow passengers. The serenity of nature's wonders in national parks is disrupted by people yakking on their phones. Bosses feel obliged to rebuke their employees whose cellphones ring in meetings.

Phone use by car drivers makes even young people drive erratically, moving and reacting more slowly and increasing their risk of accidents. People inadvertently dial numbers in their phone's address book when they've had too much to drink (a phenomenon known as "drunk dialing"). Camera-equipped phones have been used to take pictures of people in bathroom stalls, to cheat on school tests, and to allow thieves to capture credit card numbers. Pornography companies see cellphones as a new frontier. Employers can hire companies that can keep track of their employees' out-of-office locations through GPS tracking of their cellphones.

But just as technology can create unforeseen problems, perhaps technology can also provide solutions. Some countries—but not the United States yet—are permitting the use of radio-jamming equipment that keeps nearby cellphones from working whether the phone user likes it or not. This would certainly allow restaurants, theaters, and the like to impose a "cone of silence" that would provide relief to long-suffering members of the public who have been forced to unwillingly share in others' cell conversations.

7.9 VIDEOGAME SYSTEMS: The Ultimate Convergence Machine?

Video games are played on a display screen, usually by remote control, and generally emphasize fast action.

Several industries—videogame console makers, consumer-electronics companies, PC companies, cable companies, and telephone companies—are interested in videogames. Here let us consider just the first: the makers of gameboxes. The big videogame hardware makers are Microsoft (until now mainly a software rather than hardware business), Sony, and Nintendo. Let's see how their consoles compare.

Because the main intended use of the Xbox is for online videogames, Microsoft has invested heavily in its subscription service, Xbox LIVE, which allows Xbox players to meet online—and also to talk to people with whom they are playing via voice chat. However, Microsoft really is trying to make the device a living-room hub for all kinds of digital media—not only videogames but also movies, music, and online content. The Xbox enables users to connect cameras, digital music players, high-definition televisions, surround-sound stereo systems, and the like via Wi-Fi, and a 250-gigabyte hard drive is available on which users can copy music CDs, photos, and other digital content.

Sony's PlayStation 3, or PS3, is designed to exploit the dominance of the TV-console market that Sony established with the PlayStation 2. The PS3 uses an ultra-powerful multiprocessor, the Cell chip; it's called a "cell" because software instructions can be divided up in cells and distributed among different processors and devices (TVs, music players, and the like). This means a network can be organized without human intervention, such as, in one demonstration, 48 separate high-definition video feeds to a single display screen. PS3 enables gamers not only to videoconference over the Internet but also to have movie-quality graphics, with lifelike textures, colors, and motion. Users

Boy playing video games on his Xbox 360

Xbox 360

are able to stream and download music and movies, handling several streams at once (so that you can play a videogame and watch a movie at the same time).

Showgoers try out games at a PlayStation 3 exhibit.

Nintendo's Wii doesn't emphasize power and graphics so much as innovative, networked game play and simpler, cheaper game development. Its one-handed remote controller, which is fitted with motion sensors, allows players to wave it around frenetically, swish it gently through the air, or kick, punch, jump, or steer their way through on-screen action. Nintendo also introduced the Nintendo DS, an advanced portable game console that enables users to wirelessly connect via Wi-Fi to other users with Wi-Fi capabilities. Unlike Microsoft's and Sony's, however, Nintendo's gamebox won't play movies on DVD unless users buy a separate device. Wii also offers popular exercise programs via motion-control sports simulations—for example. skiing, golf, archery, baseball, bowling—and dancing.

With all these personal digital devices, it's no wonder that anyone born since 1982 is called a member of the "Always On" generation. They are the generation that has for their entire lives been surrounded by and using the toys and tools of the Digital Age. If you belong to this group, does it make you different from previous generations? We consider this question in the Experience Box.

Playing baseball on the Nintendo Wii

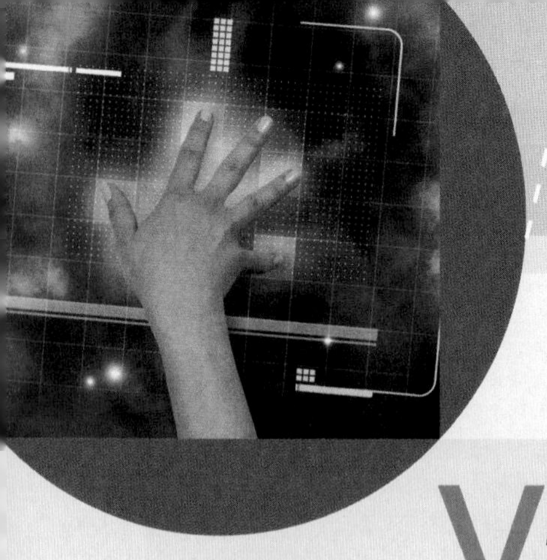

EXPERIENCE BOX

The "Always On" Generation

Videogames, computers, cellphones, portable music players, email, the Internet, instant messaging, the web, video cameras, and similar personal technology. Is this what you grew up with? Then you're a member of the Always On generation, also known as NetGeners (for "Net Generation") and Millennials (for "Millennial Generation").

Members of this cohort "have never known life without computers and the Internet," says one report. "To them the computer is not a technology—it is an assumed part of life."[41] As a result, say observers such as Marc Prensky, "today's students *think and process information fundamentally differently* from their predecessors" (his emphasis).[42]

Those most likely to have the mindset and characteristics of Always On were born on or after the year 1982. Unlike older students, Millennials tend to exhibit distinct learning styles. "Their learning preferences tend toward teamwork, experiential activities, structure, and the use of technology," says Diana Oblinger, executive director of higher education for Microsoft Corporation.[43] With such students, listening to music, sending instant messages, chatting on the phone, and doing homework all at the same time is second nature.

Let's consider some of the characteristics of these students.

Staying Connected Is Essential

After a college class lets out, students step into the hallway and immediately activate their cellphones, iPads, or notebook computers, talking to or texting friends or checking their email. At rock concerts, when the lights dim, one may see the glow of tiny blue screens, as concert goers text-message friends or have them listen to music via their cellphones—or observe the action through camera phones.

"Connecting is what the current generation of students is all about," says one report. "College students use the Internet as much for social reasons as for academic reasons."[44] Besides maintaining social contacts, students get homework assignments and lecture outlines online and participate in class discussions. They instant-message friends to brainstorm class projects and other assignments. They email professors with questions at any time. All in all, the lines between work, social life, and studying are blurring.

Multitasking Is a Way of Life

Multitasking is second nature. "It's perfectly normal for a group of college students to watch TV with their laptops in front of them," said one recent college graduate. "They'll check their campus mailbox once a day but their email every five minutes."[45] Says Prensky, such students "are used to receiving information really fast. They like to parallel process and multitask. They prefer their graphics *before* their text rather than the opposite. They prefer random access (like hypertext)."[46] They are also, having grown up with videogames, accustomed to learning how to take in many sources of information at once and how to incorporate peripheral information. Finally, games have taught them how to use and manage a large database of information.[47]

Students Are Impatient & Results-Oriented

Today's students have grown up on the "twitch speed" of videogames, instant messaging, MTV, and a customer-service kind of culture. Thus, they "have a strong demand for immediacy and little tolerance for delays," says one analysis. "They expect that services will be available 24×7 in a variety of modes (web, phone, in person) and that responses will be quick."[48] One result of this is that many students prefer typing to handwriting: It's faster. Another result: Students expect to be engaged, which is why online forums, blogs, and use of RSS aggregators to update subjects are popular.[49] They don't want to be preached to, ignored, or bored. They are also experiential learners—they prefer to learn by doing rather than learn by listening.[50]

They Respect Differences & Gravitate toward Group Activity

NetGeners are racially and ethnically diverse and consequently "accept differences that span culture, ability—or disability—and style," says one report. Indeed, they "are more comfortable with their learning differences than any other generation has been."[51] They also gravitate toward group and team activities, owing to their group-gaming experiences and their constant communication with friends through cellphones, texting, and email.

TERMS & EXPLANATIONS

convergence (p. 374) Also known as *digital convergence;* the combining of several industries—computers, communications, consumer electronics, entertainment, and mass media—through various devices that exchange data in digital form. Why it's important: *Convergence has led to electronic products that perform multiple functions, such as TVs with Internet access, cellphones that are also digital cameras, GPS units, and video players and refrigerators that allow you to send email.*

digital television (DTV) (p. 392) Television standard adopted in 1996 that uses a digital signal, or series of 0s and 1s. It uses digital cameras, digital transmission, and digital receivers and is capable of delivering movie-quality pictures and CD-quality sound. The Federal Communications Commission mandated that all TV stations be capable of broadcasting DTV by 2009. Why it's important: *DTV is much clearer and less prone to interference than analog TV. It may allow viewers to receive various kinds of information services, such as announcements from public safety and fire departments.*

e-book (p. 394) Also known as *electronic book;* electronic text, the digital-media equivalent of a conventional printed book. Why it's important: *Allows users to more easily read text, such as books, on personal computer, smartphone, iPad, or e-book reader.*

e-book reader (p. 395) A handheld device specifically designed to allow people to read electronic books. Why it's important: *Allows users to download electronic books (text), wired or wirelessly, and read them as conveniently as printed books.*

HD (hybrid digital) radio (p. 383) Form of radio that provides CD-quality sound and allows broadcasters to squeeze one analog and two digital stations on the same frequency. Why it's important: *HD radio combines digital and analog broadcast signals, enabling stations to offer an analog main channel and digital "sidebands," so that multiple types of content can be broadcast from the same position on the dial.*

high-definition television (HDTV) (p. 392) A form of television that works with digital broadcasting signals. Why it's important: *HDTV has a wider screen and higher resolution than analog television had. Whereas analog TV has a width-to-height ratio, or aspect ratio, of 4 to 3, HDTV has an aspect ratio of 16 to 9, which is similar to the wide-screen approach used in movies. In addition, compared to analog display screens, an HDTV display has 10 times more pixels on a screen—1,920 × 1,080 pixels or more. Thus, HDTV could have 1,080 lines on a screen, compared with 525-line resolution for analog TV.*

Internet radio (p. 383) Continuous streaming of audio over the Internet; listeners have no control over the stream—just as with regular radio. Why it's important: *Dedicated hardware devices, commonly called web radio or Internet radio appliances, can be purchased that connect to a home network and then to the Internet to play audio streams. Internet radio can also be played on computers and on portable devices, such as smartphones and media players, connected wirelessly to the Internet.*

megapixels (p. 387) In a digital camera, the millions of picture elements, the electronic dots making up an image; the number of megapixels expresses the camera's resolution, or image sharpness. The millions of pixels are tightly packed together on the camera's image sensor, a half-inch-wide silicon chip. When light strikes a pixel, it generates an electric current that is converted into the digital data that becomes your photograph. Why it's important: *The more megapixels a digital camera has, the better the resolution and the higher the quality of the image.*

MP3 (p. 378) Format that allows audio files to be compressed. MP3 files are about one-tenth the size of uncompressed audio files. For example, a 4-minute song on a CD takes about 40 megabytes of space, but an MP3 version of that song takes only about 4 megabytes. Why it's important: *MP3 allows audio files to be made small enough to be sent over the Internet or stored as digital files. (MP4 is the format used for video.)*

MP3 digital audio player *See* **portable media player.**

multitasking (p. 377) Performing several tasks at once, such as studying while eating, listening to music, talking on the phone, and handling email. Why it's important: *Medical and learning experts say the brain has limits and can do only so much at one time. For instance, it has been found that people who do two demanding tasks simultaneously, such as driving in heavy traffic and talking on a cellphone, do neither task as well as they do each alone. Indeed, the result of constantly shifting attention is a sacrifice in quality for any of the tasks with which one is engaged.*

podcasting (p. 384) The recording and downloading of Internet radio or similar Internet audio programs. Why it's important: *Podcasting software allows amateur deejays and hobbyists to create their own radio shows and offer them free over the Internet. Listeners can then download shows onto their MP3 players, such as the iPod, or other media players and computers.*

portable media players (PMPs) (p. 378) Small portable devices that enable you to play digital audio, video, and/or still-image files. Why it's important: *Also known as MP3 players, portable devices for playing digital audio files. PMPs differ from MP3 players in that they can handle not only audio but also video and image files. Thus, you may be able to carry several hours of music or video.*

ringtone (p. 399) The audible sound a phone makes to announce that a call is coming in. A ringtone may be an old-fashioned "ring, ring" or a clip from a popular song. Why it's important: *Users can customize the ringtones on their cellphones and even use different ringtones to identify different callers.*

sampling rate (p. 380) The number of times, expressed in kilobits per second, that a song is measured (sampled) and converted to a digital value when it is being recorded as a digital file. Why it's important: *The sampling rate affects the audio quality. For instance, a song sampled at 192 kilobits per second is three times the size of a song sampled at 64 kilobits per second and will be of better sound quality.*

satellite radio (p. 382) Also called *digital radio*; a radio service in which signals are sent from satellites in orbit around the earth or by earth-based repeaters to subscribers owning special radios that can decode the encrypted signals. Why it's important: *The CD-quality sound is much better than that of regular radio, and because the signals are digital, there are many more channels available than those on traditional radio. Also, unlike standard broadcasters, satellite radio broadcasters are for the most part not regulated by the Federal Communications Commission.*

smartphone (p. 398) Cellular telephone with microprocessor, memory, display screen, and built-in modem. Why it's important: *Some types of this multimedia phone, which combine some of the capabilities of a PC with a handset, offer a wealth of functions: text messaging, cameras, music players, videogames, email access, digital TV viewing, search tools, personal information management, GPS locators, Internet phone service, and even credit-card processing.*

standard-definition television (SDTV) (p. 393) A TV standard that has a lower resolution than HDTV, a minimum of 480 vertical lines, and a picture quality similar to that required to watch DVD movies. Why it's important: *The SDTV standard enables broadcasters to transmit more information within the HDTV bandwidth, allowing them to multicast their products, transmitting up to five SDTV programs simultaneously—and getting perhaps five times the revenue—instead of just one HDTV program. (Analog broadcasts only one program at a time.) Thus, instead of beaming high-definition pictures, some broadcasters are splitting their digital streams into several SDTV channels.*

tablet computer (p. 397) General-purpose computer contained in a single panel; it is a combination of smartphone and laptop computer with wireless connections and a multitouch screentext messaging. Why it's important: *A tablet computer offers the same portability as a laptop, but you can write on the screen just as you would on a notepad. You can then save what you have written in a digital file for safekeeping or sharing.*

text messaging (p. 398) Also known as *texting;* the sending of short messages, generally no more than 160 characters in length, to a pager, smartphone, or other handheld device, including notebook computer, as well as to desktop computers and fixed-line phones. Why it's important: *Text messaging combines the portability of cellphones with the convenience of email and instant messaging. Text messaging is particularly appropriate for situations in which making a cellphone call is intrusive.*

video on demand (VOD or VoD) (p. 394) Set of technologies that enable viewers to select videos or TV programs from a central server to watch when they want. Why it's important: *VOD allows viewers to watch programs when they want rather than when TV programmers offer them.*

CHAPTER REVIEW

stage 1 LEARNING MEMORIZATION

"I can recognize and recall information."

Self-Test Questions

1. The combining of several industries through various devices that exchange data in digital form is called __________.
2. __________ allows amateur deejays and hobbyists to create their own radio shows and offer them free over the Internet.
3. The sending of short messages generally no longer than 160 characters is called __________.
4. The electronic dots that make up a digital-camera image are called __________.
5. Performing several tasks at once is called __________.
6. The digital-media equivalent of a conventional printed book is called a(n) __________.
7. __________ is a format that allows files to be compressed so they are small enough to be sent over the Internet as digital files.
8. __________ are small portable devices that enable you to play/display digital audio, video, and/or still-image files.
9. __________ works with digital broadcasting signals and has a wider screen and higher resolution than standard TV.
10. A(n) __________ camera is one that automatically adjusts settings such as exposure and focus.

Multiple-Choice Questions

1. The number of times that a song is measured and converted to a digital value is called
   a. SLR.
   b. ripping.
   c. sampling rate.
   d. mash-up.
2. A digital camera's resolution is expressed in
   a. dpi.
   b. rpm.
   c. pda.
   d. megapixels.
   e. betapixels.
3. Smartphones have
   a. a microprocessor.
   b. a display screen.
   c. memory.
   d. a modem.
   e. all of these

4. Which of the following concerns does *not* apply to smartphone use?
   a. often causes erratic driving
   b. people can track users' movements without their knowledge
   c. users can take photos in inappropriate situations
   d. signals can open locked car doors
   e. loud conversations and ringtones can irritate people in the user's vicinity
5. __________ are the electronic dots making up an image in a digital camera.
   a. megabytes
   b. megapixels
   c. digital points per inch
   d. vectors
   e. zettabytes

True/False Questions

T F 1. The increased availability of broadband connections slowed down the process of digital convergence.

T F 2. MP3 increases the size of digital audio files in order to improve the sound quality.

T F 3. For 8 × 10 photo prints, 2-megapixel digital cameras are best.

T F 4. Memory stick is a type of flash memory card.

T F 5. Sending photos as email attachments to many people is more efficient than using an online photo-sharing service.

T F 6. One cannot transfer files from a smartphone to a desktop computer.

T F 7. HDTV uses analog signals.

LEARNING COMPREHENSION

"I can recall information in my own terms and explain it to a friend."

Short-Answer Questions

1. Briefly explain how satellite radio works. What are two advantages of satellite radio?
2. What could you use a mash-up for?
3. Why are MP3 files smaller than regular audio files, such as a purchased CD?
4. Why would you use an online photo-sharing service?
5. How does sampling rate relate to the size of MP3 files?
6. What is the difference between satellite radio and high-definition radio?
7. Which digital camera would you choose: point-and-shoot or single-lens reflex? Why?

LEARNING APPLYING, ANALYZING, SYNTHESIZING, EVALUATING

"I can apply what I've learned, relate these ideas to other concepts, build on other knowledge, and use all these thinking skills to form a judgment."

Knowledge in Action

1. Does almost everyone you know download and listen to MP3 files? Describe a few ways in which the iPod users whom you have observed are being distracted from certain activities and some responsibilities. Do you perceive a problem?
2. List five situations in which you often find yourself multitasking. How many things have you done at once? How do you think your manner of multitasking affects the quality of what you achieve?
3. What questions would you ask a friend in order to determine which digital camera, with which characteristics, you would advise her or him to buy?
4. Describe the ways that one can transfer images from a digital camera to a computer.

Web Exercises

1. Current rules of both the FCC and the U.S. Federal Aviation Administration ban in-flight cellular calling. The primary FCC concern has been possible disruption of cellphone communication on the ground. The FAA's worry is how cellphones might interfere with a plane's navigation and electrical systems. However, plans are in the works to assign new bandwidths to allow cellphone use in the air.

   Do an Internet search on the pros and cons of using cellphones during flights. Are you in favor of such use?

2. Nine states, D.C., and the Virgin Islands prohibit all drivers from using handheld cellphones while driving; but many states prohibit *all* cellphone use by certain drivers. Thirty-four states, D.C., and Guam ban text messaging for all drivers.

   Do an Internet search and find out what the law says about driving and cellphone use in the state where you are going to school and in the state where you come from.

   The rules on driving and cellphone use in many other countries are much stricter than they are in the United States; for more information, go to *http://reviews.ebay.com/list-of-states-and-countries-that-ban-driving-on-phone_WoQQugidZ10000000002960730*.

   According to the Automobile Association of America (AAA), hands-free phones are not risk free. The hands-free feature is simply a convenience: it does not increase safety. Studies show that hands-free cellphones distract drivers the same as handheld phones do. Why? Because it's the conversation that distracts the driver, not the device. Search the Internet and find some reports that support this view.

Why do you think people don't just turn off their cellphones while they are driving and let voicemail collect messages to be retrieved later?

3. The Convergence Center (*http://dcc.syr.edu/digital-convergence/*) supports research on and experimentation with media convergence. The Center is a joint effort of the Syracuse University School of Information Studies and the Newhouse School of Public Communications. Its mission is to understand the future of digital media and to engage students and faculty in the process of defining and shaping that future. Go to their site and click on What's New, Digital Convergence; choose one article to read; then write a couple of paragraphs that summarize the article.

4. Now that cellphones have cameras, camera voyeurism is becoming a problem. The U.S. Video Voyeurism Prevention Act of 2004 has made this behavior a federal offense. This act prohibits photographing or videocapturing (including with cellphones) a naked person without his or her consent in any place where there can be "a reasonable expectation of privacy." Punishment includes fines of up to $100,000 or up to a year in prison, or both.

   Cellphone vendors say this law may be hard to enforce and may even be a deterrent to promising technology and create a false sense of security. Some cellphone manufacturers deny that voyeurs are any more likely to snoop using a cellphone camera than using other technologies such as digital cameras. But other people say the opportunity differs, that most people don't carry digital cameras around with them. With a cellphone camera there is more opportunity to take snapshots of interesting images, and unfortunately this can include images that can threaten privacy. Voyeurs using cellphone cameras could easily pretend to be doing something else, such as dialing or talking.

   Some state legislators have proposed legislation requiring camera phones sold to emit an audible noise or flash a light when users press the shutter. But such noise and light would disturb happy occasions such as weddings, where people use cellphone cameras to take pictures and send them instantly to loved ones who couldn't attend.

   Research the cameraphone voyeurism problem on the Internet. How could you protect your privacy in public situations?

5. The Cellular Telecommunications & Internet Association (CTIA) reminds us that text messaging can be a fast, efficient, and reliable way to communicate in the event of an emergency. And if more wireless users rely on text messaging in crisis situations, the people who need to make voice calls the most—emergency responders and 911 callers—can get through more easily.

   "Everyone should have a plan for communicating in times of emergencies, and text messaging can be an efficient way to reach your friends, family or loved ones. In the time it takes one person to make a 1-minute voice call, hundreds of thousands of text messages can be exchanged," said the president and CEO of CTIA. "In these days of increased terrorist threats and heightened awareness, learning all the options on your wireless phone is an important piece of being prepared."

   Text messages have also been used around the world to alert citizens in times of danger. In Kuwait, during the 1990 conflict, Kuwaitis were warned about imminent attacks from Iraq via text messaging. And in Hong Kong, some years ago, a wireless carrier set up a system to provide SARS updates via mobile phone. Users punched in a three-digit number and received a text message indicating if they were near any buildings where SARS victims lived or worked. The information was obtained from a daily list released by the Health Department.

   In the frantic days leading up to the landfall of Hurricane Rita in September 2005, Houston radio station KRBE offered to deliver hurricane alerts via text messaging across cellphones to listeners, enabling information to be delivered anytime, anywhere, regardless of whether a person was near a radio or a computer. At a time when traditional media networks experienced coverage issues from storm damage, power lines were down, and cars were running out of gas, KRBE was able to provide a continuous two-way stream of information via the cellphone. Many listeners expressed gratitude for information on road closures, fuel availability, evacuation orders, and storm damage during a frightening experience.

   Do an Internet search on how text messaging has been used more recently to help in various types of emergencies around the world. What types of suppliers have provided the messages? Using what types of systems? How do cellphone users know where/how to retrieve the messages?

DATABASES ARE IN YOUR LIFE

Digital Engines for Today's Economy

Chapter Topics & Key Questions

8.1 **Managing Files: Basic Concepts** What are the data storage hierarchy, the key field, types of files, and some methods of data access and storage?

8.2 **Database Management Systems** What are the benefits of database management systems, and what are the main types of database access?

8.3 **Database Models** What are the main types of database models?

8.4 **Data Mining** How does data mining work, and how could it be useful to me?

8.5 **Databases & the Digital Economy: E-Business & E-Commerce** What are e-business and e-commerce, and what are three types of e-commerce systems?

8. 6 **Information Systems in Organizations: Using Databases to Help Make Decisions** How does information flow within an organization, and what are different types of information systems?

8.7 **Artificial Intelligence** What are the main areas of artificial intelligence?

8.8 **Databases: Concerns about Privacy & Identity Theft** What are two main concerns about the uses of databases?

Download the free UIT 10e App for key term flash cards, quizzes, and a game, *Over the Edge*

The Library of Congress is the largest library in the world, with more than 147 million items on approximately 838 miles of bookshelves. The collections include more than 33 million books and other print materials, 3 million recordings, 12.5 million photographs, 5.4 million maps, 6 million pieces of sheet music, and 64.5 million manuscripts.[1]

The Library of Congress is huge, but it is able to house its collection. However, in 2011 if the amount of digital information in existence were to be stored permanently (on hard drives, tapes, CDs, DVDs and memory devices), it would have exceeded the total storage space available by almost 50%. In 2007 the "digital universe" comprised 281 exabytes (281 billion gigabytes), and there was almost 45 gigabytes of data for every person on the planet. However, there are about 1.8 zettabytes (1,800 billion billion gigabytes) of data in 2011.[2] The biggest growth in data has been "visual in nature, from devices such as digital cameras, digital surveillance cameras, and digital televisions. Other fast-growing elements include social networks, data centers supporting cloud computing, sensor-base applications and the growth of the Internet in developing countries."[3]

Regardless of the storage problems, how will all such information be organized and made accessible? The answer has to do with databases. The arrival of databases has changed the nature of many of our business and social institutions. Today, for instance, because of the huge increase in online Internet sales, credit card fraud has boomed, and so slight changes in your spending patterns—buying much more clothing than usual or filling your car's gas tank twice in one day—will trigger an alert that may freeze your card.[4] But databases are everywhere now and promise to bring even more changes in the future. Wikipedia *(www.wikipedia.org)*, for instance, is a web-based, free-content, multilingual encyclopedia that anyone can log on to and add to or edit as he or she sees fit; it has more than 13 million articles in approximately 250 languages.[5] The National Geographic Society and IBM's Watson Research Labs launched a massive database called the Genographic Project (*https://genographic.nationalgeographic.com/genographic/index.htm*) that is cataloging genetic markers and is capable of tracing the geographic origins of your and other people's ancestors back more than 10,000 years. Google has created a database consisting of millions of digitally scanned books from several university libraries (*http://books.google.com/*).

Instant ID. The IBIS Mobile Identification System can verify a person's identity in minutes from a remote location. It uses fingerprint information captured by the handheld device; the information is transmitted to the Automated Fingerprint Identification System (AFIS), a huge database used by law enforcement officers, among others.

Traditional electronic databases include those that handle airline reservation systems, many library catalogs, magazine subscriptions for large publishing companies, patient tracking in large hospitals, and inventories for supermarkets and big-box stores such as Walmart. These databases typically use text- and numeric-based data. Newer types of databases include multimedia data and formulas for data analysis.

Before we discuss traditional types of databases and recent innovations in database management, we need to discuss some basic concepts of file management.

8.1 MANAGING FILES: Basic Concepts

A database is a computer-based collection of related data organized so that it can be conveniently accessed, managed, and updated.

An electronic database is not just the computer-based version of what used to go into manila folders and filing cabinets. **A *database* is a logically organized collection of related data designed and built for a specific purpose,** a technology for pulling together facts that allows the slicing and dicing and mixing and matching of unprocessed data in all kinds of ways and turning it into useful information. A database can be of any size and of any degree of complexity, and it can be maintained manually or by software on computers. This chapter, of course, covers computer databases.

more info!

Library of Congress Database

Go to the Library of Congress website at:

www.loc.gov

Click on Researchers (under "Especially for"), and look at the research tools offered. Could any help you with your research work? Explore a few that interest you.

How Data Is Organized: The Data Storage Hierarchy

"Hierarchy" refers to a graded series of ordered groupings—usually a pyramid-like ranking, with the largest or most important entities on the top.

Data in a traditional database can be grouped into a hierarchy of categories, each increasingly more complex. **The *data storage hierarchy* consists of the levels of data stored in a computer database: bits, characters (bytes), fields, records, and tables (files).** (• *See Panel 8.1, next page.*) An alternative concept in database design is known as *hypertext*. In a hypertext database, any object, whether it be a piece of text, a picture, or a film, can be linked to any other object. Hypertext databases are particularly useful for organizing large amounts of disparate information, but they are not designed for numerical analysis.[6]

BITS Computers, as we have said, are based on the principle that electricity may be on or off. Thus, the *bit* is the smallest unit of data the computer can store in a database—represented by 0 for off or 1 for on. Next is the byte.

CHARACTERS **A *character* (byte) is a letter, number, or special character.** *A, B, C, 1, 2, 3, #, $, %* are all examples of single characters. A combination of bits represents a character.

Bits and bytes are the building blocks for representing data, whether it is being processed, telecommunicated, or stored in a database. The computer deals with the bits and bytes; you, however, will need to deal mostly with fields (columns), records (rows), and tables (files).

Feline phrasing database. The toy maker Takara of Japan has marketed a "cat's words translator," which uses a database of cat voices to output cat "phrases." Humans can use these translators to "communicate" with their cats.

panel 8.1

How data is organized

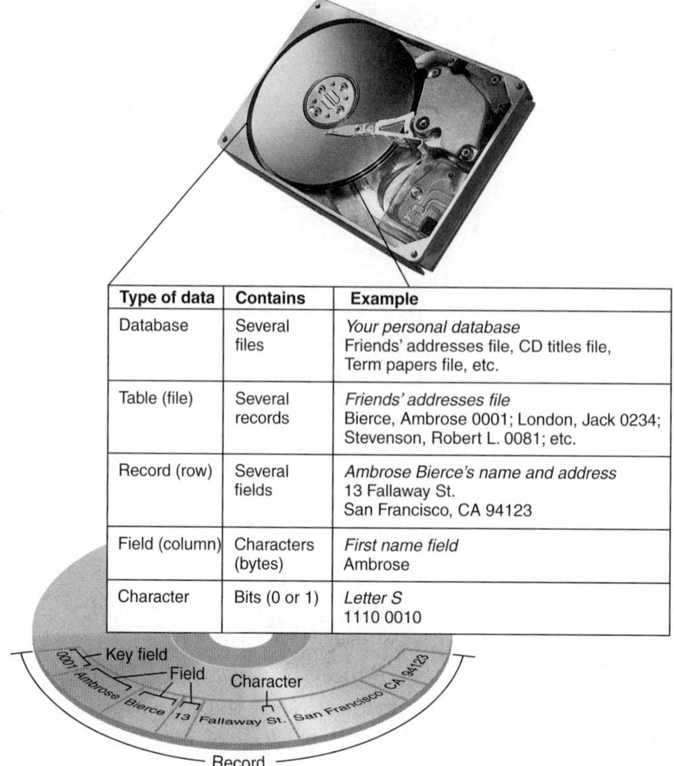

Type of data	Contains	Example
Database	Several files	*Your personal database* Friends' addresses file, CD titles file, Term papers file, etc.
Table (file)	Several records	*Friends' addresses file* Bierce, Ambrose 0001; London, Jack 0234; Stevenson, Robert L. 0081; etc.
Record (row)	Several fields	*Ambrose Bierce's name and address* 13 Fallaway St. San Francisco, CA 94123
Field (column)	Characters (bytes)	*First name field* Ambrose
Character	Bits (0 or 1)	*Letter S* 1110 0010

FIELD **A *field (column)* is a unit or category of data consisting of one or more characters (bytes).** It is the smallest unit of meaningful information in the database. Each field has a *field name* that describes the kind of data that should be entered into the field. An example of a field is your first name, *or* your street address, *or* your Social Security number.

Fields can be designed to be a certain maximum length or a variable length, and they can also be designed to hold different types of data, such as text only, numbers only, dates only, time, a "yes" or "no" answer only, web links only, or pictures, sound, or video.

RECORD **A *record (row)* is a collection of related fields;** it represents one entry in a table. Each record stores data about only one entity, which can be a person, a place, a thing, an occurrence, or a phenomenon. An example of a record would be your name *and* address *and* Social Security number.

FILE **A *file* (often called *table*) is a collection of related records.** An example of a table is data collected on everyone employed in the same department of a company, including all names, addresses, and Social Security numbers. You use tables a lot because the table is the collection of data or information that is treated as a unit by the computer.

The table is at the top of the data hierarchy. A collection of related tables forms the database. A company database might include tables on all past and current employees in all departments. There would be various records for each employee in various tables: payroll, retirement benefits, sales quotas and achievements (if in sales), and so on.

The Key Field

A key field (primary key) is a field in a record that holds unique data that identifies that record from all the other records in the table and in the database

An important concept in data organization is that of the key field. *(See Panel 8.1.)* As we said in Chapter 3, in the section on database applications, a *primary key* (*key field*) is, in general, a field that is chosen to uniquely identify a record so that it can be easily retrieved and processed. The primary key is often an identification number, Social Security number, customer account number, or the like or a combination of letters and numbers set up as a meaningful code. The primary characteristic of the key field is that it is *unique*. Thus, numbers are clearly preferable to names as primary keys, because there are many people with common names such as James Johnson, Susan Williams, Ann Wong, or Roberto Sanchez, whose records might be confused. Student records are often identified by student ID numbers used as primary keys.

As we also mentioned in Chapter 3, the *foreign key* (p. 167) is a field (or fields) in a table that matches the primary key of another table; in other words, it points to the primary key of another table. Foreign keys thus can be used to cross-reference tables. For example, in a Student table (contains general data about all students), the primary key could be Student ID, because each student has a unique ID number. But in the Courses table, many students would be listed many times, because most students take many courses. Their Student IDs would be the foreign keys that would link each student to the primary key in the master Student table.

Survival Tip

Guard Your Social Security Number

The Social Security number is an important key field to records about you. Don't carry it with you. Don't print it on checks. Don't give it out unless really necessary. See also *www.ssa.gov/pubs/10064.html* regarding Social Security numbers and ID theft.

8.2 Database Management Systems

A database management system is software that enables users to store, modify, and extract information from a database. The system manages incoming data, organizes it, and provides ways for information to be modified or extracted by users or other programs.

As we've said, a database is an organized collection of related (integrated) tables (files). A database may be small, contained entirely within your own personal computer, or it may be massive, available through online connections or on supercomputers. Such massive databases are of particular interest, because they offer phenomenal resources that until recently were unavailable to most ordinary computer users.

In the 1950s, when commercial use of computers was just beginning, a large organization would have different files for different purposes. For example, a university might have one file (called a "flat file") for course grades, another for student records, another for tuition billing, and so on. In a corporation, people in the accounting, order-entry, and customer-service departments all had their own separate files. Thus, if an address had to be changed, for example, each file would have to be updated separately. The files (now called tables, or relations) were stored on magnetic tape and had to be accessed in sequence in what was called a *file-processing system*.

Later, magnetic-disk technology came along, allowing any file to be accessed randomly (out of sequence). This permitted the development of new technology and new software: the database management system. **A *database management system (DBMS)*, or *database manager*, is software written specifically to control the structure of a database and access to the data.** In a DBMS an address change need be entered only once, and the updated information is then available in any relevant table (file). (Strictly speaking, the *database* is the collection of the data, and the *database management system* is the software—but many professionals use "database" to cover both the data and the software.)

The Benefits of Database Management Systems

Information technology has dramatically improved the creation and management of data and information systems.

The advantages of database management systems are these:

REDUCED DATA REDUNDANCY *Data redundancy*, or *repetition*, means that the same data fields (a person's address, say) appear over and over again in different files and often in different formats. In the old file-processing system, separate files would repeat the same data, wasting storage space. In a database management system, the information appears just once, freeing up more storage capacity. In the old data storage systems, if one field needed to be updated, someone had to make sure that it was updated in *all* the places it appeared—an invitation to error and to wasted time.

This process of structuring data to minimize duplication and inconsistencies is called *normalization*.

SPEED Modern DBMSs are obviously much faster than manual data-organization systems and faster than older computer-based database arrangements.

IMPROVED DATA INTEGRITY *Data integrity* means that data is accurate, consistent, and up to date. In the old system, when a change was made in one file, it might not have been made in other necessary files. The result was that some reports were produced with erroneous information. In a DBMS, reduced redundancy increases the likelihood of data integrity—the chances that the data is accurate, consistent, and up to date—because each updating change is made in only one place.

Also, many DBMSs provide built-in check systems that help ensure the accuracy of the data that is input. The expression "garbage in, garbage out" (abbreviated *GIGO*) refers to the fact that a database with incorrect data cannot generate correct information.

TIMELINESS The speed and the efficiency of DBMSs generally ensure that data can be supplied in a timely fashion—when people need it.

EASE OF SHARING The data in a database belongs to and is shared, usually over a network, by an entire organization. The data is independent of the programs that process the data and it is easy for nontechnical users to access data (if they have authorization to do so). Individual computer users can also develop their own small databases, using a database application package (p. 165).

EASE OF DATA MAINTENANCE Database management systems offer standard procedures for adding, editing, and deleting records, as well as validation checks to ensure that the appropriate type of data is being entered properly and completely into each field type. Data backup utilities ensure availability of data in case of primary system failure.

FORECASTING CAPABILITIES DBMSs can hold massive amounts of data that can be manipulated, studied, and compared in order to forecast behaviors in markets and other areas that can affect sales and marketing managers' decisions as well as the decisions of administrators of educational institutions, hospitals, and other organizations.

INCREASED SECURITY Although various departments may share data, access to specific information can be limited to selected users—called *authorization control*. Thus, for example, through the use of passwords, a student's financial, medical, and grade information in a university database is made available only to those who have a legitimate need to know.

Database Disadvantages

Some drawback of databases are these:

- Database systems are complex, difficult, and time-consuming to design.
- Substantial hardware and software start-up costs.
- Damage to database affects virtually all applications programs.
- Possible extensive conversion costs when changing database systems
- Initial training required for all programmers and users.

(From *http://wiki.answers.com/Q/Disadvantages_of_database_management_system; www.cl500.net/pros_cons.html*.)

Three Database Components

A database management system may have three components integrated into the software—a data dictionary, DBMS utilities, and a report generator.

DATA DICTIONARY: FOR DEFINING DATA DEFINITIONS & STRUCTURE **A *data dictionary*, also called a *repository*, is a document or file that stores the data definitions and descriptions of the structure of data used in the database.** Data dictionaries contain no actual data from the database, only information for managing it. Without a data dictionary, however, a DBMS

PRACTICAL ACTION

Accuracy & Completeness

As we have mentioned, databases—including online encyclopedias such as Wikipedia—can provide you with more facts and faster facts but not always better facts. A former professor of broadcast journalism at Buffalo State College in New York suggests five limitations to bear in mind when using databases for research:[7]

- **You Can't Get the Whole Story:** For some purposes, databases are only a foot in the door. There may be many facts or facets of the topic that are not in a database. Reporters, for instance, find a database is a starting point. It may take intensive investigation to get the rest of the story.
- **It's Not the Gospel:** Just because you see something on a computer screen doesn't mean it's accurate. Numbers, names, and facts must be verified in other ways. For instance, because in the past nearly anyone could contribute to Wikipedia, physicians have questioned the reliability of medical entries on that site.[8]
- **Know the Boundaries:** One database service doesn't have it all. For example, you might find full text articles from *The New York Times* on one service, from *The Wall Street Journal* on another, and from *The Los Angeles Times* on yet another, but no service carrying all three.
- **Find the Right Words**: You have to know which keywords (search words) to use when searching a database for a topic.
- **History Is Limited**: Most public databases have information going back to 1980, and a few into the 1970s, but this may pose problems if you're trying to research something that happened—or was written about—earlier.

cannot access data from the database. The data dictionary defines the basic organization of the database and contains a list of all tables in the database, the number of records in each file, and the names and types of each field. The data dictionary may also help protect the security of the database by indicating who has the right to access it. Most database management systems keep the data dictionary hidden from users to prevent them from accidentally destroying its contents.

UTILITIES: FOR MAINTAINING THE DATABASE ***DBMS utilities*** **are programs that allow you to maintain the database by creating, editing, and deleting data, records, and files.** The utilities enable you to monitor the types of data being input and to sort your database by key fields, making searching and organizing information much easier.

REPORT GENERATOR: FOR PRODUCING DOCUMENTS **A *report generator* is a program for producing an on-screen or printed document from all or part of a database.** You can specify the format of the report in advance—row headings, column headings, page headers, and so on. With a report generator, even nonexperts can create attractive, readable reports on short notice.

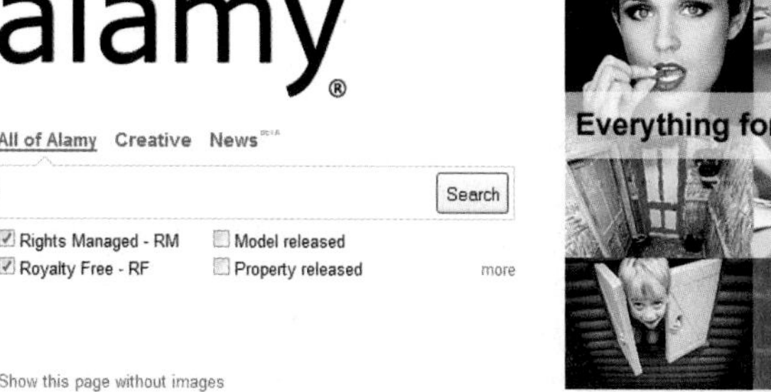

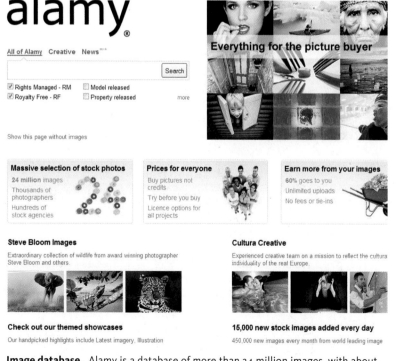

Image database. Alamy is a database of more than 24 million images, with about 450,000 images added every other month. Many of them are available for free to be used in many types of documents and publications.

The Database Administrator

Database administrators use database software to organize, store, and manage data. They identify user needs, set up computer databases, test systems, maintain data integrity, and set up backup and security. They ensure that systems perform as they should and add people to the system as needed.

Large databases are managed by a specialist called a database administrator. **The *database administrator (DBA)* coordinates all related activities and needs for an organization's database,** ensuring the database's recoverability, integrity, security, availability, reliability, and performance. Database administrators determine user access privileges; set standards, guidelines, and control procedures; assist in establishing priorities for requests; prioritize conflicting user needs; and develop user documentation and input procedures. They are also concerned with security—establishing and monitoring ways to prevent unauthorized access and making sure data is backed up and recoverable should a failure occur—and to establish and enforce policies about user privacy.

8.3 Database Models

A database model determines what information is to be contained in a database, how the information will be used, and how the items in the database will be related to one another.

Organizations may use one kind of DBMS for daily processing of transactions (such as sales figures) and then move the processed data into another DBMS that's better suited for random inquiries and analysis. Older DBMS models, introduced in the 1960s, are *hierarchical* and *network*. Commonly used new models are *relational, object-oriented, and multidimensional.* (● *See Panel 8.2.*)

Hierarchical Database

The hierarchical database model was one of the first models to be widely used.

In a *hierarchical database*, fields or records are arranged in related groups resembling a family tree, with child (lower-level) records subordinate to parent (higher-level) records. The parent record at the top of the database is called the *root record* or *root parent*. (● *See Panel 8.3, p. 418.*)

The hierarchical database is the oldest and simplest of the five models. It lent itself well to the tape storage systems used by mainframes in the 1960s–1970s. It is still used in some types of passenger reservation systems, and many banks and insurance companies, as well as government departments and hospitals (for inventory and accounting systems), still use them.

panel 8.2

Timeline: Developments in database technology

4000–1200 BCE	3000 BCE–1400 CE	1086	1621	1642	1666
Inhabitants of the first known civilization in Sumer keep records of commercial transactions on clay tablets	Inca civilization creates the khipu coding system to store the results of mathematical calculations	Domesday Book: William I orders a survey of England to assess value for taxing purposes	Slide rule invented (Edmund Gunther)	First mechanical adding machine (Blaise Pascal)	First mechanical calculator that can add and subtract (Samuel Morland)

Requisition Number:	DY8352
Job Title:	Database Administrator
Location:	Chicago, IL - O'Hare
City:	Chicago
State:	Illinois
Country:	US
Description:	Welcome to the new Allscripts, formed through the merger of Allscripts and Eclipsys! • Our Mission is to be the most trusted provider of innovative solutions that empower all stakeholders across the healthcare continuum to deliver world-class outcomes. • Our Vision is a connected community of health. With the largest connected community of clients in healthcare, Allscripts is able to deliver an integrated platform of clinical, financial, connectivity and information solutions to facilitate enhanced collaboration and exchange of critical patient information. Allscripts offers exciting new career opportunities in various locations throughout the U.S. We are passionate about our mission to improve healthcare. We work to make a difference and this is an exciting time to join us! We are currently seeking talented, bright and hard working individuals with a proven track record of success. We are currently recruiting for a Database Administrator. The Enterprise solutions SWAT team is seeking a bright, energetic, and process driven Database Programmer to join our team. Overview: The SWAT team is responsible for the continued Level 3 support of all Enterprise applications for existing releases. Responsibilities also include providing occasional off-cycle enhancements and support for the release currently in development. The ideal candidate must have proven experience in data analysis, database design, SQL programming, ability to program in Visual Basic and C# is ideal. A strong background programming on SQL and/or Oracle databases would be preferred. The candidate must have excellent organization and communication skills. Ability and flexibility to get things done is a must! Responsibilities • Provide Level 3 support for technical issues in the Enterprise applications. This includes working very closely with the Level 2 support team. • Implementation of new features into the Enterprise product
Job Requirements:	Database Skills • A comprehensive understanding of SQL Server 2000 and 2005. Understanding of Oracle databases would also be acceptable. • A understanding of relational database design, data modeling, and stored procedures. • Experience in writing optimized queries, stored procedures, and triggers. • Tuning for performance of existing stored procedures and reports. • Physical design and implementation of databases a plus Other Requirements • Previous experience supporting managing a customer database, marketing data, and associated queries and analysis is a plus • Excellent written and verbal communications skills required to be able to explain technical concepts to non-technical audiences. • Ability to work in a fast paced team environment and meet deadlines. Education A Bachelor's degree in Computer Science, Information Systems, Software Engineering or other related scientific or technical discipline is required. Professional certification may be substituted.

Job listing for a database administrator (DBA) Here is an example of the requirements for a DBA (from Allscripts). (SQL is a database query language that we discuss shortly.)

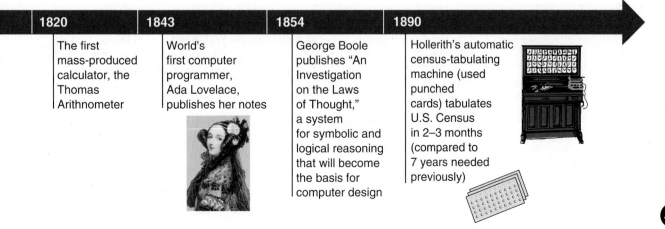

1820 The first mass-produced calculator, the Thomas Arithnometer

1843 World's first computer programmer, Ada Lovelace, publishes her notes

1854 George Boole publishes "An Investigation on the Laws of Thought," a system for symbolic and logical reasoning that will become the basis for computer design

1890 Hollerith's automatic census-tabulating machine (used punched cards) tabulates U.S. Census in 2–3 months (compared to 7 years needed previously)

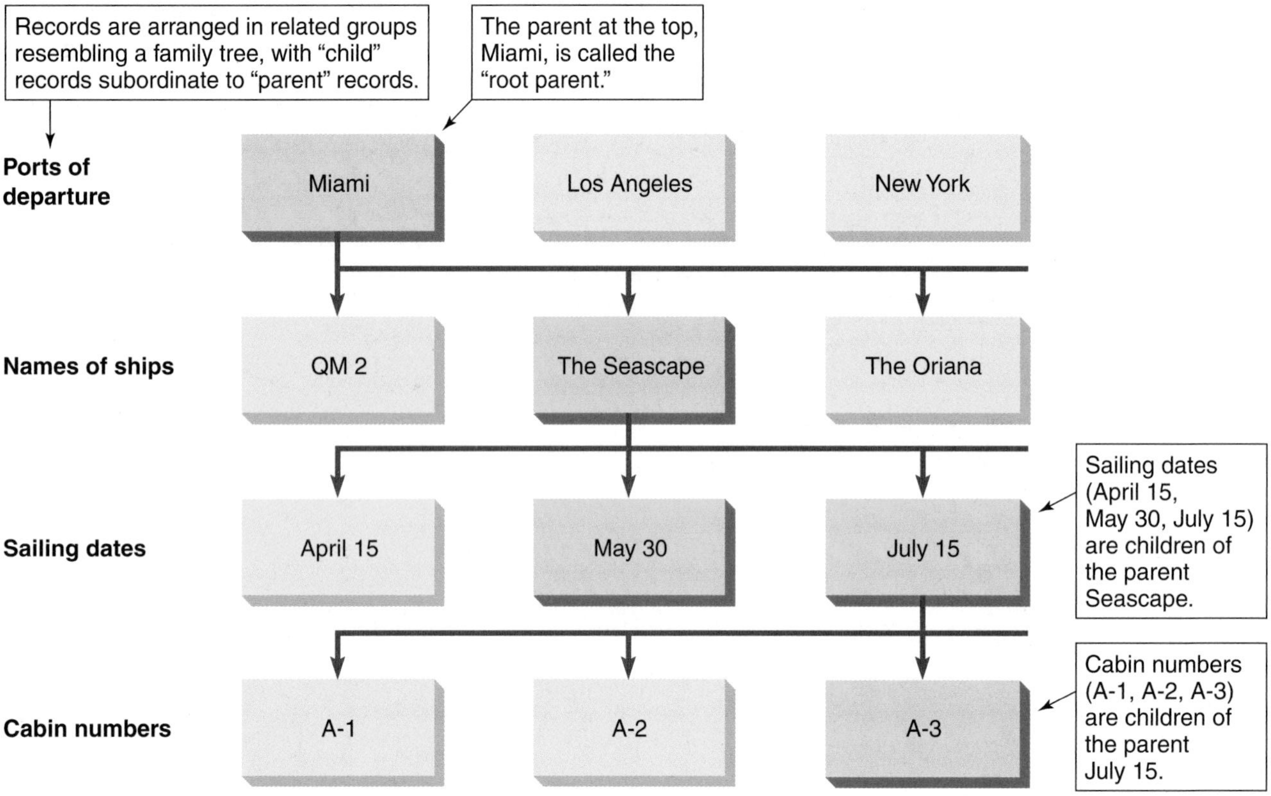

Records are arranged in related groups resembling a family tree, with "child" records subordinate to "parent" records.

The parent at the top, Miami, is called the "root parent."

Ports of departure	Miami	Los Angeles	New York
Names of ships	QM 2	The Seascape	The Oriana
Sailing dates	April 15	May 30	July 15
Cabin numbers	A-1	A-2	A-3

Sailing dates (April 15, May 30, July 15) are children of the parent Seascape.

Cabin numbers (A-1, A-2, A-3) are children of the parent July 15.

panel 8.3

Hierarchical database

Example of a cruise ship reservation system

In hierarchical databases, accessing or updating data is very fast, because the relationships have been predefined. However, because the structure must be defined in advance, it is quite rigid. There can be only one parent per child, and no relationships among the child records are possible. Moreover, adding new fields to database records requires that the entire database be redefined. A new database model was needed to address the problems of data redundancy and complex data relationships.

Network Database

The network database model was created to represent a more complex data relationship effectively, improve database performance, and impose a database standard.

The *network database* was in part developed to solve some of the problems of the hierarchical database model. A network database is similar to a

1960	1961	1962	1967	1967–1968	1969	1970
Evolution of the database concept	Prototype of first DBMS—IBM developed hierarchical model	Stanford and Purdue Universities establish the first departments of computer science	Hand-held calculator 	National Crime Information Center (NCIC) goes online with 95,000 pieces of information in five databases, handling 2 million transactions in its first year	ARPANet established, led to Internet	Micro-processor chips come into use; floppy disk introduced for storing data; E.F. Codd develops the relational database, which evolved into IBM's System R project, which in turn evolved into SQL 

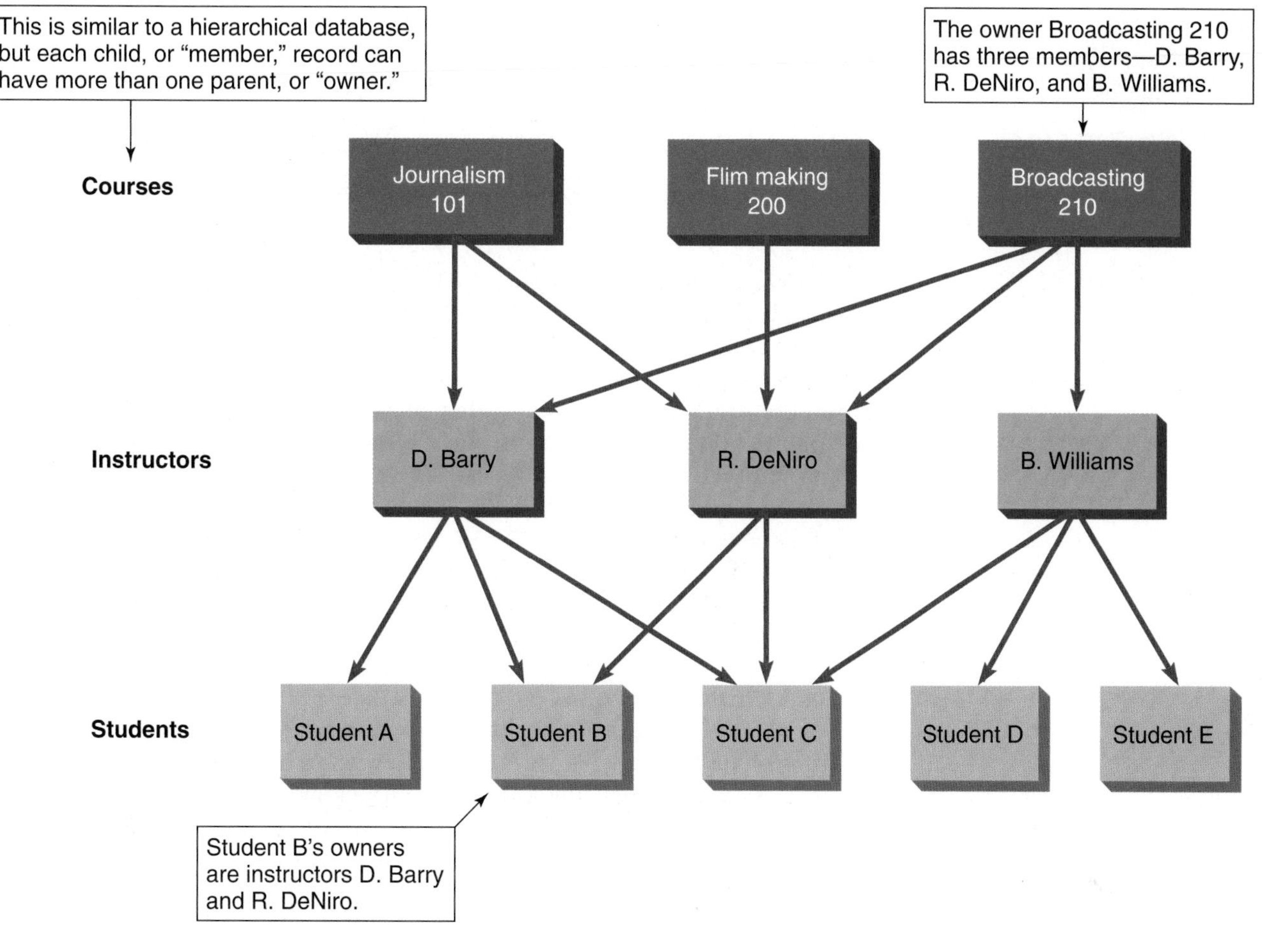
This is similar to a hierarchical database, but each child, or "member," record can have more than one parent, or "owner."
The owner Broadcasting 210 has three members—D. Barry, R. DeNiro, and B. Williams.
Courses
Journalism 101
Flim making 200
Broadcasting 210
Instructors
D. Barry
R. DeNiro
B. Williams
Students
Student A
Student B
Student C
Student D
Student E
Student B's owners are instructors D. Barry and R. DeNiro.

hierarchical database, but each child record can have more than one parent record. (● *See Panel 8.4.*) Thus, a child record, which in network database terminology is called a *member,* may be reached through more than one parent, which is called an *owner*.

panel 8.4

Network database

Example of college class-scheduling system

Established in 1971, and also used principally with mainframes, the network database is more flexible than the hierarchical arrangement, because different relationships may be established between different branches of data. However, it still requires that the structure be defined in advance, and, as with the hierarchical model, the user must be familiar with the structure of the database. Moreover, there are limits to the number of possible links among records, and to examine a field one must retrieve the entire record.

1971	1975	1976	1976	1978	1980	1981
First pocket calculator; all U.S. states and Washington, D.C. can access NCIC criminal data; network database model	First micro-computer (MITS Altair 8800)	Queen Elizabeth sends the first royal email	Apple I computer (first personal computer sold in assembled form)	Introduction of SQL (Structured Query Language); publication of OSI model by the International Standards Organization	dBASE II, the first database program for personal computers; during the 1980s, the hierarchical and network database models fade into the background and the relational model becomes popular	IBM introduces personal computer

Who Was E. F. Codd?

To learn about him and others who influenced database technology, go to:

www.ida.liu.se/~juhta/publications/famous_cs_related_to_iislab.pdf

Although the network database was an improvement over the hierarchical database, some people in the database community believed there had to be a better way to manage large amounts of data.

Relational Database

The relational database model grew out of the hierarchical and network database models.

The **relational database** was born in 1970 when E. F. Codd, a researcher at IBM, wrote a paper outlining the model. Since then, relational databases grew in popularity in the 1980s to become the standard today. More flexible than hierarchical and network database models, the ***relational database*** **relates, or connects, data in different tables of rows and columns through the use of primary keys, or common data elements;** the tables are also called relations—tables of related data. *(• See Panel 8.5.)* The data in different tables can be assembled and reassembled in many different ways without having to reorganize the database tables.

Examples of relational microcomputer DBMS programs are Access and QuickBase. Examples of relational models used on larger computer systems are Oracle, Informix, MS SQL Server, and Sybase.

HOW A RELATIONAL DATABASE WORKS In the relational database, there are no access paths down through a hierarchy. Instead, data elements are stored in different tables made up of rows and columns. In database terminology, the tables are called *relations* (files), the rows are called *tuples* (records), and the columns are called *attributes* (fields). Whereas in the hierarchical and network database models data is arranged according to physical address (location in storage), in the relational model data is arranged logically, by content. Hence, the physical order of the records or fields in a table is completely immaterial. Each record in the table is identified by a field—the primary key—that contains a unique value. These two characteristics allow the data in a relational database to exist independently of the way it is physically stored on the computer. Thus, unlike with the older models, a user is not required to know the physical location of a record in order to retrieve its data. And a database search does not have to go through an entire string of data before reaching the wanted data.

A typical large database, such as Amazon.com's, contains hundreds or thousands of tables all used together to quickly find the exact information needed at any given time.

Relational databases are created using a special computer language, *structured query language (SQL)*, that is the standard for database interoperability. SQL is the foundation for all of the popular database applications available today, from Access to Oracle.

1984	1985	1990s	1994	2003	2006	2008	2011
Apple Macintosh; first personal laser printer; release of Ashton-Tate dBase III	Object-oriented database model	Development of the multi-dimensional database	Apple and IBM introduce PCs with full-motion video built in; wireless data transmission for small portable computers; web browser first invented	Human Genome Project completes mapping all 90,000 or so genes for massive database	Google claims a searchable database of 25 billion web pages	Google reaches 1 trillion searchable pages	World's largest database = U.S. Library of Congress; #2 = Amazon.com; #3 = ChoicePoint; #4 = Sprint; #5 = Google

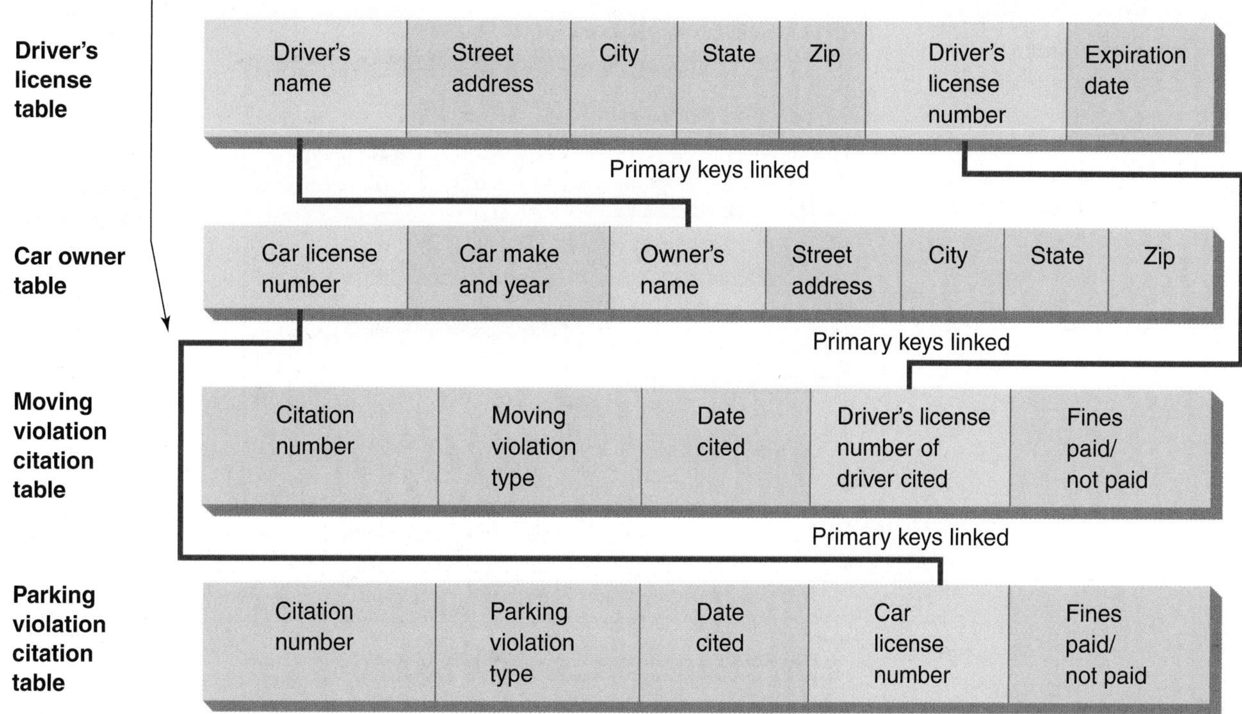

panel 8.5

Relational database

Example of a state department of motor vehicles database

USING STRUCTURED QUERY LANGUAGE To retrieve data in a relational database, you specify the appropriate fields and the tables to which they belong in a query to the database, using a query language. ***Structured query language* (*SQL*, pronounced "sequel") is the standard query language used to create, modify, maintain, and query relational databases.** The three components of a basic SQL query are the SELECT . . . FROM statement, the WHERE clause, and the ORDER BY clause. The fields used in the query are specified with SELECT, and the tables to which they belong are specified with FROM. Selection criteria are determined by WHERE, and the query results can be sorted in any sequence with ORDER.

Most popular database programs provide a graphical query-building tool, so the user does not need to have a thorough knowledge of SQL. (• *See Panel 8.6, next page.)*

Here is an example of a SQL query:

```
SELECT PRODUCT-NUMBER, PRODUCT-NAME
FROM PRODUCT
WHERE PRICE < 100.00
ORDERBY PRODUCT-NAME;
```

This query selects all records in the product file for products that cost less than $100.00 and displays the selected records alphabetically according to product name and including the product number—for example:

C-50	Chair
A-34	Mirror
D-168	Table

QUERY BY EXAMPLE One feature of most query languages is query by example. Often a user will seek information in a database by describing a procedure for finding it. However, in ***query by example (QBE)*, the user asks for information in a database by using a sample record form, or table, to define the qualifications he or she wants for selected records;** in other words, the user fills in a form. (• *See Panel 8.7, next page.)*

panel 8.6

Database queries: SQL

Query Wizard

Access's Query Wizard will easily assist you in creating a select query.

Query Wizard

Access' Query Wizard will easily assist you to begin creating a select query.

- Click the **Create query by using wizard** icon in the database window to have Access step you through the process of creating a query.

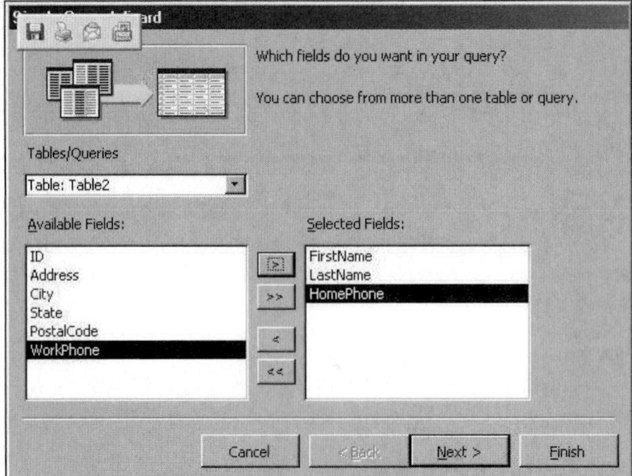

- From the first window, select fields that will be included in the query by first selecting the table from the drop-down **Tables/Queries** menu. Select the fields by clicking the > button to move the field from the Available Fields list to Selected Fields. Click the double arrow button >> to move all of the fields to Selected Fields. Select another table or query to choose from more fields and repeat the process of moving them to the Selected Fields box. Click **Next** > when all of the fields have been selected.

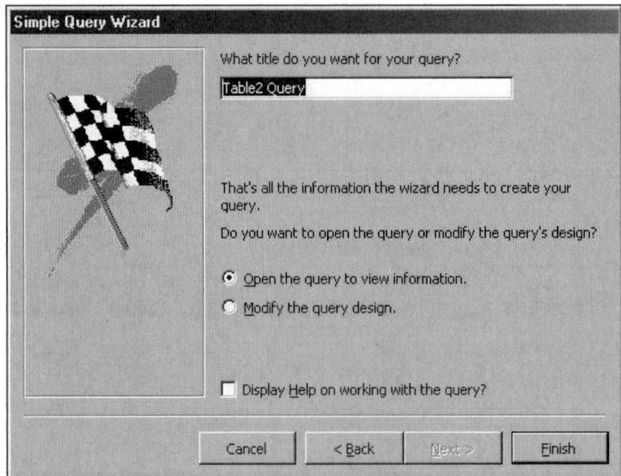

- On the next window, enter the name for the query and click **Finish**.

panel 8.7

Database queries: QBE

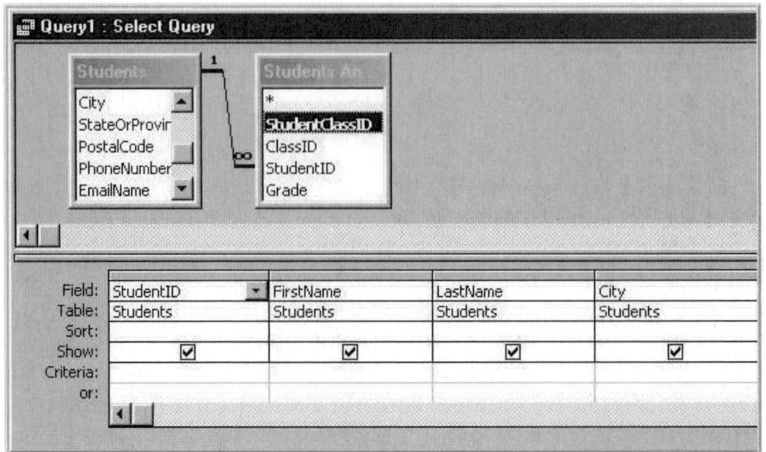

For example, a university's database of its student-loan records might have the column headings (field names) NAME, ADDRESS, CITY, STATE, ZIP, AMOUNT OWED. When you use the QBE method, the database would display an empty record with these column headings. You would then type in the search conditions that you want in the appropriate columns.

Thus, if you wanted to find all Beverly Hills, California, students with a loan balance due of $3,000 or more, you would type *BEVERLY HILLS* in the CITY column, *CA* in the STATE column, and *>=3000* ("greater than or equal to $3,000") in the AMOUNT OWED column.

Some DBMSs, such as Symantec's Q&A, use natural language interfaces, which allow users to make queries in any spoken language, such as English. With this software, you could ask your questions—either typing or speaking (if the system has voice recognition)—in a natural way, such as "How many sales reps sold more than one million dollars' worth of books in the Western Region in January?"

Database technology is crucial to managing inventory in large warehouses.

Object-Oriented Database

An object-oriented database management system supports the modeling and creation of data as objects.

Traditional database models, including the relational model, still work well in traditional business situations. However, they fall short in areas such as engineering design and manufacturing, scientific experiments, telecommunications, geographic information systems, and multimedia. The object-oriented database model was developed to meet the needs of these applications. **An *object-oriented database* uses "objects," software written in small, reusable chunks, as elements within database files.** An *object* consists of (1) data in any form, including text, numbers, graphics, audio, and video, and (2) instructions on the action to be taken on the data. In this kind of DBMS the operations carried out on information items (data objects) are considered part of their definition. Examples of object-oriented databases are FastObjects, GemStone, Objectivity DB, Jasmine Object Database, and KE Texpress. Many high-tech companies exist that can create custom databases.

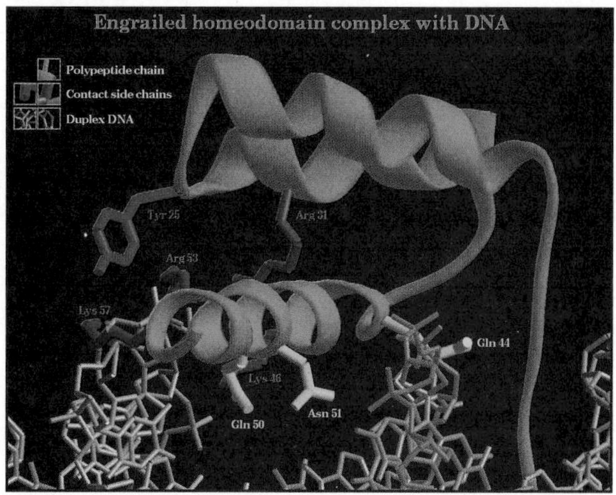

Computer-generated model of DNA; it was constructed from data in a multimedia database.

An object-oriented database is a *multimedia database*; it can store more types of data than a relational database can. For example, an object-oriented student database might contain each student's photograph, a "sound bite" of his or her voice, and even a short piece of video, in addition to grades and personal data. Moreover, the object would store operations, called *methods,* the programs that objects use to process themselves. For example, these programs might indicate how to calculate the student's grade-point average or how to display or print the student's record.

TYPES OF OBJECT-ORIENTED DATABASES One type of object-oriented database is a *hypertext database,* or *web database,* which contains text links to other documents. Another type is a *hypermedia database,* which contains these links as well as graphics, sound, and video. These two types of object-oriented databases, which are created by software such as Adobe ColdFusion, are accessible via the web.

In addition, companies such as Microsoft, IBM, Informix, Sybase, and Oracle have developed *object-relational,* or *enhanced-relational,* database models. Examples are DB2, Cloudscape, ASE, Sybase IQ, SQL Anywhere, and Oracle. These handle both hierarchical and network data (structured data) and relational and object-oriented data.

Multidimensional Database

A multidimensional database (MDB) is a type of database that is optimized for data warehouse and online analytical processing applications.

The multidimensional database was developed during the 1990s for use when the purpose is to analyze data rather than perform online transactions. **A *multidimensional database (MDB)* models data as facts, dimensions, or numerical measures for use in the interactive analysis of large amounts of data for decision-making purposes.** Multidimensional databases are frequently created using input from existing relational databases. Examples are InterSystems Caché, ContourCube, and Cognos PowerPlay.

A multidimensional database uses the idea of a cube to represent the dimensions of data available to a user, using up to four dimensions. *(• See Panel 8.8.)* For example, "sales" could be viewed in the dimensions of (1) product model, (2) geography, (3) time, or (4) some additional dimension. In this case, "sales" is known as the main attribute (or measure) of the data cube and the other dimensions are seen as "feature" attributes.

Unlike relational databases, which often require SELECT . . . FROM and other types of SQL queries to provide information, multidimensional databases allow users to ask questions in more colloquial English, such as "How many type Z dog leashes have been sold in New Jersey so far this year?" The

more info!

Cool, Clear Water?

The Environmental Protection Agency uses data on drinking water to help manage environmental programs. For public access to EPA databases, go to:

www.epa.gov/safewater/databases.html

panel 8.8

Multidimensional database cube

Sample cube capturing sales data. Data cubes support viewing of up to four dimensions simultaneously.

Sample sales spreadsheet

Product	Number of purchases by city			
	Aalborg	Copenhagen	Los Angeles	New York City
Milk	123	555	145	5,001
Bread	102	250	54	2,010
Jeans	20	89	32	345
Light bulbs	22	213	32	9,450

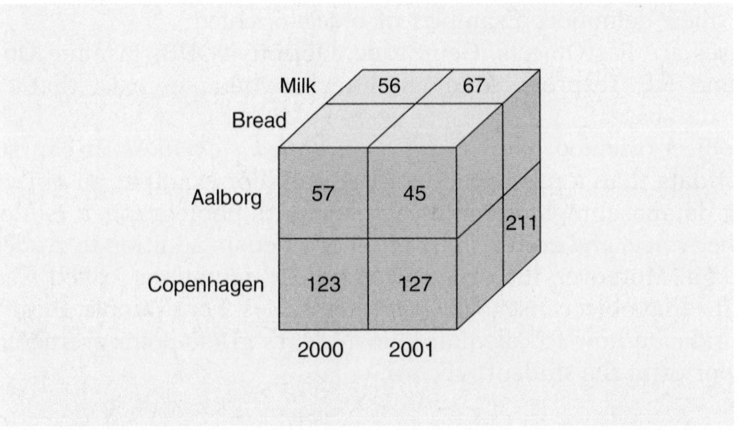

Sample cube capturing sales data. Data cubes support viewing of up to four dimensions simultaneously. In this case, the cube generalizes the spreadsheet from the table to three dimensions—product, city, year.

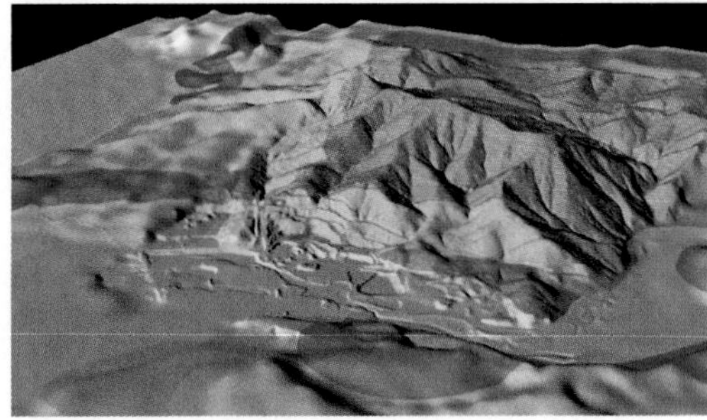

(*Left*) Geological multimedia databases are used in the mining industry. (*Right*) A weather map generated from a multimedia meteorological database.

means for doing so is *online analytical processing (OLAP) software,* which can quickly provide answers to complex database queries. OLAP software is used in business reporting for sales, marketing, management reporting, trend analysis, and similar areas. An OLAP application that accesses data from a multidimensional database is known as a *MOLAP (multidimensional OLAP)* application.

8.4 Data Mining

Data mining (DM) is sorting through data to identify patterns and establish relationships, analyzing data from different perspectives and summarizing it into useful information.

A personal database, such as the address list of friends you have on your microcomputer, is generally small. But some databases are almost unimaginably vast, involving records for millions of households and trillions of bytes of data. Some record-keeping activities require the use of so-called massively parallel database computers that cost $1 million or more. "These machines gang together scores or even hundreds of the fastest microprocessors around," says one description, "giving them the oomph to respond in minutes to complex database queries."[9]

These large-scale efforts go under the name "data mining." ***Data mining (DM)* is the computer-assisted process of sifting through and analyzing vast amounts of data in order to extract hidden patterns and meaning and to discover new knowledge.** The purpose of DM is to describe past trends and predict future trends. Thus, data-mining tools might sift through a company's immense collections of customer, marketing, production, and financial data and identify what's worth noting and what's not. Data-mining techniques are used in many research areas, including mathematics, cybernetics, genetics, and marketing.

The Process of Data Mining

Data mining prepares data for a data warehouse.

In data mining, data is acquired and prepared for what is known as a "data warehouse" through the following steps. (● *See Panel 8.9, next page.*)

1. DATA SOURCES Data may come from a number of sources: (a) point-of-sale transactions in files (flat files) managed by file management systems on mainframes, (b) databases of all kinds, and (c) other—for example, news articles transmitted over newswires or online sources such as the internet. To the mix may also be added (d) data from data warehouses, as we describe.

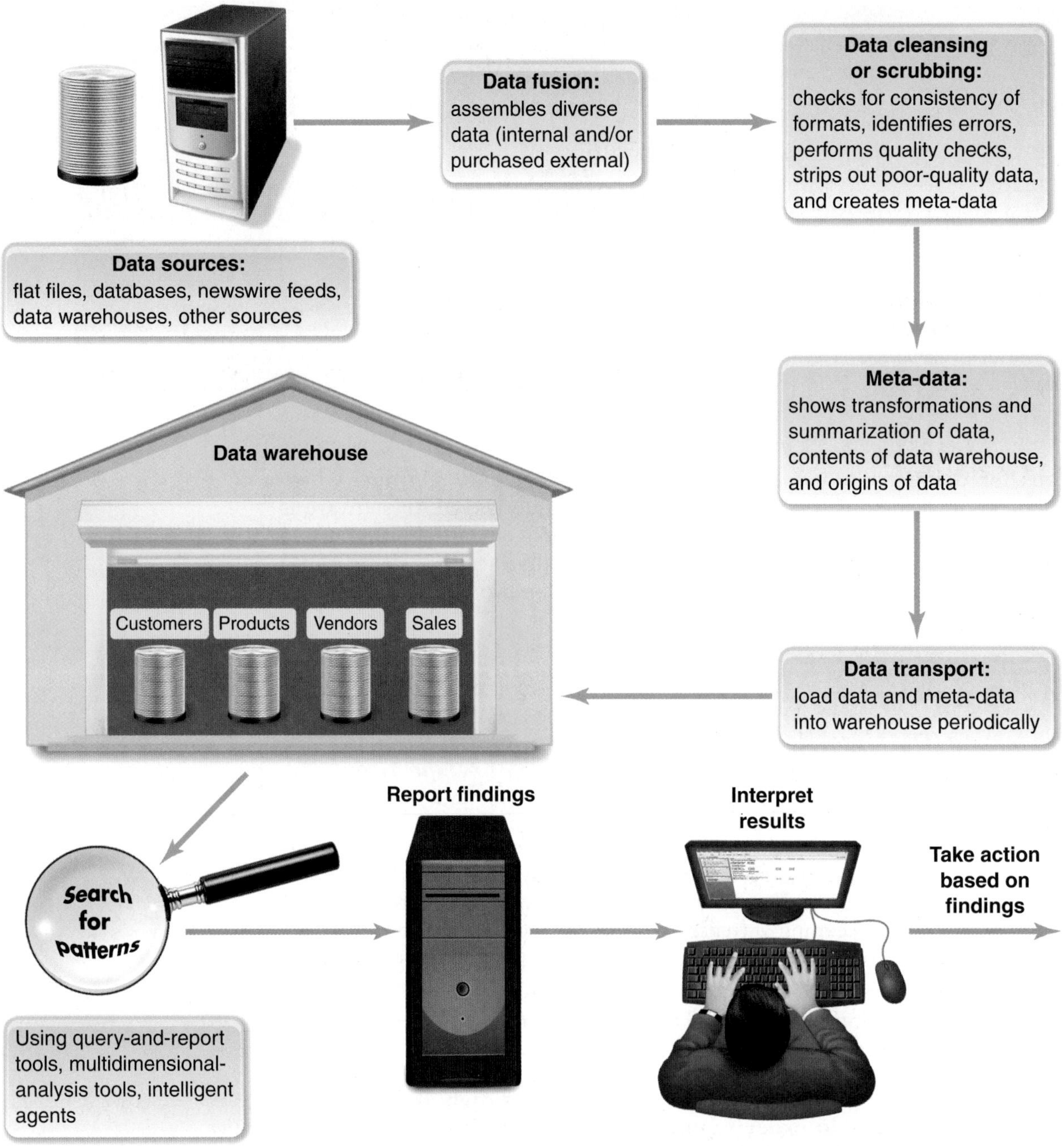

Data sources: flat files, databases, newswire feeds, data warehouses, other sources

Data fusion: assembles diverse data (internal and/or purchased external)

Data cleansing or scrubbing: checks for consistency of formats, identifies errors, performs quality checks, strips out poor-quality data, and creates meta-data

Meta-data: shows transformations and summarization of data, contents of data warehouse, and origins of data

Data transport: load data and meta-data into warehouse periodically

Data warehouse

Customers | Products | Vendors | Sales

Search for Patterns

Using query-and-report tools, multidimensional-analysis tools, intelligent agents

Report findings

Interpret results

Take action based on findings

panel 8.9

The data-mining process

Database of Culturally Significant Plants

What are "culturally significant plants"? Go to:

http://plants.usda.gov/java/factSheet

2. DATA FUSION & CLEANSING Data from diverse sources, whether from inside the company (internal data) or purchased from outside the company (external data), must be fused together and then put through a process known as *data cleansing,* or *scrubbing*. Even if the data comes from just one source, such as one company's mainframe, the data may be of poor quality, full of errors and inconsistencies. Therefore, for data mining to produce accurate results, the source data has to be "scrubbed"—that is, cleaned of errors and checked for consistency of formats.

3. DATA & META-DATA The cleansing process yields both the cleaned-up data and a variation of it called meta-data. *Meta-data* is essentially data about data; it describes how and when and by whom a particular set of data was collected and how the data is formatted. (The data in a data dictionary, for example, is meta-data.)

Meta-data is essential for understanding information stored in data warehouses. Meta-data shows the origins of the data, the transformations it has undergone, and summary information about it, which makes it more useful than the cleansed but unintegrated, unsummarized data. The meta-data also describes the contents of the data warehouse.

4. DATA TRANSPORT TO THE DATA WAREHOUSE Both the data and the meta-data are sent to the data warehouse. **A *data warehouse* is a special database of cleaned-up data and meta-data.** It is a replica, or close reproduction, of a mainframe's data.

The data warehouse is stored on disk using storage technology such as RAID (redundant arrays of independent disks). Small data warehouses may hold 100 gigabytes of data or less; large ones may store terabytes of data.

MINING THE DATA: SEARCHING FOR PATTERNS & INTERPRETING THE RESULTS Data in the warehouse is usually analyzed—or mined—using one of two popular *algorithms,* or step-by-step problem-solving procedures:

- **Regression analysis:** Basically, *regression analysis* takes a particular set of numerical data and develops a mathematical formula that fits the data. This formula is then applied to new sets of data of the same type to predict future situations.
- **Classification analysis:** *Classification analysis* is a statistics pattern-recognition process that is applied to data sets with more than just numerical data.

SOME APPLICATIONS OF DATA MINING Some short-term payoffs from data mining can be dramatic. One telephone company, for instance, mined its existing billing data to identify 10,000 supposedly "residential" customers who spent more than $1,000 a month on their phone bills. When it looked more closely, the company found that these customers were really small businesses trying to avoid paying the more expensive business rates for their telephone service.[10] The Internal Revenue Service has a program designed to catch tax cheaters by locating inconsistencies between mortgage payments and income.[11] However, the payoffs in the long term could be truly astonishing. Sifting subatomic-particle information may reveal new insights into the nature of the universe. Mining medical research data may reveal new knowledge about diseases. Text-mining programs, which build on data-mining principles, may scour 250,000 pages an hour of scholarly articles, automatically categorizing information, making links between unconnected documents, and providing visual maps.[12]

Some other applications of data mining are as follows.[13]

- *Data Mining & Cancer Detection*—The important goal in cancer detection and treatment is to understand the relationship between variations in human DNA sequences and variability in disease susceptibility. The data-mining technique used to perform this task is known as *multifactor dimensionality reduction.*
- *Sports*—Brian James, coach of the Toronto Raptors, has used data mining to "rack and stack" his team against the rest of the National Basketball Association (NBA). A coach in the U.S. Gymnastics Federation used a DM tool called *IDIS* (Iowa Drug Information Service) to discover what long-term factors contributed to athletes' performance, so as to know what problems to treat early on. Miami Heat officials contend that data mining delivers an even more effective targeted audience than traditional advertising or traditional mass-media marketing.[14]
- *Marketing* —Marketers use DM tools to mine point-of-sale databases of retail stores, which contain facts (such as prices, quantities sold, and dates

of sale) for thousands of products in hundreds of geographic areas. By understanding customer preferences and buying patterns, marketers hope to target consumers' individual needs.

One way that grocery stores create profiles is by the use of data mining. Data mining is a process that is used to predict future behaviors and trends by discerning patterns and relationships from large amounts of warehoused raw (from disparate sources) data through the use of statistics and other mathematical techniques.

IDIS & IDIN

The University of Iowa's Division of Drug Information Service, within the College of Pharmacy, offers IDIS, a bibliographic database, and IDIN (Iowa Drug Information Network), which provides drug information. Go to:

www.uiowa.edu/~idis

- *Health*—A Los Angeles hospital used IDIS to see what subtle factors affect success and failure in back surgery. Another system helps health care organizations pinpoint groups whose costs are likely to increase in the near future, so that medical interventions can be made. Researchers have used data mining to generate treatment plans to handle the error and complexity of treatment process for healthcare providers.
- *Science*—DM techniques are being employed to find new patterns in genetic data, molecular structures, global climate changes, and more. For instance, one DM tool (called SKICAT, for "SKy Image CATaloging") has been used to catalog more than 50 million galaxies. Given the release of the Galaxy Zoo Data Release 1 researchers have begun to explore the myriad ways that one can use the most accurate database of galaxy morphology ever compiled.[15]
- *Counterterrorism*—The U.S. federal government has used data-mining tools to look through databases for clues on terrorism. Counterterrorism experts analyze records "on travel habits, calling patterns, email use, financial transactions, and other data to pinpoint possible terrorist activity," according to one report, although there is some question as to how effective the effort is.[16]
- *Sentiment Analysis*—Companies concerned about how online opinion among users of blogs and social networks can make or break their products in the marketplace have used "sentiment analysis" tools to analyze what is being said online.[17]
- *Exploring the "Deep Web"*—In summer 2008 Google's search engine added the one-trillionth address to the list of addresses it knows about—but that represents only a fraction of the entire World Wide Web, and no one search engine is capable of reaching it all. Beyond Google's trillion pages, says one report, is a vaster Web of hidden data: "financial information, shopping catalogs, flight schedules, medical research, and all kinds of other material stored in databases that remains largely invisible to search engines."[18] New search tools are now being devised to match searches with the databases most likely to produce the relevant information—this is called data mining.

8.5 DATABASES & THE DIGITAL ECONOMY: E-Commerce & E-Business

"Digital economy" refers to the marketplace that exists on the Internet.

At one time there was a difference between the Old Economy and the New Economy. The first consisted of traditional companies—car makers, pharmaceuticals, retailers, publishers. The second consisted of computer, telecommunications, and Internet companies (AOL, Amazon, eBay, and a raft of "dot-com" firms). Now, however, most Old Economy companies have absorbed the new Internet-driven technologies, and the differences between the two sectors have dwindled. In other words, most companies are now engaged in *e-business,* using the Internet to facilitate every aspect of running a business. As one article puts it: "At bottom the Internet is a tool that dramatically lowers the cost of communication. That means it can radically alter any industry or activity that depends on the flow of information."[19]

One sign of growth is that the number of Internet host computers has been almost doubling every year. But the mushrooming of computer networks and the booming popularity of the World Wide Web are only the most obvious signs of the digital economy. Behind them lies something equally important: the growth of vast stores of information in databases.

How are databases underpinning the digital economy? Let us consider two aspects: *e-commerce* and *types of e-commerce systems—B2B, B2C,* and *C2C.*

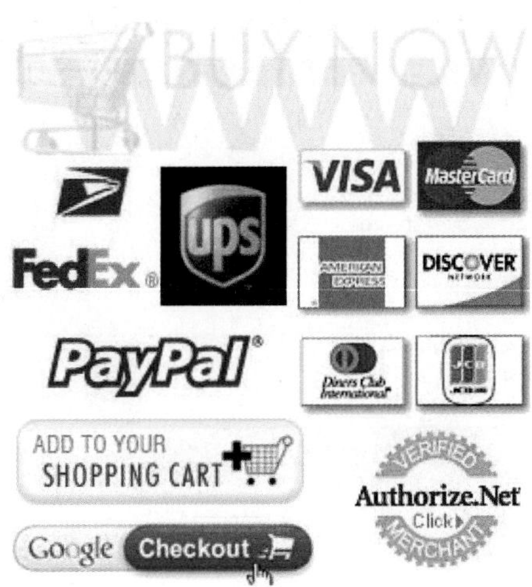

A great many entities support e-commerce (*www.mexabet.biz/articles/article-95.html*).

E-Commerce: Online Buying & Selling

E-commerce refers to online transactions—buying and selling of goods and/or services over the Internet; e-business covers online transactions but also extends to all Internet-based interactions with business partners, suppliers, and customers.

The Internet might have remained the text-based province of academicians and researchers had it not been for the creative contributions of Tim Berners-Lee, whom we introduced in Chapter 2 (p. 65). He was the computer scientist who came up with the coding system (hypertext markup language, or HTML), linkages, and addressing scheme (URLs) that debuted in 1991 as the graphics-laden and multimedia World Wide Web. "It's hard to overstate the impact of the global system he created," states one technology writer. "He took a powerful communications system [the Internet] that only the elite could use, and turned it into a mass medium."[20]

The arrival of the web, aided by the growth and the increasing sophistication of enormous databases, has led to ***e-commerce*, or *electronic commerce*, the buying and selling of products and services through computer networks.** E-commerce is reshaping entire industries and revamping the very notion of what a company is. Indeed, online shopping is growing even faster than the increase in computer use, which has been fueled by the falling price of personal computers.

Two well-known e-firms are Amazon.com, which sells books and many other goods, and priceline.com, which lets you name the price you're willing to pay for airline tickets and hotel rooms. (eBay is considered an online shopping bazaar, or auction place, rather than an online retailer.) Probably the foremost example of e-commerce is Amazon.com.

Comparing Prices at the Local Mall

Some online companies allow you to compare prices in local stores:

www.shoplocal.com

AN EXAMPLE OF E-COMMERCE: AMAZON.COM In 1994, seeing the potential for electronic retailing on the World Wide Web, Jeffrey Bezos left a successful career on Wall Street to launch an online bookstore called Amazon.com. Why the name "Amazon"?

"Earth's biggest river, Earth's biggest bookstore," said Bezos in a 1996 interview. "The Amazon River is ten times as large as the next largest river, which is the Mississippi, in terms of volume of water. Twenty percent of the world's fresh water is in the Amazon River Basin, and we have six times as many titles as the world's largest physical bookstore."[21] A more hardheaded reason is that, according to consumer tests, words starting with "A" show up on search-engine lists first.[22]

Still, Bezos realized that no bookstore with four walls could possibly stock the more than 2.5 million titles that were active and in print. Moreover, he saw that an online bookstore wouldn't have to make the same investment in retail clerks, store real estate, or warehouse space (in the beginning, Amazon.com

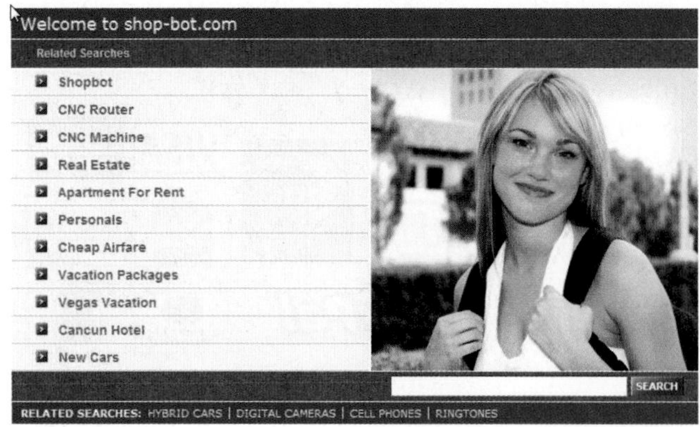

Shop bot

ordered books from the publisher *after* it took the book buyer's order), so it could pass savings along to customers in the form of discounts. In addition, he appreciated that there would be opportunities to obtain demographic information about customers in order to offer personalized services. For example, Amazon could let customers know of books that might be of interest to them. Such personalized attention is difficult for traditional large bookstores. Finally, Bezos saw that there could be a good deal of online interaction: customers could post reviews of books they read and could reach authors by email to provide feedback. All this was made possible on the web by the recording of information on giant databases.

Amazon.com sold its first book in July 1995, and by 2008 was No. 1 in the Internet Retailer Top 500 Guide, with sales of $4.06 billion.[23] (It was still No. 1 in 2010.) What began as Earth's biggest bookstore also has rapidly become Earth's biggest anything store, offering CDs, DVDs, videos, electronics, toys, tools, home furnishings, clothing, prescription drugs, film-processing services, and more. For a long time the company put market share ahead of profits, but now it's focusing on profits.

ONLINE RETAILERS: E-TAILERS Some e-commerce businesses are also known as *e-tailers,* or electronic retailers. The effectiveness of e-tailing was evident as early as 1997, when Dell Computer reported taking multimillion-dollar orders at its website. E-tailing has resulted in the development of *e-tailware,* software tools for creating online catalogs and managing the business connected with doing online retailing. Some e-commerce groups (such as shopping.com and shopzilla) offer price-comparison websites that can quickly compare prices from a number of different e-tailers and link you to them.

Some particularly interesting technologies that have helped online retailers survive are the following:

- **360-degree images:** People might well buy a book or a computer off the web on the basis of a blurry photograph, but a sweater or a sofa? Today zoom technologies allow for close inspection of nearly anything, from the detail on jewelry to the rooms in a house. With technology from iPix, 360-degree images can be created using just two standard photographs.
- **Order tracking:** The average FedEx package is scanned between 15 and 20 times between pickup and delivery, with the location of each package stored in a database. For a long time, FedEx used such order tracking strictly for internal use, but in 1994 the company turned it into a customer-service application—a brilliant marketing stroke. Now all customers can track their orders.
- **Shop bots:** The buying of online wares has also been facilitated by the arrival of shopping robots—*shop bots,* or *trading agents,* concierge programs that help users search the Internet for a particular product or service, then bring up price comparisons, locations, and other information. Examples of shop bots are mySimon, DealTime, PriceGrabber.com, Shopzilla.com, and BookFinder.com.

TYPES OF E-COMMERCE SYSTEMS: B2B, B2C, & C2C Three main types of e-commerce systems are business-to-business (B2B), business-to-consumer (B2C), and consumer-to-consumer (C2C).

- *Business-to-Business (B2B) Systems*—In a ***business-to-business (B2B) system*****, a business sells to other businesses, using the Internet or a**

private network to cut transaction costs and increase efficiencies. Besides selling products, a business might sell advertising, employee training, market research, technical support, banking services, and other business support services.

Online B2B exchanges have been developed to serve a variety of businesses, from manufacturers of steel and airplanes to convenience stores to olive oil producers. B2B exchanges help business by moving beyond pricing mechanisms and encompassing product quality, customer support, credit terms, and shipping reliability, which often count for more than price. The name given to this system is the *business web,* or *b-web,* in which suppliers, distributors, customers, and e-commerce service providers use the Internet for communications and transactions. In addition, b-webs are expected to provide extra revenue from ancillary services, such as financing and logistics. (● *See Panel 8.10.)*

more info!
What Are the World's Largest Databases?
www.focus.com/fyi/operations/10-largest-databases-in-the-world/

None of these innovations is possible without databases and the communications lines connecting them. B2B used to be conducted mostly over leased communications lines; now, however, many B2B businesses use the Internet, an extranet, and/or a virtual private network.

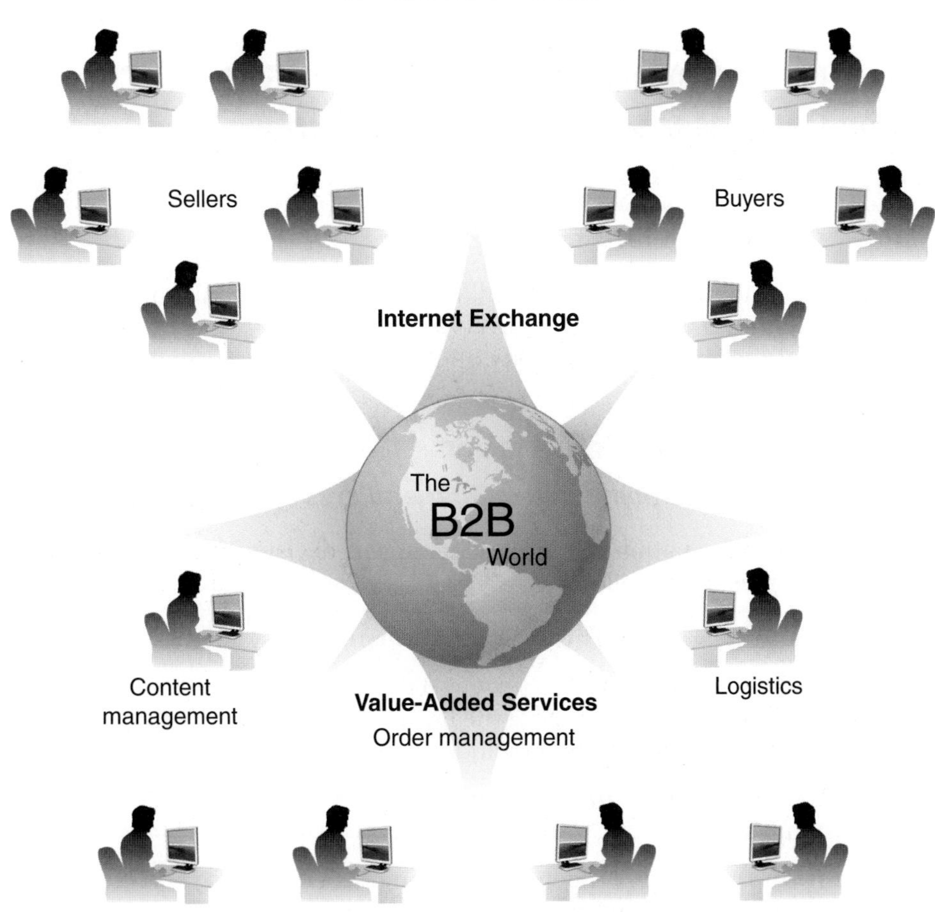

panel 8.10

B2B exchanges

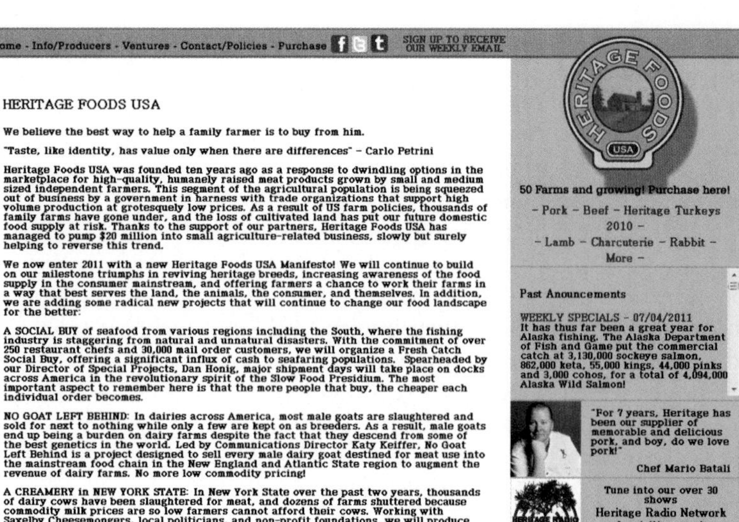

Home - Info/Producers - Ventures - Contact/Policies - Purchase
SIGN UP TO RECEIVE OUR WEEKLY EMAIL
HERITAGE FOODS USA
We believe the best way to help a family farmer is to buy from him.
"Taste, like identity, has value only when there are differences" – Carlo Petrini
Heritage Foods USA was founded ten years ago as a response to dwindling options in the marketplace for high-quality, humanely raised meat products grown by small and medium sized independent farmers. This segment of the agricultural population is being squeezed out of business by a government in harness with trade organizations that support high volume production at grotesquely low prices. As a result of US farm policies, thousands of family farms have gone under, and the loss of cultivated land has put our future domestic food supply at risk. Thanks to the support of our partners, Heritage Foods USA has managed to pump $20 million into small agriculture-related business, slowly but surely helping to reverse this trend.
We now enter 2011 with a new Heritage Foods USA Manifesto! We will continue to build on our milestone triumphs in reviving heritage breeds, increasing awareness of the food supply in the consumer mainstream, and offering farmers a chance to work their farms in a way that best serves the land, the animals, the consumer, and themselves. In addition, we are adding some radical new projects that will continue to change our food landscape for the better:
A SOCIAL BUY of seafood from various regions including the South, where the fishing industry is staggering from natural and unnatural disasters. With the commitment of over 250 restaurant chefs and 30,000 mail order customers, we will organize a Fresh Catch Social Buy, offering a significant influx of cash to seafaring populations. Spearheaded by our Director of Special Projects, Dan Honig, major shipment days will take place on docks across America in the revolutionary spirit of the Slow Food Presidium. The most important aspect to remember here is that the more people that buy, the cheaper each individual order becomes.
NO GOAT LEFT BEHIND: In dairies across America, most male goats are slaughtered and sold for next to nothing while only a few are kept on as breeders. As a result, male goats end up being a burden on dairy farms despite the fact that they descend from some of the best genetics in the world. Led by Communications Director Katy Keiffer, No Goat Left Behind is a project designed to sell every male dairy goat destined for meat use into the mainstream food chain in the New England and Atlantic State region to augment the revenue of dairy farms. No more low commodity pricing!
A CREAMERY in NEW YORK STATE: In New York State over the past two years, thousands of dairy cows have been slaughtered for meat, and dozens of farms shuttered because commodity milk prices are so low farmers cannot afford their cows. Working with Saxelby Cheesemongers, local politicians, and non-profit foundations, we will produce and sell an affordable cheese intended for sandwiches and everyday use, while paying farmers significantly more than commodity pricing for their milk. The goal of this project is that no dairy farmer living close to New York will ever be paid an unfair price for milk.
HERITAGE FOODS USA
50 Farms and growing! Purchase here!
– Pork – Beef – Heritage Turkeys 2010 –
– Lamb – Charcuterie – Rabbit – More –
Past Anouncements
WEEKLY SPECIALS - 07/04/2011
It has thus far been a great year for Alaska fishing. The Alaska Department of Fish and Game put the commercial catch at 3,130,000 sockeye salmon, 862,000 keta, 55,000 kings, 44,000 pinks and 3,000 cohos, for a total of 4,094,000 Alaska Wild Salmon!
"For 7 years, Heritage has been our supplier of memorable and delicious pork, and boy, do we love pork!"
Chef Mario Batali
Tune into our over 30 shows
Heritage Radio Network
by visiting us at
HeritageRadioNetwork.com
phone# 718 - 389 - 0985

A B2C business

- *Business-to-Consumer (B2C) Systems*—In a ***business-to-consumer (B2C) system***, **a business sells goods or services to consumers, or members of the general public.** This kind of e-commerce system essentially removes the middleman and often the need for a physical ("bricks-and-mortar") store. Examples of B2C systems are Amazon.com and BarnesandNoble.com, as well as many financial institutions and the U.S. government.
- *Consumer-to Consumer (C2C) Systems*—In a ***consumer-to-consumer (C2C) system***, **consumers sell goods or services directly to other consumers,** often with the help of a third party, such as eBay, the online auction company. Such intermediaries mediate between consumers who want to buy and sell, taking a small percentage of the seller's profit as a fee. Examples of C2C exchanges are classified ads (such as TradingPost.com), career and job websites (monster.com), social or dating websites (match.com, friendster.com, facebook.com), and online communities (craigslist.org). The advantage of C2C e-commerce is most often the reduced costs and a smaller but profitable customer base. It also gives many small business owners a way to sell their goods without running a costly bricks-and-mortar store.

8.6 INFORMATION SYSTEMS IN ORGANIZATIONS: Using Databases to Help Make Decisions

An information system is a combination of people, hardware, software, communication devices, and databases that processes data and information for a specific purpose.

The data in databases is used to build information, and information—and how it is used—lies at the heart of every organization. Of course, how useful information is depends on the quality of it, as well as the information systems used to distribute it.

The Qualities of Good Information

Having good information is critical to the success of any organization.

In general, all information to support intelligent decision making within an organization must be as follows:

- **Correct and verifiable:** This means information must be accurate and checkable.
- **Complete yet concise:** *Complete* means information must include *all* relevant data. *Concise* means it includes *only* relevant data.
- **Cost effective:** This means the information is efficiently obtained and understandable.
- **Current:** *Current* means timely yet also time sensitive, based on historical, present, or future information needs.
- **Accessible:** This means the information is quickly and easily obtainable.

Information Flows within an Organization

Information flows horizontally between departments and vertically between management levels.

Consider any sizable organization with which you are familiar. Its purpose is to perform a service or deliver a product. If it's nonprofit, for example, it may deliver the service of educating students or the product of food for famine victims. If it's profit-oriented, it may, for example, sell the service of fixing computers or the product of computers themselves. Information—whether computer-based or not—has to flow within an organization in a way that will help managers, and the organization, achieve their goals. To this end, organizations are often structured horizontally and vertically—horizontally to reflect functions and vertically to reflect management levels.

THE HORIZONTAL FLOW OF INFORMATION BETWEEN SIX DEPARTMENTS Depending on the services or products they provide, most organizations have departments that perform six functions: *research and development (R&D), production* (or *operations), marketing and sales, accounting and finance, human resources (personnel),* and *information systems (IS).* (• *See Panel 8.11, next page.)*

- **Research and development:** The research and development (R&D) department does two things: (1) It conducts basic research, relating discoveries to the organization's current or new products. (2) It does product development and tests and modifies new products or services created by researchers. Special software is available to aid in these functions.
- **Production (operations):** The production department makes the product or provides the service. In a manufacturing company, it takes the raw materials and has people or machinery turn them into finished goods. In many cases, this department uses CAD/CAM software and workstations, as well as robots (described on p. 445). In another type of company, this department might manage the purchasing, handle the inventories, and control the flow of goods and services.
- **Marketing and sales:** The marketing department oversees advertising, promotion, and sales. The people in this department plan, price, advertise, promote, package, and distribute the services or goods to customers or clients. The sales reps may use laptop computers, cellphones, wireless email, and faxes in their work while on the road.
- **Accounting and finance:** The accounting and finance department handles all financial matters. It handles cash management, pays bills and taxes, issues paychecks, records payments, makes investments, and compiles financial statements and reports. It also produces financial budgets and forecasts financial performance after receiving information from other departments.
- **Human resources:** The human resources, or personnel, department finds and hires people and administers sick leave and retirement matters. It is also concerned with compensation levels, professional development, employee relations, and government regulations.
- **Information systems (IS):** The IS department manages the organization's computer-based systems and plans for and purchases new ones.

THE VERTICAL FLOW OF INFORMATION BETWEEN MANAGEMENT LEVELS Large organizations traditionally have three levels of management—*strategic management, tactical management,* and *operational management.* These levels can be shown on an *organization chart,* a schematic drawing showing the hierarchy of formal relationships among an organization's employees. Managers on each of the three levels have different levels of responsibility and are therefore required to make different kinds of decisions. *(See Panel 8.11.)*

- **Strategic-level management:** Top managers are concerned with long-range, or strategic, planning and decisions. This top level is headed by the chief executive officer (CEO) along with several vice presidents or managers with such titles as chief financial officer (CFO), chief operating officer (COO), and chief information officer (CIO). *Strategic* decisions are complex decisions rarely based on predetermined routine procedures; they involve the subjective judgment of the decision maker. For instance, strategic decisions relate to how growth should be financed and what new markets should be tackled first. Determining the company's 5-year goals, evaluating future financial resources, and formulating a response to competitors' actions are also strategic decisions.
- **Tactical-level management:** Tactical, or middle-level managers, make tactical decisions to implement the strategic goals of the organization. A *tactical* decision is made without a base of clearly defined informational procedures; it may require detailed analysis and computations. Examples of tactical-level managers are plant manager, division manager, sales manager, branch manager, and director of personnel.
- **Operational-level management:** Operational, or low-level (supervisory level), managers make *operational* decisions—predictable decisions that can be made by following well-defined sets of routine procedures. These managers focus principally on supervising nonmanagement employees, monitoring day-to-day events, and taking corrective action where necessary. An example of an operational-level manager is a warehouse manager in charge of inventory restocking.

Note that, because there are fewer people at the level of top management and many people at the bottom, this management structure resembles a pyramid. It's also a hierarchical structure because most of the power is concentrated at the top.

panel 8.11

Organization chart
The six functional responsibilities are shown on the opposite page at the bottom of the pyramid. The three management levels are shown along the sides.

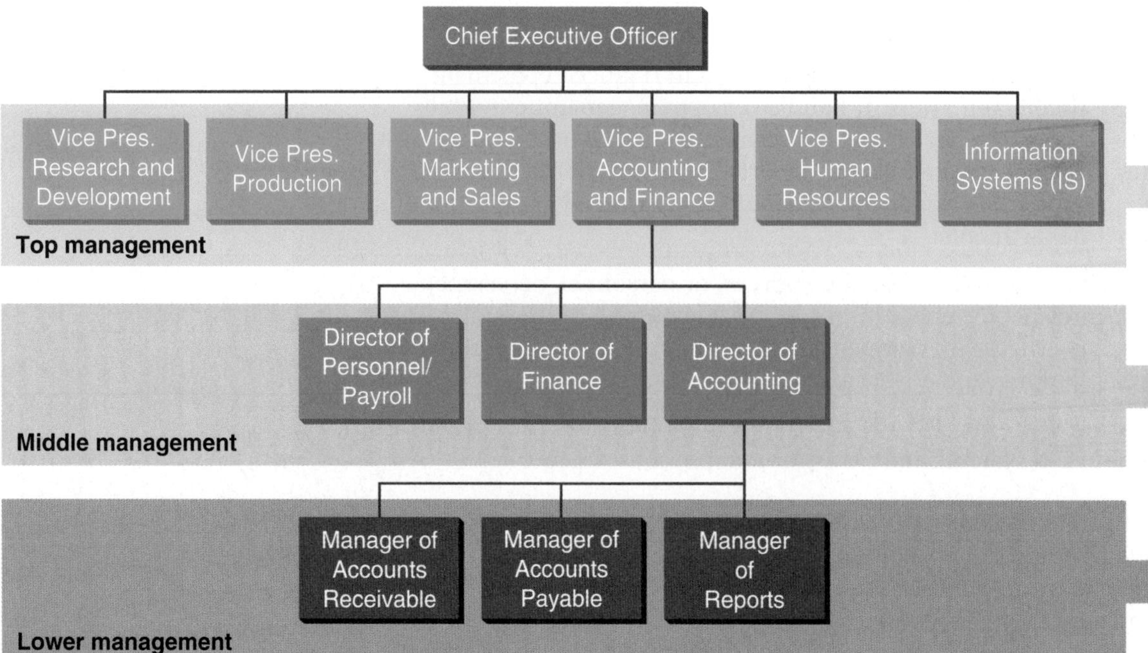

NEW INFORMATION FLOW: THE DECENTRALIZED ORGANIZATION The hierarchical, pyramid-oriented structure is changing in the computer-network era to a decentralized form in which employees are linked to a centralized database. Although the different responsibilities of the various types of managers remain, the pyramid is flattened somewhat owing to increased participation of all employees via computer-enabled systems.

Nowadays, for instance, organizations that have computer networks often use groupware to enable cooperative work by groups of people—what are known as *computer-supported cooperative work (CSCW) systems*. Through the shared use of databases, software, videoconferencing, email, intranets, organization forms and reports, and so on, many people can work together from different locations to manage information.

Computer-Based Information Systems

An information system is a combination of people, hardware, software, communication devices, network, and databases that processes data and information for a specific purpose.

The purpose of a computer-based information system is to provide managers (and various categories of employees) with the appropriate kind of information to help them make decisions. It is used to collect and analyze data from all departments and is designed to provide an organization's management with up-to-date information at any time. There are several types of computer-based information systems, which serve different levels of management:

- Office information systems
- Transaction processing systems

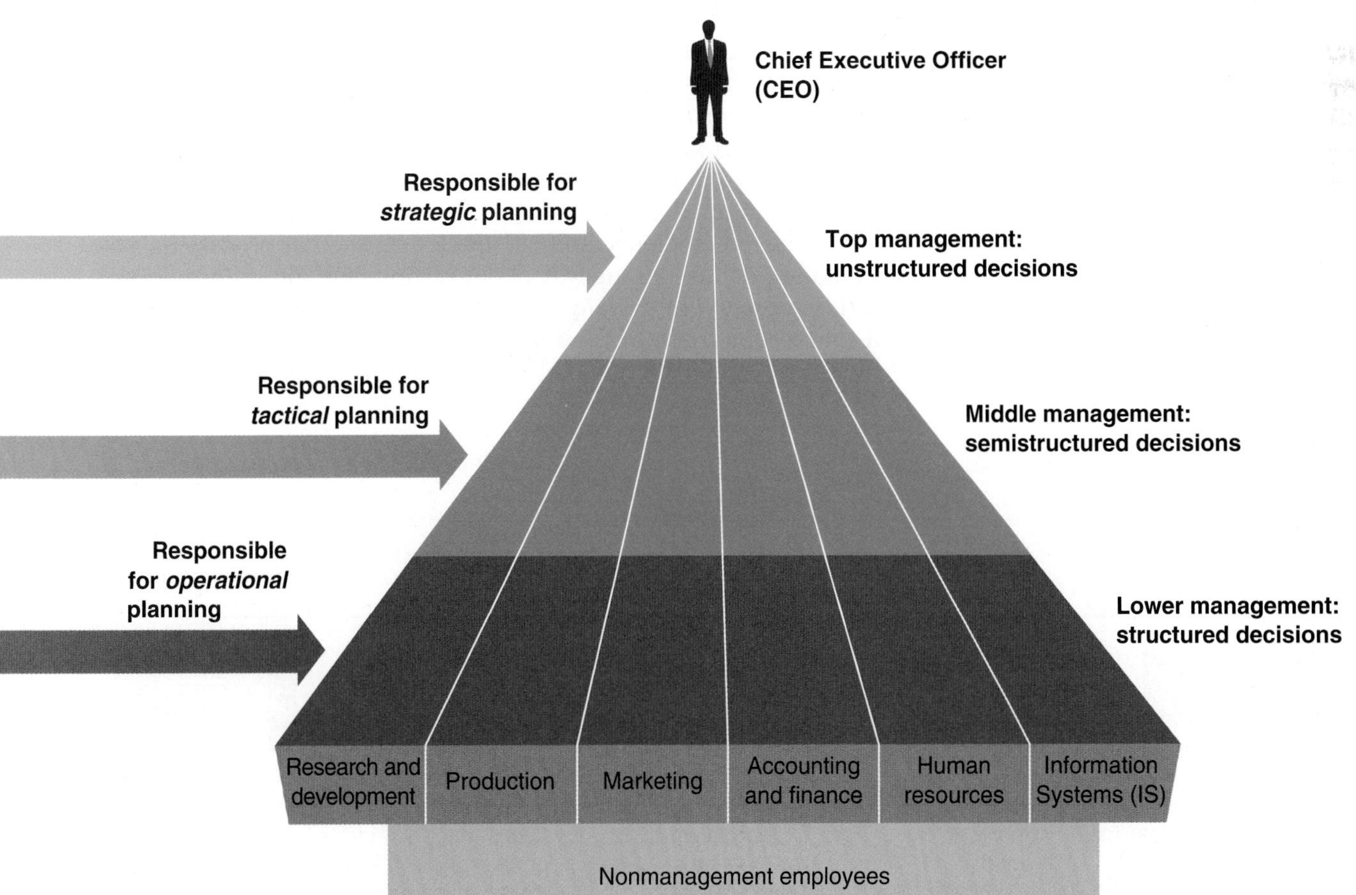

- Management information systems
- Decision support systems
- Executive support systems
- Expert systems

Office Information Systems

Office information systems facilitate communication and collaboration between the members of an organization and between organizations.

***Office information systems (OISs),* also called *office automation systems (OASs),* combine various technologies to reduce the manual labor required in operating an efficient office environment and to increase productivity.** Used throughout all levels of an organization, OIS technologies include fax, voice mail, email, scheduling software, word processing, and desktop publishing, among others. *(● See Panel 8.12.)*

The backbone of an OIS is a network—LAN, intranet, extranet—that connects everything. All office functions—dictation, typing, filing, copying, fax, microfilm and records management, telephone calls and switchboard operations—are candidates for integration into the network.

Transaction Processing Systems

Transaction processing systems are computer-based systems that take transaction-related information that is time sensitive and immediately process it and keep it current.

In most organizations, particularly business organizations, most of what goes on consists largely of structured information known as transactions. A *transaction* is a recorded event having to do with routine business activities. A transaction may be recorded manually or via a computer system and includes everything concerning the product or service in which the organization is engaged: production, distribution, sales, orders. It also includes materials purchased, employees hired, taxes paid, and so on. Today in most organizations, the bulk of such transactions is recorded in a computer-based information system. These systems tend to have clearly defined inputs and outputs, and there is an emphasis on efficiency and accuracy. Transaction processing systems record data but do little in the way of converting data into information.

A *transaction processing system (TPS)* is a computer-based information system that keeps track of the transactions needed to conduct business. The transactions can be handled via *batch processing,* also known as

panel 8.12

Office information systems

The backbone is a network linking these technologies.

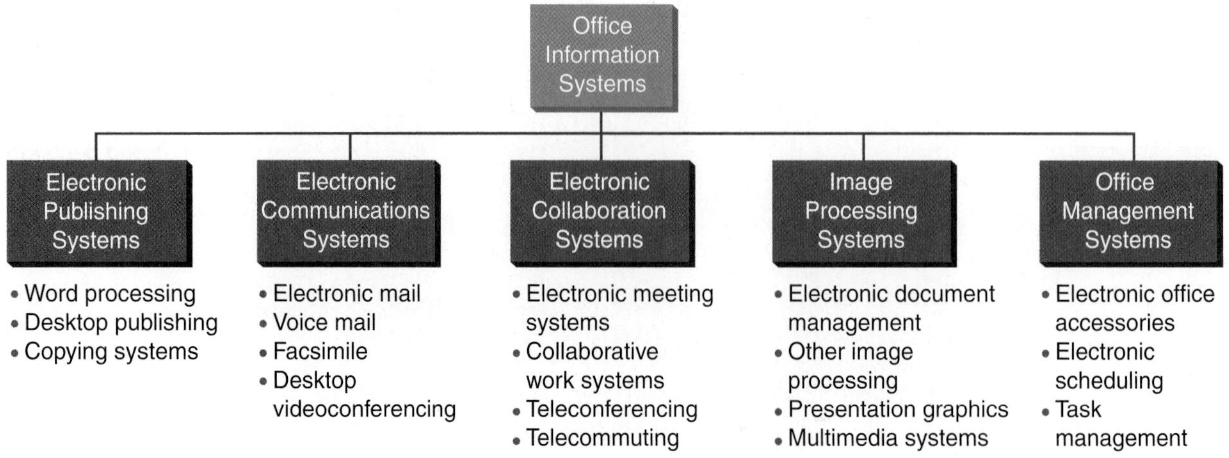

Office Information Systems

Electronic Publishing Systems	Electronic Communications Systems	Electronic Collaboration Systems	Image Processing Systems	Office Management Systems
• Word processing • Desktop publishing • Copying systems	• Electronic mail • Voice mail • Facsimile • Desktop videoconferencing	• Electronic meeting systems • Collaborative work systems • Teleconferencing • Telecommuting	• Electronic document management • Other image processing • Presentation graphics • Multimedia systems	• Electronic office accessories • Electronic scheduling • Task management

offline processing—that is, the data is gathered and processed in batches at periodic intervals, such as at the end of the day or once a week. Or they may be handled via *real-time processing,* also known as *online transaction processing (OLTP)*—that is, each transaction is processed immediately as it is entered. The data collected by a TPS is typically stored in databases.

FEATURES OF A TPS Some features of a TPS are as follows:

- **Input and output:** The inputs to the system are transaction data: bills, orders, inventory levels, and the like. The output consists of processed transactions: bills, paychecks, and so on.
- **For operational managers:** Because the TPS deals with day-to-day matters, it is principally of use to operational-level or supervisory managers, although it can also be helpful to tactical-level managers.
- **Produces detail reports:** A manager at the operational level typically receives information in the form of detail reports. A *detail report* contains specific information about routine activities. An example might be the information needed to decide whether to restock inventory.
- **One TPS for each department:** Each department or functional area of an organization usually has its own TPS. For example, the accounting and finance TPS handles order processing, accounts receivable, inventory and purchasing, accounts payable, and payroll.
- **Basis for MIS and DSS:** The database of transactions stored in a TPS provides the basis for management information systems and decision support systems, as we describe next.

Management Information Systems

Management information systems transform data into information useful in the support of decision making, principally at the tactical level.

The next level of information system after the TPS is the management information system. **A *management information system (MIS)*** (pronounced "em-eye-ess") **is a computer-based information system that uses data recorded by a TPS as input into programs that produce routine reports as output.**

FEATURES OF AN MIS Features of an MIS are as follows:

- **Input and output:** Inputs consist of processed transaction data, such as bills, orders, and paychecks, plus other internal data. Outputs consist of summarized, structured reports: budget summaries, production schedules, and the like.
- **For tactical managers:** An MIS is intended principally to assist tactical-level managers. It enables them to spot trends and get an overview of current business activities.
- **Draws from all departments:** The MIS draws from all six departments or functional areas, not just one.
- **Produces several kinds of reports:** Managers at this level usually receive information in the form of several kinds of reports: *summary, exception, periodic, demand.*

Summary reports show totals and trends. An example is a report showing total sales by office, by product, and by salesperson, as well as total overall sales.

Exception reports show out-of-the-ordinary data. An example is an inventory report listing only those items of which fewer than 10 are in stock.

Periodic reports are produced on a regular schedule. Such daily, weekly, monthly, quarterly, or annual reports may contain sales figures, income statements, or balance sheets. They are usually produced on paper, such as computer printouts.

Demand reports produce information in response to an unscheduled demand. A director of finance might order a demand credit-background report on an unknown customer who wants to place a large order. Demand reports are often produced on a terminal or microcomputer screen, rather than on paper.

Decision Support Systems

Decision support systems are a specific class of computer-based information system that supports business and organizational decision-making activities generally at the managerial level.

A more sophisticated information system is the decision support system. **A *decision support system (DSS)* is a computer-based information system that provides a flexible tool for analysis and helps managers focus on the future.** A DSS aims to produce collected information known as *business intelligence,* gathering data from a wide range of sources in a way that can be interpreted by humans and used to support better business decision making. Some decision support systems come very close to acting as artificial intelligence agents (covered in the next section). DSS applications are not single information resources, such as a database or a program that graphically represents sales figures, but a combination of integrated resources working together. Whereas a TPS records data and an MIS summarizes data, a DSS analyzes data. To reach the DSS level of sophistication in information technology, an organization must have established TPS and MIS systems first.

FEATURES OF A DSS Some features of a DSS are as follows:

- **Inputs and outputs:** Inputs include internal data—such as summarized reports and processed transaction data—and also data that is external to the organization. External data may be produced by trade associations, marketing research firms, the U.S. Bureau of the Census, and other government agencies. The outputs are demand reports on which a top manager can make decisions about unstructured problems.
- **Mainly for tactical managers:** A DSS is intended principally to assist tactical-level managers in making tactical decisions. Questions addressed by the DSS might be, for example, whether interest rates will rise or whether there will be a strike in an important materials-supplying industry.
- **Produces analytic models:** The key attribute of a DSS is that it uses models. A *model* is a mathematical representation of a real system. The models use a DSS database, which draws on the TPS and MIS files, as well as external data such as stock reports, government reports, and national and international news. The system is accessed through DSS software. The model allows the manager to do a simulation—play a "what-if" game—to reach decisions. Thus, the manager can simulate an aspect of the organization's environment in order to decide how to react to a change in conditions affecting it. By changing the hypothetical inputs to the model, the manager can see how the model's outputs are affected.

SOME USES OF DSSs Many DSSs are developed to support the types of decisions faced by managers in specific industries, such as airlines or real estate. Curious how airlines decide how many seats to sell on a flight when so many passengers are no-shows? American Airlines developed a DSS, the yield management system, that helps managers decide how much to overbook and how to set prices for each seat so that a plane is filled and profits are maximized. Wonder how owners of those big apartment complexes set rents and lease

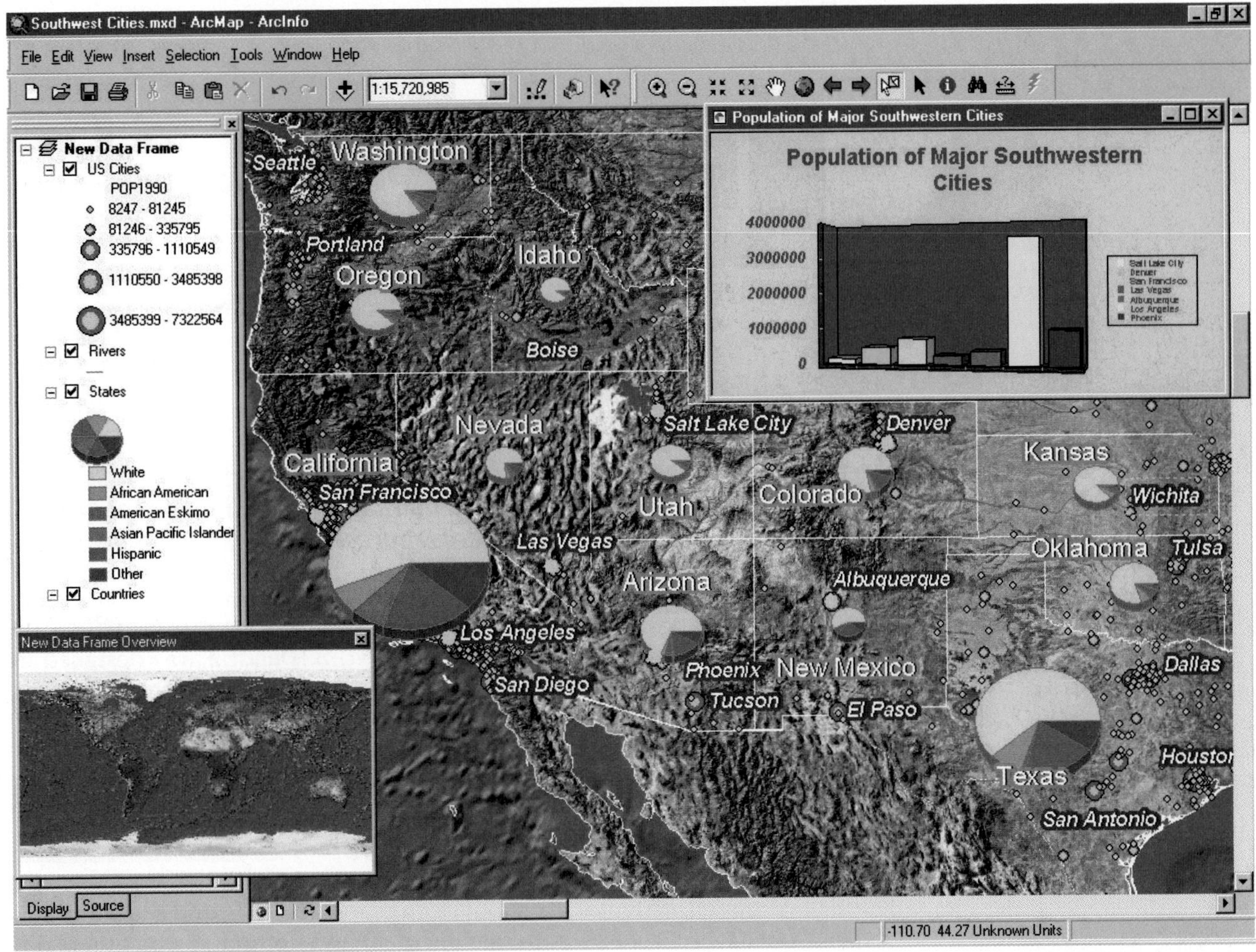

terms? Investors in commercial real estate have used DSSs to forecast property values up to 40 years into the future, based on income, expense, and cash-flow projections. Ever speculate about how insurance carriers set different rates or how Subway and McDonald's decide where to locate a store? Many companies use DSSs called *geographic information systems (GISs),* such as MapInfo and Atlas GIS, which integrate geographic databases with other business data and display maps. *(● See Panel 8.13.)*

panel 8.13

Geographic DSS for earthquake insurance

Using geographic information systems, such as MapInfo, insurance underwriters can set rates and examine potential liability in the event of a natural disaster. This one presents a visual analysis of policyholders living near earthquake fault lines.

Executive Support Systems

Executive support systems are reporting tools that allow organizations to turn their data into useful summarized reports. These reports are generally used by executive level managers for quick access to reports coming from all company levels.

Also called an *executive information system (EIS),* an **executive support system (ESS) is an easy-to-use DSS made especially for strategic managers; it specifically supports strategic decision making.** It draws on data not only from systems internal to the organization but also from those outside, such as news services or market-research databases. *(● See Panel 8.14, next page.)*

An ESS might allow senior executives to call up predefined reports from their personal computers, whether desktops or laptops. They might, for instance, call up sales figures in many forms—by region, by week, by anticipated year, by projected increases. The ESS includes capabilities for analyzing data and doing "what-if" scenarios. ESSs also have the capability to browse through summarized information on all aspects of the organization and then zero in on ("drill down" to) detailed areas the manager believes require attention.

ESSs are relatively user-friendly and require little training to use.

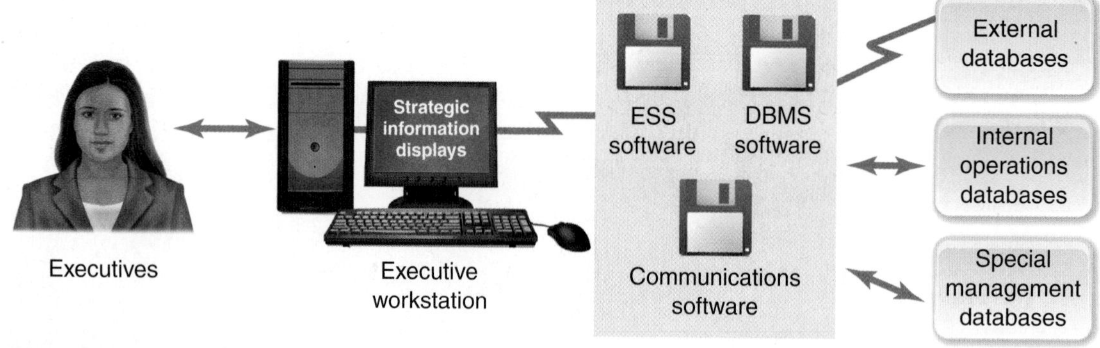

panel 8.14
Components of an ESS

Expert Systems

Expert systems are computer programs that use artificial intelligence to solve problems within a specialized domain that ordinarily requires human expertise. These expert systems represent the expert knowledge as data or rules within the computer system.

The first expert system was developed in 1965 by Edward Feigenbaum and Joshua Lederberg of Stanford University in California—U.S. Dendral was designed to analyze chemical compounds. **An *expert system*, or *knowledge-based system*, is a set of interactive computer programs that helps users solve problems that would otherwise require the assistance of a human expert.** Expert systems are created on the basis of knowledge collected on specific topics from human specialists, and they imitate the reasoning process of a human being. As we describe in the next section, expert systems have emerged from the field of artificial intelligence, the branch of computer science that is devoted to the creation of computer systems that simulate human reasoning and sensation.

Expert systems are used by both management and nonmanagement personnel to solve specific problems, such as how to reduce production costs, improve workers' productivity, or reduce environmental impact. Because of their giant appetite for memory, expert systems are usually run on large computers, although some microcomputer expert systems also exist. For example, Negotiator Pro helps executives plan effective negotiations by examining the personality types of the other parties and recommending negotiating strategies. These systems also have commercial applications in such fields as medical diagnosis, petroleum engineering, and financial investing.

8.7 Artificial Intelligence

Artificial intelligence is the branch of computer science concerned with making computers behave like humans.

You're having trouble with your new computer program. You call the customer "help desk" at the software maker. Do you get a busy signal or get put on hold to listen to music (or, worse, advertising) for several minutes? Technical support lines are often swamped, and waiting is commonplace. Or, to deal with your software difficulty, do you find yourself dealing with . . . other software?

The odds are good that you will. For instance, a software technology called *automated virtual representatives*, or *vReps*, offers computer-generated images (animation or photos of real models) that answer customer questions in real time, using natural language. vReps, which are becoming more and more common on self-service websites, are examples of expert systems, which, as we suggested above, are programs that can walk you through a problem and help solve it. Expert systems are one of the most useful applications of ***artificial intelligence (AI)*****, a group of related technologies used for developing machines to emulate human qualities, such as learning, reasoning, communicating, seeing, and hearing.** As will become clear, AI would not be possible without developments in database technology.

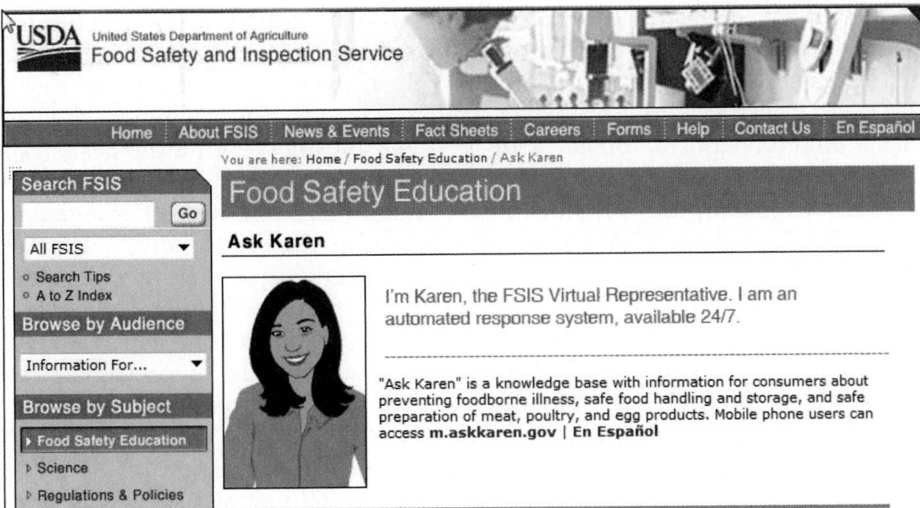

Karen, the U.S. Food Safety and Inspection Service (FSIS) virtual representative

Today the main areas of AI are these:

- Expert systems
- Natural language processing
- Intelligent agents
- Pattern recognition
- Fuzzy logic
- Virtual reality and simulation devices
- Robotics

We also consider an area known as *artificial life.*

Expert Systems

An expert system has three parts: knowledge base, inference engine, and user interface.

As we said in the last section, an *expert system* is an interactive computer program used to solve problems that would otherwise require the assistance of a human specialist. As the name suggests, it is a system imbued with knowledge by human experts.

Exsys Inc - The Expert System Experts

Capture problem-solving knowledge of top experts to provide online advice to prospects, customers and employees.

Organizations can now optimize their most valuable asset, expert knowledge, through powerful interactive Web-enabled knowledge automation expert systems. Online sessions emulate a conversation with a human expert asking focused questions and producing customized recommendations and advice. The decision making skills of your top experts can now be made available to everyone.

Exsys Corvid® development software provides non-programmers a new way to easily build interactive Web applications that capture the logic and processes used to solve problems and deliver it online, in stand-alone applications and embedded in other technologies.

Some of the most common application areas are:

- Regulatory and Compliance Requirements
- Diagnosing and Repairing Equipment and Processes
- Web Self-Service Customer or Technical Support
- Pre-Sales Advice for Prospects
- Configuration of Complex Systems
- Technical or Engineering "Best Practices"
- Capturing Corporate Knowledge Before it is Lost
- Smart CRM
- Creating Web Site Concierge Systems
- Smart Questionnaires

Expert systems. These software companies offer strategic-planning software that uses expert knowledge bases in various areas.

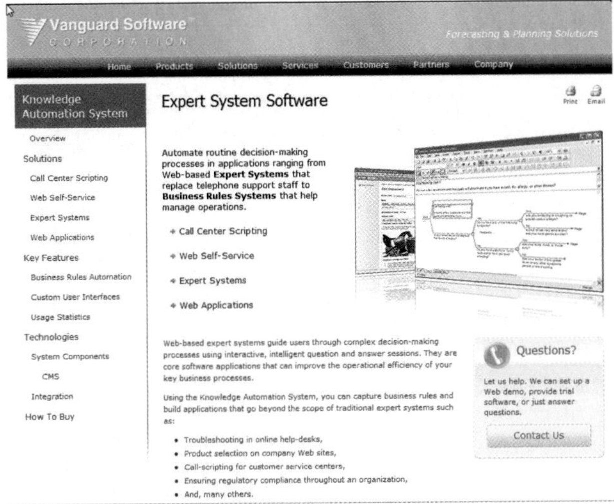

Build an Expert System

You can build an expert system for your own company. For example, go to:

www.vanguardsw.com/solutions/application/expert-systems/

http://year12ipt.ash.com/untitled-8.html

www.trade2win.com/boards/forex-strategies-systems/114796-create-your-own-expert-advisor-mql5-wizard.html

EXAMPLES OF EXPERT SYSTEMS Expert systems have been designed both for microcomputers and for larger computer systems with huge databases. One of the earliest expert systems, MYCIN helped diagnose infectious diseases. PROSPECTOR was the first expert system for assessing geological data to locate mineral deposits. Business Insight helps businesses find the best strategies for marketing a product. CARES (Computer Assisted Risk Evaluation System) helps nonprofit organizations evaluate risks and protect clients and staff. CLUES (Countrywide Loan Underwriting Expert System) evaluates home-mortgage loan applications. CLIPS (C Language Integrated Production System), widely used in government, industry, and academia, is an expert system used to build other expert systems. Whale Watcher is an expert system used to identify whales. STREAMES assists water managers to evaluate the effect of large stream nutrient loads on stream nutrient retention.

HOW EXPERT SYSTEMS DRAW ON KNOWLEDGE All these programs simulate the reasoning process of experts in certain well-defined areas. That is, professionals called *knowledge engineers* interview the experts and determine the rules and knowledge that must go into the system. For example, to develop Muckraker, an expert system to assist newspaper reporters with investigative reporting, the knowledge engineers interviewed journalists.

Programs incorporate not only the experts' surface knowledge ("textbook knowledge") but also their deep knowledge ("tricks of the trade"). What, exactly, is *deep knowledge*? "An expert in some activity has by definition reduced the world's complexity by his or her specialization," say some authorities. One result is that "much of the knowledge lies outside direct conscious awareness."[24]

THE THREE COMPONENTS OF AN EXPERT SYSTEM An expert system consists of three components. (● *See Panel 8.15.*)

- **Knowledge base:** A *knowledge base* is an expert system's database of knowledge about a particular subject, including relevant facts, information, beliefs, assumptions, and procedures for solving problems. The basic unit of knowledge is expressed as an IF-THEN-ELSE rule. ("IF this happens, THEN do this, ELSE do that.") Programs can have many thousands of rules. A system called ExperTAX, for example, which helps accountants figure out a client's tax options, consists of more than 3,000 rules. Other systems have 80,000 or 100,000 rules, which means that very large computer systems are required.
- **Inference engine:** The *inference engine* is the software that controls the search of the expert system's knowledge base and produces conclusions. It takes the problem posed by the user and fits it into the rules in the knowledge base. It then derives a conclusion from the facts and rules contained in the knowledge base.

panel 8.15

Components of an expert system

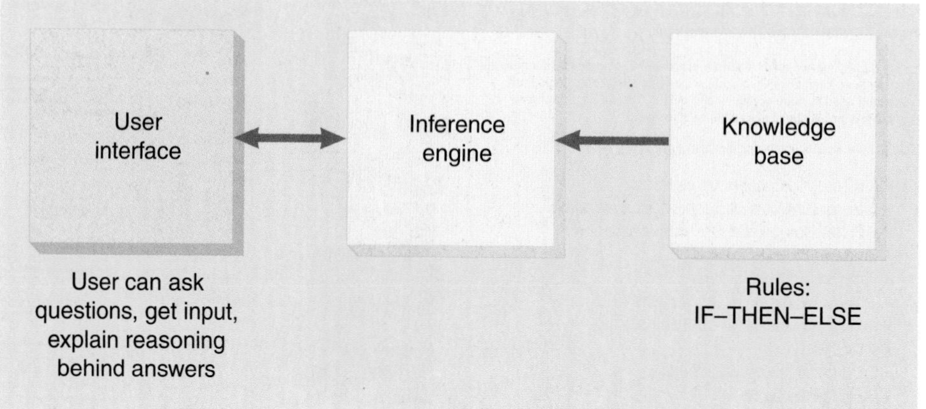

- **User interface:** The *user interface* is the display screen. It gives the user the ability to ask questions and get answers. It also explains the reasoning behind the answer.

People fearful about machines taking over our lives need to understand that expert systems are designed to be users' assistants, not replacements. Also, the success of these systems depends on the quality of the data and rules obtained from the human experts.

Natural Language Processing

Natural language processing involves designing and building software that will analyze, understand, and generate human languages, so that eventually you will be able to address your computer as though you were addressing another person.

Natural languages are ordinary human languages, such as English. (A second definition, discussed in Chapter 10, is that natural languages are fifth-generation programming languages.) ***Natural language processing*** **is the study of ways for computers to recognize and understand human language,** whether in spoken or written form. Major advances in natural language processing have occurred in *speech recognition,* in which computers translate spoken speech into text.

Think how challenging it is to make a computer translate English into another language. In one instance, the English sentence "The spirit is willing, but the flesh is weak" came out in Russian as "The wine is agreeable, but the meat is spoiled." The problem with human language is that it is often ambiguous; different listeners may arrive at different interpretations. Most existing language systems run on large computers, although scaled-down versions are now available for microcomputers.

Misunderstanding . . .

Here are some English phrases that a natural-language computer system might have trouble understanding.

www.transmachina.com/en/content/some-natural-language-examples-computers-may-have-trouble-understanding

Intelligent Agents

An intelligent agent is software that assists people and acts on their behalf, allowing them to delegate work to the agent.

How do you find information in the vast sea of the Internet? As one solution, computer scientists have developed so-called intelligent agents to find information on computer networks and filter it. **An *intelligent agent* is a form of software with built-in intelligence that monitors work patterns, asks questions, and performs work tasks on your behalf,** such as roaming networks and compiling data. Agents can perform repetitive tasks, remember things you forgot, intelligently summarize complex data, and even make recommendations to you. One type of intelligent agent is a kind of electronic assistant that will filter messages, scan news services, and perform similar secretarial chores. For example, Assistant Editor will reorganize your notes into a competently edited, logical, narrative sequence. We mentioned another kind in the shop bots, or shopping robots, used in online shopping. Also known as *bots* or *network agents,* these intelligent agents search the Internet and online databases for information and bring the results back to you.

Pattern Recognition

Pattern recognition is the computer-based identification of objects and images by their shapes, forms, outlines, color, surface texture, temperature, or other attribute.

Pattern recognition **involves a camera and software that identify recurring patterns in what they are seeing and recognize the connections between the perceived patterns and similar patterns stored in a database.** Pattern recognition is used in data mining to discover previously unnoticed patterns from massive amounts of data. Another principal use is in facial-recognition software, which allows computers to identify faces, using a digital "faceprint." Video surveillance cameras have been used to pick out suspicious individuals in crowds. Pattern recognition is also used for handwriting recognition, fingerprint identification, robot vision, and automatic voice recognition.

SECURITY

Fuzzy Logic

Fuzzy logic recognizes more than simple true and false values. Although it is used in computers, which make only yes-no "decisions," fuzzy logic works with ranges of values, solving problems in a way that more resembles human logic.

The traditional logic behind computers is based on either-or, yes-no, true-false reasoning. Such computers make "crisp" distinctions, leading to precise decision making. ***Fuzzy logic*** **is a method of dealing with imprecise data and uncertainty, with problems that have many answers rather than one.** Unlike classical logic, fuzzy logic is more like human reasoning: It deals with probability and credibility. That is, instead of being simply true or false, a proposition is mostly true or mostly false, or more true or more false.

For example, fuzzy logic has been applied in running elevators. How long will most people wait for an elevator before getting antsy? About a minute and a half, say researchers at the Otis Elevator Company. The Otis artificial intelligence division has thus done considerable research into how elevators may be programmed to reduce waiting time. Ordinarily, when someone on a floor in the middle of the building pushes the call button, the system will send whichever elevator is closest. However, that car might be filled with passengers, who will be delayed by the new stop (perhaps making them antsy), whereas another car that is farther away might be empty. In a fuzzy-logic system, the computer assesses not only which car is nearest but also how full the cars are before deciding which one to send.

Fuzzy-logic circuitry also enables handheld autofocus video cameras to focus properly. If your hand is unsteady, the circuitry in the camera determines which parts in the visual field should stand still and which should move and makes the necessary adjustments in the image. And fuzzy logic is used in many digital cooking appliances, such as rice cookers and some steamers. The built-in fuzzy-logic system on a chip senses fluctuations in cooking and automatically adjusts operation to ensure perfect results.

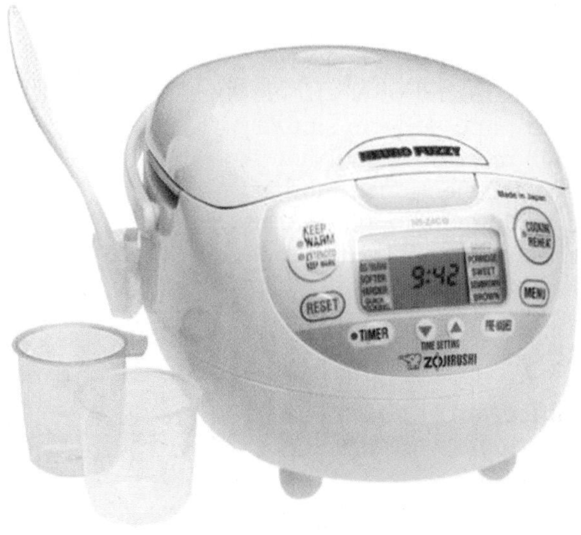

A fuzzy-logic Zojirushi rice cooker and a Haier fuzzy-logic washing machine

Virtual Reality & Simulation Devices

Virtual reality is an artificial environment that is created with hardware and software and presented to the user as a "real" environment; it allows the user to perform operations on the simulated environment and shows the effects in real time.

***Virtual reality (VR)*, a computer-generated artificial reality, projects a person into a sensation of three-dimensional space.** *(• See Panel 8.16.)* To put yourself into virtual reality, you need software and special headgear; then you can add gloves, and later perhaps a special suit. The headgear—which is called a *head-mounted display* (marketed as a VR Headset)—has two small video display screens, for each eye, to create the sense of three-dimensionality. Headphones pipe in stereophonic sound or even 3-D sound so that you think you are hearing sounds not only near each ear but also in various places all around you. The glove has sensors for collecting data about your hand movements. Once you are wearing this equipment, software gives you interactive sensory feelings similar to real-world experiences.

You may have seen virtual reality used in arcade-type games, such as Star Wars Encounter. However, there are far more important uses—for example, in simulators for training. ***Simulators* are devices that represent the behavior of physical or abstract systems.** Virtual-reality simulation technologies are applied a great deal in training. For instance, to train bus drivers, they create lifelike bus control panels and various scenarios such as icy road conditions. They are used to train pilots on various aircraft and to prepare air-traffic controllers for equipment failures. Surgeons in training can develop their skills through simulation on "digital patients." Architects create virtual walk-throughs of the structures they are designing. Virtual-reality therapy has been used for autistic children and in the treatment of phobias, such as extreme fear of public speaking or of being in public places or high places, and psychotic disorders, such as paranoia, and social disorders. And many athletes train with simulators.

Virtual reality is also being used to study people's feelings about conservation of forests. "New findings from Stanford researchers show that people who were immersed in a three-dimensional virtual forest and told to saw through a towering sequoia until it crashed in front of them later used less paper in the real world than people who only imagined what it's like to cut down a tree. 'We found that virtual reality can change how people behave,' said Sun Joo Ahn, whose doctoral dissertation outlines the findings.'"[25]

Be a Train Engineer

How does it feel to drive a train? You can find out with Microsoft's Train Simulator, pretending to direct trains over routes in the United States, United Kingdom, Austria, and Japan:

www.railserve.com/Computers/

www.ea.com/rail-simulator

How does it feel to fly? Read about it at:

www.sciencedaily.com/releases/2011/05/110505164535.htm

Virtual Reality Products

For more about VR products:

www.vrealities.com/main.html

www.cwonline.com/

http://nvisinc.com/products2009.php

Robotics

Robotics is a branch of engineering that involves the conception, design, manufacture, and operation of robots, automatic devices that perform functions normally ascribed to humans.

In the 1956 film *Forbidden Planet,* Robby the Robot could sew, distill bourbon, and speak 187 languages. We haven't caught up with science-fiction movies, but maybe we'll get there yet.

***Robotics* is the development and study of machines that can perform work that is normally done by people.** The machines themselves are called *robots*. *(• See Panel 8.17.)* As we said in Chapter 1, a *robot* is an automatic device that performs functions ordinarily executed by human beings or that operates with what appears to be almost human intelligence. (The word *robot,* derived from the Czech word for "compulsory labor," was first used by Karel Câpek in an early 1920s play.)

Shakey, developed in 1970, was the first robot to use artificial intelligence to navigate. Today Rosie and Roscoe are R2D2-like robots that perform a variety of courier duties for hospitals, saving nurses from having to make trips to supply areas, pharmacies, and cafeterias. ScrubMate—a robot equipped

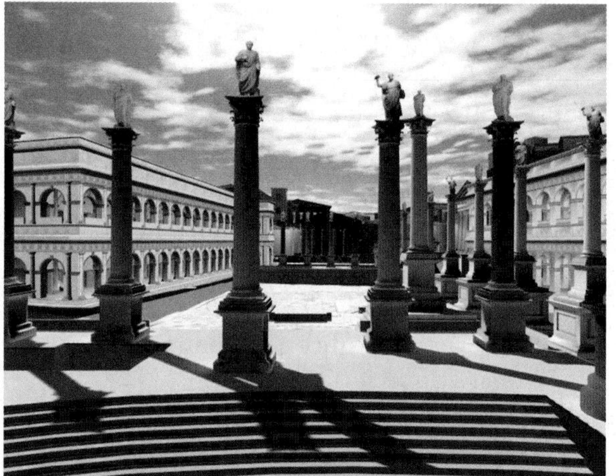

panel 8.16

Virtual reality

(*Top left*) A research assistant works on a virtual reality program at the Virtual Reality in Medicine laboratory at the University of Illinois at Chicago. Surgeons use such programs to practice surgery on patients' "virtual organs" before making the first real cut. (*Top right*) Although it may look realistic, the pilot shown here is flying a conceptual aircraft. In Grumman's simulation system development laboratory, the pilot sees high-resolution images projected onto the interior of a simulation dome. (*Middle right*) This digital reconstruction, from Virginia's Institute for Advanced Technology in the Humanities, shows the steps on the back side of the Caesarian speakers' platform, the Aemilia Basilica law court at left, and the Basilica Julia law court at right, part of the ancient Roman Forum, used for the simulation of the historic city at its peak in 400 C. E. (*Above*) This experimental virtual-reality computer simulation at Madigan Army Medical Center at Fort Lewis, Washington, shows a first-person view of a simulated attack on a military convoy in Iraq. Psychologists plan to begin using virtual reality in the future to treat soldiers suffering from posttraumatic stress disorder. (*Bottom right*) Passenger airline flight simulation that allows people who are afraid to fly to experience an airplane trip without leaving the ground.

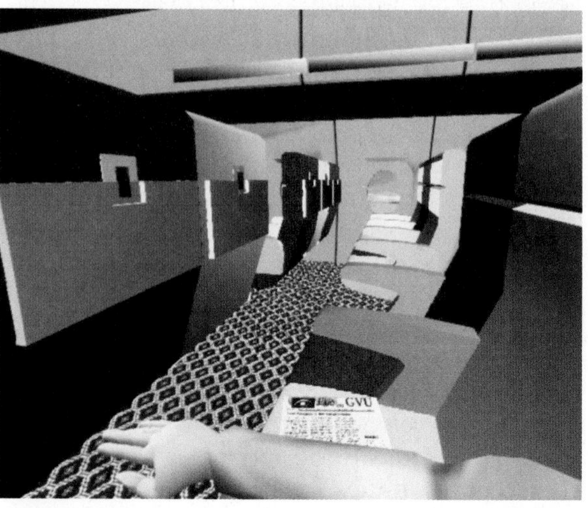

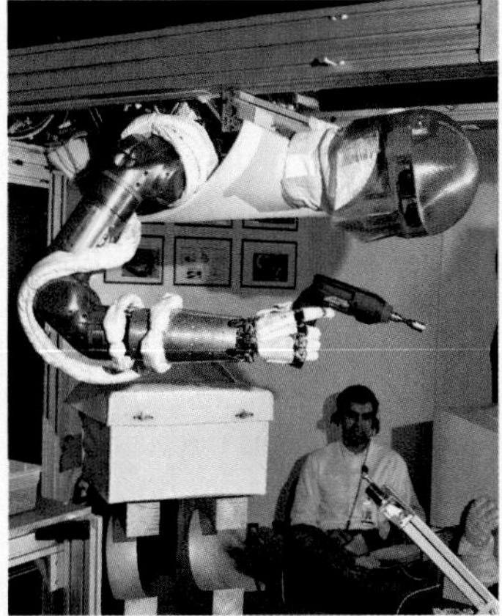

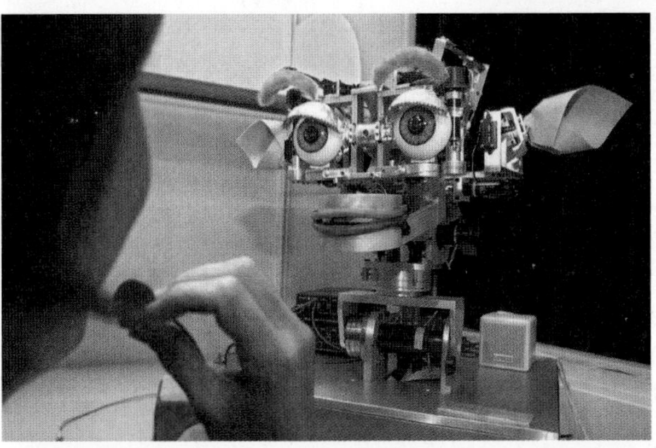

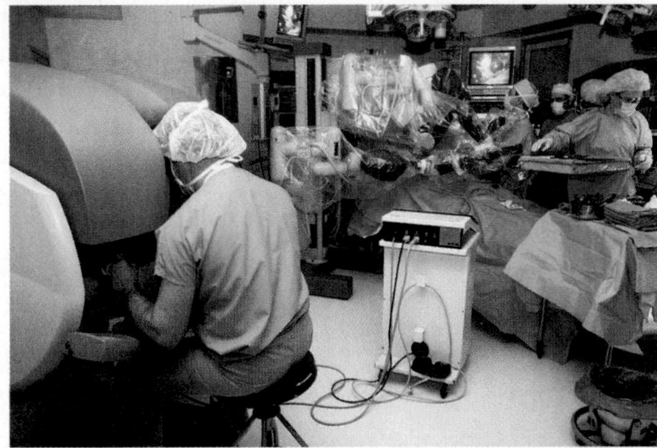

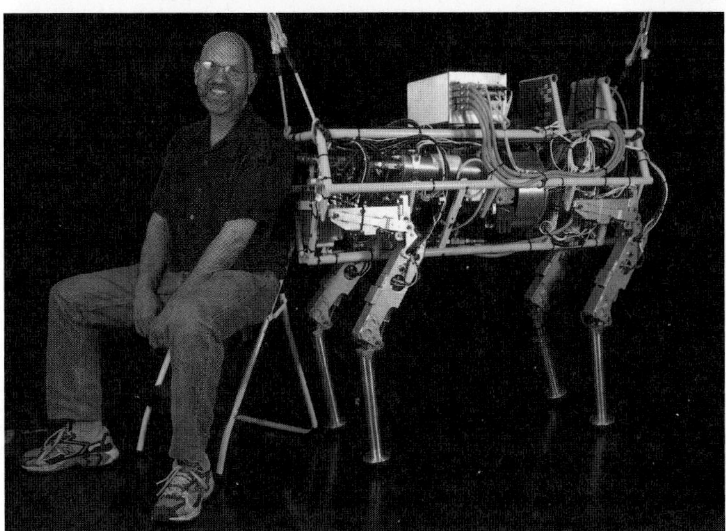

panel 8.17

Robots

(*Top left*) Many Japanese people are fond of robotic pets, such as this Sega Poochi. (*Top middle*) This Robonaut is a robotic system aimed at giving spacewalking astronauts a hand in space station construction. (*Top right*) The Robo-Soldier is an armed, unmanned ground vehicle that never gets tired, hungry, or scared. (*Middle left*) Dr. Cynthia Breazeal, at the Massachusetts Institute of Technology's Artificial Intelligence Laboratory, interacts with Kismet, a robotic head that interacts with humans in a humanlike way. (*Middle right*) A robotic surgery device, called the Da Vinci Surgical System, manipulates robotic arms during a gallbladder operation at a hospital in New Jersey. (*Bottom left*) Marc Raibert with a running quadriped, a biomimetic robot called BigDog. (*Bottom right*) "Mei Mei," a waitress robot in Chinese dress, carries a couple of glasses of water to a table in a Tokyo restaurant. The robot moves to tables using an infrared sensor and serves water and delivers menus to customers with a bow and words of welcome.

with computerized controls, ultrasonic "eyes," sensors, batteries, three different cleaning and scrubbing tools, and a self-squeezing mop—can clean bathrooms. ROBODOC is used in surgery to bore the thighbone so that a hip implant can be attached. A driverless harvester, guided by satellite signals and an artificial vision system, is used to harvest alfalfa and other crops. A robot dog named AIBO is able to learn how to sit, roll over, fetch, and do other activities. You can buy your own robot vacuum cleaner, Roomba, or the more advanced Scooba, which will not just pick up dirt but also wash, scrub, and dry the floor. At the Massachusetts Institute of Technology, a robot will water a tomato plant when the soil needs it. Roborier ("robot" + "interior") is a robot house sitter that rolls around a house and uses infrared sensors to detect suspicious movements and transmit images to absent owners.

Robots are also used for more exotic purposes such as fighting oil-well fires, doing nuclear inspections and cleanups, and checking for land mines and booby traps. An eight-legged, satellite-linked robot called Dante II was used to explore the inside of Mount Spurr, an active Alaskan volcano, sometimes without human guidance. A six-wheeled robot vehicle called Sojourner was used in NASA's 1997 Pathfinder exploration of Mars to sample the planet's atmosphere and soil and to radio data and photos back to Earth. The robot Rovers Spirit and Opportunity are currently traversing the surface of Mars (*http://marsrover.nasa.gov/home/*).

Two Approaches to Artificial Intelligence: Weak versus Strong AI

Weak AI focuses on making machines act as if they were intelligent. Strong AI focuses on making machines that really think—that represent human minds.

Two principal approaches to artificial intelligence are *weak AI* and *strong AI.*

WEAK AI *Weak AI* makes the claim that computers can be programmed to *simulate* human cognition—that some "thinking-like" features can be added to computers to make them more useful tools. We have already seen this kind of AI—call it "AI lite"—in expert systems, speech-recognition software, computer games, and the like.

A useful concept for considering weak AI is that of brute force. In programming and in AI, *brute force* is a technique for solving a complex problem by using a computer's fast processing capability to repeat a simple procedure many times. For example, a spelling checker in a word processing program doesn't really check the spelling of words; rather, it compares all the words you type into your document to a dictionary of correctly spelled words. Similarly, a chess-playing program will calculate all the possible moves that can apply to a given situation and then choose the best one; it will not analyze and strategize the way a human chess player would. Even IBM's Deep Blue program, which defeated Russian chess master Garry Kasparov in May 1997, basically took advantage of a supercomputer's fast processing abilities to examine 200 million possible plays per second—plays that had been input via a human-knowledge-based expert system.

STRONG AI *Strong AI* makes the claim that computers can be made to think on a level that is at least equal to humans and possibly even be conscious of themselves. So far, most AI advances have been piecemeal and single-purpose, such as factory robots, but proponents of strong AI believe that it's possible for computers to have the kind of wide-ranging, problem-solving ability that people have. Some researchers believe that strong AI promises a lot because of the recent developments in nanotechnology (Chapter 1, p. 23). Nanobots, which can help us fight diseases and also make us more intelligent, are being designed. Furthermore, the development of an artificial neural network (covered shortly) is being looked at as a future application of strong AI.

Some other forms of strong AI are described in the box at right. *(• See Panel 8.18.)*

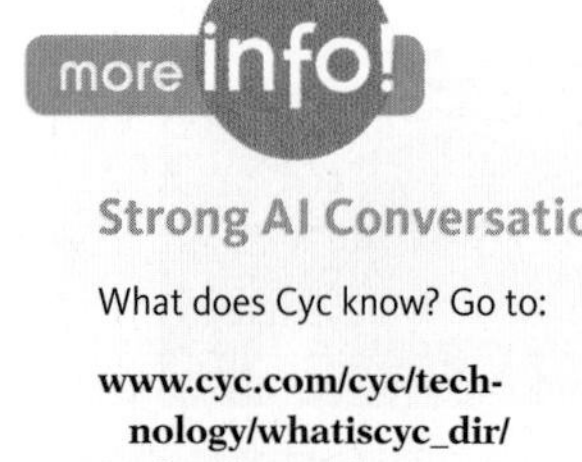

Strong AI Conversation

What does Cyc know? Go to:

www.cyc.com/cyc/technology/whatiscyc_dir/whatdoescycknow

more info!

Strong AI: COGnition

What is Cog?

www.ai.mit.edu/projects/humanoid-robotics-group/

Neural Networks. *Neural networks* use physical electronic devices or software to mimic the neurological structure of the human brain. Because they are structured to mimic the rudimentary circuitry of the cells in the human brain, they learn from example and don't require detailed instructions.

To understand how neural networks operate, we may compare them to the operation of the human brain.

- *The human neural network:* The human body has a neural network consisting of neurons, or nerve cells. The neurons are connected by a three-dimensional lattice called *axons*. Electrical connections between neurons are activated by *synapses*. The human brain is made up of about 100 billion neurons. However, these cells do not act as "computer memory" sites. No cell holds a picture of your dog or the idea of happiness. You could eliminate any cell—or even a few million—in your brain and not alter your "mind." Where do memory and learning lie? In the electrical connections between cells, the synapses. Using electrical pulses, the neurons send on/off messages along the synapses.
- *The computer neural network:* In a hardware neural network, the nerve cell is replaced by a transistor, which acts as a switch. Wires connect the cells (transistors) with one another. The synapse is replaced by an electronic component called a *resistor*, which determines whether a cell should activate the electricity to other cells. A software neural network emulates a hardware neural network, although it doesn't work as fast. Computer-based neural networks use special AI software and complicated fuzzy-logic processor chips to take inputs and convert them to outputs with a kind of logic similar to human logic.

Neural networks are already being used in a variety of situations. At a San Diego hospital emergency room in which patients complained of chest pains, the same information was given to a neural-network program and to doctors. The network correctly diagnosed patients with heart attacks 97% of the time, compared to 78% for the human physicians. Banks that use neural-network software to spot irregularities in purchasing patterns within individual accounts often notice when a credit card is stolen before its owner does.

Genetic Algorithms. A *genetic algorithm* is a program that uses Darwinian principles of random mutation to improve itself. The algorithms are lines of computer code that act like living organisms. Different sections of code haphazardly come together, producing programs. As in Darwin's rules of evolution, many chunks of code compete to see which can best fulfill the goal of the program. Some chunks will even become extinct. Those that survive will combine with other survivors to produce offspring programs.

Expert systems can capture and preserve the knowledge of expert specialists, but they may be slow to adapt to change. Neural networks can sift through mountains of data and discover obscure causal relationships, but if there is too much data, or too little, they may be ineffective. Genetic algorithms, by contrast, use endless trial and error to learn from experience—to discard unworkable approaches and grind away at promising approaches with the kind of tireless energy of which humans are incapable.

In 2000 scientists at Brandeis University reached a major milestone when they created a computerized robot that designs and builds other robots, automatically evolving without any significant human intervention. The "robotic life forms" are only a few inches long and are composed of a few plastic parts with rudimentary nervous systems made of wire. They do only one thing: inch themselves, worm-like, along a horizontal surface, using miniature motors. With no idea what a successful design might look like, the Brandeis computer was given the goal of moving on a horizontal surface; a list of possible parts to work with; a group of 200 randomly constructed, nonworking designs; and the physical laws of gravity and friction. Mimicking evolution through classic survival-of-the-fittest selection, the computer changed pieces in the designs, mutated the programming instructions for controlling movements, and ran simulations to test the designs. After 300–600 generations of evolution, the computer sent the design to a machine to build the robot. The robots currently have the brainpower of bacteria, say researchers, who say they hope to get up to insect level in a couple of years.

Cyborgs. *Cyborgs* are hybrids of machine and organisms. One example is a hockey-puck-sized robot on wheels controlled by living tissue, an immature lamprey eel brain. The brain had been removed from the eel, kept alive in a special solution, and attached to the robot by wires. The brain is thus able to receive signals from the robot's electronic eyes and in turn can send commands to move the machine's wheels.

A number of cyborgs are in existence today—for instance, the estimated 10% of the American population with electronic heart pacemakers, artificial joints, implanted corneal lenses, and drug implant systems. Future cyborgs, however, might consist of bacteria attached to computer chips to map pollutants, insects used as parts of sensors to detect land mines and chemical weapons, and rodent brains to help identify new medicines. In his book *I, Cyborg,* British cybernetics professor Kevin Warwick described having an electrode in his arm pick up neural signals and send them to a computer, which converted them into instructions for a three-fingered robot hand elsewhere.

panel 8.18

Three types of strong AI: Neural networks, genetic algorithms, and cyborgs

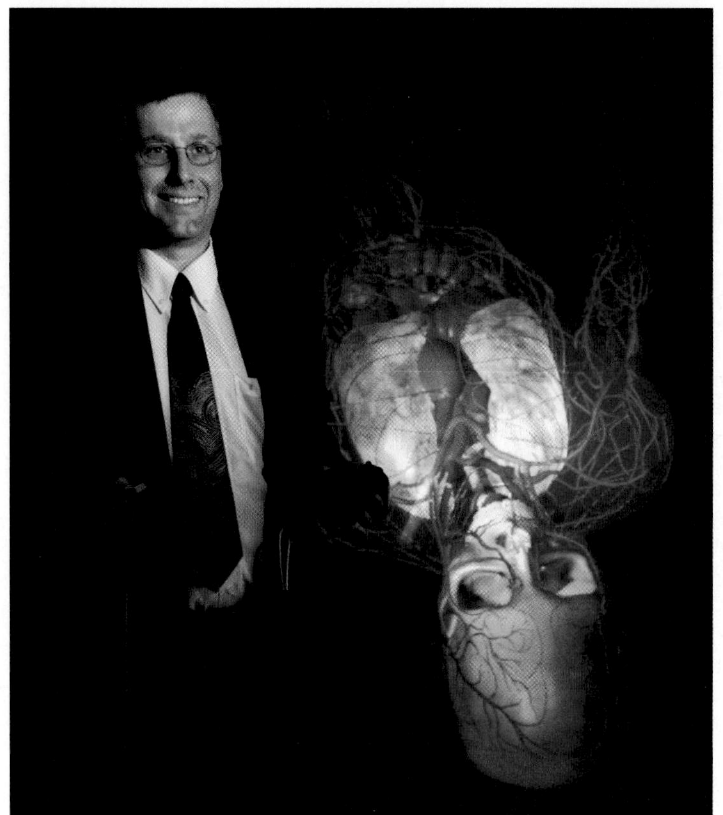

Cyber human. With the help of new scanning and computing technologies, medical imaging technology can now show real-time activities inside the human body. Dr. Christoph Sensen unveils the CAVEman, a 4D human atlas created by University of Calgary, Canada, scientists.

Artificial Life, the Turing Test, & AI Ethics

The development of artificial intelligence involves some not-yet-well-defined ethical concerns.

What is life, and how can we replicate it in silicon chips, networks, and software? We are dealing now not with artificial intelligence but with artificial life. *Artificial life,* or *A-life,* is the field of study concerned with "creatures"—computer instructions, or pure information—that are created, replicate, evolve, and die as if they were living organisms. Thus, A-life software tries to simulate the responses of a human being.

Of course, "silicon life" does not have two principal attributes associated with true living things—it is not water- and carbon-based. Yet in other respects such creatures mimic life: If they cannot learn or adapt, then they perish.

HOW CAN WE KNOW A MACHINE IS TRULY INTELLIGENT? How can we know when we have reached the point at which computers have achieved human intelligence? How will you know, say, whether you're talking to a human being on the phone or to a computer? Clearly, with the strides made in the fields of artificial intelligence and artificial life, this question is no longer just academic.

Alan Turing, an English mathematician and computer pioneer, addressed this very question in 1950. Turing predicted that by the end of the century computers would be able to mimic human thinking and to conduct conversations indistinguishable from a person's. Out of these observations came the *Turing test,* which is intended to determine whether a computer possesses "intelligence" or "self-awareness."

In the Turing test, a human judge converses by means of a computer terminal with two entities hidden in another location—one a person typing on a keyboard, the other a computer program. Following the conversation, the judge must decide which entity is human. In this test, intelligence—the ability to think—is demonstrated by the computer's success in fooling the judge. *(• See Panel 8.19.)* In 1990 Hugh Loebner established the Loebner Prize, which would award $100,000 to the first computer that could pass the Turing test (*www.loebner.net/Prizef/loebner-prize.html*).

Judith Anne Gunther participated as one of eight judges in the third annual Loebner Prize Competition, which is based on Turing's ideas. The "conversations"—each limited to 15 minutes—are restricted to predetermined topics, such as baseball, because even today's best programs have neither the databases nor the syntactical ability to handle an unlimited number of subjects.

Gunther found that she wasn't fooled by any of the computer programs ("chatterbots"). The winning program, for example, relied as much on deflection and wit as it did on responding logically and conversationally. (For example, to a judge trying to discuss a federally funded program, the computer said: "You want logic? I'll give you logic: shut up, shut up, shut up, shut up, shut up, now go away! How's that for logic?") However, Gunther *was* fooled by one of the five humans, a real person discussing abortion. "He was so uncommunicative," wrote Gunther, "that I pegged him for a computer."[26]

Human or Computer?

Make your guess as to whether it's from a human or a computer:

http://knopfdoubleday.com/2011/04/07/human-or-not-read-this-turing-test-script-and-take-a-guess/

"**Computer:** As a psychoanalyst, I am familiar with discussing such marital troubles with you as the patient on the couch. If you don't have a bad marriage just pretend that you do. Please start with 'My wife . . .' or 'My husband . . .'.
Judge: OK, I'll pretend I have a bad marriage. Let's say the reason is because he never picks up his dirty underwear. Is this marriage irreparable?
Computer: Well, if you think I'm hopeless, you can always just swear at me."

—Judith Anne Gunther, "An Encounter with A.I.," *Popular Science,* June 1994.

panel 8.19

Example of the Turing test

The Turing test is held every year. (Go to *www.loebner.net/Prizef/loebner-prize.html* for more information and for transcripts of the human/computer interactions.)

A newer sort of "reverse" Turing test, one that's simple for humans but that can baffle sophisticated computer programs, has been devised in the form of cognitive puzzles called *Captchas,* an acronym for "Completely Automated Public Turing Test to Tell Computers and Humans Apart." Captchas are most commonly used to prevent rogue bots from spamming comments or signing up for web services. Yahoo!, for example, uses a Captcha for screening when a user signs up for an account. Before being allowed to perform an action on the website, the user is presented with alphanumerical characters in a distorted graphic image (a Captcha) and asked to type them into an onscreen box. This works to prevent automated systems from abusing the site, because software does not yet exist that can read and reproduce the distorted image accurately (or such software is not available to the average user); so if the reading of and typing in of the distorted graphic are accurate, the user is likely to be a human.

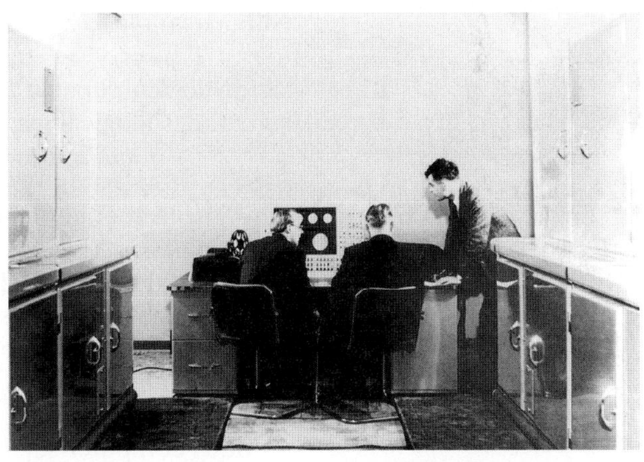

Alan Turing (*right*) in 1951, working on the Mark I computer.

Take a Few Captcha Tests

To get a feel for Captchas and learn more about what Captcha can do, go to:

www.captcha.net

reCaptcha is a new version of Captcha; besides doing what Captcha does, it helps to clarify scrambled scanned files of poor-quality old books:

www.google.com/recaptcha

SMARTER-THAN-HUMAN COMPUTERS: THE CONCEPT OF "THE SINGULARITY" Several research projects are under way that have the aim of making computers think and act more like humans. The U.S. military, for example, is spending billions to develop robots that aid or replace human soldiers. Other efforts concentrate on making driverless cars, software-based personal assistants, and an artificial brain that mimics the actions of 100 million brain neurons. All these seem to be part of a march toward a theoretical future point that scientist and science fiction writer Vernor Vinge called, in 1993, ***the Singularity*****, or *the technological singularity,* a moment when humans would have created self-aware, smarter-than-human machines that are capable of designing computers and robots that are better than humans can make today** (Chapter 1, p. 39). At this point, Vinge suggested, technological progress would have accelerated so much that machine intelligence would dominate, and the "human era would be ended." [27] Vinge thought that computers would become powerful enough by 2030 to allow the rise of such superintelligent, self-aware machines.

Others, such as Raymond Kurzweil, have taken the Singularity idea a great leap further, envisioning transferring the contents of human brains and thought processes into a computing environment, making a form of immortality possible. Thinkers such as Kevin Kelly take another tack, visualizing "the emergence of a global brain—the idea that the planet's interconnected computers might someday act in a coordinated fashion and perhaps exhibit intelligence," in one description. [28]

Will the machines take over the world? "Science is nowhere close to understanding what human intelligence is," notes one writer, "much less coming up with a formula to repeat it in silicon and electrons." We can program computers to say "I'm sorry" when they hear certain words, he points out, but they remain rigidly logical, unable to match the human mind "in its uniquely holistic and sometimes illogical ways." [29]

more info!

More on AI & Ethics

- www.nickbostrom.com/ethics/ai.html
- www.cs.swarthmore.edu/~eroberts/cs91/projects/ethics-of-ai/index.html
- www.nhpr.org/node/26435
- http://singularity-utopia.blogspot.com/2011/01/ai-ethics-to-avoid-suffering-of-human.html
- www.aaai.org/aitopics/pmwiki/pmwiki.php/AITopics/Ethics
- http://ethics.csc.ncsu.edu/risks/ai/

ETHICS IN AI Behind everything to do with artificial intelligence and artificial life—just as it underlies everything we do—is the whole matter of ethics. In his book *Ethics in Modeling,* William A. Wallace, professor of decision sciences at Rensselaer Polytechnic Institute, pointed out that computer software, including expert systems, is often subtly shaped by the ethical judgments and assumptions of the people who create it.[30] In one instance, he noted, a bank had to modify its loan-evaluation software on discovering that the software rejected certain applications because it unduly emphasized old age as a negative factor.

Many computer scientists are also concerned that developments in artificial intelligence might lead to loss of human control over computer systems, causing profound social disruptions, destruction of jobs, and even dangerous consequences.[31] For example, criminals might be able to exploit AI systems, as in using speech synthesis systems to masquerade as human beings or in mining personal information from smartphones.

Clearly, there is no such thing as completely "value-free" technology. Human beings build it, use it, and have to live with the results.

8.8 DATABASES: Concerns about Privacy & Identity Theft

Databases have facilitated loss of privacy and identity theft, which have become significant concerns for many people.

If you're under 30, maybe you're at ease in sharing your activities and locations with your friends, as through Facebook or Twitter. But are you comfortable about having your movements tracked, as through GPS-locator phones, E-ZPasses, and satellite high-definition imagery (Google Earth)? Do you care if you're leaving a digital trail behind you that may wind up in corporate or government databases—or that that data might be widely disseminated, used for advertising, or stolen?

ethics

The Threat to Privacy

The proliferation of networks and databases, of the Internet and websites, of e-commerce, of online storage of medical and insurance records, of information left exposed or poorly protected or inadvertently exposed on social networking sites such as Facebook—all of these have robbed many of us of our privacy.

Privacy is the right of people not to reveal information about themselves. Whom you vote for in a voting booth and what you say in a letter sent through the U.S. mail are private matters. However, the ease of pulling together information from databases and disseminating it over the Internet has put privacy under extreme pressure. Many people are worried about the loss of their right to privacy—and there are good reasons for this concern, as the following discussion shows.

NAME MIGRATION Once you're in a database, your name can easily migrate to other databases. For example, many school districts and colleges are allowed to sell or share student lists that contain names, ages, addresses and so on.[32] Parents installing software (Sentry, FamilySafe) to monitor their children's online activities unwittingly may have allowed the software developer to gather marketing data from children as young as 7 and to sell that information.[33] Making certain purchases, such as flowers, through your smartphone may put your name on the mailing list of 1-800-FLOWERS.com and lead to targeted ads for flowers on your phone, a form of advertising known as behavioral targeting.[34] No wonder the Federal Trade Commission has expressed sharp words to Internet companies, saying they are not explaining to users clearly enough what information they collect about them and how they are using it.[35]

RÉSUMÉ RUSTLING & ONLINE SNOOPING When you post your résumé on an Internet job board, you assume that it's private, and indeed it is supposed to be restricted to recruiters and other employers. But job boards that are just starting up may poach résumés from other job websites as a way of building up their own databases. Another problem is that much of your life may already be online and available to anyone. For instance, Camberley Crick, a part-time computer tutor, went to the apartment of a prospective client and discovered he had pulled all kinds of facts about her simply by typing her name into the search engine Google. Among the things he found: "her family website, a computer game she had designed for a freshman college class, a program from a concert she had performed in, and a short story she wrote in elementary school called 'Timmy the Turtle.'"[36]

GOVERNMENT PRYING & SPYING As part of its war on terrorism, the government has been taking steps that make defenders of privacy worried. One, for instance, was a controversial data-mining project for the U.S. Defense Department's Total Information Awareness program that would have compiled electronic dossiers on Americans. The U.S. Senate forced restrictions on the TIA program, saying that it would amount to a domestic spying apparatus.

Another concern to some is the Secure Flight program, which is meant to replace the canceled Computer Assisted Passenger Prescreening Program (CAPPS II), designed to screen out supposedly dangerous commercial airline passengers. This program involves looking through commercial and government data on all air travelers without their knowledge or permission and using the information to give every flyer a security-risk ranking.

Librarians and booksellers worry that the USA PATRIOT Act, passed by Congress six weeks after the September 11, 2001, attacks, allows FBI agents (through Section 215 of the act) to obtain a warrant from a secret federal court for library or bookstore records of anyone connected to an investigation of

Ways to Guard Your Privacy

The following websites offer ways to guard your privacy:

www.epic.org

www.identitytheft.org

www.privacyfoundation.org

www.eff.org

www.ftc.gov/privacy/index.html

www.consumerreports.org/cro/money/consumer-protection/big-brother-is-watching/overview/index.htm

www.security.mtu.edu/guard-privacy/index.php

http://gpsmaestro.com/10-ways-to-guard-your-privacy-on-a-smartphone/

Right to Privacy?

There is no explicit right to privacy in the United States Constitution. The Supreme Court has ruled that there is a limited constitutional right of privacy based on several provisions in the Bill of Rights. This includes a right to privacy from government surveillance into an area where a person has a "reasonable" expectation of privacy and also in matters relating to marriage, procreation, contraception, sexual activity, family relationships, child rearing, and education. The Supreme Court has also recognized a right of anonymity and the right of political groups to prevent disclosure of their members' names to government agencies. Some states within the United States have incorporated explicit privacy protections into their constitutions. For more details, go to:

www.privacyinternational.org/article.shtml?cmd[347]=x-347-559478

international terrorism or spying. The law prohibits librarians and booksellers from telling patrons that the FBI has requested their records. Unlike conventional search warrants, agents need not show that the target is suspected of a crime or possesses evidence of a crime.

PRIVACY LAWS Over the years, concerns about privacy have led to the enactment of a number of laws to protect individuals from invasions of privacy. (● *See Panel 8.20.*) Still, the tension between security and privacy worries many observers. Recently, an idea has been to use *cost-benefit analysis* to weigh the benefits of tighter domestic security against the costs of lost privacy and freedom. The idea has attracted an unusual array of supporters, ranging from conservatives who fret about "big government" to civil-liberties lawyers.

A NATIONAL ID CARD? Demand for photo identification has transformed driver's licenses into a primary identification document, with a number of states now using digital fingerprinting and facial-recognition security systems for their licenses. Although there is no present nationwide identity card, Congress has required (under the 2002 Enhanced Border Security and Visa Entry Reform Act) the definition of a standard under which the State Department and immigration service can issue machine-readable documents that can be used at most porous border entry points. Foreign governments are also required to use improved identity-system (biometric) technology in their passports.

Does this mean that we're on our way to some national ID card, a sort of internal passport like those carried by citizens in some European countries? Critics from conservatives to civil-liberties defenders so dislike the idea that even efforts to get state governments to standardize driver's licenses have been met with extreme resistance. One answer, perhaps, is to have a voluntary nationally accepted ID card: private companies would issue cards that adhere to strict government standards, and anyone who signs up for one would be

panel 8.20

Important federal privacy laws

For further information on these laws, go to *www.epic.org*

Freedom of Information Act (1970)
Fair Credit Reporting Act (1970)
Privacy Act (1974)
Family Educational Rights and Privacy Act (1974)
Right to Financial Privacy Act (1978)
Privacy Protection Act (1980)
Cable Communications Policy Act (1984)
Computer Fraud and Abuse Act (1984)
Electronic Communications Privacy Act (ECPA) (1986)
Computer Security Act (1987)
Computer Matching and Privacy Protection Act (1988)
Video Privacy Protection Act (1988)
Telephone Consumer Protection Act (1988)
Cable Act (1992)
Computer Abuse Amendments Act (1994)
Communications Assistance for Law Enforcement Act (1994)
National Information Infrastructure Protection Act (1996)
No Electronic Theft (NET) Act (1997)
Children's Online Privacy Protection Act (1998)
Identity Theft and Assumption Deterrence Act (1998)
Digital Millennium Copyright Act (1998)
Financial Services Modernization Act (1999)
Children's Online Privacy Protection Act (COPPA) (2000)
USA PATRIOT Act (2001)
Health Insurance Portability and Accountability Act (2003)

FIGHTING BACK AGAINST
IDENTITY THEFT
FEDERAL TRADE COMMISSION
DETER
DETECT
DEFEND
CONSUMERS
BUSINESSES
LAW ENFORCEMENT
MILITARY
MEDIA
WELCOME TO THE FTC'S IDENTITY THEFT SITE
This website is a one-stop national resource to learn about the crime of identity theft. It provides detailed information to help you deter, detect, and defend against identity theft.
On this site, consumers can learn how to avoid identity theft – and learn what to do if their identity is stolen. Businesses can learn how to help their customers deal with identity theft, as well as how to prevent problems in the first place. Law enforcement can get resources and learn how to help victims of identity theft.
Read on to find out more about identity theft and what you can do about it.
If your information has been stolen and used by an identity thief
more
If your information may have been stolen, but may or may not have been used by an identity thief
more
Learn more about identity theft
more

U.S. Federal Trade Commission's anti-ID theft site

checked against government criminal and watch-list databases that are constantly updated. Still, Congress has weighed legislation in which applicants for driver's licenses would be required to show four types of identification, such as a photo ID, a birth certificate or passport, a Social Security card, or some other document that would prove name, address, and residency. The purpose would be to turn state-issued driver's licenses into a kind of national identity card.

Checking Your Personal Records

Browse the full text of FBI documents and files released under the Freedom of Information Act at:

www.usdoj.gov/oip/index.html

For instructions on how to check and repair your personal credit reports, go to:

www.frbsf.org/publications/consumer/creditrights.html

For more information on the privacy of personal health records, go to the U.S. Department of Health and Human Services at:

www.hhs.gov/ocr/hipaa

Identity Theft

Identity theft is a crime in which an imposter obtains key pieces of personal information, such as Social Security, driver's license, mortgage account, insurance card, and/or credit card numbers in order to impersonate someone else, usually for fraudulent purposes.

It seems that people are ever increasingly at risk for identity theft. ***Identity (ID) theft*****, or *****theft of identity (TOI)*****, is a crime in which thieves hijack your name and identity and use your information and credit rating to get cash or buy things.** Often this begins with someone getting hold of your Social Security number. We discuss identity theft further in the Experience Box.

EXPERIENCE BOX

Preventing Your Identity from Getting Stolen

One day, a special-events planner in California learned that she had a new $35,000 sports utility vehicle listed in her name, along with five credit cards, a $3,000 loan, and even an apartment—none of which she'd asked for. "I cannot imagine what would be weirder, or would make you angrier, than having someone pretend to be you, steal all this money, and then leave you to clean up all their mess later," she said.[37] *Added to this was the eerie matter of constantly having to prove that she was, in fact, herself: "I was going around saying, 'I am who I am!'"*[38]

Identity Theft: Stealing Your Good Name—and More

Theft of identity is a crime in which thieves hijack your name and identity and use your good credit rating to get cash or to buy things. To begin, all they need is your full name and Social Security number. Using these, they tap into Internet databases and come up with other information—your address, phone number, employer, driver's license number, mother's maiden name, and so on. Then they're off to the races, applying for credit everywhere.

In the event planner's case, someone had used information lifted from her employee-benefits form. The spending spree went on for months, unbeknownst to her. The reason it took so long to discover the theft was that the victim never saw any bills. They went to the address listed by the impersonator, a woman, who made a few payments to keep creditors at bay while she ran up even more bills. For the victim, straightening out the mess required months of frustrating phone calls, time off from work, court appearances, and legal expenses.

In 2009 and 2010 there were nearly 20 million victims of identity theft in the United States—more than the total number of burglaries, attempted burglaries, petty thefts, purse snatchings, pickpocketings, arsons, shoplifting, check fraud, and auto thefts combined. That works out to an average of more than 20,000 ID-thefts victims every seven days.[39]

The U.S. Federal Trade Commission (FTC; *www.ftc.gov/bcp/edu/microsites/idtheft/*) tracks identity theft statistics, helps victims, and coordinates responses by various governmental agencies. They estimate that recovering from identity theft takes an average of six months and 200 hours of work. One survey found that a third of victims of identity theft had still been unable to repair their tainted identities even a year after the information was stolen.[40]

How Does Identity Theft Start?

Identity theft typically starts in one of several ways:

- ***Wallet or purse theft:*** *There was a time when a thief would steal a wallet or purse, take the cash, and toss everything else. No more. Everything from keys to credit cards can be used for theft. (One famous victim of identity theft was then-Federal Reserve chairman Ben Bernanke, whose wife, Anna, had her purse stolen in a Starbucks coffee shop. The thief, it turned out, made as much as $50,000 a day on identity theft scams.)*
- ***Mail theft:*** *Thieves also consider mailboxes fair game. The mail will yield them bank statements, credit card statements, new checks, tax forms, and other personal information. (So it's best to receive your "snailmail" in a locked box—and mail your outgoing letters at a postbox.)*
- ***Mining the trash:*** *You might think nothing of throwing away credit card offers, portions of utility bills, or old canceled checks. But "dumpster diving" can produce gold for thieves. Credit card offers, for instance, may have limits of $5,000 or more.*
- ***Telephone solicitation:*** *Prospective thieves may call you up and pretend to represent a bank, credit card company, government agency, or the like in an attempt to pry loose essential data about you. Do not give out information over the phone unless predetermined passwords and identifying phrases are used; and never give your entire Social Security number under any circumstances.*
- ***Insider access to databases:*** *You never know who has, or could have, access to databases containing your personnel records, credit records, car-loan applications, bank documents, and so on. This is one of the harder ID-theft methods to guard against.*
- ***Outsider access to databases:*** *In recent years, data burglars and con artists have tapped into big databases at such companies as ChoicePoint, Reed Elsevier, DSW Shoe Warehouse, and Bank of America/Wachovia. Other institutions, such as CitiFinancial, the University of California at Berkeley, Time Warner, and MCI, have exposed files of data through carelessness. These losses have put millions of people at risk.*

Also, public use of debit cards has become very risky. Experts recommend that you use them only inside banks and other such secure places and, if necessary, only at bank ATM machines, being careful about covering your card while using it and your hand while typing in your PIN number.

What to Do Once Theft Happens

If you're the victim of a physical theft (or even loss), as when your wallet is snatched, you should immediately contact—first by phone, and then in writing—all your credit card companies, other financial institutions, the Department of Motor Vehicles, and any other organizations whose cards you use that are now compromised. Be sure to call utility companies—telephone, cellphone, electricity, and gas; identity thieves can run up enormous phone bills. Also call the local police and your insurance company to report the loss. File a complaint with the Federal Trade Commission (1-877-ID-THEFT, or *www.ftc.gov/bcp/edu/microsites/idtheft/consumers/form-filling-instructions.html*), which maintains an ID theft database.

Notify financial institutions within 2 days of learning of your loss, because then you usually are legally responsible for only the first $50 of any theft. If you become aware of fraudulent

panel 8.21

The three major credit bureaus

Equifax	Experian	TransUnion
To check your credit report: 800-685-1111	To check your credit report: 800-397-3742	To check your credit report: 800-493-2392
www.equifax.com	*www.experian.com*	*www.transunion.com*

transactions, immediately contact the fraud units of the three major credit bureaus: Equifax, Experian, and TransUnion. (● *See Panel 8.21.*)

If your Social Security number has been fraudulently used, alert the Social Security Administration (800-772-1213).

If you have a check guarantee card that was stolen, if your checks have been lost, or if a new checking account has been opened in your name, call your bank immediately.

If your mail has been used for fraudulent purposes or if an identity thief filed a change of address form, look in the phone directory under U.S. Government Postal Service for your local postal inspector's office and call them. In some states, you can freeze your credit reports, preventing lenders and others from reviewing your credit history, which will prevent identity thieves from opening fraudulent accounts using your name. (The FTC identity theft website explains how to do this.)

How to Prevent Identity Theft

One of the best ways to keep your finger on the pulse of your financial life is, on a regular basis—once a year, say—to get a copy of your credit report from one or all three of the main credit bureaus. This will show you whether there is any unauthorized activity. Reports are free from the major credit bureaus (Equifax, Experian, and Transunion). To learn more, go to *www.annualcreditreport.com* or call toll-free 877-322-8228.

In addition, there are some specific measures you can take to guard against personal information getting into the public realm.

- ***Check your credit card billing statements:*** *If you see some fraudulent charges, report them immediately. If you don't receive your statement, call the creditor first. Then call the post office to see if a change of address has been filed under your name.*
- ***Treat credit cards and other important papers with respect:*** *Make a list of your credit cards and other important documents and a list of numbers to call if you need to report them lost. (You can photocopy the cards front and back, but make sure the numbers are legible.)*

  Carry only one or two credit cards at a time. Carry your Social Security card, passport, or birth certificate only when needed.

  Don't dispose of credit card receipts in a public place.

  Don't give out your credit card numbers or Social Security number over the phone or on the Internet unless you have some sort of trusted relationship with the party on the other end.

  Tear up credit card offers before you throw them away. Even better, buy a shredder and shred these and other such documents.

  Keep a separate credit card for online transactions, so that if anything unusual happens you're more likely to notice it and you can more easily close the account.

  Keep tax records and other financial documents in a safe place.
- ***Treat passwords with respect:*** *Memorize passwords and PINs. Don't use your birth date, mother's maiden name, or similar common identifiers, which thieves may be able to guess (see* *p. 361* *on passwords).*
- ***Treat checks with respect:*** *Pick up new checks at the bank. Shred canceled checks before throwing them away. Don't let merchants write your credit card number on the check.*
- ***Watch out for "shoulder surfers" when using phones and ATMs:*** *When using PINs and passwords at public telephones and automated teller machines, shield your hand so that anyone watching through binoculars or using a video camera—"shoulder surfers"—can't read them.*
- ***Don't bother signing up for ID-theft protection programs:*** *Companies such as LifeLock and Invisus offer to keep watch on your credit reports and public records and to alert credit bureaus if they encounter fraud activity. Such companies have been sued for misleading advertising and misleading customers.*

TERMS & EXPLANATIONS

artificial intelligence (p. 440) Group of related technologies used for developing machines to emulate human qualities, such as learning, reasoning, communicating, seeing, and hearing. Why it's important: *Today the main areas of AI are expert systems, natural language processing, intelligent agents, pattern recognition, fuzzy logic, virtual reality and simulation devices, and robotics.*

business-to-business (B2B) system (p. 430) Direct sales between businesses that involve using the Internet or a private network to cut transaction costs and increase efficiencies. Why it's important: *Business-to-business activity helps business by moving beyond pricing mechanisms and encompassing product quality, customer support, credit terms, and shipping reliability, which often count for more than price.*

business-to-consumer (B2C) system (p. 431) System in which a business sells goods or services to consumers, or members of the general public. An example is Amazon.com. Why it's important: *This kind of e-commerce system essentially removes the middleman and often even the need for a physical ("bricks-and-mortar") store.*

character (p. 411) Also called *byte;* a single letter, number, or special character. Why it's important: *Characters—such as A, B, C, 1, 2, 3, #, $, %—are part of the data storage hierarchy.*

consumer-to-consumer (C2C) system (p. 432) System in which consumers sell goods or services directly to other consumers, often with the help of a third party, such as eBay. Why it's important: *The advantage of C2C e-commerce is most often the reduced costs and a smaller but profitable customer base. It also gives many small business owners a way to sell their goods without running a costly bricks-and-mortar store.*

data dictionary (p. 414) Also called *repository;* a procedures document or disk file that stores data definitions and descriptions of database structure. It may also monitor new entries to the database as well as user access to the database. Why it's important: *The data dictionary monitors the data being entered to make sure it conforms to the rules defined during data definition. The data dictionary may also help protect the security of the database by indicating who has the right to gain access to it.*

data mining (DM) (p. 425) Computer-assisted process of sifting through and analyzing vast amounts of data in order to extract hidden patterns and meaning and to discover new knowledge. Why it's important: *The purpose of DM is to describe past trends and predict future trends. Thus, data-mining tools might sift through a company's immense collections of customer, marketing, production, and financial data and identify what's worth noting and what's not.*

data storage hierarchy (p. 411) The levels of data stored in a computer database: bits, bytes (characters), fields (columns), records (rows), and tables (files). Why it's important: *Understanding the data storage hierarchy is necessary to understand how to use a database.*

data warehouse (p. 427) A database containing cleaned-up data and meta-data (information about the data) stored using high-capacity-disk storage technology. Why it's important: *Data warehouses combine vast amounts of data from many sources in a database form that can be searched, for example, for patterns not recognizable with smaller amounts of data.*

database (p. 411) Logically organized collection of related data designed and built for a specific purpose, a technology for pulling together facts that allows the slicing and dicing and mixing and matching of data. Why it's important: *Businesses and organizations build databases to help them keep track of and manage their affairs. In addition, online database services put enormous research resources at the user's disposal.*

database administrator (DBA) (p. 416) Person who coordinates all related activities and needs for an organization's database. Why it's important: *The DBA determines user access privileges; sets standards, guidelines, and control procedures; assists in establishing priorities for requests; prioritizes conflicting user needs; develops user documentation and input procedures; and oversees the system's security.*

database management system (DBMS) (p. 413) Also called *database manager;* software that controls the structure of a database and access to the data. It allows users to manipulate more than one file at a time. Why it's important: *This software enables sharing of data (same information is available to different users); economy of files (several departments can use one file instead of each individually maintaining its own file, thus reducing data redundancy, which in turn reduces the expense of storage media and hardware); data integrity (changes made in the files in one department are automatically made in the files in other departments); and security (access to specific information can be limited to selected users).*

DBMS utilities (p. 415) Programs that allow users to maintain databases by creating, editing, and deleting data, rows (records), and tables (files). Why it's important: *DBMS utilities allow people to establish what is acceptable input data, to monitor the types of data being input, and to adjust display screens for data input.*

decision support system (DSS) (p. 438) Computer-based information system that helps managers with nonroutine decision-making tasks. Inputs consist of some summarized reports, some processed transaction data, and other internal data plus data from sources outside the organization. The outputs are flexible, on-demand reports. Why it's important: *A DSS is installed to help top managers and middle managers make strategic decisions about unstructured problems.*

e-commerce (p. 429) Electronic commerce; the buying and selling of products and services through computer networks. Why it's important: *U.S. e-commerce and online shopping are growing even faster than the increase in computer use.*

executive support system (ESS) (p. 439) Also called an *executive information system (EIS);* DSS made especially for top managers. It draws on data from both inside and outside the organization. Why it's important: *The ESS includes capabilities for analyzing data and doing "what if" scenarios to help with strategic decision making.*

expert system (p. 440) Also called *knowledge-based system;* set of interactive computer programs that helps users solve problems that would otherwise require the assistance of a human expert. Expert systems are created on the basis of knowledge collected on specific topics from human specialists, and they imitate the reasoning process of a human being. Why it's important: *Expert systems are used by both management and nonmanagement personnel to solve specific problems, such as how to reduce production costs, improve workers' productivity, or reduce environmental impact.*

field (p. 412) Also called column; unit of data consisting of one or more characters (bytes). Examples of fields are your first name, your street address, or your Social Security number. Why it's important: *A collection of fields makes up a record.*

file (table) (p. 412) Collection of related records; the file is at the top of the data hierarchy. An example of a file is a stored listing of everyone employed in the same department of a company, including all names, addresses, and Social Security numbers. Why it's important: *A file is the collection of data or information that is treated as a unit by the computer; a collection of related files makes up a database.*

fuzzy logic (p. 444) Method of dealing with imprecise data and uncertainty, with problems that have many answers rather than one. Why it's important: *Unlike "crisp," yes/no digital logic, fuzzy logic deals with probability and credibility.*

identity theft (p. 455) ID theft; also called *theft of identity (TOI);* crime in which thieves hijack a person's name and identity and use his or her information and credit rating to get cash or buy things. Why it's important: *Identity theft is on the rise in developed countries; it can ruin a person's life for many years.*

intelligent agent (p. 443) Software with built-in intelligence that monitors work tasks, asks questions, and performs work tasks, such as roaming networks, on the user's behalf. Why it's important: *An intelligent agent can filter messages, scan news services, travel over communications lines to databases, and collect files to add to a personal database.*

management information system (MIS) (p. 437) Computer-based information system that uses data recorded by TPS as input into programs that produce summary, exception, periodic, and on-demand reports of the organization's performance. Why it's important: *An MIS principally assists middle managers, helping them make tactical decisions—spotting trends and getting an overview of current business activities.*

multidimensional database (MDB) (p. 424) Type of database that models data as facts, dimensions, or numerical measures for use in the interactive analysis of large amounts of data for decision-making purposes. A multidimensional database uses the idea of a cube to represent the dimensions of data available to a user, using up to four dimensions. Why it's important: *A multidimensional database allows users to ask questions in colloquial English.*

natural language processing (p. 443) Study of ways for computers to recognize and understand human language, whether in spoken or written form. Why it's important: *Natural languages make it easier to work with computers.*

object-oriented database (p. 423) Database that uses "objects," software written in small, reusable chunks, as elements within database files. An object consists of (1) data in any form, including graphics, audio, and video, and (2) instructions for the action to be taken on the data. Why it's important: *A hierarchical or network database might contain only numeric and text data. By contrast, an object-oriented database might also contain photographs, sound bites, and video clips. Moreover, the object would store operations, called methods, the programs that objects use to process themselves.*

office information system (OIS) (p. 436) Also called *office automation system (OAS);* computer information system that combines various technologies to reduce the manual labor needed to operate an office efficiently and increase productivity; used at all levels of an organization. Why it's important: *An OIS uses a network to integrate such technologies as fax, voice mail, email, scheduling software, word processing, and desktop publishing, among others, and make them available throughout the organization.*

pattern recognition (p. 443) Use of camera and software to identify recurring patterns and to recognize the connections between the perceived patterns and similar patterns stored in a database. Why it's important: *Pattern recognition is used in data mining to discover previously unnoticed patterns; in facial recognition software to identify faces; and in handwriting recognition, fingerprint identification, robot vision, and automatic voice recognition.*

query by example (QBE) (p. 421) Feature of query-language programs whereby the user asks for information in a database by using a sample record to define the qualifications he or she wants for selected records. Why it's important: *QBE simplifies database use.*

record (row) (p. 412) Collection of related fields. An example of a record is your name and address and Social Security number. Why it's important: *Related records make up a table (file).*

relational database (p. 420) Database that relates, or connects, data in different tables of rows and columns through the use of primary keys, or common data elements. In this arrangement there are no access paths down through a hierarchy. In database terminology, the tables are called *relations* (files), the rows are called *tuples* (records), and the columns are called *attributes* (fields). Why it's important: *The relational database is now the most common database structure; it is more flexible than hierarchical and network database models.*

report generator (p. 415) In a database management system, a program users can employ to produce on-screen or printed-out documents from all or part of a database. Why it's important: *Report generators allow users to easily produce finished-looking reports.*

robotics (p. 445) Development and study of machines that can perform work normally done by people. Why it's important: *Commercial and industrial robots perform jobs more cheaply or with greater accuracy and reliability than humans. They are also used for jobs that are too dirty, dangerous, or dull to be suitable for humans. Robots are widely used in manufacturing, assembly and packing, transport, earth and space exploration, surgery, weaponry, laboratory research, and mass production of consumer and industrial goods.*

simulator (p. 445) Device that represents the behavior of physical or abstract systems. Why it's important: *Virtual-reality simulation technologies are widely applied for training purposes.*

the Singularity (p. 451) Also called *the technological singularity,* a moment when humans would have created self-aware, smarter-than-human machines that are capable of designing computers and robots that are better than humans can make today. Why it's important: *According to this concept, technological progress would have accelerated so much that machine intelligence would dominate,* *transferring the contents of human brains and thought processes into a computing environment, making a form of immortality possible.*

structured query language (SQL) (p. 420) Standard language used to create, modify, maintain, and query relational databases. Why it's important: *SQL simplifies database use.*

table (file) (p. 412) Collection of related records. An example of a table is a stored listing of everyone employed in the same department of a company, including all names, addresses, and Social Security numbers. Why it's important: *A table is the collection of data or information that is treated as a unit by the computer; a collection of related tables makes up a database.*

transaction processing system (TPS) (p. 436) Computer-based information system that keeps track of the transactions needed to conduct business. Inputs are transaction data (such as bills or orders). Outputs are processed transactions (such as bills or paychecks). Why it's important: *The TPS helps supervisory managers in making operational decisions. The data collected by a TPS is typically stored in databases.*

virtual reality (VR) (p. 445) Computer-generated artificial reality that projects a person into a sensation of three-dimensional space. Why it's important: *VR is employed in simulators for training programs.*

CHAPTER REVIEW

LEARNING MEMORIZATION

"I can recognize and recall information."

Self-Test Questions

1. According to the data storage hierarchy, databases are composed of (small to large) ________, ________, ________, ________, and ________.
2. An individual piece of data within a record is called a(n) ________.
3. A(n) ___________ coordinates all activities related to an organization's database.
4. __________ is the right of people not to reveal information about themselves.
5. The five types of database models are _________, ________, ________, ________, and ________.
6. A single letter or number is considered a(n) ________.
7. A(n) _______ is a logically organized collection of related data designed and built for a specific purpose.
8. A(n) _______ is a collection of related fields (columns).
9. A(n) _______ is an automatic device that performs functions ordinarily performed by human beings.
10. The goal of _______ is to enable the computer to communicate with the user in the user's native language.
11. _________ is a group of related technologies used for developing machines to emulate human qualities such as learning, reasoning, communicating, seeing, and hearing.
12. Devices that represent the behavior of physical or abstract systems are called ________.
13. When unauthorized persons use your name to get cash and buy things, it is called _______.
14. Most organizations have six departments: ________, ________, ________, ________, ________, and ________.
15. _________ is used to create, modify, maintain, and query relational databases.

Multiple-Choice Questions

1. Which of the following is *not* an advantage of a DBMS?
   a. file sharing
   b. reduced data redundancy
   c. increased data redundancy
   d. improved data integrity
   e. increased security
2. Which of the following qualities are necessary for information to be "good"?
   a. concise
   b. complete
   c. verifiable
   d. current
   e. all of these
3. Which of the following database models relates, or connects, data in different files through the use of a key, or common data element?
   a. hierarchical
   b. network
   c. object-oriented
   d. relational
   e. offline
4. Which of the following areas of study is *not* included in AI?
   a. pattern recognition
   b. fuzzy logic
   c. transaction processing systems
   d. natural language processing
   e. robotics

5. Which of the following levels is *not* a management level?
   a. strategic
   b. tactical
   c. hierarchical
   d. operational
   e. all of these are management levels

True/False Questions

T F 1. The use of key fields makes it easier to locate a record in a database.

T F 2. A network database models data as facts, dimensions, or numerical measures for use in interactive analysis of large amounts of data for decision-making purposes.

T F 3. A database is an organized collection of integrated files.

T F 4. Data mining is used only for small databases.

T F 5. A character is smaller than a field.

T F 6. A report generator is a machine that produces electricity by calculating complex algorithms.

T F 7. A data dictionary defines the basic organization of the database and contains a list of all files in the database.

T F 8. Most types of storage media last indefinitely.

T F 9. Expert systems are not interactive.

T F 10. You need only software to create virtual reality.

T F 11. A knowledge base is part of a natural language system.

2 LEARNING COMPREHENSION

"I can recall information in my own terms and explain it to a friend."

Short-Answer Questions

1. Name three responsibilities of a database administrator.
2. What is data mining?
3. Briefly explain what a data warehouse is.
4. List four basic advantages provided by database management systems.
5. What are expert systems used for?
6. What is SQL? QBE? Oracle? Access? DB2?
7. Explain e-commerce.
8. What are some things you can do if identity theft happens to you?
9. What are intelligent agents used for?
10. What do you need to experience virtual reality?
11. What is the main difference between weak AI and strong AI?
12. What are the four main areas of artificial intelligence?
13. What is a DSS used for? An ESS?

3 LEARNING APPLYING, ANALYZING , SYNTHESIZING, EVALUATING

"I can apply what I've learned, relate these ideas to other concepts, build on other knowledge, and use all these thinking skills to form a judgment."

Knowledge in Action

1. Interview someone who works with or manages an organization's database. What types of records make up the database? Which departments use it? What database structure is used? What are the types and sizes of storage devices? How many servers are used? Where are they? Was the database software custom-written?
2. Are you comfortable with giving away some of your privacy for increased security? Why or why not? How far would you let the government go in examining people's private lives?
3. Can identity theft be prevented? Propose some new solutions to this problem.
4. If you could design a robot, what kind would you create? What would it do?
5. If you could build an expert system, what would it do? What kinds of questions would you ask experts in order to elicit the appropriate information?
6. Should Internet-purchased products or services have a sales tax (like items purchased in regular stores)? Why or why not?
7. Do you know someone who refuses to use the Internet in any manner that requires entering any personal information whatsoever? Give some reasons for disagreeing and for agreeing with this person.

Web Exercises

1. Have you ever thought of starting your own B2C business? Search for articles on this topic. How many successful B2C businesses can you find that started with very little seed money? If you went ahead with your venture, would you use PayPal? Why or why not?
2. Visit these sites about data mining and the search for meaningfulness in large quantities of data:

   www.dmbenchmarking.com

   www.dmg.org

   www.anderson.ucla.edu/faculty/jason.frand/teacher/technologies/palace/datamining.htm

   www.dwreview.com/Data_mining/index.html

   www.laits.utexas.edu/~norman/BUS.FOR/course.mat/Alex/

www.the-modeling-agency.com/data-mining-examples.html

www.expertstown.com/data-mining-examples/

How does data mining affect you directly? How could it be used in your planned profession?

3. Grocery store loyalty cards ask consumers to trade detailed personal information in return for the promise of savings—which may in fact not exist. Some experts say the reason that stores offer cards is so that they can profile and target their customers more accurately—not to give you savings but to increase their bottom line. Also, your personal information can be sold or traded to third parties.

   One way that grocery stores create customer profiles is by the use of data mining. There are positive aspects to data mining, such as fraud detection, but there is a darker side to data mining, too.

   Stores may use the address information from your loyalty card application to match up your shopping history with data from other databases or public records (income, how much you paid for your house) so that the store knows what kinds of specials to offer you. Information about your shopping habits can be accessed with a subpoena or warrant and used against you in court proceedings. In a "trip-and-fall" case in California, a man shopping at a Southern California grocery store sued after falling in one of the aisles. It was reported (although the store denied it) that the store threatened to use his shopping history—which included large amounts of alcohol—against him in the proceedings.

   Some states limit the types of information that a grocery store can collect from you when you register for a loyalty card. For example, California state law prohibits a grocery store from requiring that you turn over your Social Security card or your driver's license number. However, data matching techniques mean that this provides very little protection to your privacy rights.

   Find out more about loyalty cards. Read the *BusinessWeek* article at *www.businessweek.com/bwdaily/dnflash/jun2002/nf20020620_7007.htm* and the About.com article at *http://couponing.about.com/od/groceryzone/a/loyaltyprograms.htm.* Also check out *http://couponing.about.com/od/groceryzone/a/disccards.htm* and *www.nytimes.com/2010/04/29/business/media/29adco.html.* Find a few more articles and then write a short report on the ethical aspects and the practical aspects of using loyalty cards.

4. How much information about you is out there? Run various search strings about yourself to see just how private your life is. Also read a few articles about how social networking sites commodify user's personal information and sell it to all sorts of entities.

5. An extensive database featuring photographs of and detailed information on each inmate of the Florida Department of Corrections can be found at this website:

   www.dc.state.fl.us/inmateinfo/inmateinfomenu.asp

   Click on Search All Corrections Offenders Databases. Then, in the text boxes, type in a common last name and a common first name, and anything else you care to enter, and click on Submit Request.

   Click on any of the following links to see the offender records that matched your search criteria:

   Inmate Population Search Results
   Inmate Release Search Results
   Supervised Population Search Results
   Absconder/Fugitive Search Results

   What kind of databases do you think these are? Do you think such databases are useful? Ethical? If you think they are useful, give your reasons.

6. What is a DNA database? Visit the following websites to learn more:

   www.familyhelix.com/articles/national-dna-database/index.php

   www.guardian.co.uk/uk/2005/apr/11/science.ukcrime

   http://ndbserver.rutgers.edu/

7. Read the following articles regarding the Homeland Security Database:

   www.dna.gov/dna-databases/

   www.dna.gov/

   www.foxnews.com/story/0,2933,70992,00.html

   www.cdispatch.com/articles/2008/07/18/local_news/area_news/area02.txt

   www.twotigersonline.com/resources.html

   www.msnbc.msn.com/id/13822662/

   http://geneticassociationdb.nih.gov/

   What is your opinion of the efficacy of such a database? Have you any concerns about the ethics or constitutionality of any aspects of this database?

8. Visit these websites for more information on identity theft:

   www.usdoj.gov/criminal/fraud/websites/idtheft.html

   www.fool.com/ccc/check/check06.htm

   http://illinoisissues.uis.edu/features/2002mar/name.html

   www.ftc.gov/bcp/edu/microsites/idtheft/

   Are you putting yourself at risk? What can you do to improve your situation?

9. Virtual reality is being used in some surprising areas. Visit:

   www.vrac.iastate.edu/

   http://vresources.org/applications/applications.shtml

   www.sciencedaily.com/news/computers_math/virtual_reality/

   http://science.howstuffworks.com/virtual-military.htm

   http://electronics.howstuffworks.com/gadgets/other-gadgets/virtual-reality6.htm

   Which area might you be interested in, and why?

9

THE CHALLENGES OF THE DIGITAL AGE Society & Information Technology Today

Chapter Topics & Key Questions

9.1 **Truth Issues: Manipulating Digital Data** What are some ways digitized output can be manipulated to fool people?

9.2 **Security Issues: Threats to Computers & Communications Systems** What are some key threats to computers?

9.3 **Security Safeguards: Protecting Computers & Communications** What are the characteristics of the five components of security?

9.4 **Quality-of-Life Issues: The Environment, Mental Health, Child Protection, & the Workplace** How does information technology create environmental, mental-health, pornography, and workplace problems?

9.5 **Economic & Political Issues: Employment & the Haves/Have-Nots** How may technology affect employment and the gap between rich and poor?

Download the free UIT 10e App for key term flash cards, quizzes, and a game, *Over the Edge*

omputers have invaluable uses for specialized work . . . but we need to question the assumption that whatever ails modern society can be cured by more information.

Indeed, Gilliam goes on, many users "are hypnotized by the computer's power to summon endless arrays of facts—information without context, data without values, knowledge without perspective."[1]

Such matters have taken on more urgency since the beginning of the war on terrorism that started on September 11, 2001, when terrorist-hijacked planes destroyed the World Trade Center Twin Towers in New York City and part of the Pentagon in Washington, D.C. The sense of urgency was reinforced by the March 2004 Madrid train bombings in Spain and the July 2005 terrorist bombings in London, considered the worst attack on that city since World War II. These attacks were followed by the shooting and bombing attacks on Mumbai, India, in 2008. And, of course, smaller attacks and unsuccessful (prevented) acts of terrorism throughout the world have continued and remain ongoing today.

Will the resulting tougher security rules imposed everywhere (including on the use of information technology) be beneficial? How can we evaluate the effect of more names in more databases, for instance, on lost privacy and even lost liberty? What kind of context or perspective will help us? One possible tool used by advocates at both ends of the political spectrum is cost-benefit analysis—to analyze the tradeoffs of heightened security on privacy, convenience, and ease of movement. Even if we can't always assign precise dollar amounts, it's important to weigh issues in a way that will prevent security goals from overtaking common sense.[2]

The Mumbai, India, terrorist attacks, November 2008, killed at least 173 people and wounded at least 308. Here firefighters try to douse the fire as smoke rises from the Taj hotel building in Mumbai.

College students continually face issues of information technology that concern which benefits need to be balanced against costs. For instance, should the U.S. Department of Defense be allowed to collect information about students for a database designed for military recruiting purposes, and does that invade your privacy rights?[3] Should your Social Security number be used as a key identifier in campus records if there's a chance low-paid clerks might steal it to apply for bogus credit cards?[4] Should laptops, cellphones, and wireless technology be allowed in classrooms if students will mainly use them to text and web surf instead of attending to the lecture? Should online instructor rating systems be allowed if prospective employers can also access them to see whether you mainly took easy courses? Should there be tighter government scrutiny of foreign students, even though this may result in their going to other countries instead of to the United States?

Such are the examples of the many infotech challenges that confront us. Elsewhere in the book we have considered ergonomics (Chapter 5) and privacy (Chapter 8). In this chapter, we consider some other major issues:

- Truth issues—manipulation of sound and images in digital data
- Security issues—accidents, natural hazards, terrorist hazards, and crime
- Quality-of-life issues—environment, mental health, child protection, the workplace
- Economic and political issues—employment and the haves/have-nots

9.1 TRUTH ISSUES: Manipulating Digital Data

Cat-erpillar? You know that such a creature does not exist. But other types of morphing are difficult to detect. Is truth an issue in such cases?

Information technology has facilitated the manipulation of all sorts of data, including text, sound, and images; this has led to big new problems in the area of credibility, especially for journalism.

The enormous capacities of today's storage devices have given photographers, graphics professionals, and others a new tool—the ability to manipulate images at the pixel level. For example, photographers can easily do *morphing*—transforming one image into another—using image-altering software such as Adobe Photoshop. In morphing, a film or video image is displayed on a computer screen and altered pixel by pixel, or dot by dot. As a result, the image metamorphoses into something else—a pair of lips morphs into the front of a Toyota, for example, or an owl into a baby.

The ability to manipulate digitized output—images and sounds—has brought a wonderful new tool to art. However, it has created some big new ethical problems. How can we know that what we're seeing or hearing is the truth? Consider the following areas of concern.

more info!

Sound Manipulation & Journalism

What is the Associated Press's policy on sound manipulation? Read under "Audio" at:

www2.sabew.org/sabewweb.nsf/8247d0ca4c256f7286256ad800773610/8381127078e05a0c862572ff00620a8b!OpenDocument

And the radio industry's?

http://prndg.org/huntsberger-qear

Manipulation of Sound

When does sound manipulation cross the line from improvement to misrepresentation?

In recent times, pop music vocals have been sounding "note- and pitch-perfect," and even some hip-hop singers have been hitting their notes with exaggerated precision, points out one writer. How is this done? Through a technology called Auto-Tune that "can take a vocal and instantly nudge it onto the proper note or move it to the correct pitch. . . . [I]t can transform wavering performance into something technically flawless."[5] Unfortunately, when most songs seem to have perfect pitch, they are harder to differentiate from one another, leading to bland sameness.

Technological manipulation of music is not new. In 2004 country music artist Anita Cochran released some new vocals, including a duet, "(I Wanna Hear) a Cheatin' Song," with Conway Twitty—who had died a decade before the song was written. The producers pulled snippets of Twitty's voice from his recording sessions, put them on a computer hard drive in digital form, and used software known as Pro Tools to patch the pieces together. Ten years earlier Frank Sinatra's 1994 album *Duets* paired him through technological tricks with such singers as Barbra Streisand, Liza Minnelli, and Bono of U2. Sinatra recorded solos live in a recording studio. His singing partners, while listening to his taped performance on earphones, dubbed in their own voices. These second voices were recorded not only at different times but often from different places. The illusion in the final recording is that the two singers are standing together in the same room. Many people think the practice of assembling bits and pieces in a studio like this drains the music of its essential flow and unity. But is this fraud?

Whatever the problems of misrepresentation in art, however, they pale beside those in journalism. What if, for example, a radio or TV news station were to edit a stream of digitized sound/video so as to misrepresent what actually happened?

"Fair Use"

This term refers to the conditions under which you can use, and manipulate, material that is copyrighted by someone else without paying royalties. When can you do this?

www.copyright.gov/fls/fl102.html

http://fairuse.stanford.edu/Copyright_and_Fair_Use_Overview/chapter9/9-a.html

http://login.vnuemedia.com/pdn/content_display/resources/is-it-legal/e3i7c8f9d806fcefe2e4a8047b1258461af

http://whatis.techtarget.com/definition/0,,sid9_gci1089600,00.html

The National Press Photographers Association's policy:

www.nppa.org/professional_development/business_practices/digitalethics.html

Manipulation of Photos

And when does photo manipulation cross the line from improvement to misrepresentation?

In one famous photo manipulation case, a Danish computer company employee created an image purporting to show a photo from a 1954 issue of *Popular Mechanics* of what a future home computer was expected to look like; it

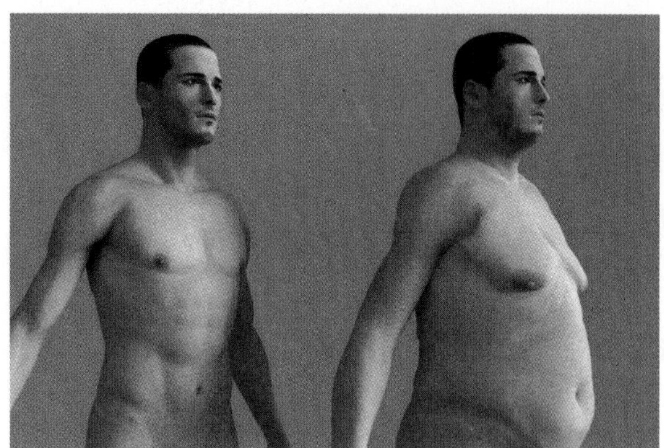

Who is the real person? Is either real?

ended up being misused by a person who believed that it was real. *(● See Panel 9.1.)* When in 2005 editors at *Newsweek* ran a cover photo of style guru Martha Stewart, who had been sent to prison for lying to federal investigators, they put a photo of her face on someone else's body, making the 63-year-old look terrific after five months behind bars. When ex–sports star O. J. Simpson was arrested in 1994 on suspicion of murder, a *Time* artist working with a computer modified the police department mug shot and darkened the image so that O. J.'s face had a sinister cast to it (go to *https://webspace.utexas.edu/cherwitz/www/ie/samples/stavchansky.pdf to see these photos*). (*Newsweek* ran the mug shot unmodified.) In May 2011, after the killing of Taliban leader Osama bin Laden by U.S. Navy Seals, the newspapers *Der Tzitung and Dee Voch* "photoshopped" U.S. Secretary of State Hillary Clinton and Director for Counterterrorism Audrey Tomason out of the White House-released "Situation Room" photo that accompanied the story—ostensibly because they are women.[6] *(● See Panel 9.2.)*

Should magazines and newspapers that report the news be taking such artistic license? At the least, shouldn't magazines be running credit lines (as *The New York Times Magazine* often does) that say something such as "Photographic illustration by X" or "Photomontage by Y, with digital manipulation by Z"?[7]

Jon Knoll, who created the image-editing program Photoshop in 1989, said later, "Mostly we saw the possibilities, the cool things, not how it would be abused."[8] But, as we have seen, Photoshop and similar programs designed to edit ("morph") digital images can obviously also be used to distort and falsify them.

Fortunately, some steps are being taken to combat this kind of digital deception. For example, Corbis, the online stock photo agency, places an imperceptible digital watermark on the more than 100 million images it makes available, which encodes information about the owner of the image within the pixels of the photograph and can be traced even if the image has been modified.

Survival Tip

Is It True?

Snopes.com, a website for debunking urban legends and hoaxes, includes a section on composite photos, some true, some fake. Go to:

www.snopes.com

panel 9.1

Photo manipulation

A manipulated photo of a typical 1950s nuclear-powered submarine console was passed off as a 1950s projection of the 2004 home computer. A well-known CEO of a computer technology company actually used the photo, believing it was real, during a speech in 2004. The image was created by a Danish hardware and software distributor, who used the submarine shot, doctored it, and entered it in a photo-manipulation contest. He said he had not intended to create a believable fake.

Scientists from the RAND Corporation have created this model to illustrate how a "home computer" could look like in the year 2004. However the needed technology will not be economically feasible for the average home. Also the scientists readily admit that the computer will require not yet invented technology to actually work, but 50 years from now scientific progress is expected to solve these problems. With teletype interface and the Fortran language, the computer will be easy to use.

panel 9.2

"Photoshopping"

In May 2011 at least two newspapers used software to erase the pictures of two important people (who happened to be women; see right) who were present in U.S. President Obama's "situation room" during the actions against terrorist Osama bin Laden (see left) (*FailedMessiah.typepad.com*).

In another technique, Dartmouth College computer science professor Hany Farid has codeveloped a program called PhotoDNA that can detect changes in photographic images.

Does Photoshopping = False Advertising, Especially for Beauty Products?

"Photoshopping and manipulating photos has become such a regular occurrence that we often see many distorted images on a daily basis without questioning them. . . . Issues that have risen with the increased use of Photoshop are seen to occur mostly in journalism and advertisement[s] and have placed an immense amount of pressure on young females to achieve the look of the technologically altered ideal . . . women" ("Maybe She's Born with It, Maybe It's Photoshop," *http://techlifepost.com/2009/02/13/photo-manipulation-false-advertising/*).

http://jennhaskins.com/images/work/photo-manipulation-paper.pdf

Manipulation of Video & Television

Any user of YouTube is already aware of how regularly software is used to edit videos.

The technique of morphing, used in still photos, takes a massive jump when used in TV news videos, and television commercials. For example, a Baltimore television reporter lost his job after acknowledging that he doctored a video to make it appear that a rival host had made a racial slur.[9] A daily news show caught another news show and one of its hosts in what appeared to be a blatant example of doctoring a report with inappropriate video to enhance an argument.[10]

And, of course, digital image manipulation has had a tremendous impact on filmmaking. It can be used to erase jet contrails from the sky in a western and to make digital planes do impossible stunts. It is used for all sorts of special effects. And it can even be used to add and erase actors. And it is possible to create virtual images during live television events. These images—such as a Coca-Cola logo in the center of a soccer field—don't exist in reality but millions of viewers see them on their TV screens.

9.2 SECURITY ISSUES: Threats to Computers & Communications Systems

Connecting to the Internet can be rewarding and interesting. However, any computer connected to the Internet is exposed to security threats.

Internet users just don't have "street smarts" about online safety and that makes them vulnerable.[11] And although some users think they are able to recognize when they are being manipulated, either legally or illegally, in fact they may be wrong. But, as we have discussed in previous chapters, there is much that we as individuals can and must do to protect our own security.

Image Analysis Software

http://lifehacker.com/5644259/how-to-detect-a-photoshopped-image

www.sqnbankingsystems.com/CAT_image_fraud.html

panel 9.3

Examples of threats to computers and communications systems

Threat Category	Types of Threats
Errors and accidents	• Human errors • Procedural errors • Software errors • Electromechanical problems • "Dirty data" problems
Natural hazards	• Flood • Hurricane • Fire • Earthquake • Tornado
Computer crimes	• Theft of hardware • Theft of software • Theft of online music and movies • Theft of time and services • Theft of information • Internet-related fraud • Taking over your PC: zombies, botnets, and blackmail • Crimes of malice: crashing entire systems
Computer criminals	• Individuals or small groups • Employees • Outside partners and suppliers • Corporate spies • Foreign intelligence services • Organized crime • Terrorists

Security issues go right to the heart of the workability of computer and communications systems. Here we discuss the following threats. *(• See Panel 9.3.)*

- Errors and accidents
- Natural hazards
- Computer crimes
- Computer criminals

Errors & Accidents

In general, errors and accidents in computer systems may be classified as human errors, procedural errors, software errors, "dirty data" problems, and electromechanical problems.

HUMAN ERRORS Which would you trust—human or computer? If you were a pilot and your plane's collision-avoidance computer told you to ascend but a human air-traffic controller told you to descend, which order would you follow? In 2001 a Russian pilot near the Swiss-German border ignored his computer (against mandatory regulations) and complied with erroneous human orders, resulting in a collision with another plane.[12]

Human errors can be of several types. Quite often, when experts speak of the "unintended effects of technology," what they are referring to are the unexpected things people do with it. Among the ways in which people can complicate the workings of a system are the following:[13]

- **Humans often are not good at assessing their own information needs:** For example, many users will acquire a computer and communications system that either is not sophisticated enough or is far more complex than they need.
- **Human emotions affect performance:** For example, one frustrating experience with a computer is enough to make some people abandon the whole system. But smashing your keyboard isn't going to get you any closer to learning how to use it better.
- **Humans act on their perceptions, which may not be fast enough to keep up:** In modern information environments, human perceptions are often too slow to keep up with the equipment. Human perception may be affected by information overload, for example, or vagueness about the value of information, as happened when English government workers carelessly lost computer disks containing personal and financial details about 25 million residents worth $2.5 billion on the black market.[14] It may also be affected by unwarranted self-assurance about one's own abilities, as happens every day when people text on their cellphones in cars hurtling along at 65 miles per hour.

PROCEDURAL ERRORS Some spectacular computer failures have occurred because someone didn't follow procedures. In 1999 the $125 million Mars Climate Orbiter was fed data expressed in pounds, the English unit of force, instead of newtons, the metric unit (about 22% of a pound). As a result, the spacecraft flew too close to the surface of Mars and broke apart. In 2009 a highly confidential document listing the U.S. nuclear sites was inadvertently posted on the Government Printing Office's website.[15]

SOFTWARE ERRORS We often hear about "software glitches" or "software bugs." A *software bug* is an error in a program that causes it not to work properly. For example, in 2008 experts found a software glitch that would have allowed attackers to gain control of water treatment plants, natural gas pipelines, and other utilities.[16] Also in 2008, patients at Veterans Administration health centers were given incorrect drug doses, were delayed in treatments, and experienced other medical errors because of software glitches in health records.[17] And it turns out that the U.S. 2012 Diversity Lottery wasn't fair. More than 12 million people applied for the green card lottery, but in a statement posted to the web, the U.S. Deputy Assistant Secretary of State for Visa Services said the results "did not represent a fair random selection of the entrants, as required by U.S. law. Although we received large numbers of entries every day during the 30-day registration period, a computer programming error caused more than 90% of the selectees to come from the first two days of the registration period."[18]

"DIRTY DATA" PROBLEMS What does GIGO mean? It means "garbage in, garbage out," which refers to "dirty data." When keyboarding a research paper, you undoubtedly make a few typing errors (which, we hope, you clean up). So do all the data-entry people around the world who feed a continual stream of raw data into computer systems. A lot of database problems in particular are caused by this kind of dirty data. *Dirty data* is incomplete, outdated, or otherwise inaccurate data.

Some common causes of dirty data:[19]

- Wrong field sizes
- Wrong and inconsistent data formats
- Logical inconsistency—for example, typing zipcodes into phone number boxes, spelling the same name different ways

- User errors resulting from lack of training, misunderstanding procedures, and the like
- Most of the problems arise when database input workers are dealing with text or spreadsheet files—especially files from many different countries

A good reason for having a look at your records—credit, medical, school—is so that you can make any corrections to them before they cause you complications. Although databases are a time-saving resource for information seekers, they can also act as catalysts, speeding up and magnifying bad data.

ELECTROMECHANICAL PROBLEMS: ARE "NORMAL ACCIDENTS" INEVITABLE? Mechanical systems, such as printers, and electrical systems, such as circuit boards, don't always work. They may be faultily constructed, get dirty or overheated, wear out, or become damaged in some other way. Two examples:

- **Electrical problems:** Power failures (brownouts and blackouts) can shut a system down. Power surges can also burn out equipment. One major area of concern is that as information technology spreads, lightning strikes that once simply made the houselights flicker will now burn out computers, phones, web connections, and servers. Since some areas experience more electrical hits than other areas do, lightning frequency could significantly affect regional economies.
- **Voting machine breakdowns:** As examples of how badly information technology can work, we have only to consider failures in voting machines, when printers jammed, servers crashed, and poorly designed touch-screen ballots led voters to make mistakes that invalidated their votes.[20]

Modern systems are made up of thousands of parts, all of which interrelate in ways that are impossible to anticipate. Because of that complexity, "normal accidents" are inevitable.[21] That is, it is almost certain that some combinations of minor failures will eventually amount to something catastrophic. Indeed, it is just such collections of small failures that led to catastrophes such as the blowing up of the *Challenger* space shuttle in 1986 and the near-meltdown of the Three Mile Island nuclear-power plant in 1979. In the Digital Age, "normal accidents" will not be anomalies but are to be expected. They will also be more global in their impact.[22]

All these considerations suggest that we need to take a hard look at the concept of storing all our information "in the cloud"—that is, online instead of on our own personal computers. Putting all our information online means we can never be quite sure who has access to it or whether it might be destroyed, either deliberately or inadvertently.

Natural Hazards

Considering the unpredictable nature of natural catastrophes and accidents, it is always best to remain prepared by backing up all data offsite.

Some disasters do not merely lead to temporary system downtime; they can wreck the entire system. Examples are natural hazards.

Whatever is harmful to property (and people) is harmful to computers and communications systems. This certainly includes natural disasters: fires, floods, earthquakes, tornadoes, hurricanes, blizzards, and the like. If they inflict damage over a wide area, as have ice storms in eastern Canada, hurricanes in the Gulf Coast states (for example, Katrina in 2005) , and earthquakes in New Zealand (2010) and Japan (2010, 2011), tsunamis (such as in Thailand in 2004 and Japan in 2011), and frequent fires in southwestern U.S. states (such as Texas), natural hazards can disable all the electronic systems we take for granted. Without power and communications connections, not just computers but cellphones, automated teller machines, credit card verifiers, and bank computers are useless.

Computer Crimes

There are many types of crimes that involve computers, but they fall into basically two types: the computer is the target or the computer is the tool.

Because of the opening of borders, the growth of low-cost international transportation, and the rise of the Internet, crime in general has become globalized, and computer crime is a big part of it. **A *computer crime* can be of two types. (1) It can be an illegal act perpetrated against computers or telecommunications,** such as hardware theft, or **(2) it can be the use of computers or telecommunications to accomplish an illegal act,** such as identity theft.

THEFT OF HARDWARE Hardware theft can range from shoplifting an accessory in a computer store to removing a laptop or cellular phone from someone's car. Professional criminals may steal shipments of microprocessor chips off a loading dock, steal desktop computers, laptops, and other devices for their parts, or even pry cash machines out of shopping-center walls.

You can make hardware theft of your electronic items harder by following some guidelines:

- Never leave the devices unattended.
- Do not use obvious or flashy carrying cases on public transportation.
- Do not publicly show off items.
- Lock devices so that others cannot activate them.
- Secure their storage area (laptops should always be equipped with security cables and locked away when not in use).
- Use ID Labels.
- Use log-in passwords on all your devices.
- Use a permanent marker or engraving on a metal, tamper-resistant tag on the laptop's outer case to record your ownership (don't use your phone number or address); ultraviolet markers are available at business supply stores.
- Pay attention in airports. Keep your eye on your laptop as you go through security. Hold onto it until the person in front of you has gone through the metal detector—and keep an eye out when it emerges on the other side of the screener.
- Be careful in hotels. If you stay in hotels, a security cable may not be enough. Try not to leave your laptop out in your room; use the safe in your room if there is one. If you're using a security cable to lock down your laptop, hang the "do not disturb" sign on your door.
- Register the laptop with its manufacturer.
- Do not leave laptops and other devices in your car or in other exposed places.
- Record the serial numbers/model numbers immediately after purchasing them and keep these numbers in a safe place, not with the devices.
- Use laptop-locating software, such as LoJack® for Laptops by Absolute® Software, which enables you to remotely locate, lock, and/or delete the data on your computer before it falls into the wrong

Survival Tip

Keeping Track of Your Cellphone

Here are some ways to avoid losing your cellphone:

- Tape your name and some kind of contact info (but not your home address) to your phone.
- Use a cellphone case that clips to your clothes or hangs around your neck; don't just stick your cellphone in your pocket or keep it in your hand when not using it.
- When traveling, check seats (plane, bus) and hotel rooms when leaving.
- Consider paying for a device-finding service in case you lose it (for example, Track It Back).
- When going through airport security, put your phone in your carry-on bag.
- Back up your phone's directory to your PC at home or with your cellphone carrier.

Laptop on a car seat. Computers left in cars are temptations for smash-and-grab thieves.

hands. Also LoJack for Laptops has a dedicated Theft Recovery Team that works with local law enforcement to recover stolen laptops and return them to their owners.

And, of course, back up all your data on something that is kept in a different place from the devices.

THEFT OF SOFTWARE *Pirated software,* as we stated in Chapter 3, is software obtained illegally, as when you make an illegal copy of a commercial videogame. This is so commonplace that software makers secretly prowl the Internet in search of purloined products and then try to get a court order to shut down the seller sites. They also look for organizations that "softlift"—companies, colleges, or other institutions that buy one copy of a program and make copies for many computers. In addition, software pirates often operate in China, Taiwan, Mexico, Russia, and various parts of Asia and Latin America, where the copying or counterfeiting of well-known software programs is practiced on a large scale. In some countries, most of the U.S. microcomputer software in use is thought to be illegally copied.

Many software pirates are reported by coworkers or fellow students to such organizations as the Software and Information Industry Association, the Interactive Digital Software Association, and the Business Software Alliance.

Survival Tip

Reporting Software Pirates

Software pirates can be reported to:

www.ic3.gov/default.aspx

https://reporting.bsa.org/r/report/add.aspx?

www.siia.net/piracy/default.asp

www.siia.net/piracy/report/report.asp

www.ehow.com/how_5266659_report-software-piracy.html

THEFT OF ONLINE MUSIC & MOVIES Many people may believe that illegally downloading music and movies is a victimless crime, but to the entertainment industry it is just plain piracy or theft. According to the U.S. Copyright Office, "copyright infringement occurs when a copyrighted work is reproduced, distributed, performed, publicly displayed, or made into a derivative work without the permission of the copyright owner." When you download or share a copyrighted song, movie, or software without the permission of the copyright holder, you are violating the copyright. You could face penalties like fines, and you could be sued by the copyright holder.

- **Stealing music:** People were quick to discover the Internet music service Napster, which in its original form allowed millions of people to exchange songs for free. Then, as illegal file swapping shifted from client/server services like Napster to peer-to-peer services such as Kazaa, Grokster, Limeware, and StreamCast and music-CD sales shrank, music companies decided to go after downloaders. They did so by getting their names and addresses from Internet access providers and by deploying electronic "robots" to monitor traffic on file-swapping networks and seek out Internet Protocol (IP) addresses.

  Then the record industry started filing copyright infringement lawsuits against students illegally downloading songs on file-sharing networks at 21 college campuses. Some settled, at fees ranging from $2,000 to $10,000 and fines of $12,000 to $17,500.[23] The U.S. Supreme Court also ruled against a pair of file-sharing networks, and two days later record companies sued 784 people for illegally distributing songs from the networks.[24] In 2009 a Minnesota woman was compelled by a federal jury to pay record companies $80,000 for each of 24 songs ($1.92 million total) that she illegally shared on a file-sharing site.[25] (Under U.S. Federal law, people who download music illegally are liable for damages as high as $150,000 per song, even if they never distribute the music.) (However, under U.S. copyright law, if you convert ["rip"] an original CD that you own to digital files, this qualifies as "fair use". As long as you use it for your own personal use and don't distribute the copyrighted material to others, then you will not be breaking the law.)

- **Stealing movies:** The film industry has also taken aggressive aim at pirated movies. For instance, in 2005 the government announced an 11-nation crackdown on organizations called "warez" (pronounced "wares"), groups that are sort of underground Internet co-ops set up to trade in copyrighted materials. Four men were charged with conspiring to violate copyright laws for operating an Internet site that offered stolen movies. Still, illegal movie downloads by digital pirates continue to cost the film industry billions every year.

  There are hundreds of movie download sites that have thousands of movies available for download. The vast majority of them are movie file-sharing (P2P) sites, and the movies available for download are pirate copies. These sites are being monitored by different agencies with the capability to trace your illegal activity right back to the server from which you downloaded. Although you may never be caught, if you are, you face a large fine or even jail time for piracy. And downloading from movie sites that provide pirate copies places your computer at high risk of receiving viruses. Since you have no idea where you are getting the files from, you have no way of knowing if they are infected with viruses or spyware. (Antivirus software will not always protect you from viruses downloaded through P2P software.)

Film Theft

For information on the different types of movie theft, go to the Motion Picture Association of America's website:

www.mpaa.org/contentprotection/types-of-content-theft

This site also gives information on legal film downloading sites.

Many websites offer video streaming legally—for example, Netflix, Blockbuster, Disney Video, Fox on Demand, Cartoon Network, FullMovies, and others.

Piracy of intellectual property, whether software, music, or movies, ultimately harms everyone, directly or indirectly, because, says one writer, "thieves do not invest in research, design, production, development, or advertising." The result is "fewer advances in science, fewer new products, fewer new music CDs, fewer new movies, less new software, and higher prices for whatever is created."[26]

THEFT OF TIME & SERVICES The theft of computer time is more common than you might think. Probably the biggest instance is people using their employer's computer time to play games, do online shopping, or dip into web pornography. Some people even operate sideline businesses.

For years "phone phreaks" have bedeviled the telephone companies. For example, they have found ways to get into company voice mail systems and then use an extension to make long-distance calls at the company's expense. They have also found ways to tap into cellular phone networks and dial for free. Satellite-TV piracy has also grown at an alarming rate.

THEFT OF INFORMATION In 2009 a cracker stole more than 500,000 patient records from a state-run database that tracked prescriptions in Virginia and demanded ransom for the return of the information.[27] In 2010 a young American and two Russian accomplices were convicted for carrying out the largest computer data theft in history, charged with stealing data from more than 130 million credit and debit cards, costing banks, companies, and insurers about $200 million.[28] Information thieves are having a field day. They have infiltrated the files of the Social Security Administration, stolen confidential personal records, and sold the information. On college campuses, they have snooped on or stolen private information such as grades. They have broken into computers of the major credit bureaus and stolen credit information and have then used the information to charge purchases or have resold it to other people. They have plundered the credit card numbers of millions of Americans and sold stolen identity data to conspirators in other countries.

INTERNET-RELATED FRAUD The U.S. Federal Trade Comssion (FTC) received 1.34 million consumer complaints during 2010, with ID theft complaints making up the largest number (19%) of reports, with complaints about Internet

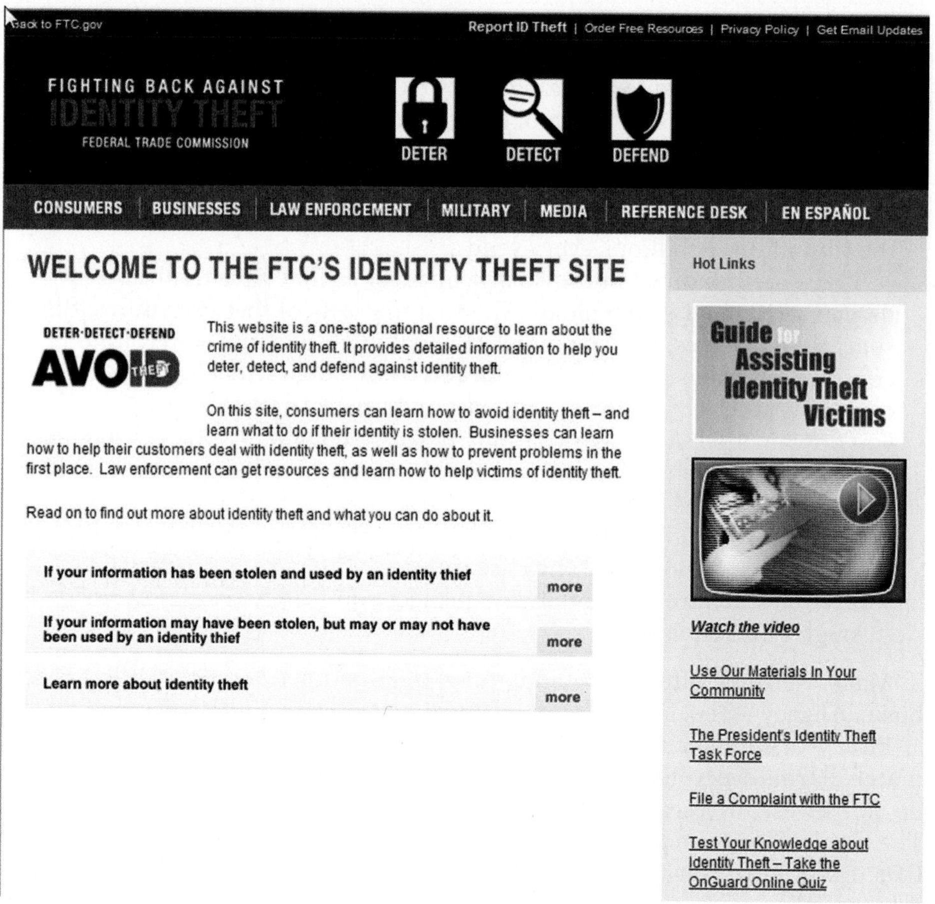
Back to FTC.gov
Report ID Theft | Order Free Resources | Privacy Policy | Get Email Updates
FIGHTING BACK AGAINST
IDENTITY THEFT
FEDERAL TRADE COMMISSION
DETER
DETECT
DEFEND
CONSUMERS | BUSINESSES | LAW ENFORCEMENT | MILITARY | MEDIA | REFERENCE DESK | EN ESPAÑOL
WELCOME TO THE FTC'S IDENTITY THEFT SITE
DETER·DETECT·DEFEND
AVOID THEFT
This website is a one-stop national resource to learn about the crime of identity theft. It provides detailed information to help you deter, detect, and defend against identity theft.
On this site, consumers can learn how to avoid identity theft – and learn what to do if their identity is stolen. Businesses can learn how to help their customers deal with identity theft, as well as how to prevent problems in the first place. Law enforcement can get resources and learn how to help victims of identity theft.
Read on to find out more about identity theft and what you can do about it.
If your information has been stolen and used by an identity thief
more
If your information may have been stolen, but may or may not have been used by an identity thief
more
Learn more about identity theft
more
Hot Links
Guide for Assisting Identity Theft Victims
Watch the video
Use Our Materials In Your Community
The President's Identity Theft Task Force
File a Complaint with the FTC
Test Your Knowledge about Identity Theft – Take the OnGuard Online Quiz

services, Internet auctions, and telephone and mobile services also in the top-10 complaint categories. About 45% of the reported fraud cases started with an e-mail contact, the FTC said.[29] At the Internet Crime Complaint Center, the most common complaints were nondelivery of merchandise and/or payment (14.4%), FBI-related scams (13.2%), and identity theft (9.8%).[30]

Here are some common Internet scams:

- **The Nigerian letter scam:** An example of a classic kind of confidence fraud is the persistent one known as the *Nigerian letter scam* (*advance-fee scam* or *419 scam*). Most Nigerian-letter perpetrators claim to have discovered inactive or delinquent accounts that hold vast amounts of money ready to be claimed. Victims are given a chance to receive nonexistent government money, often from the "Government of Nigeria," as long as they pay a fee to help transfer the money to an overseas account. Similar kinds of cyberspace fraud involve nonexistent investment deals and phony solicitations.
- **Other scams, including Evil Twin attacks:** The majority of scams involve ruses such as those we described in Chapters 2 and 6. Among them are *phishing* (sending emails that appear to come from a trusted source, which direct you to a website where you're asked to reveal personal information), *pharming* (in which malicious software is implanted in your computer that redirects you to an impostor web page), and *Trojan horses* (a program such as a screen saver that carries viruses that perpetuate mischief without your knowledge).

  A variant on conventional phishing is *Wi-Fi phishing,* known as the ***Evil Twin attack,*** **in which a hacker or cracker sets up a Wi-Fi hot spot or access point that makes your computer think it's accessing a safe public network or your home network and then monitors your communications and steals data you enter into a website,** if it

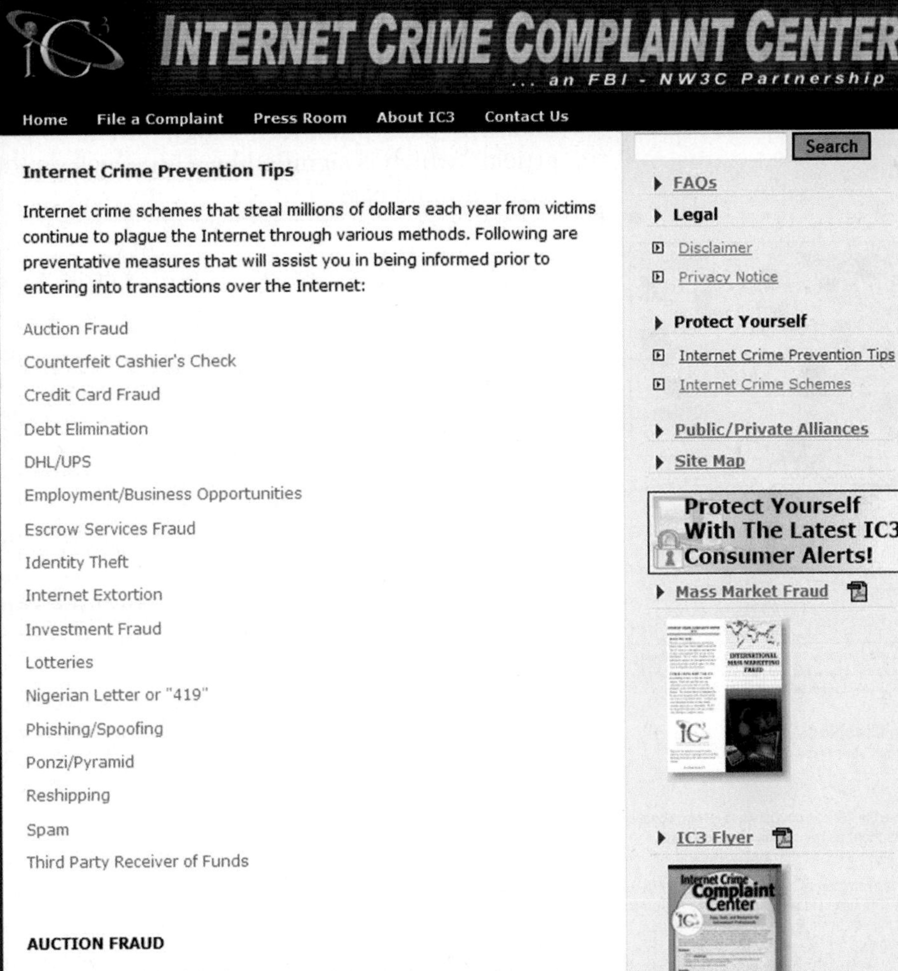

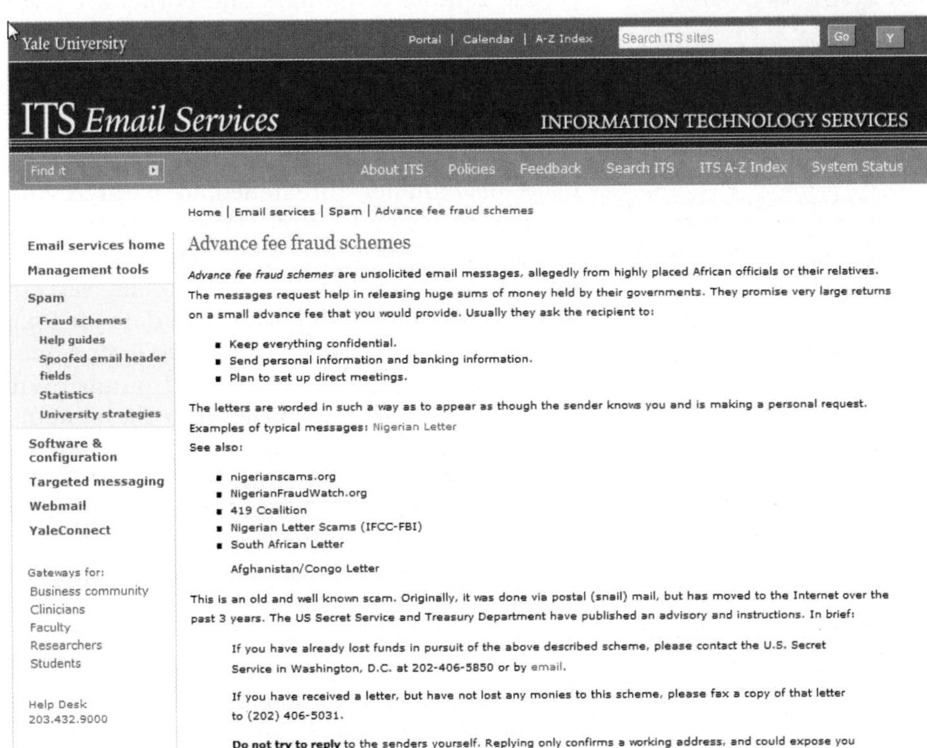

Survival Tip

Fraud Baiters

The following websites tell stories about outwitting online fraud artists. "419" refers to a section of the Nigerian legal code.

www.fbi.gov/scams-safety/fraud

www.419legal.org

www.scamvictimsunited.com

www.fraudaid.com/scamspeak/nigerian/I'veReceivedaNigerianLetter-WhatDo-I-Do.htm

Stories

Home • News • Stories • 2011 • April • Botnet Operation Disabled

Twitter (43) Facebook (911) Share

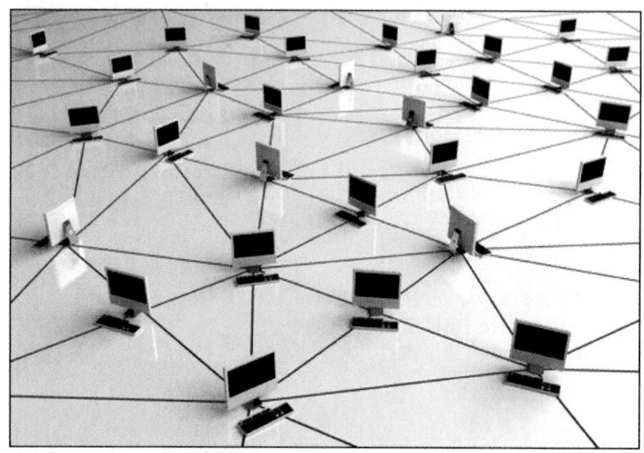

Botnets are networks of virus-infected computers controlled remotely by an attacker. The Coreflood virus is a key-logging program that allows cyber thieves to steal personal and financial information by recording unsuspecting users' every keystroke.

Botnet Operation Disabled
FBI Seizes Servers to Stop Cyber Fraud

04/14/11

In an unprecedented move in the fight against cyber crime, the FBI has disrupted an international cyber fraud operation by seizing the servers that had infected as many as two million computers with malicious software.

Botnets are networks of virus-infected computers controlled remotely by an attacker. They can be used to steal funds, hijack identities, and commit other crimes. The botnet in this case involves the potent Coreflood virus, a key-logging program that allows cyber thieves to steal personal and financial information by recording unsuspecting users' every keystroke.

Once a computer or network of computers is infected by Coreflood—infection may occur when users open a malicious e-mail attachment—thieves control the malware through remote servers. The Department of Justice yesterday received search warrants to effectively disable the Coreflood botnet by seizing the five U.S. servers used by the hackers.

"Botnets and the cyber criminals who deploy them jeopardize the economic security of the United States and the dependability of the nation's information infrastructure," said Shawn Henry, executive assistant director of the FBI's Criminal, Cyber, Response, and Services Branch. "These actions to mitigate the threat posed by the Coreflood botnet are the first of their kind in the United States," Henry noted, "and reflect our commitment to being creative and proactive in making the Internet more secure."

Now that we have interrupted the operation of the botnet servers, our cyber specialists can prevent Coreflood from sending stolen financial information to the cyber thieves. But victims' computers still remain infected. That's why we have been working closely with our private-sector partners.

Anti-virus companies are developing updated signatures to detect and remove Coreflood. To disinfect Microsoft Windows-based systems—and to keep them virus free—users are encouraged to run anti-virus software and to keep their Microsoft Windows Updates current (see sidebar).

Victimized computers that have not been disinfected using anti-virus software updates will continue to attempt to contact the Coreflood botnet servers. When this happens, we will respond by issuing a temporary stop command to the virus and then alert that user's Internet service provider (ISP), who will inform the customer that their computer is still infected. At no time will we be collecting any personal data from victim computers.

The Coreflood Virus

The Coreflood virus infects only Microsoft Windows-based computers. Generally, most users will not be able to tell if their computers are infected. It is therefore important to take the following steps:

- Make sure your Microsoft Windows Automatic Updates are turned on;

- Run anti-virus programs and ensure that theyare up to date;

- Run a security firewall on your computer; and

- Check your online banking and credit history to make sure you have not been compromised. If you have been compromised, contact your financial institution.

To learn more about what you can do to protect your computer, including how to download and receive updates on security vulnerabilities, go to the following sites operated by U.S. Computer Emergency Readiness Team (CERT) and the Federal Trade Commission, respectively: us-cert.gov/nav/nt01 and onguardonline.gov/topics/malware.aspx.

"For most infected users who are conscientious about keeping their anti-virus programs up to date, the process of disinfection will be as invisible as the Coreflood infection was itself," said one of our cyber agents. Still, there is a process in place with ISPs to make sure notification occurs if necessary.

We began our Coreflood investigation in April 2009 when a Connecticut-based company realized that hundreds of computers on its networks had been infected. Before we shut down the Coreflood operation, cyber thieves made numerous fraudulent wire transfers, costing companies hundreds of thousands of dollars.

doesn't have the right security measures. Some Internet security software offers phishing blockers. Also, "wireless users should enter private information only into sites that protect data with encryption technology," advises one article, "which is signified by a little lock on the bottom of the page."[31]

TAKING OVER YOUR PC: ZOMBIES, BOTNETS, & BLACKMAIL No too long ago a New Jersey grandmother of three was flabbergasted when her Internet access provider curtailed her outbound email privileges. The reason: an intruder had taken over her PC without her knowledge and turned it into a device for disseminating as many as 70,000 emails a day.[32]

This machine had become a ***zombie,*** **or *drone,* a computer taken over covertly and programmed to respond to instructions sent remotely,** often by instant-messaging channels (Chapter 6, p. 358). This PC, however, was only one of several home and business personal computers in what is known as a ***botnet,*** **short for "robot network," a network of computers compromised by means of a Trojan horse that plants instructions within each of the computers to wait for commands from the person controlling that network.** These remote-controlled networks are best detected by the Internet access provider, which can block the illicit network connections and help users disinfect their PCs.

The zombie computers and botnet are used to launch phishing attacks or send spam messages. They can also be used to launch denial-of-service attacks (Chapter 6, p. 355), perhaps to extort money from the targeted sites in return for halting the attacks. For instance, one cyber-blackmailer threatened to paralyze the servers of a small online-payment processing company unless it sent a $10,000 bank wire—and when the company refused, its servers were bombarded with barrages of data for four days. Blackmail has also been used in conjunction with the theft of credit card numbers or documents. One thief broke into the systems of Internet retailer CD Universe, stole 300,000 customers' credit card numbers, and when the company's executives refused to pay a ransom demand, sold them off piecemeal on the Internet (for others to illegally charge on) until he was stopped.

CRIMES OF MALICE: CRASHING ENTIRE SYSTEMS Sometimes criminals are more interested in abusing or vandalizing computers and telecommunications systems than in profiting from them. For example, a student at a Wisconsin campus deliberately and repeatedly shut down a university computer system, destroying final projects for dozens of students; a judge sentenced him to a year's probation, and he left the campus. And the website of an online seller of digital video recorders was overwhelmed by an electronic attack that knocked out its email system for weeks, the result of cyber-mercenaries allegedly hired by an entrepreneur who had been rebuffed by the company over a proposed business deal.

Other kinds of malevolent attacks could be far more serious, as follows.

- **Attacks on power-control systems:** One possibility that concerns security specialists is cyberattacks on the nation's water, power, transportation, and communications systems, causing them to crash and disrupting services to thousands, even millions, of people. This has already happened in at least one instance, when in 2009 someone severed eight fiber-optic cables in California's Silicon Valley, cutting out cellphone, landline, ATM machines, and Internet service to more than 100,000 people.[33] Also in 2009 cyberspies, probably from China and Russia, penetrated the U.S. electrical grid and left behind software programs that could be used to disrupt the system.[34] Critical infrastructure firms such as power grids and oil refineries are facing "staggering" level of cyberattacks and are not adequately prepared to defend themselves, said security firm McAfee and the Center for Strategic and International Studies (CSIS).[35]
- **Attacks on the Internet—could the entire net crash?** Also quite worrisome is the possibility of an attack on the Internet that could actually crash the whole worldwide network. This would involve crackers' tampering with something called the *border gateway protocol,* which individual networks use to announce their routes so they can carry one another's messages. By falsifying the announcements, a cracker could direct messages to nonexistent routes, thereby overloading and perhaps crashing parts of the Internet.

What were the top 10 cybercrimes in 2010?

www.inc.com/tech-blog/2010/03/top_cybercrimes_of_the_year.html

Internet Off?

For opinions on whether the Internet could really crash, go to:

www.dailymail.co.uk/sciencetech/article-1221892/Why-world-NOT-end-2012-Nasa-scientist-debunks-internet-rumours.html

www.zdnet.com/blog/networking/how-to-crash-the-internet/680

www.startribune.com/business/116513943.html

www.infosecurity-us.com/view/15136/comment-will-highspeed-malware-crash-the-internet/

www.unpan.org/Regions/Global/PublicAdministrationNews/tabid/102/mctl/ArticleView/ModuleId/1461/articleId/20089/Internet-crash--could-it-really-happen.aspx

Computer Criminals

Many types of people become computer criminals.

Known as the most remote city in the lower 48 states, Ely is a high-desert town of 4,000 or so residents located on the eastern edge of Nevada. Yet the day after the 2003 war with Iraq began, computers at a 40-bed hospital in Ely came under electronic attack. Initially this was traced to an Arab news network, suggesting cyberterrorism, but later it was pinned to a source in the former Soviet Union. "Here's tiny Ely, a place where people leave doors unlocked, and we get hacked by the Russian Mafia, who are pretending to be Arab," said a hospital technology manager. "We may be remote in geography, the most distant city from any metropolitan area, but with the Internet we might as well be in downtown New York or Los Angeles."[36]

There's almost no telling where the next threat to computer security will come from. In Chapter 6, we considered threats in the form of hackers, crackers, and cyberterrorists. Let us expand this discussion to consider some other threats.

INDIVIDUALS OR SMALL GROUPS Earlier we discussed phishers, pharmers, and creators of spyware and viruses, along with various types of crackers and hackers. These include individuals or members of small groups who use fraudulent email and websites to obtain personal information that can be exploited, either for monetary gain or sometimes simply to show off their power and give them bragging rights with other members of the hacker/cracker community.

What Is Computer Forensics?

Forensics is the process of using scientific knowledge for collecting, analyzing, and presenting evidence to the courts. (*Forensics* means "to bring to the court.") Computer forensics combines elements of law and computer science to collect and analyze data from computer systems, networks, wireless communications, and storage devices in a way that is admissible as evidence in a court of law.

http://computer.howstuffworks.com/computer-forensic.htm

www.computerforensicsworld.com/

www.computerforensicshq.com/

http://staff.washington.edu/dittrich/forensics.html

www.newyorkcomputerforensics.com/learn/common_mistakes.php

Information about a career in computer forensics:

http://jobsearchtech.about.com/od/computerjob13/a/comp_forensics_2.htm

www.legal-criminal-justice-schools.com/Criminal-Justice-Degrees/How-to-Become-a-Computer-Forensics-Investigator.html

www.computer-forensics-recruiter.com/careers.html

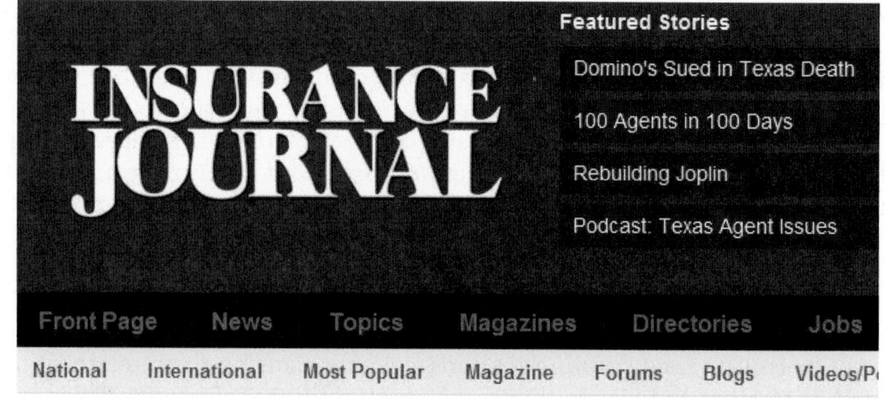

Personal Internet use Becoming Part of Employee Record

January 24, 2011

Email This Print Newsletters

Tweet 0 Share Share

Article Comments

Those photos on Facebook showing you palling around with drunks, the raunchy joke you posted on Twitter, and those links to politically incorrect groups on your personal Web site — all of this information can now become part of your job application and employment record.

The practice of employers checking employment, criminal and credit histories of job candidates is apparently no longer sufficient. A California company is helping employers collect information about job candidates and employees from Facebook, MySpace, Twitter and wherever else on the Internet the person may have posted information.

"We not only review the social networks; it's the two-thirds of user-generated content that doesn't fall into the category of Facebook, Twitter, and MySpace," said Max Drucker, co-founder and CEO of Social Intelligence Corp., in an interview with Insurance Journal. "We review blogs. We review bulletin boards. We review the microblogs. We review comments in forums. We really are looking for anything out there, personal web pages, anything out there that a person can create themselves and has posted publicly, into the public domain, online."

Drucker sees his service as a risk management tool for employers, helping them avoid liability for negligently hiring someone who later turns out to be a real mismatch, or worse. Post-hiring, it helps keep employees in line with a company's media policy.

Employees need to be aware that their personal life can affect their work life (*www.insurancejournal.com/magazines/mag-features/2011/01/24/186181.htm*)

EMPLOYEES Recently the U.S. Court of Appeals for the Ninth Circuit held that an employee "exceeds authorized access" under the federal Computer Fraud and Abuse Act (CFAA) when the employee obtains information from an employer's computer system and uses that information for a purpose that violates the employer's restrictions on the use of that information. The violation can range from obtaining information to damaging a computer or computer data.[37] What this boils down to is that employees can be criminally prosecuted for violating their employers' computer policies.

Workers may use information technology for personal profit or to steal hardware or information to sell. They may also use it to seek revenge for real or imagined wrongs, such as being passed over for promotion; indeed, the disgruntled employee is a principal source of computer crime.

OUTSIDE PARTNERS & SUPPLIERS Suppliers and clients may also gain access to a company's information technology and use it to commit crimes, especially since intranets and extranets have become more commonplace. Partners and vendors also may be the inadvertent source of hacker mischief because their systems may not be as well protected as the larger partner's networks and computers, and so a third party may penetrate their security.

CORPORATE SPIES Competing companies or individuals may break into a company's computer system to conduct industrial espionage—obtain trade secrets that they can use for competitive advantages. In France, for example, investigators stumbled on an incident in which a hacker illegally collected data on Greenpeace, which opposes nuclear power, on behalf of Électricité de France, the world's largest operator of nuclear power plants, to gather information on antinuclear campaigners.[38]

ORGANIZED CRIME Based on a 2011 Norton Cyber Crime Report, almost two-thirds of adult Internet users around the world have become some kind of cyber-crime victims.[39]

Members of organized crime rings not only steal hardware, software, and data; they also use spam, phishing, and the like to commit identity theft and online fraud. Even street gangs now have their own websites, most of them perfectly legal, but some of them possibly used as chat rooms for drug distribution. In addition, gangs use computers the way legal businesses do—as business tools—but they use them for illegal purposes, such as keeping track of gambling debts and stolen goods.

CYBERWAR FIGHTERS ***Cyberwarfare,* or *cyberwar,* is the use of computers and the Internet to attack an enemy's information systems.** Attacks on U.S. government computer networks increased 40% in 2008, according to the U.S. Computer Emergency Readiness team.[40] In April 2009 the Pentagon reported it spent more than $100 million in the previous six months responding to and repairing damage from cyberattacks and other computer network problems.[41] Computer spies even broke into the Pentagon's Joint Strike Fighter project.[42]

Cyberwar may be conducted on the level of psychological warfare, as has happened in the Middle East, for instance, where Israeli and Palestinian opponents in the Gaza war have used cellphones to warn the other side of impending attacks.[43] Or it may be conducted as a tactical maneuver in which one side hacks into the others side's computers and alters information that drives them into the first side's gunsights, as the Americans did with members of Al Qaeda in Iraq.[44] Or it may be on the scale of widespread cyberattacks on government websites, such as those North Korea inflicted on South Korea and the United States (where Treasury Department and Federal Trade Commission websites were shut down).[45] Cyberattacks include "terrorism, espionage, crime, protest, vandalism, and more. Lines between categories are often blurred, and it is usually difficult to identify the perpetrators or understand their motives. For instance, there is still debate in the cybersecurity community over whether the 2007 cyberattacks that targeted Estonian government networks (UPI) constitute cyberwarfare by Russian intelligence or acts of political protest by hackers."[46]

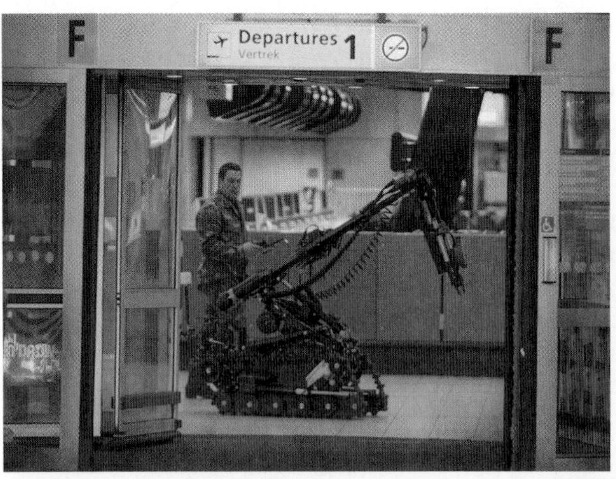

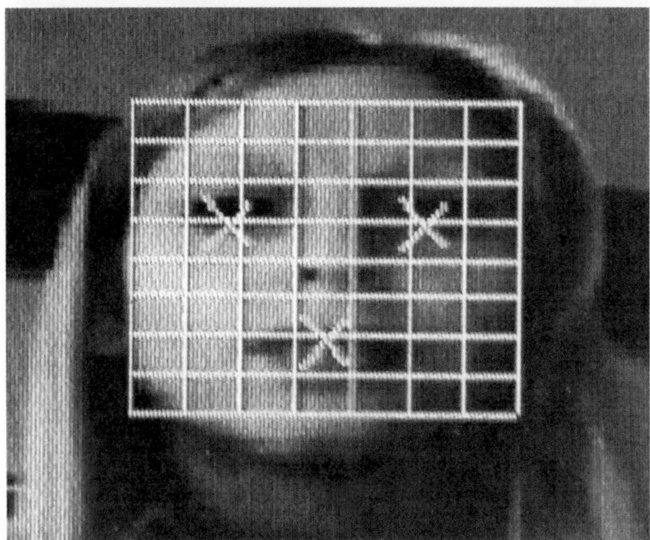

(*Above left*) A member of the Dutch bomb squad with a security robot at Schiphol Airport terminal 1 after examining a suspicious suitcase found in the luggage department. (*Above right*) A U.S. soldier makes a biometric scan of an Afghan villager during a clearance patrol in Kandahar province. (*Left*) An employee of the U.S. Federal Mint is seen on the screen of a biometric device that scanned her face at a security gate during a press conference.

Recognizing the dangers of cyberattacks, the U.S. government made online security a high priority, with President Barack Obama appointing a cybersecurity coordinator within the White House and introducing a plan for stemming cyberthreats.[47] The Pentagon also created a new agency called the Cyber Command to centralize and elevate cybersecurity.[48] A decade behind China, the United States is also now officially focused on using cyberwarfare offensively as well as defensively.[49]

A series of high-profile events in 2010 and 2011 further increased concerns about the threat of cyberattacks. These include the espionage hacks on Google and Western energy companies, the Stuxnet malware infiltration of Iranian nuclear sites, and the targeting of government networks in South Korea. "U.S. cybersecurity policy continues to evolve to meet these challenges, but critical gaps remain, including the incomplete protection of digital infrastructure vital to national security, such as power grids and financial networks."[50]

The new cybersecurity strategies implemented by President Obama supposedly will provide protections for personal privacy and civil liberties. However, Pentagon officials say these will be difficult to implement.[51]

And don't forget: many employers check your social networking profiles—for example, on Facebook—to see what employees are up to and to see what they are saying about their jobs.

PRACTICAL ACTION

Is the Boss Watching You? Trust in the Workplace

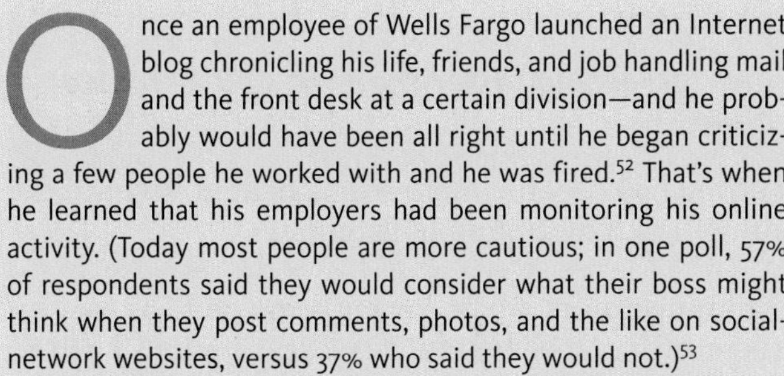

Once an employee of Wells Fargo launched an Internet blog chronicling his life, friends, and job handling mail and the front desk at a certain division—and he probably would have been all right until he began criticizing a few people he worked with and he was fired.[52] That's when he learned that his employers had been monitoring his online activity. (Today most people are more cautious; in one poll, 57% of respondents said they would consider what their boss might think when they post comments, photos, and the like on social-network websites, versus 37% who said they would not.)[53]

More and more employers are using surveillance techniques to monitor their employees, from using cameras and phone taps to recording website visits and visiting the files that employees delete. About 78% of major U.S. companies keep tabs on employees by checking their email, Internet activity, phone calls, and computer files, or by videotaping them at work.[54] In most states, the companies don't have to inform employees of this fact. In addition, software is available to measure the performance and activities of independent workers such as those working from home across the country.[55]

What are employers looking for that you should be aware of? Here are the principal areas.

Less Productivity

There's a word for all those hours employees spend each workday talking on the phone with friends, getting coffee, or gossiping—"undertime." Some such goofing off is tolerated in the name of workplace morale. The Internet, however, has created whole new ways to slack off at work. A company with 1,000 Internet users could lose more than $35 million in productivity annually from just one hour of daily web surfing by employees; non-work-related Internet surfing results in up to a 40% loss in productivity each year at American businesses. On average, office workers spend 21 hours per week online at the office, as opposed to only 9.5 hours at home.[56]

Misleading Résumés

Employers are carrying out more rigorous background checks on prospective workers since the September 11, 2001, terrorist attacks in New York City and Washington, D.C. Among the problems with (or omitted from) résumés or application forms that turned up in one study: up to 30% of applications contain false material/information; 40% of information on résumés is misrepresented; 45% of potential employees have either a criminal record, bad driving record, worker's compensation claim, or a bad credit history.[57]

Risk of Lawsuits & Viruses

One reason corporate executives are becoming more aggressive about spying on employees is that, besides ferreting out job shirkers and office-supply thieves, "they have to worry about being held accountable for the misconduct of their subordinates," says one report. "Even one offensive email message circulated around the office by a single employee can pose a liability risk for a company" under federal anticorruption and corporate governance laws.[58]

In addition, employers are worried about workers using company computers to download copyrighted music and movies, because these acts not only are a drain on corporate resources but also expose employers to the risk of lawsuits from record and movie companies as well as open company networks to viruses.

What Employers Must Do: Shred Personal Data

On the other hand, employees catch a break under part of the Fair and Accurate Credit Transactions Act passed in late 2003. Regardless of size, employers must destroy—by "shredding or burning" or "smashing or wiping"—any personal information about employees before they throw it out if they got the information from a credit report.[59]

In addition, employees transmitting text messages from devices supplied by their employer caught a break in 2008 when the Ninth U.S. Circuit Court of Appeals in San Francisco ruled that companies transmitting those messages can't disclose their contents without the recipient's consent.[60]

9.3 SECURITY SAFEGUARDS: Protecting Computers & Communications

Everyone using computers and networks must use security safeguards.

The ongoing dilemma of the Digital Age is balancing convenience against security. ***Security*** **is a system of safeguards for protecting information technology against disasters, system failures, and unauthorized access that can result in damage or loss.**

Surveillance

How do employers monitor employees' Internet usage?

www.wisegeek.com/how-do-employers-monitor-internet-usage-at-work.htm

We consider five components of security.

- Deterrents to computer crime
- Identification and access
- Encryption
- Protection of software and data
- Disaster-recovery plans

Deterrents to Computer Crime

Are computer-related crimes increasing faster than the ability to deal with them? What can be done?

As information technology crime has become more sophisticated, so have the people charged with preventing it and disciplining its outlaws.

ENFORCING LAWS Campus administrators are no longer being quite as easy on offenders and are turning them over to police. Industry organizations such as the Software Publishers Association are going after software pirates large and small. Many police departments now have officers patrolling a "cyber beat"; they regularly cruise online bulletin boards and chat rooms looking for pirated software, stolen trade secrets, child molesters, and child pornography. Interpol (the world's largest international police organization) has set up the "I-24/7" communication system to enable information-technology crime units around the world to contact Interpol 24 hours a day, 7 days a week to report cybercrimes.

More on Interpol & Cybercrime

www.itu.int/osg/csd/cybersecurity/WSIS/3rd_meeting_docs/KTAKAO%20WSIS%20INTERPOL%20NCRP%20Modified.pdf

www.interpol.int/

www.nyu.edu/intercep/lapietra/Interpol_Cyber.pdf

CERT: THE COMPUTER EMERGENCY RESPONSE TEAM In 1988, after one widespread Internet break-in, the U.S. Defense Department created the Computer Emergency Response Team (CERT, *www.us-cert.gov/*). Although it has no power to arrest or prosecute, CERT provides round-the-clock international information and security-related support services to users of the Internet. Whenever it gets a report of an electronic snooper, whether on the Internet or on a corporate email system, CERT stands ready to lend assistance. It counsels the party under attack, helps thwart the intruder, and evaluates the system afterward to protect against future break-ins.

TOOLS FOR FIGHTING FRAUDULENT & UNAUTHORIZED ONLINE USES Among the tools used to detect fraud are the following:

- **Rule-based-detection software:** In this technique, users such as merchants create a "negative file" that states the criteria each transaction must meet. These criteria include not only stolen credit card numbers but also price limits, matches of the cardholder's billing address and shipping address, and warnings if a large quantity of a single item is ordered.
- **Predictive-statistical-model software:** In this technique, tons of data from previous transactions are examined to create mathematical descriptions of what a typical fraudulent transaction is like. The software then rates incoming orders according to a scale of risk based on their resemblance to the fraud profile. Thus, for example, if some thief overhears you giving out your phone company calling-card number and he or she makes 25 calls to a country that you never have occasion to call, AT&T's software may pick up the unusual activity and call you to see if it is you who is making the calls.
- **Employee Internet management (EIM) software:** Programs made by Websense, SmartFilter, and Pearl Echo-Suite are used to monitor how much time workers spend on the web and even block access to gambling and porn sites.

- **Internet filtering software:** Some employers use special filtering software to block access to pornography, bootleg-music download, and other unwanted Internet sites that employees may want to access.
- **Electronic surveillance:** As we mentioned, employers use various kinds of electronic surveillance that includes visual and audio monitoring technologies, reading of email and blogs, and recording of keystrokes. Some companies even hire undercover agents to pretend to be coworkers.

Identification & Access

There are three main ways of authenticating a computer user's identity.

Are you who you say you are? The computer wants to know.

There are three ways a computer system can verify that you have legitimate right of access. Some security systems use a mix of these techniques. The systems try to authenticate your identity by determining (1) what you have, (2) what you know, or (3) who you are.

WHAT YOU HAVE—CARDS, KEYS, SIGNATURES, & BADGES Credit cards, debit cards, and cash-machine cards all have magnetic strips or built-in computer chips that identify you to the machine. Many require that you display your signature, which may be compared with any future signature you write. Computer rooms are always kept locked, requiring a key. Many people also keep a lock on their personal computers. A computer room may also be guarded by security officers, who may need to see an authorized signature or a badge with your photograph before letting you in.

Of course, credit cards, keys, and badges can be lost or stolen. Signatures can be forged. Badges can be counterfeited.

WHAT YOU KNOW—PINS & PASSWORDS To gain access to your bank account through an automated teller machine (ATM), you key in your PIN. A *PIN (personal identification number)* is the security number known only to you that is required to access the system. Telephone credit cards also use a PIN. If you carry either an ATM or a phone card, never carry the PIN written down elsewhere in your wallet (even disguised).

As we stated earlier in the book, *passwords* are special words, codes, or symbols required to access a computer system. Passwords are one of the weakest

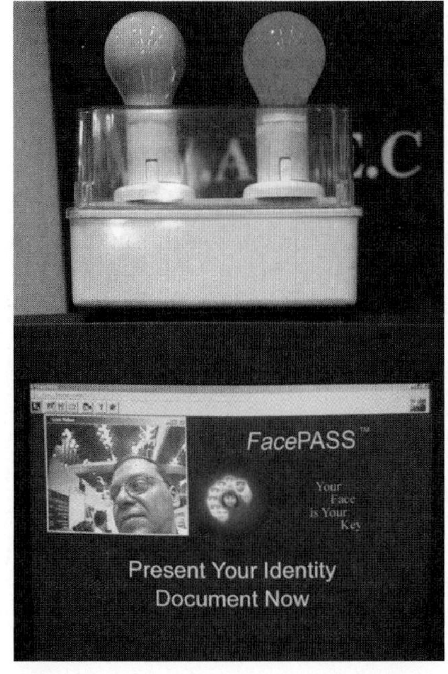

(left) Sigmatek's facial identification technology for corporate security at the International Security & Defense Exhibition in Tel Aviv, Israel. *(right)* Unattractive passport photos have become mandatory. Why? Because computers do not like smiles. A United Nations agency that sets standards for passports wants all countries to switch to a document that includes a digital representation of the bearer's face recorded on an embedded computer chip. In airports and at border crossings, a machine will read the chip—but the machine can be fooled by smiles, which introduce teeth, wrinkles, lines, and other distortions.

security links, and most can be easily guessed or stolen. We gave some suggestions on passwords in Chapters 2 and 6.

Some computer security systems have a "callback" provision. In a callback system, the user calls the computer system, punches in the password, and hangs up. The computer then calls back a certain preauthorized number. This measure will block anyone who has somehow gotten hold of a password but is calling from an unauthorized telephone.

WHO YOU ARE—PHYSICAL TRAITS Some forms of identification can't be easily faked—such as your physical traits. ***Biometrics*, the science of measuring individual body characteristics,** tries to use these in security devices, as we pointed out in Chapter 6. *Biometric authentication devices* authenticate a person's identity by verifying his or her physical or behavioral characteristics with a digital code stored in a computer system.

Encryption

Could the use of encryption lead to invasion of privacy?

SECURITY

***Encryption*,** as we said in Chapter 6, **is the process of altering readable data into unreadable form to prevent unauthorized access,** and it is what has given people confidence to do online shopping and banking. Encryption is clearly useful for some organizations, especially those concerned with trade secrets, military matters, and other sensitive data. Many financial organizations, such as Bank of America, Time Warner, and Citigroup's CitiFinancial division, stung by misplaced data of nearly 6 million people, decided to encrypt the backup tapes of customer information that they store with third-party vendors.

A very sophisticated form of encryption is used in most personal computers and is available with every late-model web browser to provide for secure communications over the Internet. However, from the standpoint of society, encryption is a two-edged sword. For instance, the 2001 attacks on the World Trade Center and Pentagon raised the possibility that the terrorists might have communicated with one another using unbreakable encryption programs. (There is no evidence they did.) Should the government be allowed to read the coded email of overseas terrorists, drug dealers, and other enemies? What about the email of all American citizens?

The U.S. government has maintained that it needs access to scrambled data for national security and law enforcement. Indeed, during the 1990s, officials urged that encryption companies be required to include a "back door" in their products that would allow the government to peek at messages exchanged by criminals and terrorists. Companies and consumers said they would not use such a product and contended that criminals surely would not either. It was also argued that many people with the most basic education in mathematics could write their own encryption systems. Ultimately, the back-door idea was dropped.

The 2001 terrorist incidents resurrected the debate. Some academics who, over the objections of the government, had freely published their research on how to make unbreakable codes were haunted by the idea that law enforcement might have figured out terrorist plans if the encryption techniques had been kept secret. Although publicly available encryption allows ordinary people to protect their privacy and businesses to protect their data, it is clear that a by-product is a limitation on the ability to fight lawbreakers and terrorists.

Protection of Software & Data

Software and data can be protected by more than antivirus programs and firewalls.

Organizations go to tremendous lengths to protect their programs and data. As might be expected, this includes educating employees about making backup disks, protecting against viruses, using firewalls, and so on. Other security procedures include these:

CONTROL OF ACCESS Access to online files is restricted to those who have a legitimate right to access—because they need them to do their jobs. Many organizations have a system for user authentication and of transaction logs for recording all accesses or attempted accesses to data.

AUDIT CONTROLS Many networks have audit controls for tracking which programs and servers were used, which files opened, and so on. This creates an audit trail, a record of how a transaction was handled from input through processing and output.

PEOPLE CONTROLS Because people are the greatest threat to a computer system, security precautions begin with the screening of job applicants. Résumés are checked to see if people did what they said they did. Another control is to separate employee functions, so that people are not allowed to wander freely into areas not essential to their jobs. Manual and automated controls—input controls, processing controls, and output controls—are used to check if data is handled accurately and completely during the processing cycle. Printouts, printer ribbons, and other waste that may reveal passwords and trade secrets to outsiders are disposed of through shredders or locked trash barrels.

Disaster-Recovery Plans

A disaster-recovery plan enables an organization to continue operating after a natural or other type of disaster.

A *disaster-recovery plan* is a method of restoring information-processing operations that have been halted by destruction or accident. "Among the countless lessons that computer users have absorbed in the hours, days, and weeks after the [1993 New York] World Trade Center bombing," wrote one reporter, "the most enduring may be the need to have a disaster-recovery plan. The second most enduring lesson may be this: even a well-practiced plan will quickly reveal its flaws."[61] Although the second (2001) attack on the World Trade Center reinforced these lessons in a spectacular way, as did Hurricane Katrina in New Orleans four years later, interestingly many companies have not gotten the message. For example, the March 2011 earthquake and tsunami disaster in Japan forced 145 companies to either go bankrupt or effectively fail.[62]

Mainframe computer systems are operated in separate departments by professionals, who tend to have disaster plans. Whereas mainframes are usually backed up, many personal computers, and even entire local area networks, are not, with potentially disastrous consequences. It has been reported that, on average, a company loses as much as 3% of its gross sales within eight days of a sustained computer outage.

A disaster-recovery plan is more than a big fire drill. It includes a list of all business functions and the hardware, software, data, and people that support those functions, as well as arrangements for alternate locations. The disaster-recovery plan also includes ways for backing up and storing programs and data in another location, ways of alerting necessary personnel, and training for those personnel.

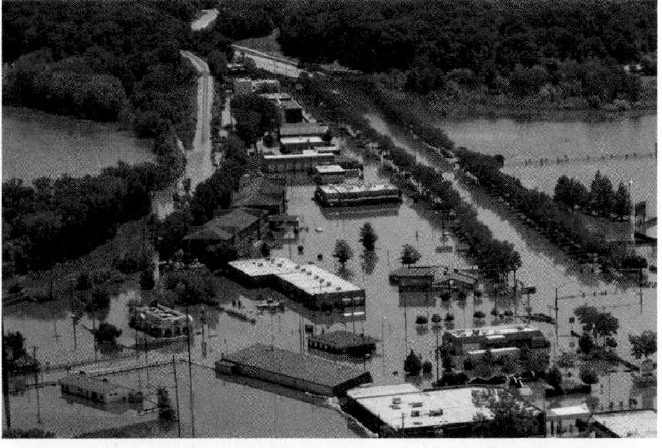

Disaster. *(Top)* Severe flooding hit Iowa in the spring of 2008; here we see Cedar Rapids. *(Bottom)* A massive tsunami engulfs a residential area after a powerful earthquake in Natori, Miyagi Prefecture, northeastern Japan, in March 2011.

9.4 QUALITY-OF-LIFE ISSUES: The Environment, Mental Health, Child Protection, & the Workplace

As we know, information technology is not without problems.

In this chapter and earlier ones we have discussed some of the worrisome effects of technology on intellectual property rights, on truth in art and journalism, on censorship issues, on health matters and ergonomics, and on privacy and security. In the following we briefly explore some other quality-of-life issues related to information technology.

Composition of a Desktop Microcomputer

Plastics Lead Aluminum Germanium Gallium Iron Tin Copper Barium Nickel Zinc Tantalum Indium Vanadium Terbium Beryllium Gold Europium Titanium Ruthenium Cobalt Palladium Manganese Silver Antimony Bismuth Chromium Cadmium Selenium Niobium Yttrium Rhodium Platinum Mercury Arsenic Silica . . .

For more information, go to:

www.eoearth.org/article/Computer_recycling

www.it-environment.org/

Environmental Problems

Among other problems, information technology leaves a larger environmental "footprint" than we might think.

The data servers that make the Internet run are huge energy hogs. A study for the Environmental Protection Agency estimated in 2007 that data centers, their servers, and their associated cooling and auxiliary infrastructure use about 1.5% of the United States' total electricity consumption.[63] And scientists estimate that the energy footprint of the net is growing by more than 10% each year.[64] Indeed, online sucks up enough energy to rank the Internet—if it were a country—fifth in the world for electricity use. That's more power than Russia uses, according to a recent report from Greenpeace.[65] Thus, many companies are taking steps to redesign their data centers to reduce the energy drain. Manufacturers of personal computers are also tackling the energy problem, adding green features such as speeding up going into power-saving sleep mode. You can also save a good deal on your household electricity bill by simply unplugging your computer when you're sleeping or not working.

Other environmental challenges remain—specifically, manufacturing and usage by-products, disposal by-products, environmental blight, and possible risks of nanotechnology.

Donating Old PCs & Cellphones

Want to get rid of that old PC or Mac? For guidance, try:

http://ww2.pcdisposal.com

www.worldcomputerexchange.org/technology

www.epa.gov/epawaste/conserve/materials/ecycling/index.htm

http://ww2.pcdisposal.com/computer-recycling.html?gclid=CPnhx97dkKkCFQQ-bAodwmckpg

http://earth911.com/recycling/electronics/

For unwanted cellphones:

http://greenphone.com/

www.crserecycling.com/main.php?p=electronics

www.shelteralliance.net/?gclid=CMGLyN3ekKkCFQkSbAoda15koQ

www.911cellphonebank.org/

www.recyclingforcharities.com/index.php

MANUFACTURING & USAGE BY-PRODUCTS Many communities are eager to have computer and chip manufacturers locate there because they perceive them to be "clean" industries. But there have been lawsuits charging that the semiconductor industry has knowingly exposed workers to a variety of hazardous toxins, some of which were linked to miscarriages, and there is speculation that others may be linked to cancer and birth defects. Wireless systems can disrupt pacemakers and other lifesaving devices in hospitals. The world's data centers are projected to surpass the airline industry as greenhouse gas polluters by 2020.[66]

DISPOSAL BY-PRODUCTS Technologies are quickly going obsolete. It has been estimated that 3% of microprocessors and memory chips, for example, go obsolete each month.[67] What to do with the "e-waste"—nearly 400 million electronic products Americans discard per year?

- According to Wirefly.org, the average cell phone user replaces his cellphone every 18 months.
- The U.S. Environmental Protection Agency (EPA) reports that over 112,000 computers are discarded every single day. That's 41.1 million desktops and laptop computers per year. And that's just in the United States (and does not include computer monitors).
- 20 million TVs are trashed in the United States every year.
- And we toss over 100 million cellphones in the trash every year.
- Only 13% of electronic waste is disposed of and recycled properly.[68]

Chemical	Source
Lead	• Cathode-ray tubes (CRTs) in amounts of 4–8 pounds. Also found in solder in circuit boards. Discarded electronics account for 30–40% of lead in the waste stream.
Cadmium	• Circuit boards, semiconductors. More than 2 million pounds estimated to exist in discarded computers in 2005.
Mercury	• Switches, batteries, fluorescent bulbs in liquid-crystal displays. By 2005, 400,000 pounds discarded.
Chromium	• Circuit boards, corrosion protection in steel. By 2005, 1.2 million pounds discarded.
PVC (polyvinyl chloride) plastics	• Connectors, cables, housings, plastic covers; about 250 million pounds discarded each year.
Brominated flame retardants	• Printed circuit boards, connectors, plastic covers, cables.

panel 9.4

Problem chemicals in PCs

Much of the electronic waste that winds up in the nation's 2,200 landfills contains large amounts of lead and other toxins that can leach into groundwater or produce dioxins and other cancer-causing agents when burned. *(• See Panel 9.4.)* The problem is worsening as new computer models are introduced on faster cycles. ABC News did a secret investigation of one e-waste recycler in Denver. This company, which claimed to safely recycle e-waste, wasn't recycling it at all. They were loading all those computer monitors, laptops, TVs, and cellphones into shipping containers and sending them to the Far East, mainly rural China and Hong Kong. This is illegal in the United States. But according to ABC News, shipping e-waste off to developing countries is not only happening, it's common. Most of our e-waste ends up in such places as Guiyu, China. The entire town has become polluted with toxins as a result of all this garbage.[69]

Many people believe that the United States should follow the lead of Europe and Japan and pass laws forcing manufacturers to reduce the use of toxic materials in new products and take back old computers for recycling.

Don't always assume you can get a school or local charity to take your old personal computer; some will, but many are tired of being stuck with junk. But there are organizations, such as the Electronic Industries Alliance Consumer Education Initiative (*www.eiae.org*), that help consumers locate donation programs and recycling companies. Dell, Gateway, and Hewlett-Packard have all created programs whereby users can send unwanted computer gear for donation, refurbishing, or recycling. Cellphones may also be turned in for recycling or reuse. Staples takes back old printer cartridges for recycling. Hewlett-Packard makes new printers from recycled material.

(*Left*) Old computers and electronic parts collect in piles at E-Parisara, an electronic waste recycling factory in Dobbspet, 45 kilometers from Bangalore, India. India's growing digital economy has contributed to the amount of e-waste it generates. According to the Karnataka, a state pollution control board, more than 10 tons of electronic waste is produced in Bangalore alone every year, and about a large percentage of the e-waste generated in the United States is exported to India, China, and Pakistan to be recycled. (*Right*) German worker sorting electronic garbage along a conveyor at a processing center. Electronic equipment, everything from cell phones to deep freezers, is collected and disposed of separately from regular trash. By law, electronics manufacturers bear the expense of recycling.

ENVIRONMENTAL BLIGHT Call it "techno-blight." This is the visual pollution represented by the forest of wireless towers, roof antennas, satellite dishes, and all the utility poles topped with transformers and strung with electric, phone, cable-TV, and other wires leading off in all directions. As the nation's electrical grid becomes more pervasive, so, people worry, will the obtrusive, ugly technology in our physical environment. Environmentalists worry about its impact on vegetation and wildlife, such as the millions of birds and bats that collide with cellular towers. Residents worry about the effect on views and property values, although antennas can be made into "stealth towers"—fake water towers, flagpoles, trees, and the like—to blend in better with the environment. Some people worry that there may be unknown health effects. Few of the thousands of miles of lines are buried underground, and most of those are in large cities. Ultimately the decision to approve or deny wireless towers resides with the Federal Communications Commission.

(*Left*) Fighting techno-blight. Environmentally friendly cellphone towers disguised as cacti. (*Right*) In Upland, California, young palm trees surround a fake palm, which is concealing a cellphone antenna.

POSSIBLE RISKS OF NANOTUBES Some environmentalists worry that the spread of nanotechnology—manipulating materials such as carbon, zinc, and gold at the molecular level—could create contaminants whose tiny size makes them especially hazardous. Many animal studies involving carbon nanotubes, superstrong carbon fibers that are now used in products such as tennis rackets and that might replace silicon in ever tinier transistors, have not found them to be risky. However, research in which nanotubes were injected into the abdomens of mice found that they developed lesions on the lungs similar to those induced by the inhalation of asbestos, which can lead to a deadly cancer. Most people are probably not endangered by nanotubes, scientists concluded, but those working with them in laboratories or at nanotube manufacturers are advised to take extra precautions.

Mental-Health Problems

Overuse of computers can increase the risk of depression and insomnia, among other health problems.

Some of the mental-health problems linked to information technology are the following ones:

ISOLATION? Automation allows us to go for days without actually speaking with or touching another person, from buying gas to playing games. Many studies have found that, as people spend more time online, they have less time for real-life relationships with family and friends. For example, a poll of 2,030 people ages 12 and older found that 28% of Americans in 2008 said they had been spending less time with members of their household as compared to 11% who said that two years earlier, a change coinciding with the rise of social networks.[70] And some studies have suggested that excessive dependence on cellphones and the Internet is like an addiction. "The deeper a technology is woven into the patterns of everyday life, the less choice we have about whether and how we use that technology."[71] With the large amount of time being spent online, some people argue that although "the social media boom is clearly on its upswing, real life social skills are ironically falling off in dramatic fashion."[72] However, a study done by Pew Internet Personal Networks and Community suggests that the Internet does not contribute to social isolation. Pew's studies found that "many Internet technologies are used as much for local contact as they are for distant communication."[73] Pew found: "Internet use does not pull people away from public places. Rather, it is associated with engagement in places such as parks, cafes, and restaurants, the kinds of locales where research shows that people are likely to encounter a wider array of people and diverse points of view."[74]

"Warning Sign of Tech Overload"

Take this short quiz (scroll down the left side to find it):

www.nytimes.com/2010/06/07/technology/07brainside.html

The difference between addiction /isolation and increased beneficial social networking seems to be *moderation* in online activity.

Recently, parents and mental-health professionals have worried that the popularity of videogames has a dark side. When Grand Theft Auto IV was announced in spring 2008, one student at the University of Northern Colorado said he was planning to spend $90 to get the collector's edition. Even though it severely pinched his budget, he said there were things he would sacrifice before a great videogame. "I'd probably give up my cellphone," he said. "Probably not food. That's really tough. I like food."[75] Earlier that year, Stanford University School of Medicine researchers showed that areas of the brain responsible for generating feelings of addiction and reward are activated during videogame play.[76]Almost one in 10 American children, ages 8 to 18, are addicted to videogames, in the same way that people are addicted to drugs and gambling.[77] Although gaming addiction is not yet officially recognized as a diagnosable disorder by the American Medical Association, "there is increasing evidence that people of all ages, especially teens and pre-teens, are facing very real, sometimes severe consequences associated with compulsive use of video and computer games."[78]

Another issue that many people have with videogames is the violence that many of them seem to celebrate. The debate over whether this violence increases the incidence of violence in the real world continues. (Read about the pros and cons of videogames at *http://videogames.procon.org/*.)

GAMBLING Gambling is already widespread in North America, but information technology makes it almost unavoidable. Instead of driving to a casino, for example, gamers can find slots, roulette, and blackjack just a mouse click away and quickly find themselves in debt.

Although gambling by wire is still basically illegal in the United States, host computers for Internet casinos and sports books have been established in Caribbean tax havens and some other places. Offshore companies taking bets from Americans for poker and casino games isn't against the law, but other types of gambling usually are against the law. Satellites, decoders, and remote-control devices allow TV viewers to do wagering from home. In these circumstances, law enforcement is extremely difficult. Despite U.S. efforts to curb gambling on the web, bettors in the United States generate a large share of global online gambling revenues, and the legal sites operating offshore are fighting back against U.S. Justice Department crackdowns as being unconstitutional. (Sometimes online gambling is legal, and sometimes it isn't—the answer depends on the circumstances.) "There's a difference between making bets, taking bets, facilitating payments to casinos, accepting advertising for it, or buying advertising for it, and even then there's a difference between casino/poker wagering and sports betting."[79]

Survival Tip

Alleviating Info-Mania

Hewlett-Packard offers a six-page "Guide to Avoiding Info-Mania" at:

http://demo.ort.org.il/clickit2/files/forums/920455712/548653262.pdf

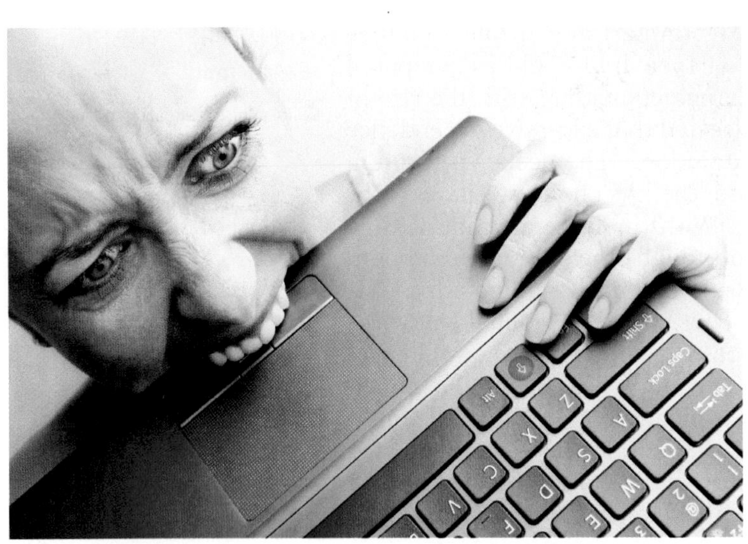

STRESS We know that there are many advantages of having on-demand information, but information technology brings stress with it. One cause of stress is the rapid change in technology—new hardware and software every year, if not more often, improved wireless connections with different standards, seemingly constant online updating, new malware, and so on. This rapid change forces all of us to continually learn new procedures. And working in IT requires a high degree of accuracy over long periods of time. A small mistake could lead to faulty information being used to make a poor decision. Hardware breakdowns and software glitches, of course, can create high levels of tension as well as sabotage work projects. Repetitive keyboard work can be boring, which is often stressful, and information overload is often cited as a cause of stress.

In the section on ergonomics (Chapter 5) we covered a few things that people can do to help to relieve IT-induced stress.

Protecting Children: Pornography, Sexual Predators, & Online Bullies

Children are the most vulnerable members of society; protecting them is a top priority.

Since computers are simply another way of communicating, it is no surprise that they are used to communicate about pornography, sexual solicitations, and threats and violence. Let's consider these.

PORNOGRAPHY One of the biggest cultural changes in the United States of the past quarter century has been the widespread distribution of sexually explicit material, making adult entertainment or pornography a business that earns upward of $12 billion yearly. Indeed, some of America's most well-known companies, such as General Motors, Time Warner, and Marriott, are now said to make millions selling pornography, as on closed-circuit TV channels in hotels.[80] Audio files called "porncasts" are available for downloading for adult podcasts. On the highways, motorists have complained of "dirty driving" as they found themselves looking at X-rated fare playing in other cars outfitted with DVD players.

As for the Internet, the number of pornography websites rose from 88,000 in 2000 to 1.6 million four years later.[81] In April 2005 it was found that two of five Internet users in the United States had visited a porn site.[82] Fully one-quarter of employees who use the Internet visit porn sites during the workday, according to 2008 figures—up 23% from a year earlier—and most such sex sites experience the most hits during office hours.[83] Some of the most innovative and experimental of web entrepreneurs, in fact, have been online pornographers, who were among the first to exploit video streaming, pop-up ads, and electronic billing.[84] Particularly bold are disseminators of child pornography, despite the efforts of Verizon, Sprint, Time Warner Cable, and others to block access to such Internet bulletin boards and websites featuring such material.

Of course, all this is of great concern to parents, who fear their children will be exposed to inappropriate sexual and also violent material, both on the web and in videogames. In 2008 the U.S. Supreme Court upheld a federal provision imposing a mandatory five-year prison term on people convicted of promoting child porn. It also upheld an earlier law prohibiting possession of child pornography.

Following are some steps being taken to shield children from adult material.

- **Online blocking software:** Some software developers have discovered a golden opportunity in making programs such as Websense, Cybersitter, Cyber Patrol, and Net Nanny. These blocking programs are designed to screen out objectionable material, typically by identifying certain unapproved keywords in a user's request or comparing the user's request for information against a list of prohibited sites. The leading online access providers also offer software filters.
- **DVD filters:** ClearPlay uses filtering technology that allows parents to edit out the inappropriate parts of films on DVDs—such as disturbing images, violence, nudity, swear words, and ethnic and social slurs.
- **Videogame rating systems:** The Entertainment Software Rating Board has a videogame ratings system that is linked to children's ages. *(• See Panel 9.5.)* To search for game ratings, go to *www.esrb.org/index-js.jsp* and type in the

Survival Tip

Beware!

Online pornography sites are infamous for injecting malware into users' browsers.

- **EC (Early Childhood):** Ages 3 and older. Contains no inappropriate material.
- **E (Everyone):** Ages 6 and older. May contain minimal or mild violence and/or infrequent mild language.
- **E10+ (Everyone 10 and older):** May contain more mild violence, mild language, and/or minimal suggestive themes.
- **T (Teen):** Ages 13 and older.May contain violence, suggestive themes, crude humor, minimal blood, and/or infrequent use of strong language.
- **M (Mature):** Ages 17 and older. May contain intense violence, blood and gore, sexual content, and/or strong language.
- **AO (Adults Only):** Ages 18 and over. May contain prolonged scenes of intense violence and/or graphic sexual content and nudity.
- **RP (Rating Pending):** Means game has been submitted to ERSB and is awaiting rating (used in advertising prior to game's release).

Source: Entertainment Software Ratings Board, ESRB Game Ratings, *www.esrb.org/esrbratings_guide.asp.*

panel 9.5

Videogame industry's rating system

These ratings are supposed to appear on videogame packages.

name of a game you are considering buying. For example, if you type in the popular "Grand Theft Auto," you will get 22 ratings, all of them T (Teen), M (Mature), or AO (Adults Only).

- **The V-chip:** The 1996 Telecommunications Law officially launched the era of the *V-chip,* a device that is required equipment in all new television sets with screen size of 13 inches or larger sold after January 2000 (*www.fcc.gov/guides/v-chip-putting-restrictions-what-your-children-watch*). The V-chip allows parents to automatically block out programs that have been labeled as high in violence, sex, or other objectionable material. Unfortunately, to turn on the controls, owners have to follow complicated instructions and menu settings, and then they have to remember their passwords when they want to watch reruns of *The Sopranos*, *X Factor, 1,000 Way to Die,* and *Criminal Minds.*
- **"xxx" web addresses:** In June 2010 the agency that controls domain names (ICANN, p. 64) said it will consider adding *.xxx* to the list of suffixes people and companies can pick when establishing their identities online. The purpose of the new domain would be to enable parents to more easily apply filtering software and so more effectively block access to porn sites. However, although the move may help parents stop their children from seeing some "porn" sites, it wouldn't force porn peddlers to use the new *.xxx* address—and some people argue that few adult-only sites will give up their existing *.com* addresses.[85]

ONLINE SEXUAL PREDATORS A task force created by 49 state attorneys general concluded in 2009 that, despite popular perceptions, sexual solicitation of children online, as on social networks like MySpace and Facebook, is really not a significant problem.[86] Even so, many parents are concerned about Internet predators reaching their children. Here are some reasons:[87]

- There is estimated to be more than 5,000,000 predators who surf the Internet. Sexual predators use forums, chat rooms, and instant messaging to locate and communicate with children.
- There is a 50% chance that if a child is in a chat room designated for under-aged children, the stranger he or she is talking to is a sexual predator logged in under a false identity.
- Surveys show that one in five of our kids will receive sexual advances while online but that less than 25% of them will inform a parent or adult.
- Approximately 5% of kids were aggressively approached by a sexual predator. This means the predator asked to meet the children offline, called them on the phone, or sent them money or gifts in the mail.
- 75% of kids are willing to share personal information with a stranger on the Internet, exactly what the sexual predator is looking for.
- 77% of the targets of online predators were 14 or older; 22% were between the ages of 10 and 13.
- 30% of those who are victimized by sexual predators are boys.
- 64% of the teens surveyed admitted they did things online that they would not want their parents to know about.
- Approximately 19% of teens say they have considered meeting someone offline that they have only known online.
- Approximately 9% of teens state that they have actually met offline a stranger they previously knew and met only online.

- The webcam is one of the favorite tools of the predator to find out what a child looks like, to try and gain personal information about him or her, and to manipulate him or her into doing things on camera that compromise his or her safety.

Some suggested prevention strategies are as follows:[88]

- **Monitor Internet use:** Parents are advised to monitor their children's Internet use and to install filters.
- **Be candid:** Parents should also make children aware that having sex with an adult is a crime and explain that molesters capitalize on teenagers' needs for acceptance.
- **Caution about revealing too much:** Children, particularly teenagers, reveal far too much about themselves online, which can make them targets for predators or bullies. For instance, 20% of teens (and a third of young adults 20–26) say they've sent or posted naked or seminaked photos or videos of themselves, mostly to be "fun or flirtatious," according to one survey.[89] This particularly risky practice is called ***sexting*****, the act of sending sexually revealing pictures of oneself through cellphone text messages or email.** Another survey found that at least a quarter of the teenagers polled had posted something they later regretted.[90]

CYBERBULLIES In yet another example of how information technology can negatively affect the social lives of children, there have been numerous reports of so-called ***cyberbullying*****, in which children in the 9–18 age range use information technologies, including the Internet, to unleash merciless taunting, nasty rumors, humiliating pictures, and other put-downs of fellow adolescents**. The tactics include stealing one another's screen names, forwarding private material to people for whom it was not intended, and posting derogatory material on blogs. "Bullies have gotten more complex and malicious as Internet access becomes more accessible with the rise of cheap, Internet-enabled mobile devices and as social networking becomes more intertwined with students' everyday lives. . . . A November 2010 government report, Indicators of School Crime and Safety: 2010, estimated that 4% of students ages 12 to 18 were cyberbullied in 2007. In a government report released May 31 [2011], about 18% of high school administrators said they had to deal with cyberbullying once a week or more. Experts say it happens more frequently than is reported."[91]

Some suggested tactics for dealing with cyberbullies are as follows:[92]

- **Save the evidence:** Children should print out offending messages and show them to their parents, who should then contact parents of the bully as well as inform school officials.
- **Block messages:** Victims should use the Block function to block further online communication from the bully. Parents should also contact email services and change the victim's screen name (and the victim should tell only his or her friends the new name).

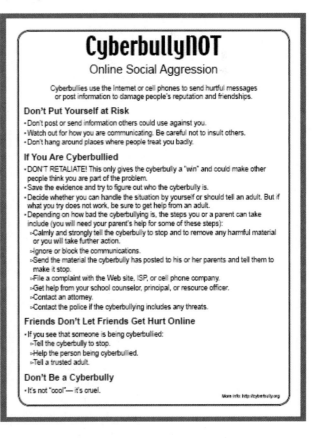

CyberbullyNOT

Online Social Aggression

Cyberbullies use the Internet or cell phones to send hurtful messages or post information to damage people's reputation and friendships.

Don't Put Yourself at Risk

- Don't post or send information others could use against you.
- Watch out for how you are communicating. Be careful not to insult others.
- Don't hang around places where people treat you badly.

If You Are Cyberbullied

- DON'T RETALIATE! This only gives the cyberbully a "win" and could make other people think you are part of the problem.
- Save the evidence and try to figure out who the cyberbully is.
- Decide whether you can handle the situation by yourself or should tell an adult. But if what you try does not work, be sure to get help from an adult.
- Depending on how bad the cyberbullying is, the steps you or a parent can take include (you will need your parent's help for some of these steps):
  - Calmly and strongly tell the cyberbully to stop and to remove any harmful material or you will take further action.
  - Ignore or block the communications.
  - Send the material the cyberbully has posted to his or her parents and tell them to make it stop.
  - File a complaint with the Web site, ISP, or cell phone company.
  - Get help from your school counselor, principal, or resource officer.
  - Contact an attorney.
  - Contact the police if the cyberbullying includes any threats.

Friends Don't Let Friends Get Hurt Online

- If you see that someone is being cyberbullied:
  - Tell the cyberbully to stop.
  - Help the person being cyberbullied.
  - Tell a trusted adult.

Don't Be a Cyberbully

- It's not "cool"— it's cruel.

More info: http://cyberbully.org

- **Contact an attorney or police:** If there are threats of violence or sexual harassment, parents should contact a lawyer or the police.

Incidentally, cyberbullying is also a problem in the workplace.[93]

Workplace Problems: Impediments to Productivity

Three types of workplace problems are misuse of technology, fussing with computers, and information overload.

MISUSE OF TECHNOLOGY Employees may look busy, as they stare into their computer screens with brows crinkled. But sometimes they're just hard at work playing videogames. Or browsing online malls (forcing corporate mail rooms to cope with a deluge of privately ordered parcels). Or looking at their investments or pornography sites.

FUSSING WITH COMPUTERS Another reason for so much wasted time is all the fussing that employees do with hardware, software, and online connections. One study in the early 1990s estimated that microcomputer users wasted 5 billion hours a year waiting for programs to run, checking computer output for accuracy, helping coworkers use their applications, organizing cluttered disk storage, and calling for technical support.[94] And that was before most people had to get involved with making online connections work or experience the frustrations of untangling complications wrought by spam, phishing, viruses, and other Internet problems. The Stanford study, referred to above, found that junk email and computer maintenance take up a significant amount of time spent online each day.

INFORMATION OVERLOAD Information technology is definitely a two-edged sword. Cellphones, pagers, and laptops may untether employees from the office, but these employees tend to work longer hours under more severe deadline pressure than do their tethered counterparts who stay at the office. Moreover, the devices that once promised to do away with annoying business travel by ushering in a new era of communications have done the opposite. They have created the office-in-a-bag that allows businesspeople to continue to work from airplane seats, hotel desks, and their own kitchen tables. The diminishing difference between work and leisure is what has been called the "blurring of life segments."[95]

Some studies have found an increase in labor productivity in the early years of the 21st century, most of it attributed to more investment in information technology and efficiency improvements made possible by this technology.[96] However, "the dirty little secret of the information age is that an increasingly large slice of work goes on outside the official work hours the government recognizes. . . . The '24/7' culture of nearly round-the-clock work is endemic to the wired economy. . . . But improving productivity is not about working longer; it's about adding more value per unit of work time."[97] An additional interesting wrinkle in the Internet age is how much work is done that is voluntary or donated work, as in all the user-generated content that is contributed to YouTube, WikiPedia, the Spore's Creature Creator universe-simulation game, and so on.[98]

Some people are concerned that "our workload and speed [do] not leave room for thoughtful reflection."[99] Adds Bill McKibben, author of *Enough: Staying Human in an Engineered Age,* "There is a real danger that one is absorbing and responding to bursts of information, rather than having time to think."[100]

The first recorded use of the phrase "information overload" was used by the futurologist Alvin Toffler in 1970, when he predicted that the rapidly increasing amounts of information being produced would eventually cause people problems. The root of the problem is that, although computer processing and memory speed and capacity are increasing all the time, the brain that humans must use to process the information is not getting any faster. Effectively, the human mind acts as a bottleneck in the process.[101] Trying to deal with all the information that bombards us is like trying to drink from a fire hose.

What are some of the signs of information overload?[102]

- Increased cardiovascular stress owing to a rise in blood pressure
- Weakened vision
- Confusion and frustration
- Impaired judgment based on overconfidence
- Irritation with others owing to an environmental input glut (which may also account for part of the "brusqueness" that is commonly attributed to big-city dwellers)

What can be done about information overload? Some suggestions:

- Spend less time on information that is nice to know and more time on information that you need to know now.
- Focus on getting relevant information, not on getting information faster, and focus on quality of information, rather than quantity.
- Learn how to create better information. Be direct in what you ask people, so that they can provide short precise answers.
- Understand the tools you have and don't switch tasks very often (single-tasking keeps the mind focused on one issue at a time).
- Avoid interruptions.
- Have quiet periods, when you disconnect.
- Take breaks.

9.5 ECONOMIC & POLITICAL ISSUES: Employment & the Haves/Have-Nots

There is an ongoing debate about whether information technology is reducing job availability and widening the gap between the rich and the poor.

In recent times, a number of critics have provided a counterpoint to the hype and overselling of information technology to which we have long been exposed. Some critics find that the benefits of information technology are balanced by a real downside. Other critics make the alarming case that technological progress is actually no progress at all—indeed, it is a curse. The two biggest charges (which are related) are, first, that information technology is killing jobs and, second, that it is widening the gap between the rich and the poor.

Technology, the Job Killer?

Increasingly intelligent machinery and automation have caused a reduction in several types of jobs.

Certainly ATMs do replace bank tellers, E-Z pass electronic systems do replace turnpike toll takers, and Internet travel agents do lure customers away from small travel agencies. Hundreds of companies are replacing service representatives with voice software. In new so-called *lights-out factories,* machines make things—for example, the tiny cutting devices you see mounted on dental-floss containers—even when no one is there; as much as possible is done with no labor. The contribution of technological advances to economic progress is steady, but the contribution to social progress is not purely positive.

A lights-out ("dark") factory. ABA-PGT plastics engineering plant; such factories have little lighting, because no or few humans work there.

But is it true, as technology critic Jeremy Rifkin has said, that intelligent machines are replacing humans in countless tasks, "forcing millions of blue-collar and white-collar workers into temporary, contingent, and part-time employment and, worse, unemployment"?[103]

This is too large a question to be fully considered in this book. We can say for sure that the U.S. economy is undergoing powerful structural changes, brought on not only by the widespread diffusion of technology but also by greater competition, increased global trade, the sending of jobs offshore, the shift from manufacturing to service employment, the weakening of labor unions, more flexible labor markets, more rapid immigration, partial deregulation, and certainly the great recession of 2008–2010. One futurist argues that by 2100 perhaps 2% of the U.S. non-farm workforce will be needed to handle white-collar "know-how" functions, such as those of most of today's office workers, but that "hyper-human" service workers, who will be required for creativity, social skills, conscious perception, positive feelings, hypothesizing, and the like, will zoom to over 90%.[104]

A counterargument is that jobs don't disappear—they just change. According to some observers, the jobs that do disappear represent drudgery. "If your job has been replaced by a computer," says Stewart Brand, "that may have been a job that was not worthy of a human."[105] Of course, that means little to someone who has no job at all.

Gap between Rich & Poor

Advances in information technology seem to lead to a widening gap between the rich and the poor.

We seem to be living through one of those difficult periods in which technology doesn't produce widely shared economic gains but instead widens the gap between those who have the right skills and those who don't.

According to the Organization for Economic Cooperation and Development (OECD), income inequality is increasing in most industrialized countries as a result of globalization and technological progress that requires greater skills from workers.[106] The gap between rich and poor is widening in countries that traditionally have a high level of inequality, such as the United States. It also is rising in countries that have been more equal, such as Denmark, Germany, and Sweden.[107] And although computer hardware is getting cheaper,

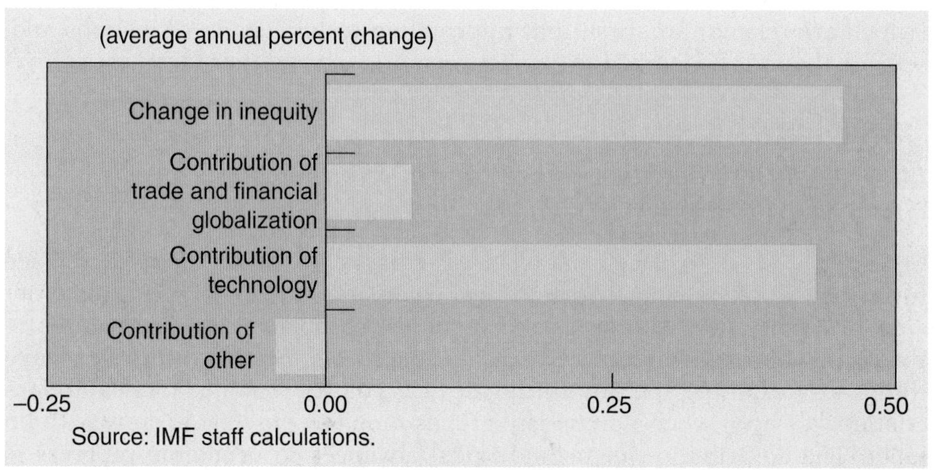

According to the International Monetary Fund, the main factor driving the recent increase in income inequality across countries has been technological progress.

high-speed Internet connections can be prohibitively expensive for poor and working-class families.

As *New York Times* columnist Thomas Friedman has written, in *The World Is Flat,* the world is "flattening," becoming more interconnected as the result of the Internet, wireless technology, search engines, file sharing, digital photography, and other cutting-edge technologies.[108] This may be good for many advanced nations. But half the world—Africa, much of Latin America, and rural areas of India and China—isn't flattening at all. And the future may be risky for America as well, because the fiber-optic cables that have been laid across the Pacific Ocean have made it easy to send offshore the jobs of all kinds of workers—accountants, radiologists, illustrators, and so on—whose work is knowledge-based.[109]

According to the International Monetary Fund, "better access to education would allow less-skilled and lower-income groups to capitalize on the opportunities from both technological progress and the ongoing process of globalization. Similarly, broadening access to finance, for instance, by improving institutions that promote pro-poor lending, could help improve the overall distribution of income even as financial development broadly continues to support overall growth."[110]

Whom Does the Internet Serve?

Do all people have equal access to the Internet?

Because of its unruly nature, perhaps the Internet truly serves no one—and that is both its blessing and its curse. Many business executives, for instance, find the public Internet so unreliable that they have moved their most critical applications to semiprivate networks, such as intranets and extranets (pp. 324–325). That means that more of the network is increasingly brought under commercial control, which for consumers might mean more fees for special services and the stifling of cultural empowerment and free speech. Despite early euphoria that the Internet would unleash a democratic spirit, nonprofit uses, and progressive websites, some see increasing corporate consolidation, at least in the United States.

For many restrictive governments outside the United States—China, Saudi Arabia, Iran, Singapore, United Arab Emirates, Bahrain, for example—that try to control Internet access by their citizens, the net poses threats to their authority. China, for instance, leads the United States in the number of people online; its nondemocratic government has cracked down on some kinds of Internet political activism but tolerated others—largely because there is so much online chatter that it can't censor it all.[111] (Some of the more than 1,000 words and phrases filtered by the Chinese instant-messaging service include "democracy," "human rights," and "oppose corruption.") But if such governments want to join the global economy, an important goal for most, perhaps they will find that less control and regulation will translate into greater e-commerce.

In a World of Breakneck Change, Can You Still Thrive?

Technological change is inevitable; adaptation is critical.

Clearly, information technology is driving the new world of jobs, services, and leisure, and nothing is going to stop it. People pursuing careers find the rules are changing very rapidly. Up-to-date skills are becoming ever more crucial. Job descriptions of all kinds are metamorphosing, and even familiar jobs are becoming more demanding.

Where will you be in all this? Today, experts advise, you must be willing to continually upgrade your skills, to specialize, and to market yourself. In a world of breakneck change, you can still thrive.

EXPERIENCE BOX

Student Use of Computers: Some Controversies

Information technology is very much a part of the college experience, of course. Elsewhere we discussed such matters as distance learning, web research, online plagiarism, and Internet addiction. Here we describe some other issues regarding students' computer use.

Using Computers in the Classroom

Although they're more expensive than desktop computers, laptops are useful because you can take them not only to libraries, to help with reading or term-paper notes, but also to class to use in taking lecture notes. You might even try using a tablet computer; be aware, however, small or virtual keyboards may pose a problem, and tablets do not support full-fledged productivity applications, such as Microsoft Office. With laptop or tablet, battery life may also be a factor.

The use of computers in classrooms is still controversial in certain quarters. Some campuses allow students to bring laptops and other electronic items to class but are imposing rules about what they are allowed to do. Too many students text one another, check their smartphones, browse the web, and visit social networking sites.

Notes Posted on the Web

Wouldn't it be nice, when you're out sick, to be able to go to a website and get the notes of lectures for the classes you missed? This is possible on campuses served by some commercial firms. Many such services are free, since the firms try to generate revenue by selling online advertising, but some charge a fee.

Such services can be a real help to students who learn best by reading rather than by hearing. They also provide additional reinforcement to students who feel they have not been able to grasp all of a professor's ideas during the lecture. However, they are no substitute for the classroom experience, with its spontaneous exchange of ideas. Moreover, "the very act of taking notes—not reading somebody else's notes, no matter how stellar—is a way of engaging the material, wrestling with it, struggling to comprehend or take issue."[112] In other words, you'll be better able to remember the lecture if you've reinforced the ideas by writing them down yourself.

Some faculty members have no problem with note-taking operations. Others disapprove, however. Among the criticisms: (1) Note-taking services don't always ask permission. (2) Instructors are reluctant to share their unpublished research in class if they think their ideas might end up posted in a public place and ripped off. (3) They might not wish to share controversial opinions with students if their views might be criticized in a worldwide forum. (4) Students might not come to class, especially if they think the lectures are boring or if they are given to chronic oversleeping or hangovers. (5) The notes may be sloppy, inaccurate, or incomplete.

Bottom line: These websites may be helpful, but they are certainly no substitute for going to class.

Online Student Evaluations

Student evaluations of courses and professors on the Internet can be useful. But since such evaluations are often expressed anonymously, they can also be inaccurate and unfair—even vicious, if students receiving poor grades take revenge by vilifying their instructors online. Many people don't understand how hard instructors work and believe that students should not be able to bash teachers in a public forum.

In reading teacher evaluations, it's useful to pay close attention to how civil and fair-minded the reports seem. And, of course, you should try to be as considerate and fair and objective as possible when writing them. Most students are not experts on teaching.

TERMS & EXPLANATIONS

biometrics (p. 484) Science of measuring individual body characteristics. Why it's important: *Biometric technology is used in some computer security systems to restrict user access. Biometric devices, such as those that use fingerprints, eye scans, palm prints, and face recognition, authenticate a person's identity by verifying his or her physical or behavioral characteristics.*

botnet (p. 476) Short for "robot network." A network of computers compromised by means of a Trojan horse that plants instructions within each of the computers to wait for commands from the person controlling that network. Why it's important: *If your PC becomes part of a botnet, it may be victimized by spam, phishing attacks, and/or denial-of-service attacks.*

computer crime (p. 471) Crime of two types: (1) an illegal act perpetrated against computers or telecommunications; (2) the use of computers or telecommunications to accomplish an illegal act. Why it's important: *Crimes against information technology include theft—of hardware, of software, of computer time, of cable or telephone services, or of information. Other illegal acts are crimes of malice and destruction. Computer crimes have very real and damaging consequences.*

cyberbullying (p. 493) Abusive behavior whereby children in the 9–18 age range use information technologies, including the Internet, to unleash merciless taunting, nasty rumors, humiliating pictures, and other put-downs of fellow adolescents. The tactics include stealing one another's screen names, forwarding private material to people for whom it was not intended, and posting derogatory material on blogs. Why it's important: *Cyberbullying may rise to the level of a misdemeanor cyberharassment charge, or if the child is young enough may result in the charge of juvenile delinquency.*

cyberwarfare (p. 479) The use of computers and the Internet to attack an enemy's information systems. Why it's important: *Attacks may be conducted as tactical maneuvers against an opponent or on the scale of widespread cyberattacks to impair government and military information systems.*

disaster-recovery plan (p. 485) Method of restoring information-processing operations that have been halted by destruction or accident. Why it's important: *Such a plan is important if an organization desires to resume computer operations quickly.*

encryption (p. 484) Process of altering readable data so that it is not usable unless the changes are undone. Why it's important: *Encryption can prevent unauthorized access and is useful to many organizations, especially those concerned with trade secrets, military matters, and other sensitive data. Some people maintain that encryption will determine the future of e-commerce, because transactions cannot flourish over the Internet unless they are secure.*

Evil Twin attack (p. 474) A variant on conventional phishing, in which a hacker or cracker sets up a Wi-Fi hot spot or access point that makes your computer think it's accessing a safe public network or your home network and then monitors your communications. Why it's important: *The hacker can steal data you enter into a website, if it doesn't have the right security measures.*

security (p. 481) System of safeguards for protecting information technology against disasters, system failures, and unauthorized access that can result in damage or loss. Five components of security are deterrents to computer crime, identification and access, encryption, protection of software and data, and disaster-recovery plans. Why it's important: *With proper security, organizations and individuals can minimize information technology losses from disasters, system failures, and unauthorized access.*

sexting (p. 493) The act of sending sexually revealing pictures of oneself through cellphone text messages or email. Why it's important: *May lead to embarrassments later in life—for example, when one is applying for a job, cause legal troubles, or draw the attention of predators.*

zombie (p. 476). Also known as a *drone*. A computer taken over covertly and programmed to respond to instructions sent remotely, often by instant-messaging channels. Why it's important: *People whose computers become zombies may be victimized by spam messages, phishing attacks, or denial-of-service attacks.*

CHAPTER REVIEW

LEARNING **MEMORIZATION**

"I can recognize and recall information."

Self-Test Questions

1. So that information-processing operations can be restored after destruction or accident, organizations should adopt a(n) __________.
2. __________ is the altering of readable data so that it is not usable unless the changes are undone.
3. __________ is incomplete, outdated, or otherwise inaccurate data.
4. An error in a program that causes it not to work properly is called a(n) __________.
5. CERT, created by the U.S. Department of Defense, stands for __________.

6. Software obtained illegally is called _________ software.
7. A variant on phishing in which someone sets up a Wi-Fi hot spot or access point that makes your computer think it's accessing a safe public network or your home network and then monitors your communications is called a(n) _______.
8. The term _______ refers to a system of safeguards for protecting information technology against disasters, system failures, and unauthorized access that can result in damage or loss.
9. A(n) ________ is a network of computers compromised by means of a Trojan horse that plants instructions within each of the computers to wait for commands from the person controlling that network.

Multiple-Choice Questions

1. Which of the following are crimes against computers and communications?
   a. natural hazards
   b. software theft
   c. information theft
   d. software bugs
   e. procedural errors
2. Which of the following methods or means is used to safeguard computer systems?
   a. signatures
   b. zombie
   c. adware
   d. worms
   e. Internet2
3. Which of the following are threats to computer systems?
   a. zombies
   b. evil twins
   c. crackers
   d. Trojan horses
   e. all of these
4. *Morphing* means
   a. programming.
   b. encrypting.
   c. changing.
   d. spying.
   e. threatening.
5. Which of these is an example of advance-fee fraud?
   a. zombie
   b. botnet
   c. phish
   d. Evil Twin attack
   e. Nigerian letter scam

True/False Questions

T F 1. The category of computer crimes includes dirty-data problems.

T F 2. Software bugs include procedural errors.

T F 3. A disaster-recovery plan is a method of encryption.

T F 4. It is impossible to detect when a photo has been morphed.

T F 5. If they got it from an employee's credit report, employers must destroy any personal information about the employee before they throw it out.

stage 2 LEARNING COMPREHENSION

"I can recall information in my own terms and explain it to a friend."

Short-Answer Questions

1. Give some examples of dirty data.
2. Briefly describe how encryption works.
3. What is a procedural error?
4. Name five threats to computers and communications systems.
5. The definition of computer crime distinguishes between two types. What are they?
6. What is phishing?
7. If your employer is checking on you, what might he or she be watching for?
8. What are three ways of verifying legitimate right of access to a computer system?
9. Name four environmental problems caused by computers.

stage 3 LEARNING APPLYING, ANALYZING, SYNTHESIZING, EVALUATING

"I can apply what I've learned, relate these ideas to other concepts, build on other knowledge, and use all these thinking skills to form a judgment."

Knowledge in Action

1. What, in your opinion, are the most significant disadvantages of using computers? What do you think can be done about these problems?
2. What's your opinion about the issue of free speech on an electronic network? Research some recent legal decisions in various countries, as well as some articles on the topic. Should the contents of messages be censored? If so, under what conditions?

3. Research the problems of stress and isolation experienced by computer users in the United States, Japan, and one other country. Write a brief report on your findings.
4. How can you ensure that information is accurate and complete? Make a list of things to remember when you are doing research on the Internet for a term paper.

Web Exercises

1. What is 128-bit encryption? Is your browser equipped? Visit the following websites to learn more about browser security:

   http://netsecurity.about.com/od/webbrowsersecurity/Web_Browser_Security_Information_and_Resources.htm

   http://iasweb.com/articles/webshopping.html

   www.us-cert.gov/cas/tips/ST05-001.html

   www.pcworld.com/businesscenter/article/221848/what_pwn2own_tells_us_about_browser_security.html

   Go to *https://browsercheck.qualys.com/*, *http://security.symantec.com/sscv6/home.asp?langid=ie&venid=sym&plfid=21&pkj=VUTVBMRSJRFSKLUKUMX*, *http://browserspy.dk/*, or *www.browserscope.org/* to run a browser security check on your computer. What are the results? What do you plan to do about any problems that were detected?

2. Here's a way to semi-encrypt an email message to a friend. In Word, type out your message; then press Ctrl+A (for *Select All*). Next go to the Format menu (or the Home tab) and select a font such as Wingdings that doesn't use letters. When your friend receives your message, he or she need only change the font back to an understandable one (such as Times New Roman) in order to read it. This certainly isn't high-level encryption, but it's a fun activity to try.

3. Visit the following websites, which discuss general Internet addiction:

   www.netaddiction.com/

   www.addictionrecov.org/internet.aspx

   www.helpguide.org/mental/internet_cybersex_addiction.htm

   www.mentalhelp.net/poc/center_index.php?id=66

   Do you have an Internet problem? Take a test:

   www.netaddiction.com/index.php?option=com_bfquiz&view=onepage&catid=46&Itemid=106

   What do you plan to do about it?

4. If you're spending too much time indoors using a computer or watching TV, you might want to consider going outside. Visit the following websites to learn about indoor air versus outdoor air:

   www.epa.gov/iaq/ia-intro.html

   www.lbl.gov/Education/ELSI/pollution-main.html

   http://eetd.lbl.gov/r-indoor.html

   Also, to read more about Internet addiction that may cause isolation from the real world, visit

   www.pewinternet.org/Reports/2009/18--Social-Isolation-and-New-Technology.aspx

   www.empowher.com/emotional-health/content/how-internet-affects-social-isolation

   http://cogsciblog.wordpress.com/2009/11/04/internet-use-does-not-increase-social-isolation-study-finds/

   www.mysocialnetwork.net/blog/410/r16/2006/10/does_internet_addiction_create.html

   http://findarticles.com/p/articles/mi_m2248/is_138_35/ai_66171001

   http://news-service.stanford.edu/news/2005/february23/internet-022305.html

   http://archives.cnn.com/2000/HEALTH/06/13/internet.addiction.wmd/

   www.newscientist.com/blog/technology/2008/03/are-we-all-internet-addicts-now.html

   What's your opinion on this issue?

   The following websites discuss computer health and safety:

   www.youtube.com/watch?v=T8qGO7XQoUw

   www.grassrootsdesign.com/intro/hs.php

   www.ics.uci.edu/~chair/comphealth2.html

   www.osha.gov/SLTC/computerworkstation/

   www.usernomics.com/workplace-ergonomics.html

5. How much do you know about the U.S. Department of Homeland Security's rules and policies concerning computer users' privacy? Go to *www.dhs.gov* and find out how you are affected.

10

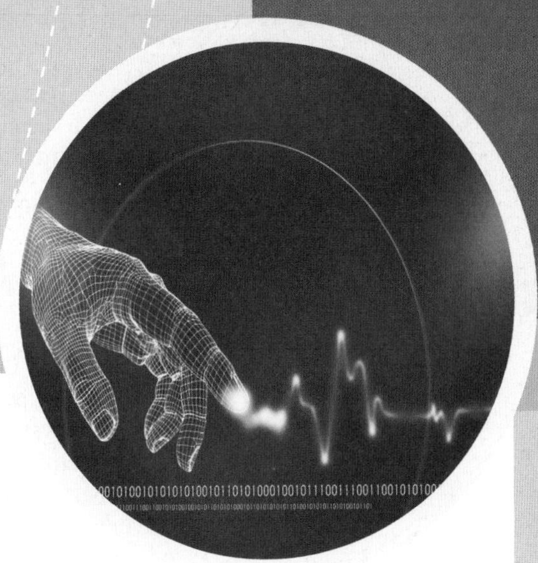

BUILDING SYSTEMS & APPLICATIONS Software Development, Programming, & Languages

Chapter Topics & Key Questions

10.1 **Systems Development and the Life Cycle of a Software Project** What are the six phases of the systems development life cycle?

10.2 **Programming: Traditionally a Five-Step Procedure** What is programming, and what are the five steps in accomplishing it?

10.3 **Five Generations of Programming Languages** What are the five generations of programming languages?

10.4 **Programming Languages Used Today** What are some third-generation languages, and what are they used for?

10.5 **Object-Oriented & Visual Programming** How do OOP and visual programming work?

10.6 **Markup & Scripting Languages** What do markup and scripting languages do?

Download the free UIT 10e App for key term flash cards, quizzes, and a game, *Over the Edge*

rganizations can make mistakes, of course, and big organizations can make really big mistakes.

In the 1990s, California's Department of Motor Vehicles' databases needed to be modernized, and Tandem Computers said it could do it. "The fact that the DMV's database system, designed around an old IBM-based platform, and Tandem's new system were as different as night and day seemed insignificant at the time to the experts involved," said one writer who investigated the project.[1] The massive driver's license database, containing the driving records of more than 30 million people, first had to be "scrubbed" of all information that couldn't be translated into the language used by Tandem computers. One such scrub yielded 600,000 errors. Then the DMV had to translate all its IBM programs into the Tandem language. "Worse, DMV really didn't know how its current IBM applications worked anymore," said the writer, "because they'd been custom-made decades before by long departed programmers and rewritten many times since." Eventually the project became a staggering $44 million loss to California's taxpayers.

Needless to say, not all mistakes are so huge. Computer foul-ups can range from minor to catastrophic. But this example shows how important planning is, especially when an organization is trying to launch a new kind of system. The best way to avoid such mistakes is to employ systems analysis and design.

10.1 Systems Development and the Life Cycle of a Software Project

Systems development involves several steps of systems analysis and design.

But, you may say, you're not going to have to wrestle with problems on the scale of motor-vehicle departments. That's a job for computer professionals. You're mainly interested in using computers and communications to increase your own productivity. Why, then, do you need to know anything about systems analysis and design?

Today every profession has an IT component, so even if you are not the programmer, you will be involved in new or updated system analysis and design at some point. In many types of jobs, you may find that your department or your job is the focus of a study by a systems analyst. Knowing how the procedure works will help you better explain how your job works or what goals your department is supposed to achieve. In progressive companies, management is always interested in suggestions for improving productivity. Systems analysis provides a method for developing such ideas.

The Purpose of a System

The purpose of a system is what it does, which does not necessarily equate with the intentions of the people who analyzed and designed it.

A *system* is defined as a collection of related components that interact to perform a task in order to accomplish a goal. A system may not work very well, but it is nevertheless a system. *The point of systems analysis and design is to ascertain how a system works and then take steps to make it better.*

An organization's computer-based information system consists of hardware, software, people, procedures, and data, as well as communications setups. These components work together to provide people with information for running the organization.

Getting the Project Going: How It Starts, Who's Involved

Several types of people are involved in getting a project going.

A single individual who believes that something badly needs changing is all it takes to get the project rolling. An employee may influence a supervisor. A customer or supplier may get the attention of someone in higher management. Top management may decide independently to take a look at a system that seems inefficient. A steering committee may be formed to decide which of many possible projects should be worked on.

Participants in the project are of three types:

- **Users:** The system under discussion should *always* be developed in consultation with users, whether floor sweepers, research scientists, or customers. Indeed, if user involvement in analysis and design is inadequate, the system may fail for lack of acceptance.
- **Management:** Managers within the organization should also be consulted about the system. They often have a higher level of understanding of what the system does and why it is used.
- **Technical staff:** Members of the company's information systems (IS) department, consisting of systems analysts and programmers, need to be involved. For one thing, they may have to execute the project. Even if they don't, they will have to work with outside IS people contracted to do the job.

Complex projects will require one or several systems analysts. **A *systems analyst* is an information specialist who performs systems analysis, design, and implementation.** The analyst's job is to study the information and communications needs of an organization and determine what changes are required to deliver better information to the people who need it. "Better" information means information that is summarized in the acronym CART—complete, accurate, relevant, and timely. The systems analyst achieves this goal through the problem-solving method of systems analysis and design.

The Six Phases of Systems Analysis & Design

Although there are different names for the stages, systems analysis and design can be broken down into six basic phases.

Systems analysis and design is a six-phase problem-solving procedure for examining an information system and improving it. The six phases make up what is called the *systems development life cycle*. **The _systems development life cycle (SDLC)_ is the step-by-step process that many organizations follow during systems analysis and design.**

Whether applied to a Fortune 500 company or a three-person engineering business, the six phases in systems analysis and design are as shown in the illustration. (● *See Panel 10.1.*) Phases often overlap,

panel 10.1

Systems development life cycle

An SDLC typically includes six phases.

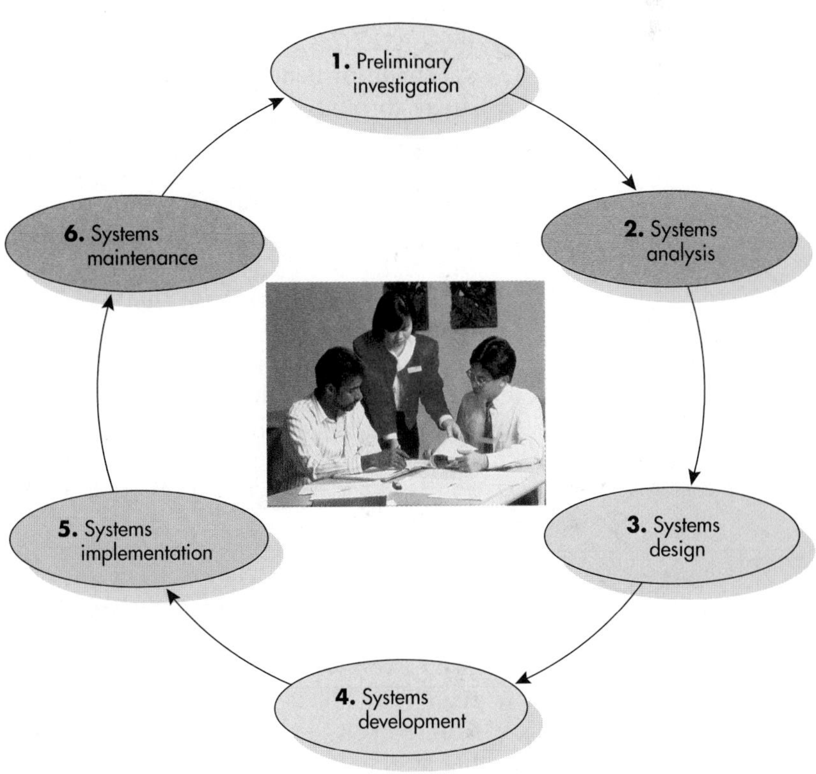

panel 10.2

First phase: Preliminary investigation

1. Conduct preliminary analysis. This includes stating the objectives, defining the nature and scope of the problem.
2. Propose alternative solutions: leave system alone, make it more efficient, or build a new system.
3. Describe costs and benefits of each solution.
4. Submit a preliminary plan with recommendations.

and a new one may start before the old one is finished, or a particular phase might not be working out well, so the analysts and designers may return to a previous phase and make adjustments. After the first four phases, management must decide whether to proceed to the next phase. User input and review are a critical part of each phase.

The First Phase: Preliminary Investigation

The first phase results in a preliminary plan.

The objective of **Phase 1, *preliminary investigation*, is to conduct a preliminary analysis, propose alternative solutions, describe costs and benefits, and submit a preliminary plan with recommendations.** (● *See Panel 10.2.*)

1. CONDUCT THE PRELIMINARY ANALYSIS In this step, you need to find out what the organization's objectives are and the nature and scope of the problem under study. Even if a problem pertains only to a small segment of the organization, you cannot study it in isolation. You need to find out what the objectives of the organization itself are. Then you need to see how the problem being studied fits in with them.

2. PROPOSE ALTERNATIVE SOLUTIONS In delving into the organization's objectives and the specific problem, you may have already discovered some solutions. Other possible solutions can come from interviewing people inside the organization, clients or customers affected by it, suppliers, and consultants. You can also study what competitors are doing. With this data, you then have three choices. You can leave the system as is, improve it, or develop a new system.

3. DESCRIBE THE COSTS & BENEFITS Whichever of the three alternatives is chosen, it will have costs and benefits. In this step, you need to indicate what these are. Costs may depend on benefits, which may offer savings. A broad spectrum of benefits may be derived. A process may be speeded up, streamlined through elimination of unnecessary steps, or combined with other processes. Input errors or redundant output may be reduced. Systems and subsystems may be better integrated. Users may be happier with the system. Customers' or suppliers' interactions with the system may be more satisfactory. Security may be improved. Costs may be cut.

4. SUBMIT A PRELIMINARY PLAN Now you need to wrap up all your findings in a written report. The readers of this report will be the executives who are in a position to decide in which direction to proceed—make no changes, change a little, or change a lot—and how much money to allow for the project. You should describe the potential solutions, costs, and benefits and indicate your recommendations.

The Second Phase: Systems Analysis

The second phase involves gathering and analyzing data.

The objective of **Phase 2, *systems analysis*, is to gather data, analyze the data, and write a report.** (● *See Panel 10.3.*) In this second phase of the SDLC, you will follow the course that management has indicated after having read your Phase 1 feasibility report. We are assuming that management has ordered you to perform Phase 2—to do a careful analysis or study of the existing system in order to understand how the new system you proposed would

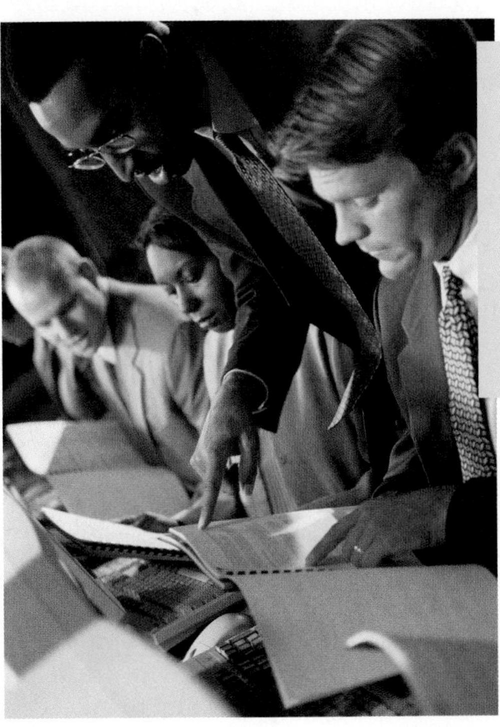

1. Gather data, using tools of written documents, interviews, questionnaires, and observations.
2. Analyze the data, using modeling tools: grid charts, decision tables, data flow diagrams, systems flowcharts, connectivity diagrams.
3. Write a report.

panel 10.3

Second phase: Systems analysis

differ. This analysis will also consider how people's positions and tasks will have to change if the new system is put into effect.

1. GATHER DATA In gathering data, you will review written documents, interview employees and managers, develop questionnaires, and observe people and processes at work.

2. ANALYZE THE DATA Once the data has been gathered, you need to come to grips with it and analyze it. Many analytical tools, or modeling tools, are available. ***Modeling tools*** **are analytical tools such as charts, tables, and diagrams used by systems analysts to present graphic, or pictorial, representations of a system.** An example of a modeling tool is a ***data flow diagram (DFD)***, **which graphically shows the flow of data through a system**—that is, the essential processes of a system, along with inputs, outputs, and files. *(• See Panel 10.4.)*

panel 10.4

Data flow diagram

(*Below left*) Symbols; (*next page*) examples of a data flow diagram (adapted from *http://visualcase.com/tutorials/about-data-flow-diagram.htm; www.hit.ac.il/staff/leonidm/information-systems/ch24.html#Heading6*)

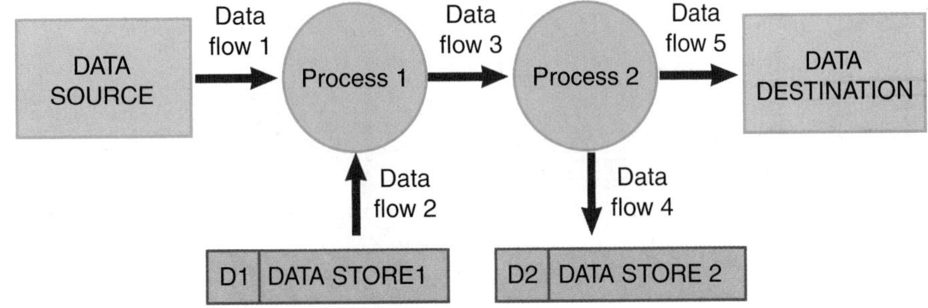

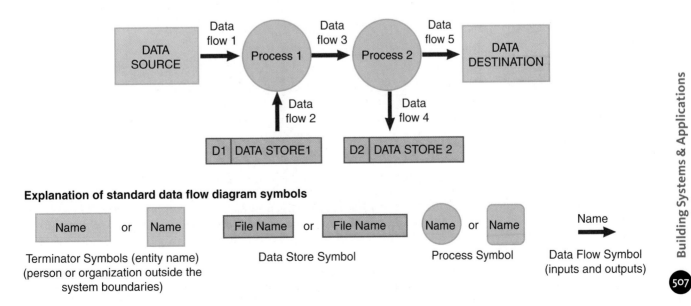

Explanation of standard data flow diagram symbols

Name or Name — Terminator Symbols (entity name) (person or organization outside the system boundaries)

File Name or File Name — Data Store Symbol

Name or Name — Process Symbol

Name → — Data Flow Symbol (inputs and outputs)

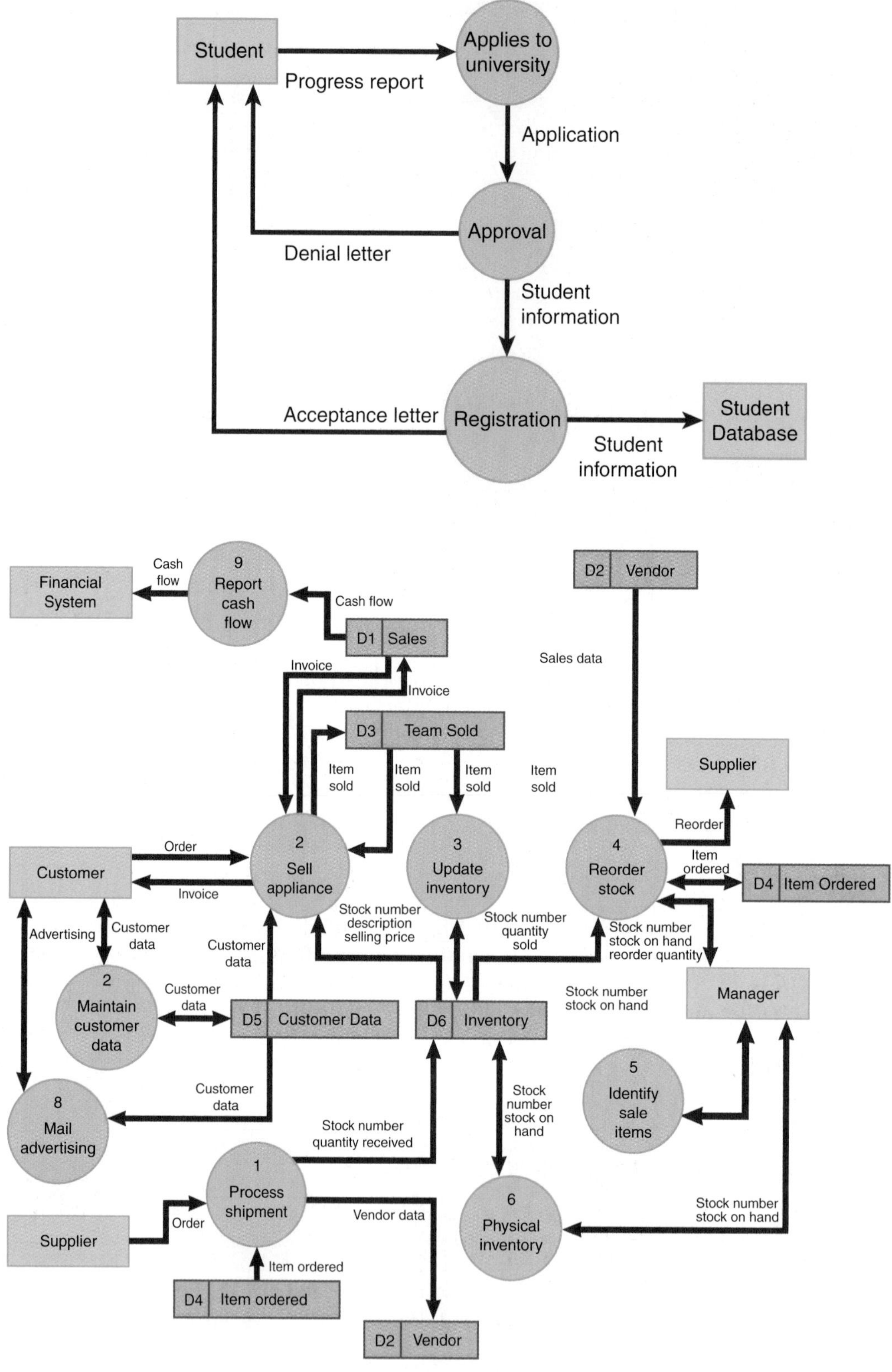

CASE tools may also be used during the analysis phase, as well as in most other phases. ***CASE (computer-aided software engineering) tools*** **are computer-automated means of designing and changing systems.** This technology is intended to speed up the process of developing systems and to improve the quality of the resulting systems. Such tools can generate and store diagrams, produce documentation, analyze data relationships, generate computer code, produce graphics, and provide project management functions. (Project management software, discussed in Chapter 3, consists of programs used to plan, schedule, and control the people, costs, and resources required to complete a project on time.)

So-called lightweight (more flexible), or "agile," team-based software and project development methodologies are also used to speed up system development; examples are Crystal Clear, Extreme Programming, Scrum, and Feature Driven Development. The agile approach supplies guiding practices that provide a framework within which to design and build a system and manage it, rather than supplying a set of rigid instructions (*http://ccpace.com/Resources/documents/AgileProjectManagement.pdf*).

Unified Modeling Language (UML) is also used to develop systems. UML is a standard language used for visual constructing software systems, as well as for business modeling. (In this case, modeling is the designing of software applications before coding.)

3. WRITE A REPORT Once you have completed the analysis, you need to document this phase. This report to management should have three parts. First, it should explain how the existing system works. Second, it should explain the problems with the existing system. Finally, it should describe the requirements for the new system and make recommendations on what to do next.

At this point, not a lot of money will have been spent on the systems analysis and design project. If the costs of going forward seem prohibitive, this is a good time for the managers reading the report to call a halt. Otherwise, you will be asked to move to Phase 3.

CASE tools and UML are important. For more information, try:

http://searchcio-midmarket.techtarget.com/definition/CASE

http://delphi.about.com/od/toppicks/tp/aatpmodelcase.htm

www.peter-lo.com/Teaching/M8034/L12.pdf

http://atlas.kennesaw.edu/~dbraun/csis4650/A&D/UML_tutorial/what_is_uml.htm

www.cragsystems.co.uk/why_use_uml.htm

www.omg.org/gettingstarted/what_is_uml.htm

For information on agile methodologies, go to:

www.niwotridge.com/PDFs/PM%20Chapter%20(short%20no%20email)%20Update%202.pdf

http://agilemethodology.org/

www.projectsmart.co.uk/agile-project-management.html

The Third Phase: Systems Design

In the third phase, the design is refined.

The objective of **Phase 3, *systems design*, is to do a preliminary design and then a detail design and to write a report.** (*● See Panel 10.5.*) In this third phase of the SDLC, you will essentially create a "rough draft" and then a "detail draft" of the proposed information system.

1. DO A PRELIMINARY DESIGN A *preliminary design* describes the general functional capabilities of a proposed information system. It reviews the system requirements and then considers major components of the system. Usually several alternative systems (called *candidates*) are considered, and the costs and the benefits of each are evaluated.

Tools used in the design phase may include CASE tools and project management software.

Prototyping is often done at this stage. ***Prototyping*** **refers to using CASE tools, UML, and other software applications to build working models of system components so that they can be quickly tested and evaluated.** Thus, **a *prototype* is a limited working system, or part of one, developed to test design concepts.** A prototype, which may be constructed in just a few days, allows users to find out immediately how a change in the system might benefit them. For example, a systems analyst might develop a menu as a possible screen display, which users could try out. The menu can then be redesigned or fine-tuned, if necessary.

2. DO A DETAIL DESIGN A *detail design* describes how a proposed information system will deliver the general capabilities described in the preliminary design. The detail design usually considers the following parts of the system in this order: output requirements, input requirements, storage requirements, processing requirements, and system controls and backup.

3. WRITE A REPORT All the work of the preliminary and detail designs will end up in a large, detailed report. When you hand over this report to senior management, you will probably also make some sort of presentation or speech.

panel 10.5

Third phase: Systems design

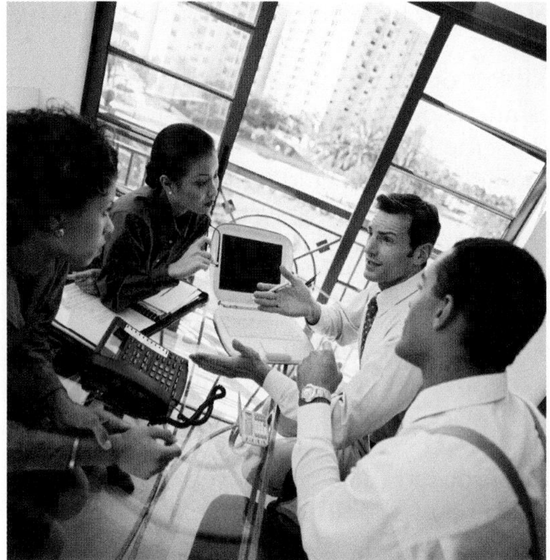

1. Do a preliminary design, using CASE tools, prototyping tools, and project management software, among others.
2. Do a detail design, defining requirements for output, input, storage, and processing and system controls and backup.
3. Write a report.

The Fourth Phase: Systems Development

In the fourth phase, the system is actually built.

In **Phase 4, *systems development*, the systems analyst or others in the organization develop or acquire the software, acquire the hardware, and then test the system.** *(• See Panel 10.6.)* Depending on the size of the project, this phase will probably involve the organization in spending substantial sums of money. It could also involve spending a lot of time. However, at the end you should have a workable system.

1. DEVELOP OR ACQUIRE THE SOFTWARE During the design stage, the systems analyst may have had to address what is called the "make-or-buy" decision, but that decision certainly cannot be avoided now. In the *make-or-buy decision*, you decide whether you have to create a program—have it custom-written—or buy it, meaning simply purchase an existing software package. Sometimes programmers decide they can buy an existing program and modify it rather than write it from scratch.

If you decide to create a new program, then the question is whether to use the organization's own staff programmers or to hire outside contract programmers (outsource it). Whichever way you go, the task could take many months.

1. Develop or acquire the software.
2. Acquire the hardware.
3. Test the system.

panel 10.6

Fourth phase: Systems development

Programming is an entire subject unto itself, which we discuss later in this chapter, along with programming languages.

2. ACQUIRE HARDWARE Once the software has been chosen, the hardware to run it must be acquired or upgraded. It's possible your new system will not require any new hardware. It's also possible that the new hardware will cost millions of dollars and involve many items: microcomputers, mainframes, monitors, modems, and many other devices. The organization may find it's better to lease than to buy some equipment, especially since, as we mentioned (Moore's law), chip capability has traditionally doubled every 18 months.

3. TEST THE SYSTEM With the software and hardware acquired, you can now start testing the system. Testing is usually done in two stages: unit testing, then system testing.

- **Unit testing:** In *unit testing,* the performance of individual parts is examined, using test (made-up or sample) data. If the program is written as a collaborative effort by multiple programmers, each part of the program is tested separately.
- **System testing:** In *system testing*, the parts are linked together, and test data is used to see if the parts work together. At this point, actual organization data may be used to test the system. The system is also tested with erroneous data and massive amounts of data to see if the system can be made to fail ("crash").

At the end of this long process, the organization will have a workable information system, one ready for the implementation phase.

The Fifth Phase: Systems Implementation

The fifth phase involves moving everything from the old system over to the new system.

Whether the new information system involves a few handheld computers, an elaborate telecommunications network, or expensive mainframes, the fifth phase will involve some close coordination in order to make the system not just workable but successful. **Phase 5, *systems implementation*, consists of converting the hardware, software, and files to the new system and training the users.** (• *See Panel 10.7.)*

1. CONVERT TO THE NEW SYSTEM Conversion, the process of transition from an old information system to a new one, involves converting hardware, software, and files. There are four strategies for handling conversion: direct, parallel, phased, and pilot.

panel 10.7

Fifth phase: Systems implementation

1. Convert hardware, software, and files through one of four types of conversions: direct, parallel, phased, or pilot.
2. Train the users.

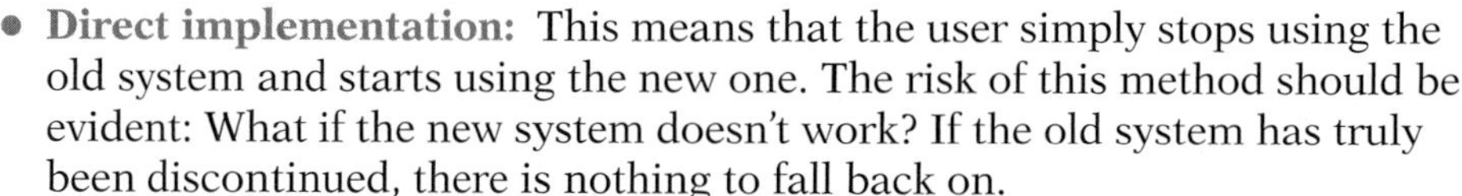

- **Direct implementation:** This means that the user simply stops using the old system and starts using the new one. The risk of this method should be evident: What if the new system doesn't work? If the old system has truly been discontinued, there is nothing to fall back on.
- **Parallel implementation:** This means that the old and new systems are operated side by side until the new system has shown it is reliable, at which time the old system is discontinued. Obviously there are benefits in taking this cautious approach. If the new system fails, the organization can switch back to the old one. The difficulty with this method is the expense of paying for the equipment and people to keep two systems going at the same time.
- **Phased implementation:** This means that parts of the new system are phased in separately—either at different times (parallel) or all at once in groups (direct).
- **Pilot implementation:** This means that the entire system is tried out, but only by some users. Once the reliability has been proved, the system is implemented with the rest of the intended users. The pilot approach still has its risks, since all of the users of a particular group are taken off the old system. However, the risks are confined to a small part of the organization.

Systemantics

Do a search: Who wrote this, and when? "Systems are seductive. They promise to do a hard job faster, better, and more easily than you could do it by yourself. But if you set up a system, you are likely to find your time and effort now being consumed in the care and feeding of the system itself. New problems are created by its very presence. Once set up, it won't go away, it grows and encroaches. It begins to do strange and wonderful things. Breaks down in ways you never thought possible. It kicks back, gets in the way, and opposes its own proper function. Your own perspective becomes distorted by being in the system. You become anxious and push on it to make it work. Eventually you come to believe that the misbegotten product it so grudgingly delivers is what you really wanted all the time. At that point encroachment has become complete . . . you have become absorbed . . . you are now a systems person!"

Hint: Check out "The Systems Bible" and the "Laws of Systematics."

2. TRAIN THE USERS Various tools are available to familiarize users with a new system—from documentation (instruction manuals) to videotapes to live classes to one-on-one, side-by-side teacher-student training. Sometimes training is done by the organization's own staffers; at other times it is contracted out.

The Sixth Phase: Systems Maintenance

All systems must be maintained and updated.

Phase 6, *systems maintenance*, adjusts and improves the system by having system audits and periodic evaluations and by making changes based on new conditions. (• *See Panel 10.8.*) Even with the conversion accomplished and the users trained, the system won't just run itself. There is a sixth—and continuous—phase in which the information system must be monitored to ensure that it is successful. Maintenance includes not only keeping the machinery running but also updating and upgrading the system to keep pace with new products, services, customers, government regulations, and other requirements.

After some time, maintenance costs will accelerate as attempts continue to keep the system responsive to user needs. At some point, these maintenance

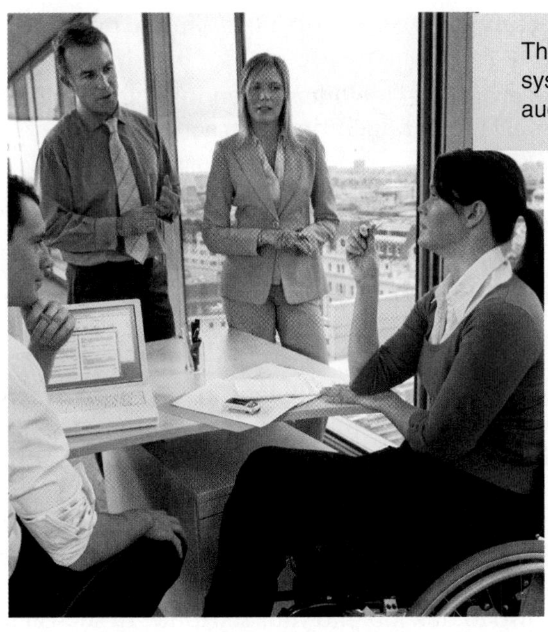
The sixth phase is to keep the system running through system audits and periodic evaluations.

panel 10.8

Sixth phase: Systems maintenance

costs become excessive, indicating that it may be time to start the entire SDLC again. (This stage is sometimes called *termination*.)

10.2 PROGRAMMING: Traditionally a Five-Step Procedure

Programming is a five-step process of software engineering.

To see how programming works, we must understand what constitutes a program. **A *program* is a list of instructions that the computer must follow to process data into information.** The instructions consist of statements used in a programming language (an artificial language used to write instructions that can be translated into machine language [Chapter 4, p. 206]). Examples are programs that do word processing, desktop publishing, or payroll processing.

The decision whether to buy or create a program forms part of Phase 4 in the systems development life cycle. Once the decision is made to develop a new system, the programmer goes to work.

A program, we said, is a list of instructions for the computer. ***Programming* is a five-step process for creating that list of instructions.** Programming is sometimes called *software engineering*; however, the latter term includes in its definition the use of best-practice processes to create and/or maintain software, whether for groups or individuals, in an attempt to get rid of the usual haphazard methods that have plagued the software industry. Software engineering involves the establishment and use of recognized engineering principles to obtain software that is reliable and works efficiently. It requires the application of a systematic, disciplined, quantifiable approach to the development, operation, and maintenance of software.

The five steps in the programming process are as follows:

1. Clarify/define the problem—include needed output, input, processing requirements.
2. Design a solution—use modeling tools to chart the program.
3. Code the program—use a programming language's syntax, or rules, to write the program.

4. Test the program—get rid of any logic errors, or "bugs," in the program ("debug" it).
5. Document and maintain the program—include written instructions for users, explanation of the program, and operating instructions.

Coding—sitting at the keyboard and typing words into a computer—is how many people view programming. As we will see, however, it is only one of the five steps.

The First Step: Clarify the Programming Needs

The first step in programming involves six smaller tasks.

The *problem clarification (definition)* step consists of six mini-steps—clarifying program objectives and users, outputs, inputs, and processing tasks; studying the feasibility of the program; and documenting the analysis. *(● See Panel 10.9.)*

1. CLARIFY OBJECTIVES & USERS You solve problems all the time. A problem might be deciding whether to take a required science course this term or next, or selecting classes that allow you also to fit a job into your schedule. In such cases, you are specifying your objectives. Programming works the same way. You need to write a statement of the objectives you are trying to accomplish—the problem you are trying to solve. If the problem is that your company's systems analysts have designed a new computer-based payroll-processing proposal and brought it to you as the programmer, you need to clarify the programming needs.

You also need to make sure you know who the users of the program will be. Will they be people inside the company, outside, or both? What kind of skills will they bring?

2. CLARIFY DESIRED OUTPUTS Make sure you understand the outputs—what the system designers want to get out of the system—before you specify the inputs. For example, what kind of reports and other forms of communication are wanted? What information should the outputs include? This step may require several meetings with systems designers and users to make sure you're creating what they want.

3. CLARIFY DESIRED INPUTS Once you know the kind of outputs required, you can then think about input. What kind of input data is needed? In what form should it appear? What is its source?

4. CLARIFY THE DESIRED PROCESSING Here you make sure you understand the processing tasks that must occur in order for input data to be processed into output data.

more info!

FBI Flop

What happens when an organization does not properly define program objectives? In 2003 the FBI started the coding for their new Virtual Case File program—and $170 million of taxpayers' money and more than 700,000 lines of error-prone commands later, they canceled the project. Why? Because they had not adequately defined the program requirements.

www.washingtonpost.com/wp-dyn/content/article/2006/08/17/AR2006081701485.html

http://spectrum.ieee.org/computing/software/who-killed-the-virtual-case-file

panel 10.9

First step: Clarify programming needs

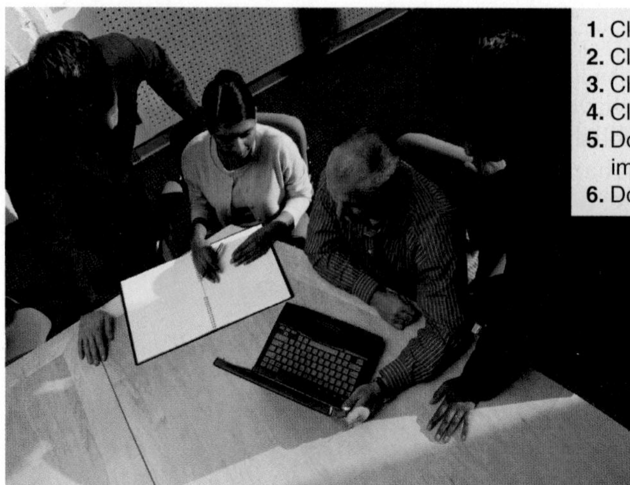

1. Clarify objectives and users.
2. Clarify desired outputs.
3. Clarify desired inputs.
4. Clarify desired processing.
5. Double-check feasibility of implementing the program.
6. Document the analysis.

5. DOUBLE-CHECK THE FEASIBILITY OF IMPLEMENTING THE PROGRAM Is the kind of program you're supposed to create feasible within the present budget? Will it require hiring a lot more staff? Will it take too long to accomplish?

Occasionally programmers suggest to managers that they buy an existing program and modify it rather than having one written from scratch.

6. DOCUMENT THE ANALYSIS Throughout program clarification, programmers must document everything they do. This includes writing objective specifications of the entire process being described.

The Second Step: Design the Program

Algorithms must be developed before the program can be designed.

Assuming the decision is to make, or custom-write, the program, you then move on to design the solution specified by the systems analysts. To design the solution, you first need to create algorithms. **An *algorithm* is a formula or set of steps for solving a particular problem.** (● *See Panel 10.10.*) To be an algorithm, a set of rules must be unambiguous and have a clear stopping point. We use algorithms every day. For example, a recipe for baking bread is an algorithm. Most programs, with the exception of some artificial intelligence applications, consist of algorithms. In computer programming, there are often different algorithms to accomplish any given task, and each algorithm has specific advantages and disadvantages in different situations. Inventing elegant algorithms—algorithms that are simple and require the fewest steps possible—is one of the principal challenges in programming.

Algorithms can be expressed in various ways. **In the *program design step*, the software is designed in two mini-steps. First, the program logic is determined through a top-down approach and modularization, using a *hierarchy chart*. Then it is designed in detail, either in narrative form, using *pseudocode*, or graphically, using *flowcharts*.** (● *See Panel 10.11.*)

It used to be that programmers took a kind of seat-of-the-pants approach to programming. Programming was considered an art, not a science. Today, however, most programmers use a design approach called *structured programming*. ***Structured programming* takes a top-down approach that breaks programs into modular forms.** It also uses standard logic tools called *control structures (sequence, selection, case, and iteration)*.

Algorithm: Calling a friend on the telephone

Input: The telephone number of your friend.

Output: None

Steps:

1. Pick up the phone and listen for a dial tone.
2. Press each digit of the phone number on the phone.
3. If busy, hang up phone, wait 5 minutes, jump to step 2.
4. If no one answers, leave a message, then hang up.
5. If no answering machine, hang up and wait 2 hours, then jump to step 2.
6. Talk to friend.
7. Hang up phone.

Assumptions:

- Step 1 assumes that you live alone and no one else could be on the phone.
- The algorithm assumes the existence of a working phone and active service.
- The algorithm assumes you are not deaf or mute.
- The algorithm assumes a normal corded phone.

panel 10.10

Example of an algorithm (www.cs.pitt.edu/~jmisurda/teaching/cs4/2064/cs0004-2064-algorithm.htm)

How Does One Go about Solving a Problem?

According to Gary Hadler, who lectures on this subject, one way is to follow four stages: recognize and define the problem, determine possible solutions, choose the best solution, implement the solution:

www.tuition.com.hk/the-stages-of-problem-solving.htm

http://jobs.monster.com/v-quality-assurance-q-software-tester-jobs.aspx

www.indeed.com/q-Software-Tester-jobs.html

In general, problems are not solved just by pondering them; specific problem-solving skills are required. For more information, try:

www.math.wichita.edu/history/men/polya.html

www.bizmove.com/skills/m8d.htm

www.wikihow.com/Solve-a-Problem

www.mindtools.com/pages/article/newTMC_00.htm

Algorithm: What's the Origin of This Word?

The word *algorithm* originates in the name of an Arab mathematician, Al-Khowarizmi, of the court of Mamun in Baghdad in the 800s. His treatises on Hindu arithmetic and on algebra made him famous. He is also said to have given algebra its name. Much of the mathematical knowledge of medieval Europe was derived from Latin translations of his works.

panel 10.11

Second step: Program design

1. Determine program logic through top-down approach and modularization, using a hierarchy chart.
2. Design details using pseudocode and/or flowcharts, preferably involving control structures.

The point of structured programming is to make programs more efficient (with fewer lines of code) and better organized (more readable) and to have better notations so that they have clear and correct descriptions.

The two mini-steps of program design are as follows.

1. DETERMINE THE PROGRAM LOGIC, USING A TOP-DOWN APPROACH Determining the program logic is like outlining a long term paper before you proceed to write it. ***Top-down program design*** **proceeds by identifying the top element, or module, of a program and then breaking it down in hierarchical fashion to the lowest level of detail.** The top-down program design is used to identify the program's processing steps, or modules. After the program is designed, the actual coding proceeds from the bottom up, using the modular approach.

- **Modularization:** The concept of modularization is important. Modularization dramatically simplifies program development, because each part can be developed and tested separately. **A *module* is a processing step of a program. Each module is made up of logically related program statements.** (Sometimes a module is called a *subprogram, subroutine, function*, or *method*.) An example of a module might be a programming instruction that simply says "Open a file, find a record, and show it on the display screen." It is best if each module has only a single function, just as an English paragraph should have a single, complete thought. This rule limits the module's size and complexity.
- **Top-down program design:** Top-down program design can be represented graphically in a hierarchy chart. **A *hierarchy chart*, or *structure chart*, illustrates the overall purpose of the program, by identifying all the modules needed to achieve that purpose and the relationships among them.** *(• See Panel 10.12.)* It works from the general down to the specific, starting with the top-level (high-level) view of what the program is to do. Then each layer refines and expands the previous one until the bottom layer can be made into specific programming modules. The program must move in sequence from one module to the next until all have been processed. There must be three principal modules corresponding to the three principal computing operations—input, processing, and output. (In Panel 10.12 they are "Read input," "Calculate pay," and "Generate output.")

2. DESIGN DETAILS, USING PSEUDOCODE AND/OR FLOWCHARTS Once the essential logic of the program has been determined, through the use of top-down programming and hierarchy charts, you can go to work on the details.

There are two basic ways to show details—write them or draw them; for example, use *pseudocode* or use *flowcharts*. Most projects use both methods.

- **Pseudocode:** ***Pseudocode*** **is a method of designing a program using normal human-language statements to describe the logic and the processing flow.** *(• See Panel 10.13.)* Pseudocode is like an outline or summary form of the program you will write.

panel 10.12

A hierarchy chart

This represents a top-down design for a payroll program. Here the modules, or processing steps, are represented from the highest level of the program down to details. The three principal processing operations—input, processing, and output—are represented by the modules in the second layer: "Read input," "Calculate pay," and "Generate output." Before tasks at the top of the chart can be performed, all the ones below must be performed. Each module represents a logical processing step.

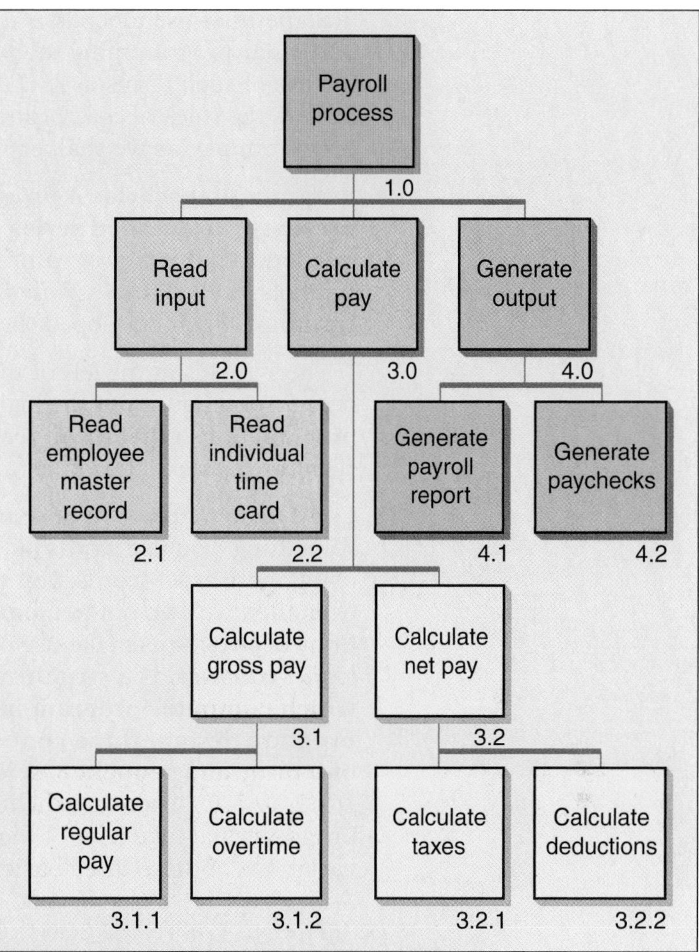

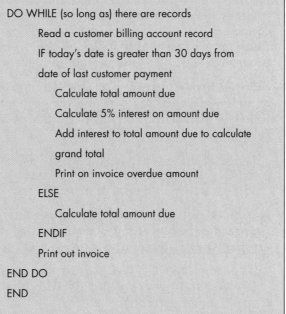

1. Each module must be of manageable size.
2. Each module should be independent and have a single function.
3. The functions of input and output are clearly defined in separate modules.
4. Each module has a single entry point (execution of the program module always starts at the same place) and a single exit point (control always leaves the module at the same place).
5. If one module refers to or transfers control to another module, the latter module returns control to the point from which it was "called" by the first module.

panel 10.13

Pseudocode

```
START
DO WHILE (so long as) there are records
      Read a customer billing account record
      IF today's date is greater than 30 days from
      date of last customer payment
          Calculate total amount due
          Calculate 5% interest on amount due
          Add interest to total amount due to calculate
          grand total
          Print on invoice overdue amount
      ELSE
          Calculate total amount due
      ENDIF
      Print out invoice
END DO
END
```

Sometimes pseudocode is used simply to express the purpose of a particular programming module in somewhat general terms. With the use of such terms as *IF, THEN,* or *ELSE,* however, the pseudocode follows the rules of *control structures,* an important aspect of structured programming, as we shall explain.

- **Program flowcharts: A *program flowchart* is a chart that graphically presents the detailed series of steps (algorithm, or logical flow) needed to solve a programming problem.** The flowchart uses standard symbols—called *ANSI symbols*, after the American National Standards Institute, which developed them. *(• See Panel 10.14.)*

  The symbols at the left of the drawing might seem clear enough. But how do you figure out the logic of a program? How do you reason the program out so that it will really work? The answer is to use control structures, as explained next.

- **Control structures:** When you're trying to determine the logic behind something, you use words like *if* and *then* and *else*. (For example, without using these exact words, you might reason along these lines: "If she comes over, then we'll go out to a movie, else I'll just stay in and watch TV.") Control structures make use of the same words. **A *control structure*, or *logic structure*, is a structure that controls the logical sequence in which computer program instructions are executed. In structured program design, three control structures are used to form the logic of a program: sequence, selection, and iteration (or loop).** *(• See Panel 10.15, p. 520.)* These are the tools with which you can write structured programs and take a lot of the guesswork out of programming. (Additional variations of these three basic structures are also used.)

COMPARING THE THREE CONTROL STRUCTURES One thing that all three control structures have in common is *one entry* and *one exit*. The control structure is entered at a single point and exited at another single point. This helps simplify the logic so that it is easier for others following in a programmer's footsteps to make sense of the program. (In the days before this requirement was instituted, programmers could have all kinds of variations, leading to the kind of incomprehensible program known as *spaghetti code*.)

Let us consider the three control structures:

- **Sequence control structure:** In the *sequence control structure,* one program statement follows another in logical order. For instance, in the example shown in Panel 10.15, there are two boxes ("Statement" and "Statement"). One box could say "Open file," the other "Read a record." There are no decisions to make, no choices between "yes" or "no." The boxes logically follow one another in sequential order.

- **Selection control structure:** The *selection control structure*—also known as an IF-THEN-ELSE *structure*—represents a choice. It offers two paths to follow when a decision must be made by a program. An example of a selection structure is as follows:

  IF a worker's hours in a week exceed 40
  THEN overtime hours equal the number of hours exceeding 40
  ELSE the worker has no overtime hours.

- **Iteration control structure:** In the *iteration,* or *loop, control structure,* a process may be repeated as long as a certain condition remains true. There are two types of iteration structures—DO UNTIL and DO WHILE.

  An example of a DO WHILE structure is as follows:
  DO read in employee records WHILE [that is, as long as] there continue to be employee records.

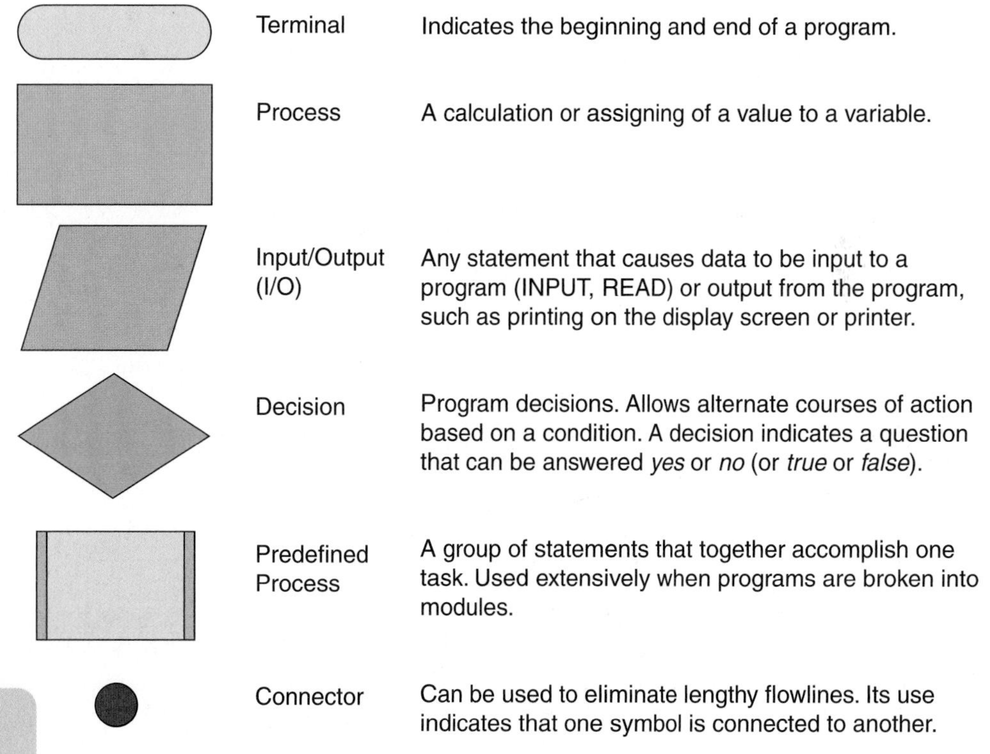

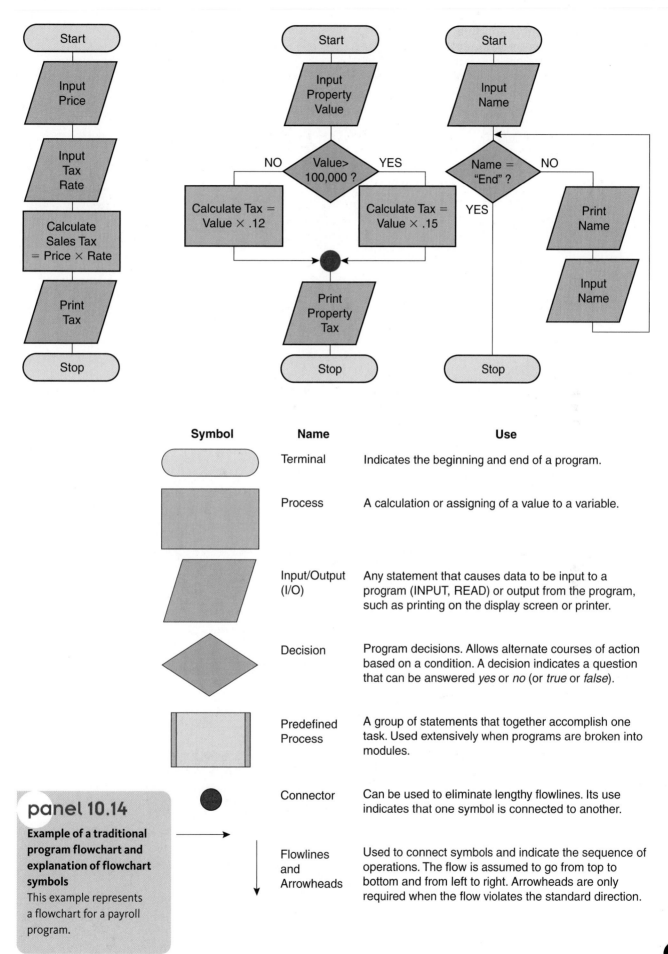

Symbol	Name	Use
	Terminal	Indicates the beginning and end of a program.
	Process	A calculation or assigning of a value to a variable.
	Input/Output (I/O)	Any statement that causes data to be input to a program (INPUT, READ) or output from the program, such as printing on the display screen or printer.
	Decision	Program decisions. Allows alternate courses of action based on a condition. A decision indicates a question that can be answered *yes* or *no* (or *true* or *false*).
	Predefined Process	A group of statements that together accomplish one task. Used extensively when programs are broken into modules.
	Connector	Can be used to eliminate lengthy flowlines. Its use indicates that one symbol is connected to another.
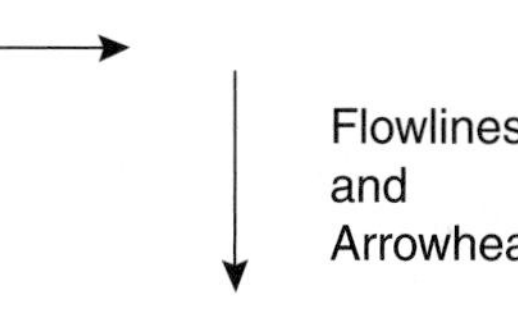	Flowlines and Arrowheads	Used to connect symbols and indicate the sequence of operations. The flow is assumed to go from top to bottom and from left to right. Arrowheads are only required when the flow violates the standard direction.

panel 10.14

Example of a traditional program flowchart and explanation of flowchart symbols

This example represents a flowchart for a payroll program.

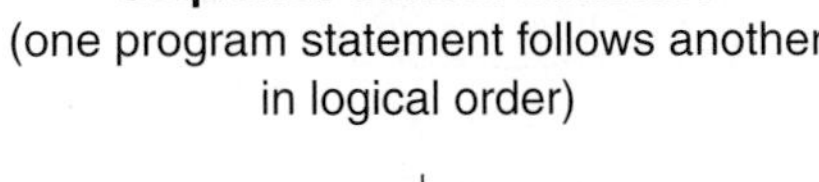

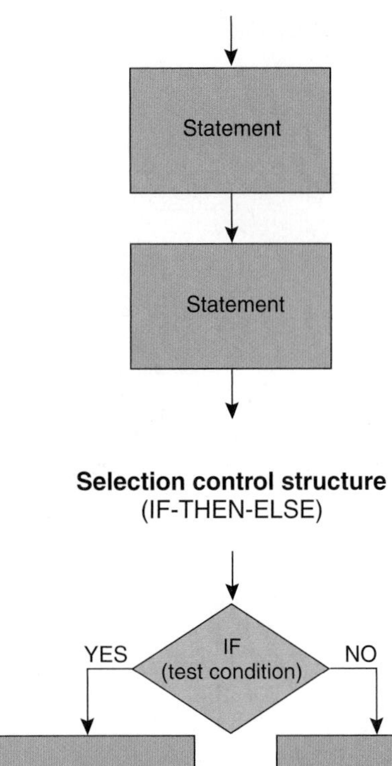

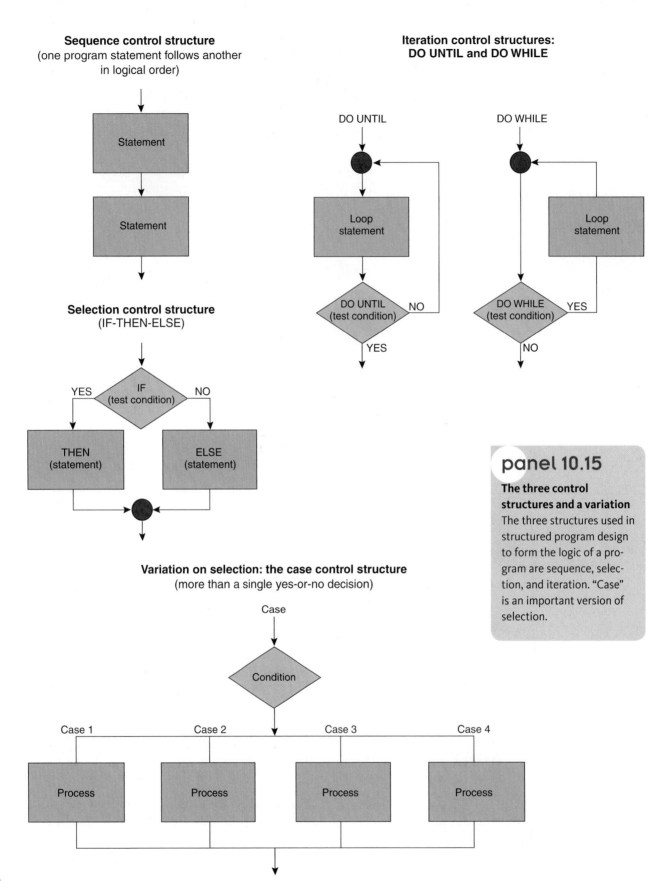

Selection control structure
(IF-THEN-ELSE)

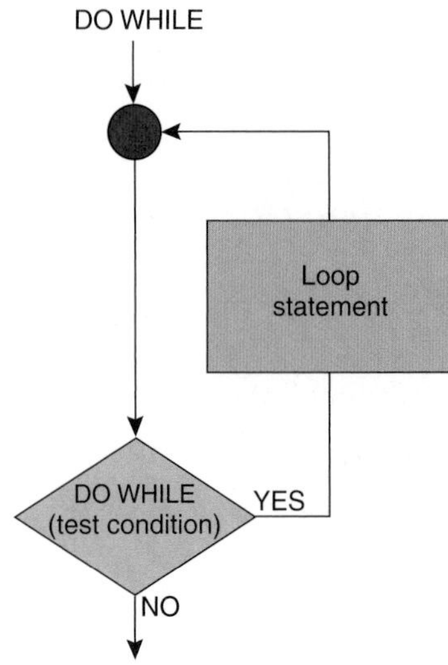

Variation on selection: the case control structure
(more than a single yes-or-no decision)

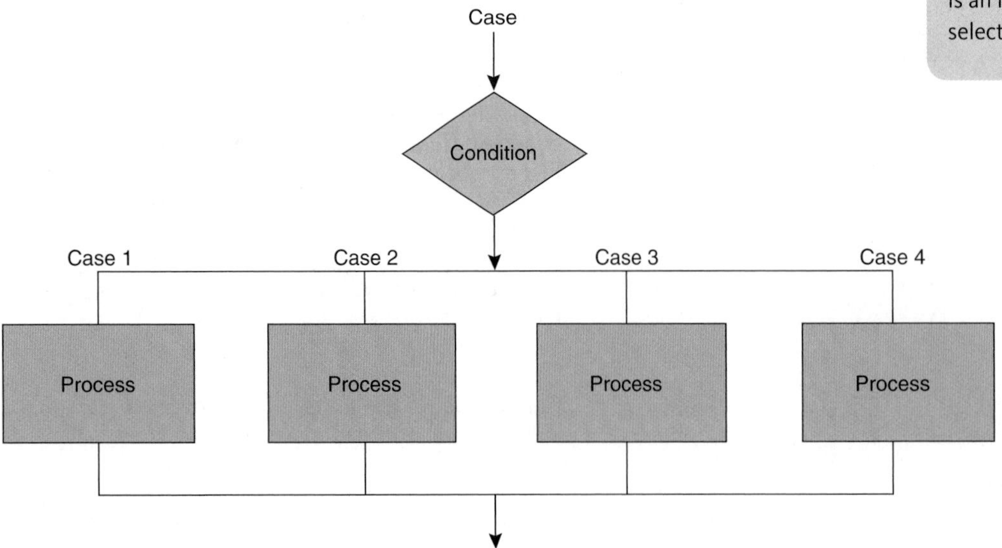

panel 10.15

The three control structures and a variation

The three structures used in structured program design to form the logic of a program are sequence, selection, and iteration. "Case" is an important version of selection.

What is the difference between the two iteration structures? It is simply this: If several statements need to be repeated, you must decide when to stop repeating them. You can decide to stop them at the beginning of the loop, using the DO WHILE structure. Or you can decide to stop them at the end of the loop, using the DO UNTIL structure. The DO UNTIL iteration means that the loop statements will be executed at least once, because in this case the iteration statements are executed before the program checks whether to stop.

Sequence, Selection, Iteration

In the 1960s it was mathematically proved that any problem that can be solved with a computer can be defined using sequence, selection, and iteration. Do an Internet search to find out who determined this and when.

The Third Step: Code the Program

Now the program is actually written.

Once the design has been developed, the actual writing, or coding, of the program begins. (*• See Panel 10.16.*) Coding is what many people think of when they think of programming, although it is only one of the five steps. ***Coding* consists of translating the logic requirements from pseudocode or flowcharts into a programming language**—the letters, numbers, and symbols that make up the program.

1. SELECT THE APPROPRIATE HIGH-LEVEL PROGRAMMING LANGUAGE

A *programming language* is a set of rules that tells the computer what operations to do. Examples of well-known programming languages are C, C++, Visual BASIC, and Java. These are called *high-level languages*, as we explain in a few pages.

Not all languages are appropriate for all uses. Some, for example, have strengths in mathematical and statistical processing. Others are more appropriate for database management or support a specific operating system, such as Unix. Some languages take more storage space than others; if you are writing code for an embedded processor (Chapter 1), for example, you would choose a language that is space efficient. And some languages are faster than others. Thus, in choosing the language, you need to consider what purpose the program is designed to serve and what languages are already being used in your organization or in your field. We consider these matters shortly in Section 10.3.

1. Select the appropriate high-level programming language.
2. Code the program in that language, following the syntax carefully.

panel 10.16

Third step: Program coding

The third step in programming is to translate the logic of the program worked out from pseudocode or flowcharts into a high-level programming language, following its grammatical rules.

2. CODE THE PROGRAM IN THAT LANGUAGE, FOLLOWING THE SYNTAX For a program to work, you have to follow the ***syntax*****, the rules of the programming language.** Programming languages have their own grammar just as human languages do. But computers are probably a lot less forgiving if you use these rules incorrectly.

The Fourth Step: Test the Program

Program testing involves both good data and bad data.

Program testing **involves running various tests and then running real-world data to make sure the program works.** (• *See Panel 10.17.*) Two principal activities are desk-checking and debugging. These steps are called *alpha testing*.

1. PERFORM DESK-CHECKING ***Desk-checking*** **is simply reading through, or checking, the program to make sure that it's free of errors and that the logic works.** In other words, desk-checking is like proofreading. This step should be taken before the program is actually run on a computer.

2. DEBUG THE PROGRAM Once the program has been desk-checked, further errors, or "bugs," will doubtless surface. **To** ***debug*** **means to detect, locate, and remove all errors in a computer program.** Mistakes may be syntax errors or logic errors. ***Syntax errors*** **are caused by typographical errors and incorrect use of the programming language.** ***Logic errors*** **are caused by incorrect use of control structures.** Programs called *diagnostics* exist to check program syntax and display syntax-error messages. Diagnostic programs thus help identify and solve problems. (*Run-time errors* may also occur when certain conditions cause the code to abort.)

Sometimes debugging is partially done in the third step, program coding, using the "buddy system," or pair programming. In this system, two people sit side by side; while one person (the "driver") codes, the other person (the "navigator") checks the code, corrects it, and offers suggestions for improvement.[2]

More about Software Testing

Go to *www.softwareqatest.com* and read the FAQs about software testing. Would you like to be a software tester? Find some job information at:

www.essortment.com/all/softwaretesting_rxng.htm

3. RUN REAL-WORLD DATA After desk-checking and debugging, the program may run fine—in the laboratory. However, it needs to be tested with real data; this is called *beta testing*. Indeed, it is even advisable to test the program not only with "good" data but also with bad data—data that is faulty, incomplete, or in overwhelming quantities—to see if you can make the system crash. Many users, after all, may be far more heavy-handed, ignorant, and careless than programmers have anticipated.

panel 10.17

Fourth step: Program testing

The fourth step is to test the program and "debug" it of errors so that it will work properly. The word "bug" dates from 1945, when a moth was discovered lodged in a relay of the Mark I computer. The moth disrupted the execution of the program.

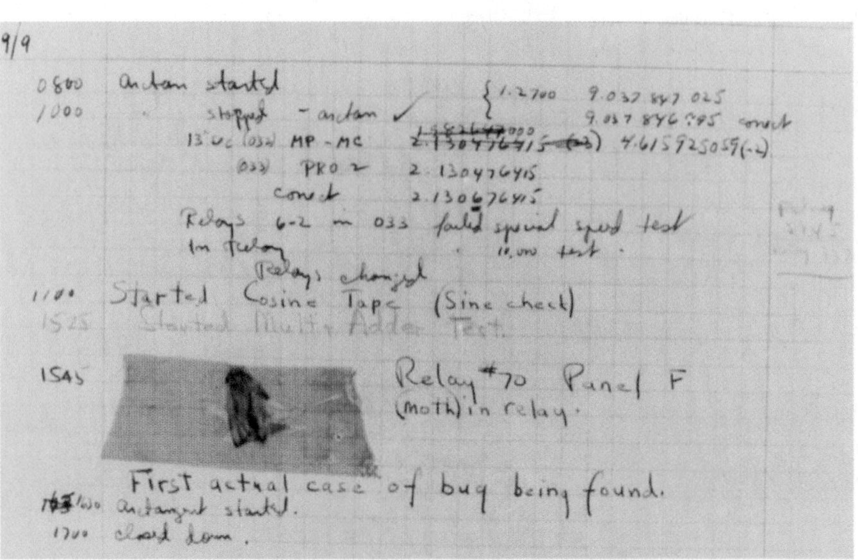

Several trials using different test data may be required before the programming team is satisfied that the program can be released. Even then, some bugs may persist, because there comes a point where the pursuit of errors is uneconomical. This is one reason why many users are nervous about using the first version (version 1.0) of a commercial software package.

Testing is done module by module and then as a whole, integrated program.

The Fifth Step: Document & Maintain the Program

Preliminary documentation should have been conducted throughout the entire programming process.

Writing the program documentation is the fifth step in programming. The resulting documentation consists of written descriptions of what a program is and how to use it. Documentation is not just an end-stage process of programming. It has been (or should have been) going on throughout all programming steps. Documentation is needed for people who will be using or be involved with the program in the future. *(• See Panel 10.18.)*

Documentation should be prepared for several different kinds of readers—users, operators, and programmers.

1. WRITE USER DOCUMENTATION When you buy a commercial software package, such as a spreadsheet, you normally get a manual with it. This is user documentation. Today manuals are usually on the software CD.

2. WRITE OPERATOR DOCUMENTATION The people who run large computers are called *computer operators*. Because they are not always programmers, they need to be told what to do when the program malfunctions. The *operator documentation* gives them this information.

3. WRITE PROGRAMMER DOCUMENTATION Long after the original programming team has disbanded, the program may still be in use. If, as is often the case, a fifth of the programming staff leaves every year, after 5 years there could be a whole new bunch of programmers who know nothing about the software. *Program documentation* helps train these newcomers and enables them to maintain the existing system.

4. MAINTAIN THE PROGRAM A word about maintenance: *Maintenance* includes any activity designed to keep programs in working condition, error-free, and up to date—adjustments, replacements, repairs, measurements, tests, and so on. The rapid changes in modern organizations—in products, marketing strategies, accounting systems, and so on—are bound to be reflected in their computer systems. Thus, maintenance is an important matter, and documentation must be available to help programmers make adjustments in existing systems.

The five steps of the programming process are summarized in the table. *(• See Panel 10.19, next page.)*

1. Write user documentation.
2. Write operator documentation.
3. Write programmer documentation.
4. Maintain the program.

panel 10.18

Fifth step: Program documentation and maintenance

The fifth step is really the culmination of activity that has been going on through all the programming steps—documentation. Written descriptions and procedures about a program and how to use it need to be developed for different people—users, operators, and programmers. Maintenance is an ongoing process.

panel 10.19

Summary of the five programming steps

Step	Activities
Step 1: Problem clarification	**1.** Clarify program objectives and program users. **2.** Clarify desired outputs. **3.** Clarify desired inputs. **4.** Clarify desired processing. **5.** Double-check feasibility of implementing the program. **6.** Document the analysis.
Step 2: Program design	**1.** Determine program logic through top-down approach and modularization, using a hierarchy chart. **2.** Design details using pseudocode and/or using flowcharts, preferably on the basis of control structures. **3.** Test design with structured walkthrough.
Step 3: Program coding	**1.** Select the appropriate high-level programming language. **2.** Code the program in that language, following the syntax carefully.
Step 4: Program testing	**1.** Desk-check the program to discover errors. **2.** Run the program and debug it (alpha testing). **3.** Run real-world data (beta testing).
Step 5: Program documentation and maintenance	**1.** Finalize user documentation. **2.** Finalize operator documentation. **3.** Finalize programmer documentation. **4.** Maintain the program.

10.3 FIVE GENERATIONS OF PROGRAMMING LANGUAGES

So far, there have been five basic generations of programming languages.

As we've said, a programming language is a set of rules that tells the computer what operations to do. Programmers, in fact, use these languages to create other kinds of software. Many programming languages have been written, some with colorful names (SNOBOL, HEARSAY, DOCTOR, ACTORS, EMERALD, JOVIAL). Each is suited to solving particular kinds of problems. What do all these languages have in common? Simply this: Ultimately they must be reduced to digital form—a 1 or 0, electricity on or off—because that is all the computer can work with.

To see how this works, one must consider the current five levels, or generations, of programming languages, ranging from low level to high level. **The five *generations of programming languages* start at the lowest level with (1) machine language (p. 206). They then range up through (2) assembly language, (3) high-level languages (procedural languages and object-oriented languages), and (4) very-high-level languages (problem-oriented languages). At the highest level are (5) natural languages.** Programming languages are said to be *lower level* when they are closer to the language that the computer itself uses—the 1s and 0s. They are called *higher level* when they are closer to the language people use—more like English, for example.

Beginning in 1945, the five levels, or generations, have evolved over the years, as programmers gradually adopted the later generations. The births of the generations are as follows. *(• See Panel 10.20.)*

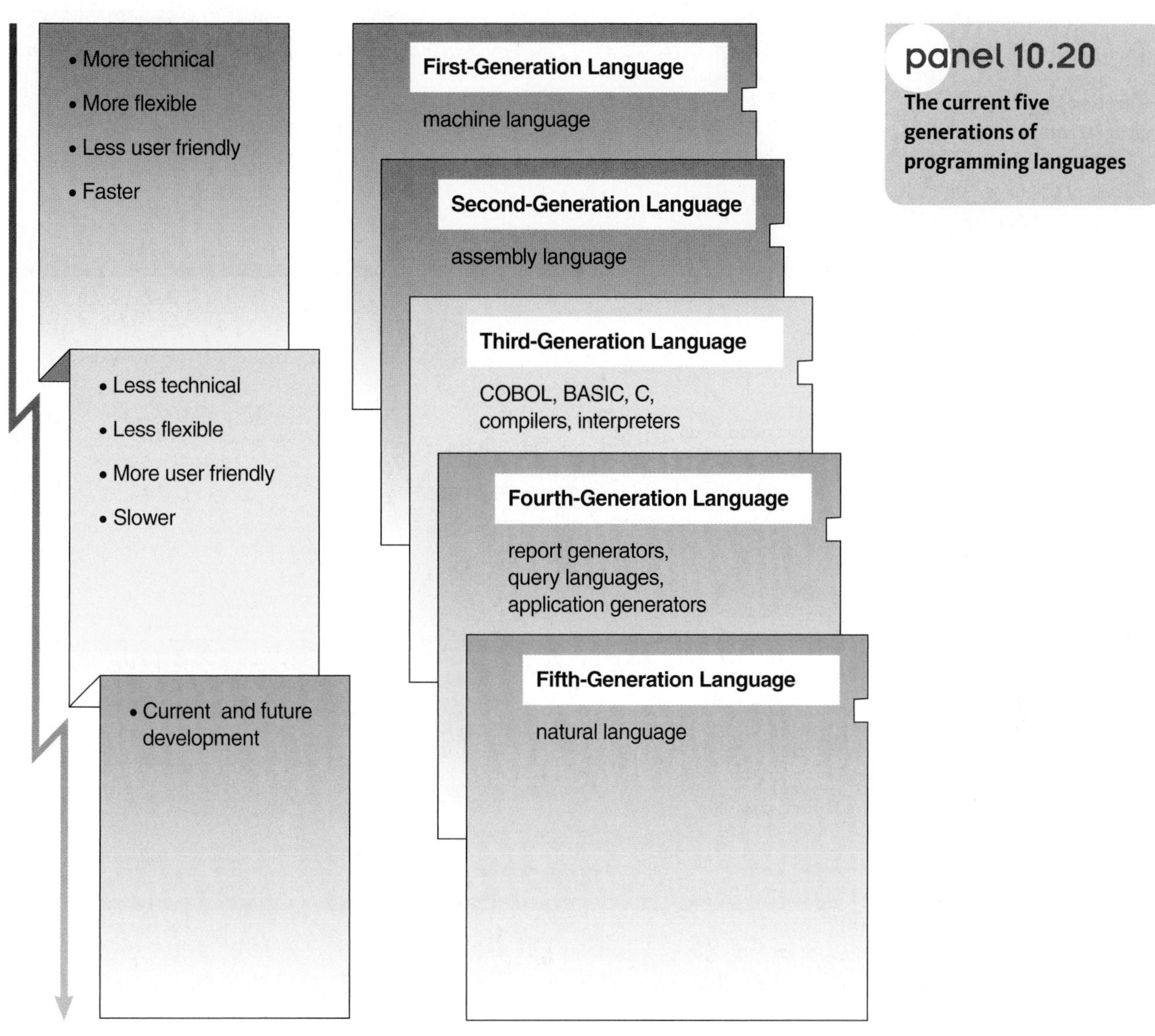

panel 10.20
The current five generations of programming languages

- First generation, 1945—*machine language*
- Second generation, mid-1950s—*assembly language*
- Third generation, mid-1950s to early 1960s—*high-level languages (procedural languages and object-oriented);* for example, FORTRAN, COBOL, BASIC, C, and C++
- Fourth generation, early 1970s—*very-high-level languages (problem-oriented languages);* for example, SQL, Intellect, NOMAD, FOCUS
- Fifth generation, early 1980s—*natural languages*

Let's consider these five generations.

First Generation: Machine Language

Machine code is the computer's "native language," the only language that a computer can "understand."

Machine language **is the basic language of the computer, representing data as 1s and 0s.** (● *See Panel 10.21, next page.*) Each CPU model has its own machine language. Machine-language programs vary from computer model to computer model; that is, they are *machine-dependent*.

panel 10.21

Three generations of programming languages

(*Top*) Machine language is all binary 0s and 1s—difficult for people to work with. (*Middle*) Assembly language uses abbreviations for major instructions (such as *MP* for "MULTIPLY"). This is easier for people to use, but still challenging. (*Bottom*) COBOL, a third-generation language, uses English words that people can understand.

First generation
Machine language

```
11110010 01110011 1101 001000010000 0111 000000101011
11110010 01110011 1101 001000011000 0111 000000101111
11111100 01010010 1101 001000010010 1101 001000011101
11110000 01000101 1101 001000010011 0000 000000111110
11110011 01000011 0111 000001010000 1101 001000010100
10010110 11110000 0111 000001010100
```

Second generation
Assembly language

```
PACK 210(8,13),02B(4,7)
PACK 218(8,13),02F(4,7)
MP   212(6,13),21D(3,13)
SRP  213(5,13),03E(0),5
UNPK 050(5,7),214(4,13)
OI   054(7),X'F0'
```

Third generation
COBOL

```
MULTIPLY HOURS-WORKED BY PAY-RATE GIVING GROSS-PAY ROUNDED.
```

Machine-language binary digits, which correspond to the on and off electrical states of the computer, are clearly not convenient for people to read and use. Believe it or not, though, programmers *did* work with these mind-numbing digits. There must have been great sighs of relief when the next generation of programming languages—assembly language—came along.

Second Generation: Assembly Language

Assembly language uses symbolic instruction codes.

Assembly language **is a low-level programming language that allows a programmer to write a program using abbreviations or more easily remembered words instead of numbers,** as in machine language; essentially, assembly language is a mnemonic version of machine language. (*Refer to Panels 10.20 and 10.21.*) For example, the letters "MP" could be used to represent the instruction MULTIPLY and STO (to represent STORE).

As you might expect, a programmer can write instructions in assembly language more quickly than in machine language. Nevertheless, it is still not an easy language to learn, and it is so tedious to use that mistakes are frequent. Moreover, assembly language has the same drawback as machine language in that it varies among processor (computer) brands—it is machine-dependent.

We now need to introduce the concept of *language translator*. Because a computer can execute programs only in machine language, a translator or converter is needed if the program is written in any other language. **A** ***language translator*** **is a type of system software that translates a program written in a second-, third-, or higher-generation language into machine language.**

Language translators are of three types:

- Assemblers
- Compilers
- Interpreters

An *assembler*, or *assembler program*, is a program that translates the assembly-language program into machine language. We describe compilers and interpreters in the next section.

Third Generation: High-Level or Procedural Languages

High-level languages are more like human language.

A *high-level*, or procedural/object-oriented, *language* resembles some human language such as English; an example is COBOL, which is used for business applications. (Refer to Panels 10.20 and 10.21.) A procedural language allows users to write in a familiar notation, rather than numbers or abbreviations. Also, unlike machine and assembly languages, most are not machine-dependent—that is, they can be used on more than one kind of computer. There are hundreds of high-level languages; however, only a few are widely used in industry. Familiar languages of this sort include FORTRAN, COBOL, and C. (We cover object-oriented languages shortly.)

For a procedural language to work on a computer, it needs a language translator to translate it into machine language. Depending on the procedural language, either of two types of translators may be used—a *compiler* or an *interpreter*.

COMPILER—EXECUTE LATER **A *compiler* is a language-translator program that converts the entire program of a high-level language into machine language *before* the computer executes the program.** The programming instructions of a procedural language are called the *source code*. The compiler translates it into machine language, which in this case is called the *object code*. The important point here is that the object code can be saved and thus can be executed later (as many times as desired), rather than run right away. *(• See Panel 10.22.)* These executable files—the output of compilers—have the .exe extension on many systems.

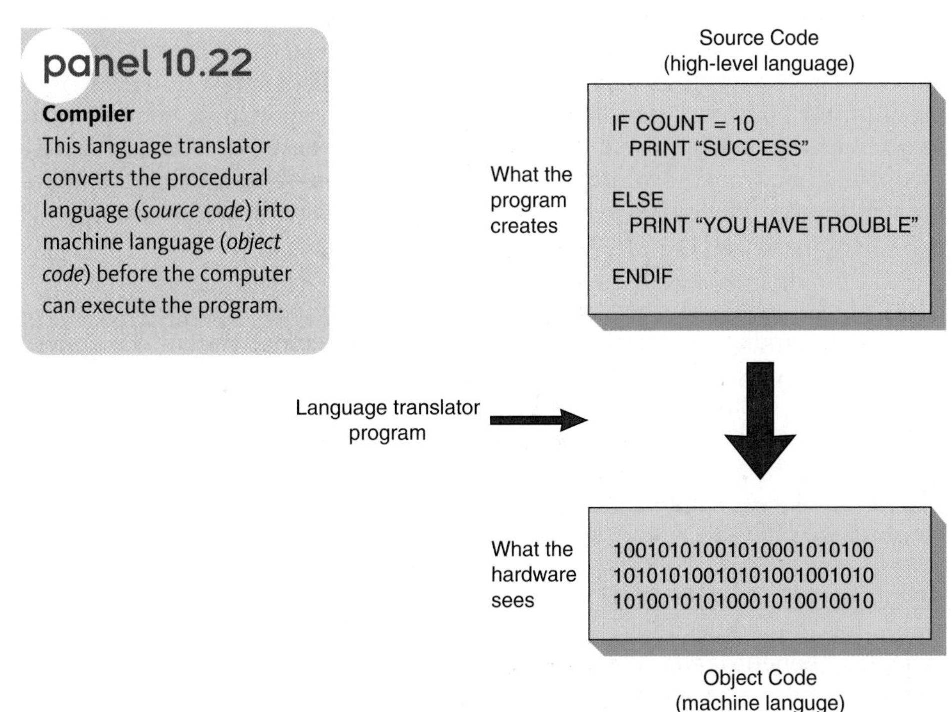

Source Code
(high-level language)
What the program creates
IF COUNT = 10
PRINT "SUCCESS"
ELSE
PRINT "YOU HAVE TROUBLE"
ENDIF
Language translator program
What the hardware sees
1001010100101000101010O
1010101001010100100101O
1010010101000101001001O
Object Code
(machine languge)

panel 10.22

Compiler

This language translator converts the procedural language (*source code*) into machine language (*object code*) before the computer can execute the program.

Examples of procedural languages using compilers are COBOL, FORTRAN, Pascal, and C. (● *See Panel 10.23.*)

INTERPRETER—EXECUTE IMMEDIATELY **An *interpreter* is a language-translator program that converts each procedural language statement into machine language and executes it *immediately*, statement by statement.** In contrast to the compiler, an interpreter does not save object code. Therefore, interpreted code generally runs more slowly than compiled code. However, the code can be tested line by line. BASIC and PERL are procedural languages using an interpreter.

WHY DOES IT MATTER? Who cares, you might say, whether you can run a program now or later? (After all, "later" could be only a matter of seconds or minutes.) Here's the significance: When a compiler is used, it requires two steps (the source code and the object code) before the program can be executed. The interpreter, however, requires only *one* step. The advantage of a compiler language is that, once you have obtained the object code, the program executes faster. The advantage of an interpreter language, on the other hand, is that programs are easier to develop. Some language translators can both compile and interpret.

SQL Example

If you were to update the data on a salesperson for all customers in a particular region, the procedural-language way might look something like this:

```
do until eof
  if rs("state") = "NH" then
    rs("salesperson") = "Mike"
  end if
  rs.next
loop
```

The SQL way would be:

```
UPDATE customers SET salesperson = "Mike" WHERE state = "NH"
```

(*www.paragoncorporation.com/ArticleDetail.aspx?ArticleID=27*)

Fourth Generation: Very-High-Level or Problem-Oriented Languages

Fourth-generation languages are even closer to human language than 3GLs; most of them are used to access databases.

Third-generation languages tell the computer *how* to do something. Fourth-generation languages, in contrast, tell the computer *what* to do. ***Very-high-level*, or problem-oriented or nonprocedural, *languages*, also called** *fourth-generation languages* **(4GLs), are much more user-oriented and allow users to develop programs with fewer commands compared with procedural languages,** although they require more computing power. These languages are called *problem-oriented* because they are designed to solve specific problems, whereas procedural languages are more general-purpose languages.

Three types of problem-oriented languages are report generators, query languages, and application generators.

REPORT GENERATORS A *report generator*, also called a *report writer*, is a program for end-users that produces a report. The report may be a printout or a screen display. It may show all or part of a database file. You can specify the format in advance—columns, headings, and so on—and the report generator will then produce data in that format. Report generators (an example is RPGIV) were the precursors to today's query languages.

What Can SQL Do?

- execute queries against a database
- retrieve data from a database
- insert records in a database
- update records in a database
- delete records from a database
- create new databases
- create new tables in a database
- create stored procedures in a database
- create views in a database
- manipulate tables

(*www.w3schools.com/SQl/sql_intro.asp*)

QUERY LANGUAGES A query language is an easy-to-use language for accessing and manipulating data from a database management system. The query may be expressed in the form of a sentence or near-English command. Or the query may be obtained from choices on a menu.

Examples of query languages are SQL (for "Structured Query Language") and Intellect. For example, with Intellect, which is used with IBM mainframes, you can make an English-language request such as "Tell me the number of employees in the sales department."

APPLICATION GENERATORS An *application generator* is a programmer's tool consisting of modules that have been preprogrammed to accomplish various tasks. The benefit is that the programmer can generate application programs from descriptions of the problem rather than by traditional programming, in which he or she has to specify how the data should be processed.

FORTRAN

```
IF (XINVO .GT. 500.00) THEN
    DISCNT = 0.07 * XINVO
ELSE
    DISCNT = 0.0
ENDIF
XINVO = XINVO – DISCNT
```

COBOL

```
OPEN-INVOICE-FILE.
    OPEN I-O INVOICE FILE.

READ-INVOICE-PROCESS.
    PERFORM READ-NEXT-REC THROUGH READ-NEXT-REC-EXIT UNTIL END-OF-FILE.
    STOP RUN.

READ-NEXT-REC.
    READ INVOICE-REC
        INVALID KEY
            DISPLAY 'ERROR READING INVOICE FILE'
            MOVE 'Y' TO EOF-FLAG
            GOTO READ-NEXT-REC-EXIT.
    IF INVOICE-AMT > 500
        COMPUTE INVOICE-AMT = INVOICE-AMT – (INVOICE-AMT * .07)
        REWRITE INVOICE-REC.

READ-NEXT-REC-EXIT.
    EXIT.
```

BASIC

```
10  REM     This Program Calculates a Discount Based on the Invoice Amount
20  REM         If Invoice Amount is Greater Than 500, Discount is 7%
30  REM         Otherwise Discount is 0
40  REM
50  INPUT "What is the Invoice Amount"; INV.AMT
60  IF INV.AMT > 500 THEN LET DISCOUNT = .07 ELSE LET DISCOUNT = 0
70  REM         Display results
80  PRINT "Original Amt", "Discount", "Amt after Discount"
90  PRINT INV.AMT, INV.AMT * DISCOUNT, INV.AMT – INV.AMT * DISCOUNT
100 END
```

Pascal

```
if INVOICEAMOUNT > 500.00 then
  DISCOUNT := 0.07 * INVOICEAMOUNT
else
  DISCOUNT := 0.0;
INVOICEAMOUNT := INVOICEAMOUNT – DISCOUNT
```

C

```
if (invoice_amount > 500.00)
  discount = 0.07 * invoice_amount;
else
  discount = 0.00;
invoice_amount = invoice_amount – discount;
```

panel 10.23

Some third-generation languages compared

This shows how five languages handle the same statement. The statement specifies that a customer gets a discount of 7% of the invoice amount if the invoice is greater than $500; if the invoice is lower, there is no discount.

Programming Language Popularity

Which are the most commonly used languages?

www.tiobe.com/index.php/content/paperinfo/tpci/index.html

www.devtopics.com/most-popular-programming-languages/

Programmers use application generators to help them create parts of other programs. For example, the software is used to construct on-screen menus or types of input and output screen formats. NOMAD and FOCUS, two database management systems, include application generators.

Fifth Generation: Natural Languages

Fifth-generation languages are used mainly for artificial intelligence and neural networks.

Natural languages are of two types. The first comprises ordinary human languages: English, Spanish, and so on. The second type comprises programming languages that use human language to give people a more natural connection with computers.

With a problem-oriented language, you can type in some rather routine inquiries, such as (in the language known as FOCUS) the following:

SUM SHIPMENTS BY STATE BY DATE.

Natural languages, by contrast, allow questions or commands to be framed in a more conversational way or in alternative forms—for example:

I WANT THE SHIPMENTS OF PERSONAL DIGITAL ASSISTANTS FOR ALABAMA AND MISSISSIPPI BROKEN DOWN BY CITY FOR JANUARY AND FEBRUARY. ALSO, MAY I HAVE JANUARY AND FEBRUARY SHIPMENTS LISTED BY CITIES FOR PERSONAL COMMUNICATORS SHIPPED TO WISCONSIN AND MINNESOTA.

Natural languages are part of the field of study known as *artificial intelligence* (discussed in Chapter 8). Artificial intelligence (AI) is a group of related technologies that attempt to develop machines capable of emulating human qualities, such as learning, reasoning, communicating, seeing, and hearing.

The dates of the principal programming languages are shown in the timeline running along the bottom of these pages. (• *See Panel 10.24.)*

10.4 PROGRAMMING LANGUAGES USED TODAY

Third-level computer languages are still the major means of communication between the digital computer and its user.

We now turn back and consider some of the third-generation, or high-level, languages in use today.

panel 10.24

Timeline: Brief history of the development of programming languages and formatting tools

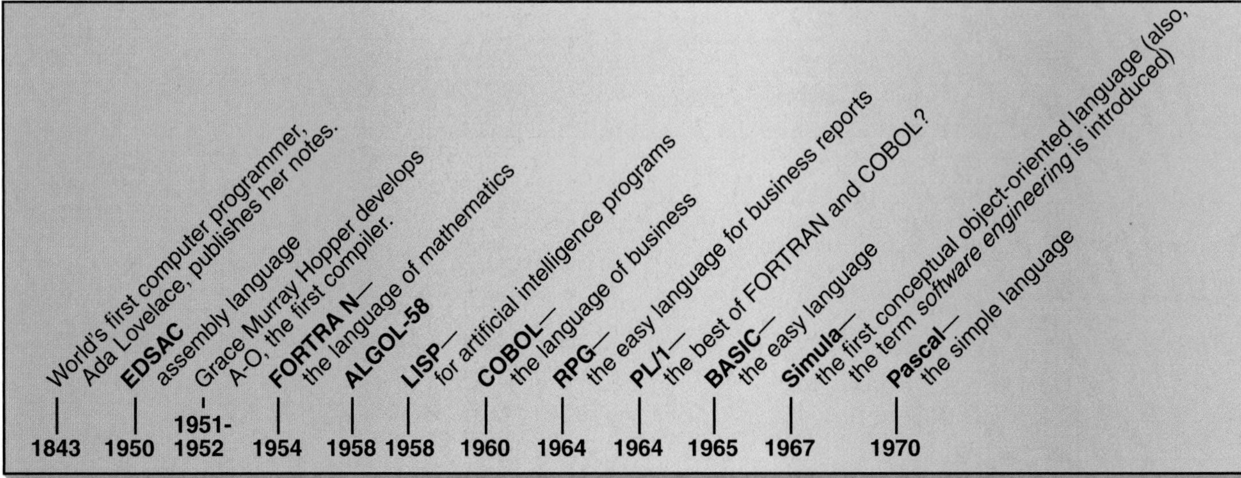

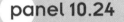

FORTRAN

The language of mathematics and the first high-level language

Developed from 1954 to 1956 by John Backus and others at IBM, *FORTRAN* (*for FORmula TRANslator*) was the first high-level language. *(Refer back to Panel 10.23.)* Originally designed to express mathematical formulas, it is still the most widely used language for mathematical, scientific, and engineering problems. It is also useful for complex business applications, such as forecasting and modeling. However, because it cannot handle a large volume of input/output operations or file processing, it is not used for more typical business problems and has become basically a legacy language. (A "legacy language" is still used by many companies, but it is an older language that is generally no longer updated or developed.)

COBOL

The first language of business

Developed under the auspices of the U.S. Department of Defense, with Grace Murray Hopper as a major contributor, and formally adopted in 1960, *COBOL* (for *COmmon Business-Oriented Language*) is the most frequently used business programming language for large computers. (Refer again to Panel 10.23.) Its most significant attribute is that it is extremely readable. For example, a COBOL line might read:

MULTIPLY HOURLY-RATE BY HOURS-WORKED GIVING GROSS-PAY

Writing a COBOL program resembles writing an outline for a research paper. The program is divided into four divisions—Identification, Environment, Data, and Procedure. The divisions in turn are divided into sections, which are divided into paragraphs, which are further divided into statements. The Identification Division identifies the name of the program and the author (programmer) and perhaps some other helpful comments. The Environment Division describes the computer on which the program will be compiled and executed. The Data Division describes what data will be processed. The Procedure Division describes the actual processing procedures.

Some people believe that COBOL is becoming obsolete. However, others disagree. Few things that were around in the IT industry in 1960 are still around today, except perhaps in museums and in basements. Yet the COBOL language, albeit highly evolved from its origins, remains relevant. The corporate assets represented by the billions (trillions?) of lines of COBOL code still running on commercial computers aren't about to be abandoned. Nor should they be. New tools that help integrate legacy (read: COBOL) systems with PC applications,

more info!

Who Was Grace Hopper?

Rear Admiral Grace Murray Hopper (1906–1992) was also a pioneer computer scientist and a developer of software concepts.

http://gracehopper.org/2011/

www.history.navy.mil/photos/pers-us/uspers-h/g-hoppr.htm

www.sdsc.edu/ScienceWomen/hopper.html

http://cs-www.cs.yale.edu/homes/tap/Files/hopper-story.html

www.thocp.net/biographies/hopper_grace.html

more info!

What's a Widget?

Widgets (*see below*) are compact, single-purpose programs. Typical Widgets include GUI buttons, dialog boxes, pull-down menus, etc. Among other things, Widgets can be used to enhance blogs. For Widget info, go to:

www.apple.com/downloads/dashboard/

www.techterms.com/definition/widget

http://widgets.yahoo.com/

www.pcmag.com/encyclopedia_term/0,2542,t=widget&i=54456,00.asp

Want to make your own Widget?

http://widgets.opera.com/widgetize/start

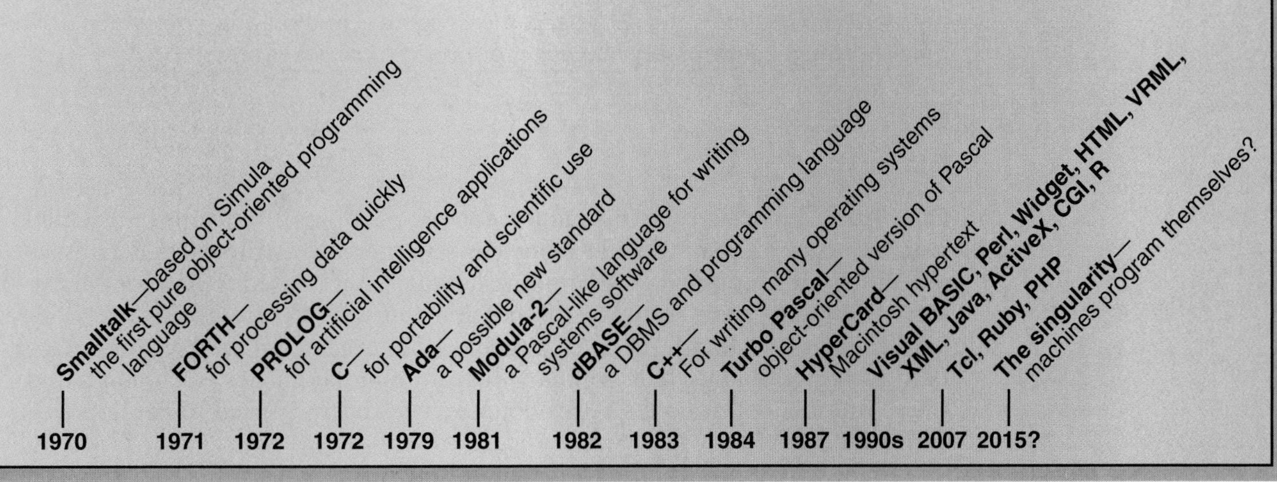

1970 Smalltalk—based on Simula the first pure object-oriented programming language
1971 FORTH—for processing data quickly
1972 PROLOG—for artificial intelligence applications
1972 C—for portability and scientific use
1979 Ada—a possible new standard
1981 Modula-2—a Pascal-like language for writing systems software
1982 dBASE—a DBMS and programming language
1983 C++—For writing many operating systems
1984 Turbo Pascal—object-oriented version of Pascal
1987 HyperCard—Macintosh hypertext
1990s Visual BASIC, Perl, Widget, HTML, VRML, XML, Java, ActiveX, CGI, R
2007 Tcl, Ruby, PHP
2015? The singularity—machines program themselves?

web services, new data formats, and protocols have been available since distributive systems emerged years ago. As today's application environment has evolved, so has COBOL's capability to link to it, merge with it, and interact with it. Stretching the lifespan of an enterprise's legacy systems increases the value and productivity of its IT development staff and of the assets they produce.[3]

more info!

Government in Action

In 2009, the governor of California fired about 10,000 temporary and part-time workers and reduced the pay levels of about 200,000 permanent employees. However, a week later, the state controller pointed out that the state payroll records could not be changed to accommodate the cuts, because they were written in COBOL—and the only state employees who knew the code were among the fired part-time employees (*www.funnytimes.com/*, February 2009).

The fact that COBOL systems have been built for more than 30 years means each one is unique and is tailored to each individual business's needs. These systems have given companies their competitive edge and have proved far harder to replace or rewrite than expected (*www.computerweekly.com/Articles/2008/08/07/231774/cobol-programmer-shortage-starts-to-bite.htm*).

BASIC

The easy language

BASIC was developed by John Kemeny and Thomas Kurtz in 1964 for use in training their students at Dartmouth College. By the late 1960s, it was widely used in academic settings on all kinds of computers, from mainframes to PCs.

BASIC (*Beginner's All-purpose Symbolic Instruction Code*) used to be the most popular microcomputer language and is considered the easiest programming language to learn. (*Refer to Panel 10.23.*) Although it is available in compiler form, the interpreter form is more popular with first-time and casual users. This is because it is interactive, meaning that user and computer can communicate with each other during the writing and running of the program. Today there is no one version of BASIC. One of the popular current evolutions is Visual BASIC (VB.net), discussed shortly.

Pascal

The simple language

Named after the 17th-century French mathematician Blaise Pascal and developed in 1970 by Niklaus Wirth, *Pascal* is an alternative to BASIC as a language for teaching purposes and is relatively easy to learn. (*Refer to Panel 10.23.*) Pascal is a simple language, and it helps to introduce beginners to other languages, such as C, C++, and JAVA.

more info!

99 Bottles of Beer

This website holds a collection of the song "99 Bottles of Beer" programmed in 1,434 different programming languages:

www.99-bottles-of-beer.net/

. . . and the number keeps growing.

C

For portability, operating systems, and scientific use

C is the successor of B, which was the successor of BCPL, which was the successor of CPL (Computer Programming Language), an early programming language that was not implemented. Developed by Dennis Ritchie at Bell Laboratories in the early 1970s, *C* is a general-purpose, compiled language that was developed for midrange computers (minicomputers) but that works well for microcomputers and is portable among many computers. It was originally developed for writing system software. The first major program written in C was the Unix operating system, and for many years C was considered to be inextricably linked with Unix. Now, however, C is an important language independent of Unix. Today it is widely used for creating operating systems and writing applications, including word processing, spreadsheets, games, robotics, and graphics programs. It is now considered a necessary language for programmers to know.

C++

Enhancement of C

C++ (for "increased C," pronounced see-plus-plus), an object-oriented language (covered shortly) developed by Bjarne Stroustrup at Bell Labs, is one of the most popular programming languages; it is used to develop Microsoft Windows system software, application software, device drivers, network applications, graphics, and entertainment software such as video games. C++ has influenced many other popular programming languages, such as C# and Java. (An offshoot of C++, C# (pronounced see-sharp) is used to develop web applications.)

C and C++ are not teaching languages; both are relatively difficult to learn.

LISP

For artificial intelligence programs

LISP (*LISt Processor*) is a third-generation language used principally to construct artificial intelligence programs. Developed at the Massachusetts Institute of Technology in 1958 by mathematician John McCarthy, LISP is used to write expert systems and natural language programs. As we saw in Chapter 8, expert systems are programs that are imbued with knowledge by a human expert; the programs can walk you through a problem and help solve it.

10.5 OBJECT-ORIENTED & VISUAL PROGRAMMING

Procedural languages focus on static data and the procedures and functions that need to be performed on the data; object-oriented languages focus on the "things" or classes of objects in a system and uses the classes as a way to organize what needs to be done; visual programming uses graphics, drawings, animation, and/or icons.

Consider how it was for the computer pioneers, programming in machine language or assembly language. Novices programming with C, for example, can breathe a collective sigh of relief that they weren't around at the dawn of the Computer Age. Even some of the simpler third-generation languages present challenges, because they are procedure-oriented, forcing the programmer to follow a predetermined path.

Fortunately, two developments have made things easier—object-oriented programming and visual programming.

Conventional Programs

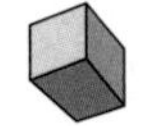

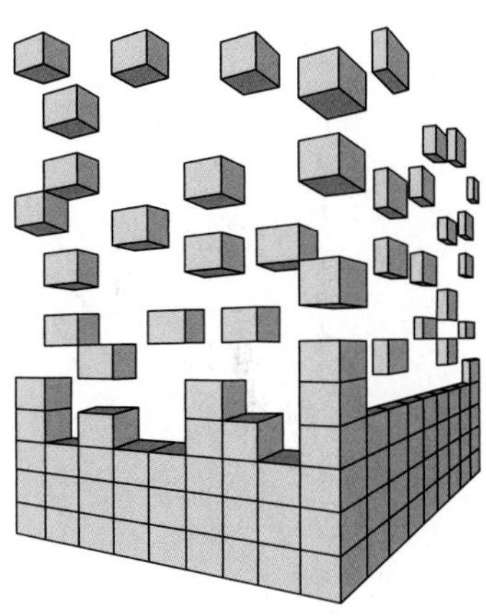

Object-Oriented Programming (OOP)

Programming by building with "classes."

Imagine you're programming in a traditional third-generation language, such as BASIC, creating your coded instructions one line at a time. As you work on some segment of the program (such as how to compute overtime pay), you may think, "I'll bet some other programmer has already written something like this. Wish I had it. It would save a lot of time." Fortunately, a kind of recycling technique exists. This is object-oriented programming, an improved version of 3GLs.

HOW OOP WORKS: OBJECT, MESSAGE, & METHOD Object-oriented programming consists of the following components:

1. ***What OOP is:* In <u>*object-oriented programming (OOP*</u>, pronounced "oop"), data and the instructions for processing that data are combined into a self-sufficient "object" that can be used in other programs.** The important thing here is the object.
2. ***What an "object" is:* An <u>*object*</u> is a self-contained module consisting of preassembled programming code.** The module contains, or encapsulates, both (1) a chunk of data and (2) the processing instructions that may be performed on that data.
3. ***When an object's data is to be processed—sending the "message":*** Once the object becomes part of a program, the processing instructions may or may not be activated. A particular set of instructions is activated only when the corresponding "message" is sent. A *message* is an alert sent to the object when an operation involving that object needs to be performed.
4. ***How the object's data is processed—the "methods":*** The message need only identify the operation. How it is actually to be performed is embedded within the processing instructions that are part of the object. These processing instructions within the object are called the *methods.*

Object-Oriented Programs

RECYCLING BLOCKS OF PROGRAM CODE Once you've written a block of program code (that computes overtime pay, for example), it can be reused in any number of programs. Thus, with OOP, unlike traditional programming, you don't have to start from scratch—that is, reinvent the wheel—each time.

Object-oriented programming takes longer to learn than traditional programming, because it means training oneself to a different way of thinking. However, the beauty of OOP is that an object can be used repeatedly in different applications and by different programmers, speeding up development time and lowering costs.

THREE IMPORTANT CONCEPTS OF OOP Object-oriented programming has three important concepts, which go under the jaw-breaking names of *encapsulation, inheritance*, and *polymorphism*. Actually, these are not as fearsome as they look:

- **ENCAPSULATION:** *Encapsulation* means an object contains (encapsulates) both (1) data and (2) the relevant processing instructions, as we have seen. Once an object has been created, it can be reused in other programs. An object's uses can also be extended through the concepts of *class* and *inheritance.*

- **INHERITANCE:** Once you have created an object, you can use it as the foundation for similar objects that have the same behavior and characteristics. All objects that are derived from or related to one another are said to form a *class*. Each class contains specific instructions (methods) that are unique to that group.

  Classes can be arranged in hierarchies—classes and subclasses. *Inheritance* is the method of passing down traits of an object from classes to subclasses in the hierarchy. Thus, new objects can be created by inheriting traits from existing classes.

  Writer Alan Freedman gives this example: "The object MACINTOSH could be one instance of the class PERSONAL COMPUTER, which could inherit properties from the class COMPUTER SYSTEMS."[4] If you were to add a new computer, such as DELL, you would need to enter only what makes it different from other computers. The general characteristics of personal computers would be inherited.

- **POLYMORPHISM:** Polymorphism means the presence of "many shapes." In object-oriented programming, *polymorphism* means that a message (generalized request) produces different results based on the object that it is sent to.

  Polymorphism has important uses. It allows a programmer to create procedures about objects whose exact type is not known in advance but will be at the time the program is actually run on the computer. Freedman gives this example: "A screen cursor may change its shape from an arrow to a line depending on the program mode." The processing instructions "to move the cursor on screen in response to mouse movement would be written for 'cursor,' and polymorphism would allow that cursor to be whatever shape is required at runtime." It would also allow a new cursor shape to be easily integrated into the program.

EXAMPLES OF OOP LANGUAGES: C++ & JAVA Two important examples of OOP languages are C++ and Java.

- **C++:** *C++* combines the traditional C programming language with object-oriented capability. With C++, programmers can write standard code in C without the object-oriented features, use object-oriented features, or do a mixture of both.

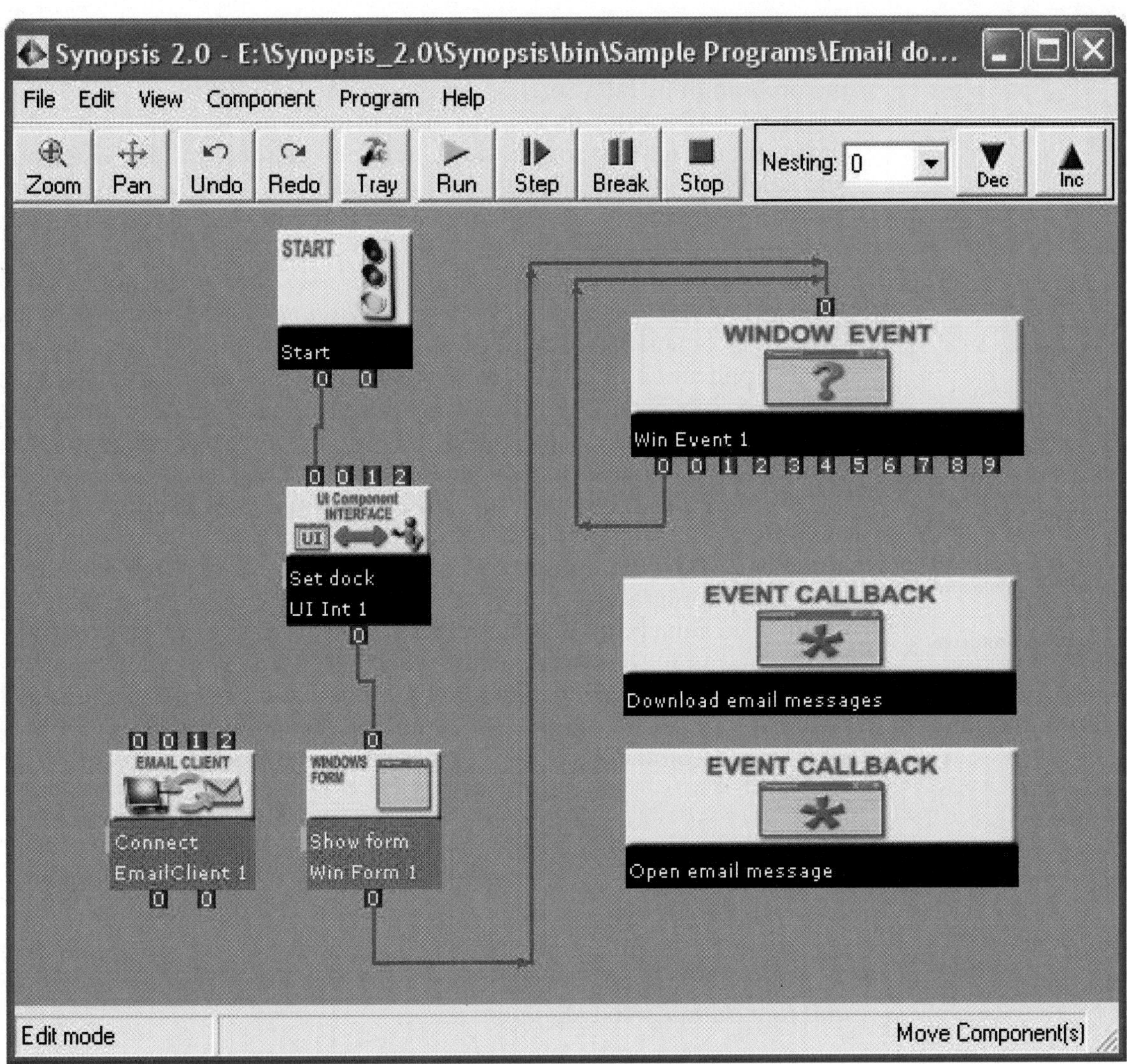

Visual programming of Windows applications with Synopsis (*www.codemorphis.com/*)

- **Java:** A high-level programming language developed by Sun Microsystems in 1995, *Java,* also an object-oriented language, is used to write compact programs that can be downloaded over the Internet and immediately executed on many kinds of computers. Java is similar to C++ but is simplified to eliminate language features that cause common programming errors. It is often used to collect information from networked computers and for web applications.

  Small Java applications are called Java *applets* and can be downloaded from a web server and run on your computer by a Java-compatible web browser, such as Mozilla Firefox or Microsoft Internet Explorer. Java applets make websites more interactive and attractive, adding features such as animation and calculators—but only if a browser is capable of supporting Java. Users also can download free Java applets from various sites on the Internet.

Visual Programming: The Example of Visual BASIC

Visual programming allows programming to be done using menus, buttons, and other graphic elements that are selected from a palette.

Essentially, visual programming takes OOP to the next level. The goal of visual programming is to make programming easier for programmers and more accessible to nonprogrammers by borrowing the object orientation of OOP

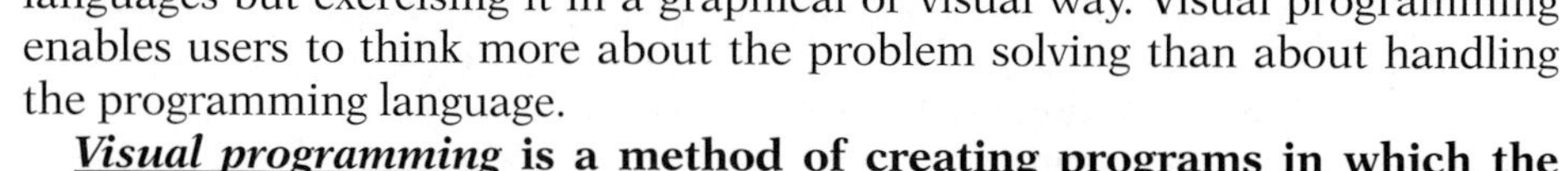

languages but exercising it in a graphical or visual way. Visual programming enables users to think more about the problem solving than about handling the programming language.

Visual programming **is a method of creating programs in which the programmer makes connections between objects by drawing, pointing, and clicking on diagrams and icons and by interacting with flowcharts.** Thus, the programmer can create programs by clicking on icons that represent common programming routines.

An example of visual programming is *Visual BASIC, now available through Microsoft's .NET framework (VB.net),* a Windows-based, object-oriented programming language from Microsoft that lets users develop Windows and Office applications by (1) creating command buttons, textboxes, windows, and toolbars, which (2) then may be linked to small BASIC programs that perform certain actions. Visual BASIC is *event-driven*, which means that the program waits for the user to do something (an "event"), such as click on an icon, and then the program responds. At the beginning, for example, the user can use drag-and-drop tools to develop a graphical user interface, which is created automatically by the program. Because of its ease of use, Visual BASIC allows even novice programmers to create impressive Windows-based applications.

Since its launch in 1990, the Visual BASIC approach has become the norm for programming languages. Now there are visual environments for many programming languages, including C, C++, Pascal, and Java. Visual BASIC is sometimes called a *rapid application development (RAD)* system because it enables programmers to quickly build prototype applications.

What is .NET?

Microsoft's .NET software framework runs primarily on Windows and allows developers to use code from several programming languages:

www.microsoft.com/net/overview.aspx

http://msdn.microsoft.com/en-us/vbasic/bb466159

http://msdn.microsoft.com/library/zw4w595w.aspx

10.6 MARKUP & SCRIPTING LANGUAGES

A markup language is a set of tags that are used to "mark up" text documents so that sections of text can be logically identified and arranged. Scripting languages are simple programming languages commonly used to add functionality to web pages.

A *markup language* is a kind of coding, or "tags," inserted into text that embeds details about the structure and appearance of the text. Markup languages have codes for indicating layout and styling (such as boldface, italics, paragraphs, insertion of graphics, and so on) within a text file—for example, HTML. The name "markup" is derived from the traditional publishing practice of "marking up" a manuscript, that is, adding printer's instructions in the margins of a paper manuscript.

Some early examples of markup languages available outside the publishing industry could be found in typesetting tools on Unix systems. In these systems, formatting commands were inserted into the document text so that typesetting software could format the text according to the editor's specifications. After a time it was seen that most markup languages had many features in common. This led to the creation of *SGML (Standard Generalized Markup Language)*, which specified a syntax for including the markup in documents, as well as another system (a so-called *metalanguage*) for separately describing what the markup meant. This allowed authors to create and use any markup they wished, selecting tags that made the most sense to them. SGML was developed and standardized by the International Organization for Standards (ISO) in 1986.

SGML is used widely to manage large documents that are subject to frequent revisions and need to be printed in different formats. Because it is a large and complex system, it was not yet widely used on personal computers. This changed dramatically when Tim Berners-Lee used some of the SGML syntax, without the metalanguage, to create HTML (Hypertext Markup Language, Chapter 2, p. 69). HTML may be the most used document format in the world today.

For some people, the term *script* may conjure up images of actors and actresses on a sound stage practicing lines from a book of text. In web terms, however, a ***script*** **is a short list of self-executing commands embedded in a web page that perform a specific function or routine.** Scripts are similar to the macros used in Microsoft Word or the batch files used in the early days of DOS (pp. 138–139), both of which performed functions ranging from generating text to displaying the date and time. Because they are self-executing, scripts can perform their work without user involvement, although some are initiated by an action on the part of the user (such as a mouse click) and others require user input to complete a task. In general, script languages are easier and faster to code in than the more structured, compiled languages such as C and C++ and are ideal for programs of very limited capability or that can reuse and tie together existing compiled programs.[5]

On web pages, scripting languages are used to perform many duties. For example, they create traffic counters and scrolling text, set cookies so that websites can remember user preferences, and switch out graphics and text when users click buttons or pass their mouse over items. They are also used for processing forms that the user fills out on screen. Any time you see something interesting occurring on a website, there is a good chance that a script is involved. Scripting languages are often designed for interactive use.

Following are some popular markup and scripting languages.

HTML

For creating 2-D web documents and links

As we discussed in Chapter 2, ***HTML (Hypertext Markup Language)*** **is a markup language that lets people create on-screen documents for the Internet that can easily be linked by words and pictures to other documents.** HTML is a type of code that embeds simple commands within standard ASCII text documents to provide an integrated, two-dimensional display of text and graphics. In other words, a document created in any word processor and stored in ASCII format can become a web page with the addition of a few HTML commands.

One of the main features of HTML is the ability to insert hypertext links into a document. *Hypertext links* enable you to display another web document simply by clicking on a link area—usually underlined or highlighted—on your current screen (Chapter 2). One document may contain links to many other related documents. The related documents may be on the same server as the first document, or they may be on a computer halfway around the world. A link may be a word, a group of words, or a picture.

HTML is often used with *CSS3* (*Cascading Style Sheet*), which is used to describe the look of a document written in a markup language. (A stylesheet is a set of instructions that tell a browser how to draw a particular element on a page.) CSS is designed primarily to enable the separation of document content (written in HTML or a similar markup language) from document presentation, including elements such as the layout, colors, and typeface sizes and styles.

The fifth revision of HTML is HTML 5, which is becoming a core web technology for developing and using online applications ("web apps"). HTML is cross-platform, meaning that it can be used for mobile devices and computers, and with any operating system.

HTML Tutorial

For easy-to-follow tutorials on using HTML, go to:

http://computer.howstuffworks.com/web-page2.htm

www.tizag.com/htmlT/

www.w3schools.com/html/

After you work through the tutorial, create a sample HTML-tagged document for what could become your personal website.

VRML Plug-In

Examples of download VRML add-ins are these:

http://cic.nist.gov/vrml/cosmo-player.html

http://cic.nist.gov/vrml/vbdetect.html

VRML

For creating 3-D web pages

Mark Pesce and Tony Parisi created VRML at Silicon Graphics in 1994. VRML rhymes with "thermal." ***VRML (Virtual Reality Modeling [or Markup] Language)*** **is a type of programming language used to create**

three-dimensional web pages including interactive animation. Even though VRML's designers wanted to let nonprogrammers create their own virtual spaces quickly and painlessly, it's not as simple to describe a three-dimensional scene as it is to describe a page in HTML. However, many existing modeling and CAD tools now offer VRML support, and new VRML-centered software tools are arriving. An example of a VRML scene might be a virtual room where the viewer can use controls to move around inside the room (or move the room itself) as though she or he were walking through it in real space.

To view VRML files, users need a special VRML browser (in addition to an Internet connection and a web browser). The VRML browser is what interprets VRML commands and lets the user interact with the virtual world. VRML browsers typically work as plug-ins for traditional web browsers, but newer browsers may already have the appropriate VRML browser plug-in installed. There are several VRML browsers available for Windows users, such as Cosmo and Cortona.

Web designers use new software such as WireFusion to create 3-D web page components that no longer require a plug-in for users to view them with their browser. (The successor to VRML is called *X3D*.)

For a more detailed description of XML, try:

http://searchsoa.techtarget.com/sDefinition/0,,sid26_gci213404,00.html

www.pcmag.com/encyclopedia_term/0,2542,t=XML&i=55048,00.asp

http://cplus.about.com/od/glossar1/g/xmldefn.htm

XML

For making the web work better

Another, newer markup language is XML, a standard maintained by the World Wide Web Consortium for creating special-purpose markup languages. ***XML (eXtensible Markup Language)*** **is a metalanguage (a language used to define another language) written in SGML that allows one to facilitate the easy interchange of documents on the Internet.**

Unlike HTML, which uses a set of "known" tags, XML allows you to create any tags you wish (thus it's extensible) and then describe those tags in a metalanguage known as the *DTD* (*Document Type Definition*). (A metalanguage is a language used to manipulate or define another language.) XML is similar to the concept of SGML, and in fact XML is a subset of SGML in general terms. The main purpose of XML (as opposed to SGML) is to keep the system simpler by focusing on a particular problem—documents on the Internet and the exchange of information among websites.

Whereas HTML makes it easy for humans to read websites, XML makes it easy for machines to read websites by enabling web developers to add more "tags" to a web page. At present, when you use your browser to locate a website, search engines can turn up too much, so it's difficult to find the specific site you want—say, one with a recipe for a low-calorie chicken dish for 12. XML makes websites smart enough to tell other machines whether they're "looking at." XML lets website developers put "tags" on their web pages that describe information in, for example, a food recipe as "ingredients," "calories," "cooking time," and "number of portions." Thus, your browser no longer has to search the entire web for a low-calorie poultry recipe for 12.

Following are examples of XML and HTML tags. Note that the XML statements define data content, whereas the HTML lines deal with fonts and display (boldface). XML defines "what it is," and HTML defines "how it looks."

```
XML
<firstName>Maria</firstName>
<lastName>Roberts</lastName>
<dateBirth>10-29-52</dateBirth>
```

```
HTML
<font size="3">Maria Roberts</font>
<b>October 29, 1952<b>
```

Survival Tip

How to Disable Add-Ons (Plug-Ins or Extensions)

Computer and device users may not want to use certain add-ons with their browsers. To disable add-ons in Internet Explorer, go to Tools, Manage Add-Ons, and then under Status, click on the add-ons that you wish to disable.

For disabling add-ons in Chrome, go to *www.google.com/support/chrome/bin/answer.py?answer=113907* or *http://blogote.com/tips-and-tricks/how-to-disable-or-uninstall-google-chrome-extensionsaddons/3986/*. For Firefox, go to *http://support.mozilla.com/en-US/kb/Uninstalling%20add-ons.*

JavaScript

For dynamic web pages

JavaScript uses some of the same ideas found in Java, the compiled object-oriented programming language derived from C++. ***JavaScript*** **is a popular object-oriented scripting language that is widely supported in web browsers. It adds interactive functions to HTML pages,** which are otherwise static, since HTML is a display language, not a programming language. JavaScript is embedded in HTML pages and interpreted by the web browser. Like other scripting languages, JavaScript cannot be used to create stand-alone programs.

JavaScript was originally developed by Netscape Communications under the name "LiveScript" but was then renamed to "JavaScript" and given a syntax closer to that of Sun Microsystems' Java language. The change of name happened at about the same time Netscape was including support for Java technology in its Netscape Navigator browser. Consequently, the change proved a source of much confusion. There is no real relation between Java and JavaScript; their only similarities are some syntax and the fact that both languages are used extensively on the World Wide Web.

Many companies' computers and mobile devices support JavaScript for interactive multimedia use in Web applications. Apple also uses HTML5 and CSS3, but so far it has refused to use Flash, which we cover next.

JavaScript Tutorial

Go to:

www.w3schools.com/js/js_intro.asp

www.javabeginner.com/

www.java2s.com/Tutorial/Java/CatalogJava.htm

for tutorials and information about using JavaScript.

Flash

Also for creating dynamic web pages

Adobe Flash Player**, like JavaScript also a browser "add-on," uses Adobe Flash, a scripting language based on ActionScript, to support web animation, streaming audio and video, and games.** Flash is used on most computers and mobile devices—but not Apple iPads, iPhones, and iTouch devices. Apple maintains that Flash is less secure than JavaScript—that is, it's easier to introduce malware via Flash than with JavaScript; other companies disagree.

Phone Apps

People buy a lot of phone apps, so developing programs for the new generation of smart mobile phones can be a money-maker:

www.usatoday.com/tech/news/2009-09-22-invent-applications-phones_N.htm

www.mutualmobile.com/

www.slideshare.net/a1technwyork/mobile-phone-java-applications

www.myprgenie.com/view-publication/mobile-application-development-develop-mobile-phone-apps-affordably

ActiveX

For creating interactive web pages

ActiveX was developed by Microsoft mainly as an alternative to Java for creating interactivity on web pages. Indeed, Java and ActiveX are the two major contenders in the web war for transforming the World Wide Web into a complete interactive environment. (One big difference between Java applets and ActiveX controls is that Java applets are used on all platforms, whereas ActiveX controls are generally limited to Windows environments.)

ActiveX **is a set of prewritten, reusable object-oriented components that enable programs or content of almost any type to be embedded within a web page.** This provides a simple way for programmers to add extra functionality to their software or website without needing to write code from scratch. (ActiveX is not a programming language but rather a set of rules for how applications should share information.) Software add-ons created with ActiveX are called ActiveX controls. These controls can be implemented in all types of programs, but they are most commonly distributed as small web applications, such as sound and animation.

Whereas Java requires that you download an applet each time you visit a website, with ActiveX the component is downloaded only once (to a Windows-based computer) and then stored on your hard drive for later and repeated use. ActiveX is built into Microsoft's Internet Explorer and is available as a plug-in for Mozilla Firefox.

ActiveX controls have full access to the Windows operating system, and the component can be reused by an attacker to run malicious code and gain access to critical files. Thus, although they are more powerful than Java applets, ActiveX controls can be risky in that they may damage software or data on your machine. To control this risk, Microsoft developed a registration system so that browsers can identify and authenticate an ActiveX control before downloading it.

Programmers can create ActiveX controls or components in a variety of programming languages, including C, C++, Visual BASIC, and Java. Thousands of ready-made ActiveX components are now commercially available from numerous software development companies.

Programming Tools

Programming tools are used for software development or system maintenance. Any program or utility that helps programmers or users develop applications or maintain their computers can be called a tool. Where can you get programming tools?

www.freewarefiles.com/category/programming.php

www.freewarefiles.com/category/programming.php

www.literateprogramming.com/tools.html

www.javaworld.com/javaworld/jw-04-2011/110418-opensource-tools-in-enterprise.html

www.freebyte.com/programming/

http://protools.winasm.net/

CGI (Common Gateway Interface)

For servicing web servers

CGI is a standard protocol for interfacing external application software with a web server; it manages the exchange of information between a web server and computer programs that are external to it. The external programs can be written in any programming language that is supported by the operating system on which the web server is running. Forms, counters, and guestbooks are common examples of CGI scripts that process data taken from the user. CGI programs can help make web pages more interactive. They can be written in any programming language, although scripting languages are often used.

Perl

For CGI scripts

Perl (Practical Extraction and Report Language) is a general-purpose programming language developed for text manipulation and now used for web development, network programming, system administration, GUI development, and other tasks. Perl is widely used to write web server programs for such tasks as automatically updating user accounts and newsgroup postings, processing removal requests, synchronizing databases, and generating reports. The major features of Perl are that it is easy to use and it supports both procedural and object-oriented programming.

Perl was developed in 1987 by Larry Wall, and it combines syntax from several Unix utilities and languages. Perl has also been adapted to non-Unix platforms.

Perl

Visit the Perl language page at:

www.perl.org/

PHP (Personal Home Page, or PHP Hypertext Preprocessor)

For interacting with databases

PHP allows web developers to create dynamic content that interacts with databases. PHP applications are normally found on Linux servers and in conjunction with MySQL databases. Originally designed for producing dynamic web pages, PHP is a widely used free, general-purpose scripting language that is especially suited for web development and can be embedded into HTML and also enable the automated writing of HTML pages. It generally runs on a web server, taking PHP code as its input and creating web pages as output.

What Are Lateral Thinking Tools?

Lateral thinking tools help people think clearly, logically, and creatively. Do a keyword search and find out what they are.

Thinking about Majoring in IT?

ACM (Association for Computing Machinery), the world's largest educational and scientific computing society, provides resources that advance computing as a science and a profession.

www.acm.org/

EXPERIENCE BOX

Critical Thinking Tools

Clear thinkers aren't born that way. They work at it.

The systems development life cycle is basically an exercise in clear thinking—critical thinking. Critical thinking is fundamental to systems analysis and design—particularly in the first phase, preliminary analysis. Reaching for the truth may not come easily; it is a stance toward the world, developed with practice. To achieve this, we have to wrestle with obstacles that are mostly of our own making: mindsets. By the time we are grown, our minds have become "set" in various patterns of thinking that affect the way we respond to new situations and new ideas. Such mindsets determine what ideas we think are important and, conversely, what ideas we ignore.

To break past mindsets, we need to learn to think critically. *Critical thinking* means sorting out conflicting claims, weighing the evidence for them, letting go of personal biases, and arriving at reasoned conclusions. Critical thinking means actively seeking to understand, analyze, and evaluate information in order to solve specific problems.

Learning to identify fallacious (incorrect) arguments will help you avoid patterns of faulty thinking in your own writing and thinking and identify these in others'.

Jumping to Conclusions. In the fallacy called *jumping to conclusions,* also known as *hasty generalization,* a decision maker reaches a conclusion before all the facts are available. *Example:* A company instituted the strategy of total quality management (TQM) 12 months ago. As a new manager of the company, you see that TQM has not improved profitability over the past year, and you order TQM junked, in favor of more traditional business strategies. However, what you don't know is that the traditional business strategies employed prior to TQM had an even worse effect on profitability.

Irrelevant Reason or False Cause. In the faulty reasoning known as *non sequitur* (Latin for "it does not follow"), which might better be called *false cause* or *irrelevant reason,* the conclusion does not follow logically from the supposed reason or reasons stated earlier. There is no causal relationship. *Example:* You receive an A on a test. However, because you felt you hadn't been well prepared, you attribute your success to your friendliness with the professor. Or to your horoscope. Or to wearing your "lucky shirt." None of these supposed reasons have anything to do with the result.

Irrelevant Attack on a Person or Opponent. Known as an *ad hominem* argument (Latin for "to the person"), the irrelevant attack on an opponent attacks a person's reputation or beliefs rather than his or her argument. *Example:* Your boss insists you may not hire a certain person as a programmer because he or she has been married and divorced nine times, although the person's marital history plainly has no bearing on his or her skills as a programmer.

Slippery Slope. *Slippery slope* is a failure to see that the first step in a possible series of steps does not lead inevitably to the rest. *Example:* The "domino theory," under which the United States waged wars against Communism for half a century, was a slippery-slope argument. It assumed that if Communism triumphed in one country (for example, Nicaragua), then it would inevitably triumph in other regions (the rest of Central America), finally threatening the borders of the United States itself.

Appeal to Authority. The *appeal-to-authority* argument (known in Latin as *argumentum ad verecundiam*) uses authority in one area in an effort to validate claims in another area where the person is not an expert. *Example:* You see the appeal-to-authority argument used all the time in advertising. But how qualified is a professional golfer to speak about headache remedies?

Circular Reasoning. In *circular reasoning,* a statement to be proved true is rephrased, and then the new formulation is offered as supposed proof that the original statement is in fact true. *Example:* You declare that you can drive safely at high speeds with only inches separating you from the car ahead because you have driven this way for years without an accident.

Straw Man Argument. In the *straw man* argument, you misrepresent your opponent's position to make it easier to attack, or you attack a weaker position while ignoring a stronger one. In other words, you sidetrack the argument from the main discussion. *Example:* Politicians use straw man arguments all the time. If you attack a legislator for being "fiscally irresponsible" in supporting funds for a gun-control bill, when what you really object to is the fact of gun control, you're using a straw man argument.

Appeal to Pity. In the *appeal-to-pity* argument, the advocate appeals to mercy rather than making an argument on the merits of the case itself. *Example:* Begging the dean not to expel you for cheating because your parents are poor and made sacrifices to put you through college would be a blatant appeal to pity.

Questionable Statistics. Statistics can be misused in many ways as supporting evidence. The statistics may be unknowable, drawn from an unrepresentative sample, or otherwise suspect. *Example*: Stating how much money is lost to taxes because of illegal drug transactions is speculation because such transactions are hidden or unrecorded.

TERMS & EXPLANATIONS

ActiveX (p. 539) A set of prewritten, reusable object-oriented controls, or components, that enable programs or content of almost any type to be embedded within a web page. Why it's important: *ActiveX features reusable components—small modules of software code that perform specific tasks, such as a spelling checker, which may be plugged seamlessly into other applications.*

algorithm (p. 515) Formula or set of steps for solving a particular problem. Why it's important: *All programs consist of algorithms.*

assembler (p. 527) Also called *assembler program;* language-translator program that translates assembly-language programs into machine language. Why it's important: *Language translators are needed to translate all upper-level languages into machine language, the language that actually runs the computer.*

assembly language (p. 526) Second-generation programming language; it allows a programmer to write a program using abbreviations instead of the 0s and 1s of machine language. Why it's important: *A programmer can write instructions in assembly language faster than in machine language.*

CASE (computer-aided software engineering) tools (p. 507) Software that provides computer-automated means of designing and changing systems. Why it's important: *CASE tools make systems design easier and can be used in almost any phase of the SDLC.*

coding (p. 521) In the programming process, the third step, consisting of translating logic requirements from pseudocode or flowcharts into a programming language. Why it's important: *Coding is the actual writing of a computer program, although it is only the third of five steps in programming.*

compiler (p. 527) Language translator that converts the entire program of a high-level language (called the *source code*) into machine language (called the *object code*) for execution later. Examples of compiler languages: COBOL, FORTRAN, Pascal, and C. Why it's important: *Unlike other language translators (assemblers and interpreters), a compiler program enables the object code to be saved and executed later rather than run right away. The advantage of a compiler is that, once the object code has been obtained, the program executes faster.*

control structure (p. 518) Also called *logic structure;* in structured program design, the programming structure that controls the logical sequence in which computer program instructions are executed. Three control structures are used to form the logic of a program: sequence, selection, and iteration (or loop). Why it's important: *One thing that all three control structures have in common is one entry and one exit. The control structure is entered at a single point and exited at another single point. This helps simplify the logic so that it is easier for others following in a programmer's footsteps to make sense of the program.*

data flow diagram (DFD) (p. 507) Modeling tool that graphically shows the flow of data through a system—essential processes, including inputs, outputs, and files. Why it's important: *A DFD diagrams the processes that change data into information.*

debug (p. 522) Part of program testing; the detection, location, and removal of syntax and logic errors in a program. Why it's important: *Debugging may take several trials using different data before the programming team is satisfied the program can be released. Even then, some errors may remain, because trying to remove them all may be uneconomical.*

desk-checking (p. 522) Form of program testing; programmers read through a program to ensure it's error-free and logical. Why it's important: *Desk-checking should be done before the program is actually run on a computer.*

documentation (p. 523) Written descriptions of what a program is and how to use it; supposed to be done during all programming steps. Why it's important: *Documentation is needed for all people who will be using or be involved with the program—users, operators, programmers, and future systems analysts.*

Flash Player (Adobe) (p. 539) Like JavaScript, Flash is also a browser "add-on"; it uses Adobe Flash, a scripting language based on ActionScript, to support web animation, streaming audio and video, and games. Why it's important: *Flash is used on most computers and mobile devices—but not Apple iPads, iPhones, and iTouch devices.*

generations of programming languages (p. 524) Five increasingly sophisticated levels (generations) of programming languages: (1) machine language, (2) assembly language, (3) high-level languages, (4) very-high-level languages, (5) natural languages. Why it's important: *Programming languages are said to be lower level when they are closer to the language used by the computer (0s and 1s) and higher level when closer to the language used by people. High-level languages are easier for most people to use than are lower-level languages.*

hierarchy chart (p. 516) Also called *structure chart;* a diagram used in programming to illustrate the overall purpose of a program, identifying all the modules needed to achieve that purpose and the relationships among them. Why it's important: *In a hierarchy chart, the program must move in sequence from one module to the next until all have been processed. There must be three principal modules corresponding to the three principal computing operations—input, processing, and output.*

high-level languages (p. 527) Also known as *procedural or object-oriented languages;* third-generation programming languages. They somewhat resemble human languages. Examples: FORTRAN, COBOL, BASIC, Pascal, and C. Why it's important: *High-level languages allow programmers to write in a familiar notation rather than numbers or abbreviations. Most can also be used on more than one kind of computer.*

HTML (Hypertext Markup Language) (p. 537) *HTML (Hypertext Markup Language)* is a markup language that lets people create on-screen documents for the Internet that can easily be linked by words and pictures to other documents. Why it's important: *HTML is used to create web pages.*

interpreter (p. 528) Language translator that converts each high-level language statement into machine language and executes it immediately, statement by statement. An example of a high-level language using an interpreter is BASIC. Why it's important: *Unlike a compiler translator, an interpreter does not save object code. The advantage of an interpreter is that programs are easier to develop.*

JavaScript (p. 539) Object-oriented scripting language used, for example, to write small interactive functions that are embedded in HTML pages and interact with the browser to perform certain tasks not possible in static HTML alone. (There is no real relationship between JavaScript and Java.) Why it's important: *JavaScript is used to create powerful dynamic web applications.*

language translator (p. 526) Type of system software that translates a program written in a second-, third-, or higher-generation language into machine language. Language translators are of three types: (1) assemblers, (2) compilers, and (3) interpreters. Why it's important: *Because computers run only using machine language, all higher-level languages must be translated.*

logic errors (p. 522) Programming errors caused by incorrect use of control structures. Why it's important: *Logic errors prevent a program from running properly.*

machine language (p. 525) Lowest-level (first-generation) programming language; the language of the computer, representing data as 1s and 0s. Most machine-language programs vary from computer to computer—they are machine-dependent. Why it's important: *Machine language is the language that actually runs the computer.*

markup language (p. 536) A kind of coding, or "tags," inserted into text that embeds details about the structure and appearance of the text within a text file—for example, HTML. The word "markup" is derived from the traditional publishing practice of "marking up" a manuscript, that is, adding printer's instructions in the margins of a paper manuscript. An example of a markup language is SGML (Standard Generalized Markup Language). Why it's important: *Markup languages have codes for indicating layout and styling, such as boldface, italics, paragraphs, and insertion of graphics.*

modeling tools (p. 507) Analytical tools such as charts, tables, and diagrams that are used by systems analysts. Examples are data flow diagrams, decision tables, systems flowcharts, and object-oriented analysis. Why it's important: *Modeling tools enable a systems analyst to present graphic, or pictorial, representations of a system.*

module (p. 516) Sometimes called *subprogram* or *subroutine;* a processing step of a program. Each module is made up of logically related program statements. Why it's important: *Each module has only a single function, which limits the module's size and complexity.*

natural languages (p. 530) (1) Ordinary human languages (for instance, English, Spanish); (2) fifth-generation programming languages that use human language to give people a more natural connection with computers. Why it's important: *Natural languages are part of the field of artificial intelligence; these languages are approaching the level of human communication.*

object (p. 533) In object-oriented programming, block of preassembled programming code that is a self-contained module. The module contains (encapsulates) both (1) a chunk of data and (2) the processing instructions that may be called on to be performed on that data. Once the object becomes part of a program, the processing instructions may be activated only when a "message" is sent. Why it's important: *The object can be reused and interchanged among programs, thus making the programming process much easier, more flexible and efficient, and faster.*

object-oriented programming (OOP) (p. 533) Programming method in which data and the instructions for processing that data are combined into a self-sufficient *object*—a piece of software that can be used in other programs. Why it's important: *Objects can be reused and interchanged among programs, producing greater flexibility and efficiency than is possible with traditional programming methods.*

preliminary investigation (p. 506) Phase 1 of the SDLC; the purpose is to conduct a preliminary analysis (determine the organization's objectives, determine the nature and scope of the problem), propose alternative solutions (leave the system as is, improve the efficiency of the system, or develop a new system), describe costs and benefits, and submit a preliminary plan with recommendations. Why it's important: *The preliminary investigation lays the groundwork for the other phases of the SDLC.*

problem clarification/definition (p. 514) Step 1 in the programming process. The problem-definition step requires performing six mini-steps: specifying objectives and users, outputs, inputs, and processing tasks and then studying the feasibility of the program and documenting the analysis. Why it's important: *Problem definition is the forerunner to step 2, program design, in the programming process.*

program (p. 513) List of instructions the computer follows to process data into information. The instructions consist of statements written in a programming language (for example, BASIC). Why it's important: *Without programs, computers could not process data into information.*

program design (p. 515) Step 2 in the programming process; programs are designed in two ministeps: (1) the program logic is determined through a top-down approach and modularization, using a hierarchy chart; (2) the program is designed in detail, using pseudocode or flowcharts with logical tools called *control structures.* Why it's important: *Program design is the forerunner to step 3, writing (coding), in the programming process.*

program flowchart (p. 518) Chart that graphically presents the detailed series of steps needed to solve a programming problem; it uses standard symbols called *ANSI symbols.* Why it's important: *The program flowchart is an important program design tool.*

program testing (p. 522) Step 4 in the programming process; involves running various tests and then running real-world data to make sure the program works. Why it's important: *The program must be tested before it is released to be sure that it works properly.*

programming (p. 513) Five-step process for creating software instructions: (1) Clarify/define the problem; (2) design a solution; (3) write (code) the program; (4) test the program; (5) document and maintain the program. Why it's important: *Programming is one step in the systems development life cycle.*

programming language (p. 521) Set of rules (words and symbols) that allow programmers to tell the computer what operations to follow. The five levels (generations) of programming languages are (1) machine language, (2) assembly language, (3) high-level (procedural) languages, (4) very-high-level (nonprocedural) languages, and (5) natural languages. Why it's important: *Not all programming languages are appropriate for all uses. Thus, languages must be chosen to suit the purpose of the program and to be compatible with other languages being used.*

prototype (p. 509) A limited working system, or part of one, developed to test design concepts. Why it's important: *A prototype, which may be constructed in just a few days, allows users to find out immediately how a change in the system might benefit them.*

prototyping (p. 509) Using workstations, CASE tools, and other software applications to build working models of system components so that they can be quickly tested and evaluated. Why it's important: *Prototyping is part of the preliminary design stage of Phase 3 of the SDLC.*

pseudocode (p. 516) Tool for designing a program in narrative form using normal human-language statements to describe the logic and processing flow. Using pseudocode is like doing an outline or summary form of the program to be written. Why it's important: *Pseudocode provides a type of outline or summary of the program.*

script (p. 537) A short list of self-executing commands embedded in a web page that perform a specific function or routine, often without user involvement. Why it's important: *Because they are self-executing, scripts can perform their work without user involvement.*

structured programming (p. 515) Method of programming that takes a top-down approach, breaking programs into modular forms and using standard logic tools called *control structures* (sequence, selection, case, iteration). Why it's important: *Structured programming techniques help programmers write better-organized programs, using standard notations with clear, correct descriptions.*

syntax (p. 522) "Grammar" rules of a programming language. Why it's important: *Each programming language has its own syntax, just as human languages do.*

syntax errors (p. 522) Programming errors caused by typographical errors and incorrect use of the programming language. Why it's important: *If a program has syntax errors, it will not run correctly or perhaps not run at all.*

system (p. 504) Collection of related components that interact to perform a task in order to accomplish a goal. Why it's important: *Understanding a set of activities as a system allows one to look for better ways to reach the goal.*

systems analysis (p. 506) Phase 2 of the SDLC; the purpose is to gather data (using written documents, interviews, questionnaires, and observation), analyze the data, and write a report. Why it's important: *The results of systems analysis determine whether the system should be redesigned.*

systems analysis and design (p. 505) Problem-solving procedure for examining an information system and improving it; consists of the six-phase systems development life cycle. Why it's important: *The point of systems analysis and design is to ascertain how a system works and then take steps to make it better.*

systems analyst (p. 505) Information specialist who performs systems analysis, design, and implementation. Why it's important: *The systems analyst studies the information and communications needs of an organization to determine how to deliver information that is complete, accurate, timely, and useful. The systems analyst achieves this goal through the problem-solving method of systems analysis and design.*

systems design (p. 509) Phase 3 of the SDLC; the purpose is to do a preliminary design and then a detail design and to write a report. Why it's important: *Systems design is one of the most crucial phases of the SDLC.*

systems development (p. 510) Phase 4 of the SDLC; consists of acquiring and testing hardware and software for the new system. This phase begins once management has accepted the report containing the design and has approved the way to development. Why it's important: *This phase may involve the organization in investing substantial time and money.*

systems development life cycle (SDLC) (p. 505) Six-phase process that many organizations follow during systems analysis and design: (1) preliminary investigation; (2) systems analysis; (3) systems design; (4) systems development; (5) systems implementation; (6) systems maintenance. Phases often overlap, and a new one may start before the old one is finished. After the first four phases, management must decide whether to proceed to the next phase. User input and review are a critical part of each phase. Why it's important: *The SDLC is a comprehensive tool for solving organizational problems, particularly those relating to the flow of computer-based information.*

systems implementation (p. 511) Phase 5 of the SDLC; consists of converting the hardware, software, and files to the new system and training the users. Why it's important: *This phase involves putting design ideas into operation.*

systems maintenance (p. 512) Phase 6 of the SDLC; consists of keeping the system working by having system audits and periodic evaluations and by making changes based on new conditions. Why it's important: *This phase is important for keeping a new system operational and useful.*

top-down program design (p. 516) Method of program design; a programmer identifies the top or principal processing step, or module, of a program and then breaks it down in hierarchical fashion to the lowest level of detail. Why it's important: *This design enables an entire program to be more easily developed, because the parts can be developed and tested separately.*

very-high-level languages (p. 528) Also known as *problem-oriented* and *nonprocedural languages* and *fourth-generation languages (4GLs)*; more user-oriented than third-generation languages, 4GLs require fewer commands. 4GLs consist of report generators, query languages, and application generators. Why it's important: *Programmers can write programs that need to tell the computer only what they want done, not all the procedures for doing it, which saves them the time and the labor of having to write many lines of code.*

visual programming (p. 536) Method of creating programs in which the programmer makes connections between objects by drawing, pointing, and clicking on diagrams and icons and by interacting with flowcharts. Programming is made easier because the orientation of object-oriented programming is used in a graphical or visual way. Why it's important: *Visual programming enables users to think more about the problem solving than about handling the programming language.*

VRML (Virtual Reality Modeling [Markup] Language) (p. 537) Type of programming language used to create three-dimensional (3-D) web pages. Why it's important: *VRML expands the information-delivering capabilities of the web.*

writing the program documentation (p. 523) Step 5 in the programming process; programmers write procedures explaining how the program was constructed and how it is to be used. Why it's important: *Program documentation is the final stage in the five-step programming process, although documentation should also be an ongoing task accompanying all steps.*

XML (eXtensible Markup Language) (p. 538) Metalanguage used to make it easy for machines to read websites by allowing web developers to add more "tags" to a web page. Why it's important: *XML is more powerful than HTML, allowing information on a website to be described by general tags—for example, identifying one piece of information in a recipe as "cooking time" and another as "ingredients."*

CHAPTER REVIEW

LEARNING **MEMORIZATION**

"I can recognize and recall information."

Self-Test Questions

1. The __________________ comprises six phases of examining an information system and improving it.
2. The first major program written in C was the __________ operating system.
3. ________________ is a method of creating programs in which the programmer makes connections between objects by drawing, pointing, and clicking on diagrams and icons and by interacting with flowcharts.
4. Software engineering, or __________, refers to creating instructions for computers.
5. A(n) __________ is a formula or a set of steps for solving a particular problem.
6. A(n) __________ is a collection of related components that interact to perform a task in order to accomplish a goal.
7. __________ is the basic language of the computer, representing data as 0s and 1s.

Multiple-Choice Questions

1. One of the following activities is *not* an objective of Phase 1 of the SDLC, preliminary investigation. Which one?
   a. conduct preliminary analysis
   b. describe costs and benefits
   c. acquire new software and hardware
   d. submit a preliminary plan
   e. propose alternative solutions
2. One of the following activities is *not* an objective of Phase 4 of the SDLC, systems development. Which one?
   a. convert files to the new system
   b. acquire software
   c. acquire hardware
   d. test the system
   e. address the make-or-buy decision
3. Third-generation programming languages include all the following languages except which one?
   a. FORTRAN
   b. BASIC
   c. COBOL
   d. XML
   e. C
4. All these are website markup or scripting languages except which one?
   a. Flash
   b. JavaScript
   c. HTML
   e. XML
   f. Visual BASIC

True/False Questions

T F 1. Programming errors caused by incorrect use of control structures are called logic errors.

T F 2. CASE tools—programs that automate various activities of the SDLC—are used only in Phase 3.

T F 3. Four methods of systems implementation are direct, parallel, phased, and pilot.

T F 4. User training takes place during Phase 1 of the SDLC.

T F 5. JavaScript is an object-oriented scripting language used in web browsers to add interactive functions to HTML pages.

T F 6. There are four generations of programming languages.

stage 2 LEARNING COMPREHENSION

"I can recall information in my own terms and explain it to a friend."

Short-Answer Questions

1. What is the straw man argument? Appeal to pity? What are some of the other elements of critical thinking?
2. What does a systems analyst do?
3. What are the four ways to implement a new system?
4. What are the five steps in the programming process?
5. What are the six phases of the SDLC?
6. What is a software bug?
7. What is a prototype, and what does it do?

stage 3 LEARNING APPLYING, ANALYZING, SYNTHESIZING, EVALUATING

"I can apply what I've learned, relate these ideas to other concepts, build on other knowledge, and use all these thinking skills to form a judgment."

Knowledge in Action

1. Alice is a 3-D programming environment that makes it easy to create animation for telling a story, playing an interactive game, or making a video to share on the web. Alice is also a teaching tool for learning object-oriented programming. It allows you to learn fundamental programming concepts in the context of creating animated movies and simple video games.

   In Alice, you drag and drop graphic tiles to create a program, where the instructions correspond to standard statements in a programming language such as Java or C++. Alice allows you to immediately see how your animation programs run, enabling you to easily understand the relationship between the programming statements and the behavior of objects in their animation. By manipulating the objects in their virtual world, you gain experience with all the programming constructs typically taught in an introductory programming course.

   Download Alice 2.2 from *www.alice.org/index.php?page=downloads/download_alice2.2*.

   Then watch the demonstration videos at *www.alice.org/index.php?page=what_is_alice/what_is_alice*.

   Next, give Alice a try! (Here are Alice tutorials: *www.youtube.com/watch?v=K2XA8mx3sKc* and *www.dickbaldwin.com/tocalice.htm*.)
2. Design a system that would handle the input, processing, and output of a simple form of your choice. Use a data flow diagram to illustrate the system.
3. Have you participated in a project that failed? Why did it fail? Based on what you know now, what might you have done to help the project succeed?
4. Which step of the SDLC do you find most interesting? Why?
5. Are you interested in learning how to program? Which languages would you choose to learn? Why?
6. Create a prototype invention (of anything) and have classmates test and evaluate it. Once the evaluations are received, write a detailed report, as you would at the end of Phase 3 in the SDLC process.

Web Exercises

1. The waterfall model and the spiral model are variations of the SDLC. Do keyword searches to find out how these models differ from the basic approach.
2. Compare the SDLC process to the scientific method. How are they alike? How do they differ? If you need to be refreshed on the scientific method, you can visit *http://teacher.pas.rochester.edu/phy_labs/appendixe/appendixe.html* or run a search on "scientific method."
3. Using an Internet search tool, identify a company that develops CASE tools. In a few paragraphs, describe what this company's CASE tools are used for.
4. One of the most beneficial courses you can take in college is critical thinking. The Experience Box in this chapter has an introduction to fallacious arguments. A background in logic and identification of fallacies is essential not only for making valid arguments but for life in general. After reading the Experience Box, visit the following websites:

   www.unc.edu/depts/wcweb/handouts/fallacies.html

   www.don-lindsay-archive.org/skeptic/arguments.html

   For a humorous account of how not to argue, read the Monty Python Argument sketch:

   www.youtube.com/watch?v=teMlv3ripSM

   After familiarizing yourself with the types of fallacies, watch TV for an hour (especially commercials) and identify 10 fallacies. Write them down and discuss them with your class the next day. Are our collective reality assumptions valid and cohesive? Command of logic and critical thinking will help you tremendously if you decide to get into computer programming.
5. Curious about the educational requirements for a systems designer/analyst? Go to

   http://resources.courseadvisor.com/computers-technology/systems-analyst

   www.princetonreview.com/Careers.aspx?cid=42

   www.bls.gov/oco/ocos042.htm
6. Do a keyword search for "programming" and "jobs." Which languages are most in demand now? Which of the jobs seems most interesting to you?

Extra exercise: Here is another simple example of an algorithm. Choose another simple statement and develop an algorithm for it.

Algorithm: Sorting by colors

This is an example of an algorithm for sorting cards with colors on them into piles of the same color:

1. Pick up all the cards.
2. Pick a card from your hand and look at the color of the card.
3. If there is already a pile of cards of that color, put this card on that pile.
4. If there is no pile of cards of that color, make a new pile of just this card.
5. If there is still a card in your hand, go back to the second step.
6. If there is not still a card in your hand, then the cards are sorted; you are done.

(http://simple.wikipedia.org/wiki/Algorithm)

Notes

Chapter 1

1. Study by Council for Research Excellence, reported in Brian Stelter, "8 Hours a Day Spent on Screens, Study Finds," *The New York Times,* March 27, 2009, p. B6.
2. Anthropologist Susan D. Blum, quoted in Christine Rosen, "It's Not Theft, It's Pastiche," *The Wall Street Journal,* April 16, 2009, p. A13.
3. Dana Kerr, "Overall Time Spent Online Remains Static," *cnet News,* January 28, 2009 (accessed January 29, 2011).
4. "A World Transformed: What Are the Top 30 Innovations of the Last 30 Years?" *Knowledge@Wharton,* February 18, 2009, *knowledge.wharton.upenn.edu/article.cfm?articleid=2163* (accessed May 28, 2009). See also "Life Changers," *The New York Times,* March 8, 2009, p. BU-2.5; Larry Keeley, "History's Greatest Innovations," *BusinessWeek,* February 6, 2007, *www.businessweek.com/innovate/content/feb2007/id20070216_377845.htm* (accessed January 19, 2011).
6. Josh Cantrell, "The Death of the Personal Computer," *Claris Networks,* December 8, 2010, *http://clarisnetworks.com/Blog/December-2010/The-Death-of-the-Personal-Computer* (accessed January 19, 2011).
7. Sara Rimer, "At M.I.T., Large Lectures Are Going the Way of the Blackboard," *The New York Times,* January 13, 2009, p. A12.
8. Katie Hafnet, "In Class, the Audience Weighs In," *The New York Times*, April 29, 2004, pp. E1, E6.
9. "Educational Technology in U.S. Schools," Fall 2008, Table 1, National Center for Education Statistics, Institute of Education Sciences, U.S. Department of Education, April 2010, Washington, D.C.
10. Les Smith, "Technology Can Be Useful in the Classroom," *Reno Gazette-Journal,* March 10, 2009, p. 2D. For a brilliant discussion on the use of technology in the classroom in the service of teaching science, see Carl Wieman, "Why Not Try a Scientific Approach to Science Education?" *Scientific Blogging,* March 10, 2009, and his subsequent articles, *www.scientificblogging.com/carl_wieman/why_not_try_scientific_approach_science_education* (accessed May 2, 2009).
11. Steve Jones, *Pew Internet & American Life Project: The Internet Goes to College,* September 15, 2002, *www.pewInternet.org/pdfs/PIP_College_Report.pdf* (accessed January 4, 2009).
12. "Online Learning Set for Explosive Growth as Traditional Classrooms Decline," January 27, 2011, *http://empowerlms.wordpress.com/2011/01/27/online-learning-set-for-explosive-growth-as-traditional-classrooms-decline/* (accessed June 29, 2011).
13. Greg Toppo, "Profound Shift in Home Schooling," *USA Today,* May 29, 2009, p. 1A.
14. Dan Carnevale, "Many Online Courses Work Best at No Distance at All," *The Chronicle of Higher Education,* July 30, 2004, p. A22.
15. Kim Painter, "Diagnosis by Telemedicine," *USA Today,* February 16, 2009, p. 5D. See also Christopher Lawton, "*Cough, Cough.* Is There a Doctor in the Mouse?" *The Wall Street Journal,* March 5, 2009, pp. D1, D2.
16. Stephanie Nano, "Computers Seen as Aid in X-Ray Reading," *San Francisco Chronicle,* October 2, 2008, p. A2.
17. Jesse Ellison, "A New Grip on Life," *Newsweek,* December 15, 2008, p. 64; and Pam Belluck, "In New Procedure, Artificial Arm Listens to Brain," *The New York Times,* February 11, 2001, pp. A1, A17.
18. Rebecca Boyle, "New Electric Skin Could Bring the Human Touch to Robots, Artificial Limbs," *PopSci,* September 13, 2010, *www.popsci.com/technology/article/2010-09/new-electric-skin-could-bring-human-touch-robots-and-aritifical-limbs* (accessed January 24, 2011).
19. Drew Halley, "Computer Chip Implant to Program Brian Activity, Treat Parkinsons's," *Singularity Hub,* July 21, 2010, *http://singularityhub.com/2010/07/21/computer-chip-implant-to-program-brain-activity-treat-parkinsons/* (accessed January 24, 2011).
20. Cynthia G. Wager, "Money's Digital Future," *The Futurist*, January–February 2003, pp. 14–15.
21. "North America B2C E-Commerce Report 2010," Aarkstore Enterprise Market Research Aggregation, *Capital Business, www.alianzaregioncapital.org/tag/2009-2010-e-commerce-business-statistics* (accessed January 24, 2011).
22. Jupiter Research, cited in "Online Grocery Sales a Tough Sale," *RedOrbit,* March 17, 2008, *www.redorbit.com/news/technology/1299393/online_grocery_sales_a_tough_sale/index.html* (accessed June 1, 2009).
23. Ann Plunkett, "Direct Deposit of Employee Wages, 2006," *Ezine articles, http://ezinearticles.com/?Direct-Deposit-of-Employee-Wages&id=283857* (accessed January 24, 2011).
24. Heather Green, "Kissing Off Big Labels," *BusinessWeek,* September 6, 2004, pp. 90, 92.
25. James Barron, "Best Musical Score (by a Laptop)," *The New York Times,* June 26, 2004, p. A13.
26. Bill Werde, "We've Got Algorithm, but How about Soul?" *The New York Times,* March 21, 2004, sec. 4, p. 12.
27. Peter Stack, "An Animated Future," *San Francisco Chronicle,* May 19, 1999, p. E1.
28. Jim Ericson, "Processing AVATAR," January 21, 2009, *SourceMedia* (Information Management magazine), *www.information-management.com/newsletters/avatar_data_processing-10016774-1.html* (accessed January 24, 2011).
29. William Keck, "Their World of Tomorrow Revolves around Playtime," *USA Today,* September 6, 2004, p. 10D.
30. Laura M. Holson, "Out of Hollywood, Rising Fascination with Video Games," *The New York Times,* April 10, 2004, pp. A1, B2; and Robert A. Guth and Merissa Marr, "Videogames Go Hollywood," *The Wall Street Journal,* May 10, 2004, pp. B1, B4.
31. Ellen S. Miller, "Internet Empowerment," *USA Today,* March 17, 2009, p. 9A.
32. "State Goes YouTube," *U.S. News & World Report,* December 8, 2008, p. 23.
33. "Worldwide Mobile Subscriptions to Reach 5.6 Billion by 2013," press release, Strategy Analytics, *www.strategyanalytics.com/default.aspx?mod=PressReleaseViewer&a0=4018* (accessed June 1, 2009).

34. "Cellphones and American Adults," *Pew Internet*, September 2, 2010, *www.pewInternet.org/Reports/2010/Cell-Phones-and-American-Adults/Overview.aspx* (accessed January 25, 2011).
35. Michael Specter, "Your Mail Has Vanished," *The New Yorker,* December 6, 1999, pp. 96–103.
36. "Internet 2009 in Numbers," *pingdom*, January 22, 2010, *http://royal.pingdom.com/2010/01/22/Internet-2009-in-numbers/* (accessed January 25, 2011).
37. Robert Rossney, "E-Mail's Best Asset—Time to Think," *San Francisco Chronicle,* October 5, 1995, p. E7.
38. Adam Gopnik, "The Return of the Word," *The New Yorker,* December 6, 1999, pp. 49–50.
39. Ibid.
40. Tamar Lewin, "Informal Style of Electronic Messages Is Showing Up in Schoolwork, Study Finds," *The New York Times,* April 25, 2008, p. A12.
41. *www.pewInternet.org/~/media//Files/Reports/2009/PIP_Generations_2009.pdf*, January 28, 2009 (accessed January 25, 2011).
42. Pew Internet & American Life Project, "Daily Internet Activities," February 15, 2008, *www.pewInternet.org/trends/Daily_Internet_Activities_2.15.08.htm* (accessed July 1, 2009).
43. Kevin Maney, "The Net Effect: Evolution or Revolution?" *USA Today,* August 9, 1999, pp. 1B, 2B.
44. Pew Internet & American Life Project, "Demographic of Internet Users," December 20, 2008, *www.pewInternet.org/Static-Pages/Data-Tools/Download-Data/~/media/Infographics/Trend%20Data/January%202009%20updates/Demographics%20of%20Internet%20Users%201%206%2009.jpg* (accessed June 1, 2009).
45. Sidney Jones and Susannah Fox, Pew Internet & American Life Project, "Generations Online in 2009," January 28, 2009, *www.pewinternet.org/~/media//Files/Reports/2009/PIP_Generations_2009.pdf* (accessed June 1, 2009).
46. Laurence Hooper, "No Compromises," *The Wall Street Journal,* November 16, 1992, p. R8.
47. John Markoff, "By and for the Masses," *The New York Times,* June 29, 2005, pp. C1, C5.
48. Robert D. Hof, "The Power of Us," *BusinessWeek,* June 20, 2005, pp. 74–82.
49. Verne Kopytoff, "Citizen Journalism Takes Root Online," *San Francisco Chronicle,* June 6, 2005, pp. E1, E5.
50. For a discussion of meanings of "cloud computing," see Ben Worthen, "Overuse of the Term 'Cloud Computing' Clouds Meaning of the Tech Buzz Phrase," *The Wall Street Journal,* September 23, 2008, p. B8; Daniel Lyons, "Today's Forecast: Cloudy," *Newsweek,* November 10, 2008, p. 24; Geoffrey A. Fowler and Ben Worthen, "The Internet Industry Is on a Cloud—Whatever That May Mean," *The Wall Street Journal,* March 26, 2009, pp. A1, A9; and "No Man Is an Island: The Promise of Cloud Computing," *Knowledge@Wharton,* April 1, 2009, *http://knowledge.wharton.upenn.edu/article.cfm?articleid=2190* (accessed June 1, 2009).
51. David Lagesse, "Taking a Walk in 'the Cloud,'" *U.S. News & World Report,* March 2009, pp. 71–73.
52. Tom Forester and Perry Morrison, *Computer Ethics: Cautionary Tales and Ethical Dilemmas in Computing* (Cambridge, MA: MIT Press, 1990), pp. 1–2.
53. Psychiatrist Edward M. Hallowell, quoted in Alma Tugend, "Multitasking Can Make You Lose . . . Um . . . Focus," *The New York Times,* October 25, 2008, p. B7. Hallowell is the author of *CrazyBusy: Overstretched, Overbooked, and About to Snap!* (New York: Ballantine, 2006).
54. John Tierney, "Ear Plugs to Lasers: The Science of Concentration," *The New York Times*, May 5, 2009, p. D2.
55. Winifred Gallagher, cited in Tierney, "Ear Plugs to Lasers." Gallagher is the author of *Rapt* (New York: Penguin Press, 2009).
56. Winifred Gallagher, quoted in book review, David G. Myers, "Please Pay Attention," *The Wall Street Journal,* April 20, 2009, p. A13.
57. Pam Belluck, "To Really Learn, Quit Studying and Take a Test," *The New York Times,* January 21, 2011, *www.nytimes.com/2011/01/21/science/21memory.html?partner=rss&emc=rss* (accessed January 22, 2011).
58. Francis P. Robinson, *Effective Study,* 4th ed. (New York: Harper & Row, 1970).
59. Bruce K. Broumage and Richard E. Mayer, "Quantitative and Qualitative Effects of Repetition on Learning from Technical Text," *Journal of Educational Psychology, 78,* 1982, 271–278.
60. Robin J. Palkovitz and Richard K. Lore, "Note Taking and Note Review: Why Students Fail Questions Based on Lecture Material," *Teaching of Psychology, 7,* 1980, 159–161.

Chapter 2

1. Graham T. T. Molitor, "Five Forces Transforming Communications," *The Futurist,* September–October 2001, pp. 32–37.
2. "Internet World Stats: Usage and Population Statistics," *www.internetworldstats.com/stats.htm* (accessed February 5, 2011).
3. PenPlusBytes, *http://penplusbytes.blogspot.com/2007/12/five-billion-people-will-be-connected.html* (accessed February 5, 1011).
4. Aaron Smith, "Home Broadband," *Pew Internet*, August 11, 2010, *http://pewinternet.org/Reports/2010/Home-Broadband-2010.aspx* (accessed February 5, 2011).
5. Leslie Cauley, "Rural Americans Long to Be Linked," *USA Today,* June 8, 2008, pp. 1B, 2B.
6. John Horrigan, "Mobile Access to Data and Information," *Pew Internet,* July 22, 2009, *www.pewinternet.org/Reports/2009/12-Wireless-Internet-Use/5-Mobile-access-to-data-and-information.aspx* (accessed February 5, 2011).
7. Fact Checker, "Calling It 4G Isn't Enough to Make It Faster," *Reno Gazette Journal*, January 16, 2011, p. 3A.
8. Ibid.
9. Internet2, *www.internet2.edu/about/* (accessed February 8, 2011).
10. For a short history of the development of the Internet and protocols, see Stephen D. Crocker, "How the Internet Got Its Rules," *The New York Times,* April 7, 2009, p. A25.
11. Peter Rachal, "Internet Officially Runs Out of Addresses," *PCmag.com*, February 3, 2011, *www.pcmag.com/article2/0%2C2817%2C2379327%2C00.asp* (accessed February 9, 2011).
12. *www.icann.org/en/about/* (accessed February 9, 2011).
13. Kevin J. O'Brien, "Firefox Leads in Europe, Firm Says," *The New York Times*, January 4, 2011, *www.nytimes.com/2011/01/05/technology/05browser.html* (accessed February 10, 2011).
14. Susan Wilson, "Internet Explorer Comes in Second to Firefox in Europe," *Tech.Blorge,* January 5, 2011, *http://tech.blorge.com/Structure:%20/2011/01/05/internet-explorer-comes-in-second-to-firefox-in-europe/* (accessed February 10, 2011).
15. "The Size of the World Wide Web," February 10, 2011, *www.worldwidewebsize.com/* (accessed February 10, 2011).
16. Melanie Hanes-Ramos, "Bare Bones 101: A Basic Tutorial on Searching the Web," University of South Carolina, Beaufort Library, February 5, 2009, *www.sc.edu/beaufort/library/pages/bones/bones.shtml* (accessed June 8, 2009).
17. Chris Taylor, "It's a Wiki, Wiki World," *Time,* June 6, 2005, pp. 40–42. See also Stacy Schiff, "The Interactive Truth," *The New York Times,* June 15, 2005, p. A29.

18. Ben Eisen, "Cornell Profs Slam Use of Wikipdeia," *The Cornell Daily Sun,* February 20, 2007, *www.cornellsun.com/node/21501* (accessed February 13, 2011).
19. Ellen Chamberlain, "Bare Bones 101: A Basic Tutorial on Searching the Web," University of South Carolina, Beaufort Library, September 7, 2006, *www.sc.edu/beaufort/library/pages/bones/lesson5.shtml* (accessed June 8, 2009).
20. Adam Gregerman, "Online Research Is So Easy, So Unreliable," letter, *The New York Times,* June 23, 2004, p. A26.
21. Janet Hogan, "The ABCDs of Evaluating Internet Resources," Binghamton University Libraries, November 2, 2004, *http://library.lib.binghamton.edu/search/evaluation.html;* Hope N. Tillman, "Evaluating Quality on the Net," Babson College, March 28, 2003, *www.hopetillman.com/findqual.html;* and Esther Grassian, "Thinking Critically about World Wide Web Resources," UCLA College Library, September 6, 2000, *www.library.ucla.edu/ libraries/college/help/critical/index.htm* (all accessed June 8, 2009).
22. Daniel Terdiman, "A Tool for Scholars Who Like to Dig Deep," *The New York Times,* November 25, 2004, p. B6. See also Jeffrey R. Young, "Google Unveils a Search Engine Focused on Scholarly Materials," *The Chronicle of Higher Education,* December 3, 2004, p. A34.
23. "Google's Book Scanning Project Runs into Legal Hurdles," *domain-b.com,* June 10, 2009, *www.domain-b.com/companies/companies_g/google/20090610_book_scanning_project.html* (accessed June 10, 2009).
24. Matt Lake, "Desperately Seeking Susan OR Suzie NOT Sushi," *The New York Times,* September 3, 1998, p. D1.
25. Michelle Slatalla, "The Office Meeting That Never Ends," *The New York Times,* September 23, 1999, pp. D1, D8.
26. Lee Gomes, "How the Next Big Thing in Technology Morphed into a Really Big Thing," *The Wall Street Journal,* October 4, 2004, p. B1.
27. Stephen H. Wildstrom, "Google's Magic Carpet Ride," *BusinessWeek,* July 18, 2005, p. 22.
28. Steven Levy, "The Earth Is Ready for Its Close-up," *Newsweek,* June 6, 2005, p. 13. See also James Fallows, "An Update on Stuff That's Cool (Like Google's Photo Maps)," *The New York Times,* April 17, 2005, sec. 3, p. 5; Verne Kopytoff, "Google's Free 3-D Service Brings Views of Earth Down to the PC," *San Francisco Chronicle,* June 29, 2005, pp. A1, A16; John Markoff, "Marrying Maps to Data for a New Web Service," *The New York Times,* July 18, 2005, pp. C1, C8; and Verne Kopytoff, "Microsoft, Google in Sky Fight," *San Francisco Chronicle,* July 26, 2005, pp. D1, D2.
29. Verne Koptoff, "Google Peeks Beneath the Waves," *San Francisco Chronicle,* February 3, 2009, pp. A1, A14.
30. "Google Earth's Street View: Public Boon or Privacy Invasion?," EngineeringDaily.net, *www.engineeringdaily.net/google-earths-street-view-public-boon-or-privacy-invasion* (accessed February 14, 2011).
31. Chris Taylor, "Let RSS Go Fetch," *Time,* May 30, 2005, p. 82.
32. Janet Kornblum, "Welcome to the Blogosphere," *USA Today,* July 8, 2003, p. 7D.
33. Andrew Sullivan, "Why I Blog," *The Atlantic,* November 2008, pp. 106–113.
34. Michael Agger, *Slate.com,* reported in "Blogging for Fun and Profit," *The Week,* October 17, 2008, p. 44.
35. Daniel Lyons, "Time to Hang Up the Pajamas," *Newsweek,* February 16, 2009, p. 19; and Douglas Quenqua, "Blogs Falling in an Empty Forest," *The New York Times,* June 7, 2009, Sunday Styles, pp. 1, 7.
36. Daniel Nations, "What Is Web 2.0?" About.com , 2007, *http://webtrends.about.com/od/web20/a/what-is-web20.htm* (accessed June 11, 2009).
37. "How Web 3.0 Will Work," *http://computer.howstuffworks.com/web-30.htm/printable* (accessed February 7, 2011).
38. Jeremiah Owyang, "A Collection of Social Network Stats for 2010," *Web Strategy,* January 19, 2010, *www.web-strategist.com/blog/2010/01/19/a-collection-of-social-network-stats-for-2010/* (accessed February 15, 2011).
39. Jacqui Cheng, "Popular Facebook Apps Found to Be Collecting, Selling User Info," *arstechnica.com, http://arstechnica.com/tech-policy/news/2010/10/many-faceook-apps-found-to-be-collecting-selling-user-info.ars* (accessed February 7, 2011).
40. Emily Steele and Geoffrey A. Fowler, "Facebook in Privacy Breech," October 18, 2010, *http://online.wsj.com/article/SB10001424052702304772804575558484075236968.html* (accessed February 7, 1011).
41. Stanley Fish, "Anonymity and the Dark Side of the Internet," *The New York Times,* January 3, 2011, *http://opinionator.blogs.nytimes.com/2011/01/03/anonymity-and-the-dark-side-of-the-internet/* (accessed February 8, 2011).
42. Ibid.
43. Kevin Kelly, "Achieving Techno-Literacy," *The New York Times,* September 16, 2010, *www.nytimes.com/2010/09/19/magazine/19FOB-WWLN-Kelly-t.html* (accessed February 8, 2011).
44. Brad Stone, "Friends May Be the Best Guide through the Noise," *The New York Times,* May 4, 2008, business section, p. 4.
45. Jeremiah Owyang, "A Collection of Social Network Stats for 2010," *Web Strategy,* January 19, 2010, *www.web-strategist.com/blog/2010/01/19/a-collection-of-social-network-stats-for-2010/* (accessed February 15, 2011).
46. Timothy L. O'Brien and Saul Hansell, "Barbarians at the Digital Gate," *The New York Times,* September 19, 2004, sec. 3, pp. 1, 4.
47. "Egregious Email," *Smart Computing,* October 2002, pp. 95–97.
48. "Internet in 2010:107 Trillion Emails, 262 billion Spams per Day," *Wired.CPU.com,* January 16, 2011, *http://wiredcpu.com/internet-in-2010-107-trillion-emails-262-billions-spams-per-day/* (accessed February 15, 2011).
49. Riva Richmond, "Companies Target E-Mail 'Spoofing,'" *The Wall Street Journal,* June 9, 2004, p. D9; and Amey Stone, "How to Avoid the 'Phish' Hook," *BusinessWeek online,* May 24, 2004, *www.businessweek.com/technology/content/may2004/tc20040524_8133_tc024.htm* (accessed June 12, 2009).
50. "Email Spoofing," SearchSecurity.com Definitions, November 20, 2003, *http://searchsecurity.techtarget.com/sDefinition/0,,sid14_gci840262,00.html* (accessed June 12, 2009).
51. Kim Komando, "5 Tips for Spurning Spyware and Browser Hijackers," *Microsoft Small Business Center,* 2005, *www.microsoft.com/smallbusiness/issues/marketing/privacy_spam/5_tips_for_spurning_spyware_and_browser_hijackers.mspx* (accessed June 12, 2009).
52. David Kesmodel, "Marketers Seek to Make Cookies More Palatable," *The Wall Street Journal,* June 17, 2005, pp. B1, B2.
53. "What Is Browser Hijacking?" Microsoft Safety and Security Center, *www.microsoft.com/security/resources/hijacking-whatis.aspx* (accessed February 15, 2011).
54. Joseph Telafici, quoted in Vincent Kiernan, "The Next Plague," *The Chronicle of Higher Education,* January 28, 2005, pp. A36–A38.
55. David Rothenberg, "How the Web Destroys the Quality of Students' Research Papers," *The Chronicle of Higher Education,* August 15, 1997.

Chapter 3

1. Alan Robbins, "Why There's Egg on Your Interface," *The New York Times*, December 1, 1996, sec. 3, p. 12.
2. Idris Motee, "You Think HCI Design Is Hard . . . ," *Innovation Playground*, January 14, 20102, *http://mootee.typepad.com/innovation_playground/2010/01/you-think-hci-design-is-hard-think-it-also-needs-to-consider-user-experiences-for-the-blind.html* (accessed February 21, 2011).
3. Randall Stross, "Windows Could Use a Rush of Fresh Air," *The New York Times*, June 29, 2008, Business section, p. 4.
4. "Cloud Computing: The Evolution of Software-as-a-Service," Knowledge @ W. P. Carey, June 4, 2008, *http://knowledge.wpcarey.asu.edu/article.cfm?articleid=1614* (accessed July 24, 2011).
5. Study by Kent Norman, Laboratory of Automation Psychology and Decision Processes, University of Maryland, cited in Katherine Seligman, "Computer Crashes Booming Business," *San Francisco Chronicle*, April 17, 2005, pp. A1, A21.

Chapter 4

1. Michael S. Malone, "The Tiniest Transformer," *San Jose Mercury News*, September 10, 1995, pp. 1D, 2D; excerpted from *The Microprocessor: A Biography* (New York: Telos/Springer Verlag, 1995).
2. Malone, "The Tiniest Transformer."
3. "Exabyte," The Sharpened Glossary: Definitions of Computer Terms, *www.sharpened.net/glossary/definition.php?exabyte* (accessed July 29, 2008).
4. Ernest Scheyder, "Save Some Cash, Get Unplugged," *Reno Gazette-Journal*, April 11, 2009, p. 8A.
5. Ibid.
6. Report by 1E and Alliance to Save Energy, 2009 Energy Report, reported in Jon Swartz, "Leaving PCs on Overnight Costs Companies $2.8B a Year," *USA Today*, March 25, 2009, p. 4B.
7. Stephen H. Wildstrom, "Chips with Two Brains," *BusinessWeek*, August 1, 2005, p. 20.
8. "Consumers Fail to Properly Back Up Large Digital Libraries, Says CEA," *www.reuters.com/article/pressRelease/idUS157293+18-Mar-2008+BW20080318* (accessed August 2, 2009).
9. *www.backblaze.com/press-June-is-Backup-Awareness-Month-2010.html* (accessed June 1, 2011).
10. "Solid Computing, for a Price," *The New York Times*, September 18, 2008, p. C8. See also J. Santo Domingo, "Credit-Card Hard Drives," *PC Magazine, Digital Edition*, July 2009, p. 17.
11. "Spyware Infection rates," March 2010, *www.plycomp.co.uk/virus-statistics-worldwide.html* (accessed March 17, 2012).
12. Alan Luber, "Hard Drive Backup & Restore Basics, Part 1," *Smart Computing*, August 2004, p. 96; Rachel Dodes, "Terminating Spyware with Extreme Prejudice," *The New York Times*, December 30, 2004, pp. E1, E6; Rachel Dodes, "Tools to Make Your Hard Drive Forget Its Past," *The New York Times*, December 30, 2004, p. E6; Jeff Dodd, "How to Install Operating Systems," *Smart Computing*, February 2005, pp. 60–63; and Nigel Powell, "Archive Your Drive," *Popular Science*, March 2005, pp. 73–74.
13. Michio Kaku, "What Will Replace Silicon?" *Time*, June 19, 2000, p. 99.
14. Michael Kanellos, "HP Nanotech Takes Chips beyond Transistors," CNET News.com, February 10, 2005.
15. Milan N. Stojanovic, "Columbia University: Molecular Robots on the Rise," May 14, 2010, *www.outlookseries.com/N7/Science/3864_Milan_N._Stojanovic_Columbia_University_Molecular_Robots_Milan_N._Stojanovic.htm* (accessed March 17, 2011).
16. K. Naughton, "Now We're Cooking with Batteries," *Newsweek*, December 1, 2008, pp. 42–46.
17. Daniel Lyons, "Hurry Up and Type," *Newsweek*, June 29, 2009, p. 27.
18. Don Clark, "Marvell Bets on 'Plug Computers,'" *The Wall Street Journal*, February 23, 2009, p. B4.
19. Mark Hachman, "The Bottomless DVD," *PC Magazine Digital Edition*, July 2009, p. 9.
20. Walt Mossberg, "How to Buy a Laptop," *Newser*, April 29, 2010, *www.newser.com/story/87365/how-to-buy-a-laptop.html* (accessed June 1, 2011); Walt Mossberg, "Picking Out a Laptop in the Brave, New World of Tablets," April 20, 2011, *http://allthingsd.com/20110420/picking-out-a-laptop-in-the-brave-new-world-of-tablets/* (accessed June 1, 2011).
21. "Notebooks," *PC Magazine*, November 30, 2004, pp. 121–134; "Inside Notebooks," *PC Magazine*, April 26, 2005, pp. 62–68; Bill Howard, "Multimedia Notebooks," *PC Magazine*, July 2005, pp. 89–102; Wilson Rothman, "Laptops and Desktops: Basics, Bells and Whistles," *The New York Times*, August 3, 2005, p. E6; Walter S. Mossberg, "Consider Your Needs, Then Use This Guide to Buying a Laptop," *The Wall Street Journal*, April 10, 2008, *http://ptech.allthingsd.com/20080410/consider-your-needs-then-use-this-guide-to-buying-a-laptop/* (accessed August 1, 2008); Aaron Boigon, "Several Things You Should Consider When Buying a Bargain Computer," *Reno Gazette-Journal*, March 14, 2009, p. 7A; Randall Stross, "The PC Doesn't Have to Be an Anchor," *The New York Times*, April 19, 2009, Business section, p. 4; Justin Scheck and Loretta Chao, "Leaner Laptops, Lower Prices," *The Wall Street Journal*, April 22, 2009, pp. D1, D6; Ting-I. Tsai and Ian Johnson, "As Giants Step In, Asustek Defends a Tiny PC," *The Wall Street Journal*, May 1, 2009, p. B1; "Tech Edge: Owner Tested," *Fortune Small Business*, June 2009, p. 30; Ashlee Vance, "Acer's Everywhere; How Did That Happen?" *The New York Times*, June 28, 2009, Business section, pp. 1, 6.
22. John Schwartz, "Back to School," *The New York Times*, August 3, 2005, pp. E1, E6.
23. Lyons, "Hurry Up and Type"; David Pogue, "Decoding Battery Life for Laptops," *The New York Times*, June 25, 2009, pp. B1, B6; and Walter S. Mossberg, "New Mac Laptops Use Batteries Sealed for Power," *The Wall Street Journal*, June 25, 2009, p. D1.

Chapter 5

1. David F. Gallagher, "2 Rooms, River View, ATM in Lobby," *The New York Times*, June 6, 2002, p. E1.
2. Peter Wayner, "A Keyboard That Bends to Your Needs," *The New York Times*, March 12, 2009, p. B7.
3. Julie Schmit, "Labels Will Tell Buyers Where Their Berries Grew," *USA Today*, February 2, 2009, p. 8B.
4. Larry Copeland, "Project Will Help Drivers Go More with Traffic Flow," *USA Today*, June 13, 2008, p. 1A; and Larry Copeland, "Test Project Will Gather Highway Traffic Data," *USA Today*, June 13, 2008, p. 6A.
5. Alicia Chang, "Sensors to Keep Tabs on Fault," *Reno Gazette-Journal*, March 29, 2009, pp. 1B, 3B.
6. Jeff Vining, Jerry Mechling, and Steve Bittinger, "Japan Earthquake and Tsunami Reaffirm the Need for Sensors," March 17, 2011, *www.gartner.com/DisplayDocument?id=1594915* (accessed March 28, 2011).
7. Janet Colvin, Nancy Tobler, and James A. Anderson, "Productivity and Multi-Screen Displays," *Rocky Mountain Communication Review*, Summer 2004, pp. 31–53.
8. James A. Anderson, University of Utah, quoted in "Multiple Monitor Computing Demonstrates Tangible Benefits for Corporate Workforce," NEC press release, October 6, 2003, *www.necus.com/necus/media/press_releases/template.cfm?DID=1947* (accessed July 20, 2009).
9. Farhad Manjoo, "Boss, I Need a Bigger Screen; For Work Efficiency, of Course," *The New York Times*, January 15, 2009, p. B9.

10. Danielle Weatherbee, quoted in Steve Friess, "Laptop Design Can Be a Pain in the Posture," *USA Today*, April 13, 2005, p. 8D.
11. Tom Albin, quoted in Friess, "Laptop Design Can Be a Pain in the Posture."
12. Tamara James, quoted in Friess, "Laptop Design Can Be a Pain in the Posture."
13. "Cellular Phone Health," *www.cellularphonehealth.com* (accessed March 31, 2005).
14. Siegal Sadetzki, Angela Chetrit, Avital Jarus-Hakak, Elisabeth Cardis, Yonit Deutch, Shay Duvdevani, Ahuva Zultan, Ilya Novikov, Laurence Freedman, and Michael Wolf, "Cellular Phone Use and Risk of Benign and Malignant Parotid Gland Tumors—A Nationwide Case-Control Study," *American Journal of Epidemiology* 167 (4) (2008): 457–467.
15. Minouk Schoemaker, Anthony Swerdlow et al., "Mobile Phone Use and Risk of Acoustic Neuroma: Results of the Interphone Case-Control Study in Five North European Countries," *British Journal of Cancer*, August 31, 2005, reported in Matt Moore, "No Link Between Cellphones, Tumors: Study," *GlobeandMail.com*, August 8, 2008, *www.globetechnology.com/servlet/story/RTGAM.20050831.gttumouraug31/BNStory/Technology.*
16. Danielle Dellorto, "WHO: Cell Phone Use Can Increase Possible Cancer Risk," *CNN.com*, May 31, 2011, *www.cnn.com/2011/HEALTH/05/31/who.cell.phones/index.html* (accessed June 11, 2011).
17. Leslie Berlin, "Kicking Reality Up a Notch," *The New York Times*, July 12, 2009, business section, p. 3.
18. Brooks Barnes, "Stereo Vision on the Silver Screen," *The New York Times*, January 12, 2009, pp. B1, B6; Brooks Barnes, "A Tiny Studio Enters the Third Dimension," *The New York Times*, February 8, 2009, business section, pp. 1, 5; Peter Hartlaub, "3-D Rises from the Dead," *San Francisco Chronicle*, March 20, 2009, pp. E1, E2; and Josh Quittner, "The Next Dimension," *Time*, March 30, 2009, pp. 53–62.
19. Don Clark, Ben Charny, and Jerry DiColo, "Animators Envision 3-D TV at Home," *The Wall Street Journal*, January 5, 2009, pp. B1, B6.
20. Stephen H. Wildstrom, "Coming at You: 3D on Your PC," *BusinessWeek*, January 19, 2009, p. 65.
21. Michael V. Copeland, "3-D Gets Down to Business," *Fortune*, March 30, 2009, pp. 32–40.
22. Survey by Ponemon Institute for Dell, reported in "How Workers Damage Laptops," *USA Today*, March 4, 2009, p. 1A.
23. Melinda Beck, "When Your Laptop Is a Big Pain in the Neck," *The Wall Street Journal*, December 16, 2008, p. D1.

Chapter 6

1. "What Does 'Digital' Mean in Regard to Electronics?" *Popular Science*, August 1997, pp. 91–94.
2. See Michael Fitzgerald, "Finding and Fixing a Home's Power Hogs," *The New York Times*, July 27, 2008, *www.nytimes.com/2008/07/27/technology/27proto.html?ex=1374811200&en=a965d02fc80765e1&ei=5124&partner=permalink&exprod=permalink* (accessed August 12, 2008).
3. *www.webopedia.com/TERM/P/packet_switching.html*
4. *http://whatis.techtarget.com/definition/network-topologies.html*
5. *www.networktutorials.info/topology.html*
6. Aaron Smith, "Mobile Access 2010," Pew Internet, July 7, 2010, *www.pewinternet.org/Reports/2010/Mobile-Access-2010.aspx* (accessed April 12, 2011).
7. *www.workshifting.com/2010/02/how-many-people-actually-telecommute.html*
8. *http://mobileoffice.about.com/gi/o.htm?zi=1/XJ&zTi=1&sdn=mobileoffice&cdn=gadgets&tm=6&gps=637_362_1916_798&f=20&tt=14&bt=1&bts=1&zu=http%3A//www.ivc.ca/studies/us/index.htm*
9. Jim Hopkins, "How Solo Workers Keep from Getting Depressed," *USA Today*, May 9, 2001; Stephanie Armour, "Telecommuting Gets Stuck in the Slow Lane," *USA Today*, June 25, 2001, pp. 1A, 2A; Stephanie Armour, "More Bosses Keep Tabs on Telecommuters," *USA Today*, July 24, 2001, p. 1B; Katherine Reynolds Lewis, "Working from Home Not Always the Right Fit," *San Francisco Chronicle*, July 14, 2003, p. E2; Sue Shellenbarger, "'Shed Boy Is on Line One': Some Tales from the Growing World of Home Offices," *The Wall Street Journal*, June 17, 2004, p. D1; Joyce M. Rosenberg, "Letting Staff Telecommute Changes Office," *San Francisco Chronicle*, September 7, 2008, p. H3; and Mintel Survey of 812 white-collar workers, reported in "Is Teleworking a Good Idea?" *USA Today*, October 28, 2008, p. 1B.
10. Robert Smith, quoted in Carolyn Said, "Work Is Where You Hang Your Coat," *San Francisco Chronicle*, July 18, 2005, p. E5. See also Sue Shellenbarger, "Work at Home? Your Employer May Be Watching," *The Wall Street Journal*, July 30, 2008, pp. D1, D2.
11. "Broadband," *http://searchtelecom.techtarget.com/definition/broadband* (accessed April 14, 2011).
12. "Third Annual Broadband Study Shows Global Broadband Quality Improves by 24% in One Year," October 18, 2010, Cisco, *http://newsroom.cisco.com/dlls/2010/prod_101710.html* (accessed April 14, 2011).
13. Ibid.
14. Roger Yu, "GPS Becomes a Vital Tool for Frequent Travelers," *USA Today*, July 8, 2008, p. 8B.
15. For other uses, see Marisol Bello, "Holiday Heads Up to Thieves: GPS Devices on Board the Baby Jesus," *USA Today*, December 12, 2008, p. 1A; Natalie Angier, "GPS for Forest Creatures on the Move," *The New York Times*, February 3, 2009, pp. D1, D2; David Pogue, "Peekaboo, Zoombak Sees You," *The New York Times*, April 23, 2009, pp. B1, B8; and Marian Bond, "Firm Uses GPS System to Monitor Car Fleets," *Reno Gazette-Journal*, May 5, 2009, pp. 5A, 6A.
16. Christopher Elliott, "Online Maps That Steer You Wrong," *The New York Times*, June 28, 2005, p. C8; See also Donna Leinwand, "Caution: Watch Where You're Going," *USA Today*, March 12, 2009, p. 3A.
17. *www.fcc.gov/pshs/services/911-services/*
18. Brad Tuttle, "Tough Call: If You Never Use a Landline, Why Do You Still Pay for It?" *Time*, *http://money.blogs.time.com/2010/07/26/tough-call-if-you-never-use-a-landline-why-do-you-still-pay-for-it/.*
19. Leah Christian, Scott Keeter, Kristen Purcell, and Aaron Smith, Pew Research Center, "Assessing the Cell Phone Challenge," May 20, 2010, *http://pewresearch.org/pubs/1601/assessing-cell-phone-challenge-in-public-opinion-surveys* (accessed April 15, 2011).
20. Kevin Maney, "A Very Different Future Is Calling—on Billions of Cellphones," *USA Today*, July 27, 2005, p. 3B.
21. Mathew Ingram, "Mary Meeker: Mobile Internet Will Soon Overtake Fixed Internet," Gigadom, *http://gigaom.com/2010/04/12/mary-meeker-mobile-internet-will-soon-overtake-fixed-internet/* (accessed April 15, 2011).
22. *www.itu.int/ITU-R/index.asp?category=information&rlink=imt-advanced&lang=en*
23. "USB-IF Introduced Superspeed USB (USB 3.0) Cable and Connection Certification Program," March 5, 2011, *www.allmoreinfo.com/usb-if-introduced-superspeed-usb-usb-3-0-cable-and-connector-certification-program.html* (accessed June 27, 2011).
24. "Enhancing Information and Data Security: A Never Ending Quest," *Knowledge@SMU*, June 4, 2008,

http://knowledge.smu.edu.sg/article.cfm?articleid=1144 (accessed August 9, 2009); John Markoff, "Internet Attacks Are Growing More Potent and Complex," *The New York Times,* November 10, 2008, p. B8; Deborah Gage, "Rising Threat: Online Crime," *San Francisco Chronicle,* December 9, 2008, pp. D1, D4; John Markoff, "Panel Presses to Bolster Security in Cyberspace," *The New York Times,* December 9, 2008, p. B5; Peter Eisler, "Raids on Federal Computer Data Soar," *USA Today,* February 17, 2009, p. 1A; and Byron Acohido, "Website-Infecting Attacks Spike to 450,000 a Day," *USA Today,* March 17, 2009, p. 1B.

25. *McAfee/NCSA Cyber Security Survey, Newsworthy Analysis, October 2007, http://download.mcafee.com/products/manuals/en-us/McAfeeNCSA_Analysis09-25-07.pdf?cid=36665* (accessed September 21, 2009).
26. "Symantec Internet Security Threat Report Trends for 2010," Volume 16, published April 2011, *www4.symantec.com/mktginfo/downloads/21182883_GA_REPORT_ISTR_Main-Report_04-11_HI-RES.pdf* (accessed April 17, 2011).
27. *http://answers.yahoo.com/question/index?qid=20090401094418AAlgMGk* (accessed April 15, 2011).
28. *www.security-faqs.com/what-does-the-conficker-worm-do-exactly.html* (accessed April 15, 2011).
29. Mustaque Ahamad et al., "Emerging Cyberthreats Report for 2009: Data, Mobility and Questions of Responsibility Will Drive Cyberthreats in 2009 and Beyond," Georgia Tech Information Security Center, October 2008, p. 2, *www.gtiscsecuritysummit.com/pdf/CyberThreatsReport2009.pdf* (accessed April 15, 2011).
30. Steve Boggan, "Meet the Hackers," *The Week,* September 26, 2008, pp. 44–45, originally published by *The London Times;* Lolita C. Baldor, "Officials Seek Hackers for Network Defense," *Reno Gazette-Journal,* April 19, 2009, p. 7B; and Christopher Drew and John Markoff, "Contractors Vie for Plum Work, Hacking for U.S.," *The New York Times,* May 31, 2009, main news section, pp. 1, 4.
31. Federal Bureau of Investigation, quoted in TechTarget Security Media, "Glossary," *http://searchsecurity.techtarget.com/gDefinition/0,294236,sid14_gci771061,00.html* (accessed April 14, 2008).
32. Duncan J. Watts, "Unraveling the Mysteries of the Connected Age," *The Chronicle of Higher Education,* February 14, 2003, pp. B7–B9.
33. Anick Jesdanun, "Simple Passwords Don't Suffice Online," *San Francisco Chronicle,* June 1, 2004, pp. C1, C5.
34. Victor Zapana, "Experts Offer Tips to Creating More Secure PINs, Passwords," *San Francisco Chronicle,* July 20, 2009, p. D2, reprinted from *Pittsburgh Post-Gazette.*
35. David Einstein, "The Future Is Now for Data Safety," *San Francisco Chronicle,* May 26, 2008, p. D1.
36. Randall Stross, "Goodbye, Passwords; You Aren't a Good Defense," *The New York Times,* August 10, 2008, business section, p. 4. See also Elaine Mills, "One Key Fits All," *The Wall Street Journal,* September 29, 2009, p. R11.
37. Jordan Robertson, "Citibank ATM Breach Reveals Password Security Problems," *Reno Gazette-Journal,* July 2, 2008, p. 6A.
38. Laurie J. Flynn, "Technology Leaders Favor Online ID Card over Passwords," *The New York Times,* June 24, 2008, p. C8; and Stross, "Goodbye, Passwords; You Aren't a Good Defense."

Chapter 7

1. Gary McWilliams, "It All Connects—and Converges," *The Wall Street Journal,* January 31, 2005, p. R3.
2. Jerry Yang and David Filo, cited in Cliff Edwards, "The Web's Future Is You," *BusinessWeek,* April 25, 2005, p. 18.
3. Carlos Carvajal, "The Personalization Revolution," *Digiday:Data,* April 13, 2011, *www.digidaydaily.com/data/stories/the-personalization-revolution/* (accessed April 25, 2011).
4. Barry Schwartz, *The Paradox of Choice: Why More Is Less* (New York: HarperCollins, 2005). See also Barry Schwartz, "Choice Overload Burdens Daily Modern Life," *USA Today,* January 5, 2004, p. 13A.
5. Alina Tugend, "Too Many Choices: A Problem That Can Paralyze," *The New York Times,* February 26, 2010, *www.nytimes.com/2010/02/27/your-money/27shortcuts.html* (accessed April 25, 2011).
6. Ibid.
7. Kaila Colbin, "The Danger of Personalization," *Online Spin,* March 11, 2011, *www.mediapost.com/publications/?fa=Articles.showArticle&art_aid=146543* (accessed April 25, 2011).
8. Adam Steinfield, "Why Personalization Is Dangerous for the Media," March 29, 2011, *suite101.com, www.suite101.com/content/why-personalization-is-dangerous-for-the-media-a362728* (accessed April 25, 2011).
9. Ibid.
10. Dennis K. Berman, "Technology Has Us So Plugged into Data, We Have Turned Off," *The Wall Street Journal,* November 10, 2003, p. B1; and Olivia Barker, "Got That Virtual Glow?" *USA Today,* August 3, 2009, p. 1D.
11. Roger Brown, "Multitasking Gets You There Later," *InfoQ,* June 29, 2010, *www.infoq.com/articles/multitasking-problems* (accessed April 26, 2011).
12. "MP3 Player Buying Guide," *www5.samsclub.com/Electronics/Electronics-MobileSolutions-MP3PlayerBuying-Guide.aspx* (accessed April 27, 2011).
13. Michael Bull, quoted in Benny Evangelista, "The iPod Generation," *San Francisco Chronicle,* December 27, 2004, pp. E1, E6.
14. PEW Research Center, August–September 2010, *http://pewresearch.org/databank/dailynumber/?NumberID=1117* (accessed April 28, 2011).
15. Lionel Braud, "Effect of MP3 Players on Society," *www.ehow.com/facts_5768331_effect-mp3-players-society.html* (accessed April 28, 2011).
16. Alice Park, "iPod Safety: Preventing Hearing Loss in Teens," *Time, www.time.com/time/health/article/0,8599,1881130,00.html* (accessed April 28, 2011).
17. Elizabeth Quinn,"iPods and Hearing Loss," *About.com, http://sportsmedicine.about.com/od/tipsandtricks/a/iPod_safety.htm* (accessed April 28, 2011).
18. Jocasta Williams and Michael Fardon, "Perpetual Connectivity: Lecture Recordings and Portable Media Players," *www.ascilite.org.au/conferences/singapore07/procs/williams-jo.pdf* (accessed April 28, 2011).
19. ARBITRON, "Radio Attracts Another 2.1 Million Weekly Listeners According to Radar 108," March 16, 2011, *www.allaccess.com/net-news/archive/story/88738/radio-attracts-another-2-1-million-weekly-listener* (accessed May 3, 2011).
20. Anthony Armstrong, "Satellite Radio vs. High-Definition Radio for the Layperson: The Battle for America's Ears Has Begun," *http://stereos.about.com/od/homestereotechnologies/a/radio.htm* (accessed August 17, 2008).
21. Pandora, *www.pandora.com/corporate/* (accessed May 4, 2011).
22. Todd Wallack, "Torrent of Images Is Leaving Film in the Dust," *San Francisco Chronicle,* May 23, 2005, pp. A1, A5.
23. David Einstein, "For Digital Cameras, More Megapixels May Not Mean Sharper Shots," *San Francisco Chronicle,* August 4, 2008, p. D3. See also Russ Juskalian, "Pixels Are like Cupcakes; Let Me Explain," *The New York Times,* November 13, 2008, p. B6; and David Einstein, "Cameras—Sensor Size Does Matter," *San Francisco Chronicle,* June 8, 2009, pp. C1, C2.
24. Jefferson Graham, "Tips for Buyers," *USA Today,* May 17, 2004, p. 9E.

25. Ibid.
26. "Optical vs. Digital Zoom," *www.photoxels.com/digital-photography-tutorials/optical-digital-zoom/* (accessed May 5, 2011).
27. "Evolution of Photos Creating Effects on Society," *www.seekfirst.com/node/57* (accessed May 6, 2011).
28. Maria Puente, "Memories Gone in a Snap," *USA Today,* January 21, 2005, p. 1D.
29. "India Tech Online," www.indiatechonline.com/kochi-camera-phones-for-police-173.php (accessed May 9, 2011).
30. BCM, *www.bcm.tv/about-us.html* (accessed May 9, 2011).
31. Liam McCabe, "How to Buy an Internet-Ready TV," April 22, 2010, *www.forbes.com/2010/04/22/yahoo-netflix-google-technology-breakthroughs-internet-tv.html* (accessed May 9, 2011).
32. Kevin J. O'Brien, "Mobile TV Spreading in Europe and to the U.S.," *The New York Times,* May 5, 2008, p. C2.
33. Steven Levy, "Television Reloaded," *Newsweek,* May 30, 2005, p. 50.
34. TiVo, *www.tivo.com/?WT.mc_id=PS2005&gclid=CN2Lt5-F3KgCFQkFbAodvFWfHg* (accessed May 9, 2011).
35. Nicholson Baker, "A New Page," *The New Yorker,* August 3, 2009, pp. 24–30.
36. "Technological Evolution Stirs a Publishing Revolution," *Knowledge@Wharton,* August 5, 2009, *http://knowledge.wharton.upenn.edu/article.cfm?articleid=2307* (accessed August 28, 2009).
37. PCMag.com, *www.pcmag.com/encyclopedia_term/0,2542,t=tablet+computer&i=52520,00.asp* (accessed May 9, 2011).
38. Steve Lohr, "How Much Is Too Much?" *The New York Times,* May 4, 2005, pp. E1, E9.
39. PCMag.com, *www.pcmag.com/encyclopedia_term/0,2542,t=Smartphone&i=51537,00.asp* (accessed May 9, 2011).
40. James Sullivan, "Time Waits for Everyone, Now that We've All Got Camera Phones," *San Francisco Chronicle,* May 20, 2004, p. E2.
41. Diana Oblinger, "Boomers, Gen-Xers, and Millennials: Understanding the New Students," *EDUCAUSE Review,* July/August 2003, pp. 37–47.
42. Marc Prensky, "Digital Natives, Digital Immigrants," from *On the Horizon,* October 2001, © 2001 Marc Prensky, *www.marcprensky.com/writing/Prensky%20-%20Digital%20Natives,%20Digital%20Immigrants%20-% 20Part1.pdf* (accessed May 15, 2005).
43. Oblinger, "Boomers, Gen-Xers, and Millennials," p. 38. See also Harry Hurt III, "A Generation with More than Hand-Eye Coordination," *The New York Times,* December 21, 2008, Business section, p. 5.
44. Wendy Ricard and Diana Oblinger, "The Next-Generation Student," Higher Education Leaders Symposium, Redmond, WA, June 17–18, 2003, p. 2, *http://download.microsoft.com/download/d/c/7/dc70bbbc-c5a3-48f3-855b-f01d5de42fb1/TheNextGenerationStudent.pdf* (accessed May 15, 2005).
45. Andrew Payne, quoted in Ricard and Oblinger, "The Next-Generation Student," p. 5.
46. Prensky, "Digital Natives, Digital Immigrants," p. 2.
47. Marc Prensky, "What Kids Learn That's POSITIVE from Playing Videogames," © 2002 Marc Presnsky, *www.marcprensky.com/writing/Prensky%20-%20What%20Kids%20Learn%20Thats%20POSITIVE%20From%20Playing%20Video%20Games.pdf* (accessed June 12, 2005).
48. Oblinger, "Boomers, Gen-Xers, and Millennials," p. 40, citing Jason Frand, "The Information Age Mindset: Changes in Students and Implications for Higher Education," *EDUCAUSE Review,* September/October 2000, pp. 15–24.
49. Kevin J. Delaney, "Teaching Tools," *The Wall Street Journal,* January 17, 2005, pp. R4, R5.
50. Diana G. Oblinger, "The Next Generation of Educational Engagement," *Journal of Interactive Media in Education,* May 21, 2004, pp. 1–18.
51. Ricard and Oblinger, "The Next-Generation Student," p. 4.

Chapter 8

1. Library of Congress, *www.loc.gov/about/facts.html* (accessed May 14, 2011).
2. "Universal Digital Content Set Up to Outstrip Storage, Says IDC," SCC Technology Solutions Provider, *www.scc.com/news/data-centre/digital-universe-outstrips-storage-capability* (accessed May 14, 2011).
3. Ibid.
4. Mark Lewis, "Information 2.0," Writers Summit 2008, EMC Corporation, April 4, 2008, *http://emc.typepad.com/mark/presentations/WritersSummit2008.pdf* (accessed September 12, 2009).
5. Noam Cohen, "Wikipedia," *The New York Times,* May 14, 2011, *http://topics.nytimes.com/top/news/business/companies/wikipedia/index.html* (accessed May 14, 2011).
6. *www.webopedia.com/TERM/D/database.html* (accessed May 15, 2011).
7. Peggy Williams, "Database Dangers," *Quill,* July/August 1994, pp. 37–38.
8. Kevin Pho, "Wikipedia Isn't Really the Patient's Friend," *USA Today,* July 15, 2009, p. 11A.
9. Jonathan Berry, John Verity, Kathleen Kerwin, and Gail DeGeorge, "Database Marketing," *BusinessWeek*, September 5, 1994, pp. 56–62.
10. Cheryl D. Krivda, "Data Mining Dynamite," *Byte,* October 1995, pp. 97–62.
11. Martin Vaughan, "IRS to Mine Payment Data on Mortgages," *The Wall Street Journal,* September 1, 2009, p. A5.
12. Lisa Guernsey, "Digging for Nuggets of Wisdom," *The New York Times*, October 16, 2003, pp. E1, E9; and Anne Eisenberg, "Lines and Bubbles and Bars, Oh My! New Ways to Sift Data," *The New York Times,* August 31, 2008, p. BU-4.
13. Sara Reese Hedberg, "The Data Gold Rush," *Byte*, October 1995, pp. 83–88.
14. Chen-Yueh Chen and Yi-Hsiu Lin, "A New Market Research Approach in Sport-Data Mining," *www.thesportjournal.org/article/new-market-research-approach-sport-data-mining* (accessed May 19, 2011).
15. Dr. Michael J. Way, "Galaxy Zoo Morphology Improves Photometric Redshifts in the Sloan Digital Sky Survey," *Data Mining for Astronomy,* May 5, 2011, *http://astrodatamining.net/* (accessed May 19, 2011).
16. Eric Lichtblau, "Study of Data Mining for Terrorists Is Urged," *The New York Times,* October 8, 2008, p. A20.
17. Alex Wright, "Mining the Web for Feelings, Not Facts," *The New York Times,* August 24, 2009, pp. B1, B7.
18. Alex Wright, "Exploring a 'Deep Web' That Google Can't Grasp," *The New York Times,* February 23, 2009, pp. B1, B4.
19. Michael J. Mandel and Robert D. Hof, "Rethinking the Internet," *BusinessWeek*, March 26, 2001, p. 118.
20. Joshua Quittner, "Tim Berners-Lee," *Time*, March 29, 1999, pp. 193–194.
21. Jeff Bezos, quoted in K. Southwick, interview, October 1996, *www.upside.com*.
22. D. Levy, "On-line Gamble Pays Off with Rocketing Success," *USA Today*, December 24, 1998, pp. 1B, 2B.
23. "Amazon Posts 35% Sales Growth in North America and Raises 2008 *Forecast," www.internetretailer.com/dailyNews.asp?id=2720* (accessed August 23, 2008).
24. Robert Benfer Jr., Louanna Furbee, and Edward Brent Jr., quoted in Steve Weinberg, "Steve's Brain," *Columbia Journal Review,* February 1991, pp. 50–52.
25. "Virtual Reality Lab Focuses on Conservation," *Science Daily, April 11, 2011, www.sciencedaily.com/releases/2011/04/110408163908* (accessed May 22, 2011).
26. Judith Gunther, "An Encounter with AI," *Popular Science*, June 1994, p. 90.

27. Vernor Vinge, "The Coming Technological Singularity," *Vision-21: Interdisciplinary Science & Engineering in the Era of Cyberspace,* Proceedings of Symposium Held at NASA Lewis Research Center, *NASA Conference Publication CP-10129,* March 30–31, 1993, *http://rohan.sdsu.du/faculty/vinge/misc/singularity.html* (accessed September 15, 2009).
28. John Markoff, "The Coming Superbrain," *The New York Times,* May 24, 2009, Week in Review section, pp. 1, 4.
29. Brian E. Coggins, "Human vs. Machine: Which Brain Is Ahead?" letter, *The New York Times,* July 30, 2009, p. A24.
30. William A. Wallace, *Ethics in Modeling* (New York: Elsevier Science, 1994).
31. John Markoff, "Ay Robot! Scientists Worry Machines May Outsmart Man," *The New York Times,* July 26, 2009, News section, pp. 1, 4.
32. Jeff Martin, "Privacy Concerns Arise over Student Data," *USA Today,* August 24, 2009, p. 3A.
33. Deborah Yao, "Web-Monitoring Software Gathers Data from Kids' Private Chats—Then Sells It," *San Francisco Chronicle,* September 8, 2009, p. D2.
34. Jessica E. Vascellaro and Emily Steel, "Something New Gains with Something Borrowed," *The Wall Street Journal,* June 5, 2009, p. B6; and Miguel Helft, "Google to Offer Ads Based on Interests, with Privacy Rights," *The New York Times,* March 11, 2009, p. B3.
35. Saul Hansell, "Agency Skeptical of Internet Privacy Policies," *The New York Times,* February 13, 2009, p. B5.
36. Jennifer Lee, "Trying to Elude the Google Grasp," *The New York Times,* July 25, 2001, pp. E1, E6.
37. Kathryn Rambo, quoted in Ramon G. McLeod, "New Thieves Prey on Your Very Name," *San Francisco Chronicle,* April 7, 1997, pp. A1, A6.
38. Rambo, quoted in T. Trent Gegax, "Stick 'Em Up? Not Anymore; Now It's Crime by Keyboard," *Newsweek,* July 21, 1997, p. 14.
39. Identity Theft Council, 2011, *www.identitytheftcouncil.org/about-us* (accessed May 23, 2011).
40. "Working to Resolve Identity Theft," Identity Theft Resource Center, *www.idtheftcenter.org/artman2/publish/m_facts/Facts_and_Statistics.shtml* (accessed August 25, 2009).

Chapter 9

1. Harold Gilliam, "Mind over Matter," *San Francisco Chronicle,* February 9, 2003, pp. D1, D6.
2. Edmund L. Andrews, "New Scale for Toting Up Lost Freedom vs. Security Would Measure in Dollars," *The New York Times,* March 11, 2003, p. A11.
3. Sara Lipka, "Pentagon System to Gather Student Data Raises Privacy Fears," *The Chronicle of Higher Education,* July 8, 2005, p. A30.
4. Andrea L. Foster, "ID Theft Turns Students into Privacy Activists," *The Chronicle of Higher Education,* August 2, 2002, pp. A27–A28.
5. Josh Tyrangiel, "Singer's Little Helper," *Time,* February 16, 2009, pp. 49–51.
6. *Der Tzitung* has apologized for causing any offense, claimed its photo editor didn't read the White House guidelines to not manipulate the photo, and stated that modesty guidelines bar the newspaper from publishing any photos of women.
7. Byron Calame, "Pictures, Labels, Perception and Reality," *The New York Times,* July 3, 2005, sec. 4, p. 10.
8. John Knoll, quoted in Katie Hafner, "The Camera Never Lies, but the Software Can," *The New York Times,* March 11, 2004, pp. E1, E7.
9. Howard Kurtz, "Reporter Loses Job over Altered Video of Fox's Gibson," *Washington Post,* February 25, 2009, *www.washingtonpost.com/wp-dyn/content/article/2009/02/24/AR2009022403215.html.*
10. "Hannity to Address Protest Video Question," *November 11, 2009, http://mediadecoder.blogs.nytimes.com/2009/11/11/hannity-to-address-protest-video-questions-tonight/* (accessed May 31, 2011).
11. May 2004 survey commissioned by Wells Fargo & Co, reported in Julie Dunn, "Poor 'Street Smarts' Make Web Users Vulnerable," *San Francisco Chronicle,* August 17, 2004, p. C8; reprinted from *Denver Post.*
12. Scott McCartney, "Pilots Go to 'the Box' to Avoid Midair Collisions," *The Wall Street Journal,* July 18, 2002, p. D3; and George Johnson, "To Err Is Human," *The New York Times,* July 14, 2002, sec. 4, pp. D1, D7.
13. We are grateful to Professor John Durham for contributing these ideas.
14. Ben Worthen, "Workers Losing Computer Data May Lack Awareness of Its Value," *The Wall Street Journal,* November 27, 2007, p. B3.
15. H. Josef Hebert, "Nuclear Sites Posted on Internet in Error," *San Francisco Chronicle,* June 4, 2009, p. A4.
16. Jordan Robertson, "Software Glitch Leaves Utilities Open to Attack," *San Francisco Chronicle,* June 12, 2008, p. C4.
17. Hope Yen, "VA Ordered to Explain Risky Software Flaws," *San Francisco Chronicle,* January 15, 2009, p. A8.
18. Robert McMillan, "Computer Glitch Forces U.S. to Cancel Visa Lottery Results," IDG News Service, May 13, 2011, *http://catless.ncl.ac.uk/Risks/26.45.html#subj2* (accessed May 31, 2011).
19. "The Problem of Dirty Data," August 9, 2009, *www.articlesbase.com/databases-articles/the-problem-of-dirty-data-1111299.html* (accessed May 31, 2011).
20. Richard Wolf, "Get Out Your Pencils: Paper Ballots Make a Return," *USA Today*, February 29, 2008, p. 2A; Richard Wolf, "Flawed Ballots Cited in Study," *Reno Gazette-Journal,* July 21, 2008, p. 1B; Adam Cohen, "A Tale of Three (Electronic Voting) Elections," *The New York Times,* July 31, 2008, p. A22; Deborah Hastings, "Touch-Screen Voting Machines—Store or Scrap?" *San Francisco Chronicle,* August 25, 2008, p. D3; and Gary Fineout, "Invalid Ballots in Florida Doubled in 2008," *The New York Times,* February 26, 2009, p. A19.
21. Charles Perrow, *Normal Accidents: Living with High-Risk Technologies* (New York: Basic Books, 1984).
22. Paul Virilio, reported in Alan Riding, "Expounding a New View of Accidents," *The New York Times,* December 26, 2002, pp. B1, B2.
23. Jefferson Graham, "College Students Sued over Music Downloads," *USA Today,* March 24, 2005, p. 5B.
24. Larem Gullo, "Record Industry Sues 784 Users for Illegally Sharing Music Online," *San Francisco Chronicle,* June 30, 2005, pp. C1, C2.
25. "Music Labels Win $2 Million in Web Case," *The New York Times,* June 19, 2009, p. B2.
26. Pat Choate, *Hot Property: The Stealing of Ideas in an Age of Globalization* (New York: Alfred A. Knopf, 2005), quoted in Michael Lind, "Freebooters of Industry," *The New York Times Book Review,* July 10, 2005, p. 34.
27. Ben Worthen, "New Epidemic Fears: Hackers," *The Wall Street Journal,* August 4, 2009, p. A6.
28. Siobhan Gorman, "Arrest in Epic Cyber Crime," *The Wall Street Journal,* August 18, 2009, pp. A1, A4; AP, "20-Year Sentence in Card Numbers," March 25, 2010, *www.nytimes.com/2010/03//26/technology/26hacker.html* (accessed June 3, 2011).
29. FTC, "ID Theft again Tops Consumer Complaints," March 9, 2011, *www.techworld.com.au/article/379120/ftc_id_theft_again_tops_consumer_complaints/* (accessed June 3, 2011).
30. National White Collar Crime Center, "IC3 2010 Annual Report on Internet Crime Released," February 2010, *www.ic3.gov/media/annualreports.aspx* (accessed June 3, 2011).
31. David Bank and Riva Richmond, "Where the Dangers Are," *The Wall Street Journal,* July 18, 2005, pp. R1,

R3.; see also Jon Swartz, "Hackers Want to Be Your (Malicious) Friend," *USA Today,* August 13, 2008, p. 3B.

32. Byron Acohido and Jon Swartz, "Are Hackers Using Your PC to Spew Spam and Steal?" *USA Today,* September 8, 2004, pp. 1B, 4B.
33. Nanette Asimov, Ryan Kim, and Kevin Fagan, "South Bay Phone Chaos—Vandals Slice Vital Cables," *San Francisco Chronicle,* April 10, 2009, pp. A1, A12.
34. Siobhan Gorman, "Electricity Grid in U.S. Penetrated by Spies," *The Wall Street Journal,* April 8, 2009, pp. A1, A2; and Siobhan Gorman, "Electricity Industry to Scan Grid for Spies," *The Wall Street Journal,* June 18, 2009, p. A3.
35. "Power Grids, Oil Refineries Face 'Staggering' Level of Cyberattacks," April 19, 2011, *www.securitynewsdaily.com/power-grids-oil-refineries-staggering-level-cyberattacks-0710/* (accessed June 3, 2011).
36. Frank X. Mullen Jr., "Hackers into Ely Hospital's Computers Traced to Russia," *Reno Gazette-Journal,* April 7, 2003, pp. 1A, 6A.
37. Michael F. Martin, June 1, 2011, "Expanded Protection Against Employee Computer Data Theft Under Computer Fraud and Abuse Act," *www.natlawreview.com/article/expanded-protection-against-employee-computer-data-theft-under-computer-fraud-and-abuse-act* (accessed June 4, 2011).
38. David Jolly, "In France, Intricate Tale of Corporate Espionage," *The New York Times,* August 25, 2009, p. B4.
39. "Interpol: Cybercrime Is the Biggest Criminal Threat," *PCrisk.com, www.pcrisk.com/internet-threat-news/2131-interpol-cyber-crime-is-the-biggest-criminal-threat* (accessed June 6, 2011).
40. U.S. Computer Emergency Readiness team, reported in "U.S. Computers Vulnerable," *The Week,* February 27, 2009, p. 6.
41. Lolita C. Baldor, "Pentagon Says It Spent $100 Million Fending Off 6 Months of Cyberattacks," *San Francisco Chronicle,* April 8, 2009, p. C3.
42. Jack Goldsmith, "Defend America, One Laptop at a Time," *The New York Times,* July 2, 2009, p. A21.
43. Jim Michaels, "Cellphones Put to 'Unnerving' Use in Gaza," *USA Today,* January 14, 2009, p. 4A.
44. David E. Sanger, John Markoff, and Thom Shanker, "U.S. Plans Attack and Defense in Web Warfare," *The New York Times,* April 28, 2009, pp. A1, A14.
45. "U.S. Officials Eye N. Korea in Cyber Attack," *Reno Gazette-Journal,* July 9, 2009, p. 1B.
46. Jonathan Masters, "Confronting the Cyber Threat," Council on Foreign Relations, May 23, 2011, *www.cfr.org/technology-and-foreign-policy/confronting-cyber-threat/p15577* (accessed June 6, 2011).
47. David E. Sanger, "Pentagon Plans New Arm to Wage Computer Wars," *The New York Times,* May 29, 2009, pp. A1, A17; Byron Acohido, "Obama Vows to Prioritize Cybersecurity," *USA Today,* June 1, 2009, p. 4B; and Chloe Albanesius, "Obama's Cyber-space Crackdown," *PC Magazine, Digital Edition,* July 2009, pp. 7–8.
48. Siobhan Gorman and Yochi Dreazen, "Military Command Is Created for Cyber Security," *The Wall Street Journal,* July 24, 2009, p. A6.
49. L. Gordon Crovitz, "Obama and Cyber Defense," *The Wall Street Journal,* June 29, 2009, p. A11.
50. Masters, "Confronting the Cyber Threat."
51. Thom Shanker and David E. Shanker, "Privacy May Be a Victim in Cyberdefense Plan," *The New York Times,* June 13, 2009, pp. A1, A3; and Siobhan Gorman, "Troubles Plague Cyberspy Defense," *The Wall Street Journal,* July 3, 2009, pp. A1, A10.
52. Stephanie Armour, "Beware the Blog: You May Get Fired," *Reno Gazette-Journal,* June 25, 2005, pp. 1E, 4E.
53. Deloitte's Ethics and Workplace survey, reported in "Social Networking and the Boss," *USA Today,* June 24, 2009, p. 1B.
54. Employee Computer & Internet Abuse Statistics, Snapshot Spy, *www.snapshotspy.com/employee-computer-abuse-statistics.htm*; Computer Monitoring, *www.computer-monitoring.com/employee-monitoring/stats.htm* (accessed June 6, 2011).
55. Damon Darlin, "Software That Monitors Your Work, Wherever You Are," *The New York Times,* April 12, 2009, Business section, p. 4.
56. "Office Slacker Stats," Staff Monitoring Solutions, *www.staffmonitoring.com/P32/stats.htm* (accessed June 4, 2011).
57. American Databank, *www.americandatabank.com/statistics.htm* (accessed June 6, 2011).
58. Marci Alboher Nusbaum, "New Kind of Snooping Arrives at the Office," *The New York Times,* July 13, 2003, sec. 3, p. 12.
59. Mindy Fetterman, "Employers Must Shred Personal Data," *USA Today,* June 1, 2005, p. 3B.
60. Bob Egelko, "U.S. Appeals Court Limits Release of Text Messages," *San Francisco Chronicle,* June 19, 2008, p. B3; and Jennifer Ordonez, "They Can't Hide Their Pryin' Eyes," *Newsweek,* July 7/July 14, 2008, p. 22.
61. John Holusha, "The Painful Lessons of Disruption," *The New York Times,* March 17, 1993, pp. C1, C5.
62. "March 11 Disaster Already Causes 145 Business Failures," June 3, 2011, *http://mdn.mainichi.jp/mdnnews/national/news/20110603p2g00m0dm006000c.html* (accessed June 6, 2011).
63. Environmental Protection Agency study, reported in William M. Bulkeley, "Cutting Tech's Energy Bill," *The Wall Street Journal,* September 9, 2008, p. B6; and Kent Garber, "Powering the Information Age," *U.S. News & World Report,* April 2009, pp. 46–48.
64. Bobbie Johnson, "Web Providers Must Limit Internet's Carbon Footprint, Say Experts," *guardian.co.uk,* May 3, 2009, *www.guardian.co.uk/technology/2009/may/03/internet-carbon-footprint* (accessed June 7, 2011).
65. "Cloud Computing and Internet Use Suck Energy, Emit CO2, Says Greenpeace," April 29, 2011, *High Technology Resource, http://mardiutomo.com/publication-news/2011/04/cloud-computing-and-internet-use-suck-energy-emit-co2-says-greenpeace/* (accessed June 7, 2011).
66. Steve Lohr, "Data Centers as Polluters," *The New York Times,* May 5, 2008, p. C6.
67. Lee Gomes, "Companies Struggle to Keep Up as Technologies Grow Obsolete," *The Wall Street Journal,* April 29, 2008, p. B7.
68. Heather Levin, "Electronic Waste (E-Waste) Recycling and Disposal—Fact, Statistics, & Solutions," March 25, 2011, *http://blog.macroaxis.com/2011/03/25/electronic-waste-e-waste-recycling-and-disposal-%e2%80%93-facts-statistics-solutions/* (accessed June 7, 2011).
69. Ibid.
70. Study by Annenberg Center for the Digital Future, University of Southern California, reported in "Is the Internet Behind Less Family Face Time?" *USA Today,* June 16, 2009, p. 6D. See also Brad Stone, "Coffee Can Wait. The Day's First Stop Is Online," *The New York Times,* August 10, 2009, pp. A1, A3.
71. Tara Parker-Pope, "An Ugly Toll of Technology: Impatience and Forgetfulness," *The New York Times,* June 6, 2010, *www.nytimes.com/2010/06/07/technology/07brainside.html?ref=yourbrainoncomputers* (accessed June 7, 2011).
72. "Social Networks: Growth, Isolation, and Sucking the Time Away from Us," Online Conference on Networks and Communities, April 26, 2010, *http://networkconference.netstudies.org/2010/04/social-networks-growth-isolation-and-sucking-the-time-away-from-us/* (accessed June 7, 2011).

73. Ibid.
74. Ibid.
75. Matt Richtel, "For Gamers, the Craving Won't Quit," *The New York Times,* April 29, 2008, pp. C1, C4.
76. Jennifer Seter Wagner, "When Play Turns to Trouble," *U.S. News & World Report,* May 19, 2008, pp. 51–52.
77. Study by Iowa State University, reported in Staci Hupp, "1 in 10 Kids Addicted to Video Games," *Reno-Gazette-Journal,* April 21, 2009, p. 1B.
78. "Videogame Addiction," *www.video-game-addiction.org/* (accessed June 7, 2011).
79. Michael Bluejay, "Is Online Gambling Legal in the U.S.?" VegasClick.com, May 2011, *http://vegasclick.com/online/legal.html* (accessed June 7, 2011).
80. "Porn in the USA," *60 Minutes,* CBSNews.com, September 5, 2004.
81. Websense Inc., 2004, and Nielsen/Net Ratings, 2004, reported in "Internet Porn Grows," *USA Today,* June 20, 2004, p. 12A.
82. Tracking by comScore Media Metrix, reported in Anick Jesdanun, "Will a Virtual Red-Light District on the Web Help Parents Curb Online Porn?" *San Francisco Chronicle,* June 13, 2005, p. E2.
83. Nielsen Online October 2008 figures, reported in Anna Kuchment and Karen Springen, "The Tangled Web of Porn in the Office," *Newsweek,* December 8, 2008, p. 14.
84. Jon Swartz, "Online Porn Often Leads High-Tech Way," *USA Today,* March 9, 2004, pp. 1B, 2B.
85. "Porn Sites Closer to .xxx Web Address," *msnbc.com,* June 5, 2010 (acessed June 7, 2011).
86. *Enhancing Child Safety and Online Technologies: Final Report of the Internet Safety Technical Task Force to the Multi-State Working Group on Social Networking of State Attorneys General of the United States,* The Berkman Center for Internet and Society at Harvard University, 2009, *http://cyber.law.harvard.edu/pubrelease/isttf/* (accessed September 29, 2009). See also Brad Stone, "Despite News Reports, Task Force Finds Online Threat to Children Overblown," *The New York Times,* January 14, 2009, p. A14; and Emily Steel, "No Easy Answer for Protecting Kids Online," *The Wall Street Journal,* January 14, 2009, p. B4.
87. "Internet—Online Predators Statistics—Dangers For Kids," July 10, 2010, *http://ezinearticles.com/?Internet—Online-Predators-Statistics—Dangers-For-.edu/pubrelease/isttf/* (accessed September 29, 2009).
88. Marilyn Elias, "Survey Paints Different Portrait of Online Abuser," *USA Today,* August 2, 2004, p. 8D; and Jane L. Levere, "Blunt Ads for Teenagers Warn of Net Predators," *The New York Times,* June 8, 2005, p. C10.
89. *Se and Tech: Results from a Survey of Teens and Young Adults,* The National Campaign to Prevent Teen and Unplanned Pregnancy; and *CosmoGirl.com,* survey by Teenage Research Unlimited of 1,280 teens and young adults online, September 25–October 3, 2008, *www.thenationalcampaign.org/sextech/PDF/SexTech_Summary.pdf* (accessed September 29, 2009). See also Sharon Jayson, "Flirting Goes High-Tech, Low-Taste," *USA Today,* December 10, 2008, p. 1A; and Irene Sege, "Nude Photos of Teens Getting Unexpected Play," *San Francisco Chronicle,* December 12, 2008, p. A28. Another survey by Harris Interactive also found that one in five teens had "sexted"; see Donna Leinwand, "Survey: 1 in 5 Teens 'Sext' Despite Risks," *USA Today,* June 24, 2009, p. 3A.
90. Survey by Common Sense Media, reported in Jill Tucker, "Teens Show, Tell Too Much Online," *San Francisco Chronicle,* August 10, 2009, pp. A1, A6.
91. Jason Koebler, "Cyber Bullying Growing More Malicious, Experts Say," *U.S. News,* June 3, 2011, *www.usnews.com/education/blogs/high-school-notes/2011/06/03/cyber-bullying-growing-more-malicious-experts-say* (accessed June 7, 2011).
92. Jon Swartz, "Schoolyard Bullies Get Nastier Online," *USA Today,* March 7, 2005, pp. 1A, 2A; "Cyberbullies Cause Real Pain" [letters], *The New York Times,* August 30, 2004, p. A20; Jeff Chu, "You Wanna Take This Online?" *Time,* August 8, 2005, pp. 52, 55; Cynthia G. Wagner, "Beating the Cyberbullies," *The Futurist,* September–October 2008, pp. 14–15; and Sue Shellenbarger, "Cyberbully Alert: Web Sites Make It Easier to Flag Trouble," *The Wall Street Journal,* December 17, 2008, p. D1.
93. Cari Tuna, "Lawyers and Employers Take the Fight to 'Workplace Bullies,'" *The Wall Street Journal,* August 4, 2008, p. B6.
94. STB Accounting Systems 1992 survey, reported in Del Jones, "On-line Surfing Costs Firms Time and Money," *USA Today,* December 8, 1995, pp. 1A, 2A.
95. Kevin Maney, "No Time Off? It's Tech Giants' Fault," *USA Today,* July 21, 2004, p. 4B. See also Michael Sanserino, "Suits Question After-Hours Demands of Email and Cellphones," *The Wall Street Journal,* August 10, 2009, pp. B1, B2.
96. U.S. Labor Department, reported in Sue Kirchoff, "Worker Productivity Rises at Fastest Rate since 1950," *USA Today,* February 7, 2003, p. 5B. See also Janet Rue-Dupree, "Innovation Should Mean More Jobs, Not Less," *The New York Times,* January 4, 2009, Business section, p. 3.
97. Stephen S. Roach, "Working Better or Just Harder?" *The New York Times,* February 14, 2000, p. A27.
98. N'Gai Croal, "The Internet Is the New Sweatshop," *Newsweek,* July 7/July 14, 2008, p. 54.
99. David Levy, quoted in Joseph Hart, "Technoskeptic Techie," *Utne,* January–February 2005, pp. 28–29.
100. Bill McKibben, quoted in Jeffrey R. Young, "Knowing When to Log Off," *The Chronicle of Higher Education,* April 22, 2005, pp. A34–A35.
101. "Understanding Information Overload," *infogeneering, www.infogineering.net/understanding-information-overload.htm* (accessed June 7, 2011).
102. William Van Winkle, "Information Overload," *www.gdrc.org/icts/i-overload/infoload.html* (accessed June 7, 2011).
103. Jeremy Rifkin, "Technology's Curse: Fewer Jobs, Fewer Buyers," *San Francisco Examiner,* December 3, 1995, p. C19.
104. Richard W. Samson, "How to Succeed in the Hyper-Human Economy," *The Futurist,* September–October 2004, pp. 38–43.
105. Stewart Brand, in "Boon or Bane for Jobs?" *The Futurist,* January–February 1997, pp. 13–14.
106. Sebastian Moffett, "Technology Widens Gap Between Rich and Poor," May 4, 2011, *http://online.wsj.com/article/SB10001424052748703922804576301154008155570.html* (accessed June 8, 2011).
107. Ibid.
108. Thomas L. Friedman, *The World Is Flat: A Brief History of the Twenty-First Century* (New York: Farrar, Straus & Giroux, 2005).
109. Paul Magnusson, "Globalization Is Great—Sort Of," *BusinessWeek,* April 25, 2005, p. 25. See also Fareed Zakaria, "The Wealth of Yet More Nations," *The New York Times Book Review,* May 1, 2005, pp. 10–11; Russ L. Juskalian, "Prospering in Brave New World Takes Adaptation," *USA Today,* May 2, 2005, p. 4B; and Roberto J. Gonzalez, "Falling Flat," *San Francisco Chronicle,* May 15, 2005, pp. B1, B4.
110. Moffett, "Technology Widens Gap Between Rich and Poor."
111. Charles Hutzler, "Yuppies in China Protest via the Web—and Get Away with It," *The Wall Street Journal,*

March 10, 2004, pp. A1, A8; Howard W. French, "Despite an Act of Leniency, China Has Its Eye on the Web," *The New York Times,* June 27, 2004, sec. 1, p. 6; Charles Hutzler, "China Finds New Ways to Restrict Access to the Internet," *The Wall Street Journal,* September 1, 2004, pp. B1, B2; Tom Zeller, Jr., "Beijing Loves the Web until the Web Talks Back," *The New York Times,* December 6, 2004, p. C15; Jim Yardley, "A Hundred Cellphones Bloom, and Chinese Take to the Streets," *The New York Times,* April 25, 2005, pp. A1, A6; Bruce Einhorn and Heather Green, "Blogs under Its Thumb," *BusinessWeek,* August 8, 2005, pp. 42–43; Michael Wines and Andrew Jacobs, "To Shut Off Tiananmen Talk, China Blocks More Web Sites," *The New York Times,* June 3, 2009, p. A13; Jeannie Nuss, "Web Site Tracks Online Censorship Reports," *San Francisco Chronicle,* August 24, 2009, p. D2; and Jonathan Ansfield, "China Adds Layer of Web Surveillance with a Rule Seeking Users' Names," *The New York Times,* September 6, 2009, News section, p. 4.

112. Todd Gitlin, quoted in Dora Straus, "Lazy Teachers, Lazy Students" [letter], *The New York Times,* September 12, 1999, sec. 4, p. 18.

Chapter 10

1. Gary Webb, "Potholes, Not 'Smooth Transition,' Mark Project," *San Jose Mercury News,* July 3, 1994, p. 18A.
2. Jim Remsik, "For Software Writing, a Buddy System," *The New York Times,* September 20, 2009, p. 8.
3. Jerome Garfunkel, "COBOL: Still Relevant after All These Years," December 17, 2003, *www.cobolreport.com/columnists/jermoe/02172003.asp (accessed January 10, 2008).*
4. Alan Freedman, *The Computer Glossary,* 6th ed. (New York: AMACOM, 1993), p. 370.
5. *http://searchenterpriselinux.techtarget.com/sDefinition/0,,sid39_gci213098,00.html#* (accessed August 30, 2008).

Photo Credits

Chapter 1

Page 1: Alberto Pomares/Getty Images; **3:** © Edward Bock/Corbis; **4:** Kumar Sriskandan/Alamy; **5:** Syracuse Newspapers/Greenlar/The Image Works; **8** *(left)*: Courtesy of IBM; **8** *(top right)*: David Silverman/Getty Images; **8** *(bottom right)*: © Mark Thiessen/National Geographic Society/Corbis; **9** *(top right)*: YOSHIKAZU TSUNO/AFP/Getty Images; **9** *(top left)*: Fujifotos/The Image Works; **9** *(bottom right)*: Shizuo Kambayashi/AP Images; **11** *(bottom left)*: The Kobal Collection/Twentieth Century-Fox Film Corporation; **11** *(bottom right)*: © Grand Tour/Corbis; **12:** Jeff Greenberg/The Image Works; **14** *(top)*: Courtesy of Obscura Digital; **14** *(bottom)*: Syracuse Newspapers/Jim Commentucci/The Image Works; **14** *(middle)*: Alistair Berg/Getty Images; **17** *(left)*: Courtesy of Unisys Archives; **17** *(right)*: © Lannis Waters/ZUMA Press/Corbis; **18** *(left)*: Courtesy of Apple; **18** *(middle)*: Courtesy of HTC; **18** *(right)*: Courtesy of Sprint; **19:** Alberto Pomares/Getty Images; **20:** © The Star-Ledger/Mitsu Yasukawa/The Image Works; **23:** Courtesy of RIKEN and Fujitsu; **24** *(top)*: Courtesy of IBM; **24** *(middle)*: Courtesy of Hewlett-Packard; **24** *(bottom)*: © Bernd Thissen/dpa/Corbis; **25** *(top right)*: Courtesy of Gateway Computer; **25** *(top left)*: Courtesy of Apple Computer; **25** *(top middle)*: MANPREET ROMANA/AFP/Getty Images; **25** *(bottom left)*: Courtesy of Apple; **25** *(bottom right)*: Courtesy of Dell; **25** *(bottom middle)*: Courtesy of Apple; **26** *(bottom right)*: Courtesy of Hewlett-Packard; **26** *(top left)*: Courtesy of Pantech; **26** *(bottom left)*: Courtesy of Amazon; **26** *(top right)*: Courtesy of T-Mobile; **27** *(top left)*: Courtesy of Motorola Corp.; **27** *(bottom left)*: Courtesy of Hewlett-Packard; **27** *(top right)*: David Friedman/Getty Images; **27** *(bottom right)*: Courtesy of Hewlett-Packard; **31** *(right)*: Courtesy of Intel; **31** *(left)*: Corbis Flirt/Alamy; **33:** Courtesy of Seagate; **35:** Courtesy of Apple; **36** *(bottom)*: Courtesy of Adobe Systems Inc.; **36** *(top)*: Courtesy of Microsoft Corporation: **37** *(bottom)*: Courtesy of PR NewsFoto; **37** *(top left)*: Shizuo Kambayashi/AP Images; **37** *(top right)*: Fred Greaves/AP Images; **39** *(top)*: John Foxx/Getty Images; **39** *(bottom)*: Sean Gallup/Getty Images; **41:** Alberto Pomares/Getty Images

Chapter 2

Page 51: EyeSee/Fotosearch; **58:** © amana images inc./Alamy; **59:** Courtesy of DirectTV; **60:** Courtesy of Samsung; **64:** Courtesy of Chris Harrison; **65:** NOAH SEELAM/AFP/Getty Images; **77:** EyeSee/Fotosearch; **79:** EyeSee/Fotosearch; **82:** Courtesy of Research in Motion Ltd.; **98:** YOSHIKAZU TSUNO/AFP/Getty Images; **99** *(top)*: Web 20/Fotosearch; **99** *(bottom)*: Ron Haviv/VII/Corbis; **100:** EyeSee/Fotosearch; **107:** EyeSee/Fotosearch; **108:** EyeSee/Fotosearch

Chapter 3

Page 119: John Foxx/Getty Images; **128:** John Foxx/Getty Images; **130:** Courtesy of Symantec; **141** *(bottom)*: © John Van Hasselt/Corbis; **141** *(top)*: Courtesy of Apple; **141** *(top)*: Courtesy of Apple; **142** *(bottom)*: Dan Lamont/Corbis; **148** *(left)*: Courtesy of Motorola; **148** *(middle)*: Courtesy of Apple; **148** *(right)*: Courtesy of Verizon; **177:** Tom Wagner; **181:** John Foxx/Getty Images; **187:** John Foxx/Getty Images

Chapter 4

Page 197: © Stockbyte/Getty Images; **199** *(left)*: Courtesy of IBM Archives; **199** *(right)*: © Bettmann/Corbis; **200:** Courtesy of Intel; **201** *(left)*: Courtesy of Intel; **201** *(top right)*: Courtesy of Intel; **201** *(bottom right)*: Courtesy of Intel; **208** *(top)*: Courtesy of iGo, Inc.; **208** *(bottom)*: Courtesy of www.apc.com; **210** *(bottom)*: Corbis RF/Alamy; **210** *(top)*: photolibrary.com; **211:** © Stockbyte/Getty Images; **212** *(bottom right)*: Courtesy of AMD; **212** *(top)*: Courtesy of Intel; **212** *(bottom left)*: Courtesy of Intel; **218:** Courtesy of Kingston Technology Company; **221** *(middle right)*: © Radius Images/Corbis; **221** *(bottom left)*: Courtesy of Alan Palmer; **221** *(bottom right)*: Courtesy of Lenovo; **221** *(top)*: Courtesy of Hewlett-Packard: **223** *(top left)*: Courtesy of Adaptec; **223** *(top right)*: Courtesy of Logitech; **223** *(top bottom right)*: Courtesy of Apple; **223** *(top bottom left)*: © Matthieu Spohn/PhotoAlto/Corbis; **223** *(bottom right)*: Getty Images; **224:** Courtesy of Plantronics; **225:** Courtesy of Jeff Grisso/www.sonic84.com; **226** *(top)*: oliver leedham/Alamy; **226** *(bottom)*: Thinkstock Images/Getty Images; **228:** Courtesy of Belkin; **229** *(bottom left)*: David Gee 3/Alamy; **230:** Courtesy of IBM; **231** *(top)*: Courtesy of IBM; **231** *(middle)*: Courtesy of Lacie; **231** *(bottom)*: Artur Marciniec/Alamy; **232:** Courtesy of Kprateek88; **233:** Christian Delbert/Alamy; **234:** Courtesy of Samsung; **235:** Katsumi Kasahara/AP Images; **237** *(top right)*: Tony Cenicola/New York Times/Redux Pictures; **237** *(bottom right)*: Fabian Bimmer/AP Images; **237** *(bottom)*: Courtesy of Corsair; **237** *(top left)*: Courtesy of PNY Technologies; **238:** © Stockbyte/Getty Images; **239:** © Stockbyte/Getty Images; **241** *(bottom left)*: Courtesy of Nokia; **241** *(top left)*: Courtesy of Saw-Wai Hla and Kendal Clark, Ohio University; **242:** Frank Franklin II/AP Images; **245:** © Stockbyte/Getty Images

Chapter 5

Page 255: Steve Allen/Getty Images; **256** *(right)*: Lonely Planet Images/Alamy; **256** *(left)*: © Najlah Feanny/Corbis; **258** *(right)*: Tom Rittenhouse; **258** *(left)*: Courtesy of Lenovo; **259** *(bottom)*: Jochen Luebke/AFP/Getty Images; **259** *(top)*: Courtesy of Logitech; **260** *(left)*: Ryan McVay/Getty Images; **260** *(right)*: John Slater/Taxi/Getty Images; **260** *(middle)*: Peter Cade/Getty Images; **261** *(top left)*: Comstock Images/Getty Images; **261** *(bottom left)*: Iain Masterton/Alamy; **261** *(bottom right)*: Courtesy of Sony; **261** *(top right)*: Comstock Images/Getty Images; **263** *(bottom left)*: Courtesy of Microsoft; **263** *(top right)*: Courtesy of DigiSecrets; **264** *(bottom)*: Courtesy of ID8 Mobile; **265:** Courtesy of Logitech; **266** *(top)*: Courtesy of Lenovo; **266** *(bottom left)*: Courtesy of Inamo Restaurant, London; **266** *(bottom right)*: Joe Gill/The Express Times/AP Images; **267** *(top left)*: Courtesy of MultiTouch Ltd.; **267** *(top right)*: Courtesy of Apple; **268** *(top left)*: Courtesy of HTC; **268** *(top right)*: Courtesy of Axiotron; **268** *(bottom)*: © Edward Rozzo/Corbis; **269** *(top)*: Courtesy of Wacom Technology; **269** *(bottom left)*: Courtesy of Epson; **269** *(bottom right)*: Wenatchee World, Mike Bonnicksen/AP Images; **269** *(middle)*: Courtesy of Livescribe; **272** *(bottom)*: David Williams/Alamy; **272** *(top)*: Courtesy of Intermec Technologies; **273** *(bottom left)*: Courtesy of 3D Scanners Ltd./www.3dscanners.com; **273** *(bottom right)*: Courtesy of 3D Scanners Ltd./www.3dscanners.com; **274:** Junior Gonzalez/Getty Images; **275** *(top)*: Courtesy of Hewlett-Packard; **275** *(bottom)*: Courtesy of IBM; **276** *(bottom right)*: Blend Images/Alamy; **276** *(bottom left)*: Courtesy of Lenovo; **276** *(top)*: Courtesy of Contour; **278:** Burazin/Getty Images; **281** *(left)*: William Thomas Cain/Getty Images; **281** *(middle)*: Courtesy of Nike and Hamish2K; **281** *(right)*: Eye Ubiquitous/Alamy; **282** *(top right)*: ISU/STOCK4B/Getty Images; **282** *(bottom left)*: Timo Arnall/Getty Images; **282** *(top left)*: Elaine Thompson/AP Images; **282** *(bottom right)*: © STUART WALKER/Alamy; **283** *(top right)*: © Ren√© Johnston/ZUMA Press/Corbis; **283** *(top left)*: Michael

Probst/AP Images; **283** *(bottom right)*: Justin Sullivan/Getty Images; **284** *(top)*: Tony Cenicola/New York Times/Redux Pictures; **284** *(left)*: © vario images GmbH & Co.KG/Alamy; **288:** Courtesy of Hewlett-Packard; **289** *(bottom)*: Courtesy of Dell; **290** *(top left)*: Peter Thompson/New York Times/Redux Pictures; **290** *(bottom right)*: Barry Batchelor/PA Wire/AP Images; **290** *(bottom left)*: Courtesy of JCM American Corporation/PRNewsFoto; **290** *(top right)*: Peter Thompson/New York Times/Redux Pictures; **291** *(middle)*: Courtesy of Hewlett-Packard; **291** *(top right)*: Courtesy of Samsung; **291** *(top left)*: Courtesy of Sony Corporation; **291** *(bottom left)*: Courtesy of Epson; **291** *(bottom right)*: Courtesy of Epson; **292:** Steve Allen/Getty Images; **293** *(left)*: Steven Senne/AP Images; **293** *(right)*: Courtesy of Epson; **297** *(top)*: Owen Franken/Corbis; **297** *(bottom)*: Richard T. Nowitz/Corbis; **299** *(top)*: Dr. Irfan Essa/Georgia Tech; **299** *(bottom)*: Courtesy of E-Ink Corp. and L. G. Phillips; **299** *(middle)*: Rick Friedman; **301:** Steve Allen/Getty Images

Chapter 6

Page 311: © Image Source/Corbis; **317:** Fievet Laurent/AFP/Getty Images; **328** *(top)*: Courtesy of Belkin; **328** *(middle)*: Courtesy of Sling Media; **328** *(bottom)*: Courtesy of HMS Industrial Networks; **329** *(left)*: Tetra Images/Getty Images; **329** *(right)*: artpartner-images.com/Alamy; **332** *(top)*: PETER FOLEY/epa/Corbis; **332** *(bottom)*: digerati/Alamy; **333** *(top)*: Corbis; **333** *(bottom)*: © Sergey Galushko/Alamy; **334:** Eric Myer/Getty Images; **334** *(top right)*: Steve Allen/Brand X Pictures/Corbis; **334** *(top left)*: Dorling Kindersley/Getty Images; **334** *(bottom left)*: Don Farrall/Getty Images; **334** *(middle right)*: Andy Whale/Getty Images; **334** *(bottom)*: © Seth Resnick/Science Faction/Corbis; **336:** © Image Source/Corbis; **340** *(top right)*: Brian Williams; **340** *(top left)*: Bob Rowan, Progressive Image/Corbis; **340** *(bottom)*: Liu Liqun/Corbis; **341** *(top right)*: Olivier Prevosto/Corbis; **341** *(top left)*: HO/AP Images; **341** *(bottom)*: Pallava Bagla/Corbis; **342:** Courtesy of Pulse Data; **344** *(top right)*: © Jerry McCrea/Star Ledger/Corbis; 344T *(left)*: © Dennis Drenner/Aurora Open/Corbis; **344** *(bottom)*: Courtesy of White Bear Technologies; **345:** Courtesy of Ford Media; **346:** Courtesy of Research in Motion Ltd.; **347:** Judy Mason; **349** *(bottom)*: Courtesy of Photoshop; **349** *(middle)*: Courtesy of Nikon; **349** *(top)*: Courtesy of Nikon; **355:** © Image Source/Corbis; **359:** © Image Source/Corbis; **360:** Courtesy of Symantec; **362:** Chad Hunt/Corbis; **364:** © Image Source/Corbis; **365:** © Image Source/Corbis

Chapter 7

Page 373: Maciej Frolow/Getty Images; **374:** Courtesy of LG; **375:** Shizuo Kambayashi/AP Images; **376** *(bottom)*: Courtesy of Apple; **376** *(top)*: Courtesy of Apple; **378:** Courtesy of Creative Technology Ltd.; **379** *(bottom)*: Martin Meissner/AP Images; **379** *(top)*: Courtesy of Microsoft; **380** *(top)*: Reed Saxon/AP Images; **380** *(bottom)*: Courtesy of Ford Media; **382:** Courtesy of Sirius/PRNewsFoto/NewsCom; **383:** Courtesy of JVC; **384** *(right)*: Courtesy of Sony Corp.; **385:** D-BASE/Getty Images; **388** *(left)*: Courtesy of Sony; **388** *(right)*: Courtesy of SanDisk; **391:** Maciej Frolow/Getty Images; **393:** Courtesy of Tivo; **394** *(left)*: Courtesy of Sling Media; **394** *(top right)*: Courtesy of Sling Media; **394** *(bottom right)*: Courtesy of Sling Media; **395** *(left)*: Courtesy of Amazon.com; **395** *(right)*: AP Images; **397:** Courtesy of Viewsonic; **398** *(bottom)*: Robert Wilkinson/Alamy; **398** *(top)*: Courtesy of Apple; **401:** Ronda Churchill/Bloomberg via Getty Images; **402:** ©Sylent-Press/ullstein bild/The Image Works; **403** *(top)*: David McNew/Getty Images; **403** *(bottom)*: CP, Aaron Harris/AP Images; **404:** Maciej Frolow/Getty Images

Chapter 8

Page 409: James Leynse/Corbis; **410:** Courtesy of Identix; **411:** Noboru Hashimoto/Corbis; **415:** James Leynse/Corbis; **423** *(bottom)*: Corbis; **423** *(top)*: Charlie Westerman/Getty Images; **425** *(left)*: Courtesy of TECHBASE International; **425** *(right)*: NOAA/Reuters/Corbis; **446** *(bottom right)*: Bob Mahoney/The Image Works; **446** *(top left)*: M.Spencer Green/AP Images; **446** *(bottom left)*: Ted S. Warren/AP Images; **446** *(top right)*: AP Images; **446** *(middle right)*: Courtesy of Bernard Frischer of Virginia's Institute for Advanced Technology in the Humanities/AP Images; **447** *(bottom left)*: Jodi Hilton/New York Times/Redux Pictures; **447** *(top right)*: Kim Jae-Hwan/AFP/Getty Images; **447** *(middle left)*: Lisa Poole/AP Images; **447** *(top left)*: Bertil Ericson/AP Images; **447** *(top middle)*: Brett Coomer/AP Images; **447** *(bottom right)*: Shizuo Kambayashi/AP Images; **447** *(middle right)*: Mike Derer/AP Images; **450:** Jeff McIntosh/AP Images; **451** *(bottom)*: Science Museum /SSPL/The Image Works; **451** *(top right)*: Tetra Images/Getty Images; **456:** James Leynse/Corbis

Chapter 9

Page 463: Corbis; **464:** HARISH TYAGI/epa/Corbis; **465:** Bob Elsdale/Getty Images; **466** *(bottom)*: Courtesy of Troels Eklund Andersen; **466** *(top)*: MedicalRf.com/Getty Images; **467:** Pete Souza/The White House/MCT via Getty Images; **472:** Justin Kase zsixz/Alamy; **480** *(top left)*: Michael Kooren/Reuters/Corbis; **480** *(top right)*: BEHROUZ MEHRI/AFP/Getty Images; **480** *(bottom)*: Jockel Finck/AP Images; **481:** Corbis; **483** *(left)*: Ricki Rosen/Corbis; **483** *(right)*: Tony Cenicola/New York Times/Redux Pictures; **485** *(top)*: MANDEL GAN/AFP/Getty Images; **485** *(bottom)*: © Kyodo/XinHua/Xinhua Press/Corbis; **487:** Gabe Palmer/Corbis; **488** *(bottom left)*: Courtesy of Larson, a DMB Company; **488** *(top right)*: Uriel Sinai/Getty Images; **488** *(top left)*: © Bernd Thissen/dpa/Corbis; **488** *(bottom right)*: David Butow/Corbis SABA; **490** *(top)*: Vladimir Maravic/Getty Images; **491** *(bottom right)*: Comstock/PictureQuest; **496:** David M.Russell; **498:** Corbis

Chapter 10

Page 503: John Foxx/Getty Images; **505:** PhotoDisc/Getty Images; **506:** Comstock/PictureQuest; **507:** Photodisc/Getty Images; **510** *(top)*: Stockbyte/Getty Images; **510;** Courtesy of Apple Inc./Photo by Dwight Eschilman; **511:** Photodisc/Getty Images; **512:** Photodisc/Getty Images; **513:** Image Source/PunchStock; **514:** Ryan McVay/Getty Images; **516:** Eric Audras/Photoalto/PictureQuest; **521:** fStop/Getty Images; **522:** PhotoDisc/Getty Images; **523:** Digital Vision/Getty Images; **541:** John Foxx/Getty Images

Index

Boldface *page numbers indicate pages on which key terms are defined.*

N

O